The Debt Market
Volume I

The International Library of Critical Writings in Financial Economics

Series Editor: Richard Roll
Allstate Professor of Economics
The Anderson School at UCLA, USA

This major series presents by field outstanding selections of the most important articles across the entire spectrum of financial economics – one of the fastest growing areas in business schools and economics departments. Each collection has been prepared by a leading specialist who has written an authoritative introduction to the literature.

1. The Theory of Corporate Finance (Volumes I and II)
   Michael J. Brennan

2. Futures Markets (Volumes I, II and III)
   A.G. Malliaris

3. Market Efficiency: Stock Market Behaviour in Theory and Practice (Volumes I and II)
   Andrew W. Lo

4. Microstructure: The Organization of Trading and Short Term Price Behavior (Volumes I and II)
   Hans R. Stoll

5. The Debt Market (Volumes I, II and III)
   Stephen A. Ross

Future titles will include:

Options Markets
G.M. Constantinides and A.G. Malliaris

Empirical Corporate Finance
Michael J. Brennan

Asset Pricing Theory and Tests
Robert Grauer

Emerging Markets

Continuous Time Finance
Stephen M. Schaefer

Behavioral Finance
Harold M. Shefrin

International Securities
George C. Philippatos and Gregory D. Koutmos

International Capital Markets

Wherever possible, the articles in these volumes have been reproduced as originally published using facsimile reproduction, inclusive of footnotes and pagination to facilitate ease of reference.

For a list of all Edward Elgar published titles visit our site on the World Wide Web at http://www.e-elgar.co.uk

The Debt Market

Volume I
Valuation: The General Theory

Edited by

Stephen A. Ross

Franco Modigliani Professor of Finance and Economics, Sloan School of Management and Department of Economics
Massachusetts Institute of Technology, USA

THE INTERNATIONAL LIBRARY OF CRITICAL WRITINGS IN FINANCIAL ECONOMICS

An Elgar Reference Collection
Cheltenham, UK • Northampton, MA, USA

Published by
Edward Elgar Publishing Limited
Glensanda House
Montpellier Parade
Cheltenham
Glos GL50 1UA
UK

Edward Elgar Publishing, Inc.
136 West Street, Suite 202
Northampton
Massachusetts 01060
USA

A catalogue record for this book is available from the British Library.

Library of Congress Cataloguing in Publication Data

The debt market / edited by Stephen A. Ross.
— (The International library of critical writings in financial economics ; 5)
Includes bibliographical references and index.
Contents: v. 1. Valuation, the general theory — v. 2. Testing, portfolio management, and special effects — v. 3. Fixed income instruments.
1. Bonds—Mathematical models. 2. Bond market. 3. Fixed-income securities. 4. Interest rates. 5. Investments. I. Ross, Stephen A. II. Series.

HG4651 .D43 2000
332.63'23—dc21 00–034825

ISBN 1 85278 987 5 (3 volume set)

Printed and bound in Great Britain by MPG Books Ltd, Bodmin, Cornwall

Contents

Acknowledgements vii
Foreword Richard Roll ix
Reader's Guide Stephen A. Ross xi
Introduction Stephen A. Ross xiii

PART I THE CLASSICAL EXPECTATIONS HYPOTHESIS

1. F.A. Lutz (1941), 'The Structure of Interest Rates', *Quarterly Journal of Economics*, **LV**, 36–63 3
2. J.M. Culbertson (1957), 'The Term Structure of Interest Rates', *Quarterly Journal of Economics*, **LXXI** (4), November, 485–517 31
3. John H. Wood (1964), 'The Expectations Hypothesis, the Yield Curve, and Monetary Policy', *Quarterly Journal of Economics*, **LXXVIII** (3), August, 457–70 64
4. Franco Modigliani and Richard Sutch (1966), 'Innovations in Interest Rate Policy', *American Economic Review*, **LVI** (2), May, 178–97 78
5. J. Huston McCulloch (1975), 'An Estimate of the Liquidity Premium', *Journal of Political Economy*, **83** (1), February, 95–119 98

PART II TESTING RATIONAL EXPECTATIONS HYPOTHESES

6. Robert J. Shiller (1990), 'The Term Structure of Interest Rates' with an Appendix by J. Huston McCulloch, in Benjamin M. Friedman and Frank H. Hahn (eds), *Handbook of Monetary Economics*, Volume I, Chapter 13, Amsterdam: North-Holland, 627–722 125
7. John Y. Campbell and Robert J. Shiller (1991), 'Yield Spreads and Interest Rate Movements: A Bird's Eye View', *Review of Economic Studies*, **58** (3), No. 195, May, 495–514 221
8. Robert F. Stambaugh (1988), 'The Information in Forward Rates: Implications for Models of the Term Structure', *Journal of Financial Economics*, **21**, 41–70 241
9. Eugene F. Fama (1975), 'Short-Term Interest Rates as Predictors of Inflation', *American Economic Review*, **65** (3), June, 269–82 271
10. Bradford Cornell (1978), 'Monetary Policy, Inflation Forecasting and the Term Structure of Interest Rates', *Journal of Finance*, **XXXIII** (1), March, 117–27 285
11. Eugene F. Fama (1984), 'Term Premiums in Bond Returns', *Journal of Financial Economics*, **13**, 529–46 296

12. Tadashi Kikugawa and Kenneth J. Singleton (1994), 'Modeling the Term Structure of Interest Rates in Japan', *Journal of Fixed Income*, **4** (2), September, 6–16 314

PART III THE DERIVATIVE ASSET APPROACH TO THE TERM STRUCTURE

13. Robert C. Merton (1973), 'Theory of Rational Option Pricing', *Bell Journal of Economics and Management Science*, **4** (1), Spring, 141–83 327
14. John C. Cox and Stephen A. Ross (1976), 'The Valuation of Options for Alternative Stochastic Processes', *Journal of Financial Economics*, **3**, 145–66 370
15. Oldrich Vasicek (1977), 'An Equilibrium Characterization of the Term Structure', *Journal of Financial Economics*, **5**, 177–88 392
16. John C. Cox, Jonathan E. Ingersoll, Jr. and Stephen A. Ross (1981), 'A Re-examination of Traditional Hypotheses about the Term Structure of Interest Rates', *Journal of Finance*, **XXXVI** (4), September, 769–99 404
17. John C. Cox, Jonathan E. Ingersoll, Jr. and Stephen A. Ross (1985), 'A Theory of the Term Structure of Interest Rates', *Econometrica*, **53** (2), March, 385–407 435
18. John C. Cox, Jonathan E. Ingersoll, Jr. and Stephen A. Ross (1985), 'An Intertemporal General Equilibrium Model of Asset Prices', *Econometrica*, **53** (2), March, 363–84 458
19. Michael J. Brennan and Eduardo S. Schwartz (1979), 'A Continuous Time Approach to the Pricing of Bonds', *Journal of Banking and Finance*, **3** (2), July, 133–55 480
20. David Heath, Robert Jarrow and Andrew Morton (1992), 'Bond Pricing and the Term Structure of Interest Rates: A New Methodology for Contingent Claims Valuation', *Econometrica*, **60** (1), January, 77–105 503
21. Philip H. Dybvig, Jonathan E. Ingersoll, Jr. and Stephen A. Ross (1996), 'Long Forward and Zero-Coupon Rates Can Never Fall', *Journal of Business*, **69** (1), January, 1–25 532

Name Index 557

Acknowledgements

The editor and publishers wish to thank the authors and the following publishers who have kindly given permission for the use of copyright material.

American Economic Association for articles: Franco Modigliani and Richard Sutch (1966), 'Innovations in Interest Rate Policy', *American Economic Review*, **LVI** (2), May, 178–97; Eugene F. Fama (1975), 'Short-Term Interest Rates as Predictors of Inflation', *American Economic Review*, **65** (3), June, 269–82.

Blackwell Publishers, Inc. for articles: Bradford Cornell (1978), 'Monetary Policy, Inflation Forecasting and the Term Structure of Interest Rates', *Journal of Finance*, **XXXIII** (1), March, 117–27; John C. Cox, Jonathan E. Ingersoll, Jr. and Stephen A. Ross (1981), 'A Re-examination of Traditional Hypotheses about the Term Structure of Interest Rates', *Journal of Finance*, **XXXVI** (4), September, 769–99.

Econometric Society for articles: John C. Cox, Jonathan E. Ingersoll, Jr. and Stephen A. Ross (1985), 'An Intertemporal General Equilibrium Model of Asset Prices', *Econometrica*, **53** (2), March, 363–84; John C. Cox, Jonathan E. Ingersoll, Jr. and Stephen A. Ross (1985), 'A Theory of the Term Structure of Interest Rates', *Econometrica*, **53** (2), March, 385–407; David Heath, Robert Jarrow and Andrew Morton (1992), 'Bond Pricing and the Term Structure of Interest Rates: A New Methodology for Contingent Claims Valuation', *Econometrica*, **60** (1), January, 77–105.

Elsevier Science BV for article: Michael J. Brennan and Eduardo S. Schwartz (1979), 'A Continuous Time Approach to the Pricing of Bonds', *Journal of Banking and Finance*, **3** (2), July, 133–55.

Elsevier Science Ltd for excerpt: Robert J. Shiller (1990), 'The Term Structure of Interest Rates' with an Appendix by J. Huston McCulloch, in Benjamin M. Friedman and Frank H. Hahn (eds), *Handbook of Monetary Economics*, Volume I, Chapter 13, 627–722.

Elsevier Science SA for articles: John C. Cox and Stephen A. Ross (1976), 'The Valuation of Options for Alternative Stochastic Processes', *Journal of Financial Economics*, **3**, 145–66; Oldrich Vasicek (1977), 'An Equilibrium Characterization of the Term Structure', *Journal of Financial Economics*, **5**, 177–88; Eugene F. Fama (1984), 'Term Premiums in Bond Returns', *Journal of Financial Economics*, **13**, 529–46; Robert F. Stambaugh (1988), 'The Information in Forward Rates: Implications for Models of the Term Structure', *Journal of Financial Economics*, **21**, 41–70.

Institutional Investor, Inc. for article: Tadashi Kikugawa and Kenneth J. Singleton (1994), 'Modeling the Term Structure of Interest Rates in Japan', *Journal of Fixed Income*, **4** (2), September, 6–16.

MIT Press Journals for articles: F.A. Lutz (1941), 'The Structure of Interest Rates', *Quarterly Journal of Economics*, **LV**, 36–63; J.M. Culbertson (1957), 'The Term Structure of Interest Rates', *Quarterly Journal of Economics*, **LXXI** (4), November, 485–517; John H. Wood (1964), 'The Expectations Hypothesis, the Yield Curve, and Monetary Policy', *Quarterly Journal of Economics*, **LXXVIII** (3), August, 457–70.

RAND for article: Robert C. Merton (1973), 'Theory of Rational Option Pricing', *Bell Journal of Economics and Management Science*, **4** (1), Spring, 141–83.

Review of Economic Studies Ltd for article: John Y. Campbell and Robert J. Shiller (1991), 'Yield Spreads and Interest Rate Movements: A Bird's Eye View', *Review of Economic Studies*, **58** (3), No. 195, May, 495–514.

University of Chicago Press for articles: J. Huston McCulloch (1975), 'An Estimate of the Liquidity Premium', *Journal of Political Economy*, **83** (1), February, 95–119; Philip H. Dybvig, Jonathan E. Ingersoll, Jr. and Stephen A. Ross (1996), 'Long Forward and Zero-Coupon Rates Can Never Fall', *Journal of Business*, **69** (1), January, 1–25.

Every effort has been made to trace all the copyright holders but if any have been inadvertently overlooked the publishers will be pleased to make the necessary arrangement at the first opportunity.

In addition the publishers wish to thank the Library of the London School of Economics and Political Science, the Marshall Library of Economics, Cambridge University, B & N Microfilm and the Library of Indiana University at Bloomington, USA for their assistance in obtaining these articles.

Foreword

Richard Roll

In his famous phrase 'the extent of the market', Adam Smith anticipated modern fixed income securities, for there has never been a market to equal theirs in its size and scope. As Professor Stephen Ross emphasizes in his refined introduction to these volumes, debt securities are not only of immense financial relevance, but are fascinating to a broad constituency of investors, economists and government officials, partly because they offer the hope of a peek into the future. That hope has not yet been fulfilled, but it has motivated impressive scientific developments.

The term structure of interest rates resides at the very core of fixed income analysis. Not surprisingly, Professor Ross has selected a number of seminal articles about the term structure extending back to the early 1940s, but he emphasizes the more recent derivatives approach based on continuous-time mathematics. This literature is not only elegant; it forms the foundation of much modern practice in bond valuation, trading, underwriting and portfolio management. Volume I contains Professor Ross' selections of the most important papers.

In Volume II, Professor Ross has included empirical papers testing the derivatives approach. This is followed by papers applying the derivatives approach to specific problems, such as the valuation of options on bonds. Techniques for bond portfolio management, particularly the use of duration for immunization, round out Volume II's mainly practical papers.

Volume III is devoted to the corporate bond and mortgage sub-markets, each very large in its own right and each associated with remarkable developments in theory, empirical testing and practice. These markets represent perhaps the most thorough melding of academic research and practical implementation in all of economics. The distinction is thoroughly blurred between finance departments of universities and research departments of financial institutions. Important developments are originating from both and there are many interactions between them.

Yet, as Professor Ross warns, many unanswered questions remain. Most derivatives based theories make the blatantly wrong presumption that individuals share common beliefs. If this were actually true, debt markets would undoubtedly be much smaller and exhibit markedly less trading activity. Every fixed income contract and secondary market trade has a borrower and lender, a seller and a buyer. Disagreement about value seems likely to be the predominant motive for each side. No one knows, or can yet even imagine, what fixed income models must become to accommodate this obvious reality. Perhaps the models will remain unchanged. Perhaps they will have to be altered beyond recognition. One thing is certain: whoever makes those future advances will be intimately familiar with the papers collected here by Professor Ross.

Reader's Guide

Stephen A. Ross

The introduction that follows is intended to provide an overview of the topics covered in these three volumes. The volumes are organized into separate parts. While the specific articles within each part are not referred to in the introduction, the organization of the introduction follows that of the collected papers. Each 'part' of collected papers is discussed in a particular section of the introduction which describes the central intellectual content of that part. The introduction also strives to place the individual sections in an overall intellectual and historical context. Within the parts, the articles themselves are generally, but not invariably, in chronological order. This is purposeful; the order for each part has been chosen so that the reader who is new to the subject should proceed sequentially from the first article to the last.

Introduction

Stephen A. Ross

The fixed income markets have always fascinated economists and financial experts. Governments finance their activities, corporations finance their investments and individuals finance their consumption in the debt markets. Together with the attendant swaps and derivatives markets, the debt markets dwarf the other world markets both in size and in the enormous liquidity they offer. Not surprisingly, discussion of interest rates and prognostications about central bank operations dominate popular economic discourse. Obviously, the magnitude of these markets and their pivotal role in determining investment activity, foreign exchange, and their evident centrality for macroeconomics, would always demand our attention. The lure which attracts us to study them, however, is subtler. The fixed income markets and the pricing of bonds, as expressed most naturally in the term structure of interest rates, offer us the hope of a peek into the future.

The Term Structure of Interest Rates

Finance is about the valuation of claims to assets whose payouts occur in the future. The extent to which the price of a government bond with a fixed future payout differs from the sum of the payouts themselves is called the time value of money. There is a vast array of short term bonds and notes with payouts of one or two years, as well as bonds with maturities extending out decades. The Walt Disney Company, for example, recently issued a bond with a maturity of a century and for over a century the British government has sold consols, that is, bonds with no maturity date that promise to pay a constant level coupon forever, or at least as long as there is a Britain. There is a market price for one dollar to be received at almost any specified future date and, in this sense, the fixed income markets are as complete as any markets that we have. Furthermore, since bonds of nearly all maturities are traded, we can use their prices to measure the time value of money over nearly any time span.

To understand pricing in the fixed income markets and to focus our attention in the proper place, unfortunately we have to introduce some notation. This can become quite complex, with claims to dollars being referenced by the time the claim is made as well as by the time the dollars are to be received. We begin our analysis of the debt markets with the default free government bond markets, that is, the term structure of default free bonds or 'the term structure' for simplicity. Our analysis is merely a modern restatement of the work of Macaulay (1938), Lutz (1940–41), Culbertson (1957) and Hicks (1946), who, in turn, built on the seminal contributions of Irving Fisher (1930).

Governments typically issue a full array of bonds of different maturities, with the near term bonds, a few years or less, promising fixed payments of a principal amount, say 1, at a specified future date, T, and with longer term bonds paying coupons over time. Payments are usually made at regular time intervals, and, for convenience, we will assume that all payments are made at the end of the period and denote the payment at the end of period t by $c(t)$. The last payment, $c(T)$, is received at the terminal date or maturity, T. Bonds with only a terminal payment and no intermediate coupon payments are called zeros or bullet bonds. Bonds with intermediate coupons and a terminal payment equal to the final coupon plus the principal of the bond are called balloons. Every bond can be thought of as being made up of a series of zeros. For instance, a ten year balloon bond can be thought of as being equivalent to nine zeros, each of which pays the annual coupon due in that year and a tenth zero which pays the final coupon plus the principal.

If we let $p(t)$ denote the price of a zero bond with maturity t, then the yield to maturity on this bond, $y(t)$, is defined as the annual interest rate that discounts the payment of \$1 at time t to the current price,

$$\frac{1}{(1+y(t))^t} = p(t)$$

The one year spot rate, $y(1)$, is simply the yield on a one year bond,

$$\frac{1}{(1+y(1))} = p(1)$$

The price of any coupon bond paying a string of coupons of $c(t)$ at each year t, $p(c(t))$, will be the sum of the values of each of its coupon payments,

$$\begin{aligned} p(c(t)) &= p(1)c(1) + \ldots + p(T)c(T) \\ &= \frac{c(1)}{(1+y(1))} + \ldots + \frac{c(T)}{(1+y(T))^T} \end{aligned}$$

This relation is a consequence of the absence of arbitrage, in this case the simple law of one price. If, say, the coupon bond sold for more than the sum of the values of its separate coupons, then agents could purchase the component zero bonds and then issue a coupon bond knowing that they could pay the coupon bonds as their zeros matured. At time t they would receive the payment $c(t)$ and could use it to pay the promised coupon, $c(t)$. Since the coupon bond was assumed to sell for more than the sum of the values of the coupon payments, then the agent could pocket the difference and would be prepared to undertake this riskless arbitrage at arbitrary scale. This, in turn, would enforce the equality.

Within this default free government bond market there is an implicit term structure that tells us the implied yield on any forward transaction for exchanging dollars from one point in time for dollars at another time. There are many equivalent ways to express this term structure; the sequence of yields to maturity, $y(t)$, is one, but the most common is by the forward curve, $f(t)$, derived from these yields. The current spot rate for a one year loan is simply $y(1)$ and we will label this as the spot forward rate, $f(0) = y(1)$. The rate for a one year loan that will commence one year from now and mature at time 2 is called the one year forward rate, $f(1)$. To derive $f(1)$, notice that an equivalent transaction to committing to lend for one year starting one year from now is buy a two year bond and, simultaneously, borrow the current cost, $p(2)$, with a one year loan, that is, sell one year bonds with a principal amount of $p(2)/p(1)$, which will produce proceeds of $p(2)$ today. At time 1 the current one year loan will be repaid and there will be a cash outflow of

$$\frac{p(2)}{p(1)} = \frac{(1 + y(1))}{(1 + y(2))^2}$$

At time 2, when the two year bond matures, there will be a cash inflow of \$1. The implicit forward rate for the loan, then, is a rate, $f(1)$, that equates the receipt of \$1 at time 2 discounted

$$\frac{1}{(1 + f(1))} = \frac{(1 + y(1))}{(1 + y(2))^2}$$

back to time 1 to the dollar outflow at time 1, or

$$(1 + f(1)) = \frac{(1 + y(2))^2}{(1 + y(1))}$$

By a similar argument, the forward rate, $f(t)$, on a loan to extend from period t to $t + 1$, is given by

$$(1 + f(t)) = \frac{(1 + y(t + 1))^{t+1}}{(1 + y(t))^t}$$

By rearranging these equations, we can see that

$$(1 + y(t)) = ((1 + f(0))\,(1 + f(1))\,...\,(1 + f(\mathrm{t} - 1)))^{1/t}$$

The vector of forward rates, $(f(0), \ldots, f(T))$ is called the term structure of interest rates and it extends as far as we have bonds that enable us to determine the individual rates. The dream of early researchers (and even of many current ones) is that like some prescient seer we can read these tea leaves and learn how the future will unfold. Surely the one year forward rate must be telling us something about what the spot one year interest rate will be one year from now. I think it is this hope, together, of course, with the evident commercial interest in the field, that has inspired past research and that fuels the vast current research effort in the fixed income markets.

Rational Expectations Theory: Certainty and Certainty Equivalence

The earliest theoretical work on the bond markets assumed that the future was certain and asked what determined the term structure in a world of certainty. The classical papers that begin this collection (Volume I, Part I) are consistent with a certain world, but they make a serious effort to cope with the presence of uncertainty. Recognizing that uncertainty prevents forward rates from perfectly predicting future spot rates, and reasoning by analogy with the certain case, these models assert that the actual distribution from which the spot rates are drawn is centered or biased in an estimable way from the current forward rates.

This early work posits certainty equivalent forms of the expectations hypothesis in which the market reaches equilibrium by the interplay of the demand and supply of different agents who treat their expectations as though they were certain – with, perhaps, an *ad hoc* adjustment for risk (see Wood (1964) and McCulloch (1975)). Modigliani and Sutch (1966) introduce their Preferred Habitat Theory in which demanders and suppliers have preferred habitats or maturities for their lending and borrowing. These agents are generally constrained in the positions they take, and, in some cases, have different beliefs and degrees of rationality. The requirement of certainty equivalence, in effect that forward rates are unbiased or differ by a simple constant from the mean of the distribution of future spot rates, while convenient is surprisingly strong and somewhat *ad hoc*. It is difficult to reconcile certainty equivalence with an equilibrium model of the term structure; it is not generally consistent with the standard models of individual behavior to have individuals indifferent to risk at all future maturities. (A notable and presciently modern exception is the book by Richard Roll, which, unfortunately, was too large for this collection.) This is, also, a literature that developed before the era when such models were subjected to the stronger rationality tests that we now demand of agents with asymmetric beliefs. In particular, when agents are allowed to have asymmetric beliefs no effort is made consistently to tie these beliefs back to the equilibrium that emerges or to ask what inferences they would draw from the prevailing term structure itself.

Nevertheless, these models remain important for our understanding of how individual beliefs are reflected in the equilibrium term structure and they also form the basis for the bulk of the extant empirical literature on the term structure (Volume I, Part II). Indeed, they are purposely constructed as linear to fit into the standard regression model and to permit the use of the standard tests of the efficient market hypothesis. An important consequence of these models is that the deviations of the future spot rate from the current forward rate should be unpredictable innovations, that is, that the market should be efficient. Fama (1984), Stambaugh (1988) and Campbell and Shiller (1991) are studies in this vein, and Kikugawa and Singleton (1994) extend this analysis to Japan. A common finding of this body of work is the persistence of term premia phenomena at certain future dates requiring *ad hoc* explanations. Another empirical focus is a variant of the Fisher hypothesis that the nominal observed interest rate is the sum of the real interest rate and inflationary expectations. In this work, rational expectations theory is used to disentangle the real and nominal interest rates (see Fama (1975) and Cornell (1978)).

Arbitrage and the Term Structure: The Derivatives Approach to Pricing

The absence of arbitrage is generally thought to be at the heart of what might be called neoclassical finance. Whether or not a market is in equilibrium may be a matter of semantics as much as it is one of science, but, even as science, the force of demand and supply can never be expected to be as powerful a price determinant as the simpler requirement that there be no arbitrage. In effect, this is demand and supply with infinitely elastic excess demand. In a world without uncertainty the forward rate in the term structure, say the one year forward rate two years out, is a perfect predictor of what the actual one year rate will be in two years. In a fashion very similar to the argument we used to derive the term structure of forward rates, this equality is enforced by arbitrage. If it were not so, then by arranging a forward contract commitment to lend or borrow at the forward rate two years from now, a sure profit could be made if this rate is different from the known rate that will prevail at that time. In a world of uncertainty, locking in a sure profit is no longer possible, but the work on rational expectations and the assumption of certainty equivalence is an attempt to extend by analogy the clean no arbitrage results of the certain world to the more difficult reality of uncertainty. Individuals with unwavering faith in the validity of their (common) predictions will enforce equilibria that are analytically equivalent to those for the certain case. The only distinction is the embarrassment of living in a world in which these firm predictions are only rarely true.

With the introduction of option pricing theory by Black, Scholes and Merton, a new approach to the theory of the term structure has been developed that realizes the hope of extending no arbitrage arguments in a natural way to stochastic environments, and that allows for both rational beliefs and a consistent equilibrium. We will call this the derivative approach to pricing, or the DAP, for short (Volume I, Part III). Merton (1973) provided an example of this approach to modeling the term structure and Vasicek (1977) developed the first parametric model. While on the surface the DAP would seem to have little in common with the older approaches and the rational expectations work, they are really quite close relatives. The fundamental theorem of neoclassical finance asserts (in part) that the absence of arbitrage is equivalent to the existence of a positive linear pricing operator. This is more familiarly known as risk neutral pricing (see Cox and Ross (1976)). The DAP is the implementation of the methodology of risk neutral pricing. The first step is the assumption of a stochastic mechanism for generating interest rate scenarios. These scenarios are then transformed into risk neutral scenarios, that is, interest rate scenarios in which we have removed the effects of risk aversion. The payoffs for any asset, for example, a bond of a particular maturity, are then discounted at the risk neutral term structure in each scenario and the results are averaged to get expected value, which, in the absence of arbitrage, will be the fair market value of the asset. Thus the DAP extends the term structure arguments from a sure world to an uncertain world and, as in a certain world, uses the force of arbitrage to pin down prices. Cox, Ingersoll and Ross (1985a, 1985b) develop these arguments and introduce the particular square root model in which the variance of short rates is proportional to the level. By contrast, in the Vasicek (1977) model the variance of the short interest rate is independent of the level of the rate and, consequently, negative interest rates are possible. Cox, Ingersoll and Ross (1981) compare this approach with the traditional certainty equivalent theory developed in Parts I and II.

The DAP also brings a new intuition to bear. The central intuition of the older literature was the use of current forward rates as predictors of future spot rates. Unexploited was the well known but largely ignored observation that most of the movement in the term structure of interest rates – the government or 'risk free' term structure – can be captured by a few factors or surrogates constructed from the bonds (see Cox, Ingersoll and Ross (1985a) and Brennan and Schwartz (1979)). For example, conditional on knowing next month's movement in the general level of interest rates, that is, parallel shifts in the yield curve, the change in long rates relative to short rates and the changing convexity of the curve, that is, changes in interest rate volatility, then the price change of any individual bond can be predicted with great accuracy (see Volume II, Part I). Since this information effectively completely determines the change in any individual bond price, it is, therefore, a sufficient set of statistics for the movement in the entire term structure. The absence of arbitrage and the fundamental theorem of risk neutral pricing imply that the expected rate of return on any bond will be linearly dependent on its exposures (betas) to these factors and the partial differential equations that express this relation are those that are solved to provide us with explicit term structure models. In models that admit of analytical solutions, the term structure and bond prices become functions of a set of state variables or, equivalently, a set of marketed securities, and bond prices depend on and are derived from these more primitive variables, hence the acronym, DAP (see Cox, Ingersoll and Ross (1985a, 1985b)). Heath, Jarrow and Morton (1992) build on these results to develop a framework in which specifying the volatilities of the forward rates forms the basis for term structure models and, thus, the set of state variables need not be finite. It is important to emphasize that these models are wholly rational in that prices are consistent with individual beliefs and these beliefs are predicated on the very distributions of interest rates that actually occur. It is also important to note that they provide some quite unexpected results, as, for example, in Dybvig, Ingersoll and Ross (1996) which shows that the yield to maturity on infinite bullet bonds can never fall.

The development of the DAP has been an explosive area of research. Much of this effort has focused on different approaches to backing out from the current term structure expectational variables associated with the stochastic development of the spot interest rate. Using one of the DAP rational intertemporal models, from the current term structure we should be able to retrieve the market's predictions of the distribution of future interest rates, including, for example, future volatilities. Understandably, this work is closely linked with the empirical work on testing these new theoretical option based approaches to the term structure, and it is certainly not surprising that the well articulated theories of the term structure have led to an extensive empirical literature and an enormous variety of models and approaches for applying them in the world of trading (Volume II, Parts I and II). As with all empirical efforts, this raises more questions than it answers. Perhaps a short summary of the most salient features of the empirical findings (of Volume I, Part II and Volume II, Part I) would be as follows. First, broadly speaking, the markets appear efficient with forward rates having predictive content for future spot rates. Second, it is clear that there are only a limited number of factors that are operative in describing the stochastic evolution of the term structure over time; probably more than one and, if one ignores the fine structure of individual bond prices, probably not more than three (see Litterman and Scheinkman (1991) and Litterman, Scheinkman and Weiss (1991)). Third, from a practical perspective, the DAP models provide a detailed format for the application of risk neutral pricing and for the accurate evaluation of the prices of interest sensitive securities, although no particular parametric model appears to have stable parameters (see Brown and Dybvig (1986), Gibbons and Ramaswamy (1993) and Brown and Schaefer (1994)). Not surprisingly, different implementations of these models, in particular different discrete time versions (Volume II, Part II), have become the workhorses for applications in the financial markets. Cox, Ross and Rubinstein (1979) develop a discrete time binomial model for the development of interest rates that is now widely used to model the term structure. Using variants of this model, Ho and Lee (1986) and Black, Derman and Toy (1990) show how to use the current term structure to estimate the model, and Hull and White (1990) fit the current term structure to time dependent versions of the Cox, Ingersoll and Ross (1985a) square root model and the Vasicek (1977) model.

As an aside, one of the ironies of the research on the debt markets is that this simplest of markets has given rise to some of the most sophisticated analysis in economics. Nor is this a new phenomenon. From the nineteenth century on, the mathematical analysis of the bond markets has always been much more sophisticated than the attendant analysis of the stock markets, and this despite the obvious fact that the equity markets are more complex than the bond markets. A government bond is usually assumed to have a fixed and immutable cash flow and the only thing that impacts on its value is the intertemporal cost of money, but the cash flows received by the holder of equity are impacted by a host of complications and contingencies. Indeed, when a bond becomes junky enough we call it a stock. Why, then, are our analyses of the stock market so conceptually simple with their price/earnings ratios and linear betas and factors, when compared with the modern nonlinear and continuous time term structure models we will introduce? The answer, I think, lies in the very simplicity of the fixed income markets. Since there is only one real issue on which to focus, namely what is the time value of money, it invites us to bring out all the mathematical artillery in our arsenals.

Taxes and Clientele Effects

It would be wrong, though, to give the impression that all is settled in the analysis of the term structure of interest rates; nothing could be further from the truth. Indeed, many of the old insights and theories are now being re-examined with the new methodologies. One of the earliest of these is that of the clientele effects. In the Preferred Habitat Theory (Modigliani and Sutch (1966)), in analogy with work on futures markets, it was observed that there were natural buyers and sellers of bonds of different maturities. Individuals who looked forward to retiring at a fixed age or who had large expenditures, for example, college expenses, at a fixed date in the future would be natural demanders of bonds of particular maturities. For this reason, it was argued that such individuals would bid up the prices and lower the equilibrium interest rates on such bonds and, as a consequence, forward rates would be biased downward as predictors of future spot rates. Within the context of the new option methodologies where all bonds are packages of a small number of factor exposures and, thus, ultimately perfectly substitutable, the impact of these clientele effects on interest rates is more suspect, but at least one such effect, that of taxes, would not disappear (Volume II, Part III). The certainty equivalent adjustments of the term structure for taxes focuses on finding equilibrium after tax rates (see McCulloch (1975) and Roll (1984)). Schaefer (1982) and Dybvig and Ross (1986) examine the interplay of this equilibrium with natural short sales constraints, such as those on shorting tax exempt government bonds. Dybvig and Ross (1986) show that this amends the fundamental theorem of risk neutral pricing to a nonlinear pricing operator. The DAP models of the term structure have also been extended to take account of the impact of taxes (Torous (1985)), and Constantinides and Ingersoll (1984) demonstrate that taxes on realizations and the holder's option to defer and change the character of gains and losses has an impact on the equilibrium term structure.

Uses and Applications of Term Structure Theory: Duration and Immunization

Associated with any model of the term structure of interest rates are positive implications and prescriptions for behavior. This is an old literature to which the DAP approaches to the term structure have given a new twist (Volume II, Part IV). In an effort to immunize its net value, a company or an institution that has both assets and liabilities may wish to manage its portfolio so as to ensure that changes in the value of the liabilities are offset by equal changes in the values of the assets. In the context of a life insurance company's liabilities this led to the development of measures of duration. Duration is intended to measure the impact of a change in the level of interest rates on the value of a fixed income instrument. Unfortunately, the exact meaning of the phrase 'a change in the level of interest rates' is ambiguous, and different measures of duration arise depending on whether we are considering a parallel shift in yields or a move in the current spot rate or some other such change. Redington (1952) and Fisher and Weil (1971) analyse immunization and duration for parallel shifts, and Bierwag (1977) and Ingersoll, Skelton and Weil (1978) consider some alternative stochastic movements. Ingersoll (1983) studies empirically whether immunization has actually been possible. Immunization clearly depends on the particular stochastic term structure model we are employing; in a stochastic model of the term structure a shift in a parameter is best interpreted as a movement along a particular interest rate scenario rather than as a parametric once and for all change. Using the DAP, Cox, Ingersoll and Ross (1979) examine immunization with a stochastic factor model where the term structure can shift in arbitrary ways, and Schaefer (1984) surveys the field where the term structure can shift arbitrarily. Whatever the details, though, the underlying intuition is that a company would be immunized against changes in the term structure of interest rates if the duration of the assets matched that of the liabilities. Using the DAP, the extent to which the original concept of duration is, perhaps, necessary but not sufficient for immunization is now well understood and more elaborate models for immunization have been developed.

Corporate Bonds, Mortgages and Exotics

Having extended our analysis of the term structure from a world of certainty to one of uncertainty, but with no risk of default, it is natural to extend it further to the world of risky bonds. The study of corporate bonds (Volume III, Part I) has developed as an area of its own, deeply rooted in corporate finance and with only a passing nod to the theory of the term structure of interest rates. This is unfortunate because our analysis of the term structure is now so well understood that it would be natural to meld it with the analysis of the corporate supply of bonds of different maturities. With a few notable exceptions this has not been done, but, taking the supply of corporate bonds as given, an extensive literature has grown that studies the valuation of corporate bonds. This began with the observation that the simplest corporate bond is equivalent to a default free government bond together with a short position in a put on the value of the company that issued it (see Black and Scholes (1973) and Merton (1974)) and, thus, is amenable to a DAP analysis. The literature on corporate bonds has subsequently developed with a focus on default risk and the other options embedded in most corporate bonds such as prepayment, callability and convertibility, but with only scant attention paid to term structure effects. Black and Cox (1976) examine bonds of different seniority and show that junior bonds can have stock-like features. Ingersoll (1977) studies the optimal call behavior for convertible bonds, Stulz and Johnson (1985) value secured debt, Brennan and Schwartz (1977) value bonds that have optional maturity and coupon features, and Dunn and Eades (1989) extend the study of the optimal conversion strategy. Litterman and Iben (1991) use the DAP to develop a theory of the term structure of credit spreads. The empirical likelihood of corporate bond default is estimated by Altman (1989). On the endogeneity of supply, Smith and Warner (1979) develop a contracting approach to the establishment of the convenants which define default and Diamond (1993) shows that private information can lead to a relation between the seniority and the maturity of corporate debt.

While the study of corporate bonds has proceeded largely independently of the related term structure effects, this has not been the case for other fixed income markets. The study of the mortgage markets and of more exotic interest sensitive securities has been a wonderful application of the DAP analysis to the idiosyncrasies of the instruments being studied (Volume III, Part II). In the case of mortgages, the central issue beyond the term structure itself is the possibility of early repayment. In other words, the borrower often has an option to refinance as interest rates decline and this limits the upside potential for the holder of the mortgage. Valuing mortgages is a combination of term structure valuation and the valuation of this option – often with empirical analysis of the exercise behavior of borrowers – and it is one of the most vibrant applications of risk neutral scenario term structure analysis. Pinkus, Hunter and Roll (1987) provide an introduction to this area and Richard and Roll (1989) focus on the central distinguishing feature, valuing the option to prepay the mortgage. Breeden (1991) provides a detailed analysis of fixed rate mortgages, Schwartz and Torous (1989) value bonds that are stripped from mortgages, and Titman and Torous (1989) empirically study the valuation of commercial mortgages.

The analysis of indexed bonds, that is, bonds whose cash flows change with interest rate changes or other parameter changes, is a second area of much research. Cox, Ingersoll and Ross (1980) apply the DAP to value bonds with coupons that float with movements in interest rates, and Ramaswamy and Sundaresan (1986) extend this analysis to cover additional covenant features of the bonds. Roll (1996) begins the analysis of the inflation indexed bonds recently issued by the US Treasury.

Conclusion: What We Know and What We Don't Know

We began our journey into the debt markets with the hope that we could use them to foretell the future. To some extent that naive view has been replaced by a more sophisticated one that has proven to be far more fruitful. We now know that we can value bonds and interest sensitive instruments as the discounted expected value under the risk neutral probability distribution, and this approach, the DAP, coupled with specific assumptions about the stochastic process that underlies spot rates, has cracked the puzzle. While we cannot predict the future, we can say that the bond prices we see today are discounted averages of values that would arise under different scenarios or evolutions of the future. Of course, this cannot tell us which of the scenarios will occur, but that is as it must be in an uncertain world.

While the new tools are quite powerful, as is always the case they raise more questions than they answer. For one thing, they have spotlighted how important it is for us to understand the exact stochastic motion of spot interest rates. For another, nearly all of the models of the term structure are models in which individuals have common knowledge. How this is to be reconciled with a world in which individuals have different beliefs is unknown and our study of markets in which asymmetric information is the prime driver is in its infancy. Given our empirical and practical successes, though – and fully aware of the foolishness inherent in being too smug about what we think we know – I would not expect research into these issues to fundamentally alter what we currently understand about the term structure.

More importantly, having made so much progress in understanding the workings of the bond markets, it is now time to use this new knowledge to enhance our understanding of the macroeconomic problems that provided much of the impetus for this study in the first place. To give one example, currently the bulk of macroeconomic investment analyses concerns how the level of interest rates influences aggregate investment. Work on the term structure, though, has taught us that the impact on investments may be much richer than the mere effect of interest rate levels. To the extent to which interest rates are volatile, every investment embodies an option on the financing cost and should be delayed if the cost of doing so is sufficiently low relative to the value of the option. This gives new meaning to Keynesian 'animal spirits' and provides a familiar and logical rationale for the fall-off in investment as times grow more uncertain. The flow back from the modern financial study of the term structure and, indeed, of all of finance, to the broader field of economics will be a major theme of future research.

Acknowledgement

The author is grateful to John Cox for his helpful comments and to Richard Roll, the Series Editor, for his extensive suggestions and work.

References

Fisher, Irving (1930), *The Theory of Interest*, Macmillan, New York.
Hicks, J.R. (1946), *Value and Capital*, 2nd edn, Clarendon Press, Oxford.
Macaulay, Frederick R. (1938), *Some Theoretical Problems suggested by The Movements of Interest Rates, Bond Yields and Stock Prices in the United States Since 1856*, National Bureau of Economic Research, New York.
Roll, Richard (1970), *The Behavior of Interest Rates*, Basic Books, New York.

Part I
The Classical Expectations Hypothesis

[1]

THE STRUCTURE OF INTEREST RATES

SUMMARY

I. Assumptions, 36.— Five propositions concerning the relationship between short and long rates, 37.— II. Influence of the costs of investment, 41.— Shiftability on the lenders' side, 43.— Two complications: many maturities, 44; the function of banks as changers of maturities, 45.— III. The influence of risk, 46.— IV. Expectations: the rational investor's decisions, 48; possible inconsistencies, 49. Effect of divergent expectations among members of the market, when the majority expect rising interest rates, 51; when "the market" expects rates to fall, 54.— V. Verification: movement of interest rates over time, 55; structure of yields on different maturities, 56.— VI. Bearing of this analysis on: influence of the discount rate on investment, 60; interest and the marginal efficiency of capital, 60; influence of wide gaps between short and long rates, 61; the "liquidity theory of interest," 62.

It has long been customary in works on the theory of interest to talk about *the* interest rate, and to deal with the problem of the difference between rates on different maturities by adding a footnote to the effect that the author understands by *the* interest rate the whole "family" of interest rates. Although the incompleteness of this kind of treatment was generally recognized, it was not regarded as an essential defect of the theory, because it was assumed that the whole "family" of interest rates moved up and down together, and that furthermore there was a tendency towards equalization of the different rates. The wide discrepancy between long and short rates which is at present observable, and which has existed ever since the middle of 1932 (apart from a short period during the banking crisis), has shown once again that these assumptions are not always borne out by the facts. The last few years have therefore seen new attempts to find out what determines the relationship between long and short interest rates. The present article tries to set out the theory of this relationship and to verify it so far as possible by reference to the facts.

I

In our approach to the problem of the relation between long and short-term rates, we shall start out, in this first section, by making three assumptions: (1) everybody concerned knows what the future short-term rates will be, i.e. there is accurate forecasting in the market; (2) there are no costs of investment, either for lenders or for borrowers; (3) there is complete shiftability for lenders as well as for borrowers. The lender who wants to invest for, say, ten years is equally well prepared to buy a ten-year bond or to lend on a one-year contract and to re-lend ten times. Similarly, a lender who wants to invest for only one year is in principle prepared to buy a ten-year bond or a bond of any other maturity and to sell it again after the first year. The same shiftability is assumed for the borrower.

Under these assumptions we can set out the following propositions as to the relationship between short and long rates:

(1) We can conceive of the long-term rate as a sort of average of the future short-term rates.[1] If we neglected the compound interest factor, it would be a simple arithmetic average. If we take account of that factor, the formula is more complicated.[2] The arithmetic average can, however, be used as a sufficiently close approximation for most purposes. The character of the long rate as an average of the future short rates can also be seen from the table on page 38, which shows short rates for successive years together with the yields in the same years for bonds with various maturities.

From the property of the long-term rate as the average of the future short rates propositions (2) to (5) below follow:

1. This has been pointed out by many authors. Cf. Irving Fisher, The Theory of Interest, 1930, p. 70; W. W. Riefler, Money Rates and Money Markets in the United States, 1930, p. 121; F. R. Macaulay, Some Theoretical Problems suggested by the Movement of Interest Rates, Bond Yields and Stock Prices in the United States since 1856, 1938, p. 29; R. G. Hawtrey, A Century of Bank Rate, 1938, p. 149; J. B. Williams, The Theory of Investment Value, 1938, p. 60; J. R. Hicks, Value and Capital, 1939, p. 145.

2. The exact formula, where R_n stands for the long rate on a loan which is repaid after n unit periods, r_1 for the short rate in period 1, r_2 for the short rate in period 2, etc., is:

$$R_n = \frac{(1+r_1)(1+r_2)\cdots(1+r_n)-1}{(1+r_2)(1+r_3)\cdots(1+r_n)+(1+r_3)\cdots(1+r_n)+\cdots+(1+r_n)+1}$$

This formula is based on the assumption that the long-term interest payments are made regularly at the same intervals as those at which the short rate is paid.

For a simpler formula, which is exact only for the case where all the interest on the long-term loan is paid out at the end of the loan transaction, see Hicks, op. cit., p. 145. (Cf. also Lindahl, Money and Capital, p. 188n. The latter's interpretation of the conditions under which the formula is valid is not quite accurate.)

SHORT AND LONG INTEREST RATES AND BOND PRICES[1]

I	II	III	IV	V	VI	VII	VIII
		5% BOND REDEEMABLE AT PAR AT END OF YEAR INDICATED IN COL. I			PRICES OF BONDS AT BEGINNING OF YEAR INDICATED IN COL. I		
Year	"Short" Rates (for one year) in Years Indicated in Col. I	Yield to Redemption (at beginning of first year)	Price (at beginning of first year)	Yield on Perpetual 5% Bond (at beginning of year indicated in Col. I)	Bond with 4 Years or More to Run	3-Year Bond	2-Year Bond
	%	%		%			
1	5	5	100	5.22	95.821	96.606	99.101
2	6	5.48	99.10	5.23	95.612	96.436	99.057
3	8	6.23	96.61	5.19	96.349	97.222	(100)
4	6	6.17	95.82	5.05	99.057	(100)	
5	5	5.92	95.82	5.00	100		
All following years	5	5.22[2]	95.82[2]	5.00	100		

[1] The calculations are based on the assumption of *annual* interest payments.
[2] Perpetual bond.

(2) The long rate can never fluctuate as widely as the short rate. All future changes in the short rate are already reflected in the present long rate, and the lapse of time which makes these changes in the short rate materialize affects the long rate only to the extent to which the average of these short rates becomes higher or lower by the vanishing of one short rate after the other into the past. (Compare, for instance, the movement of the yield of a perpetual bond with the movement of short-term rates, as shown in the table.)

(3) It is possible that the long rate may move temporarily contrariwise to the short rate. The long rate would rise, in spite of a simultaneous fall in the short rate, if the preceding short rate was lower than the average of the succeeding short rates, and *vice versa.* If we use the arithmetic average as a first approximation, it can easily be seen that this is so. If, for instance, the short rates in three successive years are four per cent, three per cent, and eight per cent, respectively, the yield on a bond redeemable at the end of the third year will be five per cent in the first year and will rise to five and one-half per cent in the second year, in spite of the fall in the short rate from the first to the second year.

(4) Turning now from the movement of the rates over time to the structure of the rates at a given moment of time, we see that the current yield to redemption of a long-term bond will be above the current short rate, provided the average of the future short rates up to the maturity date of the bond is above the current short rate (and *vice versa*). Such a situation also indicates that the long rate will rise later on, since the average of the short rates is bound to go up when the prevailing low short rate has passed by.

We can depict the yields to redemption, at a given date, of bonds of different maturities by drawing a graph in which the yields are plotted along the vertical axis and the redemption dates along the horizontal axis. We can, of course, obtain curves of all kinds as we assume different movements of future short-term rates. However, I will list here only a few possible patterns which are of practical significance, as we shall see later.

It is obvious that yields for bonds of different maturities will all be the same, i.e. the curve will be a straight line, if future short rates do not change. If the future short rates move in such a way that each successive short rate is above the average of the preceding ones (this condition, it may be noted, allows the short rate to fall temporarily at some point in the future without bringing about a kink in the curve), we obtain a scale of yields which is steadily ascending. The curve will, of course, flatten out if the short rates settle down at an unchanging level from a certain point onwards. In the reverse case, we obtain a scale which descends with the increasing length of the maturities and flattens out later. Finally, we obtain a scale of yields which first goes up with the increasing length of the maturities, and then goes down again when the short rates fall below the average of the preceding short rates. This is the case depicted in the table on page 38. (See columns II and III.) If we do not know the future short rates, but have a series of yields for bonds of different maturities, we can calculate from this the implied future short rates.[3]

(5) It is evident that the return on an investment for a given time is the same, no matter in what form the investment is made. The prices of bonds fluctuate in such a way as to make this result come true. An investor who wants, for instance, to invest his money for one year can either invest in the short-term market for one year, or buy a bond of any maturity and sell it after a year. For instance, if he buys a perpetual five per cent bond at the beginning of the first year for 95.821 and sells it at the beginning of the second year for 95.612, he makes exactly five per cent, which is equal to the short-term rate for one year. If he holds the bond for two years and sells it at 96.349 at the beginning of the third year, he again makes exactly the same as if he had invested short for five per cent in the first year and six per cent in the second year. Similarly, a person who bought this bond at the beginning of the second year at the price of 95.612, and sold it at the beginning of the third year at the price of 96.349, would make the six per cent which was the prevailing short rate in the second year. (A series of bond prices which move in the manner described may be found in the table on page 38.) The formula

$$\frac{\textit{Nominal interest rate} + \textit{capital gain (or} - \textit{capital loss)}}{\textit{purchasing price}}$$

always gives a return which is equivalent to what the investor would have obtained if he had invested and reinvested at short term for the same time. Thus, as long as the long-term rate expresses the

3. Cf. Keynes, General Theory, p. 168f., and Williams, op. cit., Chap. XX.

average of the future short-term rates, it does not pay to borrow short and to buy long-term bonds, even though the long-term interest rate (whether this be represented by the running yield or by the yield to redemption) may be above the short-term rate. Whoever engages in such a transaction will discover, when he sells the bond, that he loses on capital account exactly what he thought to gain on interest account. There is, therefore, no mechanism which tends to make short and long rates *equal*. However, there is a mechanism which makes short and long rates *consistent* with each other. Suppose the price of a bond were such that its yield to redemption were above the average of the future short rates for the time for which the bond has to run; then it would pay to borrow short and buy the bond. This process would lower the yield of the bond until it became equal to the "*average*" of the future short rates.[4]

II

The next step in our analysis will be to introduce the costs of investment. We shall proceed on the assumption that the costs of borrowing *per unit of time* are the smaller, the longer the time for which the money is borrowed. This assumption seems on the whole to be justified. As far as bonds are concerned, the absolute costs to

4. Macaulay in dealing with the same problem reaches a very strange result. Having postulated perfect forecasting in the market, he says, "If in a tight short-term money market in which six-month obligations of the highest grade are selling on a seven per cent per annum basis, a four per cent bond be selling at par, its *price* at the end of the six-month period must have *risen* to $101.50, if it is to show a return of seven per cent per annum for the six-month period. This, of course, means a *fall* in the 'yield' during the six months. To preserve the theoretical relationship between present long-term and future short-term interest rates, the 'yields' of bonds of the highest grade should *fall* during a period in which short-term rates are higher than the yields of the bonds and *rise* during a period in which short-term rates are lower." (Op. cit., p. 33.) Macaulay admits that experience shows more nearly the opposite result, from which he concludes that the actual forecasting done by the market is very bad. It is, however, his own theoretical deductions which are at fault. Under his assumption of correct forecasting, the initial price of 100 for a four per cent bond, when the rate in the short-term market is seven per cent, is only possible if the later short rates are going to be far below seven per cent. That is to say, the opposite movement of short-rate and yield in the example is only temporarily possible. If the short rate is above the yield to redemption on a bond, this yield will fall only under the condition that the average of the future short rates is below the current short rate. Therefore Macaulay's paradoxical conclusion that the yield of a bond has to fall if the short rate is above the yield, and *vice versa*, is not substantiated.

be paid to underwriters and other middlemen do not vary with the length of the maturity of the bond, which means that the costs per unit of time are the smaller, the longer the maturity.[5] In the case of bank loans (where the costs of borrowing are not separated out as such, but are included in the interest rate) the same assumption can be made, since the investigation of the borrower's credit worthiness requires more or less the same procedure, and therefore the same costs, no matter for how long a period the loan is granted.

The question now is: how do these costs of borrowing influence the relation of short to long rates? In order to answer this question, I shall, as a first approximation, treat these costs (of running the banking business, underwriting, etc.) as a price which has to be paid to a third party (banks, etc.) simply and solely for the service of bringing lenders and borrowers together. If we are to isolate the influence of the cost factor, we must assume that the rate of interest, once it is established in the market, will not change in the future. This assumption is necessary in order to exclude discrepancies between short and long rates which may arise merely because it is known or expected that the short rates will rise or fall in the future (cf. Section I).

As a starting point, we may think of a situation where there is no shiftability, either on the borrowers' or on the lenders' side. This means that an investor who invests long cannot withdraw his funds before the bond is redeemed, so that a person who has funds at his disposal for a shorter time than the bond has to run has no other choice than to invest in the short market. Nor can a borrower finance long-term capital requirements by borrowing short and continually renewing the loan. In such a case the long and short rates (for the time being I assume only two maturities, "long" and "short") are independent of each other. It is very likely that in this situation the long rate will be above the short, because there will be relatively few funds whose owners can part with them irrevocably for a very long time, whereas the demand for long-term

5. The costs of floating bonds do vary, however, according to the amount borrowed. An investigation by the Securities and Exchange Commission shows that they range between 9.2 per cent for issues of less than 250,000 dollars and 2.3 per cent for issues of 25,000,000 dollars and over. The reader may introduce this factor in the following way: the "costs of borrowing," as we refer to them in the text, may be regarded as the minimum costs of borrowing, to which additions have to be made on the side of the borrower if he borrows in amounts smaller than that to which the minimum applies, just as additions have to be made for increasing degrees of risk.

funds will be relatively large owing to the importance of fixed capital. By long and short rate in this connection we mean the rate which the lender gets (i.e. exclusive of the costs). The *borrower's* rate, which *includes* these costs, will be higher than this *lender's* rate, and the short rate relatively more so than the long, i.e. the difference between the long and short rates will be smaller for the borrowers than it will for the lenders.

The demand and supply conditions in the two markets which prevail under the conditions assumed above (i.e. where there is no shifting) we shall henceforth call the "original distribution," and we shall generally assume that, for the reasons indicated, this distribution is such as to give a long-term rate which is above the short-term rate.

Let us now introduce shiftability on the lenders' side. Shifting will take place from the short market to the long, since the lender's rate is higher there. In other words, those who have short funds to invest will buy bonds and sell them after a time. This process will bring the long rate down. Moving in and out of the long market, however, entails special costs, consisting of a brokerage fee for the buying transaction and a brokerage fee *plus* a transfer tax for the selling transaction. These costs of shifting, expressed as a percentage per unit of time of the funds lent, vary of course for the different "shifters" according to the length of time for which they have their funds available. Shifting will go on, then, until the lender's long rate has been brought down to a level which is above the lender's short rate by an amount equal to the costs of shifting for what we may call the "marginal shifter," i.e. the person for whom the costs of shifting per unit of time are such that it only just pays to shift into the long market.[6] For all shifters from the short into the long market we have to distinguish between the

6. To give an example. Let us suppose that the marginal shifter has his funds available for three months. If we assume a brokerage fee of $2 per $1,000 purchase price and a transfer tax of 40 cents, then the total costs of shifting (covering purchase and sale) will be $4.40 on $1,000 for three months, that is, 1.76 per cent per annum, and the lender's gross long rate must be higher than the lender's short rate by that amount. This figure is not quite accurate since the long investor has also to pay a brokerage fee (for purchasing), which must be reimbursed as part of the interest rate he receives. Thus, strictly speaking, it is only the *difference* in the costs (per unit of time) of investing for the long lender and investing and disinvesting for the short lender which has to be taken into account in calculating the effect of the costs of shifting on the gap between the lender's long and short rates. However, if we take the period of long lending long enough we can neglect this refinement.

gross long rate, which includes the costs of shifting, and the net long rate, which excludes them. The net rate which the marginal shifter receives in the long market will be the same as he could obtain in the short market. A long investor who can stay in the long market until the bond is redeemed will, of course, receive the whole of the lender's gross long rate as a net rate, and all those shifters who have their funds available for a longer time than the marginal shifter will receive as a net rate less than the long investor, but more than the marginal shifter, depending on the length of time for which they have their funds available.

As far as the *borrower's* rates are concerned, the long rate as well as the short rate will be above the corresponding lender's rates, owing to the costs of borrowing. In comparing the borrower's long rate with the borrower's short rate, we have to remember that the costs of borrowing short are higher than the costs of borrowing long. But to the latter we now have to add the costs of shifting, which, as we have seen, make the lender's gross long rate higher than the lender's short rate. Whether the net effect will be to make the borrower's long rate higher than the borrower's short rate depends on the magnitude of the costs of shifting and the time over which they have to be spread. In practice they are not likely to be such as to raise the borrower's long rate above the borrower's short rate.

The analysis made so far has to be supplemented in two respects.[7] In the first place we do not have only two maturities for which contracts can be made, but many more. This does not invalidate our previous conclusions, but it makes it possible for lenders' rates on some relatively long loans to be above the rates on shorter loans by less than the amount which corresponds to the costs of shifting between the relevant markets. Suppose, for

7. We neglect the possibility that the borrowers too may shift. If, as is most likely, the borrower's short rate is above the borrower's long rate after the shifting on the lender's side has taken place, nothing has to be added to the conclusions reached above. Shifting on the borrower's side from long to short would not pay. Shifting from short to long would not pay either, since the funds, when they were set free in the borrower's enterprise as soon as the need for them had passed, would have to be lent out by him at the lower lender's rate. If, however, the borrower's short rate were below the borrower's long rate, borrowers would shift from the long market to the short provided the costs of so doing were less than the difference between the two rates. The effect of this factor would be to restrict the amount of shifting from the short to the long market on the lender's side to smaller proportions than would obtain in the absence of shifting on the borrower's side.

instance, that we have the following three maturities: short, medium and long, and that in the "original distribution" the rates ascend with the increasing length of the maturity. Shifting will then take place from the medium into the long market, and from the short into the medium market, until the lender's long rate is above the medium rate by the marginal cost of shifting from the medium to the long market, and the medium rate above the short rate by the marginal costs of shifting from the short to the medium market. But the lender's long rate need not be sufficiently above the short rate to make it pay to shift from the short into the long market.[8] Thus in the final adjustment the gaps between some of the rates may be less than the minimum costs of shifting between the two respective markets.

Secondly, up to this point we have treated the banks as agents, the function of which is simply to bring would-be lenders into direct touch with would-be borrowers. However, the banks do more than that. They change shorter maturities into longer ones. Even though the funds of the depositors may be short funds, they are invested by the banks in commercial loans with longer maturities or even in bonds. How does this shifting activity of the banks affect the rates for different maturities? Suppose that under a direct lending system the funds of the marginal shifter into the long market would be three months funds and that all shorter funds would be lent out in the short market. If these shorter funds are deposited with a bank, the bank can shift part of them into longer maturities without incurring such high costs of shifting as the marginal shifter would incur in the case of direct lending. This is because the bank, since it can rely on the automatic replacement of one depositor by another, does not have to disinvest in three months time. The result will be that the borrower's as well as the lender's rates on longer maturities will be lower, and the discrepancy between the short and long rates smaller, than if the lenders lent directly to borrowers. The owner of three-months funds will in consequence fall below the margin of shifting and will have to become a depositor too. Shifting by lenders on their own

8. It is, of course, possible to conceive of an "original distribution" in which the long rate is so high, and/or so few medium-term funds are available, that it pays for the shortest funds to shift into the long market. In this case the long rate would be above the *medium* rate by more than the costs of shifting from the medium into the long market.

account will not pay, unless they have their funds for a much longer time than was needed before the banks intervened.

We may summarize the main points of the analysis as follows:

(1) The costs of borrowing make the borrower's short and long rates higher than the corresponding lender's rates.

(2) The costs of shifting tend to make the lender's long rate somewhat higher than the lender's short rate. There can be no doubt that the costs of shifting alone prevent people with relatively short funds from investing in bonds, and induce them to leave their funds on deposit with a bank where they receive either no interest at all or else a much lower rate than they would receive in the long market.

(3) Within each market the lenders obtain a net rate which is the higher the longer the time for which they have their funds available.

(4) The costs of borrowing make for a higher borrower's short rate than long rate. The costs of shifting for the lender, although they make for a higher long rate than short rate, are not likely to be sufficient to raise the borrower's long rate to equality with, or above, the borrower's short rate. It is not possible to prove this accurately by reference to the facts. For the difference between the rates on bank loans and the long-term rate (say on bonds) is not only dependent on the cost factor, but is also influenced by expectations as to the future course of interest rates. However, it seems safe to say that in "quiet" times, when there is no particular reason for the market to expect changes in interest rates, the customer's rates charged by the banks are considerably above high-grade bond yields,[9] even if we add to these latter a percentage figure expressing the per annum costs of borrowing through the bond market.

III

In this section uncertainty and risk will be introduced, i.e. we shall assume that the future movement of interest rates is unknown, but that people have certain expectations about their

9. Cf. W. W. Riefler, op. cit., p. 67. The chart given there, which shows that the yield on the average high-grade bond was from 1919 to 1928 (with the exception of a few months in 1924) below the average of the rates charged to customers by banks in the larger cities, is not an unimpeachable proof, since the credit risk of the two series may be different. However, the spread seems to be wide enough to warrant our conclusion that the borrower's short rate is higher than the borrower's long rate.

movement. Risk of default, however, will be excluded from the discussion; the only risk considered will be that associated with changes in interest rates.

In order to investigate the influence of this risk factor, we shall here analyze the case where all members of the market believe it most likely (i.e. expect) that the interest rate will remain what it is and that the chance of a rise and the chance of a fall are even. This assumption allows us to isolate the influence of the risk factor, because it excludes discrepancies between the rates which are due solely to the fact that the members of the market *expect* the interest rate to rise or to fall.

How, then, does the risk factor influence the equilibrium relationship between the rates on various maturities? This question has been given two conflicting answers in the literature. Williams,[1] for instance, believes that long and short rates will be equal under these conditions. Hicks[2] thinks that the long rate will be above the short.

Suppose that we have maturities for all the various lengths of time for which different investors think they have their funds available, and suppose further that in the "original distribution" the rates are higher the longer the maturities. Those who move into the latter have a chance that the return on their investment, $\frac{\text{nominal rate} + \text{capital gain or} - \text{capital loss}}{\text{purchase price}}$, may be above what they can obtain in their "original" markets for the same period, but they also run the risk that the return may be below that figure. Consequently, if the attitude of the marginal shifter into the longer market is such that he weights the unfavorable chance more heavily than the favorable one, or in other words that he demands a certain compensation for the risk of disappointment, he will not be satisfied with a rate in the longer market which is above the rate in his own market simply by the cost of shifting. It follows that in equilibrium we shall have a scale of rates which ascends with the length of the maturities more steeply than would be the case if we had the cost of shifting alone to consider. A detailed analysis of what determines the gaps between the yields on different maturities would have to follow the lines of the argument developed in section II, which may be applied to the effect of the

1. J. B. Williams, op. cit., p. 341.
2. J. R. Hicks, op. cit., p. 166.

risk premium just as well as to the effect of the costs of shifting.

The result just arrived at is, however, entirely dependent on our assumption about the "original distribution." The essence of the matter is that an investor may ask for a risk premium whenever he moves out of his "original" market, no matter whether he moves into a shorter or longer market, because in either case the return which he will obtain in the market to which he moves is uncertain. Therefore, if we assume an "original distribution" in which the scale of rates descends, or has ups-and-downs, as we pass from the shorter to the longer maturities, we obtain entirely different results. It is not legitimate, therefore, to conclude (with Hicks) that the effect of the risk factor, as such, must necessarily be to make long rates higher than shorter ones. On the other hand, the view (of Williams) that the risk factor will be without effect on the relationship between the rates is correct only provided the investors do not weight the chance of a loss more heavily than the equal chance of a gain.[3]

IV

In section I we laid down certain propositions as to the relationship between interest rates on various maturities under the assumption of complete foresight. If we were content to speak, as is customary, in the vague terms of "expectations of the market," we should now only have to replace the word "foreseen" by the word "expected," and could then repeat the propositions of section I amplified by the application of what has been said on the influence of the cost and the risk factors. However, this would be correct only if it could be assumed that all members of the market have identical expectations. Only then would it make sense to look upon the long rate as being fundamentally the average of the expected future short rates. We know, however, that the different members of the market seldom have identical expectations, and it is the analysis of this aspect to which we shall now turn.

It will be helpful, in the first instance, to set out the method which a rational investor would have to follow in deciding in which market (short or long) it pays for him to invest. (For the time being

3. In the analysis in the text we made two unrealistic assumptions, (1) that everybody knows exactly for how long he has his funds available and (2) that there are maturities for all the different lengths of time for which investors think they can invest. However, the main conclusions would not be materially altered, if we dropped these two assumptions.

we assume that there are only two maturities.) An owner of funds will go into the long market if he thinks the return he can make there over the time for which he has his funds available will be above the return he can make in the short market over the same time, and *vice versa*. His estimate of the relative profitability of the two markets will be based on his expectations[4] about future interest rates and bond prices, and will be reflected in the price he is willing to pay for the long-term bond at the present moment. In the simplest case he will determine this price by the following method. He will discount the price at which he expects to sell the bond at the date when he wants to disinvest (this price is dependent on what he anticipates the long rate will be at that date) and all the interest payments up to that time, back to the present moment, using as the discount factor for each year the short rate which he expects to prevail in that year. This procedure gives him a bond valuation which he will compare with the existing bond price in the market. If the latter is higher than the former, he will invest in the short market instead of buying the bond, since this relationship indicates that he can make more in the short market than in the long. If the bond price in the market is lower than his "subjective" bond price, he will invest long. If the two prices are identical he will be indifferent as between the long and short markets, since he expects to make the same in both.[5] In short, he is prepared to pay a price for the bond which is equal to or lower than the price obtained by discounting all the future payments in the fashion described above.

This, however, is not the end of the matter. The fact that the discounting procedure just described may give the individual investor a "subjective" bond valuation which diverges from the current price in the market implies that the current long rate does not necessarily reflect the future short rates which that investor expects. Similarly, his expectations as to the future long rates need not be consistent with his expectations as to the future short rates. In Section I, where we assumed accurate forecasting for

4. In the remainder of the discussion I shall, for brevity's sake, use the expression "expected" interest rate or bond price to denote the rate or price which the person uses in making his calculation. It thus reflects the result both of the probability estimate and of the risk premium.

5. Since it is possible for a person to adopt a different attitude towards risk with respect to different portions of his funds, it may be that an investor will invest part of his funds in the short market and part in the long.

everybody concerned, there was no need to distinguish between the two, since the course of long rates was automatically determined, once we assumed the course of future short rates to be definitely known. In the present case, however, an investor's personal expectations about the future course of short rates do not necessarily commit him as to his expectations about the long rate, since the latter depends, not on what *he* thinks about the future short rates, but what the "market," i.e. other people, think about them. The individual investor, therefore, may quite reasonably form an opinion about the future long rate which is inconsistent with his opinion about future short rates. From this it follows that an investor, if he discounts, as above, the bond price expected at the end of his entire investment period plus the interest payments up to that time, and obtains a "subjective" bond value which is below (or above) the current bond price, will not necessarily go into the short market (or the long market) now.

There are two main possibilities. First, he may expect that at some intermediate date the yield on the bond (to his personal disinvestment date) will fall below the average of the short rates which he expects to prevail from this intermediate date to the date of his final disinvestment. This means that he expects the bond price to be relatively *high* at the intermediate date. If the bond valuation obtained by discounting *this* price, along with the interest payments, exceeds the current bond price in the market, he will go into the long market now (with the intention of shifting into the short market later). If it is below, he will of course go into the short market from the start.

The second possibility is that the investor may expect the yield on the bond at some intermediate date to exceed the average of the short rates from that date onwards, i.e. he expects the market price of the bond to be relatively *low* at that date. He will then contemplate going into the short market now and into the long market later. There will, however, be some price at which it will be worth his while to go into the long market now instead of waiting. In order to calculate this price, he will discount the expected price at the contemplated buying date along with the interest payments up to that date, back to the present moment. If he were to buy the bond now at this price, he would make just as much as if he went into the short market first and waited till later before buying the bond. If the current bond price is below this "subjective" bond value, it will pay him to go into the long market now; if it is above, he will invest short now, and go into the long market later.

So we see that for any pattern[6] of expectations the investor arrives at a "subjective" bond value which constitutes the maximum price which he is prepared to bid for the bond in the market. We can now proceed to our main task: the analysis of the effect of differences in expectations among the different members of the market.

(1) We may suppose that, following a situation in which there has been equality between the long and short rates, the expectations of most of the owners of funds change in the direction of *rising* interest rates. *They change in different degrees for different persons.* On the basis of the analysis given above, all those who expect such a rise will arrive at "subjective" bond values which are below the current price in the market. We may range the owners of funds in order of the bond prices which they are willing to pay, or, what is the same thing, in order of the yields to redemption (or long rates) which these "subjective" bond prices imply. All those who now demand "subjective" long rates which are higher than the current long rate in the market will prefer to invest in the short market, their inducement to do so being the greater the wider the gap between their "subjective" long rate and the actual long rate. This will lead to an increase in the volume of funds offered in the short market and a decrease in the volume offered in the long market, as compared with the situation from which we started. The effect will be to lower the short rate and to raise the long, the degree of the movement depending on the elasticities of demand for short and long funds. The rise in the long rate will tend to check the movement from the long into the short market, since the higher long rate will now exceed the "subjective" rates of some investors, thus wiping out their preference for the short market. The long rate will rise until two conditions are fulfilled: (*a*) the supply of and demand for funds in each market are equal, and (*b*) all owners of funds whose "subjective" long rates are higher than the current long rate are in the short market. One amendment,

6. More complicated cases such as going into the long market now, getting out later, and going in again still later, etc., can be treated by the same method. They are, however, of minor importance in practice, since investors hardly ever have sufficiently definite ideas to allow them to plan such complicated investment schemes.

however, must be made to the foregoing exposition. We must suppose that the adjustment of the long and short rates in the process of shifting funds from the long into the short market will cause some slight revision of the "subjective" long rates for two reasons: (*a*) because the current short rate, which is one of the discount factors entering into the calculation of the "subjective" long rates, goes down, thus lowering the "subjective" long rates; and (*b*) because the expectations about the course of future short (and long) rates are likely to be affected. In which direction this second factor will work we cannot say *a priori*, and consequently we cannot make any definite statement about the direction in which the "subjective" long rates will be affected by the two factors combined.

The following diagram illustrates the way in which the new equilibrium is reached after expectations have changed. *ON* is the total volume of funds (assumed fixed) which is available for investment in both markets together. $D^L D^L$ is the demand curve for

FIGURE I

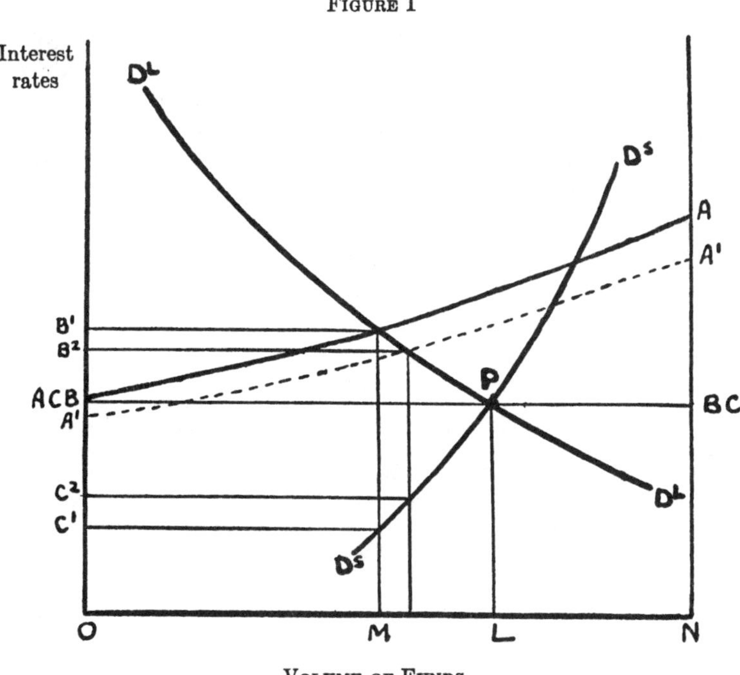

long funds and $D^S D^S$ (drawn with *N* as the origin) is the demand curve for short funds. Then in the initial situation, before expectations change, the long rate and short rate are both equal to *OB*, and *OL* is invested in the long market and *NL* in the short. *AA* is what we shall call the "expectations" curve: it represents the line-up of the "subjective" long rates which correspond to people's expectations after the latter have changed. Now assuming that this curve remains unaltered throughout the process of adjustment, we see that equilibrium will be reëstablished with the long rate *OB′*, the short rate *OC′*, *OM* invested in the long market, and *NM* in the short market. And the spread between the long and short rates will have increased from zero to *C′B′*. However, we must suppose that while the change in the rates is taking place, *AA* will tend to shift, and the final equilibrium position will give a spread between the rates which is slightly smaller or slightly larger (according to whether the expectations curve shifts to the right or to the left) than that arrived at on the basis of the original expectations curve.[7]

The analysis above shows that the final spread between the two rates will depend on two sets of factors. (1) The more elastic are the demand curves for short and long funds over the relevant range the smaller will be the spread. (2) Broadly speaking, the greater the number of investors (weighted by the volume of their funds) who have high "subjective" long rates, and the higher these rates are, the more funds will be invested in the short market and the greater will be the final spread. More accurately, the spread depends on (*a*) the shape of the expectations curve (the steeper the curve over the relevant range the greater the spread), and (*b*) the direction in which and the degree to which this curve shifts in response to changing long and short rates during the process of adjustment.[8]

7. The position of the expectations curve corresponding to the rates *OC″* and *OB′* would, let us suppose, be *A′A′*. But this curve would again give different interest rates OC^2 and OB^2, and the latter would in turn react back on the expectations curve. All that we can say, then, is that in equilibrium the long rate will be somewhere between *OB′* and OB^2 and the short rate somewhere between *OC″* and OC^2.

8. We have not taken into account the possibility that the borrowers also may shift according to their expectations about future interest rates. However, there is not likely to be much shifting on the borrowers' side in the situation analysed in the text. The borrowers, unless they have opposite ideas from the lenders about the future of interest rates, have no reason to shift.

I can do no more than briefly indicate the results that are obtained if we assume the existence of more than two maturities. An investor will calculate a "subjective" value, on the basis of his expectations, for each of the various maturities, and if he expects a rise in interest rates he will obtain a higher value the shorter the maturity. This will give the result that if most investors expect rising interest rates in the future, the rates on those maturities of which the redemption date lies within the period during which the rising interest rates are expected will ascend with the length of the maturities. In equilibrium all those owners of funds who expect the rates to rise soon and/or to a large extent will have their funds in the shorter maturities, and all those who expect the rates to rise later and/or to a smaller extent will have them in the longer maturities.[9]

(2) There is no need to give a detailed analysis of the case where "the market" expects interest rates to fall. The same sort of analysis could be applied as was used in case (1). In terms of the diagram on page 52 we should have an expectations curve which lay below *BB* over most of its length. With such a state of expectations we obtain a scale of interest rates which descends with the increasing length of the maturities. But two additional remarks are called for. First, borrowers may shift from long to short borrowing, if they too expect a fall in the interest rates. This will tend to accentuate the discrepancy between the short and the long rates which is brought about by the behavior of the lenders. Secondly, it seems likely that the short rate cannot remain above the long for such a lengthy period as the long rate can remain above the short. The reason is that in this case banks will feel more inclined to shift from the long to the short market, because the higher yield will here be combined with compliance with the traditional views about the greater liquidity of short-term paper, whereas the shift from the short to the long market contravenes the liquidity rule.[1]

Those who want funds for long-term purposes will, of course, have an additional incentive to borrow in the long market, if they think that the long rate is going to rise. Those, on the other hand, who want short-term funds are not likely to borrow long, no matter what they think about the future rates.

9. A closer analysis, which is too lengthy to be undertaken here, would also have to take account of the volume of the securities outstanding (or the demand for funds) under each of the various maturities, since this factor will influence the size of the spread between the rates on those maturities.

1. In more general terms this means that, in addition to costs and

(3) The diagram can also be used to show that we may obtain *equal* interest rates, not only if *all* members of the market expect the interest rate to remain stable[2] (I am here neglecting the cost factor), but also if different members have different expectations, provided the distribution of the latter is such as to give an "expectations curve" which goes through the point P in the diagram — an unlikely coincidence.

V

In this section we shall try to verify some of the propositions of Section I as amplified by what has been said in Sections II, III and IV. In order to simplify the terminology, we shall talk in terms of the "expectations of the market." The reader will be aware, from the analysis of Section IV, of the complicated relationships that are hidden behind this term.

(1) We turn first to the *movement* of the interest rates over time. Although the fact that different people in the market hold different opinions about the course of the rates that may be expected to prevail in the future means that there is no precise

uncertainty, certain institutional factors also influence the structure of interest rates. American banks look upon Government bonds and notes with maturities up to five years as eligible for holding in their "secondary reserve." This creates a strong demand for such bonds, and we may presume that this factor by itself makes for lower interest rates on investments with maturities up to five years than on those with longer maturities. (Compare the yields for 1938 on the chart on page 58, where a wide gap is observable between the yield on the five-year maturity and the yield on the next longer maturity.) English banks aim at keeping a certain relatively fixed percentage of their assets (the thirty per cent ratio) in the form of cash and short material. There is therefore a relatively fixed supply of funds whose owners are not prepared to shift them into the long market, even if the rate there is higher. This makes it possible for the Treasury to cause the short rate to fall below the long rate, simply by curtailing the issue of treasury bills. This discrepancy will last as long as the shortage of treasury bills continues, and it is one which cannot be explained in terms of expectations. Furthermore, within each category of short material, the banks, for a variety of institutional reasons, look upon shorter maturities as being more liquid than longer ones. For this reason three-months bills are preferred to six-months bills in the commercial paper and the bankers' acceptances markets, and call loans to time loans to the stock exchange. The result is that the rates are slightly lower on the shorter maturities than on the longer maturities within the same category of short loans. To this rule there are only very rare exceptions. Apparently only if it is practically certain that the rate on the shorter maturities is going to fall (for instance, if bankers are sure that the official discount rate is going to be lowered) will the rate on the longer term bills be below the rate on the shorter term ones (as in England in December, 1929).

2. Cf. p. 39.

sense in which we can call the long rate an average of the expected future short rates, it remains nevertheless true that the long rate (or bond yield) is, in the complicated way described in Section IV, the outcome of the whole pattern of expectations of the members of the market as to the future short rates during the time the bond has to run. This still gives the result that the long rate cannot fluctuate as widely as the short rate. That the long rate is in practice more stable than the short rate is such a familiar fact as to require no statistical proof.

The long rate can move temporarily contrariwise to the short rate. The long rate may fall while the short rate rises, provided "the market" thinks future short rates will be below the short rate from which the rise starts, and *vice versa.* Considering that "the market" does not form any very definite idea about future short rates which are still a long time ahead, we should not expect this to happen very often. Indeed, as a rule, the long rate is either entirely unaffected by changes in the short rate or else it moves very slightly in the same direction as the latter. A contrary movement of short and long rates is most likely to be found in connection with seasonal fluctuations of the short rate. The market knows that these are temporary, and if, for instance, a seasonal rise in the short rate impinges on a situation in which the general tendency is expected to be a fall in the rates, we may obtain such a contrary movement. This situation seems to have prevailed in the latter half of 1930 in London, when the market rate on three-months bank bills rose from 2.07 per cent in September to 2.18 per cent in November, while during the same time the yield on 2½ per cent Consols fell from 4.52 per cent to 4.27 per cent.[3] Since it was in the early phase of the depression, a general fall in the rates could reasonably be expected, despite the seasonal rise in the short market. Other instances of the same kind can be found.

(2) We turn now to the structure of yields on different maturities at a given date. If nobody concerned has any reason to believe that the future short rates will be higher or lower than the present rates, we shall obtain approximately[4] equal yields for different maturities. Such a situation is likely to occur at a time when busi-

3. The figures cited are the monthly averages.

4. The risk and cost factors make, as we saw previously, for rates which ascend slightly with the increasing length of the maturity. However, the differences due to these factors are probably so slight in practice that they will always be overshadowed by the expectations factor.

ness is good without, however, showing any sign of a boom. This was approximately the state of affairs in 1927. The chart on p. 58 shows that in May of that year Government bonds and notes, which for purposes of comparison have the advantage of being without default risk, show about the same yields for different maturities.[5] (There seems to be a slight tendency towards lower yields for longer maturities.) Not all yields are exactly in line. There are several reasons for this. First, Government bonds and notes are not all treated alike with respect to tax exemption.[6] Secondly, the impression gained from studying the material is that the "arbitrage" in the bond market does not work as perfectly as it does, for instance, in the foreign exchange market, so that a yield may be out of line for this reason alone.[7] Thirdly, the fact that it is not known for certain that the bond will be redeemed either at the first optional call date or else at the final maturity date (it may be redeemed at some date in between) may account for some irregularities. (Cf. footnote 8 below). But despite the influence of these factors the figures for the date we have chosen in 1927 (as depicted in the chart) are very nearly on the same level.

We shall have a line of yields descending continuously with maturities of increasing lengths and then flattening out, if the short rates are expected to fall in the near future and then to reach a certain level where they will stay. Such a situation is likely to prevail in a financial crisis at the top of a boom, or what is believed to be the top of a boom. On March 26, 1929, there was a crash on the stock exchange. For this date we obtain an almost continuous downward movement in the yields for maturities of increasing lengths, as can again be seen in the chart on p. 58.[8]

5. In conformity with the generally accepted practice, the yields are calculated to maturity, if the bonds are selling below par, and to the earliest optional call date, if they are selling above par.

6. For instance, the First Liberty Loan 3½ per cent redeemable 1932–47 shows a yield to the call date 1932 (against which year it is plotted in the chart) of 3.3 per cent, which is below the yields on the other securities redeemable at the same time. This can be explained by reference to the fact that this bond is exempt from all surtax, whereas the others are only partially exempt.

7. The high yield (3.8 per cent) on the Second Liberty Loan 4 per cent 1927–42 (calculated to the call date and plotted against the year 1927 in the chart) is difficult to explain, considering the fact that the Second Liberty Loan Converted 4¼ per cent 1927–42 with exactly the same tax features has a yield of only 3.4 per cent.

8. A glance at the chart shows that one yield (plotted against the year 1947) is very much out of line. It is the yield on the First Liberty Loan

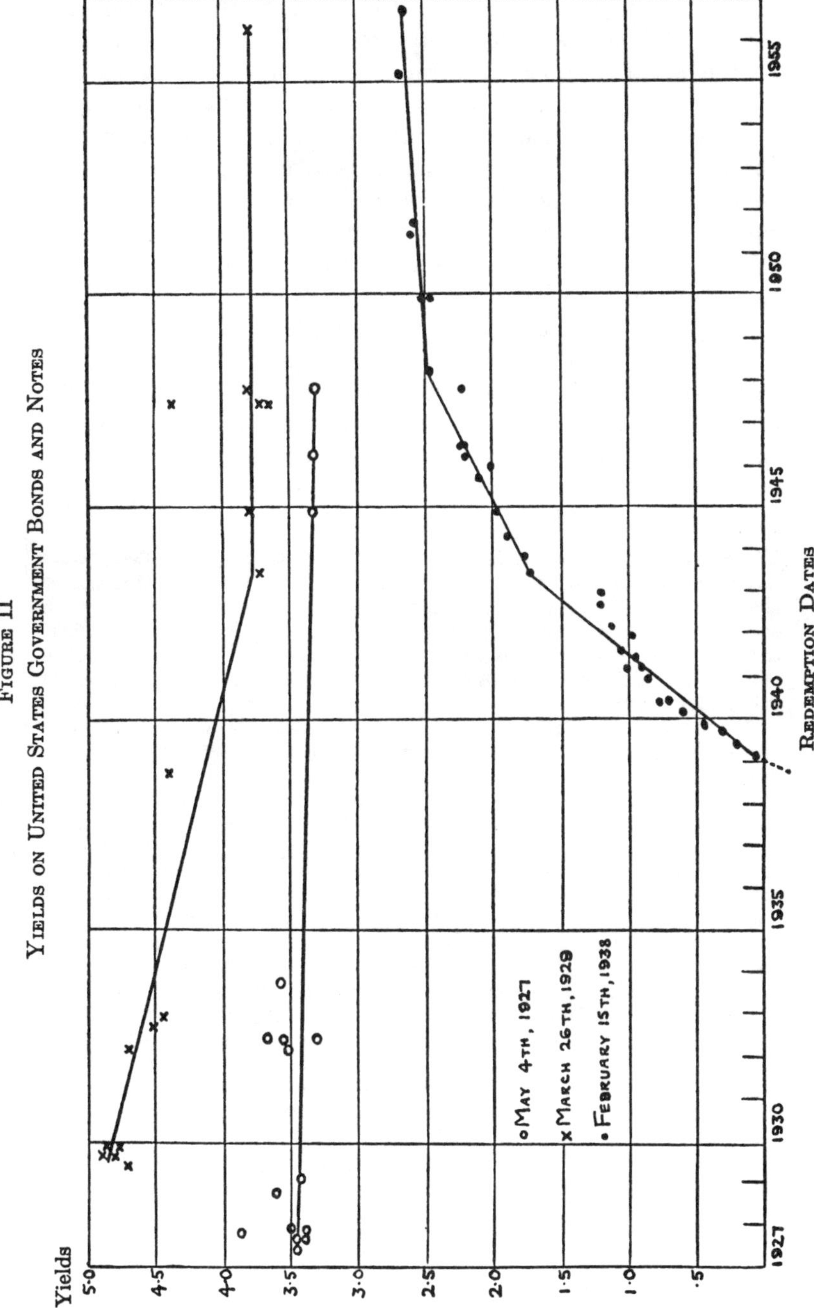

Figure II
Yields on United States Government Bonds and Notes

In recent years we have had a situation where future short rates (as well as long rates) were expected to rise, which accounts for the fact that we have a series of yields which ascends with the length of the maturities. This is shown in the chart, which gives the yields for Government securities of various maturities on February 15, 1938. Any date in the last seven or eight years gives a similarly rising series. The existence of these expectations at the present time is not proved by this ascending scale of yields alone. Direct evidence to the same effect is to be found in the financial journals, which are full of warnings that present interest rates are unusually low. There is also the evidence of the investment policy of the banks, which are reluctant to invest any substantial proportion of their assets in bonds with distant maturities for fear of a fall in their value resulting from rising interest rates. Finally, there have been numerous issues of serial bonds where the bonds which fall due later bear a higher coupon rate than those which fall due earlier.[9]

Converted 4¼ per cent bond, call date 1932 and maturity date 1947, which has a yield to maturity of 4.4 per cent, whereas other bonds (plotted against the same year) have a yield of around 3.8 per cent. As this irregularity persisted in the following weeks, it cannot be due merely to imperfect adjustment of the market. The real reason, I think, is this: the bond in question stood at $98\frac{9}{32}$, and its yield is consequently calculated to the maturity date. However, it is clearly indicated by the whole curve of the yields on securities of different maturities that the market expected a fall in interest rates in the near future. It was therefore likely that the bond would be redeemed *before* 1947 (perhaps as early as 1932), since its price was likely to rise above par before that date. (Much the same is true for the Fourth Liberty Loan 4½ per cent 1933–38, plotted against the year 1938 in the chart.) The other bonds whose yields are plotted against the same year 1947 (with the exception of the First Liberty Loan 3½ per cent, which is free from all surtax) are bonds which cannot be repaid before 1944 or 1946, so that the same argument does not apply to them. The rule according to which we calculate the yield to the maturity date, if the bond is selling below par, and to the first optional call date, if it is selling above par, is somewhat arbitrary, and in some cases obviously does not make sense.

9. Cases where the market expects the interest rates to rise first and then to fall later can also be found in the empirical material, but I must omit them here for lack of space. I have described the "curves" of the yields on different maturities for only a few selected dates. If we were to trace the movements of these curves continuously through time, they would reveal how quickly, and in response to what events, the expectations of investors change. Such an investigation would thus be a contribution towards obtaining empirical material about the behavior of expectations in a dynamic system. I hope to extend the investigation along these lines at a later date.

VI

The analysis of the relationship between long and short rates has a bearing on many problems, practical as well as theoretical. In the remainder of this article we can deal with only four of them.

(1) If it is true that only changes in the *long* rate affect investment, it seems to follow that the discount rate can only influence investment if the discount rate reacts on the long-term rate. Now one of the conclusions which can be drawn from the analysis in this article is that a change in the short rate will bring about a change in the long rate only if a general conviction is created that the short rate will remain low for a considerable time. Therefore the monetary authority has to create such a conviction,[1] if it wants to bring down the long-term rate and to induce more borrowing. Owing, however, to the fact that in the past, particularly under the gold standard, the discount rate was changed very often, partly with an eye to the external situation of the country, the public has become used to frequent changes in the short rate and is not inclined to believe that a low level of short rates is going to persist. This seems to imply that the discount rate should be altered as infrequently as possible. If this is not feasible, the central banks must try to influence the long rate directly, if they want to regulate investment.

(2) An entrepreneur who considers whether to borrow capital or not is said to compare the marginal efficiency of capital with the interest rate. Which interest rate? An entrepreneur who wants to finance long investment has to compare the existing long-term rate with the average of the expected future short-term rates (plus the costs of re-borrowing) or, if he expects the long rate to fall, with the average of the short rates for part of the time and the long rate for the rest of the time for which he wants to borrow. Whichever is the lower will be the one which he will set against the marginal efficiency of his capital or his expected profit rate.[2] As the different entrepreneurs will usually have different expectations, they will base their action with regard to investment on different rates. There is, therefore, no such thing as "the" interest rate which keeps "the" entrepreneurs from expanding, unless we

1. Cf. Keynes, General Theory, p. 203.

2. Cf. Breit, Ein Beitrag zur Theorie des Geld- und Kapitalmarktes, Zeitschrift für Nationalökonomie, 1935, p. 644.

assume very stable conditions in which there is no reason for any entrepreneur to think that the rates will change.

(3) A wide gap between short and long rates may exert a considerable influence on the amount of new borrowing that is undertaken. If the long rate is above the short, which implies an expectation that the long rate will rise, borrowers will try to borrow long in order to take advantage of the particularly low rate. The lenders, among them the banks, have an opposite interest: they prefer shorter maturities in this situation. It may therefore be difficult to float long-term securities. There are, however, several ways out of this difficulty. One way would be for the borrowers to shorten the maturities. Apparently for this reason, the British Treasury did float its Defence Loan of 1937 in the form of bonds with the comparatively short maturity of seven to ten years, and still more recently (January, 1940) a Conversion Loan has been announced with only three to five years to run.

The same problem exists, probably in even greater degree, with regard to flotations by corporations, and the difficulty may possibly be accentuated by the fact that the corporations have to make use of investment houses. The latter may be reluctant to float bond issues, either because they are afraid that the interest rate will have risen before they have sold the whole of the issue, or because they are anxious to avoid disappointing important customers (e.g. institutional investors), who may suffer a loss because the interest rate rises after the bonds have been sold to them. Here again a shortening of the maturities would facilitate borrowing operations. However, in view of the high costs of borrowing, corporations cannot adopt this procedure so easily as a government can.[3] Corporations have therefore sometimes used different methods to adapt their flotations to the situation where the interest rate is expected to rise.

First, as has been mentioned before, there have been many

3. Before the last war, particularly in the nineteenth century, governments and corporations sometimes floated perpetual bonds or bonds with maturities of a hundred years or longer. Nowadays a government or corporation would hardly issue such bonds. This is no doubt the effect of the increase in uncertainty about future economic developments (including the course of interest rates). Such an increase in uncertainty necessarily makes perpetual bonds, and bonds with very long maturities, unpopular with the investor. The shortening of the maturities is a method by which the capitalistic system adapts itself to the condition of greater uncertainty which has prevailed since the last war.

cases of serial issues where the bonds which fall due later bear higher interest rates than those which are due earlier. By issuing these serial maturities the corporation accommodates lenders who do not want to invest in long-term securities. At the same time it is enabled to take advantage, in some measure, of the low rates prevailing for shorter maturities, and to "spread" the costs of borrowing. Secondly, recourse can be had to the practice, so far not very common, of issuing securities with variable interest rates.[4] Such issues are made attractive to the lender by a rising nominal interest rate which will protect him against a loss (or at least reduce it), if and when the long rate in the market rises.

(4) The analysis of this article has shown that the relationship between interest rates on different maturities is determined in the main by the expectations as to the future course of interest rates. According to the "liquidity theory of interest," it is the degree of liquidity of securities with different maturities which determines this relationship. The most liquid asset, money, does not bear interest. Securities, being less liquid than money, bear an interest rate which is the higher the longer the maturity, since the danger of a capital loss due to a change in the interest rate in the market is supposed to be the greater (and therefore liquidity the smaller) the longer the security has to run. We know, however, that the short-term rate can be *above* the long-term rate, a fact which does not seem to fit in very well with the liquidity theory of interest. It is not possible to get out of this difficulty by calling a situation in which the short rate is above the long an exception, and ascribing it to the "technical conditions of the market" in times of financial crisis. The short rate is too frequently above the long, and often stays above it for too long a time, to warrant such a statement. In London, for instance, the short rate was above the long rate for nineteen months from the end of 1919 to the middle of 1921, and for eleven months in 1929. Before the War of 1914–1918 there are apparently[5] times where the short rate was above the long rate

4. For instance, R. H. White Co. of Boston recently executed a note for 1.5 million dollars, payable in twenty years, to the Prudential Insurance Co., for which the interest rate was as follows: 4 per cent for the first ten years, 4¼ per cent for the next five years, and 4½ per cent for the last five years. (Commercial and Financial Chronicle, Monthly Bank and Quotation Record, March, 1939.)

5. The Research Department of the London School of Economics has collected material on short and long rates in London, back to the year 1825.

for even longer periods, and the long rate cannot be said to have shown a tendency to stay more often and for longer periods above the short rate than the short rate above the long.

If we can bring ourselves to adopt a rather unusual yet logical definition of the term liquidity, we can still say, in spite of these facts, that the degree of liquidity determines the relationship between the rates on different maturities. One asset is said to be less liquid than another because the danger of a loss seems to be greater in case it is sold. Now if the owner of an asset thinks that he has a good chance of making a gain when he sells it, it seems to be logical to attribute a particularly high degree of liquidity to this asset. In times, therefore, when an investor expects the interest rate to fall, we should have to say that he regards securities with longer maturities as more liquid than those with shorter maturities, and is consequently prepared to take a lower rate on the long ones than on the short. Provided we adopt this terminology, we can say that the degree of liquidity of securities of different maturities, as understood by the marginal lenders in the different markets, determines (together with the cost factor) the relationship between the interest rates.[6]

F. A. LUTZ.

PRINCETON UNIVERSITY.

However, in this material the short rate is represented for the period before the War of 1914–1918 only by the rate on the first Friday in the month, whereas the long-term rate is the monthly average of the daily yields on Consols. The reader has to keep this in mind in appraising the following statistics. (In order to reduce the error I have eliminated from the series those months in which the two rates are relatively near to each other.) Between 1825 and 1938 the long rate was above the short in 764 months, whereas the short was above the long in 580 months. If we deduct from the first figure the months of the last years (which have no counterpart in previous times), the long rate was above the short in 677 months. The 580 months can in either case hardly be called an exception. The longest time for which the short rate was without interruption above the long is 42 months, and periods of more than 20 months are not infrequent. If we again exclude the current period, we find that the longest time over which the long rate was above the short was 44 months.

6. However, money then falls out of line. For, as far as its degree of liquidity is concerned, it would range below securities which give a chance of a capital gain; all the same, the latter bear interest whereas money does not.

[2]

THE

QUARTERLY JOURNAL
OF ECONOMICS

Vol. LXXI November, 1957 No. 4

THE TERM STRUCTURE OF INTEREST RATES

By J. M. CULBERTSON*

I. The elements of term structure theory, 489. — II. The role of debt liquidity differences in the rate structure, 491. — III. The role of speculative activity in the term structure, 496. — IV. Changes in the maturity structure of demand for funds, 502. — V. Yields on short-term and long-term U. S. government securities 1920–1957, 504. — VI. Some implications for credit policy, 516.

This paper develops a theory of the maturity structure of interest rates applicable in particular to developments in markets for U. S. government debt in modern times. It applies the theory to broad changes in the rate structure since 1920, and examines some of its implications for economic stabilization policies.

The theory of the term structure of interest rates, although it has not figured in the renowned controversies over the theory of "the interest rate," has concerned both students of credit control and active participants in debt markets. Among the earlier economists who sought to explain the interest rate structure, J. B. Say[1] and Henry Sidgwick[2] made sensible contributions that could have served as a basis for further development of a realistic theory. However, relatively little attention was paid to this area of theory until the end of the 1920's, at which time there appeared several important works dealing with it.

Karin Koch's *A Study of Interest Rates*[3] pointed out the significance of the behavior of the rate structure for monetary policy

* This paper was written while the author was a member of the staff of the Board of Governors of the Federal Reserve System. The views expressed are personal views of the author and in no way reflect the position of the Board. The writer wishes to express appreciation to colleagues for comments on a draft of this paper. The paper is based upon a doctoral dissertation submitted at the University of Michigan in 1956, "A Theory of the Term Structure of Interest Rates."

1. *A Treatise on Political Economy* (Philadelphia, 1867), pp. 344–47.
2. *The Principles of Political Economy* (3d. ed.; New York and London, 1901), pp. 251–81.
3. London, 1929.

and engaged in a detailed discussion of institutional and theoretical considerations affecting the structure of rates. Irving Fisher's *The Theory of Interest*[4] developed the relationship between short-term and long-term rates of interest under conditions of perfect foresight that later became the basis of the expectational theory of the term structure. However, his realistically oriented discussion emphasized the importance of institutional factors and the inapplicability of any precise theoretical formulation. His observations on the behavior of the rate structure suggest that short-term and long-term rates tend to move together, with short-term rates moving over a wider range.[5] Winfield W. Riefler's comprehensive study, *Money Rates and Money Markets in the United States,*[6] generally supported the same conclusion. The author pointed up the compartmentalization of debt markets; however, the general relationship assumed to exist was one of competition among debts of different maturity on the basis of relative yields. The data compiled by the author for the 1920's on average market yields on typical short-term and long-term private debt showed a general correspondence in direction and timing of movements, with short-term yields moving over a wider amplitude.[7]

Keynes in the *Treatise on Money*[8] accepted the Riefler findings and sought to support them with data on British experience. He went on to argue that changes in short-term rates, which could be brought about by central bank action, were effectively communicated to long-term markets, and that it was mainly through this channel that monetary policy was effective.[9] In the *General Theory,* however, in recognition of the reluctance of long-term rates to decline in the 1930's, he abandoned this doctrine. He sought to explain the long-term rate of interest as a "highly conventional" or a "highly psychological phenomenon," and emphasized the importance of expected future levels of long-term rates.[1] Apart from the main stream of development is Hawtrey's argument that changes in short-term rates caused by central bank action have little effect upon long-term rates, and that it is directly through the action of short-term rates upon the economy that monetary policy is effective.[2]

4. New York, 1930.
5. See pp. 313–14, and chap. IX (particularly pp. 209–10) on these points.
6. New York, 1930.
7. See particularly pp. 7–9 and 116–23.
8. London, 1930.
9. See particularly II, 352–64.
1. New York, 1936, pp. 202–4.
2. *A Century of Bank Rate* (London, 1938), pp. 184–95.

The doctrine on the term structure of rates most influential recently among English and American theorists, which we will term the expectational theory, was based upon the theoretical consideration of the implications of confidently held expectations and was made credible by the experience of the 1930's. As developed by John R. Hicks[3] and Friedrich A. Lutz,[4] the theory argues that the interest rate on a long-term debt tends to equal the average of short-term rates expected over the duration of the long-term debt.[5]

The influence of the expectational theory seems to have been confined mainly to academic economists. The view most common among those close to debt markets seems to be the older one, that interest rates generally move up and down together because of overlapping among debt markets. Some also have emphasized the role of "arbitrage" of specialists in debt markets in bringing about such behavior.[6]

Different theories of the rate structure necessarily imply different views as to the effectiveness of monetary policy and the manner in which it should be conducted. The expectational theory, since it makes long-term rates of interest depend upon the long-run expectations of the public, has naturally supported a pessimistic view as to the effectiveness of monetary policy. It has led some to conclude that if the monetary authority wants to affect long-term interest rates, it should attempt to do so directly by buying and selling long-

3. *Value and Capital*, (2d. ed.; Oxford, 1946), chap. XI.

4. "The Structure of Interest Rates," this *Journal*, LV (Nov. 1940), 36–63.

5. This is not the same expectational relationship as that emphasized by Keynes in the *General Theory*. It assumes operations based upon long-run expectations regarding short-term rates, while Keynes's approach is based upon short-run expectations regarding long-term rates. Keynes was aware of the other way of formulating the problem, mentioning it before setting it aside in both the *Treatise* (II, 352–53) and the *General Theory* (pp. 168–69)

6. For a discussion of this see the *Report of the Ad Hoc Subcommittee on Open Market Operations of the Federal Open Market Committee* and the *Comments* by the Federal Reserve Bank of New York. *Hearings Before the Subcommittee on Economic Stabilization of the Joint Committee on the Economic Report*, 83d Congress, Second Session (1954), pp. 257–331.

Among other recent contributions to the theory of the rate structure is an unpublished manuscript by W. Braddock Hickman, which points out some shortcomings of the expectational theory as an explanation of the actual behavior of the rate structure and develops anew the importance of institutional factors governing the interconnections among debt markets. "The Term Structure of Interest Rates, An Exploratory Analysis," mimeographed preliminary draft, 1942, Financial Research Program, National Bureau of Economic Research. An unpublished doctoral dissertation by Mona E. Dingle also emphasizes the importance of such institutional considerations, and provides a thorough historical review of factors affecting the interest rate structure in the United States. "The Structure of Interest Rates; A Study of Market Influences," University of California, 1951.

term debt,[7] though the theory itself would not dispose one to be optimistic regarding the efficacy even of such actions.

A good deal of recent debate over monetary policies reflects our uncertainties regarding broader questions of economic fact and theory: What behavior of the term structure of rates has, in fact, been "normal" in recent times, and what should we expect for the future? Have long-term rates been "sticky" or unresponsive to current conditions? If not, why has our recent experience been different from that of the 1930's? Do we have any standards that permit us to indicate how behavior of the interest rate structure different from that of recent years would have been more helpful to economic stability? This paper does not undertake to answer all of these questions, but it offers a first approximation to a realistic theory of the behavior of the term structure of rates. Such a theory must be the starting point of any attempt to answer them.

We find the expectational theory unsatisfactory on theoretical grounds and inconsistent with the behavior of the rate structure in the postwar period. We turn to a theory more closely akin to those of the 1920's in emphasizing the interconnection among debt markets, but attempt to develop more systematically than has been done in the past the role of expectations, liquidity differences among debts of different maturities, and changes in the maturity structure of debt available. This approach seems to explain satisfactorily the behavior of the term structure recently and during the 1920's, as well as the aberrant experience of the 1930's.

The theory of the term structure developed in this paper can be summarized briefly in the following manner: Rates on short-term and long-term U. S. government securities, which are tied to rates on related private debt, characteristically move simultaneously in the same direction in the short run (over periods of weeks and months), with short-term rates changing over the wider range. The general coincidence of movement in rates reflects basically the simultaneous impact in various credit markets of changes in general credit conditions resulting from changes in business conditions and monetary policy, and substitutability between short-term and long-term debt on the part of both borrowers and lenders. However, this substitutability is limited in extent, and when the maturity structure of debt supplied to the economy undergoes a substantial short-run change, either because of Treasury debt management operations or actions of private borrowers, this is reflected in the

7. This is one of the conclusions that Lutz drew from his analysis (see *op. cit.*, p. 60).

rate structure. Yields on short-term debt average lower than those on long-term debt because of the advantage of the superior liquidity of such debt to the holder and the liquidity disadvantage of issuing such debt to private borrowers. The amount of the liquidity premiums reflected in the term structure can vary with changes in the maturity structure of outstanding debt and with other factors affecting marginal preferences for liquidity in investment assets. Behavior based upon interest rate expectations is important mainly as a factor determining very short-run movements in long-term rates. Such behavior is based mainly on near-term expectations, and is ordinarily of little importance in determining average rate levels, and relationships, over considerable periods of time. This theory is summarized in the following section, and then explored in greater detail.

I. The Elements of Term Structure Theory

The decisions of borrowers and of lenders as to the maturity of the debt that they create or hold, and the factors underlying them, determine the relative market valuation of debts of different maturities, in conjunction with government monetary and debt management policies. Four major factors underlying the market's relative valuation of short-term and long-term debt are described in this section, and explored somewhat further in later sections. These are: (1) the liquidity difference between long-term and short-term debt; (2) the attractiveness of debts of different maturities on the basis of expected future changes in debt prices; (3) short-run effects of changes in the maturity structure of supply of debt coupled with rigidities in the maturity structure of demand for it; and (4) differences in lending costs related to debt maturity.

Short-term debt is more liquid than long-term debt. This fact compels some lenders to choose short-term debt, and induces others to prefer it. If there are limitations on the ability or willingness of debtors to do their borrowing by short-term debt, this factor can thus result in a marginal lender preference for, and lower yields on, short-term debt. In fact, it is clear that the ability of private borrowers to finance their activities by short-term borrowing is subject to limitations. Average yields on short-term debt lower than those on long-term debt can be explained, therefore, as representing the market's marginal evaluation of the superior liquidity of existing short-term debt. This liquidity premium should be affected by changes in the maturity structure of debt supplied to lenders, in lender attitudes toward liquidity, and in other factors affecting the liquidity balance in the economy.

To turn to the second factor, expectations of lenders and borrowers regarding future changes in interest rates, where these exist, evidently must affect inducements to hold and to issue debt of different maturities. However, the behavior of most borrowers and lenders is not ordinarily governed by such expectations. The effect upon the rate structure of those patterns of speculative (i.e., expectationally governed) behavior that do exist depends upon the nature of their planning periods, characteristic timing of operations, and other such details, as well as upon the interrelationship among individual patterns of activity. Thus, both the relative importance as a price-determining factor and the characteristic effect of speculative activity are matters that finally must be settled by reference to the facts regarding the particular market during the particular period. In general, however, in debt markets such behavior is more prominent in the market for debt that is more unstable in price, that is, long-term debt, and it is predominantly based upon near-term expectations, rather than upon those related to the more distant future. These considerations do not support the view that long-term rates should tend to equal the average of short-term rates expected over the period to maturity of the long-term debt, or the view that "market expectations" can logically be inferred from the actual structure of interest rates.

In short-run analysis, or in explanation of actual interest rates, changes in the maturity structure of supply of debt, coupled with imperfect elasticity of demand for particular types of debt, must affect the term structure of rates, creating a structure different from that which would exist with the same pattern of available debt if a longer period of time were allowed for adjustment. It is clear that the mobility of funds among debt of different maturities is limited by a variety of factors, and it is a matter of record that there have been considerable shifts in the maturity structure of debt outstanding. This factor, then, must be credited with a role in explaining actual term structure developments. Enumeration of those influences that would be significant within a framework of long-run equilibrium analysis is not sufficient.

Finally, costs of acquiring and administering debt may bear some systematic relationship to its maturity. In so far as they do, this would have to be a part of the theory of the term structure of rates. Differences in lenders' costs of evaluating, acquiring, administering, and liquidating debt of different types affect their net returns, and should be reflected in the normal market structure of (gross) interest rates. Some interest rate differentials evidently are to be explained mainly on this basis, for example that between certain U. S. bonds and U. S.-guaranteed mortgages.

However, such costs evidently are mainly related to other characteristics of debt than its maturity as such. Investigative, costs would be larger per dollar-year of debt for unknown, small and infrequent borrowers, but would not depend directly on the maturity of the debt itself. Administrative costs of maintaining a debt would be related to the type of debt — for example, whether there are instalment payments to be processed — but not significantly to its maturity. Costs per dollar-year of acquiring and terminating debt would be related to the average period that it was held, which in turn would tend to be related to its maturity; however, for high-grade open market debt such costs would not be large enough to enter significantly into a discussion of the term structure of rates. For some comparisons of particular debts of different maturity, the major explanation of yield difference may be differences in lending costs, but systematic differences in yield among debts differing in maturity but similar in other respects evidently are not to be explained in any considerable part on this basis. Therefore, the cost factor is not considered further in this paper, but the other three factors listed above are discussed at greater length.

II. The Role of Debt Liquidity Differences in the Rate Structure

The liquidity of a debt may be defined as its ability to be turned into cash on short notice on definite and favorable terms. "Liquidity" must not be based upon any specific expectations regarding future debt prices or market conditions, but rather on the general characteristics of the asset. If reference is made to specific price expectations, which must be proved right or wrong in individual cases, then what is involved is not analysis of liquidity, but rather "speculative" analysis, which it is useful to distinguish and to discuss separately.

The bases of the superior liquidity of debt that is short-term are two: (1) the period until the debt liquidates itself at maturity is shorter, and (2) fluctuations in prices of short-term debt are characteristically smaller than those of long-term debt, and thus the price at which the debt can be sold is more certain. Considerations other than the maturity of particular debts also affect their liquidity; but where these other factors are equal, debt of shorter maturity is the more liquid.

Lender behavior and liquidity premiums. The lender with perfect foresight would be unconcerned with liquidity. He would know for each future point in time what assets he would hold and what cash requirements would arise; no worrisome "ifs" would plague his calculations. The lender not blessed with omniscience, however, generally desires liquidity in his debt holdings for the protection and financial flexibility that it confers. The holder of a sufficient volume of liquid debt will not have to fear large liquidation losses if forced to meet unexpectedly large external cash demands. Also, he can count on being able to raise cash to take advantage of unforeseen profit opportunities without incurring offsetting losses in liquidating debt holdings.

No investor has perfect foresight, and it is doubtful that many act as if they thought that they did. However, for some investors, such as active speculators in debt markets, liquidity is a quite minor consideration in choices. For some others, such as life insurance companies, the proportion of investment assets that needs to be in liquid form is very small. However, most investors must be sensitive to liquidity considerations when considering the disposition of a significant portion of their debt-invested funds.

The possible cash needs with which lenders are concerned arise from a variety of situations: the bank's concern is with withdrawals of deposits; businesses provide reserves for taxes and contingencies; individuals may have in mind a variety of possible opportunities and calamities in considering the need of ready availability of their savings. The concern of many financial institutions with their ability to meet possible liquidation needs is reinforced by a variety of legal and customary requirements intended to insure that they will hold assets of adequate liquidity.

Particular future cash needs differ in (1) the degree to which their timing is certain, ranging from definite liabilities to pay given taxes on a certain day to completely uncertain contingencies, and in (2) the nearness or remoteness of the time at which they will arise or are most likely to arise. Those cash needs that are definite in timing may call for the holding of debt of a specific maturity, debt that has a liquidity of the particular "quality" that matches the cash need. The Treasury tax anticipation bill held against definite tax liabilities is an example of such a situation. If all cash needs were so definite, a generalized concept of liquidity might not be a very useful one; liquidity of each variety might have to be considered by itself — although the various liquidities would in any case have some degree of substitutability. However, in fact a large part of the possible cash needs against which assets are held are not definite in timing. To these needs that may arise at some unknown time in the future, a generalized concept of debt liquidity is appropriate. The existence of some cash needs that are definite and relate to the near future and a large volume of needs that are indefinite but may have to be met in the near future creates a demand for liquidity in general, a preference for debt that can be liquidated on short notice on relatively certain terms.

Such general liquidity preference is a matter of degree, and the extent to which it exists is not a matter of logic, but of institutional arrangements, economic conditions, and national temperament. A people with a gambling disposition would tend to put less emphasis upon liquidity; a more stable economy or one in which more personal contingencies were provided for by insurance or government programs would have less need for liquidity in investment assets. Further, the emphasis that is placed upon liquidity may sometimes change over relatively short periods of time as a result of new conditions or new experience. Many Americans took a much greater interest in liquidity in 1933 than they did in 1928.

Even though many investors have a preference for liquidity in their holdings of debt and other assets, it would not necessarily command a premium at the margin if there were no limitations on the ability and readiness of the economy to provide liquidity in its investment assets. In fact, however, the degree of liquidity provided in the asset stock is restricted.[8] The volume of most highly liquid assets — currency, bank deposits, short-term government securities, savings bonds — is controlled by the government. Limitations on the ability of private borrowers to provide liquid debt are discussed below.

Borrower behavior and liquidity premiums. A borrower with perfect foresight and the credit standing required to be able to borrow on debt of any maturity would naturally choose the maturity that would minimize his borrowing costs. If short-term debt tended to bear lower yields than long-term debt because of lenders' preference for liquidity, such borrowers would tend to do their borrowing on the basis of short-term debt to the point at which lenders' liquidity demands were satiated, liquidity in debt was deprived of marginal significance, and debt yields included no liquidity premiums.

Most actual borrowers, however, are not in a position to behave

8. What is directly relevant to the determination of liquidity premiums, of course, is the liquidity of available assets as perceived by investors. They may be guilty of systematic errors, sometimes perceiving assets as more liquid than they are and vice versa, and this must be kept in mind in explaining actual liquidity premiums.

in this manner. They are not possessed of perfect foresight, and in most cases do not wish to take a speculative position in debt markets. Also, they must, in quite the same way as lenders, be concerned with the adequacy of their liquidity positions, and this restricts their ability to assume short-term obligations.

From the viewpoint of the effect on his liquidity position, the debtor should borrow for the longest maturity possible, within the limit of his need for funds. The further in the future the cash need involved in repayment is placed, the more favorable is the liquidity position of the debtor. However, reasonable debtor behavior does not involve seeking the most favorable liquidity position possible, but rather one that balances the costs of maintaining a liquid position with the dangers and possible costs of not maintaining one. Thus, the general rule in business borrowing is to relate the maturity of the debt to the period of time that the funds are needed for a particular purpose, or the type of phsyical assets to be purchased with the funds.

For a business to finance plant construction by short-term borrowing impairs its liquidity position. If short-term credit to refund its maturing obligations were ever unavailable, it would be placed in an untenable position. The immediate interests of the lender could be well enough protected under such an arrangement. The short-term debt would be liquid, and his position could be secure for the same reason that the borrower's is insecure: he could always decline to renew the credit at maturity if the deal began to look risky. However, most lenders take upon themselves some responsibility for the continued financial health of their borrowers, and are unwilling to make a loan that may be ruinous to the borrower even though their own interests are adequately protected. Thus, though there are exceptions and there is a significant area within which practice is flexible, lenders as much as borrowers generally insist upon a maturity of debt that is related to the purpose of borrowing. Given the structure of uses of borrowed funds, and the predominant role of fixed investment, the application of this rule limits the ability of private borrowers to procure their funds by supplying the economy with liquid short-term debt. Thus, changes in the relative proportions of long- and short-term private debt outstanding are largely associated with shifts in importance among activities characteristically financed by different types of credit — changes in business inventory holdings, in fixed investment expenditures, developments in securities speculation — rather than with changes in the characteristic maturity of the debt used to finance given activities.

Some other factors affect the liquidity structure of existing debt. Intermediary financial institutions can offer to their creditors debt more liquid than that which they themselves hold. By careful management of portfolio maturities, by relying on the law of large numbers to regularize withdrawals and upon funds provided by growth as a potential reserve, they can borrow on shorter term than they lend. Thus, changes in the degree to which the services of such institutions are utilized may affect the liquidity situation. As a rule, such changes would proceed slowly, but in the event of widespread failures or closings of such institutions this would not be the case. Another factor that would affect the liquidity of debt supplied would be changes in economic and financial conditions affecting default risks. An increase in estimated default risks would adversely affect the liquidity of debt subject to such risks. Changes in government loan-guarantee or asset-price-support programs also would affect the liquidity situation.

A final determinant of the average liquidity of outstanding debt, one that is not only variable in the short run but also subject to control, is the maturity structure of the debt of the U. S. government. The government is not subject to the limitations that apply to other borrowers and, limited only by administrative problems (and fears of violating accepted canons of "sound finance"), it can alter at will the maturity structure of its outstanding debt. Such action can be a very powerful force to produce desired changes, or to offset undesired changes, in the maturity structure of other debt, or in other factors affecting the liquidity situation of the economy.

The role of liquidity premiums in the U. S. term structure. The above analysis suggests that in the absence of offsetting forces yields on short-term debt would be expected to average lower than those on long-term debt because of liquidity premiums. The rate differentials arising out of liquidity differences (which are not the whole of actual rate differentials) should tend to be widened, for example, during periods in which the proportion of outstanding debt that is short term is unusually small or in which other factors operate to increase demands for liquidity or to reduce the availability of liquid investment assets. U. S. experience supports this view, as is illustrated below. Yields on short-term U. S. government debt have averaged well below those on such long-term debt during the period since 1920, and this differential was particularly great during the 1930's, when a number of factors were operating to make short-term debt especially scarce and liquidity especially prized.

III. The Role of Speculative Activity in the Term Structure

Speculative activity in debt markets may be defined for present purposes as that based upon particular expectations regarding the future behavior of debt prices and yields. The term "speculative" is used descriptively, with no derogatory implications intended. Under conditions of perfect foresight, such behavior evidently would determine the maturity structure of interest rates, as, indeed, it would determine price interrelationships among investment assets of all types. Under more realistic assumptions, however, the predominance of and the nature of speculation in particular markets is a matter that must be determined on the facts of the case; no direct link between the price structure at a particular time and assumed expected future prices can be asserted *a priori* to exist.

The description of the speculative activity present in a given market can be a complex matter. Consider some of the factors that must be taken into account: Speculative planning of an individual must be described in terms of the particular alternative assets among which choices are made, the time periods over which comparisons are made, and the scale of potential operations. All of these can differ for different speculators, and for a given speculator at different times. Also, the expectations of individual speculators are not ordinarily unanimous or self-consistent. For these reasons, the net effect of speculative activity is not usually something that is clear and definite, but is rather the net result of individual patterns of operation that are diverse and in many cases inconsistent.

The scale of speculative activity is limited by the resources of speculators, and by the factors that prevent many market participants from behaving as speculators. Thus, it cannot simply be taken as *the* determinant of price, but rather its net effect must be weighed against the other motives and forces simultaneously governing the purchases and sales of nonspeculators. Speculative activity dominates some markets, and is insignificant in others; the question of its role in a given market is one that must be faced directly. Further, speculation may govern some price-time relationships within a market and not others; it may be the marginal factor determining prices at one time but not at another.

The terms of reference of speculative activity in debt. Two distinctive features of debt have shaped theorizing about interest rates and expectations: (1) it is a contract (salable, in the case of open market debt) with a definite duration, and (2) attention ordinarily focuses on the computed yield of the contract if held to maturity. These characteristics have led some writers to assume that speculative operations involving debts of different maturities must be based upon a comparison of yields to maturity. Therefore, it is assumed that a speculator considering buying a 20-year bond or a 90-day bill would base his choice on a comparison of the yield to maturity of the bond with the expected average bill yield over the same period, thus, perforce basing his choice on a 20-year planning period. He would thus be assuming implicitly that if bills were purchased in the first instance they would then be held through the 20-year period. But this would, in fact, be an irrational way of formulating the choice. At the least, the speculator must take account of the fact that if he buys the bills he will have a chance of recommitting his funds elsewhere at their maturity on the basis of a known rate of return for the period that they were held; the buyer of 3-month bills is not obligated to keep replacing them for twenty years because he made a choice at the outset between buying them and buying a 20-year bond.

The broader objection to this approach is that it assumes that the planning period of speculative operations is determined by the life of the longest investment asset being considered. Such an assumption is both unreasonable and contrary to common practice. A 20-year bond can be bought with the expectation of selling it at a profit within two days. A 90-day futures contract may be bought (or sold) with the expectation of closing the deal profitably within a week.

Prices of debt, as is illustrated in a following section, fluctuate appreciably from day to day, and from month to month. The speculator who can correctly anticipate these changes can earn a large annual rate of return from his funds. Even the investor who is basically not a speculator must sometimes be tempted to try to anticipate such short-period price changes. No one takes pleasure in finding a price of 98 on something that he bought the week before at 99. Why then should the speculator ignore these short-period movements, look far into the uncertain future, and bet on a long-period change in debt prices that is certain to produce a time-rate of return that is virtually insignificant?

Thus, it is to be expected that speculation in debt markets will be primarily based upon short planning periods, because near-term expectations are usually better formulated than those related to the more distant future, and because maximum time-rates of return are obtained by making use of short-period price fluctuations. The planning period of speculative operations is necessarily related to the amplitude of price movements of the asset involved. The time-rate of return that can be earned by operations based on a particular planning period must be sufficient to justify the investment of funds, skill, and effort. Because debt prices fluctuate within a relatively narrow range, and because average prices and yields over longer periods vary by even less, speculative operations in debt markets, even more than in some others, should be based upon short planning periods. The evidence of investor interests provided by the choice of subject matter of the financial press and market letters strongly suggests that, in fact, their preoccupation is with the near-term future.

Nonspeculative investment in debt. Is there such a thing as nonspeculative investment, or is there only investment that is wisely or foolishly speculative? Economists sometimes are disposed to argue that all decisions may be treated as if based upon expectations; at least, that certain expectations are necessarily "implicit" in the decisions. Thus, it is argued that the buyer of a 20-year bond is showing, at least implicitly, his conviction that short-term rates over the coming 20 years will average lower than the yield on his bond. Is this an acceptable line of analysis? There seem to be two types of difficulty with it.

In the first place, if we are to ignore the investor's limitations and his actual decision-making process and impute to him behavior consistent with perfect foresight, then something more — and something different — is "implicit" in his choice than the comparison indicated above. His choice of the bond implies that he considers it the most profitable investment in the whole economy. The relevant time period, however, is the immediate future, not the coming twenty years. The ideal investor maximizes the rate of return to his funds over each day and hour.

If, however, we leave this sterile-looking approach and try to consider our investor realistically, we must recognize a shift in our terms of reference. The problem becomes a factual one of what is the investor's actual decision-making process — among what alternatives does he really choose, and upon what basis — in view of his limitations, objectives, and external constraints. In this kind of analysis, it is misleading to see as "logically implicit" in the investor's decision a choice other than the choice actually made, and then to proceed to analyze the decision on the basis of this inferred choice. If we grant that what is at issue is the actual decision-making process of the investor, this could involve any of a large number of patterns of speculative activity. But it also could involve decisions that are, in fact, nonspeculative. Indeed, this is probably the predominant type of debt market behavior.

Investment governed by expectations regarding future interest rates is a gamble, just as is speculative behavior in other markets. If expectations usually prove to be correct, the speculation will be profitable; if they usually prove to be wrong, it will produce results less favorable than would have been earned by nonspeculative decisions, and may produce losses. For many investors, including the more important financial institutions, it is not irrational to so operate as to avoid this gamble. Actual investors, indeed, are rational enough to know that their foresight is not perfect, and that they would be foolish to act as if it were. Further, nonspeculative behavior is in many cases understood to be required by the position of the investor, and is demanded by custom and law.

Nonspeculative investment behavior involves making choices on some basis that is independent of any particular expectations regarding the future course of debt prices and interest rates. This can be done in a number of possible ways. A common one is to select a portfolio maturity structure suited to the liquidity needs of the investor and justified on an earnings basis by average past experience, and then hold to this portfolio structure through whatever short-run shifts may occur in expectations or interest rates. The behavior of most financial institutions is of this general character, with investment concentrated in long-term debt except in so far as liquidity needs require the holding of short-term debt. The maintenance of a relatively constant portfolio structure insures the institution that its earnings will not vary extremely, and will not turn out disastrously lower (or embarrassingly larger) than those of competitors.

Choices among debts of different maturity on the basis of a direct comparison of their relative yields to maturity is also nonspeculative behavior, since it does not involve planning over any future period. Behavior of this type also seems to be important in debt markets.[9]

Maturity yields and holding-period yields. If speculators do not ordinarily operate over a planning period equal to the period to

9. Some discussions have emphasized "arbitrage" of dealers and professional investors as an important factor affecting the behavior of the term structure and the performance of debt markets. However, the expression seems to be used by different people to refer to several types of speculative and nonspeculative behavior (none of which is arbitrage in the strict meaning of that word). Although the operations of dealers (and other active traders) are extremely important in determining day-to-day movements in debt prices and the stability or instability of the market, it seems that the type of broad changes in the rate structure on which this paper focuses must be attributed mainly to more basic forces.

maturity of the debt involved, then their choices cannot be based upon a comparison of debt "yields," as these are ordinarily defined. These measure the rate of return from holding the debt over only one time span, that until maturity (or in some cases until first call, in the case of callable bonds). The speculator using some other time span as his planning period should, rather, make his choice on the basis of a comparison of analogous "holding-period yields," which measure the rates of return that would be earned on each debt if it were sold at the price expected to prevail at the end of the planning period.

In retrospect, also, a holding-period yield can be computed that measures the rate of return earned on a debt during the period over which it actually was held, including, of course, capital gains and losses as well as interest accruals during the holding period. Such holding-period yields can be computed for all varieties of debt, for holding periods of any duration, for any period of history. Study of the behavior of actual holding-period yields permits the drawing of some important conclusions about speculation in debt markets, for it indicates in clear terms the nature of the opportunities for successful speculation that were not taken. It indicates the extent to which speculation of the market was imperfect, because speculative activity was insufficient in scope or incorrect in form and did not succeed in bringing to equality the rates of return earned on different debts.

Holding-period yields can be computed analogously to maturity yields. The holding-period yield can be defined as that annual rate of return at which the discounted value of interest payments and the sale price of the debt is equal to the initial price. For holding periods of less than a year, a compounding period equal to the holding period could be assumed; however, we will follow the convention that is applied to bond yields and assume no compounding within the year. Thus, we define the holding-period yield as the rate of return for the holding period times the number of such periods in a year. For example, if a 3 per cent bond were purchased for $100, held for one week, and sold for $100.50 plus accrued interest of $0.6, the dollar yield would be $.56, just over 1/2 per cent, for the one-week holding period, or an annual rate of 29 per cent.

The characteristic behavior of actual holding-period yields, debt prices, and maturity yields in relation to debt maturity is an important part of the background against which speculative operations in debt markets take place. As a matter of arithmetic, the change in the price of a debt required to cause a given change in its maturity yield is directly related to its term to maturity. For example, to cause a 3 per cent bond to fall from a maturity yield of 3 per cent to one of 2.8 per cent requires an increase in price of $.04 if its term to maturity is three months, $0.20 if it is one year, and $4.79 if it is forty years. Therefore, if debts of different maturities characteristically underwent changes of the same amplitude in maturity yields, the price changes involved for long-term debt would be a large multiple of those for short-term debt — say, on the order of 100 times as large. And if debts of longer maturity did undergo such larger price fluctuations, their holding-period yields evidently would fluctuate over a similarly wider range. Or, to state the relationship in the opposite manner, if holding-period yields for short holding periods for debt of all maturities were held to equality, or to the same range of fluctuation, then maturity yields on long-term debts would change over a range only a small fraction as large as that applying to short-term debt.

The effectiveness of debt speculation. If debt markets were fully speculated on the basis of perfect foresight (that is, if the rate structure were the self-consistent reflection of a single, and correct, pattern of expectations) then holding-period yields on debts of all maturities should be equal for any and all holding periods. This is rather a farfetched condition, of course, as is apparent if one stops to consider its implications for a debt structure including a wide range of maturities. If debt markets were dominated by speculative activity based upon approximately unanimous expectations and upon a single predominant planning period, discrepancies over the planning period in actual holding-period yields for debts of different maturities would reflect errors in the expectations. In fact, there is no basis for assuming as a general rule — though it may sometimes occur — a near unanimity of expectations and planning periods. However, examination of the behavior of past holding-period yields on debts of different maturities may still tell us something, albeit only something negative, about the effectiveness with which debt markets were speculated.

The behavior of some such actual holding-period yields is examined below. It appears that holding-period yields for short holding periods of long- and short-term debt have diverged widely, in a manner that seems to have been characteristically repeated during up and down swings in interest rates and that does not seem to be explainable on the basis of prevalence of particular errors of expectations. This appears to indicate that debt markets are not dominated by expectationally oriented behavior in such manner that broad changes in the term structure of interest rates can generally be interpreted as reflecting changes in market expectations. The prevalence of such a pattern of behavior of holding-period yields suggests that the explanation of broad movements in the term structure of rates must be sought principally in factors other than behavior governed by interest rate expectations.[1]

IV. Changes in the Maturity Structure of Demand for Funds

It is generally recognized that changes occur over time in the maturity structure of demand for funds. Such changes are important in day-to-day market developments, occurring in an irregular manner that depends upon such factors as the timing of new security issues. They occur also over longer periods of time, in part on the basis of more regular factors, as is indicated below. Once it is admitted that such changes in the maturity structure of demand for funds do occur, and that the maturity structure of debt holdings is not a matter of indifference to lenders — that funds are not perfectly mobile among debts differing in maturity — it is clear that such changes must be one factor influencing the maturity structure of interest rates existing at any moment. In part this influence is to be related to factors discussed above. That is, changes in the maturity structure of demand for funds and in the structure of outstanding debt affect marginal liquidity premiums and marginal lending costs applicable to debts of different maturities; also they could affect the market impact, at the margin, of speculative operations. However, in addition to these factors, rigidities in the structure of supply, or impediments to perfect mobility of funds among debts of different maturity can, in themselves, be important determinants of the actual interest rate structure.

Short-run changes can occur not only in the maturity structure of demand for funds, but also in the structure of supply. Such changes would be mainly in response to the factors discussed above, shifts in liquidity estimates and preferences, in relative lending costs, and in lender expectations and patterns of speculative activity. Some other factors, such as changes in the pattern of financial institutions on account of legal, political, or sociological factors, would affect the structure of supply of funds but are not discussed here

1. However, it is undeniable that over short periods of time, periods measured in days or weeks, expectations, and even amorphous psychological reactions, can be a powerful force affecting interest rates. Expectational factors undoubtedly played an important role in the sharp peaking of long-term rates in May 1953, and in several short-run movements in yields of intermediate-term and long-term Treasury securities in 1956.

because they would not ordinarily be important in the short run. Changes in monetary policy or other developments affecting the relative role of commercial bank funds (mainly short-term and intermediate-term) in the total supply could cause a short-run shift in the structure of supply of funds.

To return, then, to the causes of such shifts in the maturity structure of demand for funds as would affect the term structure of rates (other than on a day-to-day basis), these appear to be caused mainly by shifts in the purposes of borrowing, and by Treasury debt management operations. It was argued above that the maturity of private borrowing is generally closely related to its purpose. Thus, shifts in business and financial developments tend to be reflected in changes in the maturity structure of borrowing. Business inventory developments and securities speculation are reflected in changes in short-term borrowing; changes in automobile sales affect extensions of the intermediate-term credit commonly used in this area; changes in sales of new houses, in business fixed investment, in state and local government construction are reflected in demands for new long-term credit.

There are a variety of impediments to mobility of funds in debt markets: legal restrictions on some types of borrowing and on debt holdings of institutional investors, desire of investors for portfolio diversification, customary investment standards applied to financial institutions, lags in establishment or revision of financial institutions, specialization of investors on technical grounds, impediments to geographical movement of funds in cases requiring judgment or administrative activity, etc. The burden of making the shift in the allocation of loan funds required by a change in the structure of demand for funds may fall principally upon one group of lenders which bridges the major markets involved. In shifts in the balance of demands between short-term and other markets, the commercial banks necessarily play a crucial role.

In both of the two postwar recessions, the banks made important shifts in the allocation of their funds, replacing declining business loans with government securities. This maintained the volume of bank credit in use and the money supply, and helped to limit the recessions and to provide a financial climate that encouraged recovery. Following 1929, an unusual combination of circumstances brought a remarkable shift in the maturity structure of demand for funds away from the short-term end, as is indicated below. The impact of this shift, and its implications for the liquidity position of creditors, is a major factor in the explanation of the abnormal term structure of the early 1930's. Some of the major changes that have taken place in the maturity structure of demand for funds, and their implications, are discussed below.

V. Yields on Short-term and Long-term U. S. Government Securities: 1920–1957

The past behavior of the maturity structure of yields on U. S. government debt is examined below to see how it can be described and how it is to be interpreted in terms of the above discussion. This investigation deals with changes in the term structure over periods of months rather than with day-to-day and week-to-week movements. The latter should be explainable also in terms of the same framework of analysis, but haphazard variations in the structure of demand for and supply of funds and day-to-day changes in market sentiment and expectations should be more important than over longer periods.

The term structure of rates for the period since 1920 is examined as a whole with reference successively to several aspects of its behavior. First, the broad relationship between changes in long-term and short-term interest rates is described. Second, characteristic behavior of holding-period yields from short-term and long-term debt is examined. Finally, periods during which shifts in the maturity structure of demands for funds were of particular importance are considered.

The general behavior of the term structure. Some general observations applying to the behavior of yields (monthly averages) on Treasury bills in relation to those on long-term bonds may be gathered from a chart showing their movements over a considerable period of time.[2] The short-term rates were characteristically below the long-term rates. They were above them only for two relatively short periods, both of which coincided with peak levels of interest rates generally. Thus, experience seems clearly consistent with the view that in modern times the superior liquidity of short-term debt has had marginal significance. Short-run movements in yields on short-term and long-term debt have generally been simultaneous and in the same direction. Movements in short-term rates have been much the wider in amplitude, both in absolute and relative terms. There is no evidence of a lead-lag relationship. Short-term rates were generally closest to long-term rates, or above them, at times when both were relatively high. While this was the general

2. See that in the *Federal Reserve Chart Book, Historical Supplement*, 1956, pp. 38–39.

character of the relative behavior of short-term and long-term rates, there clearly were some important developments that were not in conformity with this pattern.

It may help to define more closely the nature of the relationship between changes in long-term and short-term rates if data for some periods during which they moved characteristically together are arrayed in a scatter diagram. This will indicate the nature of the interrelationship that existed during these periods of consonant movement, and disclose whether it is the same in one as in another such period. It will also indicate the nature of the shifts that took place in intervals between such periods.

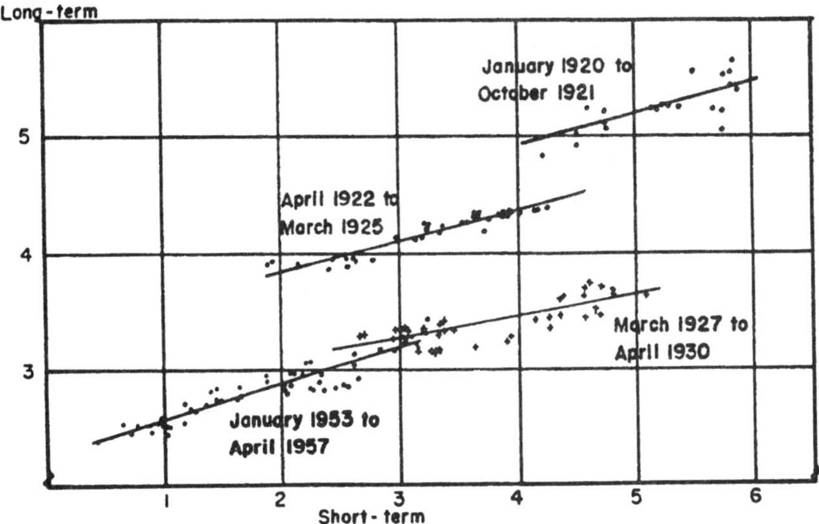

CHART I

Relation Between Yields on Long-Term and Short-Term U. S. Government Securities, Selected Periods
Monthly average yields, per cent per year

Note. Long-term yields shown are those included as "bonds: long-term, old series" on the chart mentioned in the text; they apply to bonds mostly due or callable in 10–20 years. Short-term yields shown are those on 3–6 month certificates and notes for periods through 1930 and average issuing yields of Treasury bills in 1953–57.

Chart I indicates that long-term and short-term rates were subject to fairly close short-run relationships during a number of periods since 1920, relationships that shifted during some intervening periods. The short-run relationships indicated for most of these periods have roughly the same slope (though the 1927–30 period shows less responsiveness of long-term rates than the others), but there were

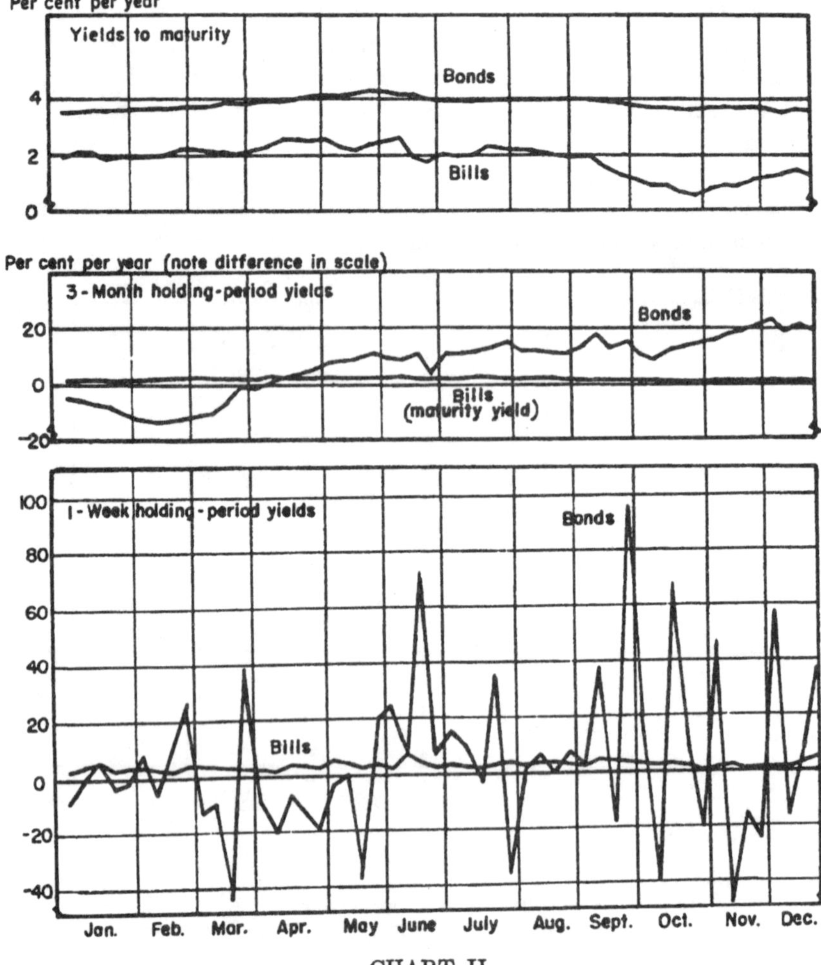

CHART II

MATURITY YIELDS AND 3-MONTH AND 1-WEEK HOLDING-PERIOD YIELDS FOR BONDS AND BILLS: 1953
(Weekly)

Note. Bills are longest issue outstanding of Treasury bills. Bonds are Treasury 12/67-72's. Holding-period yields are annual rates of return including capital gain or loss for indicated holding periods beginning with dates shown.

shifts during the 1920's that brought long-term rates lower relative to short-terms. It is interesting to note that in very broad terms the relationship for the period beginning with 1953 is consistent with that for the latter 1920's, though the relative amplitude of movement of long-term rates is greater in the recent period.

The least-squares relationship plotted for the earliest period, including 1920 and most of 1921, is as follows: long-term rate = 3.9 + .27 short-term rate. That for the most recent period, 1953 through April 1957, is as follows: long-term rate = 2.3 + .31 short-term rate. These relationships are consistent with the observations suggested above. They indicate that short-term rates are more volatile than long-term rates, showing fluctuations between three and four times as large in absolute terms. While short-term rates are below long-term rates at interest rate levels such have existed in recent years, the relationships would suggest that if the pressure of demand on available loan funds became sufficiently great they would tend to rise above them, as they did on some occasions during the 1920's. According to the relationship given for the recent period, the level to which rates would have to rise before long-term and short-term rates would be equal would be about 3.3 per cent. At the other extreme, according to the same relationship, the minimum level to which long-term rates would fall in the short run in the event that short-term rates were reduced to zero would be about 2.3 per cent.

The behavior of holding-period yields and the role of speculative activity. The year 1953, which included a rather sharp rise and subsequent decline in interest rates, is taken as a basis for illustrations of the behavior of holding-period yields. Chart II shows maturity yields on a long-term bond and on Treasury bills during 1953, and shows the annual rate of return, including capital gains and losses, earned by holding these securities for 3-month and for 1-week periods throughout the year.[3]

The chart illustrates that such holding-period yields fluctuated over a much wider range than maturity yields, that holding-period yields on long-term debt fluctuated over a much wider range than those on short-term debt, and that the shorter the period of time over which holding-period yields are computed the wider was the range of fluctuation. While existence of these general relationships is common knowledge, it is useful to have a definite measure of the

3. No allowance has been made for transactions costs in computing holding-period yields; thus these somewhat overstate the actual rate of return that could be earned, particularly for short holding periods that would involve frequent turnover of debt holdings. However, transactions costs on U. S. securities are very low, ordinarily running less than 1/10 per cent on a purchase and sale, and the general conclusions drawn would not be affected by allowing for them.

extent of the differences among holding-period yields, and between holding-period yields and maturity yields.

Thus, while maturity yields on the bonds shown ranged between 2.75 and 3.13 per cent, yield rates for 3-month holding periods ranged between minus 13 and plus 23 per cent, and yields for 1-week holding periods ranged between 97 per cent and minus 48 per cent. Holding-period yields on the bonds were generally negative during the early months of the year, when yields were rising and bond prices were falling; they were generally positive and quite large during the remainder of the year, when falling yields predominated and capital gains were earned by bondholders. In the case of yields for 1-week holding periods, the erratic changes in bond prices overshadowed the broader movements, and such yields showed extreme fluctuations.

Thus, it appears that during periods in which the level of interest rates is changing — which includes most of the postwar period to date — yields for short holding periods on long-term debt characteristically differ greatly from those on short-term debt; evidence of anything approaching perfect speculation is absent. Holding-period yields for long-term debt fluctuate over a much wider range than those for short-term debt, and thus long-term debt offers the more tempting target for speculative activity.

This pattern of behavior of holding-period yields illustrates some of the difficulties in the way of an attempt to explain the behavior of the rate structure in terms of expectations. What sort of expectations, one must ask, could possibly have produced this result? Was the extended 1952–53 rise in interest rates, indeed, a matter of continuing surprise to investors, and the decline from mid-1953 to mid-1954, and the subsequent rise? A group of speculators so uniformly wrong in their expectations would not seem a good bet to remain in business. The traditional expectational theory, of course, assumed the very long, rather than the short, planning — or holding — period. But how many investors in a position to behave on the basis of expectations would be content to hold bonds in a month, say, when they were losing money on them at the rate of 25 per cent a year because they believed that over the coming twenty years bill yields would average a bit lower than the maturity yield on their bonds? If the movements in long-term rates were caused by changes in the public's long-run expectations regarding short-term rates, then is it a coincidence that these conformed so closely with changes in current economic conditions and monetary policy? The conclusion to which one seems forced to turn is that speculative activity, dominant though it can be in very short-run movements, does not determine the broad course of interest rates or of interest-rate interrelationships.

Changes in the maturity structure of demand for funds. Short-run changes in the maturity structure of private demand for funds have reflected mainly the impact of changes in the economic and financial situation upon the pre-existing pattern of demands for credit. The volume of commercial loans of banks has always been closely responsive to ups and downs in business. In some part, perhaps, it has reflected shifts in the optimism or pessimism of banks and in the credit standards that they applied to prospective borrowers. However, its primary cause has been changes in the demand for business loans associated mainly with changes in business expenditures for inventories and fixed capital. Commerical and agricultural loans of weekly reporting member banks declined about 18 per cent in the 1949 recession and 12 per cent in the 1953 recession (excluding changes in holdings of Commodity Credit Corporation obligations), although neither of these periods was attended by liquidity panic or by any pressure on banks to liquidate their assets. In fact, the marked decline in loans was accompanied by reductions in interest rates, and banks simultaneously were adding to their holdings of U. S. securities in order to keep their funds employed.

Similarly, changes in the volume of stock market credit have been related to the broad behavior of stock prices, and in more recent times, to changes in margin requirements, and have reflected mainly changes on the side of demand for funds. Also, short-run changes in consumer credit have been closely related to changes in sales of consumer durable goods, and demand for such credit.

Long-term debt generally has shown much less responsiveness to changes in business conditions, as is indicated by Chart III. This difference in behavior has not reflected merely the fact that the slower turnover of long-term debt implies a lesser maximum rate of decline; rather, it has resulted from greater stability in the demand for new funds. Thus, the volume of outstanding long-term debt continued to rise (on an end-of-year basis) through the 1921 recession, and in the postwar period its continued growth has not been significantly interrupted by moderate recessions.[4] This suggests that one factor explaining the wider swings in short-term rates associated with economic fluctuations is the fact that the related changes in demand for short-term funds are greater than in those

4. The 1951 decline in "other debt" shown in Chart III reflected a very large, and partially temporary, shift in U. S. government debt from bonds and notes to certificates and bills.

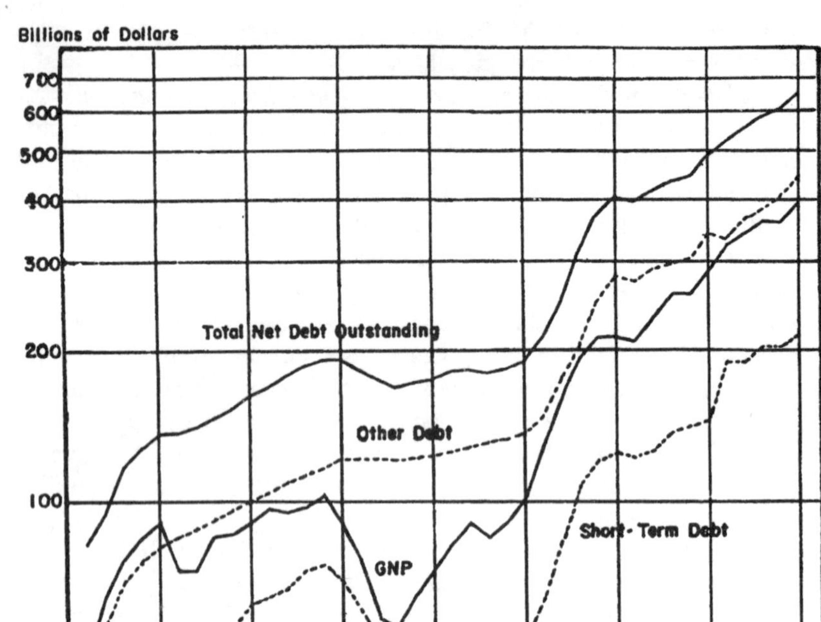

CHART III

NET DEBT OUTSTANDING IN THE UNITED STATES, SHORT-TERM AND OTHER
Ratio scale: 1916–1955

Note. Debt data are as of the end of the year indicated, except that state and local debt is as of June 30; gross national product data are annual totals. Net debt excludes that issued by and held within (1) the federal government and its corporations and agencies (not including Federal Reserve Banks), (2) state and local governments as a group, and (3) affiliated corporate systems under a single management. The classification of debt is generally on the basis of original maturity. Debt classified as short-term includes Treasury bills and certificatse of indebtedness, corporate debt of original maturity less than one year, and all nonmortgage debt of individuals and unincorporated business. "Other" debt includes federal and corporate debt not included as short-term, mortgage debt, and all state and local debt. Except for the breakdown of federal debt, concepts and data are those of the Department of Commerce; see *Survey of Current Business*, Oct. 1950, pp. 9–15, May 1956, pp. 6–14.

for long-term funds. It also suggests that a drop in the supply of short-term debt during an economic decline could be such as to affect the liquidity position of lenders and the interest rate structure. Such a development seems to have been an important factor in the failure of long-term rates to accompany the sharply declining short-term rates during the early 1930's, and in the unfavorable liquidity conditions of that period.

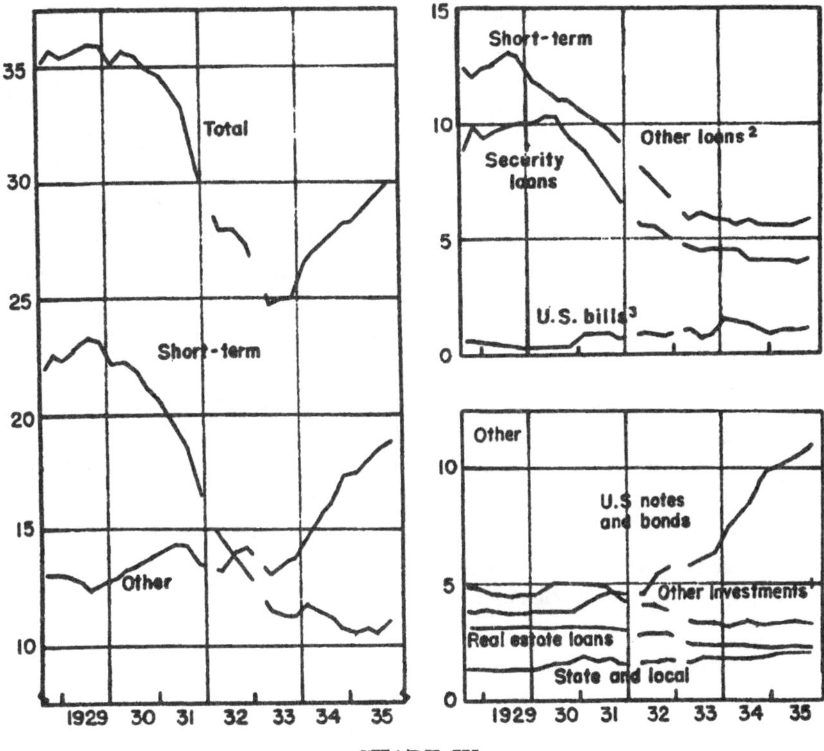

CHART IV

Member Bank Loans and Investments: 1928–1935
(Billions of dollars)

1 Includes U. S.-nonguaranteed and corporate bonds, notes, and debentures, corporate stocks, and foreign securities.

2 Includes all loans other than real estate loans and those on securities.

3 Includes certificates of indebtedness.

Note. The definitions of short-term and other debt, definitions that are far from ideal, are indicated by the charts in the right hand panel. Data are as of call report dates; they are from *Banking and Monetary Statistics*, Board of Governors, Federal Reserve System, 1943, pp. 72–77.

Private short-term borrowing began a rapid and extended decline after 1929, both security loans — which were particularly important in the liquidity position of banks and other lenders — and business and consumer loans. The volume of private long-term borrowing reacted to the financial crash by increasing sharply. From the end of 1929 to the end of 1930, debt other than short-term ("other debt" as defined in Chart III) increased $5 billion, or 5 per cent, reflecting in part a shift in corporate fund-raising from stocks to bonds. It was not until 1933 that private long-term debt outstanding dropped below its 1929 level, which contrasts sharply with the behavior of short-term borrowing. Total outstanding debt other than short-term never did show any considerable decline during the 1930's, as the Treasury financed the bulk of its deficit in the bond market and thus offset what reduction did take place in private debt. From 1931 through 1939 (fiscal years), the Treasury issued $23.2 billion of bonds for cash and in refundings and the outstanding amount rose $13.3 billion (excluding savings bonds); from 1920 through 1929, the Treasury had issued a total of only $3.2 billion in bonds and the volume outstanding had declined $4.1 billion. Debt management policy during the depression did not offset the shift in the maturity structure of private debt that made short-term debt, particularly liquid very short-term debt, abnormally scarce, while illiquid long-term debt continued in very large quantity.

The shift in the maturity structure of outstanding debt necessarily was reflected in commercial bank assets, and in bank liquidity positions. Practically the entire decline in loans and investments of member banks was in security loans and in other loans (excluding real estate), as may be seen from Chart IV. Such loans fell by more than one-half from 1929 to 1933, while other assets rose somewhat. The situation that faced banks, then, was this: Reserve positions after early 1930 (except during the short periods of bank runs) were easier than they had been in years, and by 1932 abnormal excess reserve balances began to accumulate. However, the liquidity position of banks had been dealt a heavy blow by the collapse in holdings of short-term credit, particularly call loans. Therefore, while they were willing to make secure short-term loans at very low yields, and in some cases at no yield at all, there was a limit to the rate at which they were willing to expand their holdings of less liquid debt. After the early 1930's, a large volume of bank reserves remained unused and was not made the basis for expansion in bank credit in use and in the money supply.[5]

5. It is sometimes argued that the banks were in an extremely liquid position after about 1933 because of their very large holdings of excess reserves, which undoubtedly are some sort of a liquid asset. However, there are two reservations to be made against this position. (1) It is questionable that bankers considered excess reserves as dollar-for-dollar substitutes for liquid earning assets. Some of their traditional ways of looking at things would not dispose them to be content with an asset position consisting, say, of long-term bonds and

This imbalance between the maturity structure of demand for and supply of funds coincided with events that tended to raise demands for liquidity in investment assets: the disappointment of expectations in the 1929 crash, continued declines in prices of many investment assets, the spreading wave of defaults abroad and at home. Under these extremely unfavorable conditions, the mobility of funds was not sufficient to convert "easy money" in markets for liquid short-term debt into generally easy credit conditions, or to maintain a normal relation between short-term and long-term rates. Yields on short-term Treasury securities were abnormally low because banks had ample funds that they were willing to invest in liquid short-term debt, and the supply of such debt was very limited. Long-term yields declined belatedly because demands for such funds continued large, savings declined, and banks because of liquidity considerations had to limit the rate at which they were willing to move into such debt. The wide differential between short-term and long-term rates can be interpreted as consisting mainly of an unusual liquidity premium associated with the peculiar conditions of the times.

Bond yields dropped somewhat in late 1929 and eased off further through mid-1931, finally about regaining the lows reached in 1928 — at which time short-term rates, of course, had been much higher. Then bond yields were pushed up sharply by the financial crisis of late 1931 and did not get back down to the earlier levels again until 1934. Thereafter, they declined irregularly until 1941, eventually reaching levels that probably were not out of line with the depressed short-term rates (assuming the sort of relationship indicated by the scatter diagrams above).

What is truly singular about the behavior of the rate structure during the 1930's is the fact that long-term rates did not show larger declines during the earlier part of the period. It was four years before long-term rates began to show a full response to the remarkable drop in short-term rates in 1930. An effective program

excess reserves. (2) There is a danger of double-counting the excess reserves. In so far as they are doing service as a liquid asset, they are not really "excess" in the sense of being available to support acquisition of additional earning assets. Thus, if a higher level of bank credit would have been desirable, perhaps what was needed was a still larger volume of excess reserves — though this hardly seems the best way of going about the matter. (If excess reserves in this period are to be regarded as partially serving as liquid assets, the banks' reaction to the 1936–37 decline in excess reserves was not so unreasonable as is commonly supposed). In the text discussion, we are focusing attention on the liquidity of banks' *earning assets*, and asking what prevented their excess reserves from being used to support expansion of bank credit.

for economic stabilization cannot tolerate such a lag. The Keynesian argument that declines in long-term rates are impeded, beyond a certain point, by expectations that rates will again rise to "normal" levels, entailing capital losses to holders of such debt,[6] clearly was increasingly applicable after, say, about 1936, as long-term rates continued to set new record lows. However, this factor was not sufficient to prevent continued declines during this period. The argument is not particularly applicable to the earlier 1930's, when rates were not low by the standards of the late 1920's, and in relation to current short-term rates were obviously peculiarly high.

What would have been an effective government financial policy during this period (neglecting the impediments to action represented by existing conceptions of "sound finance" and by the gold standard)? Such a policy would not have permitted so large a decline in commercial bank credit and the money supply, and would have provided an effective bridge between the easy conditions created in short-term markets and those in long-term markets. This could have been done by making available a larger volume of commercial bank reserves earlier in the period, and by a properly conceived debt management policy. The Treasury should have issued short-term debt in such volume as to meet all needs of commercial banks (at positive yields, rather than the zero and negative yields that developed). This would have given banks a suitable asset to acquire in order to use the reserves that were made available to them, thus sustaining the money supply and the liquidity condition of the economy generally. It also would have strengthened the liquidity position of the banks themselves against the adversities that developed. As the counterpart of this action, the Treasury should have made drastically smaller offerings to the intermediate-term and long-term sectors of the market. This would have left more investment funds to seek employment in private debt, driving yields down (since Treasury offerings were a major factor keeping them up) and presenting more favorable financing terms to private borrowers. This would have meant rising bond prices, which would also have improved the balance-sheet position of investors. With such a policy, the "pushing on a string" doctrine of monetary policy should not have had an occasion to develop. Prompt creation following 1929 of financial conditions more favorable to recovery might have done much to prevent the subsequent descent into the depths of financial chaos and depression.

The behavior of the maturity structure of debt in the moderate

6. *General Theory*, pp. 202–4.

recessions of the postwar period has been quite different from that following 1929, and from that of the 1921 and 1937 contractions. Substantial reductions in commercial loans of banks occurred during both of the postwar recessions; however, the importance of these relative to the total volume of bank credit was much less than in prewar experience. Other types of short- and intermediate-term credit did not show the same sort of cyclical responsiveness to these moderate recessions, mainly continuing upward or holding stable in response to factors more specifically related to individual areas. Stock market credit declined somewhat in 1949 (comparisons on a monthly basis) but rose in 1953–54; consumer credit rose in 1949, but leveled off in 1953–54; agricultural loans of banks increased in both periods, a sharp rise in 1953 reflecting a change in the manner of financing the activities of the Commodity Credit Corporation. So far in the postwar period, thus, the impact of recession on the structure of debt has been different from that of prewar years, as a result of basic changes in the structure of debt and in the response of the economy to setbacks in demand.

The implications of a given shift in the structure of private debt also would be different now than in the prewar period. War finance created a large volume of liquid short-term U. S. government debt, and this has displaced short-term private debt as the cornerstone of the liquidity position of banks and other financial institutions. With liquidity desires now mainly focused on government debt, changes in call loans and in other short-term private debt do not have the same significance that they once had.

This review of the behavior of the structure of rates on U. S. government securities, thus, supports the generalizations made in the introduction: Short-term rates have averaged lower and have moved over a wider range than, but generally together with, long-term rates. The behavior of the rate structure does not seem explainable in terms of long-run expectations, though near-term expectations can temporarily govern the behavior of rates. The fundamental factors underlying the general coincidence of short-run movements in short-term and long-term rates seem to be the fact that debts of different maturities are to some degree substitutes for both borrowers and lenders (on the basis of their relative yields to maturity), and the fact that demands for funds of all types tend to be affected to some degree by changes in business conditions. Long-term yields move within the narrower range because the debt price changes and speculative implications of a given yield change are greater for long-term debt, and because demand for long-term funds is less responsive to business fluctuations. Short-run changes in the maturity structure of debt supplied can produce corresponding changes in yields.

VI. Some Implications for Credit Policy

This interpretation of the behavior of the rate structure, taken together with the facts of our postwar experience, has implications for the conduct of monetary policy and its role in the over-all economic stabilization program quite at variance with those of the expectational theory. Some of these implications are summarized below.

1. Direct government action in debt markets is not ordinarily necessary to produce roughly simultaneous upward and downward movements of long-term and short-term interest rates in response to changes in business conditions and in monetary policy (assuming debt management policies of at least some minimum degree of appropriateness.) Such behavior has been characteristic of interest rates in recent years. More broadly, the period since 1920 generally has been characterized by such congruous movements of long-term and short-term rates except for some apparently structural shifts in the relationship between long-term and short-term rates during the 1920's, the abnormal rate structure of the earlier 1930's, and some short periods of panic reactions in debt markets during the 1930's.

2. The regular behavior of the term structure and even some of its moderate departures from regular behavior seem to reflect supply and demand forces that can claim to be relevant to the term structure and perhaps to have some adaptive significance for the economy. Some theorists have assumed that the natural behavior of the term structure has little economic meaning or function. Explanations of the term structure on the basis of psychological or long-run expectational factors naturally tend to lead to such a view.

Any attempt at close administrative control over the rate structure, therefore, ought to be based upon a rather clear understanding of what objectives are sought, what private forces are being overridden, and what will be the effect of overriding them. For example, if a short-run movement in long-term yields were being caused by an irregularity in the flow of private security issues, government buying or selling to smooth out yields might be at the expense of encouraging fluctuation in the rate of private long-term borrowing. Is it clear that this would promote stability? Or, government action to offset the effects of an anticipatory movement in long-term yields based upon correctly informed speculative activity might have the twofold result of delaying an appropriate adjustment in yields and contributing directly to the profits of the speculators.

3. Our experience has been that, except under the special conditions of the 1930's, debt markets have been generally free of panic reaction and excessive and self-feeding instability — though in the early postwar period many feared that such behavior would develop. Our recent experience reinforces the view that debt markets have the necessary adaptability and resilience to adjust effectively to changes in economic conditions and in active anticyclical monetary and debt management policies.

4. Among the factors that can cause changes in the term structure of rates are shifts in the liquidity premiums reflected in the rate structure. These may result from changes in the maturity structure of available debt, from other factors affecting the liquidity structure of the stock of investment assets, or from changes in investor attitudes toward liquidity. Properly interpreted, thus, the behavior of the interest rate structure can be one indication of the liquidity situation of the economy, which, together with other evidence, can help to guide the conduct of monetary and debt management policies in maintaining liquidity conditions suited to the needs of economic stabilization. In particular, abnormally low yields on liquid short-term debt during a depression may be an indication that the economy is starved for liquidity, and abnormally high yields on such debt during prosperity may indicate that the supply of liquidity instruments is excessive for the conditions of the times.

5. If used actively in a co-ordinated manner, monetary and debt management policies can play an essential role in dealing with both inflationary and deflationary problems, by enforcing an appropriate behavior of interest rates, through their impact upon conditions in debt markets, and through their influence upon the liquidity position of the economy.

J. M. Culbertson.

School of Commerce
University of Wisconsin

[3]

THE EXPECTATIONS HYPOTHESIS, THE YIELD CURVE, AND MONETARY POLICY *

JOHN H. WOOD

Introduction, 457. — I. Elasticity of expectations and empirical and policy implications of the expectations hypothesis, 459. — II. A simplified elastic expectations model, 462; the model, 462; an empirical estimate of responsiveness of expected rates to current short rates, 463. — III. Effects of a swapping operation on the yield curve, 469.

The expectations hypothesis of the term structure of interest rates, as formulated by Fisher [1] and restated by Hicks and Lutz,[2] is usually understood to imply (1) that interest rates on long-term securities will move less, on the average, than rates on short-term securities, (2) that the monetary authority cannot reasonably expect to influence significantly long-term rates by means of open market operations in either the short- or long-term end of the market, (3) that an open market operation involving securities of different term-to-maturity which leaves the money stock unchanged — a swap — will leave the structure of rates unaltered; i.e., will affect neither the level nor the slope of the yield curve.[3]

* Work on this paper was partly supported by a Federal Reserve Bank of Chicago Research Fellowship. I wish to acknowledge the helpful suggestions and criticisms of George Horwich, Purdue University, Edwin S. Mills, Johns Hopkins University, Myron A. Grove, University of Oregon, and Frank deLeeuw and Henry Goldstein, Federal Reserve Board. The views expressed are my own.

1. See, for example, the following works by Irving Fisher: "Appreciation and Interest," *Publications of the American Economic Association*, Vol. 11 (Aug. 1896), pp. 23–29, 88–92; *The Nature of Capital and Income* (New York: Macmillan, 1906), pp. 273–74; and *The Theory of Interest* (New York: Macmillan, 1930), p. 70.

2. See J. R. Hicks, *Value and Capital* (2d ed.; Oxford: Clarendon Press, 1946), pp. 144–47; and F. A. Lutz, "The Structure of Interest Rates," *Readings in the Theory of Income Distribution*, eds. William Fellner and Bernard Haley (Philadelphia: Blakiston, 1951), pp. 499–529. (Reprinted from this *Journal*, LV (Nov. 1940), 36–63.) According to the Hicks formulation, long-term rates plus unity are expressed as geometric averages of current and expected short rates plus unity extending over the maturity of the longest-term rate being considered. Although the Lutz expression is somewhat more complicated, reflecting different assumptions with respect to discount factors and reinvestment of coupons, the implications discussed here are identical to those for the Hicks equation.

3. These implications of the expectations hypothesis have been discussed extensively, both in the literature of the 1930's and, more recently, since the mid-1950's. For some of the more prominent representatives of the earlier discussions, see J. M. Keynes, *A Treatise on Money*, II (London: Macmillan, 1930), 352–62; W. W. Riefler, *Money Rates and Money Markets in the United States* (New York: Harper and Brothers, 1930), p. 121; R. G. Hawtrey, *A Century of Bank Rate* (London: Longman's, Green and Co.,

The expectations hypothesis as a descriptive theory of relationships among rates on default-free securities differing only with respect to term-to-maturity, although under frequent attack in recent years,[4] has recently been given substantial empirical support by Meiselman,[5] who found that the Hicks expectations model, supplemented by an error-learning mechanism for the formulation of (directly unobservable) expectations, is consistent with the data.[6] Meiselman has, in effect, thrown the burden of proof onto the critics of the expectations theory.[7] It behooves us, in view of the added plausibility which must now be attributed to the expectations theory, to examine its implications more closely.

Meiselman has, in his error-learning model,[8] placed unprecedented emphasis on the elasticity of expectations of future rates of interest with respect to current rates. Earlier writers, although not unaware of the theoretical and empirical importance of the extent to which expectations of future rates are elastic or inelastic,[9] directed most of their attention to the case in which it was assumed that expectations of future short rates were perfectly, or at least highly, inelastic; i.e., were not responsive to changes in current rates. It

1938), pp. 184–206; J. R. Hicks, "Mr. Hawtrey on Bank Rate and the Long-Term Rate of Interest," *The Manchester School*, IX (April 1939), 21–37; and Lutz, *op. cit.*, pp. 520–29.

Among the more recent contributors have been C. E. Walker, "Federal Reserve Policy and the Structure of Interest Rates on Government Securities," this *Journal*, LXVIII (Feb. 1954), 19-42; J. M. Culbertson, "The Term Structure of Interest Rates," this *Journal*, LXXI (Nov. 1957), 485–517; J. W. Conard, *Introduction to the Theory of Interest* (Berkeley: University of California Press, 1959), pp. 289–360; and David Meiselman, *The Term Structure of Interest Rates* (Englewood Cliffs: Prentice-Hall, 1962), pp .31–49.

4. See, for example, Culbertson, *op. cit.*, pp. 496–98, 507–9; Dudley G. Luckett, "Professor Lutz and the Structure of Interest Rates," this *Journal*, LXXIII (Feb. 1959), 131–44.

5. *Op. cit.*, pp. 18–42.

6. The data used by Meiselman are the "basic yields of corporate bonds" compiled by Durand and Winn. See David Durand, *Basic Yields of Corporate Bonds, 1900–1942* (New York: National Bureau of Economic Research, 1947); David Durand and Willis J. Winn, *Basic Yields of Bonds, 1926–1947: Their Measurement and Pattern* (New York: National Bureau of Economic Research, 1947); and *The Economic Almanac.*

7. For a discussion of empirical investigations by Meiselman and others of alternative theories of the rate structure, see J. H. Wood, "Expectations, Errors, and the Term Structure of Interest Rates," *Journal of Political Economy*, LXXI (April 1963), 160–71.

8. Meiselman's model will be described in some detail in Section I below.

9. See, for example, Lutz, *op. cit.*, p. 520; Hicks, "Mr. Hawtrey on Bank Rate and the Long-Term Rate of Interest," *op. cit.*, p. 26; and T. de Scitovszky, "A Study of Interest and Capital," *Economica*, N.S., VII (Aug. 1940), 304–5. Hicks (*Value and Capital*, *op. cit.*, p. 205) defines "the elasticity of a particular person's expectations of the price of a commodity X as the ratio of the proportional rise in expected future prices of X to the proportional rise in its current price." We use an analogous definition, substituting "rate on a default-free bond" for "price of a commodity."

is this inelastic-expectations case from which the implications enumerated at the beginning of the present paper are drawn. These implications are greatly attenuated or even reversed if expectations of future rates are highly elastic.

In the following pages, I will, within the framework of the Hicks expectations model, (1) develop more precisely the empirical and policy implications of elastic as opposed to inelastic expectations of future short-term rates of interest, (2) derive empirical estimates, with the aid of certain simplifying assumptions, of the responsiveness of expectations of future short rates to changes in current short rates, and (3) show that a Federal Reserve open market swap will cause the equilibrium structure of yields to be altered when expectations are not perfectly inelastic.

I. Elasticity of Expectations and Empirical and Policy Implications of the Expectations Hypothesis

The relationship between the current rate on securities with n periods to run until maturity and the current one-period rate may be written, following the Hicks approach,

$$(1)\quad R_{nt} = [(1 + R_{1t})(1 + {}_{t+1}r_{1t})(1 + {}_{t+2}r_{1t}) \ldots (1 + {}_{t+n-1}r_{1t})]^{\frac{1}{n}} - 1,$$

where t is the current period, R_{nt} is the rate prevailing at time t on a security maturing in n periods, and ${}_{t+i}r_{1t}$ is the rate expected at time t to prevail on a one-period security at time $t + i$.[1]

If the monetary authority wishes to influence interest rates generally,[2] and if expectations of future short rates are perfectly inelastic (i.e., independent of the current short-term rate), then the amount by which R_{nt} should be expected to be changed relative to the change in R_{1t} is given by the partial derivative of R_{nt} with respect to R_{1t}:

1. Throughout this paper, upper-case R's refer to currently observed rates while lower-case r's indicate expected rates.

2. The expectations hypothesis implies nothing with respect to the monetary authority's ability to influence the level of rates generally, only its ability to influence rates relative to each other. Only the Federal Reserve's resources, its strength of will, and institutional and behavioral factors apart from those inherent in the expectations hypothesis limit the Federal Reserve's ability to exert any influence desired on any rate, regardless of term-to-maturity — as long as it is willing to accept, along with movements in the rate which is the direct object of policy, relative movements in other rates implied by the expectations theory.

$$(2)\quad \frac{\delta R_{nt}}{\delta R_{1t}} = \frac{[(1+R_{1t})(1+{}_{t+1}r_{1t})(1+{}_{t+2}r_{1t})}{n(1+R_{1t})}$$

$$\frac{\ldots(1+{}_{t+n-1}r_{1t})]^{\frac{1}{n}}}{n(1+R_{1t})} = \frac{(1+R_{nt})}{n(1+R_{1t})}.$$

The derivative of R_{nt} with respect to R_{1t} decreases as n increases (i.e., $\frac{\delta^2 R_{nt}}{\delta R_{1t}\delta n} < 0$) and lies between zero and one for all interest rates which may reasonably be expected to occur.[3]

It is apparent from equation (2) that actions undertaken to influence the level of rates will, unless expectations of future rates are affected, leave long rates changed little relative to short rates. This is true whether it is long-term or short-term securities which are acted upon directly. It is the model that is formally expressed in equations (1) and (2) from which the implications mentioned at the outset of this paper are derived.

But, it is unreasonable to suppose that short-term rates which are expected to prevail in the near future are unrelated to the short-term rate currently prevailing. It would seem that investors adjust their expectations of future rates in response to, among other factors, recent movements in rates as well as in response to the current short rate relative to what is conceived to be the "normal" rate. A related concept of elastic interest-rate expectations underlies Meiselman's model. Meiselman sets forth the hypothesis that investors revise their expectations of short rates "on the basis of errors made in forecasting the current short-term rate":[4]

$$(3)\quad {}_{t+n}r_{1t} - {}_{t+n}r_{1t-1} = f_n(R_{1t} - {}_{t}r_{1t-1}).$$

Writing equation (3) in linear form, solving for ${}_{t+n}r_{1t}$, and substituting the result into equation (1), we have

3. The general forms of equations (1) and (2) are, respectively,

$$R_{nt} = (1+R_{mt})^{\frac{m}{n}}[(1+{}_{t+m}r_{1t})(1+{}_{t+m+1}r_{1t})\ldots(1+{}_{t+n-1}r_{1t})]^{\frac{1}{n}} - 1$$

and

$$\frac{\delta R_{nt}}{\delta R_{mt}} = \frac{m(1+R_{nt})}{n(1+R_{mt})}.$$

The relationship between current short and long rates can also be expressed, within the framework of the Hicks equation, as a function of the expected long rate:

$$R_{nt} = (1+R_{1t})^{\frac{1}{n}}(1+{}_{t+1}r_{n-1t})^{\frac{n-1}{n}} - 1.$$

4. Meiselman, *op. cit.*, p. 20. The one-period rate expected at time t to prevail at the beginning of period t + n is implied, according to the expectations theory, by the structure of rates observed at time t:

$$r_{1t+n} = \frac{(1+R_{n+1t})^{n+1}}{(1+R_{nt})^{n}} - 1.$$

$$(4)\quad R_{nt} = \{(1 + R_{1t})[1 + a_2 + b_2(R_{1t} - {}_tr_{1t-1}) + {}_{t+1}r_{1t-1}][1 + a_3 + b_3(R_{1t} - {}_tr_{1t-1}) + {}_{t+2}r_{1t-1}] \ldots [1 + a_n + b_n(R_{1t} - {}_tr_{1t-1}) + {}_{t+n-1}r_{1t-1}]\}^{\frac{1}{n}} - 1,$$

where the forecasting error, $R_{1t} - {}_tr_{1t-1}$, enters the equation $n - 1$ times.

When $n = 2$, the derivative of R_{nt} with respect to R_{1t} is

$$(5)\quad \frac{\delta R_{2t}}{\delta R_{1t}} = \frac{2b_2R_{1t}+b_2(1-{}_tr_{1t-1})+{}_{t+1}r_{1t-1}+1+a_2}{2(1+R_{2t})}.$$

This derivative varies with current and expected rates, but in the special case where $a = 0$ and $R_{2t} = R_{1t} = {}_tr_{1t-1} = {}_{t+1}r_{1t-1}$ (i.e., the yield curve is horizontal),[5]

$$(6)\quad \frac{\delta R_{2t}}{\delta R_{1t}} = \frac{b_2 + 1}{2} \gtreqless 1 \text{ for } b_2 \gtreqless 1.$$

These results are not changed substantially when interest rates vary within normal ranges and for n greater than 2, so that we may say that the Meiselman model implies that long-term rates may be expected to move less than short-term rates only if expectations of future rates are revised by amounts, on the average, less than the error in forecasting the current one-period rate. Although Meiselman's b terms were all 0.7 or less, we can see that it is not inconceivable that investors might be highly responsive to past forecasting errors, so that it is consistent with the expectations hypothesis for long rates to be fully as volatile as short rates. The relationships on which Meiselman's model is based and the estimates derived from empirical testing of this model indicate that, while the monetary authority cannot expect to influence long rates as much as short rates, it may expect to have a greater impact on long rates, given the magnitude of its operations, than might be supposed from an examination of the implications of the expectations hypothesis where expectations are thought to be inelastic.[6]

5. Meiselman's (*op. cit.*, pp. 22, 25, 27–29) regressions found the constant term, a, not significantly different from zero.

6. These considerations are reminiscent of the Keynes (*op. cit.*, pp. 352–53), Hawtrey (*op. cit.*, pp. 185–87), Hicks ("Mr. Hawtrey on Bank Rate and the Long-Term Rate of Interest," *op. cit.*, pp. 22–33) discussions concerning the central bank's ability to influence long-term rates. Keynes interpreted the data to indicate that it was reasonable to expect the long rate to be susceptible to monetary policy, while Hawtrey took the opposite view. Hicks believed the data to be somewhat more consistent with Hawtrey than with Keynes, but differed with Hawtrey in supposing expectations to have an elasticity somewhat greater than zero.

II. A Simplified Elastic Expectations Model

A. The Model

Meiselman's model may be considered a special case of a more general expression of the expectations hypothesis in which expectations of future short rates are, for whatever behavioral reasons, linearly related to current short rates. This more general model may be written

$$(7)\quad R_{nt} = [(1+R_{1t})(1+a_{2t}+b_2R_{1t})(1+a_{3t}+b_3R_{1t}) \ldots (1+a_{nt}+b_nR_{1t})]^{\frac{1}{n}} - 1,$$

where $b_2, b_3, \ldots, b_n$ are measures of the responsiveness to R_{1t} of ${}_{t+1}r_{1t}, {}_{t+2}r_{1t}, \ldots, {}_{t+n-1}r_{1t}$, and $a_{2t}, a_{3t}, \ldots, a_{nt}$ encompass all of the factors other than R_{1t} (including the usual constant term entering linear expressions) which influence expectations of future short rates. In the Meiselman case, equation (4), a_{nt} corresponds to $a_n - b_n({}_tr_{1t-1}) + {}_{t+n-1}r_{1t-1}$. In other models, a_{nt} may include factors relating to such economic phenomena as income, "normal" rates, and Federal Reserve and Treasury activities.

Equation (7) may be approximated very closely by the linear expression

$$(8)\quad R_{nt}' = \frac{R_{1t}\left(1 + \sum_{i=2}^{n} b_i\right) + \sum_{i=2}^{n} a_{it}}{n}.$$

An example of the closeness of this approximation is given in Table I for the case in which $n = 2$. If we let ${}_{t+1}r_{1t} = .03$ and R_{1t} vary between zero and .06, the values of R_{2t} and R_{2t}', the approximation to R_{2t}, are given in columns two and three, respectively. The derivatives of R_{2t} and R_{2t}' with respect to R_{1t} are given for the inelastic expectations case in the last two columns. As one can see, the approximations are very close and continue so for n greater than two and for varying expected short rates. R_{nt}' and $\delta R_{nt}'/\delta R_{1t}$ become better approximations of R_{nt} and $\delta R_{nt}/\delta R_{1t}$ as n increases.[7]

The derivative of the linear approximation, R_{nt}', with respect to R_{1t} is, in the elastic expectations case,

$$(9)\quad \frac{\delta R_{nt}'}{\delta R_{1t}} = \frac{1}{n}\left(1 + \sum_{i=2}^{n} b_i\right) \gtreqless 1 \text{ as } \bar{b}_i \gtreqless 1,$$

where $\bar{b}_i = \frac{1}{n-1}\sum_{i=2}^{n} b_i$ is the mean of the b_i:

7. In fact, in the case where ${}_{t+1}r_{1t} = {}_{t+2}r_{1t} = \ldots = {}_{t+n-1}r_{1t}$, $R_{nt}' \rightarrow R_{nt}$ and $\delta R_{nt}'/\delta R_{1t} \rightarrow \delta R_{nt}/\delta R_{1t}$ as $n \rightarrow \infty$.

TABLE I

LINEAR APPROXIMATIONS OF R_{2t} AND $\frac{\delta R_{2t}}{\delta R_{1t}}$ WHERE ${}_{t+1}r_{1t} = .03$

R_{1t}	$R_{2t}=[(1+R_{1t})(1.03)]^{1/2}-1$	$R_{2t}'=\frac{R_{1t}+.03}{2}$	$\delta R_{2t}/\delta R_{1t}$	$\delta R_{2t}'/\delta R_{1t}$
0	.01489	.015	.507	.5
.01	.01995	.020	.505	.5
.02	.02499	.025	.502	.5
.03	.03	.030	.500	.5
.04	.03499	.035	.498	.5
.05	.03995	.040	.495	.5
.06	.04489	.045	.493	.5

B. An Empirical Estimate of Responsiveness of Expected Rates to Current Short Rates

I will develop in this section a model from which we may estimate the values of the b_i entering the linear equations presented above. The estimates derived are intended neither to prove nor disprove the expectations hypothesis as a valid descriptive theory of the term structure of rates.[8] Rather, the model derived below will enable us, if we take the expectations hypothesis as given (and Meiselman's results suggest this may not be an outlandish assumption),[9] to evaluate the empirical and policy implications of this theory.

We may write equation (8) in terms of first differences in n- and one-period rates as follows, where $\triangle R_{nt}' = R_{nt}' - R_{nt}'_{-1}$ and $\triangle R_{1t} = R_{1t} - R_{1t-1}$:

$$\triangle R_{nt}' = \frac{(1 + \sum_{i=2}^{n} b_i)\triangle R_{1t} + \sum_{i=2}^{n} (a_{it} - a_{it-1})}{n}. \tag{10}$$

If the a_{it} and a_{it-1} are assumed to have equal expectations, the expected value of $\triangle R_{nt}'$ is

$$E\triangle R_{nt}' = \frac{(1 + \sum_{i=2}^{n} b_i)}{n} E\triangle R_{1t}, \tag{11}$$

8. If the data are found to be consistent with the model based on the expectations theory derived below, however, the expectations theory is thereby indirectly lent additional empirical support.

9. A recent study by Jacob B. Michaelsen also appears to lend support to the expectations hypothesis as an empirically valid descriptive theory. "The Term Structure of Interest Rates: Comment," this *Journal*, LXXVII (Feb. 1963), 166–74.

which may be written

$$(12)\quad \frac{E\Delta R_{nt}'}{E\Delta R_{1t}} = \frac{1 + \Sigma\, b_i}{n}.$$

The assumption necessary to the conversion of (10) into (11), i.e., $E(a_{it} - a_{it-1}) = 0$, is satisfied if those factors other than current short rates influencing current long rates, a_{it}, are compositely equally as likely to rise as to decline between successive periods, and if the distribution of that change is symmetric around zero. That this assumption is valid at least in the Meiselman version (where $a_{nt} = a_n - b_n\,[{}_tr_{1t-1}] + {}_{t+n-1}r_{1t-1}$) of our model is indicated by a sample mean for Δa_{2t} of .02668 compared with a sample standard error of .08584 for a sample of 53 observations from the years 1902–54.[1]

Now write a regression equation, with the classical assumptions regarding the disturbance terms, u_t, where $\hat{a}$ and $\hat{\beta}$ are least-squares estimators of the true parameters,

$$(13)\quad \Delta R_{nt} = \hat{a}_n + \hat{\beta}_n \Delta R_{1t} + e_t.$$

The expectation of ΔR_{nt} is

$$(14)\quad E\Delta R_{nt} = a_n + \beta_n E\Delta R_{1t},$$

which may be written, where a_n is zero,

$$(15)\quad \frac{E\Delta R_{nt}}{E\Delta R_{1t}} = \beta_n\,.$$

Equating the right-hand sides of equations (12) and (15), i.e., assuming R_{nt}' to be a "sufficiently good" estimate of R_{nt}, we have

$$(16)\quad \frac{1 + \sum_{i=2}^{n} b_i}{n} = \beta_n\,,$$

or

$$(17)\quad \sum_{i=2}^{n} b_i = n\beta_n - 1.$$

Thus, given observations on a sufficient variety of interest rates of different term, we can solve for estimates of the b_i, b_i', from estimates of the β_i, $\hat{\beta}_i$. We have, for example, from equation (16),

$$(17.1)\quad b_2' = 2\hat{\beta}_2 - 1,$$

$$(17.2)\quad b_3' = 3\hat{\beta}_3 - b_2' - 1 = 3\hat{\beta}_3 - 2\hat{\beta}_2,$$

and, in general,

1. The sample mean and standard error are in terms of interest rates measured in percentage points.

$$\text{(17.3)} \quad b_n' = n\hat{\beta}_n - (n-1)\hat{\beta}_{n-1}.$$

Columns two through four of Table II list the regression results based on equation (13), with the standard errors of the regression coefficients in parentheses under the corresponding coefficients. Column five lists estimates of the b_n, b_n', based on the $\hat{\beta}_n$ shown in column three. The data used are Durand's [2] annual "basic yields of corporate bonds" for the period 1900–1954. Since not all yields up to the longest term, R_{40}, are estimated by Durand, we must resort in some cases to estimates of means of the b_n. Such a mean is indicated, for example, by $\bar{b}_{16,20}' = (b_{16}' + b_{17}' + b_{18}' + b_{19}' + b_{20}')/5$.

The estimated constant terms, $\hat{a}_n$, are not significantly different from zero, as assumed for purposes of equation (15), validating the relationships expressed in equation (17). The multiple coefficients of determination, R^2, are high and vary inversely with the maturity of the dependent variable, and the $\hat{\beta}_n$ are all significantly different from zero at the 1 per cent level. The b_n' tend to decline as maturity increases up to fourteen years, indicating that expectations, at least in the moderately distant future, are less responsive[3] to current rates than are near-term expectations. But the b_n' show an unmistakable tendency to rise between $n = 15$ and $n = 40$.

A possible explanation of the rising b_n' for $n > 14$ stems from

2. From Durand (*op. cit.*, pp. 5–6) and *The Economic Almanac*. It is appropriate to indicate here that, as Durand points out ("A Quarterly Series of Corporate Basic Yields, 1952–57, and Some Attendant Reservations," *Journal of Finance*, XIII (Sept. 1958), 348–56), his basic yield data are subject to substantial error, and analyses using these data must be interpreted accordingly. Errors in variables, when occurring in conjunction with the use of least-squares regression, will cause estimates of the coefficients to be biased toward zero even for large samples (See J. Johnston, *Econometric Methods* (New York: McGraw-Hill, 1963), pp. 148–50). Assuming observation errors to be mutually and serially independent of the true values of the variables, $\hat{\beta} = \beta/(1 + k)$, where $\hat{\beta}$ is the estimated coefficient, β is the true coefficient and k is the ratio of the variance of the observation errors to the variance of the true value of the independent variable. Thus, our results understate to an unknown extent the responsiveness of long-term to short-term rates. It can be shown, however, that since the independent variable is the same for each of the regressions shown in Table II, ratios of the estimated coefficients, $\hat{\beta}_i/\hat{\beta}_j$ $(i, j = 2,3, \ldots, 40)$ are unbiased, and also that ratios of the b''s, b_i'/b_j', are unbiased except where b_2' enters the ratio, since b_2' is biased downward relative to $b_3', b_4', \ldots$.

3. It is desirable to use a term such as "responsiveness" here rather than elasticity since, for any two-variable linear equation in which the constant term is zero, elasticity is always unitary. Thus, in the model used here, long-term rates are more or less responsive to movements in the short-term rate as the b_j are larger or smaller, with the elasticity of ΔR_{nt} with respect to ΔR_{1t} remaining equal to unity throughout. Elasticity would be the appropriate measure of responsiveness in a model in which, for example, ${}_{t+j}r_{1t} = a_{j-1t}R_{1t}^{b_{j-1}}$.

the "liquidity premium" version of the expectations hypothesis, according to which, because of the greater variability in prices of long-term securities and the higher costs of converting long-term securi-

TABLE II

ESTIMATES OF THE b_n USING DURAND'S DATA: INDEPENDENT VARIABLE ΔR_{1t}

Dependent Variables, ΔR_{nt}	$\hat{a}_n$	$\hat{\beta}_n$	R^2	b_n'
ΔR_2	.0029	.8274	.970	$b_2' = .6548$
	(.0138)	(.0200)		
ΔR_3	.0009	.6988	.914	$b_3' = .4416$
	(.0204)	(.0297)		
ΔR_4	.0004	.6110	.850	$b_4' = .3476$
	(.0244)	(.0355)		
ΔR_5	.0051	.5411	.793	$b_5' = .2615$
	(.0264)	(.0383)		
ΔR_6	.0014	.4930	.744	$b_6' = .2525$
	(.0276)	(.0401)		
ΔR_7	.0007	.4546	.710	$b_7' = .2242$
	(.0277)	(.0403)		
ΔR_8	.0021	.4260	.686	$b_8' = .2258$
	(.0275)	(.0399)		
ΔR_9	.0000	.4023	.670	$b_9' = .2127$
	(.0269)	(.0391)		
ΔR_{10}	.0000	.3828	.655	$b_{10}' = .2073$
	(.0265)	(.0385)		
ΔR_{12}	.0000	.3528	.648	$\bar{b}_{11,12}' = .2028$
	(.0248)	(.0360)		
ΔR_{14}	.0017	.3272	.637	$\bar{b}_{13,14}' = .1736$
	(.0235)	(.0342)		
ΔR_{15}	.0002	.3192	.641	$b_{15}' = .2072$
	(.0228)	(.0331)		
ΔR_{20}	.0006	.2883	.633	$\bar{b}_{16,20}' = .1952$
	(.0209)	(.0304)		
ΔR_{25}	.0020	.2734	.620	$\bar{b}_{21,25}' = .2142$
	(.0204)	(.0296)		
ΔR_{30}	.0027	.2680	.615	$\bar{b}_{26,30}' = .2410$
	(.0202)	(.0294)		
ΔR_{40}	.0037	.2696	.611	$\bar{b}_{31,40}' = .2744$
	(.0205)	(.0298)		

ties into cash, investors will be induced to hold long-term securities only if a positive yield differential, or liquidity premium, exists between long- and short-term yields. It is not unreasonable to suppose that these liquidity premiums, in addition to being associated positively with term-to-maturity, also vary directly with the level of interest rates. Such will be the case if, when interest rates rise (bond prices fall), the riskiness associated with holdings of securities generally, and long-term securities in particular, looms larger in the minds of investors. Further, transactions costs rise relative to bond prices as these prices fall, especially long-term prices since these usually fall farther than short-term prices. These considerations imply that, not only are liquidity premiums positively related to the level of rates, but also that the responsiveness of liquidity premiums to current rates is greater for long-term than for short-term securities.

Thus, the forward rates used in our analysis, ${}_{t+j}r_{1t}$, may each be composed of two elements, an expected future short-term rate, ${}_{t+j}r_{1t}^e$, and a liquidity premium, ${}_{t+j}L_{1t}$, such that ${}_{t+j}r_{1t} = {}_{t+j}r_{1t}^e + {}_{t+j}L_{1t}$, where each of the terms on the right-hand side of the equation are linearly and positively related to R_{1t}: ${}_{t+j}r_{1t}^e = a_{j+1t}^e + b_{j+1}^e R_{1t}$ and ${}_{t+j}L_{1t} = a_{j+1t}^L + b_{j+1}^L R_{1t}$, where $a_{j+1t}^e + a_{j+1t}^L = a_{j+1t}$ and $b_{j+1}^e + b_{j+1}^L = b_{j+1}$. It may be seen that, from these assumed relationships, even when the responsiveness of expected rates to changes in current rates declines monotonically as maturity increases, b_n will exceed b_{n-m}, for example, when $b_n^L - b_{n-m}^L > b_{n-m}^e - b_n^e$.

The results in Table II imply, then, that the responsiveness of expected rates to current rates dominates changes in liquidity premiums resulting from changes in current rates for short- and intermediate-term securities, but that the relative magnitudes of these responses are reversed for longer term securities.[4]

Table III shows estimates of the b_n using monthly observations of monthly averages of daily rates on U.S. Government securities during the period January 1947–December 1962.[5] The unit in which term-to-maturity is measured is taken to be 3 months instead of 1 year as for purposes of Table II. Term-to-maturity here is less neatly defined than for the Durand data and the maturities used here approximate mid-points of the range of terms-to-maturity in the data: 3 month Treasury bill rates are taken to be 1 period rates; 9–12 month rates are defined as 4 period rates; 3 to 5 year rates are defined as 16 period rates; and rates on securities maturing in 10 years or over are taken to be 50 period rates.

Characteristics of the results in Table III are similar to those

4. This discussion has drawn heavily from Reuben Kessel, "The Cyclical Behavior of the Term Structure of Interest Rates" (New York: National Bureau of Economic Research, 1962), unpublished MS., pp. 40–80.

5. As reported in the *Federal Reserve Bulletin*.

in Table II:[6] $\hat{\beta}_n$ and R^2 vary inversely with maturity (more dependably, for $\hat{\beta}_n$, in Table III than in Table II), and $\hat{a}_n$ is never significantly different from zero. The R^2 terms, however, are lower in Table III than in Table II, indicating that first-differences in interest rates of different maturities are less closely related when observed at monthly intervals than annually. This may be an indication of a fairly lengthy response period on the part of investors.

TABLE III

ESTIMATES OF THE b_n USING GOVERNMENT YIELDS: INDEPENDENT VARIABLE ΔR_{1t}

Dependent Variables, ΔR_{nt}	$\hat{a}_n$	$\hat{\beta}_n$	R^2	b_n'
ΔR_4	.0003 (.0074)	.8212 (.0384)	.708	$\bar{b}_{2,4}' = .7616$
ΔR_{16}	.0002 (.0078)	.4972 (.0403)	.446	$\bar{b}_{5,16}' = .3892$
ΔR_{50}	.0063 (.0044)	.1867 (.0227)	.263	$\bar{b}_{17,50}' = .0406$

These results lend some support to the validity of the expectations hypothesis as a descriptive theory of the rate structure in that the model expressed in equation (16), which is derived from an approximation of the expectations equation (7), is found generally to fit the data well. We should not place too much emphasis on the support given by these results to the expectations theory relative to competing theories, however, since most theories of the term structure imply larger movements in short-term than in long-term rates. The objective of this study lies in another sphere. We have taken the expectations theory as given as a point of departure in order to derive its empirical implications for the monetary authority's ability to influence various segments of the yield curve. The results indicate that, while long-term rates may be expected to change less than short-term rates as a result of actions by the Federal Reserve (or indeed as a result of any other set of policy or nonpolicy events

6. A difference between the results presented in Tables II and III is that, in Table II, unlike Table III, no autocorrelation of the residuals exists. The Durbin-Watson ratios for the first and last regressions, for example, in Table II, are 2.14 and 1.91, respectively, indicating no significant autocorrelation in the residuals. Durbin-Watson ratios for the three regressions in Table III are, respectively, 1.96, 1.69, and 1.58, allowing us, for 191 observations and one independent variable, to accept the hypothesis of serial independence of the residuals for the first two regressions, but not permitting us to accept this hypothesis at the 1 per cent level for the third regression.

affecting interest rates), movements in long rates will not by any means be insignificant. We see, for example, from Table II that movements in rates on securities maturing between 5 and 40 years in the future may be expected to be from .54 to .27 as great as movements in the 1-year rate, given sufficient time for adjustment. Looking at Table III, we see that rates on government securities maturing in 3 to 5 years and over 10 years can be expected to move only slightly less than one-half and one-fifth as much as the rate on 3-month Treasury bills, even given the relatively short adjustment period implied by monthly observations.

Certain sets of policy objectives with respect to the level and structure of rates continue to be inconsistent when viewed within the framework of the expectations hypothesis. The results presented here imply, as also does the expectations theory with zero elasticity of expectations, that the Federal Reserve will find it very difficult, for example, to induce simultaneously a decrease in interest rates generally and a decline in the differential between long and short rates, $R_L - R_s$.

III. Effects of a Swapping Operation on the Yield Curve

The expectations hypothesis, when expectations of future rates are inelastic with respect to current rates, implies that a Federal Reserve swap will leave the equilibrium yield curve unaltered. A swap may be defined as a simultaneous purchase and sale by the Federal Reserve of securities of different term-to-maturity such that total bank reserves are not changed.

Let the Federal Reserve buy long-terms and sell short-terms such that bank reserves and, we shall assume, the stock of money are left unchanged. If the market is in equilibrium prior to these operations, prices of long-term and short-term securities must initially rise and fall, respectively, if investors are to be induced to sell their long-terms to the Federal Reserve and to take on additional short-terms. Thus, in the first instance, the swap results in lower long rates and higher short rates than in the original equilibrium. But such a situation cannot prevail for long because the stock of money, the total market value of securities held by the public, and all other aspects of the public's portfolio have been left unaltered, given that long and short securities are perfect substitutes. Thus, nothing has happened to change the public's preferences for securities holdings relative to other types of investments or expenditures so that bond prices will not have changed relative to other prices in the new equilibrium compared with the original equilibrium — meaning that they will not have changed at all since nothing has occurred to cause other prices to change. If expectations have not been affected by these events, then the precise relationship between long and short rates existing prior to the swap must continue, in equilibrium, to exist. Consequently, given no change in the level of rates and no change in long relative to short rates, we must, in the new equilibrium, have precisely the same rate structure as that which held in the initial equilibrium.

If expectations of future rates are responsive to changes in current rates, however, as in the models specified in equations (4) and (7), then the initial impact on long and short rates of the Federal Reserve's operation, no matter how brief these effects might be, will induce investors to alter their expectations of future rates of interest. That is, in a circumstance such as that described above, where short-term rates rise as one of the immediate responses to the Federal Reserve induced disturbance, expectations of future short rates will rise, causing equilibrium long rates to rise relative to equilibrium short rates.

Investors will readjust their portfolios subsequent to the swap, mitigating these effects somewhat. But part of the initial impact on expectations will endure, so that the relationship between long and short rates which prevails in the new equilibrium will be different from that which held in the initial equilibrium.

Thus, the elastic expectations version of the expectations theory, in addition to modifying substantially the first two implications of this theory stated at the outset of this paper, completely invalidates the third.

Board of Governors, Federal Reserve System
Washington, D.C.

[4]

INNOVATIONS IN INTEREST RATE POLICY*

By Franco Modigliani *and* Richard Sutch
Massachusetts Institute of Technology

This paper is an examination of the success, or we should say lack of success, of the policy launched at the beginning of 1961 by the incoming Kennedy Administration, which has become known as "Operation Twist." This was an attempt to twist the maturity structure of interest rates by raising yields on securities with short term to maturity while simultaneously lowering, or at least holding the line on, long-term rates. Higher short-term rates were expected to contribute significantly toward stemming the outflow of capital and thus helping the United States balance-of-payments problem, while low long-term rates were considered desirable to stimulate the economy by increasing the flow of private investment. We are not concerned, however, with the broad issue of whether Operation Twist contributed to improving the balance of payments while sustaining domestic activity. Our focus is, rather, on Operation Twist per se. We direct ourselves to a review of the techniques used by the government and Federal Reserve to affect the term structure and attempt to assess how far they succeeded in achieving the stated goal of twisting the yield curve.

As far as we can see there were two main actions aimed directly at such a twisting:

1. Federal Reserve open market operations and Treasury debt management operations directed toward shortening the average term to maturity of the outstanding government debt held by the public. An increase in the relative supply of short-term securities was expected to exert upward pressure on short-term rates, while the corresponding decrease in the availability of long-term securities should have tended to lower long-term yields, thus twisting the term structure in the desired direction.

2. Beginning in January, 1962, the successive increases in the struc-

* The authors wish to express their thanks to Charles Bischoff, of Massachusetts Institute of Technology, for his invaluable assistance in the application of the Almon interpolation technique used in this paper. All computations were performed at the Computation Center of the Sloan School of Management, M.I.T., utilizing the "REGRT" regression program written by Robert Hall. The research was supported in part by a grant from the Ford Foundation to the Sloan School of Management for research in business finance, and by National Science Foundation funds. The authors have had the benefit of discussion with several colleagues, and in particular with Professor Eli Shapiro, of Harvard University, and Professor Paul Samuelson, of Massachusetts Institute of Technology.

ture of ceiling rates payable on commercial banks' time and saving deposits under Regulation Q. According to the *Economic Report of the President* of January, 1962, this "action was taken to promote competition for saving and to encourage retention of foreign funds by member banks and thus moderate pressures on this country's balance of payments" [3, p. 88, Table 8]. Also under this heading one should include the recent acquiescence by the Federal Reserve Board to the issuance of unsecured notes and debentures by commercial banks.[1]

An examination of the behavior of key short- and long-term rates between early 1961 and the third quarter of 1965, summarized in Table 1, reveals that short-term rates have risen substantially while long-term rates moved relatively little, some moderately up (government bonds, corporate Aaa) others moderately down (municipals, coporate Baa's, mortgage rates). As a result, the spread between rates on long-term government bonds and the bills rate has declined from 150 base points down to 35 base points, while the difference between Aaa corporate bonds and the commercial paper rate shrank from 125 to 12 base points. These figures would seem to provide impressive evidence that Operation Twist was a remarkable success. To make such an interpretation (as has been frequently done) would be much too hasty, for as historical experience has shown, the spread typically tends to close in a period of recovery and rising short-term rates, such as prevailed between 1961 and the present. Indeed, currently prevailing spreads are still appreciably larger than they were at the peak of the previous cycle in 1959 and early 1960, as can be seen from the last row of Table 1, Part B. Thus the closing of the spreads between the turn of 1960 and the present might reflect merely the normal tendency for spreads to close as short-term rates advance. This hunch can be tested by estimating the historical relationship between the spread and short rates with ordinary regression techniques, and then comparing the actual relation between short and long rates with that predicted by the least square regression. Using government securities we estimated the relation between the spread (S) and the Treasury three month bills rate (r) with quarterly data for the period 1952-I to 1961-IV, obtaining

[1] Other tools were brought to bear on the problem but were not designed to twist yield curves; rather, they were policies that were intended to change the reaction of the economy to a given yield curve. These can be broadly summarized under two headings: (1) Measures directly aimed at reducing capital exports for a given structure of long- and short-term rates: these measures include primarily (*a*) the interest equalization tax and (*b*) the Johnson Administration program of voluntary restraint in bank lending to foreigners and to domestic firms for foreign operations, and in direct foreign investments. (2) Fiscal measures aimed at increasing the rate of domestic long-term investments for a given level of long-term rates: these measures include (*a*) the Internal Revenue Department's revised depreciation guide lines and (*b*) the investment credit provisions. An assessment of these policies is beyond the province of this study, which will concentrate only on those techniques designed to change the shape of the yield curve.

$$R_t - r_t \equiv S_t = \underset{(0.17)}{2.16} - \underset{(0.070)}{0.495 r_t} = .495(4.37 - r_t)$$

$$S_e = .39$$

Since in the third quarter of 1965 the bill rate was 3.85 percent, this equation would predict a spread between the long rate and the bill rate of 33 points, almost identical with the spread actually prevailing of 35 base points. Very similar negative conclusions about the effectiveness of Operation Twist can be reached by extrapolating the relation between the commercial paper rate and the spread between this rate and Moody's Aaa bond yields, whether the relation is estimated for the postwar period alone or going back to the beginning of the 1920's.

Are we, then, to conclude that Operation Twist was a total failure, at least with respect to the structure of yields on marketable securities—that the changes which occurred since the inception of that operation are not noticeably different from what might have been expected in its absence? Clearly, to draw such a conclusion from the rudimentary evidence presented above would be no more warranted than to infer from the figures of Table 1 that the policy was a howling success. The point of these simple tests is rather to emphasize that the task of assessing the success of the operation is far from trivial and can only be adequately tackled with the help of a theoretically grounded and empirically tested understanding of the basic forces which tend to shape the yield structure and its variations in time. It is, then, to this challenging task that we must turn first.

I. *Recent Theoretical Developments in the Analysis of the Maturity Structure*

There is by now general agreement that in an ideal world of no transaction costs or taxes, rational behavior and certainty (about future rates), the maturity structure of yields must be controlled by the simple principle that all outstanding instruments, regardless of maturity, must produce identical returns over any given interval of time—where the return is defined as the sum of cash payments plus any increase (or minus any decrease) in the market value of the instrument. This principle in turn implies that at any date t the spread between the yield of an n period bond and the short rate, $S(n, t) = R(n, t) - R(1, t)$, is equal to minus the capital gain from holding the n period instrument. The capital gain in turn is inversely related to the change in yield: $\Delta R(n, t) = R(n-1, t+1) - R(n, t)$. Consequently, $R(n, t)$ can be expressed in terms of the current short rate $R(1, t)$ and the future long rate $R(n-1, t+1)$. Moreover, since $R(n-1, t+1)$ can in turn be expressed in terms of $R(1, t+1)$ and $R(n-2, t+2)$, and so on, recursively, it is readily apparent that $R(n, t)$ can also be expressed in terms of the current and

TABLE 1

BEHAVIOR OF SOME KEY SHORT- AND LONG-TERM RATES FROM 1960–61 TO THE THIRD QUARTER OF 1965

Year and Quarter	Bills Rate	Commercial Paper Rate	Average Rate on Time Deposits	Average Yield on S&L Shares	Long-term Government Bonds	Corporate Bonds (Moody's) Aaa	Corporate Bonds (Moody's) Baa	High Grade Municipals	Conventional Mortgage Yields
A. Levels (%)									
	(1)	(2)	(3)	(4)	(5)	(6)	(7)	(8)	(9)
1960–3	2.36	3.37	2.57	3.86*	3.82	4.31	5.10	3.60	6.25
1961–1	2.35	3.01	2.65	3.90*	3.83	4.27	5.06	3.34	6.05
1965–3	3.85	4.38	4.15†	4.19‡	4.20	4.50	4.89	3.27	5.85§
B. Changes									
1960–3 to 1965–3	1.49	1.01	1.58†	0.35*,‡	.37	.19	−.21	−.33	−.40§
1961–1 to 1965–3	1.50	1.37	1.50†	0.29*,‡	.36	.23	−.17	−.26	−.20§
1960–1 to 1965–3	−.09	−.31	1.64†	0.35*,‡	−.02	−.05	−.42	−.72	−.45§

* Average for the year.
† Second quarter of 1965.
‡ Average for 1964.
§ Last quarter of 1964.
SOURCES: Columns 1, 2, 5, 6, 7, 8, *Economic Indicators*.
Column 4, Savings and Loan League.
Column 3, Frank de Leeuw and the Federal Reserve Bank of St. Louis.
Column 9, Federal Housing Administration.

future rates for one period loans prevailing in each of the n periods to maturity, $R(1, t)$, $R(1, t+1)$, $\cdots$ $R(1, t+n-1)$, although the precise form of the functional relation will depend on the shape of the stream of cash payments promised by the bond until maturity. Finally, because the return to the lender and the cost to the borrower over any interval will be the same regardless of the maturity of the instrument held or issued, neither would have a special incentive to match the maturity structure of his assets or liabilities to the length of time for which he intends to remain a creditor or debtor.

There is unfortunately much less agreement as to the determinants of the yield structure in the "real" world. The prevailing points of view may be summarized as follows.

1. At one end of the spectrum is the Pure Expectation Hypothesis, which holds that the certainty model provides an adequate approximation to the real world, except that the equality of returns of the certainty world must now be replaced by the equality of "expected" returns, where the expected returns may be thought of as the mean value (or some other analogous measure of central tendency) of the subjective probability distribution of possible returns. In particular, for every n, $R(n, t)$ must equal $R(1, t)$ minus the expected capital gain, determined by the expected change in the n period rate, say $\Delta R^e(n, t)$. For otherwise holders of bonds with lower expected returns would try to sell them, bidding down their price and raising their yield, and to acquire higher yielding instruments, bidding up their price and reducing their yields, until the postulated relation would come to hold.

2. A variant of the expectation hypothesis, of Keynesian inspiration [10] but articulated largely by Hicks [8], which has wide support at the present, may be labeled the Risk Premium Model. It basically accepts the view that yields on various maturities are related to each other by the expectations of future long rates, and hence also short rates, but it calls attention to differences in the degree of uncertainty which attaches to the expected return to be obtained, in the short run, from holding securities of different length. While the return on short-term securities is certain (since the value of the principal is guaranteed by repayment at the end of the period), the return on longer maturities is not guaranteed because of the uncertainty of future rates and hence of the end of period market value of the bond. Furthermore, the uncertainty tends to be greater the longer the maturity, since a given change in the long rate tends to produce a greater variation in terminal value the longer the remaining life to maturity. If, then, investors are prevailingly risk averters, as a good deal of other evidence suggests, one should expect that if the expected return were the same on all maturities, they would tend to prefer the safer short-term instruments. Hence, in order to induce the market to hold the longer-term maturities supplied by long-

term borrowers, the expected return on these maturities must exceed that on shorter-term instruments by an expected risk or liquidity premium. According to this view, the yield curve will tend to rise more than the curve implied by the pure expectation hypothesis because of the increasing risk premium as the term to maturity increases. The size of these risk premiums might be expected to depend on the relative supplies of longer maturities and the strength of investors' risk aversion.

3. Finally, there is the view that might be labeled the Market Segmentation Hypothesis. The proponents of this approach suggest that both lenders and borrowers have definite preferences for instruments of a specific maturity, and for various reasons, partly due to institutional factors and regulations constraining financial intermediaries, will tend to stick to securities of the corresponding maturity, without paying attention to rates of return on other maturities.[2] Hence the rates for different terms to maturity tend to be determined, each in its separate market, by their independent supply and demand schedules. The rates so set might well imply wide differences in the expected return obtainable in the current period, or over some sequence of periods, by investing in different maturities, but such differences, it is argued, would not induce traders to move out of their preferred maturity—or maturity habitat, as we shall call it—except possibly when the discrepancies become extreme and glaring.

In our view, each of the three models has its merits, but also suffers from shortcomings. We propose, therefore, an alternative model which, in essence, blends the previous three, and which we label the Preferred Habitat Theory. This model shares with the Hicksian approach the notion that the yield structure is basically controlled by the principle of the equality of expected returns, but modified by the risk premiums. Yet it differs from it in one fundamental respect. The Hicksian model assumes that all traders are concerned with the short period return and that, therefore, anybody going long is bearing the risk associated with the uncertainty of the short period return from longer-term instruments. But this view would be correct only if we could assume that every lender desires to turn his portfolio back into cash at the end of the short period; i.e., that he has a short habitat (cf. Meiselman [14]). In reality, however, different transactors are likely to have different habitats, as the segmentation theory points out. Suppose that a person has an n period habitat; that is, he has funds which he will not need for n periods and which, therefore, he intends to keep invested in bonds for n periods. If he invests in n period bonds, he will know exactly the outcome of his investments as measured by the terminal value of his wealth (this being only approximately true if he were to invest in a conventional loan and precisely true for a pure n period loan; that is, a loan that was

[2] This view has been stressed by a number of authors, in particular Culbertson [3].

issued on a discount basis). If, however, he stays short, his outcome is uncertain, as it will depend on the future course of the short rates in periods 2, 3, . . . , n-1. Furthermore, he is likely to have to incur greater transaction costs. Thus, if he has risk aversion, he will prefer to stay long unless the average of the expected short rates exceeds the long rate by an amount sufficient to cover extra transaction costs-and to compensate him for the extra risk of going short. Similarly, if he should invest in maturities longer than n, he would also be exposing himself to risk, this time to the Hicks-Keynesian uncertainty as to the price he can fetch for his not-yet-matured bonds. Thus, risk aversion should not lead investors to prefer to stay short but, instead, should lead them to hedge by staying in their maturity habitat, unless other maturities (longer or shorter) offer an expected premium sufficient to compensate for the risk and cost of moving out of one's habitat. Similar considerations will clearly apply, *mutatis mutandis*, to the borrower's side of the market.

Under this model the rate for a given maturity, n, could differ from the rate implied by the Pure Expectation Hypothesis by positive or negative "risk premiums," reflecting the extent to which the supply of funds with habitat n differs from the aggregate demand for n period loans forthcoming at that rate. If the n period demand exceeded the funds with n period habitat, there would tend to arise a premium in the n period maturity, and conversely.[3] Such premiums or discounts would tend to bring about shifts in funds between different maturity markets, both through the "speculation" of investors tempted out of their natural habitat by the lure of higher expected returns and through "arbitrage" by intermediaries induced to "take a position" by borrowing in the maturity range where the expected return is low, and lending where the expected return is high.

In summary, then, the Habitat Model implies that the spread $S(n, t)$ between the long rate $R(n, t)$ and the short rate $R(1, t)$ should depend primarily on the expected change in the long rate, $\Delta R^e(n, t)$. But it suggests that the spread could also be influenced by the supply of long- and short-term securities by primary borrowers (i.e., by borrowers other than arbitrageurs) relative to the corresponding demand of primary lenders, to an extent reflecting prevailing risk aversion, transaction costs, and facilities for effective arbitrage operations.

These conclusions can be conveniently summarized in the following equations.

$$\begin{aligned}&\text{Expected current return on an } n \text{ period bond}\\&\equiv R(n, t) + \text{Expected capital gain}\\&= R(1, t) + F_t\end{aligned}$$

[3] This is only approximately true, for under risk aversion, funds of habitat n would not be indifferent as to where they would move but would tend to spill, preferably into neighboring maturities where the risk would tend to be smaller.

where F_t stands for the net effect of relative supply factors and could in principle be positive or negative. Solving for $R(n, t)$, and taking the Expected Capital Gain as proportional to the expected fall in the long rate, i.e., to $-\Delta R^e(n, t)$, we can also write

$$\begin{aligned} (1) \qquad R(n, t) &= R(1, t) - \text{Expected capital gain} + F_t \\ &= R(1, t) + \beta \Delta R^e(n, t) + F_t \end{aligned}$$ [4]

II. *An Operational Formulation of the Habitat Model*

Before we can test our hypothesis we must recast equation (1) into an operational form suitable for empirical estimation. This entails specifying both a theory of how expectations are formed and a functional form for the summary term "F." For a model of expectations we draw on the highly imaginative approach of Frank de Leeuw [4] who synthesized two currently held views as to the determinants of the expected change in long-term rates.[5]

One widely held hypothesis associated with Keynes [11] holds that the market expects the interest rate to regress toward a "normal" level based on past experience. Modifying slightly De Leeuw's formulation, we approximate this normal level, denoted by $\overline{R}_t$, by some average of the long rates for the past m periods and a constant which could be thought of as a very long-run normal level. Thus:

$$\overline{R}_t = v \sum_{i=1}^{m} \mu_i R_{t-i} + (1 - v)c \qquad 0 < v < 1$$

where R_t is used hereafter as a symbol for the long-term rate and the μ_i's are weights adding up to one. Since the recent experience should be more salient we should expect the μ_i's to decline toward zero as i rises from one to m. This regressive hypothesis can thus be formalized as

$$(2) \qquad \Delta R_t^e = \alpha_1(\overline{R}_t - R_t) = \alpha_1 \left[v \sum_{i=1}^{m} \mu_i R_{t-i} + (1 - v)c - R_t \right]$$ [6]

where α_1 is a measure of the speed with which R_t is expected to return to $\overline{R}$.

[4] The substitution of $-\beta\Delta R^e(n, t)$ for the expected capital gain should be recognized as an approximation, if β is taken as constant. Strictly speaking, β can be shown to be a function both of the length to maturity n and of $R(n, t)$ (as well as possibly future short rates). However, the dependence on n need not be neglected if we deal with a fixed maturity n; and the effect of $R(n, t)$ can be shown to be sufficiently small to be neglected to a first approximation within the range of variation of $R(n, t)$ prevailing in the period with which we are concerned.

[5] Meiselman [14] and Kessel [9] have also made important contributions in this area, but while their work provides impressive support for the expectations model, their approach is not directly applicable to our problem.

[6] This hypothesis could also be derived by replacing the notion of a normal level with the notion of a normal range (cf., Malkiel [13]).

A quite different hypothesis, advanced by James Duesenberry, suggests that expectations might be extrapolative: "a rise in rates [leading] to an expectation of a further rise and vice versa" ([5], p. 318). De Leeuw suggests that the recent trend in rates might be approximated by the difference between the current rate and some weighted average of recent past rates and accordingly expresses the extrapolative hypothesis as

$$\Delta R_t^e = \alpha_2 \left(R_t - \sum_{i=1}^{n} \delta_i R_{t-i} \right); \qquad \alpha_2 > 0 \tag{3}$$

where n should be appreciably smaller than m and the weights, δ_i, would probably decline rather rapidly.

Now, as De Leeuw rightly points out, it is quite credible that both hypotheses contain an important element of truth—that expectations contain both extrapolative and regressive elements. If so, we can combine the right-hand side of (2) and (3) to obtain

$$\Delta R_t^e = -aR_t + \sum_{i=1}^{m} b_i R_{t-i} + dc \tag{4}$$

where $a=(\alpha_1-\alpha_2)$, $b_i=\alpha_1 v\mu_i-\alpha_2\delta_i$, with δ_i defined to be zero for $i>n$, and $d=\alpha_1(1\text{-}v)$. Since the term in the summation now represents the difference of two lag structures, we can no longer expect it to be of a simple geometric form. Indeed, if the extrapolative element is at all significant (i.e., α_2 is not zero or small compared with $\alpha_1 v$) we should find that initially, since δ_i falls faster than μ_i, b_i rises (possibly even from negative values), reaching a peak in the neighborhood of n and then declines back toward zero.

We are ready now to substitute equation (4) into the basic hypothesis (1) which yields

$$R_t = r_t - \beta a R_t + \sum_{i=1}^{m} \beta b_i R_{t-i} + \beta dc + F_t$$

where r_t is used hereafter to denote the short rate $R(1, t)$. As it now stands, this equation involves the current long rate on both sides; but this can be readily handled by solving the equation for R_t, obtaining finally

$$R_t = Ar_t + \sum_{i=1}^{m} B_i R_{t-i} + C + F_t' + \epsilon_t \tag{5}$$

where

$A = \dfrac{1}{1+\beta a}$, $B_i = \dfrac{\beta}{1+\beta a} b_i$, $C = \dfrac{\beta dc}{1+\beta a}$ and ϵ_t is the error term.

We note that, since β and a are supposed to be positive, the coefficient A should be positive but distinctly below unity, and that, since the lag coefficients, B_i, are proportional to the b_i of (4), our earlier inferences about the b_j's—which define the lag structure—applies equally to the B_i's.

III. *Estimation of the Model*

If we disregard for the moment the nondescript supply term F', equation (5) contains only observables and is in principle ready for estimation and testing. In so doing, however, we must face two rather difficult problems. Since the distributed lag on the previous long rates should be quite long and not of the familiar exponentially declining type, it poses estimation problems. These De Leeuw solved with an ingenious technique that involved estimation of only a small number of coefficients rather than a separate coefficient for each lagged value of R (an alternative which would undoubtedly lead to severe multicolinearity problems). However, since his writing, an alternative, more powerful and far more flexible technique for estimating lag structures has been developed by Shirley Almon [1] and pursued by Charles Bischoff in work currently in progress at the Massachusetts Institute of Technology. This procedure imposes very little a priori restriction on the lag structure, requiring merely that it can be approximated by a polynomial. Since our formulation suggests that the lag distribution should rise to a single peak and then fall, we concluded that a fourth degree polynomial would be sufficiently flexible to closely reproduce the true structure.

The Almon Interpolation Distribution involves the calculation of Lagrangian interpolation polynomials, which are used to weight a specified number of past values of the variable whose lag is to be estimated. These weighted averages, or Almon variables, are then entered in the ordinary least squares regression equation. For a fourth degree polynomial, five Lagrangian polynomials would be needed to define the structure. However, since we have a priori reasons to believe that the lag structure will taper off to negligible values at some finite distance in the past, we further impose the restriction that the polynomial to be estimated should assume a zero value at a finite lag. This allows us to use only four Lagrangian polynomials and hence also four Almon variables.[7] The four coefficients estimated for these variables in the regression plus

[7] This is a modification of the procedure which Mrs. Almon followed in her paper on lags between capital appropriations and expenditures [1]. She specified that the lag distribution began as well as ended with a zero value, and thus only three Almon variables were necessary to estimate the fourth degree polynomial. For our purposes the requirement that the polynomial pass through zero at t plus one seemed to place an unwarranted restriction on the shape of the distributed lag. Experiments with several alternative restrictions indicated that a free estimation of the head of the distribution yielded more sensible lag structures and closer fits.

the a priori specification of the intercept yield the five points necessary to define a fourth degree polynomial.

However, before we attempt to apply this technique, we must face another difficulty. Equation (5) purports to explain the dependent variable R_t in terms of lagged values of itself. It is well known that in the presence of serial correlation of the error term, ϵ_t, such a procedure will lead to biased estimates of the coefficients [7].

The problem is particularly serious for our present purposes, as it can be shown that if, in fact, Operation Twist was successful, then an equation of the form (5) estimated by ordinary least squares would very likely tend to conceal and understate the true effectiveness.

One way to handle this difficulty would be to estimate (5) using recently developed techniques for consistent estimation of equations which include a lagged dependent variable.[8] However, we propose an alternative approach. As is well known, an equation in the form of (5) implies that R_t can also be expressed as a function only of r_t and a weighted sum of all previous short rates, r_{t-i}. This result can derived by using equation (5) to express R_{t-1} in terms of r_{t-1}, and R_{t-2} to R_{t-m-1}, and so on, recursively. The final result involves only r_{t-j}, with j extending indefinitely into the past, but with the coefficients of the far removed r_{t-j} approaching zero. Hence, to a first approximation R_t can be expressed as an average of a finite and reasonably small number of lagged values of r:

$$R_t = \alpha + \beta_o r_t + \sum_{i=1}^{m} \beta_i r_{t-i} + \eta_t \tag{6}$$[9]

This equation is very similar to (5), from which it differs only because the distributed lag on the long rate is replaced by a distributed lag on the short rate. This substitution is in essence equivalent to hypothesizing that the expected long rate R_t^e can be approximated as a weighted average of past short rates rather than past long rates. This is certainly as sensible a hypothesis as De Leeuw's original. Indeed, it is basically an implication of that hypothesis, and conversely. Whether it is more convenient and efficient to approximate the basic model by a long lag on the long rate or on the short rate is, in the last analysis, a purely pragmatic and empirical issue.[10] But even if (6) should fit the data less well than

[8] Such a technique would be similar to that suggested by Liviatan [12].

[9] Ideally, one might wish to estimate an infinite lag on r_t. Estimation techniques for the Pascal-Solow lag distribution [15] now being developed by Robert Hall look to be suitable for such a model, but this will have to wait for a later date. It is very unlikely, however, that refined estimation techniques could substantially alter our conclusions. Incidentally, equation (6) can be recognized as simply the first stage of the Liviatan technique as applied to this model (see footnote 8 above).

[10] The only statistically significant difference between (5) and (6) lies in the stochastic properties of the error term hypothesized for the two models. If (5) holds with nonserially correlated error, then (6) will have an error vector which is autoregressive, and conversely.

(5), it has two significant advantages: (1) because it does not involve the lagged dependent variable, an unbiased estimate of its coefficients can be obtained by ordinary regression techniques; and (2) it provides a more reliable tool for testing Operation Twist, free of the bias noted above.

The basic hypothesis (6) was estimated using the Almon technique described above for the forty quarters spanning the pre-Operation Twist period, 1952-I to 1961-IV, with R_t defined as the yield on long-term government bonds (i.e., due or callable in ten years or later) and r_t defined as the three-months Treasury bills rate. Since we are particularly interested in the behavior of the spread, we have found it convenient to subtract r_t from both sides of the equation. This transformation converts the dependent variable into the spread $S_t = R_t - r_t$ without affecting the right-hand side of the equation or its statistical properties except for changing the coefficient of r_t on the right-hand side from β_o to $-(1\text{-}\beta_o)$.

Lags of between two and seven years were tested with the most satisfactory results obtained for lags of around four years. The 16-quarter lag produced lower standard errors, smaller serial correlation, and the most sensible lag structure, although the multiple correlation and DW statistics[11] were not very sensitive to the length of lag, at least beyond four years. The result can be summarized as follows, omitting for the moment variables besides the short rate:

$$(7) \qquad S_t = \underset{(0.028)}{1.239} - \underset{(0.030)}{0.684}\, r_t + \sum_{i=1}^{16} \beta_i r_{t-i}$$

$$R^2 = .975 \qquad S_e = .093 \qquad DW = 1.42$$

The expression

$$\sum_{i=1}^{16} \beta_i R_{t-i}$$

represents the finite lag. The 16 coefficients of r_{t-i} (the β_i's) are plotted within a band of plus and minus one standard error, in Figure 1.[12]

These results are rather striking. The coefficient of r_t has the predicted sign and order of magnitude, the lag structure has the predicted shape, and its initial rising segment provides impressive support for the hypothesis that expectations involve significant extrapolative as well as the

[11] The symbol DW denotes the Durbin-Watson statistic, a measure of the estimated first order serial correlation of the residual error [6].

[12] The actual least squares regression entered four Almon variables, each of which received highly significant coefficients. These coefficients were unscrambled to obtain the lag structure and its standard error plotted in Figure 1. Because there is no unique way of selecting the interpolation polynomials to be used in the estimation of the lag distribution, the presentation of these four coefficients was thought not to be as helpful to the reader as the summary statistics presented.

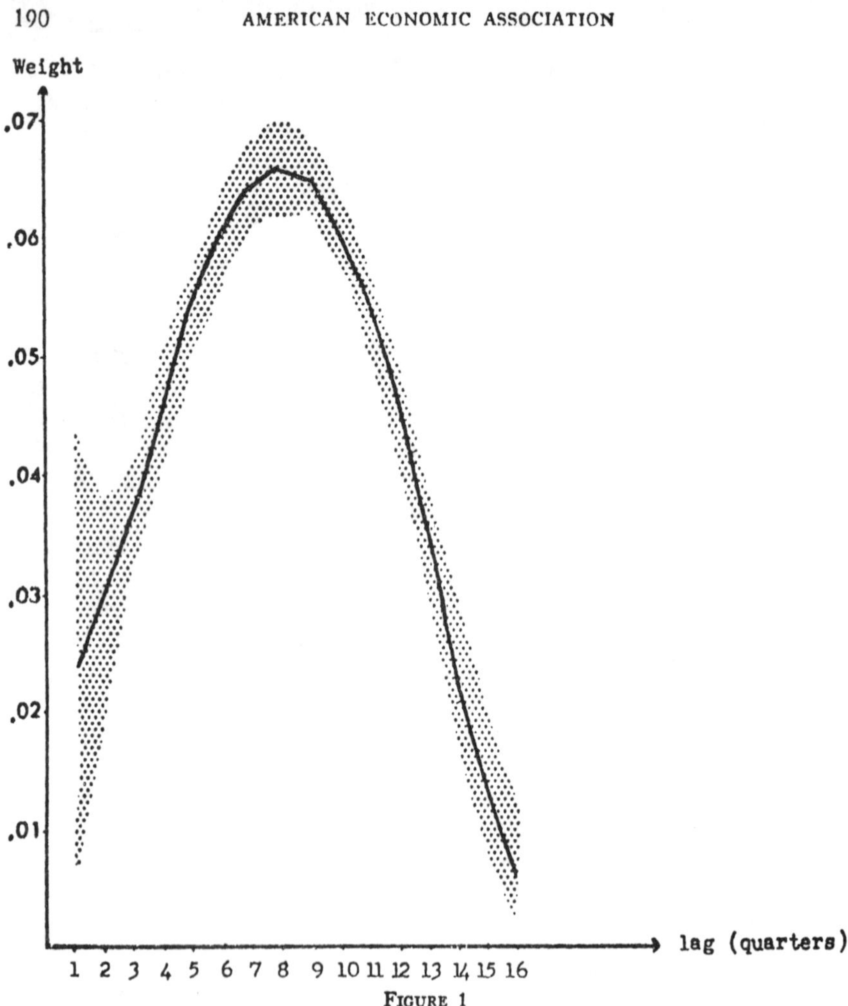

FIGURE 1

LAG STRUCTURE ON THE SHORT RATE PLUS AND MINUS ONE STANDARD ERROR (EQUATION 7)*

* The coefficients and their standard errors plotted are, from left to right: .0229(.0215), .0293(.0091), .0373(.0054), .0458(.0060), .0536(.0058), .0599(.0048), .0641(.0044), .0656(.0049), .0644(.0055), .0603(.0056), .0537(.0053), .0449(.0051), .0347(.0058), .0239(.0070), .0136(.0074), .0514(.0056).

widely recognized regressive elements. The multiple correlation is quite high and the standard error remarkably low, less than 10 base points. (This, incidentally, is a vast improvement over De Leeuw's original model, which for the same period, even with additional significant variables, has a standard error of 34 base points and a *DW* of .79.)

There remains to examine whether the small residual error might reflect in some measure supply effects, subsumed under F'_t in equation (5); or more precisely variation in supply conditions for, to some extent, the rather large constant term of (7) may already reflect a risk premium resulting from supply effects. Unfortunately, the measurement of supply-demand effects poses formidable problems, even if we are prepared to limit ourselves to variations in supply, on the assumption that the demand side is not subject to significant variations. The problem arises not only from shortage of data but even more from the statistical and conceptual difficulties of separating the total supply from the relevant primary supply. For this reason, most authors have ended up by measuring supply effects by the composition of the outstanding supply of marketable federal debt outside the Federal Reserve and Government Trust Accounts. De Leeuw in particular tried to test the effect of both the composition and the change in the composition of the debt outstanding in each of four maturity classes. He could find no evidence that the proportion outstanding in the various classes had any effect, but found some evidence that an increase in the proportion of both short (less than one year) and intermediate debt (one to five years) tended to reduce the spread.

We have repeated the tests of De Leeuw and others, and we find that none of the many debt variables we have tested obtains a significant coefficient with the predicted sign.[13] This is somewhat surprising in light of our a priori expectations, but does confirm the findings of most other authors. We must conclude that neither the maturity structure of the government debt nor changes in the maturity structure exert any significant, lasting or transient, influence on the relation between the two rates. This conclusion is supported by lack of positive evidence that these variables affect the spread in the generally supposed direction, and is reinforced by the consideration that the behavior of the spread can be accounted for quite closely without any reference to such variables, implying that their effect, if at all present, could be only of a secondary order of magnitude. This is not to say, of course, that there are no supply-demand effects, but merely that we could find no evidence that operations on the government component of the supply have a noticeable effect on the term structure as defined.

Ironically enough, this finding should be a source of relief to the authorities concerned with debt management because it turns out that,

[13] To illustrate, when we add to (7) the two variables that De Leeuw found to have significant effects in the predicted direction, namely, the change in the proportion of short-term debt, $\Delta[D_S/D_T]$, and the change in the proportion of intermediate debt, $\Delta[D_I/D_T]$, we find

$$S_t = \underset{(0.061)}{1.233} - \underset{(0.040)}{0.709}r_t + \sum_{i=1}^{16} \beta_i r_{t-i} + \underset{(1.20)}{0.93}\,\Delta\left[\frac{D_S}{D_T}\right] - \underset{(1.49)}{0.97}\,\Delta\left[\frac{D_I}{D_T}\right]$$

The variables D_S and D_I were calculated with an elaborate averaging technique by the flow-of-funds section of the Federal Reserve Board, who generously made them available to us. We have also tried using the proportion of short and long debt, the changes in these proportions, the average length to maturity of publicly-held debt, and other such variables, and in no case were significant supply effects in evidence. This leads us to suspect that the significant coefficients that De Leeuw found in his original studies must be a spurious result.

with a very few and fleeting exceptions, the combined result of Federal Reserve-Treasury debt management since the last quarter of 1961 was to lengthen steadily the maturity of the debt held by the public, reversing a previous trend. While in the first quarter of 1960 the average maturity stood at 4.3 years, the lowest figure on record until that time, by the second quarter of 1965 it stood at 5.7 years. Thus, if lengthening the maturity had the usually supposed effect of increasing the spread, then debt management would have pretty consistently worked toward defeating the goal of Operation Twist.

IV. *Testing the Effects of Operation Twist*

Since equation (7) has sound theoretical underpinnings, as well as strong empirical support, it should provide a sensible basis for a test of the effectiveness of Operation Twist. To this end we extrapolated this equation from the first quarter of 1962 to 1965-II, and the result is graphed as a dashed curve in the top panel of Figure 2. It is apparent that, through the middle of 1964, there is very little evidence that these policies produced an appreciable effect on the term structure. With but a couple of exceptions, the error is within ten base points, or less than the standard error; beginning with the second quarter of 1962, however, the spread is consistently smaller than the computed value and, beginning with 1964-IV, the difference becomes impressive, four to six times the standard error. Thus the best that could be said on the basis of (7) is that the twist policy was slightly to moderately successful.

Since our results indicate that this success is not attributable to debt management by the Treasury or the Federal Reserve, we must consider whether the only other major tool applied might be responsible for what twisting took place. That was, as we noted, the successive increases in the ceiling rates on time deposits under Regulation Q. Particularly noteworthy is the fact that the major increases in the ceiling rate came precisely at the beginning of 1962 and again in the last quarter of 1964. But while the coincidence of dates is suggestive, it is at best circumstantial evidence. To put our case on a solid footing, we must specify the mechanism by which an increase in the ceilings on interest payable to savings deposits could be expected to affect the spread, and then look for direct evidence that this mechanism was actually at work in the period under consideration.

To see what light the Habitat Theory can shed on the nature of the mechanism, we note once more that the rather large constant term in (7) suggests that during the postwar period the expected return from long-term bonds tended to exceed the short rate by a positive premium. According to the Habitat model the prevalence of such a positive premium would indicate a systematic tendency for the primary supply of

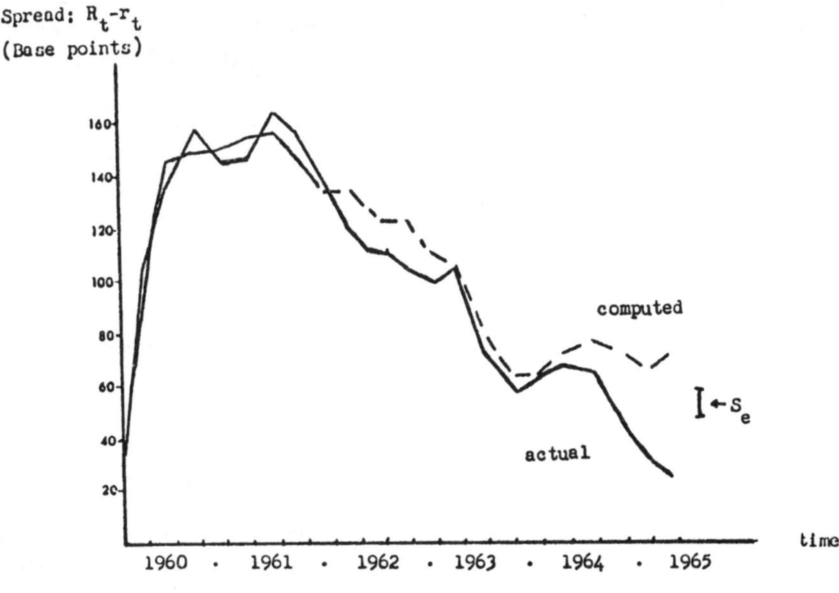

Equation (7) Extrapolated

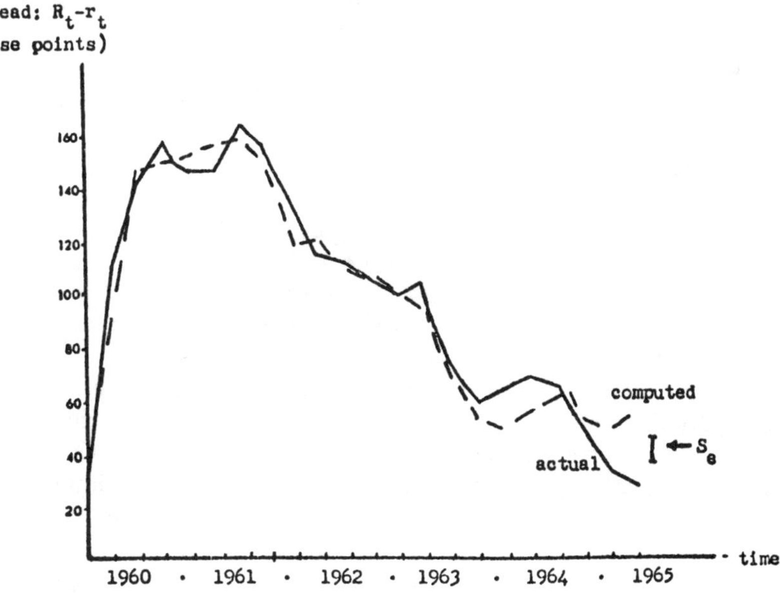

Equation (8) Actual and Fitted Values

FIGURE 2

funds to exceed the primary demand in the short market and to fall short of the primary demand in the long market. We have further seen that under these conditions the size of the premium on longs would depend, among other things, on the "facilities for effective arbitrage operations." In particular, we should expect that any significant impediment to arbitrage, such as a curtailment of the ability of a certain class of would-be arbitrageurs to attract short-term funds with a rate as high as they would otherwise be prepared to pay, would tend to raise the premium. Among such potential arbitrageurs one presumably would include commercial banks, hence the Regulation Q ceiling on time deposit rates (if sufficiently low to be effective) would be a force creating an artificially large premium. Thus, we would presume that increases in the ceiling rate would tend to reduce the spread by allowing banks to arbitrage away part of this premium.

This theoretical formulation suggests that to measure the effect of Regulation Q we need to introduce a variable which (1) should treat the successive lifting of the ceilings, not as positive forces contributing to twist, but rather as the removal of an interference with normal arbitrage operations; and (2) should play the largest role when other short-term rates are very close to or above ceiling; while it should cease to have effect once the ceiling is sufficiently above these rates. Beyond that level, changes in the ceiling should no longer affect the spread. Thus we define a variable, Q, as follows:

$$Q_t = r_t - (q_t - a) \qquad \text{if positive, zero otherwise}$$

where q_t is the ceiling rate under Regulation Q and $(r_t + a)$ is a threshold level such that any higher ceiling would be irrelevant at time t. Just how high the gap, a, should be is hard to guess a priori, and depends in a large measure upon what rate is used for r_t. Since we are dealing with the market for government securities it seems sensible to use the treasury bills rate itself for r_t. For a we assumed somewhat arbitrarily a value of one hundred base points.[14]

When we fit our regression model, including the variable Q, for the entire period from 1952 to mid-1965, we find that the coefficient of the variable Q has the expected positive sign, although it is on the borderline of statistical significance.[15] It is also rather small, as it implies that when r_t equals the ceiling, the premium is only ten base points higher than it would be in the absence of an effective ceiling. The marginal

[14] We use the ceiling rate q_t rather than the average rate actually offered by banks because q_t is the policy variable whose effect we wish to estimate. See also footnote 15.

[15] Nearly identical results are obtained if Q is entered with a one-quarter lag, raising the possibility that a short distributed lag on Q might improve the results, although we have not investigated this approach. It was also found that if the threshold level, a, was chosen to be 50 base points rather than 100, the same qualitative results were obtained.

statistical significance and the small magnitude of the coefficient estimated for Q raises the possibility that other events in the period after 1961 are causing a spurious effect. One such major development, and one that could have affected the ability of commercial banks to attract short-term funds, was the introduction in 1961 of negotiable Time Certificates of Deposit (CD's). To be sure, the spectacular growth of this instrument after 1962 could not have occurred had not the ceiling been raised that year, so that banks could offer CD's at rates competitive with other short-term instruments. Nonetheless, the CD must be regarded as a true financial innovation which could have enhanced the capacity of banks to arbitrage even if Regulation Q had never existed.

To test the effect, if any, of this innovation, one could rely on the dummy variable technique, adding to (7) a variable taking the value one after 1962 and zero everywhere else. This would allow the constant term of the equation (which is a measure of the risk premium) to assume two values: one value for pre-1962 and a second, lower value (the sum of the constant term and the coefficient of the dummy variable) after 1962.

When we entered into the regression such a dummy—denoted by Z in the equation below—its coefficient has the expected negative sign and is significant in relation to its standard error:

$$(8) \qquad S_t = \underset{(0.064)}{1.278} - \underset{(0.031)}{0.695}r_t + \sum_{i=1}^{16} \alpha_i r_{t-i} - \underset{(0.043)}{0.124}Z^{16}$$

$$R^2 = 0.964 \qquad S_e = 0.103 \qquad DW = 1.02$$

Actual and computed values for this equation are shown in panel 2 of Figure 2.

When Q is added along with Z in a similar regression, the coefficient of Q not only loses its statistical significance but actually becomes negative. This result is confirmed by rerunning (7) with Q but not Z for the period before 1962, thereby excluding the CD years altogether. The coefficient of Q is again negative. This outcome suggests that the successive increases in the ceiling contributed to twist solely by permitting

[16] The use of a dummy variable in (8) may appear less than satisfactory, failing to bring out the fact that the contribution of the newly introduced CD's depends on whether the ceiling rate is sufficiently high to enable banks to offer rates competitive with other short-term instruments. With these considerations in mind, we had actually defined the variable Z to take (1) the value 1 only when the ceiling q_t exceeds r_t by at least 50 base points, a gap which we assumed to be sufficiently large to give banks the needed elbow room; (2) the value zero when r_t equals the ceiling, by which time banks would likely lose nearly all power of attracting CD funds; and (3) to decrease linearly between these limits as $(q_t - r_t)$ shrinks from 50 base points to zero. As it turns out, however, from 1962 to 1965-II the ceiling was consistently kept at least 50 base points above r_t. (Note in this connection that for the last quarter of 1964 the ceiling was taken as 4.25, a simple average of the 4 percent rate ruling up to November 24 and the 4.5 rate ruling thereafter.) Therefore, the variable defined above always has the value one, and is undistinguishable from an ordinary dummy. But in extrapolating (8) beyond the period of observation, care should be taken if r_t gets too close to the ceiling, as it has done very recently.

the invention of CD's—for which Operation Twist cannot properly claim credit—to exercise its maximum effect, some twelve base points according to the estimate of equation (8).[17] It should be acknowledged, however, that our results do not effectively enable us to ascertain whether the coefficient of the dummy variable Z measures just the effect of CD's, as intended, or whether it also picks up other, yet unspecified effects of Operation Twist, including possibly psychological effects modifying expectations.

In concluding, we wish to emphasize that the results we have reported represent but the preliminary findings of a continuing study of the determinants of the maturity structure of interest rates. We can indicate, however, that these results are broadly supported by a similar study of the behavior of the spread in the corporate market between the yield on Aaa rated bonds and the commercial paper rate, both for the postwar period and for the longer span beginning with the inception of the Federal Reserve System. At this stage we feel that the following conclusions can be advanced with considerable confidence.

1. The expectation model can account remarkably well for the relation between short- and long-term rates in the United States. Furthermore, the prevailing expectations of long-term rates involve a blending of extrapolation of very recent changes and regression toward a long-term normal level.

2. There is no evidence that the maturity structure of the federal debt, or changes in this structure, exert a significant, lasting or transient, influence on the relation between the two rates.

3. The spread between long and short rates in the government market since the inception of Operation Twist was on the average some twelve base points below what one might infer from the pre-Operation Twist relation. This discrepancy seems to be largely attributable to the successive increase in the ceiling rate under Regulation Q which enabled the newly invented CD's to exercise their maximum influence.

4. Any effects, direct or indirect, of Operation Twist in narrowing the spread which further study might establish, are most unlikely to exceed some ten to twenty base points—a reduction that can be considered moderate at best.

[17] Note that if Z is interpreted along the lines of footnote 16, then for the initial period 1962-I to 1963-II when r_t remained below the old ceiling rate of 3 percent, the introduction of CD's would have contributed some to the closing of the spread even if the ceiling had not been raised. Thus for this initial span the contribution of the increase in ceiling as such must be estimated at somewhat less than 12 points, although how much less it is not really possible to say with confidence.

REFERENCES

1. S. Almon, "The Distributed Lag Between Capital Appropriations and Expenditures," *Econometrica*, Jan., 1965.

2. *Brookings Quarterly Econometric Model of the United States Economy*, J. Duesenberry, G. Fromm, L. Klein, E. Kuh, eds. (Rand McNally and North Holland, 1965).
3. J. Culbertson, "The Term Structure of Interest Rates," *Q.J.E.*, Nov., 1957.
4. F. de Leeuw, "A Model of Financial Behavior," Chap. 13 in [2].
5. J. Duesenberry, *Business Cycles and Economic Growth* (McGraw-Hill, 1958).
6. J. Durbin and G. Watson, "Testing for Serial Correlation in Least Squares Regression, II," *Biometrika*, June, 1951.
7. Z. Griliches, "A Note on Serial Correlation Bias in Estimates of Distributed Lags," *Econometrica*, Jan., 1961.
8. J. Hicks, *Value and Capital* (Oxford Univ. Press, 1939).
9. R. Kessel, *The Cyclical Behavior of the Term Structure of Interest Rates* (N.B.E.R., Occasional Paper 91, 1965).
10. J. Keynes, *A Treatise on Money*, Vol. II (Harcourt, Brace and Co., 1930).
11. ———, *The General Theory of Employment, Interest and Money* (Harcourt, Brace and Co., 1936).
12. N. Liviatan, "Consistent Estimation of Distributed Lags," *Int. Econ. Rev.* Jan., 1963.
13. B. Malkiel, "Expectations, Bond Prices and the Term Structure of Interest Rates," *Q.J.E.*, May, 1962.
14. D. Meiselman, *The Term Structure of Interest Rates* (Prentice-Hall, 1962).
15. R. Solow, "On a Family of Lag Distributions," *Econometrica*, Apr., 1960.

[5]

An Estimate of the Liquidity Premium

J. Huston McCulloch

Boston College and Harvard University

The liquidity premium on U.S. government securities is quantitatively estimated and tabulated, using maturities from 1 month to 30 years. Unbiased forecasting by the market is assumed in order to get at expectations. The premium is estimated, first allowing it to take any shape and then constraining it to conform to a functional form which implies that the "normal" shape of the yield curve is monotonically increasing toward an asymptote. Tests for constancy of the premium over the post-Accord period, normality of the forecasting errors, and monotonicity of the premium with respect to maturity are performed, and the dependence of the premium on the level of interest rates is discussed.

I. Introduction

It has long been known that short-term interest rates tend to lie below long-term rates on securities with equal default risk. As early as 1935, Charles C. Abbott referred to the reversals in the usual relationship that occurred from June 1920 to January 1921 and from May 1928 to November 1929 as "the more striking in that they contradict the well-known tendency for obligations of short maturity to sell consistently at higher prices and with lower yields than obligations of equal security but longer maturity."[1]

This paper is based on the author's Ph.D. dissertation, Economics Department, University of Chicago. He is indebted to Lester G. Telser, the chairman of his thesis committee, for encouragement and guidance. He also benefited from discussions with, and suggestions from, the other members of his committee, Reuben A. Kessel and Merton H. Miller. In addition, he wishes to acknowledge helpful comments at various stages in this research from Fischer Black, Eugene F. Fama, James Meginnis, Charles R. Nelson, members of the Applied Price Theory and Money and Banking Workshops at the University of Chicago, and the referees. The author was supported by a fellowship from the Earhart Foundation.

[1] Abbott (1935, p. 9). As it happens, the evidence Abbott cited was not statistically strong enough to demonstrate the existence of a liquidity premium (McCulloch 1973, pp. 62–63).

[*Journal of Political Economy*, 1975, vol. 83, no. 1]

A number of questions regarding this "liquidity premium" need to be answered. How large is it for various pairs of maturities? Does the premium increase monotonically with maturity? Does it vary with the level of interest rates? Is it the same for different periods in time? And is it large enough to imply that holders of longer-term bonds have a systematically higher holding period yield, after taking into account transactions costs as reflected by bid-asked spreads?

The liquidity premium is defined as the difference between a forward interest rate and the market's expectation of the corresponding future spot rate. Measurement of this premium is complicated by the fact that expectations are not directly observable. A straightforward, but in practice unreliable and limited, method is to ask market participants what they believe future interest rates will be (Kane and Malkiel 1967). Another approach is to build a model of expectation generation based on the past behavior of interest rates and, in some instances, of other variables.[2] However, these models entail strong assumptions about the set of information people take into account in forming their expectations. A third approach simply assumes that forecasting errors have mean zero, so that the subsequent realization gives us an unbiased estimator of the forecast. In one variation on this third approach, Kessel (1965) actually compares the forward rate to the subsequent spot rate. However, this variation does not make the most efficient use of the data available. Under the same basic assumption, Cagan (1969) and Roll (1970) have been able to use the term structure for two nearby points in time to obtain observations on the liquidity premium all the way out to the longest maturity observed.

Unfortunately, neither Cagan's paper nor Roll's book tells us about the size of the liquidity premium applicable to forecasts for periods longer than a few months. For instance, at the end of June 1953, the forward rate on a 10-year loan to begin 5 years in the future was 3.16 ($\pm$0.01) percent per year. Five years later, the corresponding 10-year spot rate was 2.94 ($\pm$0.02) percent per year.[3] It would be interesting to know whether such a fall was unanticipated, whether it is about the size one would expect given liquidity preference, or whether the difference was less than the mean liquidity premium, so that it actually represents an unanticipated rise. The answer has not been given in the literature for maturities of this duration.

In this paper we use a modification of the Cagan-Roll method to estimate the size of the post-Accord liquidity premium for all available maturities, together with the relevant measurement errors implied by

[2] E.g., Meiselman (1962), Diller (1969), Nelson (1972), Modigliani and Shiller (1973), Modigliani and Sutch (1966).

[3] Calculated by the author, using bid-asked mean prices of U.S. government securities and the technique described in McCulloch (1971).

this procedure, and to attack the other questions posed above. The results are compared with those obtained by other investigators.

II. The Behavior of the Postwar Liquidity Premium

In this section, we define an estimator of the liquidity premium. Its values for three pilot maturities are used to test the premium and the variance of the forecasting errors for constancy over the postwar period. The forecasting errors are tested for normality, and the dependence of the liquidity premium on the level of interest rates is discussed.

An Estimator of the Liquidity Premium

In the real world, observed bond maturities do not lie at evenly spaced discrete intervals, even though this would make our calculations easier. Nevertheless, we would expect the price of any security to be governed by a smooth discount function $\delta(t, s)$, which gives the value at time t of a dollar to be repaid at time s in the future, that is, after maturity $m = s - t$.

Corresponding to the discount function we observe at time t is a two-dimensional complex of forward interest rates $r(t, s_1, s_2)$ on hypothetical point-payment forward loans to begin at time s_1 and be repaid at time s_2, where $t \leq s_1 \leq s_2$. Most past investigators have taken m_2 (where $m_2 = s_2 - s_1$, the duration of the forward loan) as a constant with some convenient value, usually a week, month, quarter, or year, and have considered the liquidity premium corresponding only to a one-dimensional complex of forward rates as m_1 varies (where $m_1 = s_1 - t$, the period until the forward loan begins). We, on the other hand, are interested in all values of m_2, from the limit as m_2 approaches zero out to several years or even decades. In the next section, we will treat both forward rates and the liquidity premium in terms of the two variables m_1 and m_2.

However, the forward rates for different values of m_2 are far from independent. In general, forward rates with large m_2 can be obtained by averaging together appropriate forward rates with smaller m_2. It is therefore convenient for our investigation of the qualitative properties of the liquidity premium to single out a one-dimensional complex of independent forward rates, taking m_2 equal to its smallest value of interest. In our case, this is the limit as m_2 goes to zero. This "marginal" or "instantaneous" forward rate $\rho(t, s)$, where $s = t + m_1$, is related to the discount function by

$$\rho(t, s) = -100 \frac{\partial \delta(t, s)/\partial s}{\delta(t, s)}. \tag{1}$$

Because we fit a smooth curve to the discount function, we are able to evaluate this derivative. When t and s coincide, $\rho(t, t)$ becomes a "spot" rate of interest on a hypothetical loan of very short maturity, in effect a "call money" rate.

We define the liquidity premium $\pi(m)$ to be the difference between the forward rate and the expected value of the future spot rate:

$$\rho(t, s) = E_t\rho(s, s) + \pi(m), \qquad m = s - t, \tag{2}$$

where E_t denotes the expected value as of time t.[4] Of course, not all participants have the same expectations about the future. We must regard $E_t\rho(t, s)$ as some sort of market average of individual expectations.[5]

If forecasting errors are unbiased, we could compare the forward rate with the actual subsequent spot rate to get an estimator of $\pi(m)$. However, for large values of m, we would have very few such pairs of observations. We can get around this problem by observing that today's forecast of some distant future variable must be an unbiased estimator of all future forecasts of that variable. Thus, if we have observations on the term structure at points in time Δt apart, we must have:

$$E_t\rho(s, s) = E_t[E_{t+\Delta t}\rho(s, s)], \tag{3}$$

where s is some time later than $t + \Delta t$. This seems like a reasonable assertion; if we had any reason at time t to believe that our next period expectation of $\rho(s, s)$ would be any different from our current expectation, we would already have incorporated this information into our current expectation, bringing the two expectations into equality.[6]

Given observations on the term structure at times $t_1, t_2, \ldots t_j \ldots,$ where $t_j - t_{j-1} = \Delta t$, we define $\Delta\pi_j(i\Delta t)$ by

$$\Delta\pi_j(i\Delta t) = \rho(t_j, t_j + i\Delta t) - \rho(t_j + \Delta t, t_j + i\Delta t). \tag{4}$$

Putting (2), (3), and (4) together, we have

$$\Delta\pi_j(i\Delta t) = \pi(i\Delta t) - \pi[(i - 1)\Delta t] + u_{i,j}, \tag{5}$$

[4] Two slightly different possible definitions of the liquidity premium are discussed in McCulloch (1973, pp. 18–19).

[5] See Williams (1938), chap. 10. Bierwag and Grove (1967) develop an ingenious model in which the market behaves as if governed by a market expectation which is an arithmetic average of individual expectations, weighted in proportion to the individuals' audacity (negative risk aversion), certainty, and wealth. Unfortunately, they deal in terms of price uncertainty, instead of consumption uncertainty. Compare Stiglitz (1970), who correctly deals with consumption uncertainty, although he assumes homogeneous expectations.

[6] This is essentially the point Samuelson makes (1965, pp. 41–49). His analysis is unnecessarily complicated by assumptions about the relation between anticipations and current forward prices. The real crux of his argument is that anticipations themselves must fluctuate randomly. The proof of our assertion is similar to the proofs he gives. Once we have identified the psychological anticipation with the mathematical expected value by our unbiased forecasting assumption, the remainder of the proof is a purely mathematical consequence of the properties of probability distributions.

where $u_{i,j}$ is a random forecasting error with mean zero. When we sum (5) over i from one to n, we obtain the following estimator of $\pi(m)$ for $m = n\Delta t$:

$$\begin{aligned} \pi_j(m) &= \sum_{i=1}^{n} \Delta\pi_j(i\Delta t), \\ &= \pi(m) - \pi(0) + \sum_{i=1}^{n} u_{i,j}, \\ &= \pi(m) + v_{m,j}. \end{aligned} \tag{6}$$

Since the $u_{i,j}$ have mean zero, the $v_{m,j}$ also have mean zero.[7]

The discount function $\delta(t, s)$ was fit for the close of each month from December 1946 to March 1966 by means of a quadratic spline.[8] The prices used were the means of bid-and-asked monthly closing offers for most fully taxable U.S. government bills, notes, and bonds.[9] Forward rates were derived from these discount curves, and from them the values $\pi_j(m)$ were calculated. Figure 1 shows monthly observations on $\pi_j(m)$ for $m = 1$ year, along with the average yield to maturity

$$\begin{aligned} \eta(t_j, m) &= \frac{1}{m} \int_{t_j}^{t_j+m} \rho(t_j, s)\, ds \\ &= -\frac{100}{m} \ln \delta(t_j, t_j + m). \end{aligned} \tag{7}$$

For ease of comparison, both are shown relative to the same origin, but with different scales.

Likelihood Ratio Tests for Homogeneity

For the purpose of analysis, we divided this interval into four approximately equal periods, as shown in table 1. These periods correspond roughly to the pre-Accord period, the first Eisenhower administration,

[7] Roll (1970, pp. 98–99) estimates the liquidity premium as the sum of first differences of forward rates, so this is basically the same method as his. However, he used forward rates spanning 1 week, while we have taken the limit as the period spanned goes to zero.

[8] See McCulloch (1971) for details of this procedure, and Rice (1969, 2:123–67) for a discussion of splines in general. Compare Williams (1938, pp. 120–24), who gives an algorithm that fits security prices exactly. His method yields a step-function forward curve (see his chart 4, p. 355), instead of one that is continuous. The method proposed by Bryan and Carleton (1972) is similar to his in this respect. Weingartner (1966) proposes a method based on successive approximations to the coupon-free yield curve. Buse (1970) raises objections that apply to a large number of other studies.

[9] These data were collected by Reuben A. Kessel from the quotation sheets of Salomon Brothers and Hutzler, Inc., of New York, and were processed under the supervision of Merton H. Miller and Myron Scholes. Reduction of these data into discount curves and forward rates was supported by a grant from the University of Chicago, Graduate School of Business.

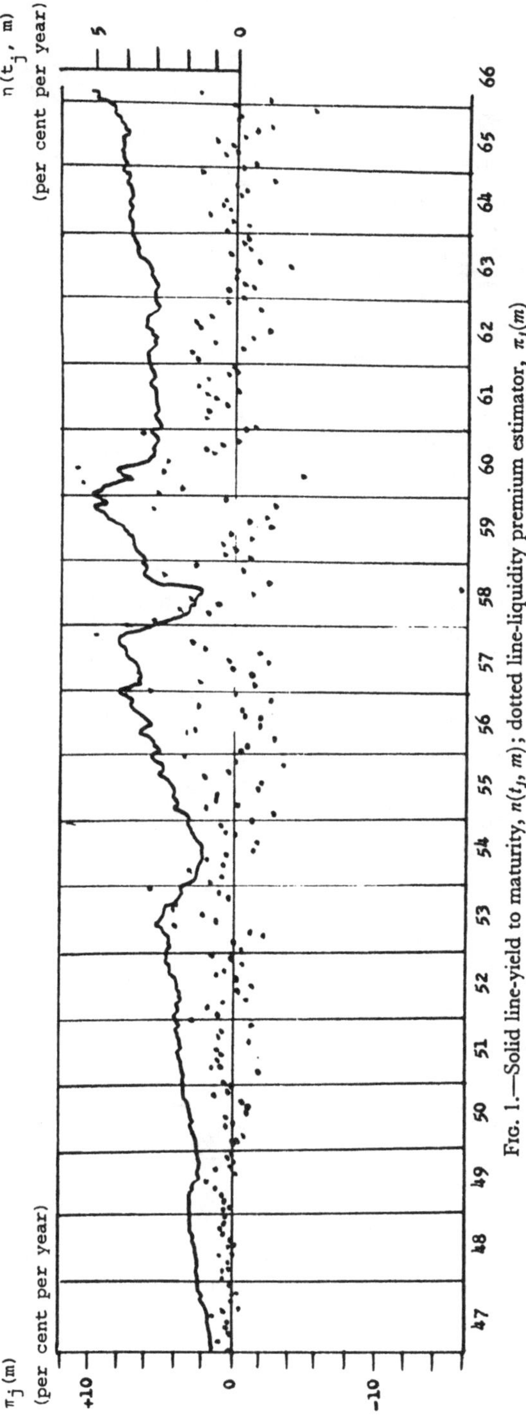

FIG. 1.—Solid line-yield to maturity, $\eta(t_j, m)$; dotted line-liquidity premium estimator, $\pi_j(m)$

TABLE 1

DEFINITION OF PERIODS FOR HOMOGENEITY TESTS

Period	Number of Even-numbered Observations
1. December 31, 1946–March 4, 1951	25
2. March 4, 1951–December 31, 1955	29
3. December 31, 1955–December 31, 1960...........	30
4. December 31, 1960–March 31, 1966	31

the second Eisenhower administration, and the Kennedy/Johnson administration.

Although we would expect the pure forecasting errors to be serially uncorrelated, the errors we observe may not be because of additional errors introduced in measuring $\pi_j(m)$. The term structure cannot be measured exactly, and measurement errors for forward rates of different maturities are strongly correlated. Adjacent estimators $\pi_{j-1}(m)$ and $\pi_j(m)$ are both dependent on the term structure for time t_j, so their measurement errors will not be independent. However, the measurement errors for alternate estimators are completely independent, so that if we discard alternate observations, we should satisfy the serial independence assumption necessary to estimate the mean. Using all the data would give us smaller, but erroneous, confidence intervals. In order to avoid the month of the Accord, we will use the even-numbered observations, that is, starting with the month January 31, 1947 to February 29, 1947.[10]

The premium seems to be small with a small variance during period 1, definitely positive with an intermediate variance during periods 2 and 4, and perhaps larger with the largest variance during period 3. This suggests the following hypotheses: H_1—a common mean and variance for all four periods (one mean, one variance); H_2—one mean and variance for period 1, and a second mean and variance for periods 2–4 (two means, two variances); H_3—one mean for all four periods, but separate variances for each period (one mean, four variances); H_4—one mean for period 1, a second mean for periods 2–4, and separate variances for each period (two means, four variances); H_5—a different mean and variance for each period (four means, four variances).

These hypotheses were compared to one another using the likelihood ratio test. The asymptotically χ^2 statistics are shown in table 2, along with the relevant critical values of the appropriate χ^2 distribution.

We see that we may easily reject H_1 in favor of H_2, and H_2 in favor of H_4. We may reject H_3 in favor of H_4 for m = 3 months but get insignificant values for this test for 1 year and 15 years. We may not,

[10] It will be shown below, in table 3, that while all the observations taken together exhibit autocorrelation, alternate ones do not.

TABLE 2

LIKELIHOOD RATIO χ^2 STATISTICS

Hypothesis		Maturity			Degrees of Freedom	Critical Levels of χ^2				
						Degrees of Freedom	Confidence Level			
Null	Alternative	3-month	1-year	15-year			.995	.99	.90	.80
H_1	H_2	48.3	53.6	34.0	2	1	7.9	6.6	2.7	1.6
H_2	H_4	51.9	44.2	19.8	2	2	10.6	9.2	4.6	3.2
H_3	H_4	14.7	1.2	0.0	1					
H_4	H_5	3.8	1.2	4.4	2					

NOTE.—Based on 115 even observations.

TABLE 3

MAXIMUM-LIKELIHOOD ESTIMATES OF MEANS AND STANDARD DEVIATIONS UNDER H_4

STATISTIC	PERIOD	OBSERVATIONS	MATURITY: 3 months	1 year	15 years
$\hat{\mu}$	1	Evens	0.052 (0.046)	0.06 (0.12)	−0.8 (1.2)
$\hat{\mu}$	2–4	Evens	0.357 (0.057)	0.33 (0.22)	−0.7 (1.7)
$\hat{\mu}$	2–4	Odds	0.394 (0.054)	0.50 (0.22)	0.1 (1.5)
$\hat{\sigma}$	1	Evens	0.23	0.61	5.88
$\hat{\sigma}$	2	Evens	0.58	1.67	14.03
$\hat{\sigma}$	3	Evens	1.42	4.67	27.06
$\hat{\sigma}$	4	Evens	0.38	1.68	13.25
vNR	1–4	All (231 observations)	1.33 (0.999999+)	1.67 (0.989)	1.90 (0.58)
vNR	1–4	Evens (115 observations)	1.82 (0.71)	1.82 (0.70)	1.77 (0.82)

NOTE.—Means "μ" are in percent per year. Standard deviations "σ" are in (percent per year) per (month)$^{1/2}$. Confidence levels shown in parentheses beneath the von Neumann ratios (vNR) are for a two-tailed test against no autocorrelation, based on the normal approximation for large samples given in Hart (1942).

however, reject H_4 in favor of H_5. We interpret these results as meaning that there has been a fairly constant liquidity premium since the Accord, although the variance of forecasting errors has not been constant. We may not treat the pre-Accord liquidity premium as equal to the post-Accord premium, but this is to be expected, since prior to the Accord the Federal Reserve System explicitly supported the prices of government securities, so that forward rates did not necessarily reflect market forces. The difference between the pre- and post-Accord means for 1 year and 15 years is not significant due to the greater accumulation of forecasting errors for these maturities, but we assume that the same is true for these maturities as for 3 months.[11]

Table 3 shows the maximum-likelihood estimates of the means and standard deviations for the different periods under H_4. The pre-Accord premium, at least for 3 months, was significantly lower than the post-Accord premium. Standard deviations increase with maturity and are higher for period 3 and lower for period 1 than they are for periods 2 or 4. For comparison, the post-Accord means for the omitted odd observations are shown. They run a little higher than the means for the even observations, but not significantly so. Also shown are von Neumann ratios based on the H_4 residuals divided by their estimated standard deviations. As predicted above, autocorrelation is highly significant when we use all the observations (at least for 3 months and 1 year), but becomes insignificant when we use only alternative observations.

[11] Wallace (1964, pp. 25–26) also finds significantly different behavior prior to the accord than after.

TABLE 4

STANDARDIZED RANGE TESTS FOR NORMALITY

	3 months	1 year	15 years
Raw data:			
Standardized range	9.48	8.85	6.41
$\hat{\alpha}_{.96}$	1.34	1.47	1.47
After adjustment for heteroskedasticity:			
Standardized range	5.38	5.74	5.53

Confidence Intervals for Normality—90 Observations*
(Two-tailed Test)

.80..........	4.36–5.60
.90..........	4.23–5.82
.98..........	4.01–6.27
.99..........	3.95–6.44

NOTE.—Based on 90 even post-Accord observations.
* Interpolated from David, Hartley, and Pearson (1954).

Tests for Normality

Table 4 shows the "standardized range" statistic for our post-Accord observations $\pi_j(m)$. It is defined as the ratio of the sample range to the estimate of the standard deviation of the errors. When the standard deviation is treated as if it were constant, we find that we may easily reject normality at the 99 percent level for 3 months and 1 year, and at the 98 percent level for 15 years. This finding might lead us to reject, as Roll does (1970, chap. 4), normality in favor of the class of symmetric stable distributions. If so, we would arrive at the estimates for the characteristic exponent α of the stable distributions shown in the second line of table 4.[12] Our estimates of α are on the same order as those obtained by Roll.[13] However, when we allow for different variances in periods 2, 3, and 4, and divide the maximum-likelihood residuals by their respective estimated standard deviations before calculating the standardized range, we find that the resulting statistics are never significant at the 90 percent level, and only once at the 80 percent level. Although we can reject homoskedastic normality, we are unable to reject heteroskedastic normality. Provided we allow for this heteroskedasticity, we seem to be justified in using tests based on the more familiar normal distribution.[14]

[12] See Fama and Roll (1968; 1971) for techniques of estimating α. The estimator $\hat{\alpha}_{.96}$, which is used here, is based on the .04 and .96 fractiles of the sample distribution. Our "standardized range" is the same as Fama and Roll's "Studentized range."

[13] Roll finds values of $\hat{\alpha}$ from 1.22 to 1.72, mostly around 1.4, for 1949–64 weekly data. For 17–22 weeks to maturity, he finds some as low as 1.00 for 1959–64 (1970, p. 70). A Cauchy distribution has $\alpha = 1$, while a normal distribution has $\alpha = 2$.

[14] Press (1967) and Praetz (1972) also offer interpretations of leptokurtic residuals in terms of mixtures of normals with different variances. However, the compound distributions they suggest are homogeneous over time, in contrast with the one we propose.

Dependence of the Liquidity Premium on the Level of Interest Rates

Van Horne (1965) and Nelson (1972, p. 93) offer evidence which, they contend, supports the view that the liquidity premium decreases with the level of interest rates. On the other hand, Kessel (1965, p. 25) and Cagan (1969, p. 93) give evidence intended to show that the liquidity premium increases with the level of rates. These tests have been called into question by Telser (1967) and McCulloch (1973, pp. 36–39).

Any direct comparison between our liquidity premium estimator and the level of rates is open to two objections. First, in deriving it, we assumed the underlying premium was constant. This can bias any comparison to the extent that the unforeseen change in rates has been correlated with the level of rates. Second, the premium estimator and the level are both calculated with measurement error from the same data. This can lend some inconsistency to any regression coefficients.

Although it should be interpreted with caution, the comparison is still worth making. Figure 1 and similar charts (not shown here) for m = 3 months and m = 16 years show no obvious relation between our liquidity premium estimator and the level of interest rates. If there had been a pronounced relation, it would have been picked up by our maximum-likelihood test for nonconstancy of the premium since the Accord, in view of the fairly steady rise in interest rates over this period. Furthermore, direct regressions of the premium estimator on the level show no significant correlation either way for the post-Accord period.[15]

In view of the inconclusive nature of our own findings and the lack of consensus in the literature, we will assume that the post-Accord liquidity premium has been approximately independent of the level of interest rates.

III. The Post-Accord Liquidity Premium

Using the information we gathered in Section II about the behavior of the liquidity premium and the forecasting errors, we are ready to estimate the liquidity premium for a variety of maturities. We first estimate it without imposing any particular functional form on it. We find no evidence to contradict monotonicity or boundedness, so we then estimate it under the assumption that the premium monotonically approaches an asymptote. Since we are interested primarily in how free-market forces (relatively speaking) shape the term structure, and since the pre-Accord liquidity premium has been shown to be significantly different from that since the Accord, we restrict ourselves in this section to our 90 alternate post-Accord observations.

[15] See McCulloch (1973, p. 35). If period 1 is included in the regressions, the level has a positive and significant slope for m = 3 months. However, it is questionable whether this is the direct effect of the lower pre-Accord rates themselves, or if the low rates are only acting as a proxy for the higher level of intervention in the securities market prior to the Accord.

TABLE 5

FREE-FORM ESTIMATES OF LIQUIDITY PREMIUM
(POST-ACCORD EVEN OBSERVATIONS)

m	n	$\hat{\pi}(m)$	$\hat{\bar{\pi}}(m)$
0	0	0.0	0.0
		(0.0)	(0.0)
1 month	90	0.19	0.09
		(0.03)	(0.02)
2 months	90	0.32	0.17
		(0.05)	(0.03)
3 months	90	0.36	0.23
		(0.06)	(0.03)
6 months	90	0.37	0.31
		(0.11)	(0.06)
9 months	90	0.32	0.32
		(0.16)	(0.08)
1 year	90	0.33	0.32
		(0.21)	(0.11)
2 years	90	0.34	0.33
		(0.40)	(0.20)
3 years	90	0.37	0.33
		(0.56)	(0.29)
5 years	90	0.47	0.39
		(0.82)	(0.44)
10 years	90	−0.68	0.15
		(1.40)	(0.75)
20 years	87	0.59	0.23
		(2.10)	(1.24)
30 years*	67	−5.24	−2.47
		(3.81)	(2.02)

NOTE.—Standard errors in parentheses.
* Periods 2 and 3 treated as if they had the same variance, due to shrinking sample size.

The Liquidity Premium and the Average Liquidity Premium

Table 5 gives our free-form estimates of the liquidity premium $\pi(m)$ and of the average liquidity premium,

$$\bar{\pi}(m) = \int_0^m \pi(x)\, dx. \tag{8}$$

The function $\pi(m)$ gives us the "typical" shape of the marginal forward interest rate curve $\rho(t, s)$, for if we expected to have the same marginal forward rates (as a function of maturity $m = s - t$) forever, we would find

$$\rho(t, s) = \rho(t, t) + \pi(s - t). \tag{9}$$

In this case, we would also expect to have the same yield curve forever and would have

$$\eta(t, m) = \eta(t, 0) + \bar{\pi}(m). \tag{10}$$

Thus, the average liquidity premium shown in table 5 gives us the "typical" shape of the yield curve. This average liquidity premium was estimated by averaging together the values

$$\bar{\pi}_j(m) = \frac{1}{m}\int_0^m \pi_j(x)\,dx, \tag{11}$$

again allowing for heteroskedasticity.[16]

The Mean Liquidity Premium

One of the most important applications of the liquidity premium is to evaluate the market's expectation of future interest rates spanning a positive interval in the future, on the basis of current forward rates. We define the mean forward rate observed at time t corresponding to a loan to begin at time $t + m_1$ and to be repaid at time $t + m_1 + m_2$ by

$$r(t, t + m_1, t + m_1 + m_2) = \frac{1}{m_2}\int_{m_1}^{m_1+m_2} \rho(t, t + m)\,dm. \tag{12}$$

In order to calculate the market's expectation of the future m_2-year yield to maturity $\eta(t + m_1, m_2)$ from this forward rate, we need to know the mean liquidity premium:

$$p(m_1, m_2) = r(t, t + m_1, t + m_1 + m_2) - E_t\eta(t + m_1, m_2). \tag{13}$$

It can be shown that

$$p(m_1, m_2) = [(m_1 + m_2)\bar{\pi}(m_1 + m_2) - m_1\bar{\pi}(m_1) - m_2\bar{\pi}(m_2)]/m_2. \tag{14}$$

Consequently,

$$p_j(m_1, m_2) = [(m_1 + m_2)\bar{\pi}_j(m_1 + m_2) - m_1\bar{\pi}_j(m_1) - m_2\bar{\pi}_j(m_2)]/m_2 \tag{15}$$

is an unbiased observation on $p(m_1, m_2)$. These observations were averaged together heteroskedastically to obtain the estimates of $p(m_1, m_2)$ shown in table 6.

It happens that when m_2 equals the observation interval Δt (1 month in our case), our estimator of the mean liquidity premium is identically equal to the difference between the 1-month holding period yield on a security of maturity $m + \Delta t$ and the certain yield on a security of Δt

[16] The integral in eq. (11) was evaluated by summing trapezoids with width $\Delta t = 1/12$ year.

TABLE 6

FREE-FORM ESTIMATES OF MEAN LIQUIDITY PREMIUM $p(m_1, m_2)$

(Post-Accord Even Observations--Standard Errors in Parentheses)

m_1 \ m_2	0	1 mo.	2 mos.	3 mos.	6 mos.	9 mos.	1 year	2 years	3 years	5 years	10 yrs.	20 yrs.	30 yrs.
0	0.0 (0.0)	0.0 (0.0)	0.0 (0.0)	0.0 (0.0)	0.0 (0.0)	0.0 (0.0)	0.0 (0.0)	0.0 (0.0)	0.0 (0.0)	0.0 (0.0)	0.0 (0.0)	0.0 (0.0)	0.0 (0.0)
1 month	0.19 (0.03)	0.16 (0.02)	0.12 (0.02)	0.10 (0.02)	0.04 (0.02)	0.03 (0.02)	0.02 (0.02)	0.01 (0.02)	0.01 (0.02)	0.01 (0.01)	-0.01 (0.01)	-0.00 (0.01)	-0.01 (0.01)
2 months	0.32 (0.05)	0.25 (0.04)	0.19 (0.03)	0.15 (0.04)	0.06 (0.04)	0.03 (0.04)	0.03 (0.03)	0.01 (0.03)	0.01 (0.03)	0.01 (0.03)	-0.01 (0.02)	-0.00 (0.02)	-0.03 (0.02)
3 months	0.36 (0.06)	0.29 (0.05)	0.22 (0.05)	0.16 (0.05)	0.06 (0.05)	0.04 (0.05)	0.03 (0.05)	0.02 (0.05)	0.01 (0.05)	0.01 (0.04)	-0.02 (0.03)	-0.00 (0.03)	-0.05 (0.03)
6 months	0.37 (0.11)	0.27 (0.11)	0.18 (0.11)	0.12 (0.11)	0.04 (0.11)	0.04 (0.11)	0.04 (0.10)	0.01 (0.10)	0.02 (0.09)	0.01 (0.08)	-0.05 (0.07)	-0.01 (0.06)	-0.10 (0.06)
9 months	0.32 (0.16)	0.23 (0.16)	0.15 (0.16)	0.11 (0.16)	0.05 (0.16)	0.05 (0.16)	0.05 (0.15)	0.01 (0.15)	0.02 (0.14)	0.01 (0.12)	-0.08 (0.10)	-0.01 (0.08)	-0.15 (0.10)
1 year	0.33 (0.21)	0.25 (0.21)	0.18 (0.21)	0.13 (0.21)	0.08 (0.21)	0.06 (0.20)	0.05 (0.20)	0.02 (0.20)	0.03 (0.18)	0.00 (0.16)	-0.11 (0.14)	-0.01 (0.11)	-0.20 (0.13)
2 years	0.34 (0.40)	0.24 (0.39)	0.17 (0.39)	0.12 (0.39)	0.05 (0.40)	0.04 (0.39)	0.03 (0.39)	0.03 (0.38)	0.05 (0.35)	-0.07 (0.32)	-0.24 (0.27)	0.04 (0.23)	-0.42 (0.25)
3 years	0.37 (0.56)	0.28 (0.56)	0.21 (0.56)	0.16 (0.56)	0.10 (0.55)	0.09 (0.55)	0.09 (0.55)	0.08 (0.53)	0.05 (0.51)	-0.20 (0.48)	-0.38 (0.40)	0.09 (0.34)	-0.53 (0.38)
5 years	0.47 (0.82)	0.37 (0.82)	0.29 (0.81)	0.23 (0.81)	0.12 (0.82)	0.07 (0.81)	0.02 (0.81)	-0.17 (0.80)	-0.34 (0.80)	-0.65 (0.79)	-0.66 (0.64)	-0.83 (0.62)	-1.28 (0.68)
10 years	-0.68 (1.40)	-0.77 (1.40)	-0.86 (1.40)	-0.92 (1.40)	-1.02 (1.40)	-1.07 (1.39)	-1.09 (1.39)	-1.21 (1.36)	-1.26 (1.34)	-1.33 (1.27)	-0.48 (1.16)	-1.91 (1.31)	--
20 years	0.59 (2.10)	-0.14 (2.24)	-0.21 (2.24)	-0.25 (2.25)	-0.30 (2.25)	-0.28 (2.24)	-0.24 (2.23)	0.36 (2.31)	0.60 (2.27)	-3.31 (2.49)	-3.82 (2.62)	--	--
30 years	-5.24 (3.81)	-5.38 (3.81)	-5.52 (3.81)	-5.62 (3.81)	-5.84 (3.81)	-5.95 (3.80)	-6.03 (3.79)	-6.29 (3.75)	-5.30 (3.81)	-7.67 (4.08)	--	--	--

(McCulloch 1973, pp. 43–45). Thus, our estimator is the same as Cagan's difference in holding period yields, except that we use an observation interval of 1 month, while he used 1 week. By developing it as we have, however, we are able to estimate the typical shape of the yield and forward curves exactly.[17]

Transactions Costs

If there were no transactions costs, it would follow from table 6 that for many pairs of maturities, it is worth the while of a lender who desires a short holding period to buy a longer maturity and to sell it before maturity, rather than simply to buy the shorter maturity in the first place. However, he cannot really both buy and sell at the bid-asked mean prices as implicitly assumed so far.

We cannot quantify all the components of the cost to an investor or borrower of going in and out of securities. However, the quoted bid-asked spread gives us a fair estimate of the external component of this cost, at least for large institutional investors. Subject, then, to the condition that he must buy high at the asked price and sell low at the bid price, we may investigate whether the short-term lender does better or worse to buy a longer maturity initially and sell it before maturity than simply to buy a short security.

We found that a lender who wished to lend for only 1, 2, or 3 months would have done significantly better to have bought a 2-, 4-, or 6-month security, respectively, even though it would mean having to go into the market twice instead of only once (McCulloch 1973, pp. 46–50). When we compared these differentials with the comparable values from table 6, we found that the bid-asked spread eats up only about one-third of the liquidity premium for these three pairs of maturities. However, the essentially short-term nature of the liquidity premium is evidenced by the fact that a lender who wished to lend for 4 months would not have done significantly better to have bought an 8-month security.

Miller and Orr (1967, pp. 133–51) have estimated the cost to one large nonfinancial corporation of going into and out of a given security as about \$20–\$50. Half this internal transaction cost just equals the premium (after bid-asked spread cost) on a 6-month bill held for 3 months, for investments of \$36,000–\$91,000. Therefore, a transaction would have to be in the hundreds to thousands of dollars before it definitely pays to try to exploit the liquidity premium.

[17] Culbertson (1957, p. 506) also works in terms of the difference in holding-period yields. Roll (1970, pp. 98–99) estimates the liquidity premium by a sum of differences of forward rates that is also equal to the difference in holding-period yields. In McCulloch (1973, p. 45), we show that interpolating from our table 6 for m_1 = 6 months and m_2 = 1 week gives an estimate not significantly different from Roll's.

Exponential Form Estimates of the Liquidity Premium

In tables 5 and 6 we made no assumptions about the form of the liquidity premium as a function of m. Since we put relatively little in, we got relatively little out in return. Thus, for longer maturities, where the variance of the forecasting errors is high, our estimators have very high standard errors. To return to the example we cited in Section I, the forward rate for a 10-year loan 5 years in the future from June 30, 1953 was 3.16 percent per annum. From table 6 ,we see that the premium on this rate would be -0.66 (± 0.64) percent per annum, so that a 95 percent confidence interval for the market expectation of the future 10-year spot rate extends from 2.54 percent per annum to 5.10 percent per annum (2.0 standard errors in each direction from $3.16 - [-0.66]$). The subsequently observed spot rate was 2.94 percent per annum, which lies within this interval, so we may not say for certain whether there was an unanticipated rise or fall, or no unanticipated change at all.

In order to pin the liquidity premium down with greater precision, we must make stronger assumptions. Kessel (1965) has argued that the liquidity premium should be such as to give the "typical" shape of the yield curve a monotonically increasing shape that approaches a horizontal asymptote.[18] If so, this information would eliminate much of our present uncertainty as to the behavior of $\pi(m)$ for m greater than 1 year or so.

Our free-form estimate of $\pi(m)$ rises in the first few months and then levels off. Although it falls off after 5 years, its final value (-5.24 ± 3.81 percent per year) is not significantly lower than its highest value (0.59 ± 2.10 percent per year), so its downward slope for long maturities is not necessarily significant.[19] The low values for long maturities may simply reflect the rise in interest rates over the period studied, which was probably largely unanticipated.

Since the observed liquidity premium seems not to differ significantly from the monotonically increasing-to-an-asymptote shape, we will try fitting it under that assumption. A simple two-parameter function that has these properties is

$$\pi(m) = b(1 - e^{-am}). \tag{16}$$

The parameters a and b were fit to our data by the maximum-likelihood technique as follows: free-form estimates of $\pi(m)$ for the six maturities 1 month, 3 months, 6 months, 1 year, 5 years, and 15 years were obtained

[18] Hicks (1946, p. 147) argues in favor of a monotonically increasing liquidity premium due to risk aversion in the face of interest-rate uncertainty. However, this is a non sequitur (Long 1972 and McCulloch 1973, pp. 4–10). Nevertheless, we give two alternative justifications of Kessel's monotonic shape, based on considerations involving the uncertain timing of receipts and expenditures and on the nature of a fractional reserve banking system (McCulloch 1973, pp. 10–15).

[19] A more powerful test of monotonicity is performed below.

as in table 5. Then intermaturity covariances were estimated about these means, producing a different 6 × 6 covariance matrix for each of the three post-Accord periods. The likelihood function was computed and maximized with respect to a and b based on the assumption that each set of six $\pi_j(m)$ constituted a multinormal drawing about the means given in (16). Given a, the maximizing value of b can be written in closed form. Different values of a were tried, until upper and lower bounds were found within .0005 of one another. The final estimator of a was placed halfway between these bounds, and the estimator of b calculated for this $\hat{a}$. The covariance matrix of the estimators of a and b was estimated by evaluating at $\hat{a}$ and $\hat{b}$ the second partial derivatives with respect to a and b of the logarithm of the likelihood function and inverting the negative of the matrix of these derivatives (Goldberger 1964, p. 131). The estimates thus obtained and their standard errors and covariance are

$$\begin{aligned} \hat{a} &= 6.059(\text{yr})^{-1}, \\ &\quad (1.068) \\ \hat{b} &= 0.4335 \text{ percent per year}, \\ &\quad (0.0738) \\ \hat{\text{cov}}(\hat{a}, \hat{b}) &= 0.06262. \end{aligned} \tag{17}$$

Given our formula for $\pi(m)$, we may compute $\bar{\pi}(m)$ and $p(m_1, m_2)$ by:

$$\bar{\pi}(m) = b[1 - (1 - e^{-am})/(am)], \tag{18}$$

$$p(m_1, m_2) = b(1 - e^{-am_1})(1 - e^{-am_2})/(am_2). \tag{19}$$

Standard errors for these nonlinear functions of a and b were approximated using the formula for asymptotic variances (Goldberger 1964, pp. 122–25). The results are shown in tables 7 and 8. Figures 2 and 3 show typical forward curves and yield curves incorporating the estimated values of $\pi(m)$ and $\bar{\pi}(m)$. Figure 2 uses the free-form estimates, while figure 3 uses the exponential-form estimates.

Table 6 can be used to answer a number of questions. The first column of figures tells us how much more return we would make, on average, by turning over daily in securities of maturity m than we would by turning over in "call money." (These comparisons ignore transactions costs, which of course would make it prohibitively expensive to buy a 30-year bond, hold it for a day, and then replace it by a new bond with a full 30 years to run. Our "call money" rate is the limit as maturity goes to zero of the bid-asked mean rate on Treasury bills.) The second column tells us how much more we would make by holding securities of maturity m to maturity than we would make by turning over in call money. By subtraction we also obtain the difference in yield to maturity we would obtain over a given period by holding securities of different maturities.

TABLE 7

EXPONENTIAL-FORM ESTIMATE OF LIQUIDITY PREMIUM (POST-ACCORD EVEN OBSERVATIONS)

m	$\hat{\pi}(m)$	$\hat{\hat{\pi}}(m)$	$\hat{\pi}(\infty) - \hat{\pi}(m)$	$\hat{\hat{\pi}}(\infty) - \hat{\hat{\pi}}(m)$
0	0.000	0.000	0.433	0.433
	(0.000)	(0.000)	(0.074)	(0.074)
1 month	0.172	0.093	0.262	0.340
	(0.018)	(0.010)	(0.065)	(0.069)
2 months	0.276	0.161	0.158	0.273
	(0.030)	(0.017)	(0.052)	(0.064)
3 months	0.338	0.210	0.095	0.223
	(0.040)	(0.023)	(0.040)	(0.058)
6 months	0.413	0.297	0.021	0.136
	(0.062)	(0.037)	(0.014)	(0.041)
9 months	0.429	0.339	0.005	0.094
	(0.070)	(0.046)	(0.004)	(0.030)
1 year	0.432	0.362	0.001	0.071
	(0.073)	(0.052)	(0.001)	(0.023)
2 years	0.433	0.398	0.000	0.036
	(0.074)	(0.063)	(0.000)	(0.012)
3 years	0.433	0.410	0.000	0.024
	(0.074)	(0.066)	(0.000)	(0.008)
5 years	0.433	0.419	0.000	0.014
	(0.074)	(0.069)	(0.000)	(0.005)
10 years	0.433	0.426	0.000	0.007
	(0.074)	(0.072)	(0.000)	(0.002)
20 years	0.433	0.430	0.000	0.004
	(0.074)	(0.073)	(0.000)	(0.001)
30 years	0.433	0.431	0.000	0.002
	(0.074)	(0.073)	(0.000)	(0.001)

NOTE.—Standard errors in parentheses.

For example, by holding 3-year notes to maturity, we would expect to get $0.410 - 0.210 = 0.200$ percent per year more than we would by holding a sequence of 3-month bills to maturity. The standard error of this figure depends on a covariance not shown, but it must lie between $|0.066 + 0.023| = 0.089$ and $|0.066 - 0.023| = 0.043$.

The third column of figures in table 6 tells us how much more we would make by turning over daily in long maturities ($m \to \infty$) than by turning over daily in maturity m. Note that on this score there is no perceptible difference between 2-year bonds and perpetuities. The last column tells us how much more we get if we hold longs to maturity than if we hold securities of maturity m to maturity. Comparable free-form estimates do not appear in table 5 because without our exponential-form assumption (or something comparable), we have no information about what happens at infinity.

Our exponential-form estimates are never significantly different from our free-form estimates. Indeed, it is only rarely that they differ by more than 1 free-form standard error. However, our assumption of the exponential form greatly reduces the standard errors. The premium on

TABLE 8

EXPONENTIAL-FORM ESTIMATES OF MEAN LIQUIDITY PREMIUM $p(m_1, m_2)$

(Post-Accord Even Observations--Standard Errors in Parentheses)

m_1 \ Mm_2	0	1 mo.	2 mos.	3 mos.	6 mos.	9 mos.	1 year	2 years	3 years	5 years	10 yrs.	20 yrs.	30 yrs.
0	0.0 (0.0)	0.0 (0.0)	0.0 (0.0)	0.0 (0.0)	0.0 (0.0)	0.0 (0.0)	0.0 (0.0)	0.0 (0.0)	0.0 (0.0)	0.0 (0.0)	0.0 (0.0)	0.0 (0.0)	0.0 (0.0)
1 month	0.17 (0.02)	0.13 (0.01)	0.11 (0.01)	0.09 (0.01)	0.05 (0.01)	0.04 (0.01)	0.03 (0.01)	0.01 (0.00)	0.01 (0.00)	0.01 (0.00)	0.00 (0.00)	0.00 (0.00)	0.00 (0.00)
2 months	0.28 (0.03)	0.22 (0.03)	0.17 (0.03)	0.14 (0.02)	0.09 (0.02)	0.06 (0.01)	0.05 (0.01)	0.02 (0.01)	0.02 (0.00)	0.01 (0.00)	0.00 (0.00)	0.00 (0.00)	0.00 (0.00)
3 months	0.34 (0.04)	0.27 (0.04)	0.21 (0.04)	0.17 (0.03)	0.11 (0.02)	0.07 (0.02)	0.06 (0.01)	0.03 (0.01)	0.02 (0.00)	0.01 (0.00)	0.01 (0.00)	0.00 (0.00)	0.00 (0.00)
6 months	0.41 (0.06)	0.32 (0.06)	0.26 (0.05)	0.21 (0.05)	0.13 (0.04)	0.09 (0.03)	0.07 (0.02)	0.03 (0.01)	0.02 (0.01)	0.01 (0.00)	0.01 (0.00)	0.00 (0.00)	0.00 (0.00)
9 months	0.32 (0.07)	0.34 (0.07)	0.27 (0.06)	0.22 (0.06)	0.13 (0.04)	0.09 (0.03)	0.07 (0.02)	0.04 (0.01)	0.02 (0.01)	0.01 (0.00)	0.01 (0.00)	0.00 (0.00)	0.00 (0.00)
1 year	0.43 (0.07)	0.34 (0.07)	0.27 (0.06)	0.22 (0.06)	0.14 (0.04)	0.09 (0.03)	0.07 (0.02)	0.04 (0.01)	0.02 (0.01)	0.01 (0.00)	0.01 (0.00)	0.00 (0.00)	0.00 (0.00)
2 years	0.43 (0.07)	0.34 (0.07)	0.27 (0.06)	0.22 (0.06)	0.14 (0.04)	0.09 (0.03)	0.07 (0.02)	0.04 (0.01)	0.02 (0.01)	0.01 (0.00)	0.01 (0.00)	0.00 (0.00)	0.00 (0.00)
3 years	0.43 (0.07)	0.34 (0.07)	0.27 (0.06)	0.22 (0.06)	0.14 (0.04)	0.09 (0.03)	0.07 (0.02)	0.04 (0.01)	0.02 (0.01)	0.01 (0.00)	0.01 (0.00)	0.00 (0.00)	0.00 (0.00)
5 years	0.43 (0.07)	0.34 (0.07)	0.27 (0.06)	0.22 (0.06)	0.14 (0.04)	0.09 (0.03)	0.07 (0.02)	0.04 (0.01)	0.02 (0.01)	0.01 (0.00)	0.01 (0.00)	0.00 (0.00)	0.00 (0.00)
10 years	0.43 (0.07)	0.34 (0.07)	0.27 (0.06)	0.22 (0.06)	0.14 (0.04)	0.09 (0.03)	0.07 (0.02)	0.04 (0.01)	0.02 (0.01)	0.01 (0.00)	0.01 (0.00)	0.00 (0.00)	0.00 (0.00)
20 years	0.43 (0.07)	0.34 (0.07)	0.27 (0.06)	0.22 (0.06)	0.14 (0.04)	0.09 (0.03)	0.07 (0.02)	0.04 (0.01)	0.02 (0.01)	0.01 (0.00)	0.01 (0.00)	0.00 (0.00)	0.00 (0.00)
30 years	0.43 (0.07)	0.34 (0.07)	0.27 (0.06)	0.22 (0.06)	0.14 (0.04)	0.09 (0.03)	0.07 (0.02)	0.04 (0.01)	0.02 (0.01)	0.01 (0.00)	0.01 (0.00)	0.00 (0.00)	0.00 (0.00)

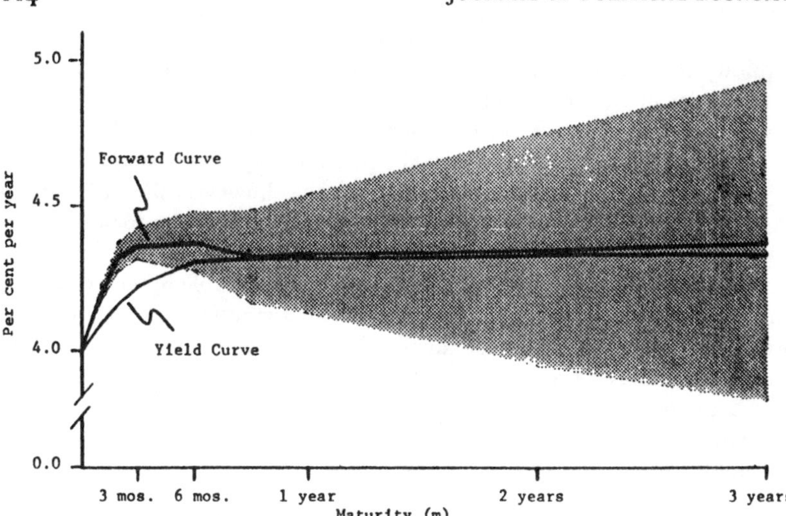

FIG. 2.—Typical shape of forward curve and yield curve under free-form assumption. Short rate assumed to be 4 percent per year. Forward curve shown with band extending ±1 standard error.

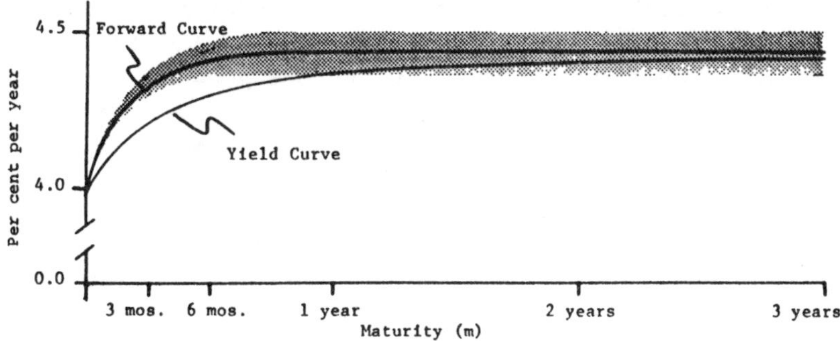

FIG. 3.—Typical shape of forward curve and yield curve under exponential form assumption. Short rate assumed to be 4 percent per year. Forward curve shown with band extending ±1 standard error.

a 10-year rate 5 years forward is now 0.01 (± less than 0.005). Our estimate of the June 30, 1953 forecast of the June 30, 1958 10-year spot rate becomes 3.16 − 0.01 = 3.15 percent per annum. The measurement errors of the forward rate and the premium combine to give a standard error of about 0.01, so our 95 percent confidence interval now extends from 3.13 to 3.17 percent per year. The subsequent spot rate was 2.94 (±0.02) percent, so we may definitely say that the fall was unanticipated—provided, of course, we are willing to accept the assumptions of monotonicity and boundedness that led us to the exponential form.

The striking aspect of table 8 is the very low values for the mean liquidity premium when m_2 (the duration of the forward loan) is larger than a year or so. Previous investigations have given the impression that the liquidity premium is on the order of 0.5 percent per year. Our results are not inconsistent with these levels, provided m_2 is very small, as it has been in other studies. When m_2 becomes large, however, the premium in the subsequent spot rate is almost as large as that in the forward rate. The two nearly cancel out, leaving only a small residual. If we make no assumptions about the form of the premium, as in table 6, we get a very large confidence interval that gives us little information, due to the large amount of "noise" at these maturities. But then we impose monotonicity and boundedness, the additional information closes the confidence interval about a value very near zero.

Under our exponential assumption, $p(m_1, m_2)$ as defined in (19) obeys the following inequality:

$$p(m_1, m_2) < (b/a)/m_2. \tag{20}$$

This inequality gives us a convenient upper bound for the liquidity premium. The value of b/a is 0.072 percent (standard error = 0.023), so we may state at the 95 percent confidence level that the mean premium is less than $0.101/m_2$ percent per year, when m_2 is measured in years.[20] If m_2 is a small fraction of a year, the liquidity premium can be substantial. But when m_2 is larger than 3 years or so, the premium is less than the precision with which forward rates can be measured.[21]

We are able to test the exponential-form estimates against the free-form estimates by means of the likelihood ratio test. With the free form we are estimating six independent means. With the exponential form, we are constraining these six values to conform to a two-parameter function, so twice the logarithm of the likelihood ratio should be compared with the χ_4^2 distribution.[22] Since its value was 4.71, which is not significant at even the 70 percent level, we may not reject the exponential form. Incidentally, this test provides a test for monotonicity. Since we may not reject this specific monotonic form, it follows a fortiori that we may not reject monotonicity in general.

[20] For a one-tailed test, the boundary of the 95 percent confidence region is approximately 1.70 standard errors above the mean.

[21] The logit form $\pi(m) = bm/(a + m)$ was tried in addition to the exponential form. Even though it increases monotonically to an asymptote, it does not imply an upper bound such as that given in eq. (20). However, the exponential form gave a slightly higher likelihood and therefore was preferred.

[22] The relevant free-form estimates for this test are ones which maximize the joint likelihood, taking into account the intermaturity covariances. These estimates are slightly different from those given in table 5, which take each maturity by itself.

Comparison with Survey Study

A survey of market expectations conducted by Kane and Malkiel[23] on April 1, 1965, affords us an opportunity to check our liquidity premium estimates against estimates that do not depend on our assumption of unbiased forecasting. Their sample consisted of 200 banks, life insurance companies, and nonfinancial corporations. Respondents varying in number from 77 to 90 ventured opinions as to the 90-day bill rate and 10-year bond rate on the various future dates listed in table 9. The standard errors of the mean market forecasts are remarkably small. For the 90-day-bill forecasts, they are actually considerably smaller than our measurement errors for the corresponding forward rates.

The survey premia are never significantly different from our free-form estimates from table 6, thanks to the high errors on the latter. And the survey premia are not significantly different from our exponential-form estimates for loans of 90 days' duration. In large measure this is due to the ambiguity of the forward rates. However, we run into trouble when we try to compare the survey premia on 10-year bonds to our table 8 estimates. For the bond 1 year in the future, the survey premium exceeds ours by four basis points or 1 standard error, and for 2 years, by 21 basis points, or 4 standard errors. This discrepancy casts some doubt on the validity of either our exponential form or the survey responses. It may be that the exponential form approaches its asymptote too quickly. In defense of our results, however, it should be noted that the survey results (taken together with the forward rates we have computed) strongly suggest that p(2 years, 10 years) is about four times p(1 year, 10 years), contradicting the widely accepted hypothesis that the premium increases with distance into the future at a decreasing rate.[24] The comparison of survey estimates of expectations with unbiased forecasting estimates like ours appears to be a fruitful field for future research.

IV. Conclusion

Without imposing any particular form on the liquidity premium, we were able to demonstrate the following: there is a liquidity premium, significantly greater than zero. This premium has been large enough since the Accord to imply that for some maturities, borrowers or lenders who desire one borrowing or lending period would do better in a different maturity, in spite of the extra costs incurred. The premium has been larger since the Accord than it was during the 4 years before the Accord.

[23] (1967). I am grateful to Malkiel for a letter explaining some of the figures given in that paper.

[24] The problem cannot be that the questionnaires were not filled out promptly on April 1, but only after a delay of variable length, for the forward rates in question were actually higher on April 30 and May 31 than they had been at the close of March.

TABLE 9

COMPARISON OF PREMIA FROM TABLES 6 AND 8 WITH THOSE DERIVED FROM KANE-MALKIEL SURVEY

Future Date	Security	Forward Rate*	Survey Expected Rate†	Survey Premium	Exponential-Form Premium	Free-Form Premium
July 1, 1965	90-day bill	4.07	3.99	.06	.17	.16
		(.13)	(.01)	(.13)	(.03)	(.05)
October 1, 1965	90-day bill	4.04	4.01	.03	.21	.12
		(.18)	(.01)	(.18)	(.05)	(.11)
January 1, 1966	90-day bill	3.84	3.96	−.12	.22	.11
		(.18)	(.02)	(.18)	(.06)	(.16)
April 1, 1966	90-day bill	3.81	3.86	−.05	.22	.13
		(.19)	(.02)	(.19)	(.06)	(.21)
April 1, 1967	90-day bill	3.93	3.66	.27	.22	.12
		(.10)	(.04)	(.11)	(.06)	(.39)
April 1, 1966	10-year bond	4.17	4.12	.05	.01	−.11
		(.03)	(.02)	(.04)	(.00)	(.14)
April 1, 1967	10-year bond	4.20	3.98	.22	.01	−.24
		(.04)	(.03)	(.05)	(.00)	(.27)

NOTE.—Standard errors in parentheses.

* Rates computed from U.S. Government security prices as of March 31, 1965, by method of McCulloch (1971). Logarithmic rates converted to banker's discount basis for comparison to bills.

† Mean of "most likely" rate for all respondents. Standard error equals standard deviation given by Kane and Malkiel (1967), divided by the square root of the number of respondents.

Finally, the variance of forecasting errors has not been constant over the period since the Accord.

We were unable to demonstrate any variation in the liquidity premium itself since the Accord, either as a function of time or as a function of the level of interest rates. We were also unable to detect nonnormality in the distribution of the forecasting errors (provided we allow for heteroskedasticity), or nonmonotonicity in the behavior of the premium as a function of maturity.

However, if we do not impose a particular form, our estimates of the mean term premium on long-term forward rates are very inaccurate. When we postulate the monotonic and bounded exponential form of (16) we obtain the relatively precise estimates contained in tables 7 and 8. In particular, we may then say that the forward rate corresponding to a future loan of duration *m* years is greater than the expected future spot rate, but by no more than 0.101/*m* percent per year.

References

Abbott, Charles C. "A Note on the Government Bond Market, 1919–1930." *Rev. Econ. and Statis.* 17 (January 1935): 7–12.

Bierwag, G. O., and Grove, M. A. "A Model of the Term Structure of Interest Rates." *Rev. Econ. and Statis.* 40 (1967): 50–62.

Bryan, William R., and Carleton, Willard T. "A Method of Estimating the Term Structure of Interest Rates." Unpublished paper given at meetings of the American Finance Association, Toronto, December 1972.

Buse, Adolf. "Expectations, Prices, Coupons, and Yields." *J. Finance* 25 (September 1970): 809–18.

Cagan, Phillip. "A Study of Liquidity Premiums on Federal and Municipal Government Securities." In *Essays on Interest Rates*, vol. 1, edited by J. M. Guttentag and P. Cagan. New York: Nat. Bur. Econ. Res., 1969.

Culbertson, John M. "The Term Structure of Interest Rates." *Q.J.E.* 71 (November 1957): 485–517.

David, H. A.; Hartley, H. O.; and Pearson, E. S. "The Distribution of the Ratio, in a Single Normal Sample, of Range to Standard Deviation." *Biometrika* 41 (1954): 482–93.

Diller, Stanley. "Expectations in the Term Structure of Interest Rates." *Economic Forecasts and Expectations: Analysis of Forecasting Behavior and Performance.* Edited by J. Mincer. New York: Nat. Bur. Econ. Res., 1969.

Fama, Eugene F., and Roll, Richard. "Some Properties of Symmetric Stable Distributions." *J. American Statis. Assoc.* 63 (September 1968): 817–36.

———. "Parameter Estimates for Symmetric Stable Distributions." *J. American Statis. Assoc.* 66 (June 1971): 331–38.

Goldberger, Arthur S. *Econometric Theory.* New York: Wiley, 1964.

Hart, B. I. "Tabulation of the Probabilities for the Ratio of the Mean Square Successive Difference to the Variance." *Ann. Math. Statis.* 13 (1942): 207–14.

Hicks, John R. *Value and Capital.* 2d ed. Oxford: Clarendon Press, 1946.

Kane, Edward J., and Malkiel, Burton G. "The Term Structure of Interest Rates: An Analysis of a Survey of Interest Rate Expectations." *Rev. Econ. and Statis.* 69 (August 1967): 343–55.

Kessel, Reuben A. *The Cyclical Behavior of the Term Structure of Interest Rates.* New York: Nat. Bur. Econ. Res., 1965. Reprinted in *Essays on Interest Rates.* Vol. 2. Edited by J. M. Guttentag. New York: Nat. Bur. Econ. Res., 1971.

Long, John B., Jr. "Consumption-Investment Decisions and Equilibrium in the Securities Market." In *Studies in the Theory of Capital Markets,* edited by M. C. Jensen. New York: Praeger, 1972.

McCulloch, J. Huston. "Measuring the Term Structure of Interest Rates." *J. Bus.* 44 (January 1971): 19–31.

———. "An Estimate of the Liquidity Premium." Ph.D. dissertation, Univ. Chicago, 1973.

Meiselman, David. *The Term Structure of Interest Rates.* Englewood Cliffs, N.J.: Prentice-Hall, 1962.

Miller, Merton H., and Orr, Daniel. "An Application of Control-Limit Models to the Management of Corporate Cash Balances." *Financial Research and Management Decisions.* Edited by A. A. Robichek. New York: Wiley, 1967.

Modigliani, Franco, and Shiller, Robert J. "Inflation, Rational Expectations, and the Term Structure of Interest Rates." *Economica,* n.s. 40 (February 1973): 12–43.

Modigliani, Franco, and Sutch R. "Innovations in Interest Rate Policy." *A.E.R.* 56 (May 1966): 178–97.

Nelson, Charles R. *The Term Structure of Interest Rates.* New York: Basic Books, 1972.

Praetz, Peter D. "The Distribution of Share Price Changes." *J. Bus.* 45 (January 1972): 49–55.

Press, S. James. "A Compound Events Model for Security Prices." *J. Bus.* 40 (July 1967): 317–35.

Rice, John R. *The Approximation of Functions.* Vol. 2. Reading, Mass.: Addison-Wesley, 1969.

Roll, Richard. *The Behavior of Interest Rates: The Application of the Efficient Market Model to U.S. Treasury Bills.* New York: Basic Books, 1970.

Samuelson, Paul A. "Proof That Properly Anticipated Prices Fluctuate Randomly." *Indus. Management Rev.* 6 (Spring 1965): 41–49.

Stiglitz, Joseph E. "A Consumption-oriented Theory of the Demand for Financial Assets and the Term Structure of Interest Rates." *Rev. Econ. Studies* 37 (July 1970): 321–51.

Telser, Lester G. "A Critique of Some Recent Empirical Research on the Explanation of the Term Structure of Interest Rates." *J.P.E.* 75, no. 4, pt. II (August 1967): 546–68.

Van Horne, James. "Interest Rate Risk and the Term Structure of Interest Rates." *J.P.E.* 73, no. 4 (August 1965): 344–51.

Wallace, Neil. "The Term Structure of Interest Rates and the Maturity Composition of the Federal Debt." Ph.D. dissertation, Univ. Chicago, 1964.

Weingartner, H. Martin. "The Generalized Rate of Return." *J. Financial and Quantitative Analysis* 1 (September 1966): 1–29.

Williams, John Burr. *The Theory of Investment Value.* Cambridge, Mass.: Harvard Univ. Press, 1938.

Part II
Testing Rational Expectations Hypotheses

[6]

THE TERM STRUCTURE OF INTEREST RATES

ROBERT J. SHILLER*

Yale University

with an Appendix by

J. HUSTON McCULLOCH

Ohio State University

Contents

1. Introduction 629
2. Simple analytics of the term structure: Discount bonds 630
3. Fundamental concepts 633
    3.1. Bonds: Their definition 633
    3.2. Interest rates: Their definition 634
    3.3. Par bonds 635
    3.4. Instantaneous and perpetuity rates 636
    3.5. Estimates of the term structure 636
    3.6. Duration 637
    3.7. Forward rates 639
    3.8. Holding period rates 644
4. Theories of the term structure 644
    4.1. Expectations theories of the term structure 644
    4.2. Risk preferences and the expectations hypothesis 645
    4.3. Definitions of term premia 647
    4.4. Early presumptions pertaining to the sign of the term premium 649
    4.5. Risk preferences and term premia 651
5. Empirical studies of the term structure 653
    5.1. Empirical expectations hypotheses for the term structure 653
    5.2. The rational expectations hypothesis in empirical work 654

*The author is indebted to John Campbell, Benjamin Friedman, Jonathan Ingersoll, Edward Kane, Stephen LeRoy, Jeffrey Miron, and J. Huston McCulloch for helpful comments and discussions, and to Jeeman Jung, Sejin Kim, Plutarchos Sakellaris, and James Robinson for research assistance. Research was supported by the National Science Foundation.

The research reported here is part of the NBER's research program in Financial Markets and Monetary Economics. Any opinions expressed are those of the authors and not those of the National Bureau of Economic Research.

Handbook of Monetary Economics, Volume I, Edited by B.M. Friedman and F.H. Hahn

5.3. The volatility of long-term interest rates 658
5.4. Encouraging results for the rational expectations hypothesis 660
5.5. Interpreting departures from the expectations theory 664
5.6. Seasonality and interest rates 665
5.7. The sign of term premia 666
5.8. Modelling time-varying term premia 667
5.9. Flow of funds models 668
6. Some concluding observations 670
Appendix A: Mathematical symbols 671
Appendix B: U.S. term structure data, 1946–87 (by J. Huston McCulloch) 672
References 716

1. Introduction

The term of a debt instrument with a fixed maturity date is the time until the maturity date. The term structure of interest rates at any time is the function relating interest rate to term. Figure 13.1 shows the U.S. term structure of nominal interest rates according to one definition for each year since 1948. Usually the term structure is upward sloping; long-term interest rates are higher than short-term interest rates and the interest rate rises with term. Sometimes the term structure is downward sloping. Sometimes it is hump shaped, with intermediate terms having highest interest rates.

The study of the term structure inquires what market forces are responsible for the varying shapes of the term structure. In its purest form, this study considers only bonds for which we can disregard default risk (that interest or principal will not be paid by the issuer of the bond), convertibility provisions (an option to convert the bond to another financial instrument), call provisions (an option of the issuer to pay off the debt before the maturity date), floating rate provisions (provisions that change the interest payments according to some rule) or other special features.[1] Thus, the study of the term structure may be regarded as the study of the market price of time, over various intervals, itself.

What follows is an effort to consolidate and interpret the literature on the term structure as it stands today. The notation adopted is a little more complicated than usual, to allow diverse studies to be treated in a uniform notation. Definitions of rates of return, forward rates and holding returns for all time intervals are treated here in a uniform manner and their interrelations, exact or approximate, delineated. The concept of duration is used throughout to simplify mathematical expressions. Continuous compounding is used where possible to avoid arbitrary distinctions based on compounding assumptions. The relations described here can be applied approximately to conventionally defined interest rates or exactly to the continuously compounded McCulloch data in Appendix B. The McCulloch data, published here for the first time, are the cleanest interest rate data available in that they are based on a broad spectrum of government bond prices and are corrected for coupon and special tax effects.

Section 2 is a brief introduction to some key concepts in the simplest case, namely that of pure discount bonds. Section 3 sets forth the full definitions and concepts and their interrelations. Section 4 sets forth theories of the term

[1]The U.S. government bonds used to produce Figure 13.1 are in some dimensions good approximations to such bonds: default risk must be considered very low, the bonds are not convertible, and there are no floating rate provisions. However, many long-term U.S. bonds are callable five years before maturity, and some bonds are given special treatment in estate tax law.

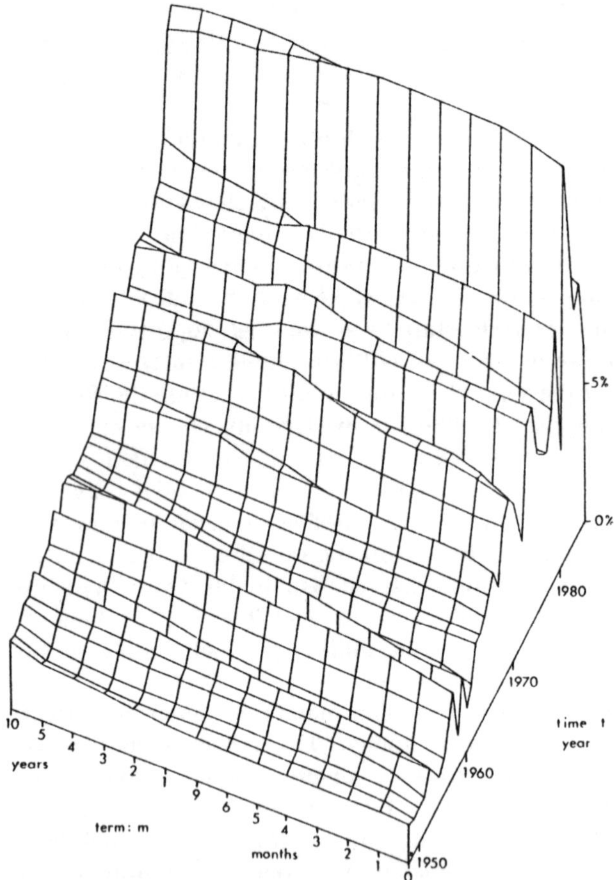

Figure 13.1. The term structure of interest rates. Data plotted are par bond yields to maturity, $r_p(t, t+m)$, against time t and term m, annual data, end of June 1948–85. Curves on the surface parallel to the m-axis show the term structure for various years. Curves on the surface parallel to the t-axis show the path through time of interest rates of various maturities. Maturities shown are 0, 1, 2, 3, 4, 5, 6, and 9 months and 1, 2, 3, 4, 5, and 10 years. Note that longer maturities are at the left, the reverse of the usual plot of term structures, so an "upward sloping" term structure slopes up to the left. Source of data: Table 13.A.3 of Appendix B.

structure, and Section 5 the empirical work on the term structure. Section 6 is an overview and interpretation of the literature.

2. Simple analytics of the term structure: Discount bonds

A discount bond is a promise by the issuer of the bond of a single fixed payment (the "principal") to the holder of the bond at a given date (the "maturity"). There are no intervening interest payments; thus the bond sells for less than the principal before the maturity date, i.e. it is expected to sell at a discount. The issuer of the bond has no other obligation than to pay the principal on the maturity date. An investment in a discount bond is not illiquid because the holder can sell it at any time to another investor. Let us denote by $p_d(t, T)$ the market price at time t of a discount bond whose principal is one dollar and whose maturity date is T, $t \leq T$. The subscript d denotes discount bond, to contrast this price from the par bond price to be defined below. The "term" of the bond (which will be represented here by the letter m) is the time to maturity, $m = T - t$. Thus, the term of any given bond steadily shrinks through time: a three-month bond becoming a two-month bond after one month and a one-month bond after two months.

All discount bonds maturing at date T for which there is no risk of default by the issuer ought to be perfectly interchangeable, and to sell at time t for $p_d(t, T)$ times the principal. The price $p_d(t, T)$ is thus determined by the economy-wide supply and demand at time t for credit to be repaid at time T. The determination of $p_d(t, T)$ is thus macroeconomic in nature, and is not at the discretion of any individual issuer or investor.

The price $p_d(t, T)$ of a discount bond may be generally expected to increase gradually with time t until the maturity date T, when it reaches its maximum, equal to one dollar. The increase in price for any holder of the bond over the period of time that he or she holds it is the return to holding it. The actual increase in price, since it is determined by market forces, may not be steady and may vary from time to time. It is useful to have some measure of the prospective increase in price that is implicit in the price $p_d(t, T)$. The yield to maturity (or interest rate) $r_d(t, T)$ at time t on the discount bond maturing at time T can be defined, given $p_d(t, T)$, as the *steady* rate at which the price should increase if the bond is to be worth one dollar at time T. If the growth of price is to be steady, then the price at time t', $t \leq t' \leq T$, should be given by $p_d(t, T)\,e^{(t'-t)r_d(t,T)}$. Setting this price equal to one dollar where $t' = T$, and solving for $r_d(t, T)$, we find that the yield to maturity is given by

$$r_d(t, T) = -\log_n(p_d(t, T))/(T - t)\,.$$

The term structure of interest rates, for discount bonds, is the function relating $r_d(t, t + m)$ to m. We may also refer to $r_d(t, t + m)$ as the "m-period rate"; if m is very small as the "short rate" and if m is very large as the "long rate".

Note that the term structure at any given date is determined exclusively by bond prices quoted on that day; there is a term structure in every daily newspaper. Those making plans on any day might well consult the term structure on that day. We can all lend (that is, invest) at the rates shown in the paper, and while we cannot all borrow (that is, issue bonds) at these rates, the rates shown are likely to be indicative of the rates at which we can borrow. If the one-year interest rate is high and the two-year interest rate is low (i.e. if there is a descending term structure in this range), then individual firms, or governments, who plan to borrow for one year may be rather discouraged, and inclined to defer their borrowing plans for another year. Those who plan to lend this year rather than next would be encouraged. The reverse would happen if the term structure were ascending. Most individuals, of course, do not pay close attention to the term structure, but many do, and firms and governments do as well. The term structure on any day is determined by those who enter their preferences in the market on that day. A descending term structure on that day means that if the term structure had been flat there would be an excess supply of one-year bonds or an excess demand for two-year bonds. The descending term structure arises, of course, to choke off this excess supply or demand.

In making plans using the term structure it is helpful to realize that the term structure on any given date has in it implicit future interest rates, called forward rates. In the above example, where the term structure is descending between one and two years, it is implicit in the term structure that the one-year interest rate can be guaranteed to be lower next year than it is this year. To guarantee the forward rate one must be able both to buy and to issue bonds at quoted prices. One achieves this by trading in bonds of different maturities available today. One buys a discount bond at time t maturing at time T at price $p_d(t, T)$ and issues an amount of discount bonds maturing at t' at price $p_d(t, t')$, where $t < t' < T$. If the number of bonds issued equals $p_d(t, T)/p_d(t, t')$, then one will have broken even, at time t. That is, one will not have acquired or lost any cash today in the transaction. However, at time t' one must pay the principal on the bonds issued, equal to $p_d(t, T)/p_d(t, t')$. At time T one will receive the principal on the $(T-t)$-period bond, equal to 1. Thus, the outcome of the transaction is in effect that one is committing oneself at time t to buy a discount bond at time t' maturing at time T with price $p_d(t, T)/p_d(t, t')$. The forward rate $f_d(t, t', T)$ at time t applying to the time interval t' to T is the yield to maturity on this contract:

$$f_d(t, t', T) = -\log_n(p_d(t, T)/p_d(t, t'))/(T-t'), \quad t < t' < T .$$

This may also be called the $t'-t$ period ahead forward rate of term $T-t'$. One can also guarantee that one can borrow at the forward rate $f_d(t, t', T)$ by buying discount bonds maturing at t' and issuing bonds maturing at T.

One might thus consider, in deciding whether or not to defer borrowing or lending plans, a comparison of the spot rate $r_d(t, T)$ with the forward rate of corresponding maturity k periods in the future, $f_d(t, t+k, T+k)$. There is also another margin to consider. One might hold one's borrowing or lending plans fixed, deciding, let us say, to invest at time $t+k$, but to consider whether to tie down the interest rate today at $f_d(t, t+k, T+k)$ or to wait and take one's chances with regard to the future spot rate $r_d(t+k, T+k)$.

The subject of the literature surveyed here is how people who are making decisions at the various margins interact to determine the term structure. Before embarking on this, it is important to broaden our definitions and concepts.

3. Fundamental concepts

3.1. Bonds: Their definition

The term "bond" will be used here for any debt instrument, whether technically bond, bill, note, commercial paper, etc. and whether or not payments are defined in nominal (money) terms or in real terms (that is, tied to a commodity price index).

A bond represents a claim on a prespecified sequence of payments. A bond which is issued at time I and matures at time T is defined by a w-element vector of payment dates $(t_1, t_2, \ldots, t_{w-1}, T)$, where $I < t_i \leq T$ for all i, and by a w-element vector of corresponding positive payments $(s_1, s_2, s_3, \ldots, s_w)$. In theoretical treatments of the term structure, payments may be assumed to be made continually in time, so that the payment stream is represented by a positive function of time $s(t)$, $I < t \leq T$.

Two kinds of payment sequences are common. For the discount bond referred to above the vector of payment dates contains a single element T and the vector of payments contains the single element called the principal. A coupon bond, in contrast, promises a payment at regular intervals of an amount c called the coupon and a payment of the last coupon and principal (the latter normalized here at 1) at the maturity date. Thus, for example, a coupon bond that will mature in an integer number of periods and whose coupons are paid at integer intervals has vector of payment dates $(I+1, I+2, \ldots, I+w-1, I+w)$, and vector of payments $(c, c, \ldots, c, c+1)$. A perpetuity or consol is a special case of a coupon bond for which T, the maturity date, is infinity.

The purchaser at time t of a bond maturing at time T pays price $p(t, T)$ and is entitled to receive those payments corresponding to the t_i that are greater than t, so long as the purchaser continues to hold the bond.[2] A coupon bond is

[2]In the United States coupon bonds are typically traded "and accrued interest" (rather than "flat") which means that the price $p(t, T)$ actually paid for a coupon bond between coupon dates is equal to its quoted price plus accrued interest which is a fraction of the next coupon. The fraction is the time elapsed since the last coupon payment divided by the time interval between coupons.

said to be selling at par at time t if $p(t, T)$ is equal to the value of the principal, by our convention equal to 1.00.

A coupon bond may be regarded as a portfolio of discount bonds. If coupons are paid once per time period, for example, then the portfolio consists of an amount c of discount bonds maturing at time $I + 1$, an amount c discount bonds maturing at time $I + 2$, etc. and an amount $c + 1$ of discount bonds maturing at time T. Should all such discount bonds be traded, we would expect, by the law of one price, that (disregarding discrepancies allowed by taxes, transactions costs and other market imperfections) the price of the portfolio of discount bonds should be the same as the price of the coupon bond.[3]

There is thus (abstracting from market imperfections) a redundancy in bond prices, and if both discount and coupon bonds existed for all maturities, we could arbitrarily confine our attention to discount bonds only or coupon bonds only. In practice, we do not generally have prices on both kinds of bonds for the same maturities. In the United States, for example, discount bonds were until recently available only for time to maturity of one year or less. There is also redundancy among coupon bonds, in that one can find coupon bonds of differing coupon for the same maturity date.

3.2. *Interest rates: Their definition*

The *yield to maturity* (or, loosely, interest rate) at time t of a bond maturing at time T is defined implicitly as the rate $r(t, T)$ that discounts its vector of payments s to the price $p(t, T)$:

$$p(t, T) = \sum_{t_i > t} s_i \, e^{-(t_i - t) r(t, T)} . \tag{1}$$

The right-hand side of this expression is just the present value, discounted at rate $r(t, T)$, of the remaining payments accruing to bond holders. For discount bonds, this expression reduces to the expression given in Section 2 above. The yield to maturity may also be given an interpretation as above. Given the price $p(t, T)$, $r(t, T)$ is that steady rate of appreciation of price between payment dates so that if the price falls by the amount s_i at each t_i before T, the price equals S_T at time T. In theoretical treatments of the term structure in which the

[3]Conversely, a discount bond may be considered a portfolio of coupon bonds, though in this case the portfolio involves negative quantities. For example, a two-period discount bond may be regarded as a portfolio of one- and two-period coupon bonds whose coupons are c_1 and c_2, respectively. The portfolio would consist of $-(c_2)/[(c_1 + 1)(c_2 + 1)]$ of the one-period coupon bonds and $1/(c_2 + 1)$ of the two-period coupon bonds.

payments are assumed to be made continually in time, the summation in (1) is replaced by an integral.

The expression (1) gives the continuously compounded yield to maturity $r(t, T)$. One can define a yield to maturity with any compounding interval h: $r(t, T, h) = (e^{hr(t,T)} - 1)/h$. In the United States, where coupons are traditionally paid semiannually, it is customary to express yields to maturity at annual rates with semiannual compounding.[4] Continuous compounding will be assumed here for consistency, as we do not wish to allow such things as the interval between coupon dates to dictate the compounding interval.[5]

For coupon bonds it is customary to define the *current yield* as the total coupons paid per year divided by the price. Current yield is not used to represent the interest rate and should not be confused with the yield to maturity.

If coupon payments are made once per period, then equation (1) is a $(T-t)$-order polynomial equation in $e^{-r(t,T)}$ which therefore has $T-t$ roots. However, given that $s_i \geq 0$ for all i, there is only one real positive root, and this is taken for the purpose of computing the yield to maturity $r(t, T)$.

Roots of polynomials of order n can be given an explicit formula in terms of the coefficients of the polynomial only if n is less than five. Thus, yields to maturity for $T-t$ greater than or equal to five can be determined from price only by iterative or other approximation procedures, or with the use of bond tables.

The term structure of interest rates at time t is the function relating yield to maturity $r(t, t+m)$ to term m. A plot of $r(t, t+m)$ against m is also known as a yield curve at time t. There is a term structure for discount bonds and a term structure for coupon bonds. If we assume the law of one price as described in the preceding section, then, given the coupons, there is a relation between the different term structures.

3.3. *Par bonds*

Consider a bond that pays coupons continuously at rate c per period until the maturity date T when a lump-sum payment of 1 is made. If we disregard taxes and other market imperfections, the law of one price implies that the price of

[4]Thus, computing yield by solving (1) and converting to semiannual compounding (using $h = 0.5$) gives us exactly the yields in bond value tables, as in Financial Publishing Company (1970), so long as the term m is an integer multiple of $h = 0.5$. Whether or not m is an integer multiple of h, this also gives exactly yields to maturity as presented in Stigum (1981, p. 111) if $p(t, T)$ is represented as price plus accrued interest.

[5]Continuously compounded yield to maturity has also been referred to as "instantaneous compound interest", "force of interest", or "nominal rate convertible instantaneously". See, for example, Skinner (1913).

this bond in terms of $p_d(t, T)$ is given by

$$p_p(t, T) = \int_t^T c p_d(t, s)\, ds + p_d(t, T)\,. \tag{2}$$

The yield $r_p(t, T)$ of a par bond is found from $p_p(t, T)$ by setting the left-hand side of this expression to 1 and solving for c:[6]

$$r_p(t, T) = \frac{1 - p_d(t, T)}{\int_t^T p_d(t, s)\, ds}\,. \tag{3}$$

3.4. *Instantaneous and perpetuity rates*

The interest rate of term zero is $r_p(t, t)$, defined as the limit of $r_p(t, T)$ as $T \to t$, or as $r_d(t, t)$ defined as the limit of $r_d(t, T)$ as T approaches t. It is the instantaneous interest rate, which is of course not directly observed in any market. Since $r_p(t, t) = r_d(t, t)$ we can adopt the simpler notation r_t to refer to this instantaneous rate of interest. At the other extreme is $r_p(t, \infty)$, the limit of $r_p(t, T)$ as T approaches ∞. This is the consol or perpetuity yield, which is just the inverse of the integral of $p_d(t, s)$ from $s = t$ to $s = \infty$.[7]

3.5. *Estimates of the term structure*

At any point of time t there will be an array of outstanding bonds differing by term, $m = T - t$, and by payment streams. Of course, not all possible times to maturity will be observed on available bonds at any given time t, and for some terms there will be more than one bond available. There has long been interest in estimates of rates of interest on standard bonds in terms of a standard list of times to maturity, interpolated from the rates of interest on bonds of those maturities that are actively traded.

[6]Note that for a par bond the yield to maturity equals the coupon. Note also that in the presence of taxes the law of one price need not imply (2) or (3). McCulloch's (1975b) formula for $r_p(t, T)$ collapses to (3) if the income tax rate is zero.

[7]Corresponding to the consol yield, we may also define the yield of a discount bond of infinite term, $r_d(t, \text{infinity})$, defined as the limit of $r_d(t, T)$ as T goes to infinity. Dybvig, Ingersoll and Ross (1986) have a curious result concerning $r_d(t, \text{infinity})$ in the context of a state price density model. They show that if $r_d(t, \text{infinity})$ exists for all t, then $r_d(t, \text{infinity}) \leq r_d(s, \text{infinity})$ with probability one when $t < s$. Otherwise, arbitrage profits would obtain. Thus, the long-term interest rate so defined can never fall. Intuitively, this seemingly strange result follows from the fact that for large enough T the price $p_d(t, T)$ is virtually zero and hence cannot decline, but will rise dramatically if there is any decline in $r_d(t, T)$.

The U.S. Treasury reports constant maturity yields for its own securities, that appear regularly in the *Federal Reserve Bulletin*. Salomon Brothers (1983) provides yield curve data for government bonds of a wide range of maturities. Durand (1942, and updated) provides yield curve data for corporate bonds. These data are interpolated judgmentally.[8]

McCulloch (1971, 1975b) used a spline interpolation method that deals statistically with the redundancy of bonds and deals systematically with some differences among bonds, such as tax provisions pertaining to them. His method produced an estimate of an after-tax discount function and from that the price $p_d(t, T)$ of a taxable discount bond as a continuous function of T. Expression (1) was then used to convert this estimated function into a function $r_d(t, T)$. Values of his estimated continuous function for various values of t and T appear in Table 13.A.1. His method allows for the fact that, in the U.S. personal income tax law, capital gains are not taxable until the bond is sold and that, until the 1986 Tax Act, capital gains on bonds originally issued at par were taxed at a rate which was lower than the income tax rate. He describes his function in Appendix B. Other functional forms for estimation of the term structure have been discussed by Chambers, Carlton and Waldman (1984), Jordan (1984), Nelson and Siegel (1985), Schaefer (1981), Shea (1984, 1985), and Vasicek and Fong (1982).

McCulloch used his estimated $p_d(t, T)$ to produce an estimate of the term structure of par bond yields, using an equation differing from (3) above only for tax effects.

3.6. *Duration*

The term $m = T - t$ of a bond is the time to the last payment, and is unrelated to the times or magnitudes of intervening payments $s_1, s_2, \ldots, s_{w-1}$. Since bonds can be regarded as portfolios of discount bonds, it may be more useful to describe bonds by a weighted average of the terms of the constituent bonds rather than by the term of the longest bond in the portfolio. The duration of a bond, as defined by Macaulay (1938), is such a weighted average of the terms of the constituent discount bonds, where the weights correspond to the amount of the payments times a corresponding discount factor.[9] The use of the discount factor in the definition implies that terms of very long-term constituent bonds

[8]Other important sources of historical data may be noted. Homer (1963) and Macaulay (1938) provide long historical time series. Amsler (1984) has provided a series of high quality preferred stock yields that might proxy for a perpetuity yield in the United States, a series which is much longer than that supplied by Salomon Brothers (1983).

[9]Hicks (1946) independently defined "average period", which is equivalent to Macaulay's first definition of duration.

will tend to have relatively little weight in the duration formula. Thus, 30-year coupon bonds and 40-year coupon bonds have similar durations; indeed, they are similar instruments since the payments beyond 30 years into the future are heavily discounted and not important today relative to the coupons that come much sooner.

Macaulay actually gave two different definitions of duration that differed in the specification of the discount factor. The first definition of the duration of a bond of term m at time t uses the yield to maturity of the bond:[10]

$$D(m, t) = \frac{\sum_{t_i > t} (t_i - t) s_i \, e^{-(t_i - t) r(t, t+m)}}{\sum_{t_i > t} s_i \, e^{-(t_i - t) r(t, t+m)}} . \tag{4}$$

The second definition of duration of a bond of term m at time t uses prices of discount bonds as discount factors:

$$D'(m, t) = \frac{\sum_{t_i > t} (t_i - t) s_i p_d(t, t_i)}{\sum_{t_i > t} s_i p_d(t, t_i)} . \tag{4'}$$

By either definition of duration, if the bond is a discount bond, then the duration equals the term m, that is, we shall write $D_d(m, t) = m$. Otherwise, (since payments s_i are positive) the duration is less than the time to maturity.

If a bond is selling at par and coupons are paid continually, then duration using (4) is:

$$D_p(m, t) = \frac{1 - e^{-m r_p(t, t+m)}}{r_p(t, t+m)} . \tag{5}$$

Thus, the duration of a perpetuity, whose term is infinite, is $1/r_p(t, \infty)$.

The duration using yields to maturity to discount $D(m, t)$ is the derivative of the log of $p(t, T)$, using (1), with respect to the yield to maturity $r(t, T)$.[11] Thus, duration may be used as an index of the "risk" of a bond. The concept of duration has thus played a role in the literature on "immunization" from interest rate risk of portfolios of financial intermediaries. A portfolio is fully immunized if there is complete cash-flow matching, that is, if the payments

[10]The second argument, t, of duration will be dropped below in contexts where the interest rate $r(t, t+m)$ is replaced by a constant.

[11]This fact was used by Hicks and was rediscovered by Samuelson (1945), Fisher (1966), Hopewell and Kaufman (1973), and others.

received on assets exactly equal payments paid on liabilities. When such cash-flow matching is infeasible, portfolio managers may instead try to match the overall duration of their assets with the duration of their liabilities. As long as the term structure makes only parallel shifts, the yields on bonds of all terms being increased or decreased by the same amount, then duration matching will perfectly immunize the portfolio and there is no uncertainty about net worth. However, the term structure rarely makes a parallel shift, long-term interest rates being more stable than short-term interest rates, and so duration tends to overstate the relative riskiness of long-term bonds. Other methods of immunization have been proposed that take this into account [see Ingersoll, Skelton and Weil (1978)].

3.7. *Forward rates*[12]

The time t discount bond forward rate applying to the interval from t' to T, $f_d(t, t', T)$, alluded to in Section 2 above, is defined in terms of yields to maturity and duration in Table 13.1, expression (a). Using (1) one verifies that this expression is the same as the expression given in Section 2 above. The forward rate compounded once per h periods is $f_d(t, t', T, h) = (\exp(hf_d(t, t', T)) - 1)/h$.

The limit of expression (a) of Table 13.1 as t' approaches T, denoted $f_d(t, T, T)$ or just $f(t, T)$ is the instantaneous forward rate:[13]

$$f(t, T) = r_d(t, T) + (T - t)\,\mathrm{d}r_d(t, T)/\mathrm{d}T \tag{6}$$

[12]The earliest use of the term "forward rate", and the first indication that it can be thought of as a rate on a forward contract that can be computed from the term structure, appears to be in Hicks (1946) [first published (1939)]. Kaldor (1939) speaks of forward rates and their interpretation as rates in forward contracts, but attributes the idea to Hicks. Macaulay (1938) speaks of computing "implicit interest rates" without making an analogy to forward contracts (p. 30). Of course, the notion that long rates are averages of future short rates has a longer history; the earlier authors appear not to have written of computing forward rates from the long rates, or of showing an analogy of such rates to rates in forward contracts.

I wrote to Sir John Hicks asking if he had coined the term forward rate in the term structure. He replied that he only remembers being influenced by a 1930 paper in Swedish by Lindahl, later published in English (1939), which is couched, Hicks writes, "in terms of expected rates rather than forward rates; it is likely that the change from one to the other is my own contribution".

[13]McCulloch, who was concerned with the effects of taxation, writes (1975b, p. 823) what appears to be a different expression for the instantaneous forward rate. If we adopt some of the notation of this paper this is:

$$f(t, T) = -\{\partial\delta(t, T)/\partial T\}/\{(1 - z)\delta(t, T)\},$$

where $\delta(t, T)$ is the price at time t of an *after-tax* dollar at time T, and z is the marginal tax rate. However, since $\delta(t, T) = \exp(-(1 - z)(T - t)r_d(t, T))$, his formula is identical to the one shown here, i.e. the tax rate drops out of the formula expressed in terms of $r_d(t, T)$. The tax rate *should* drop out because both the interest rate $r_d(t, T)$ and the forward rate are taxable.

Table 13.1
Formulas for computation of forward rates and holding rates

I. Time t forward rate applying to interval from t' to T, $t \leq t' \leq T$:

$$\text{(a)}\quad f_i(t, t', T) = \frac{D_i(T-t)r_i(t, T) - D_i(t'-t)r_i(t, t')}{D_i(T-t) - D_i(t'-t)} .$$

II. Holding period rate or return from t to t' on bond maturing at time T, $t \leq t' \leq T$:

$$\text{(b)}\quad h_i(t, t', T) = \frac{D_i(T-t)r_i(t, T) - [D_i(T-t) - D_i(t'-t)]r_i(t', T)}{D_i(t'-t)} .$$

III. Holding period rate of return from t to t' rolling over bonds of term $m = T - t$, $t \leq T \leq t'$:

$$\text{(c)}\quad h_i(t, t', T) = \left\{ \sum_{k=0}^{s-1} (D_i(km+m) - D_i(km))r_i(t+km, t+km+m) \right.$$
$$\left. + [D_i(t'-t) - D_i(sm)]h_i(t+sm, t', t+sm+m) \right\} \Big/ D_i(t'-t) ,$$

where s = largest integer $\leq (t'-t)/m$.

Note: In the above formulas, substitute $i = \mathrm{d}$ for discount bonds, $i = \mathrm{p}$ for par bonds. Par bond formulas give linear approximation to true rates. Duration (from which the second argument, t, has been dropped here) is given by $D_{\mathrm{d}}(m) = m$, $D_{\mathrm{p}}(m) = (1 - \mathrm{e}^{-R_t m})/R_t$, where R_t is the point of linearization, which might be taken as $r_{\mathrm{p}}(t, T)$. These formulas may be applied to data in Tables 13.A.1 and 13.A.3.

or

$$f(t, t+m) = r_{\mathrm{d}}(t, t+m) + m\, \mathrm{d}r_{\mathrm{d}}(t, t+m)/\mathrm{d}m . \tag{7}$$

It follows that the instantaneous forward rate follows the same relation to the spot rate as does marginal cost to average cost. To see this relation, think of m as output produced and $r_{\mathrm{d}}(t, t+m)$ as price of a unit of output. As with the familiar cost curves, the instantaneous forward rate (marginal) equals the instantaneous spot rate (average) when m equals zero, that is, $f(t, t) = r_t$. The forward rate is less than the spot rate where the slope of the term structure is negative, and is greater than the spot rate where the slope of the term structure is positive. An example showing a term structure and forward rate curve is shown in Figure 13.2.[14]

Solving the differential equation (7) we can show:

$$f_{\mathrm{d}}(t, t', T) = (T - t')^{-1} \int_{t'}^{T} f(t, s)\, \mathrm{d}s . \tag{8}$$

[14]Instantaneous forward rates computed using McCulloch's data for large $T - t$ seem to be very erratic. Vasicek and Fong (1982) have suggested that the problem would be eliminated if McCulloch had used exponential splines instead of the ordinary splines of his procedure; however, McCulloch (1984) has disputed whether this would solve the problem.

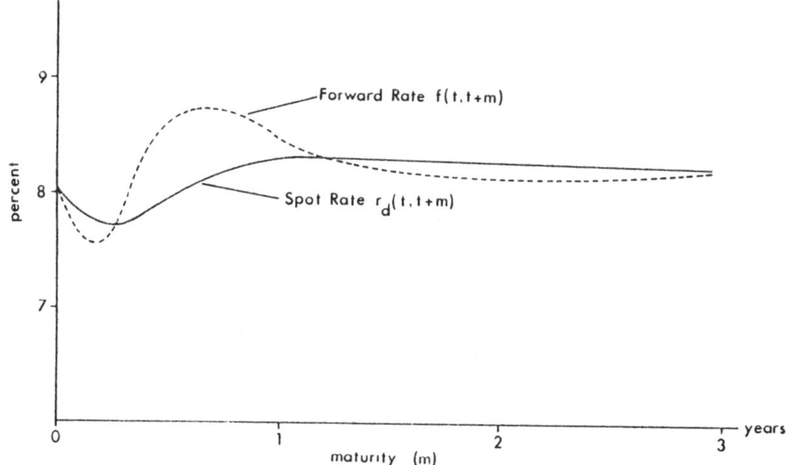

Figure 13.2. The term structure of interest rates $r_d(t, t+n)$ (solid line) and the instantaneous forward rate $f(t, t+n, t+n)$ (dashed line) for the end of August 1978. Source of data: Tables 13.A.1 and 13.A.2 in Appendix B.

Thus, the forward rate $f_d(t, t', T)$ is a simple average of the instantaneous forward rates between t' and T (see Figure 13.3).

Par bond forward rates can also be computed. These are especially useful if one wishes to make comparisons with spot interest rates as commonly quoted, since longer-term bonds usually trade near par. At time t one can guarantee for oneself a par bond issued at time t' and maturing at time T ($t \leq t' \leq T$) by buying at time t one discount bond maturing at time T, buying discount bonds maturing continually between t' and T whose principal accrues at rate c, and selling a discount bond maturing at date t' such that the proceeds of the sale exactly equal the total purchases made. If one then chooses c such that the number of bonds maturing at time t' sold is 1, one will have guaranteed for oneself, in effect, the rate of interest on a par bond at time t' maturing at T. The par forward rate $F_p(t, t', T)$ equals c or:[15]

$$F_p(t, t', T) = \frac{p_d(t, t') - p_d(t, T)}{\int_{t'}^{T} p_d(t, s)\, ds} . \tag{9}$$

[15]This formula for the forward rate differs slightly from that in McCulloch (1975b, p. 825). His formula replaces $p_d(x, y)$ with $\delta(x, y) = p_d(x, y)^{1-z}$ and divides by $(1 - z)$, where z is the marginal tax rate. His formula is *not* quite identical to the one shown here if $z > 0$. However, the Volterra–Taylor linearization (like that which follows immediately in the text) of his expression in terms of instantaneous forward rates *is* identical to equation (10) below, and the tax rate drops out of that.

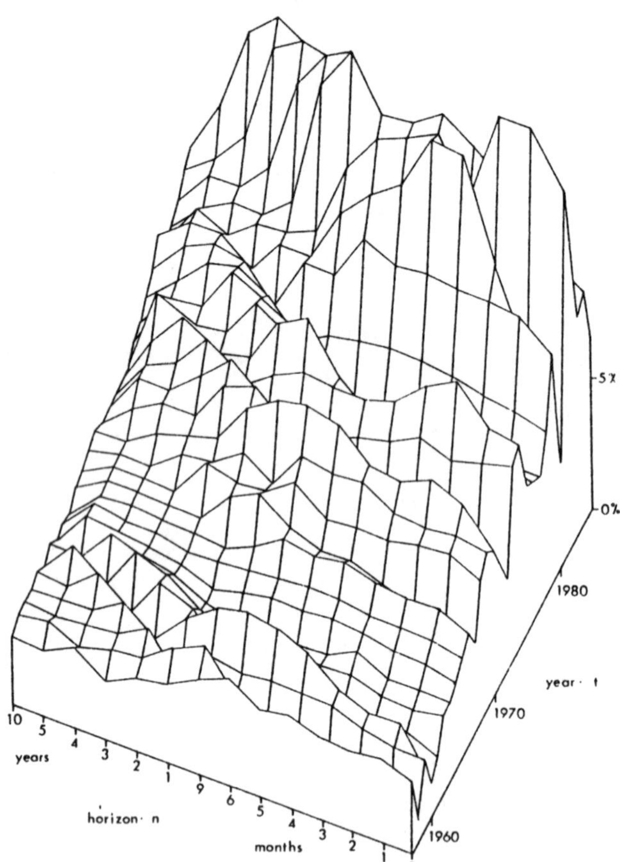

Figure 13.3. Instantaneous forward rates. Data plotted are $f(t-n, t, t)$ against time t and horizon n. The annual data series $f(t, t, t) = r_t$ seen at the far right of the surface is the instantaneous interest rate for the end of June of each year, 1957 to 1985. Curves on the surface parallel to the n axis show the path through time of the "forecast" implicit in the term structure of the instantaneous forward rate applying to the date shown on the t axis. If there were perfect foresight, we would expect these curves to be horizontal straight lines. In the expectations theory of the term structure with zero risk premium, they should be random walks. Curves on the surface parallel to the t-axis show the path through time of a forward rate of fixed forecast horizon. Data plotted here are from Table 13.A.2 of Appendix B.

Note the similarity between this expression and expression (3) for the par spot rate, above.

The limit of expression (9) as t' approaches T is the same as the values given by expressions (6) or (7) above for the instantaneous discount forward rate, hence the omission in those expressions of the d or p subscript.

It can be shown that the par bond forward rate is a *weighted* average of instantaneous forward rates, where the weights are proportional to the prices of the discount bond maturing at the date to which the instantaneous forward rate applies:[16]

$$F_p(t, t', T) = \frac{\int_{t'}^{T} p_d(t, s) f(t, s)\, ds}{\int_{t'}^{T} p_d(t, s)\, ds}\,. \tag{9'}$$

This expression may be compared with the corresponding expression for discount bonds, expression (8) above. This expression gives more weight to instantaneous forward rates in the near future, rather than equal weight to all forward rates as in expression (8).

Using (8) for $t = t'$ and substituting for $p_d(t, s)$ in the above expression makes $F_d(t, t', T)$ a functional of $f(t, s)$ considered as a function of s. Following Campbell (1984, 1986b), this functional can be linearized around $f(t, s) = R$ using a Volterra–Taylor expansion [Volterra (1959)]. We will refer to the linear approximation to the forward rate $F_p(t, t', T)$ as $f_p(t, t', T)$. This is:[17]

$$f_p(t, t', T) = \frac{R}{e^{-(t'-t)R} - e^{-(T-t)R}} \int_{t'}^{T} e^{-R(s-t)} f(t, s)\, ds\,. \tag{10}$$

Using expression (10) and that $f_p(t, t, T) = r_p(t, T)$ gives us again expression (a) in Table 13.1 for this forward rate in terms of par interest rates only.[18] The expression for forward rates on par bonds is the same as that on discount bonds except that duration on par bonds, $D_p(s - t)$, replaces the duration on discount bonds, $D_d(s - t) = s - t$, where $s = t', T$. It might also be noted that expression (a) in Table 13.1 gives the true par forward rate $F_p(t, t', T)$ exactly if a slightly different but less convenient, definition of duration is used.[19]

[16]See McCulloch (1977).

[17]The lower case f here denotes a linear approximation to the upper case F above. In contrast, for discount bonds the linear approximation is no different from the true forward rate, so lower case f is used for both. A discrete time version of (10) appears in Shiller (1979).

[18]The quality of this approximation to $F_p(t, t', T)$ is discussed in Shiller, Campbell and Schoenholtz (1983). The approximation is good except when both $t' - t$ and $T - t'$ are large.

[19]If we use Macaulay's definition of duration using prices of discount bonds as discount factors, (4'), and compute duration at time t of a bond whose continuous coupon is not constant through time but at time $t + i$ always equals $f(t, t + i)$, then one finds that duration is given by:

$$D'(m) = \int_{t}^{t+m} p_d(t, s)\, ds\,.$$

Using expression (9) [and the fact that $F_p(t, t, T) = r_p(t, T)$] one finds that $F_p(t, t', T)$ equals the right-hand side of expression (a) in Table 13.1, where the above $D'(m)$ replaces $D_p(m)$.

3.8. *Holding period rates*

A holding period rate is a rate of return to buying a bond (or sequence of bonds) and selling at a later date. The simple discount bond holding period rate, $h_d(t, t', T)$, where $t \leq t' \leq T$, is the rate of return from buying at time t a discount bond maturing at date T and selling it at date t'; see Table 13.1, expression (b). The rollover discount bond holding period rate, $h_d(t, t', T)$, where $t < T < t'$, is the rate of return from buying at time t a discount bond of term $m = T - t$, reinvesting ("rolling over") the proceeds in another m-period discount bond at time $t + m$, and continuing until time t' when the last m-period discount bond is sold [Table 13.1, expression (c)].

The par bond holding period rate, $H_p(t, t', T)$, where $t \leq t' \leq T$, is the yield to maturity on the stream of payments accruing to someone who buys at time t a par bond maturing at T, receives the stream of coupons between t' and T, and sells the bond at time T. This holding period rate can be defined as an implicit function of the coupon on the bond $r_p(t, T)$ and the selling price, which in turn is a function of $r_p(t', T)$ as well as the coupon $r_p(t, T)$. This implicit function may be linearized around $H_p(t, t', T) = r_p(t, T) = r_p(t', T) = R$ to yield the approximate $h_p(t, t', T)$ shown in Table 13.1, expression (b).[20] The rollover par bond holding period rate, $H_p(t, t', T)$, $t < T < t'$, is the yield to maturity on the stream of payments accruing to someone who buys at time t a par bond maturing at time $T = t + m$, reinvests proceeds in a par bond maturing at time $t + 2m$, and continues until time t' when the last par bond is sold. The linear approximation $h_p(t, t', T)$ appears in Table 13.1, expression (c).

4. Theories of the term structure

4.1. *Expectations theories of the term structure*

The expectations hypothesis, in the broadest terms, asserts that the slope of the term structure has something to do with expectations about future interest rates. The hypothesis is certainly very old, although it apparently did not receive an academic discussion until Fisher (1896).[21] Other important early

[20]The quality of this linear approximation to $H_p(t, t', T)$ is generally quite good; see Shiller, Campbell and Schoenholtz (1983) and Campbell (1986b).

[21]Fisher (1896) appears to say that the market has perfect foresight (p. 91). I have been unable to find any earlier discussion of the expectations theory of the term structure. Bohm-Bawerk (1891) discussed how expectations of future short rates affect today's long rate, but appears to conclude that the term structure is always flat (p. 280). Perhaps there is a hint of the expectations theory in Clark (1895, p. 395). Malkiel (1966) claims (p. 17) that "one can find anticipations of the expectations theory" in Sidgwick (1887) and Say (1853). In reading any of these works, one is led to conclude that the hint of the expectations theory is very slight.

discussions were in Fisher (1930), Williams (1938), Lutz (1940), and Hicks (1946). The expectations hypothesis probably derives from observing the way people commonly discuss choices between long and short debt as investments. They commonly speak of the outlook for future interest rates in deciding whether to purchase a long-term bond rather than a short-term bond as an investment. If interest rates are expected to decline, people may advise "locking in" the high long-term interest rate by buying a long-term bond. If everyone behaves this way, it is plausible that the market yield on long-term interest rates would be depressed in times when the short rate is expected to decline until the high demand for long-term interest rates is eliminated. Thus, relatively downward-sloping term structures are indicative of expectations of a decline in interest rates, and relatively upward-sloping term structures of a rise.

Early term structure theorists apparently could not think of any formal representation of the expectations hypothesis other than that forward rates equalled actual future spot rates (plus possibly a constant).[22] Early empirical work finding fault with the expectations hypothesis for the inaccuracy of the forecasts [Macaulay (1938), Hickman (1942), and Culbertson (1957)] were later dismissed by subsequent writers who thought that the issue should instead be whether the forward rates are in accord with a model of expectations [Meiselman (1962), Kessel (1965)]. Since the efficient markets revolution in finance in the 1960s, such a model has generally involved the assumption of rational expectations.

4.2. *Risk preferences and the expectations hypothesis*

Suppose economic agents can be characterized by a representative individual whose utility function has the simple form:

$$U = \sum_{t=0}^{\infty} u(C_t)/(1+\mu)^t \,, \tag{11}$$

where C_t is consumption at time t, μ is the subjective rate of time preference, and $u(C_t)$ is momentary utility or "felicity". Calling v_t the real value (value in terms of the consumption good rather than money) of any asset or portfolio of assets including reinvested coupons or dividends, a first-order condition for maximization of expected utility is that

$$u'(C_t)v(t) = \mathrm{E}_t\{(1+\mu)^{t-t'}u'(C_{t'})v(t')\} \,, \quad t < t' < T \,. \tag{12}$$

[22]Conard (1959) wrote: "I assume not only that expectations concerning future rates are held with confidence by all investors, but also that these expectations are realized. Only by adding this last assumption is it possible to build a theory whose predictions can be meaningfully tested empirically" (p. 290).

If there is risk neutrality, then $u(C_t)$ is linear in C_t and $u(C_t) = a + bC_t$. It follows from (12) that

$$\frac{\mathrm{E}_t v(t')}{v(t)} = (1+\mu)^{t'-t}. \tag{13}$$

If the asset is a discount index bond maturing at time T, then $v(t') = p_\mathrm{d}(t', T)$ and the left-hand side of this expression is one plus the expected holding return compounded every $t'-t$ periods, i.e. it is one plus $\mathrm{E}_t(\mathrm{e}^{xh_\mathrm{d}(t,t',T)} - 1)/x$, where x equals $t'-t$. This means that under risk neutrality expected holding period returns as computed in the left-hand side of (13) will be equalized, i.e. will not depend on T. This in turn suggests that a particular formal expectations theory of the term structure follows from risk neutrality. Of course, risk neutrality may not seem a very attractive assumption, but approximate risk neutrality might be invoked to justify the intuitive expectations hypothesis described in the preceding section. Invoking risk neutrality to justify an expectations theory of the term structure was done by Meiselman (1962), Bierwag and Grove (1967), Malkiel (1966), Richard (1978), and others.

There are, however, fundamental problems with the expectations hypothesis as derived from risk neutrality. It is not possible for all expected holding period returns as defined in the left-hand side of (13) to be equalized if future interest rates are uncertain. This point was emphasized by Stiglitz (1970), who also attributed it to C.C. von Weizsacker. If one-period expected holding period returns are equalized for a one-period compounding interval, then $1/p_\mathrm{d}(0,1) = \mathrm{E}_0 p_\mathrm{d}(1,2)/p_\mathrm{d}(0,2)$. If two-period expected holding period returns are equalized for a two-period compounding interval, then $1/p_\mathrm{d}(0,2) = \mathrm{E}_0(1/p_\mathrm{d}(1,2))/p_\mathrm{d}(0,1)$. It follows that $\mathrm{E}_0 p_\mathrm{d}(1,2) = 1/\mathrm{E}_0(1/(p_\mathrm{d}(1,2))$. This is a contradiction, since Jensen's inequality states that for any random variable x that is always greater than zero, unless x is nonstochastic, $\mathrm{E}(x) > 1/\mathrm{E}(1/x))$.

For index bonds, equation (13) implies that interest rates are *not* random, and that therefore Jensen's inequality does not come into play [Cox, Ingersoll and Ross (1981), LeRoy (1982a)]. This can be easily seen by substituting $p_\mathrm{d}(t, t')$ for $v(t)$ in (13). Since t' is the maturity date, and the real value of the index bond at maturity is specified as $v(t') = 1$, it follows that $v(t')$ is not random. Clearly, (13) then implies that $p_\mathrm{d}(t, t')$ is not random either. It will be known with certainty at any date before t. Thus, while risk neutrality gives us an expectations hypothesis, it gives us a perfect foresight version that is extreme and uninteresting. It would be possible to alter the utility function (11) to allow the subjective rate of time preference μ to vary through time, and that would give us a time varying yield curve. Still, we would have a perfect foresight model and a model in which preferences alone determine interest rates.[23]

Risk neutrality is of course not a terribly attractive assumption, given various evidence on human behavior. The theoretical literature does not appear to contain any argument for appealing simple restrictions on preferences or technology that singles out for us an attractive version of the expectations hypothesis; see LeRoy (1982a) for a discussion. Cox, Ingersoll and Ross (1981) offered two sets of assumptions other than risk neutrality that can produce an expectations hypothesis for the term structure: one involving locally certain consumption changes, the other involving state-independent logarithmic utility. But by offering such special cases they are not giving any reason to suspect that the expectations hypothesis should be taken seriously in applied work.

Applied workers, actually, have rarely taken seriously the risk neutrality expectations hypothesis as it has been defined in the theoretical literature, and so the theoretical discussion of this expectations hypothesis may be something of a red herring. The applied literature has defined the expectations hypothesis to represent constancy through time of differences in expected holding returns, or constancy through time of the difference between forward rates and expected spot rates, and not that these constants are zero. We shall see in the next subsection that these theories can be described as assuming constancy of the "term premia". Campbell (1986b) has stressed that some of the important conclusions of this theoretical literature do not carry over to the definitions of the expectations hypothesis in the empirical literature.[24]

4.3. *Definitions of term premia*[25]

There is little agreement in the empirical literature on definitions of term premia, and often term premia are defined only for certain special cases. Here,

[23]Cox, Ingersoll and Ross (1981) emphasize that risk neutrality itself does not necessarily imply that interest rates are nonstochastic. Utility is not concave, and investors could be at a corner solution to their maximization problem in which (13) does not hold. However, they argued that in this case the expectations hypothesis will not generally be valid.

LeRoy (1983) showed [correcting errors in his own papers (1982a, 1982b)] a sense in which when there is "near risk neutrality", that is, when utility functions are nearly linear, the expectations hypothesis is approximately satisfied.

[24]Cox, Ingersoll and Ross (1981) showed that if there are fewer relevant state variables in an economy than there are bond maturities outstanding and if bond prices follow Itô processes, then only one version of the rational expectations hypothesis, what they called the "local expectations hypothesis", can obtain in a rational expectations equilibrium. Campbell showed that this conclusion hinges on the assumption of a zero, not just constant, risk premium. He also showed a sense in which the other versions of the expectations hypothesis (which they claimed to reject as inconsistent with rational expectations equilibrium) may not be importantly different from their local expectations hypothesis.

[25]Much of this subsection follows Campbell and Shiller (1984) and Campbell (1986b).

some definitions will be adopted which are clarifications and generalizations of definitions already commonplace. As suggested in the discussion in the preceding subsection, economic theory does not give us guidance as to how to define term premia, and so choices will be made here to retain essential linearity, which will simplify discussion.

The forward term premium, $\Phi_{f,i}(t, t', T)$, $i = \mathrm{p, d}$, will be defined as the difference between the forward rate and the expectation of the corresponding future spot rate. Unless otherwise noted, this expectation will be defined as a rational expectation, i.e. E_t is the mathematical expectation conditional on information available at time t. Thus we have:

$$\Phi_{f,i}(t, t', T) = f_i(t, t', T) - \mathrm{E}_t r_i(t', T)\,, \quad t < t' < T\,, \quad i = \mathrm{p, d}\,. \tag{14}$$

The holding period term premium, $\Phi_{h,i}(t, t', T)$, for $t < t' < T$, will be defined as the difference between the conditional expected holding period yield and the corresponding spot rate:

$$\Phi_{h,i}(t, t', T) = \mathrm{E}_t h_i(t, t', T) - r_i(t, t')\,, \quad t < t' < T\,, \quad i = \mathrm{p, d}\,. \tag{15}$$

The rollover term premium, $\Phi_{r,i}(t, t', m)$, for $t < t + m < t'$, will be defined as the difference between the yield on a bond maturing at time t' and the conditional expected holding period return from rolling over a sequence of m-period bonds:[26]

$$\Phi_{r,i}(t, t', m) = r_i(t, t') - \mathrm{E}_t h_i(t, t', t + m)\,, \quad t < t + m < t'\,, \quad i = \mathrm{p, d}\,. \tag{16}$$

Although earlier authors did not always clearly intend rational expectations and often used different conventions about compounding, we can loosely identify the above definitions with definitions given by earlier authors. Hicks (1946), who is commonly credited with first defining these in the term structure literature, referred to both $\Phi_f(t, t', T)$ and $\Phi_r(t, t', m)$ as the "risk premium".[27] Because of a subsequent liquidity theory of interest by Lutz (1940), and analogy with the Keynes' (1936) liquidity preference theory, the risk premium has also become known as the "liquidity premium". In this survey, the phrase "term premium" will be used throughout as synonymous with risk premium and liquidity premium; it is preferred to these because the phrase does not

[26]Note that this risk premium has the form interest rate minus expected holding yield, in contrast to expected holding period yield minus interest rate in the preceding expression. This way of defining risk premia seems to be conventional; the rate on the longer asset comes first with a positive sign.

[27]See Hicks (1946, p. 147).

have an association with a specific theory of the term structure. The holding period term premium $\Phi_{h,i}(t, t', T)$ is referred to as the expected "excess return" in finance textbooks.

From the definitions in Table 13.1, there are simple proportional relations between holding period term premia and forward rate term premia:

$$\Phi_{h,i}(t, t', T) = \{D_i(T-t)/D_i(t'-t) - 1\}\Phi_{f,i}(t, t', T)\,, \quad t < t' < T\,. \tag{17}$$

We also have the following relations for the rollover term premium, where $t < t + m < t'$, $t' - t = sm$, s integer:

$$\Phi_{r,i}(t, t', m) = (1/D_i(t'-t)) \sum_{k=0}^{s-1} [D_i(km+m) - D_i(km)]\Phi_{f,i}(t, t+km, t+km+m)\,, \tag{18}$$

$$\Phi_{r,i}(t, t', m) = (1/D_i(t'-t)) \sum_{k=0}^{s-1} [D_i(km+m) - D_i(km)]\mathrm{E}_t\Phi_{h,i}(t+km, t+km+m, t+sm)\,, \tag{19}$$

4.4. Early presumptions pertaining to the sign of the term premium

Hicks (1946) thought that there was a tendency for term premia to be positive. In this context he referred to the forward rate term premium, $\Phi_{f,i}(t, t', T)$, but if this term premium is always positive, then by (17) above so must the holding period term premium $\Phi_{h,i}(t, t', T)$ and, by (18), the rollover term premium $\Phi_{r,i}(t, t', m)$.

Hicks' reasons to expect that term premia should be positive had their motivation in the theory of "normal backwardation" in commodity forward markets of Keynes (1930). Hicks wrote:[28]

> . . . the forward market for loans (like the forward market for commodities) may be expected to have a constitutional weakness on one side, a weakness which offers an opportunity for speculation. If no extra return is offered for long lending, most people (and institutions) would prefer to lend short, at least in the sense that they would prefer to hold their money on deposit in some way or other. But this situation would leave a large excess demand to borrow long which would not be met. Borrowers would thus tend to offer better terms in order to persuade lenders to switch over into the long market.

[28] Hicks (1946, p. 146).

He offered no evidence (other than that on average risk premia themselves) that would support such a "constitutional weakness" on one side of the forward market.

Lutz (1940) offered a "liquidity theory of interest" that also predicted positive term premia:

> ... The most liquid asset, money, does not bear interest. Securities, being less liquid than money, bear an interest rate which is higher the longer the maturity, since the danger of capital loss due to a change in the interest rate in the market is supposed to be the greater (and therefore liquidity the smaller) the longer the security has to run.[29]

His theory appears to ascribe term premia to own-variance, contrary to received wisdom in finance theory today.

Such theories were disputed by Modigliani and Sutch (1966) by merely pointing out that it is not clearly rational for individuals to prefer to lend short or to be concerned with short-term capital losses. If one is saving for a child's college education 10 years ahead, it is least risky to put one's savings in the form of a (real) 10-year bond rather than roll over short bonds. They proposed as an alternative to Hicks' theory the "preferred habitat theory". A trader's habitat is the investment horizon he or she is most concerned about, and that person will prefer to borrow or lend at that term. There is a separate supply and demand for loanable funds in each habitat, which could give rise to any pattern of term premia. Traders may be "tempted out of their natural habitat by the lure of higher expected returns"[30] but because of risk aversion this will not completely level term premia. The idea that individuals have a single habitat must be described as heuristic.[31] The intertemporal capital asset pricing model typically assumes maximization of an intertemporal utility function that involves the entire future consumption stream, with exponentially declining weights, and thus no single "habitat". However, the Modigliani–Sutch conclusion that term premia might as well, on theoretical grounds, be positive as negative seems now to be generally accepted.[32]

[29]Lutz (1940, p. 62).

[30]Modigliani and Sutch (1966, p. 184).

[31]Cox, Ingersoll and Ross (1981) consider an economy in which all investors desire to consume at one fixed date. They find that the risk premium, defined as the expected instantaneous return minus the instantaneous interest rate, may not be lowest for bonds maturing at this date. Still, they argue that a preferred habitat theory holds if the habitat is defined in terms of a "stronger or weaker tendency to hedge against changes in the interest rate" (p. 786).

[32]LeRoy (1982b) has argued that the risk premia are likely to be positive on theoretical grounds in a model without production, but had no results on the sign of the risk premium when production is introduced.

4.5. Risk preferences and term premia

If the representative agent maximizes the utility function (11), and therefore satisfies the first-order condition (12), then it follows that:[33]

$$e^{-(\tau_2-\tau_1)r_d(\tau_1,\tau_2)} = E_{\tau_1} S(\tau_1, \tau_2)\,, \tag{20}$$

where $S(\tau_1, \tau_2)$ is the marginal rate of substitution between time τ_1 and τ_2.[34] For equation (20), the precise definition of $S(\tau_1, \tau_2)$ will depend on whether we are dealing with index bonds or bonds whose principal is defined in nominal terms, that is, on whether $r_d(\tau_1, \tau_2)$ is a real or nominal rate. With index bonds, $S(\tau_1, \tau_2)$ is defined as $u'(C(\tau_2))/(u'(C(\tau_1))(1+\mu)^{(\tau_2-\tau_1)})$. With bonds whose principal is defined in nominal terms, $S(\tau_1, \tau_2)$ is defined as $u'(C(\tau_2))/u'(C(\tau_1)) \times (\pi(\tau_1)/\pi(\tau_2))/(1+\mu)^{(\tau_2-\tau_1)}$. Here $\pi(\tau)$ is a commodity price index at time τ, that is, the price of the consumption good in terms of the unit of currency. Thus, $S(\tau_1, \tau_2)$ is the marginal rate of substitution between consumption at time τ_1 and consumption at time τ_2 if the bond is an index bond, and between a nominal dollar at time τ_1 and a nominal dollar at time τ_2 if the bond is a conventional nominal bond.[35]

It follows from equation (20) for $t < t' < T$ [setting (τ_1, τ_2) in (20) as (t, t'), (t, T) and (t', T)] that:

$$\begin{aligned} e^{-(T-t)r_d(t,T)} &= e^{-(t'-t)r_d(t,t')} E_t\, e^{-(T-t')r_d(t',T)} \\ &\quad + \mathrm{cov}_t(S(t, t'), S(t', T))\,. \end{aligned} \tag{21}$$

In order to put this in terms of the above definitions of term premia, we use the linearization $e^x \approx (1 + x)$ for small x to derive from the above:

$$\Phi_{f,d}(t, t', T) \approx -\mathrm{cov}_t(S(t, t'), S(t', T))/(T - t')\,. \tag{22}$$

The term premium $\Phi_{f,d}(t, t', T)$ depends on the covariance between the marginal rate of substitution between t and t' and the marginal rate of substitution between t' and T.[36] If this covariance is negative, then forward

[33]To show this, use $v(t') = v(\tau_2) = 1$ and $v(t) = v(\tau_1) = p_d(\tau_1, \tau_2) = \exp(-(\tau_2 - \tau_1)\; r_d(\tau_1, \tau_2))$ in (12) where $\tau_1 < \tau_2$ so that $r_d(\tau_1, \tau_2)$ as well as $v(\tau_1)$ is known at time τ_1.

[34]It follows that increasing the uncertainty at time τ_1 about consumption at τ_2 will, if there is diminishing marginal utility, lower $r_d(r_1, \tau_2)$. This point was made by Fisher (1907, p. 214).

[35]Benninga and Protopapadakis (1983) describe the relation of risk premia on nominal bonds to risk premia on index bonds.

[36]LeRoy (1984) gives an expression for the term premium defined as the expected real j-period return on an i-period nominal bond minus the return to maturity of a j-period real bond.

rates tend to be above expected spot rates, as Hicks originally hypothesized, and the risk premium is positive.[37] In the case of index bonds, a negative covariance means that if real consumption should increase faster than usual between t and t', it tends to increase less fast than usual between t' and T. In the case of nominal bonds, the interpretation of the sign of the term premium is less straightforward. But consider the utility function $u(C_t) = \log(C_t)$. Then for nominal bonds $S(t, t')$ equals nominal consumption at time t divided by nominal consumption at time $t+1$. Then, the nominal term premium $\Phi_{f,d}(t, t', T)$ would tend to be positive if it happens that when nominal consumption increases faster than usual between t and t' it tends to increase less fast than usual between t' and T.

One can also derive [taking unconditional expectations of (20)] an expression like (21) for unconditional expectations:

$$\mathrm{E}\,\mathrm{e}^{-(T-t)r_d(t,T)} = \mathrm{E}\,\mathrm{e}^{-(t'-t)r_d(t,t')}\mathrm{E}\,\mathrm{e}^{-(T-t')r_d(t',T)} + \mathrm{cov}(S(t, t'), S(t', T))\,. \tag{23}$$

From which, by a linearization, we have:

$$\mathrm{E}(\Phi_{f,d}(t, t', T)) \approx -\mathrm{cov}(S(t, t'), S(t', T))/(T - t')\,. \tag{24}$$

Thus, the mean term premium $\Phi_{f,d}(t, t', T)$ is positive if the unconditional covariance between $S(t, t')$ and $S(t', T)$ is negative. Such a negative covariance might be interpreted as saying that marginal utility is "unsmooth" between $\tau = t$ and $\tau = T$. This means that when detrended marginal utility increases between $\tau = t$ and $\tau = t'$ it tends to decrease between t' and T. A positive covariance, and hence a negative term premium, would tend to occur if marginal utility is "smooth" between $\tau = t$ and $\tau = T$.

If the values of bonds of all maturities are assumed to be deterministic functions of a small number of state variables that are continuous diffusion processes, then theoretical restrictions on risk premia beyond those defined here can also be derived [e.g. Brennan and Schwartz (1980), Cox, Ingersoll and Ross (1981), Dothan (1978), Langetieg (1980), Marsh (1980), Richard (1978) and Vasicek (1978)]. When bond values are such deterministic functions of diffusion processes, if the restrictions did not hold there would be riskless

[37] Woodward (1983) discusses term premia in terms of the serial correlation of marginal utility of consumption rather than the serial correlation of marginal rates of substitution. Her principal result is that in a case where the correlation conditional on information at t between $u'(c_{t'})$ and $u'(c_T)$ is negative, then the sign of the term premium may be sensitive to the definition of the premium. She defines as an alternative definition of the term premium, the "solidity premium", based on forward and actual discounts. The negative correlation she defines is an unlikely special case. Actual aggregate consumption in the United States roughly resembles a random walk [Hall (1978)] for which the correlation she defines is positive.

arbitrage opportunities. The assumption of such a state variable representation has been convenient for theoretical models. It has even led to a complete general equilibrium model of the term structure in a macro economy [Cox, Ingersoll and Ross (1985a, 1985b)], a model subjected to empirical testing by Brown and Dybvig (1986).

5. Empirical studies of the term structure

5.1. Empirical expectations hypotheses for the term structure

One need not assume rational expectations to proceed with studying an expectations theory of the term structure if one has data on expectations or can infer expectations from other data. The first study of the term structure using an expectations model was performed by Meiselman (1962). Meiselman proposed the "error learning hypothesis" that economic agents revise their expectations in proportion to the error just discovered in their last period expectation for today's one-period rate. This hypothesis then implies that $f_i(t, t+n, t+n+1) - f_i(t-1, t+n, t+n+1) = a_n + b_n(r_i(t, t+1) - f_i(t-1, t, t+1))$. He estimated a_n and b_n by regression analysis using U.S. Durand's annual data 1901–54 for $n = 1, 2, \ldots, 8$. He took as encouraging for the model that the signs of the estimated b_n were all positive and declined with n. However, Buse (1967) criticized his conclusion, saying that "...such results are implied by any set of smoothed yield curves in which the short-term interest rates have shown a greater variability than long-term interest rates".

It was pointed out later by Diller (1969) and Nelson (1970a) that the error learning principle is a property of optimal linear forecasts. They found that the coefficients b_n that Meiselman estimated compared rather favorably with the coefficients implied by an estimated linear forecasting equation. However, the univariate form of the error learning principle proposed by Meiselman applies only to univariate optimal linear forecasts [Shiller (1978)], and thus the Meiselman theory is unfortunately restrictive.

Other authors have used survey expectations data for market expectations of future interest rates. Survey methods seem particularly attractive since surveys can be focused on the institutional investors who hold most government and corporate bonds, and who are probably not well described in terms of the expected utility of consumption models described in the preceding section.[38]

Friedman (1979) used data 1969–78 from a quarterly survey of financial market participants by the *Goldsmith–Nagan Bond and Money Market Letter*.

[38]See Board of Governors (1985, pp. 20 and 54). Of course, individuals ultimately have claims on the assets of these institutions; still there is an institutional layer between them and the bonds held on their behalf.

He found that the term premium on U.S. Treasury bills, $\Phi_d(t, t+1, t+2)$ and $\Phi_d(t, t+2, t+3)$ (where time is measured in months), was positive on average and depended positively on the level of interest rates. He showed [Friedman (1980c)] that his model differed substantially from a rational expectations model, in that the survey expectations could be improved upon easily. Kane and Malkiel (1967) conducted their own survey of banks, life insurance companies and nonfinancial corporations to learn about the relation of expectations to the term structure of interest rates. They learned that many investors seemed not to formulate specific interest rate expectations (especially for the distant future) and those that did, did not have uniform expectations. Kane (1983) found using additional Kane–Malkiel survey data 1969–72 that term premia appear positively related to the level of interest rates.

5.2. *The rational expectations hypothesis in empirical work*

Although the rational expectations hypothesis regarding the term structure has had many forms, it has its simplest form used in empirical work in terms of the continuously compounded yields discussed here. Often, the other forms of the hypothesis do not differ importantly from that discussed here [see Shiller, Campbell and Schoenholtz (1983) and Campbell (1986b)]. In the definition to be used here, the rational expectations hypothesis is that all term premia, $\Phi_{h,i}(t, t+n, t+m+n)$, $0<m$, $0<n$, $\Phi_{f,i}(t, t+n, t+m+n)$, $0<m$, $0<n$, and $\Phi_{r,i}(t, t+n, m)$, $0<m<n$, do not depend on time t.[39] This means that all term premia depend only on maturity and not time, and the changing slope of the term structure can only be interpreted in terms of the changing expectations for future interest rates.[40]

The literature testing forms of the rational expectations hypothesis like that defined here is enormous.[41] It is difficult to summarize what we know about the expectations hypothesis from this literature. We are studying a two-dimensional array of term premia; term premia depend on m (the maturity of the

[39]When dealing with par bonds, the expectations model defined here relates to the linearized model. The assumption here is that the point of linearization R does not depend on the level of interest rates, otherwise the model will not be linear in interest rates.

[40]Note that in this expectations hypothesis, stated in terms of continuously compounded yields, it is possible for all risk premia to be zero. We do not encounter the Jensen's inequality problem alluded to above in connection with risk neutrality. The problem alluded to by von Weizsaecker and Stiglitz was essentially one of compounding, and is eliminated when we couch the model in terms of continuously compounded interest rates.

[41]The literature has to do almost entirely with nominal interest rates, as a term structure of index bonds is observed only for brief periods in certain countries. Campbell and Shiller (1988) in effect looked at the real term structure in the postwar U.S. corporate stock price data by correcting the dividend price ratio for predictable changes in real dividends, leaving a long-term real consol component of the dividend price ratio. The expectations hypothesis was not supported by the evidence.

forward instrument) and n (the time into the future that the forward instrument begins). Term premia may be approximately constant for some m and n and not for others; certain functions of term premia may be approximately constant and not others. Term premia may be approximately constant for some time periods and not others, or in some countries and not others.

Testing for the constancy of term premia ultimately means trying to predict the right-hand side of the equations defining term premia [equations (14), (15) or (16) above] from which the conditional expectations operator E_t is deleted, in terms of information at time t. This means predicting either excess holding period returns or the difference between forward rates and corresponding spot rates in terms of information at time t. Because of the relations between the definitions of term premia [equations (17), (18), or (19) above] it does not matter whether the regression has excess holding yields or the difference between forward rates and corresponding spot rates as the variable explained; the difference has to do only with a multiplicative constant for the dependent variable. Of course, most studies do not use the exact definitions of term premia defined here, in terms of continuously compounded rates or, in the case of par bonds, linearized holding yields, but the differences in definition are generally not important.

Some studies may report some tests of the rational expectations hypothesis that have the appearance of something very different; for example, Roll (1970) tested (and rejected using 1–13 week U.S. Treasury bill data 1949–64) the martingale property of forward rates by testing whether changes in forward rates $f_d(t, t', T) - f_d(t-1, t', T)$ are serially correlated through time t. But in fact testing the hypothesis that there is no such serial correlation is no different from testing the hypothesis that *changes* in the difference between forward rates and corresponding spot rates cannot be predicted based on information consisting of past changes in forward rates. For another example, some researchers have noted that for large m and small n the holding return $h_t(t, t+n, t+m)$ is approximately equal to $r_i(t, t+m) - r_i(t+n, t+n+m)$, the change in the long rate, divided by $D_i(n)$. If n is very small, $1/D_t(n)$ is a very large number, and the excess holding return is heavily influenced by the change in the long rate. The rational expectations hypothesis thus suggests that $r_t(t, t+m) - r_i(t+n, t+n+m)$ is approximately unforecastable, and hence that long rates are in this sense approximately random walks. The random walk property for long-term interest rates was tested by Phillips and Pippenger (1976, 1979), Pesando (1981, 1983), and Mishkin (1978).[42]

[42]The random walk property is an approximation useful only under certain assumptions [see Mishkin (1980) and Begg (1984)]. Phillips and Pippenger (1976, 1979) used the random walk approximation to assert that the Modigliani and Sutch (1966) and Modigliani and Shiller (1973) distributed lag regressions explaining the long rate must be spurious. Looking at the out-of-sample fit of the equation does not suggest that term-structure equations like that in Modigliani–Shiller are completely spurious: see Ando and Kennickell (1983).

Of all the studies of the rational expectations hypothesis for the term structure, of greatest interest are the results in which the explanatory variable is approximately (or approximately proportional to) the spread between a forward rate $f_i(t, m, n)$ and the spot rate of the same maturity as the forward rate, $r_i(t, t+m)$. This spread forecasts the change in $r_i(t, t+m)$ over the next n periods. Regressions in the literature that can be interpreted at least approximately as regressions of the actual change in spot rates $r_i(t+n, t+m+n) - r_i(t, t+m)$ on the predicted change $f_i(t, m, n) - r_i(t, t+m)$ and a constant are shown in Table 13.2.

What is clear from Table 13.2 is that the slope coefficient is quite far below one – and often negative – for low forecast horizon n, regardless of the maturi-

Table 13.2
Regressions of changes in m-period interest rates on changes predicted by the term structure: $r_i(t+n, t+m+n) - r_i(t, t+m)$ on $f_i(t, t+n, t+m+n) - r_i(t, t+m)$ and constant

Study	Country	Sample	m (years)	n (years)	Slope coef.	Std. error	R^2
Shiller	U.S.	1966–77	>20.0	0.25	−5.56	1.67	0.201
(1979)[a]	U.S.	1919–58	>20.0	1.00	−0.44	0.75	0.01
	U.K.	1956–77	∞	0.25	−5.88	2.09	0.09
Shiller,	U.S.	1959–74	0.25	0.25	0.27	0.18	0.03
Campbell and Schoenholtz (1983)[b]	U.S.	1959–73	30.0	0.50	−1.46	(1.79)	0.02
Mankiw	Canada	1961–84	0.25	0.25	0.10	(0.07)	0.02
(1986)[c]	W. Germany	1961–84	0.25	0.25	0.14	(0.07)	0.03
Fama	U.S.	1959–82	1/12	1/12	0.46	(0.07)	0.13
(1984a)[d]			1/12	2/12	0.25	(0.10)	0.02
			1/12	3/12	0.26	(0.12)	0.02
			1/12	4/12	0.17	(0.10)	0.01
			1/12	5/12	0.11	(0.10)	0.00
Fama and Bliss	U.S.	1964–84	1.00	1.00	0.09	(0.28)	0.00
(1987)[e]			1.00	2.00	0.69	(0.26)	0.08
			1.00	3.00	1.30	(0.10)	0.24
			1.00	4.00	1.61	(0.34)	0.48
Shiller (1986)[f]	U.S.	1953–86	0.25	rollover*	0.61	(0.17)	0.090

Note: Expectations theory of the term structure asserts that the slope coefficient should be 1.00. Not all regressions summarized here were in exactly the form shown here; in some cases a linearization was assumed to transform results to the form shown here. Significance level refers to a test of hypothesis that the coefficient is 1.00.

*Dependent variable is approximately $S^*(m, n)$ and the independent variable is $S(m, n)$ as defined in expression (26) in text.

[a]Page 1210, table 3, rows 1, 4 and 5. Column 2 coefficient was converted using duration implicit in γ_n given in Table 13.1 rows 1, 4 and 5 column 1.

[b]Page 192, table 3, rows 4 and 10, columns 5 and 6.

[c]Page 81, table 9, rows 2 and 4, columns 3 and 4.

[d]Page 517, table 4, rows 6–10, columns 1–2.

[e]Page 686, table 3, rows 1–4, columns 3–4.

[f]Page 103.

ty m of the forward interest rate, but rises closer to one for higher n. This result may at first seem counterintuitive. One might have thought that forecasts into the near future would be more accurate than forecasts into the more distant future; the reverse seems to be true.

When both n and m are small, both less than a year or so, the slope coefficients are positive (the right sign) but substantially lower than one. Thus, for example, when two-month interest rates exceed one-month rates by more than the average term premium, $\Phi_{r,i}(t, 2, 1)$, the one-month rate does tend to increase as predicted, but by substantially less than the predicted amount.[43]

The results in Table 13.2 look especially bad for the rational expectations hypothesis when the forecast horizon n is small (a year or less in the table) and the maturity of the forward rate m is large (20 or more years in the table). Here, the spread between the forward rate and spot rate predicts the wrong direction of change of interest rates. One might consider it the "essence" of the rational expectations hypothesis that an unusually high spread between the forward rate and current spot rate portends increases in interest rates, not the decreases as observed.

It is helpful in interpreting this result to consider a caricature, the case of a perpetuity (for which $m = \infty$) paying coupon c once per period, and where, for simplicity, the term premium is zero. Then the price of the perpetuity $p_p(t, \infty)$ equals coupon over yield $c/r_p(t, \infty, 1)$, and the spread between the one-period-ahead forward consol yield and the one-period spot rate is proportional to the spread between the consol yield and the one-period rate. When the consol yield is above the one-period interest rate, $r(t, t+1, 1)$, then its current yield $c/p_p(t, \infty)$ is greater than the one-period rate $r(t, t+1, 1)$. This would suggest that consols are then a better investment for the short run than is short debt. Since the rational expectations hypothesis with zero term premium would deny this, it follows that the consol yield $r_p(t, \infty, 1)$ should be expected to increase over the next period, producing a decline in price, a capital loss that offsets the high current yield. But, in fact when the consol yield is high relative to the short rate the consol yields tends to fall subsequently and not rise.[44] The capital gain tends to augment rather than offset the high current yield. The naive rule that long bonds are a better investment (in an expected value sense) whenever long rates are above short rates is thus confirmed.

[43]Regressions for large n and small m are not in Table 13.2. Since such forward rates are very sensitive to rounding error or small noise in the long-term interest rates, we cannot accurately measure such forward rates.

Some more favorable results for the expectations theory with small n were reported in Shiller (1981a); however, these results were later found to be related to a couple of anomalous observations [Shiller, Campbell and Schoenholtz (1983)].

[44]That long rates tend to move opposite the direction indicated by the expectations theory was first noted by Macaulay (1938, p. 33): "the yields of bonds of the highest grade should *fall* during a period when short rates are higher than the yields of bonds and *rise* during a period in which short rates are the lower. Now experience is more nearly the opposite."

Froot (1987) attempted a decomposition of the departure from 1.00 of the coefficient in Table 13.2 here into two parts: a part due to expectation error and a part due to time-varying term premium. He used survey data published in the investor newsletter *Reporting on Governments* (continuing the Goldsmith–Nagan data series) to represent expectations. He found that for three-month-ahead forecasts of three-month rates, the departure from 1.00 is due primarily to time-varying term premium. But for forecasts of changes in 30-year mortgage rates, the expectations error bears most of the blame for the departure of the coefficient from 1.00.[45]

5.3. *The volatility of long-term interest rates*

According to the rational expectations theory of the term structure, n-period interest rates are a weighted moving average of one-period interest rates plus a constant term premium; that is, from (16) and Table 13.1:[46]

$$r_i(t, t+m) = D_i(m)^{-1} \sum_{k=0}^{m-1} (D_i(k+1) - D_i(k)) \times \mathrm{E}_t r_i(t+k, t+k+1) + \Phi_m\,, \quad i = \mathrm{p}, \mathrm{d}\,, \tag{25}$$

where $\Phi_m = \Phi_{r,i}(t, t+m, 1)$ is constant through time. Since long moving averages tend to smooth the series averaged, one might expect to see that long rates are a very smooth series. Are long-term rates too "choppy" through time to accord with the expectations theory? It is natural to inquire whether this is so and, if so, whenever it is possibly related to the poor results for the expectations hypothesis that were obtained in the Table 13.2 regressions.

Because of the choppiness of long-term interest rates, short-term holding returns on long-term bonds, which are related to the short-term change in long-term interest rates, are quite variable. Culbertson (1957), in his well-known critique of expectations models of interest rates, thought the volatility of holding yields was evidence against the model. He showed a time-series plot of holding yields on long bonds and, noting their great variability, remarked "what sort of expectations, one might ask, could possibly have produced this result?".[47]

It is possible, using the expectations hypothesis, to put limits on the variability of both long-term interest rates themselves and on short-term

[45] See Froot (1987, table 3). Note that his regressions are run in a slightly different form than in Table 13.2 here, but that our Table 13.2 coefficients can be inferrred from his.

[46] For par bonds, it is necessary to evaluate $D_\mathrm{p}(k)$ with (5) using a fixed point of linearization r, so that (25) will be linear in interest rates.

[47] Culbertson (1957, p. 508).

holding returns on long-term debt. The expectations hypothesis implies that $r_t(t, t+m) = \mathrm{E}_t r_i^*(t, t+m) + \Phi_m$, where $r_i^*(t, t+m)$ is the "perfect foresight" or "ex post rational" long-term interest rate defined as:

$$r_i^*(t, t+m) = D_i(m)^{-1} \sum_{k=0}^{m-1} (D_i(k+1) - D_i(k)) \times \mathrm{E}_t r_i(t+k, t+k+1)\,, \quad i = \mathrm{p}, \mathrm{d}\,. \tag{26}$$

It follows that $r_i^*(t, t+m) = r_i(t, t+m) + \Phi_m + u_{mt}$, where u_{mt} is a forecast error made at time t and observed at time $t+m$. Since u_{mt} is a forecast error, if forecasts are rational, u_{mt} cannot be correlated with anything known at time t; otherwise the forecast could be improved. Hence, u_{mt} must be uncorrelated with $r_t(t, t+m)$. Since the variance of the sum of two independent variables is the sum of their variances it follows that $\mathrm{var}(r_i^*(t, t+m)) = \mathrm{var}(r_i(t, t+m)) + \mathrm{var}(u_{mt})$, and since $\mathrm{var}(u_{mt})$ cannot be negative, the rational expectations model implies [Shiller (1979)]:[48]

$$\mathrm{var}(r_i(t, t+m)) \le \mathrm{var}(r_i^*(t, t+m))\,, \quad i = \mathrm{p}, \mathrm{d}\,, \tag{27}$$

so there is an upper bound to the variance of m-period rates given by the variance of $r_i^*(t, t+m)$. One can also put an upper bound to the variance of the holding period return in terms of the one-period rate [Shiller (1981a)]:

$$\mathrm{var}(h_i(t, t+1, t+m)) \le (D(m)/D(1))\,\mathrm{var}(r_i(t, t+1))\,, \quad i = \mathrm{p}, \mathrm{d}\,, \tag{28}$$

where in the case $i = \mathrm{p}$ of par bonds, $D(m)$ and $D(1)$ are computed from equation (5) above with interest rate $2r$, where r is the point of linearization.

Both of the above inequalities were found to be violated using U.S. data and m of 2 or more years [Shiller (1979, 1981a, 1986) and Singleton (1980b)]. Their rejection could have either of two interpretations: the rational expectations hypothesis could be wrong, in such a way as to make long rates much more volatile than they should be, or the measures of the upper bound in the inequalities could be faulty: the measures of $\mathrm{var}(r_i^*(t, t+m))$ or $\mathrm{var}(r_i(t, t+1))$ could understate the true variance.

The latter view of the violation of the inequalities was argued by Flavin (1983) who showed with Monte Carlo experiments that if the one-period interest rate $r_i(t, t+1)$ is a first-order autoregressive process with the autoregressive parameter close to one (see the next subsection), the inequalities are likely to be violated in small samples even if the rational expectations model is true. Such a process shows a great deal of persistence, and $r_i(t, t+1)$ may thus

[48] LeRoy and Porter (1981) also noted this inequality in a different context.

stay on one side of the true mean throughout the sample. Thus, the sample variance around the sample mean of $r_i(t, t+1)$ or of $r_i^*(t, t+m)$ may be a strikingly downward biased measure of their true variance.

Flavin's is apparently a variable interpretation of the excess volatility results. The volatility tests do not allow us to tell whether there is too much variability in long rates or just nonstationarity in short rates. They *do* allow us to reject the idea that movements in long rates can be interpreted in terms of rational expectations of movements in short rates within the range historically observed.

5.4. Encouraging results for the rational expectations hypothesis

It does not follow from the Table 13.2 results with small n that the spread between very long-term interest rates and short-term interest rates is totally wrong from the standpoint of the expectations hypothesis. One way of summarizing the relatively good results [Shiller (1986)] for this spread for larger n is to compute both actual and perfect foresight spreads between very long-term interest rates and short-term interest rates. Defining the spread $S_{ti}(m) = r_i(t, t+m) - r_i(t, t+1)$ (m integer>1), then the rational expectations hypothesis implies:

$$S_{ti}(m) = \mathrm{E}_t S_{ti}^*(m) + \Phi_m, \quad i = \mathrm{p, d}, \tag{29}$$

$$S_{ti}^*(m) = r_i^*(t, t+m) - r_i(t, t+1). \tag{30}$$

From the definition (26) of $r_i^*(t, t+m)$, it can be shown that $S_{ti}^*(m)$ is the duration weighted average of expected changes in the n-period rate. Equation (29) thus asserts that when long rates are high relative to short rates the weighted average of increases in short rates should tend to be high. The values of $S_{td}(m)$ and $S_{td}^*(m)$ are plotted for $m = 10$ in Figure 13.4 for those years for which data are available in Appendix B. The correspondence between $S_{td}^*(m)$ and $S_{td}(m)$ is apparent. This might be viewed as a striking confirmation of some element of truth in the expectations hypothesis. Moreover, a variance inequality analogous to (28) above is that $\mathrm{var}(S_{ti}(m)) \leq \mathrm{var}(S_{ti}^*(m))$. This variance inequality is satisfied by the data. This result does not by itself establish whether or not Flavin's view of the variance inequality violation described in the preceding section is correct.[49]

[49]Indeed, even if $S_{ti}(m)$ and $S_{ti}^*(m)$ look good by this criterion, there could be some small noise contaminating $S_{ti}(m)$ which, if the noise is not highly serially uncorrelated, could cause holding period yields to be much more volatile than would be implied by the expectations model. Moreover, the appearance of $S_{ti}(m)$ and $S_{ti}^*(m)$ may also be relatively little affected by a gross overstatement of the variability of $r_i(t, t+m)$, so long as it is substantially less variable than the short rate [see Shiller (1986)].

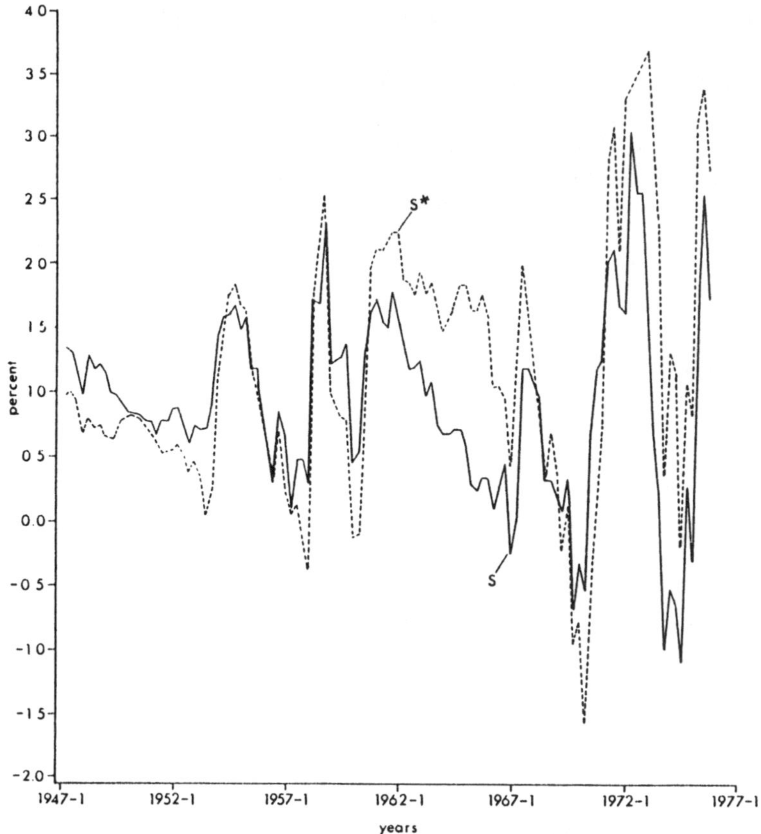

Figure 13.4. The long-short spread $S_{td}(n) = r_d(t, t+n) - r_d(t, t+1)$, solid line, and the perfect-foresight spread $S^*_{td}(n) = r^*_d(t, t+n) - r_d(t, t+1)$, dashed line, where $r^*_d(t, t+n)$ is the perfect foresight n-period rate defined by expression (26), $n = 40$ quarters. Thus, $r^*_d(t, t+n) = (\Sigma\ (\tau = t, t+39) r(\tau, \tau+1))/40$. Data plotted are quarterly series for the end of the first month of each quarter using McCulloch's three-month and ten-year discount bond yield series, Table 13.A.1, Appendix B. $S_{td}(n)$ is plotted for 1947 first quarter to 1975 third quarter at annual rates.

One must consider, though, whether this apparent confirmation of the expectations theory for large m could also be described in a less inspiring way: as reflecting largely just that the long rate is much smoother than the short rate. In fact, the correspondence in postwar U.S. data between $S^*_{td}(10, 1)$ and $S_{td}(10, 1)$ would still be apparent if the long rate $r(t, t+10)$ had been a simple trend through the path of short rates. Short-term interest rates have shown an apparent tendency to revert to trend; thus, a duration weighted average of future changes in the short rate is approximately minus the detrended short rate.

It was shown by Modigliani and Shiller (1973) and Shiller (1972) [following

Sutch (1968)] that a regression of a long rate on a distributed lag of short rates produces distributed lag coefficients that crudely resembled the "optimal" distributed lag coefficients implied by an autoregression in first differences for the short rate. Similarly, a regression of the long rate on a distributed lag of short rates and a distributed lag of inflation rates is consistent with a vector autoregression in first differences using the short rate and the inflation rate.[50] The basic principle of these analyses can be illustrated by assuming for simplicity here (as in Flavin) that the short rate $r_p(t, t+1)$ follows a first-order autoregressive (AR-1) process around a mean μ: $r_p(t+1, t+2) - \mu = \lambda(r_p(t, t+1) - \mu) + \varepsilon_t$, $0 < \lambda < 1$, where ε_t is a realization of a random variable with zero mean independent of ε_{t-k}, $k \neq 0$. The optimal forecast at time t of $r_p(t+k, t+k+1)$ is:

$$\mathrm{E}_t r_p(t+k, t+k+1) = \mu + \lambda^k(r_p(t, t+1) - \mu)\,. \tag{31}$$

From (25) and (5) for $m = \infty$ and $i = \mathrm{p}$ the consol yield is given by:

$$r_p(t, t+\infty) = (1-\gamma) \sum_{k=0}^{\infty} \gamma^k \mathrm{E}_t r_p(t+k, t+k+1) + \Phi\,, \tag{32}$$

where $\gamma = \mathrm{e}^{-r}$ and r is the point of linearization. Thus, the consol yield is a sort of present value of expected future one period rates. Together, (31) and (32) imply:

$$r_p(t, t+\infty) = \frac{(1-\gamma)}{(1-\gamma\lambda)}\, r_p(t, t+1) + \Phi\,. \tag{33}$$

One can therefore evaluate the rational expectations model by first regressing $r_p(t+1, t+2)$ on $r_p(t, t+1)$ and a constant [i.e. estimating λ in (31)], and computing the theoretical coefficient of $r(t)$ using (33). This theoretical coefficient can be compared with the slope coefficient in a regression of $r_p(t, t+\infty)$ onto $r_p(t, t+1)$ and a constant. Now, in fact, our assumption that $r_p(t, t+1)$ was forecast by the market according to (31) would imply that (33) should hold without error. However, it can be shown that whether or not $r_p(t, t+1)$ is an AR-1 process if $\mathrm{E}_t r_p(t+k, t+k+1)$ is the optimal forecast of $r_p(t+k, t+k+1)$ conditional on an information set that includes $r_p(t, t+1)$, then a theoretical regression of $r_p(t, t+\infty)$ on $r_p(t, t+1)$ and a constant should produce the coefficient $(1-\gamma)/(1-\gamma\lambda)$, where λ is the slope coefficient in a theoretical regression of $r_p(t+1, t+2)$ on $r_p(t, t+1)$, [Shiller (1972)]. With

[50]Distributed lag regressions explaining the term structure have had different functional forms: see, for example, Bierwag and Grove (1967), Cargill and Meyer (1972) or Malkiel (1966). A comparison of eight different distributed lag models of the term structure is in Dobson, Sutch and Vanderford (1976).

this assumption there is an error term in (33) reflecting information held by market participants beyond $r(t, t+1)$. Comparing such estimated coefficients using more complicated autoregressive models was the method used in the aforementioned papers.

Note that if γ and λ are both near one, then $(1-\gamma)/(1-\gamma\lambda)$ may be very sensitive to λ. When data are limited, we cannot tell with much accuracy what λ is, and hence cannot pin down what the value of $(1-\gamma)/(1-\gamma\lambda)$ is. Thus, we cannot say with much assurance whether the consol yield in fact is or is not too volatile.

Such simple comparisons of estimated coefficients are not formal tests of the rational expectations model. Rather, they are indications of the "fit" of the model. If we are given data on a consol yield $r_p(t, \infty)$ and the one-period rate $r_p(t, 1)$, then a likelihood ratio test of all restrictions of the model [except for a restriction implied by the stationarity of $r_p(t, \infty)$] amounts to nothing more than a regression of the excess return $h_p(t, t+1, \infty) - r_p(t, t+1) = (r_p(t, \infty) - \gamma r_p(t+1, \infty))/(1-\gamma) - r_p(t, t+1)$ on information at time t. [Shiller (1981a), Campbell and Shiller (1987)].

Note that such tests may not have much power to determine whether long rates are too volatile to accord with market efficiency. Suppose, for example, that the short rate $r_p(t, t+1)$ is a first-order autoregressive process as above, and suppose that the long rate overreacts to the short rate, $r_p(t, \infty) = (\mu + \Phi) + b(r_p(t, 1) - \mu)$, where $b > (1-\gamma)/(1-\gamma\lambda)$. Then the excess holding return $h_p(t, t+1, \infty) - r_p(t, t+1)$, defined as $(r_p(t, \infty) - \gamma r_p(t+1, \infty))/(1-\gamma) - r_p(t, t+1)$, is equal (up to a constant) to $(c-1)r_p(t, t+1) - \gamma c r_p(t+1, t+2)$, where $c = b/(1-\gamma)$. If γ is close to one and c large, then this excess return is approximately proportional to b, and changing b would do little more than scale it up or down. If the excess return is not very forecastable for one b, it is likely also to be not very forecastable for another b. Then, a regression of excess holding returns on the short rate may have little power to detect even major departures of b from $(1-\gamma)/(1-\gamma\lambda)$.

Tests of the rational expectations model are not so straightforward when using data on a single long rate that is not a consol yield and a short rate. Sargent (1979) showed how, using a companion-form vector autoregression, it is readily possible to test the restrictions implied by the rational expectations model even with such data. He was unable to reject these restrictions on the vector autoregression of long and short rates using a likelihood ratio test. However, it was later discovered that Sargent's paper did not test all restrictions, and when the additional restrictions were incorporated into the analysis, the hypothesis was rejected [Hansen and Sargent (1981), Shiller (1981a)]. These rejections, however, do not deny the *similarity* between actual and optimal distributed lag coefficients. Campbell and Shiller (1987) used a cointegrated vector autoregressive framework, where the vector contained two elements, the long rate and the short rate, and confirmed both that the rational expectations model is rejected with a Wald test and that the model is of some value in describing how long rates respond to short rates and their own lagged values.

There is also some evidence that the relation of long rates to lagged interest rates changes approximately appropriately when the stochastic properties of interest rates change. It was shown by Shiller (1987) that such a correspondence between the distribution lag coefficients holds up crudely speaking even when one uses nineteenth-century U.S. data, or nineteenth- or twentieth-century British data. In the nineteenth century in Britain, for example, short rates appeared to be sharply mean reverting, so that long rates should have been nearly constant: indeed the distributed lag regressions of the British consol yield on the short rates showed sharply reduced coefficients relative to the twentieth-century coefficients in a distributed lag regression of long rates on short rates. Mankiw, Miron and Weil (1987) found an abrupt, and they interpreted appropriate, given the rational expectations model, change in the distributed lag coefficients, at the time of the founding of the Federal Reserve.

How is it then that the forward-spot spread $f(t, t+m, t+m+n) - r_p(t, t+m)$ seems to predict well only for large n and not small n? Fama and Bliss (1987) interpreted this finding as reflecting the fact that interest rates are not very forecastable into the near future, but better forecastable into the more distant future. He gave as an example the story of AR-1 Model described in connection with equations (31)–(33) above. The expectation as of time t or the change $r(t+n, t+n+1) - r(t, t+1)$ is $(\gamma^n - 1)(r(t, t+1) - \mu)$. For γ close to, but below, one, the variance of the expected change is quite small for small n, and grows with n. Thus, for small n any noise in the term premium might swamp out the component in the forward-spot spread $F(t, t+n, t+m+n) - r(t, t+m)$ that is due to predictable change in interest rates.

5.5. *Interpreting departures from the expectations theory*

Of course, as a matter of tautology, the fact that the coefficients in Table 13.2 do not all equal one has something to do with time-varying term premia. But the nature of the time varying term premia has not been given an ample description for all n and m.

One story for the negative coefficients in Table 13.2 for large m ($\geq$20 years) and small n ($\leq$one year) is that there might be noise in term premia on long-term interest rates unrelated to short-term interest rates. The noise might be due to exogenous shift to investor demand, or even to changing fashions and fads in investing. Suppose, for example, that this "noise" is serially uncorrelated, as though it were due to an error in measuring long-term interest rates.[51] Consider for simplicity consols, $m = \infty$, for which $f_p(t, t+n, \infty) - r_p(t, \infty) = (D_p(n)/(D_p(\infty) - D_p(n))(r_p(t, \infty) - r_p(t, n))$. If one regresses $r_p(t+n, \infty) - r_p(t, \infty)$ on this, then one has $r_p(t, \infty)$ on both sides of the equation with opposite signs. Thus, any "noise" in $r_p(t, \infty)$ might give a negative slope coefficient in the regression.

This simple story about extraneous noise like measurement error in long rates, while suggestive, is not completely adequate in explaining the wrong signs in the Table 13.2 regressions for large m and small n. If the problem were just exogenous noise in long rates then an instrumental variables approach to the estimation of the above regressions with economic variables as instruments would correct the wrong sign; yet it does not [Mankiw (1986)].

A different story for the wrong sign in the regression is that long rates do not react properly to short rates. The distributed lag regressions noted above of long rates on short rates, while similar to the distributed lag implied by an autoregressive forecasting regression for short rates, are not quite the same. In fact, the distributed lag coefficients of long rates on short rates tend to show too simple a pattern, like a simple exponential decay pattern instead of a relatively choppy pattern seen in the optimal responses of long rates to short rates implied by the forecasting equation [Shiller (1987)]. This result might come about because people who price long bonds tend to blur the past somewhat in their memories, or because people use a simple "conventional" pricing rule for long bonds.[52]

5.6. Seasonality and interest rates

The above discussion suggests that the expectations hypothesis works best when interest rate movements are well forecastable. With many economic variables seasonal movements are forecastable far into the future. If there is any seasonality in interest rates, one would expect to see a seasonal pattern to the term structure. We would not expect that long rates and short rates should show the same seasonal pattern, that is, reach their highest point in the same month. Instead, the expectations theory would predict a phase shift between

[51] Just as well, the wrong signs in some regressions could be due to measurement error in interest rates, a point considered and rejected as the main explanation for the wrong signs by Shiller (1979) and Mankiw (1986). However, measurement error is taken more seriously by Brown and Dybvig (1986). They needed measurement error to study the one-factor version of the Cox–Ingersoll–Ross model because without it there would be a perfect dependence among the interest rates of different maturity.

[52] Keynes (1936) said that the long rate is "highly conventional . . . its actual value is largely governed by the prevailing view as to what its value is expected to be". The idea here is apparently that a simple rule of thumb used to price long-term bonds may become validated when market prices appear to follow the rule.

long and short rates. Macaulay (1938) investigated whether this occurred using data on call money and time rates 1890 to 1913, and concluded that there was "evidence of definite and relatively successful forecasting",[53] for seasonal movements, though not for movements other than seasonals.

Sargent (1971) noted that the maturity on the call rates was not well defined, and in fact the actual maturities of the call loans are likely to have had a seasonality themselves. He thus sought to reproduce Macaulay's work using more recent data for which maturity can be defined more precisely. Sargent showed that in a perfect foresight model the simple expectations theory for discount bonds implies that the m-period rate $r_d(t, t+m)$ should lead the one-period rate $r_d(t, t+1)$ by $(m-1)/2$ periods across all frequencies. He used U.S. Treasury Bill rates on one to thirteen week bills for 1953 to 1960. He found that long rates did tend to lead short rates at the seasonal frequencies, but by much less than the theoretical $(m-1)/2$.

The post World War II data set that Sargent used, however, contained a much milder seasonal than was evident in the prewar data that Macaulay had used. The Federal Reserve was founded in 1913 to "provide an elastic currency" and this clearly meant that one of their missions was to eliminate seasonals, which they then largely did [see Shiller (1980) and Miron (1984, 1986)].[54] Mankiw and Miron (1986), using a time series on pre-1913 U.S. interest rates of three and six months maturity, found more encouraging results for the expectations theory.

5.7. *The sign of term premia*

Kim (1986) investigated whether the observed term premium between nominal three- and six-month treasury bills in the United States 1959–86 could be reconciled with the covariance between $S(t, t+3)$ and $S(t+3, t+6)$ as described by equation (22) or (24) as the theory prescribes. He used a co-integrated vector autoregressive model for the two log interest rates, log consumption and a log price index, and a lognormality assumption for the error term. He transformed the vector with the co-integrating vector so that the transformed vector has as elements the spread between the two log interest rates, the change in one of the interest rates, the change in log real consumption and the change in the log price index. For the model, the covariance in equation (22) is constant through time. He tested the restrictions across the

[53] Macaulay (1938, p. 36).

[54] Clark (1986) questioned whether the decline in seasonality was due to the founding of the Fed. He noted that seasonals disappeared in the United States and other countries at about the same time, and that seasonals disappeared approximately three years before the seasonals in currency and high powered money changed.

mean vector, coefficient vector, and variance matrix of residuals using a Wald test. The test rejected the restrictions; on the other hand, the sign of the term premium is as predicted by the sign of the covariance.

Other studies of consumption and the term structure of interest rates looked at short-term real returns on long and short bonds and their correlation with real consumption changes to see if the difference in mean real returns between long and short bonds could be reconciled with the covariance of real returns with real marginal rates of substitution. Grossman, Melino and Shiller (1987) found that the excess real one-period returns between long-term debt and short-term debt had negligible correlation with real per capita consumption changes with annual U.S. data 1890–1981 and with U.S. quarterly data 1953–83. They rejected at high significance levels the covariance restrictions using a vector autoregression model including real returns on long-term debt, short-term debt, and corporate stocks.[55]

5.8. *Modelling time-varying term premia*

Since the rational expectations hypothesis can be rejected, as discussed above, it follows that the term premium is time varying. Although the term premium is not observed itself without error, we can study its projection onto any information set by regressing the variables represented on the right-hand sides of the expressions defining term premia, i.e. (14), (15), and (16) above, from which the expectations operators have been deleted, onto information available at time t. The above discussion of the projection onto the forward-spot spread concerns only one possible such regression. There is no theory of the term structure well-developed enough to allow us to predict what variables to use, so the empirical literature here often looks like a "fishing expedition".

Kessel (1965) regressed the forward-spot spread $f_d(t, t+1, t+2) - r_d(t+1, t+2)$ on $r_d(t, t+1)$, where the time unit is four weeks, to test whether term premia are related to the level of interest rates. He found, using monthly U.S. Treasury Bill data 1949–61, that there was a positive coefficient on $r_d(t, t+1)$. However, Nelson (1972b), using analogous methodology, found the opposite sign for the coefficient of the interest rate. Both Kessel and Nelson gave theories why risk considerations should imply the sign they got. Shiller (1979) in effect regressed $f_p(t, t+1, t+m+1) - r_p(t+1, t+m+1)$ on $r_p(t, t+m)$ for m very large with quarterly, monthly, and annual time periods for U.S. and U.K. history and found a consistently positive coefficient, which was interpreted as a sign of possible excess volatility of long rates. Campbell and Shiller

[55]Mankiw (1986) inquired whether the time variation in the covariance could be reconciled with time variation in the spread between long and short rates in the United States, Canada, the United Kingdom, and Germany 1961–84. He concluded that it could not.

(1984) in effect found a negative slope coefficient in a regression (in effect) of $f_d(t, t+1, t+241) - r_d(t+1, t+241)$ on $r_d(t, t+1)$, where time is measured in months, and interpreted this result as reflecting a possible underreaction of long rates to short rates. It is difficult to produce a useful summary of these conflicting results.

Other researchers have used some indicators of time-varying risk premia in such regressions. Modigliani and Shiller (1973) and Shiller, Campbell and Schoenholtz (1983) used a moving standard deviation of interest rates. Fama (1976), Mishkin (1982), and Jones and Roley (1983) used other measures of the variability in interest rates. Such measures were often statistically significant. Engle, Lilien and Robins (1987) used an ARCH model to model time-varying variance of interest rates, and concluded that the risk premium so modelled helps to explain the failures of the expectations theory.

Still other variables have been used to explain time-varying term premia. Nelson (1972b) used an index of business confidence. Shiller, Campbell and Schoenholtz (1983) used a measure of the volume of trade in bonds. Keim and Stambaugh (1986) used a low-grade yield spread variable (the difference between yields on long-term under-BAA-rated corporate bonds and short-term Treasury bills), and a small-firm variable (the log of the share price, averaged equally across the quintile of smallest market value on the New York Stock Exchange). Campbell (1987) used a latent variable model of the returns on bills, bonds and common stocks to infer time-varying risk premia in all three markets.

5.9. Flow of funds models

Clearly, term premia do vary and are correlated with observable economic variables. But what kind of structural model might clarify why they vary? One might expect that when the federal government issues a large amount of long-term debt, the supply of long-term debt should rise and, other things equal, term premia should rise. One might also expect that in time when funds flow into life insurance companies, major purchasers of long-term bonds, then the demand for long-term debt should rise and, other things equal, term premia should decline. Thus, the term structure might be related to such flows of funds.[56]

[56]Conversely, when the government attempts to peg the term structure, there should be consequential flows of demand across maturities. Walker (1954) noted that when the Federal Reserve attempted to peg an upward-sloping term structure there was a great shift out of short-term securities into long-term securities by the holders of government debt. Such a shift is implied by the expectations hypothesis.

There was a flurry of research on the effects of government debt policy on the term structure following the policy, brought in by the Kennedy Administration in the United States in 1961, known as "Operation Twist". Operation Twist consisted of Federal Reserve open market operations and Treasury debt management operations directed toward shortening the average term to maturity of outstanding public debt, with the intention of "twisting" the term structure.[57] Okun (1963) and Scott (1965) correlated the term structure with federal debt measures without accounting for expectations. Modigliani and Sutch (1966, 1967) added dummy or debt composition variables to their distributed lag regressions of long rates on short rates, but found evidence of only a "weak" effect of national debt on the term structure. Indeed, the simple distributed lag on short rates explained long rates so well that there was little room for much improvement of fit using debt policy variables.[58] The Modigliani–Sutch conclusions were criticized by Wallace (1967) for the assumption that government debt policy is exogenous over the sample period.

There is a substantial literature on models that relate interest rates to such flows of funds; see, for example, Ando and Modigliani (1975), Brainard and Tobin (1968), De Leeuw (1965), Friedman (1977a, 1980a), Hendershott (1971), or Backus, Brainard, Smith and Tobin (1980). But much of this literature makes no explicit use of expectations of future interest rates that ought to play a pivotal role in the term structure of interest rates. Many of the models are not complete, e.g. providing estimates of some demands for funds, and not providing a general equilibrium that might give a theory of the term structure.

Friedman and Roley (1979) and Roley (1982) estimated a flow of funds model [along the lines of Friedman (1977a, 1980b), and Roley (1977)] but incorporating as determinants of the demand functions not yields to maturity but rational expectations of short-run returns.

Flow of funds modelling has offered the promise of estimating consistently general equilibrium models of the determination of interest rates, but such modelling has to date been hampered by the same problems that have prevented any consensus on other macroeconometric models. A lot of subjective judgment goes into specifying the identifying restrictions, exogeneity specifications and other assumptions that lie behind a complicated simultaneous equation model. Hence, there is a lot of uncertainty about the validity of particular models.

[57]Operation Twist also involved relaxing some interest rate ceilings. The federal debt structure during the early 1960s in fact went in exactly the opposite direction to what was implied by Operation Twist, as the Treasury's debt policy was contradicting the Fed's. See Friedman (1981).

[58]Friedman (1977a, 1981) did find a significant coefficient in a term structure equation for a variable which was the ratio of outstanding federal long-term securities to outstanding federal short-term securities.

6. Some concluding observations

There has been a lot of progress in our understanding of the term structure in the last twenty years. We now have formal heuristic theoretical models of the term structure in terms of the ultimate objectives of economic agents and the stochastic properties of forcing variables. These models are beginnings that have changed our way of thinking about the term structure. We now have an extensive empirical literature describing in great detail how the term structure is correlated with other economic variables. But we could hope for still more progress.

It is of course very difficult to say where the actual opportunities for productive research lie, but it is possible to say where there are problems to be solved.

Theoretical work on the term structure, while it has offered many insights, still does not allow us to say much about the term structure we observe. Most theorists are currently using a representative individual utility of consumption model, while most corporate and government bonds in the United States are held by institutions. Even if institutions were somehow behaving as if they were representative consumers, we must face the fact that the expected present value of utility of consumption model has not held up well in tests of the returns on assets other than bonds. Probably, the theoretical model is just not a good descriptor of human behavior.

Most of the theoretical work on the expectations hypothesis has worked on the term structure of index bonds, but freely tradable true index bonds of varying maturity are virtually nonexistent. The theoretical literature has tried to find justifications for a zero term premia model, while the assumption of zero term premia has never been an issue for empirical researchers. That term premia are not zero and change through time has not suggested any well-posed problems for theoretical researchers working in the current paradigm that would produce any idea as to how to expect them to change.

Empirical work on the term structure has produced consensus on little more than that the rational expectations model, while perhaps containing an element of truth, can be rejected. There is no consensus on why term premia vary. There does not seem even to be agreement on how to describe the correlation of the term premia with other variables. A lot more research could be done leading to consensus on, for example, the senses in which long rates may be influenced by government fiscal policy, term premia are related to some measures of risk, interest rates overreact or underreact to short rates, or be influenced by or depend on rules of thumb or "satisficing" behavior. Flow of funds models have some interest, but seem to have been largely dropped by researchers in the wake of the rational expectations revolution, just when they should have been integrated with it.

Appendix A: Mathematical symbols

$D_i(m, t)$ = Duration of an m-period bond at time t. Second argument will sometimes be omitted, i = d: discount bond, i = p: par bond.

$f_d(t, t', T)$ = The forward discount interest rate at time t applying to the interval from t' to T, $t \leq t' \leq T$. The term of the forward instrument is $m = T - t'$.

$F_p(t, t', T)$ = The forward par interest rate at time t applying to the interval from t' to T, $t \leq t' \leq T$. The term of the forward instrument is $m = T - t'$.

$f_p(t, t', T)$ = Linear approximation to $F_p(t, t', T)$.

$h_d(t, t', T)$ = The discount holding period return. If $t \leq t' \leq T$ it is the return from buying a discount bond at time t that matures at time T and selling it at time t'. If $t \leq T \leq t'$, it is the rate of return from rolling over discount bonds of maturity $m = T - t$, until time t'.

$H_p(t, t', T)$ = The par holding period return. If $t \leq t' \leq T$, it is the return from buying a par bond at time t that matures at time T, receiving coupons between t and t' and selling it at time t'. If $t \leq T \leq t'$, it is the rate of return from rolling over par bonds of maturity $m = T - t$ until time t'.

$h_p(t, t', T)$ = Linear approximation to $H_p(t, t', T)$.

m = the term of a bond, equal to the time to maturity $T - t$.

$p(t, T)$ = The price at time t of a bond that matures at time T, whose principal is 1.

$p_i(t, T)$ = The price at time t of a bond that matures at time T, whose principal is 1, i = d: discount bond, i = p: par bond.

$r(t, T)$ = The interest rate (yield to maturity) at date t on a bond that matures at date T, continuous compounding.

r(t, T, h) = The interest rate (yield to maturity), compounded every h periods, at date t on a bond that matures at date T.

$r_d(t, T)$ = The interest rate (yield to maturity) at date t on a discount bond that matures at date T, continuous compounding.

$r_p(t, T)$ = The interest rate (yield to maturity) at date t on a par bond that matures at date T, continuous compounding.

s_i = The amount of the ith payment made on a bond, made at date t_i on a coupon bond $s_i = c$, $i < T$, $s_T = 1 + c$.

t_i = The date of the ith payment on a bond.

T = The date on which a bond matures.

$\Phi_{f,i}(t, t', T)$ = Forward term premium, equal to $f_i(t, t', T) - E_t r_i(t', T)$, $t < t' < T$, i = p, d.

$\Phi_{h,i}(t, t', T)$ = Holding period term premium, equal to $E_t h_i(t, t', T) - r_i(t, t')$, $t < t' < T$, i = p, d.

$\Phi_{r,i}(t, t', m)$ = Rollover term premium, equal to $r_i(t, t') - E_t h_i(t, t', t+m)$, $t < t+m < t'$, i = p, d.

w = The number of payments promised by a bond when it was issued.

Appendix B: U.S. term structure data, 1946–87[59] (by J. Huston McCulloch)

The three tables that follow summarize the term structure of interest rates on U.S. Treasury securities from December 1946 to February 1987.

Table 13.A.1 shows the zero-coupon yield curve on an annual percentage, continuously compounded basis. This yield curve is inferred from the prices of whole securities, rather than being based on the recently developed (but much less liquid) market for stripped Treasury securities. In Shiller's notation, this is $100r_d(t, t+m)$, as used in his (1).

Table 13.A.2 shows the instantaneous forward rate curve on the same annual percentage, continuous compounding basis. This curve shows the marginal return to lengthening an investment in m-year zeroes by one instant. The zero coupon yield for maturity m is the unweighted average of these forward rates between 0 and m. In Shiller's notation, these forward rates are $100f(t, t+m)$, as used in his (7).

Table 13.A.3 shows the par bond yield curve, again on an annual percentage, continuously compounded basis. This is defined as the (unique) coupon rate that would make a bond of maturity m be quoted at par, and gives a precise meaning to the ambiguous conventional concept of a "yield curve" for coupon bonds. The par bond yield for maturity m is a weighted average, with declining weights, of the forward rates between 0 and m. The tabulated values are essentially $100r_p(t, t+m)$, as used in Shiller's (3).

These values were computed by fitting the discount function that gives the present value of a future dollar to Treasury security prices. This discount function [$p_d(t, T)$ in Shiller's nomenclature] was curve fit with a cubic spline, as described in McCulloch (1975b), and as modified at NBER-West during 1977–78.[60]

Briefly, the data sets include most of the marketable U.S. government bills, notes and bonds. Closing bid and asked quotations for the last working day of

[59]Written by J. Huston McCulloch while he was Visiting Professor at l'Ecole Superieure des Sciences Economiques et Commerciales (ESSEC), Cergy, France, on professional leave from the Ohio State University Economics Department.

[60]This NBER version fits the actual "flat" price to the sum of the values of the individual payments. This is slightly more accurate than the version I developed at the Treasury in 1973 and described in McCulloch (1975b), which fit the "and interest" price to an idealized continuous coupon flow. McCulloch (1971) contains further background information on this procedure.

In only one instance prior to March 1986, namely the zero-maturity rates for May 1958, did the cubic spline indicate a negative interest rate, of −0.11 percent. This value was not significantly negative, however (its estimated standard error was 0.54 percent), and so it was replaced with a zero in the tables. The zero at $m = 0$ for May 1947 is the actually estimated value. Since March 1986 forward rates in the range 27 to 29 years have often been negative, but these maturities are beyond the range of the tables.

the month indicated, as reported in dealer quote sheets or the next day's *Wall Street Journal*, were averaged. These observations were given weights inversely proportional to the bid-asked spread. Callable bonds were treated as if maturing on their call dates, if currently selling above par, and as if running to final maturity, if currently selling below par. "Flower bonds" (redeemable at par in payment of estate taxes if owned by the decedent at the time of death) could not all be eliminated, as they constituted the bulk of the observations for many maturities during the earlier part of the period. Accordingly, they were selectively eliminated during these years if the estate feature appeared to be active. For further details see McCulloch (1981, pp. 229–230). Since August 1985, callables are not used.

During the early 1970s, a legislative ceiling on the interest rates the Treasury could pay on long-term debt effectively prevented the issue of new bonds. As existing bonds approached maturity, the longest available maturity therefore fell to under 15 years, so that values over 10 years are occasionally missing during this period. The longest available maturity sometimes also fluctuates by five years from month to month if the longest securities are callable and hovering near par. Since the cubic spline does not lend itself to extrapolation, this methodology cannot be used to infer longer term interest rates than those shown.[61]

The curve-fitting procedure was adjusted for tax effects, as described in McCulloch (1975b). The capital gains advantage on deep discount bonds could not be ignored during the earlier part of the period, when most of the long-term bonds were heavily discounted. The importance of this adjustment greatly diminished after 1969, however, when the tax laws were changed so that commercial banks were required to treat capital gains and losses symetrically. After this date, the best fitting apparent marginal tax rate generally was much lower than before, and was often less than 10 percent.[62]

The par bond yields in Table 13.A.3 are based on hypothetical continuous-coupon bonds, and therefore are on a continuous-compounding basis directly comparable to the rates in Tables 13.A.1 and 13.A.2. "Bond yields" quoted in the press and elsewhere are instead on a semiannual compounding basis. Following Shiller's terminology (Section 2), each continuously compounded value, $r_{\mathrm{p}}(t, t+m)$, in Table 13.A.3 may be converted to its semiannually compounded equivalent value, $r_{\mathrm{p}}(t, t+m, 0.5)$, by means of

$$r_{\mathrm{p}}(t, t+m, 0.5) = 2(\mathrm{e}^{0.5 r_{\mathrm{p}}(t, t+m)} - 1)\,.$$

This adjustment would make the rates several basis points higher than in the tables.

[61] The exponential spline approach proposed by Vasicek and Fong (1982) has the considerable virtue of making such as extrapolation meaningful. Chen (1986) has implemented the VF approach along with a modification proposed by the present author, with mixed preliminary results; the forward curves are better behaved at the long end, but often the rèstrictions implicit in the VF model and in the modified model can be formally rejected with a likelihood ratio test.

[62] It should be noted that the identity (9′) holds for the values in Table 13.A.3, but only using the discount function that applies to *after-tax* payments. Cf. Shiller's footnote 12.

Table 13.A.1

McCulloch zero coupon yield curve series, continuous compounding, end of month data, 12/46–2/87

Year	Month	0 mo	1 mo	2 mo	3 mo	4 mo	5 mo	6 mo	9 mo	1 yr	2 yr	3 yr	4 yr	5 yr	10 yr	15 yr	20 yr	25 yr
1946																		
	12	0.18	0.32	0.42	0.48	0.52	0.55	0.58	0.65	0.72	0.95	1.15	1.30	1.41	1.82	2.16	2.32	
1947																		
	1	0.16	0.32	0.43	0.49	0.52	0.56	0.58	0.65	0.72	0.94	1.12	1.27	1.39	1.82	2.16	2.33	
	2	0.19	0.33	0.42	0.47	0.51	0.54	0.57	0.65	0.71	0.95	1.14	1.29	1.41	1.82	2.14	2.32	
	3	0.13	0.32	0.44	0.51	0.55	0.58	0.61	0.68	0.74	0.94	1.10	1.25	1.36	1.80	2.13	2.31	
	4	0.08	0.30	0.44	0.52	0.57	0.61	0.64	0.71	0.78	1.00	1.17	1.31	1.42	1.81	2.14	2.32	
	5	0.00	0.29	0.47	0.57	0.63	0.67	0.70	0.77	0.83	1.02	1.17	1.30	1.40	1.81	2.14	2.31	
	6	0.08	0.33	0.49	0.57	0.62	0.65	0.68	0.76	0.82	1.02	1.19	1.32	1.43	1.85	2.19	2.34	
	7	0.06	0.38	0.58	0.67	0.73	0.77	0.80	0.87	0.93	1.10	1.23	1.34	1.43	1.83	2.21	2.33	
	8	0.16	0.53	0.75	0.86	0.92	0.95	0.98	1.02	1.05	1.12	1.19	1.26	1.35	1.81	2.19	2.30	
	9	0.52	0.74	0.88	0.95	0.99	1.01	1.02	1.06	1.08	1.15	1.22	1.31	1.40	1.85	2.21	2.32	
	10	0.45	0.73	0.91	1.00	1.05	1.08	1.10	1.15	1.18	1.28	1.37	1.45	1.54	1.95	2.30	2.37	
	11	0.60	0.81	0.95	1.02	1.06	1.09	1.11	1.16	1.20	1.32	1.43	1.53	1.63	2.06	2.36	2.43	
	12	0.93	0.90	0.90	0.91	0.93	0.95	0.98	1.04	1.11	1.34	1.52	1.66	1.78	2.18	2.41		
1948																		
	1	1.04	0.96	0.92	0.91	0.92	0.94	0.96	1.02	1.08	1.32	1.52	1.66	1.78	2.19	2.41		
	2	1.02	0.97	0.94	0.95	0.96	0.97	0.99	1.05	1.11	1.33	1.51	1.64	1.76	2.17	2.41		
	3	1.00	0.98	0.97	0.98	1.00	1.01	1.03	1.08	1.14	1.33	1.50	1.63	1.74	2.17	2.43		
	4	0.98	0.98	0.99	1.01	1.02	1.04	1.05	1.10	1.15	1.33	1.48	1.60	1.72	2.16	2.45		
	5	0.97	0.99	1.00	1.02	1.03	1.04	1.05	1.09	1.12	1.25	1.37	1.48	1.60	2.08	2.40		
	6	0.95	0.98	1.00	1.02	1.03	1.05	1.06	1.11	1.15	1.32	1.46	1.58	1.70	2.18	2.45		
	7	1.02	0.99	0.98	0.99	1.01	1.02	1.04	1.10	1.16	1.37	1.53	1.65	1.77	2.19	2.43		
	8	1.13	1.06	1.03	1.03	1.05	1.07	1.09	1.15	1.21	1.43	1.59	1.71	1.81	2.20	2.43		
	9	1.09	1.08	1.09	1.10	1.12	1.14	1.16	1.22	1.28	1.48	1.62	1.73	1.82	2.19	2.43		
	10	1.11	1.08	1.08	1.09	1.11	1.13	1.16	1.22	1.29	1.51	1.65	1.77	1.86	2.22	2.43		
	11	1.10	1.10	1.11	1.12	1.14	1.15	1.17	1.23	1.28	1.46	1.59	1.70	1.80	2.20	2.46		
	12	1.06	1.11	1.14	1.16	1.18	1.19	1.21	1.24	1.28	1.40	1.52	1.63	1.74	2.18	2.44		
1949																		
	1	1.09	1.13	1.15	1.17	1.18	1.19	1.20	1.22	1.25	1.35	1.46	1.57	1.68	2.14	2.43		
	2	1.16	1.14	1.13	1.14	1.14	1.15	1.16	1.20	1.23	1.36	1.48	1.59	1.69	2.13	2.40		
	3	1.03	1.11	1.16	1.19	1.20	1.21	1.22	1.24	1.26	1.34	1.43	1.53	1.64	2.10	2.41		
	4	1.10	1.12	1.14	1.15	1.16	1.17	1.18	1.20	1.23	1.33	1.43	1.54	1.64	2.10	2.42		
	5	1.00	1.09	1.15	1.18	1.19	1.20	1.21	1.23	1.24	1.31	1.40	1.50	1.60	2.09	2.42		
	6	0.81	1.02	1.13	1.18	1.19	1.20	1.20	1.19	1.18	1.17	1.24	1.34	1.46	2.00	2.35		
	7	0.80	0.96	1.05	1.08	1.10	1.10	1.10	1.10	1.09	1.10	1.19	1.31	1.43	1.98	2.30		

		0 mo	1 mo	2 mo	3 mo	4 mo	5 mo	6 mo	9 mo	1 yr	2 yr	3 yr	4 yr	5 yr	10 yr	15 yr	20 yr	25 yr
	8	0.86	0.98	1.05	1.08	1.09	1.09	1.10	1.10	1.10	1.12	1.20	1.30	1.40	1.91	2.26		
	9	0.88	1.01	1.08	1.10	1.11	1.11	1.11	1.10	1.09	1.10	1.18	1.29	1.40	1.92	2.23		
	10	0.82	0.99	1.07	1.10	1.11	1.11	1.11	1.11	1.11	1.12	1.20	1.31	1.42	1.92	2.23		
	11	0.82	1.01	1.12	1.16	1.17	1.18	1.17	1.16	1.15	1.14	1.21	1.31	1.42	1.91	2.23		
	12	0.93	1.03	1.09	1.11	1.12	1.12	1.12	1.12	1.12	1.14	1.22	1.31	1.40	1.87	2.19		
1950		0 mo	1 mo	2 mo	3 mo	4 mo	5 mo	6 mo	9 mo	1 yr	2 yr	3 yr	4 yr	5 yr	10 yr	15 yr	20 yr	25 yr
	1	0.97	1.07	1.13	1.15	1.16	1.16	1.16	1.15	1.15	1.16	1.25	1.36	1.47	1.96	2.25		
	2	1.00	1.10	1.16	1.18	1.19	1.19	1.19	1.18	1.17	1.17	1.25	1.36	1.48	1.99	2.28		
	3	0.89	1.08	1.19	1.23	1.24	1.24	1.24	1.23	1.21	1.20	1.28	1.39	1.51	2.02	2.31		
	4	0.92	1.11	1.22	1.25	1.27	1.27	1.27	1.26	1.26	1.26	1.34	1.45	1.56	2.05	2.34		
	5	0.93	1.14	1.25	1.29	1.31	1.31	1.30	1.28	1.27	1.24	1.32	1.43	1.55	2.07	2.36		
	6	0.90	1.13	1.25	1.29	1.30	1.31	1.31	1.30	1.29	1.30	1.39	1.49	1.60	2.10	2.36		
	7	0.86	1.16	1.31	1.36	1.37	1.37	1.36	1.33	1.29	1.25	1.33	1.44	1.56	2.11	2.39		
	8	1.00	1.25	1.37	1.41	1.43	1.42	1.42	1.39	1.36	1.34	1.41	1.51	1.62	2.12	2.39		
	9	1.10	1.29	1.40	1.43	1.44	1.45	1.45	1.44	1.43	1.44	1.52	1.61	1.70	2.15	2.42		
	10	0.83	1.18	1.37	1.44	1.48	1.49	1.50	1.52	1.52	1.56	1.64	1.72	1.80	2.19	2.42		
	11	1.07	1.31	1.43	1.48	1.49	1.50	1.50	1.49	1.49	1.52	1.60	1.70	1.80	2.22	2.43		
	12	0.79	1.25	1.49	1.57	1.60	1.61	1.61	1.58	1.55	1.52	1.59	1.68	1.78	2.23	2.45		
1951		0 mo	1 mo	2 mo	3 mo	4 mo	5 mo	6 mo	9 mo	1 yr	2 yr	3 yr	4 yr	5 yr	10 yr	15 yr	20 yr	25 yr
	1	0.80	1.21	1.44	1.54	1.57	1.59	1.60	1.59	1.57	1.57	1.63	1.70	1.77	2.18	2.44		
	2	0.78	1.21	1.45	1.55	1.58	1.59	1.59	1.57	1.55	1.55	1.62	1.71	1.81	2.25	2.46		
	3	1.24	1.44	1.56	1.61	1.64	1.66	1.68	1.73	1.76	1.87	1.96	2.03	2.08	2.31	2.48	2.58	
	4	0.93	1.33	1.55	1.63	1.68	1.70	1.72	1.75	1.77	1.85	1.92	2.00	2.07	2.40	2.61	2.70	
	5	0.96	1.34	1.56	1.65	1.69	1.72	1.74	1.78	1.81	1.89	1.97	2.06	2.16	2.56	2.76	2.71	
	6	0.90	1.38	1.64	1.73	1.77	1.79	1.81	1.81	1.81	1.84	1.93	2.02	2.11	2.51	2.72	2.70	
	7	1.29	1.49	1.61	1.65	1.67	1.68	1.69	1.70	1.70	1.77	1.85	1.94	2.02	2.40	2.64	2.68	
	8	1.32	1.54	1.65	1.68	1.69	1.70	1.70	1.69	1.68	1.73	1.81	1.90	1.99	2.35	2.53	2.60	
	9	1.49	1.60	1.66	1.69	1.71	1.73	1.75	1.78	1.82	1.92	2.00	2.07	2.14	2.43	2.63	2.65	
	10	0.81	1.26	1.53	1.65	1.71	1.74	1.76	1.80	1.82	1.91	2.01	2.09	2.17	2.51	2.70	2.68	
	11	1.05	1.39	1.58	1.66	1.70	1.72	1.73	1.76	1.78	1.88	1.98	2.07	2.16	2.53	2.72	2.73	
	12	1.55	1.70	1.79	1.84	1.86	1.88	1.89	1.92	1.94	2.02	2.09	2.17	2.24	2.54	2.70	2.75	
1952		0 mo	1 mo	2 mo	3 mo	4 mo	5 mo	6 mo	9 mo	1 yr	2 yr	3 yr	4 yr	5 yr	10 yr	15 yr	20 yr	25 yr
	1	0.94	1.33	1.54	1.62	1.66	1.69	1.72	1.76	1.79	1.88	1.97	2.06	2.14	2.49	2.70	2.74	
	2	0.90	1.34	1.56	1.65	1.70	1.73	1.75	1.81	1.85	1.97	2.08	2.18	2.28	2.64	2.79	2.78	
	3	1.10	1.37	1.52	1.59	1.63	1.66	1.68	1.73	1.77	1.90	2.01	2.10	2.18	2.52	2.74	2.79	
	4	1.39	1.58	1.68	1.72	1.75	1.76	1.77	1.80	1.81	1.87	1.94	2.02	2.10	2.44	2.61	2.63	
	5	1.43	1.64	1.75	1.79	1.82	1.83	1.84	1.87	1.89	1.95	2.00	2.06	2.12	2.39	2.58	2.65	
	6	1.65	1.75	1.80	1.83	1.85	1.87	1.88	1.92	1.95	2.05	2.13	2.19	2.24	2.42	2.61	2.68	
	7	1.72	1.80	1.86	1.89	1.91	1.92	1.94	1.98	2.01	2.13	2.22	2.28	2.32	2.47	2.61	2.68	
	8	1.46	1.71	1.85	1.91	1.95	1.98	2.00	2.05	2.09	2.21	2.30	2.36	2.41	2.56	2.69	2.74	
	9	1.06	1.46	1.70	1.81	1.87	1.91	1.94	2.00	2.04	2.17	2.27	2.35	2.43	2.70	2.83	2.83	

Table 13.A.1 (cont.)

Year	Month	0 mo	1 mo	2 mo	3 mo	4 mo	5 mo	6 mo	9 mo	1 yr	2 yr	3 yr	4 yr	5 yr	10 yr	15 yr	20 yr	25 yr
1952	10	1.32	1.59	1.75	1.82	1.86	1.89	1.92	1.97	2.01	2.13	2.22	2.28	2.34	2.54	2.69	2.75	
	11	1.55	1.78	1.92	1.99	2.02	2.05	2.07	2.11	2.13	2.21	2.27	2.31	2.35	2.52	2.69	2.77	
	12	1.82	1.94	2.02	2.06	2.08	2.09	2.11	2.14	2.16	2.24	2.30	2.34	2.38	2.56	2.76		
1953		0 mo	1 mo	2 mo	3 mo	4 mo	5 mo	6 mo	9 mo	1 yr	2 yr	3 yr	4 yr	5 yr	10 yr	15 yr	20 yr	25 yr
	1	1.63	1.82	1.93	1.97	2.00	2.02	2.03	2.06	2.09	2.18	2.26	2.33	2.40	2.66	2.80		
	2	1.86	2.02	2.11	2.15	2.16	2.18	2.19	2.20	2.22	2.26	2.31	2.37	2.44	2.73	2.90		
	3	1.95	1.99	2.01	2.03	2.05	2.06	2.07	2.10	2.13	2.24	2.33	2.41	2.48	2.76	2.92		
	4	1.78	2.06	2.23	2.30	2.34	2.37	2.39	2.43	2.46	2.55	2.63	2.70	2.76	3.00	3.10	3.14	3.19
	5	1.43	1.94	2.23	2.35	2.42	2.47	2.50	2.58	2.63	2.79	2.91	3.01	3.09	3.31	3.29	3.22	3.19
	6	1.18	1.61	1.89	2.03	2.11	2.17	2.20	2.28	2.33	2.48	2.59	2.69	2.76	3.01	3.06	3.06	3.12
	7	1.72	1.94	2.06	2.12	2.16	2.19	2.21	2.26	2.31	2.45	2.57	2.66	2.74	2.99	3.05	3.11	
	8	1.62	1.79	1.89	1.95	1.99	2.03	2.06	2.14	2.21	2.45	2.64	2.77	2.86	3.09	3.13	3.15	
	9	0.86	1.22	1.46	1.59	1.67	1.72	1.77	1.87	1.95	2.18	2.34	2.43	2.49	2.65	2.80	2.98	
	10	0.65	0.98	1.19	1.31	1.39	1.44	1.49	1.60	1.70	1.99	2.20	2.34	2.44	2.71	2.88	2.99	
	11	1.36	1.44	1.49	1.53	1.56	1.59	1.62	1.69	1.76	1.98	2.16	2.30	2.40	2.75	2.95	3.04	
	12	1.09	1.25	1.35	1.42	1.46	1.49	1.52	1.60	1.66	1.88	2.03	2.13	2.21	2.48	2.71	2.88	
1954		0 mo	1 mo	2 mo	3 mo	4 mo	5 mo	6 mo	9 mo	1 yr	2 yr	3 yr	4 yr	5 yr	10 yr	15 yr	20 yr	25 yr
	1	1.05	0.96	0.92	0.93	0.95	0.97	1.00	1.10	1.19	1.53	1.78	1.95	2.09	2.49	2.69	2.82	
	2	0.84	0.89	0.92	0.94	0.97	0.99	1.01	1.06	1.12	1.34	1.56	1.78	1.98	2.47	2.53	2.61	
	3	0.99	0.99	0.99	1.00	1.01	1.02	1.04	1.09	1.14	1.34	1.55	1.75	1.93	2.42	2.54	2.63	
	4	0.62	0.67	0.71	0.75	0.78	0.81	0.83	0.91	0.99	1.23	1.42	1.60	1.77	2.38	2.51	2.60	
	5	0.51	0.60	0.66	0.69	0.73	0.76	0.79	0.87	0.96	1.28	1.58	1.84	2.03	2.51	2.61	2.67	
	6	0.67	0.62	0.60	0.62	0.63	0.66	0.69	0.77	0.85	1.15	1.41	1.65	1.85	2.43	2.51	2.56	
	7	0.64	0.68	0.71	0.73	0.75	0.77	0.79	0.84	0.90	1.16	1.44	1.69	1.89	2.39	2.48	2.53	
	8	1.30	1.11	1.00	0.96	0.95	0.95	0.96	0.99	1.04	1.25	1.49	1.71	1.91	2.46	2.51	2.54	
	9	0.90	0.90	0.92	0.94	0.97	1.00	1.03	1.12	1.20	1.45	1.64	1.81	1.98	2.46	2.50	2.55	
	10	0.72	0.85	0.93	0.98	1.02	1.06	1.09	1.18	1.26	1.55	1.79	1.98	2.12	2.44	2.52	2.59	
	11	0.86	0.93	0.98	1.02	1.05	1.08	1.10	1.18	1.25	1.53	1.79	1.99	2.14	2.49	2.63	2.68	
	12	0.92	0.95	0.98	1.01	1.04	1.07	1.10	1.20	1.29	1.61	1.88	2.08	2.21	2.51	2.64	2.69	
1955		0 mo	1 mo	2 mo	3 mo	4 mo	5 mo	6 mo	9 mo	1 yr	2 yr	3 yr	4 yr	5 yr	10 yr	15 yr	20 yr	25 yr
	1	1.19	1.10	1.07	1.09	1.13	1.17	1.22	1.35	1.47	1.85	2.05	2.19	2.29	2.65	2.79	2.82	2.82
	2	0.91	1.14	1.29	1.38	1.45	1.51	1.56	1.70	1.82	2.16	2.32	2.40	2.47	2.71	2.83	2.88	2.90
	3	1.33	1.33	1.35	1.39	1.43	1.48	1.52	1.65	1.78	2.13	2.30	2.40	2.47	2.70	2.80	2.84	2.85
	4	1.44	1.50	1.55	1.60	1.65	1.69	1.73	1.85	1.95	2.25	2.38	2.46	2.53	2.76	2.86	2.86	2.85
	5	0.91	1.15	1.32	1.43	1.51	1.57	1.62	1.76	1.87	2.19	2.35	2.46	2.53	2.73	2.80	2.82	2.83
	6	1.04	1.27	1.43	1.53	1.60	1.66	1.71	1.85	1.96	2.29	2.47	2.58	2.66	2.86	2.90	2.88	2.85

		0 mo	1 mo	2 mo	3 mo	4 mo	5 mo	6 mo	9 mo	1 yr	2 yr	3 yr	4 yr	5 yr	10 yr	15 yr	20 yr	25 yr
	7	1.56	1.67	1.75	1.82	1.87	1.92	1.96	2.08	2.19	2.49	2.66	2.76	2.83	2.99	3.01	2.97	2.93
	8	1.83	1.95	2.04	2.10	2.15	2.19	2.23	2.33	2.41	2.66	2.78	2.85	2.90	2.96	2.96	2.94	2.94
	9	2.16	2.15	2.14	2.15	2.16	2.17	2.19	2.23	2.28	2.46	2.62	2.72	2.79	2.89	2.91	2.92	2.93
	10	2.03	2.05	2.07	2.10	2.13	2.15	2.18	2.25	2.31	2.50	2.60	2.66	2.70	2.81	2.85	2.86	2.88
	11	1.80	2.11	2.31	2.41	2.47	2.51	2.55	2.63	2.69	2.81	2.83	2.84	2.85	2.89	2.92	2.93	2.95
	12	2.34	2.42	2.49	2.53	2.56	2.59	2.61	2.68	2.73	2.84	2.86	2.87	2.88	2.92	2.92	2.90	2.89

1956		0 mo	1 mo	2 mo	3 mo	4 mo	5 mo	6 mo	9 mo	1 yr	2 yr	3 yr	4 yr	5 yr	10 yr	15 yr	20 yr	25 yr
	1	2.24	2.28	2.31	2.33	2.35	2.36	2.38	2.41	2.45	2.56	2.64	2.69	2.73	2.81	2.84	2.85	2.86
	2	1.60	1.97	2.18	2.28	2.34	2.38	2.41	2.49	2.55	2.66	2.71	2.74	2.77	2.84	2.87	2.88	2.88
	3	2.13	2.20	2.26	2.32	2.38	2.43	2.48	2.62	2.73	2.98	3.04	3.05	3.06	3.07	3.04	2.99	2.95
	4	2.61	2.63	2.66	2.70	2.74	2.78	2.83	2.94	3.04	3.23	3.21	3.16	3.13	3.06	3.04	3.05	3.06
	5	2.13	2.37	2.53	2.62	2.67	2.71	2.74	2.81	2.86	2.95	2.96	2.95	2.94	2.89	2.90	2.93	2.97
	6	2.24	2.33	2.40	2.45	2.48	2.52	2.55	2.63	2.69	2.85	2.92	2.96	2.97	2.97	2.94	2.93	2.93
	7	1.88	2.08	2.24	2.35	2.44	2.53	2.60	2.79	2.94	3.20	3.27	3.28	3.27	3.19	3.11	3.06	3.04
	8	2.12	2.40	2.58	2.69	2.78	2.86	2.93	3.10	3.24	3.48	3.54	3.55	3.54	3.40	3.29	3.22	3.17
	9	2.50	2.70	2.84	2.93	3.00	3.06	3.11	3.23	3.34	3.51	3.49	3.45	3.42	3.34	3.24	3.14	3.07
	10	2.27	2.56	2.76	2.89	2.98	3.05	3.11	3.24	3.34	3.46	3.48	3.50	3.51	3.47	3.33	3.22	3.21
	11	2.53	2.81	3.01	3.15	3.27	3.36	3.44	3.62	3.69	3.74	3.70	3.66	3.63	3.49	3.39	3.31	3.28
	12	3.10	3.08	3.15	3.29	3.43	3.54	3.63	3.76	3.80	3.77	3.72	3.71	3.71	3.71	3.63	3.52	3.42

1957		0 mo	1 mo	2 mo	3 mo	4 mo	5 mo	6 mo	9 mo	1 yr	2 yr	3 yr	4 yr	5 yr	10 yr	15 yr	20 yr	25 yr
	1	3.05	3.06	3.10	3.14	3.18	3.21	3.23	3.26	3.27	3.26	3.24	3.24	3.25	3.21	3.14	3.12	3.23
	2	2.39	2.94	3.19	3.29	3.35	3.39	3.42	3.46	3.47	3.45	3.42	3.40	3.39	3.36	3.30	3.25	3.23
	3	2.81	2.89	2.95	3.01	3.07	3.11	3.16	3.28	3.36	3.45	3.44	3.43	3.42	3.37	3.25	3.19	3.25
	4	3.05	3.02	3.03	3.07	3.12	3.17	3.21	3.34	3.43	3.54	3.56	3.56	3.57	3.53	3.38	3.30	3.39
	5	3.14	3.21	3.26	3.30	3.33	3.36	3.38	3.44	3.49	3.56	3.60	3.64	3.68	3.68	3.49	3.35	3.40
	6	2.81	3.08	3.26	3.36	3.44	3.49	3.54	3.65	3.71	3.75	3.74	3.77	3.83	3.90	3.63	3.42	3.49
	7	2.66	3.06	3.30	3.42	3.51	3.57	3.63	3.74	3.80	3.84	3.84	3.87	3.92	3.88	3.59	3.41	3.54
	8	2.50	3.07	3.40	3.58	3.71	3.82	3.90	4.06	4.11	3.99	3.84	3.80	3.82	3.80	3.57	3.44	3.59
	9	2.78	3.23	3.53	3.70	3.81	3.89	3.95	4.10	4.19	4.21	4.10	4.02	4.00	4.01	3.80	3.59	3.58
	10	3.10	3.36	3.54	3.65	3.72	3.78	3.83	3.94	4.01	4.05	4.01	3.97	3.95	3.91	3.79	3.67	3.64
	11	2.06	2.64	3.01	3.19	3.28	3.34	3.37	3.43	3.46	3.48	3.48	3.45	3.42	3.34	3.57	3.72	3.45
	12	2.06	2.71	2.77	2.78	2.79	2.79	2.79	2.78	2.77	2.77	2.70	2.81	2.85	3.06	3.20	3.25	

1958		0 mo	1 mo	2 mo	3 mo	4 mo	5 mo	6 mo	9 mo	1 yr	2 yr	3 yr	4 yr	5 yr	10 yr	15 yr	20 yr	25 yr
	1	1.53	1.46	1.44	1.49	1.56	1.64	1.72	1.95	2.14	2.54	2.70	2.80	2.89	3.17	3.27	3.30	3.35
	2	1.10	1.14	1.20	1.27	1.34	1.41	1.48	1.66	1.81	2.15	2.36	2.52	2.65	3.06	3.21	3.26	3.30
	3	0.94	0.99	1.05	1.11	1.18	1.25	1.31	1.49	1.66	2.10	2.32	2.47	2.58	2.92	3.13	3.28	3.37
	4	1.18	1.15	1.16	1.18	1.21	1.24	1.27	1.37	1.46	1.80	2.06	2.26	2.41	2.84	3.05	3.17	3.24
	5	0.00	0.25	0.49	0.63	0.74	0.83	0.92	1.14	1.32	1.77	2.00	2.18	2.34	2.92	3.12	3.16	3.17
	6	0.84	0.75	0.72	0.74	0.79	0.85	0.92	1.11	1.30	1.90	2.23	2.41	2.55	3.02	3.21	3.28	3.30
	7	0.54	0.70	0.83	0.92	1.00	1.07	1.13	1.31	1.47	2.02	2.45	2.74	2.91	3.19	3.40	3.57	3.66

Table 13.A.1 (cont.)

Year	Month	0 mo	1 mo	2 mo	3 mo	4 mo	5 mo	6 mo	9 mo	1 yr	2 yr	3 yr	4 yr	5 yr	10 yr	15 yr	20 yr	25 yr
1958	8	1.35	1.87	2.20	2.38	2.49	2.58	2.65	2.82	2.96	3.36	3.55	3.65	3.70	3.76	3.74	3.73	3.72
	9	1.00	1.95	2.57	2.89	3.04	3.14	3.20	3.31	3.36	3.50	3.62	3.71	3.75	3.75	3.72	3.72	3.76
	10	1.08	1.82	2.30	2.53	2.67	2.76	2.83	2.98	3.09	3.38	3.54	3.64	3.68	3.71	3.69	3.68	3.71
	11	0.83	1.90	2.58	2.91	3.07	3.16	3.23	3.33	3.38	3.48	3.55	3.60	3.63	3.64	3.65	3.68	3.71
	12	2.13	2.42	2.62	2.74	2.84	2.91	2.97	3.10	3.19	3.46	3.64	3.75	3.82	3.90	3.85	3.78	3.77
1959		0 mo	1 mo	2 mo	3 mo	4 mo	5 mo	6 mo	9 mo	1 yr	2 yr	3 yr	4 yr	5 yr	10 yr	15 yr	20 yr	25 yr
	1	2.32	2.47	2.61	2.76	2.90	3.01	3.09	3.27	3.40	3.74	3.90	3.97	4.00	3.99	4.00	4.02	4.02
	2	2.04	2.38	2.64	2.83	2.97	3.07	3.15	3.29	3.38	3.60	3.72	3.77	3.79	3.80	3.90	4.02	4.07
	3	2.44	2.57	2.72	2.89	3.06	3.19	3.29	3.48	3.59	3.83	3.92	3.97	3.98	3.97	3.97	3.98	3.99
	4	2.78	2.74	2.80	2.94	3.10	3.23	3.32	3.49	3.61	3.88	4.04	4.13	4.18	4.20	4.12	4.02	3.97
	5	2.80	2.75	2.82	3.03	3.27	3.47	3.60	3.79	3.86	3.98	4.10	4.18	4.21	4.18	4.11	4.05	4.02
	6	2.70	2.77	2.93	3.16	3.42	3.62	3.75	3.91	3.97	4.14	4.33	4.41	4.41	4.23	4.14	4.10	4.07
	7	1.97	2.40	2.75	3.04	3.31	3.56	3.79	4.26	4.41	4.34	4.40	4.53	4.58	4.41	4.20	4.05	3.98
	8	3.14	3.48	3.74	3.95	4.13	4.27	4.39	4.55	4.56	4.44	4.52	4.63	4.67	4.49	4.25	4.07	4.00
	9	3.43	3.64	3.90	4.22	4.53	4.77	4.90	4.99	4.93	4.69	4.70	4.71	4.69	4.47	4.26	4.09	4.00
	10	2.14	3.17	3.79	4.06	4.20	4.32	4.42	4.56	4.55	4.36	4.44	4.61	4.69	4.48	4.23	4.06	3.98
	11	2.31	3.53	4.23	4.52	4.68	4.77	4.84	4.93	4.95	4.87	4.81	4.77	4.73	4.52	4.31	4.14	4.06
	12	4.02	4.08	4.28	4.56	4.77	4.88	4.94	5.01	5.02	4.95	4.88	4.83	4.81	4.70	4.51	4.30	4.20
1960		0 mo	1 mo	2 mo	3 mo	4 mo	5 mo	6 mo	9 mo	1 yr	2 yr	3 yr	4 yr	5 yr	10 yr	15 yr	20 yr	25 yr
	1	3.28	3.54	3.82	4.11	4.33	4.47	4.56	4.68	4.71	4.69	4.72	4.74	4.76	4.63	4.36	4.34	
	2	3.58	3.81	4.05	4.25	4.35	4.38	4.38	4.38	4.40	4.49	4.57	4.61	4.60	4.40	4.25	4.16	4.16
	3	2.40	2.68	2.91	3.10	3.23	3.34	3.41	3.55	3.63	3.79	3.91	3.99	4.03	4.07	4.06	4.05	4.03
	4	2.89	2.97	3.02	3.07	3.18	3.34	3.53	3.98	4.16	4.25	4.36	4.46	4.49	4.34	4.27	4.25	4.23
	5	1.82	2.60	3.02	3.16	3.24	3.34	3.45	3.76	3.93	4.14	4.25	4.31	4.31	4.15	4.16	4.20	4.18
	6	1.25	1.65	1.97	2.20	2.38	2.52	2.65	2.95	3.18	3.70	3.89	3.94	3.99	4.20	4.10	3.93	3.84
	7	1.65	1.83	2.02	2.21	2.38	2.50	2.60	2.79	2.91	3.17	3.28	3.37	3.47	3.82	3.83	3.75	3.70
	8	1.45	1.97	2.36	2.61	2.77	2.85	2.87	2.85	2.88	3.14	3.32	3.45	3.56	3.87	3.88	3.82	3.81
	9	2.69	2.34	2.31	2.53	2.75	2.86	2.89	2.83	2.80	3.05	3.30	3.48	3.59	3.81	3.86	3.86	3.86
	10	1.22	1.61	1.93	2.19	2.38	2.52	2.61	2.76	2.85	3.14	3.36	3.54	3.66	3.90	3.93	3.91	3.88
	11	1.24	1.79	2.19	2.44	2.59	2.69	2.77	2.91	3.01	3.31	3.53	3.70	3.81	4.00	4.02	3.98	3.94
	12	1.87	2.03	2.16	2.27	2.36	2.41	2.44	2.51	2.58	2.87	3.12	3.30	3.44	3.75	3.83	3.85	3.85
1961		0 mo	1 mo	2 mo	3 mo	4 mo	5 mo	6 mo	9 mo	1 yr	2 yr	3 yr	4 yr	5 yr	10 yr	15 yr	20 yr	25 yr
	1	1.88	2.04	2.18	2.30	2.40	2.47	2.52	2.64	2.76	3.15	3.40	3.55	3.65	3.85	3.91	3.93	3.93
	2	2.47	2.48	2.54	2.62	2.69	2.75	2.80	2.90	2.97	3.19	3.34	3.46	3.53	3.73	3.80	3.83	3.84
	3	2.02	2.19	2.32	2.42	2.50	2.57	2.64	2.78	2.86	3.05	3.25	3.43	3.56	3.82	3.87	3.85	3.82
	4	1.42	1.93	2.20	2.27	2.30	2.38	2.48	2.73	2.85	3.04	3.20	3.35	3.47	3.76	3.82	3.80	3.77

		0 mo	1 mo	2 mo	3 mo	4 mo	5 mo	6 mo	9 mo	1 yr	2 yr	3 yr	4 yr	5 yr	10 yr	15 yr	20 yr	25 yr
	5	2.10	2.24	2.34	2.40	2.46	2.53	2.60	2.79	2.92	3.20	3.37	3.50	3.59	3.83	3.85	3.80	3.74
	6	1.80	2.08	2.24	2.31	2.37	2.45	2.54	2.75	2.90	3.28	3.50	3.64	3.73	3.90	3.94	3.93	3.90
	7	1.12	1.74	2.10	2.24	2.32	2.41	2.50	2.73	2.88	3.26	3.56	3.76	3.87	4.00	3.99	3.95	3.91
	8	1.74	2.05	2.24	2.36	2.48	2.60	2.71	2.93	3.05	3.37	3.61	3.77	3.87	4.01	4.01	4.00	4.02
	9	1.89	1.99	2.15	2.34	2.50	2.62	2.70	2.88	3.00	3.32	3.53	3.66	3.74	3.87	3.93	3.98	4.06
	10	1.74	1.96	2.15	2.32	2.47	2.58	2.67	2.85	2.96	3.24	3.46	3.61	3.71	3.90	3.92	3.93	4.00
	11	2.00	2.28	2.47	2.60	2.68	2.75	2.80	2.93	3.03	3.33	3.53	3.68	3.80	4.04	4.01	3.96	4.00
	12	2.32	2.48	2.63	2.75	2.84	2.90	2.94	3.06	3.15	3.42	3.59	3.73	3.84	4.09	4.07	4.01	4.04
1962		0 mo	1 mo	2 mo	3 mo	4 mo	5 mo	6 mo	9 mo	1 yr	2 yr	3 yr	4 yr	5 yr	10 yr	15 yr	20 yr	25 yr
	1	2.20	2.48	2.66	2.75	2.82	2.89	2.95	3.10	3.21	3.52	3.72	3.85	3.95	4.15	4.12	4.06	4.06
	2	2.24	2.48	2.65	2.76	2.84	2.89	2.93	3.02	3.09	3.30	3.47	3.62	3.75	4.11	4.14	4.10	4.12
	3	2.65	2.63	2.70	2.83	2.90	2.90	2.87	2.85	2.89	3.15	3.35	3.51	3.62	3.91	3.99	4.00	3.99
	4	2.67	2.69	2.73	2.78	2.82	2.85	2.87	2.93	3.00	3.26	3.42	3.54	3.64	3.93	3.98	3.96	3.94
	5	2.10	2.45	2.66	2.72	2.74	2.76	2.79	2.88	2.94	3.11	3.32	3.52	3.66	3.94	3.98	3.96	3.93
	6	2.98	2.93	2.92	2.95	2.98	2.99	2.99	3.00	3.03	3.28	3.49	3.65	3.77	3.99	4.02	4.00	3.97
	7	2.53	2.69	2.81	2.90	2.97	3.03	3.08	3.19	3.26	3.42	3.60	3.75	3.86	4.07	4.09	4.09	4.18
	8	2.52	2.66	2.77	2.85	2.92	2.98	3.02	3.09	3.11	3.15	3.34	3.54	3.68	3.98	4.03	4.02	4.03
	9	2.68	2.69	2.74	2.84	2.91	2.93	2.93	2.92	2.93	3.09	3.32	3.53	3.68	3.97	4.01	3.99	3.99
	10	2.38	2.53	2.65	2.74	2.81	2.84	2.85	2.85	2.88	3.10	3.32	3.50	3.64	3.97	3.99	3.95	3.94
	11	2.35	2.67	2.86	2.93	2.95	2.96	2.97	2.98	3.01	3.17	3.32	3.46	3.59	3.96	3.98	3.93	3.95
	12	2.98	2.94	2.94	2.97	3.00	3.01	3.00	2.98	3.01	3.22	3.35	3.44	3.53	3.92	3.94	3.90	3.95
1963		0 mo	1 mo	2 mo	3 mo	4 mo	5 mo	6 mo	9 mo	1 yr	2 yr	3 yr	4 yr	5 yr	10 yr	15 yr	20 yr	25 yr
	1	2.95	2.93	2.94	2.98	3.02	3.02	3.01	2.98	2.99	3.15	3.33	3.50	3.63	3.92	3.95	3.94	4.00
	2	2.82	2.84	2.88	2.94	2.97	2.97	2.95	2.92	2.94	3.16	3.38	3.55	3.69	3.99	4.04	4.03	4.01
	3	1.83	2.20	2.55	2.85	3.04	3.12	3.12	3.03	2.99	3.15	3.38	3.56	3.70	4.02	4.06	4.04	4.03
	4	2.83	2.85	2.89	2.94	2.99	3.02	3.03	3.05	3.08	3.28	3.46	3.60	3.71	4.00	4.08	4.09	4.09
	5	2.91	2.95	3.00	3.06	3.10	3.12	3.12	3.10	3.11	3.31	3.51	3.65	3.76	4.00	4.06	4.06	4.06
	6	2.99	2.98	3.00	3.05	3.10	3.12	3.12	3.11	3.13	3.33	3.53	3.69	3.81	4.02	4.06	4.06	4.05
	7	2.88	3.05	3.19	3.29	3.36	3.40	3.42	3.44	3.46	3.58	3.70	3.81	3.88	4.01	4.03	4.02	4.01
	8	3.08	3.26	3.38	3.44	3.48	3.50	3.53	3.58	3.60	3.63	3.71	3.83	3.92	4.04	4.04	4.02	4.01
	9	3.53	3.44	3.42	3.47	3.52	3.56	3.57	3.59	3.59	3.65	3.75	3.86	3.94	4.10	4.10	4.06	4.07
	10	3.25	3.36	3.46	3.54	3.60	3.64	3.65	3.66	3.67	3.75	3.85	3.94	4.01	4.19	4.16	4.11	4.09
	11	3.01	3.27	3.46	3.57	3.64	3.67	3.70	3.72	3.74	3.79	3.85	3.92	3.98	4.13	4.14	4.13	4.13
	12	3.52	3.51	3.53	3.59	3.64	3.69	3.72	3.78	3.81	3.91	3.97	4.03	4.07	4.18	4.20	4.19	4.18
1964		0 mo	1 mo	2 mo	3 mo	4 mo	5 mo	6 mo	9 mo	1 yr	2 yr	3 yr	4 yr	5 yr	10 yr	15 yr	20 yr	25 yr
	1	3.35	3.42	3.49	3.55	3.60	3.64	3.67	3.73	3.78	3.88	3.94	4.00	4.05	4.21	4.21	4.17	4.14
	2	3.51	3.53	3.58	3.65	3.72	3.77	3.80	3.86	3.90	3.98	4.03	4.07	4.11	4.24	4.22	4.18	4.14
	3	3.57	3.51	3.52	3.60	3.68	3.73	3.77	3.85	3.91	4.07	4.14	4.18	4.20	4.26	4.25	4.22	4.19
	4	3.18	3.32	3.43	3.51	3.57	3.62	3.66	3.75	3.81	3.97	4.06	4.13	4.17	4.21	4.21	4.21	4.20
	5	3.00	3.29	3.46	3.52	3.55	3.60	3.64	3.76	3.82	3.92	3.98	4.03	4.07	4.20	4.19	4.15	4.13

Table 13.A.1 (cont.)

Year	Month	0 mo	1 mo	2 mo	3 mo	4 mo	5 mo	6 mo	9 mo	1 yr	2 yr	3 yr	4 yr	5 yr	10 yr	15 yr	20 yr	25 yr
1964																		
	6	3.28	3.46	3.54	3.55	3.55	3.59	3.63	3.72	3.75	3.83	3.92	4.00	4.06	4.16	4.16	4.14	4.13
	7	3.02	3.32	3.46	3.51	3.54	3.60	3.65	3.73	3.74	3.75	3.88	4.00	4.08	4.21	4.21	4.19	4.18
	8	3.21	3.40	3.51	3.56	3.60	3.65	3.69	3.77	3.79	3.84	3.93	4.02	4.08	4.23	4.23	4.21	4.18
	9	3.50	3.53	3.57	3.63	3.69	3.74	3.78	3.85	3.87	3.89	3.95	4.01	4.06	4.19	4.21	4.20	4.18
	10	3.39	3.45	3.53	3.62	3.70	3.75	3.79	3.85	3.88	3.92	3.97	4.02	4.06	4.17	4.19	4.17	4.16
	11	3.37	3.63	3.81	3.90	3.97	4.03	4.08	4.14	4.15	4.13	4.13	4.14	4.15	4.19	4.20	4.20	4.18
	12	3.13	3.56	3.80	3.89	3.94	3.98	4.00	4.02	4.00	3.99	4.04	4.08	4.12	4.22	4.23	4.22	4.19
1965		0 mo	1 mo	2 mo	3 mo	4 mo	5 mo	6 mo	9 mo	1 yr	2 yr	3 yr	4 yr	5 yr	10 yr	15 yr	20 yr	25 yr
	1	3.81	3.85	3.89	3.93	3.97	4.02	4.06	4.06	4.03	3.98	4.02	4.06	4.10	4.19	4.21	4.20	4.19
	2	3.61	3.87	4.00	4.04	4.07	4.11	4.13	4.15	4.14	4.09	4.08	4.10	4.13	4.23	4.23	4.20	4.18
	3	3.60	3.82	3.94	3.98	4.01	4.05	4.07	4.10	4.09	4.07	4.09	4.12	4.14	4.20	4.21	4.20	4.19
	4	3.82	3.89	3.94	3.99	4.02	4.05	4.07	4.08	4.07	4.07	4.10	4.12	4.14	4.20	4.21	4.20	4.19
	5	3.74	3.86	3.93	3.95	3.98	4.00	4.03	4.06	4.07	4.07	4.08	4.11	4.14	4.23	4.23	4.21	4.19
	6	3.71	3.79	3.84	3.87	3.89	3.92	3.93	3.94	3.93	3.95	4.02	4.07	4.11	4.20	4.22	4.20	4.19
	7	3.81	3.81	3.84	3.89	3.93	3.96	3.98	3.99	4.00	4.06	4.11	4.15	4.17	4.22	4.23	4.22	4.21
	8	3.70	3.81	3.88	3.93	3.98	4.04	4.09	4.12	4.10	4.13	4.17	4.20	4.23	4.28	4.27	4.25	4.24
	9	3.93	3.95	4.01	4.11	4.19	4.24	4.28	4.33	4.35	4.34	4.33	4.34	4.36	4.41	4.37	4.31	4.28
	10	3.85	3.92	4.02	4.13	4.22	4.26	4.29	4.33	4.35	4.38	4.40	4.43	4.44	4.46	4.40	4.33	4.29
	11	3.67	3.93	4.09	4.18	4.25	4.32	4.37	4.42	4.44	4.50	4.54	4.55	4.56	4.54	4.49	4.44	4.37
	12	4.31	4.44	4.52	4.57	4.66	4.75	4.82	4.92	4.96	5.08	5.10	5.04	4.97	4.70	4.59	4.51	4.45
1966		0 mo	1 mo	2 mo	3 mo	4 mo	5 mo	6 mo	9 mo	1 yr	2 yr	3 yr	4 yr	5 yr	10 yr	15 yr	20 yr	25 yr
	1	4.50	4.52	4.61	4.72	4.79	4.82	4.84	4.87	4.90	5.04	5.10	5.08	5.02	4.79	4.64	4.54	4.50
	2	4.24	4.50	4.65	4.74	4.82	4.90	4.97	5.08	5.13	5.18	5.21	5.25	5.28	5.20	4.94	4.72	4.66
	3	4.19	4.40	4.53	4.61	4.70	4.79	4.85	4.94	4.97	5.02	5.01	4.99	4.96	4.82	4.70	4.61	4.57
	4	4.44	4.63	4.69	4.70	4.74	4.82	4.87	4.93	4.95	5.04	5.04	5.02	5.02	4.95	4.81	4.67	4.60
	5	4.21	4.49	4.65	4.69	4.75	4.86	4.95	5.02	5.06	5.25	5.26	5.18	5.11	4.94	4.82	4.73	4.68
	6	4.22	4.49	4.60	4.62	4.69	4.80	4.87	4.95	5.02	5.36	5.39	5.31	5.26	5.11	4.97	4.83	4.73
	7	4.09	4.58	4.78	4.81	4.90	5.01	5.09	5.17	5.21	5.40	5.48	5.48	5.46	5.26	5.01	4.80	4.71
	8	4.21	4.79	5.06	5.12	5.28	5.56	5.76	5.89	5.94	6.30	6.28	6.14	6.01	5.57	5.29	5.08	4.97
	9	5.00	5.20	5.35	5.48	5.61	5.74	5.83	5.92	5.91	5.79	5.68	5.56	5.42	5.07	4.96	4.89	4.77
	10	4.24	4.85	5.19	5.36	5.50	5.62	5.70	5.74	5.72	5.61	5.53	5.46	5.38	5.08	4.86	4.71	4.65
	11	3.66	4.62	5.15	5.28	5.32	5.37	5.41	5.43	5.48	5.68	5.55	5.41	5.37	5.27	5.05	4.86	4.76
	12	4.60	4.70	4.82	4.94	5.02	5.07	5.08	5.05	5.03	5.02	4.98	4.93	4.87	4.72	4.67	4.63	4.59
1967		0 mo	1 mo	2 mo	3 mo	4 mo	5 mo	6 mo	9 mo	1 yr	2 yr	3 yr	4 yr	5 yr	10 yr	15 yr	20 yr	25 yr
	1	4.37	4.54	4.61	4.61	4.61	4.63	4.64	4.63	4.63	4.68	4.70	4.70	4.69	4.62	4.56	4.51	4.48
	2	3.77	4.37	4.59	4.60	4.61	4.64	4.66	4.64	4.68	4.91	4.86	4.79	4.80	4.87	4.83	4.75	4.68
	3	3.91	4.01	4.10	4.16	4.18	4.17	4.16	4.14	4.14	4.24	4.30	4.35	4.42	4.60	4.64	4.63	4.60

	4	3.01	3.54	3.74	3.77	3.82	3.89	3.93	3.99	4.06	4.44	4.57	4.63	4.72	4.94	4.96	4.90	4.80
	5	3.20	3.35	3.43	3.49	3.61	3.74	3.84	3.95	4.04	4.53	4.64	4.62	4.71	4.96	4.97	4.92	4.88
	6	3.32	3.75	3.96	4.05	4.17	4.35	4.54	4.93	5.08	5.22	5.25	5.33	5.42	5.44	5.23	5.06	5.06
	7	3.29	3.79	4.04	4.18	4.38	4.60	4.78	5.06	5.16	5.14	5.08	5.11	5.20	5.35	5.25	5.13	5.08
	8	3.49	3.93	4.26	4.49	4.67	4.82	4.95	5.21	5.31	5.39	5.38	5.40	5.44	5.42	5.29	5.18	5.19
	9	4.34	4.25	4.35	4.59	4.83	5.02	5.16	5.36	5.40	5.39	5.40	5.45	5.51	5.52	5.39	5.27	5.22
	10	3.80	4.19	4.45	4.63	4.82	5.04	5.22	5.44	5.50	5.61	5.63	5.64	5.68	5.71	5.60	5.50	5.49
	11	3.57	4.27	4.76	5.04	5.23	5.43	5.60	5.81	5.75	5.62	5.67	5.73	5.78	5.82	5.77	5.72	
	12	3.90	4.43	4.85	5.16	5.40	5.59	5.72	5.90	5.90	5.88	5.89	5.84	5.79	5.77	5.81	5.78	5.58
1968		0 mo	1 mo	2 mo	3 mo	4 mo	5 mo	6 mo	9 mo	1 yr	2 yr	3 yr	4 yr	5 yr	10 yr	15 yr	20 yr	25 yr
	1	4.64	4.74	4.84	4.95	5.04	5.11	5.17	5.33	5.45	5.58	5.59	5.63	5.68	5.73	5.68	5.56	5.41
	2	4.37	4.79	5.01	5.12	5.21	5.28	5.34	5.45	5.51	5.65	5.71	5.72	5.70	5.69	5.69	5.63	
	3	4.52	4.94	5.18	5.28	5.34	5.41	5.47	5.60	5.69	5.86	5.92	5.91	5.90	5.97	6.02	5.94	
	4	5.06	5.34	5.51	5.61	5.68	5.75	5.80	5.90	5.94	6.02	6.06	6.06	6.03	5.93	5.81	5.68	5.56
	5	5.20	5.57	5.76	5.84	5.92	6.01	6.08	6.15	6.17	6.17	6.03	5.93	5.94	5.98	5.89	5.72	5.49
	6	5.27	5.29	5.34	5.42	5.51	5.60	5.69	5.87	5.94	5.94	5.86	5.83	5.82	5.75	5.66	5.55	5.44
	7	4.92	5.10	5.19	5.23	5.30	5.38	5.44	5.46	5.46	5.50	5.51	5.51	5.52	5.53	5.49	5.43	5.35
	8	4.60	5.05	5.24	5.26	5.29	5.36	5.41	5.43	5.41	5.37	5.41	5.47	5.51	5.56	5.50	5.41	5.33
	9	5.13	5.20	5.24	5.28	5.33	5.40	5.45	5.44	5.41	5.46	5.47	5.49	5.53	5.65	5.68	5.62	5.45
	10	5.25	5.34	5.46	5.59	5.64	5.66	5.67	5.70	5.70	5.63	5.61	5.63	5.65	5.79	5.87	5.83	5.61
	11	4.32	5.07	5.47	5.60	5.67	5.73	5.78	5.87	5.86	5.65	5.66	5.70	5.74	5.95	6.08	6.02	5.64
	12	5.98	6.14	6.24	6.31	6.39	6.49	6.56	6.63	6.62	6.59	6.55	6.48	6.43	6.42	6.47	6.41	
1969		0 mo	1 mo	2 mo	3 mo	4 mo	5 mo	6 mo	9 mo	1 yr	2 yr	3 yr	4 yr	5 yr	10 yr	15 yr	20 yr	25 yr
	1	5.87	5.95	6.10	6.29	6.41	6.48	6.51	6.52	6.48	6.39	6.32	6.27	6.24	6.34	6.50	6.55	
	2	5.34	5.89	6.18	6.30	6.39	6.49	6.55	6.56	6.51	6.59	6.68	6.57	6.45	6.37	6.48	6.47	
	3	4.66	5.64	6.08	6.12	6.12	6.19	6.27	6.34	6.31	6.26	6.27	6.28	6.29	6.42	6.51	6.46	6.17
	4	6.51	6.11	5.97	6.01	6.08	6.12	6.15	6.20	6.24	6.36	6.43	6.41	6.39	6.34	6.30	6.23	6.10
	5	5.83	5.97	6.09	6.20	6.31	6.40	6.48	6.58	6.60	6.74	6.82	6.73	6.63	6.57	6.67	6.63	
	6	5.89	6.26	6.44	6.49	6.63	6.90	7.20	7.66	7.67	7.49	7.35	7.15	6.97	6.59	6.43	6.33	
	7	5.54	6.55	7.05	7.19	7.27	7.37	7.47	7.62	7.65	7.55	7.31	7.04	6.84	6.48	6.36	6.24	
	8	6.84	7.05	7.10	7.07	7.12	7.25	7.39	7.54	7.53	7.42	7.26	7.09	6.95	6.54	6.26	6.10	
	9	7.10	7.03	7.07	7.19	7.33	7.45	7.54	7.72	7.81	7.90	7.80	7.72	7.66	7.20	6.62	6.24	
	10	6.22	6.69	6.93	7.05	7.22	7.41	7.52	7.53	7.40	7.20	7.31	7.20	7.04	6.72	6.57	6.40	
	11	6.00	6.89	7.41	7.67	7.85	7.99	8.06	8.02	7.84	7.52	7.55	7.42	7.27	7.02	6.91	6.66	
	12	5.90	7.28	8.00	8.14	8.15	8.22	8.27	8.14	7.94	8.06	8.16	7.97	7.78	7.32	6.99	6.63	
1970		0 mo	1 mo	2 mo	3 mo	4 mo	5 mo	6 mo	9 mo	1 yr	2 yr	3 yr	4 yr	5 yr	10 yr	15 yr	20 yr	25 yr
	1	6.95	7.62	7.93	8.01	8.05	8.07	8.06	7.99	7.96	7.97	7.96	7.95	7.92	7.44	6.77	6.43	
	2	6.10	6.68	6.94	7.01	7.02	7.01	6.98	6.90	6.89	7.07	7.18	7.17	7.13	6.81	6.44	6.22	
	3	6.64	6.43	6.39	6.48	6.57	6.59	6.59	6.61	6.65	6.85	7.00	7.09	7.11	6.84	6.80		
	4	6.29	6.52	6.78	7.03	7.20	7.28	7.33	7.44	7.53	7.71	7.79	7.82	7.83	7.71	7.35	6.83	
	5	6.28	6.56	6.82	7.04	7.16	7.19	7.21	7.32	7.45	7.73	7.73	7.64	7.59	7.70			

Table 13.A.1 (cont.)

Year	Month	0 mo	1 mo	2 mo	3 mo	4 mo	5 mo	6 mo	9 mo	1 yr	2 yr	3 yr	4 yr	5 yr	10 yr	15 yr	20 yr	25 yr
1970																		
	6	5.46	6.12	6.45	6.52	6.58	6.68	6.80	7.06	7.22	7.52	7.61	7.63	7.63	7.50			
	7	4.32	5.92	6.50	6.43	6.38	6.50	6.66	6.86	6.89	7.29	7.45	7.46	7.48	7.60			
	8	6.07	6.24	6.33	6.38	6.45	6.56	6.67	6.79	6.78	7.15	7.31	7.32	7.35	7.57			
	9	5.61	5.56	5.71	6.03	6.32	6.48	6.54	6.59	6.60	6.68	6.82	6.97	7.08	7.30			
	10	5.05	5.45	5.76	5.96	6.09	6.17	6.23	6.30	6.34	6.52	6.71	6.86	6.97	7.20			
	11	4.40	4.75	4.97	5.07	5.08	5.06	5.05	5.10	5.16	5.39	5.62	5.88	6.08	6.49	6.52	6.32	
	12	3.98	4.57	4.84	4.90	4.92	4.93	4.91	4.89	4.99	5.47	5.74	5.89	6.00	6.34	6.51	6.39	
1971		0 mo	1 mo	2 mo	3 mo	4 mo	5 mo	6 mo	9 mo	1 yr	2 yr	3 yr	4 yr	5 yr	10 yr	15 yr	20 yr	25 yr
	1	3.99	4.11	4.15	4.17	4.22	4.25	4.25	4.19	4.24	4.73	5.23	5.62	5.87	6.17	6.04	5.98	
	2	3.13	3.25	3.35	3.43	3.50	3.56	3.61	3.69	3.75	4.23	4.78	5.20	5.49	6.12	6.32	6.32	
	3	3.46	3.46	3.54	3.64	3.69	3.69	3.69	3.74	3.81	4.15	4.52	4.86	5.15	5.72	5.85	5.91	
	4	3.49	3.81	3.97	4.04	4.14	4.24	4.33	4.51	4.64	5.20	5.63	5.90	6.05	6.15			
	5	3.92	4.20	4.35	4.38	4.40	4.44	4.51	4.75	4.97	5.49	5.78	5.97	6.12	6.53			
	6	4.52	4.95	5.13	5.12	5.15	5.29	5.47	5.83	6.06	6.49	6.66	6.74	6.80	6.83			
	7	4.78	5.21	5.33	5.31	5.42	5.64	5.82	6.02	6.06	6.50	6.77	6.86	6.91	6.95			
	8	4.49	4.46	4.42	4.40	4.47	4.64	4.82	5.12	5.27	5.55	5.70	5.82	5.93	6.30			
	9	4.55	4.47	4.52	4.65	4.78	4.89	4.99	5.17	5.27	5.51	5.70	5.87	5.95	5.97			
	10	3.56	4.06	4.29	4.37	4.44	4.47	4.48	4.49	4.60	5.06	5.19	5.49	5.76	5.96	6.12		
	11	3.67	4.06	4.28	4.35	4.39	4.45	4.50	4.63	4.75	5.07	5.27	5.60	5.84	5.85			
	12	3.24	3.33	3.51	3.70	3.87	3.99	4.03	4.11	4.29	4.84	5.04	5.29	5.49	5.97			
1972		0 mo	1 mo	2 mo	3 mo	4 mo	5 mo	6 mo	9 mo	1 yr	2 yr	3 yr	4 yr	5 yr	10 yr	15 yr	20 yr	25 yr
	1	2.41	3.02	3.28	3.38	3.53	3.68	3.78	3.99	4.18	4.84	5.29	5.56	5.76	6.40			
	2	3.36	3.25	3.29	3.44	3.60	3.72	3.82	4.05	4.24	4.83	5.23	5.49	5.68	6.26			
	3	3.32	3.42	3.64	3.93	4.16	4.33	4.47	4.78	5.00	5.52	5.78	5.94	6.04	6.22			
	4	3.30	3.28	3.44	3.67	3.86	4.01	4.12	4.34	4.50	5.15	5.55	5.72	5.83	6.21			
	5	3.31	3.50	3.67	3.81	3.95	4.09	4.21	4.43	4.56	5.00	5.34	5.56	5.73	6.14			
	6	3.39	3.68	3.91	4.11	4.31	4.51	4.69	5.02	5.17	5.48	5.68	5.83	5.94	6.24			
	7	3.41	3.56	3.70	3.86	4.04	4.25	4.43	4.74	4.88	5.36	5.72	5.86	5.97	6.40			
	8	4.27	4.35	4.42	4.51	4.65	4.85	5.02	5.28	5.37	5.67	5.89	6.02	6.13	6.51			
	9	4.65	4.48	4.52	4.74	4.98	5.17	5.31	5.53	5.63	5.86	5.97	6.01	6.09	6.62			
	10	4.49	4.54	4.65	4.82	4.97	5.10	5.19	5.36	5.48	5.81	5.98	6.04	6.10	6.45			
	11	4.82	4.79	4.83	4.92	5.04	5.16	5.26	5.36	5.36	5.67	5.88	5.93	5.99	6.34			
	12	4.77	4.93	5.08	5.22	5.34	5.43	5.48	5.56	5.59	5.90	6.04	6.07	6.12	6.41			
1973		0 mo	1 mo	2 mo	3 mo	4 mo	5 mo	6 mo	9 mo	1 yr	2 yr	3 yr	4 yr	5 yr	10 yr	15 yr	20 yr	25 yr
	1	5.22	5.44	5.62	5.77	5.87	5.93	5.97	6.02	6.06	6.26	6.35	6.34	6.34	6.45	6.65	6.94	
	2	5.49	5.59	5.73	5.90	6.03	6.11	6.16	6.29	6.39	6.61	6.66	6.64	6.62	6.55	6.60		
	3	5.77	6.08	6.34	6.53	6.70	6.82	6.91	6.99	6.96	6.79	6.71	6.6R	6.65	6.58	6.60		

		0 mo	1 mo	2 mo	3 mo	4 mo	5 mo	6 mo	9 mo	1 yr	2 yr	3 yr	4 yr	5 yr	10 yr	15 yr	20 yr	25 yr
	4	5.95	6.01	6.17	6.39	6.55	6.64	6.68	6.73	6.72	6.65	6.62	6.61	6.61	6.57	6.61		
	5	6.00	6.53	6.86	7.01	7.07	7.10	7.10	7.09	7.05	6.80	6.64	6.63	6.66	6.78	6.86	6.94	
	6	7.30	7.45	7.56	7.62	7.69	7.76	7.81	7.79	7.59	7.04	6.87	6.79	6.76	6.79	6.91	7.04	
	7	7.96	8.29	8.39	8.36	8.39	8.52	8.65	8.77	8.66	8.17	7.88	7.70	7.59	7.34	7.25	7.32	
	8	8.41	8.64	8.71	8.68	8.67	8.70	8.74	8.67	8.47	7.71	7.30	7.13	7.06	7.04	7.13	7.22	
	9	7.59	7.13	7.04	7.25	7.49	7.67	7.78	7.77	7.58	6.93	6.69	6.62	6.62	6.76	6.91	7.01	
	10	6.74	7.15	7.36	7.41	7.48	7.63	7.69	7.35	6.98	6.82	6.93	6.91	6.84	6.89	7.21	7.41	
	11	7.85	7.49	7.43	7.62	7.85	8.02	8.07	7.80	7.43	6.73	6.72	6.70	6.67	6.79	7.06	7.25	
	12	7.13	7.29	7.45	7.57	7.64	7.63	7.59	7.34	7.11	6.72	6.70	6.67	6.63	6.79	7.19	7.49	
1974		0 mo	1 mo	2 mo	3 mo	4 mo	5 mo	6 mo	9 mo	1 yr	2 yr	3 yr	4 yr	5 yr	10 yr	15 yr	20 yr	25 yr
	1	7.36	7.52	7.62	7.66	7.63	7.55	7.47	7.23	7.02	6.73	6.75	6.76	6.77	7.00	7.32	7.53	
	2	7.18	7.58	7.65	7.59	7.56	7.54	7.48	7.19	6.99	6.76	6.80	6.83	6.85	7.09	7.41	7.62	
	3	8.01	8.51	8.65	8.64	8.61	8.58	8.56	8.45	8.29	7.82	7.69	7.61	7.55	7.49	7.58	7.74	
	4	8.52	8.73	8.90	9.01	9.01	8.98	8.99	9.06	8.94	8.28	8.16	8.09	8.03	7.89	7.86	7.94	
	5	7.55	7.66	7.95	8.29	8.46	8.47	8.51	8.75	8.73	8.02	7.98	7.95	7.89	7.83	7.91	8.02	
	6	7.65	7.65	7.69	7.76	7.88	8.04	8.21	8.62	8.68	8.19	8.27	8.22	8.11	7.84	7.80	7.86	
	7	7.04	7.55	7.74	7.74	7.86	8.07	8.26	8.61	8.65	8.42	8.45	8.39	8.28	8.01	7.91	7.97	
	8	9.17	9.20	9.23	9.30	9.43	9.59	9.73	9.92	9.74	8.76	8.51	8.44	8.40	8.27	8.11	8.16	
	9	6.26	6.06	6.07	6.32	6.79	7.31	7.70	8.24	8.29	7.95	8.01	7.97	7.90	7.89	8.11	8.43	
	10	6.37	7.12	7.70	8.09	8.17	8.09	8.02	7.94	7.86	7.72	7.85	7.85	7.80	7.75	7.85	8.05	
	11	7.44	7.45	7.52	7.63	7.73	7.81	7.83	7.69	7.51	7.26	7.41	7.49	7.52	7.70	7.89	7.97	
	12	6.51	6.77	7.00	7.18	7.26	7.26	7.23	7.16	7.13	7.18	7.23	7.21	7.17	7.43	7.90	8.10	
1975		0 mo	1 mo	2 mo	3 mo	4 mo	5 mo	6 mo	9 mo	1 yr	2 yr	3 yr	4 yr	5 yr	10 yr	15 yr	20 yr	25 yr
	1	5.47	5.53	5.67	5.84	5.94	6.00	6.02	6.05	6.15	6.71	6.98	7.13	7.24	7.48	7.58	7.71	8.11
	2	4.48	4.98	5.33	5.55	5.67	5.73	5.77	5.85	5.92	6.26	6.59	6.85	7.06	7.49	7.59	7.68	
	3	5.06	5.27	5.48	5.66	5.76	5.82	5.86	6.01	6.16	6.70	7.00	7.22	7.40	7.93	8.21	8.31	
	4	4.77	5.15	5.41	5.60	5.80	6.01	6.20	6.58	6.86	7.59	7.79	7.89	7.97	8.13	8.16	8.25	
	5	4.66	4.94	5.14	5.28	5.40	5.50	5.60	5.85	6.07	6.84	7.20	7.41	7.56	7.97	8.15	8.18	8.03
	6	5.59	5.67	5.83	6.04	6.18	6.26	6.32	6.62	6.85	7.21	7.48	7.63	7.70	7.87	7.96	8.04	
	7	5.97	6.00	6.13	6.34	6.56	6.75	6.90	7.13	7.26	7.65	7.83	7.91	7.94	8.03	8.12	8.18	8.24
	8	5.73	5.98	6.24	6.50	6.74	6.93	7.08	7.34	7.46	7.70	7.89	8.00	8.02	8.09	8.23	8.36	8.44
	9	6.24	6.31	6.47	6.69	6.91	7.09	7.23	7.46	7.62	8.03	8.19	8.26	8.28	8.37	8.49	8.56	8.59
	10	5.25	5.36	5.49	5.63	5.73	5.81	5.86	6.07	6.29	6.96	7.24	7.41	7.55	7.93	8.10	8.18	
	11	4.67	5.13	5.46	5.68	5.86	6.02	6.15	6.38	6.57	7.23	7.49	7.66	7.82	8.22	8.32	8.32	8.32
	12	4.98	5.06	5.16	5.29	5.42	5.53	5.63	5.89	6.10	6.68	7.04	7.27	7.42	7.80	7.98	8.08	
1976		0 mo	1 mo	2 mo	3 mo	4 mo	5 mo	6 mo	9 mo	1 yr	2 yr	3 yr	4 yr	5 yr	10 yr	15 yr	20 yr	25 yr
	1	4.52	4.52	4.63	4.79	4.92	5.02	5.11	5.33	5.56	6.39	6.90	7.23	7.45	7.89	7.97	7.98	
	2	4.46	4.67	4.89	5.10	5.29	5.47	5.61	5.90	6.11	6.76	7.09	7.29	7.43	7.80	7.96	8.04	
	3	4.77	4.78	4.89	5.05	5.22	5.37	5.50	5.80	6.04	6.65	6.98	7.18	7.33	7.69	7.82	7.89	
	4	4.86	4.70	4.80	4.99	5.17	5.31	5.43	5.74	6.01	6.58	6.88	7.11	7.28	7.69	7.87	7.95	
	5	4.86	5.24	5.48	5.61	5.78	5.96	6.11	6.40	6.66	7.25	7.46	7.60	7.68	7.89	8.04	8.13	

Table 13.A.1 (cont.)

		0 mo	1 mo	2 mo	3 mo	4 mo	5 mo	6 mo	9 mo	1 yr	2 yr	3 yr	4 yr	5 yr	10 yr	15 yr	20 yr	25 yr
1976	6	5.26	5.30	5.36	5.48	5.63	5.80	5.93	6.15	6.36	6.91	7.17	7.36	7.49	7.81	7.94	8.02	
	7	5.09	5.10	5.16	5.27	5.41	5.55	5.65	5.85	6.08	6.69	6.97	7.20	7.39	7.85	7.97	8.02	
	8	4.80	4.98	5.09	5.17	5.28	5.41	5.50	5.65	5.83	6.43	6.67	6.90	7.11	7.66	7.82	7.88	
	9	5.13	5.07	5.09	5.18	5.28	5.38	5.47	5.59	5.73	6.27	6.54	6.80	7.01	7.56	7.74	7.82	
	10	4.69	4.74	4.85	4.98	5.08	5.15	5.20	5.30	5.46	6.02	6.27	6.50	6.73	7.46	7.72	7.82	
	11	4.37	4.41	4.46	4.51	4.56	4.63	4.68	4.77	4.88	5.39	5.66	5.79	6.01	7.09	7.64	7.80	
	12	4.22	4.26	4.34	4.45	4.53	4.59	4.63	4.72	4.84	5.35	5.66	5.90	6.11	6.83	7.15	7.32	
1977		0 mo	1 mo	2 mo	3 mo	4 mo	5 mo	6 mo	9 mo	1 yr	2 yr	3 yr	4 yr	5 yr	10 yr	15 yr	20 yr	25 yr
	1	4.58	4.57	4.66	4.81	4.95	5.06	5.15	5.34	5.55	6.17	6.46	6.72	6.91	7.38	7.62	7.73	
	2	4.41	4.52	4.65	4.78	4.90	4.99	5.07	5.30	5.52	6.11	6.46	6.76	6.98	7.44	7.69	7.86	7.94
	3	4.54	4.51	4.55	4.65	4.75	4.83	4.91	5.17	5.41	5.97	6.38	6.69	6.91	7.42	7.68	7.82	7.85
	4	4.33	4.44	4.58	4.72	4.85	4.95	5.05	5.30	5.51	6.07	6.40	6.70	6.92	7.45	7.67	7.77	7.79
	5	4.80	4.90	5.00	5.11	5.21	5.30	5.37	5.55	5.70	6.13	6.38	6.64	6.84	7.39	7.64	7.76	7.76
	6	4.98	4.96	5.01	5.12	5.23	5.32	5.39	5.52	5.64	6.06	6.29	6.53	6.73	7.27	7.45	7.56	
	7	5.16	5.25	5.36	5.48	5.60	5.72	5.81	5.97	6.09	6.41	6.63	6.84	6.99	7.38	7.55	7.63	7.69
	8	5.35	5.38	5.49	5.65	5.82	5.94	6.03	6.18	6.26	6.47	6.65	6.78	6.89	7.25	7.47	7.61	
	9	5.75	5.74	5.85	6.04	6.19	6.28	6.34	6.47	6.57	6.75	6.85	6.97	7.06	7.33	7.53	7.66	7.73
	10	6.27	6.11	6.16	6.37	6.55	6.65	6.71	6.88	7.01	7.20	7.29	7.38	7.42	7.55	7.72	7.86	7.90
	11	5.31	5.67	5.97	6.19	6.36	6.48	6.58	6.76	6.87	7.07	7.18	7.24	7.28	7.51	7.71	7.84	7.87
	12	5.38	5.82	6.13	6.32	6.46	6.55	6.63	6.81	6.92	7.10	7.25	7.37	7.45	7.68	7.86	7.98	8.03
1978		0 mo	1 mo	2 mo	3 mo	4 mo	5 mo	6 mo	9 mo	1 yr	2 yr	3 yr	4 yr	5 yr	10 yr	15 yr	20 yr	25 yr
	1	5.69	6.07	6.35	6.53	6.67	6.77	6.86	7.02	7.12	7.28	7.42	7.53	7.61	7.81	8.01	8.16	8.20
	2	5.98	6.23	6.41	6.56	6.68	6.81	6.92	7.08	7.16	7.44	7.58	7.69	7.76	7.92	8.09	8.22	8.27
	3	6.84	6.56	6.51	6.52	6.76	6.87	6.97	7.18	7.32	7.58	7.69	7.78	7.85	8.02	8.19	8.29	8.29
	4	5.86	6.03	6.25	6.51	6.74	6.93	7.09	7.37	7.52	7.78	7.83	7.88	7.93	8.10	8.27	8.36	8.32
	5	6.33	6.44	6.60	6.81	7.02	7.21	7.36	7.64	7.78	7.96	8.01	8.08	8.13	8.27	8.44	8.50	8.30
	6	6.24	6.61	6.95	7.25	7.48	7.63	7.75	8.02	8.20	8.29	8.34	8.32	8.31	8.45	8.56	8.53	8.40
	7	6.40	6.55	6.76	7.01	7.24	7.44	7.62	8.00	8.20	8.26	8.29	8.28	8.29	8.39	8.47	8.46	8.36
	8	8.05	7.88	7.76	7.70	7.73	7.84	7.95	8.20	8.30	8.26	8.23	8.21	8.20	8.20	8.23	8.29	8.31
	9	7.89	8.00	8.15	8.32	8.48	8.59	8.66	8.68	8.66	8.45	8.30	8.27	8.29	8.43	8.51	8.48	8.38
	10	8.35	8.65	8.84	8.94	9.09	9.31	9.50	9.74	9.66	9.25	9.07	8.93	8.83	8.66	8.65	8.69	8.67
	11	8.95	8.99	9.06	9.17	9.31	9.45	9.58	9.79	9.76	9.25	8.86	8.68	8.63	8.62	8.60	8.51	8.41
	12	7.63	8.63	9.25	9.55	9.70	9.77	9.86	10.22	10.33	9.79	9.33	9.09	9.01	8.86	8.75	8.65	8.53
1979		0 mo	1 mo	2 mo	3 mo	4 mo	5 mo	6 mo	9 mo	1 yr	2 yr	3 yr	4 yr	5 yr	10 yr	15 yr	20 yr	25 yr
	1	9.64	9.51	9.49	9.56	9.63	9.68	9.73	9.86	9.80	9.34	8.87	8.68	8.67	8.72	8.67	8.63	8.55
	2	9.58	9.63	9.65	9.67	9.73	9.82	9.90	10.00	9.97	9.58	9.20	9.02	8.98	8.97	8.90	8.78	8.65

		0 mo	1 mo	2 mo	3 mo	4 mo	5 mo	6 mo	9 mo	1 yr	2 yr	3 yr	4 yr	5 yr	10 yr	15 yr	20 yr	25 yr
	3	9.54	9.59	9.65	9.71	9.76	9.80	9.83	9.86	9.77	9.49	9.12	8.93	8.89	8.90	8.86	8.79	8.68
	4	9.54	9.58	9.67	9.78	9.86	9.90	9.93	9.99	9.91	9.63	9.24	9.08	9.08	9.12	9.06	8.95	8.83
	5	9.80	9.78	9.78	9.80	9.80	9.79	9.78	9.72	9.61	9.27	8.91	8.77	8.76	8.87	8.91	8.90	8.80
	6	8.73	8.98	9.13	9.19	9.23	9.24	9.25	9.23	9.11	8.71	8.57	8.50	8.50	8.63	8.70	8.67	8.54
	7	9.22	9.14	9.22	9.40	9.53	9.59	9.63	9.64	9.48	9.02	8.82	8.74	8.74	8.82	8.82	8.76	8.63
	8	9.98	10.11	10.10	10.02	10.02	10.10	10.19	10.30	10.21	9.56	9.28	9.16	9.10	8.99	8.89	8.80	8.68
	9	9.99	10.22	10.34	10.39	10.44	10.48	10.52	10.57	10.48	9.78	9.45	9.30	9.22	9.16	9.11	8.88	8.63
	10	11.24	11.73	12.15	12.49	12.67	12.72	12.73	12.68	12.44	11.59	11.23	10.96	10.77	10.31	10.02	9.74	9.43
	11	10.27	11.23	11.69	11.77	11.83	11.95	12.03	11.72	11.33	10.80	10.34	10.24	10.21	10.11	9.86	9.69	9.50
	12	7.12	10.27	11.88	12.28	12.35	12.35	12.30	11.82	11.41	10.86	10.39	10.12	10.03	10.02	9.96	9.79	9.51
1980		0 mo	1 mo	2 mo	3 mo	4 mo	5 mo	6 mo	9 mo	1 yr	2 yr	3 yr	4 yr	5 yr	10 yr	15 yr	20 yr	25 yr
	1	11.03	11.87	12.28	12.36	12.39	12.43	12.43	12.05	11.73	11.31	10.90	10.74	10.72	10.90	10.89	10.76	10.52
	2	13.29	13.92	14.26	14.32	14.37	14.54	14.73	14.92	14.90	14.46	13.65	13.19	12.91	12.28	11.93	11.47	10.93
	3	13.89	15.07	15.44	15.24	15.19	15.53	15.92	15.85	15.28	14.15	13.25	12.71	12.38	12.02	12.17	11.70	10.87
	4	10.28	10.39	10.52	10.68	10.82	10.95	11.04	11.07	10.96	10.50	10.38	10.40	10.44	10.71	10.85	10.73	10.40
	5	8.22	7.85	7.76	7.91	8.10	8.25	8.36	8.52	8.69	9.02	9.14	9.49	9.70	10.21	10.48	10.44	10.17
	6	4.09	6.66	7.94	8.16	8.11	8.13	8.20	8.34	8.43	8.95	9.09	9.26	9.42	10.02	10.26	10.04	9.65
	7	6.47	7.84	8.57	8.80	8.87	8.90	8.93	9.01	9.14	9.65	9.77	9.95	10.11	10.70	11.00	10.89	10.40
	8	8.27	9.20	9.86	10.26	10.50	10.64	10.71	10.90	11.14	11.26	11.27	11.43	11.48	11.20	11.28	11.06	10.48
	9	10.98	11.20	11.42	11.63	11.79	11.89	11.95	11.96	11.89	11.84	11.68	11.62	11.59	11.55	11.78	11.55	10.90
	10	10.23	11.66	12.58	12.99	13.14	13.21	13.27	13.27	13.11	12.69	12.56	12.46	12.36	11.99	12.13	11.87	11.24
	11	13.63	14.39	14.80	14.86	14.77	14.75	14.83	14.92	14.45	13.64	13.16	12.87	12.66	12.06	12.19	11.84	11.02
	12	10.88	12.90	14.20	14.76	14.75	14.58	14.40	13.84	13.20	12.52	12.27	12.16	12.10	11.94	11.92	11.41	10.65
1981		0 mo	1 mo	2 mo	3 mo	4 mo	5 mo	6 mo	9 mo	1 yr	2 yr	3 yr	4 yr	5 yr	10 yr	15 yr	20 yr	25 yr
	1	13.97	14.72	15.06	15.02	14.86	14.69	14.54	14.10	13.65	12.80	12.49	12.40	12.36	12.19	12.17	11.74	10.96
	2	13.60	14.20	14.56	14.70	14.68	14.62	14.56	14.31	14.00	13.52	13.46	13.38	13.29	12.91	12.78	12.22	11.43
	3	13.10	13.03	12.94	12.82	12.72	12.66	12.65	12.74	12.86	12.81	12.93	13.00	13.01	12.69	12.65	12.16	11.14
	4	12.57	14.11	14.99	15.20	15.10	15.00	14.96	14.87	14.67	14.30	14.12	14.00	13.90	13.50	13.39	12.68	11.65
	5	16.27	16.21	16.01	15.67	15.31	15.06	14.95	14.86	14.69	14.15	13.82	13.54	13.31	12.89	12.80	12.31	11.41
	6	14.03	14.41	14.61	14.65	14.65	14.65	14.66	14.56	14.42	14.19	13.93	13.87	13.74	13.29	13.11	12.60	11.57
	7	14.50	14.98	15.27	15.41	15.52	15.67	15.80	15.88	15.75	15.33	15.04	14.90	14.66	13.89	13.67	12.93	11.62
	8	15.40	15.64	15.84	16.00	16.15	16.33	16.51	16.63	16.35	16.15	15.60	15.60	15.46	14.61	14.39	13.96	12.61
	9	12.64	13.68	14.38	14.76	15.04	15.35	15.65	16.02	15.91	16.11	15.82	15.85	15.70	15.06	15.14	14.41	12.43
	10	12.75	12.97	13.09	13.13	13.21	13.42	13.69	14.12	14.10	14.16	14.25	14.35	14.36	14.21	14.21	13.61	12.21
	11	10.17	10.24	10.37	10.57	10.78	10.94	11.06	11.31	11.56	12.23	12.53	12.59	12.72	12.95	12.79	12.59	11.86
	12	8.26	9.71	10.79	11.51	11.97	12.30	12.55	13.05	13.33	13.51	13.58	13.72	13.77	13.67	13.70	13.27	11.88
1982		0 mo	1 mo	2 mo	3 mo	4 mo	5 mo	6 mo	9 mo	1 yr	2 yr	3 yr	4 yr	5 yr	10 yr	15 yr	20 yr	25 yr
	1	11.73	12.14	12.51	12.84	13.11	13.29	13.41	13.64	13.81	13.85	13.91	13.94	13.90	13.80	13.87	13.26	12.10
	2	11.85	11.98	12.27	12.72	13.19	13.47	13.56	13.55	13.75	13.88	13.82	13.80	13.71	13.58	13.85	13.42	12.35
	3	14.57	13.96	13.66	13.66	13.77	13.84	13.86	13.88	13.95	14.11	14.06	13.98	13.94	13.64	13.51	13.19	12.00
	4	12.31	12.32	12.46	12.71	12.94	13.09	13.16	13.29	13.46	13.64	13.61	13.48	13.46	13.31	13.04	12.76	12.16

Table 13.A.1 (cont.)

		0 mo	1 mo	2 mo	3 mo	4 mo	5 mo	6 mo	9 mo	1 yr	2 yr	3 yr	4 yr	5 yr	10 yr	15 yr	20 yr	25 yr
1982		0 mo	1 mo	2 mo	3 mo	4 mo	5 mo	6 mo	9 mo	1 yr	2 yr	3 yr	4 yr	5 yr	10 yr	15 yr	20 yr	25 yr
	5	11.56	11.62	11.72	11.85	12.01	12.14	12.24	12.55	12.87	13.23	13.37	13.45	13.49	13.30	13.22	12.96	12.15
	6	10.65	11.74	12.57	13.12	13.46	13.68	13.81	14.03	14.21	14.32	14.43	14.35	14.27	13.84	13.65	13.25	12.07
	7	8.49	9.15	9.82	10.50	11.08	11.50	11.77	12.26	12.65	12.93	13.31	13.34	13.35	13.28	13.27	13.05	12.18
	8	7.54	7.51	7.78	8.33	8.96	9.48	9.84	10.56	11.17	11.89	12.26	12.34	12.47	12.44	12.23	12.25	11.79
	9	6.88	6.94	7.24	7.77	8.39	8.90	9.23	9.82	10.37	11.21	11.56	11.61	11.65	11.74	11.59	11.40	11.11
	10	7.81	7.72	7.83	8.11	8.41	8.63	8.73	8.97	9.45	10.01	10.52	10.60	10.75	10.87	10.82	10.95	10.41
	11	7.67	7.87	8.11	8.39	8.65	8.81	8.87	8.95	9.32	9.84	10.33	10.52	10.71	10.97	10.96	11.19	10.65
	12	8.05	8.07	8.11	8.17	8.25	8.31	8.34	8.45	8.79	9.45	9.92	10.17	10.33	10.59	10.67	10.79	10.37
1983		0 mo	1 mo	2 mo	3 mo	4 mo	5 mo	6 mo	9 mo	1 yr	2 yr	3 yr	4 yr	5 yr	10 yr	15 yr	20 yr	25 yr
	1	8.01	8.07	8.15	8.26	8.38	8.46	8.52	8.67	8.96	9.60	10.09	10.32	10.55	11.04	11.18	11.52	11.13
	2	7.90	7.91	7.96	8.06	8.17	8.23	8.24	8.28	8.61	9.20	9.70	9.78	9.86	10.36	10.63	11.08	10.35
	3	8.36	8.56	8.72	8.86	8.95	9.01	9.02	9.06	9.25	9.73	10.01	10.18	10.31	10.64	10.83	11.00	10.45
	4	8.01	8.10	8.19	8.28	8.35	8.39	8.41	8.49	8.72	9.23	9.63	9.81	9.97	10.32	10.52	10.69	10.15
	5	8.38	8.56	8.71	8.83	8.93	9.00	9.05	9.16	9.32	9.89	10.18	10.36	10.52	10.86	11.11	11.29	10.85
	6	8.25	8.57	8.81	8.98	9.09	9.18	9.24	9.39	9.58	10.13	10.40	10.57	10.69	[illegible]	11.21	11.22	10.72
	7	8.63	8.95	9.22	9.43	9.60	9.72	9.81	10.04	10.35	10.98	11.16	11.35	11.53	11.78	11.84	11.82	11.59
	8	8.74	9.01	9.25	9.46	9.65	9.80	9.91	10.13	10.36	11.01	11.35	11.56	11.69	11.79	11.89	12.08	11.44
	9	8.77	8.77	8.83	8.92	9.04	9.15	9.24	9.48	9.70	10.36	10.66	10.92	11.13	11.38	11.43	11.53	10.94
	10	8.46	8.49	8.58	8.72	8.87	9.01	9.12	9.38	9.62	10.38	10.83	11.10	11.29	11.64	11.77	11.81	11.37
	11	8.17	8.58	8.88	9.07	9.19	9.28	9.37	9.58	9.71	10.44	10.77	11.09	11.26	11.47	11.55	11.62	11.14
	12	8.18	8.63	8.97	9.20	9.33	9.42	9.50	9.71	9.89	10.63	10.93	11.25	11.43	11.66	11.74	11.85	11.36
1984		0 mo	1 mo	2 mo	3 mo	4 mo	5 mo	6 mo	9 mo	1 yr	2 yr	3 yr	4 yr	5 yr	10 yr	15 yr	20 yr	25 yr
	1	8.87	8.94	9.02	9.10	9.18	9.25	9.32	9.49	9.63	10.39	10.69	11.03	11.20	11.53	11.58	11.69	11.45
	2	8.45	8.86	9.17	9.37	9.51	9.60	9.68	9.85	9.98	10.77	11.05	11.43	11.61	11.85	11.91	12.06	11.85
	3	9.22	9.50	9.76	9.97	10.12	10.22	10.27	10.39	10.61	11.30	11.58	11.91	12.07	12.31	12.21	12.29	12.16
	4	9.26	9.49	9.73	9.96	10.15	10.27	10.34	10.53	10.81	11.56	11.89	12.17	12.34	12.60	12.52	12.64	12.44
	5	9.65	9.56	9.69	10.04	10.46	10.79	11.01	11.43	11.93	12.69	13.29	13.31	13.44	13.62	13.43	13.26	13.25
	6	8.83	9.39	9.84	10.18	10.47	10.73	10.98	11.60	11.99	12.85	13.09	13.31	13.40	13.51	13.26	13.23	13.31
	7	9.67	10.03	10.33	10.57	10.76	10.91	11.03	11.32	11.63	12.29	12.34	12.44	12.52	12.65	12.56	12.59	12.24
	8	10.78	10.74	10.76	10.82	10.92	11.02	11.13	11.41	11.67	12.21	12.28	12.41	12.49	12.47	12.35	12.14	12.29
	9	10.52	10.44	10.44	10.50	10.60	10.69	10.76	10.94	11.16	11.77	11.96	12.14	12.21	12.15	12.00	11.88	11.74
	10	8.07	8.57	8.96	9.25	9.44	9.57	9.65	9.83	10.15	10.89	11.13	11.28	11.39	11.55	11.48	11.41	11.21
	11	7.47	8.00	8.38	8.62	8.77	8.88	8.99	9.29	9.53	10.31	10.69	10.96	11.23	11.43	11.49	11.60	11.20
	12	6.30	7.23	7.84	8.13	8.19	8.25	8.37	8.81	9.13	9.93	10.44	10.76	11.11	11.46	11.55	11.59	11.20
1985		0 mo	1 mo	2 mo	3 mo	4 mo	5 mo	6 mo	9 mo	1 yr	2 yr	3 yr	4 yr	5 yr	10 yr	15 yr	20 yr	25 yr
	1	7.29	7.73	8.03	8.19	8.27	8.35	8.44	8.73	8.98	9.76	10.22	10.53	10.78	11.12	11.31	11.18	10.93
	2	6.77	7.67	8.32	8.71	8.91	9.04	9.13	9.36	9.65	10.46	10.93	11.24	11.50	11.86	12.03	11.96	11.87

	3	7.67	8.04	8.32	8.51	8.66	8.77	8.87	9.14	9.42	10.30	10.68	11.03	11.28	11.59	11.73	11.84	11.39
	4	7.24	7.52	7.76	7.98	8.16	8.30	8.39	8.62	8.94	9.79	10.28	10.60	10.90	11.40	11.61	11.71	11.46
	5	6.69	7.00	7.20	7.32	7.39	7.43	7.48	7.67	8.01	8.84	9.31	9.58	9.86	10.33	10.82	10.80	10.62
	6	6.49	6.72	6.90	7.03	7.13	7.20	7.25	7.45	7.75	8.64	9.16	9.56	9.85	10.29	10.65	10.91	10.35
	7	6.82	7.06	7.25	7.40	7.51	7.60	7.66	7.84	8.09	8.98	9.51	9.91	10.17	10.65	10.99	11.11	10.67
	8	7.35	7.24	7.22	7.27	7.36	7.46	7.55	7.76	7.93	8.80	9.33	9.58	9.80	10.33	10.90	10.82	10.07
	9	7.02	7.11	7.19	7.26	7.31	7.38	7.44	7.70	8.02	8.74	9.26	9.54	9.85	10.46	11.02	10.98	10.38
	10	6.95	7.16	7.30	7.35	7.39	7.44	7.51	7.68	7.81	8.58	9.00	9.22	9.53	10.08	10.73	10.47	9.57
	11	5.66	6.59	7.16	7.38	7.40	7.41	7.46	7.65	7.75	8.32	8.65	8.97	9.24	9.59	10.12	10.31	9.79
	12	5.19	6.24	6.90	7.17	7.23	7.26	7.30	7.42	7.50	7.88	8.22	8.39	8.56	9.02	9.60	9.82	9.35
1986		0 mo	1 mo	2 mo	3 mo	4 mo	5 mo	6 mo	9 mo	1 yr	2 yr	3 yr	4 yr	5 yr	10 yr	15 yr	20 yr	25 yr
	1	6.38	6.81	7.06	7.16	7.19	7.22	7.27	7.40	7.48	7.92	8.19	8.46	8.66	9.28	9.78	9.56	9.90
	2	6.51	6.89	7.12	7.20	7.20	7.20	7.22	7.29	7.33	7.65	7.76	7.90	8.02	8.12	8.47	8.53	8.27
	3	6.73	6.58	6.49	6.46	6.47	6.47	6.47	6.56	6.72	6.92	7.06	7.24	7.32	7.43	7.61	7.88	7.90
	4	5.82	5.98	6.10	6.18	6.23	6.27	6.30	6.39	6.49	6.91	7.07	7.22	7.31	7.48	7.73	8.11	8.11
	5	6.11	6.23	6.34	6.43	6.50	6.55	6.60	6.71	6.87	7.39	7.76	7.98	8.02	8.21	8.49	9.03	8.95
	6	5.96	6.01	6.06	6.11	6.15	6.17	6.17	6.23	6.41	6.86	7.15	7.30	7.37	7.49	7.90	8.67	8.63
	7	5.08	5.50	5.77	5.88	5.92	5.93	5.94	6.03	6.18	6.61	6.89	7.10	7.22	7.64	8.22	8.69	8.34
	8	4.37	4.86	5.15	5.24	5.23	5.23	5.26	5.40	5.48	5.99	6.25	6.51	6.65	7.35	7.79	8.11	7.88
	9	5.14	5.20	5.26	5.32	5.38	5.45	5.53	5.70	5.82	6.44	6.79	7.07	7.24	7.86	8.38	8.73	8.47
	10	4.65	5.03	5.24	5.30	5.32	5.36	5.41	5.57	5.69	6.20	6.51	6.76	6.93	7.64	8.23	8.33	7.84
	11	5.06	5.24	5.37	5.46	5.51	5.54	5.56	5.61	5.70	6.13	6.40	6.60	6.74	7.28	8.01	8.53	8.16
	12	4.07	5.00	5.57	5.80	5.81	5.78	5.77	5.82	5.95	6.37	6.70	6.70	6.81	7.33	8.03	8.62	8.32
1987		0 mo	1 mo	2 mo	3 mo	4 mo	5 mo	6 mo	9 mo	1 yr	2 yr	3 yr	4 yr	5 yr	10 yr	15 yr	20 yr	25 yr
	1	5.23	5.51	5.67	5.70	5.70	5.71	5.74	5.84	5.88	6.25	6.46	6.63	6.78	7.35	7.94	8.33	8.04
	2	5.44	5.49	5.53	5.55	5.58	5.61	5.65	5.77	5.89	6.29	6.48	6.64	6.76	7.27	7.82	8.20	7.98

Table 13.A.2.
McCulloch instantaneous forward rate data, continuous compounding, end of month data, 12/46–2/87

Year	Month	0 mo	1 mo	2 mo	3 mo	4 mo	5 mo	6 mo	9 mo	1 yr	2 yr	3 yr	4 yr	5 yr	10 yr	15 yr	20 yr	25 yr
1946																		
	12	0.18	0.45	0.57	0.61	0.65	0.70	0.74	0.87	0.98	1.38	1.66	1.83	1.94	2.53	3.05	2.26	
1947		0 mo	1 mo	2 mo	3 mo	4 mo	5 mo	6 mo	9 mo	1 yr	2 yr	3 yr	4 yr	5 yr	10 yr	15 yr	20 yr	25 yr
	1	0.16	0.45	0.58	0.62	0.66	0.70	0.74	0.86	0.96	1.34	1.61	1.79	1.93	2.57	3.01	2.49	
	2	0.19	0.44	0.56	0.60	0.65	0.69	0.74	0.86	0.98	1.37	1.65	1.81	1.93	2.52	3.00	2.49	
	3	0.13	0.47	0.62	0.66	0.69	0.73	0.76	0.87	0.96	1.30	1.57	1.76	1.91	2.55	2.93	2.60	
	4	0.08	0.49	0.65	0.69	0.73	0.77	0.81	0.92	1.03	1.39	1.64	1.78	1.91	2.52	2.98	2.49	
	5	0.00	0.52	0.74	0.78	0.81	0.84	0.87	0.96	1.05	1.35	1.58	1.75	1.88	2.53	3.00	2.45	
	6	0.08	0.53	0.71	0.75	0.78	0.82	0.85	0.96	1.05	1.39	1.64	1.80	1.94	2.59	3.07	2.15	
	7	0.06	0.64	0.85	0.88	0.91	0.94	0.97	1.05	1.13	1.40	1.59	1.73	1.87	2.60	3.17	1.80	
	8	0.16	0.82	1.07	1.08	1.09	1.09	1.10	1.11	1.14	1.25	1.40	1.60	1.81	2.68	3.09	1.79	
	9	0.52	0.92	1.08	1.09	1.09	1.10	1.11	1.13	1.16	1.29	1.45	1.66	1.86	2.69	3.01	2.03	
	10	0.45	0.96	1.17	1.18	1.19	1.21	1.22	1.26	1.30	1.46	1.63	1.80	1.97	2.73	3.08	1.70	
	11	0.60	0.99	1.15	1.17	1.19	1.21	1.23	1.28	1.33	1.54	1.74	1.93	2.10	2.81	2.99	2.06	
	12	0.93	0.89	0.91	0.96	1.01	1.06	1.11	1.24	1.36	1.76	2.00	2.16	2.31	2.80	2.85		
1948		0 mo	1 mo	2 mo	3 mo	4 mo	5 mo	6 mo	9 mo	1 yr	2 yr	3 yr	4 yr	5 yr	10 yr	15 yr	20 yr	25 yr
	1	1.04	0.90	0.88	0.93	0.98	1.02	1.07	1.21	1.34	1.76	2.02	2.18	2.32	2.80	2.86		
	2	1.02	0.93	0.93	0.97	1.02	1.06	1.10	1.23	1.34	1.73	1.98	2.14	2.29	2.82	2.88		
	3	1.00	0.96	0.98	1.02	1.06	1.10	1.14	1.24	1.35	1.69	1.93	2.11	2.27	2.86	2.94		
	4	0.98	0.99	1.01	1.05	1.09	1.12	1.15	1.26	1.35	1.66	1.88	2.07	2.25	2.91	2.97		
	5	0.97	1.01	1.03	1.06	1.08	1.10	1.12	1.19	1.25	1.49	1.72	1.94	2.14	2.91	3.01		
	6	0.95	1.00	1.04	1.07	1.10	1.13	1.16	1.24	1.33	1.62	1.85	2.07	2.27	2.95	2.93		
	7	1.02	0.97	0.98	1.03	1.07	1.12	1.16	1.28	1.39	1.73	1.94	2.13	2.29	2.85	2.85		
	8	1.13	1.02	1.01	1.06	1.11	1.16	1.21	1.34	1.46	1.80	1.99	2.15	2.30	2.81	2.84		
	9	1.09	1.08	1.11	1.15	1.20	1.24	1.28	1.40	1.51	1.81	1.98	2.13	2.28	2.81	2.86		
	10	1.11	1.07	1.09	1.14	1.19	1.24	1.29	1.43	1.54	1.86	2.03	2.18	2.31	2.78	2.81		
	11	1.10	1.10	1.13	1.17	1.21	1.25	1.28	1.39	1.48	1.76	1.94	2.12	2.28	2.88	2.90		
	12	1.06	1.15	1.19	1.22	1.24	1.26	1.28	1.35	1.41	1.65	1.87	2.07	2.25	2.90	2.88		
1949		0 mo	1 mo	2 mo	3 mo	4 mo	5 mo	6 mo	9 mo	1 yr	2 yr	3 yr	4 yr	5 yr	10 yr	15 yr	20 yr	25 yr
	1	1.09	1.16	1.19	1.21	1.22	1.24	1.25	1.30	1.35	1.57	1.80	2.01	2.21	2.92	2.89		
	2	1.16	1.12	1.13	1.15	1.18	1.20	1.23	1.30	1.37	1.61	1.82	2.01	2.19	2.86	2.87		
	3	1.03	1.18	1.23	1.24	1.25	1.26	1.27	1.30	1.33	1.51	1.73	1.94	2.14	2.92	2.90		
	4	1.10	1.14	1.17	1.18	1.20	1.21	1.23	1.28	1.33	1.53	1.75	1.95	2.14	2.93	2.92		
	5	1.00	1.17	1.23	1.24	1.24	1.25	1.25	1.27	1.30	1.47	1.69	1.92	2.13	2.95	2.94		
	6	0.81	1.18	1.27	1.25	1.23	1.21	1.20	1.16	1.14	1.23	1.52	1.79	2.04	2.95	2.87		
	7	0.80	1.09	1.16	1.14	1.13	1.11	1.10	1.08	1.07	1.21	1.51	1.79	2.04	2.89	2.81		

Year	Month	0 mo	1 mo	2 mo	3 mo	4 mo	5 mo	6 mo	9 mo	1 yr	2 yr	3 yr	4 yr	5 yr	10 yr	15 yr	20 yr	25 yr
	8	0.86	1.07	1.14	1.13	1.12	1.11	1.10	1.09	1.10	1.22	1.47	1.71	1.93	2.83	2.84		
	9	0.88	1.11	1.16	1.14	1.13	1.11	1.10	1.07	1.06	1.20	1.48	1.74	1.98	2.79	2.80		
	10	0.82	1.11	1.17	1.15	1.14	1.13	1.11	1.09	1.09	1.23	1.50	1.74	1.97	2.77	2.80		
	11	0.82	1.16	1.25	1.22	1.20	1.18	1.16	1.13	1.10	1.22	1.48	1.73	1.96	2.76	2.77		
	12	0.93	1.12	1.15	1.15	1.14	1.13	1.12	1.11	1.12	1.24	1.48	1.69	1.90	2.70	2.77		
1950		0 mo	1 mo	2 mo	3 mo	4 mo	5 mo	6 mo	9 mo	1 yr	2 yr	3 yr	4 yr	5 yr	10 yr	15 yr	20 yr	25 yr
	1	0.97	1.15	1.20	1.19	1.17	1.16	1.15	1.13	1.13	1.28	1.55	1.80	2.03	2.77	2.73		
	2	1.00	1.18	1.24	1.22	1.20	1.19	1.17	1.14	1.13	1.27	1.56	1.82	2.06	2.82	2.70		
	3	0.89	1.24	1.32	1.29	1.27	1.24	1.22	1.18	1.15	1.30	1.58	1.85	2.09	2.86	2.71		
	4	0.92	1.26	1.34	1.32	1.30	1.28	1.27	1.23	1.22	1.37	1.63	1.88	2.10	2.91	2.67		
	5	0.93	1.30	1.39	1.36	1.33	1.30	1.28	1.22	1.19	1.33	1.62	1.89	2.13	2.95	2.62		
	6	0.90	1.30	1.38	1.36	1.34	1.32	1.30	1.27	1.25	1.42	1.69	1.94	2.16	2.91	2.60		
	7	0.86	1.39	1.48	1.43	1.39	1.34	1.31	1.22	1.17	1.33	1.64	1.92	2.17	3.01	2.59		
	8	1.00	1.43	1.52	1.48	1.44	1.40	1.37	1.31	1.27	1.43	1.69	1.93	2.15	2.98	2.54		
	9	1.10	1.44	1.52	1.49	1.47	1.45	1.44	1.40	1.39	1.56	1.78	1.98	2.18	2.97	2.58		
	10	0.83	1.46	1.60	1.58	1.57	1.56	1.55	1.53	1.54	1.69	1.88	2.05	2.21	2.92	2.51		
	11	1.07	1.49	1.57	1.55	1.53	1.51	1.50	1.47	1.47	1.66	1.88	2.09	2.28	2.92	2.46		
	12	0.79	1.60	1.77	1.71	1.66	1.61	1.57	1.48	1.44	1.61	1.84	2.06	2.26	3.00	2.42		
1951		0 mo	1 mo	2 mo	3 mo	4 mo	5 mo	6 mo	9 mo	1 yr	2 yr	3 yr	4 yr	5 yr	10 yr	15 yr	20 yr	25 yr
	1	0.80	1.53	1.74	1.70	1.67	1.64	1.61	1.55	1.52	1.65	1.82	1.99	2.16	3.02	2.42		
	2	0.78	1.55	1.76	1.70	1.65	1.61	1.57	1.49	1.46	1.66	1.88	2.09	2.28	3.01	2.38		
	3	1.24	1.60	1.71	1.73	1.75	1.77	1.79	1.84	1.89	2.07	2.19	2.27	2.35	2.70	2.91	2.76	
	4	0.93	1.64	1.81	1.81	1.81	1.81	1.81	1.82	1.85	2.00	2.16	2.30	2.44	2.95	3.04	2.81	
	5	0.96	1.64	1.82	1.83	1.83	1.84	1.85	1.87	1.90	2.05	2.23	2.44	2.62	3.19	2.96	2.08	
	6	0.90	1.75	1.94	1.91	1.89	1.86	1.85	1.81	1.80	1.98	2.19	2.39	2.57	3.15	2.97	2.26	
	7	1.29	1.65	1.76	1.74	1.73	1.72	1.71	1.71	1.74	1.93	2.11	2.28	2.44	3.04	3.13	2.29	
	8	1.32	1.70	1.77	1.74	1.72	1.70	1.69	1.66	1.67	1.88	2.08	2.26	2.43	2.89	2.85	2.82	
	9	1.49	1.68	1.74	1.77	1.79	1.81	1.84	1.89	1.94	2.09	2.23	2.35	2.47	2.93	3.02	2.24	
	10	0.81	1.61	1.89	1.88	1.88	1.88	1.87	1.89	1.91	2.10	2.27	2.43	2.57	3.05	2.99	2.16	
	11	1.05	1.65	1.82	1.81	1.81	1.81	1.81	1.83	1.87	2.07	2.27	2.45	2.61	3.11	3.02	2.39	
	12	1.55	1.82	1.92	1.93	1.94	1.95	1.96	1.99	2.03	2.17	2.32	2.46	2.59	3.01	3.02	2.72	
1952		0 mo	1 mo	2 mo	3 mo	4 mo	5 mo	6 mo	9 mo	1 yr	2 yr	3 yr	4 yr	5 yr	10 yr	15 yr	20 yr	25 yr
	1	0.94	1.63	1.78	1.79	1.80	1.81	1.83	1.86	1.90	2.06	2.23	2.40	2.55	3.07	3.10	2.42	
	2	0.90	1.67	1.81	1.83	1.85	1.87	1.89	1.94	1.99	2.20	2.39	2.57	2.73	3.16	2.96	2.50	
	3	1.10	1.58	1.71	1.73	1.76	1.78	1.80	1.86	1.92	2.14	2.31	2.45	2.58	3.08	3.21	2.44	
	4	1.39	1.73	1.81	1.81	1.82	1.82	1.83	1.85	1.88	2.00	2.15	2.34	2.49	2.95	2.89	2.41	
	5	1.43	1.80	1.87	1.88	1.89	1.90	1.90	1.93	1.95	2.06	2.18	2.31	2.42	2.86	2.99	2.66	
	6	1.65	1.82	1.88	1.90	1.92	1.94	1.96	2.02	2.07	2.23	2.34	2.39	2.44	2.82	3.05	2.53	
	7	1.72	1.87	1.94	1.96	1.98	2.00	2.02	2.09	2.15	2.33	2.44	2.48	2.52	2.74	2.95	2.72	
	8	1.46	1.90	2.02	2.05	2.07	2.09	2.11	2.18	2.23	2.42	2.53	2.57	2.61	2.83	3.05	2.55	
	9	1.06	1.78	2.02	2.04	2.06	2.07	2.09	2.15	2.20	2.39	2.54	2.67	2.78	3.11	2.98	2.71	

Table 13.A.2 (cont.)

1952		0 mo	1 mo	2 mo	3 mo	4 mo	5 mo	6 mo	9 mo	1 yr	2 yr	3 yr	4 yr	5 yr	10 yr	15 yr	20 yr	25 yr
	10	1.32	1.80	1.96	1.98	2.00	2.02	2.04	2.10	2.15	2.33	2.45	2.52	2.59	2.88	3.02	2.81	
	11	1.55	1.97	2.11	2.13	2.14	2.15	2.16	2.20	2.23	2.35	2.42	2.47	2.53	2.88	3.11	2.81	
	12	1.82	2.04	2.12	2.14	2.15	2.17	2.18	2.22	2.26	2.38	2.45	2.49	2.55	2.97	3.28		
1953		0 mo	1 mo	2 mo	3 mo	4 mo	5 mo	6 mo	9 mo	1 yr	2 yr	3 yr	4 yr	5 yr	10 yr	15 yr	20 yr	25 yr
	1	1.63	1.97	2.06	2.07	2.08	2.10	2.11	2.15	2.19	2.35	2.48	2.61	2.72	3.05	3.11		
	2	1.86	2.15	2.22	2.22	2.22	2.23	2.23	2.24	2.26	2.35	2.48	2.64	2.77	3.18	3.23		
	3	1.95	2.02	2.06	2.08	2.10	2.12	2.14	2.19	2.25	2.44	2.59	2.71	2.82	3.19	3.28		
	4	1.78	2.29	2.44	2.45	2.47	2.48	2.49	2.53	2.57	2.71	2.84	2.97	3.07	3.33	3.26	3.29	3.53
	5	1.43	2.33	2.59	2.62	2.64	2.67	2.69	2.76	2.83	3.06	3.24	3.35	3.44	3.48	3.07	2.95	3.33
	6	1.18	1.96	2.31	2.34	2.36	2.38	2.40	2.47	2.52	2.73	2.90	3.02	3.12	3.27	3.05	3.14	3.76
	7	1.72	2.11	2.23	2.26	2.28	2.31	2.33	2.40	2.47	2.71	2.89	3.01	3.11	3.26	3.15	3.52	
	8	1.62	1.93	2.04	2.09	2.14	2.19	2.23	2.36	2.49	2.88	3.11	3.19	3.26	3.31	3.17	3.34	
	9	0.86	1.52	1.82	1.88	1.92	1.97	2.01	2.13	2.23	2.56	2.71	2.72	2.73	2.92	3.29	3.77	
	10	0.65	1.25	1.52	1.58	1.64	1.69	1.75	1.90	2.05	2.49	2.72	2.79	2.84	3.12	3.31	3.33	
	11	1.36	1.50	1.59	1.64	1.68	1.73	1.77	1.89	2.01	2.39	2.64	2.77	2.89	3.26	3.37	3.20	
	12	1.09	1.38	1.52	1.56	1.61	1.65	1.69	1.81	1.91	2.24	2.40	2.47	2.55	2.97	3.30	3.41	
1954		0 mo	1 mo	2 mo	3 mo	4 mo	5 mo	6 mo	9 mo	1 yr	2 yr	3 yr	4 yr	5 yr	10 yr	15 yr	20 yr	25 yr
	1	1.05	0.89	0.90	0.97	1.05	1.12	1.19	1.39	1.57	2.12	2.40	2.55	2.68	3.03	3.17	3.24	
	2	0.84	0.92	0.98	1.01	1.05	1.09	1.12	1.23	1.34	1.78	2.23	2.62	2.89	2.77	2.64	3.13	
	3	0.99	0.98	1.00	1.03	1.06	1.10	1.13	1.23	1.34	1.75	2.17	2.53	2.79	2.82	2.77	3.08	
	4	0.62	0.72	0.78	0.84	0.89	0.95	1.00	1.14	1.27	1.64	1.96	2.30	2.62	2.91	2.81	3.01	
	5	0.51	0.67	0.74	0.80	0.85	0.91	0.96	1.13	1.29	1.92	2.42	2.73	2.90	2.90	2.78	2.99	
	6	0.67	0.59	0.61	0.67	0.73	0.79	0.84	1.01	1.17	1.71	2.15	2.53	2.83	2.84	2.57	2.94	
	7	0.64	0.72	0.76	0.79	0.82	0.86	0.29	1.01	1.13	1.73	2.25	2.59	2.78	2.77	2.60	2.83	
	8	1.30	0.96	0.87	0.90	0.94	0.97	1.01	1.12	1.23	1.72	2.17	2.57	2.88	2.79	2.52	2.87	
	9	0.90	0.91	0.96	1.03	1.09	1.15	1.20	1.36	1.50	1.87	2.15	2.50	2.83	2.73	2.53	2.96	
	10	0.72	0.95	1.06	1.12	1.17	1.23	1.28	1.43	1.58	2.07	2.43	2.63	2.73	2.70	2.70	2.93	
	11	0.86	0.99	1.07	1.12	1.17	1.21	1.26	1.40	1.54	2.08	2.49	2.68	2.75	2.91	2.87	2.80	
	12	0.92	0.98	1.04	1.10	1.17	1.23	1.29	1.47	1.64	2.22	2.59	2.72	2.74	2.86	2.91	2.69	
1955		0 mo	1 mo	2 mo	3 mo	4 mo	5 mo	6 mo	9 mo	1 yr	2 yr	3 yr	4 yr	5 yr	10 yr	15 yr	20 yr	25 yr
	1	1.19	1.04	1.08	1.19	1.29	1.39	1.48	1.73	1.95	2.38	2.53	2.66	2.79	3.14	2.98	2.82	2.83
	2	0.91	1.33	1.51	1.60	1.70	1.78	1.87	2.09	2.27	2.63	2.63	2.70	2.79	3.07	3.04	2.98	2.98
	3	1.33	1.34	1.41	1.51	1.61	1.71	1.80	2.04	2.24	2.61	2.66	2.73	2.80	3.02	2.97	2.91	2.94
	4	1.44	1.55	1.65	1.74	1.82	1.90	1.98	2.18	2.35	2.64	2.67	2.74	2.84	3.09	2.95	2.81	2.81
	5	0.91	1.36	1.60	1.69	1.77	1.85	1.92	2.13	2.29	2.62	2.74	2.81	2.85	2.97	2.90	2.86	2.90
	6	1.04	1.47	1.68	1.77	1.85	1.93	2.01	2.22	2.39	2.75	2.89	2.96	3.00	3.06	2.89	2.76	2.77

		0 mo	1 mo	2 mo	3 mo	4 mo	5 mo	6 mo	9 mo	1 yr	2 yr	3 yr	4 yr	5 yr	10 yr	15 yr	20 yr	25 yr
	7	1.56	1.77	1.90	1.99	2.07	2.15	2.22	2.43	2.59	2.92	3.04	3.10	3.12	3.13	2.94	2.80	2.78
	8	1.83	2.05	2.19	2.26	2.32	2.39	2.45	2.60	2.74	3.00	3.06	3.06	3.05	2.99	2.92	2.90	2.94
	9	2.16	2.13	2.14	2.18	2.21	2.24	2.27	2.37	2.46	2.81	3.02	3.05	3.03	2.96	2.94	2.94	2.99
	10	2.03	2.07	2.12	2.18	2.23	2.28	2.32	2.45	2.56	2.76	2.83	2.86	2.88	2.93	2.92	2.93	2.99
	11	1.80	2.36	2.59	2.63	2.67	2.71	2.74	2.83	2.90	2.91	2.86	2.87	2.89	2.97	2.97	2.98	3.01
	12	2.34	2.50	2.59	2.63	2.68	2.72	2.76	2.85	2.92	2.93	2.90	2.91	2.93	2.97	2.88	2.82	2.85
1956		0 mo	1 mo	2 mo	3 mo	4 mo	5 mo	6 mo	9 mo	1 yr	2 yr	3 yr	4 yr	5 yr	10 yr	15 yr	20 yr	25 yr
	1	2.24	2.31	2.36	2.38	2.41	2.43	2.45	2.52	2.58	2.74	2.83	2.86	2.88	2.91	2.88	2.88	2.94
	2	1.60	2.26	2.45	2.49	2.53	2.57	2.60	2.68	2.74	2.80	2.82	2.85	2.87	2.93	2.91	2.90	2.95
	3	2.13	2.27	2.39	2.49	2.59	2.69	2.77	2.99	3.15	3.20	3.11	3.10	3.10	3.05	2.90	2.80	2.81
	4	2.61	2.65	2.73	2.82	2.91	3.00	3.07	3.26	3.39	3.30	3.06	3.01	3.00	2.99	3.03	3.08	3.12
	5	2.13	2.58	2.77	2.81	2.85	2.88	2.91	2.99	3.03	3.01	2.95	2.91	2.88	2.84	2.97	3.09	3.16
	6	2.24	2.41	2.51	2.57	2.62	2.67	2.72	2.84	2.93	3.04	3.07	3.05	3.02	2.91	2.90	2.90	2.95
	7	1.88	2.26	2.51	2.65	2.79	2.91	3.02	3.29	3.45	3.43	3.35	3.29	3.23	3.01	2.93	2.91	2.95
	8	2.12	2.62	2.85	2.99	3.11	3.22	3.33	3.56	3.70	3.69	3.63	3.54	3.45	3.13	3.03	2.97	2.99
	9	2.50	2.87	3.06	3.16	3.24	3.32	3.40	3.57	3.69	3.57	3.37	3.31	3.30	3.17	2.93	2.78	2.82
	10	2.27	2.81	3.09	3.19	3.28	3.36	3.44	3.58	3.62	3.55	3.53	3.55	3.55	3.23	2.91	2.95	3.57
	11	2.53	3.04	3.34	3.53	3.69	3.81	3.90	3.96	3.90	3.69	3.57	3.51	3.46	3.26	3.12	3.09	3.25
	12	3.10	3.10	3.40	3.71	3.93	4.05	4.07	3.97	3.88	3.64	3.62	3.70	3.75	3.60	3.33	3.08	2.94
1957		0 mo	1 mo	2 mo	3 mo	4 mo	5 mo	6 mo	9 mo	1 yr	2 yr	3 yr	4 yr	5 yr	10 yr	15 yr	20 yr	25 yr
	1	3.05	3.09	3.19	3.27	3.32	3.34	3.34	3.31	3.28	3.21	3.23	3.26	3.27	3.06	2.95	3.25	4.28
	2	2.39	3.33	3.47	3.52	3.55	3.56	3.56	3.52	3.48	3.38	3.35	3.36	3.36	3.25	3.14	3.10	3.23
	3	2.81	2.96	3.08	3.18	3.27	3.35	3.43	3.57	3.61	3.47	3.40	3.40	3.40	3.17	2.93	3.12	4.03
	4	3.05	3.01	3.09	3.21	3.31	3.41	3.49	3.66	3.71	3.61	3.57	3.59	3.60	3.27	2.99	3.25	4.48
	5	3.14	3.27	3.35	3.40	3.45	3.49	3.53	3.61	3.64	3.65	3.71	3.79	3.84	3.38	2.92	3.07	4.35
	6	2.81	3.31	3.52	3.61	3.69	3.76	3.82	3.90	3.87	3.72	3.77	3.98	4.13	3.51	2.78	2.99	4.94
	7	2.66	3.38	3.63	3.72	3.80	3.87	3.92	3.99	3.95	3.84	3.88	4.06	4.16	3.37	2.77	3.17	5.44
	8	2.50	3.52	3.86	4.03	4.18	4.28	4.35	4.35	4.16	3.64	3.54	3.81	3.98	3.40	2.95	3.36	5.40
	9	2.78	3.60	3.98	4.09	4.17	4.25	4.32	4.44	4.45	4.02	3.78	3.82	3.97	3.80	3.03	3.03	4.31
	10	3.10	3.58	3.82	3.91	3.98	4.05	4.10	4.20	4.22	3.99	3.86	3.86	3.90	3.74	3.37	3.32	3.87
	11	2.06	3.11	3.55	3.56	3.56	3.55	3.55	3.54	3.53	3.49	3.43	3.32	3.23	3.56	4.34	3.63	0.74
	12	2.66	2.78	2.82	2.81	2.80	2.79	2.77	2.75	2.74	2.79	2.86	2.96	3.06	3.43	3.49	3.24	
1958		0 mo	1 mo	2 mo	3 mo	4 mo	5 mo	6 mo	9 mo	1 yr	2 yr	3 yr	4 yr	5 yr	10 yr	15 yr	20 yr	25 yr
	1	1.53	1.41	1.48	1.68	1.87	2.05	2.20	2.59	2.83	2.98	3.06	3.17	3.28	3.54	3.39	3.41	3.71
	2	1.10	1.19	1.34	1.49	1.63	1.76	1.87	2.15	2.31	2.65	2.91	3.09	3.24	3.57	3.45	3.42	3.53
	3	0.94	1.04	1.17	1.31	1.45	1.58	1.70	2.01	2.27	2.68	2.85	2.97	3.06	3.43	3.68	3.76	3.61
	4	1.18	1.14	1.18	1.26	1.33	1.40	1.46	1.66	1.84	2.39	2.74	2.95	3.06	3.41	3.51	3.55	3.50
	5	0.00	0.55	0.84	1.00	1.14	1.28	1.41	1.74	1.98	2.34	2.59	2.86	3.12	3.66	3.38	3.20	3.21
	6	0.84	0.69	0.71	0.87	1.02	1.17	1.31	1.70	2.03	2.82	2.92	3.03	3.19	3.65	3.54	3.43	3.35
	7	0.54	0.85	1.05	1.17	1.28	1.39	1.50	1.81	2.10	3.00	3.52	3.64	3.54	3.58	4.00	4.13	3.76

Table 13.A.2 (cont.)

1958		0 mo	1 mo	2 mo	3 mo	4 mo	5 mo	6 mo	9 mo	1 yr	2 yr	3 yr	4 yr	5 yr	10 yr	15 yr	20 yr	25 yr
	8	1.35	2.30	2.68	2.78	2.87	2.96	3.05	3.28	3.48	3.92	3.95	3.94	3.90	3.75	3.68	3.67	3.79
	9	1.00	2.73	3.48	3.52	3.52	3.51	3.52	3.52	3.55	3.76	3.96	3.96	3.88	3.66	3.66	3.79	4.16
	10	1.08	2.43	2.98	3.04	3.10	3.15	3.20	3.35	3.48	3.80	3.91	3.91	3.85	3.66	3.63	3.71	4.04
	11	0.83	2.78	3.55	3.56	3.55	3.54	3.54	3.53	3.53	3.64	3.75	3.74	3.71	3.65	3.70	3.80	3.96
	12	2.13	2.66	2.93	3.06	3.16	3.24	3.29	3.41	3.53	3.89	4.07	4.11	4.08	3.87	3.64	3.58	3.93
1959		0 mo	1 mo	2 mo	3 mo	4 mo	5 mo	6 mo	9 mo	1 yr	2 yr	3 yr	4 yr	5 yr	10 yr	15 yr	20 yr	25 yr
	1	2.32	2.61	2.92	3.19	3.38	3.48	3.55	3.72	3.87	4.21	4.22	4.16	4.09	3.94	4.07	4.08	3.88
	2	2.04	2.68	3.09	3.32	3.45	3.49	3.53	3.62	3.70	3.91	3.97	3.90	3.83	3.90	4.27	4.42	4.09
	3	2.44	2.70	3.04	3.43	3.67	3.77	3.80	3.90	3.98	4.10	4.12	4.08	4.02	3.95	3.99	4.02	4.06
	4	2.78	2.75	3.02	3.43	3.68	3.76	3.80	3.90	3.99	4.27	4.40	4.40	4.35	4.09	3.81	3.68	3.92
	5	2.80	2.76	3.10	3.78	4.20	4.28	4.23	4.11	4.05	4.24	4.43	4.38	4.30	4.03	3.91	3.85	4.02
	6	2.70	2.89	3.32	3.96	4.37	4.43	4.34	4.16	4.10	4.57	4.75	4.53	4.32	3.97	3.98	3.97	3.96
	7	1.97	2.79	3.39	3.85	4.34	4.79	5.10	5.07	4.68	4.17	4.82	4.90	4.68	3.91	3.66	3.59	3.90
	8	3.14	3.78	4.21	4.53	4.77	4.92	4.97	4.73	4.50	4.36	4.89	4.93	4.73	3.97	3.62	3.52	3.99
	9	3.43	3.87	4.48	5.22	5.67	5.68	5.46	4.92	4.55	4.60	4.79	4.68	4.55	4.01	3.67	3.53	3.87
	10	2.14	3.99	4.62	4.60	4.70	4.88	4.95	4.66	4.39	4.19	4.98	5.15	4.86	3.88	3.60	3.53	3.91
	11	2.31	4.49	5.10	5.12	5.15	5.18	5.17	5.05	4.94	4.70	4.69	4.63	4.53	4.08	3.73	3.59	3.93
	12	4.02	4.21	4.80	5.36	5.38	5.27	5.21	5.11	5.02	4.78	4.70	4.69	4.70	4.39	3.85	3.61	4.11
1960		0 mo	1 mo	2 mo	3 mo	4 mo	5 mo	6 mo	9 mo	1 yr	2 yr	3 yr	4 yr	5 yr	10 yr	15 yr	20 yr	25 yr
	1	3.28	3.81	4.42	4.91	5.04	5.03	4.99	4.85	4.75	4.70	4.81	4.84	4.81	4.07	3.77	5.18	
	2	3.58	4.04	4.53	4.72	4.56	4.40	4.36	4.42	4.47	4.68	4.77	4.64	4.48	4.03	3.91	3.95	4.40
	3	2.40	2.94	3.32	3.57	3.71	3.78	3.82	3.84	3.86	4.07	4.23	4.22	4.18	4.07	4.02	3.97	3.96
	4	2.89	3.04	3.11	3.29	3.72	4.27	4.66	4.84	4.57	4.36	4.74	4.71	4.49	4.10	4.18	4.18	4.05
	5	1.82	3.20	3.52	3.41	3.56	3.89	4.16	4.47	4.40	4.39	4.53	4.41	4.21	4.01	4.31	4.31	3.71
	6	1.25	2.02	2.51	2.79	3.02	3.20	3.36	3.74	3.96	4.36	4.14	4.12	4.29	4.26	3.59	3.32	3.81
	7	1.65	2.02	2.40	2.76	2.96	3.04	3.10	3.23	3.32	3.50	3.55	3.72	3.95	4.11	3.62	3.42	3.73
	8	1.45	2.42	2.99	3.23	3.23	3.04	2.90	2.86	3.07	3.61	3.77	3.92	4.06	4.09	3.73	3.62	4.00
	9	2.69	2.15	2.58	3.27	3.44	3.18	2.92	2.61	2.85	3.64	3.94	4.05	4.05	4.00	3.91	3.85	3.90
	10	1.22	1.96	2.51	2.86	3.04	3.06	3.05	3.09	3.20	3.63	3.96	4.13	4.15	4.09	3.91	3.78	3.77
	11	1.24	2.27	2.84	3.01	3.09	3.11	3.14	3.24	3.38	3.83	4.11	4.23	4.23	4.14	3.96	3.80	3.74
	12	1.87	2.17	2.41	2.57	2.63	2.61	2.61	2.72	2.88	3.41	3.77	3.93	3.99	4.06	3.95	3.85	3.81
1961		0 mo	1 mo	2 mo	3 mo	4 mo	5 mo	6 mo	9 mo	1 yr	2 yr	3 yr	4 yr	5 yr	10 yr	15 yr	20 yr	25 yr
	1	1.88	2.19	2.44	2.64	2.74	2.77	2.80	3.00	3.22	3.78	3.97	4.03	4.05	4.06	4.01	3.96	3.93
	2	2.47	2.52	2.69	2.87	2.97	3.01	3.05	3.15	3.24	3.55	3.75	3.83	3.87	3.95	3.94	3.90	3.83
	3	2.02	2.35	2.54	2.67	2.81	2.94	3.03	3.07	3.11	3.42	3.85	4.04	4.07	4.05	3.89	3.72	3.62
	4	1.42	2.32	2.49	2.35	2.52	2.87	3.11	3.21	3.19	3.35	3.70	3.88	3.97	4.02	3.85	3.68	3.56

		0 mo	1 mo	2 mo	3 mo	4 mo	5 mo	6 mo	9 mo	1 yr	2 yr	3 yr	4 yr	5 yr	10 yr	15 yr	20 yr	25 yr
	5	2.10	2.35	2.49	2.57	2.72	2.90	3.04	3.24	3.33	3.62	3.80	3.93	4.01	4.01	3.76	3.54	3.45
	6	1.80	2.30	2.45	2.47	2.66	2.89	3.06	3.28	3.43	3.85	4.00	4.07	4.09	4.05	3.95	3.84	3.77
	7	1.12	2.23	2.56	2.51	2.65	2.88	3.05	3.27	3.39	3.91	4.34	4.36	4.27	4.05	3.90	3.77	3.72
	3	1.74	2.30	2.52	2.72	2.96	3.18	3.31	3.40	3.48	3.91	4.24	4.26	4.22	4.07	3.96	3.99	4.36
	9	1.89	2.12	2.51	2.89	3.07	3.11	3.16	3.30	3.42	3.83	4.05	4.05	4.02	4.02	4.09	4.22	4.50
	10	1.74	2.16	2.52	2.80	2.98	3.08	3.14	3.25	3.34	3.73	4.02	4.09	4.12	4.02	3.91	4.04	4.68
	11	2.00	2.51	2.78	2.89	2.98	3.05	3.11	3.27	3.40	3.81	4.06	4.20	4.29	4.12	3.83	3.87	4.65
	12	2.32	2.64	2.90	3.06	3.12	3.15	3.20	3.36	3.49	3.84	4.04	4.21	4.34	4.20	3.88	3.87	4.62

1962		0 mo	1 mo	2 mo	3 mo	4 mo	5 mo	6 mo	9 mo	1 yr	2 yr	3 yr	4 yr	5 yr	10 yr	15 yr	20 yr	25 yr
	1	2.20	2.72	2.89	2.97	3.10	3.22	3.30	3.48	3.63	3.99	4.19	4.31	4.38	4.22	3.92	3.87	4.39
	2	2.24	2.69	2.92	3.03	3.09	3.12	3.15	3.24	3.34	3.66	3.94	4.19	4.38	4.36	4.05	4.00	4.51
	3	2.65	2.66	2.94	3.16	3.04	2.78	2.70	2.91	3.11	3.63	3.89	4.04	4.12	4.19	4.09	4.00	3.95
	4	2.67	2.72	2.81	2.91	2.97	2.98	3.00	3.12	3.28	3.68	3.82	3.97	4.12	4.18	3.99	3.86	3.85
	5	2.10	2.73	2.91	2.81	2.81	2.89	2.96	3.10	3.15	3.48	3.96	4.20	4.24	4.16	3.96	3.83	3.85
	6	2.98	2.90	2.95	3.05	3.06	3.02	2.99	3.06	3.23	3.76	4.06	4.20	4.22	4.16	4.00	3.88	3.90
	7	2.53	2.82	3.02	3.14	3.23	3.30	3.36	3.44	3.47	3.75	4.11	4.28	4.31	4.20	4.07	4.22	4.92
	8	2.52	2.78	2.96	3.08	3.17	3.22	3.25	3.20	3.13	3.41	3.98	4.23	4.29	4.21	4.03	3.98	4.23
	9	2.68	2.72	2.91	3.10	3.11	2.98	2.90	2.92	3.01	3.51	4.02	4.27	4.30	4.18	4.00	3.93	4.08
	10	2.38	2.67	2.87	2.98	3.00	2.94	2.88	2.86	3.03	3.59	3.92	4.14	4.26	4.20	3.90	3.80	4.10
	11	2.35	2.93	3.12	3.04	2.99	2.99	2.99	3.04	3.14	3.50	3.76	3.99	4.18	4.22	3.86	3.81	4.35
	12	2.98	2.92	2.97	3.07	3.08	3.01	2.96	2.99	3.17	3.58	3.65	3.79	4.05	4.20	3.80	3.84	4.66

1963		0 mo	1 mo	2 mo	3 mo	4 mo	5 mo	6 mo	9 mo	1 yr	2 yr	3 yr	4 yr	5 yr	10 yr	15 yr	20 yr	25 yr
	1	2.95	2.93	3.01	3.11	3.09	3.00	2.94	2.96	3.08	3.52	3.87	4.10	4.19	4.12	3.93	3.99	4.53
	2	2.82	2.88	2.99	3.07	3.02	2.92	2.85	2.92	3.09	3.62	3.97	4.18	4.26	4.23	4.06	3.95	4.00
	3	1.83	2.56	3.21	3.60	3.57	3.28	3.05	2.77	2.96	3.62	4.00	4.22	4.31	4.26	4.04	3.94	4.07
	4	2.83	2.88	2.99	3.10	3.15	3.12	3.10	3.11	3.23	3.69	3.94	4.10	4.20	4.28	4.17	4.09	4.09
	5	2.91	3.00	3.11	3.21	3.22	3.15	3.10	3.08	3.23	3.75	4.01	4.16	4.22	4.22	4.12	4.04	4.05
	6	2.99	2.98	3.09	3.21	3.22	3.16	3.11	3.10	3.25	3.77	4.08	4.25	4.28	4.19	4.09	4.03	4.05
	7	2.88	3.21	3.43	3.54	3.58	3.54	3.50	3.49	3.56	3.83	4.05	4.16	4.18	4.11	4.03	3.97	3.97
	8	3.08	3.41	3.55	3.57	3.60	3.63	3.66	3.68	3.65	3.72	4.06	4.26	4.26	4.09	3.99	3.93	4.02
	9	3.53	3.38	3.46	3.64	3.70	3.68	3.64	3.60	3.62	3.81	4.08	4.26	4.31	4.18	4.00	3.98	4.28
	10	3.25	3.47	3.64	3.76	3.79	3.76	3.71	3.68	3.73	3.93	4.13	4.28	4.36	4.25	3.99	3.93	4.24
	11	3.01	3.50	3.75	3.82	3.84	3.81	3.79	3.77	3.79	3.90	4.06	4.18	4.25	4.23	4.11	4.07	4.24
	12	3.52	3.52	3.61	3.77	3.85	3.87	3.88	3.91	3.94	4.06	4.15	4.21	4.25	4.27	4.21	4.15	4.14

1964		0 mo	1 mo	2 mo	3 mo	4 mo	5 mo	6 mo	9 mo	1 yr	2 yr	3 yr	4 yr	5 yr	10 yr	15 yr	20 yr	25 yr
	1	3.35	3.49	3.61	3.71	3.78	3.81	3.84	3.89	3.92	4.03	4.11	4.21	4.30	4.31	4.12	4.01	4.09
	2	3.51	3.56	3.71	3.88	3.95	3.96	3.96	3.99	4.02	4.10	4.16	4.24	4.32	4.30	4.10	3.99	4.09
	3	3.57	3.49	3.62	3.85	3.95	3.95	3.96	4.05	4.14	4.29	4.27	4.28	4.31	4.29	4.17	4.08	4.07
	4	3.18	3.44	3.61	3.71	3.79	3.85	3.90	3.97	4.02	4.20	4.31	4.34	4.30	4.23	4.21	4.17	4.13
	5	3.00	3.52	3.68	3.63	3.69	3.83	3.94	4.01	4.01	4.05	4.13	4.22	4.29	4.27	4.10	4.01	4.13

Table 13.A.2 (cont.)

1964	0 mo	1 mo	2 mo	3 mo	4 mo	5 mo	6 mo	9 mo	1 yr	2 yr	3 yr	4 yr	5 yr	10 yr	15 yr	20 yr	25 yr
6	3.28	3.59	3.60	3.54	3.63	3.78	3.87	3.88	3.86	3.99	4.19	4.28	4.28	4.21	4.11	4.07	4.16
7	3.02	3.54	3.61	3.60	3.73	3.86	3.93	3.82	3.73	3.94	4.29	4.41	4.39	4.28	4.17	4.11	4.16
8	3.21	3.55	3.65	3.68	3.77	3.89	3.95	3.89	3.84	4.00	4.22	4.32	4.36	4.31	4.18	4.09	4.11
9	3.50	3.56	3.68	3.81	3.91	3.98	4.00	3.95	3.90	3.99	4.12	4.22	4.29	4.30	4.20	4.13	4.15
10	3.39	3.52	3.70	3.88	3.97	3.99	3.99	3.96	3.94	4.02	4.12	4.20	4.26	4.26	4.17	4.10	4.12
11	3.37	3.85	4.07	4.13	4.22	4.30	4.31	4.21	4.14	4.12	4.14	4.17	4.20	4.23	4.21	4.16	4.10
12	3.13	3.90	4.08	4.07	4.12	4.14	4.11	3.99	3.93	4.07	4.19	4.25	4.29	4.30	4.22	4.13	4.07
1965	0 mo	1 mo	2 mo	3 mo	4 mo	5 mo	6 mo	9 mo	1 yr	2 yr	3 yr	4 yr	5 yr	10 yr	15 yr	20 yr	25 yr
1	3.81	3.89	3.95	4.05	4.19	4.25	4.20	3.97	3.87	4.02	4.15	4.22	4.27	4.28	4.21	4.14	4.10
2	3.61	4.06	4.14	4.13	4.22	4.27	4.25	4.14	4.07	4.03	4.09	4.20	4.29	4.29	4.18	4.10	4.13
3	3.60	3.99	4.08	4.06	4.14	4.21	4.21	4.09	4.02	4.10	4.18	4.22	4.25	4.25	4.20	4.15	4.15
4	3.82	3.94	4.04	4.11	4.15	4.16	4.14	4.06	4.02	4.12	4.19	4.22	4.23	4.24	4.21	4.17	4.14
5	3.74	3.96	4.00	4.01	4.08	4.13	4.14	4.11	4.09	4.08	4.14	4.23	4.31	4.29	4.18	4.11	4.15
6	3.71	3.85	3.91	3.94	3.99	4.03	4.01	3.90	3.88	4.08	4.20	4.25	4.29	4.27	4.20	4.14	4.13
7	3.81	3.83	3.92	4.03	4.07	4.07	4.06	4.01	4.03	4.18	4.26	4.27	4.28	4.26	4.21	4.17	4.16
8	3.70	3.90	4.00	4.08	4.22	4.31	4.28	4.10	4.07	4.21	4.29	4.32	4.34	4.29	4.21	4.18	4.24
9	3.93	3.99	4.19	4.37	4.45	4.47	4.47	4.42	4.39	4.30	4.33	4.42	4.48	4.37	4.20	4.13	4.25
10	3.85	4.00	4.26	4.44	4.46	4.44	4.43	4.41	4.41	4.42	4.47	4.51	4.53	4.37	4.18	4.09	4.20
11	3.67	4.14	4.33	4.40	4.54	4.62	4.59	4.49	4.51	4.60	4.61	4.59	4.58	4.47	4.33	4.19	4.09
12	4.31	4.55	4.62	4.77	5.06	5.20	5.16	5.08	5.13	5.21	5.00	4.76	4.58	4.39	4.30	4.23	4.22
1966	0 mo	1 mo	2 mo	3 mo	4 mo	5 mo	6 mo	9 mo	1 yr	2 yr	3 yr	4 yr	5 yr	10 yr	15 yr	20 yr	25 yr
1	4.50	4.58	4.85	4.99	4.98	4.95	4.93	4.94	5.04	5.27	5.11	4.90	4.74	4.44	4.26	4.23	4.51
2	4.24	4.70	4.86	4.98	5.16	5.27	5.29	5.31	5.28	5.22	5.32	5.40	5.41	4.75	4.16	4.09	5.01
3	4.19	4.57	4.71	4.85	5.07	5.18	5.15	5.09	5.08	5.03	4.96	4.89	4.82	4.57	4.37	4.33	4.59
4	4.44	4.75	4.71	4.76	5.02	5.16	5.12	5.00	5.04	5.14	4.98	4.97	5.01	4.70	4.37	4.23	4.47
5	4.21	4.72	4.82	4.79	5.14	5.40	5.31	5.10	5.23	5.49	5.04	4.88	4.84	4.67	4.51	4.43	4.54
6	4.22	4.68	4.65	4.72	5.11	5.28	5.17	5.10	5.39	5.76	5.16	5.05	5.06	4.83	4.54	4.33	4.34
7	4.09	4.32	4.91	4.94	5.36	5.53	5.43	5.28	5.41	5.68	5.55	5.44	5.34	4.77	4.29	4.14	4.66
8	4.21	5.22	5.29	5.34	6.31	6.87	6.55	5.96	6.31	6.65	5.91	5.56	5.38	4.92	4.56	4.42	4.71
9	5.00	5.37	5.61	5.87	6.16	6.31	6.23	5.98	5.85	5.54	5.34	5.03	4.77	4.75	4.73	4.53	4.08
10	4.24	5.32	5.63	5.77	6.06	6.14	5.99	5.69	5.62	5.43	5.32	5.15	4.98	4.60	4.31	4.24	4.62
11	3.66	5.37	5.75	5.42	5.50	5.64	5.56	5.48	5.74	5.71	5.00	5.07	5.33	4.89	4.40	4.21	4.64
12	4.60	4.81	5.07	5.25	5.27	5.21	5.09	4.96	4.99	4.98	4.85	4.70	4.60	4.57	4.53	4.48	4.43
1967	0 mo	1 mo	2 mo	3 mo	4 mo	5 mo	6 mo	9 mo	1 yr	2 yr	3 yr	4 yr	5 yr	10 yr	15 yr	20 yr	25 yr
1	4.37	4.65	4.65	4.60	4.67	4.69	4.65	4.62	4.67	4.75	4.72	4.66	4.61	4.49	4.39	4.35	4.44
2	3.77	4.78	4.70	4.56	4.74	4.78	4.67	4.64	4.94	5.05	4.56	4.69	4.96	4.85	4.64	4.44	4.34
3	3.91	4.11	4.26	4.28	4.18	4.12	4.10	4.11	4.20	4.41	4.44	4.61	4.77	4.76	4.67	4.54	4.36

		0 mo	1 mo	2 mo	3 mo	4 mo	5 mo	6 mo	9 mo	1 yr	2 yr	3 yr	4 yr	5 yr	10 yr	15 yr	20 yr	25 yr
	4	3.01	3.91	3.87	3.86	4.08	4.17	4.12	4.14	4.41	4.98	4.74	4.92	5.20	5.09	4.86	4.57	4.24
	5	3.20	3.46	3.54	3.74	4.17	4.35	4.26	4.16	4.50	5.22	4.55	4.76	5.27	5.10	4.87	4.71	4.77
	6	3.32	4.07	4.19	4.33	4.79	5.31	5.63	5.64	5.48	5.29	5.40	5.73	5.81	5.10	4.57	4.61	5.78
	7	3.29	4.16	4.34	4.65	5.28	5.63	5.67	5.56	5.37	4.95	5.02	5.42	5.69	5.27	4.88	4.73	5.15
	8	3.49	4.31	4.81	5.09	5.33	5.53	5.66	5.68	5.60	5.37	5.37	5.58	5.61	5.19	4.88	4.91	5.67
	9	4.34	4.25	4.72	5.37	5.73	5.82	5.84	5.63	5.45	5.38	5.51	5.70	5.71	5.32	4.98	4.88	5.33
	10	3.80	4.51	4.87	5.14	5.64	6.13	6.12	5.70	5.67	5.72	5.63	5.77	5.89	5.56	5.24	5.20	5.89
	11	3.57	4.87	5.51	5.68	5.99	6.39	6.53	5.85	5.40	5.66	5.88	5.94	5.94	5.78	5.60	5.58	
	12	3.90	4.90	5.58	5.99	6.25	6.38	6.40	6.04	5.81	5.92	5.83	5.61	5.61	5.86	5.86	5.37	4.07
1968		0 mo	1 mo	2 mo	3 mo	4 mo	5 mo	6 mo	9 mo	1 yr	2 yr	3 yr	4 yr	5 yr	10 yr	15 yr	20 yr	25 yr
	1	4.64	4.84	5.06	5.26	5.36	5.42	5.51	5.77	5.85	5.61	5.65	5.83	5.85	5.70	5.42	5.02	4.55
	2	4.37	5.11	5.30	5.39	5.54	5.63	5.64	5.67	5.71	5.84	5.82	5.65	5.63	5.70	5.62	5.28	
	3	4.52	5.27	5.48	5.49	5.59	5.72	5.81	5.91	5.98	6.06	5.97	5.86	5.90	6.13	6.03	5.28	
	4	5.06	5.56	5.77	5.85	5.95	6.05	6.10	6.07	6.04	6.16	6.13	5.97	5.91	5.71	5.44	5.16	4.99
	5	5.20	5.85	5.98	6.04	6.30	6.44	6.39	6.23	6.22	6.01	5.57	5.82	6.08	5.90	5.48	4.90	4.25
	6	5.27	5.33	5.47	5.67	5.88	6.09	6.21	6.20	6.13	5.78	5.68	5.76	5.77	5.59	5.35	5.10	4.94
	7	4.92	5.24	5.29	5.37	5.64	5.75	5.65	5.44	5.49	5.53	5.51	5.55	5.58	5.49	5.34	5.13	4.88
	8	4.60	5.37	5.38	5.26	5.56	5.71	5.61	5.38	5.33	5.38	5.60	5.66	5.68	5.50	5.27	5.05	4.92
	9	5.13	5.26	5.31	5.40	5.61	5.71	5.59	5.32	5.39	5.54	5.50	5.62	5.71	5.79	5.65	5.18	4.24
	10	5.25	5.44	5.75	5.86	5.75	5.71	5.75	5.75	5.65	5.54	5.62	5.71	5.79	6.03	5.96	5.36	3.93
	11	4.32	5.64	5.92	5.85	5.92	6.01	6.05	5.98	5.68	5.48	5.81	5.87	5.94	6.33	6.25	5.23	2.77
	12	5.98	6.27	6.40	6.51	6.77	6.95	6.91	6.65	6.54	6.56	6.36	6.20	6.23	6.54	6.52	5.85	
1969		0 mo	1 mo	2 mo	3 mo	4 mo	5 mo	6 mo	9 mo	1 yr	2 yr	3 yr	4 yr	5 yr	10 yr	15 yr	20 yr	25 yr
	1	5.87	6.06	6.48	6.78	6.78	6.70	6.62	6.44	6.34	6.24	6.13	6.10	6.18	6.67	6.88	6.42	
	2	5.34	6.31	6.52	6.58	6.79	6.89	6.81	6.41	6.31	6.95	6.56	6.02	5.98	6.56	6.73	5.92	
	3	4.66	6.35	6.44	6.07	6.27	6.61	6.64	6.33	6.17	6.25	6.30	6.33	6.39	6.67	6.62	5.85	3.92
	4	6.51	5.84	5.94	6.22	6.30	6.28	6.28	6.33	6.38	6.57	6.48	6.31	6.26	6.28	6.16	5.83	5.28
	5	5.83	6.10	6.33	6.52	6.70	6.83	6.87	6.70	6.65	7.07	6.73	6.28	6.23	6.76	6.85	5.87	
	6	5.89	6.53	6.62	6.69	7.50	8.44	8.89	8.08	7.41	7.28	6.78	6.33	6.23	6.18	6.06	5.98	
	7	5.54	7.30	7.56	7.43	7.61	7.90	8.00	7.82	7.68	7.16	6.49	6.08	6.05	6.15	6.06	5.64	
	8	6.84	7.18	7.06	7.05	7.54	8.00	8.08	7.63	7.43	7.16	6.74	6.45	6.35	5.90	5.54	5.95	
	9	7.10	7.01	7.24	7.62	7.85	7.97	8.02	8.10	8.11	7.78	7.50	7.47	7.33	6.07	4.98	5.80	
	10	6.22	7.05	7.20	7.44	8.05	8.19	7.91	7.22	6.84	7.46	7.27	6.56	6.36	6.38	6.13	5.58	
	11	6.00	7.60	8.09	8.29	8.51	8.50	8.28	7.60	7.09	7.61	7.36	6.77	6.66	6.80	6.46	5.25	
	12	5.90	8.33	8.77	8.16	8.35	8.61	8.37	7.48	7.33	8.71	7.81	7.11	7.01	6.65	5.93	5.24	
1970		0 mo	1 mo	2 mo	3 mo	4 mo	5 mo	6 mo	9 mo	1 yr	2 yr	3 yr	4 yr	5 yr	10 yr	15 yr	20 yr	25 yr
	1	6.95	8.11	8.22	8.15	8.17	8.09	7.95	7.82	7.93	7.95	7.93	7.89	7.70	6.14	4.97	6.62	
	2	6.10	7.10	7.19	7.11	7.00	6.88	6.79	6.76	6.98	7.42	7.29	7.02	6.86	6.08	5.41	6.09	
	3	6.64	6.30	6.49	6.80	6.78	6.60	6.58	6.73	6.85	7.21	7.36	7.31	7.08	6.22	8.02		
	4	6.29	6.77	7.32	7.67	7.66	7.57	7.59	7.73	7.82	7.95	7.94	7.90	7.85	7.23	5.96	4.64	
	5	6.28	6.83	7.31	7.57	7.43	7.26	7.33	7.73	7.95	7.96	7.49	7.33	7.49	7.97			

Table 13.A.2 (cont.)

Year	Month	0 mo	1 mo	2 mo	3 mo	4 mo	5 mo	6 mo	9 mo	1 yr	2 yr	3 yr	4 yr	5 yr	10 yr	15 yr	20 yr	25 yr
1970	6	5.46	6.61	6.77	6.64	6.91	7.26	7.48	7.64	7.73	7.87	7.72	7.63	7.59	7.06			
	7	4.32	7.01	6.69	6.07	6.61	7.28	7.52	7.03	7.07	7.99	7.56	7.46	7.67	7.20			
	8	6.07	6.37	6.44	6.53	6.81	7.17	7.27	6.80	6.82	7.86	7.43	7.35	7.58	7.54			
	9	5.61	5.60	6.23	7.03	7.23	6.95	6.77	6.66	6.63	6.91	7.28	7.49	7.55	7.27			
	10	5.05	5.81	6.26	6.44	6.51	6.51	6.48	6.44	6.49	6.90	7.24	7.40	7.42	7.37			
	11	4.40	5.04	5.28	5.21	5.02	4.95	5.06	5.30	5.42	5.81	6.41	6.85	6.90	6.83	6.26	5.09	
	12	3.98	5.00	5.08	4.99	4.99	4.90	4.80	5.03	5.54	6.18	6.34	6.36	6.46	6.85	6.68	5.14	
1971		0 mo	1 mo	2 mo	3 mo	4 mo	5 mo	6 mo	9 mo	1 yr	2 yr	3 yr	4 yr	5 yr	10 yr	15 yr	20 yr	25 yr
	1	3.99	4.19	4.18	4.27	4.41	4.31	4.14	4.17	4.57	5.80	6.58	6.91	6.83	6.09	5.55	6.50	
	2	3.13	3.36	3.51	3.66	3.78	3.83	3.84	3.86	4.00	5.40	6.26	6.62	6.68	6.79	6.59	6.01	
	3	3.46	3.50	3.76	3.88	3.76	3.69	3.74	3.92	4.11	4.88	5.60	6.15	6.36	6.20	6.06	6.24	
	4	3.49	4.05	4.15	4.28	4.55	4.75	4.83	4.90	5.16	6.25	6.66	6.71	6.60	5.82			
	5	3.92	4.42	4.49	4.42	4.53	4.73	4.95	5.48	5.74	6.23	6.44	6.65	6.84	6.55			
	6	4.52	5.26	5.22	5.09	5.50	6.15	6.43	6.67	6.80	7.00	6.99	7.02	7.05	6.36			
	7	4.78	5.48	5.31	5.38	6.19	6.72	6.71	6.19	6.32	7.34	7.19	7.10	7.13	6.59			
	8	4.49	4.42	4.35	4.44	5.01	5.59	5.74	5.72	5.74	5.91	6.10	6.28	6.44	6.66			
	9	4.55	4.46	4.73	5.05	5.28	5.42	5.48	5.57	5.62	5.89	6.29	6.38	6.20	6.07			
	10	3.56	4.42	4.54	4.57	4.65	4.58	4.48	4.65	5.22	5.36	5.83	6.79	6.75	5.82	7.81		
	11	3.67	4.37	4.53	4.45	4.60	4.76	4.81	4.99	5.21	5.43	6.13	6.86	6.61	5.63			
	12	3.24	3.47	3.91	4.27	4.47	4.38	4.19	4.53	5.11	5.33	5.73	6.24	6.34	6.53			
1972		0 mo	1 mo	2 mo	3 mo	4 mo	5 mo	6 mo	9 mo	1 yr	2 yr	3 yr	4 yr	5 yr	10 yr	15 yr	20 yr	25 yr
	1	2.41	3.46	3.52	3.72	4.20	4.31	4.30	4.57	4.94	5.96	6.32	6.44	6.68	7.07			
	2	3.36	3.22	3.51	3.94	4.15	4.27	4.37	4.66	4.95	5.82	6.15	6.36	6.56	6.86			
	3	3.32	3.58	4.20	4.74	4.96	5.07	5.20	5.56	5.79	6.22	6.38	6.43	6.43	6.32			
	4	3.30	3.36	3.89	4.33	4.53	4.64	4.70	4.85	5.13	6.29	6.28	6.21	6.35	6.64			
	5	3.31	3.68	3.97	4.23	4.52	4.75	4.85	4.90	5.02	5.81	6.15	6.32	6.42	6.55			
	6	3.39	3.94	4.33	4.69	5.13	5.48	5.67	5.64	5.64	5.94	6.19	6.36	6.46	6.43			
	7	3.41	3.70	4.00	4.37	4.84	5.25	5.42	5.29	5.33	6.32	6.36	6.29	6.52	6.80			
	8	4.27	4.42	4.56	4.85	5.37	5.81	5.92	5.69	5.65	6.25	6.35	6.47	6.68	6.76			
	9	4.65	4.42	4.81	5.49	5.86	5.98	6.01	5.94	5.94	6.22	6.10	6.22	6.60	7.22			
	10	4.49	4.62	4.94	5.32	5.53	5.62	5.67	5.77	5.89	6.33	6.23	6.26	6.49	6.76			
	11	4.82	4.80	4.96	5.25	5.55	5.75	5.73	5.41	5.40	6.39	6.14	6.10	6.35	6.66			
	12	4.77	5.08	5.38	5.61	5.75	5.79	5.76	5.67	5.76	6.47	6.17	6.20	6.44	6.57			
1973		0 mo	1 mo	2 mo	3 mo	4 mo	5 mo	6 mo	9 mo	1 yr	2 yr	3 yr	4 yr	5 yr	10 yr	15 yr	20 yr	25 yr
	1	5.22	5.64	5.96	6.14	6.18	6.15	6.14	6.14	6.21	6.63	6.39	6.29	6.35	6.77	7.36	8.39	
	2	5.49	5.71	6.06	6.37	6.44	6.41	6.43	6.63	6.77	6.82	6.67	6.55	6.52	6.50	7.05		
	3	5.77	6.37	6.78	7.07	7.27	7.37	7.32	6.99	6.76	6.55	6.57	6.58	6.56	6.48	6.92		

		0 mo	1 mo	2 mo	3 mo	4 mo	5 mo	6 mo	9 mo	1 yr	2 yr	3 yr	4 yr	5 yr	10 yr	15 yr	20 yr	25 yr
	4	5.95	6.13	6.59	6.98	7.03	6.95	6.89	6.75	6.65	6.56	6.58	6.60	6.58	6.53	6.98		
	5	6.00	6.96	7.32	7.29	7.23	7.17	7.11	6.99	6.86	6.31	6.44	6.72	6.83	6.96	7.06	7.41	
	6	7.30	7.59	7.71	7.80	7.97	8.09	8.07	7.34	6.74	6.49	6.55	6.60	6.66	6.99	7.29	7.61	
	7	7.96	8.50	8.38	8.29	8.74	9.26	9.37	8.64	8.09	7.42	7.23	7.14	7.11	7.05	7.16	8.18	
	8	8.41	8.78	8.70	8.60	8.73	8.91	8.88	8.16	7.58	6.55	6.54	6.71	6.83	7.18	7.43	7.51	
	9	7.59	6.85	7.24	8.02	8.38	8.36	8.20	7.33	6.69	6.13	6.30	6.54	6.71	7.08	7.30	7.26	
	10	6.74	7.46	7.59	7.51	8.01	8.26	7.62	5.98	6.04	7.09	7.03	6.67	6.52	7.45	8.11	7.67	
	11	7.85	7.28	7.64	8.32	8.70	8.59	8.00	6.65	6.04	6.50	6.71	6.57	6.55	7.29	7.86	7.48	
	12	7.13	7.45	7.75	7.86	7.74	7.50	7.19	6.57	6.32	6.58	6.64	6.50	6.49	7.48	8.39	8.01	
1974		0 mo	1 mo	2 mo	3 mo	4 mo	5 mo	6 mo	9 mo	1 yr	2 yr	3 yr	4 yr	5 yr	10 yr	15 yr	20 yr	25 yr
	1	7.36	7.65	7.78	7.67	7.38	7.15	6.97	6.55	6.30	6.70	6.79	6.79	6.86	7.63	8.22	7.83	
	2	7.18	7.81	7.56	7.42	7.53	7.36	6.97	6.41	6.39	6.75	6.92	6.91	6.96	7.72	8.31	7.97	
	3	8.01	8.83	8.69	8.55	8.50	8.45	8.40	8.03	7.59	7.40	7.43	7.32	7.28	7.59	7.96	8.60	
	4	8.52	8.92	9.20	9.18	8.89	8.90	9.14	9.03	8.18	7.73	7.95	7.83	7.76	7.76	7.85	8.77	
	5	7.55	7.86	8.68	9.12	8.67	8.51	8.93	9.21	8.10	7.56	7.98	7.73	7.62	7.94	8.21	8.52	
	6	7.65	7.68	7.78	8.03	8.45	8.89	9.25	9.38	8.31	8.12	8.38	7.83	7.52	7.64	7.80	8.49	
	7	7.04	7.90	7.79	7.86	8.62	9.12	9.29	9.14	8.46	8.44	8.40	7.98	7.76	7.72	7.77	8.88	
	8	9.17	9.23	9.30	9.59	10.06	10.36	10.47	9.89	8.59	7.83	8.14	8.25	8.29	7.95	7.74	9.52	
	9	6.26	5.96	6.34	7.41	8.93	9.65	9.60	8.95	7.99	7.97	8.04	7.71	7.59	8.21	8.93	9.86	
	10	6.37	7.78	8.72	8.80	8.03	7.62	7.69	7.78	7.48	7.97	8.05	7.68	7.53	7.87	8.27	9.18	
	11	7.44	7.49	7.71	7.96	8.13	8.07	7.77	7.12	6.88	7.42	7.80	7.67	7.64	8.11	8.34	7.98	
	12	6.51	7.02	7.43	7.58	7.37	7.16	7.07	6.99	7.07	7.35	7.28	7.04	7.04	8.33	9.16	7.61	
1975		0 mo	1 mo	2 mo	3 mo	4 mo	5 mo	6 mo	9 mo	1 yr	2 yr	3 yr	4 yr	5 yr	10 yr	15 yr	20 yr	25 yr
	1	5.47	5.64	6.02	6.26	6.24	6.17	6.10	6.20	6.72	7.46	7.56	7.63	7.68	7.74	7.85	8.56	11.49
	2	4.48	5.40	5.89	6.05	5.99	5.94	5.96	6.06	6.23	6.96	7.49	7.79	7.95	7.84	7.76	8.35	
	3	5.06	5.48	5.90	6.08	6.05	6.06	6.14	6.46	6.81	7.46	7.75	8.02	8.22	8.67	8.80	8.28	
	4	4.77	5.47	5.81	6.16	6.66	7.05	7.20	7.50	7.92	8.32	8.15	8.23	8.29	8.26	8.24	9.09	
	5	4.66	5.18	5.47	5.65	5.83	6.01	6.16	6.52	6.98	7.88	7.96	8.10	8.21	8.50	8.47	7.95	6.87
	6	5.59	5.79	6.24	6.59	6.59	6.57	6.81	7.49	7.50	7.82	8.11	8.04	7.99	8.09	8.19	8.44	
	7	5.97	6.08	6.49	7.01	7.38	7.60	7.66	7.59	7.74	8.18	8.18	8.08	8.03	8.23	8.33	8.38	8.71
	8	5.73	6.24	6.77	7.27	7.60	7.80	7.86	7.83	7.83	8.12	8.36	8.23	8.05	8.35	8.66	8.78	8.77
	9	6.24	6.42	6.87	7.39	7.72	7.87	7.92	7.99	8.20	8.51	8.50	8.41	8.34	8.63	8.78	8.72	8.80
	10	5.25	5.48	5.76	6.01	6.08	6.10	6.21	6.73	7.18	7.77	7.85	8.02	8.15	8.41	8.46	8.35	
	11	4.67	5.52	6.00	6.26	6.54	6.76	6.82	6.94	7.35	8.02	8.06	8.31	8.53	8.61	8.42	8.24	8.62
	12	4.98	5.15	5.41	5.67	5.89	6.07	6.22	6.59	6.86	7.56	7.92	8.00	8.04	8.29	8.39	8.28	
1976		0 mo	1 mo	2 mo	3 mo	4 mo	5 mo	6 mo	9 mo	1 yr	2 yr	3 yr	4 yr	5 yr	10 yr	15 yr	20 yr	25 yr
	1	4.52	4.58	4.94	5.24	5.38	5.47	5.58	5.99	6.51	7.67	8.12	8.28	8.36	8.24	8.05	8.02	
	2	4.46	4.89	5.31	5.71	6.03	6.26	6.38	6.60	6.92	7.66	7.83	7.95	8.04	8.24	8.31	8.24	
	3	4.77	4.84	5.19	5.55	5.86	6.07	6.22	6.59	6.89	7.52	7.72	7.87	7.98	8.09	8.07	8.08	
	4	4.86	4.67	5.17	5.58	5.78	5.95	6.11	6.61	7.03	7.22	7.70	7.90	7.98	8.18	8.24	8.14	
	5	4.86	5.55	5.81	6.02	6.52	6.84	6.88	7.14	7.72	7.74	7.99	8.02	7.99	8.25	8.40	8.36	

Table 13.A.2 (cont.)

Year	Month	0 mo	1 mo	2 mo	3 mo	4 mo	5 mo	6 mo	9 mo	1 yr	2 yr	3 yr	4 yr	5 yr	10 yr	15 yr	20 yr	25 yr
1976	6	5.26	5.35	5.54	5.88	6.34	6.58	6.55	6.70	7.26	7.49	7.85	7.99	8.03	8.19	8.22	8.28	
	7	5.09	5.14	5.33	5.64	6.00	6.18	6.17	6.44	7.00	7.37	7.73	8.02	8.23	8.28	8.15	8.24	
	8	4.80	5.13	5.25	5.43	5.79	5.99	5.96	6.06	6.65	7.02	7.39	7.80	8.04	8.21	8.08	8.04	
	9	5.13	5.05	5.23	5.48	5.70	5.86	5.86	5.92	6.39	6.91	7.35	7.75	7.96	8.13	8.09	8.06	
	10	4.69	4.82	5.11	5.34	5.42	5.44	5.44	5.65	6.19	6.66	6.94	7.43	7.89	8.24	8.19	8.03	
	11	4.37	4.45	4.55	4.66	4.82	4.94	4.94	5.03	5.40	6.19	6.09	6.48	7.28	8.57	8.76	7.49	
	12	4.22	4.33	4.54	4.75	4.82	4.80	4.82	5.02	5.40	6.14	6.42	6.78	7.19	7.71	7.85	7.77	
1977	1	4.58	4.61	4.94	5.28	5.44	5.53	5.60	5.91	6.43	6.85	7.31	7.64	7.68	8.01	8.15	7.85	
	2	4.41	4.65	4.92	5.17	5.31	5.40	5.54	5.98	6.32	6.91	7.43	7.84	7.86	8.05	8.30	8.35	8.10
	3	4.54	4.51	4.73	4.97	5.10	5.22	5.40	5.95	6.22	6.90	7.45	7.74	7.81	8.09	8.27	8.16	7.66
	4	4.33	4.56	4.86	5.13	5.31	5.46	5.60	5.98	6.29	6.82	7.36	7.75	7.84	8.08	8.13	7.98	7.76
	5	4.80	5.00	5.21	5.42	5.58	5.71	5.81	6.02	6.27	6.68	7.17	7.58	7.72	8.08	8.16	7.99	7.58
	6	4.98	4.97	5.20	5.46	5.63	5.73	5.75	5.84	6.18	6.53	7.04	7.42	7.61	7.84	7.80	8.05	
	7	5.16	5.35	5.60	5.86	6.09	6.24	6.30	6.33	6.53	6.82	7.30	7.56	7.65	7.85	7.88	7.87	8.07
	8	5.35	5.45	5.77	6.18	6.39	6.45	6.48	6.50	6.53	6.88	7.11	7.25	7.38	7.79	8.01	8.01	
	9	5.75	5.79	6.19	6.57	6.66	6.63	6.65	6.81	6.89	6.94	7.22	7.37	7.43	7.78	8.03	8.08	7.83
	10	6.27	6.06	6.48	6.99	7.10	7.04	7.06	7.33	7.42	7.36	7.59	7.64	7.56	7.88	8.21	8.26	7.76
	11	5.31	6.00	6.49	6.78	6.94	7.00	7.06	7.18	7.21	7.38	7.40	7.41	7.52	7.94	8.21	8.19	7.65
	12	5.38	6.20	6.61	6.80	6.91	6.98	7.06	7.25	7.23	7.41	7.68	7.78	7.80	8.07	8.32	8.32	8.09
1978	1	5.69	6.40	6.80	7.00	7.14	7.24	7.31	7.39	7.39	7.56	7.82	7.91	7.92	8.21	8.56	8.55	8.07
	2	5.98	6.44	6.74	6.94	7.19	7.42	7.49	7.36	7.46	7.79	7.97	8.06	8.03	8.24	8.58	8.60	8.21
	3	6.84	6.40	6.62	7.03	7.27	7.40	7.50	7.70	7.79	7.86	8.01	8.09	8.10	8.36	8.62	8.51	8.09
	4	5.86	6.22	6.75	7.26	7.60	7.80	7.91	7.96	8.02	7.94	7.99	8.08	8.13	8.47	8.69	8.46	7.90
	5	6.33	6.58	6.98	7.47	7.83	8.05	8.18	8.20	8.19	8.06	8.21	8.33	8.33	8.59	8.87	8.32	6.47
	6	6.24	6.96	7.60	8.05	8.24	8.28	8.36	8.73	8.67	8.45	8.32	8.24	8.36	8.76	8.69	8.12	7.87
	7	6.40	6.74	7.23	7.73	8.11	8.39	8.60	8.85	8.68	8.34	8.29	8.27	8.34	8.61	8.60	8.17	7.94
	8	8.05	7.73	7.57	7.65	8.05	8.43	8.61	8.72	8.46	8.14	8.18	8.17	8.18	8.21	8.41	8.48	8.29
	9	7.89	8.13	8.50	8.83	9.02	9.05	8.93	8.60	8.58	7.98	8.07	8.31	8.42	8.67	8.60	8.17	7.85
	10	8.35	8.90	9.07	9.28	9.89	10.40	10.48	9.87	8.98	8.88	8.59	8.43	8.44	8.54	8.74	8.82	8.20
	11	8.95	9.05	9.25	9.54	9.89	10.16	10.26	10.03	9.31	8.44	7.94	8.32	8.53	8.63	8.44	8.04	8.17
	12	7.63	9.44	10.11	10.19	10.09	10.10	10.49	11.11	10.07	8.92	8.16	8.56	8.74	8.64	8.45	8.18	8.07
1979	1	9.64	9.43	9.57	9.80	9.87	9.91	10.05	9.99	9.27	8.53	7.75	8.43	8.78	8.68	8.56	8.39	8.08
	2	9.58	9.66	9.69	9.77	10.05	10.30	10.32	10.06	9.69	8.77	8.30	8.68	8.93	8.89	8.63	8.23	8.25

3	9.54	9.64	9.77	9.88	9.94	9.97	9.99	9.77	9.29	9.04	8.08	8.58	8.88	8.87	8.71	8.39	8.23
4	9.54	9.65	9.90	10.08	10.06	10.06	10.13	9.98	9.40	9.11	8.29	8.87	9.18	9.08	8.81	8.41	8.45
5	9.80	9.77	9.81	9.83	9.78	9.72	9.70	9.48	9.10	8.64	8.12	8.55	8.85	9.02	8.98	8.68	8.10
6	8.73	9.18	9.32	9.33	9.31	9.29	9.29	9.04	8.42	8.46	8.21	8.40	8.56	8.87	8.79	8.28	7.94
7	9.22	9.14	9.55	9.91	9.88	9.82	9.80	9.42	8.66	8.66	8.36	8.63	8.82	8.89	8.75	8.37	7.91
8	9.98	10.17	9.96	9.87	10.24	10.56	10.61	10.32	9.57	8.71	8.77	8.84	8.88	8.81	8.63	8.33	8.18
9	9.99	10.39	10.48	10.52	10.62	10.70	10.73	10.52	9.87	8.75	8.83	8.88	8.94	9.17	8.71	7.70	8.06
10	11.24	12.19	12.94	13.28	13.07	12.82	12.74	12.29	11.08	10.91	10.25	10.09	9.96	9.69	9.24	8.50	8.04
11	10.27	11.94	12.10	11.88	12.21	12.52	12.25	10.21	10.48	9.14	9.79	10.02	10.13	9.69	9.23	9.02	8.39
12	7.12	12.66	13.55	12.73	12.43	12.25	11.74	10.27	10.25	9.99	9.15	9.50	9.82	9.99	9.66	8.82	8.07

1980	0 mo	1 mo	2 mo	3 mo	4 mo	5 mo	6 mo	9 mo	1 yr	2 yr	3 yr	4 yr	5 yr	10 yr	15 yr	20 yr	25 yr
1	11.03	12.50	12.67	12.44	12.53	12.58	12.17	10.71	11.06	10.16	10.09	10.46	10.80	11.07	10.68	9.91	9.56
2	13.29	14.41	14.63	14.38	14.78	15.54	15.77	14.90	14.95	12.36	11.89	11.79	11.73	11.56	10.78	9.32	8.62
3	13.89	15.85	15.37	14.61	15.82	17.71	17.71	14.10	13.56	11.82	11.18	11.07	11.11	12.33	11.95	8.45	8.06
4	10.28	10.51	10.82	11.13	11.38	11.51	11.44	10.86	10.43	9.95	10.32	10.53	10.69	11.17	10.91	9.72	8.61
5	8.22	7.62	7.89	8.48	8.79	8.91	8.93	8.85	9.65	8.47	10.23	10.59	10.56	10.98	10.86	9.65	8.82
6	4.09	8.60	9.19	8.13	7.99	8.40	8.64	8.54	8.97	9.25	9.58	9.92	10.19	10.89	10.27	8.46	8.38
7	6.47	8.89	9.41	9.14	9.04	9.06	9.10	9.28	9.80	9.80	10.29	10.65	10.86	11.61	11.35	9.52	7.72
8	8.27	9.99	10.90	11.16	11.24	11.14	11.09	11.63	11.95	11.01	11.73	11.90	11.44	11.16	11.32	9.23	7.66
9	10.98	11.43	11.85	12.19	12.33	12.27	12.16	11.79	11.68	11.47	11.41	11.48	11.40	11.99	12.02	9.37	8.19
10	10.23	12.83	13.90	13.69	13.51	13.51	13.53	12.91	12.39	12.32	12.25	12.06	11.82	12.00	12.29	9.65	8.89
11	13.63	14.98	15.26	14.64	14.47	14.98	15.47	14.02	12.45	12.53	12.08	11.92	11.69	11.86	12.34	8.94	7.63
12	10.88	14.56	16.07	15.34	14.22	13.67	13.37	11.90	10.97	11.96	11.78	11.87	11.85	11.91	11.34	8.32	8.03

1981	0 mo	1 mo	2 mo	3 mo	4 mo	5 mo	6 mo	9 mo	1 yr	2 yr	3 yr	4 yr	5 yr	10 yr	15 yr	20 yr	25 yr
1	13.97	15.26	15.32	14.62	14.14	13.91	13.70	12.68	12.07	11.82	12.00	12.22	12.18	12.11	11.76	8.87	7.78
2	13.60	14.68	15.06	14.79	14.48	14.30	14.16	13.39	12.83	13.31	13.27	13.01	12.84	12.54	12.07	8.82	9.18
3	13.10	12.95	12.73	12.46	12.39	12.52	12.68	13.14	13.20	12.88	13.27	13.15	12.90	12.35	12.40	8.34	7.34
4	12.57	15.33	16.06	15.14	14.58	14.66	14.83	14.35	13.91	13.87	13.69	13.58	13.42	13.15	12.64	8.07	9.40
5	16.27	16.08	15.47	14.53	14.05	14.19	14.56	14.48	13.92	13.40	12.91	12.50	12.39	12.64	12.25	8.95	8.03
6	14.03	14.70	14.82	14.66	14.63	14.71	14.68	14.04	14.11	13.23	13.72	13.47	12.99	12.78	12.50	8.85	7.97
7	14.50	15.37	15.65	15.74	16.04	16.41	16.48	15.56	15.30	14.28	14.67	14.13	13.32	13.26	12.79	7.71	7.85
8	15.40	15.86	16.20	16.44	16.81	17.28	17.47	15.93	15.46	14.61	15.31	15.40	14.43	13.58	14.19	9.68	7.17
9	12.64	14.55	15.42	15.66	16.19	16.95	17.31	15.90	15.66	15.40	15.78	15.62	14.62	14.83	15.20	7.26	5.77
10	12.75	13.14	13.22	13.26	13.77	14.72	15.30	14.38	13.88	14.30	14.62	14.54	14.24	14.04	14.06	8.15	9.07
11	10.17	10.34	10.71	11.22	11.54	11.62	11.64	12.09	12.52	13.21	12.83	12.95	13.52	12.38	12.68	10.53	8.37
12	8.26	10.98	12.59	13.18	13.51	13.72	13.88	14.15	14.11	13.54	14.00	14.10	13.84	13.45	13.88	8.43	7.72

1982	0 mo	1 mo	2 mo	3 mo	4 mo	5 mo	6 mo	9 mo	1 yr	2 yr	3 yr	4 yr	5 yr	10 yr	15 yr	20 yr	25 yr
1	11.73	12.53	13.22	13.75	14.01	14.00	14.00	14.26	14.26	13.94	14.09	13.91	13.61	14.03	13.49	8.54	9.42
2	11.85	12.19	13.01	14.23	14.78	14.32	13.66	13.92	14.65	13.68	13.76	13.59	13.12	14.27	13.97	9.56	8.81
3	14.57	13.51	13.39	13.93	14.17	14.06	13.92	14.02	14.22	14.15	13.81	13.71	13.78	12.83	13.59	9.41	7.71
4	12.31	12.39	12.89	13.49	13.71	13.57	13.46	13.79	14.06	13.74	13.25	13.13	13.55	12.39	12.63	10.60	10.40

Table 13.A.2 (cont.)

Year	Month	0 mo	1 mo	2 mo	3 mo	4 mo	5 mo	6 mo	9 mo	1 yr	2 yr	3 yr	4 yr	5 yr	10 yr	15 yr	20 yr	25 yr
1982	5	11.56	11.70	11.96	12.31	12.58	12.73	12.85	13.52	14.02	13.48	13.72	13.67	13.61	12.65	13.31	9.99	10.38
	6	10.65	12.70	13.94	14.40	14.56	14.52	14.44	14.59	14.84	14.48	14.45	13.89	14.01	12.68	13.71	8.69	9.82
	7	8.49	9.81	11.19	12.44	13.11	13.17	13.09	13.54	13.92	13.66	13.81	13.21	13.65	12.51	13.81	9.60	11.17
	8	7.54	7.63	8.61	10.26	11.33	11.62	11.66	12.54	13.27	12.70	12.79	12.63	13.34	11.04	12.62	11.01	10.26
	9	6.88	7.12	8.08	9.65	10.71	10.95	10.83	11.46	12.40	12.07	12.07	11.61	12.05	11.20	11.34	10.03	10.88
	10	7.81	7.73	8.24	9.07	9.48	9.41	9.18	10.12	11.39	11.04	11.21	10.80	11.87	9.68	11.69	10.06	6.60
	11	7.67	8.09	8.64	9.24	9.51	9.36	9.01	9.65	10.99	10.41	11.42	11.00	12.05	9.74	12.13	10.45	6.96
	12	8.05	8.10	8.22	8.40	8.53	8.52	8.46	9.16	10.26	10.20	11.10	10.84	11.15	10.25	11.41	10.21	7.21
1983		0 mo	1 mo	2 mo	3 mo	4 mo	5 mo	6 mo	9 mo	1 yr	2 yr	3 yr	4 yr	5 yr	10 yr	15 yr	20 yr	25 yr
	1	8.01	8.14	8.35	8.63	8.79	8.80	8.78	9.35	10.15	10.61	11.13	11.07	11.98	10.40	12.56	11.55	7.54
	2	7.90	7.94	8.12	8.40	8.52	8.41	8.22	8.84	10.14	9.88	10.73	9.69	10.98	9.39	12.86	10.15	5.94
	3	8.36	8.74	9.02	9.20	9.25	9.17	9.06	9.40	10.10	10.27	10.72	10.68	11.13	10.38	11.96	10.04	7.10
	4	8.01	8.19	8.37	8.53	8.59	8.52	8.47	9.02	9.69	10.01	10.52	10.34	10.96	9.97	11.74	9.65	6.98
	5	8.38	8.73	8.98	9.16	9.26	9.29	9.29	9.54	10.02	10.69	10.82	10.98	11.34	10.88	12.21	10.65	7.85
	6	8.25	8.85	9.23	9.38	9.47	9.52	9.56	9.88	10.45	10.73	11.06	11.12	11.25	11.29	11.83	10.06	7.86
	7	8.63	9.25	9.70	9.99	10.17	10.23	10.27	10.83	11.64	11.41	11.68	12.15	12.26	11.82	11.98	11.42	9.76
	8	8.74	9.26	9.70	10.07	10.33	10.45	10.47	10.76	11.34	11.79	12.17	12.20	12.30	11.24	12.98	11.06	7.84
	9	8.77	8.80	8.98	9.27	9.51	9.65	9.76	10.15	10.57	11.14	11.49	11.88	12.01	11.09	12.16	10.48	7.80
	10	8.46	8.55	8.81	9.19	9.48	9.63	9.71	10.10	10.59	11.50	11.89	11.98	12.11	11.64	12.34	10.89	9.11
	11	8.17	8.93	9.37	9.51	9.61	9.74	9.88	10.02	10.27	11.27	11.82	12.07	11.87	11.33	12.19	10.64	8.93
	12	8.18	9.03	9.54	9.69	9.75	9.85	9.97	10.28	10.64	11.44	11.95	12.26	12.05	11.40	12.52	10.94	9.08
1984		0 mo	1 mo	2 mo	3 mo	4 mo	5 mo	6 mo	9 mo	1 yr	2 yr	3 yr	4 yr	5 yr	10 yr	15 yr	20 yr	25 yr
	1	8.87	9.02	9.18	9.34	9.49	9.61	9.70	9.92	10.29	11.15	11.80	12.02	11.84	11.35	12.13	11.40	10.14
	2	8.45	9.22	9.68	9.85	9.95	10.04	10.12	10.24	10.61	11.36	12.31	12.49	12.23	11.62	12.54	11.91	10.66
	3	9.22	9.77	10.22	10.53	10.63	10.54	10.49	10.91	11.61	11.91	12.65	12.87	12.61	11.74	12.46	12.23	11.41
	4	9.26	9.73	10.21	10.61	10.77	10.70	10.69	11.29	11.94	12.36	12.85	13.03	13.06	11.96	12.94	12.51	11.39
	5	9.65	9.58	10.18	11.31	12.02	12.16	12.03	12.82	13.80	14.16	13.83	13.47	14.27	13.15	12.94	12.79	13.72
	6	8.83	9.89	10.63	11.10	11.55	12.01	12.43	13.07	13.28	13.64	13.82	13.95	13.60	12.79	12.96	13.51	13.03
	7	9.67	10.36	10.86	11.21	11.45	11.57	11.67	12.23	12.81	12.61	12.57	12.84	12.81	12.44	12.71	12.12	9.94
	8	10.78	10.73	10.84	11.09	11.34	11.55	11.72	12.21	12.67	12.51	12.55	12.91	12.73	12.36	11.71	11.88	12.57
	9	10.52	10.40	10.50	10.79	11.00	11.09	11.14	11.54	12.07	12.31	12.55	12.66	12.39	11.84	11.68	11.23	11.74
	10	8.07	9.02	9.64	9.95	10.08	10.07	10.02	10.58	11.51	11.57	11.66	11.79	11.89	11.48	11.36	10.78	10.70
	11	7.47	8.46	9.01	9.15	9.26	9.42	9.63	10.09	10.43	11.44	11.55	12.03	12.44	11.35	12.02	10.93	9.97
	12	6.30	8.00	8.74	8.52	8.35	8.68	9.22	10.00	10.18	11.23	11.52	12.08	12.84	11.47	11.99	10.76	9.80
1985		0 mo	1 mo	2 mo	3 mo	4 mo	5 mo	6 mo	9 mo	1 yr	2 yr	3 yr	4 yr	5 yr	10 yr	15 yr	20 yr	25 yr
	1	7.29	8.10	8.50	8.51	8.55	8.75	9.02	9.56	9.91	10.94	11.30	11.65	11.83	11.58	11.46	10.08	10.55
	2	6.77	8.45	9.35	9.53	9.55	9.57	9.60	10.12	10.89	11.55	12.05	12.32	12.73	12.23	12.20	11.52	10.76

	3	7.67	8.36	8.79	9.01	9.17	9.29	9.42	9.96	10.55	11.36	11.76	12.26	12.31	11.80	12.37	11.30	8.07
	4	7.24	7.78	8.23	8.58	8.79	8.85	8.87	9.44	10.31	10.95	11.40	11.79	12.37	11.84	12.16	11.59	8.87
	5	6.69	7.25	7.53	7.56	7.60	7.66	7.76	8.47	9.52	9.79	10.39	10.56	11.34	11.17	11.74	10.12	9.23
	6	6.49	6.92	7.20	7.38	7.47	7.49	7.56	8.24	8.97	9.89	10.53	10.89	11.14	10.50	12.06	10.29	6.56
	7	6.82	7.27	7.59	7.79	7.92	7.96	7.99	8.50	9.16	10.27	10.90	11.20	11.25	11.26	11.90	10.56	7.12
	8	7.35	7.18	7.24	7.52	7.76	7.92	8.04	8.28	8.73	9.69	10.86	10.10	11.32	11.22	12.22	8.58	6.55
	9	7.02	7.20	7.34	7.44	7.55	7.69	7.87	8.58	9.29	9.89	10.29	10.72	11.32	11.74	11.91	9.49	6.90
	10	6.95	7.34	7.48	7.46	7.55	7.75	7.95	8.00	8.62	9.07	10.23	9.95	11.51	11.10	12.07	7.11	6.49
	11	5.66	7.34	7.95	7.60	7.40	7.54	7.84	8.02	8.19	8.82	9.87	10.01	10.61	10.25	11.73	9.51	6.22
	12	5.19	7.09	7.82	7.53	7.34	7.43	7.57	7.68	7.83	8.31	9.30	8.71	9.80	9.90	11.27	9.25	5.68
1986		0 mo	1 mo	2 mo	3 mo	4 mo	5 mo	6 mo	9 mo	1 yr	2 yr	3 yr	4 yr	5 yr	10 yr	15 yr	20 yr	25 yr
	1	6.38	7.15	7.42	7.29	7.26	7.43	7.61	7.65	7.86	8.39	9.09	9.39	9.51	10.50	10.51	7.14	6.57
	2	6.51	7.19	7.43	7.28	7.18	7.24	7.37	7.43	7.49	8.18	7.92	8.60	8.27	8.72	9.34	7.93	6.74
	3	6.73	6.46	6.38	6.45	6.49	6.48	6.51	7.02	7.31	7.13	7.58	7.86	7.36	7.80	8.25	8.85	6.25
	4	5.82	6.12	6.29	6.37	6.42	6.44	6.48	6.68	6.91	7.64	7.31	7.91	7.38	7.96	8.66	9.48	5.41
	5	6.11	6.35	6.53	6.66	6.75	6.79	6.82	7.14	7.52	8.08	8.89	8.30	8.18	8.60	9.73	10.97	4.22
	6	5.96	6.06	6.16	6.26	6.28	6.21	6.19	6.65	7.14	7.43	7.92	7.59	7.83	7.84	9.79	11.57	2.16
	7	5.08	5.84	6.15	6.06	5.99	5.98	6.04	6.43	6.77	7.28	7.59	7.79	7.55	8.75	9.96	9.63	2.81
	8	4.37	5.25	5.53	5.29	5.17	5.31	5.52	5.70	5.88	6.35	7.29	7.20	7.29	8.47	8.94	8.79	3.96
	9	5.14	5.27	5.38	5.50	5.65	5.82	5.96	6.06	6.36	7.08	7.88	7.90	7.99	8.97	9.80	9.33	4.58
	10	4.65	5.33	5.48	5.38	5.42	5.60	5.76	5.96	6.21	6.91	7.34	7.62	7.58	9.06	9.43	7.50	4.20
	11	5.06	5.39	5.59	5.65	5.67	5.67	5.66	5.81	6.14	6.37	7.51	6.88	7.98	8.33	10.32	9.29	3.03
	12	4.07	5.75	6.38	6.03	5.69	5.65	5.76	6.14	6.44	7.40	7.06	6.61	8.03	8.33	10.37	9.79	3.15
1987		0 mo	1 mo	2 mo	3 mo	4 mo	5 mo	6 mo	9 mo	1 yr	2 yr	3 yr	4 yr	5 yr	10 yr	15 yr	20 yr	25 yr
	1	5.23	5.73	5.85	5.71	5.69	5.81	5.96	6.02	6.06	6.77	7.02	7.28	7.49	8.52	9.62	8.91	4.00
	2	5.44	5.53	5.59	5.62	5.68	5.78	5.90	6.13	6.35	6.53	7.23	7.03	7.48	8.31	9.39	8.88	4.50

Table 13.A.3
McCulloch par bond yield curve series, continuous compounding, end of month data, 12/46–2/87

Year	Month	0 mo	1 mo	2 mo	3 mo	4 mo	5 mo	6 mo	9 mo	1 yr	2 yr	3 yr	4 yr	5 yr	10 yr	15 yr	20 yr	25 yr
1946																		
	12	0.18	0.32	0.42	0.48	0.52	0.55	0.58	0.65	0.72	0.95	1.14	1.29	1.41	1.80	2.10	2.25	
1947		0 mo	1 mo	2 mo	3 mo	4 mo	5 mo	6 mo	9 mo	1 yr	2 yr	3 yr	4 yr	5 yr	10 yr	15 yr	20 yr	25 yr
	1	0.16	0.32	0.43	0.48	0.52	0.56	0.58	0.65	0.72	0.94	1.12	1.26	1.38	1.80	2.10	2.26	
	2	0.19	0.33	0.42	0.47	0.51	0.54	0.57	0.65	0.71	0.95	1.14	1.28	1.40	1.79	2.09	2.25	
	3	0.13	0.32	0.44	0.51	0.55	0.58	0.61	0.68	0.74	0.94	1.10	1.24	1.36	1.78	2.07	2.23	
	4	0.08	0.30	0.45	0.52	0.57	0.61	0.64	0.71	0.78	1.00	1.17	1.30	1.41	1.79	2.08	2.24	
	5	0.00	0.29	0.47	0.57	0.63	0.67	0.70	0.77	0.83	1.02	1.17	1.29	1.39	1.78	2.08	2.24	
	6	0.08	0.33	0.49	0.57	0.62	0.65	0.68	0.76	0.82	1.02	1.19	1.32	1.43	1.82	2.13	2.27	
	7	0.06	0.38	0.58	0.67	0.73	0.77	0.80	0.87	0.92	1.10	1.23	1.34	1.43	1.80	2.15	2.26	
	8	0.16	0.53	0.76	0.86	0.92	0.95	0.97	1.02	1.05	1.12	1.18	1.26	1.35	1.78	2.13	2.23	
	9	0.52	0.74	0.88	0.95	0.98	1.01	1.02	1.06	1.08	1.15	1.22	1.30	1.39	1.82	2.14	2.25	
	10	0.45	0.73	0.91	1.00	1.05	1.08	1.10	1.14	1.18	1.28	1.36	1.45	1.53	1.92	2.24	2.31	
	11	0.59	0.81	0.95	1.02	1.06	1.09	1.11	1.16	1.20	1.32	1.42	1.52	1.62	2.03	2.30	2.37	
	12	0.93	0.90	0.90	0.91	0.93	0.95	0.97	1.04	1.11	1.34	1.52	1.66	1.77	2.17	2.40		
1948		0 mo	1 mo	2 mo	3 mo	4 mo	5 mo	6 mo	9 mo	1 yr	2 yr	3 yr	4 yr	5 yr	10 yr	15 yr	20 yr	25 yr
	1	1.04	0.96	0.92	0.91	0.92	0.94	0.96	1.02	1.08	1.32	1.51	1.66	1.78	2.18	2.40		
	2	1.02	0.97	0.94	0.95	0.96	0.97	0.99	1.05	1.11	1.33	1.50	1.64	1.76	2.16	2.40		
	3	1.00	0.98	0.97	0.98	1.00	1.01	1.03	1.08	1.14	1.33	1.49	1.62	1.73	2.14	2.38		
	4	0.98	0.98	0.99	1.00	1.02	1.04	1.05	1.10	1.15	1.33	1.48	1.60	1.71	2.13	2.39		
	5	0.97	0.99	1.00	1.02	1.03	1.04	1.05	1.09	1.12	1.25	1.37	1.48	1.59	2.05	2.34		
	6	0.95	0.98	1.00	1.02	1.03	1.05	1.06	1.11	1.15	1.31	1.45	1.58	1.69	2.14	2.39		
	7	1.02	0.99	0.98	0.99	1.01	1.02	1.04	1.10	1.16	1.37	1.53	1.65	1.76	2.18	2.41		
	8	1.13	1.06	1.03	1.04	1.05	1.07	1.09	1.15	1.21	1.43	1.58	1.71	1.81	2.19	2.41		
	9	1.09	1.08	1.09	1.10	1.12	1.14	1.16	1.22	1.28	1.48	1.61	1.72	1.82	2.19	2.41		
	10	1.11	1.08	1.08	1.09	1.11	1.13	1.16	1.22	1.29	1.51	1.65	1.76	1.86	2.21	2.41		
	11	1.11	1.10	1.11	1.12	1.14	1.16	1.17	1.23	1.28	1.46	1.59	1.69	1.79	2.17	2.40		
	12	1.06	1.11	1.14	1.16	1.18	1.19	1.21	1.24	1.28	1.40	1.52	1.63	1.73	2.15	2.38		
1949		0 mo	1 mo	2 mo	3 mo	4 mo	5 mo	6 mo	9 mo	1 yr	2 yr	3 yr	4 yr	5 yr	10 yr	15 yr	20 yr	25 yr
	1	1.09	1.13	1.15	1.17	1.18	1.19	1.20	1.22	1.25	1.35	1.46	1.57	1.67	2.11	2.37		
	2	1.16	1.14	1.13	1.13	1.14	1.15	1.16	1.20	1.23	1.36	1.48	1.58	1.68	2.10	2.34		
	3	1.03	1.11	1.16	1.19	1.20	1.21	1.22	1.24	1.26	1.33	1.43	1.53	1.63	2.07	2.35		
	4	1.10	1.12	1.14	1.15	1.16	1.17	1.18	1.20	1.23	1.33	1.43	1.53	1.63	2.07	2.35		
	5	1.00	1.09	1.15	1.18	1.19	1.20	1.21	1.23	1.24	1.31	1.40	1.50	1.60	2.06	2.35		
	6	0.81	1.02	1.13	1.18	1.19	1.20	1.20	1.19	1.18	1.17	1.24	1.34	1.45	1.97	2.28		
	7	0.79	0.96	1.05	1.08	1.10	1.10	1.10	1.10	1.09	1.10	1.19	1.30	1.42	1.94	2.24		

Year	Month	0 mo	1 mo	2 mo	3 mo	4 mo	5 mo	6 mo	9 mo	1 yr	2 yr	3 yr	4 yr	5 yr	10 yr	15 yr	20 yr	25 yr
	8	0.86	0.98	1.05	1.08	1.09	1.09	1.10	1.10	1.10	1.12	1.19	1.29	1.40	1.88	2.20		
	9	0.88	1.01	1.08	1.10	1.11	1.11	1.11	1.10	1.09	1.10	1.18	1.28	1.40	1.89	2.18		
	10	0.82	0.98	1.07	1.10	1.11	1.11	1.11	1.11	1.11	1.12	1.20	1.31	1.41	1.89	2.18		
	11	0.82	1.01	1.12	1.16	1.17	1.17	1.17	1.16	1.15	1.14	1.21	1.31	1.41	1.88	2.17		
	12	0.93	1.03	1.09	1.11	1.12	1.12	1.12	1.12	1.12	1.14	1.21	1.30	1.40	1.84	2.14		
1950		0 mo	1 mo	2 mo	3 mo	4 mo	5 mo	6 mo	9 mo	1 yr	2 yr	3 yr	4 yr	5 yr	10 yr	15 yr	20 yr	25 yr
	1	0.97	1.07	1.13	1.15	1.16	1.16	1.16	1.15	1.15	1.16	1.25	1.35	1.46	1.93	2.19		
	2	1.00	1.10	1.16	1.18	1.19	1.19	1.19	1.18	1.17	1.17	1.25	1.36	1.47	1.96	2.22		
	3	0.89	1.08	1.19	1.23	1.24	1.24	1.24	1.23	1.21	1.20	1.28	1.39	1.50	1.99	2.25		
	4	0.92	1.11	1.22	1.25	1.27	1.27	1.27	1.26	1.25	1.26	1.34	1.44	1.55	2.02	2.28		
	5	0.93	1.14	1.25	1.29	1.30	1.31	1.30	1.28	1.26	1.25	1.32	1.43	1.54	2.04	2.30		
	6	0.90	1.13	1.25	1.29	1.30	1.31	1.31	1.30	1.29	1.30	1.38	1.49	1.60	2.08	2.33		
	7	0.86	1.16	1.31	1.36	1.37	1.37	1.36	1.33	1.29	1.25	1.33	1.44	1.56	2.07	2.33		
	8	1.00	1.25	1.37	1.41	1.42	1.42	1.42	1.39	1.36	1.34	1.41	1.51	1.61	2.08	2.33		
	9	1.10	1.29	1.40	1.43	1.44	1.45	1.45	1.44	1.43	1.44	1.52	1.61	1.70	2.12	2.37		
	10	0.83	1.18	1.37	1.44	1.48	1.49	1.50	1.52	1.52	1.56	1.64	1.72	1.80	2.18	2.39		
	11	1.07	1.31	1.43	1.47	1.49	1.50	1.50	1.49	1.49	1.52	1.60	1.70	1.79	2.20	2.39		
	12	0.79	1.25	1.49	1.57	1.60	1.61	1.61	1.58	1.55	1.52	1.59	1.68	1.77	2.19	2.40		
1951		0 mo	1 mo	2 mo	3 mo	4 mo	5 mo	6 mo	9 mo	1 yr	2 yr	3 yr	4 yr	5 yr	10 yr	15 yr	20 yr	25 yr
	1	0.80	1.21	1.44	1.54	1.57	1.59	1.60	1.59	1.57	1.57	1.63	1.70	1.77	2.16	2.39		
	2	0.78	1.21	1.45	1.55	1.58	1.59	1.59	1.57	1.54	1.55	1.62	1.71	1.80	2.21	2.41		
	3	1.24	1.44	1.55	1.61	1.64	1.66	1.68	1.73	1.76	1.87	1.96	2.02	2.08	2.29	2.45	2.53	
	4	0.93	1.33	1.55	1.63	1.68	1.70	1.72	1.75	1.77	1.84	1.92	2.00	2.07	2.37	2.56	2.64	
	5	0.96	1.34	1.56	1.64	1.69	1.72	1.74	1.78	1.81	1.89	1.97	2.06	2.15	2.53	2.72	2.69	
	6	0.90	1.38	1.64	1.73	1.77	1.79	1.80	1.81	1.81	1.84	1.92	2.01	2.10	2.48	2.67	2.66	
	7	1.29	1.49	1.61	1.65	1.67	1.68	1.69	1.70	1.70	1.77	1.85	1.93	2.01	2.37	2.59	2.64	
	8	1.32	1.54	1.65	1.68	1.69	1.70	1.70	1.69	1.68	1.72	1.81	1.90	1.98	2.33	2.49	2.57	
	9	1.49	1.60	1.66	1.69	1.71	1.73	1.75	1.78	1.82	1.92	1.99	2.07	2.13	2.41	2.59	2.62	
	10	0.81	1.26	1.53	1.65	1.71	1.74	1.76	1.80	1.82	1.91	2.00	2.09	2.17	2.49	2.67	2.67	
	11	1.05	1.39	1.58	1.66	1.70	1.72	1.73	1.76	1.78	1.88	1.97	2.07	2.16	2.51	2.68	2.70	
	12	1.55	1.70	1.79	1.84	1.86	1.88	1.89	1.92	1.94	2.02	2.09	2.16	2.23	2.51	2.66	2.71	
1952		0 mo	1 mo	2 mo	3 mo	4 mo	5 mo	6 mo	9 mo	1 yr	2 yr	3 yr	4 yr	5 yr	10 yr	15 yr	20 yr	25 yr
	1	0.94	1.33	1.54	1.62	1.66	1.69	1.71	1.76	1.79	1.88	1.97	2.05	2.13	2.46	2.65	2.69	
	2	0.91	1.34	1.56	1.65	1.70	1.73	1.75	1.81	1.85	1.97	2.08	2.18	2.27	2.62	2.76	2.76	
	3	1.10	1.37	1.52	1.59	1.63	1.66	1.68	1.73	1.77	1.90	2.01	2.10	2.18	2.51	2.72	2.76	
	4	1.39	1.58	1.68	1.72	1.75	1.76	1.77	1.79	1.81	1.87	1.94	2.01	2.09	2.42	2.59	2.61	
	5	1.43	1.64	1.75	1.79	1.82	1.83	1.84	1.87	1.89	1.95	2.00	2.06	2.12	2.38	2.56	2.63	
	6	1.65	1.75	1.80	1.83	1.85	1.87	1.88	1.92	1.95	2.05	2.13	2.19	2.23	2.42	2.59	2.66	
	7	1.72	1.80	1.86	1.89	1.91	1.92	1.94	1.98	2.01	2.13	2.21	2.28	2.32	2.47	2.59	2.65	
	8	1.46	1.71	1.85	1.91	1.95	1.97	2.00	2.05	2.09	2.21	2.30	2.36	2.41	2.55	2.68	2.72	
	9	1.06	1.46	1.70	1.81	1.87	1.91	1.94	2.00	2.04	2.17	2.27	2.35	2.42	2.68	2.80	2.81	

Table 13.A.3 (cont.)

1952		0 mo	1 mo	2 mo	3 mo	4 mo	5 mo	6 mo	9 mo	1 yr	2 yr	3 yr	4 yr	5 yr	10 yr	15 yr	20 yr	25 yr
	10	1.32	1.59	1.75	1.82	1.86	1.89	1.92	1.97	2.00	2.12	2.21	2.28	2.33	2.53	2.66	2.72	
	11	1.55	1.78	1.92	1.99	2.02	2.05	2.07	2.11	2.13	2.21	2.27	2.31	2.35	2.51	2.66	2.74	
	12	1.82	1.94	2.02	2.05	2.08	2.09	2.11	2.14	2.16	2.24	2.30	2.34	2.38	2.55	2.73		

1953		0 mo	1 mo	2 mo	3 mo	4 mo	5 mo	6 mo	9 mo	1 yr	2 yr	3 yr	4 yr	5 yr	10 yr	15 yr	20 yr	25 yr
	1	1.63	1.82	1.92	1.97	2.00	2.02	2.03	2.07	2.09	2.18	2.26	2.33	2.39	2.64	2.77		
	2	1.86	2.02	2.11	2.14	2.16	2.18	2.18	2.20	2.21	2.26	2.31	2.37	2.44	2.71	2.86		
	3	1.95	1.99	2.01	2.03	2.05	2.06	2.07	2.10	2.13	2.24	2.33	2.41	2.48	2.74	2.88		
	4	1.78	2.06	2.23	2.30	2.34	2.37	2.39	2.43	2.46	2.55	2.62	2.69	2.75	2.99	3.08	3.11	3.16
	5	1.43	1.93	2.22	2.35	2.42	2.47	2.50	2.58	2.63	2.79	2.91	3.00	3.08	3.29	3.28	3.22	3.20
	6	1.18	1.61	1.89	2.03	2.11	2.17	2.20	2.28	2.33	2.48	2.59	2.68	2.75	2.99	3.03	3.04	3.09
	7	1.72	1.94	2.06	2.12	2.16	2.19	2.21	2.26	2.31	2.45	2.57	2.66	2.74	2.97	3.03	3.09	
	8	1.62	1.79	1.89	1.95	1.99	2.03	2.06	2.14	2.21	2.45	2.63	2.76	2.85	3.07	3.12	3.14	
	9	0.86	1.22	1.46	1.59	1.67	1.72	1.77	1.87	1.94	2.18	2.33	2.42	2.48	2.64	2.77	2.93	
	10	0.65	0.97	1.19	1.31	1.39	1.44	1.49	1.60	1.69	1.99	2.20	2.34	2.43	2.69	2.86	2.96	
	11	1.36	1.44	1.49	1.53	1.56	1.59	1.62	1.69	1.75	1.98	2.16	2.29	2.40	2.74	2.92	3.01	
	12	1.09	1.25	1.35	1.42	1.46	1.49	1.52	1.60	1.66	1.88	2.03	2.13	2.20	2.47	2.68	2.83	

1954		0 mo	1 mo	2 mo	3 mo	4 mo	5 mo	6 mo	9 mo	1 yr	2 yr	3 yr	4 yr	5 yr	10 yr	15 yr	20 yr	25 yr
	1	1.05	0.96	0.92	0.92	0.95	0.97	1.00	1.10	1.19	1.53	1.78	1.95	2.08	2.48	2.68	2.80	
	2	0.84	0.89	0.92	0.94	0.97	0.99	1.01	1.06	1.12	1.34	1.56	1.78	1.97	2.45	2.52	2.59	
	3	0.99	0.99	0.99	1.00	1.01	1.02	1.04	1.09	1.14	1.34	1.54	1.75	1.93	2.41	2.52	2.61	
	4	0.62	0.67	0.71	0.75	0.78	0.81	0.83	0.91	0.99	1.23	1.42	1.59	1.77	2.33	2.49	2.58	
	5	0.51	0.60	0.66	0.69	0.73	0.76	0.79	0.87	0.96	1.28	1.58	1.83	2.03	2.50	2.60	2.66	
	6	0.67	0.62	0.60	0.61	0.63	0.66	0.68	0.77	0.85	1.15	1.41	1.64	1.85	2.42	2.49	2.54	
	7	0.64	0.68	0.71	0.73	0.75	0.77	0.79	0.84	0.90	1.16	1.44	1.69	1.89	2.38	2.47	2.51	
	8	1.30	1.11	1.00	0.96	0.95	0.95	0.96	0.99	1.04	1.25	1.48	1.71	1.91	2.44	2.50	2.53	
	9	0.90	0.90	0.92	0.94	0.97	1.00	1.03	1.12	1.20	1.45	1.64	1.80	1.98	2.45	2.49	2.53	
	10	0.72	0.85	0.93	0.98	1.02	1.06	1.09	1.18	1.26	1.55	1.78	1.97	2.11	2.43	2.51	2.58	
	11	0.86	0.93	0.98	1.02	1.05	1.08	1.10	1.18	1.25	1.53	1.79	1.99	2.13	2.48	2.62	2.67	
	12	0.92	0.95	0.98	1.01	1.04	1.07	1.10	1.20	1.29	1.61	1.88	2.08	2.20	2.49	2.62	2.67	

1955		0 mo	1 mo	2 mo	3 mo	4 mo	5 mo	6 mo	9 mo	1 yr	2 yr	3 yr	4 yr	5 yr	10 yr	15 yr	20 yr	25 yr
	1	1.19	1.10	1.07	1.09	1.13	1.17	1.22	1.35	1.47	1.84	2.05	2.18	2.29	2.63	2.77	2.80	2.80
	2	0.91	1.14	1.29	1.38	1.45	1.51	1.56	1.70	1.82	2.16	2.31	2.40	2.46	2.70	2.81	2.85	2.87
	3	1.33	1.33	1.35	1.39	1.43	1.47	1.52	1.65	1.78	2.13	2.29	2.39	2.46	2.69	2.78	2.81	2.83
	4	1.44	1.50	1.55	1.60	1.65	1.69	1.73	1.85	1.95	2.25	2.38	2.46	2.52	2.75	2.84	2.84	2.84
	5	0.91	1.15	1.32	1.43	1.50	1.57	1.62	1.75	1.87	2.18	2.35	2.45	2.52	2.72	2.79	2.81	2.82
	6	1.04	1.27	1.43	1.53	1.60	1.66	1.71	1.84	1.96	2.28	2.46	2.58	2.65	2.84	2.88	2.87	2.85

		0 mo	1 mo	2 mo	3 mo	4 mo	5 mo	6 mo	9 mo	1 yr	2 yr	3 yr	4 yr	5 yr	10 yr	15 yr	20 yr	25 yr
	7	1.55	1.67	1.75	1.82	1.87	1.92	1.96	2.08	2.19	2.49	2.65	2.75	2.82	2.97	2.99	2.97	2.94
	8	1.83	1.95	2.04	2.10	2.15	2.19	2.23	2.33	2.41	2.66	2.78	2.85	2.89	2.95	2.95	2.94	2.94
	9	2.16	2.15	2.14	2.15	2.16	2.17	2.19	2.23	2.28	2.46	2.61	2.72	2.78	2.88	2.90	2.91	2.92
	10	2.03	2.05	2.07	2.10	2.13	2.15	2.18	2.25	2.31	2.50	2.59	2.66	2.70	2.80	2.83	2.85	2.87
	11	1.80	2.11	2.31	2.41	2.47	2.51	2.55	2.63	2.69	2.81	2.83	2.84	2.85	2.89	2.91	2.93	2.94
	12	2.34	2.42	2.49	2.53	2.56	2.59	2.61	2.68	2.73	2.84	2.86	2.87	2.88	2.92	2.92	2.90	2.89
1956		0 mo	1 mo	2 mo	3 mo	4 mo	5 mo	6 mo	9 mo	1 yr	2 yr	3 yr	4 yr	5 yr	10 yr	15 yr	20 yr	25 yr
	1	2.24	2.28	2.31	2.33	2.35	2.36	2.37	2.41	2.45	2.55	2.63	2.68	2.72	2.81	2.83	2.84	2.85
	2	1.60	1.97	2.18	2.28	2.34	2.38	2.41	2.49	2.54	2.66	2.71	2.74	2.76	2.83	2.86	2.87	2.88
	3	2.13	2.20	2.26	2.32	2.38	2.43	2.48	2.62	2.73	2.98	3.03	3.05	3.06	3.07	3.04	3.00	2.97
	4	2.61	2.63	2.66	2.70	2.74	2.78	2.82	2.94	3.04	3.22	3.21	3.16	3.13	3.06	3.05	3.05	3.06
	5	2.13	2.37	2.53	2.62	2.67	2.71	2.74	2.81	2.86	2.95	2.96	2.95	2.94	2.90	2.90	2.92	2.96
	6	2.24	2.33	2.40	2.45	2.48	2.52	2.55	2.63	2.69	2.85	2.92	2.95	2.97	2.97	2.95	2.94	2.93
	7	1.88	2.08	2.24	2.35	2.44	2.52	2.60	2.79	2.93	3.20	3.26	3.27	3.27	3.19	3.13	3.08	3.06
	8	2.12	2.40	2.58	2.69	2.78	2.86	2.93	3.10	3.23	3.47	3.53	3.54	3.54	3.41	3.32	3.25	3.21
	9	2.50	2.70	2.84	2.93	3.00	3.05	3.11	3.23	3.33	3.50	3.49	3.45	3.42	3.34	3.26	3.17	3.11
	10	2.27	2.56	2.76	2.89	2.98	3.05	3.10	3.24	3.33	3.46	3.48	3.50	3.51	3.47	3.35	3.26	3.25
	11	2.53	2.81	3.01	3.15	3.26	3.36	3.44	3.61	3.69	3.74	3.70	3.66	3.63	3.50	3.41	3.35	3.32
	12	3.10	3.08	3.15	3.29	3.42	3.54	3.63	3.76	3.80	3.77	3.72	3.71	3.71	3.71	3.64	3.56	3.47
1957		0 mo	1 mo	2 mo	3 mo	4 mo	5 mo	6 mo	9 mo	1 yr	2 yr	3 yr	4 yr	5 yr	10 yr	15 yr	20 yr	25 yr
	1	3.05	3.06	3.10	3.14	3.18	3.21	3.23	3.26	3.27	3.26	3.24	3.24	3.25	3.22	3.15	3.13	3.21
	2	2.39	2.94	3.18	3.29	3.35	3.39	3.42	3.46	3.47	3.45	3.42	3.40	3.39	3.36	3.31	3.27	3.25
	3	2.81	2.89	2.95	3.01	3.07	3.11	3.16	3.27	3.36	3.45	3.44	3.43	3.42	3.37	3.27	3.21	3.25
	4	3.05	3.02	3.03	3.07	3.12	3.17	3.21	3.33	3.42	3.54	3.56	3.56	3.57	3.53	3.41	3.34	3.40
	5	3.14	3.21	3.26	3.30	3.33	3.36	3.38	3.44	3.49	3.56	3.60	3.64	3.67	3.68	3.52	3.41	3.43
	6	2.81	3.08	3.26	3.36	3.44	3.49	3.54	3.65	3.71	3.74	3.74	3.77	3.82	3.89	3.67	3.50	3.54
	7	2.66	3.06	3.30	3.42	3.51	3.57	3.62	3.74	3.80	3.84	3.84	3.87	3.92	3.89	3.65	3.49	3.57
	8	2.50	3.07	3.40	3.58	3.71	3.82	3.90	4.06	4.11	3.99	3.85	3.80	3.82	3.81	3.62	3.51	3.60
	9	2.78	3.23	3.53	3.70	3.81	3.89	3.95	4.10	4.18	4.21	4.10	4.03	4.00	4.01	3.83	3.66	3.64
	10	3.10	3.36	3.54	3.65	3.72	3.78	3.83	3.94	4.01	4.05	4.01	3.97	3.95	3.92	3.81	3.72	3.69
	11	2.06	2.63	3.01	3.19	3.28	3.34	3.37	3.43	3.45	3.48	3.48	3.45	3.42	3.35	3.55	3.67	3.47
	12	2.66	2.73	2.77	2.78	2.79	2.79	2.79	2.78	2.77	2.77	2.78	2.81	2.85	3.05	3.17	3.22	
1958		0 mo	1 mo	2 mo	3 mo	4 mo	5 mo	6 mo	9 mo	1 yr	2 yr	3 yr	4 yr	5 yr	10 yr	15 yr	20 yr	25 yr
	1	1.53	1.46	1.44	1.49	1.56	1.64	1.72	1.95	2.14	2.54	2.69	2.79	2.88	3.15	3.25	3.28	3.32
	2	1.10	1.14	1.20	1.27	1.34	1.41	1.48	1.66	1.80	2.14	2.36	2.52	2.64	3.04	3.18	3.24	3.27
	3	0.94	0.99	1.05	1.11	1.18	1.25	1.31	1.49	1.66	2.09	2.32	2.46	2.57	2.90	3.10	3.24	3.32
	4	1.18	1.16	1.16	1.18	1.21	1.24	1.27	1.37	1.46	1.79	2.05	2.25	2.40	2.81	3.01	3.12	3.19
	5	0.00	0.25	0.49	0.63	0.74	0.83	0.92	1.14	1.32	1.76	1.99	2.17	2.33	2.90	3.09	3.13	3.14
	6	0.84	0.75	0.72	0.74	0.79	0.85	0.91	1.11	1.30	1.90	2.22	2.40	2.54	2.98	3.16	3.23	3.25
	7	0.54	0.70	0.83	0.92	1.00	1.07	1.13	1.30	1.47	2.02	2.44	2.72	2.89	3.17	3.36	3.51	3.58

Table 13.A.3 (cont.)

1958		0 mo	1 mo	2 mo	3 mo	4 mo	5 mo	6 mo	9 mo	1 yr	2 yr	3 yr	4 yr	5 yr	10 yr	15 yr	20 yr	25 yr
	8	1.35	1.87	2.20	2.38	2.49	2.58	2.65	2.82	2.96	3.35	3.54	3.64	3.69	3.75	3.74	3.73	3.72
	9	1.00	1.95	2.57	2.88	3.04	3.14	3.20	3.30	3.36	3.50	3.62	3.70	3.74	3.74	3.72	3.72	3.75
	10	1.08	1.82	2.30	2.53	2.67	2.76	2.83	2.98	3.09	3.37	3.53	3.62	3.67	3.70	3.68	3.68	3.70
	11	0.83	1.90	2.58	2.91	3.07	3.16	3.23	3.33	3.38	3.47	3.55	3.60	3.62	3.64	3.65	3.67	3.70
	12	2.13	2.42	2.62	2.75	2.84	2.91	2.97	3.09	3.19	3.45	3.63	3.74	3.80	3.88	3.85	3.80	3.79
1959		0 mo	1 mo	2 mo	3 mo	4 mo	5 mo	6 mo	9 mo	1 yr	2 yr	3 yr	4 yr	5 yr	10 yr	15 yr	20 yr	25 yr
	1	2.32	2.47	2.61	2.76	2.89	3.00	3.09	3.27	3.40	3.73	3.89	3.96	3.99	3.99	3.99	4.01	4.01
	2	2.04	2.38	2.64	2.83	2.97	3.07	3.14	3.29	3.38	3.60	3.71	3.76	3.78	3.79	3.87	3.96	4.01
	3	2.44	2.57	2.72	2.89	3.06	3.19	3.29	3.48	3.59	3.82	3.92	3.96	3.98	3.97	3.97	3.98	3.99
	4	2.78	2.74	2.80	2.94	3.10	3.22	3.32	3.49	3.61	3.87	4.03	4.12	4.16	4.19	4.13	4.05	4.01
	5	2.80	2.75	2.82	3.03	3.27	3.47	3.60	3.79	3.86	3.97	4.10	4.17	4.20	4.18	4.12	4.08	4.05
	6	2.70	2.77	2.93	3.16	3.42	3.62	3.75	3.91	3.96	4.13	4.31	4.39	4.40	4.24	4.17	4.14	4.11
	7	1.97	2.40	2.75	3.04	3.30	3.56	3.79	4.25	4.40	4.34	4.39	4.52	4.57	4.42	4.24	4.12	4.06
	8	3.14	3.48	3.74	3.95	4.13	4.27	4.38	4.54	4.56	4.45	4.51	4.62	4.66	4.51	4.32	4.17	4.11
	9	3.43	3.64	3.90	4.21	4.53	4.76	4.90	4.99	4.92	4.69	4.70	4.71	4.70	4.50	4.32	4.19	4.12
	10	2.14	3.17	3.79	4.06	4.20	4.32	4.42	4.55	4.55	4.36	4.44	4.60	4.67	4.50	4.29	4.15	4.08
	11	2.31	3.53	4.23	4.52	4.67	4.77	4.84	4.93	4.94	4.87	4.81	4.78	4.74	4.55	4.37	4.23	4.16
	12	4.02	4.08	4.27	4.56	4.77	4.88	4.94	5.01	5.02	4.95	4.88	4.84	4.81	4.72	4.56	4.41	4.33
1960		0 mo	1 mo	2 mo	3 mo	4 mo	5 mo	6 mo	9 mo	1 yr	2 yr	3 yr	4 yr	5 yr	10 yr	15 yr	20 yr	25 yr
	1	3.28	3.54	3.82	4.11	4.33	4.47	4.56	4.68	4.71	4.69	4.71	4.74	4.76	4.65	4.43	4.39	
	2	3.58	3.81	4.05	4.25	4.35	4.37	4.37	4.38	4.40	4.48	4.57	4.60	4.59	4.42	4.30	4.23	4.21
	3	2.40	2.68	2.91	3.09	3.23	3.33	3.41	3.55	3.62	3.78	3.90	3.98	4.02	4.06	4.06	4.05	4.04
	4	2.89	2.97	3.02	3.08	3.18	3.34	3.53	3.97	4.15	4.24	4.35	4.45	4.48	4.35	4.29	4.27	4.25
	5	1.82	2.60	3.02	3.16	3.24	3.33	3.45	3.76	3.92	4.13	4.24	4.30	4.30	4.16	4.16	4.20	4.18
	6	1.25	1.66	1.97	2.20	2.37	2.52	2.65	2.95	3.18	3.69	3.88	3.93	3.98	4.18	4.10	3.97	3.90
	7	1.65	1.83	2.02	2.21	2.37	2.50	2.60	2.79	2.91	3.16	3.28	3.36	3.45	3.79	3.81	3.75	3.71
	8	1.45	1.97	2.36	2.61	2.77	2.85	2.87	2.85	2.88	3.13	3.31	3.44	3.55	3.84	3.86	3.81	3.81
	9	2.68	2.34	2.31	2.53	2.75	2.86	2.89	2.83	2.80	3.04	3.29	3.46	3.57	3.79	3.83	3.84	3.84
	10	1.22	1.61	1.93	2.18	2.38	2.51	2.60	2.76	2.85	3.13	3.35	3.52	3.64	3.87	3.91	3.89	3.88
	11	1.24	1.79	2.19	2.44	2.59	2.69	2.77	2.90	3.00	3.30	3.52	3.68	3.78	3.97	3.99	3.97	3.94
	12	1.87	2.03	2.16	2.27	2.36	2.41	2.44	2.51	2.58	2.87	3.11	3.29	3.41	3.71	3.79	3.81	3.82
1961		0 mo	1 mo	2 mo	3 mo	4 mo	5 mo	6 mo	9 mo	1 yr	2 yr	3 yr	4 yr	5 yr	10 yr	15 yr	20 yr	25 yr
	1	1.88	2.04	2.18	2.30	2.40	2.47	2.52	2.64	2.76	3.14	3.38	3.53	3.63	3.82	3.88	3.90	3.91
	2	2.47	2.48	2.54	2.62	2.69	2.75	2.80	2.90	2.97	3.18	3.34	3.45	3.52	3.71	3.77	3.80	3.81
	3	2.02	2.19	2.32	2.42	2.50	2.57	2.64	2.78	2.86	3.05	3.24	3.42	3.54	3.79	3.84	3.83	3.81
	4	1.42	1.93	2.20	2.27	2.30	2.38	2.48	2.72	2.84	3.03	3.20	3.34	3.45	3.72	3.78	3.78	3.76

		0 mo	1 mo	2 mo	3 mo	4 mo	5 mo	6 mo	9 mo	1 yr	2 yr	3 yr	4 yr	5 yr	10 yr	15 yr	20 yr	25 yr
	5	2.10	2.24	2.34	2.40	2.46	2.53	2.60	2.79	2.91	3.20	3.37	3.49	3.58	3.80	3.83	3.79	3.75
	6	1.80	2.08	2.24	2.31	2.37	2.45	2.54	2.75	2.90	3.28	3.49	3.62	3.71	3.88	3.91	3.91	3.89
	7	1.12	1.74	2.10	2.24	2.32	2.41	2.50	2.73	2.88	3.25	3.54	3.74	3.85	3.98	3.98	3.95	3.92
	8	1.74	2.05	2.24	2.36	2.48	2.60	2.71	2.92	3.05	3.36	3.60	3.75	3.84	3.98	3.99	3.98	4.00
	9	1.89	1.99	2.15	2.34	2.50	2.62	2.70	2.88	3.00	3.31	3.52	3.65	3.72	3.85	3.90	3.94	4.00
	10	1.74	1.96	2.15	2.32	2.47	2.58	2.67	2.84	2.96	3.24	3.45	3.59	3.69	3.87	3.89	3.90	3.95
	11	2.00	2.28	2.47	2.60	2.68	2.75	2.80	2.93	3.03	3.32	3.52	3.67	3.78	4.00	3.99	3.96	3.99
	12	2.32	2.48	2.63	2.75	2.83	2.89	2.94	3.05	3.14	3.41	3.58	3.71	3.82	4.06	4.05	4.01	4.03
1962		0 mo	1 mo	2 mo	3 mo	4 mo	5 mo	6 mo	9 mo	1 yr	2 yr	3 yr	4 yr	5 yr	10 yr	15 yr	20 yr	25 yr
	1	2.20	2.48	2.66	2.75	2.82	2.88	2.95	3.09	3.21	3.52	3.70	3.83	3.93	4.12	4.11	4.06	4.06
	2	2.24	2.49	2.65	2.76	2.84	2.89	2.93	3.02	3.09	3.29	3.46	3.60	3.73	4.07	4.11	4.08	4.10
	3	2.64	2.63	2.71	2.83	2.90	2.90	2.87	2.85	2.89	3.14	3.34	3.49	3.60	3.87	3.95	3.97	3.97
	4	2.67	2.69	2.73	2.78	2.82	2.85	2.87	2.93	3.00	3.25	3.42	3.53	3.63	3.91	3.96	3.95	3.93
	5	2.10	2.45	2.66	2.72	2.74	2.76	2.79	2.87	2.94	3.11	3.31	3.50	3.64	3.91	3.95	3.94	3.92
	6	2.98	2.93	2.92	2.95	2.98	2.99	2.99	3.00	3.03	3.27	3.48	3.64	3.75	3.96	3.99	3.98	3.97
	7	2.53	2.68	2.81	2.90	2.97	3.03	3.08	3.19	3.26	3.42	3.59	3.74	3.84	4.04	4.07	4.07	4.13
	8	2.52	2.66	2.77	2.85	2.92	2.98	3.02	3.09	3.11	3.15	3.34	3.53	3.66	3.95	3.99	3.99	4.00
	9	2.68	2.69	2.74	2.83	2.90	2.93	2.93	2.92	2.93	3.08	3.31	3.51	3.66	3.94	3.98	3.97	3.97
	10	2.38	2.53	2.65	2.75	2.81	2.84	2.85	2.85	2.88	3.10	3.32	3.49	3.63	3.94	3.97	3.94	3.93
	11	2.35	2.67	2.86	2.93	2.95	2.96	2.97	2.98	3.01	3.17	3.32	3.45	3.57	3.92	3.95	3.92	3.93
	12	2.98	2.94	2.94	2.97	3.00	3.00	3.00	2.99	3.01	3.21	3.34	3.43	3.52	3.88	3.91	3.88	3.92
1963		0 mo	1 mo	2 mo	3 mo	4 mo	5 mo	6 mo	9 mo	1 yr	2 yr	3 yr	4 yr	5 yr	10 yr	15 yr	20 yr	25 yr
	1	2.95	2.93	2.94	2.98	3.02	3.02	3.01	2.98	2.99	3.15	3.33	3.49	3.62	3.89	3.93	3.93	3.97
	2	2.82	2.84	2.88	2.94	2.97	2.97	2.95	2.92	2.94	3.15	3.37	3.54	3.67	3.96	4.01	4.01	4.00
	3	1.83	2.20	2.55	2.85	3.04	3.12	3.12	3.03	2.99	3.15	3.37	3.55	3.69	3.99	4.03	4.02	4.02
	4	2.83	2.85	2.89	2.94	2.99	3.02	3.03	3.05	3.08	3.27	3.45	3.59	3.70	3.97	4.04	4.06	4.06
	5	2.91	2.95	3.00	3.06	3.10	3.12	3.12	3.10	3.11	3.31	3.50	3.64	3.74	3.98	4.03	4.04	4.04
	6	2.99	2.98	3.00	3.05	3.10	3.12	3.12	3.11	3.12	3.32	3.52	3.68	3.79	3.99	4.04	4.04	4.04
	7	2.88	3.05	3.19	3.29	3.36	3.40	3.42	3.44	3.46	3.58	3.70	3.80	3.87	4.00	4.02	4.02	4.01
	8	3.08	3.26	3.38	3.44	3.47	3.50	3.53	3.57	3.60	3.63	3.71	3.82	3.91	4.02	4.03	4.01	4.01
	9	3.53	3.44	3.42	3.47	3.52	3.56	3.57	3.59	3.59	3.65	3.74	3.85	3.93	4.09	4.08	4.06	4.07
	10	3.25	3.36	3.46	3.54	3.60	3.64	3.65	3.66	3.67	3.75	3.84	3.93	4.00	4.17	4.15	4.11	4.10
	11	3.01	3.27	3.46	3.57	3.64	3.67	3.69	3.72	3.74	3.79	3.85	3.92	3.97	4.11	4.13	4.12	4.12
	12	3.52	3.51	3.53	3.58	3.64	3.69	3.72	3.78	3.81	3.91	3.97	4.02	4.06	4.16	4.19	4.19	4.18
1964		0 mo	1 mo	2 mo	3 mo	4 mo	5 mo	6 mo	9 mo	1 yr	2 yr	3 yr	4 yr	5 yr	10 yr	15 yr	20 yr	25 yr
	1	3.35	3.42	3.49	3.55	3.60	3.64	3.67	3.73	3.78	3.88	3.94	3.99	4.04	4.19	4.20	4.17	4.15
	2	3.51	3.53	3.58	3.65	3.72	3.77	3.80	3.86	3.89	3.98	4.02	4.07	4.11	4.22	4.22	4.18	4.16
	3	3.57	3.51	3.52	3.60	3.67	3.73	3.77	3.85	3.91	4.07	4.14	4.17	4.19	4.26	4.25	4.23	4.20
	4	3.18	3.32	3.43	3.50	3.57	3.62	3.66	3.75	3.81	3.96	4.06	4.13	4.16	4.20	4.21	4.20	4.20
	5	3.00	3.29	3.46	3.52	3.55	3.60	3.64	3.76	3.82	3.92	3.98	4.02	4.07	4.18	4.18	4.16	4.14

Table 13.A.3 (cont.)

		0 mo	1 mo	2 mo	3 mo	4 mo	5 mo	6 mo	9 mo	1 yr	2 yr	3 yr	4 yr	5 yr	10 yr	15 yr	20 yr	25 yr
1964																		
	6	3.28	3.46	3.54	3.54	3.55	3.58	3.62	3.71	3.75	3.83	3.91	3.99	4.05	4.14	4.15	4.14	4.13
	7	3.02	3.32	3.46	3.51	3.54	3.60	3.65	3.73	3.74	3.75	3.87	3.99	4.07	4.20	4.20	4.19	4.18
	8	3.21	3.40	3.51	3.56	3.60	3.64	3.69	3.77	3.79	3.83	3.93	4.01	4.08	4.21	4.22	4.20	4.18
	9	3.50	3.53	3.57	3.63	3.69	3.74	3.78	3.85	3.87	3.89	3.95	4.00	4.05	4.18	4.20	4.19	4.18
	10	3.39	3.45	3.53	3.62	3.70	3.75	3.79	3.85	3.88	3.92	3.97	4.02	4.06	4.16	4.18	4.17	4.16
	11	3.37	3.63	3.81	3.90	3.97	4.03	4.08	4.14	4.15	4.13	4.13	4.14	4.15	4.18	4.19	4.19	4.18
	12	3.13	3.56	3.80	3.89	3.94	3.98	4.00	4.02	4.00	3.99	4.04	4.08	4.12	4.21	4.22	4.21	4.20
1965		0 mo	1 mo	2 mo	3 mo	4 mo	5 mo	6 mo	9 mo	1 yr	2 yr	3 yr	4 yr	5 yr	10 yr	15 yr	20 yr	25 yr
	1	3.81	3.85	3.89	3.92	3.97	4.02	4.06	4.06	4.03	3.98	4.02	4.06	4.09	4.18	4.20	4.20	4.19
	2	3.61	3.87	4.00	4.04	4.07	4.11	4.13	4.15	4.14	4.09	4.08	4.10	4.12	4.22	4.22	4.20	4.19
	3	3.60	3.82	3.94	3.98	4.01	4.04	4.07	4.10	4.08	4.07	4.09	4.12	4.14	4.20	4.21	4.20	4.19
	4	3.82	3.88	3.94	3.99	4.02	4.05	4.07	4.08	4.07	4.07	4.10	4.12	4.14	4.19	4.20	4.20	4.19
	5	3.74	3.86	3.93	3.95	3.98	4.00	4.03	4.06	4.07	4.07	4.08	4.11	4.14	4.23	4.23	4.21	4.20
	6	3.71	3.79	3.84	3.87	3.89	3.92	3.93	3.94	3.93	3.95	4.01	4.07	4.10	4.19	4.21	4.20	4.19
	7	3.81	3.81	3.84	3.89	3.93	3.96	3.97	3.99	4.00	4.05	4.11	4.15	4.17	4.22	4.22	4.22	4.21
	8	3.70	3.81	3.88	3.93	3.98	4.04	4.09	4.12	4.10	4.13	4.17	4.20	4.23	4.27	4.27	4.25	4.24
	9	3.93	3.95	4.01	4.11	4.18	4.24	4.28	4.33	4.35	4.34	4.33	4.34	4.36	4.40	4.37	4.33	4.31
	10	3.85	3.92	4.02	4.13	4.22	4.26	4.29	4.33	4.35	4.38	4.40	4.42	4.44	4.45	4.40	4.35	4.32
	11	3.67	3.92	4.09	4.18	4.25	4.32	4.37	4.42	4.44	4.50	4.54	4.55	4.56	4.54	4.50	4.45	4.41
	12	4.31	4.44	4.52	4.57	4.66	4.75	4.82	4.92	4.96	5.07	5.09	5.04	4.97	4.73	4.62	4.55	4.50
1966		0 mo	1 mo	2 mo	3 mo	4 mo	5 mo	6 mo	9 mo	1 yr	2 yr	3 yr	4 yr	5 yr	10 yr	15 yr	20 yr	25 yr
	1	4.50	4.52	4.61	4.72	4.79	4.82	4.84	4.87	4.90	5.04	5.09	5.07	5.03	4.82	4.68	4.60	4.56
	2	4.24	4.50	4.65	4.74	4.82	4.90	4.96	5.08	5.13	5.18	5.21	5.24	5.27	5.21	4.99	4.81	4.76
	3	4.19	4.40	4.53	4.61	4.70	4.78	4.85	4.94	4.97	5.01	5.01	4.99	4.96	4.84	4.73	4.66	4.62
	4	4.44	4.63	4.69	4.70	4.74	4.82	4.87	4.93	4.95	5.04	5.04	5.02	5.02	4.96	4.83	4.73	4.67
	5	4.21	4.50	4.65	4.69	4.75	4.86	4.95	5.02	5.05	5.25	5.25	5.18	5.12	4.96	4.85	4.78	4.73
	6	4.22	4.50	4.60	4.62	4.69	4.79	4.87	4.94	5.02	5.35	5.38	5.31	5.26	5.13	5.00	4.90	4.81
	7	4.08	4.58	4.78	4.81	4.90	5.01	5.09	5.17	5.21	5.40	5.47	5.48	5.46	5.28	5.07	4.90	4.82
	8	4.21	4.79	5.06	5.12	5.28	5.56	5.75	5.88	5.94	6.29	6.28	6.14	6.02	5.62	5.37	5.20	5.10
	9	5.00	5.20	5.35	5.48	5.61	5.74	5.83	5.92	5.91	5.80	5.68	5.57	5.44	5.11	5.01	4.95	4.86
	10	4.24	4.85	5.19	5.35	5.49	5.62	5.69	5.73	5.71	5.61	5.54	5.47	5.39	5.11	4.93	4.79	4.74
	11	3.66	4.62	5.15	5.28	5.32	5.37	5.41	5.43	5.48	5.68	5.56	5.42	5.38	5.28	5.11	4.95	4.86
	12	4.60	4.70	4.82	4.94	5.02	5.07	5.08	5.05	5.03	5.02	4.99	4.94	4.88	4.74	4.69	4.65	4.62
1967		0 mo	1 mo	2 mo	3 mo	4 mo	5 mo	6 mo	9 mo	1 yr	2 yr	3 yr	4 yr	5 yr	10 yr	15 yr	20 yr	25 yr
	1	4.37	4.54	4.61	4.61	4.62	4.63	4.63	4.63	4.63	4.68	4.70	4.70	4.68	4.62	4.57	4.53	4.51
	2	3.77	4.37	4.59	4.59	4.61	4.64	4.66	4.64	4.68	4.91	4.86	4.79	4.80	4.86	4.83	4.77	4.72
	3	3.91	4.01	4.10	4.16	4.18	4.17	4.16	4.14	4.14	4.24	4.29	4.35	4.41	4.58	4.62	4.62	4.60

		0 mo	1 mo	2 mo	3 mo	4 mo	5 mo	6 mo	9 mo	1 yr	2 yr	3 yr	4 yr	5 yr	10 yr	15 yr	20 yr	25 yr
	4	3.01	3.54	3.74	3.77	3.82	3.88	3.93	3.99	4.06	4.43	4.56	4.62	4.70	4.92	4.94	4.90	4.83
	5	3.21	3.34	3.43	3.49	3.61	3.74	3.84	3.95	4.04	4.52	4.63	4.62	4.70	4.94	4.95	4.92	4.89
	6	3.32	3.75	3.96	4.05	4.17	4.35	4.54	4.92	5.08	5.21	5.25	5.32	5.41	5.44	5.27	5.13	5.12
	7	3.29	3.79	4.04	4.18	4.38	4.60	4.77	5.05	5.15	5.13	5.08	5.11	5.20	5.33	5.26	5.17	5.13
	8	3.49	3.93	4.26	4.49	4.67	4.82	4.95	5.20	5.31	5.39	5.37	5.40	5.44	5.42	5.31	5.23	5.22
	9	4.34	4.25	4.34	4.59	4.83	5.02	5.16	5.35	5.40	5.38	5.40	5.45	5.50	5.51	5.41	5.32	5.28
	10	3.80	4.18	4.45	4.63	4.81	5.03	5.22	5.44	5.49	5.60	5.62	5.64	5.67	5.71	5.63	5.55	5.53
	11	3.57	4.27	4.76	5.04	5.23	5.42	5.60	5.80	5.75	5.62	5.67	5.73	5.77	5.81	5.78	5.74	
	12	3.90	4.43	4.84	5.16	5.40	5.58	5.72	5.89	5.89	5.88	5.88	5.84	5.80	5.77	5.80	5.78	5.66
1968		0 mo	1 mo	2 mo	3 mo	4 mo	5 mo	6 mo	9 mo	1 yr	2 yr	3 yr	4 yr	5 yr	10 yr	15 yr	20 yr	25 yr
	1	4.64	4.74	4.84	4.95	5.04	5.11	5.17	5.33	5.45	5.58	5.59	5.63	5.67	5.72	5.68	5.60	5.49
	2	4.37	4.79	5.01	5.12	5.21	5.28	5.34	5.44	5.51	5.64	5.71	5.71	5.70	5.69	5.69	5.65	
	3	4.52	4.94	5.18	5.28	5.34	5.41	5.47	5.60	5.68	5.86	5.91	5.91	5.90	5.96	6.00	5.95	
	4	5.07	5.33	5.51	5.61	5.68	5.75	5.80	5.90	5.94	6.01	6.06	6.06	6.03	5.94	5.84	5.74	5.65
	5	5.20	5.57	5.76	5.84	5.92	6.01	6.08	6.15	6.17	6.17	6.03	5.94	5.95	5.99	5.91	5.78	5.63
	6	5.27	5.29	5.34	5.42	5.51	5.60	5.69	5.87	5.94	5.94	5.87	5.83	5.82	5.76	5.68	5.60	5.52
	7	4.92	5.10	5.19	5.23	5.30	5.38	5.43	5.46	5.46	5.50	5.50	5.51	5.52	5.53	5.50	5.45	5.39
	8	4.59	5.05	5.24	5.26	5.29	5.36	5.41	5.43	5.41	5.37	5.41	5.46	5.50	5.55	5.51	5.44	5.38
	9	5.13	5.20	5.24	5.28	5.33	5.40	5.44	5.44	5.41	5.45	5.47	5.49	5.52	5.63	5.66	5.62	5.50
	10	5.25	5.34	5.46	5.59	5.64	5.66	5.67	5.70	5.70	5.63	5.61	5.63	5.65	5.78	5.85	5.82	5.67
	11	4.32	5.07	5.47	5.60	5.67	5.73	5.78	5.87	5.86	5.65	5.66	5.70	5.74	5.93	6.04	6.01	5.76
	12	5.98	6.14	6.24	6.31	6.39	6.48	6.56	6.63	6.62	6.59	6.56	6.49	6.44	6.42	6.46	6.42	
1969		0 mo	1 mo	2 mo	3 mo	4 mo	5 mo	6 mo	9 mo	1 yr	2 yr	3 yr	4 yr	5 yr	10 yr	15 yr	20 yr	25 yr
	1	5.87	5.95	6.10	6.28	6.41	6.48	6.51	6.51	6.48	6.39	6.32	6.27	6.25	6.33	6.45	6.50	
	2	5.34	5.89	6.18	6.30	6.39	6.48	6.55	6.56	6.50	6.59	6.67	6.57	6.46	6.38	6.46	6.46	
	3	4.66	5.64	6.08	6.12	6.12	6.19	6.27	6.34	6.31	6.26	6.27	6.28	6.29	6.40	6.47	6.45	6.29
	4	6.51	6.11	5.97	6.01	6.08	6.12	6.14	6.20	6.23	6.36	6.42	6.41	6.39	6.34	6.31	6.26	6.17
	5	5.83	5.97	6.09	6.20	6.31	6.40	6.47	6.58	6.60	6.74	6.81	6.73	6.64	6.58	6.65	6.63	
	6	5.89	6.26	6.44	6.49	6.62	6.90	7.20	7.65	7.66	7.49	7.36	7.17	7.00	6.66	6.52	6.44	
	7	5.54	6.55	7.05	7.19	7.27	7.36	7.46	7.61	7.64	7.55	7.32	7.08	6.90	6.56	6.45	6.36	
	8	6.84	7.05	7.10	7.07	7.12	7.25	7.39	7.53	7.53	7.42	7.28	7.12	6.99	6.63	6.40	6.28	
	9	7.10	7.03	7.07	7.19	7.33	7.45	7.54	7.71	7.81	7.90	7.81	7.74	7.68	7.31	6.88	6.61	
	10	6.22	6.69	6.93	7.05	7.22	7.41	7.51	7.52	7.40	7.20	7.30	7.21	7.07	6.79	6.67	6.56	
	11	6.00	6.89	7.40	7.66	7.85	7.98	8.05	8.02	7.85	7.53	7.56	7.44	7.31	7.08	6.99	6.85	
	12	5.90	7.28	7.99	8.13	8.15	8.22	8.27	8.14	7.94	8.06	8.15	7.98	7.82	7.43	7.18	6.95	
1970		0 mo	1 mo	2 mo	3 mo	4 mo	5 mo	6 mo	9 mo	1 yr	2 yr	3 yr	4 yr	5 yr	10 yr	15 yr	20 yr	25 yr
	1	6.95	7.62	7.93	8.01	8.05	8.07	8.06	7.99	7.96	7.97	7.96	7.95	7.93	7.55	7.07	6.82	
	2	6.10	6.68	6.94	7.01	7.02	7.00	6.98	6.90	6.89	7.07	7.17	7.16	7.12	6.87	6.60	6.44	
	3	6.64	6.43	6.39	6.48	6.57	6.59	6.59	6.61	6.65	6.84	6.98	7.07	7.09	6.88	6.83		
	4	6.29	6.52	6.78	7.03	7.19	7.27	7.32	7.44	7.52	7.70	7.78	7.81	7.82	7.74	7.50	7.18	
	5	6.28	6.56	6.82	7.03	7.16	7.19	7.20	7.31	7.44	7.72	7.72	7.64	7.60	7.68			

Table 13.A.3 (cont.)

Year	Month	0 mo	1 mo	2 mo	3 mo	4 mo	5 mo	6 mo	9 mo	1 yr	2 yr	3 yr	4 yr	5 yr	10 yr	15 yr	20 yr	25 yr
1970	6	5.46	6.12	6.44	6.52	6.57	6.68	6.79	7.05	7.21	7.51	7.60	7.61	7.61	7.52			
	7	4.32	5.92	6.50	6.43	6.38	6.50	6.66	6.86	6.89	7.27	7.43	7.44	7.46	7.57			
	8	6.07	6.24	6.33	6.38	6.44	6.56	6.67	6.79	6.78	7.13	7.29	7.30	7.33	7.52			
	9	5.62	5.56	5.71	6.03	6.32	6.47	6.53	6.59	6.60	6.67	6.81	6.94	7.04	7.24			
	10	5.05	5.45	5.76	5.96	6.09	6.17	6.22	6.30	6.34	6.51	6.69	6.83	6.93	7.13			
	11	4.40	4.75	4.97	5.07	5.08	5.06	5.05	5.09	5.16	5.38	5.60	5.84	6.02	6.39	6.44	6.34	
	12	3.98	4.57	4.84	4.90	4.92	4.93	4.91	4.89	4.99	5.46	5.72	5.86	5.96	6.26	6.39	6.35	
1971		0 mo	1 mo	2 mo	3 mo	4 mo	5 mo	6 mo	9 mo	1 yr	2 yr	3 yr	4 yr	5 yr	10 yr	15 yr	20 yr	25 yr
	1	3.99	4.11	4.15	4.17	4.22	4.25	4.25	4.19	4.24	4.72	5.19	5.56	5.79	6.09	6.01	5.98	
	2	3.12	3.25	3.34	3.42	3.50	3.56	3.61	3.69	3.74	4.21	4.74	5.14	5.41	5.97	6.15	6.17	
	3	3.46	3.46	3.54	3.64	3.69	3.69	3.69	3.74	3.81	4.15	4.50	4.83	5.09	5.62	5.74	5.80	
	4	3.49	3.81	3.97	4.04	4.13	4.24	4.33	4.50	4.63	5.18	5.60	5.85	6.00	6.11			
	5	3.92	4.20	4.35	4.38	4.40	4.44	4.51	4.75	4.96	5.47	5.75	5.93	6.07	6.43			
	6	4.52	4.95	5.12	5.12	5.15	5.29	5.46	5.82	6.05	6.47	6.64	6.72	6.77	6.81			
	7	4.79	5.21	5.33	5.31	5.42	5.63	5.82	6.01	6.06	6.48	6.74	6.83	6.88	6.93			
	8	4.49	4.46	4.42	4.40	4.47	4.64	4.82	5.11	5.26	5.54	5.69	5.80	5.90	6.22			
	9	4.55	4.47	4.52	4.65	4.78	4.89	4.99	5.16	5.27	5.50	5.68	5.84	5.92	5.95			
	10	3.56	4.06	4.29	4.37	4.43	4.47	4.48	4.49	4.60	5.04	5.17	5.46	5.71	5.91	6.03		
	11	3.67	4.06	4.28	4.35	4.39	4.45	4.50	4.63	4.75	5.06	5.26	5.56	5.78	5.82			
	12	3.24	3.33	3.50	3.70	3.87	3.98	4.03	4.11	4.29	4.82	5.02	5.25	5.44	5.87			
1972		0 mo	1 mo	2 mo	3 mo	4 mo	5 mo	6 mo	9 mo	1 yr	2 yr	3 yr	4 yr	5 yr	10 yr	15 yr	20 yr	25 yr
	1	2.41	3.02	3.28	3.38	3.53	3.68	3.78	3.99	4.18	4.83	5.26	5.52	5.70	6.28			
	2	3.36	3.25	3.29	3.44	3.60	3.72	3.82	4.05	4.23	4.82	5.20	5.45	5.63	6.15			
	3	3.32	3.42	3.64	3.92	4.16	4.33	4.46	4.77	5.00	5.50	5.76	5.91	6.00	6.17			
	4	3.30	3.28	3.44	3.67	3.86	4.01	4.12	4.33	4.49	5.12	5.52	5.68	5.79	6.13			
	5	3.32	3.50	3.67	3.81	3.95	4.09	4.21	4.43	4.56	4.98	5.31	5.53	5.68	6.06			
	6	3.39	3.67	3.91	4.11	4.31	4.51	4.69	5.01	5.16	5.47	5.66	5.80	5.91	6.19			
	7	3.41	3.56	3.70	3.86	4.04	4.25	4.43	4.73	4.87	5.35	5.69	5.83	5.93	6.32			
	8	4.27	4.35	4.42	4.51	4.65	4.84	5.02	5.27	5.36	5.66	5.87	6.00	6.10	6.44			
	9	4.64	4.48	4.52	4.74	4.98	5.17	5.31	5.53	5.63	5.85	5.96	6.00	6.07	6.53			
	10	4.49	4.54	4.65	4.82	4.97	5.09	5.18	5.36	5.47	5.80	5.96	6.02	6.08	6.38			
	11	4.82	4.79	4.83	4.92	5.04	5.16	5.26	5.36	5.36	5.65	5.86	5.91	5.97	6.27			
	12	4.77	4.93	5.08	5.22	5.34	5.42	5.48	5.55	5.59	5.89	6.03	6.06	6.10	6.36			
1973		0 mo	1 mo	2 mo	3 mo	4 mo	5 mo	6 mo	9 mo	1 yr	2 yr	3 yr	4 yr	5 yr	10 yr	15 yr	20 yr	25 yr
	1	5.22	5.44	5.62	5.77	5.87	5.93	5.96	6.02	6.06	6.26	6.34	6.34	6.33	6.42	6.57	6.75	
	2	5.49	5.59	5.73	5.90	6.03	6.11	6.16	6.28	6.39	6.60	6.65	6.64	6.62	6.56	6.59		
	3	5.77	6.08	6.33	6.53	6.69	6.82	6.91	6.99	6.96	6.79	6.72	6.69	6.67	6.60	6.60		

	4	5.95	6.01	6.17	6.39	6.55	6.63	6.68	6.72	6.72	6.65	6.62	6.62	6.61	6.58	6.60		
	5	6.00	6.53	6.86	7.01	7.07	7.10	7.10	7.09	7.05	6.81	6.66	6.64	6.67	6.76	6.82	6.87	
	6	7.30	7.45	7.56	7.62	7.68	7.75	7.81	7.79	7.60	7.06	6.89	6.82	6.78	6.80	6.88	6.96	
	7	7.96	8.29	8.39	8.36	8.38	8.51	8.65	8.77	8.66	8.19	7.91	7.75	7.64	7.41	7.33	7.35	
	8	8.41	8.64	8.70	8.68	8.67	8.70	8.74	8.67	8.47	7.74	7.35	7.19	7.11	7.07	7.12	7.17	
	9	7.59	7.13	7.04	7.25	7.49	7.67	7.77	7.77	7.58	6.96	6.71	6.65	6.65	6.75	6.86	6.92	
	10	6.74	7.15	7.36	7.41	7.48	7.63	7.69	7.35	6.99	6.83	6.93	6.91	6.85	6.88	7.14	7.29	
	11	7.85	7.49	7.43	7.62	7.85	8.02	8.06	7.80	7.44	6.75	6.74	6.71	6.68	6.77	6.97	7.09	
	12	7.13	7.29	7.45	7.57	7.63	7.63	7.59	7.34	7.12	6.74	6.72	6.68	6.65	6.76	7.03	7.21	
1974		0 mo	1 mo	2 mo	3 mo	4 mo	5 mo	6 mo	9 mo	1 yr	2 yr	3 yr	4 yr	5 yr	10 yr	15 yr	20 yr	25 yr
	1	7.36	7.52	7.62	7.66	7.63	7.55	7.47	7.24	7.03	6.74	6.76	6.76	6.77	6.96	7.18	7.30	
	2	7.18	7.58	7.65	7.59	7.56	7.54	7.48	7.19	7.00	6.77	6.80	6.83	6.85	7.04	7.26	7.40	
	3	8.01	8.51	8.65	8.64	8.61	8.58	8.56	8.46	8.30	7.84	7.72	7.64	7.58	7.51	7.57	7.65	
	4	8.51	8.73	8.90	9.01	9.01	8.98	8.99	9.06	8.94	8.31	8.18	8.12	8.06	7.93	7.90	7.93	
	5	7.55	7.66	7.95	8.29	8.45	8.47	8.51	8.74	8.73	8.04	8.00	7.97	7.91	7.85	7.90	7.96	
	6	7.65	7.65	7.69	7.76	7.87	8.03	8.20	8.61	8.67	8.20	8.27	8.23	8.13	7.90	7.86	7.88	
	7	7.04	7.55	7.74	7.74	7.86	8.07	8.26	8.60	8.64	8.42	8.45	8.39	8.30	8.07	8.00	8.01	
	8	9.17	9.20	9.23	9.29	9.43	9.59	9.72	9.91	9.74	8.80	8.56	8.48	8.45	8.33	8.21	8.22	
	9	6.26	6.06	6.07	6.32	6.79	7.30	7.68	8.22	8.28	7.95	8.01	7.97	7.92	7.89	8.03	8.20	
	10	6.37	7.12	7.70	8.08	8.17	8.09	8.02	7.94	7.86	7.72	7.84	7.85	7.80	7.75	7.82	7.92	
	11	7.44	7.45	7.52	7.63	7.73	7.81	7.83	7.69	7.52	7.27	7.40	7.48	7.51	7.66	7.79	7.86	
	12	6.51	6.77	7.00	7.18	7.26	7.26	7.23	7.16	7.13	7.18	7.23	7.21	7.18	7.37	7.70	7.84	
1975		0 mo	1 mo	2 mo	3 mo	4 mo	5 mo	6 mo	9 mo	1 yr	2 yr	3 yr	4 yr	5 yr	10 yr	15 yr	20 yr	25 yr
	1	5.47	5.53	5.67	5.84	5.94	6.00	6.02	6.05	6.15	6.69	6.95	7.10	7.20	7.42	7.50	7.59	7.77
	2	4.48	4.98	5.33	5.55	5.67	5.73	5.76	5.84	5.92	6.25	6.56	6.81	7.00	7.39	7.49	7.56	
	3	5.06	5.27	5.48	5.66	5.76	5.82	5.86	6.00	6.16	6.68	6.97	7.18	7.35	7.82	8.05	8.13	
	4	4.77	5.15	5.41	5.59	5.79	6.01	6.20	6.57	6.85	7.55	7.76	7.85	7.92	8.08	8.11	8.16	
	5	4.66	4.94	5.14	5.28	5.40	5.50	5.60	5.84	6.06	6.82	7.16	7.36	7.50	7.86	8.02	8.05	8.00
	6	5.59	5.67	5.83	6.03	6.18	6.25	6.32	6.62	6.84	7.20	7.45	7.60	7.67	7.82	7.90	7.96	
	7	5.97	6.00	6.13	6.34	6.56	6.74	6.89	7.13	7.25	7.64	7.81	7.88	7.91	8.00	8.07	8.11	8.14
	8	5.73	5.98	6.24	6.50	6.74	6.93	7.08	7.33	7.45	7.69	7.87	7.97	8.00	8.06	8.16	8.24	8.29
	9	6.25	6.31	6.47	6.69	6.91	7.09	7.22	7.46	7.61	8.01	8.17	8.23	8.25	8.34	8.42	8.47	8.49
	10	5.25	5.36	5.49	5.63	5.73	5.80	5.86	6.06	6.29	6.94	7.21	7.37	7.50	7.84	7.98	8.04	
	11	4.67	5.12	5.46	5.68	5.86	6.02	6.15	6.38	6.56	7.21	7.46	7.63	7.77	8.13	8.23	8.24	8.25
	12	4.99	5.06	5.16	5.29	5.41	5.53	5.63	5.89	6.09	6.66	7.01	7.23	7.37	7.71	7.87	7.94	
1976		0 mo	1 mo	2 mo	3 mo	4 mo	5 mo	6 mo	9 mo	1 yr	2 yr	3 yr	4 yr	5 yr	10 yr	15 yr	20 yr	25 yr
	1	4.52	4.52	4.63	4.79	4.92	5.02	5.10	5.33	5.55	6.37	6.86	7.18	7.39	7.80	7.89	7.91	
	2	4.46	4.67	4.88	5.09	5.29	5.46	5.61	5.89	6.10	6.74	7.06	7.26	7.39	7.73	7.87	7.94	
	3	4.77	4.78	4.89	5.05	5.22	5.37	5.50	5.80	6.03	6.63	6.95	7.14	7.28	7.62	7.74	7.79	
	4	4.86	4.70	4.79	4.99	5.17	5.30	5.42	5.73	6.01	6.56	6.85	7.08	7.23	7.61	7.76	7.83	
	5	4.86	5.24	5.48	5.61	5.77	5.96	6.11	6.39	6.65	7.23	7.43	7.57	7.64	7.84	7.95	8.02	

Table 13.A.3 (cont.)

		0 mo	1 mo	2 mo	3 mo	4 mo	5 mo	6 mo	9 mo	1 yr	2 yr	3 yr	4 yr	5 yr	10 yr	15 yr	20 yr	25 yr
1976	6	5.26	5.30	5.36	5.47	5.63	5.80	5.93	6.14	6.35	6.90	7.14	7.32	7.44	7.73	7.84	7.90	
	7	5.09	5.10	5.16	5.27	5.41	5.55	5.65	5.85	6.07	6.67	6.94	7.16	7.33	7.75	7.86	7.90	
	8	4.80	4.98	5.09	5.17	5.28	5.40	5.50	5.65	5.82	6.41	6.65	6.87	7.06	7.56	7.70	7.76	
	9	5.13	5.07	5.09	5.18	5.28	5.38	5.46	5.59	5.73	6.25	6.52	6.77	6.96	7.46	7.62	7.69	
	10	4.69	4.75	4.85	4.98	5.08	5.15	5.20	5.30	5.45	6.01	6.25	6.47	6.69	7.34	7.56	7.65	
	11	4.37	4.41	4.46	4.50	4.56	4.63	4.68	4.77	4.88	5.38	5.63	5.76	5.96	6.85	7.25	7.38	
	12	4.22	4.26	4.34	4.45	4.53	4.59	4.63	4.72	4.84	5.34	5.64	5.87	6.07	6.72	7.00	7.14	
1977		0 mo	1 mo	2 mo	3 mo	4 mo	5 mo	6 mo	9 mo	1 yr	2 yr	3 yr	4 yr	5 yr	10 yr	15 yr	20 yr	25 yr
	1	4.58	4.57	4.66	4.81	4.95	5.06	5.14	5.34	5.54	6.15	6.43	6.68	6.85	7.27	7.46	7.55	
	2	4.41	4.52	4.65	4.79	4.90	4.99	5.07	5.30	5.51	6.09	6.42	6.71	6.92	7.34	7.54	7.66	7.72
	3	4.54	4.51	4.55	4.65	4.75	4.83	4.91	5.17	5.40	5.95	6.35	6.64	6.84	7.31	7.52	7.63	7.66
	4	4.33	4.44	4.58	4.72	4.84	4.95	5.05	5.30	5.50	6.05	6.37	6.65	6.86	7.33	7.52	7.60	7.63
	5	4.80	4.90	5.00	5.11	5.21	5.29	5.37	5.55	5.70	6.12	6.36	6.60	6.79	7.28	7.49	7.58	7.60
	6	4.98	4.96	5.01	5.12	5.23	5.32	5.39	5.52	5.63	6.04	6.27	6.50	6.69	7.17	7.33	7.42	
	7	5.16	5.25	5.36	5.48	5.60	5.72	5.81	5.97	6.08	6.40	6.61	6.80	6.95	7.30	7.44	7.51	7.55
	8	5.35	5.38	5.49	5.65	5.82	5.94	6.02	6.18	6.26	6.46	6.63	6.76	6.86	7.17	7.35	7.45	
	9	5.75	5.74	5.85	6.03	6.18	6.28	6.33	6.47	6.56	6.74	6.84	6.95	7.03	7.27	7.43	7.53	7.57
	10	6.28	6.11	6.16	6.37	6.54	6.65	6.71	6.87	7.00	7.20	7.28	7.36	7.40	7.51	7.64	7.74	7.77
	11	5.30	5.67	5.97	6.19	6.36	6.48	6.57	6.75	6.86	7.06	7.17	7.22	7.27	7.47	7.62	7.72	7.75
	12	5.38	5.82	6.13	6.32	6.45	6.55	6.63	6.80	6.91	7.08	7.23	7.35	7.42	7.62	7.75	7.83	7.87
1978		0 mo	1 mo	2 mo	3 mo	4 mo	5 mo	6 mo	9 mo	1 yr	2 yr	3 yr	4 yr	5 yr	10 yr	15 yr	20 yr	25 yr
	1	5.69	6.07	6.35	6.53	6.67	6.77	6.85	7.02	7.11	7.27	7.40	7.51	7.58	7.75	7.89	7.98	8.01
	2	5.98	6.22	6.41	6.55	6.68	6.81	6.91	7.08	7.15	7.42	7.56	7.67	7.73	7.87	7.99	8.07	8.10
	3	6.84	6.56	6.51	6.62	6.75	6.87	6.96	7.18	7.32	7.56	7.68	7.76	7.82	7.97	8.09	8.15	8.17
	4	5.86	6.03	6.25	6.50	6.74	6.93	7.08	7.36	7.51	7.77	7.82	7.87	7.91	8.05	8.17	8.22	8.22
	5	6.33	6.44	6.60	6.81	7.02	7.20	7.35	7.63	7.77	7.95	7.99	8.06	8.10	8.22	8.33	8.38	8.32
	6	6.24	6.61	6.94	7.24	7.47	7.63	7.74	8.01	8.19	8.28	8.33	8.31	8.31	8.41	8.49	8.48	8.44
	7	6.40	6.55	6.76	7.00	7.23	7.43	7.61	7.98	8.18	8.25	8.28	8.28	8.28	8.36	8.42	8.42	8.39
	8	8.04	7.87	7.76	7.70	7.73	7.84	7.95	8.19	8.29	8.26	8.23	8.21	8.21	8.20	8.22	8.25	8.26
	9	7.89	8.00	8.15	8.32	8.47	8.59	8.65	8.68	8.66	8.46	8.32	8.29	8.30	8.41	8.46	8.46	8.42
	10	8.34	8.65	8.84	8.94	9.09	9.30	9.49	9.73	9.65	9.26	9.10	8.96	8.87	8.72	8.70	8.71	8.70
	11	8.95	8.99	9.06	9.17	9.30	9.45	9.58	9.78	9.75	9.27	8.91	8.74	8.69	8.66	8.64	8.59	8.55
	12	7.63	8.63	9.24	9.55	9.70	9.77	9.85	10.21	10.31	9.82	9.39	9.16	9.08	8.94	8.86	8.80	8.74
1979		0 mo	1 mo	2 mo	3 mo	4 mo	5 mo	6 mo	9 mo	1 yr	2 yr	3 yr	4 yr	5 yr	10 yr	15 yr	20 yr	25 yr
	1	9.64	9.51	9.49	9.56	9.63	9.68	9.73	9.85	9.80	9.36	8.93	8.75	8.73	8.74	8.71	8.69	8.65
	2	9.58	9.63	9.65	9.67	9.73	9.82	9.90	10.00	9.97	9.60	9.25	9.08	9.04	9.00	8.95	8.89	8.84

Year	Month	0 mo	1 mo	2 mo	3 mo	4 mo	5 mo	6 mo	9 mo	1 yr	2 yr	3 yr	4 yr	5 yr	10 yr	15 yr	20 yr	25 yr
	3	9.54	9.59	9.65	9.71	9.76	9.80	9.83	9.86	9.78	9.50	9.16	8.98	8.94	8.93	8.90	8.86	8.82
	4	9.54	9.58	9.67	9.78	9.86	9.90	9.93	9.99	9.91	9.64	9.29	9.14	9.12	9.14	9.10	9.05	8.99
	5	9.80	9.78	9.78	9.79	9.80	9.79	9.78	9.72	9.62	9.29	8.96	8.82	8.80	8.87	8.90	8.90	8.86
	6	8.73	8.98	9.13	9.19	9.23	9.24	9.25	9.23	9.11	8.73	8.59	8.53	8.52	8.61	8.66	8.65	8.61
	7	9.22	9.14	9.22	9.40	9.53	9.59	9.62	9.63	9.49	9.04	8.85	8.77	8.77	8.82	8.82	8.79	8.74
	8	9.98	10.11	10.10	10.03	10.03	10.10	10.19	10.29	10.21	9.59	9.33	9.21	9.15	9.04	8.97	8.92	8.86
	9	9.99	10.22	10.34	10.39	10.43	10.48	10.52	10.57	10.48	9.82	9.51	9.37	9.29	9.21	9.17	9.07	8.96
	10	11.24	11.73	12.15	12.48	12.66	12.72	12.72	12.68	12.45	11.64	11.30	11.06	10.89	10.50	10.30	10.15	10.02
	11	10.27	11.23	11.69	11.77	11.83	11.94	12.02	11.73	11.35	10.84	10.41	10.31	10.27	10.18	10.02	9.93	9.84
	12	7.12	10.27	11.87	12.27	12.34	12.34	12.29	11.84	11.44	10.90	10.46	10.21	10.12	10.08	10.03	9.96	9.85
1980		0 mo	1 mo	2 mo	3 mo	4 mo	5 mo	6 mo	9 mo	1 yr	2 yr	3 yr	4 yr	5 yr	10 yr	15 yr	20 yr	25 yr
	1	11.03	11.87	12.28	12.36	12.38	12.42	12.42	12.06	11.75	11.35	10.97	10.82	10.79	10.90	10.89	10.84	10.77
	2	13.29	13.92	14.25	14.32	14.37	14.53	14.72	14.91	14.90	14.50	13.77	13.36	13.11	12.57	12.33	12.10	11.89
	3	13.89	15.07	15.44	15.24	15.19	15.53	15.91	15.85	15.31	14.25	13.43	12.94	12.65	12.26	12.30	12.13	11.88
	4	10.28	10.39	10.52	10.67	10.82	10.95	11.04	11.07	10.96	10.52	10.41	10.41	10.45	10.65	10.74	10.71	10.59
	5	8.22	7.85	7.76	7.91	8.10	8.25	8.36	8.51	8.68	9.01	9.12	9.43	9.62	10.05	10.25	10.26	10.18
	6	4.09	6.66	7.94	8.15	8.11	8.13	8.19	8.33	8.42	8.93	9.06	9.22	9.36	9.85	10.03	9.96	9.82
	7	6.47	7.83	8.57	8.80	8.87	8.90	8.93	9.01	9.13	9.63	9.74	9.91	10.05	10.52	10.73	10.72	10.57
	8	8.27	9.20	9.85	10.25	10.49	10.63	10.70	10.89	11.12	11.25	11.26	11.40	11.44	11.25	11.29	11.21	11.02
	9	10.98	11.20	11.42	11.62	11.78	11.89	11.94	11.95	11.89	11.84	11.70	11.65	11.61	11.57	11.68	11.62	11.44
	10	10.23	11.65	12.57	12.99	13.13	13.20	13.26	13.27	13.11	12.72	12.60	12.51	12.42	12.12	12.17	12.08	11.91
	11	13.63	14.39	14.80	14.85	14.77	14.75	14.83	14.92	14.47	13.70	13.26	13.00	12.81	12.30	12.33	12.19	11.93
	12	10.88	12.90	14.19	14.74	14.74	14.58	14.41	13.86	13.25	12.57	12.34	12.23	12.18	12.03	12.01	11.82	11.56
1981		0 mo	1 mo	2 mo	3 mo	4 mo	5 mo	6 mo	9 mo	1 yr	2 yr	3 yr	4 yr	5 yr	10 yr	15 yr	20 yr	25 yr
	1	13.97	14.72	15.05	15.02	14.86	14.69	14.55	14.12	13.69	12.87	12.57	12.48	12.43	12.29	12.26	12.10	11.86
	2	13.60	14.20	14.56	14.69	14.68	14.62	14.56	14.32	14.02	13.56	13.50	13.42	13.34	13.06	12.97	12.75	12.49
	3	13.10	13.03	12.94	12.82	12.72	12.67	12.65	12.74	12.86	12.81	12.91	12.98	12.99	12.77	12.74	12.56	12.24
	4	12.57	14.11	14.98	15.20	15.10	15.00	14.96	14.87	14.69	14.33	14.17	14.06	13.98	13.67	13.59	13.35	13.04
	5	16.27	16.21	16.01	15.68	15.32	15.08	14.97	14.87	14.70	14.20	13.89	13.65	13.45	13.09	13.02	12.83	12.55
	6	14.03	14.41	14.61	14.65	14.64	14.65	14.66	14.57	14.43	14.21	13.97	13.92	13.81	13.46	13.34	13.15	12.82
	7	14.50	14.98	15.27	15.40	15.52	15.66	15.79	15.87	15.75	15.36	15.10	14.98	14.78	14.19	14.04	13.77	13.36
	8	15.39	15.64	15.84	16.00	16.15	16.32	16.50	16.62	16.35	16.17	15.68	15.67	15.56	14.95	14.79	14.64	14.29
	9	12.63	13.68	14.37	14.75	15.03	15.33	15.63	15.99	15.90	16.09	15.85	15.86	15.75	15.30	15.29	15.10	14.60
	10	12.75	12.97	13.09	13.12	13.21	13.41	13.68	14.10	14.08	14.14	14.23	14.31	14.32	14.24	14.23	14.07	13.72
	11	10.17	10.24	10.37	10.57	10.77	10.94	11.05	11.30	11.55	12.19	12.47	12.53	12.65	12.87	12.79	12.72	12.48
	12	8.26	9.71	10.79	11.50	11.96	12.28	12.53	13.02	13.29	13.48	13.55	13.67	13.71	13.67	13.68	13.56	13.19
1982		0 mo	1 mo	2 mo	3 mo	4 mo	5 mo	6 mo	9 mo	1 yr	2 yr	3 yr	4 yr	5 yr	10 yr	15 yr	20 yr	25 yr
	1	11.73	12.14	12.51	12.84	13.10	13.28	13.40	13.63	13.79	13.83	13.90	13.92	13.90	13.82	13.85	13.67	13.34
	2	11.85	11.98	12.27	12.71	13.17	13.46	13.54	13.54	13.73	13.87	13.82	13.80	13.73	13.61	13.74	13.62	13.35
	3	14.57	13.96	13.67	13.66	13.77	13.84	13.86	13.88	13.94	14.10	14.06	13.99	13.96	13.75	13.66	13.55	13.21
	4	12.31	12.32	12.46	12.71	12.94	13.08	13.15	13.28	13.44	13.62	13.60	13.50	13.48	13.38	13.23	13.12	12.93

Table 13.A.3 (cont.)

Year	Month	0 mo	1 mo	2 mo	3 mo	4 mo	5 mo	6 mo	9 mo	1 yr	2 yr	3 yr	4 yr	5 yr	10 yr	15 yr	20 yr	25 yr
1982	5	11.56	11.62	11.72	11.85	12.00	12.13	12.24	12.53	12.84	13.20	13.34	13.41	13.45	13.34	13.28	13.19	12.95
	6	10.65	11.74	12.56	13.11	13.45	13.67	13.80	14.01	14.19	14.30	14.40	14.35	14.28	14.00	13.87	13.72	13.36
	7	8.49	9.15	9.82	10.49	11.07	11.48	11.75	12.23	12.61	12.90	13.25	13.28	13.30	13.29	13.27	13.21	12.94
	8	7.54	7.51	7.78	8.33	8.96	9.46	9.82	10.53	11.12	11.84	12.18	12.27	12.39	12.44	12.30	12.31	12.16
	9	6.88	6.94	7.24	7.77	8.39	8.88	9.21	9.80	10.34	11.16	11.50	11.55	11.60	11.70	11.62	11.53	11.41
	10	7.80	7.72	7.83	8.11	8.41	8.62	8.73	8.96	9.44	9.99	10.47	10.56	10.69	10.85	10.81	10.90	10.64
	11	7.67	7.87	8.11	8.39	8.64	8.81	8.87	8.95	9.31	9.82	10.28	10.46	10.64	10.93	10.91	11.05	10.82
	12	8.05	8.07	8.11	8.17	8.25	8.31	8.33	8.45	8.78	9.42	9.87	10.11	10.25	10.51	10.58	10.66	10.49
1983		0 mo	1 mo	2 mo	3 mo	4 mo	5 mo	6 mo	9 mo	1 yr	2 yr	3 yr	4 yr	5 yr	10 yr	15 yr	20 yr	25 yr
	1	8.01	8.07	8.15	8.26	8.38	8.46	8.51	8.67	8.95	9.57	10.04	10.26	10.47	10.93	11.03	11.23	11.10
	2	7.90	7.91	7.96	8.06	8.17	8.23	8.24	8.28	8.60	9.18	9.65	9.74	9.81	10.28	10.45	10.71	10.45
	3	8.36	8.56	8.72	8.86	8.95	9.00	9.02	9.06	9.24	9.71	9.98	10.13	10.25	10.56	10.68	10.79	10.60
	4	8.01	8.10	8.19	8.28	8.35	8.39	8.41	8.49	8.71	9.21	9.59	9.76	9.91	10.24	10.38	10.49	10.29
	5	8.38	8.56	8.71	8.83	8.93	9.00	9.05	9.16	9.31	9.87	10.14	10.31	10.45	10.76	10.93	11.04	10.90
	6	8.25	8.57	8.81	8.98	9.09	9.17	9.23	9.38	9.57	10.11	10.36	10.52	10.63	10.90	11.05	11.08	10.91
	7	8.63	8.95	9.22	9.43	9.60	9.72	9.80	10.03	10.33	10.95	11.12	11.29	11.45	11.68	11.73	11.73	11.67
	8	8.74	9.01	9.25	9.46	9.65	9.80	9.91	10.12	10.35	10.97	11.29	11.48	11.61	11.73	11.78	11.88	11.71
	9	8.77	8.78	8.83	8.92	9.04	9.15	9.24	9.47	9.69	10.32	10.60	10.85	11.03	11.27	11.32	11.38	11.20
	10	8.46	8.49	8.58	8.72	8.87	9.01	9.12	9.37	9.61	10.34	10.76	11.01	11.18	11.50	11.59	11.63	11.51
	11	8.17	8.58	8.87	9.07	9.19	9.28	9.37	9.57	9.70	10.40	10.70	10.99	11.15	11.36	11.42	11.46	11.33
	12	8.18	8.63	8.97	9.19	9.32	9.42	9.50	9.70	9.88	10.58	10.87	11.16	11.31	11.54	11.59	11.66	11.54
1984		0 mo	1 mo	2 mo	3 mo	4 mo	5 mo	6 mo	9 mo	1 yr	2 yr	3 yr	4 yr	5 yr	10 yr	15 yr	20 yr	25 yr
	1	8.87	8.94	9.02	9.10	9.18	9.25	9.32	9.48	9.62	10.35	10.63	10.94	11.09	11.39	11.44	11.50	11.44
	2	8.45	8.86	9.17	9.37	9.50	9.60	9.68	9.84	9.98	10.73	10.98	11.32	11.48	11.72	11.77	11.84	11.80
	3	9.22	9.50	9.75	9.96	10.12	10.21	10.26	10.38	10.60	11.25	11.52	11.80	11.94	12.18	12.14	12.18	12.15
	4	9.25	9.49	9.73	9.96	10.15	10.26	10.33	10.52	10.79	11.51	11.82	12.06	12.21	12.46	12.44	12.49	12.45
	5	9.65	9.56	9.69	10.04	10.45	10.78	10.99	11.41	11.89	12.63	13.18	13.22	13.32	13.52	13.44	13.39	13.38
	6	8.83	9.39	9.83	10.18	10.46	10.72	10.96	11.57	11.95	12.78	13.00	13.20	13.29	13.41	13.31	13.29	13.31
	7	9.67	10.03	10.32	10.56	10.76	10.91	11.02	11.31	11.61	12.24	12.30	12.39	12.46	12.58	12.54	12.55	12.48
	8	10.78	10.74	10.76	10.82	10.92	11.02	11.12	11.39	11.65	12.17	12.25	12.36	12.43	12.45	12.39	12.32	12.34
	9	10.52	10.44	10.44	10.50	10.60	10.69	10.76	10.94	11.15	11.73	11.91	12.07	12.14	12.13	12.06	12.01	11.97
	10	8.07	8.57	8.96	9.24	9.44	9.57	9.64	9.83	10.13	10.85	11.08	11.21	11.31	11.47	11.44	11.42	11.37
	11	7.47	8.00	8.38	8.62	8.76	8.88	8.98	9.28	9.51	10.26	10.62	10.87	11.10	11.32	11.37	11.43	11.32
	12	6.30	7.23	7.84	8.12	8.19	8.25	8.36	8.80	9.11	9.88	10.36	10.65	10.95	11.30	11.38	11.41	11.31
1985		0 mo	1 mo	2 mo	3 mo	4 mo	5 mo	6 mo	9 mo	1 yr	2 yr	3 yr	4 yr	5 yr	10 yr	15 yr	20 yr	25 yr
	1	7.29	7.72	8.03	8.19	8.27	8.34	8.43	8.72	8.97	9.72	10.15	10.43	10.65	10.96	11.10	11.07	11.00
	2	6.77	7.67	8.32	8.70	8.91	9.04	9.13	9.35	9.63	10.41	10.86	11.13	11.36	11.70	11.82	11.81	11.80

	3	7.67	8.04	8.32	8.51	8.65	8.77	8.86	9.13	9.40	10.25	10.61	10.92	11.14	11.43	11.54	11.60	11.49
	4	7.24	7.52	7.76	7.98	8.16	8.29	8.38	8.61	8.93	9.74	10.20	10.49	10.76	11.20	11.35	11.42	11.37
	5	6.69	7.00	7.20	7.32	7.38	7.43	7.48	7.67	8.00	8.80	9.25	9.50	9.75	10.17	10.49	10.52	10.48
	6	6.50	6.72	6.90	7.03	7.13	7.20	7.25	7.44	7.74	8.60	9.09	9.45	9.71	10.11	10.34	10.49	10.35
	7	6.82	7.06	7.25	7.40	7.51	7.60	7.66	7.83	8.08	8.93	9.44	9.80	10.04	10.46	10.69	10.78	10.66
	8	7.35	7.24	7.22	7.27	7.36	7.46	7.54	7.75	7.92	8.76	9.25	9.49	9.68	10.15	10.49	10.51	10.30
	9	7.02	7.11	7.19	7.25	7.31	7.37	7.44	7.69	8.00	8.70	9.19	9.45	9.72	10.23	10.59	10.62	10.47
	10	6.95	7.16	7.30	7.35	7.39	7.44	7.51	7.67	7.81	8.54	8.93	9.14	9.41	9.89	10.27	10.23	9.97
	11	5.66	6.59	7.16	7.38	7.40	7.41	7.46	7.64	7.74	8.29	8.60	8.89	9.12	9.45	9.75	9.87	9.76
	12	5.19	6.24	6.89	7.16	7.23	7.25	7.29	7.41	7.49	7.86	8.17	8.33	8.48	8.87	9.22	9.36	9.25
1986		0 MO	1 MO	2 MO	3 MO	4 MO	5 MO	6 MO	9 MO	1 YR	2 YR	3 YR	4 YR	5 YR	10YR	15YR	20YR	25YR
	1	6.38	6.80	7.06	7.16	7.19	7.21	7.27	7.40	7.48	7.89	8.15	8.39	8.57	9.07	9.38	9.35	9.15
	2	6.51	6.89	7.11	7.20	7.20	7.20	7.22	7.29	7.33	7.63	7.74	7.87	7.97	8.07	8.29	8.34	8.26
	3	6.73	6.58	6.49	6.46	6.47	6.47	6.47	6.56	6.72	6.91	7.04	7.21	7.28	7.38	7.51	7.65	7.68
	4	5.82	5.98	6.10	6.18	6.23	6.27	6.30	6.39	6.49	6.89	7.05	7.19	7.27	7.41	7.58	7.78	7.81
	5	6.11	6.23	6.34	6.43	6.50	6.55	6.59	6.71	6.86	7.37	7.73	7.94	7.98	8.16	8.36	8.69	8.70
	6	5.96	6.01	6.06	6.11	6.15	6.17	6.17	6.23	6.40	6.84	7.11	7.25	7.33	7.44	7.70	8.07	8.12
	7	5.08	5.50	5.76	5.88	5.92	5.93	5.94	6.03	6.17	6.60	6.86	7.05	7.16	7.51	7.88	8.14	8.07
	8	4.37	4.86	5.15	5.24	5.23	5.23	5.26	5.39	5.48	5.97	6.22	6.46	6.59	7.17	7.48	7.67	7.63
	9	5.14	5.20	5.26	5.32	5.38	5.45	5.53	5.69	5.81	6.42	6.76	7.03	7.19	7.74	8.15	8.40	8.31
	10	4.65	5.03	5.24	5.30	5.32	5.36	5.41	5.57	5.69	6.18	6.47	6.70	6.86	7.44	7.84	7.94	7.80
	11	5.07	5.24	5.37	5.45	5.51	5.54	5.56	5.61	5.70	6.12	6.37	6.55	6.68	7.16	7.62	7.91	7.84
	12	4.08	5.00	5.57	5.80	5.81	5.78	5.76	5.82	5.94	6.35	6.66	6.68	6.77	7.22	7.67	7.98	7.94
1987		0 MO	1 MO	2 MO	3 MO	4 MO	5 MO	6 MO	9 MO	1 YR	2 YR	3 YR	4 YR	5 YR	10YR	15YR	20YR	25YR
	1	5.23	5.51	5.66	5.70	5.70	5.71	5.74	5.84	5.88	6.24	6.44	6.60	6.73	7.20	7.60	7.82	7.77
	2	5.44	5.49	5.53	5.55	5.58	5.61	5.64	5.77	5.88	6.27	6.45	6.61	6.71	7.14	7.51	7.73	7.69

References

Amsler, C. (1984). 'A "pure" long-term interest rate and the demand for money', *Journal of Economics and Business*, 36: 359–370.

Ando, A. and A. Kennickell (1983) 'A reappraisal of the Phillips curve and the term structure of interest rates', University of Pennsylvania.

Ando, A. and F. Modigliani (1975) 'Some reflections on describing structures in financial sectors', in: G. Fromm and L. Klein, eds., *The Brookings model: Perspectives and recent developments*. Amsterdam: North-Holland.

Backus, D., W.C. Brainard, G. Smith and J. Tobin (1980) 'A model of U.S. financial and nonfinancial economic behavior', *Journal of Money, Credit and Banking*, 12: 259–293.

Begg, D.K.H. (1984) 'Rational expectations and bond pricing: Modelling the term structure with and without certainty equivalence', *Economic Journal*, 94: 45–58.

Benninga, S. and A. Protopapadakis (1983) 'Real and nominal interest rates under uncertainty: The Fisher theorem and the term structure', *Journal of Political Economy* 91: 856–867.

Bierwag, G.O. and M.A. Grove (1967) 'A model of the term structure of interest rates', *Review of Economics and Statistics*, 49: 50–62.

Bohm-Bawerk, E.V. (1891) *The positive theory of capital*. G.E. Stechert & Co.

Board of Governors of the Federal Reserve System (1985) *Flow of funds accounts financial assets and liabilities year-end, 1961–84*. Washington.

Bodie, Z., A. Kane and R. McDonald (1984) 'Why haven't nominal rates declined?', *Financial Analysts Journal*, 40: 16–27.

Brainard, W.C. and J. Tobin (1968) 'Pitfalls in financial model building', *American Economic Review Papers and Proceedings*, 58: 99–122.

Brealey, R. and S. Schaefer (1977) 'Term structure with uncertain inflation', *Journal of Finance*, 32: 277–289.

Brennan, M.J. and E.S. Schwartz (1980) 'Conditional predictions of bond prices and returns', *Journal of Finance*, 35: 405–417.

Brown, S. and P. Dybvig (1986) 'The empirical implications of the Cox, Ingersoll, Ross theory of the term structure of interest rates', *Journal of Finance*, 41: 616–630.

Buse, A. (1967) 'Interest rates, the Meiselman model and random numbers', *Journal of Political Economy*, 75: 49–62.

Campbell, J.Y. (1984) 'Asset duration and time-varying risk premia', unpublished Ph.D. dissertation, Yale University.

Campbell, J.Y. (1986a) 'Bond and stock returns in a simple exchange model', *Quarterly Journal of Economics*, 101: 786–803.

Campbell, J.Y. (1986b) 'A defense of traditional hypotheses about the term structure of interest rates', *Journal of Finance*, 41: 183–193.

Campbell, J.Y. (1987) 'Stock returns and the term structure', *Journal of Financial Economics*, 18: 373–399.

Campbell, J.Y. and R.J. Shiller (1984) 'A simple account of the behavior of long-term interest rates', *American Economic Review Papers and Proceedings*, 74: 44–48.

Campbell, J.Y. and R.J. Shiller (1987) 'Cointegration and tests of present value models', *Journal of Political Economy*, 95: 1062–1088.

Campbell, J.Y. and R.J. Shiller (1988) 'The dividend price ratio and expectations of future dividends and discount factors', *Review of Financial Studies*, 1: 195–228.

Cargill, T.F. and R.A. Meyer (1972) 'A spectral approach to estimating the distributed lag relationship between long-term and short-term interest rates', *International Economic Review*, 13: 223–238.

Chambers, D.R., W.T. Carlton and D.W. Waldman (1984) 'A new approach to the estimation of the term structure of interest rates', *Journal of Financial and Quantitative Analysis*, 19: 233–252.

Chen, E.T. (1986) 'Estimation of the term structure of interest rates via cubic exponential spline functions', unpublished doctoral dissertation draft, The Ohio State University.

Clark, J.B. (1895) 'The gold standard of currency in light of recent theory', *Political Science Quarterly*, 10: 389–403.

Clark, T.A. (1986) 'Interest rate seasonals and the Federal Reserve', *Journal of Political Economy*, 94: 76–125.
Conard, J.W. (1959) *An introduction to the theory of interest*. Berkeley and Los Angeles: University of California Press.
Cox, J.C., J.E. Ingersoll, Jr. and S.A. Ross (1981) 'A reexamination of traditional hypotheses about the term structure of interest rates', *Journal of Finance*, 36: 769–799.
Cox, J.C., J.E. Ingersoll, Jr. and S.A. Ross (1985a) 'An intertemporal general equilibrium model of asset prices', *Econometrica*, 53: 363–384.
Cox, J.C., J.E. Ingersoll, Jr. and S.A. Ross (1985b) 'A theory of the term structure of interest rates', *Econometrica*, 53: 385–408.
Culbertson, J.M. (1957) 'The term structure of interest rates', *Quarterly Journal of Economics*, 71: 485–517.
De Leeuw, F. (1965) 'A Model of Financial Behavior', in: J. Duesenberry et al., eds., *The Brookings quarterly economic model of the United States*. Chicago: Rand McNally, pp. 465–530.
Diller, S. (1969) 'Expectations and the term structure of interest rates', in: J. Mincer, ed., *Economic forecasts and expectations*. New York: National Bureau of Economic Research.
Dobson, S.W. (1978) 'Estimating term structure equations with individual bond data', *Journal of Finance*, 33: 75–92.
Dobson, S.W., R.C. Sutch and D.E. Vanderford (1976) 'An evaluation of alternative empirical models of the term structure of interest rates', *Journal of Finance*, 31: 1035–1065.
Dothan, L.U. (1978) 'On the term structure of interest rates', *Journal of Financial Economics*, 6: 59–69.
Durand, D. (1942) *Basic yields of corporate bonds, 1900–1942*, Technical Paper No. 3, NBER.
Dybvig, P.H., J.E. Ingersoll Jr. and S.A. Ross (1986) 'Long forward rates can never fall', Unpublished paper, Yale University.
Dunn, K.B. and K.J. Singleton (1984) 'Modelling the term structure of interest rates under nonseparable utility and durability of goods', NBER Working Paper 1415.
Echols, M.E. and J.W. Elliott (1976) 'A quantitative yield curve model for estimating the term structure of interest rates', *Journal of Financial and Quantitative Analysis*, 11: 87–114.
Engle, R.F., D.M. Lilien and R.P. Robins (1987) 'Estimating time varying risk premia in the term structure: The ARCH-M model', *Econometrica*, 55: 391–407.
Fama, E.F. (1976) 'Inflation uncertainty and expected return on Treasury bills', *Journal of Political Economy*, 84: 427–448.
Fama, E.F. (1984a) 'The information in the term structure', *Journal of Financial Economics*, 13: 509–528.
Fama, E.F. (1984b) 'Term premiums in bond returns', *Journal of Financial Economics*, 13: 529–546.
Fama, E.F. (1986) 'Term premiums and default premiums in money markets', *Journal of Financial Economics*, 17: 175–196.
Fama, E.F. and R.R. Bliss (1987) 'The information in long-maturity forward rates', *American Economic Review*, 77: 680–692.
Financial Publishing Company (1970) *Expanded bond values tables*. London: Routledge & Kegan Paul, Ltd.
Fisher, I. (1896) 'Appreciation and interest', Publications of the American Economic Association, pp. 23–29 and 88–92.
Fisher, I. (1907) *The rate of interest, its nature, determination and relation to economic phenomena*. New York: Macmillan.
Fisher, I. (1930) *Theory of interest*. New York: Macmillan.
Fisher, L. (1966) 'An algorithm for finding exact rates of return', *Journal of Business*, 39: 111–118.
Flavin, M. (1983) 'Excess volatility in the financial markets: A reassessment of the empirical evidence', *Journal of Political Economy*, 91: 929–956.
Flavin, M. (1984a) 'Excess sensitivity of consumption to current income: Liquidity constraints or myopia?', NBER Working Paper 1341.
Flavin, M. (1984b) 'Time series evidence on the expectations hypothesis of the term structure', *Carnegie-Rochester Conference Series on Public Policy*, 20: 211–238.

Friedman, B.M. (1977a) 'Financial flow variables and the short-run determination of long-run interest rates', *Journal of Political Economy*, 85: 661–689.
Friedman, B.M. (1977b) 'The inefficiency of short-run monetary targets for monetary policy', *Brookings Papers on Economic Activity*, 2: 293–335.
Friedman, B.M. (1979) 'Interest rate expectations versus forward rates: Evidence from an expectations survey', *Journal of Finance*, 34: 965–973.
Friedman, B.M. (1980a) 'The determination of long-term interest rates: Implications for fiscal and monetary policies', *Journal of Money, Credit and Banking*, 12(Part 2): 331–352.
Friedman, B.M. (1980b) 'The effect of shifting wealth ownership on the term structure of interest rates: The case of pensions', *Quarterly Journal of Economics*, 94: 567–590.
Friedman, B.M. (1980c) 'Survey evidence on the rationality of interest rate expectations', *Journal of Monetary Economics*, 6: 453–465.
Friedman, B.M. (1981) 'Debt management policy, interest rates and economic activity', NBER Working Paper.
Friedman, B.M. and V.V. Roley (1979) 'Investors portfolio behavior under alternative models of long-term interest rate expectations: Unitary, rational or autoregressive', *Econometrica*, 47: 1475–1497.
Froot, K.A. (1987) 'New hope for the expectations hypothesis of the term structure of interest rates', Sloan School of Management.
Grossman, S.J., A. Melino and R.J. Shiller (1987) 'Estimating the continuous time consumption based asset pricing model', *Journal of Business and Economic Statistics*, 5: 315–327.
Hall, R.E. (1978) 'Stochastic implications of the life cycle-permanent income hypothesis', *Journal of Political Economy*, 6: 971–988.
Hamburger, M.J. and E.N. Platt (1975) 'The expectations hypothesis and the efficiency of the Treasury bill market', *Review of Economics and Statistics*, 57: 190–199.
Hansen, L.P. and T.J. Sargent (1981) 'Exact linear rational expectations models: Specification and estimation', Staff Report, Federal Reserve Bank of Minneapolis.
Hansen, L.P. and K.J. Singleton (1983) 'Stochastic consumption, risk aversion, and the temporal behavior of asset returns', *Journal of Political Economy*, 91: 249–265.
Hendershott, P.H. (1971) 'A flow of funds model estimated for the non-bank finance sector', *Journal of Money, Credit and Banking*, 3: 815–832.
Hickman, W.B. (1942) 'The term structure of interest rates: An exploratory analysis', NBER. Results shown in Kessel (1965, Appendix A, pp. 103–105).
Hicks, J.R. (1946) *Value and capital*, 2nd edn. Oxford: Oxford University Press.
Homer, S. (1963) *A history of interest rates*. New Brunswick: Rutgers University Press.
Hopewell, M. and G. Kaufman (1973) 'Bond price volatility and term to maturity: A generalized respecification', *American Economic Review*, 63: 749–753.
Huizinga, J. and F.S. Mishkin (1984) 'The measurement of ex-ante real interest rates on assets with different risk characteristics', unpublished paper, Graduate School of Business, University of Chicago.
Ingersoll, J.E., Jr., J. Skelton and R.L. Weil (1978) 'Duration forty years later', *Journal of Financial and Quantitative Analysis*, 13: 627–650.
Jarrow, R.A. (1981) 'Liquidity premiums and the expectations hypothesis', *Journal of Banking and Finance*, 5: 539–546.
Jones, D.S. and V.V. Roley (1983) 'Rational expectations and the expectations model of the term structure: A test using weekly data', *Journal of Monetary Economics*, 12: 453–465.
Jordan, J.V. (1984) 'Tax effects in term structure estimation', *Journal of Finance*, 39: 393–406.
Kaldor, N. (1939) 'Speculation and instability', *Review of Economic Studies*, 7: 1–27.
Kane, E.J. (1970) 'The term structure of interest rates: An attempt to reconcile teaching with practice', *The Journal of Finance*, 25: 361–374.
Kane, E.J. (1980) 'Market incompleteness and divergences between forward and future interest rates', *Journal of Finance*, 35: 221–234.
Kane, E.J. (1983) 'Nested tests of alternative term structure theories', *Review of Economics and Statistics*, 65: 115–123.
Kane, E.J. and B.G. Malkiel (1967) 'The term structure of interest rates: An analysis of a survey of interest rate expectations', *Review of Economics and Statistics*, 49: 343–355.

Keim, D.B. and R.F. Stambaugh (1986) 'Predicting returns in the stock and bond markets', *Journal of Financial Economics*, 17: 357–390.

Kessel, R.A. (1965) *The cyclical behavior of the term structure of interest rates*. New York: NBER.

Keynes, J.M. (1930) *Treatise on money*. New York: Macmillan.

Keynes, J.M. (1936) *The general theory of employment, interest and money*. London: Macmillan & Co. Ltd.

Kim, S.-J. (1986) 'Explaining the risk premium: Nominal interest rates, inflation and consumption', Yale University.

Langetieg, T.C. (1980) 'A multivariate model of the term structure', *Journal of Finance*, 35: 71–97.

LeRoy, S.F. (1982a) 'Expectations models of asset prices: A survey of theory', *Journal of Finance*, 37: 185–217.

LeRoy, S.F. (1982b) 'Risk aversion and the term structure of real interest rates', *Economics Letters*, 10: 355–361.

LeRoy, S.F. (1983) 'Risk aversion and the term structure of real interest rates: A correction', *Economics Letters*, 12: 339–340.

LeRoy, S.F. (1984) 'Nominal prices and interest rates in general equilibrium: Endowment shocks', *Journal of Business*, 57: 197–213.

LeRoy, S.F. and R.D. Porter (1981) 'The present value relation: Tests based on implied variance bounds', *Econometrica*, 49: 555–574.

Lindahl, E. (1939) *Studies in the theory of money and capital*. New York: Rinehart and Company.

Long, J.B. (1974) 'Stock prices, inflation and the term structure of interest rates', *Journal of Financial Economics*, 1: 131–170.

Lutz, F.A. (1940) 'The structure of interest rates', *Quarterly Journal of Economics*, 55: 36–63.

Macaulay, F.R. (1938) *Some theoretical problems suggested by the movements of interest rates, bond yields, and stock prices in the Unites States since 1856*. New York: NBER.

Malkiel, B.G. (1966) *The term structure of interest rates: Expectations and behavior patterns*. Princeton: Princeton University Press.

Mankiw, N.G. (1986) 'The term structure of interest rates revisited', *Brookings Papers on Economic Activity*, 1986, 1: 61–96.

Mankiw, N.G. and J.A. Miron (1986) 'The changing behavior of the term structure of interest rates', *Quarterly Journal of Economics*, 101: 211–228.

Mankiw, N.G and L.H. Summers (1984) 'Do long-term interest rates overreact to short-term interest rates?, *Brookings Papers on Economic Activity*, 00: 223–242.

Mankiw, N.G., J.A. Miron and D.N. Weil (1987) 'The adjustment of expectations of a change in regime: A study of the founding of the Federal Reserve, *American Economic Review*, 77: 358–374.

Marsh, T.A. (1980) 'Equilibrium term structure models: Test methodology', *Journal of Finance*, 35: 421–435.

Marsh, T.A. and E.R. Rosenfeld (1983) 'Stochastic processes for interest rates and equilibrium bond prices', *Journal of Finance*, 38: 635–646.

McCallum, J.S. (1975) 'The expected holding period return, uncertainty and the term structure of interest rates', *Journal of Finance*, 30: 307–323.

McCulloch, J.H. (1971) 'Measuring the term structure of interest rates', *Journal of Business*, 44: 19–31.

McCulloch, J.H. (1975a) 'An estimate of the liquidity premium', *Journal of Political Economy*, 83: 95–119.

McCulloch, J.H. (1975b) 'The tax adjusted yield curve', *Journal of Finance*, 30: 811–830.

McCulloch, J.H. (1977) 'Cumulative unanticipated changes in interest rates', NBER Working Paper 222.

McCulloch, J.H. (1981) 'Interest rate risk and capital adequacy for traditional banks and financial intermediaries', in: S.J. Maisel, ed., *Risk and capital adequacy in commercial banks*. Chicago: University of Chicago Press and NBER, pp. 223–248.

McCulloch, J.H. (1984) 'Term structure modeling using constrained exponential splines', Ohio State University.

Meiselman, D. (1962) *The term structure of interest rates*. Englewood Cliffs: Prentice-Hall.
Melino, A. (1983) 'Estimation of a rational expectations model of the term structure', in: *Essays on estimation and inference in linear rational expectations models*, unpublished Ph.D. Dissertation, Harvard University.
Melino, A. (1986) 'The term structure of interest rates: Evidence and theory', NBER Working Paper 1828.
Michaelsen, J.B. (1965) 'The term structure of interest rates and holding period yields on government securities', *Journal of Finance*, 20: 444–463.
Miron, J.A. (1984) 'The economics of seasonal time series', Ph.D. dissertation, M.I.T.
Miron, J.A. (1986) 'Financial panics, the seasonality of the nominal interest rate, and the founding of the fed', *American Economic Review*, 76: 125–140.
Mishkin, F.S. (1978) 'Efficient markets theory: Implications for monetary policy', *Brookings Papers on Economic Activity*, 1978, 2: 707–752.
Mishkin, F.S. (1980) 'Is the preferred habitat model of the term structure inconsistent with financial market efficiency?', *Journal of Political Economy*, 88: 406–411.
Mishkin, F.S. (1982) 'Monetary policy and short-term interest rates: An efficient markets–rational expectations approach', *Journal of Monetary Economics*, 37: 63–72.
Modigliani, F. and R.J. Shiller (1973) 'Inflation, rational expectations and the term structure of interest rates', *Economica*, 40: 12–43.
Modigliani, F.R. and R. Sutch (1966) 'Innovations in interest rate policy', *American Economic Review*, 56: 178–197.
Modigliani, F. and R. Sutch (1967) 'Debt management and the term structure of interest rates: An analysis of recent experience', *Journal of Political Economy*, 75: 569–589.
Nelson, C.R. (1970a) 'A critique of some recent empirical research in the explanation of the term structure of interest rates', *Journal of Political Economy*, 78: 764–767.
Nelson, C.R. (1970b) 'Testing a model of the term structure of interest rates by simulation of market forecasts', *Journal of the American Statistical Association*, 65: 1163–1190.
Nelson, C.R. (1972a) 'Estimation of term premiums from average yield differentials in the term structure of interest rates', *Econometrica*, 40: 277–287.
Nelson, C.R. (1972b) *The term structure of interest rates*. New York: Basic Books.
Nelson, C.R. and A.F. Siegel (1985) 'Parsimonious modelling of yield curves for U.S. Treasury bills', NBER Working Paper 1594.
Okun, A.M. (1963) 'Monetary policy, debt management, and interest rates: A quantitative appraisal', in: Commission on Money and Credit, *Stabilization Policies*. Englewood Cliffs: Prentice-Hall, pp. 331–380.
Pesando, J.E. (1975) 'Determinants of term premiums in the market for United States Treasury bills', *Journal of Finance*, 30: 1317–1327.
Pesando, J.E. (1978) 'On the efficiency of the bond market: Some Canadian evidence', *Journal of Political Economy*, 86: 1057–1076.
Pesando, J.E. (1981) 'On forecasting interest rates: An efficient markets perspective', *Journal of Monetary Economics*, 8: 305–318.
Pesando, J.E. (1983) 'On expectations, term premiums and the volatility of long-term interest rates', *Journal of Monetary Economics*, 12: 467–474.
Phillips, L. and J. Pippenger (1976) "Preferred habitat vs. efficient market: A test of alternative hypotheses', *Federal Reserve Bank of St. Louis Review*, 58: 151–164.
Phillips, L. and J. Pippenger (1979) 'The term structure of interest rates in the MPS model: Reality or illusion?', *Journal of Money, Credit and Banking*, 11: 151–164.
Richard, S.F. (1978) 'An arbitrage model of the term structure of interest rates', *Journal of Financial Economics*, 6: 33–57.
Roley, V.V. (1977) 'A structural model of the U.S. government securities market', unpublished Ph.D. dissertation, Harvard University.
Roley, V.V. (1981) 'The determinants of the Treasury security yield curve', *Journal of Finance*, 36: 1103–1126.
Roley, V.V. (1982) 'The effect of federal debt management policy on corporate bond and equity yields', *Quarterly Journal of Economics*, 97: 645–668.
Roll, R. (1970) *The behavior of interest rates*. New York: Basic Books.

Roll, R. (1971) 'Investment diversification and bond maturity', *Journal of Finance*, 26: 51–66.
Salomon Brothers, Inc. (1983) *An analytical record of yields and yield spreads: From 1945*. New York.
Samuelson, P.A. (1945) 'The effect of interest rate increases on the banking system', *American Economic Review*, 35: 16–27.
Sargent, T.J. (1971) 'Expectations at the short end of the yield curve: An application of Macaulay's test', in: J.M. Guttentag, ed., *Essays on interest rates*, Vol. II. New York: NBER, pp. 391–412.
Sargent, T.J. (1979) 'A note on the estimation of the rational expectations model of the term structure', *Journal of Monetary Economics*, 5: 133–143.
Say, J.B. (1853) *A treatise on political economy*. Philadelphia: Lippincott Grambo & Co.
Schaefer, S.M. (1981) 'Measuring a tax-specific term structure of interest rates in the market for British Government securities', *Economic Journal*, 91: 415–438.
Scott, R.H. (1965) 'Liquidity and the term structure of interest rates', *Quarterly Journal of Economics*, 79: 135–145.
Shea, G.S. (1984) 'Pitfalls in smoothing interest rate term structure data: Equilibrium models and spline approximations', *Journal of Financial and Quantitative Analysis*, 19: 253–269.
Shea, G.S. (1985) 'Interest rate term structure equations with exponential splines: A note', *Journal of Finance*, 40: 319–325.
Shiller, R.J. (1972) 'Rational expectations and the structure of interest rates', unpublished Ph.D. dissertation, M.I.T.
Shiller, R.J. (1978) 'Rational expectations and the dynamic structure of macroeconomic models: A critical review', *Journal of Monetary Economics*, 4: 1–44.
Shiller, R.J. (1979) 'The volatility of long-term interest rates and expectations models of the term structure', *Journal of Political Economy*, 87: 1190–1219.
Shiller, R.J. (1980) 'Can the federal reserve control real interest rates?', in: S. Fischer, ed., *Rational expectations and economic policy*, Chicago: NBER and University of Chicago Press.
Shiller, R.J. (1981a) 'Alternative tests of rational expectations Models: The case of the term structure', *Journal of Econometrics*, 16: 71–87.
Shiller, R.J. (1981b) 'Do stock prices move too much to be justified by subsequent changes in dividends?', *American Economic Review*, 71: 421–436.
Shiller, R.J. (1986) 'Comments and discussion', *Brookings Papers on Economic Activity*, 1986, 1: 100–107.
Shiller, R.J. (1987) 'Conventional valuation and the term structure of interest rates', in: R. Dornbusch, S. Fischer and J. Bossons, eds., *Macroeconomics and finance: Essays in honour of Franco Modigliani*. Cambridge, Mass.: MIT Press.
Shiller, R.J., J.Y. Campbell and K.L. Schoenholtz (1983) 'Forward rates and future policy: Interpreting the term structure of interest rates', *Brookings Papers on Economic Activity*, 1983, 1: 173–217.
Sidgwick, H. (1887) *The principles of political economy*. London: Macmillan.
Singleton, K.J. (1980a) 'A latent time series model of the cyclical behavior of interest rates', *International Economic Review*, 21: 559–575.
Singleton, K.J. (1980b) 'Expectations models of the term structure and implied variance bounds', *Journal of Political Economy*, 88: 1159–1176.
Singleton, K.J. (1980c) 'Maturity-specific disturbances and the term structure of interest rates', *Journal of Money, Credit and Banking*, 12 (Part I): 603–614.
Skinner, E.B. (1913) *The mathematical theory of investment*. Boston: Ginn and Co.
Startz, R. (1982) 'Do forecast errors or term premia really make the difference between long and short rates?', *Journal of Financial Economics*, 10: 323–329.
Stiglitz, J. (1970) 'A consumption-oriented theory of the demand for financial assets and the term structure of interest rates', *Review of Economic Studies*, 37: 321–351.
Stigum, M. (1978) *The money market: Myth, reality and practice*. Homewood: Dow Jones–Irwin.
Stigum, M. (1981) *Money market calculations: Yields, break-evens and arbitrage*. Homewood: Dow Jones–Irwin.
Summers, L.H. (1982) 'Do we really know that markets are efficient?', NBER Working Paper.

Sutch, R. (1968) 'Expectations, risk and the term structure of interest rates,' unpublished Ph.D. dissertation, M.I.T.
Telser, L.G. (1967) 'A critique of some recent empirical research on the explanation of the term structure of interest rates', *Journal of Political Economy*, 75: 546–561.
Vasicek, O.A. (1978) 'An equilibrium characterization of the term structure', *Journal of Financial Economics*, 6: 33–57.
Vasicek, O.A. and H. G. Fong (1982) 'Term structure modelling using exponential splines', *Journal of Finance*, 37: 339–348.
Volterra, V. (1959) *Theory of functionals and of integral and integrodifferential equations*. New York: Dover.
Walker, C.E. (1954) 'Federal reserve policy and the structure of interest rates in government securities', *Quarterly Journal of Economics*, 68: 19–42.
Wallace, N. (1967) 'Comment', *Journal of Political Economy*, 75: 590–592.
Walsh, C.E. (1985) 'A rational expectations model of term premia with some implications for empirical asset demand functions', *Journal of Finance*, 40: 63–83.
Williams, J.B. (1938) *The theory of investment value*. Cambridge, Mass.: Harvard University Press.
Wood, J.H. (1963) 'Expectations, errors and the term structure of interest rates', *Journal of Political Economy*, 71: 160–171.
Woodward, S. (1983) 'The liquidity premium and the solidity premium', *American Economic Review*, 73: 348–361.

[7]

Review of Economic Studies (1991) 58, 495–514
0034-6527/91/00300495 $02.00

Yield Spreads and Interest Rate Movements: A Bird's Eye View

JOHN Y. CAMPBELL
Princeton University and NBER

and

ROBERT J. SHILLER
Yale University and NBER

First version received October 1989; *final version accepted August* 1990 (*Eds.*)

This paper examines postwar U.S. term structure data and finds that for almost any combination of maturities between one month and ten years, a high yield spread between a longer-term and a shorter-term interest rate forecasts rising shorter-term interest rates over the long term, but a declining yield on the longer-term bond over the short term. This pattern is inconsistent with the expectations theory of the term structure, but is consistent with a model in which the spread is proportional to the value implied by the expectations theory.

1. INTRODUCTION

Does the slope of the term structure—the yield spread between longer-term and shorter-term interest rates—predict future changes in interest rates? And if so, is the predictive power of the yield spread in accordance with the expectations theory of the term structure?

These questions are important, both for forecasting interest rates and for interpreting shifts in the yield curve. If the expectations theory is an adequate description of the term structure, then rational expectations of future interest rates are the dominant force determining current long-term interest rates. On the other hand, if the expectations theory is very far from accurate, then predictable changes in excess returns must be the main influence moving the term structure. It makes sense to thoroughly explore the validity of the simple expectations theory before undertaking a detailed study of the sources of predictable time-variation in excess returns.[1]

The literature on the term structure contains a bewildering variety of answers to these questions. Almost all studies statistically reject the expectations theory of the term structure; but some studies suggest that the yield spread does predict interest rate movements in roughly the way one would expect if the expectations theory is true, while other studies reach the opposite conclusion. Different studies use different econometric methods, test different implications of the expectations theory, and look at different interest rate maturities.

1. We refer to "the" expectations theory of the term structure. One problem that has hampered empirical work is that in fact there are many different versions of the expectations theory, as emphasized by Cox, Ingersoll, and Ross (1981) and others. We have however argued elsewhere that these different expectations theories are in important respects very similar, and are all closely approximated by a single linear expectations theory (Shiller (1979), Shiller, Campbell, and Schoenholtz (1983), Campbell (1986)). Note also that we are including the hypothesis of rational expectations in our definition of the expectations theory. This contrasts with the usage of some authors (e.g. Froot (1989)).

In this paper we show that certain statements can be made quite generally. For almost any pair of maturities between one month and ten years, the following is true: When the yield spread between the longer-term interest rate and the shorter-term interest rate is relatively high, the yield on the longer-term bond tends to fall over the life of the shorter-term bond. This runs counter to the expectations theory. At the same time, shorter-term rates tend to rise over the life of the longer-term bond, in accordance with the expectations theory. In a nutshell, when the spread is high the long rate tends to fall and the short rate tends to rise.

The data set used here consists of continuously compounded yields on riskless pure discount bonds. These yields were calculated by McCulloch (1990) from raw data on U.S. Treasury bill, note and bond prices, measured over the period 1952:1-1987:2 at the end of each month.[2] We will present results for all possible pairs of maturities in the range 1, 2, 3, 4, 6, and 9 months and 1, 2, 3, 4, 5, and 10 years. Thus, the results in this paper are two-dimensional tables of evaluations of the linear expectations theory. While the main findings hold over all possible sets of maturities, there are some interesting differences between the behaviour of the short end of the term structure (maturities less than one year) and the long end of the term structure (maturities greater than one year). We discuss these further below.

The organization of the paper is as follows. In Section 2 we derive the implications of the expectations theory of the term structure for the relation between yield spreads and subsequent interest rate movements. We discuss several ways in which these implications can be tested, including regression methods and a modification of the vector autoregressive approach of Campbell and Shiller (1987). In Section 3 we apply these methods to the McCulloch term-structure data. We also use a Monte Carlo study to check the finite-sample properties of our procedures. In Section 4 we try to interpret our results further. We argue that one simple alternative, in which the yield spread equals its value under the expectations theory plus orthogonal noise, is not consistent with the data. We suggest another alternative, which makes the yield spread a constant multiple of its value under the expectations theory. This model could be generated by time-varying risk premia which are correlated with expected increases in short-term interest rates, or by a failure of rational expectations in our sample period.

2. THE EXPECTATIONS THEORY OF THE TERM STRUCTURE

The expectations theory of the term structure of interest rates is a relationship between a longer-term n-period interest rate $R_t^{(n)}$ and a shorter-term m-period interest rate $R_t^{(m)}$, where n/m is an integer. In the case of pure discount bonds, as with our data here, this is:

$$R_t^{(n)} = (1/k)\sum_{i=0}^{k-1} E_t R_{t+mi}^{(m)} + c, \qquad k = n/m. \tag{1}$$

Equation (1) states that the n-period rate is a constant, plus a simple average of the current and expected future m-period rates up to $n-m=(k-1)m$ periods in the future. Note that the sum of the coefficients of the m-period interest rates is one. The parameter c reflects a term premium, that is a predictable excess return on the n-period bond over the m-period bond. The term premium may vary with m and n but is assumed to be constant through time.

2. McCulloch's data actually begin in 1946:12, but we drop the data from the period before the Treasury Accord of 1951.

Equation (1) can be obtained directly if one assumes that expected continuously compounded yields to maturity on all discount bonds are equal, up to a constant; this is the approach taken by Fama (1984). Equation (1) can also be derived as a linear approximation to any of several different nonlinear expectations theories of the term structure. The approximation is quite adequate for most purposes (Shiller, Campbell, and Schoenholtz (1983), Campbell (1986)). For example, if one assumes that the expected total return over m periods on buying an n-period bond and selling it m periods later equals the return on holding an m-period bond to maturity plus a constant, then one finds that the expectation of a nonlinear expression in $R_t^{(n)}$ and $R_{t+m}^{(n-m)}$ equals $R_t^{(m)}$ plus a constant. Linearizing this expression around $R_t^{(n)} = R_{t+m}^{(n-m)} = 0$, one gets a rational expectations model that if solved forward yields (1).

It should be noted that (1) is a time-consistent model. If the model holds for $m = 1$ and all n, then it holds for all $m \geqq 1$ and all n. This is an important property which many time-series models do not possess. An AR (2) model with monthly data is not consistent with an AR (2) model with quarterly data, for example. There is no such problem here.

The spread as a forecast of changes in interest rates

Our purpose is to state as simply as possible what elements of truth can be found in the expectations theory of the term structure. We therefore concentrate our attention on the behaviour through time of a simple measure of the shape of the term structure: the spread between the n-period rate and the m-period rate, $S_t^{(n,m)} = R_t^{(n)} - R_t^{(m)}$. The spread is of course proportional to the slope of the term structure between m and n.

The expectations theory of the term structure implies that the spread is a constant risk premium, plus an optimal forecast of changes in future interest rates. We can test the model by regressing the appropriate changes onto the spread and testing whether the coefficient equals one. And we can, apart from testing the model, evaluate its usefulness by checking to what extent the spread resembles an optimal forecast of the changes in interest rates.

There are several ways to write the spread as a forecast of future changes in interest rates. First, the spread predicts the m-period change in yield on the longer-term bond. This bond has n periods to maturity at time t, so it has $n - m$ periods to maturity at time $t + m$. According to the expectations theory,

$$s_t^{(n,m)} \equiv (m/(n-m)) S_t^{(n,m)} = E_t R_{t+m}^{(n-m)} - R_t^{(n)}, \tag{2}$$

where we use $s_t^{(n,m)}$ to denote a maturity-specific multiple of the yield spread, and we are suppressing constant terms for simplicity. The intuition behind equation (2) is that if the yield on the n-period bond is expected to rise over the next m periods, this will give a capital loss to holders of the bond. To equate expected returns over m periods, the n-period bond has to have a higher current yield than the m-period instrument. One may test (2) by regressing $R_{t+m}^{(n-m)} - R_t^{(n)}$ onto a constant and its predicted value $s_t^{(n,m)}$ defined in (2) as: $s_t^{(n,m)} \equiv (m/(n-m)) S_t^{(n,m)}$. Since we are assuming that expectations are rational, the slope coefficient should be one.

Second, by subtracting $R_t^{(m)}$ from both sides of equation (1) and rearranging terms, one can show that the spread forecasts a weighted average $S_t^{(n,m)*}$ of changes in shorter-term (m-period) interest rates over n periods:

$$S_t^{(n,m)} = E_t S_t^{(n,m)*},$$

$$S_t^{(n,m)*} \equiv (1/k) \textstyle\sum_{i=1}^{k-1} (\sum_{j=1}^{i} \Delta^m R_{t+jm}^{(m)}) = \sum_{i=1}^{k-1} (1 - i/k) \Delta^m R_{t+im}^{(m)}. \tag{3}$$

The notation Δ^m indicates that a change is measured over m periods, so for example $\Delta^m R_{t+m}^{(m)} = R_{t+m}^{(m)} - R_t^{(m)}$.

The variable $S_t^{(n,m)*}$ may be called the "perfect-foresight spread", since it is the spread that would obtain, given the model, if there were perfect foresight about future interest rates. With perfect foresight, if m-period rates are going to rise over the life of the n-period bond, then the n-period yield needs to be higher than the current m-period yield to equate the returns on the n-period bond, held to maturity, and a sequence of m-period bonds. Below we shall regress the perfect-foresight spread onto a constant and the actual spread to evaluate the model. Again, because of the rational expectations assumption, the slope coefficient should be one.

Equations (2) and (3) are complete characterizations of the expectations theory of the term structure; if (2) holds for all m and n, then (3) holds for all m and n, and vice versa. However it is important to note that for any *particular* values of m and n, the validity of (2) does not generally imply the validity of (3) or vice versa.

An exception to this statement occurs when $n = 2m$, a case that is often studied in empirical work.[3] In this case equations (2) and (3) take particularly simple forms because $R_{t+m}^{(n-m)}$ equals $R_{t+m}^{(m)}$ in equation (2), while the weighted sum on the right hand side of (3) has only one element. Equation (2) becomes

$$S_t^{(n,m)} = E_t R_{t+m}^{(m)} - R_t^{(n)}, \tag{4}$$

and (3) becomes

$$S_t^{(n,m)} = (1/2) E_t \Delta^m R_{t+m}^{(m)} = (1/2) E_t [R_{t+m}^{(m)} - R_t^{(m)}]. \tag{5}$$

Equation (4) says that the spread equals the difference between the optimal forecast of the m-period rate m periods from now and the n-period rate today, while equation (5) says that the spread equals one-half the optimal forecast of the change in the m-period rate over the next m periods. If (4) holds for a particular m and n, then (5) must also hold, and vice versa. (To see this, just subtract $R_t^{(m)}$ from both sides of (4) and rearrange.)

Since (4) and (5) are special cases of (2) and (3), they can be tested using the same regression approach. If the regression coefficient for the test of (4) is written b, the regression coefficient for the test of (5) will be $(1+b)/2$.

The theoretical spread

Regression tests of the expectations theory have the great merit of simplicity. But they also have some serious disadvantages. First, the regression of the perfect-foresight spread onto the actual spread involves n-period overlapping errors. One only has an entirely independent observation of the forecast power of the term structure every n periods. While econometric methods are available to correct regression standard errors for overlap, they do not work well when the degree of overlap is large relative to the sample size. (See for example Stock and Richardson (1989) and Hodrick (1990).) Since n can be as large as 10 years, and we have only 35 years of data, this is a worrisome problem.

Second, regression tests do not tell us how similar are the movements of the actual spread to the movements implied by the expectations theory. We would like to evaluate the ability of the expectations theory to explain the shape of the term structure, and regression tests are not well suited for this purpose.

3. See for example Shiller, Campbell, and Schoenholtz (1983), who looked at 3- and 6-month Treasury bills.

In earlier work (Campbell and Shiller (1987)), we proposed a vector-autoregressive (VAR) approach for evaluating present value models. That paper dealt with the case in which n is infinite, but the approach can easily be modified to handle a finite value of n. The VAR approach avoids the need to estimate regressions with overlapping errors. The VAR includes the 1-period change in the m-period interest rate, and the actual yield spread. From the estimated VAR coefficients, one can compute the optimal forecast of m-period interest rate changes over any horizon; the long-run behaviour of interest rates is inferred from their short-run behaviour in the sample period, rather than being estimated directly. The appropriate weighted average of forecast interest rate changes (the "theoretical spread") can be calculated, and compared with the actual spread. If the expectations theory is true, the two variables should be the same.

The details of the VAR approach are given in Campbell and Shiller (1987); here we merely summarize the method and show how we can apply it to the expectations theory with a finite horizon n. The first step in the analysis is to note that equation (3) can be projected onto a subset of the information set used by market participants. This is necessary because of course the true information set of the market is unobservable. Provided that we use an information subset that includes the yield spread $S_t^{(n,m)}$ itself, equation (3) takes the same form when projected onto the subset. It says that the observed yield spread should equal the optimal forecast of future increases in short-term rates, conditional on the information subset used in our test.

Next we specify the form of the information subset more precisely. We assume that $\Delta R_t^{(m)}$ is a stationary stochastic process, and that the expected excess return on an n-period bond over an m-period bond is stationary. These assumptions imply that $x_t \equiv [\Delta R_t^{(m)}, S_t^{(n,m)}]$ is a stationary vector-stochastic process. We shall use the history of x_t as our information subset.

We assume that x_t can be represented as a p-th-order VAR. This system can be rewritten as a first-order VAR in the companion form $z_t = Az_{t-1} + u_t$, where z_t has $2p$ elements, first $\Delta R_t^{(m)}$ and $p-1$ lags and then $S_t^{(n,m)}$ and $p-1$ lags. The vector z_t summarizes the whole history of x_t. Multi-period interest rate forecasts are easily computed from the companion form, since $E[z_{t+k}|x_t, x_{t-1}, \ldots] = E[z_{t+k}|z_t] = A^k z_t$.

We next define vectors g and h such that $g'z_t = S_t^{(n,m)}$ and $h'z_t = \Delta R_t^{(m)}$. (These vectors have $2p$ elements, all of which are zero except for the first element of h and the $p+1$-st element of g, which equal one.) Then we can use (3) to compute the VAR forecast of the perfect-foresight spread; we write this forecast $S_t'^{(n,m)}$. Tedious algebra shows that $S_t'^{(n,m)}$ can be expressed as[4]

$$S_t'^{(n,m)} \equiv h'A[I-(m/n)(I-A^n)(I-A^m)^{-1}](I-A)^{-1}z_t. \tag{6}$$

We call $S_t'^{(n,m)}$ the "theoretical spread", since it is the spread which would obtain if the expectations theory were true. Equation (3), projected onto the information subset z_t, implies that

$$S_t^{(n,m)} = g'z_t = S_t'^{(n,m)}. \tag{7}$$

Note that if the expectations theory of the term structure is true, (7) should hold whatever information set economic agents are using. The intuitive explanation is that if term premia are constant, all the relevant information of market participants is embodied in the yield spread $S_t^{(n,m)}$, which is included in the VAR system. Of course, if the expectations theory

4. Note that this expression reduces to the much simpler formula in Campbell and Shiller (1987) when n is infinite.

is not true, then the VAR system may not adequately summarize the information available to the market.

The equality of the actual spread and the theoretical spread puts a set of nonlinear restrictions on the coefficients of the estimated VAR. These can be tested formally using a Wald test (Campbell and Shiller (1987)). We do not pursue this approach here, since the regression methods discussed above are simpler if one's purpose is merely to test the model. Instead, we use the VAR to compare the historical behaviour of $S_t^{(n,m)}$ and $S_t'^{(n,m)}$. We compute the correlation of $S_t^{(n,m)}$ and $S_t'^{(n,m)}$, and the ratio of their standard deviations. If $S_t^{(n,m)}$ equals $S_t'^{(n,m)}$, of course, the correlation and the standard deviation ratio should both equal one.

Some previous results

We found in our earlier work (Shiller (1979), Shiller, Campbell and Schoenholtz (1983)) that for very large n and small m when $R_{t+m}^{(n-m)} - R_t^{(n)}$ is regressed on $s_t^{(n,m)}$ then the coefficient of $s_t^{(n,m)}$ tends often to be significantly different from one. In fact, the point estimate is negative. We concluded that the theory was very far off-track; that the expectations theory of the term structure is just wrong.[5]

In later work (Campbell and Shiller (1987)), we used a different metric to evaluate the expectations theory for large n and small m, and we found that the expectations theory seemed to work fairly well. We computed the correlation between $S_t^{(n,m)}$ and $S_t'^{(n,m)}$ and found it to be quite high. This suggests that the actual spread behaves much as it should according to the expectations model.[6] The correlation between $S_t^{(n,m)}$ and $S_t'^{(n,m)}$ can be high and still we may get a wrong sign in a regression test of equation (2). This can happen, for example, if $S_t^{(n,m)}$ equals $S_t'^{(n,m)}$ plus a small serially uncorrelated noise term, because the noise term appears on the left- and right-hand sides of (2) with opposite signs.

Other recent work has also emphasized the ability of the yield spread to forecast short rate changes over long horizons. Fama and Bliss (1987) set $m = 1$ year and $n = 2$, 3, and 4 years. They worked with "forward premia", which are linear combinations of two different yield spreads. According to the expectations theory, forward premia should forecast unweighted averages of changes in short rates, as opposed to the weighted averages forecast by yield spreads. Fama and Bliss regressed the appropriate short rate changes onto forward premia, and found that the forecasting power of the term structure improves as the horizon n increases. They attributed this to a slowly mean-reverting interest rate process that is more easily forecast over long time periods than over short intervals.

A largely unrelated literature has looked at the short end of the term structure, with n up to 12 months. Shiller, Campbell, and Schoenholtz (1983) found that the yield spread between 3- and 6-month Treasury bill rates helps to forecast the change in the 3-month bill rate, but not as strongly as the expectations theory requires. Fama (1984) found some evidence that the slope of the term structure predicts interest rate changes over a few months, but the predictive power seemed to decay rapidly with the horizon.[7]

5. See also Mankiw and Summers (1984) and Froot (1989).

6. Shiller (1989) has used plots of the actual spread and the perfect foresight spread to make the same point.

7. Mishkin (1988*a*) has updated the results in Fama (1984). Fama (1990) and Mishkin (1988*b*, 1990) have extended the analysis to look at the forecast power of the yield curve, at both short and long horizons, for future inflation rates. See Shiller (1990) for a survey of other research on the term structure.

3. DATA AND EMPIRICAL RESULTS

The McCulloch monthly term structure data (1990) give pure discount (zero coupon) bond yields for U.S. Government securities over the period 1946:12–1987:2. We use the sample 1952:1–1987:2, to allow for lags and to exclude data from before the Treasury Accord of 1951. The data include maturities of 0, 1, 2, 3, 4, 5, 6, and 9 months, and 1, 2, 3, 4, 5, and 10 years. Longer maturities are available only for part of the sample. These data are continuously compounded yields to maturity.

Of course, pure discount government bonds of long maturity do not exist. But existing government bonds may be regarded as portfolios of pure discount bonds, bonds maturing on all coupon dates and the maturity date. One may suppose that they are priced, except for some tax considerations, as the sum of the values of the constituent bonds in the portfolio. One can therefore infer the prices (and thus the yields) of the constituent bonds. There are problems in making this inference: there may be more than one way to infer the yield of a certain discount bond (giving possibly different answers in practice) and no way to infer the yield of other discount bonds (since coupon and maturity dates may not be evenly spaced through time). Thus, McCulloch (1990) inferred the discount yields by an interpolation method using cubic splines.[8]

McCulloch's data are very clean in the sense that they are unaffected by differing coupons, coupon dates, or differing compounding conventions across maturities. They are ideally suited to the kind of analysis we wish to do here over a broad range of maturities. The data are not interval averaged, but are observed at the end of each month.

Forecasting the change in the longer-term yield

Table 1(a) confirms that the slope of the term structure between almost *any two* maturities gives the wrong direction of forecast for the change in yield of the longer-term (n-period) bond over the life of the shorter-term (m-period) bond.[9] Asymptotic standard errors, which have been corrected for heteroskedasticity and equation error overlap in the manner of Hansen and Hodrick (1980) and White (1984), show that almost all the coefficients are significantly different from one at conventional significance levels. Thus, earlier conclusions in Shiller (1979) and Shiller, Campbell and Schoenholtz (1983) for some maturities are found to extend to just about all maturity pairs m and n. By this metric, the expectations theory of the term structure is a resounding failure.

The general tendency for wrong signs to appear throughout the table is robust to the sample period. In Table 1(b) we report results for the case $m = 1$ over a variety of subsamples, including the 1952–1978 period (the longest possible subsample which avoids the 1979 monetary policy regime shift) and the shorter periods 1952–1959, 1960–1969, 1970–1978 and 1979–1987. We find a predominance of wrong signs in every period except 1952–1959.

As a check on the McCulloch data, these results can be compared with earlier results using different monthly data on U.S. Treasury obligations. Shiller, Campbell, and Schoenholtz (1983) found that when the three-month change in the three-month rate is regressed on the predicted change implicit in the spread between six-month and three-month rates, with data January 1959 to June 1979, the slope coefficient was 0·285. Here, the slope

8. Fama and Bliss (1987) inferred yields on pure discount bonds using the assumption that instantaneous forward rates are step functions of maturity. This is an alternative to McCulloch's procedure. Our results below are similar to those of Fama and Bliss for the maturities they consider.

9. The lower left-hand part of the table, where n is large and m is small, uses the approximation that $R_{t+m}^{(n-m)} = R_{t+m}^{(n)}$. In the rest of the table we give results only where we observe $R_{t+m}^{(n-m)}$ directly.

TABLE 1(*a*)

Regression of $R_{t+m}^{(n-m)} - R_t^{(n)}$ *on predicted change* $s_t^{(n,m)}$

	m							
n	1	2	3	4	6	12	24	60
2	0·002 (0·238) 0·000 0·000	—	—	—	—	—	—	—
3	−0·176 (0·362) 0·001 0·001	−0·361 (0·502)	—	—	—	—	—	—
4	−0·437 (0·469) 0·000 0·002	−0·611 (0·562) 0·011 0·005	−0·452 (0·366)	—	—	—	—	—
6	−1·029 (0·537) 0·000 0·000	−1·276 (0·557) 0·000 0·000	−1·294 (0·400) 0·001 0·000	−1·203 (0·309)	—	—	—	—
9	−1·219[a] (0·598) 0·019 0·000	—	−1·682 (0·486) 0·004 0·000	−1·482 (0·311)	−0·654 (0·508)	—	—	—
12	−1·381[a] (0·683) 0·038 0·000	−1·592[a] (0·712) 0·064 0·000	−1·967 (0·601) 0·003 0·000	—	−0·913 (0·657) 0·056 0·013	—	—	—
24	−1·815[a] (1·151) 0·122 0·017	−1·919[a] (1·142) 0·099 0·011	−1·694[a] (0·939) 0·114 0·007	−1·482[a] (0·842) 0·150 0·010	−0·893[a] (0·743) 0·134 0·041	−1·034 (0·620) 0·047 0·042	—	—
36	−2·239[a] (1·444) 0·122 0·037	−2·164[a] (1·462) 0·104 0·032	−1·922[a] (1·210) 0·109 0·022	−1·692[a] (1·065) 0·128 0·035	−1·184[a] (0·877) 0·128 0·034	−1·396 (0·883) 0·034 0·034	−0·465 (1·086)	—
48	−2·665[a] (1·634) 0·087 0·023	−2·561[a] (1·662) 0·055 0·046	−2·208[a] (1·392) 0·091 0·028	−1·960[a] (1·206) 0·093 0·032	−1·447[a] (0·991) 0·129 0·033	−1·736 (1·027) 0·019 0·033	−0·725 (1·233) 0·115 0·353	—
60	−3·099[a] (1·749) 0·079 0·019	−2·941[a] (1·795) 0·070 0·043	−2·525[a] (1·523) 0·080 0·030	−2·276[a] (1·318) 0·088 0·028	−1·750[a] (1·096) 0·099 0·038	−2·022 (1·205) 0·024 0·049	−0·811 (1·369)	—
120	−5·024[a] (2·316) 0·029 0·009	−4·695[a] (2·424) 0·032 0·024	−4·298[a] (2·107) 0·028 0·015	−3·944[a] (1·851) 0·047 0·019	−3·198[a] (1·673) 0·060 0·027	—	—	4·575 (1·926) 0·146 0·331

Notes. The first number in any set is the estimated regression slope coefficient of $R_{t+m}^{(n-m)} - R_t^{(n)}$ onto $s_t^{(n,m)} \equiv (m/(n-m))S_t^{(n,m)}$. According to the expectations theory, this coefficient should equal one. Constant terms (not shown) are included in all regressions. Hansen-Hodrick standard errors are below estimated coefficients, in parentheses. For each regression, the sample is the longest possible using data from 1952:1 through 1987:2. Where n/m is an integer the table also gives, below the standard errors, two numbers from a Monte Carlo experiment. The first is the fraction of 1000 runs which produced an estimated regression coefficient which was further away from one in the same direction than the coefficient obtained in the data. The second number is the fraction of 1000 runs in which a 2-sided t-test of the hypothesis that the coefficient equals one rejected the null more strongly than the t-test on the actual data.

[a] Uses the approximation that $R_{t+m}^{(n-m)} = R_{t+m}^{(n)}$.

TABLE 1(b)

Regression of $R_{t+1}^{(n-1)} - R_t^{(n)}$ on predicted change $s_t^{(n,1)}$: subsamples

n	1952–1987 (421)	1952–1978 (323)	1952–1959 (95)	1960–1969 (119)	1970–1978 (107)	1979–1987 (97)
	Sample period (number of observations)					
2	0·002 (0·238)	−0·267 (0·151)	−0·261 (0·193)	−0·089 (0·253)	−0·436 (0·419)	0·347 (0·342)
3	−0·176 (0·362)	−0·471 (0·223)	−0·194 (0·284)	−0·381 (0·311)	−0·855 (0·691)	0·167 (0·577)
4	−0·437 (0·469)	−0·509 (0·283)	−0·101 (0·388)	−0·481 (0·333)	−0·850 (0·893)	−0·287 (0·789)
6	−1·029 (0·537)	−0·537 (0·340)	−0·121 (0·542)	−0·567 (0·393)	−0·981 (0·982)	−1·345 (0·902)
9	−1·219[a] (0·598)	−0·394[a] (0·458)	0·590[a] (0·633)	−0·598[a] (0·544)	−0·907[a] (1·124)	−1·826[a] (1·066)
12	−1·381[a] (0·683)	−0·672[a] (0·598)	0·771[a] (0·752)	−1·044[a] (0·661)	−1·216[a] (1·307)	−1·778[a] (1·237)
24	−1·815[a] (1·151)	−1·031[a] (0·986)	1·796[a] (1·557)	−2·876[a] (1·284)	−1·063[a] (1·594)	−2·218[a] (2·052)
36	−2·239[a] (1·444)	−1·210[a] (1·187)	3·021[a] (2·379)	−3·840[a] (1·891)	−1·245[a] (1·774)	−2·791[a] (2·431)
48	−2·665[a] (1·634)	−1·272[a] (1·326)	3·807[a] (2·852)	−4·373[a] (2·254)	−1·293[a] (1·936)	−3·468[a] (2·714)
60	−3·099[a] (1·749)	−1·483[a] (1·442)	4·138[a] (3·264)	−4·886[a] (2·535)	−1·424[a] (2·083)	−4·052[a] (2·894)
120	−5·024[a] (2·316)	−2·263[a] (1·869)	3·099[a] (4·801)	−6·029[a] (3·796)	−2·103[a] (2·650)	−6·830[a] (3·817)

Notes. This table gives the same regression coefficients and standard errors as Table 1(a), except that $m = 1$ throughout the table and results are reported for subsamples. No Monte Carlo results are reported.
[a] See notes to Table 1(a).

coefficient in Table 1(a) for $m = 3$ and $n = 6$ is $b = -1{\cdot}279$. The implied slope coefficient for the regression run by Shiller, Campbell, and Schoenholtz is $(1+b)/2 = -0{\cdot}140$. If we use the January 1959 to June 1979 sample our estimated b is $-0{\cdot}302$ so that $(1+b)/2 = 0{\cdot}348$, which compares reasonably well with the earlier result. Fama (1984) found that when the actual change over one month in the one-month rate is regressed using data 1959–1982 on the predicted change the slope coefficient is 0·46. Our $(1+b)/2$ from Table 1(a) is 0·51, and if b is reestimated using their sample period $b = -0{\cdot}302$ and $(1+b)/2 = 0{\cdot}54$. Fama and Bliss (1987) found that when the actual change in the one-year rate over one year is regressed 1964–1984 on the predicted change the slope coefficient is 0·09. Using our Table 1(a), $(1+b)/2 = -0{\cdot}14$, using their sample period $b = -0{\cdot}882$ and $(1+b)/2 = 0{\cdot}06$. These comparisons show that the McCulloch data give similar results to results with other data sets.

Forecasting changes in short rates

Table 2 shows the results of regressing $S_t^{(n,m)*}$ on $S_t^{(n,m)}$ for combinations of n and m that are represented in the McCulloch data, for which n is an integer multiple of m. The

TABLE 2

Slope coefficients in regression of $S_t^{(n,m)*}$ on $S_t^{(n,m)}$

	m							
n	1	2	3	4	6	12	24	60
2	0·501	—	—	—	—	—	—	—
	(0·119)							
	0·000							
	0·000							
3	0·446	—	—	—	—	—	—	—
	(0·190)							
	0·000							
	0·006							
4	0·436	0·195	—	—	—	—	—	—
	(0·238)	(0·281)						
	0·001	0·011						
	0·022	0·005						
6	0·237	0·021	−0·147	—	—	—	—	—
	(0·167)	(0·163)	(0·200)					
	0·000	0·010	0·001					
	0·000	0·001	0·000					
9	0·151	—	−0·008	—	—	—	—	—
	(0·165)		(0·147)					
	0·001		0·015					
	0·000		0·000					
12	0·161	0·078	0·044	−0·056	0·044	—	—	—
	(0·228)	(0·192)	(0·189)	(0·185)	(0·329)			
	0·006	0·033	0·023	0·022	0·056			
	0·019	0·004	0·005	0·000	0·013			
24	0·302	0·287	0·269	0·229	0·186	−0·017	—	—
	(0·212)	(0·210)	(0·230)	(0·262)	(0·324)	(0·372)		
	0·031	0·096	0·116	0·117	0·073	0·047		
	0·067	0·063	0·086	0·098	0·100	0·042		
36	0·614	0·642	0·610	0·568	0·526	0·257	—	—
	(0·230)	(0·243)*	(0·101)	(0·174)	(0·225)	(0·408)		
	0·151	0·211	0·225	0·210	0·193	0·119		
	0·318	0·368	0·070	0·194	0·223	0·250		
48	0·873	0·929	0·951	0·959	0·942	0·720	0·137	—
	(0·291)	(0·271)	(0·240)	(0·205)	(0·088)	(0·335)	(0·617)	
	0·256	0·289	0·299	0·321	0·299	0·230	0·115	
	0·817	0·868	0·898	0·913	0·697	0·613	0·353	
60	1·232	1·289	1·292	1·297	1·242	1·130	—	—
	(0·182)	(0·168)	(0·161)	(0·141)	(0·161)	(0·193)		
	0·581	0·574	0·576	0·594	0·630	0·677		
	0·501	0·418	0·370	0·334	0·474	0·698		
120	1·157	1·207	1·223	1·227	1·228	1·274	1·345	2·788
	(0·094)	(0·093)	(0·095)	(0·097)	(0·101)	(0·113)	(0·169)	(0·963)
	0·713	0·685	0·667	0·681	0·690	0·673	0·618	0·146
	0·583	0·463	0·437	0·443	0·429	0·423	0·429	0·331

Notes. $S_t^{(n,m)*}$, the perfect-foresight spread, is defined in equation (3) in the text. The first element in each set is the slope coefficient in a regression with a constant term, and that in parentheses is the Hansen-Hodrick standard error. By the expectations theory, the slope coefficient should be one. The sample period for each element is the longest possible sample using data from 1952:1 to 1987:2. Since computation of $S_t^{(n,m)*}$ requires data extending $n-m$ periods into the future, the sample in the regression ends $n-m$ months before 1987:2. The table also gives two numbers from a Monte Carlo experiment. These are constructed in the same way as the Monte Carlo results reported in Table 1(a).

* Newey-West (1987) correction used because Hansen-Hodrick procedure gave a negative standard error on constant or spread.

regression coefficients should be one if the expectations hypothesis is valid. In fact, the coefficients are almost always positive but also deviate substantially from one when the maturity n of the longer-term bond is below 3 or 4 years. At this short end of the term structure, asymptotic standard errors imply rejection of the expectations theory at conventional significance levels. At the long end of the term structure, the regression coefficients are very close to one and the expectations theory is not rejected.

We thus see an apparent paradox: the slope of the term structure almost always gives a forecast in the wrong direction for the short-term change in the yield on the longer bond, but gives a forecast in the right direction for long-term changes in short rates. We next use our VAR procedures in order to judge how the spread moves through time in relation to an unrestricted forecast of changes in short rates.

Table 3(a) reports correlations between the actual spread $S_t^{(n,m)}$ and the estimated theoretical spread $S_t'^{(n,m)}$. For each estimated correlation we first ran a fourth-order vector autoregression for the vector $[\Delta R_t^{(m)}, S_t^{(n,m)}]'$ using monthly data from January 1952 to February 1987 and used the result to form the A matrix for the companion form. This estimate of A was then substituted into equation (7) to arrive at $S_t'^{(n,m)}$, and the correlation with $S_t^{(n,m)}$ computed. An asymptotic standard error was calculated in the way described in Campbell and Shiller (1987). The correlation is almost always positive and often very high. This result also holds up in subsamples, as shown in Table 3(b).

Table 4(a) shows the standard deviation of $S_t'^{(n,m)}$ divided by that of $S_t^{(n,m)}$. We find that the coefficient is typically around one-half, regardless of m and n. Thus, the spread is too variable to accord with the simple expectations model.[10] Similar results hold in all subsamples (Table 4(b)), except for large n in the 1952–1959 period.

These results can be compared to results in Table 2 in the following way. The product of an element in Table 3(a) (the correlation of $S_t'^{(n,m)}$ and $S_t^{(n,m)}$) and the corresponding element in Table 4(a) (the standard deviation of $S_t'^{(n,m)}$ divided by the standard deviation of $S_t^{(n,m)}$) is the regression coefficient when $S_t'^{(n,m)}$ is regressed on $S_t^{(n,m)}$. This regression coefficient should be (except for sampling error) the same as that in Table 2. We find that they are about the same when n is small, but diverge substantially when n is large.

There are several possible explanations for this discrepancy. First, in order to regress $S_t^{(n,m)*}$ on $S_t^{(n,m)}$ we must truncate the sample enough to allow computation of $S_t^{(n,m)*}$ which requires data $n-m$ periods into the future. (For this reason we do not try to apply the approach of Table 2 in subsamples.) To do the calculations in Tables 3 and 4 there is no such need to truncate the sample. Thus, the discrepancy in results might just be due to different sample periods, and our estimates with shorter samples in Tables 3(b) and 4(b) show that this is a large part of the explanation. In Tables 3(b) and 4(b), the expectations theory performs noticeably better in the shorter sample period 1952–1978 than in the full sample period 1952–1987; but at the bottom of Table 2 the full sample has been truncated by almost ten years, so the effective sample period is roughly 1952–1978.[11]

A second possible reason for the discrepancy is that perhaps our vector autoregression truncated after four months is too short, and thus our estimate of $S_t'^{(n,m)}$ is subject to error. In our previous work we have suggested that long lags may be useful in forecasting interest rates (Campbell and Shiller (1984)). When we increase the lag length to eight

10. This statement is subject to a caveat. As discussed above, if the expectations theory of the term structure is false, then the VAR system is not guaranteed to summarize all the relevant information available to market participants. For more on this point, see Beltratti and Shiller (1990).

11. Campbell and Shiller (1987) also found that the expectations theory performed better in the pre-1979 period.

TABLE 3(a)

Correlation of $S_t'^{(n,m)}$ and $S_t^{(n,m)}$

	m							
n	1	2	3	4	6	12	24	60
2	0·736	—	—	—	—	—	—	—
	(0·148)							
	0·000							
	0·094							
3	0·761	—	—	—	—	—	—	—
	(0·190)							
	0·002							
	0·437							
4	0·720	0·502	—	—	—	—	—	—
	(0·213)	(0·451)						
	0·001	0·063						
	0·285	0·545						
6	0·486	0·058	−0·355	—	—	—	—	—
	(0·373)	(0·566)	(0·556)					
	0·003	0·012	0·000					
	0·210	0·118	0·015					
9	0·374	—	−0·156	—	—	—	—	—
	(0·421)		(0·904)					
	0·005		0·008					
	0·181		0·269					
12	0·391	0·282	0·126	−0·072	−0·111	—	—	—
	(0·468)	(0·909)	(1·211)	(1·309)	(1·494)			
	0·007	0·049	0·017	0·017	0·015			
	0·237	0·603	0·663	0·576	0·514			
24	0·543	0·629	0·612	0·512	0·409	0·212	—	—
	(0·764)	(0·941)	(1·148)	(1·565)	(1·960)	(1·865)		
	0·021	0·088	0·102	0·108	0·062	0·023		
	0·749	0·920	0·953	0·964	0·980	0·930		
36	0·770	0·851	0·860	0·833	0·776	0·645	—	—
	(0·531)	(0·431)	(0·442)	(0·594)	(0·917)	(1·311)		
	0·021	0·088	0·102	0·108	0·062	0·023		
	0·749	0·920	0·953	0·964	0·980	0·930		
48	0·867	0·920	0·930	0·923	0·900	0·839	0·896	—
	(0·328)	(0·210)	(0·189)	(0·231)	(0·363)	(0·580)	(0·348)	
	0·101	0·192	0·232	0·249	0·224	0·182	0·301	
	0·861	0·801	0·763	0·804	0·885	0·908	0·852	
60	0·912	0·948	0·956	0·954	0·939	0·893	—	—
	(0·218)	(0·128)	(0·109)	(0·128)	(0·209)	(0·375)		
	0·115	0·213	0·271	0·270	0·232	0·206		
	0·810	0·737	0·731	0·766	0·863	0·869		
120	0·979	0·986	0·988	0·988	0·984	0·975	0·983	0·990
	(0·045)	(0·027)	(0·021)	(0·023)	(0·038)	(0·062)	(0·041)	(0·020)
	0·159	0·250	0·290	0·315	0·284	0·235	0·312	0·624
	0·667	0·642	0·568	0·593	0·698	0·680	0·708	0·623

Notes. This table gives the correlation coefficients of $S_t'^{(n,m)}$ with $S_t^{(n,m)}$ and estimated standard errors (in parentheses). $S_t'^{(n,m)}$ is computed from equation (6) in the text based on a vector autoregression starting in 1952:1 and ending in 1987:2. The vector autoregression had four lags. The table also gives two numbers from a Monte Carlo experiment. The first number is the fraction of 1000 runs in which the difference between the estimated correlation and one was larger than in the actual data. The second number is the fraction of 1000 runs in which the difference between the estimated correlation and one, divided by its standard error, was larger than in the actual data.

TABLE 3(*b*)

Correlation of $S_t'^{(n,1)}$ and $S_t^{(n,1)}$: subsamples

	Sample period (number of observations)					
n	1952–1987 (421)	1952–1978 (323)	1952–1959 (95)	1960–1969 (119)	1970–1978 (107)	1979–1987 (97)
2	0·738 (0·148)	0·626 (0·115)	0·668 (0·134)	0·785 (0·170)	0·303 (0·169)	0·696 (0·138)
3	0·763 (0·189)	0·585 (0·172)	0·717 (0·192)	0·687 (0·218)	0·256 (0·378)	0·707 (0·184)
4	0·723 (0·212)	0·604 (0·204)	0·729 (0·254)	0·589 (0·283)	0·538 (0·406)	0·675 (0·228)
6	0·493 (0·372)	0·583 (0·279)	0·712 (0·353)	0·513 (0·421)	0·657 (0·495)	0·395 (0·348)
9	0·386 (0·419)	0·561 (0·394)	0·742 (0·382)	0·417 (0·646)	0·628 (0·638)	0·282 (0·383)
12	0·404 (0·463)	0·587 (0·468)	0·801 (0·342)	0·240 (0·839)	0·695 (0·653)	0·301 (0·504)
24	0·558 (0·743)	0·829 (0·349)	0·963 (0·088)	−0·145 (0·986)	0·925 (0·241)	0·260 (0·984)
36	0·779 (0·509)	0·922 (0·180)	0·987 (0·021)	−0·129 (1·254)	0·971 (0·103)	0·388 (1·203)
48	0·872 (0·313)	0·968 (0·079)	0·991 (0·009)	−0·087 (1·623)	0·991 (0·035)	0·513 (1·181)
60	0·914 (0·210)	0·986 (0·037)	0·993 (0·007)	0·116 (2·087)	0·997 (0·011)	0·626 (1·006)
120	0·979 (0·044)	0·997 (0·007)	0·996 (0·004)	0·800 (1·048)	0·999 (0·003)	0·867 (0·356)

Notes. This table gives the same statistics as Table 3(*a*), except that $m = 1$ throughout the table and results are reported for subsamples. No Monte Carlo results are reported.

months, we find that the estimated standard deviation ratio is roughly unchanged; the estimated correlation tends to fall, but is less precisely estimated. Overall, the increase in lag length does not reduce the discrepancy between the results in Table 2 and those in Tables 3 and 4.

A third explanation for the discrepancy is that the asymptotic standard errors reported in Table 2 may understate the possible effects of sampling error on the regression slope coefficients in this table. Below we use a Monte Carlo experiment to confirm that this point is also important.

The effect of the forecast horizon

Fama and Bliss (1987) have emphasized that the forecast power of the term structure for changes in short rates improves as the forecast horizon increases from 2 years to 5 years. Our study of the full range of maturities confirms this result, but shows that in fact below 1 year the forecast power deteriorates with the horizon. The forecast power reaches its minimum at 9 to 12 months, and then starts to improve. This effect can be seen in the "U-shaped" pattern of coefficients as one moves down the first column of Table 2, Table 3(*a*), or Table 4(*a*). It is evident also in most of the subsamples in Tables 3(*b*) and 4(*b*).

TABLE 4(*a*)

$\sigma(S_t'^{(n,m)})/\sigma(S_t^{(n,m)})$

	m							
n	1	2	3	4	6	12	24	60
2	0·681 (0·136) 0·000 0·022	—	—	—	—	—	—	—
3	0·586 (0·145) 0·000 0·008	—	—	—	—	—	—	—
4	0·607 (0·162) 0·000 0·024	0·388 (0·216) 0·000 0·009	—	—	—	—	—	—
6	0·501 (0·145) 0·000 0·004	0·357 (0·196) 0·000 0·002	0·404 (0·225) 0·001 0·024	—	—	—	—	—
9	0·424 (0·129) 0·000 0·000	—	0·317 (0·168) 0·000 0·001	—	—	—	—	—
12	0·382 (0·119) 0·000 0·000	0·280 (0·158) 0·000 0·000	0·263 (0·153) 0·000 0·000	0·285 (0·151) 0·000 0·001	0·332 (0·155) 0·000 0·000	—	—	—
24	0·303 (0·135) 0·000 0·000	0·255 (0·249) 0·000 0·017	0·236 (0·283) 0·000 0·020	0·224 (0·262) 0·000 0·013	0·238 (0·217) 0·000 0·004	0·272 (0·135) 0·000 0·000	—	—
36	0·308 (0·225) 0·000 0·020	0·289 (0·353) 0·000 0·116	0·279 (0·398) 0·001 0·130	0·264 (0·417) 0·000 0·185	0·266 (0·427) 0·000 0·141	0·273 (0·346) 0·000 0·091	—	—
48	0·334 (0·274) 0·000 0·070	0·336 (0·382) 0·001 0·188	0·335 (0·422) 0·006 0·212	0·325 (0·449) 0·004 0·217	0·323 (0·481) 0·002 0·239	0·321 (0·444) 0·001 0·188	0·376 (0·526) 0·008 0·286	—
60	0·357 (0·291) 0·000 0·093	0·365 (0·381) 0·017 0·168	0·367 (0·415) 0·036 0·219	0·358 (0·441) 0·018 0·250	0·353 (0·476) 0·011 0·261	0·340 (0·450) 0·003 0·215	—	—
120	0·474 (0·285) 0·043 0·129	0·481 (0·337) 0·053 0·205	0·488 (0·356) 0·070 0·228	0·487 (0·372) 0·068 0·236	0·485 (0·398) 0·079 0·281	0·478 (0·383) 0·070 0·232	0·523 (0·379) 0·081 0·255	0·552 (0·385) 0·136 0·275

Notes. This table gives first the standard deviation of $S_t'^{(n,m)}$ divided by the standard deviation of $S_t^{(n,m)}$ and then estimated standard errors of this ratio (in parentheses). $S_t'^{(n,m)}$ is computed from equation (6) in the text based on a vector autoregression starting in 1952:1 and ending in 1987:2. The vector autoregression had four lags. The table also gives two numbers from a Monte Carlo experiment. The first is the fraction of 1000 runs which produced an estimated standard deviation ratio which was further away from one in the same direction than the ratio obtained in the data. The second number is the fraction of 1000 runs in which a 2-sided t test of the hypothesis that the ratio equals one rejected the null more strongly than the t test on the actual data.

TABLE 4(b)

$\sigma(S_t'^{(n,1)})/\sigma(S_t^{(n,1)})$: *Subsamples*

	Sample period (number of observations)					
n	1952–1987 (421)	1952–1978 (323)	1952–1959 (95)	1960–1969 (119)	1970–1978 (107)	1979–1987 (97)
2	0·681 (0·136)	0·585 (0·128)	0·545 (0·123)	0·581 (0·112)	0·931 (0·365)	0·986 (0·148)
3	0·586 (0·144)	0·503 (0·132)	0·483 (0·117)	0·582 (0·112)	0·674 (0·389)	0·922 (0·144)
4	0·607 (0·162)	0·508 (0·125)	0·472 (0·142)	0·551 (0·128)	0·679 (0·376)	0·948 (0·170)
6	0·500 (0·144)	0·461 (0·099)	0·489 (0·180)	0·429 (0·102)	0·599 (0·277)	0·824 (0·200)
9	0·424 (0·129)	0·427 (0·101)	0·554 (0·217)	0·329 (0·085)	0·508 (0·234)	0·714 (0·181)
12	0·382 (0·119)	0·400 (0·100)	0·649 (0·275)	0·309 (0·103)	0·441 (0·235)	0·627 (0·165)
24	0·304 (0·138)	0·416 (0·219)	1·170 (0·566)	0·328 (0·222)	0·459 (0·408)	0·470 (0·123)
36	0·311 (0·227)	0·473 (0·272)	1·510 (0·575)	0·316 (0·238)	0·504 (0·411)	0·392 (0·142)
48	0·338 (0·274)	0·541 (0·295)	1·578 (0·471)	0·277 (0·218)	0·579 (0·401)	0·370 (0·202)
60	0·360 (0·290)	0·589 (0·293)	1·539 (0·406)	0·235 (0·115)	0·637 (0·378)	0·365 (0·260)
120	0·476 (0·284)	0·717 (0·231)	1·288 (0·238)	0·266 (0·351)	0·743 (0·282)	0·428 (0·354)

Notes. This table gives the same statistics as Table 4(a), except that $m = 1$ throughout the table and results are reported for subsamples.

The movements of longer-term yields, however, do not display this U-shaped pattern. In Tables 1(a) and 1(b) the coefficients become increasingly negative as the horizon increases. The tendency of the long rate to fall when the spread is high is quite robust to the maturity of the longer-term instrument.

Monte Carlo results

Our VAR approach can also be used to generate artificial data for Monte Carlo simulations. It is known that there can be small-sample bias in standard errors of regressions with predetermined but not exogenous variables. (See Mankiw and Shapiro (1986) and Stambaugh (1986) for a discussion of this in the context of rational expectations models.) The problem is particularly serious when asymptotic corrections are used to handle equation-error overlap which is large relative to the sample size (Stock and Richardson (1989), Hodrick (1990)). Monte Carlo simulations are an appealing way to avoid excessive reliance on asymptotic distribution theory.

To generate data which match the moments of the actual data while obeying the restrictions of the expectations theory, we start by drawing normal random errors and feeding them through the VAR system estimated on the actual data. This gives us artificial time series for $\Delta R_t^{(m)}$ and $S_t^{(n,m)}$. We then replace $S_t^{(n,m)}$ with $S_t'^{(n,m)}$, calculated using the true VAR coefficients (those estimated on the actual data and which generate the artificial data). This procedure can be used whenever n/m is an integer. It gives us artificial data which obey the expectations theory in population, but the estimated VAR coefficients do not necessarily obey the restrictions of the theory in each artificial sample.

Tables 1(a), 2(a), 3(a), and 4 give two numbers for each entry which summarize the results of the Monte Carlo experiment. The first number is the fraction of 1000 runs which produced an estimated regression coefficient (or correlation, or standard deviation ratio) which was further away from one in the same direction (that is, usually, smaller) than the coefficient obtained in the data. This is a "one-sided" empirical significance level for the coefficient. The second number is the fraction of 1000 runs in which a t-test of the expectations theory, computed using the asymptotic standard error on the coefficient, rejected the null more strongly than the t-test on the actual data. This is a "two-sided" empirical significance level for the expectations theory t-test. One can compare the empirical significance level with the significance level from the normal distribution to evaluate the quality of the asymptotic standard errors in the tables.

The Monte Carlo results show that there is some finite-sample bias in asymptotically valid regression tests of the expectations theory. The bias is particularly noticeable when the order of equation error overlap is large (that is, for large m on the right hand side of Table 1 and for large n at the bottom of Table 2). In these parts of the tables, the asymptotic standard errors greatly understate the true uncertainty about the regression coefficients.

However this bias is not enough to overturn our conclusions about the expectations theory. In Table 1 the expectations theory is rejected very strongly at the short end, and comfortably at the long end. In Table 2 the theory is rejected at the short end but not the long end. The VAR procedures generally give weak evidence that the actual and theoretical spreads are imperfectly correlated, and stronger evidence that the actual spread has higher variability than the theoretical spread.

One interesting feature of the Monte Carlo results is that the two empirical significance levels are sometimes quite different from one another. For example, in Table 3(a) with $m=1$ and $n=24$, only 21 out of 1000 runs delivered a correlation between $S_t^{(n,m)}$ and $S_t'^{(n,m)}$ that was lower than the one estimated in the data. But 749 out of 1000 runs delivered a correlation which was further from one when normalized by its asymptotic standard error. In this table, it seems that the artificial data sets tended to deliver higher correlations between $S_t^{(n,m)}$ and $S_t'^{(n,m)}$ and smaller standard errors than are found in the actual data. We conjecture that this is due to heteroskedasticity in the actual data which is not captured by our Monte Carlo experiment.

4. FURTHER INTERPRETATION

We have documented the fact that for any pair of maturities the yield spread fails to correctly predict subsequent movements in the yield on the longer-term bond, yet it does forecast short rate movements in roughly the way implied by the expectations theory. The purpose of this section is to explore some possible explanations for this fact. The explanations we will consider are not finance-theoretic models of time-varying risk premia, but simply econometric descriptions of ways in which the expectations theory might fail.

One obvious alternative to the expectations theory is a model of the form

$$S_t^{(n,m)} = E_t S_t^{(n,m)*} + c + v_t, \tag{8}$$

where v_t is an error term which is orthogonal to $E_tS_t^{(n,m)*}$. Equation (8) can generate a negative coefficient when $R_{t+m}^{(n-m)}-R_t^{(n)}$ is regressed on $s_t^{(n,m)}$, since the error term v_t appears positively in the independent variable and negatively in the dependent variable of this regression. The numerator of the regression coefficient, the covariance between the right-hand and left-hand side variables, has a term $\text{Cov}(v_t, v_{t+m})-\text{Var}(v_t)$ added to it. This can make the regression coefficient negative if v_t is variable and not too highly serially correlated.

Equation (8) also implies that the regression coefficient when $S_t^{(n,m)*}$ is regressed on $S_t^{(n,m)}$ is $1/(1+VR)$, where VR is the ratio of the variance of v_t to the variance of $S_t^{(n,m)*}$. The correlation coefficient between $E_tS_t^{(n,m)*}$ and $S_t^{(n,m)}$ and the ratio of the standard deviation of $E_tS_t^{(n,m)*}$ to the standard deviation of $S_t^{(n,m)}$ both equal the square root of $1/(1+VR)$.

The VAR results in Tables 3 and 4 do not suggest that this model fits the data, since we found that the correlation coefficient was very close to one while the ratio of standard deviations was roughly one half. It is also possible to test (8) more directly, if we impose extra orthogonality conditions on the error term v_t. For example, if we assume that v_t is white noise, then any variables dated $t-1$ or earlier can be used as instruments in an instrumental variables regression of $R_{t+m}^{(n-m)}-R_t^{(n)}$ onto $s_t^{(n,m)}$. These lagged variables will be orthogonal to v_t, so the IV coefficient should be one as implied by the expectations theory. Alternatively, if we assume that v_t follows an MA (q) process, then any variables dated $t-q-1$ or earlier can be used as instruments.

In Table 5 we report the results of instrumental variables regressions of $R_{t+m}^{(n-m)}-R_t^{(n)}$ onto $s_t^{(n,m)}$. We set $m=1$ and use the full 1952-1987 sample. For comparison, the first column reports the OLS regression results from Table 1(a). The next three columns give IV regression coefficients with standard errors, where the instruments are the spread lagged 1 month, 6 months, and 12 months respectively. The results are not encouraging for the model (8); the IV coefficients are always negative and often more so than the OLS coefficients. Standard errors increase with the lag length of the instrument, but this does not provide any positive evidence in favour of (8).[12]

An alternative orthogonality condition would be that v_t is orthogonal to current and past short-term interest rates. If this is so, then the projection of the yield spread onto the history of short rates has the form implied by the expectations theory; the failure of the expectations theory is caused by the behaviour of the error term in this projection. We can test this idea by using current and lagged short rates as instruments in the IV regression of $R_{t+m}^{(n-m)}-R_t^{(n)}$ onto $s_t^{(n,m)}$. In the last two columns of Table 5 we use the level of $R_t^{(1)}$, less a 12-month or 60-month backwards moving average of $R_t^{(1)}$, as an instrument. We write these variables as $X_{t,12}$ and $X_{t,60}$, respectively. $X_{t,12}$ is a better instrument for shorter-term yield spreads, while $X_{t,60}$ is a better instrument for longer-term yield spreads. But neither set of results is very encouraging for the model. At least over the period 1952-1987, it appears that the component of the yield spread which is correlated with past short rates is at least partly responsible for the failure of the expectations theory.[13]

12. These results are consistent with those reported in Campbell and Shiller (1987) using a VAR approach to test (8).

13. We analyzed this question earlier in Campbell and Shiller (1984). Using a different approach, we reached a similar conclusion for the period 1959-1982. Over the period 1959-1979, however, we found no evidence against equation (9) with an error term orthogonal to short rates. Indeed an IV regression of the type reported in the last column of Table 5 does give some positive coefficients over the shorter sample period, but the standard errors are quite large.

TABLE 5

Instrumental variables regression of $R_{t+1}^{(n-1)} - R_t^{(n)}$ on predicted change $s_t^{(n,1)}$

	Instruments					
n	None (OLS)	$s_{t-1}^{(n,1)}$	$s_{t-6}^{(n,1)}$	$s_{t-12}^{(n,1)}$	$X_{t,12}$	$X_{t,60}$
2	0·002 (0·238)	−1·687 (1·134)	−1·997 (1·484)	−0·106 (0·563)	0·309 (1·561)	−4·578 (4·921)
3	−0·176 (0·362)	−1·373 (1·160)	−3·491 (2·166)	−0·363 (0·747)	−0·164 (1·374)	— (—)
4	−0·437 (0·469)	−1·223 (1·046)	−4·490 (2·179)	−0·733 (1·017)	−0·309 (1·380)	4·610 (10·931)
6	−1·029 (0·537)	−1·678 (0·953)	−5·071 (2·461)	−1·664 (1·574)	−0·142 (1·772)	4·199 (10·071)
9	−1·219[a] (0·598)	−2·089[a] (1·027)	−6·937[a] (3·453)	−2·395[a] (2·283)	0·060[a] (2·089)	2·200[a] (5·364)
12	−1·381[a] (0·683)	−2·146[a] (0·959)	−6·000[a] (2·901)	−2·997[a] (3·144)	−0·061[a] (1·919)	0·990[a] (3·155)
24	−1·815[a] (1·151)	−2·262[a] (1·127)	−4·392[a] (2·552)	−4·219[a] (3·692)	−0·269[a] (2·049)	0·078[a] (2·367)
36	−2·239[a] (1·444)	−2·328[a] (1·398)	−4·850[a] (2·588)	−4·586[a] (4·106)	−0·611[a] (2·153)	−0·559[a] (2·255)
48	−2·665[a] (1·634)	−2·719[a] (1·598)	−5·767[a] (2·865)	−4·477[a] (4·251)	−1·067[a] (2·376)	−1·095[a] (2·313)
60	−3·099[a] (1·749)	−3·058[a] (1·728)	−6·205[a] (3·039)	−4·513[a] (4·433)	−1·518[a] (2·539)	−1·632[a] (2·384)
120	−5·024[a] (2·316)	−4·908[a] (2·405)	−8·063[a] (3·968)	−4·909[a] (6·256)	−3·524[a] (3·394)	−3·839[a] (2·992)

Notes. Table 5 gives estimated regression slope coefficients of $R_{t+1}^{(n-1)} - R_t^{(n)}$ onto $s_t^{(n,m)} \equiv (m/(n-m))S_t^{(n,m)}$. Regressions were estimated using instrumental variables, which are identified at the top of each column. The first three columns use lagged spreads, the last two use the difference between the current short rate and a 12-month backwards moving average ($X_{t,12}$) and the difference between the current short rate and a 60-month backwards moving average ($X_{t,60}$). According to the model given in equation (8), the slope coefficients should equal one. Constant terms (not shown) are included in all regressions. Hansen-Hodrick standard errors are below estimated coefficients, in parentheses. For each regression, the sample is the longest possible using data from 1952:1 through 1987:2

[a] Uses approximation that $R_{t+m}^{(n-m)} = R_{t+m}^{(n)}$.

These results suggest that equation (8) may be too restrictive to explain the data. A more promising model may be

$$S_t^{(n,m)} = kE_tS_t^{(n,m)*} + c, \tag{9}$$

where the coefficient k is greater than one. This model can also generate a negative coefficient when $R_{t+m}^{(n-m)} - R_t^{(n)}$ is regressed on $s_t^{(n,m)}$. Now the covariance between the left-hand and right-hand side variables of the regression has a term

$$k(k-1)\operatorname{Cov}(E_{t+m}S_{t+m}^{(n,m)*}, E_tS_t^{(n,m)*}) - k(k-1)\operatorname{Var}(E_tS_t^{(n,m)*})$$

added to it. This can make the regression coefficient negative if $E_tS_t^{(n,m)*}$ is not too serially correlated and k is large enough.

The model (9) also implies that the regression of $S_t^{(n,m)*}$ on $S_t^{(n,m)}$ will give a coefficient of $1/k$. The correlation of $E_tS_t^{(n,m)*}$ and $S_t^{(n,m)}$ will be one, but the ratio of their standard deviations will be $1/k$. This model roughly fits the results from Tables 2, 3, and 4, except that the Table 2 regression coefficients tend to exceed the Table 4 standard deviation ratios for long horizons.[14]

Equation (9) could be described as an *overreaction* model of the yield spread. It says that the long rate differs from the short rate in the direction implied by the expectations theory; however, the spread between the two rates is larger than can be justified by rational expectations of future short rate changes.

An alternative way to describe equation (9) is to say that long rates *underreact* to short-term interest rates. This interpretation was offered in Campbell and Shiller (1984), although the empirical results in that paper were not as comprehensive as those here. We argued there that long rates are fairly well described as a distributed lag on short rates, where the distributed lag weights are all positive and their sum is very close to one. (It should be exactly one if predictable excess returns are stationary and the short-term interest rate follows a stochastic process with a unit root.) Relative to the predictions of the expectations theory, the estimated distributed lag gives too little weight to the current short rate, and too much weight to lagged short rates. In this sense the long rate underreacts to the current level of the short rate.[15]

To see that the Campbell and Shiller (1984) model is consistent with our results here, consider its implications for the spread between the long rate and the short rate. The spread will be a distributed lag on past short rates with negative weight on the current short rate and positive weight on the distributed lag of past short rates, where all weights sum to zero. The Campbell and Shiller (1984) model implies that the spread's distributed lag representation would conform more closely to the expectations theory if the absolute value of all weights were scaled down towards zero. This also follows from equation (9).[16]

The deviation from the expectations theory described by equation (9) could be caused by time-varying risk premia which are correlated with expected increases in short-term interest rates. Alternatively, it is possible that in our sample period the bond market underestimated the persistence of movements in short rates (and thus overestimated the predictability of future short rate changes). Variations in the long-short spread were due primarily to sudden movements in short rates, and in this sample period long rates reacted too sluggishly to these sudden movements, so that the consequential movements in the spread were too large to be in accordance with the expectations theory.

Acknowledgement. We are grateful to Ludger Hentschel for able and dedicated research assistance, to the National Science Foundation for financial support, and to the LSE Financial Markets Group for its hospitality.

REFERENCES

BELTRATTI, A. and SHILLER, R. J. (1990), "Actual and Warranted Relations Between Asset Prices" (Unpublished paper, University of Turin and Yale University).

CAMPBELL, J. Y. (1986) "A Defense of Traditional Hypotheses about the Term Structure of Interest Rates", *Journal of Finance*, **41**, 183–193.

14. As discussed above, this discrepancy is largely due to the difference in sample periods caused by the truncation of the sample in Table 2.

15. Mankiw and Summers (1984) described a similar underreaction model in which the long rate gives too much weight to *expected future* short rates, as opposed to lagged short rates. The underreaction story is not what one would expect given the evidence for "excess volatility" of long rates presented by one of the authors (Shiller (1979)). However that evidence depended on the assumption that the short-term interest rate is stationary, which is probably inappropriate for the postwar period in the U.S. See Shiller (1989) for further discussion.

16. Equation (9) is stronger in that it implies that the component of the spread which is orthogonal to current and lagged short rates should also be scaled down.

CAMPBELL, J. Y. and SHILLER, R. J. (1984), "A Simple Account of the Behavior of Long-Term Interest Rates", *American Economic Review, Papers and Proceedings*, 74, 44-48.

CAMPBELL, J. Y. and SHILLER, R. J. (1987), "Cointegration and Tests of Present Value Models", *Journal of Political Economy*, **95**, 1062-1088.

COX, J. C., INGERSOLL, J. E. and ROSS, S. A. (1981), "A Reexamination of Traditional Hypotheses about the Term Structure of Interest Rates", *Journal of Finance*, **36**, 769-799.

FAMA, E. F. (1984), "The Information in the Term Structure", *Journal of Financial Economics*, **13**, 509-528.

FAMA, E. F. (1990), "Term Structure Forecasts of Interest Rates, Inflation, and Real Returns", *Journal of Monetary Economics*, **25**, 59-76.

FAMA, E. F. and BLISS, R. R. (1987), "The Information in Long-Maturity Forward Rates", *American Economic Review*, **77**, 680-692.

FROOT, K. A. (1989), "New Hope for the Expectations Hypothesis of the Term Structure of Interest Rates", *Journal of Finance*, **44**, 283-305.

HANSEN, L. P. and HODRICK, R. J. (1980), "Forward Rates as Optimal Predictors of Future Spot Rates", *Journal of Political Economy*, **88**, 829-853.

HODRICK, R. J. (1990), "Dividend Yields and Expected Stock Returns: Alternative Procedures for Inference and Measurement" (Unpublished paper, Northwestern University).

MCCULLOCH, J. (1990), "U.S. Government Term Structure Data", in Friedman, B. and Hahn, F. (eds.), *The Handbook of Monetary Economics* (Amsterdam: North Holland).

MANKIW, N. G. and SHAPIRO, M. D. (1986), "Do We Reject Too Often? Small Sample Properties of Tests of Rational Expectations Models", *Economics Letters*, **20**, 139-145.

MANKIW, N. G. and SUMMERS, L. H. (1984), "Do Long-Term Interest Rates Overreact to Short-Term Interest Rates?", *Brookings Papers on Economic Activity*, **1**, 223-242.

MISHKIN, F. S. (1988*a*), "The Information in the Term Structure: Some Further Results", *Journal of Applied Econometrics*, **3**, 307-314.

MISHKIN, F. S. (1988*b*), "The Information in the Longer-Maturity Term Structure About Future Inflation" (Unpublished paper, Columbia University).

MISHKIN, F. S. (1990), "What Does the Term Structure Tell Us About Future Inflation?", *Journal of Monetary Economics*, **25**, 77-95.

NEWEY, W. K. and WEST, K. D. (1987), "A Simple, Positive Definite, Heteroscedasticity and Autocorrelation Consistent Covariance Matrix", *Econometrica*, **55**, 703-708.

SHILLER, R. J. (1979), "The Volatility of Long-Term Interest Rates and Expectations Theories of the Term Structure", *Journal of Political Economy*, **87**, 1190-1219.

SHILLER, R. J. (1989) *Market Volatility* (Cambridge, Mass.: MIT Press).

SHILLER, R. J. (1990), "The Term Structure of Interest Rates", in Friedman, B. and Hahn, F. (eds.), *The Handbook of Monetary Economics* (Amsterdam: North Holland).

SHILLER, R. J., CAMPBELL, J. Y. and SCHOENHOLTZ, K. L. (1983), "Forward Rates and Future Policy: Interpreting the Term Structure of Interest Rates", *Brookings Papers on Economic Activity*, **1**, 173-217.

STAMBAUGH, R. F. (1986), "Bias in Regressions with Lagged Stochastic Regressors" (Unpublished paper, Graduate School of Business, University of Chicago).

STOCK, J. H. and RICHARDSON, M. (1989), "Drawing Inferences from Statistics Based on Multi-Year Asset Returns" (Unpublished paper, Harvard University and Stanford University).

WHITE, H. (1984) *Asymptotic Theory for Econometricians* (New York: Academic Press).

Journal of Financial Economics 21 (1988) 41–70. North-Holland

THE INFORMATION IN FORWARD RATES
Implications for Models of the Term Structure

Robert F. STAMBAUGH*

University of Chicago, Chicago, IL 60637, USA

Received November 1986, final version received June 1987

Term-structure models from Cox, Ingersoll, and Ross (1985) imply that conditional expected discrete-period returns on discount instruments are linear functions of forward rates. Tests reject a single-latent-variable model of expected returns on U.S. Treasury bills, but two or three latent variables appear to describe expected returns on bills of all maturities. Expected returns estimated using two-latent-variables exhibit variation with business cycles similar to what Fama (1986) observes for forward rates. Inverted term structures precede recessions and upward-sloping structures precede recoveries.

1. Introduction

Empirical work in finance during the past ten years has devoted increased attention to variation through time in expected asset returns. Evidence produced by numerous studies, viewed collectively, indicates that returns on many types of assets can be predicted by a variety of variables observed ex ante.[1] A number of studies use variation in expected returns to make inferences about theories of the relative pricing of assets, e.g., Hansen and Singleton (1982, 1983), Hansen and Hodrick (1983), Gibbons and Ferson (1985), Campbell (1987), and Ferson, Kandel, and Stambaugh (1987). These studies illustrate that asset pricing theories often provide a richer set of empirical implications when expected returns are changing.

Forward rates for U.S. Treasury bills can reliably predict returns on bills of various maturities [e.g., Fama (1976, 1984a) and Startz (1982)]. For example,

*I thank Nai-fu Chen, Eugene Fama, Wayne Ferson, Campbell Harvey, Gur Huberman, Ravi Jagannathan, Krishna Ramaswamy, John Campbell (the referee), René Stulz (the editor), and participants in workshops at the University of Chicago, Duke University, University of Michigan, University of Minnesota, University of Pennsylvania, Vanderbilt University, and National Bureau of Economic Research for helpful discussions and comments. Financial support was provided by the Center for Research in Security Prices, and much of the research was conducted while the author was a Batterymarch Fellow.

[1]A partial list includes Fama and Schwert (1977), Hall (1981), Huizinga and Mishkin (1984), Keim and Stambaugh (1986), Campbell (1987), French, Schwert, and Stambaugh (1987), and Fama and French (1988).

Fama (1984a) regresses monthly bill returns in excess of the one-month rate on forward premiums (forward rates in excess of the one-month rate) and finds reliable predictive power for bills having maturities of two to six months, with up to 39% of the variance explained for two-month bills. Fama submits (p. 520) that 'the rich patterns of variation in expected returns uncovered here stand as challenges to be explained by more explicit models of market equilibrium'.

This study asks whether the information about expected Treasury bill returns in forward rates is consistent with various models of the term structure, primarily the one- and two-factor general equilibrium models developed by Cox, Ingersoll, and Ross (1985). The role of forward premiums as predictors of discrete-period excess returns is developed within the framework of Cox, Ingersoll, and Ross (hereafter CIR). Two convenient properties of the CIR models are exploited. First, the continuously compounded yield on a discount bond is a linear function of the relevant underlying state variables. Second, the dynamic processes of those state variables imply linear conditional expectations of future values given current values. Together these properties imply that forward premiums are linear predictors of excess returns. The likely effects of measurement error make the proposed investigation of expected returns more reasonable than an examination of other implications (such as perfect correlation of price changes in the one-factor model).

Restrictions on expected returns implied by the CIR models are tested using a multivariate latent-variable specification and the generalized method of moments (GMM) approach of Hansen (1982) and Hansen and Singleton (1982). The number of latent variables required to describe expected excess returns equals the number of state variables that enter the CIR pricing relation. A single-variable model of the term structure is rejected, but the evidence suggests that two, perhaps three, latent variables are sufficient to describe the expected excess returns on bills with maturities from two to twelve months.[2] This inference is obtained, however, only after steps are taken to avoid possible spurious effects due to measurement error. Tests on data more susceptible to problems of measurement error make it appear that the number of latent variables required to describe expected excess returns is no less than the number of maturities considered.

Fama (1986) concludes that although the term structure of expected returns on Treasury bills, as measured by the structure of forward rates, has been humped on average over the past 20 years, periods of upward-sloping term

[2]Brennan and Schwartz (1980, 1982), using a different approach, conclude that there are probably three factors present in prices of U.S. and Canadian Government bonds of various maturities. Rather than examining expected returns, they examine the deviations between actual bond prices and bond prices implied by a specific model containing two state variables represented by the short rate and the consol rate. Brennan and Schwartz conclude that the correlation structure of these deviations across different bonds indicates the presence of a third factor.

structures tend to coincide with periods of economic expansion and periods of humps tend to surround recessions. This study finds that a two-latent-variable model also produces shifts in the term structure of expected returns that appear to be related to the business cycle. Specifically, downward-sloping term structures tend to precede peaks and upward-sloping structures tend to precede troughs. One interpretation of such behavior in expected returns, implied by a model proposed by Rubinstein (1974) and reconsidered by Breeden (1986), involves differences between variances of expected aggregate consumption at different dates in the future.

2. Conditional expected returns in the Cox–Ingersoll–Ross models

In addition to providing a framework for modeling the term structure of interest rates in a general equilibrium setting, CIR also develop several specific models as illustrations. Two of these models are particularly suited to analyzing expected returns in discrete time.

In the first model, production opportunities in the economy depend on a single state variable summarized by the equilibrium (instantaneous) rate of interest $r(t)$, which follows the process

$$\mathrm{d}r = \kappa(\theta - r)\,\mathrm{d}t + \sigma\sqrt{r}\,\mathrm{d}z_1, \tag{1}$$

with $\kappa\theta \geq 0$ and $\sigma > 0$, and where $\mathrm{d}z_1$ is the increment of a standard Wiener process.[3] Let $P(\tau, t)$ denote the price at time t of a default-free discount bond with time to maturity τ and face value equal to unity, and define $p(\tau, t) \equiv \ln P(\tau, t)$. Then $p(\tau, t)$ is given by

$$p(\tau, t) = \alpha(\tau) + \beta(\tau) r(t), \tag{2}$$

where $\alpha(\tau)$ and $\beta(\tau)$ also depend on κ, θ, σ, and a constant risk premium parameter, λ.[4]

The second model introduces a distinction between nominal and real values and assumes that the price level $\pi(t)$ follows the process

$$\mathrm{d}\pi = y\pi\,\mathrm{d}t + \sigma_\pi \pi\sqrt{y}\,\mathrm{d}z_2, \tag{3}$$

and that the expected inflation rate $y(t)$ follows the process

$$\mathrm{d}y = \kappa_2(\theta_2 - y)\,\mathrm{d}t + \sigma_2\sqrt{y}\,\mathrm{d}z_3, \tag{4}$$

[3]See Marsh and Rosenfeld (1983) and Oldfield and Rogalski (1987) for empirical investigations of the validity of the process in (1).

[4]See Cox, Ingersoll, and Ross (1985, pp. 390–394).

where dz_2 and dz_3 are increments of Wiener processes (assumed to be uncorrelated with dz_1) and $\mathrm{cov}(y, \pi) \equiv \rho\sigma_2\sigma_\pi y\pi$. If $P(\tau, t)$ now represents the nominal price of a discount bond with maturity τ that is default-free in nominal terms, then $p(\tau, t)$ [$= \ln P(\tau, t)$] is given by

$$p(\tau, t) = \alpha^*(\tau) + \beta(\tau)r(t) + \delta(\tau)y(t), \tag{5}$$

where $\beta(\tau)$ is the same as in (2) and $\alpha^*(\tau)$ and $\delta(\tau)$ also depend on κ, θ, σ, λ, σ_π, κ_2, θ_2, σ_2, and ρ.[5] [The real price of a bond that is default-free in real terms (an index bond) is still given by (2).]

A convenient characteristic of both (2) and (5) is that, for a given maturity, the relation between $p(\tau, t)$ and the state variables is linear with constant coefficients. Such a property might be conjectured for more general models. For example, Oldfield and Rogalski (1987) apply a no-arbitrage approach [e.g., Vasicek (1977) and Richard (1978)] to obtain relations of the general form

$$p(\tau, t) = a_0(\tau) + \sum_{i=1}^{K} a_i(\tau)x_i(t), \tag{6}$$

where the a's are constants for a given τ and the x's are realizations of K state variables (factors).[6] As those authors point out, however, obtaining such a relation through the no-arbitrage approach requires joint assumptions about the processes governing the factors as well as the risk 'prices' associated with the factors. In general, one cannot be sure that such assumptions are consistent with an underlying model of equilibrium.[7] This study entertains (6) as an empirical representation of the term structure but recognizes that, beyond the one- and two-factor CIR models in (2) and (5), theoretical support is tenuous.

The square root processes in (1) and (4) possess the convenient property that conditional expectations of the state variables are linear functions of their past realizations.[8] That is, if $\boldsymbol{x}(t) \equiv [r(t), y(t)]'$, then

$$\mathrm{E}\{\boldsymbol{x}(t+1)|\boldsymbol{x}(t)\} = \boldsymbol{d}_1 + \boldsymbol{D}_2\boldsymbol{x}(t), \tag{7}$$

[5] See Cox, Ingersoll, and Ross (1985, pp. 401–404), where the process for y is given by their 'Model 2'.

[6] Richard (1978) assumes the same dynamics as in (1), (3), and (4), and he obtains the pricing relation in (5) using the no-arbitrage approach. Richard also makes assumptions about the functional forms of the prices of risk, whereas Cox, Ingersoll, and Ross make an assumption about individuals' utility functions and derive such prices endogenously.

[7] See Cox, Ingersoll, and Ross (1985, pp. 397–398) for a discussion of this point.

[8] These properties are given by Cox, Ingersoll, and Ross (1985, p. 392). The bivariate relation in (7) follows immediately, given the assumed independence of dz_1 and dz_3 (and $\boldsymbol{D}_2$ is in fact diagonal). The conditional distribution of $\boldsymbol{x}(t+1)$ is bivariate noncentral chi-square [see Johnson and Kotz (1972, pp. 230–231)].

where $\boldsymbol{d}_1$ and $\boldsymbol{D}_2$ are constant. The deviations from these conditional means are heteroskedastic, however. In models with more than two factors, eq. (7) is assumed to describe conditional expectations of a $K \times 1$ vector of state variables, $\boldsymbol{x}$. For other than the CIR models described above, such an assumption is not necessarily consistent with (6) as an equilibrium pricing relation. The remainder of this section shows that (7), when combined with the pricing equations represented generally by (6), implies that conditional expected excess returns over discrete periods are linear functions of forward premiums.

Let $H(\tau, t+1)$ denote the continuously compounded rate of return from t to $t+1$ (one month) on a bill with τ months to maturity at t, and let $h(\tau, t+1)$ denote the return in excess of the one-month rate. That is,

$$\begin{aligned} h(\tau, t+1) &= H(\tau, t+1) - H(1, t+1) \\ &= p(\tau-1, t+1) - p(\tau, t) + p(1, t) \end{aligned} \tag{8}$$

[noting that $p(0, t+1) = 0$]. Let $F(\tau, t)$ denote the forward rate for the month ending at $t+\tau$ observed at the end of month t, and define the forward premium $f(\tau, t)$ as the forward rate in excess of the one-month rate. That is,

$$\begin{aligned} f(\tau, t) &= F(\tau, t) - H(1, t+1) \\ &= p(\tau-1, t) - p(\tau, t) + p(1, t). \end{aligned} \tag{9}$$

Let $\boldsymbol{h}(t+1) \equiv [h(\tau_1^h, t+1), \ldots, h(\tau_N^h, t+1)]'$ denote an $N \times 1$ vector of excess returns, where the N maturities are held constant for all t. Given (8) and the pricing relation in (6), $\boldsymbol{h}(t+1)$ can be written as

$$\boldsymbol{h}(t+1) = \boldsymbol{c}_1 + \boldsymbol{C}_2 \boldsymbol{x}(t+1) + \boldsymbol{C}_3 \boldsymbol{x}(t), \tag{10}$$

where $\boldsymbol{c}_1$, $\boldsymbol{C}_2$, and $\boldsymbol{C}_3$ are constant. Let $\boldsymbol{f}(t) \equiv [f(\tau_1^f, t), \ldots, f(\tau_M^f, t)]'$ denote an $M \times 1$ vector of forward premiums, where the M maturities are held constant for all t but may be different from the maturities used in constructing $\boldsymbol{h}(t+1)$. Given (6) and (9), $\boldsymbol{f}(t)$ can be written as

$$\boldsymbol{f}(t) = \boldsymbol{g}_1 + \boldsymbol{G}_2 \boldsymbol{x}(t), \tag{11}$$

where $\boldsymbol{g}_1$ and $\boldsymbol{G}_2$ are constant. Assume $M \geq K$, where K is the dimension of $\boldsymbol{x}$ (number of state variables), and assume that $\boldsymbol{G}_2$ has full column rank.[9] Then there exist $\boldsymbol{g}_1^*$ and $\boldsymbol{G}_2^*$ (not unique if $M > K$) such that

$$\boldsymbol{x}(t) = \boldsymbol{g}_1^* + \boldsymbol{G}_2^* \boldsymbol{f}(t). \tag{12}$$

[9] The latter condition will hold in the CIR models.

Combining (7), (10), and (12) gives the result

$$\mathrm{E}\{\boldsymbol{h}(t+1)|\boldsymbol{f}(t)\} = \boldsymbol{b}_1 + \boldsymbol{B}_2\boldsymbol{f}(t), \tag{13}$$

where

$$\boldsymbol{b}_1 = \boldsymbol{c}_1 + \boldsymbol{C}_2\boldsymbol{d}_1 + [\boldsymbol{C}_2\boldsymbol{D}_2 + \boldsymbol{C}_3]\boldsymbol{g}_1^*, \tag{14}$$

and

$$\boldsymbol{B}_2 = [\boldsymbol{C}_2\boldsymbol{D}_2 + \boldsymbol{C}_3]\boldsymbol{G}_2^*. \tag{15}$$

The $N \times M$ matrix $\boldsymbol{B}_2$ in (13) has rank of at most K, the number of state variables, since $\boldsymbol{G}_2^*$ in (15) has dimensions $K \times M$. In other words, at least $M - K$ of the forward premiums are redundant for determining conditional expected excess returns. The linear relation in (13), with the accompanying rank condition on $\boldsymbol{B}_2$, serves as the primary focus of this study's empirical work.

3. Empirical considerations

The previous section discusses expectations of excess returns conditioned on forward premiums, but the selection of forward premiums as the conditioning variables is arbitrary. For example, the same models allow conditional expected excess returns to be stated as linear functions of yields to maturity. Forward premiums are selected primarily to provide a link to previous studies that document variation in expected excess returns on Treasury bills [Fama (1984a, 1986)].

The condition that the rank of $\boldsymbol{B}_2$ in (13) is at most K can be viewed as a restriction on the coefficient matrix in the multivariate regression,

$$\boldsymbol{h}(t+1) = \boldsymbol{b}_1 + \boldsymbol{B}_2\boldsymbol{f}(t) + \boldsymbol{u}(t+1), \qquad t = 1,\ldots,T. \tag{16}$$

Tests of similar rank restrictions are discussed by Hansen and Hodrick (1983) and by Gibbons and Ferson (1985). [See also Campbell (1987).] To derive testable rank restrictions, those studies assume expectations conditioned on the set of information variables are linear with constant coefficients and the conditional betas of the underlying pricing relation are constant, although these assumptions are not necessarily part of the pricing theory being tested. The essential point of the previous section is that the CIR models imply such econometric restrictions.

Although the models of the term structure discussed above lead to apparently testable implications about the behavior of expected excess returns, a strict interpretation of these models produces less appealing implications. For example, the vector of yield changes should lie in a K-dimensional subspace (e.g., yield changes should be perfectly correlated across maturities in the one-factor model). Similarly, the covariance matrix of $\boldsymbol{u}(t+1)$ in (16) should have rank of at most K. Such strong implications surely fail in the data, but rejecting the models on these grounds is probably unreasonable. Given the likely quotation errors, the averaging of bid and ask prices, and other imperfections in the price data, it seems reasonable to design statistical tests that allow for the presence of measurement error.

Although measurement error can render some of the strictest implications of the CIR models empirically uninteresting, the implications about expected returns can offer legitimate tests if one makes assumptions about the nature of the measurement errors. The approach here makes three assumptions. First, measurement errors in both $\boldsymbol{h}(t+1)$ and $\boldsymbol{f}(t)$ add noise to $\boldsymbol{u}(t+1)$ sufficient to give the covariance matrix of $\boldsymbol{u}(t+1)$ full rank. A specific distribution for the measurement errors is not assumed, and in general $\boldsymbol{u}(t+1)$ remains non-normal and heteroskedastic.[10] Second, if $\boldsymbol{f}(t)$ denotes the observed forward premiums and $\boldsymbol{f}^*(t)$ denotes the true (unobservable) forward premiums, assume that

$$\mathrm{E}\{\boldsymbol{f}^*(t)|\boldsymbol{f}(t)\} = \boldsymbol{w}_1 + \boldsymbol{W}_2\boldsymbol{f}(t), \tag{17}$$

where $\boldsymbol{w}_1$ and $\boldsymbol{W}_2$ are constant. Third, assume that the measurement errors in $\boldsymbol{h}(t+1)$ are uncorrelated with $\boldsymbol{f}(t)$. These assumptions preserve the original properties of (16), except that the disturbance covariance matrix becomes nonsingular. The rank of the coefficient matrix $\boldsymbol{B}_2$ is still at most K. Thus, the relation between expected excess returns and forward rates can still be used to test the models. Satisfying the assumption that errors in $\boldsymbol{h}(t+1)$ are uncorrelated with $\boldsymbol{f}(t)$ requires some care in selecting the data used to construct excess returns and forward rates. As will be seen, inferences about the rank of $\boldsymbol{B}_2$ are sensitive to violations of this assumption.

Since both the continuously compounded returns and forward premiums used here to investigate (16) are stated in excess of the one-month rate, the distinction between real and nominal values disappears insofar as measuring bill prices. The real/nominal distinction is important, however, in defining the characteristics of the bills being investigated. The bills used here are nominally default-free, as opposed to index bonds. Thus, for example, rejection of $K=1$ would reject a one-factor CIR model in which a distinction between real and

[10]Another approach is to allow specific assumptions about the distribution of measurement errors to determine the stochastic specification of the econometric model. Brown and Dybvig (1986), in an investigation of the one-factor CIR model, assume that the measurement errors are normally and identically distributed and use this specification to obtain maximum likelihood estimates of the model's parameters.

nominal values is either not recognized or assumed to be unimportant. A rejection of $K=1$ would not reject the same model if the real/nominal distinction is important. When inflation is appended to such a model in the manner described in the previous section, then the rank of $\boldsymbol{B}_2$ equals two when the bills used are nominally default-free.[11]

The rank restriction on $\boldsymbol{B}_2$ is not the only restriction on (16) imposed by a particular pricing model. For example, in the absence of measurement errors, the coefficients in (16) are functions (albeit complicated) of four parameters in the one-factor CIR model and of nine parameters in the two-factor CIR model. The introduction of additional unknown parameters to account for measurement errors, such as $\boldsymbol{w}_1$ and $\boldsymbol{W}_2$ in (17), further complicates the analysis, but imposing additional restrictions in (16) might prove to be an interesting direction for future work.

4. Data and empirical results

4.1. The unique role of the matched-maturity forward premium

The data set to be investigated first was constructed by Fama (1984a) using the U.S. Government Securities File of the Center for Research in Security Prices (CRSP) at the University of Chicago. This data set provides month-end prices of U.S. Treasury bills for each of six maturities from one to six months. The data begin in March 1959 and have been updated by CRSP through 1985. Each month, the bill with maturity closest to six months is selected. This bill is then followed to maturity, providing in subsequent months the prices for maturities of five months, four months, etc. The prices, which are averages of bid and ask quotations, are then used to compute both excess returns and forward premiums for each of five maturities from two to six months. Since there are both five excess returns (N) and five forward premiums (M), the coefficient matrix $\boldsymbol{B}_2$ in (16) has dimensions 5×5.

Before proceeding directly to formal tests of the rank of the coefficient matrix $\boldsymbol{B}_2$ in (16), a more descriptive examination of this hypothesis is presented. Fama (1984a) estimates, for each of five maturities, regressions of the form

$$h(\tau, t+1) = b_{1,\tau} + b_{2,\tau} f(\tau, t) + u(\tau, t+1). \tag{18}$$

In other words, the maturity used in computing the forward premium is the same as that used in computing the excess return. A useful starting point for this study is to ask whether the forward premium with the same maturity

[11] Gibbons and Ramaswamy (1986) use a different approach to test a model with inflation uncertainty where (2) prices an index bond.

Table 1

Correlations between excess returns and forward premiums on Treasury bills with maturities of two to six months, March 1959 to November 1985. $h(\tau, t+1)$ is the excess return on a bill with τ months to maturity at the end of month t, and $f(\tau, t)$ is the forward premium for month $t+\tau$ observed at the end of month t.

Excess return $h(\tau, t+1)$	Forward premium				
	$f(2, t)$	$f(3, t)$	$f(4, t)$	$f(5, t)$	$f(6, t)$
Panel A. Forward premiums with matching maturities; the five maturities used to construct the forward rates are the same as those used to compute the excess returns (i.e., the same set of bills is used to compute both forward rates and excess returns).					
$h(2, t+1)$	0.48	0.30	0.29	0.32	0.19
$h(3, t+1)$	0.29	0.34	0.27	0.28	0.21
$h(4, t+1)$	0.20	0.26	0.32	0.19	0.16
$h(5, t+1)$	0.19	0.23	0.29	0.31	0.19
$h(6, t+1)$	0.16	0.19	0.25	0.28	0.26
Panel B. Forward premiums with nonmatching maturities; the forward-rate maturity is in each case about one week less than the maturity used to compute the excess return (i.e., a different set of bills is used to compute the forward rates).					
$h(2, t+1)$	0.25	0.25	0.26	0.28	0.14
$h(3, t+1)$	0.17	0.26	0.30	0.26	0.19
$h(4, t+1)$	0.07	0.18	0.29	0.17	0.12
$h(5, t+1)$	0.11	0.18	0.30	0.27	0.20
$h(6, t+1)$	0.12	0.15	0.29	0.27	0.20

contains more information, in terms of correlation, about the expected excess return than does a forward premium for another maturity. In the one-factor CIR model, for example, a single forward premium for any maturity is sufficient to capture all of the information in the current term structure. In that case, there would be no particular reason to select the forward premium whose maturity matches that of the excess return. We do observe, however, that forward premiums are not perfectly correlated across maturities; indeed, for the overall March 1959 to November 1978 period, the pairwise correlations among forward premiums for the five maturities range from only 0.49 to 0.66.

Panel A of table 1 displays the sample correlations between excess returns and forward premiums for all of the possible pairings. In virtually all cases, for the overall period and both subperiods, the correlation between the excess return for a given maturity and the forward premium for any of the five maturities is highest when the maturity of the forward premium matches that of the excess return. That is, the largest number in each row tends to lie on the diagonal. The only exceptions occur for $h(6, t+1)$ in the overall period and in the first subperiod, in which cases the correlation is highest for $f(5, t)$. All of the other cases suggest that the forward premium with the matching maturity possesses the greatest ability to forecast next month's excess return.

Table 2

Regressions of excess returns on forward premiums for Treasury bills with maturities of two to six months, March 1959 to November 1985. $h(\tau^h, t+1)$ is the excess return on a bill with τ^h months to maturity at the end of month t, and $f(\tau, t-s)$ is the forward rate for the one-month period ending at $t-s+\tau$. The t-statistics reflect comparisons of the coefficient estimates to zero and are computed using heteroskedasticity-consistent estimates of standard errors.

$$h(\tau^h, t+1) = b_1 + \sum_{\tau=2}^{6} b_\tau f(\tau, t-s) + u(t+1).$$

Months to maturity τ^h	Estimated coefficients $\hat{b}_1$[a]	$\hat{b}_2$	$\hat{b}_3$	$\hat{b}_4$	$\hat{b}_5$	$\hat{b}_6$	$t(\hat{b}_1)$	$t(\hat{b}_2)$	$t(\hat{b}_3)$	$t(\hat{b}_4)$	$t(\hat{b}_5)$	$t(\hat{b}_6)$	R^2	$\rho_1(u)$[b]
Panel A. Forward premiums with matching maturities, not lagged ($s=0$); the five values of τ^h match exactly the five values of τ														
2	0.17	0.58	−0.04	−0.00	0.10	−0.05	2.43	4.70	−0.34	−0.01	1.49	−0.75	0.236	0.14
3	0.11	0.15	0.46	0.04	0.18	−0.04	0.89	0.75	2.49	0.22	1.48	−0.29	0.134	0.13
4	−0.04	−0.10	0.33	0.80	0.03	−0.05	−0.23	−0.33	1.19	2.99	0.16	−0.27	0.107	0.12
5	−0.12	−0.24	0.06	0.73	0.70	−0.03	−0.51	−0.61	0.17	2.16	2.99	−0.11	0.118	0.14
6	−0.30	−0.32	−0.23	0.71	0.62	0.52	−1.06	−0.66	−0.53	1.80	2.27	1.49	0.106	0.13
Panel B. Forward premiums with nonmatching maturities, not lagged ($s=0$); each value of τ is about one week less than a value of τ^h														
2	0.24	0.13	0.14	0.12	0.15	−0.13	2.79	0.82	0.63	0.54	1.59	−1.65	0.107	0.29
3	0.19	−0.09	0.23	0.41	0.18	−0.07	1.36	−0.46	0.64	1.16	1.36	−0.52	0.103	0.15
4	0.07	−0.37	0.13	1.02	0.10	−0.10	0.35	−1.30	0.25	2.04	0.47	−0.54	0.097	0.14
5	−0.03	−0.47	−0.21	1.10	0.54	0.10	−0.11	−1.40	−0.32	1.72	2.13	0.43	0.116	0.17
6	−0.13	−0.46	−0.53	1.24	0.70	0.24	−0.46	−1.16	−0.68	1.60	2.40	0.89	0.110	0.14
Panel C. Lagged forward premiums ($s=1$); the same sets of bills are used to compute excess returns and forward premiums, but the forward premiums are lagged one month														
2	0.19	0.12	0.35	−0.02	−0.01	−0.00	3.14	1.15	3.27	−0.19	−0.25	−0.01	0.116	0.29
3	0.24	−0.07	0.24	0.01	0.18	0.09	2.21	−0.39	1.36	0.08	1.93	0.70	0.059	0.16
4	0.14	−0.33	0.30	0.10	0.39	−0.00	0.90	−1.15	1.17	0.41	2.79	−0.00	0.045	0.12
5	0.16	−0.55	0.36	0.04	0.48	0.28	0.76	−1.28	0.97	0.11	2.58	1.08	0.058	0.15
6	0.18	−0.70	0.39	−0.18	0.69	0.30	0.68	−1.34	0.93	−0.45	2.73	0.97	0.052	0.11

[a] The numbers in this column are multiplied by 1,000.
[b] $\rho_1(u)$ is the estimated first-order autocorrelation of the residuals.

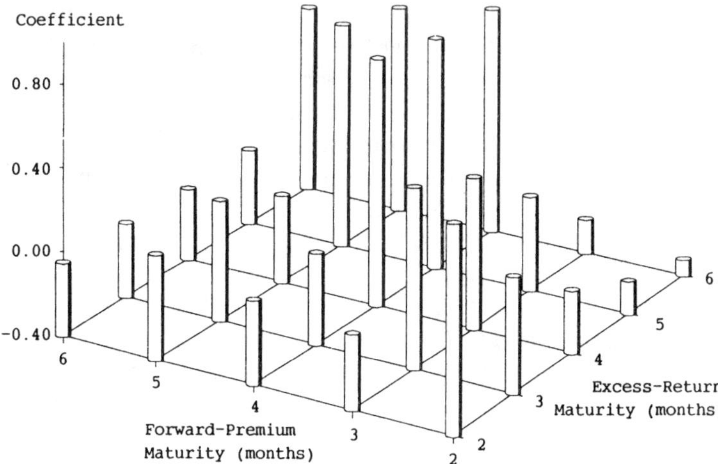

Fig. 1. Plot of coefficients estimated in regressions of excess returns on matched-maturity forward premiums of Treasury bills with maturities of two to six months, March 1959 to November 1985.

Perhaps a more striking illustration of the above phenomenon occurs when the excess return for each maturity is regressed simultaneously on the five forward premiums. Panel A of table 2 reports results of the regression

$$h(\tau^h, t+1) = b_1 + \sum_{\tau=2}^{6} b_\tau f(\tau, t) + u(t+1), \tag{19}$$

for $\tau^h = 2,\ldots,6$. With few exceptions, the coefficient on the forward premium for month $t+\tau^h$ is more than two standard errors above zero, but the coefficients for the other forward premiums are not reliably different from zero. [The t-statistics reported are based on heteroskedasticity-consistent estimates of the standard errors. See White (1980) and Hsieh (1983).] Fig. 1 plots the estimated coefficients on the five forward premiums for each of the five excess-return regressions in the overall period. The pattern of larger coefficients for the matched-maturity forward premiums is illustrated by the taller symbols on the diagonal of the grid, although adjacent values are also large in the regressions with excess returns of maturities five and six.

4.2. Possible explanations and alternative sets of forward premiums

The dominant contribution of the matched-maturity forward premium in the above results might be viewed as casual evidence against the one-factor CIR model of the term structure. As noted earlier, that model assigns no unique role to the matched-maturity premium – any other maturity should serve as well. In contrast, fig. 1 suggests that each of the forward premiums plays a unique role in predicting one of the excess returns, and this observation is confirmed more formally in the latent-variable tests presented below. One could argue that such results are consistent with a model in which a larger number of state variables are important for pricing. If each of the state variables is highly autocorrelated, then the matched-maturity forward premium is likely to have the greatest predictive ability. If $x_i(t)$ is approximately equal to the conditional expectation of $x_i(t+1)$, then the right-hand side of (6) gives a good approximation to the expected value of $p(\tau-1, t+1)$. In that case, comparing (8) and (9) reveals that the conditional expectation of $h(\tau, t+1)$ is approximately $f(\tau, t)$, since the conditional expectation of $p(\tau-1, t+1)$ is approximately $p(\tau-1, t)$. Forward premiums for other maturities do not possess this property. Thus, with a large number of highly autocorrelated state variables, the matched-maturity forward premium could play a unique role in predicting the excess return.

There is, however, a second possible explanation for these empirical regularities. From (8) and (9), observe that both $h(\tau, t+1)$ and $f(\tau, t)$ contain the (log) prices $p(\tau, t)$ and $p(1, t)$. As Fama (1984a) notes, measurement errors in these prices can produce spurious, self-fulfilling components of predicted excess returns. This possibility is investigated here by constructing an alternative set of forward premiums using bills different from those used to compute excess returns. Although the measurement errors in two disjoint sets of bill prices are not necessarily independent, this approach might provide some information about which, if either, of the above two explanations is more likely.

As explained above, Fama selects each month the bill with maturity closest to six months. An alternative set of bills is formed here by instead selecting each month the bill that matures immediately before the original bill selected by Fama. In most cases, the alternative bill has one week less until maturity than the original bill. As in the original data set, the bill selected is used in subsequent months to provide prices for successively lower maturities. When last used, the bill's maturity is approximately three weeks. The alternative set of bills generated by this procedure is used to compute forward rates for maturities from one to six months (less one week in each case); forward premiums for maturities two through six are computed as the forward rates minus the three-week rate.[12] These alternative forward premiums are hereafter referred to as those with nonmatching maturities, as opposed to the original set with matching maturities, in which the maturity of each forward premium matches the maturity of a bill used to compute excess returns.

[12]As in Fama's original data, all rates are standardized by multiplying the continuously compounded daily rates by 30.4.

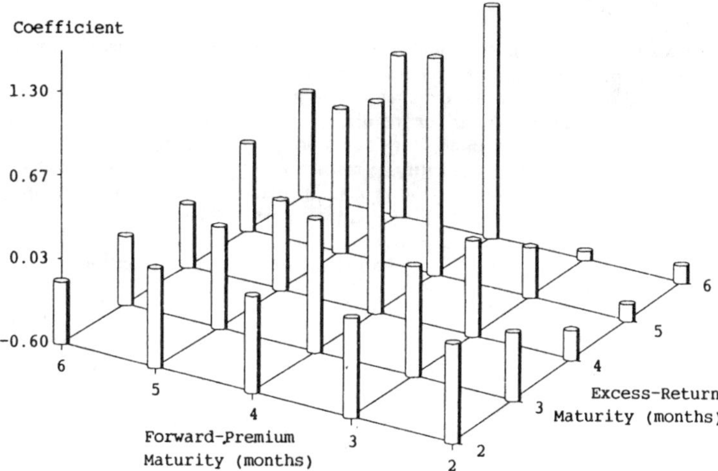

Fig. 2. Plot of coefficients estimated in regressions of excess returns on nonmatched-maturity forward premiums of Treasury bills with maturities of two to six months, March 1959 to November 1985.

Panel B of table 1 contains the estimated correlations between the excess returns and the set of nonmatching forward premiums. Unlike what we observe with the original data in panel A, the diagonal elements in panel B show little if any tendency to be the largest in a given row. Although many of the correlations in panel B are slightly lower than their counterparts in panel A, the differences are largest for the diagonal elements.

Panel B of table 2 reports results of regression (19) using the nonmatching forward premiums. The same decrease in the importance of the diagonal elements is evident in the regression coefficients. Fig. 2 plots the regression coefficients for the overall period, and the contrast with fig. 1 is clear. The forward premium whose maturity is closest to that of the excess return does not, in general, appear to play a special role in predicting the excess return. In fact, the coefficient on the forward premium for four months (less one week) tends to be large in all of the regressions.

The differences between the results in tables 2 and 3 are somewhat inconsistent with the first explanation offered above, wherein a large number of autocorrelated state variables enter as in (6). In that scenario, one might expect the close-maturity (one-week difference) forward premium to be a reasonably good substitute for the matched-maturity forward premium, so that the close-maturity forward premium would still make the dominant contribution in the multiple regression. On the other hand, the difference in the results produced by the two data sets is consistent with the presence of measurement error that is uncorrelated across different bills. If the measurement error in

Table 3

Chi-square statistic for tests of the number of latent variables in expected excess returns of Treasury bills with maturities up to six months, March 1959 to November 1985. The tests use the generalized method of moments with excess returns for monthly maturities 2,3,...,6 as dependent variables and with forward premiums for maturities 2,3,...,6 as instruments (in addition to a constant). Heteroskedasticity is allowed, but the disturbances are assumed serially uncorrelated. The chi-square statistic tests the overidentifying restrictions implied by the latent-variable specification. The p-value (in parentheses) is the probability under the null hypothesis that the test statistic would exceed the reported value.

	Latent variables (degrees of freedom)			
Dates	1 (16)	2 (9)	3 (4)	4 (1)
Panel A. Forward premiums with matching maturities as instruments				
3/1959–11/1985	66.28 (0.000)	53.69 (0.000)	31.22 (0.000)	8.73 (0.003)
3/1959–7/1972	53.62 (0.000)	33.37 (0.001)	24.36 (0.000)	10.59 (0.001)
8/1972–11/1985	38.70 (0.001)	29.62 (0.001)	17.57 (0.001)	5.01 (0.025)
3/1959–8/1979	67.38 (0.000)	53.31 (0.000)	34.77 (0.000)	10.65 (0.001)
Panel B. Forward premiums with nonmatching maturities as instruments				
3/1959–11/1985	47.66 (0.000)	23.55 (0.005)	6.41 (0.171)	1.06 (0.303)
3/1959–7/1972	37.35 (0.002)	20.99 (0.013)	9.52 (0.049)	2.16 (0.142)
8/1972–11/1985	31.89 (0.010)	17.54 (0.041)	2.55 (0.636)	0.08 (0.782)
3/1959–8/1979	49.42 (0.000)	27.60 (0.001)	15.17 (0.004)	6.51 (0.011)
Panel C. Lagged forward premiums as instruments				
4/1959–11/1985	38.02 (0.002)	18.57 (0.029)	7.38 (0.117)	2.62 (0.105)
4/1959–7/1972	26.33 (0.050)	9.49 (0.394)	3.87 (0.424)	0.00 (0.975)
8/1972–11/1985	21.77 (0.151)	8.44 (0.491)	3.43 (0.488)	0.26 (0.611)
4/1959–8/1979	22.45 (0.129)	12.74 (0.692)	1.70 (0.790)	0.18 (0.676)

$p(\tau, t)$ [cf. (8) and (9)] is uncorrelated with errors in prices of other bills, then the errors in the nonmatched forward premiums are uncorrelated with the errors in the excess returns. In that case, the close-maturity forward premium need not play a unique role in a model with, for example, one state variable, whereas the matched-maturity premium would appear to make a unique contribution because of the correlation between its measurement error and the measurement error in the excess return. The latent-variable tests presented below in section 4.3 produce different inferences depending on the set of forward premiums used as instruments to predict excess returns. Whether measurement errors of plausible magnitudes can account for these differences is discussed in section 4.4.

Another approach to the measurement error problem is to use lagged values of the forward premiums, so that the prices used to compute the forward premiums are observed before any of the prices used to compute the excess returns. The linearity of the conditional means in (7) also holds for lagged values. That is, $\mathrm{E}\{\boldsymbol{x}(t+1)|\boldsymbol{x}(t-s)\}$ is linear in $\boldsymbol{x}(t-s)$ for $s>0$. Therefore, the linearity of (13) and the accompanying rank restriction on the coefficient matrix $\boldsymbol{B}_2$ also obtain with $\boldsymbol{f}(t-s)$ in place of $\boldsymbol{f}(t)$ (although the values of the coefficients will in general be different). Panel C of table 2 reports the results of regressions using the excess returns and forward premiums from the original set of bills but with the forward premiums lagged one month. In general, these regressions explain less variance than in the previous cases. Nevertheless, for each equation the hypothesis that the coefficients on the forward premiums jointly equal zero can be rejected at conventional significance levels. The patterns of the estimated coefficients do not suggest the strong linear independence that is evident in the results with the nonlagged forward premiums in panel A. This set of lagged forward premiums, as well as the two sets of nonlagged forward premiums, is used below in formal tests of this linear independence.

4.3. Tests of the number of latent variables in expected returns

As shown earlier, the pricing models discussed in section 2 imply that the $N \times M$ coefficient matrix $\boldsymbol{B}_2$ in (16) has rank K, where N is the number of assets and K is the number of state variables in the pricing relation. Assume that the first K rows of $\boldsymbol{B}_2$ are linearly independent. That is, the first K equations relate expected excess returns on a set of K 'reference assets' to $\boldsymbol{f}(t)$, the vector of forward premiums.[13] Then the matrix $\boldsymbol{B}_2$, given that it has rank K, can be written as

$$\boldsymbol{B}_2 = \begin{bmatrix} \boldsymbol{L} \\ \boldsymbol{QL} \end{bmatrix}, \tag{20}$$

where $\boldsymbol{L}$ is a $K \times M$ matrix of rank K and $\boldsymbol{Q}$ is $(N-K) \times K$. In other words, the last $N-K$ rows of $\boldsymbol{B}_2$ are linear combinations of the first K rows.

[13] In this application, the reference assets are chosen to have nonadjacent maturities.

The restriction in (20) is tested using the generalized method of moments [Hansen (1982)], which exploits the condition that the disturbance vector $\boldsymbol{u}(t+1)$ in (16) must be orthogonal to a vector of instruments. The instruments are the variables used to form conditional expectations at time t. Given the representation of conditional expectations in (13), the instruments in this case consist of a constant plus the M forward premiums, thus yielding $N \cdot (M+1)$ orthogonality conditions. Hansen (1982) provides a test statistic that is distributed in large samples as χ^2 if a set of overidentifying restrictions holds. The degrees of freedom equal the number of orthogonality conditions minus the number of parameters estimated, and for the restrictions in (20) the degrees of freedom equal $(N-K) \cdot (M-K)$. With five assets $(N=5)$ and five forward premiums $(M=5)$, the degrees of freedom equal $(5-K)^2$.

Given the processes assumed for the state variables [(1) and (4)], the disturbance vector $\boldsymbol{u}(t+1)$ is nonnormal and heteroskedastic. As applied here, the GMM approach allows such behavior, although the disturbances are assumed to be serially uncorrelated. Campbell (1987) applies this same test to different data, and Hansen and Hodrick (1983) use the GMM approach to test a similar restriction assuming serially correlated but homoskedastic disturbances. Gibbons and Ferson (1985) test a similar restriction using a likelihood ratio test, where the disturbances are assumed to obey the conditions of the standard normal regression model. The null hypotheses tested in the latter two studies include restrictions in addition to those represented in (20). Hansen and Hodrick test whether the rank of $[\boldsymbol{b}_1\ \boldsymbol{B}_2]$ equals K, where $K=1$ in their case.[14] Gibbons and Ferson test whether

$$[\boldsymbol{b}_1\ \boldsymbol{B}_2] = \begin{bmatrix} \boldsymbol{L}^* \\ \boldsymbol{Q}^*\boldsymbol{L}^* \end{bmatrix} \quad \text{and} \quad \boldsymbol{Q}^*\boldsymbol{1}_{(K+1)} = \boldsymbol{1}_{N-(K+1)}, \tag{21}$$

where $\boldsymbol{L}^*$ is a $(K+1) \times M$ matrix of rank $K+1$, $\boldsymbol{1}_p$ denotes a p-vector of ones, and the dependent variables are raw returns rather than excess returns. These additional restrictions involving the intercept vector $\boldsymbol{b}_1$ arise from assuming that a pricing relation with K betas holds for expected discrete-period returns. The models of the term structure considered here restrict the rank of $\boldsymbol{B}_2$, but the intercept restrictions included in (21) are not implied for discrete-period returns.[15]

Tests are conducted for the overall period from March 1959 through November 1985 as well as for three subperiods. The first two subperiods are simply the first and second halves of the overall period, and the remaining

[14] Campbell reports results both with and without this additional restriction.

[15] These restrictions would be appropriate, however, for expected instantaneous rates of return.

subperiod runs from March 1959 through August 1979.[16] This last subperiod is chosen to exclude the period beginning in October 1979, when the Federal Reserve announced a change in operating procedure. Some researchers argue that the interest-rate process experienced structural shifts associated with this event.[17]

Panel A of table 3 reports the chi-square statistics and the associated p-values for tests of one, two, three, and four latent variables in expected returns, where the original forward premiums with matching maturities are used as instruments. The first three hypotheses ($K = 1, 2, 3$) are rejected strongly, with p-values of 0.001 or less in the overall period and in both subperiods. The hypothesis $K = 4$, which restricts only one parameter, also produces p-values of 0.003 or less in all but the August 1972 to November 1985 subperiod, where the p-value is 0.025. In general, these results suggest that the number of latent variables required to describe expected excess returns is no less than the number of assets considered (five). In other words, these tests indicate that the five rows of $\boldsymbol{B}_2$, whose estimated values are plotted in fig. 1, are linearly independent.

Panel B of table 3 reports the same tests as conducted in table 2, except that the alternative nonmatched-maturity forward premiums are used as instruments. The hypotheses $K = 3$ and $K = 4$ generally are not rejected at conventional significance levels. Exceptions occur in the March 1959 to August 1979 subperiod, where the p values are 0.004 and 0.011 for tests of $K = 3$ and $K = 4$. The hypothesis $K = 2$ produces p-values of 0.013 and 0.041 in the two equal-length subperiods, but the p-values are 0.005 and 0.001 in the overall period and the March 1959 to August 1979 subperiod. Whether one views these results as supporting $K = 2$ may depend in part on how strongly one maintains the assumption that the parameters underlying the maturity-dependent coefficients in the pricing relations [e.g., (2) and (5)] remain constant over the longer sample periods. It seems reasonable to conclude that evidence against $K = 2$ is, at best, mixed. The evidence against $K = 1$ remains strong, although the p-value in the second subperiod is 0.010.

Panel C of table 3 reports results of the same tests using forward premiums lagged one month. For a given hypothesis, the p-value in panel C generally exceeds the p-value in panel B. The hypotheses $K = 1$ and $K = 2$ produce p-values of 0.002 and 0.029 in the overall period, but all other p-values exceed conventional significance levels. In considering these results, however, the reader should bear in mind that the R^2s are also typically smaller in the regressions of excess returns on lagged forward premiums (cf. panel C of table

[16]Recall that, in the notation used here, the observation for $t = 8/79$ corresponds to the excess return during 9/79 [cf. eq. (16)].

[17]See, for example, Huizinga and Mishkin (1984) and Huizinga and Leiderman (1985).

2). Thus, the power to reject higher values of K might be less than in the previous cases.

Inferences about the number of latent variables in expected excess returns differ sharply depending on whether the maturities of the forward premiums used as instruments match the maturities of the excess returns. With the first set of matching-maturity forward premiums, the tests reject the hypothesis that the number of latent variables required is less than five, the number of assets considered. Using the nonmatching set, the tests suggest that the number of latent variables required to describe expected returns on bills with maturities up to six months equals two, possibly three. These differences in the results for the latent-variable tests confirm the differences in the patterns of the regression coefficients observed in the previous section. Again, the greater number of latent variables apparently required with the matching-maturity forward premiums could reflect asset-specific measurement errors.

4.4. A closer look at the effects of measurement error

An obvious question raised by the previous discussion is whether measurement errors with plausible characteristics can account for the differences in results. Although it is difficult to specify the precise nature of the measurement errors, a rough feel for reasonable magnitudes might be gained by examining bid–ask spreads. The pricing models discussed earlier pertain to a single equilibrium price and do not include a framework in which to handle separate bid and ask prices. The price data used here are constructed by averaging bid and ask quotations. Suppose that the equilibrium price that is appropriate for the pricing model lies somewhere within the quoted bid–ask range but is not necessarily the average. It would be useful to know whether such measurement errors would be sufficient to affect inferences about the number of latent variables.

Let $P(\tau, t)$ denote the average of the bid and ask prices, which is used here as the observed price (with τ and t as defined earlier). Let $P^*(\tau, t)$ denote the true equilibrium price, and let $P^{\mathrm{b}}(\tau, t)$ and $P^{\mathrm{a}}(\tau, t)$ denote the bid and ask prices. As before, lower-case letters denote logs of these prices. Define the relative pricing error and the relative bid–ask spread:

$$\eta(\tau, t) \equiv p(\tau, t) - p^*(\tau, t), \tag{22}$$

$$s(\tau, t) \equiv p^{\mathrm{a}}(\tau, t) + p^{\mathrm{b}}(\tau, t). \tag{23}$$

For each of maturities two through six, $s(\tau, t)$ was computed each month using the reported bid and ask prices of the bills in the original (Fama's) data set. For maturities two through six, the average values of $s(\tau, t)$ are 0.00027, 0.00023, 0.00041, 0.00047, and 0.00041. Given these magnitudes, the arithmetic average of the bid and ask prices is very close to the geometric average. That is, $p(\tau, t)$ is well approximated by

$$p(\tau, t) = p^{\mathrm{b}}(\tau, t) + 0.5s(\tau, t). \tag{24}$$

Assume that the true price is given by

$$p^{*}(\tau, t) = p^{\mathrm{b}}(\tau, t) + \nu(\tau, t)s(\tau, t), \tag{25}$$

where $\nu(\tau, t)$ is distributed uniformly on the interval $[0,1]$ and independently across τ and t. This essentially amounts to an assumption that the true price is distributed uniformly over the bid–ask interval and that measurement errors are independent across bills. Combining (22), (24), and (25) gives

$$\eta(\tau, t) = [0.5 - \nu(\tau, t)]s(\tau, t). \tag{26}$$

Note that the excess return on the τ-maturity bill, $h(\tau, t+1)$, and the forward premium with the matched maturity, $f(\tau, t+1)$, both contain the error $\eta(\tau, t)$ [cf. eqs. (8) and (9)].[18] It is easily verified that

$$\mathrm{var}\{\eta(\tau, t)\} = \tfrac{1}{12}\mathrm{E}\{[s(\tau, t)]^2\}. \tag{27}$$

Based on sample means of $s(\tau, t)^2$, the values of (27) for maturities two through six (times 10^7) are 0.103, 0.075, 0.196, 0.278, and 0.253. The variances of the monthly excess returns for the same maturities (times 10^7) are 5.19, 14.42, 30.85, 53.38, and 79.62. The variances of the forward premiums (times 10^7) are 3.35, 3.60, 3.47, 6.34, and 6.85. Thus, the variances of the errors are 6% or less of the variances of the forward premiums and much less than the variances of the excess returns.

To investigate whether errors of this nature could affect the latent-variable tests in the manner suggested earlier, the following experiment was performed. For each month and maturity, the relative spread $s(\tau, t)$ was combined with a uniform random number $\nu(\tau, t)$, using (26), to produce an error $\eta(\tau, t)$. These errors were then added to the excess returns for maturities two through six and to the corresponding forward premiums constructed from the alternative (nonmatching) set of bills. Latent-variable tests of $K = 3$ and $K = 4$ were then conducted for the overall 1959–1985 period using these new excess returns and forward premiums.

The above procedure was repeated ten times. For the tests of $K = 3$, the p-values range from 0.008 to 0.040 and average 0.019 across the ten trials.

[18]In addition, the excess return contains $\eta(\tau - 1, t+1)$ and the forward premium contains $\eta(\tau, t)$. Both quantities also contain $\eta(1, t)$, but this same error is present in forward premiums for all maturities and therefore should not induce a maturity-specific contribution.

Recall that, without the additional generated errors, the same data produce a p-value of 0.171 for the hypothesis $K = 3$ (table 4, panel B). The tests of $K = 4$ produce p-values that range from 0.007 to 0.066 and average 0.039 across the ten trials with the additional generated errors. Again, recall that a test of $K = 4$ using the same data, but without the added errors, produces a p-value of 0.303.

The above experiments suggest that errors induced by fluctuations of true prices within the bid–ask range are sufficient to produce rejections of hypotheses that would otherwise not be rejected. Indeed, it appears that one would be led to the same inference obtained with the original set of matched-maturity data – that there are as many latent variables as maturities. The errors modeled include no errors in the bid and ask quotations themselves, and thus seem to represent a fairly conservative specification of the magnitudes of possible measurement errors.[19]

4.5. Results for bills with longer maturities

This section extends the previous analysis of expected excess returns on bills with maturities up to six months to bills with maturities from seven to twelve months. Returns and forward rates for the longer-maturity bills are taken from a data set constructed by Fama (1984b) and updated by CRSP. The file is constructed like the data set described in section 4.1. Each month the bill with maturity closest to twelve months is selected; this bill provides the prices for maturities eleven through seven in subsequent months. The data cover the period December 1963 through November 1985.[20]

The longer maturities are analyzed separately here because the data available for maturities seven through twelve differ from the data for the shorter maturities in an important way. Since one-year bills are issued only once a month, the longer-maturity data set already uses all outstanding bills with maturities greater than six months. Thus, unlike for the shorter maturities, an alternative set of forward premiums with nonmatching maturities cannot be constructed for maturities seven through twelve.

Regressions of excess returns on forward premiums for maturities seven through twelve produce patterns similar to those reported earlier for the matching-maturity forward premiums with the shorter maturities: the coeffi-

[19]The experiments reported probably understate somewhat the effect of errors limited to the kind specified in (26). In the above framework, the excess returns and forward premiums to which the generated errors are added already contain (uncorrelated) errors of similar magnitudes. Thus, the relative increases in explanatory power produced by adding the matching errors would be less than if the other errors were absent.

[20]There are 14 months during this period in which data for one or more of the longer maturities are unavailable. These months are omitted in the subsequent tests.

cient on the forward premium whose maturity matches that of the excess return tends to be large. Given the strong possibility that measurement error is the source of these patterns, forward premiums for the longer maturities are not attractive instruments for the latent-variable tests. Nevertheless, the excess returns on these longer maturities can be used with the previous set of instruments to investigate the number of latent variables necessary to describe expected excess returns on a wider array of maturities.

Panel A of table 4 reports results of the latent-variables tests using excess returns for maturities two through twelve. The instruments used are the nonmatching-maturity forward premiums for maturities two through six, the same instruments used in panel B of table 3. In general, the p-value for a given hypothesis is larger for the eleven-asset case (table 4, panel A) than for the five-asset case (table 3, panel B). Indeed, even the p-values for a model with two latent variables are 0.11 or more, whereas they ranged from 0.001 to 0.041 in panel B of table 3. Thus, if a hypothesis is not rejected at a given significance level using excess returns on five maturities, that hypothesis is not rejected using eleven maturities.

The increases in p-values obtained with the larger set of maturities should probably not lead one to accept hypotheses that would have been rejected using fewer maturities. The tests using the larger set of maturities use a somewhat smaller sample, in both total number of time-series observations and the number of observations per estimated parameter. Differences in finite-sample behavior of the test statistic could account for the larger p-values. For example, the Monte Carlo results of Tauchen (1985) suggest, in a different application, that the GMM chi-square test of overidentifying restrictions shows a slight tendency to accept the null hypothesis too often in smaller samples. It seems reasonable to conclude that increasing the number of maturities considered does not increase the number of latent variables that are required to describe expected excess returns.

As discussed above, the forward premiums for the longer maturities are less attractive as instruments because of the potential problems arising from common measurement errors in matching-maturity forward premiums and excess returns. The longer-maturity forward premiums, however, may contain true information about expected excess returns that is not captured by shorter-maturity forward premiums. As a partial check of the latter possibility, part B of table 4 reports latent-variable tests where the nine-month forward premium is added to the set of instruments and the nine-month excess return is excluded (to eliminate the matching-maturity problem). In multiple regressions of the longer-maturity excess returns on the longer-maturity forward premiums, the nine-month forward premium appears to contain significant explanatory power for all maturities, whereas the other forward premiums tend to contribute reliably only in predicting the matched-maturity excess return. Thus, the nine-month forward premium is selected on the basis of its

Table 4

Chi-square statistic for tests of the number of latent variables in expected excess returns of Treasury bills with maturities up to twelve months, December 1963 to November 1985. The tests are conducted using the generalized method of moments with monthly excess returns as dependent variables and with forward premiums as instruments (in addition to a constant). Heteroskedasticity is allowed, but the disturbances are assumed serially uncorrelated. The chi-square statistic tests the overidentifying restrictions implied by the latent-variable specification. The p-value (in parentheses) is the probability under the null hypothesis that the test statistic would exceed the reported value.

	Latent variables			
Dates	1	2	3	4
Panel A. Excess returns for eleven maturities (2–12); five forward premiums as instruments (maturities 2–6)				
12/1963–11/1985	64.80 (0.008)	31.05 (0.269)	14.37 (0.571)	2.99 (0.886)
12/1963–11/1974	55.95 (0.048)	35.78 (0.120)	19.40 (0.248)	9.08 (0.247)
12/1974–11/1985	50.46 (0.124)	26.47 (0.493)	10.24 (0.854)	2.26 (0.944)
12/1963–8/1979	65.56 (0.007)	36.19 (0.111)	21.04 (0.177)	10.32 (0.171)
Degrees of freedom	40	27	16	7
Panel B. Excess returns for ten maturities (2–8, 10–12); six forward premiums as instruments (maturities 2–6, 9)				
12/1963–11/1985	79.50 (0.001)	45.93 (0.053)	22.12 (0.392)	7.55 (0.819)
12/1963–11/1974	61.73 (0.049)	46.65 (0.046)	28.16 (0.136)	17.67 (0.126)
12/1974–11/1985	49.73 (0.291)	30.77 (0.529)	18.51 (0.617)	7.28 (0.839)
12/1963–8/1979	69.24 (0.012)	49.28 (0.026)	30.40 (0.084)	18.13 (0.112)
Degrees of freedom	45	32	21	12
Panel C. Excess returns for eleven maturities (2–12); eleven lagged forward premiums as instruments (maturities 2–12)				
1/1964–11/1985	126.39 (0.038)	93.56 (0.161)	78.96 (0.099)	52.18 (0.351)
1/1964–8/1979	114.47 (0.153)	100.33 (0.072)	79.82 (0.088)	64.91 (0.063
Degrees of freedom	100	81	64	49

in-sample ability to predict excess returns on various maturities. In spite of this preselection method, inferences about the number of latent variables are similar to those obtained previously. The overall-period p-values are 0.053 for $K=2$ and 0.392 for $K=3$. Thus, it still appears that two or three latent variables are sufficient to describe expected excess returns on bills with maturities of two through twelve months.

Table 5

Comparisons of within-sample and one-step-ahead forecasts of excess returns on Treasury bills with maturities up to twelve months, December 1963 to November 1985.

	Two latent variables[a]		Two adjacent maturities[b]		Maturities 2–6[c]	
Maturity	Mean square error[d]	Percent explained[e]	Mean square error[d]	Percent explained[e]	Mean square error[d]	Percent explained[e]
	Panel A. Within-sample forecasts, 12/1963–11/1985					
2	0.060	4.64	—	—	0.056	10.01
3	0.156	9.10	0.156	8.62	0.154	9.87
4	0.338	8.86	0.353	4.91	0.335	9.66
5	0.578	11.10	0.600	7.73	0.578	11.22
6	0.862	10.94	0.891	7.94	0.861	11.08
7	1.035	10.09	1.107	3.79	1.034	10.17
8	1.413	9.43	1.482	5.01	1.413	9.45
9	1.962	10.37	2.093	4.35	1.960	10.44
10	2.491	10.56	2.634	5.40	2.489	10.63
11	2.964	10.18	3.163	4.14	2.963	10.21
12	3.481	10.64	—	—	3.480	10.65
	Panel B. One-step-ahead forecasts, 12/1974–11/1985					
2	0.120	−29.33	—	—	0.122	−31.32
3	0.280	−8.30	0.256	1.21	0.286	−10.33
4	0.607	−5.95	0.575	−0.04	0.606	−5.85
5	1.015	0.96	0.992	3.16	1.035	−0.97
6	1.531	2.79	1.550	1.56	1.577	−0.02
7	1.752	1.90	1.757	1.61	1.773	0.74
8	2.456	0.80	2.497	−0.09	2.499	−0.95
9	3.448	0.80	3.393	2.36	3.503	−0.80
10	4.327	0.45	4.199	3.37	4.339	0.17
11	5.192	2.06	5.153	2.79	5.243	1.11
12	6.056	2.47	—	—	6.115	1.51

[a] The results labeled 'Two latent variables' are obtained using the generalized method of moments, with excess returns for maturities 2–12 as dependent variables and forward premiums for maturities 2–6 (in addition to a constant) as instruments.

[b] The results labeled 'Two adjacent maturities' are obtained from ordinary least-squares regression of the excess return for each maturity τ on two forward premiums, one for maturity $\tau-1$ and one for maturity $\tau+1$.

[c] The results labeled 'Maturities 2–6' are obtained from ordinary least-squares regression of the excess return for each maturity on the set of nonmatching forward premiums for maturities 2–6.

[d] The numbers in this column are multiplied by 100,000.

[e] $(VAR\text{-}MSE)/VAR \times 100$, where VAR is the total variance of the excess return and MSE is the mean square error.

Panel C of table 4 reports results using lagged forward premiums. In this case it is possible to use forward premiums for all eleven maturities as instruments. That is, since the forward premiums are lagged, it is not necessary to have an alternative set of bills for the longer maturities to avoid the measurement-error problem discussed earlier. The test of $K=1$ produces a p-value of 0.038 in the overall period, but all other p-values are 0.063 or higher. Again, the inclusion of longer maturities does not lead to the rejection of hypotheses that are not rejected by the shorter-maturity tests.

Table 5 provides additional descriptive evidence on the relative explanatory power of the model with two latent variables. Panel A compares the within-sample fit for the overall period with two alternatives. In the first alternative, the excess return for maturity τ is regressed on the forward premiums for maturities $\tau-1$ and $\tau+1$. (Recall that the own-maturity forward premium would introduce possible spurious explanatory power as a result of measurement error.) This alternative allows more maturity-specific information to enter the conditional expected excess return. The second alternative uses the same instruments as the two-latent-variable model – forward premiums with maturities of two through six months – but no latent-variable restriction is imposed. In other words, the excess return for a given maturity is simply regressed on the five forward premiums for maturities two through six. Panel B of table 5 presents results for the same three cases, except the models are estimated using data only up to the month preceding the forecast month. The first subperiod is used as the base period for the initial forecast, so the one-step-ahead monthly forecasts cover the second subperiod, December 1974 through November 1985. Both panels (A and B) report, for each model and maturity, the mean squared forecast error (MSE) and the percentage difference between the total excess return variance and the MSE.[21] The two-latent-variable model outperforms the adjacent-maturity specification for all maturities within the sample but only three maturities (6, 7, and 8) in the one-step-ahead forecasts. The latent-variable model performs marginally worse than the unrestricted model within the sample (as it must) but outperforms it for all but one maturity (four months) in the one-step-ahead forecasts.

5. Changes in the term structure of expected excess returns

5.1. Business cycles and the slope of the term structure

As Fama (1984b) observes, average bill returns over the sample period of this study increase with maturity up to about nine months and then decline with maturity, and this same humped term structure is present in average

[21] The negative numbers in table 5 represent cases in which the variance of the forecast error exceeds the variance of the excess return.

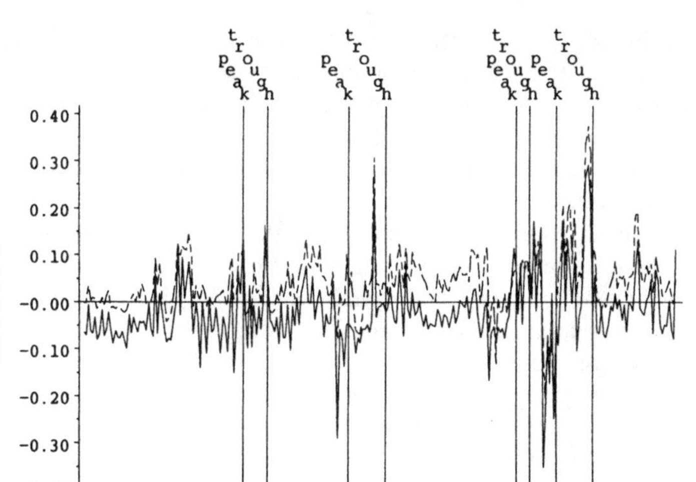

Fig. 3. Differences in expected monthly percent returns on Treasury bills with maturities of two, six, and twelve months estimated in a model with two latent variables. The solid line plots the difference for twelve months minus six months, and the dashed line plots the difference for six months minus two months. Vertical lines indicate business-cycle peaks and troughs.

forward premiums. In a subsequent paper, Fama (1986) observes that, although the structure of forward premiums is humped on average, the shape of that structure shifts over time. Forward premiums tend to be upward sloping during periods of economic expansion and humped or downward sloping around recessions. Since Fama argues that forward premiums are approximately equal to expected excess returns, the same behavior is attributed to the term structure of expected excess returns.

If a model with, say, two latent variables is to be an adequate description of expected excess returns on bills of all maturities, then such a model should produce similar shifts in the shape of the term structure. Although a two-variable model can produce shifts in the shape of the term structure (indeed, so can a one-variable model), it remains to be investigated here whether the model estimated in the previous section does so.

Shifts in the shape of the estimated term structure can be seen fig. 3, which plots differences in the fitted expected returns between twelve-month and six-month bills (solid line) and between six-month and two-month bills (dashed line). The fitted values are obtained from the two-latent-variable model with forward premiums for maturities two through six as instruments (the model used for $K = 2$ in panel A of table 4). As shown in the figure, the two-latent-variable model produces rich variation in the term structure of expected excess returns. Although the term structure is humped on average (the average fitted values essentially reproduce the sample average excess returns), periods of both upward- and downward-sloping structures are common. When the dashed line plots above zero and the solid line plots below zero, the term structure is humped. When both lines plot above (below) zero, the term structure slopes upward (downward).

The plots in fig. 3 suggest that changes in the shape of the term structure of expected returns are related to business cycles. Vertical rules on the graph indicate business-cycle peaks and troughs, as reported by the National Bureau of Economic Research [see Moore and Zarnowitz (1984)]. Periods in which the solid line (twelve months minus six months) is most prominently negative precede business-cycle peaks, especially the peaks beginning the most severe recessions, in 1973–1975 and 1982–1983. In other words, the term structure of expected returns is often downward sloping, at least for the longer maturities, as the economy heads into recessions.

The largest positive values of the solid line (twelve months minus six months) precede the troughs ending the two most severe recessions, and relatively large positive slopes also surround the trough in 1980. That is, the term structure of expected returns slopes upward as the economy heads into recoveries. Thus, although the term structure is somewhat humped on average over the sample period, the sharpest departures from this average pattern appear to accompany turning points in economic activity.

The estimates of expected returns in fig. 3 are functions of two latent variables extracted from forward premiums with maturities *up to only six months*. That is, in addition to restricting the vector of expected returns to lie in two dimensions, the model uses only information in prices of bills with maturities of six months or less to estimate expected monthly returns on bills with longer maturities. It is noteworthy that this model produces shifts in the term structure of expected returns similar to those Fama (1986) observes based on forward premiums for the entire range of maturities.

5.2. A variance-based interpretation

One framework in which to analyze the above shifts in the pattern of expected returns is a model developed by Breeden (1986) using the time–state preference approach. This discrete-period framework has a close analogue in the continuous-time framework of Cox, Ingersoll, and Ross. As Breeden (1986, pp. 21–22) observes, however, the discrete-period framework relates yields on finite-maturity instruments to the conditional distribution of consumption at specific future dates, whereas the continuous-time framework provides a relation between the instantaneous rate of interest and the instantaneous mean and variance of consumption. This characteristic of the discrete-period model provides a convenient framework in which to analyze the business-cycle-related shifts in the term structure described above.

Breeden (1986) shows that the price of a τ-period discount instrument can be approximated by a 'mean–variance' formulation involving the mean and variance of aggregate consumption,

$$p(\tau, t) = -\tau\rho - \gamma[\mathrm{E}_t\{c_{t+\tau}\} - c_t] + \frac{\gamma^2}{2}\,\mathrm{var}_t\{c_{t+\tau}\}, \tag{28}$$

where $p(\tau, t)$ is the (log) price of a τ-period bill, c_t is the natural log of aggregate consumption at time t, ρ is the rate of pure time preference, γ is the coefficient of relative risk aversion, and E_t and var_t denote the mean and the variance conditioned on information available at time t. As Breeden notes, obtaining (28) as an exact representation requires stronger assumptions, such as constant relative risk aversion and lognormally distributed consumption [Rubinstein (1974)], but the equation may also provide a useful approximation in more general models.

The above model is used here to analyze the differences between expected holding-period returns on bills of different maturities. Substituting (28) into the expression for the holding-period return $H(\tau, t+1)$ [$= p(\tau-1, t+1) - p(\tau, t)$] and taking the expectation conditional on information at time t gives

$$\begin{aligned}\mathrm{E}_t\{H(\tau, t+1)\} &= \rho + \gamma[\mathrm{E}_t\{c_{t+1}\} - c_t] \\ &\quad + \frac{\gamma^2}{2}[\mathrm{E}_t\{\mathrm{var}_{t+1}\{c_{c+\tau}\}\} - \mathrm{var}_t\{c_{t+\tau}\}] \\ &= \rho + \gamma[\mathrm{E}_t\{c_{t+1}\} - c_t] \\ &\quad - \frac{\gamma^2}{2}\,\mathrm{var}_t\{\mathrm{E}_{t+1}\{c_{t+\tau}\}\}.\end{aligned} \tag{29}$$

Eq. (29) then implies that the difference between expected holding-period returns on bills with different maturities, say τ and s, can be written

$$\begin{aligned}&\mathrm{E}_t\{H(\tau, t+1) - H(s, t+1)\} \\ &= \frac{\gamma^2}{2}[\mathrm{var}_t\{\mathrm{E}_{t+1}\{c_{t+s}\}\} - \mathrm{var}_t\{\mathrm{E}_{t+1}\{c_{t+\tau}\}\}].\end{aligned} \tag{30}$$

That is, the difference between expected returns on bills of different maturities is the difference between variances of expected consumption for two different times in the future.

Assume that $\tau > s$ in eq. (30). When the expected return on the shorter-maturity bill exceeds that of the longer-maturity bill, then future expected consumption for time $t + \tau$ has greater variance than future expected consumption for time $t + s$. This situation would correspond to a downward-sloping structure of expected returns, and recall from fig. 3 that such behavior typically occurs during the year preceding a business-cycle peak. In other words, expected consumption for the more distant month is more variable entering a recession. The reverse occurs with upward-sloping structures. In that case, expected consumption for the closer month is more variable. Recall again from fig. 3 that such behavior of expected returns typically precedes recoveries. Together, both cases suggest that the variance of expected consumption is greater for months during a recession. Although this exercise is very preliminary, the implied behavior of variability of expected consumption in relation to the business cycle seems plausible.

6. Conclusions

Models of the term structure developed by Cox, Ingersoll, and Ross (1985) – CIR – imply that expected excess returns are linear functions of forward premiums, where the number of latent variables captured by the forward premiums equals the number of state variables in the pricing relation. Restrictions on the number of latent variables can be tested using the generalized method of moments, which allows for the heteroskedasticity and nonnormality of the unexpected excess returns implied by the CIR models.

Forward premiums are used to predict excess returns in the latent-variable tests. When the maturities of the forward premiums match those of the excess returns, the number of state variables required to describe expected excess returns can appear to be large because of measurement errors. An alternative set of forward premiums with nonmatching maturities is likely to reduce the problems arising from measurement error.

Based on forward premiums with nonmatching maturities, the generalized method-of-moments latent-variable tests reject a CIR single-variable specification of the term structure for nominally default-free bonds, but two or three latent variables appear to be sufficient to describe expected excess returns on bills with maturities from two to twelve months. A two-latent-variable model is consistent with a two-factor CIR model that incorporates inflation uncertainty.

The term structure of expected excess returns fitted from a two-latent-variable model appears to shift over time in relation to turning points in business cycles. Downward-sloping structures tend to precede recessions, and upward-sloping structures tend to precede recoveries. Such behavior is consistent with an explanation in which the variance of expected consumption is greater for months during recessions. This behavior of expected returns for bills with maturities of up to twelve months is produced using information in prices of bills with maturities of six months or less. Business-cycle-related shifts in the shape of the term structures of expected returns are also observed by Fama (1986) based on forward rates for the full range of maturities.

By examining expected returns conditional on forward premiums, this study focuses on the number of relevant state variables in the term structure of Treasury bills, but the identity of the state variables is not investigated. An interesting direction for future research would be to investigate whether similar behavior in expected returns can be explained by models in which identities for the state variables are imposed. An investigation of the number of latent variables in expected returns on discount bonds of longer maturities would also be useful (although prices on such bonds would have to be estimated from prices of coupon bonds). It is possible that some state variables may have little impact on short-maturity instruments but could affect longer-maturity prices significantly.

References

Breeden, Douglas T., 1986, Consumption, production, inflation, and interest rates: A synthesis, Journal of Financial Economics 16, 3–39.

Brennan, Michael J. and Eduardo S. Schwartz, 1980, Conditional predictions of bond prices and returns, Journal of Finance 35, 405–419.

Brennan, Michael J. and Eduardo S. Schwartz, 1982, An equilibrium model of bond pricing and a test of market efficiency, Journal of Financial and Quantitative Analysis 17, 301–329.

Brown, Stephen J. and Philip H. Dybvig, 1986, The empirical implications of the Cox, Ingersoll, Ross theory of the term structure of interest rates, Journal of Finance 41, 617–630.

Campbell, John Y., 1987, Stock returns and the term structure, Journal of Financial Economics 18, 373–399.

Cox, John C., Jonathan E. Ingersoll, and Stephen A. Ross, 1985, A theory of the term structure of interest rates, Econometrica 53, 385–407.

Fama, Eugene F., 1976, Forward rates as predictors of future spot rates, Journal of Financial Economics 3, 361–377.

Fama, Eugene F., 1984a, The information in the term structure, Journal of Financial Economics 13, 509–528.

Fama, Eugene F., 1984b, Term premiums in bond returns, Journal of Financial Economics 13, 529–546.

Fama, Eugene F., 1986, Term premiums and default premiums in money markets, Journal of Financial Economics, 17, 175–196.

Fama, Eugene F. and Kenneth R. French, 1988, Permanent and temporary components of stock prices, Journal of Political Economy, forthcoming.

Fama, Eugene F. and G. William Schwert, 1977, Asset returns and inflation, Journal of Financial Economics 5, 115–146.

Ferson, Wayne E., Shmuel Kandel, and Robert F. Stambaugh, 1987, Tests of asset pricing with time-varying expected risk premiums and market betas, Journal of Finance 42, 201–220.

French, Kenneth R., G. William Schwert, and Robert F. Stambaugh, 1987, Expected stock returns and volatility, Journal of Financial Economics 19, 3–29.

Gibbons, Michael R. and Wayne Ferson, 1985, Testing asset pricing models with changing expectations and an unobservable market portfolio, Journal of Financial Economics 14, 217–236.

Gibbons, Michael R. and Krishna Ramaswamy, 1986, The term structure of interest rates: Empirical evidence, Working paper (Stanford University, Stanford, CA).

Hall, Robert E., 1981, Intertemporal substitution in consumption, Working paper (Stanford University, Stanford, CA).
Hansen, Lars Peter, 1982, Large sample properties of the generalized method of moments estimators, Econometrica 50, 1029–1054.
Hansen, Lars Peter and Robert J. Hodrick, 1983, Risk averse speculation in the forward foreign exchange market: An econometric analysis of linear models, in Jacob A. Frenkel, ed., Exchange rates and international macroeconomics (University of Chicago Press, Chicago, IL).
Hansen, Lars Peter and Kenneth J. Singleton, 1982, Generalized instrumental variables estimation of nonlinear rational expectation models, Econometrica 50, 1269–1286.
Hansen, Lars Peter and Kenneth J. Singleton, 1983, Stochastic consumption, risk aversion, and the temporal behavior of asset returns, Journal of Political Economy 91, 249–265.
Hsieh, David A., 1983, A heteroscedasticity-consistent covariance matrix estimator for time series regressions, Journal of Econometrics 22, 281–290.
Huizinga, John and Leonardo Leiderman, 1985, Interest rates, money supply announcements and monetary base announcements, Working paper (University of Chicago, Chicago, IL and Tel Aviv University, Tel Aviv).
Huizinga, John and Frederick S. Mishkin, 1984, Inflation and real interest rates on assets with different risk characteristics, Journal of Finance 39, 699–712.
Johnson, Norman L. and Samuel Kotz, 1972, Distributions in statistics: Continuous multivariate distributions (Wiley, New York).
Keim, Donald B. and Robert F. Stambaugh, 1986, Predicting returns in the stock and bond markets, Journal of Financial Economics 17, 357–390.
Marsh, Terry A. and Eric R. Rosenfeld, 1983, Stochastic processes for interest rates and equilibrium bond prices, Journal of Finance 38, 635–646.
Moore, Geoffrey H. and Victor Zarnowitz, 1984, The development and role of the National Bureau's business cycle chronologies, Working paper no. 1394 (National Bureau of Economic Research, Cambridge, MA).
Oldfield, George S. and Richard J. Rogalski, 1987, Stationary properties of Treasury bill term structure movements, Journal of Monetary Economics 19, 229–254.
Richard, Scott F., 1978, An arbitrage model of the term structure of interest rates, Journal of Financial Economics 6, 33–57.
Rubinstein, Mark, 1974, An aggregation theorem for securities markets, Journal of Financial Economics 1, 225–244.
Startz, Richard, 1982, Do forecast errors or term premia really make the difference between long and short rates?, Journal of Financial Economics 10, 323–329.
Tauchen, George, 1985, Statistical properties of generalized method of moments estimates of structural parameters using financial market data, Working paper (Duke University, Durham, NC).
Vasicek, Oldrich, 1977, An equilibrium characterization of the term structure, Journal of Financial Economics 5, 177–188.
White, Halbert, 1980, A heteroskedasticity-consistent covariance matrix estimator and a direct test for heteroskedasticity, Econometrica 48, 817–838.

[9]

Short-Term Interest Rates as Predictors of Inflation

By EUGENE F. FAMA*

Irving Fisher pointed out that with perfect foresight and a well-functioning capital market, the one-period nominal rate of interest is the equilibrium real return plus the fully anticipated rate of inflation. In a world of uncertainty where foresight is imperfect, the nominal rate of interest can be thought of as the equilibrium expected real return plus the market's assessment of the expected rate of inflation.

The relationships between interest rates and inflation have been tested extensively.[1] In line with Fisher's initial work, the almost universal finding is that there are no relationships between interest rates observed at a point in time and rates of inflation subsequently observed. Although the market does not do well in predicting inflation, the general finding is that there are relationships between current interest rates and past rates of inflation. This is interpreted as evidence in favor of the Fisherian view. Thus Fisher concludes:

> We have found evidence, general and specific, . . . that price changes do, generally and perceptibly, affect the interest rate in the direction indicated by *a priori* theory. But since forethought is imperfect, the effects are smaller than the theory requires and lag behind price movements, in some periods, very greatly. [p. 451]

Fisher's empirical evidence, and that of most other researchers, is in fact inconsistent with a well-functioning or "efficient" market.[2] An efficient market correctly uses all relevant information in setting prices. If the inflation rate is to some extent predictable, and if the one-period equilibrium expected real return does not change in such a way as to exactly offset changes in the expected rate of inflation, then in an efficient market there will be a relationship between the one-period nominal interest rate observed at a point in time and the one-period rate of inflation subsequently observed. If the inflation rate is to some extent predictable and no such relationship exists, the market is inefficient: in setting the nominal interest rate, it overlooks relevant information about future inflation.

This paper is concerned with efficiency in the market for one- to six-month U.S. Treasury Bills. Unlike Fisher and most of the rest of the literature, the results presented here indicate that, at least during the 1953–71 period, there are definite relationships between nominal interest rates and rates of inflation subsequently observed. Moreover, during this period the bill market seems to be efficient in the sense that nominal interest rates summarize all the information about future inflation rates that is in time-series of past inflation rates. Finally, another interesting result is that the substantial variation in nominal bill rates during the 1953–71

* Professor of finance, Graduate School of Business, University of Chicago. This research was supported by the National Science Foundation. I am grateful to F. Black, N. Gonedes, M. Jensen, A. Laffer, M. Miller, C. Nelson, H. Roberts, and C. Upton for helpful comments, and to J. MacBeth and D. Garren for computational assistance.

[1] For a summary, see Richard Roll.

[2] For a discussion of the theory of efficient capital markets and related empirical work, see the author.

period seems to be due entirely to variation in expected inflation rates; in other words, expected real returns on bills seem to be constant during the period.

The theory and tests of bill market efficiency are first presented for one-month bills. The results are then extended to bills with longer maturities.

I. Inflation and Efficiency in the Bill Market: Theory

A. *Returns and the Inflation Rate*

The nominal return from the end of month t−1 to the end of month t on a Treasury Bill with one month to maturity at t−1 is

$$(1) \qquad R_t = \frac{v_t - v_{t-1}}{v_{t-1}} = \frac{\$1{,}000 - v_{t-1}}{v_{t-1}}$$

where $v_t = \$1{,}000$ is the price of the bill at t, and v_{t-1} is its price at t−1. Since the bill has one month to maturity at t−1, once v_{t-1} is set, R_t is known and can be interpreted as the one-month nominal rate of interest set in the market at t−1 and realized at t.

Let p_t be the price level at t, that is, p_t is the price of consumption goods in terms of money, so that the purchasing power of a unit of money, the price of money in terms of goods, is $\pi_t = 1/p_t$. The real return from t−1 to t on a one-month bill is then

$$(2) \qquad \tilde{r}_t = (v_t\tilde{\pi}_t - v_{t-1}\pi_{t-1})/v_{t-1}\pi_{t-1}$$

$$(3) \qquad = R_t + \tilde{\Delta}_t + R_t\tilde{\Delta}_t$$

where tildes (~) are used to denote random variables, and

$$(4) \qquad \tilde{\Delta}_t = (\tilde{\pi}_t - \pi_{t-1})/\pi_{t-1}$$

is the rate of change in purchasing power from t−1 to t. In monthly data, R_t and $\tilde{\Delta}_t$ are close to zero, so that although the equality only holds as an approximation, no harm is done if (3) is reduced to

$$(5) \qquad \tilde{r}_t = R_t + \tilde{\Delta}_t$$

Thus the real return from the end of month t−1 to the end of month t on a Treasury Bill with one month to maturity at t−1 is the nominal return plus the rate of change in purchasing power from t−1 to t.

The fact that $\tilde{r}_t$ is a random variable at t−1 only because $\tilde{\Delta}_t$ is a random variable explains why bills are attractive for studying how well the market uses information about future inflation in setting security prices. It seems reasonable to assume that investors are concerned with real returns on securities. Since all uncertainty in the real return on a one-month bill is uncertainty about the change in the purchasing power of money during the month, one-month bills are the clear choice for studying how well the market absorbs information about inflation one month ahead. For the same reason, n-month bills are best for studying n-month predictions of inflation.

B. *The General Description of an Efficient Market*

Market efficiency requires that in setting the price of a one-month bill at t−1, the market correctly uses all available information to assess the distribution of $\tilde{\Delta}_t$. Formally, in an efficient market,

$$(6) \qquad f_m(\Delta_t \mid \phi^m_{t-1}) = f(\Delta_t \mid \phi_{t-1})$$

where ϕ_{t-1} is the set of information available at t−1, ϕ^m_{t-1} is the set of information used by the market, $f_m(\Delta_t \mid \phi^m_{t-1})$ is the market assessed density function for $\tilde{\Delta}_t$, and $f(\Delta_t \mid \phi_{t-t})$ is the true density function implied by ϕ_{t-1}.

When the market sets the equilibrium price of a one-month bill at t−1, R_t is also set. Given the relationship among $\tilde{r}_t$, R_t, and $\tilde{\Delta}_t$ of (5), the market's assessed distribution for $\tilde{r}_t$ is implied by R_t and its assessed distribution for $\tilde{\Delta}_t$. If (6) holds, then the market's assessed distribution for $\tilde{r}_t$ is the true distribution

$$(7) \qquad f_m(r_t \mid \phi^m_{t-1}, R_t) = f(r_t \mid \phi_{t-1}, R_t)$$

In short, if the market is efficient, then in setting the nominal price of a one-month bill at t−1, it correctly uses all available information to assess the distribution of $\tilde{\Delta}_t$. In this sense v_{t-1} fully reflects all available information about $\tilde{\Delta}_t$. Since an equilibrium value of v_{t-1} implies an equilibrium value of R_t, the one-month nominal rate of interest set in the market at t−1 likewise fully reflects all available information about $\tilde{\Delta}_t$. Finally, when an efficient market sets R_t, the distribution of the real return $\tilde{r}_t$ that it perceives is the true distribution.

C. *A Simple Model of Market Equilibrium*

The preceding specification of market efficiency is so general that it is not testable. Since we cannot observe $f_m(\Delta_t \mid \phi^m_{t-1})$, we cannot determine whether (6) holds, and so we cannot determine whether the the bill market is efficient. What the model lacks is a more detailed specification of the link between $f_m(\Delta_t \mid \phi^m_{t-1})$ and v_{t-1}; that is, we must specify in more detail how the equilibrium price of a bill at t−1 is related to the market-assessed distribution of $\tilde{\Delta}_t$. This is a common feature of tests of market efficiency. A test of efficiency must be based on a model of equilibrium, and any test is simultaneously a test of efficiency and of the assumed model of equilibrium.

The first assumption of the model of bill market equilibrium is that in their decisions with respect to one-month bills, the primary concern of investors is the distribution of the real return on a bill. A market equilibrium depends visibly on a market-clearing value of the nominal price v_{t-1}, but it is assumed that what causes investors to demand the outstanding supply of bills is the implied "equilibrium distribution" of the real return. Testable propositions about market efficiency then require propositions about the characteristics of the market assessed distribution $f_m(r_t \mid \phi^m_{t-1}, R_t)$ that results from an equilibrium price v_{t-1} at t−1. As is common in tests of market efficiency, we concentrate on the mean of the distribution, and the proposition about $E_m(\tilde{r}_t \mid \phi^m_{t-1}, R_t)$ is that for all t and ϕ^m_{t-1},

$$(8) \qquad E_m(\tilde{r}_t \mid \phi^m_{t-1}, R_t) = E(\tilde{r})$$

Thus the model of bill market equilibrium is the statement that each month the market sets the price of a one-month bill so that it perceives the expected real return on the bill to be $E(\tilde{r})$. In short, the equilibrium expected real return on a one-month bill is assumed to be constant through time.

II. Testable Implications of Market Efficiency When the Equilibrium Expected Real Return Is Constant Through Time

A. *The Real Return*

In an efficient market (7) holds, and (7) implies

$$(9) \qquad E_m(\tilde{r}_t \mid \phi^m_{t-1}, R_t) = E(\tilde{r}_t \mid \phi_{t-1}, R_t)$$

If market equilibrium is characterized by (8), then with (9) we have

$$(10) \qquad E(\tilde{r}_t \mid \phi_{t-1}, R_t) = E(\tilde{r})$$

Thus at any time t−1 the market sets the price of a one-month bill so that its assessment of the expected real return is the constant $E(\tilde{r})$. Since an efficient market correctly uses all available information, $E(\tilde{r})$ is also the true expected real return on the bill.

The general testable implication of this combination of market efficiency with a model of market equilibrium is that there is no way to use ϕ_{t-1}, the set of information available at t−1, or any subset of ϕ_{t-1}, as the basis of a correct assessment of the expected real return on a one-month bill which is other than $E(\tilde{r})$. One subset of ϕ_{t-1} is the time-series of past real returns. If (10) holds,

(11) $$E(\tilde{r}_t \mid r_{t-1}, r_{t-2}, \ldots) = E(\tilde{r})$$

That is, there is no way to use the time-series of past real returns as the basis of a correct assessment of the expected real return which is other than $E(\tilde{r})$. If (11) holds, the autocorrelations of $\tilde{r}_t$ for all lags are equal to zero, so that sample autocorrelations provide tests of (11).

Sample autocorrelations of $\tilde{r}_t$ are presented later, but it is well to make one point now. The autocorrelations are joint tests of market efficiency and of the model for the equilibrium expected real return. Thus nonzero autocorrelations of $\tilde{r}_t$ are consistent with a world where the equilibrium expected real return is constant and the market is inefficient, but nonzero autocorrelations are also consistent with a world where the market is efficient and equilibrium expected real returns change through time as a function of the sequence of past real returns. Market efficiency in no way rules out such behavior of the equilibrium expected return.

B. *The Nominal Interest Rate as a Predictor of Inflation*

There are tests that distinguish better between the hypothesis that the market is efficient and the hypothesis that the expected real return is constant through time. From (5), the relationship between the market's expectation of the rate of change in purchasing power, the nominal rate of interest, and the market's expectation of the real return is

(12) $$E_m(\tilde{\Delta}_t \mid \phi^m_{t-1}) = E_m(\tilde{r}_t \mid \phi^m_{t-1}, R_t) - R_t$$

If the expected real return is the constant $E(\tilde{r})$, then (12) becomes

(13) $$E_m(\tilde{\Delta}_t \mid \phi^m_{t-1}) = E(\tilde{r}) - R_t$$

If the market is also efficient,

(14) $$E(\tilde{\Delta}_t \mid \phi_{t-1}) = E(\tilde{r}) - R_t$$

Thus a constant expected real return implies that all variation through time in the nominal rate R_t is a direct reflection of variation in the market's assessment of the expected value of $\tilde{\Delta}_t$. If the market is also efficient, then all variation in R_t mirrors variation in the best possible assessment of the expected value of $\tilde{\Delta}_t$. Moreover, once R_t is set at time t−1, the details of ϕ_{t-1}, the information that an efficient market uses to assess the expected value of $\tilde{\Delta}_t$, become irrelevant. The information in ϕ_{t-1} is summarized completely in the value of R_t. In this sense, the nominal rate R_t observed at t−1 is the best possible predictor of the rate of inflation from t−1 to t.

To test these propositions, it is convenient to introduce a new class of models of market equilibrium that includes (8) as a special case. Suppose that at any time t−1 the market always sets the price of a one-month bill so that it perceives the expected real return to be

(15) $$E_m(\tilde{r}_t \mid \phi^m_{t-1}, R_t) = \alpha_0 + \gamma R_t$$

If the market is also efficient, we have

(16) $$E(\tilde{r}_t \mid \phi_{t-1}, R_t) = \alpha_0 + \gamma R_t$$

With (5), (15) and (16) imply that

(17) $$E_m(\tilde{\Delta}_t \mid \phi^m_{t-1}) = \alpha_0 + \alpha_1 R_t, \quad \alpha_1 = \gamma - 1$$

(18) $$E(\tilde{\Delta}_t \mid \phi_{t-1}) = \alpha_0 + \alpha_1 R_t, \quad \alpha_1 = \gamma - 1$$

In the new model, γ is the proportion of the change in the nominal rate from one month to the next that reflects a change in the equilibrium expected real return, and $-\alpha_1 = 1-\gamma$ is the proportion of the change in R_t that reflects a change in the expected value of $\tilde{\Delta}_t$. In the special case where the expected real return is constant through time, $\gamma=0$, $\alpha_1=-1$, and all variation in R_t mirrors variation in $E(\tilde{\Delta}_t|\phi_{t-1})$.

Estimates of α_0 and α_1 in (18) can be obtained by applying least squares to

$$\tilde{\Delta}_t = \alpha_0 + \alpha_1 R_t + \tilde{\epsilon}_t \tag{19}$$

If the coefficient estimates are inconsistent with the hypothesis that

$$\alpha_0 = E(\tilde{r}) \quad \text{and} \quad \alpha_1 = -1 \tag{20}$$

the model of a constant equilibrium expected real return is rejected. The more general interpretation of (15), that is, with unrestricted values of the coefficients, can then be taken as the model for the equilibrium expected real return, and other results from the estimates of (19) can be used to test market efficiency. Thus, like (14), (18) says that in an efficient market R_t summarizes all the information about the expected value of $\tilde{\Delta}_t$ which is in ϕ_{t-1}. For example, given R_t, the sequence of past values of the disturbance $\tilde{\epsilon}_t$ in (19) should be of no additional help in assessing the expected value of $\tilde{\Delta}_t$ which implies that the autocorrelations of the disturbance should be zero for all lags.

The approach is easily generalized to obtain other tests of (14). For example, one item of information available at $t-1$ is Δ_{t-1}. If periods of inflation or deflation tend to persist, then Δ_{t-1} is relevant information for assessing the expected value of $\tilde{\Delta}_t$. If the information in Δ_{t-1} is not correctly used by the market in setting R_t, then the coefficient α_2 in

$$\tilde{\Delta}_t = \alpha_0 + \alpha_1 R_t + \alpha_2 \Delta_{t-1} + \tilde{\epsilon}_t \tag{21}$$

is nonzero. On the other hand, if (14) holds, the market is efficient and the value of R_t set at $t-1$ summarizes all the information available about the expected value of $\tilde{\Delta}_t$, which includes any information in Δ_{t-1} and any information in the past values of $\tilde{\epsilon}_t$. Thus, in this case, $\alpha_2=0$ and the autocorrelations of the disturbance $\tilde{\epsilon}_t$ in (21) are zero for all lags. Moreover, if (14) holds, the expected real return is constant through time, so that the values of α_0 and α_1 in (21) are as in (20). All of these propositions are tested below with least squares estimates of (21).

C. *Reinterpretation of the Proposed Tests*

It is well to recognize that all of the tests of market efficiency are different ways to examine whether in assessing the expected value of $\tilde{\Delta}_t$, the market correctly uses any information in the past values $\Delta_{t-1}, \Delta_{t-2}, \ldots$. The point is obvious with respect to tests based on the coefficient α_2 in (21). The argument is also direct for the autocorrelations of the disturbances $\tilde{\epsilon}_t$ in (19) and (21). The disturbance $\tilde{\epsilon}_t$ in (19) is the deviation of $\tilde{\Delta}_t$ from the market's assessment of its conditional expected value, when $E_m(\tilde{\Delta}_t|\phi^m_{t-1})$ is given by (17). The autocorrelations of $\tilde{\epsilon}_t$ tell us whether the past values of these deviations are used correctly by the market when it assesses the expected value of $\tilde{\Delta}_t$. Nonzero autocorrelations imply that the market is inefficient; one can improve on the market's assessment of the expected value of $\tilde{\Delta}_t$ by making correct use of information in past values of Δ_t. Likewise the disturbance $\tilde{\epsilon}_t$ in (21) is the deviation of $\tilde{\Delta}_t$ from its conditional expected value when the latter is allowed to be a function of Δ_{t-1} as well as of R_t. Finally, if the equilibrium expected real return is constant through time, then the market's assessment of the expected value of $\tilde{\Delta}_t$ is described by (13). From (5) it then follows that

$$\tilde{r}_t - E(\tilde{r}) = \tilde{\Delta}_t + R_t - E(\tilde{r}) \tag{22a}$$

$$= \tilde{\Delta}_t - E_m(\tilde{\Delta}_t \,|\, \phi^m_{t-1}) \tag{22b}$$

Thus, the deviation of $\tilde{r}_t$ from its expected value is the deviation of $\tilde{\Delta}_t$ from the market's assessment of its expected value, when the latter is described by (13). Tests of market efficiency based on the autocorrelations of $\tilde{r}_t$, like all the other proposed tests, are concerned with whether the market correctly uses any information in the time-series of past values, $\Delta_{t-1}, \Delta_{t-2}, \ldots,$ when it assesses $E_m(\tilde{\Delta}_t | \phi_{t-1}^m)$ on which the nominal rate R_t is then based. Any such test must assume some model of market equilibrium, that is, some proposition about the equilibrium expected real return $E_m(\tilde{r}_t | \phi_{t-1}^m)$, which in turn implies some proposition about $E_m(\tilde{\Delta}_t | \phi_{t-1}^m)$, and this is where the tests differ.

There is, however, no need to apologize for the fact that the tests of market efficiency concentrate on the reaction of the market to information in the time-series of past rates of change in the purchasing power of money. Beginning with the pioneering work of Fisher, researchers in this area have long contended, and the results below substantiate the claim, that past rates of inflation are important information for assessing future rates. Moreover, previous work almost uniformly suggests that the market is inefficient; in assessing expected future rates of inflation, much of the information in past rates is apparently ignored. This conclusion, if true, indicates a serious failing of a free market. The value of a market is in providing accurate signals for resource allocation, which means setting prices that more or less fully reflect available information. If the market ignores the information from so obvious a source as past inflation rates, its effectiveness is seriously questioned. The issue deserves further study.

III. The Data

The one-month nominal rate of interest R_t used in the tests is the return from the end of month t−1 to the end of month t on the Treasury Bill that matures closest to the end of month t. The data are from the quote sheets of Salomon Brothers. In computing R_t from (1), the average of the bid and asked prices at the end of month t−1 is used for the nominal price v_{t-1}. The Bureau of Labor Statistics Consumer Price Index (*CPI*) is used to estimate Δ_t, the rate of change in the purchasing power of money from the end of month t−1 to the end of month t. The use of any index to measure the level of prices of consumption goods can be questioned. There is, however, no need to speculate about the effects of shortcomings of the data on the tests. If the results of the tests seem meaningful, the data are probably adequate.

The tests cover the period from January 1953 through July 1971. Tests for periods prior to 1953 would be meaningless. First, during World War II and up to the Treasury-Federal Reserve Accord of 1951, interest rates on Treasury Bills were pegged by the government. In effect, a rich and obstinate investor saw to it that Treasury Bill rates did not adjust to predictable changes in inflation rates. Second, at the beginning of 1953 there was a substantial upgrading of the *CPI*.[3] The number of items in the Index increased substantially, and monthly sampling of major items became the general rule. For tests of market efficiency based on monthly data, monthly sampling of major items in the *CPI* is critical. Sampling items less frequently than monthly, the general rule prior to 1953, means that some of the price changes for month t show up in the Index in months subsequent to t. Since nominal prices of goods tend to move together, spreading price changes for month t into following months creates spurious positive autocorrelation in monthly changes in the Index. This gives the appearance that there is more information about future inflation rates in past inflation rates than is really the case. Since the spurious component of the information in measured inflation rates is not easily isolated, test of market efficiency on pre-

[3] See ch. 10 of the *BLS* reference.

1953 data would be difficult to interpret.

The values of the *CPI* from August 1971 to the present (mid-1974) are also suspect. During this period the Nixon Administration made a series of attempts to fix prices. The controls were effective in creating "shortages" of some important goods (who can forget the gas queues of the winter of 1973–74?), so that for this period there are nontrivial differences between the observed values of the *CPI* and the true costs of goods to consumers. For this reason, the tests concentrate on the "clean" precontrols period January 1953 to July 1971.

IV. Results for One-Month Bills

Table 1 shows sample autocorrelations $\hat{\rho}_\tau$ of Δ_t for lags τ of from one to twelve months. The table also shows sample means and standard deviations of Δ_t, and

$$\sigma(\hat{\rho}_1) = 1/(T-1)^{1/2} \tag{23}$$

where $T-1$ is the number of observations used to compute $\hat{\rho}_1$, and $\sigma(\hat{\rho}_1)$ is the approximate standard error of $\hat{\rho}_1$ under the hypothesis that the true autocorrelation is zero. Table 2 shows sample autocorrelations and other statistics for the real return r_t. Although, for simplicity, the development of the theory is in terms of the approximation given by (5), the exact expression (3) is used to compute r_t in the empirical work.

Table 3 shows summary statistics for the estimated version of (19). In addition to the least squares regression coefficient estimates a_0 and a_1, the table shows the sample standard errors of the estimates $s(a_0)$ and $s(a_1)$; the coefficient of determination, adjusted for degrees of freedom; $s(e)$, the standard deviation of the residuals; and the first three residual autocorrelations, $\hat{\rho}_1(e)$, $\hat{\rho}_2(e)$, and $\hat{\rho}_3(e)$. Table 4 shows similar summary statistics for the estimated version of (21).

A. *The Information in Past Inflation Rates*

The market efficiency hypothesis to be tested is that the one-month nominal interest rate R_t set in the market at the end of month t−1 is based on correct utilization of all the information about the expected value of $\tilde{\Delta}_t$, which is in the time-series of past values $\Delta_{t-1}, \Delta_{t-2}, \ldots$. The hypothesis is only meaningful, however, if past rates of change in purchasing power do indeed have information about the expected future rate of change. The predominance

TABLE 1—AUTOCORRELATIONS OF Δ_t: ONE-MONTH INTERVALS

	1/53–7/71	1/53–2/59	3/59–7/64	8/64–7/71
$\hat{\rho}_1$	.36	.21	−.09	.35
$\hat{\rho}_2$	.37	.28	−.09	.34
$\hat{\rho}_3$	.27	.10	−.25	.26
$\hat{\rho}_4$	.30	.16	−.05	.23
$\hat{\rho}_5$	.29	.01	.03	.33
$\hat{\rho}_6$	.29	−.01	.09	.30
$\hat{\rho}_7$	.25	.05	−.06	.18
$\hat{\rho}_8$	.34	.18	−.20	.37
$\hat{\rho}_9$	.36	.21	.13	.24
$\hat{\rho}_{10}$	.34	.20	.04	.21
$\hat{\rho}_{11}$	.27	.09	−.09	.18
$\hat{\rho}_{12}$	.37	.18	.17	.30
$\sigma(\hat{\rho}_1)$	.07	.12	.13	.11
$\bar{\Delta}$	−.00188	−.00111	−.00108	−.00321
$s(\Delta)$	.00234	.00258	.00169	.00195
$T-1$	222	73	64	83

TABLE 2—AUTOCORRELATIONS OF r_t: ONE-MONTH BILLS

	1/53–7/71	1/53–2/59	3/59–7/64	8/64–7/71
$\hat{\rho}_1$	.09	.11	−.04	.10
$\hat{\rho}_2$	.13	.17	.01	.08
$\hat{\rho}_3$	−.02	−.02	−.20	−.01
$\hat{\rho}_4$	−.01	.01	−.06	−.10
$\hat{\rho}_5$	−.02	−.14	.00	.08
$\hat{\rho}_6$	−.02	−.18	.07	.07
$\hat{\rho}_7$	−.07	−.09	−.09	−.15
$\hat{\rho}_8$	.04	.05	−.23	.17
$\hat{\rho}_9$	.11	.11	.09	.04
$\hat{\rho}_{10}$	.10	.12	.07	−.02
$\hat{\rho}_{11}$	.03	.03	−.10	−.07
$\hat{\rho}_{12}$	.19	.16	.19	.15
$\sigma(\hat{\rho}_1)$	.07	.12	.13	.11
$\bar{r}$	.00074	.00038	.00111	.00075
$s(r)$	.00197	.00240	.00172	.00168
$T-1$	222	73	64	83

TABLE 3—REGRESSION TESTS ON ONE-MONTH BILLS

$\Delta_t = a_0 + a_1 R_t + e_t$

Period	a_0	a_1	$s(a_0)$	$s(a_1)$	Coefficient of Determination	$s(e)$	$\hat{\rho}_1(e)$	$\hat{\rho}_2(e)$	$\hat{\rho}_3(e)$
1/53–7/71	.00070	−.98	.00030	.10	.29	.00196	.09	.13	−.02
1/53–2/59	.00116	−1.49	.00069	.42	.14	.00240	.09	.15	−.05
3/59–7/64	−.00038	−.33	.00095	.42	−.01	.00168	−.09	−.08	−.26
8/64–7/71	.00118	−1.10	.00083	.20	.26	.00167	.09	.06	−.02

of large estimated autocorrelations of Δ_t in Table 1 indicates that this is the case.

In fact, especially for the longer periods 1/53–7/71 and 8/64–7/71, the sample autocorrelations of Δ_t for different lags are similar in size with individual estimates in the neighborhood of .30. This finding is discussed later when the behavior through time of Δ_t is studied in more detail.

B. *Market Efficiency*

Given that the equilibrium expected real return is constant through time, the market efficiency hypothesis says that the autocorrelations of the real return $\tilde{r}_t$ are zero for all lags. The sample autocorrelations of r_t in Table 2 are close to zero. Recall from (5) that the real return r_t is approximately the rate of change in purchasing power Δ_t plus the nominal interest rate R_t. The evidence from the sample autocorrelations of Δ_t and r_t in Tables 1 and 2 is that adding R_t to Δ_t brings the substantial autocorrelations of Δ_t down to values close to zero. This is consistent with the hypothesis that R_t, the nominal rate set at t−1, summarizes completely the information about the expected value of $\tilde{\Delta}_t$ which is in the time-series of past values, Δ_{t-1}, Δ_{t-2}, ...

Tables 3 and 4 give further support to the market efficiency hypothesis. When applied to (21), the hypothesis says that α_2, the coefficient of Δ_{t-1}, is zero, and the autocorrelations of the disturbance $\tilde{\epsilon}_t$ are likewise zero for all lags. The residual autocorrelations in Table 4 are close to zero. The values of a_2, the sample estimates of α_2 in (21), are also small and always less than two standard errors from zero. When applied to (19), the market efficiency hypothesis is again that the autocorrelations of the disturbance $\tilde{\epsilon}_t$ should be zero. The residual autocorrelations in Table 3 are close to zero. Moreover, comparing the results for the estimated versions of (19) and (21) in Tables 3 and 4 shows that dropping Δ_{t-1} from the model has almost no effect on the coefficients of determination, which is consistent with the implication of market efficiency that the value of R_t set at time t−1 summarizes any information in Δ_{t-1} about the expected value of $\tilde{\Delta}_t$.

Closer inspection of the tables seems to

TABLE 4—REGRESSION TESTS ON ONE-MONTH BILLS

$\Delta_t = a_0 + a_1 R_t + a_2 \Delta_{t-1} + e_t$

Period	a_0	a_1	a_2	$s(a_0)$	$s(a_1)$	$s(a_2)$	Coefficient of Determination	$s(e)$	$\hat{\rho}_1(e)$	$\hat{\rho}_2(e)$	$\hat{\rho}_3(e)$
1/53–7/71	.00059	−.87	.11	.00030	.12	.07	.30	.00195	−.05	.13	−.04
1/53–2/59	.00108	−1.40	.11	.00069	.44	.11	.14	.00238	−.09	.17	−.07
3/59–7/64	−.00054	−.30	−.08	.00097	.42	.13	−.02	.00170	−.01	−.11	−.25
8/64–7/71	.00073	−.89	.14	.00084	.24	.11	.24	.00164	−.04	.05	−.01

provide slight evidence against market efficiency. Except for the 3/59–7/64 period, the first-order sample autocorrelations of r_t, though small, are nevertheless all positive. The estimated regression coefficients a_2 of Δ_{t-1} in Table 4 are likewise small but generally positive, as are the first-order residual autocorrelations in Table 3. It is well to note, however, that even after the upgrading of the *CPI* in 1953, there are some items whose prices are sampled less frequently than monthly; and items that are sampled monthly are not sampled at the same time during the month. Again, since prices of goods tend to move together, these quirks of the sampling process induce spurious positive autocorrelation in measured rates of change in purchasing power. Since an efficient market does not react to "information" that is recognizably spurious, the small apparent discrepancies from efficiency provide more "reasonable" evidence in favor of the efficiency hypothesis than if the data suggested that the hypothesis does perfectly well.

C. *The Expected Real Return*

The evidence is also consistent with the hypothesis that the expected real return on a one-month bill is constant during the 1953–71 period. First, the sample autocorrelations of the real return r_t are joint tests of the hypotheses that the market is efficient and that the expected real return is constant through time. Since the sample autocorrelations of r_t in Table 2 are close to zero, the evidence is consistent with a world where both hypotheses are valid.

The regression coefficient estimates for (19) and (21) in Tables 3 and 4 are, however, more direct evidence on the hypothesis that the expected value of $\tilde{r}_t$ is constant. The hypothesis implies that in (19) and (21), the intercept α_0 is the constant expected real return $E(\tilde{r})$ and the coefficient α_1 of R_t is -1.0. The coefficient estimates a_1 of α_1 in (19) and (21) are always well within two standard errors of -1.0. And statistical considerations aside, the estimate $a_1=-.98$ for (19) for the overall period 1/53–7/71 is impressively close to -1.0. Given estimates a_1 of α_1 in (19) and (21) that are close to -1.0, and given the earlier observation that the estimates a_2 of α_2 in (21) are close to zero, equation (5) and the least squares formulas guarantee that the intercept estimates a_0 for (19) and (21) in Tables 3 and 4 are close to the sample means of the real return in Table 2.

Finally, the sample autocorrelations of r_t in Table 2 and the regression coefficient estimates a_0 and a_1 in Tables 3 and 4 are consistent with the world of equation (13) where the equilibrium expected real return is constant and all variation through time in the nominal interest rate R_t mirrors variation in the market's assessment of the expected value of $\tilde{\Delta}_t$. There is, however, another interesting way to check this conclusion. From the discussion of (22) it follows that the standard deviation of the real return $\tilde{r}_t$ is the standard deviation of the disturbance $\tilde{\epsilon}_t$ in (19) when the coefficients α_0 and α_1 in (19) are constrained to have the values $\alpha_0=E(r)$ and $\alpha_1=-1.0$ that are appropriate under the hypothesis that the expected real return is constant through time. If this hypothesis is incorrect, letting the data choose values of α_0 and α_1, as in Table 3, should produce lower estimates of the disturbance variance than when the values of the coefficients are constrained. But the results indicate that, especially for the longer periods, not only are the values of $s(r)$ in Table 2 almost identical to the values of $s(e)$ in Table 3, but the sample autocorrelations of r_t and e_t are almost identical. In short, the hypothesis that the expected real return is constant fits the data so well that the residuals from the estimated version of (19) are more or less identical to the deviations of r_t from its sample mean.

V. The Behavior of $\tilde{\Delta}_t$

The results allow some interesting insights into the behavior through time of $\tilde{\Delta}_t$. The rate of change in purchasing power can always be written as

$$(24) \qquad \tilde{\Delta}_t = E(\tilde{\Delta}_t \mid \phi_{t-1}) + \tilde{\epsilon}_t$$

Since the evidence is consistent with the hypothesis that the expected real return is constant through time, we can substitute (14) into (24) to get

$$(25) \qquad \tilde{\Delta}_t = E(\tilde{r}) - R_t + \tilde{\epsilon}_t$$

The conclusion drawn from the residual autocorrelations in Table 3 and the sample autocorrelations of r_t in Table 2 is that the disturbance $\tilde{\epsilon}_t$ in (25) is uncorrelated through time. The time-series of past values of $\tilde{\epsilon}_t$ is no real help in predicting the next value. Quite the opposite sort of behavior characterizes the expected value of $\tilde{\Delta}_t$ in (24). Since, as stated in (25), variation in R_t through time mirrors variation in the expected value of $\tilde{\Delta}_t$, the time-series properties of R_t are the time-series properties of $E(\tilde{\Delta}_t \mid \phi_{t-1})$. For the 1/53–7/71 period, the first four sample autocorrelations of R_t are all in excess of .93, and only one of the first twenty-four is less than .9. Sample autocorrelations close to 1.0 are consistent with the representation of R_t as a random walk. Thus in contrast with the evidence for the disturbance $\tilde{\epsilon}_t$ in (24), the autocorrelations of R_t indicate that there is much persistence through time in the level of R_t and thus in the level of $E(\tilde{\Delta}_t \mid \phi_{t-1})$. The time-series of past values of R_t has substantial information about future values.

This discussion helps explain the behavior of the sample autocorrelations of $\tilde{\Delta}_t$ in Table 1. As stated in (24), $\tilde{\Delta}_t$ has two components. One component of $\tilde{\Delta}_t$, its expected value, behaves like a random walk. The other component of $\tilde{\Delta}_t$, the disturbance $\tilde{\epsilon}_t$, is essentially random noise. The autocorrelations of its expected value cause the autocorrelations of $\tilde{\Delta}_t$ to likewise have approximately the same magnitude for different lags. The uncorrelated disturbance $\tilde{\epsilon}_t$, however, causes the autocorrelations of $\tilde{\Delta}_t$, unlike those of R_t, to be far below 1.0.

The sample autocorrelations of R_t suggest that the expected value of $\tilde{\Delta}_t$ behaves through time much like a random walk. The sample autocorrelations of the month-to-month changes in R_t, shown in Table 5, suggest, however, that we can improve on this description of the behavior of $E(\tilde{\Delta}_t \mid \phi_{t-1})$. For example, the first-order autocorrelations of $R_t - R_{t-1}$ are consistently negative. From the first-order autocorrelations for the longer periods, the change in R_t might reasonably be represented as

$$(26) \quad \tilde{R}_{t+1} - R_t = -.25(R_t - R_{t-1}) + \tilde{\eta}_t$$

Thus the process that generates the nominal rate is no longer just a random walk. The process is slightly regressive so that on average the change in the expected inflation rate from one month to the next reverses itself by about 25 percent.

Table 5—Autocorrelations of $R_t - R_{t-1}$

	1/53–7/71	1/53–2/59	3/59–7/64	8/64–7/71
$\hat{\rho}_1$	−.25	−.14	−.41	−.18
$\hat{\rho}_2$	.06	.05	.07	.06
$\hat{\rho}_3$	.01	.07	−.03	.00
$\hat{\rho}_4$	.15	.23	.08	.18
$\hat{\rho}_5$	−.03	−.04	.07	−.13
$\hat{\rho}_6$	−.06	.01	−.12	−.01
$\hat{\rho}_7$	−.13	−.35	−.11	−.05
$\hat{\rho}_8$	.10	.17	.13	.02
$\hat{\rho}_9$	.06	−.03	−.06	.18
$\hat{\rho}_{10}$	−.24	−.26	−.07	−.42
$\hat{\rho}_{11}$	−.05	−.16	−.10	.08
$\hat{\rho}_{12}$	.09	.13	.06	.04
$\sigma(\hat{\rho}_1)$	.07	.12	.13	.11
$\overline{dR}$	.00001	.00000	.00001	.00001
$s(dR)$	.00032	.00028	.00035	.00033
$T-1$	221	72	63	82

VI. Results for Bills with Longer Maturities

The presentation of theory and tests of bill market efficiency has concentrated so far on one-month bills and one-month rates of change in the purchasing power of money. As far as the theory is concerned, the interval of time over which the variables are measured is arbitrary. In testing the theory, the fact that the *CPI* is only reported monthly limits us to tests based on intervals that cover an integral number of months. Tests are presented now for one- to six-month intervals. Thus, in these tests the interval from t−1 to t is one, or two, . . . , or six months; R_t is the sure one-, or two-, . . . , or six-month nominal rate of interest from t−1 to t on a bill with one, or two, . . . , or six months to maturity at t−1; and the real return $\tilde{r}_t$ and the rate of change in the purchasing power of money $\tilde{\Delta}_t$ are likewise measured for nonoverlapping one- to six-month intervals.

Since the theory and tests are the same for bills of all maturities, the market efficiency hypothesis is that in setting the nominal rate R_t at time t−1, the market correctly uses any information about the expected value of $\tilde{\Delta}_t$ which is in the time-series of past values Δ_{t-1}, Δ_{t-2}, ... The model of market equilibrium on which the tests are based is the assumption that the expected real returns on bills with one to six months to maturity are constant through time. The tests of these propositions are in Tables 6 to 9, and the tests are the same as those for one-month bills in Tables 1 to 4. Results for the one- to three-month versions of the variables are shown for the 1/53–7/71 and 3/59–7/71 periods. Since the data for four- to six-month bills are only available beginning in March 1959, results for the four- to six-month versions of the variables are only shown for the 3/59–7/71 period.

Implicit in the tests of market efficiency is the assumption that past rates of change in purchasing power have information about expected future rates of change. The autocorrelations of Δ_t in Table 6 support this assumption. The autocorrelations are large for all six intervals used to measure Δ_t. But consistent with the hypotheses that the market is efficient and that the equilibrium expected real returns on bills with different maturities are constant through time, the autocorrelations of the real returns shown in Table 7 are close to zero. Remember from (5) that the n-month real return on an n-month bill is approximately the n-month rate of change in purchasing power plus the n-month nominal return on the bill. Thus the evidence from the autocorrelations of Δ_t and r_t in Tables 6 and 7 is that when R_t is added to Δ_t, the substantial autocorrelations of Δ_t drop to values close to zero. This is consistent with a world where R_t, the n-month nominal rate set at t−1, summarizes all the information about the expected value of the rate of change in purchasing power over the n months from t−1 to t which is in the time-series of past rates of changes in purchasing power.

The model gets further support from the regression tests in Table 8. Consistent with the hypothesis that expected real returns are constant through time, the estimates a_1 of α_1 in (19) in Table 8 are all impressively close to −1.0. Consistent with the hypothesis that the market is efficient, the residual autocorrelations in Table 8 are close to zero for bills of all maturities.

The only hint of evidence against the model is in the estimates of (21) for five- and six-month bills in Table 9. As predicted by the model, the values of a_1 and a_2 for one- to four-month bills are close to −1.0 and 0.0, and the residual autocorrelations are close to 0.0. For the five- and six-month bills, however, the values of a_1 are rather far from −1.0 and the values of a_2

TABLE 6—AUTOCORRELATIONS OF Δ_t: ONE- TO-SIX-MONTH INTERVALS

	1/53–7/71 Interval			3/59–7/71 Interval					
	1	2	3	1	2	3	4	5	6
$\hat{\rho}_1$	.36	.50	.53	.40	.55	.58	.67	.84	.86
$\hat{\rho}_2$	.37	.39	.57	.39	.50	.74	.72	.78	.83
$\hat{\rho}_3$	.27	.43	.59	.32	.66	.64	.71	.74	.74
$\hat{\rho}_4$	.30	.45	.54	.36	.57	.70	.71	.73	.81
$\hat{\rho}_5$	.29	.52	.48	.43	.58	.66	.63	.76	.90
$\hat{\rho}_6$	.29	.41	.38	.44	.56	.65	.76	.77	1.03[a]
$\hat{\rho}_7$	.25	.40	.39	.34	.53	.65	.61	.89	.98
$\hat{\rho}_8$	.34	.32	.27	.40	.60	.58	.73	.83	.95
$\hat{\rho}_9$	.36	.36	.32	.44	.55	.73	.70	.94	.45
$\hat{\rho}_{10}$	.34	.30	.08	.40	.49	.42	.65	.79	.32
$\hat{\rho}_{11}$	.27	.28	.35	.34	.54	.84	.54	.14	−.07
$\hat{\rho}_{12}$	.37	.28	.29	.47	.56	.55	.82	.11	.23
$\sigma(\hat{\rho}_1)$	.07	.10	.12	.08	.12	.14	.17	.19	.21
$\bar{\Delta}$	−.00188	−.00368	−.00550	−.00228	−.00445	−.00656	−.00881	−.01105	−.01319
$s(\Delta)$	.00234	.00386	.00521	.00211	.00348	.00485	.00628	.00735	.00857
$T-1$	222	110	73	148	73	49	36	29	24

[a] The sample autocorrelations are estimated as linear regression coefficients. Thus the estimates can be greater than 1.0.

are rather far from 0.0. In conducting so many different tests for so many different bills, however, some results are likely to turn out badly even though the model is a valid approximation to the world. This argument gains force from the fact that the autocorrelations of the real returns in Table 7 and the estimates of (19) in Table 8 do not produce evidence for five- and six-month bills that contradicts the model.

VII. Interest Rates as Predictors of Inflation: Comparisons with the Results of Others

In a world where equilibrium expected real returns on bills are constant through

TABLE 7—SAMPLE AUTOCORRELATIONS OF r_t: ONE- TO SIX-MONTH BILLS

	1/53–7/71 Bill			3/59–7/71 Bill					
	1	2	3	1	2	3	4	5	6
$\hat{\rho}_1$	.09	.15	.00	.05	.03	−.16	−.17	.02	.07
$\hat{\rho}_2$	.13	−.09	.02	.05	−.15	.16	−.06	−.13	.07
$\hat{\rho}_3$	−.02	−.03	.08	−.08	.18	−.14	.20	−.03	−.05
$\hat{\rho}_4$	−.01	.01	.26	−.07	−.06	.25	.14	.03	.26
$\hat{\rho}_5$	−.02	.18	.16	.06	.00	.11	−.08	.15	.11
$\hat{\rho}_6$	−.02	.10	−.09	.10	.10	.04	.30	−.19	.43
$\hat{\rho}_7$	−.07	.15	.06	−.10	.07	.06	−.22	.33	−.04
$\hat{\rho}_8$	.04	−.01	−.01	.00	.14	.02	.17	−.02	.49
$\hat{\rho}_9$	.11	.06	.08	.09	.08	.18	.16	.25	−.60
$\hat{\rho}_{10}$	.10	.00	−.32	.05	−.07	−.33	−.09	.04	.27
$\hat{\rho}_{11}$	.03	.04	.11	−.04	.08	.36	−.02	−.69	.32
$\hat{\rho}_{12}$	.19	.09	.19	.20	.20	.10	.32	.13	.07
$\sigma(\hat{\rho}_1)$	.07	.10	.12	.08	.12	.14	.17	.19	.21
$\bar{r}$	.00074	.00185	.00306	.00090	.00224	.00373	.00514	.00706	.00882
$s(r)$	.00197	.00292	.00371	.00169	.00236	.00307	.00379	.00375	.00444
$T-1$	222	110	73	148	73	49	36	29	24

TABLE 8—REGRESSION TESTS ON ONE- TO SIX-MONTH BILLS
$\Delta_t = a_0 + a_1 R_t + e_t$

Period	Bill	a_0	a_1	$s(a_0)$	$s(a_1)$	Coefficient of Determination	$s(e)$	$\hat{\rho}_1(e)$	$\hat{\rho}_2(e)$	$\hat{\rho}_3(e)$
1/53–7/71	1	.00070	− .98	.00030	.10	.29	.00196	.09	.13	−.02
	2	.00161	− .96	.00066	.11	.42	.00296	.15	−.08	−.03
	3	.00228	− .92	.00105	.11	.48	.00380	.00	.03	.10
3/59–7/71	1	.00120	−1.09	.00041	.12	.36	.00169	.04	.05	−.08
	2	.00269	−1.08	.00086	.12	.52	.00245	.02	−.16	.14
	3	.00397	−1.03	.00145	.13	.55	.00330	−.16	.12	−.16
	4	.00543	−1.03	.00216	.14	.58	.00413	−.18	−.10	.14
	5	.00635	− .97	.00236	.12	.68	.00416	.01	−.10	−.02
	6	.00879	−1.01	.00344	.14	.65	.00505	.01	−.01	−.11

time, then, aside from the additive constant $E(\tilde{r})$ in (13), the nominal rate R_t set at time t−1 is in effect the market's prediction of the rate of change in purchasing power from t−1 to t. The coefficients of determination in Table 8 indicate that variation through time in these predictions accounts for 30 percent of the variance of subsequently observed values of Δ_t in the case of one-month bills, and the proportion of the sample variance of Δ_t accounted for by R_t increases to about 65 percent for five- and six-month bills. Thus, nominal interest rates observed at t−1 contain nontrivial information about the rate of change in purchasing power from t−1 to t. Moreover, the evidence on market efficiency suggests that the market's prediction of $\tilde{\Delta}_t$ is the best that can be made on the basis of information available at time t−1; or, more precisely, it is the best that can be done on the basis of information in past rates of change in purchasing power.

As noted earlier, the results reported here differ substantially from those of the rest of the literature on interest rates and inflation. In line with the early work of Fisher, the almost universal finding in other studies is that the market does not perform efficiently in predicting inflation. But the earlier studies, including, of course, Fisher's, are based primarily on pre-1953 data, and the negative results on market efficiency may to a large extent just reflect poor commodity price data. By

TABLE 9—REGRESSION TESTS ON ONE- TO SIX-MONTH BILLS
$\Delta_t = a_0 + a_1 R_t + a_2 \Delta_{t-1} + e_t$

Period	Bill	a_0	a_1	a_2	$s(a_0)$	$s(a_1)$	$s(a_2)$	Coefficient of Determination	$s(e)$	$\hat{\rho}_1(e)$	$\hat{\rho}_2(e)$	$\hat{\rho}_3(e)$
1/53–7/71	1	.00059	− .87	.11	.00030	.12	.07	.30	.00195	−.05	.13	−.04
	2	.00115	− .78	.17	.00064	.13	.09	.44	.00280	.03	−.06	.02
	3	.00173	− .79	.11	.00107	.15	.12	.48	.00372	−.06	.07	.05
3/59–7/71	1	.00109	−1.01	.07	.00042	.14	.08	.35	.00169	−.03	.05	−.07
	2	.00252	−1.02	.05	.00094	.18	.12	.51	.00248	−.02	−.16	.15
	3	.00390	−1.06	−.04	.00169	.23	.17	.53	.00334	−.10	.11	−.17
	4	.00520	− .97	.07	.00261	.26	.20	.57	.00423	−.23	−.06	.12
	5	.00359	− .57	.40	.00301	.27	.23	.71	.00404	−.13	−.08	−.02
	6	.00263	− .39	.58	.00406	.28	.23	.72	.00461	−.29	.18	−.32

the same token, the success of the tests reported here is probably to a nonnegligible extent a consequence of the availability of good data beginning in 1953.

Poor commodity price data also probably explain why the empirical literature is replete with evidence in support of the so-called Gibson Paradox—the proposition that there is a positive relationship between the nominal interest rate and the level of commodity prices, rather than the relationship between the interest rate and the rate of change in prices posited by Fisher.[4] With a poor price index, the Fisherian relationship between the nominal interest rate and the true inflation rate can be obscured by noise and by spurious autocorrelation in measured inflation rates. But over long periods of time—and the Gibson Paradox is usually posited as a long-run phenomenon—even a poor index picks up general movements in prices. Thus if inflations and deflations tend to persist (an implication of the evidence presented here that $E(\tilde{\Delta}_t | \phi_{t-1})$ is close to a random walk), there may well appear to be a relationship between the level of interest rates and the measured level of prices, which merely reflects the more fundamental Fisherian relationship between the interest rate and the rate of change of prices that is obscured by poor data. In this study, which is based on the relatively clean data of the 1953–71 period, the Fisherian relationship shows up clearly.

[4] For a discussion of the Gibson Paradox and a review of previous evidence, see Roll. A more recent study is Thomas Sargent.

VIII. Conclusions

The two major conclusions of the paper are as follows. First, during the 1953–71 period, the bond market seems to be efficient in the sense that in setting one- to six-month nominal rates of interest, the market correctly uses all the information about future inflation rates that is in time-series of past inflation rates. Second, one cannot reject the hypothesis that equilibrium expected real returns on one- to six-month bills are constant during the period. When combined with the conclusion that the market is efficient, this means that one also cannot reject the hypothesis that all variation through time in one- to six-month nominal rates of interest mirrors variation in correctly assessed one- to six-month expected rates of change in purchasing power.

REFERENCES

E. F. Fama, "Efficient Capital Markets: A Review of Theory and Empirical Work," *J. Finance*, May 1970, *25*, 383–417.

I. Fisher, *The Theory of Interest*, New York 1930, reprinted A. M. Kelley, 1965.

R. Roll, "Interest Rates on Monetary Assets and Commodity Price Index Changes," *J. Finance*, May 1972, *27*, 251–77.

T. J. Sargent, "Interest Rates and Prices in the Long Run: A Study of the Gibson Paradox," *J. Money, Credit, Banking*, Feb. 1973, *5*, 385–449.

U.S. Bureau of Labor Statistics, *Handbook of Methods for Surveys and Studies*, Bull. 1458, Washington 1971.

Salomon Brothers, "United States Treasury Securities," New York, issued daily.

THE JOURNAL OF FINANCE VOL. XXXIII, NO. 1 MARCH 1978

MONETARY POLICY, INFLATION FORECASTING AND THE TERM STRUCTURE OF INTEREST RATES

BRADFORD CORNELL*

I. INTRODUCTION

THE THEORETICAL AND EMPIRICAL literature on the term structure of interest rates seeks to explain the pattern of nominal returns on securities of differing maturity [see for example (21, 22, 24, 25, 26)]. Variation in nominal rates, however, can be due either to variation in the real return on capital or variation in the expected rate of inflation. This distinction is crucial because it turns out that the source of variation in the nominal rate has important implications for the term structure. The purpose of this paper is to outline the differential impact on the term structure of fluctuating inflationary expectations as opposed to fluctuation in the real rate.

In carrying out the analysis it is assumed that the demand for money function is stable. Given this assumption, varying rates of inflation must be associated with similar variation in the money stock. Real shocks cannot have a continuing impact on the price level unless they lead to a shift in the supply of money. The importance of this assumption is noted at the relevant points.

The next section briefly reviews the literature on both the term structure and the relationship between interest rates and inflationary expectations. In the following section a unified model is derived under the assumption that the real rate is constant. The fourth section extends the model to cover the case of a variable real rate and discusses the model's empirical relevance. The final section summarizes the paper.

II. INFLATIONARY EXPECTATIONS AND THE TERM STRUCTURE

Most prominent among the theories of the term structure is the expectations hypothesis [see (22, 26)]. The hypothesis states that nominal rates on long-term securities will depend on the expected nominal rate on short-term securities in the manner given by equation (1)

$$(1+i_m)^m = (1+{}_1i_1)(1+E({}_2i_1))\ldots(1+E({}_mi_1)) \tag{1}$$

i_m = the nominal rate on m-period debt.
${}_ki_1$ = the nominal rate on one-period debt for period k.
E = the expectation operator.

Many theorists, however, have rejected the pure form of the expectations

* Assistant Professor of Finance, University of Arizona. I would like to thank Michael Hurd, R. I. McKinnon, John Scadding and William F. Sharpe for comments on this paper. Detailed critiques of earlier versions by Anthony M. Santomero, a referee for the *Journal*, also proved most beneficial. Any errors that have persevered must be attributed to me.

hypothesis. As early as 1946, Hicks [18] argued that the hypothesis would underpredict the long-term rate. He felt that risk averse investors would favor short-term over long-term securities while the reverse would be true of borrowers. To induce savers to lengthen their maturities, Hicks claimed, would require borrowers to pay a liquidity premium on long-term securities. For this reason the weighted average of short rates given by (1) would underestimate the long rate by an amount equal to the liquidity premium.

Modigliani and Sutch (henceforth M-S) [22, 24] offered a straightforward generalization of Hicks' argument which they called the "preferred habitat theory." The basis of the theory was the hypothesis that

> Both final wealth holders and final borrowers have definite preferences as to the length of time they want to keep their funds invested or for which they require financing (that is, they have a preferred habitat).

In terms of these preferred habitats the authors conclude that

> It follows that the only way a transactor with an m-period habitat can acquire certainty of return or cost is for him to invest or borrow only through m-period instruments. Going shorter would expose him to uncertainty concerning the borrowing or lending terms prevailing for the balance of the period; going longer would expose him to uncertainty about the market value of the unexpired instrument at the time of its intended liquidation.

As the above quote demonstrates, M-S failed to adequately distinguish between real and nominal rates of return. If we make the usual assumption that the utility function is defined over real wealth, the transactor with a preferred habitat of m periods would desire a certain real return or cost over the m periods. Quite clearly, this goal cannot be achieved by holding securities with a fixed nominal return, unless the rate of inflation is known with certainty. It is thus necessary to more carefully distinguish real and nominal interest rates.

Writers in the tradition of Irving Fisher [4, 5, 7, 9, 15, 17, 31], have substantiated the theory that nominal interest rates respond to inflationary expectations according to the relationship[1]

$$i = r + \pi. \tag{2}$$

$r =$ the real rate of return to capital.
$\pi =$ the expected rate of inflation over the life of the security.

In terms of equation (2), the transactor with a preferred habitat of m periods desires certainty of real m-period return, r_m. If he issues or buys m-period debt the ex-ante expected real return will equal the real return on capital, so that

$$E(r_m) = i_m - \pi_m$$

On the other hand, his ex-post realized real return is

$$r_m = i_m - p_m$$

1. This is the continuous time version of the Fisher equation. If discrete time rates of return are used the term, $r\pi$, must be added to the right-hand side.

where p_m refers to the rate of inflation that actually occured over the m-periods. The difference between the ex-ante and ex-post real return is,

$$r_m - E(r_m) = \pi_m - p_m$$

the inflation forecasting error. The variability of realized real return thus depends on the accuracy of the inflation forecast over the maturity of the security.

One possible means of reducing the forecast error is to transact in short-term securities. Over the short-run, the actual and forecast rate of inflation should not diverge substantially. For this reason it may be optimal for a risk averse transactor with an m-period preferred habitat to purchase or issue a sequence of m, one-period, securities. The next two sections mathematically evaluate this proposition and explore its implications for term structure theory.

III. The Constant Real Rate Case

All of the models derived in this paper share the following assumptions:

1. All transactors in the securities market are rational, risk averse and have homogenous expectations regarding the future course of inflation.
2. All securities are discounted instruments and there is no possibility of default.
3. There are no taxes or transaction costs.

At the outset it is also assumed that the real rate is constant. By redefining all rates of return net of this constant, we can proceed as if the real rate were zero. This added condition will be relaxed in the next section.

The behavior of transactors with m-period preferred habitats will depend on the statistical properties of the random variable representing the real amount that must be repaid after m periods to borrow one dollar today or, from the point of view of the lender, the real wealth after m periods which results from the investment of one dollar today. Transactors have two alternatives: the sale or purchase of one m-period bond or the sale or purchase of a sequence of m one-period bonds. To analyze the problem we introduce the following notation (all rates of return are in terms of continuous time):

Y_s = The real wealth, after m-periods, that results from investing one dollar in the short-term market and rolling over the investment m times (this is also the borrower's real cost per dollar borrowed).

Y_L = The real wealth that results from investing one dollar in the m-period bond.

${}_k\pi_k$ = The rate of inflation forecast for the kth period at the beginning of the kth period.

${}_1\pi_k$ = The rate of inflation forecast for the kth period at the beginning of the first period.

p_k = The rate of inflation that actually occurs during the kth period.

With the real rate zero, equation (2) implies that the short rate at the beginning of each period will be

$$i_k = {}_k\pi_k.$$

It follows that the nominal wealth accumulated by rolling over a one dollar investment in short-term bonds is[2]

$$\exp\left(\sum i_k\right)=\exp\left(\sum {}_k\pi_k\right),$$

so that the real wealth is

$$Y_s=\frac{\exp\left(\sum {}_k\pi_k\right)}{\exp\left(\sum p_k\right)}=\exp\left[\sum ({}_k\pi_k-p_k)\right]=\exp\left(\sum u_k\right) \tag{3}$$

where $u_k={}_k\pi_k-p_k$ is the inflation forecasting error.

In the case of the long-term market, equation (2) implies that the nominal rate should equal the average inflation rate expected over the m-periods, or

$$i_m=\bar{\pi}=\frac{{}_1\pi_1+{}_1\pi_2+{}_1\pi_3+\dots{}_1\pi_m}{m} \tag{4}$$

Thus

$$Y_L=\frac{\exp(mi_m)}{\exp\left(\sum p_k\right)}=\frac{\exp(m\bar{\pi})}{\exp\left(\sum p_k\right)}=\frac{\exp\left(\sum {}_1\pi_k\right)}{\exp\left(\sum p_k\right)} \tag{4}$$

$$Y_L=\exp\left[\sum ({}_1\pi_k-p_k)\right]=\exp\left(\sum w_k\right) \tag{5}$$

where w_k = the error in the inflation forecast, made at the beginning of the first period, for period k.

In light of equations (3) and (5), transactors will base their decision on whether to enter the long-or short-term market on the properties of the inflation forecasting errors.

If the financial market is efficient and transactors are rational—both of which we take as given—the u's will have the following properties:[3]

$$\begin{aligned} E(u_k)&=0 \qquad \text{for all } k \\ \operatorname{cov}(u_i,u_j)&=0 \qquad \text{for all } i\neq j \end{aligned} \tag{6}$$

To simplify the analysis we make the additional assumption that

$$u_k \sim n(0,\sigma_k^2)$$

2. The exponential notation arises because of the use of continuous time rates of return. In continuous time the value of one dollar invested at rate r for time t is e^{rt}.

3. For a proof that the u's will have these properties in an efficient market see Samuelson [29]. Evidence regarding the efficiency of the financial markets, and in particular the government securities market, is presented by Fama [8,9], Hamburger [16], Hess and Bicksler [17] and Roll [27].

This assumption greatly simplifies the exposition, because the problem can be analyzed in terms of mean and variance.[4] The assumption of normality, furthermore, is reasonable in light of the fact that the forecast errors are most likely the net result of a large number of independent random shocks.

Turning to the *w*'s, rationality again implies that

$$E(w_k)=0 \qquad \text{for all } k. \tag{7}$$

It is no longer necessarily true, however, that

$$\text{cov}(w_i, w_k)=0 \qquad \text{for all } i \neq j.$$

If, for example, inflation suddenly accelerated during period k; $w_k, w_{k+1}, w_{k+2} \cdots w_m$ would all tend to be negative, because the increase in the rate of inflation was not foreseen at the beginning of period 1. In this case

$$\text{cov}(w_k, w_j)>0 \qquad \text{for } j>k.$$

Because the covariance of the *w*'s plays an important role in future computations, it is worth inquiring under what conditions the covariances might be negative. As noted in the example, if the inflationary trend unexpectedly accelerates or decelerates the covariances will be positive. On the other hand, if the inflation rate follows an Ito process with a fixed trend, as many recent theorists such as Fisher [12] have assumed, the covariances will be zero. Only if the rate of growth in the monetary base were known could covariances be negative.[5]

Assume, for example, that the rate of growth of the monetary base is expected to be n for all future time and that real income is expected to grow at rate g. If the economy is characterized by a stable demand function for money with unitary income elasticity, rational transactors would predict an inflation rate of n-g for all future periods from the vantage point of time zero. In response to shocks to the real economy or random variation in the money multipliers, the rate of inflation may diverge from n-g. As long as the supply of money remains unchanged and the demand for money function is stable, the inflation rate will revert back to the trend. In this case it is easy to see that the *w*'s are going to be negatively correlated. A period of higher than average inflation causes a negative w and a fall in real money balances. For the economy to return to its equilibrium growth path, real balances must increase at a rate greater than g, this requires an inflation rate below n-g and thus produces a positive w.

The question of the correlation of the *w*'s thus turns on the source of inflation. If inflation comes from the real sector and is not accompanied by a change in monetary policy, as for example under a gold standard, the *w*'s will tend to be negatively correlated. If inflation is primarily a monetary phenomenon, the *w*'s will

4. Without this assumption a detailed expected utility analysis is required. Such added detail, however, provides little additional insight.

5. I assume that there is no trend in the money multiplier over time so that the expected growth rate of the base and the money stock are equal. The money multiplier may, however, be affected by short-run shocks.

tend to be positively correlated. For the remainder of this analysis, I assume that inflation is primarily a monetary phenomenon and that the w's will not be negatively correlated. The literature supporting this position is both voluminous and well-known.[6] It should be emphasized that calling inflation a monetary phenomenon does not imply that only monetary shocks can affect the price level, but that any effect on the price level will be self-terminating if not underwritten by the monetary authority.

From the stated properties of the series (u_k) and (w_k), the distributions of Y_s and Y_L can be derived. In both equations (3) and (5) the expected value of the exponent is zero. In equation (3) the independence property of the u's implies that

$$\operatorname{Var}\left(\sum_k u_k\right) = \sum_k \operatorname{Var}(u_k) \tag{8}$$

For the w's, however,

$$\operatorname{Var}\left(\sum_k w_k\right) = \sum_k \operatorname{Var}(w_k) + \sum_{i \neq j} \sum \operatorname{Cov}(w_i, w_j) \tag{9}$$

Since all of the information available at the beginning of the first period is also available at the beginning of period k, it follows that

$$\operatorname{Var}(u_k) \leqslant \operatorname{Var}(w_k) \qquad \text{for all } k \tag{10}$$

On the basis of (10) and the assumption that the w's are not negatively correlated we can conclude that

$$\operatorname{Var}\left(\sum w_k\right) \geqslant \operatorname{Var}\left(\sum u_k\right)$$

Thus

$$\begin{aligned} &\sum_k u_k \sim n(0, \alpha^2) \\ &\sum_k w_k \sim n(0, \beta^2) \end{aligned} \tag{11}$$

for some α and β such that $\beta \geqslant \alpha$.

From (11) it is possible to write down the distributions of Y_s and Y_L—both are lognormal with mean and variance given by (12) and (13).

$$Y_s \sim L\left[\exp(1/2\alpha^2), e^{\alpha^2}(e^{\alpha^2} - 1)\right] \tag{12}$$

$$Y_L \sim L\left[\exp(1/2\beta^2), e^{\beta^2}(e^{\beta^2} - 1)\right] \tag{13}$$

6. The most famous works are Cagan (2, 3) and Friedman and Schwartz (14). Other studies testing the relationship between money and prices in various countries include Klein (20) and Vogel (30).

At first glance (12) and (13) appear to imply that no general statement regarding transactor behavior can be made. The long-term bond offers both a higher mean real return and a larger variance of real wealth. In this case it is impossible to say which distribution an *investor* would prefer. This conclusion, however, ignores the other side of the market.

Borrowers interpret (12) and (13) to say that issuing long-term bonds promises them both higher mean borrowing costs, in real terms, and a larger variance. Under such circumstances it is evident that risk-averse borrowers would not issue long-term debt. Before an individual would consider selling long-term debt, the bonds would have to sell at a premium sufficiently large to insure that the mean borrowing cost was less than the mean borrowing cost of issuing the less risky sequence of short-term securities. Yet if such a premium were to exist, risk-averse lenders would then unambiguously prefer to invest in a succession of short-term instruments. Finally, at the midpoint, where the mean real returns are the same because of a premium on long-term bonds, *both* borrowers and lenders would prefer to transact in the short-term market where the ex-ante variability of real return or cost is less.

The surprising conclusion is that the long-term market should cease to exist. Even borrowers and lenders with a preferred habitat of m-periods would prefer a sequence of m, one-period, contracts to one, m-period, contract, because the short-term market offers a partial hedge against unexpected changes in the rate of inflation.

IV. The Variable Real Rate Case

When the real rate is variable, transactors can hedge against its fluctation by entering the long-term market. In the long-term market, the nominal yield, given by equation (14), is fixed no matter what the subsequent variation in the real rate

$$i_m = \bar{r} + \bar{\pi} \tag{14}$$

$\bar{r}$ = the average real rate expected to prevail over the next m-periods.

$\bar{\pi}$ = the average rate of inflation expected to prevail over the next m-periods (as given by equation (4)).

Thus

$$Y_L = \frac{\exp(mi)}{\exp\left(\sum p_k\right)} = \frac{\exp\left(m\bar{r} + \sum {}_1\pi_k\right)}{\exp\left(\sum p_k\right)}$$

$$Y_L = \exp\left(m\bar{r} + \sum {}_1\pi_k - p_k\right) = \exp\left[m\bar{r} + \sum w_k\right] \tag{15}$$

Due to the fact that $\bar{r}$ is an expected value rather than a random variable

$$E\left(m\bar{r} + \sum w_k\right) = m\bar{r} \tag{16}$$

$$\mathrm{Var}\left(m\bar{r} + \sum w_k\right) = \mathrm{Var}\left(\sum w_k\right) \tag{17}$$

Once again letting $\beta^2 = \text{Var}(\Sigma w_k)$, (16) and (17) imply that Y_L is lognormally distributed with mean and variance given by equation (18).

$$Y_L \sim L\left[e^{m\bar{r}+1/2\beta^2}, e^{2m\bar{r}+\beta^2}(e^{\beta^2}-1)\right] \tag{18}$$

In the short-term market transactors are exposed to fluctation in the real rate every time refinancing or reinvestment occurs. Denoting the real rate expected for period k by r_k, the nominal rate at the beginning of each period will be

$$i_k = r_k + \pi_k$$

Thus

$$Y_s = \frac{\exp\left(\sum i_k\right)}{\exp\left(\sum p_k\right)} = \exp\left[\sum (r_k + \pi_k - p_k)\right]$$

$$Y_s = \exp\left[\sum (r_k + u_k)\right] \tag{19}$$

Focusing on the exponent and taking expectations as of the beginning of the first period,

$$E\left[\left(\sum r_k + \sum u_k\right)\right] = m\bar{r} \tag{20}$$

$$\text{Var}\left[\sum (r_k + u_k)\right] = \text{Var}\left(\sum r_k\right) + \text{Var}\left(\sum u_k\right) + \sum_{i \neq j} \sum \text{Cov}(r_i, u_j) \tag{21}$$

Making the assumption that r_k is normally distributed, the only problem equation (21) presents is interpretation of the covariance term. Once again the key factor in determining the sign of the covariance is the source of inflation. If the unexpected inflation is caused by a shock to the real economy, the real rate will rise and u will be negative, so that r_k and u_k will be negatively correlated. On the other hand, assuming that inflation is caused by increased monetary growth rates, the real rate should fall, at least initially, and r_k and u_k will be positively correlated. Under the assumption that the main source of variation in the rate of inflation is varying monetary policy, it is safe to conclude that r_k and u_k will not be negatively correlated.

To simplify the notation define

$$\gamma^2 = \text{Var}\left(\sum r_k\right) + \text{Var}\left(\sum u_k\right) + \sum_{i,j} \sum \text{Cov}(r_i, u_j) \tag{22}$$

In this notation, the distribution of Y_s is lognormal as

$$Y_s \sim L\left[e^{m\bar{r}+1/2\gamma^2}, e^{2m\bar{r}+\gamma^2}(e^{\gamma^2}-1)\right] \tag{23}$$

Comparing equations (19) and (23) two distinct cases emerge:

1. $\gamma^2 < \beta^2$
2. $\gamma^2 > \beta^2$

The first case is identical to the constant real rate problem previously analyzed. If the long-term bonds were to sell at a premium so that the expected real return was equal in (19) and (23), both borrowers and lenders would prefer to operate in the short-term market due to the smaller ex-ante variability of real wealth. If the bonds did not sell at such a premium, either borrowers or lenders would shun them depending on which way the priced moved. Thus only short-term securities would be traded.

Case two corresponds to the situation M-S apparently had in mind. If $\gamma^2 > \beta^2$ then the variability of real return on the sequence of one-period securities will be higher. Transactors with a preferred habitat of m-periods would thus prefer to deal in the m-period market. Only if paid a liquidity premium would they issue or buy securities of a different maturity.

The distinction between the two cases can be made intuitively clearer by once again considering the limits. As the variation in the real rate goes to zero, risk becomes identified with inflation risk. If indexed bonds do not exist, the best inflation hedge is to stay in the short-term market, because each period the nominal interest rate will be adjusted to reflect the new inflationary environment. Due to this readjustment, the short-term market provides the least variance of real wealth over all horizons and is thus preferred by transactors of *every* preferred habitat. Long-term debt should disappear.

At the other extreme, when the rate of inflation is known with certainty, transactors will want to match the maturity of their securities to their preferred habitat, because by so doing they can assure a certain real return or cost over their preferred habitat. Liquidity premiums, which depend on the distribution of preferred habitats in the population, should appear to clear the market as predicted by M-S.

It is interesting to ask which of the two cases is the best approximation to reality. The answer to this question clearly depends on the source of inflation during the period of concern. Looking at the U.S. over the period 1951–1973, Fama (9, 10, 11) found that almost all the variation in Treasury Bill rates was due to changing inflationary expectations. This being the case, one would expect periods of highly variable inflation to be characterized by a fall in long-term financing.

While a detailed test of the model is beyond the scope of this paper, it is worth noting that its plausibility is supported by recent experience. The highly variable inflation rate of the 1972–1974 period greatly depressed the long-term bond markets in Canada, Britain and the United States. Corporations turned instead to short-term bank loans and the commercial paper market. The corporate bonds that were issued were of unusually short maturity.[7] Furthermore, there is no precedent of a country which has been able to maintain long-term, fixed interest rate markets in the face of a highly variable rate of inflation. The recent experience of Chile, Brazil and Israel provide examples, as do all the hyperinflations.

The analysis also casts doubt on the old saw that a company or an economy with a high ratio of short- to long-term debt is "risky, poorly managed and overextended." Raising the ratio of short- to long-term debt is the optimal response to an

7. This period also saw the introduction of indexed corporate bonds.

uncertain inflation rate. It is prudent for a firm to fund investment in plant and equipment, which offers a given real rate of return, with short-term debt, which via continuous roll-over assures the borrower of the least variable real borrowing cost.

V. Conclusions

This paper has shown that the source of variation in nominal interest rates has important implications for the term structure. When the main source of variation is fluctuation of the real rate, Modigliani and Sutch's interpretation of the preferred habitat theory is correct. With each transactor trying to match the maturity of his securities to his preferred habitat, liquidity premiums will appear to clear the bond market. The distribution of these premiums, in turn, will depend on the distribution of preferred habitats among borrowers and lenders in the population.

When the main source of variation in nominal rates is a fluctuating inflation rate caused by a variable monetary policy, the situation is radically different. If indexed bonds do not exist, transactors of *every* preferred habitat will attempt to hedge against inflation by dealing exclusively in the short-term market. No transactor will be willing to enter the long-term market unless he is paid a liquidity premium. Since premiums cannot be paid to both borrowers and lenders, trading in long-term bonds will cease.

REFERENCES

1. G. E. P. Box and G. M. Jenkins. *Time Series Analysis*, Holden-Day, 1970.
2. P. Cagan. "The Monetary Dynamics of Hyperinflation," in Friedman, ed., *Studies in the Quantity Theory of Money*, University of Chicago Press, 1956.
3. ———. *Determinants and Effects of Changes in the Stock of Money: 1875–1960*, Columbia University Press, 1965.
4. T. F. Cargill. "Interest Rates and Prices Since 1950," *International Economic Review*, (December 1973), pp. 348–371.
5. G. Chamberlain and M. Feldstein. "Multimarket Expectations and the Rate of Interest," *Journal of Money Credit and Banking*, (November 1973), pp. 873–902.
6. W.B. Cornell. *Essays on the Relationship between Interest Rates and Inflationary Expectations*, Unpublished Ph.D. dissertation, Stanford University, 1975.
7. O. Eckstein and M. Feldstein. "The Fundamental Determinants of Interest Rates," *Review of Economics and Statistics*, (November 1970) pp. 363–375.
8. E. F. Famma. "Efficient Capital Markets: A Review of Theory and Empirical Work," *Journal of Finance*, Volume 25 (May 1970), pp. 383–417.
9. ———. "Short-term Interest Rates as Predictors of Inflation," *American Economic Review*, Volumn 65 (June 1975), pp. 265–282.
10. ———. "Inflation Uncertainty and the Expected Returns on Treasury Bills," *Journal of Political Economy*, Volume 84 (June 1976), pp. 427–448.
11. ———. "Forward Rates as Predictors of Future Spot Rates," *Journal of Financial Economics*, Volume 3 (October 1976), pp. 361–377.
12. I. Fisher. *The Theory of Interest*, Macmillan Co., 1930.
13. S. Fisher. "The Demand for Indexed Bonds," *Journal of Political Economy*, Volume 83 (June 1975), pp. 509–534. .
14. M. Friedman and A. J. Schwartz. *A Monetary History of the United States: 1867–1960*, Princeton: National Bureau of Economic Research, 1963.
15. W. E. Gibson. "Interest Rates and Inflationary Expectations," *American Economic Review*, (December 1972), pp. 854–865.

16. M. J. Hamburger and E. N. Platt. "The Expectations Hypothesis and the Efficiency of the Treasury Bill Market," *The Review of Economics and Statistics* (May 1975), pp. 341–360.
17. P. J. Hess and J. L. Bicksler. "Capital Asset Prices Versus Time Series Models as Predictors of Inflation," *Journal of Financial Economics*, Volume 2 (June 1975), pp. 341–360.
18. J. R. Hicks. *Value and Capital*, 2nd edition, Clarendon Press, 1946.
19. B. Klein. "The Social Cost of the Recent Inflation and Our New Monetary Standard: The Mirage of Anticipated Inflation," Unpublished manuscript, UCLA, 1974.
20. J. J. Klein. "German Money and Prices, 1932–44," in Friedman, ed., *Studies in the Quantity Theory of Money*, University of Chicago Press, 1956.
21. J. H. McCulloch. "An Estimate of the Liquidity Premium," *Journal of Political Economy*, (February 1975), pp. 95–119.
22. D. Meiselman. *The Term Structure of Interest Rates*, Prentice-Hall, 1962.
23. F. Modigliani and R. Sutch. "Innovations in Interest Rate Policy," *American Economic Review*, (May 1966), pp. 178–197.
24. ——— and ———. "Debt Management and the Term Structure of Interest Rates," *Journal of Political Economy*, (August 1967).
25. R. A. Mundell. "Inflation and the Real Interest Rate," *Journal of Political Economy*, (June 1963), pp. 280–283.
26. C. R. Nelson. *The Term Structure of Interest Rates*, Basic Books, 1972.
27. R. Roll. *The Behavior of Interest Rates*, New York: Basic Books, 1970.
28. J. Rutledge. *A Monetarist Model of Inflationary Expectations*, Lexington, 1974.
29. P. Samuelson. "Proof that Properly Anticipated Prices Fluctuate Randomly," *Industrial Management Review*, Volume 6 (Spring 1965), pp. 41–49.
30. R. C. Vogel. "The Dynamics of Inflation in Latin America, 1950–1969," *The American Economic Review*, Volume 64 (March 1974), pp. 102–114.
31. W. P. Yohe and D. Kornosky. "Interest Rates and Price Level Changes: 1952–1969," *Review of the Federal Reserve Bank of St. Louis*, (December 1969) pp. 19–36.

[11]

Journal of Financial Economics 13 (1984) 529–546. North-Holland

TERM PREMIUMS IN BOND RETURNS

Eugene F. FAMA*

University of Chicago, Chicago, IL 60637, USA

Received November 1983, final version received June 1984

This paper examines expected returns on U.S. Treasury bills and on U.S. Government bond portfolios. Expected bill returns are estimated from forward rates and from sample average returns. Both estimation methods indicate that expected returns on bills tend to peak at eight or nine months and never increase monotonically out to twelve months. Reliable inferences are limited to Treasury bills and thus to maturities up to a year. The variability of longer-term bond returns preempts precise conclusions about their expected returns.

1. Introduction

In the early literature on the term structure of interest rates there is controversy about the existence of risk premiums in the expected returns on longer-term bonds. [See, for example Meiselman (1962) and Kessel (1965).] Recent empirical work documents reliable premiums in the expected returns on longer- versus shorter-maturity instruments. [See, for example, Roll (1970), McCulloch (1975), Fama (1976a, 1976b, 1984) and Startz (1982).] Except for McCulloch (1975), however, the recent work focuses on short-maturity instruments, in particular, U.S. Treasury bills.

This paper examines returns on bills and on portfolios of U.S. Government bonds that cover the maturity spectrum. Consistent with the liquidity preference hypothesis advanced by Kessel (1965) and others, we find statistically reliable evidence that expected returns on longer-term bills exceed the returns on one-month bills. We also find reliable evidence that expected returns on bills do not increase monotonically with maturity and generally tend to peak at eight or nine months. This conclusion is first obtained in tests on average returns, and it is then reinforced by estimates of expected returns from forward rates. The conclusion is inconsistent with the liquidity preference hypothesis which predicts that expected returns increase monotonically with maturity

*Theodore O. Yntema Professor of Finance, Graduate School of Business, University of Chicago. The comments of David Booth, Stephen Buser, Nai-Fu Chen, George Constantinides, Wayne Ferson, Robert Holthausen, David Hsieh, G. William Schwert, Rex Sinquefield, Robert Stambaugh, and the referee, Michael Gibbons, are gratefully acknowledged. This research is supported by the National Science Foundation.

because return variability increases monotonically. Moreover, since the *ex ante* estimates of expected returns from forward rates peak at the same maturities as *ex post* average returns, the non-monotonicity of average returns cannot be attributed to unexpected increases in the level of interest rates during the sample period.

During the five-year subperiods of 1953–82 covered by the bond portfolios, bonds with maturities greater than four years never have the highest average returns. During periods where the bond file overlaps with the bill file, the highest average return on a bond portfolio never exceeds the highest average return on a bill. We cannot conclude, however, that longer-term bonds have lower expected returns than short-term instruments. Like McCulloch (1975), but with the advantage of an exhaustive data base, we find that the high variability of longer-term bond returns preempts precise conclusions about their expected returns. The bond data are consistent with maturity structures of expected returns that are flat, upward sloping or downward sloping beyond a year.

The non-monotonicity of expected bill returns documented here is inconsistent with either the pure expectations hypothesis or the liquidity preference hypothesis of the classical term structure literature. It is not necessarily inconsistent with the more sophisticated models of capital market equilibrium of Sharpe (1964), Lintner (1965), Merton (1973) or Breeden (1979). I offer no direct tests. Rather, the descriptive evidence presented here, and the evidence of rich patterns of variation through time in expected bill returns presented by Fama (1984), Startz (1982) and others, stand as challenges or 'stylized facts' to be explained by candidate models.

2. The data

The U.S. Government bond file of the Center for Research in Security Prices (CRSP) of the University of Chicago contains monthly price and return information on all outstanding publicly traded U.S. Treasury securities. Two return files are created from these data, covering (1) bills with maturities up to twelve months, and (2) portfolios of bonds and notes covering all maturities.

Treasury bills with twelve months to maturity are consistently available beginning in 1964. On the last trading day of each month the bill with maturity closest to twelve months is chosen. At the end of the next month, this bill is chosen as the eleven-month bill, and at the end of the following month it becomes the ten-month bill, etc. In this way monthly returns on bills with one to twelve months to maturity are obtained at the end of each month.

Because the Treasury issues bonds and notes on an irregular basis, they must be grouped into portfolios to get unbroken time series of monthly returns. For maturities up to three years, grouping within six-month maturity intervals produces six unbroken time series of monthly returns for the 1953–82 period.

Continuous time series are also obtained for portfolios that contain maturities between three and four years, four and five years, and five to ten years. These portfolios contain only ordinary bonds and notes. Bills, 'flower' bonds (bonds redeemable at par to satisfy Federal estate taxes) and other bonds with special tax features are excluded.

To represent the behavior of the longest-term Government bonds, the Government bond return series of Ibbotson and Sinquefield (1983) is used. They choose the ordinary bond closest to twenty years to maturity. No ordinary bond with more than ten years to maturity is available during the October 1962 to January 1972 period. During this period they choose the long-term 'flower' bond with the highest price relative to par, since the returns on such bonds are likely to behave most like those on ordinary bonds.

3. Statistical issues[1]

We test vectors of average returns on bills and bonds against expected return vectors implied by hypotheses about the term structure. We also test individual average returns against their hypothetical expected values. Consistent probability statements require a multiple-comparisons framework.

3.1. Hotelling T^2 tests

The two files of bill and bond returns are treated as separate data sets rather than as a single data set to be viewed in a unified multiple-comparisons framework. The justification is that the two data sets cover different (but overlapping) periods. For each file, Hotelling T^2 statistics are used to test the hypothesis that all expected premiums in bill or bond returns are zero. A premium is defined as the difference between the one-month return on an instrument with a given maturity and the return on a one-month bill. Premiums rather than returns are used as the basic data elements because premiums are less autocorrelated than returns [Fama (1976a, 1984)].[2]

The T^2 tests on the vectors of average premiums for the two data sets produce strong evidence against the hypothesis that all expected premiums are zero in favor of the hypothesis that expected premiums are positive. Next we test the hypothesis that the structure of expected returns is flat beyond two

[1]Later sections of this paper are comprehensible without a detailed understanding of this section.

[2]For example, for the 1964–82 time period covered by the twelve-month bill file, the premiums in two- to twelve-month bill returns show first-order autocorrelation in the neighborhood of 0.2 and no systematic higher-order autocorrelation. For the 1953–82 period covered by the bond portfolio file, the premiums in the returns on shorter-term bond portfolios also show first-order autocorrelation of about 0.2. Premiums in longer-term bond returns show no systematic autocorrelation. Contemporaneous differences or spreads between the returns on adjacent maturity bills or bonds are also important in the tests that follow. These return spreads show little autocorrelation.

months. This involves a T^2 test on the vector of average differences between returns on instruments with successively longer maturities. At least for bill returns, the hypothesis that the structure of expected returns is flat beyond two months is rejected. The final step is to use a multiple-comparisons framework to examine the term structure of expected returns in detail.

The T^2 statistic is the square of the maximum possible t statistic that can be generated from any linear combination of the elements of a vector of means. The multiple-comparisons logic underlying the test is that the distribution of T^2 provides type I error protection for all possible t tests on linear combinations of the means. Thus, the distributional umbrella of the T^2 statistic can be used in an unrestricted search for differences in the expected returns on bills or bonds with different maturities. The right to conduct such a search has a cost. Because an indefinite number of tests is allowed, the differences between expected returns must be large to be identified reliably. Morrison (1976, ch. 4) and Miller (1981, ch. 5) discuss this approach to multiple comparisons, which is due to Roy and Bose (1953).

3.2. Bonferroni multiple comparisons

In contrast to the Roy–Bose approach, Bonferroni multiple comparisons require a specification that limits the relevant number of t tests on a vector of means. In particular, the Bonferroni inequality says that when p univariate t statistics are compared to 0.0 and the null hypothesis about the means is true, the probability that one or more of the t statistics is greater than the $1-\alpha$ fractile of the t distribution with $N-1$ degrees of freedom is equal to or less than $p\alpha$.

Table 1 shows large (∞) sample upper fractiles of the t statistic for Bonferroni comparisons of p means for $p = 1, 5, 10, 11$. As intuition suggests, the probability level for a given value of t is smaller the larger the number of means to be compared to zero. It is possible to specify the tests so that the relevant number of means compared to zero is the number of average bill or bond returns calculated. As a consequence, the critical values of t statistics for multiple comparisons carried out under the Bonferroni method are smaller than for the Roy–Bose approach. For example, for large-sample tests on 10 means, the 0.95 fractile of the Bonferroni t statistic is 2.58 (table 1), whereas the Roy–Bose t statistic corresponding to the 0.95 fractile of T^2 for 10 and ∞ degrees of freedom is 4.33. This higher t statistic under the Roy–Bose approach is the price one pays for the right to search over an arbitrary number of linear combinations of means.

To judge the behavior of expected returns for increasing maturities, Bonferroni fractiles are applied to the t statistics for the average differences or spreads between contemporaneous returns on adjacent maturity bills or adja-

Table 1
Upper fractiles of the t distribution for Bonferroni comparisons of p means in large (∞) samples.[a]

	t statistic value				
	1.65	1.96	2.33	2.58	3.29
			Probability level		
$p=1$	0.95	0.975	0.99	0.995	0.9995
$p=5$	0.75	0.875	0.95	0.975	0.9975
$p=10$	0.50	0.75	0.90	0.95	0.995
$p=11$	0.45	0.725	0.89	0.945	0.9945

[a] The Bonferroni inequality says that when p univariate t statistics are compared to 0.0 and the null hypothesis about the means is true, the probability that one or more of the t statistics is greater than the $1-\alpha$ fractile of the t distribution with $N-1$ degrees of freedom is equal to or less than $p\alpha$. Thus, the entries in the table for $p>1$ follow directly from those for $p=1$.

cent maturity bond portfolios. These tests are the basis of the conclusions summarized earlier about the behavior of expected returns as a function of maturity.

3.3. Subperiod results

For each of the return files, results for the overall period covered by the data and for subperiods are presented. One can argue that, if subperiod results are evaluated with the Bonferroni approach, the relevant number of comparisons is the number of means to be tested each period times the number of periods, and generally the power of the approach is lost. On the other hand, decisions about what constitute relevant 'families' of tests are to some extent at the option of the researcher. [See Miller (1981, pp. 31–35).] One can argue that subperiods can be treated individually under either the Bonferroni approach or the Roy–Bose approach to multiple comparisons.

I follow a middle-of-the-road approach to the subperiod results. Probability statements are limited to the tests for the overall sample period, and subperiod results are used for perspective and diagnostic checks on the tests for the overall period. Although the same summary statistics are used, the subperiod results are not interpreted with the same kinds of probability statements as the results for the overall period.

4. Evidence from average returns on the term structure of expected returns

Let $H\tau_{t+1}$ be the continuously compounded return from (the end of month) t to (the end of month) $t+1$ on a bill or bond portfolio with maturity τ at t. For bills, τ is a given number of months to maturity, but for bonds τ is the interval of maturities covered by a portfolio. The continuously compounded return on a bill is just the natural log of the ratio of its prices at $t+1$ and t, adjusted to a 30.4 day basis. [See Fama (1984) for details and rationale.] For a bond portfolio, the simple monthly returns on the CRSP file (which properly take account of coupons and accumulated interest) are averaged across bonds to get an equal weighted simple return. The continuously compounded portfolio return is the natural log of one plus the simple return. The premium in the return on a bill or bond portfolio with maturity τ is defined as

$$P\tau_{t+1} \equiv H\tau_{t+1} - H1_{t+1}, \tag{1}$$

where $H1_{t+1}$ is the continuously compounded return or rate of interest (later denoted R_{t+1}) calculated from the price of a bill with one month to maturity at t.

4.1. T^2 tests

Tables 2 and 3 summarize the evidence on average returns for the bills (table 2) and the bond portfolios (table 3).

The T^2 tests on the vectors of average premiums for the overall periods of available data provide no support for the hypothesis that all expected premiums are zero. The sample F statistics for the two T^2 statistics correspond to fractiles of the F distribution almost indistinguishable from 1.0. Likewise, the hypothesis that the structure of expected returns (or premiums) is flat beyond two months gets no support in the bill return data. The T^2 statistic for the vector of average values of the contemporaneous return spreads, $H\tau_{t+1} - H(\tau-1)_{t+1}$, $\tau = 3,\ldots,12$, in table 2 produces an F statistic so large that the computer program, which calculates probability levels to six decimals, rounds the probability level to 1.00.

At this point, however, the bills and the bond portfolios part company. The T^2 test on the vector of average differences between returns on adjacent maturity bond portfolios in table 3 is consistent with the hypothesis that the expected premiums in bond returns do not differ across portfolio maturities. Indeed, this T^2 test produces an F statistic just about at the median of the distribution of the F statistic under the hypothesis that expected premiums do not differ by maturity.

Most of the bond portfolios cover longer maturities than the bills. Thus, the inference from the T^2 tests that there are systematic differences in the expected returns on multi-month bills but not on bond portfolios suggests some systematic behavior of expected returns, or return variability, as a function of maturity. The results for individual maturities in tables 2 and 3 are relevant evidence.

Table 2

Average premiums, *t* statistics and T^2 tests for bills with up to twelve months to maturity.

Bill	$N = 211^a$ 8/64–12/82	$N = 101$ 8/64–12/72	$N = 110^a$ 1/73–12/82	$N = 56^a$ 1/73–12/77	$N = 54^a$ 1/78–12/82
		Average premiums			
P2	0.032	0.028	0.035	0.016	0.056
P3	0.057	0.045	0.067	0.042	0.094
P4	0.063	0.046	0.078	0.056	0.101
P5	0.074	0.061	0.086	0.065	0.108[b]
P6	0.073	0.066	0.079	0.062	0.097
P7	0.069	0.071	0.067	0.060	0.074
P8	0.088	0.084	0.091	0.083[b]	0.100
P9	0.089[b]	0.086	0.092[b]	0.082	0.102
P10	0.057	0.025	0.086	0.077	0.096
P11	0.064	0.066	0.063	0.066	0.059
P12	0.074	0.103[b]	0.047	0.040	0.054
		t statistics for average premiums			
P2	6.40	6.97	4.03	2.70	3.38
P3	6.40	7.17	4.21	3.42	3.15
P4	4.70	5.18	3.23	2.78	2.26
P5	4.14	5.12	2.64	2.43	1.78
P6	3.34	4.35	2.01	1.92	1.32
P7	2.75	3.68	1.50	1.58	0.90
P8	3.04	3.86	1.76	1.95	1.04
P9	2.59	3.27	1.49	1.69	0.88
P10	1.49	0.83	1.26	1.41	0.75
P11	1.54	2.09	0.83	1.10	0.42
P12	1.61	2.87	0.57	0.59	0.36
		t statistics for average values of $H\tau - H(\tau - 1)$			
$H3 - H2$	4.68	4.40	3.33	3.27	2.14
$H4 - H3$	1.05	0.08	1.10	1.58	0.42
$H5 - H4$	1.93	3.01	0.76	0.97	0.35
$H6 - H5$	−0.27	0.74	−0.79	−0.38	−0.69
$H7 - H6$	−0.72	0.81	−1.41	−0.33	−1.40
$H8 - H7$	3.20	2.32	2.40	2.35	1.43
$H9 - H8$	0.10	0.19	0.01	−0.13	0.07
$H10 - H9$	−4.15	−5.66	−0.50	−0.42	−0.33
$H11 - H10$	1.06	5.00	−2.41	−1.20	−2.10
$H12 - H11$	1.28	4.27	−1.41	−1.60	−0.34
		T^2 *tests for average premiums*			
T^2	130.41	152.59	69.33	49.64	56.37
F	11.29	12.48	5.72	3.69	4.18
P-level	1.00	1.00	1.00	0.9994	0.9998
		T^2 *tests for average values of* $H\tau - H(\tau - 1)$			
T^2	80.23	95.90	52.11	46.87	35.39
F	6.95	7.85	4.30	3.49	2.61
P-level	1.00	1.00	1.00	0.999	0.990

[a] Twelve-month bills are not available for eight months of the 1973–82 period, and ten- and eleven-month bills are each missing for one month. These months are deleted for all maturities.

[b] Largest average premium. Average premiums are multiplied by 100. Thus, they are percents per month.

Table 3

Average premiums, t statistics and T^2 tests for bond portfolios.

Portfolio number	Maturity range (months)	$N = 360$ 1953–82	$N = 60$ 1953–57	$N = 60$ 1958–62	$N = 60$ 1963–67	$N = 60$ 1968–72	$N = 60$ 1973–77	$N = 60$ 1978–82
				Average premiums				
1	$M < 6$	0.036	0.017	0.045	0.002[a]	0.040	0.051	0.063[a]
2	$6 \leq M < 12$	0.042	0.032	0.082	−0.008	0.062	0.049	0.034
3	$12 \leq M < 18$	0.048[a]	0.039	0.095	−0.013	0.069	0.062[a]	0.034
4	$18 \leq M < 24$	0.037	0.042	0.099	−0.036	0.072	0.040	0.002
5	$24 \leq M < 30$	0.026	0.066[a]	0.086	−0.053	0.060	0.050	−0.053
6	$30 \leq M < 36$	0.034	0.050	0.117	−0.066	0.093[a]	0.053	−0.044
7	$36 \leq M < 48$	0.012	0.046	0.120[a]	−0.082	0.041	0.028	−0.080
8	$48 \leq M < 60$	−0.024	0.043	0.059	−0.133	0.030	−0.029	−0.112
9	$60 \leq M < 120$	−0.012	0.052	0.085	−0.118	0.083	0.017	−0.190
10	$M \cong 240$	−0.128	0.015	0.001	−0.331	−0.032	−0.054	−0.068
				t statistics for average premiums				
1	$M < 6$	3.86	1.52	3.42	0.18	2.34	2.62	1.38
2	$6 \leq M < 12$	1.97	1.73	3.23	−0.50	1.54	1.07	0.32
3	$12 \leq M < 18$	1.47	1.29	1.94	−0.46	1.09	0.85	0.22
4	$18 \leq M < 24$	0.88	0.96	1.60	−0.89	0.78	0.45	0.01
5	$24 \leq M < 30$	0.53	1.19	1.20	−1.10	0.56	0.49	−0.22
6	$30 \leq M < 36$	0.60	0.78	1.33	−1.25	0.74	0.46	−0.16
7	$36 \leq M < 48$	0.18	0.65	1.14	−1.20	0.28	0.22	−0.26
8	$48 \leq M < 60$	−0.32	0.45	0.46	−1.61	0.18	−0.20	−0.32
9	$60 \leq M < 120$	−0.13	0.43	0.62	−1.11	0.39	0.10	−0.46
10	$M \cong 240$	−0.99	0.08	0.01	−1.84	−0.09	−0.20	−0.66
				t statistics for average differences between adjacent-maturity portfolio returns				
2 − 1		0.42	1.29	2.37	−0.80	0.78	−0.04	−0.43
3 − 2		0.43	0.41	0.43	−0.32	0.26	0.40	−0.00
4 − 3		−0.90	0.16	0.17	−1.46	0.07	−0.91	−0.69
5 − 4		−0.79	0.93	−0.64	−1.15	−0.42	0.33	−0.93
6 − 5		0.78	−0.68	1.19	−0.54	0.75	0.12	0.16
7 − 6		−1.33	−0.20	0.09	−0.60	−1.04	−0.64	−0.61
8 − 7		−1.52	−0.06	−1.58	−1.87	−0.18	−0.94	−0.33
9 − 8		0.34	0.17	0.51	0.33	0.46	0.46	−0.65
10 − 9		−1.72	−0.40	−0.98	−2.20	−0.47	−0.51	−0.72
				T^2 tests for average premiums				
T^2		36.80	8.96	22.45	14.79	13.99	17.50	13.03
F		3.59	0.76	1.90	1.25	1.19	1.48	1.10
P-level		0.9998	0.33	0.94	0.72	0.68	0.83	0.626
				T^2 tests for average differences between adjacent-maturity portfolio returns				
T^2		9.75	4.29	11.93	14.71	3.71	4.88	4.39
F		0.95	0.36	1.01	1.25	0.31	0.41	0.37
P-level		0.51	0.04	0.55	0.72	0.03	0.07	0.05

[a] Largest average premium. Average premiums are multiplied by 100. Thus, they are percents per month.

4.2. The behavior of average returns by maturity

4.2.1. Bills

It is impressive that the average premiums in the returns on two- to twelve-month bills in table 2 are all positive in all periods. Moreover, the maximum average return never occurs at a maturity less than five months.

The t statistics for the average values of $P2 = H2 - H1$ and $H\tau - H(\tau - 1)$, $\tau = 3, \ldots, 12$, allow us to make probability statements about the structure of expected bill returns as a function of maturity. The t statistics for the positive average values of $P2$, $H3 - H2$ and $H8 - H7$ for the overall sample period are well beyond the 0.95 fractile for t for Bonferroni probability statements about 11 means. The t statistic (1.93) for the average value of $H5 - H4$ is less impressive but nevertheless in the upper part of the right tail of the null distribution. On the other hand, the t statistic for the average value of $H10 - H9$ is negative (-4.15) and far into the left tail (below the 0.005 fractile) of the null distribution.[3]

The straightforward inference from the t statistics for the overall period is that there are expected premiums in the returns on multi-month bills, and they increase with maturity out to eight or nine months. The expected premium drops at ten months but shows no reliable movement thereafter.

The subperiod results support the conclusion that expected premiums increase out to eight or nine months, but the conclusion that expected returns on ten-month bills are lower than on nine-month bills becomes more anomalous. In the post-1972 subperiods the average premiums decline monotonically with maturity after nine months, but the average value of $P10$ is never much less than the average value of $P9$. The only period when the ten-month bill has a much lower average return than the nine-month bill is August 1964 to December 1972, but during this period the twelve-month bill provides the highest average return! In other words, most of the reliably negative average value of $H10 - H9$ observed for the overall sample period is due to a subperiod during which average returns show a 'bow' between nine and twelve months.

The behavior of ten-month bill returns during the pre-1973 period is not due to a few extreme monthly returns. A screen of the month-by-month returns indicates that during this period ten-month bills often have lower returns than nine- and twelve-month bills. Later we examine estimates of expected returns extracted from forward rates. These *ex ante* estimates confirm (but likewise do not explain) the bow observed between nine and twelve months in the *ex post* average returns of the pre-1973 period. The *ex ante* estimates of expected

[3] Since we also make probability statements about T^2 statistics for the vector of average premiums and the vector of average differences between adjacent maturity bill returns, strictly speaking we should use Bonferroni fractiles for tests on thirteen rather than eleven t statistics. This refinement has no effect on our inferences. A similar comment is relevant in the analysis of table 3.

returns from forward rates also confirm the downward slope of longer-maturity average bill returns observed during the 1973–82 period.

4.2.2. The bond portfolios

The bond portfolios cover longer maturities and a longer time period (1953–82) than the bill returns. The additional results from the bond portfolios in table 3 complement those for bills at the short end of the maturity spectrum, but the bond portfolios provide ambiguous evidence about the behavior of expected returns on longer-maturity instruments.

As noted earlier, the T^2 statistic for the vector of average bond return premiums rejects the hypothesis that expected premiums are all zero. Unlike bills, however, the T^2 test on the vector of average differences or spreads between returns on adjacent maturity bond portfolios is consistent with the hypothesis that expected premiums do not differ by maturity. These results are corroborated by the detailed evidence from the t statistics for the average return spreads. Using the Bonferroni fractiles in table 1 which are relevant when ten means are tested against zero, the average premium for the bond portfolio covering maturities up to six months is reliably greater than zero, but none of the other average differences between returns on adjacent maturity portfolios are reliably different from zero. Indeed, except for the two shortest maturity portfolios, none of the t statistics for average premiums for the 1953–82 period are large.[4]

The bond data are consistent with the hypothesis that the structure of expected premiums in bond portfolio returns is flat. The data are also consistent with a wide range of alternative hypotheses. For example, during the 1953–82 period the 20 year bond portfolio has an average premium of -0.00128 per month or about -1.5 percent per year. In univariate terms, this average premium is less than one standard error from zero. A positive average premium of the same magnitude would likewise be less than one standard error from zero – but it would be almost three times the maximum average premium observed among shorter-maturity portfolios.

Though the evidence lacks statistical precision, it is interesting that there is no five-year subperiod of the 1953–82 sample period during which average bond returns increase systematically with maturity. The shortest-maturity portfolio (< 6 months) produces the largest average return in two of the five-year subperiods. Average returns never peak in maturity intervals beyond four years. At least on an *ex post* basis, the thirty-year period 1953–82 was not propitious for long-term bonds.

[4]Since they are based on different assumptions about the relevant number of tests on means (unspecified for the T^2 statistic but specified under the Bonferroni approach), the T^2 and Bonferroni tests need not lead to the same inferences. This problem does not arise in our data.

4.2.3. The variability of returns by maturity

The obvious source of the imprecision of inferences about expected returns on longer-term bonds – high return variability – is documented in table 4. The standard deviation of the longest-term bond return premiums, 2.47 percent per month, is about fourteen times the standard deviation of the premiums for the shortest-maturity (up to six months) bond portfolio, 0.18 percent per month. Even the bond portfolio covering the eighteen- to twenty-four-month maturity range produces premiums more than four times as variable as the shortest-maturity portfolio.

The standard deviations of the differences or spreads between adjacent-maturity bill returns and adjacent-maturity bond portfolio returns show even more clearly why inferences about expected bill returns are more precise than

Table 4

Standard deviations of premiums and differences between adjacent-maturity bill and bond portfolio returns.[a]

8/64–12/82		1953–82		
Bill (1)	Std. dev. bills (2)	Bond portfolio number (3)	Maturity range (months) (4)	Std. dev. bonds (5)
		Premiums		
P2	0.07	1	$M < 6$	0.18
P3	0.13	2	$6 \leq M < 12$	0.40
P4	0.19	3	$12 \leq M < 18$	0.62
P5	0.26	4	$18 \leq M < 24$	0.79
P6	0.32	5	$24 \leq M < 30$	0.93
P7	0.36	6	$30 \leq M < 36$	1.08
P8	0.42	7	$36 \leq M < 48$	1.23
P9	0.50	8	$48 \leq M < 60$	1.42
P10	0.56	9	$60 \leq M < 120$	1.70
P11	0.61	10	$M \cong 240$	2.47
P12	0.67			
		Differences between adjacent-maturity returns		
$H3 - H2$	0.08	$2 - 1$		0.26
$H4 - H3$	0.08	$3 - 2$		0.26
$H5 - H4$	0.09	$4 - 3$		0.24
$H6 - H5$	0.08	$5 - 4$		0.25
$H7 - H6$	0.08	$6 - 5$		0.27
$H8 - H7$	0.09	$7 - 6$		0.31
$H9 - H8$	0.10	$8 - 7$		0.44
$H10 - H9$	0.11	$9 - 8$		0.67
$H11 - H10$	0.10	$10 - 9$		1.29
$H12 - H11$	0.11			

[a] The standard deviations for bills in column (2) and those for the bond portfolios in column (5) should be read as percents per month.

inferences about expected bond returns. Bill return premiums have low absolute variability, but the premium on a twelve-month bill is nevertheless about nine times more variable than the premium on a two-month bill. Because of the high correlation of adjacent maturity bill returns, however, $H12 - H11$ is only about forty percent more variable than $P2 = H2 - H1$. Positive correlation between adjacent maturity portfolio returns also causes the standard deviations of bond portfolio return spreads to increase less rapidly with maturity than the standard deviations of premiums, but the standard deviations of bond portfolio return spreads are nevertheless large relative to those for adjacent-maturity bills. For example, the standard deviation of the difference between the return on the longest-term bonds and the bond portfolio that includes five- to ten-year maturities is 1.29 percent per month, whereas the standard deviation of the difference between the returns on twelve- and eleven-month bills is only 0.11 percent per month.

4.3. Simple versus continuously compounded returns

The continuously compounded monthly returns used in the preceding tests are always less than simple returns. Since the variances of returns increase with maturity, we can predict that the differences between average simple and continuously compounded returns increase with maturity. Thus, the tendency for average premiums in bill returns to peak at eight or nine months, and the low average returns on longer-term bonds, may be due to the use of continuously compounded returns. Finally, one can interpret the arguments in Cox, Ingersoll and Ross (1981) as calling for simple returns in tests for the existence of premiums.

Table 5 shows average premiums calculated from simple returns for the overall sample periods covered by the bills and by the bond portfolios. Average premiums calculated from continuously compounded returns are also shown. The simple average premiums are always larger than the continuously compounded average premiums, and the differences indeed increase with maturity. However, for bills the differences are trivial even at the longest maturities (the largest is 0.3 basis points per month), and they are small even for the longest-maturity bond portfolios. The use of simple returns does not change the maturities that produce the largest average returns (9 months for bills and 12–18 months for the bond portfolios). The use of simple returns also has no effect of consequence on the t statistics for average premiums and average spreads between adjacent maturity returns.

5. Estimates of expected bill premiums from forward rates

Prices of longer-maturity bills and bonds move opposite to interest rates, and changes in interest rates are on average positive during the sample period.

Table 5

Comparisons of average premiums, t statistics and T^2 tests for continuously compounded and simple returns.

Bill	$N = 211$[a] 8/64–12/82 Continuous	Simple	Portfolio number	Maturity range (months)	$N = 360$ 1953–82 Continuous	Simple
			Average premiums			
P2	0.032	0.032	1	$M < 6$	0.036	0.036
P3	0.057	0.058	2	$6 \leq M < 12$	0.042	0.043
P4	0.063	0.063	3	$12 \leq M < 18$	0.048[b]	0.050[b]
P5	0.074	0.075	4	$18 \leq M < 24$	0.037	0.040
P6	0.073	0.074	5	$24 \leq M < 30$	0.026	0.031
P7	0.069	0.070	6	$30 \leq M < 36$	0.034	0.040
P8	0.088	0.090	7	$36 \leq M < 48$	0.012	0.020
P9	0.089[b]	0.091[b]	8	$48 \leq M < 60$	−0.024	−0.014
P10	0.057	0.059	9	$60 \leq M < 120$	−0.012	0.003
P11	0.064	0.067	10	$M \cong 240$	−0.128	−0.098
P12	0.074	0.077				
			t statistics for average premiums			
P2	6.40	6.38	1	$M < 6$	3.86	3.87
P3	6.40	6.38	2	$6 \leq M < 12$	1.97	2.00
P4	4.70	4.69	3	$12 \leq M < 18$	1.47	1.52
P5	4.14	4.14	4	$18 \leq M < 24$	0.88	0.95
P6	3.34	3.34	5	$24 \leq M < 30$	0.53	0.61
P7	2.75	2.77	6	$30 \leq M < 36$	0.60	0.69
P8	3.04	3.05	7	$36 \leq M < 48$	0.18	0.30
P9	2.59	2.61	8	$48 \leq M < 60$	−0.32	−0.18
P10	1.49	1.52	9	$60 \leq M < 120$	−0.13	0.03
P11	1.54	1.57	10	$M \cong 240$	−0.99	−0.75
P12	1.61	1.65				
			t statistics for average differences between adjacent-maturity returns			
H3 − H2	4.68	4.68	2 − 1		0.42	0.47
H4 − H3	1.05	1.07	3 − 2		0.43	0.51
H5 − H4	1.93	1.95	4 − 3		−0.90	−0.80
H6 − H5	−0.27	−0.24	5 − 4		−0.79	−0.70
H7 − H6	−0.72	−0.69	6 − 5		0.78	0.65
H8 − H7	3.20	3.23	7 − 6		−1.33	−1.23
H9 − H8	0.10	0.15	8 − 7		−1.52	−1.39
H10 − H9	−4.15	−4.10	9 − 8		0.34	0.46
H11 − H10	1.06	1.09	10 − 9		−1.72	−1.48
H12 − H11	1.28	1.33				
			T^2 test for average premiums			
T^2	130.41	129.48			36.80	35.24
F	11.29	11.21			3.59	3.44
P-level	1.00	1.00			0.9998	0.9997
			T^2 tests for average differences between adjacent-maturity returns			
T^2	80.23	79.45			9.75	8.53
F	6.95	6.88			0.95	0.83
P-level	1.00	1.00			0.51	0.40

[a] Twelve-month bills are not available for eight months of the 1973–82 period, and ten- and eleven-month bills are each missing for one month. These months are deleted for all maturities.

[b] Largest average premium. Average premiums should be read as percents per month.

A common claim of readers faced with the results above is that the higher sensitivity of returns on longer-term instruments to unexpected upward shifts in the level of interest rates explains their lower average realized returns.

One way to purge the effects of unexpected shifts in the term structure from estimates of expected premiums is to estimate expected premiums from forward rates. This approach can only be applied to bills since good estimates of forward rates are not possible for our (mixed maturity) bond portfolios.

5.1. Spot and forward interest rates

Define $V\tau_t$ as the price at time t (the end of month t) of a bill that has τ months to maturity at t and pays \$1 for certain at the end of month $t+\tau$. Define R_{t+1}, the one-month spot rate of interest from t to $t+1$, observed in the market at t, as

$$V1_t = \exp(-R_{t+1}). \tag{2}$$

The price $V\tau_t$ can then be expressed as

$$V\tau_t = \exp(-R_{t+1} - F2_t - \cdots - F\tau_t), \tag{3}$$

where $F\tau_t$, the forward rate for month $t+\tau$ observed at t, is

$$F\tau_t \equiv \ln(V(\tau-1)_t / V\tau_t). \tag{4}$$

Note that the spot rate R_{t+1} and the forward rates $F2_t, \ldots, F\tau_t$ can be calculated from bill prices observed in the market at time t.

Fama (1976b) shows that forward rates can be expressed as

$$\begin{aligned} F\tau_t = {} & \mathrm{E}_t(P\tau_{t+1}) + [\mathrm{E}_t(P(\tau-1)_{t+2}) - \mathrm{E}_t(P(\tau-1)_{t+1})] + \cdots \\ & + [\mathrm{E}_t(P2_{t+\tau-1}) - \mathrm{E}_t(P2_{t+\tau-2})] + \mathrm{E}_t(R_{t+\tau}), \end{aligned} \tag{5}$$

where E_t indicates an expected value at time t. Thus, the forward rate for month $t+\tau$, observed at t, contains $\mathrm{E}_t(R_{t+\tau})$, the expected value of the future spot rate for month $t+\tau$. The forward rate also contains $\mathrm{E}_t(P\tau_{t+1})$, the expected premium in the return on a τ-month bill from t to $t+1$, and current expected changes in future premiums.

Table 6 shows average values of $F\tau_t - R_{t+1}$, $\tau = 2, \ldots, 12$, for various periods of the twelve-month bill file. Forward rates are calculated from (4) and are adjusted to a 30.4 day monthly basis, as described in Fama (1984). The time t spot rate is subtracted from the time t forward rate to focus better on the expected premium component of $F\tau_t$. That is, although the expected

Table 6

Comparisons of average premiums (P_T) and average differences between contemporaneous forward and spot rates ($F_T - R$).

Maturity	8/64–12/82		8/64–12/72		1/73–12/82		1/73–12/77		1/78–12/82	
T	P_T	$F_T - R$	P_T	$F_T - R$	P_T	$F_T - R$	P_T	$F_T - R$	P_T	$F_T - R$
					Average values					
2	0.032	0.033	0.028	0.029	0.035	0.036	0.016	0.019	0.056	0.054
3	0.057	0.058	0.045	0.048	0.067	0.068	0.042	0.050	0.094	0.087
4	0.063	0.066	0.046	0.050	0.078	0.081	0.056	0.067	0.101	0.096
5	0.074	0.081	0.061	0.067	0.086	0.094	0.065	0.076	0.108[a]	0.112[a]
6	0.073	0.082	0.066	0.073	0.079	0.090	0.062	0.074	0.097	0.106
7	0.069	0.081	0.071	0.079	0.067	0.082	0.060	0.074	0.074	0.090
8	0.088	0.100	0.084	0.095	0.091	0.104	0.083[a]	0.098	0.100	0.110
9	0.089[a]	0.101[a]	0.086	0.097	0.092[a]	0.105[a]	0.082	0.099[a]	0.102	0.110
10	0.057	0.073	0.025	0.038	0.086	0.105[a]	0.077	0.099[a]	0.096	0.112[a]
11	0.064	0.082	0.066	0.080	0.063	0.084	0.066	0.091	0.059	0.077
12	0.074	0.097	0.103[a]	0.118[a]	0.047	0.078	0.040	0.085	0.054	0.070
					t statistics for average values of P_T and $F_T - R$					
2	6.40	8.60	6.97	6.66	4.03	5.93	2.70	5.66	3.38	4.69
3	6.40	13.77	7.17	12.34	4.21	9.46	3.42	9.45	3.15	6.59
4	4.70	14.50	5.18	12.23	3.23	10.63	2.78	15.00	2.26	6.56
5	4.14	14.40	5.12	10.72	2.64	10.44	2.43	9.14	1.78	7.06
6	3.34	14.29	4.35	11.42	2.01	9.72	1.92	8.81	1.32	6.44
7	2.75	12.44	3.68	12.07	1.50	7.51	1.58	9.48	0.90	4.33
8	3.04	17.92	3.86	15.22	1.76	11.55	1.95	10.43	1.04	7.06
9	2.59	16.41	3.27	14.58	1.49	10.35	1.69	11.27	0.88	5.95
10	1.49	10.07	0.83	4.73	1.26	9.59	1.41	7.99	0.75	6.08
11	1.54	12.92	2.09	10.88	0.83	8.26	1.10	7.95	0.42	4.52
12	1.61	12.63	2.87	12.86	0.57	6.57	0.59	5.49	0.36	3.88
					t statistics for average values of $H_T - H(T-1)$ and $F_T - F(T-1)$					
3 – 2	4.68	7.12	4.40	3.77	3.33	6.23	3.27	5.32	2.14	3.85
4 – 3	1.05	2.05	0.08	0.39	1.10	2.28	1.58	3.13	0.42	0.89
5 – 4	1.93	3.18	3.01	2.71	0.76	1.85	0.97	1.26	0.35	1.36
6 – 5	−0.27	0.19	0.74	0.78	−0.79	−0.56	−0.38	−0.24	−0.69	−0.51
7 – 6	−0.72	−0.17	0.81	0.78	−1.41	−0.85	−0.33	0.01	−1.40	−0.94
8 – 7	3.20	3.55	2.32	2.36	2.40	2.67	2.35	2.92	1.43	1.38
9 – 8	0.10	0.34	0.19	0.39	0.01	0.12	−0.13	0.11	0.07	0.06
10 – 9	−4.15	−3.96	−5.66	−5.41	−0.50	0.05	−0.42	−0.01	−0.33	0.07
11 – 10	1.06	1.20	5.00	3.83	−2.41	−2.57	−1.20	−0.74	−2.10	−2.98
12 – 11	1.28	2.08	4.27	3.69	−1.41	−0.68	−1.60	−0.41	−0.34	−0.57

[a]Largest average value. Means should be read as percents per month.

changes in future premiums and the expected change in the spot rate $E(R_{t+\tau}) - R_{t+1}$ in $F\tau_t - R_{t+1}$ can vary from month to month, over long sample periods, the average values of these expected changes should be close to zero. Thus, the average value of $F\tau_t - R_{t+1}$ should be close to the average value of the expected premium $E_t(P\tau_{t+1})$ in $F\tau_t$.

In setting up the comparisons in table 6, my strong prior was that the averages of $F\tau_t - R_{t+1}$ would increase monotonically with τ in all periods and allow us to infer the effects of unexpected shifts in the term structure in explaining the typically non-monotonic behavior of the average values of the premiums. Table 6 indicates, however, that the market's expectations are realized while mine are not. The average values of $F\tau_t - R_{t+1}$ and $P\tau_{t+1}$ peak at the same or adjacent maturities. This is true for the overall sample period and, perhaps more impressive, it is also true for every subperiod. The average values of $F\tau_t - R_{t+1}$ also replicate most of the details of the behavior of the average values of $P\tau_{t+1}$, for example, the bow in the average values of $P\tau_{t+1}$ observed for the nine- to twelve-month maturities during the August 1964 to December 1972 period.

The estimates of expected premiums from forward rates do not alter the general view obtained from average premiums, but the picture from the forward rates is more precise. Because the forward rate spreads, $F\tau_t - R_{t+1}$ and $F\tau_t - F(\tau - 1)_t$, are less variable than the realized premiums, $P\tau_{t+1}$, and return spreads, $H\tau_{t+1} - H(\tau - 1)_{t+1}$, the t statistics for the average values of $F\tau_t - R_{t+1}$ and $F\tau_t - F(\tau - 1)_t$ are generally larger in absolute value than those for the means of $P\tau_{t+1}$ and $H\tau_{t+1} - H(\tau - 1)_{t+1}$. As a consequence, the t statistics from the forward rate estimates for the overall sample period in table 6 provide stronger indications that expected returns on bills increase with maturity up to eight or nine months. However, the t statistic for the average value of $F10 - F9$ also reinforces the conclusion that during the overall sample period, the expected return on a ten-month bill is reliably less than that for a nine-month bill.

The straightforward inference from table 6 is that expected returns on bills do not increase monotonically with maturity. The one period (August 1964 to December 1972) when twelve-month bills produce the largest average values of $P\tau_{t+1}$ and $F\tau_t - R_{t+1}$ nevertheless shows a curious dip in the two averages for the ten- and eleven-month maturities. For all other subperiods and for the overall sample period, the largest average values of $P\tau_{t+1}$ and $F\tau_t - R_{t+1}$ occur at ten months or less.

6. Conclusions

This paper examines expected returns on U.S. Treasury bills and U.S. Government bond portfolios that cover the maturity spectrum.

Expected bill returns are estimated from forward rates and from sample average returns. Both estimation methods indicate that expected returns on bills tend to peak at eight or nine months and never increase monotonically out to twelve months. Since the estimates of expected premiums from *ex ante* forward rates peak at the same maturities as the *ex post* average premiums, the non-monotonicity of the average premiums cannot be attributed to unexpected shifts in the term structure.

During the five-year subperiods of 1953–82 covered by our bond portfolios, bonds with maturities greater than four years never have the highest average returns. During periods where the bond file overlaps with the twelve-month bill file, the highest average return on a bond portfolio never exceeds the highest average return on a bill. We cannot conclude, however, that longer-term bonds have lower expected returns than short-term instruments. The high variability of longer-term bond returns preempts precise conclusions about their expected returns. The bond data are consistent with maturity structures of expected returns that are flat, upward sloping or downward sloping beyond a year. Thus, longer-maturity bond portfolios do not provide much evidence on the behavior of expected returns.

The non-monotonicity of expected bill returns documented here is inconsistent with either the pure expectations hypothesis or the liquidity preference hypothesis of the classical term structure literature. However, it is not necessarily inconsistent with the more sophisticated models of capital market equilibrium of Sharpe (1964), Lintner (1965), Merton (1973) or Breeden (1979). I offer no direct tests. Rather, the descriptive evidence presented here, and the evidence or rich patterns of variation through time in expected bill returns presented by Fama (1984), Startz (1982) and others, stand as challenges or 'stylized facts' to be explained by candidate models.

References

Breeden, Douglas T., 1979, An intertemporal asset pricing model with stochastic consumption and investment opportunities, Journal of Financial Economics 7, 265–296.

Cox, John C., Jonathan E. Ingersoll, Jr. and Stephen A. Ross, 1981, A reexamination of traditional hypotheses about the term structure of interest rates, Journal of Finance 36, 769–799.

Fama, Eugene F., 1976a, Forward rates as predictors of future spot rates, Journal of Financial Economics 3, 361–377.

Fama, Eugene F., 1976b, Inflation uncertainty and expected returns on treasury bills, Journal of Political Economy 84, 427–448.

Fama, Eugene F., 1984, The information in the term structure, Journal of Financial Economics, this issue.

Ibbotson, Roger G. and Rex A. Sinquefield, 1983, Stocks, bonds, bills and inflation: The past and the future (Financial Analysts Research Foundation, Charlottesville, VA).

Kessel, Reuben A., 1965, The cylical behavior of the term structure of interest rates, National Bureau of Economic Research occasional paper no. 91.

Lintner, John, 1965, The valuation of risk assets and the selection of risky investments in stock portfolios and capital budgets, Review of Economics and Statistics 47, 13–27.

McCulloch, J. Huston, 1975, An estimate of the liquidity premium, Journal of Political Economy 83, 95–119.

Meiselman, David, 1962, The term structure of interest rates (Prentice-Hall, Englewood Cliffs, NJ).

Merton, Robert C., Jr., 1973, An intertemporal capital asset pricing model, Econometrica 41, 867–887.

Miller, Rupert G., Jr. 1981, Simultaneous statistical inference (Springer-Verlag, New York).

Morrison, Donald F., 1976, Multivariate statistical methods (McGraw-Hill, New York).

Roll, Richard, 1970, The behavior of interest rates (Basic Books, New York).

Roy, S.N. and R.C. Bose, 1953, Simultaneous confidence interval estimation, Annals of Mathematical Statistics 24, 513–536.

Sharpe, William F., 1964, Capital asset prices: A theory of market equilibrium under conditions of risk, Journal of Finance 19, 425–442.

Startz, Richard, 1982, Do forecast errors or term premia really make the difference between long and short rates?, Journal of Financial Economics 10, 323–329.

[12]

MODELING THE TERM STRUCTURE OF INTEREST RATES IN JAPAN

TADASHI KIKUGAWA AND KENNETH J. SINGLETON

The term structure of interest rates on Japanese government bonds (JGBs) is shaped by several important institutional forces that have arisen, in part, out of the historical development of Japanese markets.

Most of the daily volume in the JGB market represents trading in one bond, the benchmark. Furthermore, because of various accounting conventions and because insurance companies pay policyholder dividends from coupon and not capital gain income, bonds with identical maturities and different coupon rates may trade at notably different bond-equivalent yields. These differences are much greater than can be explained by differences in durations of these bonds, and they suggest that the market is effectively using different discount functions to value the associated cash flows of bonds with different coupon rates.

Equally challenging from the point of view of model evaluation using historical data is the fact that liberalization of financial markets in Japan during the past two decades has resulted in the introduction of many new securities and changes in the composition of investors within existing markets. Thus, an assumption of stationary distributions for returns over extended periods of time may not be tenable.

In light of these complications, the application of traditional term structure models to the JGB markets has been limited, and researchers instead have often pursued a descriptive approach to understanding JGB yield movements. They have focused attention on the correlations between short- and long-term rates with other variables, and on the properties of vector autoregressive representations of yields.

For instance, the Bank of Japan [1986, 1988] and Kool and Tatom [1988] estimate forecast equations for

TADASHI KIKUGAWA is vice president in the fixed income research group at Goldman Sachs (Japan) Ltd. in Tokyo.

KENNETH J. SINGLETON is vice president in the fixed income research group at Goldman Sachs (Japan) Ltd., and professor of finance at the Graduate School of Business of Stanford University in Stanford, California.

long-term bond yields based on contemporaneous and lagged values of Japanese interest rates and other domestic and foreign macroeconomic variables. Singleton [1990] examines time series models of both the means and variances of long- and short-term bond yields in Japan, placing primary emphasis on the relations between the volatilities of long- and short-term rates.

As Japanese financial markets have been liberalized and further integrated with other foreign government bond markets, JGB yields have increasingly moved sympathetically with yields in the United States and Europe. Therefore, it is natural to ask whether the term structure models that have been widely applied to other markets might now be usefully applied to the JGB markets. General equilibrium or "arbitrage-free" models of the term structure, which have been widely used for the U.S. Treasury market, have not been extensively applied to Japanese data in the published literature. (See, for example, Cox, Ingersoll, and Ross [1985], Ho and Lee [1986], or Heath, Jarrow, and Morton [1990].)

On the other hand, Shikano [1985], Shirakawa [1987], and Campbell and Hamao [1992] investigate whether various versions of the expectations theory of the term structure are useful for explaining changes in JGB yields. These studies typically reject the restrictions implied by the expectations theory, although Campbell and Hamao show that short-term rates do have considerable explanatory power for the spreads between long- and short-term yields. Furthermore, the explanatory power of these expectations models appears to have increased over time, which is consistent with the increased liberalization of the Japanese markets.

Though liberalization has been extensive, illiquidity, coupon effects, and other institutional features of JGB markets continue to be important ingredients in the price discovery process in Japan. Therefore, we proceed largely in the first tradition and attempt to document further the empirical properties of the JGB yield curve with the goal of better understanding how the "market" sets prices of JGBs.

Specifically, we investigate the distributional properties of bond-equivalent yields on bonds that were benchmark bonds (the "benchmark yield curve").[1] There is a marked change in the autocorrelation pattern of ex-benchmark bonds at #99: Changes in yields of bonds with longer maturities are nearly serially uncorrelated, while those of bonds with shorter maturities evidence substantial autocorrelation. Furthermore, the volatilities of JGB yields have the interesting pattern of being relatively low for short-maturity ex-benchmarks. We interpret both of these findings, which are notably different from the comparable statistics for the U.S. Treasury market, in terms of the relative liquidities of the various bonds.

While the average trading volumes of long- and short-term ex-benchmark bonds differ, these differences are small compared with the differences between all ex-benchmarks and the current benchmark. Thus, to a significant degree, all bonds are illiquid relative to the current benchmark.

There is, however, another very liquid market in Japan — namely, the ten-year futures contract. In Section II we argue that in response to the difficulty of effective price discovery with little depth and trading volume, the market has assigned a central role to the futures in pricing cash bonds. Indeed, over prolonged periods during 1992, the prices on the bonds that were deliverable into the futures contract were approximately equal to their conversion factor-adjusted futures prices.

Variations in price discovery mechanisms along the yield curve and over time, as well as the persistence and high kurtoses of bond yields for certain sectors, result in part from the accounting and regulatory guidelines in Japan. Our analysis suggests that these institutional forces continue to have significant effects on JGB yields and, therefore, that assessments of relative value within the JGB market should take explicit account of these elements.

A key feature of our JGB yield curve model is its adjustment of prices for coupon and par effects in the process of computing fitted yields. Moreover, it chooses the fitted yields such that the deviations between fitted and actual yields are informative about future yield levels.

II. TIME SERIES PROPERTIES OF YIELDS ON EX-BENCHMARK BONDS

We begin our empirical analysis by investigating some of the distributional properties of the yields on ex-benchmark JGBs that a term structure theory should explain. We focus attention on the ex-benchmark yields and #99, because these are often the relatively more liquid bonds, and they increasingly serve as the sectoral benchmarks for the respective nearby bonds.[2]

Our sample period extends from the end of

April 1990 through the end of May 1992; we look at daily, end-of-week, and end-of-month data (513, 110, and 26 observations, respectively). In all cases, we examine the properties of the first difference in the logarithm of the bond-equivalent yield.

The term structure of volatilities (annualized standard deviations of changes in the logarithms of yields) is presented in the column headed "V" in Exhibit 1 and graphed in Exhibit 2. For the daily sampling interval, the volatilities are approximately flat from #53 to #89 at about 8%, then increase to between 11% and 12% for #99 through the recent benchmark #129, and finally decline again for the super-long bonds S02 and S10. This pattern differs from the generally downward-sloping volatility curve found in the U.S. Treasury market.

To interpret this finding, note that #99 through #129 were deliverable into the JGB futures for at least part of our sample period. In addition, these bonds have consistently been more readily available in the market and have therefore registered relatively larger trading volumes.

These two observations are not independent, as deliverability into the futures implies that the price risk on the bond may be effectively hedged with the ten-year JGB futures contract, which is the primary hedging instrument for the entire JGB market. Although #99 through #111 recently have not been deliverable into the futures, they have maintained their relative liquidity.

The shorter-term ex-benchmark bonds are, on the other hand, relatively illiquid, as are the super-long bonds. Thus, it seems that the relatively illiquid bonds are also those with low volatilities of yield changes.

In Exhibit 3 and in the column headed "K" in Exhibit 1, we show the kurtoses of the yield changes (which measure the thickness of the tails of the distributions). The most striking feature of Exhibit 3 is the very large kurtoses for daily changes in #53 through #78 that shrink to virtually the same levels of change as all other bonds in the monthly data.

Exhibit 3 suggests that, for daily data, the yield distribution for the short-term bonds has much fatter tails than the normal distribution (which has a kurtosis of 3). Consequently, there are larger probabilities of daily changes in yields that are away from the mean change.

A plausible interpretation of these findings is that, because of thin and infrequent trading in these bonds, recorded prices may not in fact be transaction prices. When trades do occur, the yield changes may be quite large, as recorded prices "catch up" with underlying changes in value.

Over weekly and monthly intervals, on the other hand, the recorded yield changes are likely to be large compared with mismeasurement resulting from infrequent trading. Therefore, large differences in kurtosis across bonds would not be induced by such measurement problems.

Next, we estimate first-order autoregressive representations of the yield changes.[3] Exhibit 4 displays the coefficient of determination (R-squared), and Exhibit 5 shows the autoregressive coefficient (b). The tabulated results are in columns five through eight (R^2, b, e, and T) in Exhibit 1.

For the relatively liquid #99 through #129, the estimated values of b are small and insignificantly different from zero. The U.S. Treasury market shows similarly low autocorrelations for changes in the on-the-run bond yields. In contrast, the more illiquid short-term and super-long bonds have both larger autocorrelation coefficients and higher coefficients of determination.

The significant autocorrelations of the short-term bond yields explain the changes in shape of the term structure of volatilities in Exhibit 2 as the sampling interval is increased. Annualized daily volatilities understate the yield volatility when there is positive autocorrelation in the process, since the correlations between consecutive yield changes are not counted.

With monthly data, these cross-correlations are included out to one month, so the monthly volatilities would be expected to be larger. The autocorrelations for monthly data are similar to those reported by Campbell and Hamao [1992] over a longer sample period.

Anecdotal evidence suggests that the prices of the illiquid short-term bonds remain in a narrow trading range for periods of time, but that when they do move in one direction, there is a tendency for volume to increase and for there to be trading pressure on prices in the same direction. The positive autocorrelation reflects such tendencies.

Another way of summarizing this notion is to calculate the proportion of times that positive yield changes are followed by positive ones and negative yield changes by negative ones. We display this "same direction ratio" in the last column of Exhibit 1. In the absence of persistence, this ratio should be 50%, but it is about 17% larger for bonds #53 through #78 and over 7% larger for #89 and the super-longs.

EXHIBIT 1 ■ Time Series Properties ■ Log Change of Bond-Equivalent Yield (April 27, 1990–May 29, 1992)

Maturity	Issue Number	V (%)	K	R^2	b	e	T	SDR (%)
Daily Data								
01/20/93	53	8.42	10.05	0.161	0.401	0.041	9.86	65.07
12/20/93	59	8.17	10.49	0.214	0.462	0.039	11.76	67.51
12/20/94	68	8.13	7.53	0.159	0.399	0.041	9.80	67.23
07/20/95	78	8.11	8.21	0.157	0.397	0.041	9.75	67.03
06/20/96	89	8.50	4.97	0.076	0.275	0.043	6.45	57.45
06/20/97	99	10.44	4.76	0.007	0.082	0.044	1.84	50.33
12/22/97	105	11.42	4.97	0.002	0.039	0.044	0.89	50.75
06/22/98	111	11.52	4.89	0.000	0.011	0.044	0.25	50.32
06/21/99	119	11.66	4.54	0.000	0.006	0.044	0.14	49.26
03/20/00	129	11.35	4.62	0.002	0.045	0.044	1.00	50.31
03/20/07	S02	6.70	5.27	0.034	0.184	0.044	4.22	57.48
03/20/09	S10	6.12	5.06	0.029	0.170	0.044	3.88	58.66
Weekly Data								
01/20/93	53	12.71	4.53	0.162	0.401	0.089	4.51	70.48
12/20/93	59	12.35	5.23	0.159	0.399	0.089	4.46	75.24
12/20/94	68	11.70	3.72	0.152	0.388	0.090	4.34	71.03
07/20/95	78	11.64	3.32	0.140	0.373	0.090	4.14	74.77
06/20/96	89	10.94	3.73	0.044	0.205	0.093	2.20	59.81
06/20/97	99	11.11	3.75	0.008	0.086	0.093	0.92	55.14
12/22/97	105	11.68	3.68	0.000	0.010	0.095	0.11	51.40
06/22/98	111	11.57	4.08	0.000	0.013	0.094	0.14	49.53
06/21/99	119	11.60	4.55	0.001	0.036	0.095	0.38	55.14
03/20/00	129	12.06	4.11	0.000	0.019	0.096	0.20	55.14
03/20/07	S02	8.47	3.15	0.172	0.412	0.088	4.67	59.81
03/20/09	S10	7.70	2.86	0.200	0.444	0.087	5.13	60.75
Monthly Data								
01/20/1993	53	19.58	2.18	0.020	0.143	0.211	0.68	62.50
12/20/1993	59	19.39	2.32	0.052	0.230	0.209	1.10	62.50
12/20/1994	68	17.65	2.46	0.082	0.282	0.202	1.40	62.50
07/20/1995	78	17.46	2.13	0.077	0.276	0.203	1.36	62.50
06/20/1996	89	14.85	2.30	0.110	0.316	0.192	1.65	70.83
12/22/1997	105	14.20	2.63	0.033	0.174	0.202	0.86	58.33
06/22/1998	111	14.05	2.36	0.022	0.146	0.204	0.72	58.33
06/21/1999	119	14.49	2.08	0.003	0.054	0.210	0.26	58.33
03/20/2000	129	14.80	2.10	0.023	0.148	0.203	0.73	58.33
03/20/2007	S02	13.65	2.36	0.055	0.220	0.196	1.13	58.33
03/20/2009	S10	12.70	1.99	0.033	0.175	0.201	0.87	50.00

V = Annualized Volatility
K = Kurtosis
R^2 = Coefficient of Determination (R-squared)
b = Autoregressive Coefficient (beta)
e = Standard Error of Beta
T = T-Statistic
SDR = Same Direction Ratio

EXHIBIT 2 ■ Term Structure of Volatility (April 27, 1990–May 29, 1992)

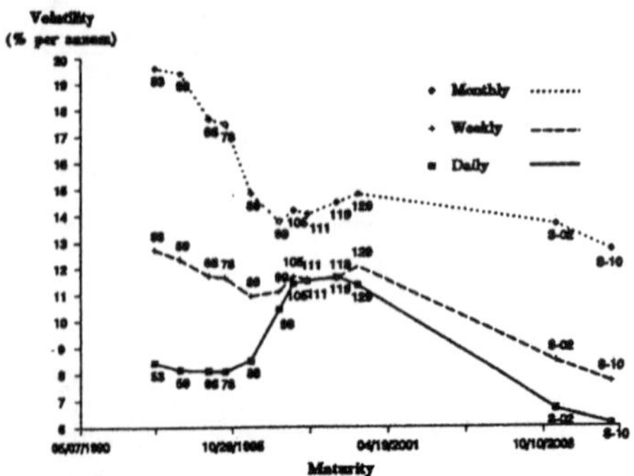

III. RELATION BETWEEN FUTURES PRICES AND YIELDS ON DELIVERABLE JGB BONDS

Our analysis suggests that the ten-year area of the JGB yield curve is most like the corresponding sector of the U.S. Treasury curve, in that volatilities are comparable, and there is little evidence of autocorrelation in yield changes. At first glance, these similarities suggest that term structure models developed for the United States and other markets may be applicable to this sector of the JGB curve.

Yet there are a priori reasons for doubting such applicability. Perhaps the most important reason is that the off-the-run bonds in the ten-year sector, although relatively liquid, have trading volumes that are small fractions of the benchmark's volume. In addition, it remains very expensive to short JGBs, so the shifts along the curve to take advantage of apparent mispricing — which are presumed in arbitrage-free term structure relations — may be costly to implement in Japan.

On the other hand, market participants do have access to another very liquid market in this sector: the JGB futures market. We argue that the futures market is

EXHIBIT 3 ■ Term Structure of Kurtosis (April 27, 1990–May 29, 1992)

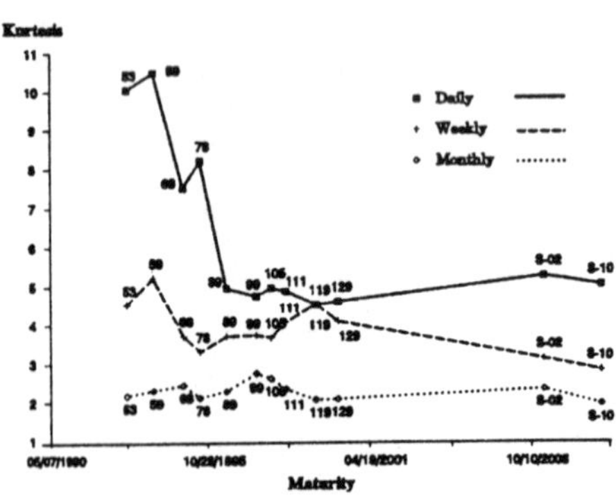

EXHIBIT 4 ■ Term Structure of Autocorrelation ■ Coefficients of Determination (April 27, 1990–May 29, 1992)

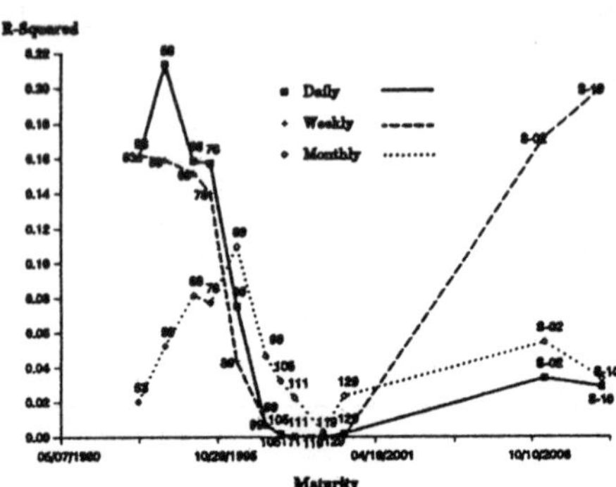

EXHIBIT 5 ■ Term Structure of Autocorrelation ■ Autocorrelation Coefficients (April 27, 1990–May 29, 1992)

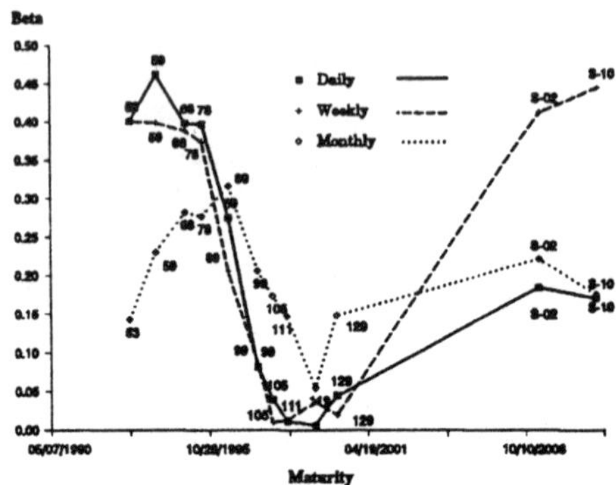

EXHIBIT 6 ■ Deliverable Yield Curve (March 1992 JGB Futures Contract)

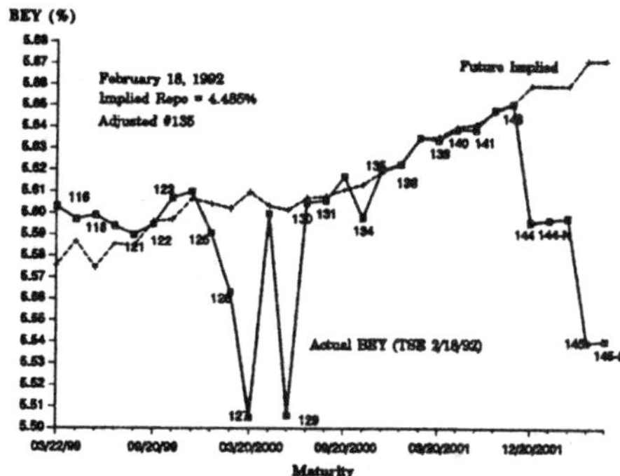

central to the pricing of bonds that are deliverable into the futures. This observation explains the relatively low autocorrelations of yield changes in this sector, since the JGB futures market is among the most liquid in the world. However, the implied term structure model is not one of the standard term structure models commonly used in, say, the United States.

To illustrate the role of futures in pricing cash instruments, we compare the actual bond-equivalent yields (BEYs) of the deliverable bonds with their counterparts implied by futures for the pricing dates February 18, 1992, and July 16, 1992. (See Asay, Kikugawa, and Singleton [1992] for a more extensive discussion of the role of futures in pricing cash bonds and some additional evidence.)

We compute the BEYs based on the futures prices as follows. We discount the closing futures price on each day by the implied repo rate of #135, we scale the discounted price by the conversion factors of the deliverable bonds, and then we compute the implied BEYs. In Exhibits 6 and 7, we display these BEYs using a plus sign (dashed line) and the actual BEYs based on TSE closing prices using a square (solid line).

Although #135 was not the cheapest-to-deliver bond on February 18, it was the cheapest-to-deliver on July 16, 1992. Therefore, for comparability, we use the implied repo rate of #135 to discount the futures on both dates.

Consistent with the model's assumption that the NBD prices are determined by the futures price, in Exhibit 6 the two lines coincide approximately over most of their length. There are, however, four notable departures from this pattern.

First, #127 is trading rich relative to its implied price based on the futures price. This seems to be a consequence of the approach of the fiscal year-end and the associated difficulty in borrowing #127 for short positions.

Also priced rich relative to the price implied by its conversion factor is #129, which is to be expected, given the bond's benchmark status. Finally, #144 and #145 are also trading rich relative to the yield curve for deliverable bonds. This may in part reflect the "market's" assessment of their potential benchmark status in the future.

Between February 1992 and our second pricing date, July 22, 1992, the JGB market experienced a substantial rally. While the prices of all bonds increased, the associated decline in yields was largest in the five- to seven-year maturity sector of the yield curve. As the market rallied, the prices of the deliverable bonds below #130 became less closely linked to the converted futures price (see Exhibit 7).

At the same time, prices of #130-#144 remained closely tied to the futures price. As #129 remained the benchmark bond, its departure from the futures-based pricing model is not surprising (but note that the benchmark premium had declined from over 9 basis points in February to about 4 bp in July).

To interpret the behavior of the shorter-maturity bonds, note first that the shortest-maturity deliverable bond on this date is #122. Furthermore, the

EXHIBIT 7 ■ Deliverable Yield Curve (September 1992 JGB Futures Contract)

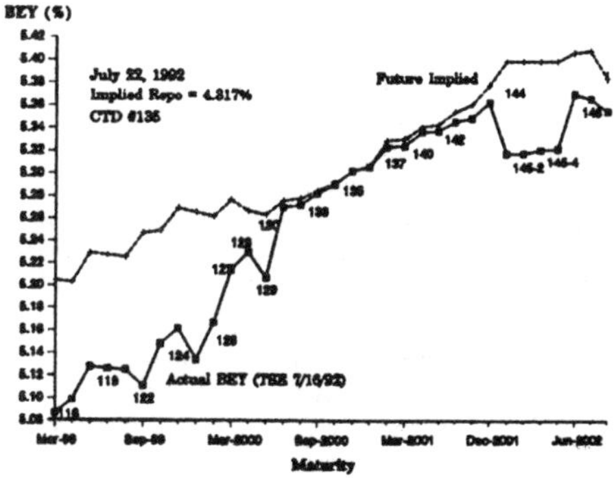

EXHIBIT 8 ■ Slope of the Deliverable Yield Curve

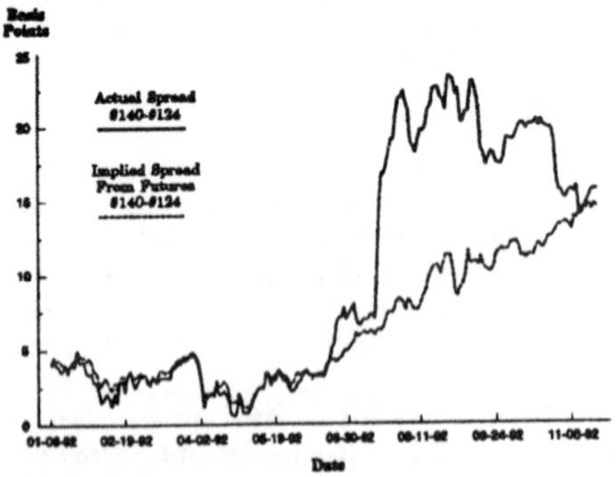

coupon rates on #127 and below are under 6%, while the coupon rates for #128–#144 are equal to or greater than 6%. In Japan there is a strong institutional preference for high-coupon bonds, resulting in part from the legal requirement that life insurance companies pay their policyholders dividends out of coupon and not capital gain income.

One consequence of this preference is that for several months prior to April 1992, the low-coupon non-deliverable bonds were trading at relatively high yields and with light trading volumes, and there was a pronounced hump in the yield curve over the five- to seven-year sector. The rally began in the ten-year sector, thereby increasing the relative cheapness of these low-coupon bonds.

Gradually, however, attention by foreign and domestic investors alike became increasingly focused on the resultant high BEYs of these bonds. At the end of 1992, the five- to seven-year sector had outperformed the other sectors of the curve.

As trading activity increased in the low-coupon non-deliverable bonds, the price discovery process changed for the similar low-coupon deliverable bonds. Instead of being based on the bond future, which had been tracking the longer-maturity higher-coupon bond prices, the prices of #122 to #128 were set in relation to the more comparable low-coupon #105, #111, and #119.

We may obtain a more complete picture of the changing nature of this relationship by comparing the actual slope of the yield curve in the deliverable sector with the slope implied by pricing of bonds off the futures. If pricing is done off the futures, these slopes should be identical.

In Exhibit 8, we display the actual and implied spreads between #140 and #124 for most of 1992. Notice that until late June 1992, the two slopes were virtually identical; this provides stronger evidence than Exhibit 6 of pricing in terms of futures. As anticipated by Exhibit 7, from July until November the difference widened substantially, primarily because the actual yield spread widened (the curve steepened) much more than the implied spread.[4] Toward the end of November 1992, the actual and implied slopes of the yield curve were once again nearly identical.

This does not necessarily imply a return to pricing of all bonds in the deliverable sector off futures, of course. The shorter-maturity deliverable bonds maintained their liquidity, so this is more a consequence of a flattening of the actual yield curve to the point where the two curves once again coincide.

This change in the price discovery process is not inconsistent with the premise of our analysis, but rather supports our argument that the price discovery process is inherently related to the relative liquidity of nearby bonds. When there is very low trading activity in the low-coupon non-deliverable ex-benchmark bonds, the price discovery for the short-maturity low-coupon deliverable bonds is based on the futures. However, starting in July 1992, the futures price was no longer the most informative indicator of value for #122–#128, given the increased trading activity in bonds with similar characteristics.

III. FITTING A JGB YIELD CURVE

The observations that bonds differ in their liquidity and that there are coupon and par effects on prices imply that JGB prices will in general not equal the present value of coupons discounted with common discount factors for coincident payment dates. Instead, the discounted values of coupons will equal market prices adjusted for the presence of these institutional influences. Furthermore, variations in price discovery mechanisms along the yield curve and over time imply that a simple model of the structure of the zero-coupon yield curve is unlikely to underlie the JGB yield curve.

Here we describe how we accommodate the various institutional considerations discussed previously in fitting the JGB yield curve. In addition, we describe briefly how we use this fitted model to assess relative value among JGBs.

Our basic approach is to determine on each trade date a discount function such that adjusted prices equal the present values of their respective coupon streams:

$$P_t^n = \sum_{j=1}^{2n} d_{t,j}\, c_{t+6j} + 100 d_{t,2n} + \text{"Adjustment Factor"}$$

where P_t^n denotes the price of an n-year bond at date t; $d_{t,j}$ denotes the discount factor for the jth coupon, c_{t+6j}, paid at month t + 6j; and the last term is the adjustment for institutional influences.

There are several institutional forces that underlie our inclusion of an adjustment factor. First, insurance companies must pay ordinary dividends to policyholders out of coupon income, not capital gains, which introduces a strong preference for coupon income. Additionally, under current accounting practices, some domestic accounts have a preference for bonds trading near par because discounts and premiums on JGBs are not accreted into accounting income until maturity of the bond. Finally, bonds purchased when interest rates were lower, and thus "under water," become more liquid as the markets rally, and losses incurred through sales are smaller. These effects tend to make bonds near par relatively rich and other coupons with similar maturities relatively cheap.

To capture these coupon and par effects, we parameterize the adjustment factor as a function of coupon level and the degree to which a bond is trading away from par. The effects are non-linear, and the magnitude of their impact on prices may vary with maturity. Furthermore, we estimate these effects daily and simultaneously with the discount factors.

Thus, the combined influence of par and coupon effects may change over time. They may also work in opposite directions. In particular, as market rates fell during the latter half of 1992, low-coupon bonds became especially unattractive to those investors seeking current yields well above the coupon rates on these bonds. Consequently, some of these bonds were trading cheap to our fitted curve, even though they were moving closer to par with the rally.

We parameterize the discount function as a series of cubic splines. The flexibility of choosing the number of segments into which the yield curve is divided and the smoothness of the functions approximating the discount function within each segment offer a large set of possible parameterizations of the discount function.

EXHIBIT 9 ■ JGB Benchmark Yield Curve (TSE Close August 12, 1992)

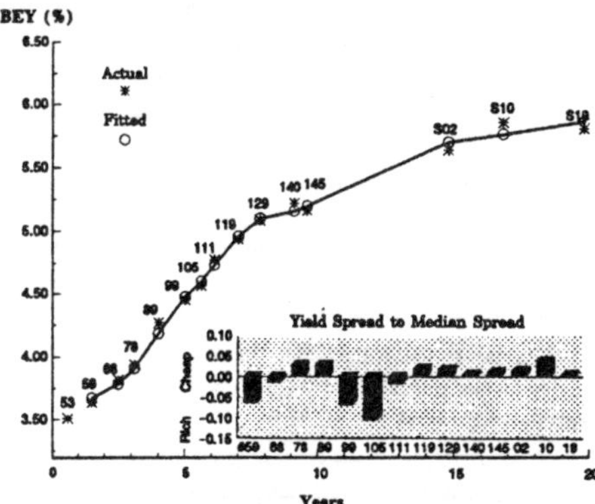

The criterion used to select our parameterization of the spline from this set is directly linked to our ultimate objective: We choose the fitted spline so that the errors in fitting the curve have predictive value for future holding-period returns. In other words, we select the fitted spline so that the model is useful for assessing the relative value of JGBs.

Exhibit 9 displays the fitted curve for August 12, 1992. The asterisks are the actual BEYs for the ex-benchmark bonds and several other key, relatively liquid bonds with one to twenty years remaining to maturity. The circles are the fitted yields from our model of the yield curve. On this particular day, #89, for instance, is trading cheap to the fitted curve (the actual yield is above the fitted yield), while #145 is trading rich to the fitted curve.

Inspection of the one-day fit alone, however, may not provide a reliable indication of the richness or cheapness of these bonds, as this spread embodies no information about the relative magnitude of this spread and historical spreads. In the JGB market, bonds may trade systematically rich or cheap to the fitted curve for institutional reasons.

The box diagram in the lower right-hand corner of Exhibit 9 represents one informative way of summarizing the recent deviations of fitted from actual BEYs for a particular bond. Consider, for example, the recent performance of the ex-benchmark #68, which is displayed in the second vertical bar from the left side of this box (#68 on the horizontal axis).

To compute this bar, we calculate the median value of the spreads (in basis points) of the actual to fitted BEY for #68 over the previous 100 days. We then subtract this median value from the spread on August 12, 1992.

This analysis accommodates the possibility that a bond persistently trades cheap or rich relative to our fitted curve. In the case of #68, the fitted BEY is below the actual BEY, and this has been true for some time. Thus, #68 has persistently traded cheap relative to the fitted curve.

Nevertheless, from a trading point of view, perhaps the more important message from Exhibit 9 is that #68 is trading at a relatively expensive level given its trading range over the previous 100 days (the current spread is less than the median spread). To the extent that there is median reversion in bond yields (a tendency for bond yields to return to their median level), we might expect that the deviation of the actual from the fitted curve will increase in the future; the bond will become cheaper.

In other words, institutional features of markets that lead bonds to trade rich or cheap relative to the curve for months clearly do not preclude sizable changes in yields over shorter intervals of time. Moreover, if there is median reversion, then investors should perhaps have considered selling #68 in favor of a relatively cheap bond (e.g., #89) in early August. The orientation of our curve analysis is, thus, toward relative value.

IV. CONCLUSIONS

We have argued that there are distinct differences among the statistical properties of the short, deliverable, and long-term sectors of the JGB yield curve. The evidence suggests that the shorter-term ex-benchmark bonds continue to lack liquidity, and as a consequence, the distributions of changes in the yields on these bonds exhibit substantial autocorrelation and very high kurtoses. Both of these statistics are symptomatic of market thinness and price pressure effects.

According to the Goldman Sachs fitted JGB yield curve, there are substantial coupon and par effects on bond yields, with the magnitudes of these effects varying across bonds and changing over time. The evidence does not support the view that coupon/par effects have become negligible in Japan. Indeed, for several reasons, investors should be sensitive to these effects when trading JGBs.

EXHIBIT 10 ■ Total Coupon Effect Over Time

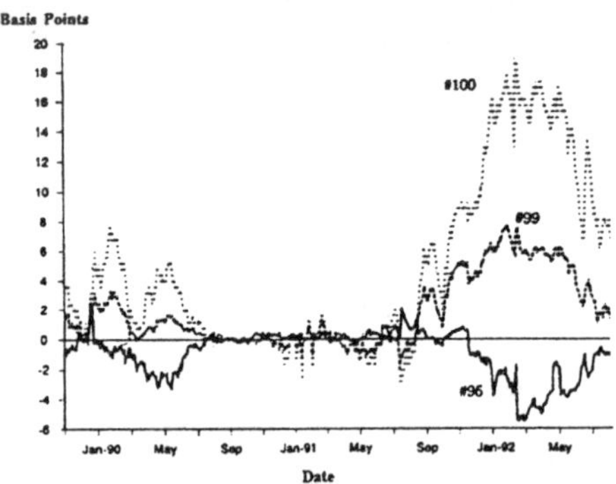

First, bonds with identical maturities but different coupons trading near par often trade at different yields because of a coupon premium in the higher-coupon bond. Historically, these differences have tended to narrow as the market has either rallied or traded off. In such circumstances, purchasing the bond nearest to par exposes investors to the possibility that market movements will cause the current-coupon premium to diminish in value and thus cause par-equivalent bonds to underperform those trading away from par. Conversely, the non-par-equivalent bonds may outperform those trading near par and so be relatively attractive to hold.

Second, when the bonds are all trading well away from par, the coupon effect tends to be small for all bonds. Purchasing higher-coupon bonds and selling the lower-coupon bonds (when all are at a discount) may be an attractive trading strategy. Since the yields are similar, the cost of carry on the trade is low. Furthermore, if the market rallies, then the higher-coupon bond may begin to reflect a current-coupon premium as its price approaches par. In this case, the higher-coupon bond will outperform the lower-coupon bond.

Finally, these observations must be qualified by the fact that there are two types of institutional effects:

1) the par effect just described, and 2) a general tendency for some market participants to shy away from low-coupon bonds. If this second effect predominates, a bond can reflect a positive coupon effect even though the par effect would suggest a richening of the bond.

The same institutional trading patterns that underlie these par and coupon effects explain in part the persistence and high kurtoses of yields. Our model of the yield curve is, by construction, designed to accommodate these institutional considerations in fitting yields, while constraining the fitted discount function to not overfit the BEYs in the following sense: If the actual BEY on a bond moves further away from our fitted curve, the change in the spread between the fitted and actual yield should be informative about value. That is, this increase in spread should be indicative of temporary developments in the market that may reverse themselves.

If, on the other hand, yields change because of a change in the general level of rates that affects the par/coupon effects, we attempt to capture this change in our adjustment factor to prices, as our relative value analysis is agnostic about the general direction of interest rates.

Nevertheless, the distributional properties of the yield changes at the short end of the yield curve should not be ignored for some aspects of trade strategy. The value of options on, for example, #68 and #78 may be influenced by both the autocorrelation and high kurtoses of these yields. In addition, assessing selling or buying pressures by domestic accounts prior to investing may be informative about potential price pressure effects underlying the positive persistence and high kurtoses of these bond yields.

Our analysis also suggests that the process by which market participants set prices based on available information has been changing with the liberalization of markets in Japan and the consequent increased liquidity of non-benchmark JGBs. Specifically, the market seems to have used the liquid futures contract for much of 1992 as the reference bond for pricing many of the non-benchmark deliverable bonds. At the end of that year, however, the short-maturity deliverable bond prices were more closely tied to the price movements of the non-deliverable bonds with six to seven years' maturity instead of the futures.

Our JGB yield curve model reflects these changes and is sufficiently flexible to accommodate the future changes in liquidity and the impact of par/coupon effects as markets are liberalized further and accounting rules change.

ENDNOTES

This article was written for Goldman, Sachs & Co. by Tadashi Kikugawa and Kenneth J. Singleton. The authors are grateful to Michael Asay, Ronald Krieger, Robert Litterman, Scott McDermott, Naho Kimoto, Scott Pinkus, and Koji Tsubouchi for helpful comments. They also wish to thank Yoko Matsunaga for assistance in preparing the charts.

[1]We include in this set #99, which is not an ex-benchmark but which has been a key reference yield for nearby bonds.

[2]These bonds are not benchmarks in the sense of the U.S. Treasury market, since they are not new issues (on-the-run bonds). Rather, they serve as benchmarks in the sense that they have relatively large trading volumes compared with nearby bonds and are closely watched by the market in setting prices on these other bonds.

[3]We estimated higher-order autoregressions, but the higher-order lags added little explanatory power.

[4]Notice that the slope of the implied curve was steepening as interest rates were falling during the latter half of 1992. This is due to a bias in the slope of the yield curve that arises from pricing bonds off of the futures. This point is developed formally in Asay, Kikugawa, and Singleton [1992].

REFERENCES

Asay, Michael, Tadashi Kikugawa, and Kenneth J. Singleton. "Futures and Price Discovery in the Japanese Government Bond Market." Goldman Sachs (Japan) Corp., 1992.

Bank of Japan. "Recent Developments in the Long-Term Bond Market." Special Paper No. 170, Research and Statistics Department, 1988.

——. "Structural Changes in the Secondary Market for Bonds and the Recent Trends in Yields on Long-Term

Bonds." Special Paper No. 132, Research and Statistics Department, 1986.

Campbell, John, and Yasushi Hamao. "Monetary Policy and the Term Structure of Interest Rates in Japan." In Kenneth J. Singleton, ed., *Japanese Monetary Policy*. Chicago: University of Chicago Press, 1992.

Cox, John C., Jonathan E. Ingersoll, Jr., and Stephen A. Ross. "A Theory of the Term Structure of Interest Rates." *Econometrica*, 53 (1985), pp. 385-407.

Heath, David, Robert Jarrow, and Andrew Morton. "Bond Pricing and the Term Structure of Interest Rates: A Discrete Time Approximation." *Journal of Financial and Quantitative Analysis*, 25 (1990), pp. 419-440.

Ho, Thomas S.Y., and Sang-Bin Lee. "Term Structure Movements and Pricing Interest Rate Contingent Claims." *Journal of Finance*, 41 (1986), pp. 1011-1030.

Kool, Clemens J.M., and John A. Tatom. "International Linkages in the Term Structure of Interest Rates." *Federal Reserve Bank of St. Louis Review*, 70 (1988), pp. 30-43.

Shikano, Yoshiaki. "Expectations Theory and Term Structure of Interest Rates." *Bank of Japan Monetary and Economic Studies*, 3 (1985), pp. 47-70.

Shirakawa, Hiromichi. "Fluctuations in Yields on Bonds: A Reassessment of the Expectations Theory Based on Japanese and U.S. Data." *Bank of Japan Monetary and Economic Studies*, 5 (1987), pp. 71-117.

Singleton, Kenneth J. "Interpreting Changes in the Volatility of Yields on Japanese Long-Term Bonds." *Bank of Japan Monetary and Economic Studies*, 8 (1990), pp. 49-77.

Part III
The Derivative Asset Approach to the Term Structure

[13]

Theory of rational option pricing

Robert C. Merton

Assistant Professor of Finance
Sloan School of Management
Massachusetts Institute of Technology

The long history of the theory of option pricing began in 1900 when the French mathematician Louis Bachelier deduced an option pricing formula based on the assumption that stock prices follow a Brownian motion with zero drift. Since that time, numerous researchers have contributed to the theory. The present paper begins by deducing a set of restrictions on option pricing formulas from the assumption that investors prefer more to less. These restrictions are necessary conditions for a formula to be consistent with a rational pricing theory. Attention is given to the problems created when dividends are paid on the underlying common stock and when the terms of the option contract can be changed explicitly by a change in exercise price or implicitly by a shift in the investment or capital structure policy of the firm. Since the deduced restrictions are not sufficient to uniquely determine an option pricing formula, additional assumptions are introduced to examine and extend the seminal Black-Scholes theory of option pricing. Explicit formulas for pricing both call and put options as well as for warrants and the new "down-and-out" option are derived. The effects of dividends and call provisions on the warrant price are examined. The possibilities for further extension of the theory to the pricing of corporate liabilities are discussed.

1. Introduction

■ The theory of warrant and option pricing has been studied extensively in both the academic and trade literature.[1] The approaches taken range from sophisticated general equilibrium models to ad hoc statistical fits. Because options are specialized and relatively unimportant financial securities, the amount of time and space devoted to the development of a pricing theory might be questioned. One justification is that, since the option is a particularly simple type of contingent-claim asset, a theory of option pricing may lead to a general theory of contingent-claims pricing. Some have argued that all such securities can be expressed as combinations of basic option contracts, and, as such, a theory of option pricing constitutes a

Robert C. Merton received the B.S. in engineering mathematics from Columbia University's School of Engineering and Applied Science (1966), the M.S. in applied mathematics from the California Institute of Technology (1967), and the Ph.D. from the Massachusetts Institute of Technology (1970). Currently he is Assistant Professor of Finance at M.I.T., where he is conducting research in capital theory under uncertainty.

The paper is a substantial revision of sections of Merton [34] and [29]. I am particularly grateful to Myron Scholes for reading an earlier draft and for his comments. I have benefited from discussion with P. A. Samuelson and F. Black. I thank Robert K. Merton for editorial assistance. Any errors remaining are mine. Aid from the National Science Foundation is gratefully acknowledged.

[1] See the bibliography for a substantial, but partial, listing of papers.

theory of contingent-claims pricing.[2] Hence, the development of an option pricing theory is, at least, an intermediate step toward a unified theory to answer questions about the pricing of a firm's liabilities, the term and risk structure of interest rates, and the theory of speculative markets. Further, there exist large quantities of data for testing the option pricing theory.

The first part of the paper concentrates on laying the foundations for a rational theory of option pricing. It is an attempt to derive theorems about the properties of option prices based on assumptions sufficiently weak to gain universal support. To the extent it is successful, the resulting theorems become necessary conditions to be satisfied by any rational option pricing theory.

As one might expect, assumptions weak enough to be accepted by all are not sufficient to determine uniquely a rational theory of option pricing. To do so, more structure must be added to the problem through additional assumptions at the expense of losing some agreement. The Black and Scholes (henceforth, referred to as B-S) formulation[3] is a significant "break-through" in attacking the option problem. The second part of the paper examines their model in detail. An alternative derivation of their formula shows that it is valid under weaker assumptions than they postulate. Several extensions to their theory are derived.

2. Restrictions on rational option pricing[4]

■ An "American"-type warrant is a security, issued by a company, giving its owner the right to purchase a share of stock at a given ("exercise") price on or before a given date. An "American"-type call option has the same terms as the warrant except that it is issued by an individual instead of a company. An "American"-type put option gives its owner the right to sell a share of stock at a given exercise price on or before a given date. A "European"-type option has the same terms as its "American" counterpart except that it cannot be surrendered ("exercised") before the last date of the contract. Samuelson[5] has demonstrated that the two types of contracts may not have the same value. All the contracts may differ with respect to other provisions such as antidilution clauses, exercise price changes, etc. Other option contracts such as strips, straps, and straddles, are combinations of put and call options.

The principal difference between valuing the call option and the warrant is that the aggregate supply of call options is zero, while the aggregate supply of warrants is generally positive. The "bucket shop" or "incipient" assumption of zero aggregate supply[6] is useful

[2] See Black and Scholes [4] and Merton [29].

[3] In [4].

[4] This section is based on Merton [34] cited in Samuelson and Merton [43], p. 43, footnote 6.

[5] In [42].

[6] See Samuelson and Merton [43], p. 26 for a discussion of "incipient" analysis. Essentially, the incipient price is such that a slightly higher price would induce a positive supply. In this context, the term "bucket shop" was coined in oral conversation by Paul Samuelson and is based on the (now illegal) 1920's practice of side-bets on the stock market.

Myron Scholes has pointed out that if a company sells a warrant against stock already *outstanding* (not just authorized), then the incipient analysis is valid as well. (E.g., Amerada Hess selling warrants against shares of Louisiana Land

because the probability distribution of the stock price return is unaffected by the creation of these options, which is not in general the case when they are issued by firms in positive amounts.[7] The "bucket-shop" assumption is made throughout the paper although many of the results derived hold independently of this assumption.

The notation used throughout is: $F(S, \tau; E)$ — the value of an American warrant with exercise price E and τ years before expiration, when the price per share of the common stock is S; $f(S, \tau; E)$ — the value of its European counterpart; $G(S, \tau; E)$ — the value of an American put option; and $g(S, \tau; E)$ — the value of its European counterpart.

From the definition of a warrant and limited liability, we have that

$$F(S, \tau; E) \geqq 0; \quad f(S, \tau; E) \geqq 0 \tag{1}$$

and when $\tau = 0$, at expiration, both contracts must satisfy

$$F(S, 0; E) = f(S, 0; E) = \text{Max}[0, S - E]. \tag{2}$$

Further, it follows from conditions of arbitrage that

$$F(S, \tau; E) \geqq \text{Max}[0, S - E]. \tag{3}$$

In general, a relation like (3) need not hold for a European warrant.

Definition: Security (portfolio) A is *dominant* over security (portfolio) B, if on some known date in the future, the return on A will exceed the return on B for some possible states of the world, and will be at least as large as on B, in all possible states of the world.

Note that in perfect markets with no transactions costs and the ability to borrow and short-sell without restriction, the existence of a dominated security would be equivalent to the existence of an arbitrage situation. However, it is possible to have dominated securities exist without arbitrage in imperfect markets. If one assumes something like "symmetric market rationality" and assumes further that investors prefer more wealth to less,[8] then any investor willing to purchase security B would prefer to purchase A.

Assumption 1: A necessary condition for a rational option pricing theory is that the option be priced such that it is neither a dominant nor a dominated security.

Given two American warrants on the same stock and with the same exercise price, it follows from Assumption 1, that

$$F(S, \tau_1; E) \geqq F(S, \tau_2; E) \quad \text{if} \quad \tau_1 > \tau_2, \tag{4}$$

and that

$$F(S, \tau; E) \geqq f(S, \tau; E). \tag{5}$$

Further, two warrants, identical in every way except that one has a larger exercise price than the other, must satisfy

$$\begin{aligned} F(S, \tau; E_1) &\leqq F(S, \tau; E_2) \\ f(S, \tau; E_1) &\leqq f(S, \tau; E_2) \quad \text{if} \quad E_1 > E_2. \end{aligned} \tag{6}$$

and Exploration stock it owns and City Investing selling warrants against shares of General Development Corporation stock it owns.)

[7] See Merton [29], Section 2.

[8] See Modigliani and Miller [35], p. 427, for a definition of "symmetric market rationality."

Because the common stock is equivalent to a perpetual ($\tau = \infty$) American warrant with a zero exercise price ($E = 0$), it follows from (4) and (6) that

$$S \geqq F(S, \tau; E), \tag{7}$$

and from (1) and (7), the warrant must be worthless if the stock is, i.e.,

$$F(0, \tau; E) = f(0, \tau; E) = 0. \tag{8}$$

Let $P(\tau)$ be the price of a riskless (in terms of default), discounted loan (or "bond") which pays one dollar, τ years from now. If it is assumed that current and future interest rates are positive, then

$$1 = P(0) > P(\tau_1) > P(\tau_2) > \cdots > P(\tau_n) \quad \text{for} \quad 0 < \tau_1 < \tau_2 < \cdots < \tau_n, \tag{9}$$

at a given point in calendar time.

Theorem 1. If the exercise price of a European warrant is E and if no payouts (e.g. dividends) are made to the common stock over the life of the warrant (or alternatively, if the warrant is protected against such payments), then $f(S, \tau; E) \geqq \text{Max}[0, S - EP(\tau)]$.

Proof: Consider the following two investments:

A: Purchase the warrant for $f(S, \tau; E)$;
Purchase E bonds at price $P(\tau)$ per bond.
Total investment: $f(S, \tau; E) + EP(\tau)$.

B: Purchase the common stock for S.
Total investment: S.

Suppose at the end of τ years, the common stock has value S^*. Then, the value of B will be S^*. If $S^* \leqq E$, then the warrant is worthless and the value of A will be $0 + E = E$. If $S^* > E$, then the value of A will be $(S^* - E) + E = S^*$. Therefore, unless the current value of A is at least as large as B, A will dominate B. Hence, by Assumption 1, $f(S, \tau; E) + EP(\tau) \geqq S$, which together with (1), implies that $f(S, \tau; E) \geqq \text{Max}[0, S - EP(\tau)]$. Q.E.D.

From (5), it follows directly that Theorem 1 holds for American warrants with a fixed exercise price over the life of the contract. The right to exercise an option prior to the expiration date always has nonnegative value. It is important to know when this right has zero value, since in that case, the values of an European and American option are the same. In practice, almost all options are of the American type while it is always easier to solve analytically for the value of an European option. Theorem 1 significantly tightens the bounds for rational warrant prices over (3). In addition, it leads to the following two theorems.

Theorem 2. If the hypothesized conditions for Theorem 1 hold, an American warrant will never be exercised prior to expiration, and hence, it has the same value as a European warrant.

Proof: If the warrant is exercised, its value will be $\text{Max}[0, S - E]$. But from Theorem 1, $F(S, \tau; E) \geqq \text{Max}[0, S - EP(\tau)]$, which is larger than $\text{Max}[0, S - E]$ for $\tau > 0$ because, from (9), $P(\tau) < 1$. Hence, the warrant is always worth more "alive" than "dead." Q.E.D.

Theorem 2 suggests that if there is a difference between the American and European warrant prices which implies a positive probability of a premature exercise, it must be due to unfavorable changes in the exercise price or to lack of protection against payouts to the common stocks. This result is consistent with the findings of Samuelson and Merton.[9]

It is a common practice to refer to Max[0, $S - E$] as the *intrinsic value* of the warrant and to state that the warrant must always sell for at least its intrinsic value [condition (3)]. In light of Theorems 1 and 2, it makes more sense to define Max[0, $S - EP(\tau)$] as the intrinsic value. The latter definition reflects the fact that the amount of the exercise price need not be paid until the expiration date, and $EP(\tau)$ is just the present value of that payment. The difference between the two values can be large, particularly for long-lived warrants, as the following theorem demonstrates.

Theorem 3. If the hypothesized conditions for Theorem 1 hold, the value of a perpetual ($\tau = \infty$) warrant must equal the value of the common stock.

Proof: From Theorem 1, $F(S, \infty; E) \geqq$ Max[0, $S - EP(\infty)$]. But, $P(\infty) = 0$, since, for positive interest rates, the value of a discounted loan payable at infinity is zero. Therefore, $F(S, \infty; E) \geqq S$. But from (7), $S \geqq F(S, \infty; E)$. Hence, $F(S, \infty; E) = S$. Q.E.D.

Samuelson, Samuelson and Merton, and Black and Scholes[10] have shown that the price of a perpetual warrant equals the price of the common stock for their particular models. Theorem 3 demonstrates that it holds independent of any stock price distribution or risk-averse behavioral assumptions.[11]

The inequality of Theorem 1 demonstrates that a finite-lived, rationally-determined warrant price must be a function of $P(\tau)$. For if it were not, then, for some sufficiently small $P(\tau)$ (i.e., large interest rate), the inequality of Theorem 1 would be violated. From the form of the inequality and previous discussion, this direct dependence on the interest rate seems to be "induced" by using as a variable, the exercise price instead of the present value of the exercise price (i.e., I conjecture that the pricing function, $F[S, \tau; E, P(\tau)]$, can be written as $W(S, \tau; e)$, where $e = EP(\tau)$.[12] If this is so, then the qualitative effect of a change in P on the warrant price would be similar to a change in the exercise price, which, from (6), is negative. Therefore, the warrant price should be an increasing function of the interest rate. This finding is consistent with the theoretical models of Samuel-

[9] In [43], p. 29 and Appendix 2.

[10] In [42], [43], and [4], respectively.

[11] It is a bit of a paradox that a perpetual warrant with a positive exercise price should sell for the same price as the common stock (a "perpetual warrant" with a zero exercise price), and, in fact, the few such outstanding warrants do not sell for this price. However, it must be remembered that one assumption for the theorem to obtain is that no payouts to the common stock will be made over the life of the contract which is almost never true in practice. See Samuelson and Merton [43], pp. 30–31, for further discussion of the paradox.

[12] The only case where the warrant price does not depend on the exercise price is the perpetuity, and the only case where the warrant price does not depend on $P(\tau)$ is when the exercise price is zero. Note that in both cases, $e = 0$, (the former because $P(\infty) = 0$, and the latter because $E = 0$), which is consistent with our conjecture.

son and Merton and Black and Scholes and with the empirical study by Van Horne.[13]

Another argument for the reasonableness of this result comes from recognizing that a European warrant is equivalent to a long position in the common stock levered by a limited-liability, discount loan, where the borrower promises to pay E dollars at the end of τ periods, but in the event of default, is only liable to the extent of the value of the common stock at that time.[14] If the present value of such a loan is a decreasing function of the interest rate, then, for a given stock price, the warrant price will be an increasing function of the interest rate.

We now establish two theorems about the effect of a change in exercise price on the price of the warrant.

Theorem 4. If $F(S, \tau; E)$ is a rationally determined warrant price, then F is a convex function of its exercise price, E.

Proof: To prove convexity, we must show that if

$$E_3 \equiv \lambda E_1 + (1 - \lambda)E_2,$$

then for every λ, $0 \leq \lambda \leq 1$,

$$F(S, \tau; E_3) \leqq \lambda F(S, \tau; E_1) + (1 - \lambda)F(S, \tau; E_2).$$

We do so by a dominance argument similar to the proof of Theorem 1. Let portfolio A contain λ warrants with exercise price E_1 and $(1 - \lambda)$ warrants with exercise price E_2 where by convention, $E_2 > E_1$. Let portfolio B contain one warrant with exercise price E_3. If S^* is the stock price on the date of expiration, then by the convexity of $\text{Max}[0, S^* - E]$, the value of portfolio A,

$$\lambda \text{ Max}[0, S^* - E_1] + (1 - \lambda) \text{ Max}[0, S^* - E_2],$$

will be greater than or equal to the value of portfolio B,

$$\text{Max}[0, S^* - \lambda E_1 - (1 - \lambda)E_2].$$

Hence, to avoid dominance, the current value of portfolio B must be less than or equal to the current value of portfolio A. Thus, the theorem is proved for a European warrant. Since nowhere in the argument is any factor involving τ used, the same results would obtain if the warrants in the two portfolios were exercised prematurely. Hence, the theorem holds for American warrants. Q.E.D.

Theorem 5. If $f(S, \tau; E)$ is a rationally determined European warrant price, then for $E_1 < E_2$, $-P(\tau)(E_2 - E_1) \leqq f(S, \tau; E_2) - f(S, \tau; E_1) \leq 0$. Further, if f is a differentiable function of its exercise price, $-P(\tau) \leq \partial f(S, \tau; E)/\partial E \leq 0$.

Proof: The right-hand inequality follows directly from (6). The left-hand inequality follows from a dominance argument. Let portfolio A contain a warrant to purchase the stock at E_2 and $(E_2 - E_1)$ bonds at price $P(\tau)$ per bond. Let portfolio B contain a warrant to purchase the stock at E_1. If S^* is the stock price on the

[13] In [43], [4], and [54], respectively.

[14] Stiglitz [51], p. 788, introduces this same type loan as a sufficient condition for the Modigliani-Miller Theorem to obtain when there is a positive probability of bankruptcy.

date of expiration, then the terminal value of portfolio A,

$$\text{Max}[0, S^* - E_2] + (E_2 - E_1),$$

will be greater than the terminal value of portfolio B, $\text{Max}[0, S^* - E_1]$, when $S^* < E_2$, and equal to it when $S^* \geq E_2$. So, to avoid dominance, $f(S, \tau; E_1) \leqq f(S, \tau; E_2) + P(\tau)(E_2 - E_1)$. The inequality on the derivative follows by dividing the discrete-change inequalities by $(E_2 - E_1)$ and taking the limit as E_2 tends to E_1. Q.E.D.

If the hypothesized conditions for Theorem 1 hold, then the inequalities of Theorem 5 hold for American warrants. Otherwise, we only have the weaker inequalities, $-(E_2 - E_1) \leq F(S, \tau; E_2) - F(S, \tau; E_1) \leq 0$ and $-1 \leq \partial F(S, \tau; E)/\partial E \leq 0$.

Let $Q(t)$ be the price per share on a common stock at time t and $F_Q(Q, \tau; E_Q)$ be the price of a warrant to purchase one share of stock at price E_Q on or before a given date τ years in the future, when the current price of the common stock is Q.

Theorem 6. If k is a positive constant; $Q(t) = kS(t)$; $E_Q = kE$, then $F_Q(Q, \tau; E_Q) \equiv kF(S, \tau; E)$ for all $S, \tau; E$ and each k.

Proof: Let S^* be the value of the common stock with initial value S when both warrants either are exercised or expire. Then, by the hypothesized conditions of the theorem, $Q = Q^* \equiv kS^*$ and $E_Q = kE$. The value of the warrant on Q will be $\text{Max}[0, Q^* - E_Q] = k\,\text{Max}[0, S^* - E]$ which is k times the value of the warrant on S. Hence, to avoid dominance of one over the other, the value of the warrant on Q must sell for exactly k times the value of the warrant on S. Q.E.D.

The implications of Theorem 6 for restrictions on rational warrant pricing depend on what assumptions are required to produce the hypothesized conditions of the theorem. In its weakest form, it is a dimensional theorem where k is the proportionality factor between two units of account (e.g., $k = 100$ cents/dollar). If the stock and warrant markets are purely competitive, then it can be interpreted as a scale theorem. Namely, if there are no economies of scale with respect to transactions costs and no problems with indivisibilities, then k shares of stock will always sell for exactly k times the value of one share of stock. Under these conditions, the theorem states that a warrant to buy k shares of stock for a total of (kE) dollars when the stock price per share is S dollars, is equal in value to k times the price of a warrant to buy one share of the stock for E dollars, all other terms the same. Thus, the rational warrant pricing function is homogeneous of degree one in S and E with respect to scale, which reflects the usual constant returns to scale results of competition.

Hence, one can always work in standardized units of $E = 1$ where the stock price and warrant price are quoted in units of exercise price by choosing $k = 1/E$. Not only does this change of units eliminate a variable from the problem, but it is also a useful operation to perform prior to making empirical comparisons across different warrants where the dollar amounts may be of considerably different magnitudes.

Let $F_i(S_i, \tau_i; E_i)$ be the value of a warrant on the common stock of firm i with current price per share S_i when τ_i is the time to expiration and E_i is the exercise price.

Assumption 2. If $S_i = S_j = S$; $\tau_i = \tau_j = \tau$; $E_i = E_j = E$, and the returns per dollar on the stocks i and j are identically distributed, then $F_i(S, \tau; E) = F_j(S, \tau; E)$.

Assumption 2 implies that, from the point of view of the warrant holder, the only identifying feature of the common stock is its (*ex ante*) distribution of returns.

Define $z(t)$ to be the one-period random variable return per dollar invested in the common stock in period t. Let $Z(\tau) \equiv \prod_{t=1}^{\tau} z(t)$ be the τ-period return per dollar.

Theorem 7. If $S_i = S_j = S$, $i, j = 1, 2, \ldots, n$;

$$Z_{n+1}(\tau) \equiv \sum_1^n \lambda_i Z_i(\tau)$$

for $\lambda_i \epsilon [0, 1]$ and $\sum_1^n \lambda_i = 1$, then

$$F_{n+1}(S, \tau; E) \leq \sum_1^n \lambda_i F_i(S, \tau; E).$$

Proof: By construction, one share of the $(n + 1)$st security contains λ_i shares of the common stock of firm i, and by hypothesis, the price per share, $S_{n+1} = \sum_1^n \lambda_i S_i = S \sum_1^n \lambda_i = S$. The proof follows from a dominance argument. Let portfolio A contain λ_i warrants on the common stock of firm i, $i = 1, 2, \ldots, n$. Let portfolio B contain one warrant on the $(n + 1)$st security. Let S_i^* denote the price per share on the common stock of the ith firm, on the date of expiration, $i = 1, 2, \ldots, n$. By definition, $S_{n+1}^* = \sum_1^n \lambda_i S_i^*$. On the expiration date, the value of portfolio A, $\sum_1^n \lambda_i \operatorname{Max}[0, S_i^* - E]$, is greater than or equal to the value of portfolio B, $\operatorname{Max}[0, \sum_1^n \lambda_i S_i^* - E]$, by the convexity of $\operatorname{Max}[0, S - E]$. Hence, to avoid dominance,

$$F_{n+1}(S, \tau; E) \leq \sum_1^n \lambda_i F_i(S, \tau; E). \text{ Q.E.D.}$$

Loosely, Theorem 7 states that a warrant on a portfolio is less valuable than a portfolio of warrants. Thus, from the point of view of warrant value, diversification "hurts," as the following special case of Theorem 7 demonstrates:

Corollary. If the hypothesized conditions of Theorem 7 hold and if, in addition, the $z_i(t)$ are identically distributed, then

$$F_{n+1}(S, \tau; E) \leq F_i(S, \tau; E)$$

for $i = 1, 2, \ldots, n$.

Proof: From Theorem 7, $F_{n+1}(S, \tau; E) \leq \sum_1^n \lambda_i F_i(S, \tau; E)$. By hypothesis, the $z_i(t)$ are identically distributed, and hence, so are the $Z_i(\tau)$. Therefore, by Assumption 2, $F_i(S, \tau; E) = F_j(S, \tau; E)$ for $i, j = 1, 2, \ldots n$. Since $\sum_1^n \lambda_i = 1$, it then follows that $F_{n+1}(S, \tau; E) \leq F_i(S, \tau; E)$, $i = 1, 2, \ldots n$. Q.E.D.

Theorem 7 and its Corollary suggest the more general proposition that the more risky the common stock, the more valuable the warrant. In order to prove the proposition, one must establish a careful definition of "riskiness" or "volatility."

Definition: Security one is *more risky* than security two if $Z_1(\tau) = Z_2(\tau) + \epsilon$ where ϵ is a random variable with the property

$$E[\epsilon | Z_2(\tau)] = 0.$$

This definition of more risky is essentially one of the three (equivalent) definitions used by Rothschild and Stiglitz.[15]

Theorem 8. The rationally determined warrant price is a non-decreasing function of the riskiness of its associated common stock.

Proof: Let $Z(\tau)$ be the τ-period return on a common stock with warrant price, $F_Z(S, \tau; E)$. Let $Z_i(\tau) = Z(\tau) + \epsilon_i$, $i = 1, \ldots, n$, where the ϵ_i are independently and identically distributed random variables satisfying $E[\epsilon_i | Z(\tau)] = 0$. By definition, security i is more risky than security Z, for $i = 1, \ldots, n$. Define the random variable return $Z_{n+1}(\tau) \equiv \frac{1}{n} \sum_1^n Z_i(\tau) = Z(\tau) + \frac{1}{n} \sum_1^n \epsilon_i$. Note that, by construction, the $Z_i(\tau)$ are identically distributed. Hence, by the Corollary to Theorem 7 with $\lambda_i = 1/n$, $F_{n+1}(S, \tau; E) \leq F_i(S, \tau; E)$ for $i = 1, 2, \ldots, n$. By the law of large numbers, $Z_{n+1}(\tau)$ converges in probability to $Z(\tau)$ as $n \to \infty$, and hence, by Assumption 2, $\lim_{n \to \infty} F_{n+1}(S, \tau; E) = F_Z(S, \tau; E)$. Therefore, $F_Z(S, \tau; E) \leq F_i(S, \tau; E)$ for $i = 1, 2, \ldots, n$. Q.E.D.

Thus, the more uncertain one is about the outcomes on the common stock, the more valuable is the warrant. This finding is consistent with the empirical study by Van Horne.[16]

To this point in the paper, no assumptions have been made about the properties of the distribution of returns on the common stock. If it is assumed that the $\{z(t)\}$ are independently distributed,[17] then the distribution of the returns per dollar invested in the stock is independent of the initial level of the stock price, and we have the following theorem:

Theorem 9. If the distribution of the returns per dollar invested in the common stock is independent of the level of the stock price, then $F(S, \tau; E)$ is homogeneous of degree one in the stock price per share and exercise price.

Proof: Let $z_i(t)$ be the return per dollar if the initial stock price is S_i, $i = 1, 2$. Define $k = (S_2/S_1)$ and $E_2 = kE_1$. Then, by Theorem 6, $F_2(S_2, \tau; E_2) \equiv kF_2(S_1, \tau; E_1)$. By hypothesis, $z_1(t)$ and $z_2(t)$ are identically distributed. Hence, by Assumption 2, $F_2(S_1, \tau; E_1) = F_1(S_1, \tau; E_1)$. Therefore, $F_2(kS_1, \tau; kE_1) \equiv kF_1(S_1, \tau; E_1)$ and the theorem is proved. Q.E.D.

Although similar in a formal sense, Theorem 9 is considerably stronger than Theorem 6, in terms of restrictions on the warrant pricing function. Namely, given the hypothesized conditions of Theorem 9, one would expect to find in a table of rational warrant values for a given maturity, that the value of a warrant with exercise price E when the common stock is at S will be exactly k times as

[15] The two other equivalent definitions are: (1) every risk averter prefers X to Y (i.e., $EU(X) \geq EU(Y)$, for all concave U); (2) Y has more weight in the tails than X. In addition, they show that if Y has greater variance than X, then it need not be more risky in the sense of the other three definitions. It should also be noted that it is the *total* risk, and not the *systematic* or portfolio risk, of the common stock which is important to warrant pricing. In [39], p. 225.

[16] In [54].

[17] Cf. Samuelson [42].

valuable as a warrant on the same stock with exercise price E/k when the common stock is selling for S/k. In general, this result will not obtain if the distribution of returns depends on the level of the stock price as is shown by a counter example in Appendix 1.

Theorem 10. If the distribution of the returns per dollar invested in the common stock is independent of the level of the stock price, then $F(S, \tau; E)$ is a convex function of the stock price.

Proof: To prove convexity, we must show that if

$$S_3 \equiv \lambda S_1 + (1 - \lambda)S_2,$$

then, for every λ, $0 \leq \lambda \leq 1$,

$$F(S_3, \tau; E) \leq \lambda F(S_1, \tau; E) + (1 - \lambda)F(S_2, \tau; E).$$

From Theorem 4,

$$F(1, \tau; E_3) \leq \gamma F(1, \tau; E_1) + (1 - \gamma)F(1, \tau; E_2),$$

for $0 \leq \gamma \leq 1$ and $E_3 = \gamma E_1 + (1 - \gamma)E_2$. Take $\gamma \equiv \lambda S_1/S_3$, $E_1 \equiv E/S_1$, and $E_2 \equiv E/S_2$. Multiplying both sides of the inequality by S_3, we have that

$$S_3F(1, \tau; E_3) \leq \lambda S_1F(1, \tau; E_1) + (1 - \lambda)S_2F(1, \tau; E_2).$$

From Theorem 9, F is homogeneous of degree one in S and E. Hence,

$$F(S_3, \tau; S_3E_3) \leq \lambda F(S_1, \tau; S_1E_1) + (1 - \lambda)F(S_2, \tau; S_2E_2).$$

By the definition of E_1, E_2, and E_3, this inequality can be rewritten as $F(S_3, \tau; E) \leq \lambda F(S_1, \tau; E) + (1 - \lambda)F(S_2, \tau; E)$. Q.E.D.

Although convexity is usually assumed to be a property which always holds for warrants, and while the hypothesized conditions of Theorem 10 are by no means necessary, Appendix 1 provides an example where the distribution of future returns on the common stock is sufficiently dependent on the level of the stock price, to cause perverse local concavity.

Based on the analysis so far, Figure 1 illustrates the general shape that the rational warrant price should satisfy as a function of the stock price and time.

FIGURE 1

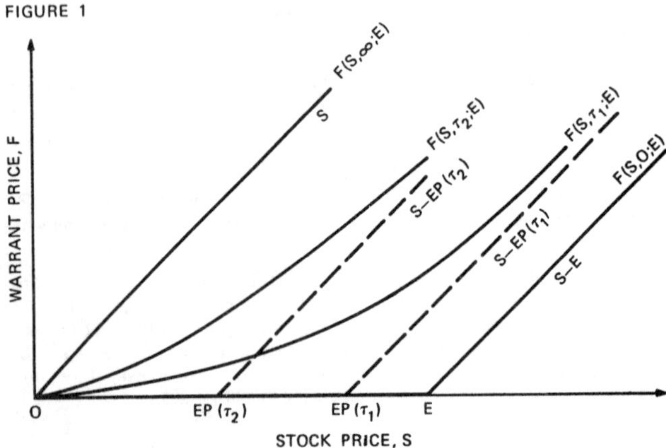

3. Effects of dividends and changing exercise price

■ A number of the theorems of the previous section depend upon the assumption that either no payouts are made to the common stock over the life of the contract or that the contract is protected against such payments. In this section, the adjustments required in the contracts to protect them against payouts are derived, and the effects of payouts on the valuation of unprotected contracts are investigated. The two most common types of payouts are stock dividends (splits) and cash dividends.

In general, the value of an option will be affected by unanticipated changes in the firm's investment policy, capital structure (e.g., debt-equity ratio), and payout policy. For example, if the firm should change its investment policy so as to lower the riskiness of its cash flow (and hence, the riskiness of outcomes on the common stock), then, by Theorem 8, the value of the warrant would decline for a given level of the stock price. Similarly, if the firm changed its capital structure by raising the debt-equity ratio, then the riskiness of the common stock would increase, and the warrant would become more valuable. If that part of the total return received by shareholders in the form of dividends is increased by a change in payout policy, then the value of an unprotected warrant would decline since the warrant-holder has no claim on the dividends.[18]

While it is difficult to provide a set of adjustments to the warrant contract to protect it against changes in investment or capital structure policies without severely restricting the management of the firm, there do exist a set of adjustments to protect the warrant holders against payouts.

Definition: An option is said to be *payout protected* if, for a fixed investment policy and fixed capital structure, the value of the option is invariant to the choice of payout policy.

Theorem 11. If the total return per dollar invested in the common stock is invariant to the fraction of the return represented by payouts and if, on each expayout date during the life of a warrant, the contract is adjusted so that the number of shares which can be purchased for a total of E dollars is increased by (d/S^x) percent where d is the dollar amount of the payout and S^x is the expayout price per share of the stock, then the warrant will be payout protected.

Proof: Consider two firms with identically distributed total returns per dollar invested in the common stock, $z_i(t)$, $i = 1, 2$, and whose initial prices per share are the same ($S_1 = S_2 = S$). For firm i, let $\lambda_i(t)(t \geq 1)$ be the return per dollar in period t from payouts and $x_i(t)$ be the return per dollar in period t from capital gains, such that $z_i(t) \equiv \lambda_i(t)x_i(t)$. Let $N_i(t)$ be the number of shares of firm i which the warrant of firm i has claim on for a total price of E, at time t where $N_1(0) = N_2(0) = 1$. By definition, $\lambda_i(t) \equiv 1 + d_i(t)/S_i^x(t)$, where $S_i^x(t) = \prod_{k=1}^{t} x_i(k)S$ is the expayout price per share at time t. Therefore, by the hypothesized conditions of the theorem, $N_i(t) = \lambda_i(t)N_i(t-1)$. On the date when the warrants are either exercised

[18] This is an important point to remember when valuing unprotected warrants of companies such as A. T. & T. where a substantial fraction of the total return to shareholders comes in the form of dividends.

or expire, the value of the warrant on firm i will be

$$\text{Max}[0, N_i(t)S_i^{x}(t) - E].$$

But, $N_i(t)S_i^{x}(t) = [\prod_{k=1}^{t} \lambda_i(t)][\prod_{k=1}^{t} x_i(t)S] = \prod_{k=1}^{t} z_i(t)S$. Since, by hypothesis, the $z_i(t)$ are identically distributed, the distribution of outcomes on the warrants of the two firms will be identical. Therefore, by Assumption 2, $F_1(S, \tau; E) = F_2(S, \tau; E)$, independent of the particular pattern chosen for the $\lambda_i(t)$. Q.E.D.

Note that if the hypothesized conditions of Theorem 11 hold, then the value of a protected warrant will be equal to the value of a warrant which restricts management from making any payouts to the common stock over the life of the warrant (i.e., $\lambda_i(t) \equiv 1$). Hence, a protected warrant will satisfy all the theorems of Section 2 which depend on the assumption of no payouts over the life of the warrant.

Corollary. If the total return per dollar invested in the common stock is invariant to the fraction of the return represented by payouts; if there are no economies of scale; and if, on each expayout date during the life of a warrant, each warrant to purchase one share of stock for exercise price E, is exchanged for $\lambda(\equiv 1 + d/S^{x})$ warrants to purchase one share of stock for exercise price E/λ, then the warrant will be payout protected.

Proof: By Theorem 11, on the first expayout date, a protected warrant will have claim on λ shares of stock at a total exercise price of E. By hypothesis, there are no economies of scale. Hence, the scale interpretation of Theorem 6 is valid which implies that the value of a warrant on λ shares at a total price of E must be identically (in λ) equal to the value of λ warrants to purchase one share at an exercise price of E/λ. Proceeding inductively, we can show that this equality holds on each payout date. Hence, a warrant with the adjustment provision of the Corollary will be payout protected. Q.E.D.

If there are no economies of scale, it is generally agreed that a stock split or dividend will not affect the distribution of future per dollar returns on the common stock. Hence, the hypothesized adjustments will protect the warrant holder against stock splits where λ is the number of postsplit shares per presplit share.[19]

The case for cash dividend protection is more subtle. In the absence of taxes and transactions costs, Miller and Modigliani[20] have shown that for a fixed investment policy and capital structure, dividend policy does not affect the value of the firm. Under their hypothesized conditions, it is a necessary result of their analysis that the total return per dollar invested in the common stock will be invariant to payout policy. Therefore, warrants adjusted according to either Theorem 11 or its Corollary, will be payout protected in the same

[19] For any particular function, $F(S, \tau; E)$, there are many other adjustments which could leave value the same. However, the adjustment suggestions of Theorem 11 and its Corollary are the only ones which do so for every such function. In practice, both adjustments are used to protect warrants against stock splits. See Braniff Airways 1986 warrants for an example of the former and Leasco 1987 warrants for the latter. λ could be less than one in the case of a reverse split.

[20] In [35].

sense that Miller and Modigliani mean when they say that dividend policy "doesn't matter."

The principal cause for confusion is different definitions of payout protected. Black and Scholes[21] give an example to illustrate "that there may not be any adjustment in the terms of the option that will give adequate protection against a large dividend." Suppose that the firm liquidates all its assets and pays them out in the form of a cash dividend. Clearly, $S^x = 0$, and hence, the value of the warrant must be zero no matter what adjustment is made to the number of shares it has claim on or to its exercise price.

While their argument is correct, it also suggests a much stronger definition of payout protection. Namely, since their example involves changes in investment policy and if there is a positive supply of warrants (the nonincipient case), a change in the capital structure, in addition to a payout, their definition would seem to require protection against all three.

To illustrate, consider the firm in their example, but where management is prohibited against making any payouts to the shareholders prior to expiration of the warrant. It seems that such a warrant would be called payout protected by any reasonable definition. It is further assumed that the firm has only equity outstanding (i.e., the incipient case for the warrant) to rule out any capital structure effects.[22]

Suppose the firm sells all its assets for a fair price (so that the share price remains unchanged) and uses the proceeds to buy riskless, τ-period bonds. As a result of this investment policy change, the stock becomes a riskless asset and the warrant price will fall to $\text{Max}[0, S - EP]$. Note that if $S < EP$, the warrant will be worthless even though it is payout protected. Now lift the restriction against payouts and replace it with the adjustments of the Corollary to Theorem 11. Given that the shift in investment policy has taken place, suppose the firm makes a payment of γ percent of the value of the firm to the shareholders. Then, $S^x = (1 - \gamma)S$ and

$$\lambda = 1 + \gamma/(1 - \gamma) = 1/(1 - \gamma).$$

The value of the warrant after the payout will be

$$\lambda \, \text{Max}[0, S^x - EP/\lambda] = \text{Max}[0, S - EP],$$

which is the same as the value of the warrant when the company was restricted from making payouts. In the B-S example, $\gamma = 1$ and so, $\lambda = \infty$ and $E/\lambda = 0$. Hence, there is the indeterminancy of multiplying zero by infinity. However, for every $\gamma < 1$, the analysis is correct, and therefore, it is reasonable to suspect that it holds in the limit.

A similar analysis in the nonincipient case would show that both investment policy and the capital structure were changed. For in this case, the firm would have to purchase γ percent of the warrants outstanding to keep the capital structure unchanged without issuing new stock. In the B-S example where $\gamma = 1$, this would require purchasing

[21] In [4].

[22] The incipient case is a particularly important example since in practice, the only contracts that are adjusted for cash payouts are options. The incipient assumption also rules out "capital structure induced" changes in investment policy by malevolent management. For an example, see Stiglitz [50].

the entire issue, after which the analysis reduces to the incipient case. The B-S emphasis on protection against a "large" dividend is further evidence that they really have in mind protection against investment policy and capital structure shifts as well, since large payouts are more likely to be associated with nontrivial changes in either or both.

It should be noted that calls and puts that satisfy the incipient assumption have in practice been the only options issued with cash dividend protection clauses, and the typical adjustment has been to reduce the exercise price by the amount of the cash dividend which has been demonstrated to be incorrect.[23]

To this point it has been assumed that the exercise price remains constant over the life of the contract (except for the before-mentioned adjustments for payouts). A variable exercise price is meaningless for an European warrant since the contract is not exercisable prior to expiration. However, a number of American warrants do have variable exercise prices as a function of the length of time until expiration. Typically, the exercise price increases as time approaches the expiration date.

Consider the case where there are n changes of the exercise price during the life of an American warrant, represented by the following schedule:

Exercise Price	*Time until Expiration* (τ)
E_0	$0 \leqq \tau \leqq \tau_1$
E_1	$\tau_1 \leqq \tau \leqq \tau_2$
$\vdots$	$\vdots$
E_n	$\tau_n \leqq \tau,$

where it is assumed that $E_{j+i} < E_j$ for $j = 0, 1, \ldots, n-1$. If, otherwise the conditions for Theorems 1–11 hold, it is easy to show that, if premature exercising takes place, it will occur only at points in time just prior to an exercise price change, i.e., at $\tau = \tau_j^+$, $j = 1, 2, \ldots, n$. Hence, the American warrant is equivalent to a *modified European warrant* which allows its owner to exercise the warrant at discrete times, just prior to an exercise price change. Given a technique for finding the price of an European warrant, there is a systematic method for valuing a modified European warrant. Namely, solve the standard problem for $F_0(S, \tau; E_0)$ subject to the boundary conditions $F_0(S, 0: E_0) = \text{Max}[0, S - E_0]$ and $\tau \leqq \tau_1$. Then, by the same technique, solve for $F_1(S, \tau; E_1)$ subject to the boundary conditions $F_1(S, \tau_1; E_1) = \text{Max}[0, S - E_1, F_0(S, \tau_1; E_0)]$ and $\tau_1 \leqq \tau \leqq \tau_2$. Proceed inductively by this dynamic-programming-like technique, until the current value of the modified European warrant is determined. Typically, the number of exercise price changes is small, so the technique is computationally feasible.

Often the contract conditions are such that the warrant will never be prematurely exercised, in which case, the correct valuation will be the standard European warrant treatment using the exercise

[23] By Taylor series approximation, we can compute the loss to the warrant holder of the standard adjustment for dividends: namely, $F(S-d, \tau; E-d) - F(S, \tau; E) = -dF_S(S, \tau; E) - dF_E(S, \tau; E) + o(d) = -[F(S, \tau; E) - (S-E)F_S(S, \tau; E)](d/E) + o(d)$, by the first-degree homogeneity of F in (S, E). Hence, to a first approximation, for $S = E$, the warrant will lose (d/S) percent of its value by this adjustment. Clearly, for $S > E$, the percentage loss will be smaller and for $S < E$, it will be larger.

price at expiration, E_0. If it can be demonstrated that

$$F_j(S, \tau_{j+1}; E_j) \geqq S - E_{j+1} \quad \text{for all } S \geqq 0 \text{ and } j = 0, 1, \ldots, N-1, \tag{10}$$

then the warrant will always be worth more "alive" than "dead," and the no-premature exercising result will obtain. From Theorem 1, $F_j(S, \tau_{j+1}; E_j) \geqq \text{Max}[0, S - P(\tau_{j+1} - \tau_j)E_j]$. Hence, from (10), a sufficient condition for no early exercising is that

$$E_{j+1}/E_j > P(\tau_{j+1} - \tau_j). \tag{11}$$

The economic reasoning behind (11) is identical to that used to derive Theorem 1. If by continuing to hold the warrant and investing the dollars which would have been paid for the stock if the warrant were exercised, the investor can with certainty earn enough to overcome the increased cost of exercising the warrant later, then the warrant should not be exercised.

Condition (11) is not as simple as it may first appear, because in valuing the warrant today, one must know for certain that (11) will be satisfied at some future date, which in general will not be possible if interest rates are stochastic. Often, as a practical matter, the size of the exercise price change versus the length of time between changes is such that for almost any reasonable rate of interest, (11) will be satisfied. For example, if the increase in exercise price is 10 percent and the length of time before the next exercise price change is five years, the yield to maturity on riskless securities would have to be less than 2 percent before (11) would not hold.

As a footnote to the analysis, we have the following Corollary.

Corollary. If there is a finite number of changes in the exercise price of a payout-protected, perpetual warrant, then it will not be exercised and its price will equal the common stock price.

Proof: applying the previous analysis, consider the value of the warrant if it survives past the last exercise price change, $F_0(S, \infty; E_0)$. By Theorem 3, $F_0(S, \infty; E_0) = S$. Now consider the value just prior to the last change in exercise price, $F_1(S, \infty; E_1)$. It must satisfy the boundary condition,

$$F_1(S, \infty; E_1) = \text{Max}[0, S - E_1, F_0(S, \infty; E_0)] = \text{Max}[0, S - E_1, S] = S.$$

Proceeding inductively, the warrant will never be exercised, and by Theorem 3, its value is equal to the common stock. Q.E.D.

The analysis of the effect on unprotected warrants when future dividends or dividend policy is known,[24] follows exactly the analysis of a changing exercise price. The arguments that no one will prematurely exercise his warrant except possibly at the discrete points in time just prior to a dividend payment, go through, and hence, the modified European warrant approach works where now the boundary conditions are $F_j(S, \tau_j; E) = \text{Max}\,[0, S - E, F_{j-1}(S - d_j, \tau_j; E)]$

[24] The distinction is made between knowing future dividends and dividend policy. With the former, one knows, currently, the actual amounts of future payments while, with the latter, one knows the conditional future payments, conditional on (currently unknown) future values, such as the stock price.

where d_j equals the dividend per share paid at τ_j years prior to expiration, for $j = 1, 2, \ldots, n$.

In the special case, where future dividends and rates of interest are known with certainty, a sufficient condition for no premature exercising is that[25]

$$E > \sum_{t=0}^{\tau} d(t)P(\tau - t)/[1 - P(\tau)]. \tag{12}$$

I.e., the net present value of future dividends is less than the present value of earnings from investing E dollars for τ periods. If dividends are paid continuously at the constant rate of d dollars per unit time and if the interest rate, r, is the same over time, then (12) can be rewritten in its continuous form as

$$E > \frac{d}{r}. \tag{13}$$

Samuelson suggests the use of discrete recursive relationships, similar to our modified European warrant analysis, as an approximation to the mathematically difficult continuous-time model when there is some chance for premature exercising.[26] We have shown that the only reasons for premature exercising are lack of protection against dividends or sufficiently unfavorable exercise price changes. Further, such exercising will never take place except at boundary points. Since dividends are paid quarterly and exercise price changes are less frequent, the Samuelson recursive formulation with the discrete-time spacing matching the intervals between dividends or exercise price changes is actually the correct one, and the continuous solution is the approximation, even if warrant and stock prices change continuously!

Based on the relatively weak Assumption 1, we have shown that dividends and unfavorable exercise price changes are the only rational reasons for premature exercising, and hence, the only reasons for an American warrant to sell for a premium over its European counterpart. In those cases where early exercising is possible, a computationally feasible, general algorithm for modifying a European warrant valuation scheme has been derived. A number of theorems were proved putting restrictions on the structure of rational European warrant pricing theory.

4. Restrictions on rational put option pricing

■ The put option, defined at the beginning of Section 2, has received relatively little analysis in the literature because it is a less popular option than the call and because it is commonly believed[27] that, given the price of a call option and the common stock, the value of a put is uniquely determined. This belief is false for American put

[25] The interpretation of (12) is similar to the explanation given for (11). Namely, if the losses from dividends are smaller than the gains which can be earned risklessly, from investing the extra funds required to exercise the warrant and hold the stock, then the warrant is worth more "alive" than "dead."

[26] See [42], pp. 25–26, especially equation (42). Samuelson had in mind small, discrete-time intervals, while in the context of the current application, the intervals would be large. Chen [8] also used this recursive relationship in his empirical testing of the Samuelson model.

[27] See, for example, Black and Scholes [4] and Stoll [52].

options, and the mathematics of put options pricing is more difficult than that of the corresponding call option.

Using the notation defined in Section 2, we have that, at expiration,

$$G(S, 0; E) = g(S, 0; E) = \text{Max}\,[0, E - S]. \tag{14}$$

To determine the rational European put option price, two portfolio positions are examined. Consider taking a long position in the common stock at S dollars, a long position in a τ-year European put at $g(S, \tau; E)$ dollars, and borrowing $[EP'(\tau)]$ dollars where $P'(\tau)$ is the current value of a dollar payable τ-years from now at the borrowing rate[28] (i.e., $P'(\tau)$ may not equal $P(\tau)$ if the borrowing and lending rates differ). The value of the portfolio τ years from now with the stock price at S^* will be: $S^* + (E - S^*) - E = 0$, if $S^* \leqq E$, and $S^* + 0 - E = S^* - E$, if $S^* > E$. The pay-off structure is identical in every state to a European call option with the same exercise price and duration. Hence, to avoid the call option from being a dominated security,[29] the put and call must be priced so that

$$g(S, \tau; E) + S - EP'(\tau) \geqq f(S, \tau; E). \tag{15}$$

As was the case in the similar analysis leading to Theorem 1, the values of the portfolio prior to expiration were not computed because the call option is European and cannot be prematurely exercised.

Consider taking a long position in a τ-year European call, a short position in the common stock at price S, and lending $EP(\tau)$ dollars. The value of the portfolio τ years from now with the stock price at S^* will be: $0 - S^* + E = E - S^*$, if $S^* \leqq E$, and $(S^* - E) - S^* + E = 0$, if $S^* > E$. The pay-off structure is identical in every state to a European put option with the same exercise price and duration. If the put is not to be a dominated security,[30] then

$$f(S, \tau; E) - S + EP(\tau) \geqq g(S, \tau; E) \tag{16}$$

must hold.

Theorem 12. If Assumption 1 holds and if the borrowing and lending rates are equal [i.e., $P(\tau) = P'(\tau)$], then

$$g(S, \tau; E) = f(S, \tau; E) - S + EP(\tau).$$

Proof: the proof follows directly from the simultaneous application of (15) and (16) when $P'(\tau) = P(\tau)$. Q.E.D.

Thus, the value of a rationally priced European put option is determined once one has a rational theory of the call option value. The formula derived in Theorem 12 is identical to B-S's equation (26), when the riskless rate, r, is constant (i.e., $P(\tau) = e^{-r\tau}$). Note

[28] The borrowing rate is the rate on a τ-year, noncallable, discounted loan. To avoid arbitrage, $P'(\tau) \leq P(\tau)$.

[29] Due to the existent market structure, (15) must hold for the stronger reason of arbitrage. The portfolio did not require short-sales and it is institutionally possible for an investor to issue (sell) call options and reinvest the proceeds from the sale. If (15) did not hold, an investor, acting unilaterally, could make immediate, positive profits with no investment and no risk.

[30] In this case, we do not have the stronger condition of arbitrage discussed in footnote (29) because the portfolio requires a short sale of shares, and, under current regulations, the proceeds cannot be reinvested. Again, intermediate values of the portfolio are not examined because the put option is European.

that no distributional assumptions about the stock price or future interest rates were required to prove Theorem 12.

Two corollaries to Theorem 12 follow directly from the above analysis.

Corollary 1. $EP(\tau) \geqq g(S, \tau; E)$.

Proof: from (5) and (7), $f(S, \tau; E) - S \leqq 0$ and from (16), $EP(\tau) \geqq g(S, \tau; E)$. Q.E.D.

The intuition of this result is immediate. Because of limited liability on the common stock, the maximum value of the put option is E, and because the option is European, the proceeds cannot be collected for τ years. The option cannot be worth more than the present value of a sure payment of its maximum value.

Corollary 2. The value of a perpetual ($\tau = \infty$) European put option is zero.

Proof: the put is a limited liability security [$g(S, \tau; E) \geqq 0$]. From Corollary 1 and the condition that $P(\infty) = 0$, $0 \geqq g(S, \infty; E)$. Q.E.D.

Using the relationship $g(S, \tau; E) = f(S, \tau; E) - S + EP(\tau)$, it is straightforward to derive theorems for rational European put pricing which are analogous to the theorems for warrants in Section 2. In particular, whenever f is homogeneous of degree one or convex in S and E, so g will be also. The correct adjustment for stock and cash dividends is the same as prescribed for warrants in Theorem 11 and its Corollary.[31]

Since the American put option can be exercised at any time, its price must satisfy the arbitrage condition

$$G(S, \tau; E) \geqq \text{Max}[0, E - S]. \tag{17}$$

By the same argument used to derive (5), it can be shown that

$$G(S, \tau; E) \geqq g(S, \tau; E), \tag{18}$$

where the strict inequality holds only if there is a positive probability of premature exercising.

As shown in Section 2, the European and American warrant have the same value if the exercise price is constant and they are protected against payouts to the common stock. Even under these assumptions, there is almost always a positive probability of premature exercising of an American put, and hence, the American put will sell for more than its European counterpart. A hint that this must be so comes from Corollary 2 and arbitrage condition (17). Unlike European options, the value of an American option is always a nondecreasing function of its expiration date. If there is no possibility of premature exercising, the value of an American option will equal the value of its European counterpart. By the Corollary to Theorem 11, the value of a perpetual American put would be zero, and by the monotonicity argument on length of time to maturity, all American puts would have zero value.

[31] While such adjustments for stock or cash payouts add to the value of a warrant or call option, the put option owner would prefer not to have them since lowering the exercise price on a put decreases its value. For simplicity, the effects of payouts are not considered, and it is assumed that no dividends are paid on the stock, and there are no exercise price changes.

This absurd result clearly violates the arbitrage condition (17) for $S < E$.

To clarify this point, reconsider the two portfolios examined in the European put analysis, but with American puts instead. The first portfolio contained a long position in the common stock at price S, a long position in an American put at price $G(S, \tau; E)$, and borrowings of $[EP'(\tau)]$. As was previously shown, if held until maturity, the outcome of the portfolio will be identical to those of an American (European) warrant held until maturity. Because we are now using American options with the right to exercise prior to expiration, the interim values of the portfolio must be examined as well. If, for all times prior to expiration, the portfolio has value greater than the exercise value of the American warrant, $S - E$, then to avoid dominance of the warrant, the current value of the portfolio must exceed or equal the current value of the warrant.

The interim value of the portfolio at T years until expiration when the stock price is S^*, is

$$S^* + G(S^*, T; E) - EP'(T) = G(S^*, T; E) + (S^* - E) + E[1 - P'(T)] > (S^* - E).$$

Hence, condition (15) holds for its American counterparts to avoid dominance of the warrant, i.e.,

$$G(S, \tau; E) + S - EP'(\tau) \geqq F(S, \tau; E). \tag{19}$$

The second portfolio has a long position in an American call at price $F(S, \tau; E)$, a short position in the common stock at price S, and a loan of $[EP(\tau)]$ dollars. If held until maturity, this portfolio replicates the outcome of a European put, and hence, must be at least as valuable at any interim point in time. The interim value of the portfolio, at T years to go and with the stock price at S^*, is

$$F(S^*, T; E) - S^* + EP(T) = (E - S^*) + F(S^*, T; E) - E[1 - P(T)] < E - S^*,$$

if $F(S^*, T; E) < E[1 - P(T)]$, which is possible for small enough S^*. From (17), $G(S^*, T; E) \geqq E - S^*$. So, the interim value of the portfolio will be less than the value of an American put for sufficiently small S^*. Hence, if an American put was sold against this portfolio, and if the put owner decided to exercise his put prematurely, the value of the portfolio could be less than the value of the exercised put. This result would certainly obtain if $S^* < E[1 - P(T)]$. So, the portfolio will not dominate the put if inequality (16) does not hold, and an analog theorem to Theorem 12, which uniquely determines the value of an American put in terms of a call, does not exist. Analysis of the second portfolio does lead to the weaker inequality that

$$G(S, \tau; E) \leqq E - S + F(S, \tau; E). \tag{20}$$

Theorem 13. If, for some $T < \tau$, there is a positive probability that $f(S, T; E) < E[1 - P(T)]$, then there is a positive probability that a τ-year, American put option will be exercised prematurely and the value of the American put will strictly exceed the value of its European counterpart.

Proof: the only reason that an American put will sell for a premium over its European counterpart is that there is a positive probability of exercising prior to expiration. Hence, it is sufficient to prove that $g(S, \tau; E) < G(S, \tau; E)$. From Assumption 1, if for some $T \leqq \tau$, $g(S^*, T; E) < G(S^*, T; E)$ for some possible value(s) of S^*, then $g(S, \tau; E) < G(S, \tau; E)$. From Theorem 12, $g(S^*, T; E) = f(S^*, T; E) - S^* + EP(T)$. From (17), $G(S^*, T; E) \geqq \text{Max}[0, E - S^*]$. But $g(S^*, T; E) < G(S^*, T; E)$ is implied if $E - S^* > f(S^*, T; E) - S^* + EP(T)$, which holds if $f(S^*, T; E) < E[1 - P(T)]$. By hypothesis of the theorem, such an S^* is a possible value. Q.E.D.

Since almost always there will be a chance of premature exercising, the formula of Theorem 12 or B-S equation (26) will not lead to a correct valuation of an American put and, as mentioned in Section 3, the valuation of such options is a more difficult analytical task than valuing their European counterparts.

5. Rational option pricing along Black-Scholes lines

■ A number of option pricing theories satisfy the general restrictions on a rational theory as derived in the previous sections. One such theory developed by B-S[32] is particularly attractive because it is a complete general equilibrium formulation of the problem and because the final formula is a function of "observable" variables, making the model subject to direct empirical tests.

B-S assume that: (1) the standard form of the Sharpe-Lintner-Mossin capital asset pricing model holds for intertemporal trading, and that trading takes place continuously in time; (2) the market rate of interest, r, is known and fixed over time; and (3) there are no dividends or exercise price changes over the life of the contract.

To derive the formula, they assume that the option price is a function of the stock price and time to expiration, and note that, over "short" time intervals, the stochastic part of the change in the option price will be perfectly correlated with changes in the stock price. A hedged portfolio containing the common stock, the option, and a short-term, riskless security, is constructed where the portfolio weights are chosen to eliminate all "market risk." By the assumption of the capital asset pricing model, any portfolio with a zero ("beta") market risk must have an expected return equal to the risk-free rate. Hence, an equilibrium condition is established between the expected return on the option, the expected return on the stock, and the riskless rate.

Because of the distributional assumptions and because the option price is a function of the common stock price, B-S in effect make use of the Samuelson[33] application to warrant pricing of the Bachelier-Einstein-Dynkin derivation of the Fokker-Planck equation, to express the expected return on the option in terms of the option price function and its partial derivatives. From the equilibrium condition on the option yield, such a partial differential equation for the option price is derived. The solution to this equation for a European call option is

$$f(S, \tau; E) = S\Phi(d_1) - Ee^{-r\tau}\Phi(d_2), \qquad (21)$$

where Φ is the cumulative normal distribution function, σ^2 is the

[32] In [4].

[33] In [42].

instantaneous variance of the return on the common stock,

$$d_1 \equiv [\log (S/E) + (r + \tfrac{1}{2}\sigma^2)\tau]/\sigma\sqrt{\tau},$$

and $d_2 \equiv d_1 - \sigma\sqrt{\tau}$.

An exact formula for an asset price, based on observable variables only, is a rare finding from a general equilibrium model, and care should be taken to analyze the assumptions with Occam's razor to determine which ones are necessary to derive the formula. Some hints are to be found by inspection of their final formula (21) and a comparison with an alternative general equilibrium development.

The manifest characteristic of (21) is the number of variables that it does *not* depend on. The option price does not depend on the expected return on the common stock,[34] risk preferences of investors, or on the aggregate supplies of assets. It does depend on the rate of interest (an "observable") and the *total* variance of the return on the common stock which is often a stable number and hence, accurate estimates are possible from time series data.

The Samuelson and Merton[35] model is a complete, although very simple (three assets and one investor) general equilibrium formulation. Their formula[36] is

$$f(S, \tau; E) = e^{-r\tau} \int_{E/S}^{\infty} (ZS - E)dQ(Z; \tau), \tag{22}$$

where dQ is a probability density function with the expected value of Z over the dQ distribution equal to $e^{r\tau}$. Equations (22) and (21) will be the same only in the special case when dQ is a log-normal density with the variance of log (Z) equal to $\sigma^2\tau$.[37] However, dQ is a risk-adjusted ("util-prob") distribution, dependent on both risk-preferences and aggregate supplies, while the distribution in (21) is the objective distribution of returns on the common stock. B-S claim that one reason that Samuelson and Merton did not arrive at formula (21) was because they did not consider other assets. If a result does not obtain for a simple, three asset case, it is unlikely that it would in a more general example. More to the point, it is only necessary to consider three assets to derive the B-S formula. In connection with this point, although B-S claim that their central assumption is the capital asset pricing model (emphasizing this over their hedging argument), their final formula, (21), depends only on the interest rate (which is exogenous to the capital asset pricing model) and on the *total* variance of the return on the common stock. It does not depend on the betas (covariances with the market) or other assets' characteristics. Hence, this assumption may be a "red herring."

Although their derivation of (21) is intuitively appealing, such an

---

[34] This is an important result because the expected return is not directly observable and estimates from past data are poor because of nonstationarity. It also implies that attempts to use the option price to estimate expected returns on the stock or risk-preferences of investors are doomed to failure (e.g., see Sprenkle [49]).

[35] In [43].

[36] *Ibid.*, p. 29, equation 30.

[37] This will occur only if: (1) the objective returns on the stock are log-normally distributed; (2) the investor's utility function is iso-elastic (i.e., homothetic indifference curves); and (3) the supplies of *both* options and bonds are at the incipient level.

important result deserves a rigorous derivation. In this case, the rigorous derivation is not only for the satisfaction of the "purist," but also to give insight into the necessary conditions for the formula to obtain. The reader should be alerted that because B-S consider only terminal boundary conditions, their analysis is strictly applicable to European options, although as shown in Sections 2 through 4, the European valuation is often equal to the American one.

Finally, although their model is based on a different economic structure, the formal analytical content is identical to Samuelson's "linear, $\alpha = \beta$" model when the returns on the common stock are log-normal.[38] Hence, with different interpretation of the parameters, theorems proved in Samuelson and in the difficult McKean appendix[39] are directly applicable to the B-S model, and vice versa.

6. An alternative derivation of the Black-Scholes model[40]

■ Initially, we consider the case of a European option where no payouts are made to the common stock over the life of the contract. We make the following further assumptions.

(1) "*Frictionless*" markets: there are no transactions costs or differential taxes. Trading takes place continuously and borrowing and short-selling are allowed without restriction.[41] The borrowing rate equals the lending rate.

(2) *Stock price dynamics:* the instantaneous return on the common stock is described by the stochastic differential equation[42]

$$\frac{dS}{S} = \alpha dt + \sigma dz, \tag{23}$$

where α is the instantaneous expected return on the common stock, σ^2 is the instantaneous variance of the return, and dz is a standard Gauss-Wiener process. α may be a stochastic variable of quite general type including being dependent on the level of the stock price or other assets' returns. Therefore, no presumption is made that dS/S is an independent increments process or stationary, although dz clearly is. However,

---

[38] In [42]. See Merton [28] for a brief description of the relationship between the Samuelson and B-S models.

[39] In [26].

[40] Although the derivation presented here is based on assumptions and techniques different from the original B-S model, it is in the spirit of their formulation, and yields the same formula when their assumptions are applied.

[41] The assumptions of unrestricted borrowing and short-selling can be weakened and still have the results obtained by splitting the created portfolio of the text into two portfolios: one containing the common stock and the other containing the warrant plus a long position in bonds. Then, as was done in Section 2, if we accept Assumption 1, the formulas of the current section follow immediately.

[42] For a general description of the theory of stochastic differential equations of the Itô type, see McKean [27] and Kushner [24]. For a description of their application to the consumption-portfolio problem, see Merton [32], [33], and [31]. Briefly, Itô processes follow immediately from the assumption of a continuous-time stochastic process which results in continuous price changes (with finite moments) and some level of independent increments. If the process for price changes were functions of stable Paretian distributions with infinite moments, it is conjectured that the only equilibrium value for a warrant would be the stock price itself, independent of the length of time to maturity. This implication is grossly inconsistent with all empirical observations.

σ is restricted to be nonstochastic and, at most, a known function of time.

(3) *Bond price dynamics:* $P(\tau)$ is as defined in previous sections and the dynamics of its returns are described by

$$\frac{dP}{P} = \mu(\tau)dt + \delta(\tau)dq(t;\tau), \tag{24}$$

where μ is the instantaneous expected return, δ^2 is the instantaneous variance, and $dq(t;\tau)$ is a standard Gauss-Wiener process for maturity τ. Allowing for the possibility of habitat and other term structure effects, it is not assumed that dq for one maturity is perfectly correlated with dq for another, i.e.,

$$dq(t;\tau)dq(t;T) = \rho_{\tau T}dt, \tag{24a}$$

where $\rho_{\tau T}$ may be less than one for $\tau \neq T$. However, it is assumed that there is no serial correlation[43] among the (unanticipated) returns on any of the assets, i.e.,

$$\begin{aligned} dq(s;\tau)dq(t;T) &= 0 \quad \text{for} \quad s \neq t \\ dq(s;\tau)dz(t) &= 0 \quad \text{for} \quad s \neq t, \end{aligned} \tag{24b}$$

which is consistent with the general efficient market hypothesis of Fama and Samuelson.[44] $\mu(\tau)$ may be stochastic through dependence on the level of bond prices, etc., and different for different maturities. Because $P(\tau)$ is the price of a discounted loan with no risk of default, $P(0) = 1$ with certainty and $\delta(\tau)$ will definitely depend on τ with $\delta(0) = 0$. However, δ is otherwise assumed to be nonstochastic and independent of the level of P. In the special case when the interest rate is nonstochastic and constant over time, $\delta \equiv 0$, $\mu = r$, and $P(\tau) = e^{-r\tau}$.

(4) *Investor preferences and expectations:* no assumptions are necessary about investor preferences other than that they

---

[43] The reader should be careful to note that it is assumed only that the *unanticipated* returns on the bonds are not serially correlated. Cootner [11] and others have pointed out that since the bond price will equal its redemption price at maturity, the total returns over time cannot be uncorrelated. In no way does this negate the specification of (24), although it does imply that the variance of the unanticipated returns must be a function of time to maturity. An example to illustrate that the two are not inconsistent can be found in Merton [29]. Suppose that bond prices for all maturities are only a function of the current (and future) short-term interest rates. Further, assume that the short-rate, r, follows a Gauss-Wiener process with (possibly) some drift, i.e., $dr = adt + gdz$, where a and g are constants. Although this process is not realistic because it implies a positive probability of negative interest rates, it will still illustrate the point. Suppose that all bonds are priced so as to yield an expected rate of return over the next period equal to r (i.e., a form of the expectations hypothesis):

$$P(\tau;r) = \exp\left[-r\tau - \frac{a}{2}\tau^2 + \frac{g^2\tau^3}{6}\right]$$

and

$$\frac{dP}{P} = rdt - g\tau dz.$$

By construction, dz is not serially correlated and in the notation of (24), $\delta(\tau) = -g\tau$.

[44] In [13] and [41], respectively.

satisfy Assumption 1 of Section 2. All investors agree on the values of σ and δ, and on the distributional characteristics of dz and dq. It is *not* assumed that they agree on either α or μ.[45]

From the analysis in Section 2, it is reasonable to assume that the option price is a function of the stock price, the riskless bond price, and the length of time to expiration. If $H(S, P, \tau; E)$ is the option price function, then, given the distributional assumptions on S and P, we have, by Itô's Lemma,[46] that the change in the option price over time satisfies the stochastic differential equation,

$$dH = H_1 dS + H_2 dP + H_3 d\tau + \tfrac{1}{2}[H_{11}(dS)^2 + 2H_{12}(dSdP) + H_{22}(dP)^2], \quad (25)$$

where subscripts denote partial derivatives, and $(dS)^2 \equiv \sigma^2 S^2 dt$, $(dP)^2 \equiv \delta^2 P^2 dt$, $d\tau = -dt$, and $(dSdP) \equiv \rho\sigma\delta SPdt$ with ρ, the instantaneous correlation coefficient between the (unanticipated) returns on the stock and on the bond. Substituting from (23) and (24) and rearranging terms, we can rewrite (25) as

$$dH = \beta H dt + \gamma H dz + \eta H dq, \quad (26)$$

where the instantaneous expected return on the warrant, β, equals $[\frac{1}{2}\sigma^2 S^2 H_{11} + \rho\sigma\delta SPH_{12} + \frac{1}{2}\delta^2 P^2 H_{22} + \alpha SH_1 + \mu PH_2 - H_3]/H$, $\gamma \equiv \sigma SH_1/H$, and $\eta \equiv \delta PH_2/H$.

In the spirit of the Black-Scholes formulation and the analysis in Sections 2 thru 4, consider forming a portfolio containing the common stock, the option, and riskless bonds with time to maturity, τ, equal to the expiration date of the option, such that the aggregate investment in the portfolio is zero. This is achieved by using the proceeds of short-sales and borrowing to finance long positions. Let W_1 be the (instantaneous) number of dollars of the portfolio invested in the common stock, W_2 be the number of dollars invested in the option, and W_3 be the number of dollars invested in bonds. Then, the condition of zero aggregate investment can be written as $W_1 + W_2 + W_3 = 0$. If dY is the instantaneous dollar return to the portfolio, it can be shown[47] that

$$\begin{aligned} dY &= W_1 \frac{dS}{S} + W_2 \frac{dH}{H} + W_3 \frac{dP}{P} \\ &= [W_1(\alpha - \mu) + W_2(\beta - \mu)]dt + [W_1\sigma + W_2\gamma]dz \\ &\quad + [W_2\eta - (W_1 + W_2)\delta]dq, \end{aligned} \quad (27)$$

where $W_3 \equiv -(W_1 + W_2)$ has been substituted out.

[45] This assumption is much more acceptable than the usual homogeneous expectations. It is quite reasonable to expect that investors may have quite different estimates for current (and future) expected returns due to different levels of information, techniques of analysis, etc. However, most analysts calculate estimates of variances and covariances in the same way: namely, by using previous price data. Since all have access to the same price history, it is also reasonable to assume that their variance-covariance estimates may be the same.

[46] Itô's Lemma is the stochastic-analog to the fundamental theorem of the calculus because it states how to differentiate functions of Wiener processes. For a complete description and proof, see McKean [27]. A brief discussion can be found in Merton [33].

[47] See Merton [32] or [33].

Suppose a strategy, $W_j = W_j^*$, can be chosen such that the coefficients of dz and dq in (27) are always zero. Then, the dollar return on that portfolio, dY^*, would be nonstochastic. Since the portfolio requires zero investment, it must be that to avoid "arbitrage"[48] profits, the expected (and realized) return on the portfolio with this strategy is zero. The two portfolio and one equilibrium conditions can be written as a 3 × 2 linear system,

$$\begin{aligned}(\alpha - \mu)W_1^* + (\beta - \mu)W_2^* &= 0\\ \sigma W_1^* + \gamma W_2^* &= 0\\ -\delta W_1^* + (\eta - \delta)W_2^* &= 0.\end{aligned} \tag{28}$$

A nontrivial solution ($W_1^* \neq 0$; $W_2^* \neq 0$) to (28) exists if and only if

$$\frac{\beta - \mu}{\alpha - \mu} = \frac{\gamma}{\sigma} = \frac{\delta - \eta}{\delta}. \tag{29}$$

Because we make the "bucket shop" assumption, μ, α, δ, and σ are legitimate exogeneous variables (relative to the option price), and β, γ, and η are to be determined so as to avoid dominance of any of the three securities. If (29) holds, then $\gamma/\sigma = 1 - \eta/\delta$, which implies from the definition of γ and in (26), that

$$\frac{SH_1}{H} = 1 - \frac{PH_2}{H} \tag{30}$$

or

$$H = SH_1 + PH_2. \tag{31}$$

Although it is not a sufficient condition, by Euler's theorem, (31) is a necessary condition for H to be first degree homogeneous in (S, P) as was conjectured in Section 2.

The second condition from (29) is that $\beta - \mu = \gamma(\alpha - \mu)/\sigma$, which implies from the definition of β and γ in (26) that

$$\tfrac{1}{2}\sigma^2 S^2 H_{11} + \rho\sigma\delta SPH_{12} + \tfrac{1}{2}\delta^2 P^2 H_{22} + \alpha SH_1 + \mu PH_2 - H_3 - \mu H = SH_1(\alpha - \mu), \tag{32}$$

or, by combining terms, that

$$\tfrac{1}{2}\sigma^2 S^2 H_{11} + \rho\sigma\delta SPH_{12} + \tfrac{1}{2}\delta^2 P^2 H_{22} + \mu SH_1 + \mu PH_2 - H_3 - \mu H = 0. \tag{33}$$

Substituting for H from (31) and combining terms, (33) can be rewritten as

$$\tfrac{1}{2}[\sigma^2 S^2 H_{11} + 2\rho\sigma\delta SPH_{12} + \delta^2 P^2 H_{22}] - H_3 = 0, \tag{34}$$

which is a second-order, linear partial differential equation of the parabolic type.

[48] "Arbitrage" is used in the qualified sense that the distributional and other assumptions are known to hold with certainty. A weaker form would say that if the return on the portfolio is nonzero, either the option or the common stock would be a dominated security. See Samuelson [44] or [45] for a discussion of this distinction.

If H is the price of a European warrant, then H must satisfy (34) subject to the boundary conditions:

$$H(0, P, \tau; E) = 0 \tag{34a}$$

$$H(S, 1, 0; E) = \text{Max}[0, S - E], \tag{34b}$$

since by construction, $P(0) = 1$.

Define the variable $x \equiv S/EP(\tau)$, which is the price per share of stock in units of exercise price-dollars payable at a *fixed date* in the future (the expiration date of the warrant). The variable x is a well-defined price for $\tau \geqq 0$, and from (23), (24), and Itô's Lemma, the dynamics of x are described by the stochastic differential equation,

$$\frac{dx}{x} = [\alpha - \mu + \delta^2 - \rho\sigma\delta]dt + \sigma dz - \delta dq. \tag{35}$$

From (35), the expected return on x will be a function of S, P, etc., through α and μ, but the instantaneous variance of the return on x, $V^2(\tau)$, is equal to $\sigma^2 + \delta^2 - 2\rho\sigma\delta$, and will depend only on τ.

Motivated by the possible homogeneity properties of H, we try the change in variables, $h(x, \tau; E) \equiv H(S, P, \tau; E)/EP$ where h is assumed to be independent of P and is the warrant price evaluated in the same units as x. Substituting (h, x) for (H, S) in (34), (34a) and (34b), leads to the partial differential equation for h,

$$\tfrac{1}{2}V^2x^2h_{11} - h_2 = 0, \tag{36}$$

subject to the boundary conditions, $h(0, \tau; E) = 0$, and $h(x, 0; E) = \text{Max}[0, x - 1]$. From inspection of (36) and its boundary conditions, h is only a function of x and τ, since V^2 is only a function of τ. Hence, the assumed homogeneity property of H is verified. Further, h does not depend on E, and so, H is actually homogeneous of degree one in $[S, EP(\tau)]$.

Consider a new time variable, $T \equiv \int_0^\tau V^2(s)ds$. Then, if we define $y(x, T) \equiv h(x, \tau)$ and substitute into (36), y must satisfy

$$\tfrac{1}{2}x^2y_{11} - y_2 = 0, \tag{37}$$

subject to the boundary conditions, $y(0, T) = 0$ and $y(x, 0) = \text{Max}\,[0, x - 1]$. Suppose we wrote the warrant price in its "full functional form," $H(S, P, \tau; E, \sigma^2, \delta^2, \rho)$. Then,

$$y = H(x, 1, T; 1, 1, 0, 0),$$

and is the price of a warrant with T years to expiration and exercise price of one dollar, on a stock with unit instantaneous variance of return, when the market rate of interest is zero over the life of the contract.

Once we solve (37) for the price of this "standard" warrant, we have, by a change of variables, the price for any European warrant. Namely,

$$H(S, P, \tau; E) = EP(\tau)y\left[S/EP(\tau), \int_0^\tau V^2(s)ds\right]. \tag{38}$$

Hence, for empirical testing or applications, one need only compute tables for the "standard" warrant price as a function of two variables, stock price and time to expiration, to be able to compute warrant prices in general.

To solve (37), we first put it in standard form by the change in variables $Z \equiv \log(x) + T/2$ and $\phi(Z, T) \equiv y(x, T)/x$, and then substitute in (37) to arrive at

$$0 = \tfrac{1}{2}\phi_{11} - \phi_2, \tag{39}$$

subject to the boundary conditions: $|\phi(Z, T)| \leqq 1$ and $\phi(Z, 0) = \text{Max}[0, 1 - e^{-Z}]$. Equation (39) is a standard free-boundary problem to be solved by separation of variables or Fourier transforms.[49] Its solution is

$$y(x, T) = x\phi(Z, T) = [x\,erfc(h_1) - erfc(h_2)]/2, \tag{40}$$

where *erfc* is the error complement function which is tabulated, $h_1 \equiv -[\log x + \tfrac{1}{2}T]/\sqrt{2T}$, and $h_2 \equiv -[\log x - \tfrac{1}{2}T]/\sqrt{2T}$. Equation (40) is identical to (21) with $r = 0$, $\sigma^2 = 1$, and $E = 1$. Hence, (38) will be identical to (21) the B-S formula, in the special case of a nonstochastic and constant interest rate (i.e., $\delta = 0$, $\mu = r$, $P = e^{-r\tau}$, and $T \equiv \sigma^2\tau$).

Equation (37) corresponds exactly to Samuelson's equation[50] for the warrant price in his "linear" model when the stock price is lognormally distributed, with his parameters $\alpha = \beta = 0$, and $\sigma^2 = 1$. Hence, tables generated from (40) could be used with (38) for valuations of the Samuelson formula where $e^{-\alpha\tau}$ is substituted for $P(\tau)$ in (38).[51] Since α in his theory is the expected rate of return on a risky security, one would expect that $e^{-\alpha\tau} < P(\tau)$. As a consequence of the following theorem, $e^{-\alpha\tau} < P(\tau)$ would imply that Samuelson's forecasted values for the warrants would be higher than those forecasted by B-S or the model presented here.

Theorem 14. For a given stock price, the warrant price is a nonincreasing function of $P(\tau)$, and hence, a nondecreasing function of the τ-year interest rate.

Proof: it follows immediately, since an increase in P is equivalent to an increase in E which never increases the value of the warrant. Formally, H is a convex function of S and passes through the origin. Hence, $H - SH_1 \leqq 0$. But from (31), $H - SH_1 = PH_2$, and since $P \geqq 0$, $H_2 \leqq 0$. By definition, $P(\tau)$ is a decreasing function of the τ-year interest rate. Q.E.D.

Because we applied only the terminal boundary condition to (34), the price function derived is for an European warrant. The correct boundary conditions for an American warrant would also include the arbitrage-boundary inequality

$$H(S, P, \tau; E) \geqq \text{Max}[0, S - E]. \tag{34c}$$

Since it was assumed that no dividend payments or exercise price changes occur over the life of the contract, we know from Theorem 1, that if the formulation of this section is a "rational" theory, then

[49] For a separation of variables solution, see Churchill [9], pp. 154–156, and for the transform technique, see Dettman [12], p. 390. Also see McKean [26].

[50] In [42], p. 27.

[51] The tables could also be used to evaluate warrants priced by the Sprenkle [49] formula. Warning: while the Samuelson interpretation of the "$\beta = \alpha$" case implies that expected returns are equated on the warrant and the stock, the B-S interpretation does not. Namely, from [29], the expected return on the warrant satisfies $\beta = r + H_1S(\alpha - r)/H$, where H_1 can be computed from (21) by differentiation.

it will satisfy the stronger inequality $H \geqq \text{Max}[0, S - EP(\tau)]$ [which is homogeneous in S and $EP(\tau)$], and the American warrant will have the same value as its European counterpart. Samuelson argued that solutions to equations like (21) and (38) will always have values at least as large as $\text{Max}[0, S - E]$, and Samuelson and Merton[52] proved it under more general conditions. Hence, there is no need for formal verification here. Further, it can be shown that (38) satisfies all the theorems of Section 2.

As a direct result of the equal values of the European and American warrants, we have:

Theorem 15. The warrant price is a nondecreasing function of the variance of the stock price return.

Proof: from (38), the change in H with respect to a change in variance will be proportional to y_2. But, y is the price of a legitimate American warrant and hence, must be a nondecreasing function of time to expiration, i.e., $y_2 \geqq 0$. Q.E.D.

Actually, Theorem 15 is a special case of the general proposition (Theorem 8) proved in Section 2, that the more risky is the stock, the more valuable is the warrant. Although Rothschild and Stiglitz[53] have shown that, in general, increasing variance may not imply increasing risk, it is shown in Appendix 2 that variance is a valid measure of risk for this model.

We have derived the B-S warrant pricing formula rigorously under assumptions weaker than they postulate, and have extended the analysis to include the possibility of stochastic interest rates.

Because the original B-S derivation assumed constant interest rates in forming their hedge positions, it did not matter whether they borrowed or lent long or short maturities. The derivation here clearly demonstrates that the correct maturity to use in the hedge is the one which matches the maturity date of the option. "Correct" is used in the sense that if the price $P(\tau)$ remains fixed while the price of other maturities changes, the price of a τ-year option will remain unchanged.

The capital asset pricing model is a sufficient assumption to derive the formula. While the assumptions of this section are necessary for the intertemporal use of the capital asset pricing model,[54] they are not sufficient, e.g., we do not assume that interest rates are nonstochastic, that price dynamics are stationary, nor that investors have homogeneous expectations. All are required for the capital asset pricing model. Further, since we consider only the properties of three securities, we do not assume that the capital market is in full general equilibrium. Since the final formula is independent of α or μ, it will hold even if the observed stock or bond prices are transient, nonequilibrium prices.

The key to the derivation is that any one of the securities' returns over time can be perfectly replicated by continuous portfolio combinations of the other two. A complete analysis would require that

[52] In [42] and [43], respectively.

[53] In [39].

[54] See Merton [31] for a discussion of necessary and sufficient conditions for a Sharpe-Lintner-Mossin type model to obtain in an intertemporal context. The sufficient conditions are rather restrictive.

all three securities' prices be solved for simultaneously which, in general, would require the examination of all other assets, knowledge of preferences, etc. However, because of "perfect substitutability" of the securities and the "bucket shop" assumption, supply effects can be neglected, and we can apply "partial equilibrium" analysis resulting in a "causal-type" formula for the option price as a function of the stock and bond prices.

This "perfect substitutability" of the common stock and borrowing for the warrant or the warrant and lending for the common stock explains why the formula is independent of the expected return on the common stock or preferences. The expected return on the stock and the investor's preferences will determine how much capital to invest (long or short) in a given company. The decision as to whether to take the position by buying warrants or by leveraging the stock depends only on their relative prices and the cost of borrowing. As B-S point out, the argument is similar to an intertemporal Modigliani-Miller theorem. The reason that the B-S assumption of the capital asset pricing model leads to the correct formula is that because it is an equilibrium model, it must necessarily rule out "sure-thing" profits among perfectly correlated securities, which is exactly condition (29). Careful study of both their derivations shows that (29) is the only part of the capital asset pricing model ever used.

The assumptions of this section are necessary for (38) and (40) to hold.[55] The continuous-trading assumption is necessary to establish perfect correlation among nonlinear functions which is required to form the "perfect hedge" portfolio mix. The Samuelson and Merton model[56] is an immediate counter-example to the validity of the formula for discrete-trading intervals.

The assumption of Itô processes for the assets' returns dynamics was necessary to apply Itô's Lemma. The further restriction that σ and δ be nonstochastic and independent of the price levels is required so that the option price change is due only to changes in the stock or bond prices, which was necessary to establish a perfect hedge and to establish the homogeneity property (31).[57] Clearly if investors did not agree on the value of $V^2(\tau)$, they would arrive at different values for the same warrant.

The B-S claim that (21) or (38) is the only formula consistent with capital market equilibrium is a bit too strong. It is not true that if the market prices options differently, then arbitrage profits are ensured. It is a "rational" option pricing theory relative to the assumptions of this section. If these assumptions held with certainty, then the B-S formula is the only one which all investors could agree on, and no deviant member could prove them wrong.[58]

---

[55] If most of the "frictionless" market assumptions are dropped, it may be possible to show that, by substituting current institutional conditions, (38) and (40) will give lower bounds for the warrant's value.

[56] In [43].

[57] In the special case when interest rates are nonstochastic, the variance of the stock price return can be a function of the price level and the derivation still goes through. However, the resulting partial differential equation will not have a simple closed-form solution.

[58] This point is emphasized in a critique of Thorp and Kassouf's [53] "sure-thing" arbitrage techniques by Samuelson [45] and again, in Samuelson [44], footnote 6.

7. Extension of the model to include dividend payments and exercise price changes

■ To analyze the effect of dividends on unprotected warrants, it is helpful to assume a constant and known interest rate r. Under this assumption, $\delta = 0$, $\mu = r$, and $P(\tau) = e^{-r\tau}$. Condition (29) simplifies to

$$\beta - r = \gamma(\alpha - r)/\sigma. \tag{41}$$

Let $D(S, \tau)$ be the dividend per share unit time when the stock price is S and the warrant has τ years to expiration. If α is the instantaneous, *total* expected return as defined in (23), then the instantaneous expected return from price appreciation is $[\alpha - D(S, \tau)/S]$. Because $P(\tau)$ is no longer stochastic, we suppress it and write the warrant price function as $W(S, \tau; E)$. As was done in (25) and (26), we apply Itô's Lemma to derive the stochastic differential equation for the warrant price to be

$$\begin{aligned} dW &= W_1(dS - D(S, \tau)dt) + W_2 d\tau + \tfrac{1}{2}W_{11}(dS)^2 \\ &= [\tfrac{1}{2}\sigma^2 S^2 W_{11} + (\alpha S - D)W_1 - W_2]dt + \sigma S W_1 dz. \end{aligned} \tag{42}$$

Note: since the warrant owner is not entitled to any part of the dividend return, he only considers that part of the expected dollar return to the common stock due to price appreciation. From (42) and the definition of β and γ, we have that

$$\begin{aligned} \beta W &= \tfrac{1}{2}\sigma^2 S^2 W_{11} + (\alpha S - D)W_1 - W_2 \\ \gamma W &= \sigma S W_1. \end{aligned} \tag{43}$$

Applying (41) to (43), we arrive at the partial differential equation for the warrant price,

$$\tfrac{1}{2}\sigma^2 S^2 W_{11} + (rS - D)W_1 - W_2 - rW = 0, \tag{44}$$

subject to the boundary conditions, $W(0, \tau; E) = 0$, $W(S, 0; E) = \text{Max}\,[0, S - E]$ for a European warrant, and to the additional arbitrage boundary condition, $W(S, \tau; E) \geqq \text{Max}\,[0, S - E]$ for an American warrant.

Equation (44) will not have a simple solution, even for the European warrant and relatively simple functional forms for D. In evaluating the American warrant in the "no-dividend" case ($D = 0$), the arbitrage boundary inequalities were not considered explicitly in arriving at a solution, because it was shown that the European warrant price never violated the inequality, and the American and European warrant prices were equal. For many dividend policies, the solution for the European warrant price will violate the inequality, and for those policies, there will be a positive probability of premature exercising of the American warrant. Hence, to obtain a correct value for the American warrant from (44), we must explicitly consider the boundary inequality, and transform it into a suitable form for solution.

If there exists a positive probability of premature exercising, then, for every τ, there exists a level of stock price, $C[\tau]$, such that for all $S > C[\tau]$, the warrant would be worth more exercised than if held. Since the value of an exercised warrant is always $(S - E)$, we have the appended boundary condition for (44),

$$W(C[\tau], \tau; E) = C[\tau] - E, \tag{44a}$$

where W satisfies (44) for $0 \leqq S \leqq C[\tau]$.

If $C[\tau]$ were a known function, then, after the appropriate change of variables, (44) with the European boundary conditions and (44a) appended, would be a semiinfinite boundary value problem with a time-dependent boundary. However, $C[\tau]$ is not known, and must be determined as part of the solution. Therefore, an additional boundary condition is required for the problem to be well-posed.

Fortunately, the economics of the problem are sufficiently rich to provide this extra condition. Because the warrant holder is not contractually obliged to exercise his warrant prematurely, he chooses to do so only in his own best interest (i.e., when the warrant is worth more "dead" than "alive"). Hence, the only rational choice for $C[\tau]$ is that time-pattern which maximizes the value of the warrant. Let $f(S, \tau; E, C[\tau])$ be a solution to (44)–(44a) for a given $C[\tau]$ function. Then, the value of a τ-year American warrant will be

$$W(S, \tau; E) = \underset{\{c\}}{\text{Max}} f(S, \tau; E, C). \quad (45)$$

Further, the structure of the problem makes it clear that the optimal $C[\tau]$ will be independent of the current level of the stock price. In attacking this difficult problem, Samuelson[59] postulated that the extra condition was "high-contact" at the boundary, i.e.,

$$W_1(C[\tau], \tau; E) = 1. \quad (44b)$$

It can be shown[60] that (44b) is implied by the maximizing behavior described by (45). So the correct specification for the American warrant price is (44) with the European boundary conditions plus (44a) and (44b).

Samuelson and Samuelson and Merton[61] have shown that for a proportional dividend policy where $D(S, \tau) = \rho S$, $\rho > 0$, there is always a positive probability of premature exercising, and hence, the arbitrage boundary condition will be binding for sufficiently large stock prices.[62] With $D = \rho S$, (44) is mathematically identical to Samuelson's[63] "nonlinear" ("$\beta > \alpha$") case where his $\beta = r$ and his $\alpha = r - \rho$. Samuelson and McKean[64] analyze this problem in great detail. Although there are no simple closed-form solutions for finite-lived warrants, they did derive solutions for perpetual warrants which are power functions, tangent to the "$S - E$" line at finite values of S.[65]

---

[59] In [42].

[60] Let $f(x, c)$ be a differentiable function, concave in its second argument, for $0 \leqq x \leqq c$. Require that $f(c, c) = h(c)$, a differentiable function of c. Let $c = c^*$ be the c which maximizes f, i.e.,

$$f_2(x, c^*) = 0,$$

where subscripts denote partial derivatives. Consider the total derivative of f with respect to c along the boundary $x = c$. Then,

$$df/dc = dh/dc = f_1(c, c) + f_2(c, c).$$

For $c = c^*, f_2 = 0$. Hence, $f_1(c^*, c^*) = dh/dc$. In the case of the text, $h = c - E$, and the "high-contact" solution, $f_1(c^*, c^*) = 1$, is proved.

[61] In [42] and [43], respectively.

[62] For $D = \rho S$, the solution to (44) for the European warrant is

$$W = [e^{-\rho\tau}S\Phi(d_1) - Ee^{-r\tau}\Phi(d_2)]$$

where Φ, d_1, and d_2 are as defined in (21). For large S,

$$W \sim [e^{-\rho\tau}S - Ee^{-r\tau}]$$

which will be less than $(S - E)$ for large S and $\rho > 0$. Hence, the American warrant can be worth more "dead" than "alive."

[63] In [42].

[64] *Ibid.* In the appendix.

[65] *Ibid.*, p. 28.

A second example of a simple dividend policy is the constant one where $D = d$, a constant. Unlike the previous proportional policy, premature exercising may or may not occur, depending upon the values for d, r, E, and τ. In particular, a sufficient condition for no premature exercising was derived in Section 3. Namely,

$$E > \frac{d}{r}. \tag{13}$$

If (13) obtains, then the solution for the European warrant price will be the solution for the American warrant. Although a closed-form solution has not yet been found for finite τ, a solution for the perpetual warrant when $E > d/r$, is[66]

$$W(S, \infty; E) = S - \frac{d}{r}\left[1 - \frac{\left(\frac{2d}{\sigma^2 S}\right)^{2r/\sigma^2}}{\Gamma\left(2 + \frac{2r}{\sigma^2}\right)} M\left(\frac{2r}{\sigma^2}, 2 + \frac{2r}{\sigma^2}, \frac{-2d}{\sigma^2 S}\right)\right] \tag{46}$$

where M is the confluent hypergeometric function, and W is plotted in Figure 2.

FIGURE 2

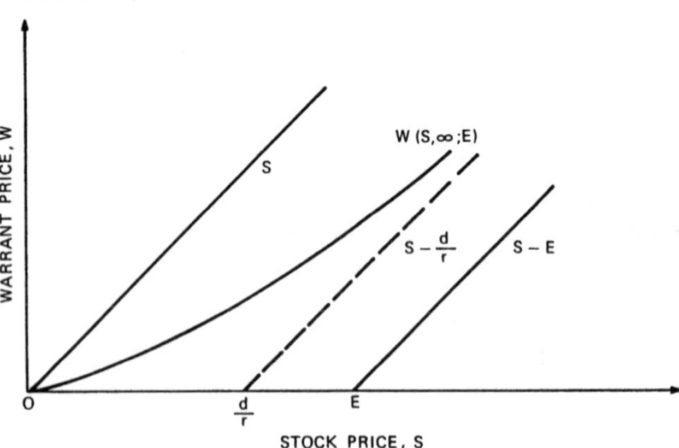

[66] Make the change in variables: $Z \equiv \delta/S$ and

$$h(Z) \equiv \exp[Z]Z^{-\gamma}W$$

where

$$\delta \equiv 2d/\sigma^2$$

and

$$\gamma \equiv 2r/\sigma^2.$$

Then, substituting in (44), we have the differential equation for h:

$$Zh'' + (\gamma + 2 - Z)h' - 2h = 0,$$

whose general solution is $h = c_1M(2, 2 + \gamma, Z) + c_2Z^{-(\gamma+1)}M(1 - \gamma, -\gamma, Z)$ which becomes (46) when the boundary conditions are applied. Analysis of (46) shows that W passes through the origin, is convex, and is asymptotic to the line $(S - d/r)$ for large S, i.e., it approaches the common stock value less the present discounted value of all future dividends forgone by holding the warrant.

Consider the case of a continuously changing exercise price, $E(\tau)$, where E is assumed to be differentiable and a decreasing function of the length of time to maturity, i.e., $dE/d\tau = -dE/dt = -\dot{E} < 0$. The warrant price will satisfy (44) with $D = 0$, but subject to the boundary conditions,

$$W[S, 0; E(0)] = \text{Max}\,[0, S - E(0)]$$

and

$$W[S, \tau; E(\tau)] \geqq \text{Max}\,[0, S - E(\tau)].$$

Make the change in variables $X \equiv S/E(\tau)$ and

$$F(X, \tau) \equiv W[S, \tau; E(\tau)]/E(\tau).$$

Then, F satisfies

$$\tfrac{1}{2}\sigma^2 X^2 F_{11} + \eta(\tau) X F_1 - \eta(\tau) F - F_2 = 0, \tag{47}$$

subject to $F(X, 0) = \text{Max}\,[0, X - 1]$ and $F(X, \tau) \geqq \text{Max}\,[0, X - 1]$ where $\eta(\tau) \equiv r - \dot{E}/E$. Notice that the structure of (47) is identical to the pricing of a warrant with a fixed exercise price and a variable, but nonstochastic, "interest rate" $\eta(\tau)$. (I.e., substitute in the analysis of the previous section for $P(\tau)$, $\exp\,[-\int_0^\tau \eta(s)ds]$, except $\eta(\tau)$ can be negative for sufficiently large changes in exercise price.) We have already shown that for $\int_0^\tau \eta(s)ds \geqq 0$, there will be no premature exercising of the warrant, and only the terminal exercise price should matter. Noting that $\int_0^\tau \eta(s)ds = \int_0^\tau [r + dE/d\tau]ds = r\tau + \log\,[E(\tau)/E(0)]$, formal substitution for $P(\tau)$ in (38) verifies that the value of the warrant is the same as for a warrant with a fixed exercise price, $E(0)$, and interest rate r. We also have agreement of the current model with (11) of Section 3, because $\int_0^\tau \eta(s)ds \geqq 0$ implies $E(\tau) \geqq E(0)\exp\,[-r\tau]$, which is a general sufficient condition for no premature exercising.

8. Valuing an American put option

■ As the first example of an application of the model to other types of options, we now consider the rational pricing of the put option, relative to the assumptions in Section 7. In Section 4, it was demonstrated that the value of an European put option was completely determined once the value of the call option is known (Theorem 12). B-S give the solution for their model in equation (26). It was also demonstrated in Section 4 that the European valuation is not valid for the American put option because of the positive probability of premature exercising. If $G(S, \tau; E)$ is the rational put price, then, by the same technique used to derive (44) with $D = 0$, G satisfies

$$\tfrac{1}{2}\sigma^2 S^2 G_{11} + rSG_1 - rG - G_2 = 0, \tag{48}$$

subject to $G(\infty, \tau; E) = 0$, $G(S, 0; E) = \text{Max}\,[0, E - S]$, and $G(S, \tau; E) \geqq \text{Max}\,[0, E - S]$.

From the analysis by Samuelson and McKean[67] on warrants, there is no closed-form solution to (48) for finite τ. However, using their techniques, it is possible to obtain a solution for the perpetual put option (i.e., $\tau = \infty$). For a sufficiently low stock price, it will be advantageous to exercise the put. Define C to be the largest value of the stock such that the put holder is better off exercising than continuing to hold it. For the perpetual put, (48) reduces to the ordinary

[67] In [42].

differential equation,

$$\tfrac{1}{2}\sigma^2 S^2 G_{11} + rSG_1 - rG = 0, \tag{49}$$

which is valid for the range of stock prices $C \leqq S \leqq \infty$. The boundary conditions for (49) are:

$$G(\infty, \infty; E) = 0, \tag{49a}$$

$$G(C, \infty; E) = E - C, \text{ and} \tag{49b}$$

choose C so as to maximize the value of the option, which follows from the maximizing behavior arguments of the previous section. (49c)

From the theory of linear ordinary differential equations, solutions to (49) involve two constants, a_1 and a_2. Boundary conditions (49a), (49b), and (49c) will determine these constants along with the unknown lower-bound, stock price, C. The general solution to (49) is

$$G(S, \infty; E) = a_1 S + a_2 S^{-\gamma}, \tag{50}$$

where $\gamma \equiv 2r/\sigma^2 > 0$. Equation (49a) requires that $a_1 = 0$, and (49b) requires that $a_2 = (E - C)C^{\gamma}$. Hence, as a function of C,

$$G(S, \infty; E) = (E - C)(S/C)^{-\gamma}. \tag{51}$$

To determine C, we apply (49c) and choose that value of C which maximizes (51), i.e., choose $C = C^*$ such that $\partial G/\partial C = 0$. Solving this condition, we have that $C^* = \gamma E/(1 + \gamma)$, and the put option price is,

$$G(S, \infty; E) = \frac{E}{(1 + \gamma)} [(1 + \gamma)S/\gamma E]^{-\gamma}. \tag{52}$$

The Samuelson "high-contact" boundary condition

$$G_1(C^*, \infty; E) = -1,$$

as an alternative specification of boundary condition (49c), can be verified by differentiating (52) with respect to S and evaluating at $S = C^*$. Figure 3 illustrates the American put price as a function of the stock price and time to expiration.

FIGURE 3

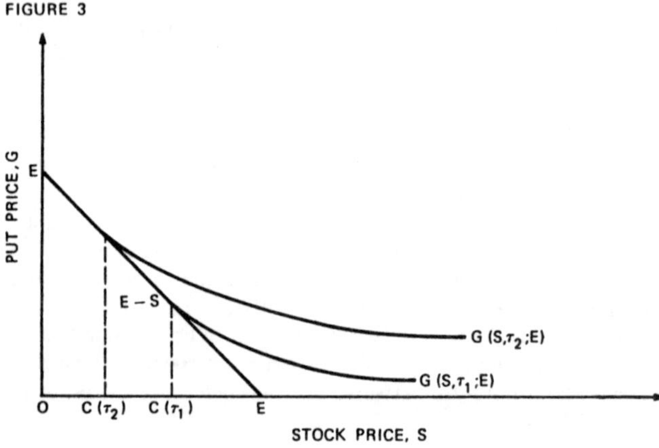

9. Valuing the "down-and-out" call option

■ As a second example of the application of the model to other types of options, we consider the rational pricing of a new type of call option called the "down-and-outer."[68] This option has the same terms with respect to exercise price, antidilution clauses, etc., as the standard call option, but with the additional feature that if the stock price falls below a stated level, the option contract is nullified, i.e., the option becomes worthless.[69] Typically, the "knock-out" price is a function of the time to expiration, increasing as the expiration date nears.

Let $f(S, \tau; E)$ be the value of an European "down-and-out" call option, and $B[\tau] = bE\exp[-\eta\tau]$ be the "knock-out" price as a function of time to expiration where it is assumed that $\eta \geqq 0$ and $0 \leqq b \leqq 1$. Then f will satisfy the fundamental partial differential equation,

$$\tfrac{1}{2}\sigma^2 S^2 f_{11} + rSf_1 - rf - f_2 = 0, \tag{53}$$

subject to the boundary conditions,

$$f(B[\tau], \tau; E) = 0$$
$$f(S, 0; E) = \text{Max}\,[0, S - E].$$

Note: if $B(\tau) = 0$, then (53) would be the equation for a standard European call option.

Make the change in variables, $x \equiv \log[S/B(\tau)]$; $T \equiv \sigma^2\tau$;

$$H(x, T) \equiv \exp[ax + \gamma\tau] f(S, \tau; E)/E,$$

and $a \equiv [r - \eta - \sigma^2/2]/\sigma^2$ and $\gamma \equiv r + a^2\sigma^2/2$. Then, by substituting into (53), we arrive at the equation for H,

$$\tfrac{1}{2}H_{11} - H_2 = 0 \tag{54}$$

subject to

$$H(0, T) = 0$$
$$H(x, 0) = e^{ax}\,\text{Max}\,[0, be^x - 1],$$

which is a standard, semiinfinite boundary value problem to be solved by separation of variables or Fourier transforms.[70]

Solving (54) and substituting back, we arrive at the solution for the "down-and-out" option,

$$\begin{aligned} f(S, \tau; E) = {} & [S\,erfc(h_1) - Ee^{-r\tau}\,erfc(h_2)]/2 \\ & -(S/B[\tau])^{-\delta}[B[\tau]\,erfc(h_3) - (S/B[\tau])\,Ee^{-r\tau}\,erfc(h_4)]/2, \end{aligned} \tag{55}$$

---

[68] See Snyder [48] for a complete description. A number of Wall Street houses are beginning to deal in this option. See *Fortune*, November, 1971, p. 213.

[69] In some versions of the "down-and-outer," the option owner receives a positive rebate, $R(\tau)$, if the stock price hits the "knock-out" price. Typically, $R(\tau)$ is an increasing function of the time until expiration [i.e., $R'(\tau) > 0$] with $R(0) = 0$. Let $g(S, \tau)$ satisfy (53) for $B(\tau) \leqq S < \infty$, subject to the boundary conditions (a) $g(B[\tau], \tau) = R(\tau)$ and (b) $g(S, 0) = 0$. Then, $F(S, \tau; E) \equiv g(S, \tau) + f(S, \tau; E)$ will satisfy (53) subject to the boundary conditions (a) $F(B[\tau], \tau; E) = R(\tau)$ and (b) $F(S, 0; E) = \text{Max}\,[0, S - E]$. Hence, F is the value of a "down-and-out" call option with rebate payments $R(\tau)$, and $g(S, \tau)$ is the additional value for the rebate feature. See Dettman [12], p. 391, for a transform solution for $g(S, \tau)$.

[70] See Churchill [9], p. 152, for a separation of variables solution and Dettman [12], p. 391, for a transform solution.

where

$$h_1 \equiv -\,[\log(S/E) + (r + \sigma^2/2)\tau]/\sqrt{2\sigma^2\tau},$$
$$h_2 \equiv -\,[\log(S/E) + (r - \sigma^2/2)\tau]/\sqrt{2\sigma^2\tau},$$
$$h_3 \equiv -\,[2\log(B[\tau]/E) - \log(S/E) + (r + \sigma^2/2)\tau]/\sqrt{2\sigma^2\tau},$$
$$h_4 \equiv -\,[2\log(B[\tau]/E) - \log(S/E) + (r - \sigma^2/2)\tau]/\sqrt{2\sigma^2\tau},$$

and $\delta \equiv 2(r - \eta)/\sigma^2$. Inspection of (55) and (21) reveals that the first bracketed set of terms in (55) is the value of a standard call option, and hence, the second bracket is the "discount" due to the "down-and-out" feature.

To gain a better perspective on the qualitative differences between the standard call option and the "down-and-outer," it is useful to go to the limit of a perpetual option where the "knock-out" price is constant (i.e., $\eta = 0$). In this case, (53) reduces to the ordinary differential equation

$$\tfrac{1}{2}\sigma^2 S^2 f'' + rSf' - rf = 0 \tag{56}$$

subject to

$$f(bE) = 0 \tag{56a}$$

$$f(S) \leqq S, \tag{56b}$$

where primes denote derivatives and $f(S)$ is short for $f(S, \infty; E)$. By standard methods, we solve (56) to obtain

$$f(S) = S - bE(S/bE)^{-\gamma}, \tag{57}$$

where $\gamma \equiv 2r/\sigma^2$. Remembering that the value of a standard perpetual call option equals the value of the stock, we may interpret $bE(S/bE)^{-\gamma}$ as the "discount" for the "down-and-out" feature. Both (55) and (57) are homogeneous of degree one in (S, E) as are the standard options. Further, it is easy to show that $f(S) \geqq \text{Max}\,[0, S - E]$, and although a tedious exercise, it also can be shown that $f(S, \tau; E) \geqq \text{Max}\,[0, S - E]$. Hence, the option is worth more "alive" than "dead," and therefore, (55) and (57) are the correct valuation functions for the American "down-and-outer."

From (57), the elasticity of the option price with respect to the stock price $[Sf'(S)/f(S)]$ is greater than one, and so it is a "levered" security. However, unlike the standard call option, it is a concave function of the stock price, as illustrated in Figure 4.

FIGURE 4

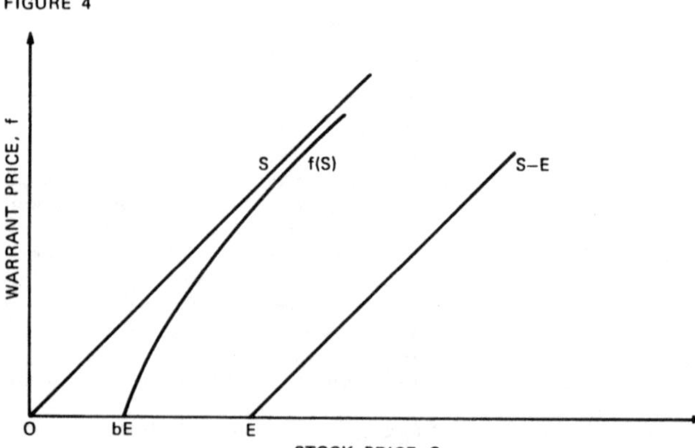

10. Valuing a callable warrant

■ As our third and last example of an application of the model to other types of options, we consider the rational pricing of a callable American warrant. Although warrants are rarely issued as callable, this is an important example because the analysis is readily carried over to the valuation of other types of securities such as convertible bonds which are almost always issued as callable.

We assume the standard conditions for an American warrant except that the issuing company has the right to ("call") buy back the warrant at any time for a fixed price. Because the warrant is of the American type, in the event of a call, the warrant holder has the option of exercising his warrant rather than selling it back to the company at the call price. If this occurs, it is called "forced conversion," because the warrant holder is "forced" to exercise, if the value of the warrant exercised exceeds the call price.

The value of a callable warrant will be equal to the value of an equivalent noncallable warrant less some "discount." This discount will be the value of the call provision to the company. One can think of the callable warrant as the resultant of two transactions: the company sells a noncallable warrant to an investor and simultaneously, purchases from the investor an option to either "force" earlier conversion or to retire the issue at a fixed price.

Let $F(S, \tau; E)$ be the value of a callable American warrant; $H(S, \tau; E)$ the value of an equivalent noncallable warrant as obtained from equation (21), $C(S, \tau; E)$ the value of the call provision. Then $H = F + C$. F will satisfy the fundamental partial differential equation,

$$\tfrac{1}{2}\sigma^2 S^2 F_{11} + rSF_1 - rF - F_2 = 0 \tag{58}$$

for $0 \leqq S \leqq \bar{S}$ and subject to

$$F(0, \tau; E) = 0,$$
$$F(S, 0; E) = \text{Max}[0, S - E]$$
$$F(\bar{S}, \tau; E) = \text{Max}[K, \bar{S} - E],$$

where K is the call price and $\bar{S}$ is the (yet to be determined) level of the stock price where the company will call the warrant. Unlike the case of "voluntary" conversion of the warrant because of unfavorable dividend protection analyzed in Section 7, $\bar{S}$ is not the choice of the warrant owner, but of the company, and hence will not be selected to maximize the value of the warrant.

Because $C = H - F$ and H and F satisfy (58), C will satisfy (58) subject to the boundary conditions,

$$C(0, \tau; E) = 0$$
$$C(S, 0; E) = 0$$
$$C(\bar{S}, \tau; E) = H(\bar{S}, \tau; E) - \text{Max}[K, \bar{S} - E].$$

Because $\bar{S}$ is the company's choice, we append the maximizing condition that $\bar{S}$ be chosen so as to maximize $C(S, \tau; E)$ making (58) a well-posed problem. Since $C = H - F$ and H is not a function of $\bar{S}$, the maximizing condition on C can be rewritten as a minimizing condition on F.

In general, it will not be possible to obtain a closed-form solution to (58). However, a solution can be found for the perpetual warrant. In this case, we known that $H(S, \tau; E) = S$, and (58) reduces to the ordinary differential equation

$$\tfrac{1}{2}\sigma^2 S^2 C'' + rSC' - rC = 0 \tag{59}$$

for $0 \leqq S \leqq \bar{S}$ and subject to

$$C(0) = 0$$
$$C(\bar{S}) = \bar{S} - \text{Max}\,(K, \bar{S} - E)$$
$$\text{Choose } \bar{S} \text{ so as to maximize } C,$$

where $C(S)$ is short for $C(S, \infty; E)$ and primes denote derivatives. Solving (59) and applying the first two conditions, we have

$$C(S) = (1 - \text{Max}[K/\bar{S}, 1 - E/\bar{S}])S. \tag{60}$$

Although we cannot apply the simple calculus technique for finding the maximizing $\bar{S}$, it is obviously $\bar{S} = K + E$, since for $\bar{S} < K + E$, C is an increasing function of $\bar{S}$ and for $\bar{S} > K + E$, it is a decreasing function. Hence, the value of the call provision is

$$C(S) = \left(\frac{E}{K + E}\right)S, \tag{61}$$

and because $F = H - C$, the value of the callable perpetual warrant is

$$F(S) = \left(\frac{K}{K + E}\right)S. \tag{62}$$

11. Conclusion

■ It has been shown that a B-S type model can be derived from weaker assumptions than in their original formulation. The main attractions of the model are: (1) the derivation is based on the relatively weak condition of avoiding dominance; (2) the final formula is a function of "observable" variables; and (3) the model can be extended in a straightforward fashion to determine the rational price of any type option.

The model has been applied with some success to empirical investigations of the option market by Black and Scholes and to warrants by Leonard.[71]

As suggested by Black and Scholes and Merton,[72] the model can be used to price the various elements of the firm's capital structure. Essentially, under conditions when the Modigliani-Miller theorem obtains, we can use the total value of the firm as a "basic" security (replacing the common stock in the formulation of this paper) and the individual securities within the capital structure (e.g., debt, convertible bonds, common stock, etc.) can be viewed as "options" or "contingent claims" on the firm and priced accordingly, So, for example, one can derive in a systematic fashion a risk-structure of interest rates as a function of the debt-equity ratio, the risk-class of the firm, and the riskless (in terms of default) debt rates.

Using the techniques developed here, it should be possible to develop a theory of the term structure of interest rates along the

[71] In [5] and [25], respectively.

[72] In [4] and [29], respectively.

lines of Cootner and Merton.[73] The approach would also have application in the theory of speculative markets.

Appendix 1[74]

■ Theorems 9 and 10 state that warrants whose common stock per dollar returns possess *distributions* that are independent of *stock price* levels (henceforth, referred to as D.I.S.P.) are: (1) homogeneous of degree one in stock price S and exercise price E—Theorem 9 and (2) convex in S—Theorem 10. This appendix exhibits via counterexample the insufficiency of the posited assumptions *sans* D.I.S.P. for the proof of Theorems 9 and 10.

First, we posit a very simple, noncontroversial, one-period European warrant pricing function, W:

$$W(S, \lambda) = K \int_{E/S}^{\infty} (S\hat{Z} - E) dP(\hat{Z}; S, \lambda), \tag{A1}$$

wherein: $1 > K > 0$ is a discounting factor which is deemed (somewhat erroneously) to be constant at this point in time (i.e., independent of S),

$\lambda \epsilon [0,1]$ is a parameter of the distribution, dP,

$$\hat{Z} \equiv Z + \lambda g(S)\epsilon \equiv Z + U(S, \lambda) \equiv \text{Common stock per dollar return,} \tag{A2}$$

Z and ϵ are independent random variables such that $E(\epsilon | Z) = 0$.

The function $g(S)$ has the following properties for our example: $g(S)\epsilon(0, 1)$, $\dfrac{dg(S)}{ds} < 0$, $dP(\hat{Z}; S, \lambda)$ is the Stieltjes integral representation of the probability density which is equivalent to the convolution of the probability densities of Z and U.

In constructing the counterexample, we choose the following uniform distributions for Z and U:

$$\begin{aligned} f(\epsilon) &= (1/2) \quad \text{for} \quad -1 \leq \epsilon \leq 1 \\ &= 0 \text{ elsewhere} \end{aligned} \tag{A3}$$

$$\begin{aligned} \rightarrow f(U) &= \frac{1}{2\lambda g(S)} \quad \text{for} \quad -\lambda g(S) \leq U \leq \lambda g(S) \\ &= 0 \text{ elsewhere} \end{aligned}$$

$$\begin{aligned} h(Z) &= (1/2) \quad \text{for} \quad 1 \leq Z \leq 3 \\ &= 0 \text{ elsewhere.} \end{aligned} \tag{A4}$$

The convoluted density would then be:

$$\frac{dP}{d\hat{Z}}(\hat{Z}; S, \lambda) = \frac{\hat{Z} - 1 + \lambda g(S)}{4\lambda g(S)} \quad \text{for} \quad 1 - \lambda g(S) \leq \hat{Z} \leq 1 + \lambda g(S) \tag{A5}$$

[73] In [11] and [29], respectively.

[74] I thank B. Goldman of M.I.T. for constructing this example and writing the appendix.

$$= (1/2) \quad \text{for} \quad 1 + \lambda g(S) \leq \hat{Z} \leq 3 - \lambda g(S)$$

$$= \frac{3 + \lambda g(S) - \hat{Z}}{4\lambda g(S)}$$

$$\text{for} \quad 3 - \lambda g(S) \leq \hat{Z} \leq 3 + \lambda g(S)$$

$$= 0 \text{ elsewhere.}$$

As a further convenience, we choose the exercise price, E, to be in the neighborhood of twice the stock price, S, and evaluate (A1):

$$W(S, \lambda) = K[E^2/4S - 3E/2 + 9S/4 + \lambda^2 g(S)^2 S/12]. \quad \text{(A6)}$$

By inspection of (A6), we notice that W is not homogeneous of degree one in S and E. Moreover, the convexity of W can be violated (locally) $\left(\text{i.e., } \frac{d^2W}{dS^2} \text{ can become negative}\right)$ by choosing a sufficiently negative $\frac{d^2g(S)}{dS^2}$:

$$\frac{d^2W}{dS^2} = \quad \text{(A7)}$$

$$K\left(E^2/2S^3 + \lambda^2/6\left[2g(S)dg/ds + \frac{S(dg)^2}{(dS)} + Sg(S)\frac{d^2g(S)}{dS^2}\right]\right) \gtreqless 0.$$

Thus, our example has shown Theorems 9 and 10 to be not generally consistent with a non-D.I.S.P. environment; however, we can verify Theorems 9 and 10 for the D.I.S.P. subcase of our example, since by construction setting $\lambda = 0$ reinstates the D.I.S.P. character of the probability distribution. By inspection, we observe that when $\lambda = 0$, the right-hand side of (A6) is homogeneous of degree one in S and E, while the right-hand side of (A7) is $KE^2/2S^3 > 0$, verifying the convexity theorem.

Appendix 2

■ It was stated in the text that Theorem 15 is really a special case of Theorem 8, i.e., variance is a consistent measure of risk in the B-S model. To prove consistency, we use the equivalent, alternative definition (Rothschild and Stiglitz')[75] of more risky that X is more risky than Y if $E[X] = E[Y]$ and $EU(X) \leq EU(Y)$ for every concave function U.

Since the B-S formula for warrant price, (21), is independent of the expected return on the stock and since the stock returns are assumed to be log normally distributed, different securities are distinguished by the single parameter, σ^2. Therefore, without loss of generality, we can assume that $\alpha = 0$, and prove the result by showing that for every concave U, $EU(Z)$ is a decreasing function of σ, where Z is a log-normal variate with $E[Z] = 1$ and the variance of

[75] In [39].

log (Z) equal to σ^2:

$$EU(Z) = \frac{1}{\sqrt{2\pi\sigma^2}} \int_0^\infty U(Z) \exp\{ - [\log Z + (1/2)\sigma^2]^2/2\sigma^2\} dZ/Z$$

$$= \frac{1}{\sqrt{2\pi}} \int_{-\infty}^\infty U(e^{\sigma x - (1/2)\sigma^2}) e^{(-1/2)x^2} dx,$$

$$\text{for} \quad x \equiv [\log Z + (1/2)\sigma^2]/\sigma;$$

$$\partial EU(Z)/\partial\sigma = \frac{1}{\sqrt{2\pi}} \int_{-\infty}^\infty U'(\quad) \exp[-(1/2)(x-\sigma)^2](x-\sigma)dx$$

$$= \frac{1}{\sqrt{2\pi}} \int_{-\infty}^\infty U'(e^{\sigma y + (1/2)\sigma^2}) y e^{-1/2 y^2} dy, \quad \text{for} \quad y \equiv x - \sigma$$

$$\equiv \text{Covariance } [U'(e^{\sigma y + (1/2)\sigma^2}), y].$$

But, $U'(\;)$ is a decreasing function of y by the concavity of U. Hence, by Theorem 236, Hardy et al.,[76] $\text{Cov}[U', y] < 0$. Therefore, $\partial EU/\partial\sigma < 0$ for all concave U

[76] In [16], p. 168.

References

1. Ayres, R. F. "Risk Aversion in the Warrant Markets." *Industrial Management Review*, Vol. 50, No. 1 (Fall 1963), pp. 45–53; reprinted in Cootner [10], pp. 497–505.
2. Bachelier, L. *Theory of Speculation* (translation of 1900 French edition), in Cootner [10], pp. 17–78.
3. Baumol, W. J., Malkiel, B. G., and Quandt, R. E. "The Valuation of Convertible Securities." *Quarterly Journal of Economics*, Vol. 80, No. 1 (February 1966), pp. 48–59.
4. Black, F. and Scholes, M. "The Pricing of Options and Corporate Liabilities," forthcoming in *Journal of Political Economy*.
5. ———. "The Valuation of Option Contracts and a Test of Market Efficiency." *Journal of Finance*, Vol. 27, No. 2 (May 1972).
6. ———. "Some Evidence on the Profitability of Trading in Put and Call Options," in Cootner [10], pp. 475–496.
7. Boness, A. J. "Elements of a Theory of Stock-Option Value," *Journal of Political Economy*, Vol. 72, No. 2 (April 1964), pp. 163–175.
8. Chen, A. H. Y. "A Model of Warrant Pricing in a Dynamic Market," *Journal of Finance*, Vol. 25, No. 5 (December 1970).
9. Churchill, R. V. *Fourier Series and Boundary Value Problems*. 2nd ed. New York: McGraw-Hill, 1963.
10. Cootner, P. H., ed. *The Random Character of Stock Market Prices*. Cambridge: M.I.T. Press, 1964.
11. ———. "The Stochastic Theory of Bond Prices." Mimeographed. Massachusetts Institute of Technology, December 1966.
12. Dettman, J. W. *Mathematical Methods in Physics and Engineering*. 2nd ed. New York: McGraw-Hill, 1969.
13. Fama, E. F. "Efficient Capital Markets: A Review of Theory and Empirical Work." *Journal of Finance*, Vol. 25, No. 2 (May 1970).
14. Giguere, G. "Warrants: A Mathematical Method of Evaluation." *Analysts Journal*, Vol. 14, No. 5 (November 1958), pp. 17–25.
15. Hallingby, P., Jr. "Speculative Opportunities in Stock Purchase Warrants." *Analysts Journal*, Vol. 3, No. 3 (1947).
16. Hardy, G. H., Littlewood, J. E. and Pölya, G. *Inequalities*. Cambridge: The University Press, 1959.

17. HAUSMAN, W. H. AND WHITE, W. L. "Theory of Option Strategy under Risk Aversion." *Journal of Financial and Quantitative Analysis*, Vol. 3, No. 3 (September 1968).
18. KASSOUF, S. T. *Evaluation of Convertible Securities*. Maspeth, N. Y.: Analytic Investors Inc., 1962.
19. ———. "Stock Price Random Walks: Some Supporting Evidence." *Review of Economics and Statistics*, Vol. 50, No. 2 (May 1968), pp. 275–278.
20. ———. *A Theory and an Econometric Model for Common Stock Purchase Warrants*. Ph.D. dissertation, Columbia University. New York: Analytical Publishers Co., 1965.
21. KRUIZENGA, R. J. "Introduction to the Option Contract," in Cootner [10], pp. 277–391.
22. ———. "Profit Returns from Purchasing Puts and Calls," in Cootner [10], pp. 392–411.
23. ———. *Put and Call Options: A Theoretical and Market Analysis*. Unpublished Ph.D. dissertation. M.I.T., 1956.
24. KUSHNER, H. J. *Stochastic Stability and Control*. New York: Academic Press, 1967.
25. LEONARD, R. J. "An Empirical Examination of a New General Equilibrium Model for Warrant Pricing." Unpublished M.S. thesis, M.I.T., September 1971.
26. MCKEAN, H. P., JR. "Appendix: A Free Boundary Problem for the Heat Equation Arising from a Problem in Mathematical Economics." *Industrial Management Review*, Vol. 6, No. 2 (Spring 1965), pp. 32–39; reprinted in [40], Chapter 199.
27. MERTON, R. C. *Stochastic Integrals*. New York: Academic Press, 1969.
28. ———. "Appendix: Continuous-Time Speculative Processes." (Appendix to Samuelson [45]), in *Mathematical Topics in Economic Theory and Computation*, SIAM, Philadelphia, 1972.
29. ———. "A Dynamic General Equilibrium Model of the Asset Market and its Application to the Pricing of the Capital Structure of the Firm." Sloan School of Management Working Paper #497–70, M.I.T., (December 1970).
30. ———. "An Empirical Investigation of the Samuelson Rational Warrant Pricing Theory," Chapter V in *Analytical Optimal Control Theory as Applied to Stochastic and Non-Stochastic Economics*, unpublished Ph.D. dissertation, M.I.T., 1970.
31. ———. "An Intertemporal Capital Asset Pricing Model," forthcoming in *Econometrica*.
32. ———. "Lifetime Portfolio Selection under Uncertainty: The Continuous-Time Case," *Review of Economics and Statistics*, Vol. 51, No. 3 (August 1969).
33. ———. "Optimum Consumption and Portfolio Rules in a Continuous-Time Model." *Journal of Economic Theory*, Vol. 3, No. 4 (December 1971).
34. ———. "Restrictions on Rational Option Pricing: A Set of Arbitrage Conditions." Mimeographed. Massachusetts Institute of Technology, August 1968.
35. MILLER, M. AND MODIGLIANI, F. "Dividend Policy, Growth, and the Valuation of Shares." *Journal of Business*, Vol. 34, No. 4 (October 1961).
36. MORRISON, R. J. "The Warrants or the Stock?" *Analysts Journal*, Vol. 13, No. 5 (November 1957).
37. PEASE, F. "The Warrant—Its Powers and Its Hazards." *Financial Analysts Journal*, Vol. 19, No. 1 (January-February 1963).
38. PLUM, V. L. AND MARTIN, T. J. "The Significance of Conversion Parity in Valuing Common Stock Warrants." *The Financial Review* (February 1966).
39. ROTHSCHILD, M. AND STIGLITZ, J. E. "Increasing Risk: I. A Definition." *Journal of Economic Theory*, Vol. 2, No. 3 (September 1970).
40. SAMUELSON, P. A. *The Collected Scientific Papers of Paul A. Samuelson*. Vol. 3. R. C. Merton, ed. Cambridge: M.I.T. Press, 1972.
41. ———. "Proof That Properly Anticipated Prices Fluctuate Randomly." *Industrial Management Review*, Vol. 6, No. 2 (Spring 1965), pp. 41–50; reprinted in [40], Chapter 198.
42. ———. "Rational Theory of Warrant Pricing." *Industrial Management Review*, Vol. 6, No. 2 (Spring 1965), pp. 13–31; reprinted in [40], Chapter 199.
43. ——— AND MERTON, R. C. "A Complete Model of Warrant Pricing That Maximizes Utility." *Industrial Management Review*, Vol. 10, No. 2 (Winter 1969), pp. 17–46; reprinted in [40], Chapter 200.

44. ———. "Mathematics of Speculative Price," in *Mathematical Topics in Economic Theory and Computation*, SIAM, Philadelphia, 1972.
45. ———. Review of [53]. *Journal of American Statistical Association*, Vol. 63, No. 323 (September 1968), pp. 1049–1051.
46. SHELTON, J. P. "The Relation of the Pricing of a Warrant to the Price of Its Associated Stock." *Financial Analysts Journal*, Vol. 23, Nos. 3–4 (Part I: May-June 1967) and (Part II: July-August 1967).
47. SLATER, L. J. "Confluent Hypergeometric Functions," Chapter 13 in *Handbook of Mathematical Functions*. National Bureau of Standards, Applied Mathematics Series, 55, August, 1966.
48. SNYDER, G. L., "Alternative Forms of Options." *Financial Analysts Journal*, Vol. 25, No. 1 (September–October 1969), pp. 93–99.
49. SPRENKLE, C. M. "Warrant Prices as Indicators of Expectations and Preferences." *Yale Economic Essays* I, pp. 172–231; reprinted in Cootner [10], pp. 412–474.
50. STIGLITZ, J. E. "On Some Aspects of the Pure Theory of Corporate Finance: Bankruptcies and Take-Overs." *The Bell Journal of Economics and Management Science*, Vol. 3, No. 2 (Autumn 1972), pp. 458–482.
51. ———. "A Re-Examination of the Modigliani-Miller Theorem." *The American Economic Review*, Vol. 59, No. 5 (December 1969).
52. STOLL, H. R. "The Relationship between Put and Call Option Prices." *Journal of Finance*, Vol. 24, No. 4 (December 1969), pp. 802–824.
53. THORP, E. O. AND KASSOUF, S. T. *Beat the Market*. New York: Random House, 1967.
54. VAN HORNE, J. C. "Warrant Valuation in Relation to Volatility and Opportunity Costs." *Industrial Management Review*, Vol. 10, No. 3 (Spring 1969), pp. 17–32.

[14]

Journal of Financial Economics 3 (1976) 145–166. © North-Holland Publishing Company

THE VALUATION OF OPTIONS FOR ALTERNATIVE STOCHASTIC PROCESSES*

John C. COX

Stanford University, Stanford, Calif. 94305, U.S.A.

Stephen A. ROSS

University of Pennsylvania, Philadelphia, Penn. 19174, U.S.A.

Received July 1975, revised version received July 1975

This paper examines the structure of option valuation problems and develops a new technique for their solution. It also introduces several jump and diffusion processes which have not been used in previous models. The technique is applied to these processes to find explicit option valuation formulas, and solutions to some previously unsolved problems involving the pricing of securities with payouts and potential bankruptcy.

1. Introduction

One of the central problems of modern finance is that of valuing claims to assets. The major result in this area is the insight of Modigliani and Miller (1958) that, in equilibrium, packages of financial claims which are, in essence, equivalent must command the same price. Modigliani and Miller recognized that in the absence of market imperfections these claims were simply financial tools for offering alternative modes of ownership of the same economic stream of returns. As a consequence, the aggregate value of the claims against the returns of a firm, for example, should be independent of the types of claims issued. Simultaneously with work on the Modigliani–Miller theorems and somewhat independently of it considerable progress was made by Samuelson (1965) and others [see Cootner (1964)] in evaluating stock options, a specialized form of financial claim. This work came to a focus in the major paper by Black and Scholes (1973) in which a complete option pricing model depending only on observable variables was derived. The Black and Scholes option pricing results can in some ways be viewed as an intertemporal analogue of the Modigliani–Miller theory. Although subsequent research has achieved greater

*The authors are grateful for the research support of the Rodney L. White Center for Financial Research at the University of Pennsylvania and the National Science Foundation Grant No. 20292. We also wish to thank Fischer Black, Michael Jensen, John Long, and Robert Merton for helpful comments.

generality and has been distinctly different in important ways, the underlying theme remains Black and Scholes' observation that in an intertemporal as well as a static setting two things which can be shown to be equivalent must sell for the same price.

It is useful to pursue this a bit further. Modigliani and Miller argue that the financial instruments issued by a firm span the returns stream, i.e., that the total package of claims on a firm, no matter how complex, is equivalent to a simple equity claim on the returns stream. A similar spanning situation is apparent in the Black and Scholes analysis. Black and Scholes assume that the value of the stock follows a particular diffusion process which will be discussed below and, as a consequence, locally in time, a stock and any option written on it will be perfectly correlated and combined with borrowing or lending at the riskless rate a position in one will be a perfect substitute for, or span, a position in the other. In this way the option is, locally, spanned by riskless bonds and the stock, and knowing the value of the stock permits us to value the option (globally by an integration argument). The critical factor in this argument and in any contingent claims valuation model is the precise description of the stochastic process governing the behavior of the basic asset. It is the characteristics of this process that determine the exact nature of the equivalence between packages of claims. The main contribution of this paper is the consideration of some alternative forms of the stochastic process governing stock prices, and the development of an approach to the option valuation problem that connects it directly to the structure of the underlying stochastic process. It will be useful, then, to give a brief and informal discussion of the stochastic processes that have previously been used.

The basic assumption employed by Black and Scholes was that the stock value followed a log-normal diffusion process,

$$\mathrm{d}S/S = \mu \mathrm{d}t + \sigma \mathrm{d}z, \tag{1}$$

where S is the value of the stock, μ is the drift term and z is a Wiener process. Eq. (1) is a short-hand notation for the following stochastic process. Let S_t be the value of the stock at time t. The percentage change in this value in the next instant, from t to $t+\mathrm{d}t$, is

$$\mathrm{d}S/S = (S_{t+\mathrm{d}t} - S_t)/St.$$

By (1) this percentage change is made up of two components, a drift term, $\mu\mathrm{d}t$, which is certain as viewed from time t and a normally distributed stochastic term $\sigma\mathrm{d}z$. The stochastic term is independent of its values in other periods and has mean zero and variance $\sigma^2\mathrm{d}t$. Put simply, eq. (1) says that the percentage change in stock value from t to $t+\mathrm{d}t$ is normally distributed with mean $\mu\mathrm{d}t$ and variance $\sigma^2\mathrm{d}t$. As $\mathrm{d}t$ gets small, then, $S_{t+\mathrm{d}t}$ will not differ much from S_t.

This is the hallmark of a diffusion process; it represents a continuous frictional sort of random walk around a trend term and, in the short run, offers no surprises.

The diffusion processes, though, are only one of two general classes of continuous time stochastic processes. The second type of stochastic process in continuous time is the jump process. A simple jump process can be written in analogy with (1) as

$$\mathrm{d}S/S = \mu\mathrm{d}t + (k-1)\mathrm{d}\pi$$

$$= \mu\mathrm{d}t + \begin{cases} \xrightarrow{\lambda\mathrm{d}t} k-1, \\ \xrightarrow[1-\lambda\mathrm{d}t]{} 0. \end{cases} \tag{2}$$

In eq. (2) π is a continuous time Poisson process, λ is referred to as the intensity of the process and $k-1$ is the jump amplitude. As with (1), eq. (2) is a short-hand notation for the stochastic process that governs the percentage change in the value of the stock on the interval from t to $t+\mathrm{d}t$. Eq. (2) says that this percentage change is composed of a drift term, $\mu\mathrm{d}t$, and a term, $\mathrm{d}\pi$, which with probability $\lambda\mathrm{d}t$ will jump the percentage stock change to $k-1$, possibly random itself, and with probability $1-\lambda\mathrm{d}t$ will do nothing. One possible interpretation is that $\lambda\mathrm{d}t$ represents the instantaneous probability of receiving a packet of information that will cause S to jump.

In contrast to the diffusion process, the jump process (2) follows a deterministic movement upon which are superimposed discrete jumps. Formally, a jump process has sample paths which are discontinuous with probability one, while those of the diffusion process are continuous with probability one. In addition, the jump processes we consider are continuous from the right almost surely, i.e., their discontinuities are simple jumps. Because of the jumps in value the local analysis of Black and Scholes for valuing options does not carry directly over to eq. (2). By assuming that k was fixed, though, Cox and Ross (1975a) showed that a riskless hedge could be formed and used to value options on jump processes.

The intent of this paper is two fold. First, we examine the rationale for assuming that stock value follows (1) or (2) and propose some plausible alternative forms. This will allow us to examine the relationships between the choice of process and the solutions to option problems, while at the same time providing additional models for empirical testing. The second central feature of this paper is the development and application of an intuitive technique, introduced in Cox and Ross (1975a), for finding the solution to option valuation problems. This approach provides new insights into the structure of option valuation problems and its application allows us to solve a previously unresolved problem, the valuation of coupon paying bonds of arbitrary finite maturity, and the complementary problem of valuing an option on a stock with constant dividend payouts. Section 2 introduces the new stochastic processes studied in this paper. Section 3 studies the general option valuation problem and develops the solution technique. Section 4 applies the technique to the processes of section 1, and section 5 briefly summarizes and concludes the paper.

2. Some alternative stochastic processes

In exploring alternative forms it is useful to construct them as jump processes. Aside from the question of whether the 'real world' follows a diffusion or a jump process, even if we use diffusion processes for their analytic conveniences, much of our intuition can be formalized with jump processes. Eq. (2), for example, describes an equity whose value drifts deterministically until a unit of information arrives. Information arrives with probability $\lambda \mathrm{d}t$ and, when it does, the stock value jumps discontinuously by $k-1$ per cent. The diffusion in (1) is the limit of such a process, where information arrives continuously and has only a differential impact.

Eq. (2) is a very special case of the general form for Markov jump processes. If x denotes the current state of the world, then a general jump process is of the form

$$\mathrm{d}S = \mu(x)\,\mathrm{d}t + \begin{cases} \tilde{k}(x)-1, & \lambda(x)\mathrm{d}t \\ 0, & 1-\lambda(x)\mathrm{d}t \end{cases} \tag{3}$$

where $\tilde{k}(x)$ has a distribution dependent on the current world state, x. We will assume that $x = S$, i.e., all state information is contained in the current stock value, S. We could, of course, also add a Wiener diffusion term, $\sigma(x)\mathrm{d}z$, to (3) to obtain a more general process, but (3) actually contains the diffusion as a limiting case (see below). The motivation for specializing (3) to (1) or (2), is that they capture two notions. First, they are in relative or percentage terms and there is some intuitive rationale for specifying the stochastic mechanism in percentage terms since this is the form of the returns. Second, by putting the process in percentage terms we can naturally include as the limited liability constraint, $S \geqq 0$. Both (1) and (2) obey this boundary condition. Beyond these not entirely compelling arguments though there does not seem to be terribly much reason for the exclusive use of (1) or (2) and doing so would overlook a number of interesting and equally defensible forms.

Suppose, for example, that in (3) we specialize the intensity, $\lambda(S)$ and the drift, $\mu(S)$, to be proportional to value, λS and μS, and choose the distribution, $k-1$, to be independent of value. Thus,

$$\mathrm{d}S = \mu S\mathrm{d}t + \begin{cases} k-1, & \lambda S\mathrm{d}t \\ 0. & 1-\lambda S\mathrm{d}t \end{cases} \tag{4}$$

With the drift term eq. (4) is a generalization of a class of stochastic processes known as birth and death processes. The local mean and variance of (4) are given by

$$E\{\mathrm{d}S\} = [\mu+\lambda E\{k-1\}]S\mathrm{d}t, \tag{5}$$

and

$$V\{\mathrm{d}S\} = \lambda E\{(k-1)^2\}S\mathrm{d}t.$$

To construct a pure birth and death process we ignore the drift in (4) and let k take on two values, $k^+ > 1$ and $k^- < 1$ with respective (conditional) probabilities π^+ and π^-,

$$\mathrm{d}S = \begin{cases} \xrightarrow{\lambda S\mathrm{d}t} \begin{cases} \xrightarrow{\pi^+} k^+-1, \\ \xrightarrow{\pi^-} k^- -1 \end{cases} \\ \xrightarrow{1-\lambda S\mathrm{d}t} \end{cases} = \begin{cases} \xrightarrow{\pi^+\lambda S\mathrm{d}t} k^+-1, \\ \xrightarrow{\pi^-\lambda S\mathrm{d}t} k^- -1, \\ \xrightarrow{1-\lambda S\mathrm{d}t} 0. \end{cases} \tag{6}$$

Eq. (6) is now an example of a simple birth and death process for a population. Imagine a firm made up of individual units (members of the population) whose sum value (population size) is S. If these units are stochastically independent of each other, we can let $\lambda \mathrm{d}t$ represent the probability of an event occurring for any one unit. An event is, with probability π^+, the 'birth' of k^+-1 additional units and with probability π^- the 'death' of $1-k^-$ units. For the whole firm (population), then, (6) describes its local movement. If $\mu = 0$ and if $\pi^+ = 1$, then (6) describes a pure birth process and if $\pi^- = 1$, (6) is called a pure death process. Eq. (2) in contrast to (6) describes the stochastic movement of a firm (population) all of whose members are perfectly dependent, that is, when one moves they all move, and the probability of such an event, $\lambda \mathrm{d}t$, is independent of the firm value (population size) although the magnitude is simply proportional.

Another interesting difference between (2) and (6) can be seen by passing to the diffusion limit in (6). The diffusion limit of (2) is the relative process (1) [see Cox and Ross (1975a)]. The limit of (6), though, as $k^+ \to 1$ and $k^- \to 1$ and $\lambda \to \infty$ in the fashion indicated in footnote 1 is a diffusion with instantaneous mean μS and variance $\sigma^2 S$, where μ and σ are given by (5), and μ is not the same as the drift in (4).[1] We could write this in the formalism of the stochastic differential as

$$\mathrm{d}S = \mu S\mathrm{d}t+\sigma\sqrt{S}\,\mathrm{d}z. \tag{7}$$

[1]To derive the diffusion limit (7) it is sufficient to demonstrate that the Kolmogorov backward equation (see discussion below in section 3) for the probability transition function

$$P_{x,y}(t,\tau) \equiv \mathrm{Prob}\,\{S_\tau = y \mid S_t = x\}, \quad \tau > t;$$

Although it is useful to consider this type of diffusion as a limiting case of an economy where firms are compositions of independent units, this interpretation is by no means necessary. Other forms of causation could lead to the same probabilistic description of events. We could in fact consider this diffusion process solely on its own merits as a description of a situation in which changes in state are small and in which the variance of price changes increases with the stock price, but more slowly than (1) so that the variance of the rate of return decreases rather than remaining constant. Considered in this way the process can certainly not be rejected on an a priori basis, and may in many situations be preferable to (1). Unlike (1) it should be noted that the diffusion process represented by (7) does permit $S = 0$, i.e., bankruptcy, to occur with positive probability (even in the absence of stock payouts).

Another specialization of (3) that is of interest is one where the firm is com-

---

for the birth and death process (6) converges to that for the diffusion (7) under an appropriate limiting argument. The backward equation for (6) is

$$-(\partial P_{x,y}/\partial t) = -\lambda x P_{x,y} + \lambda x \pi^+ P_{x+\Delta x,y} + \lambda x \pi^- P_{x-\Delta x,y},$$

where we have set $k^+ - 1 = \Delta x$ and $k^- - 1 = -\Delta x$.

Now, to maintain the instantaneous mean and variance of the diffusion process (7) in the passage to the limit we alter the intensities as $\Delta x \to 0$ in such a fashion as to maintain

$$\lambda x(\Delta x)^2 = \sigma^2 x \quad \text{and} \quad \lambda x(\pi^+ - \pi^-)\Delta x = \mu x; \quad \text{or}$$

$$\lambda = \sigma^2/(\Delta x)^2, \quad \lambda\pi^+ = \tfrac{1}{2}[\sigma^2/(\Delta x)^2 + \mu/\Delta x], \quad \lambda\pi^- = \tfrac{1}{2}[\sigma^2/(\Delta x)^2 - \mu/\Delta x].$$

Passing to the limit as $\Delta x \to 0$ in the backward equation we have the backward equation for the diffusion (7),

$$\begin{aligned} -\partial P_{x,y}/\partial t &= -\lambda x P_{x,y} + \lambda x \pi^+ [P_{x,y} + (\partial P_{x,y}/\partial x)\Delta x + \tfrac{1}{2}(\partial^2 P_{x,y}/\partial x^2(\Delta x)^2)] \\ &\quad + \lambda x \pi^- [P_{x,y} - (\partial P_{x,y}/\partial x)\Delta x + \tfrac{1}{2}(\partial^2 P_{x,y}/\partial x^2)(\Delta x)^2] \\ &= \mu x(\partial P_{x,y}/\partial x) + \tfrac{1}{2}\sigma^2 x(\partial^2 P_{x,y}/\partial x^2). \end{aligned}$$

The derivation of the absolute process (10) from the absolute jump (8) is nearly identical, but in that case we need the drift term. For the absolute process (8) the backward equation is given by

$$-\partial P_{x,y}/\partial t = -\lambda P_{x,y} + \lambda\pi^+ P_{x+\Delta x,y} + \lambda\pi^- P_{x-\Delta x,y} + \mu x(\partial P_{x,y}/\partial x).$$

Using the limiting process $\lambda\pi^+ = \lambda\pi^- = \tfrac{1}{2}(\sigma^2/(\Delta x)^2)$, we can show, as above, that the backward equation converges to the backward equation for the absolute process (10),

$$-\partial P_{x,y}/\partial t = \mu x(\partial P_{x,y}/\partial x) + \tfrac{1}{2}\sigma^2(\partial^2 P_{x,y}/\partial x^2).$$

These derivations are intended to be heuristic and only prove pointwise convergence, but they can be rigorously extended to show uniform convergence. A detailed treatment of a similar argument can be found in Feller (1951a). We should also add that since S is considered to be a value we append to (7) and (10) an absorbing barrier at $S = 0$. This recognizes that both (7) and (10) will drive a positive S to zero with positive probability.

posed of dependent units as in (2), so that intensity, λ, is constant, and where the value increment is also constant. In this case

$$dS = \mu S dt + \begin{cases} \xrightarrow{\lambda dt} \begin{cases} \xrightarrow{\pi^+} k^+ - 1, \\ \xrightarrow{\pi^-} k^- - 1, \end{cases} \\ \xrightarrow{1-\lambda dt} 0, \end{cases} \quad (8)$$

and we have jettisoned proportionality altogether. This is a case where value grows endogenously at the exponential rate μ, and where lump exogenous increments to value of size, $k-1$, occur with intensity λ. For reference we can call this the absolute process.

The local mean and variance of the absolute process are given by

$$E\{dS\} = \{\mu S + \lambda[\pi^+(k^+ - 1) + \pi^-(k^- - 1)]\} \, dt,$$

and

$$V\{dS\} = \lambda[\pi^+(k^+ - 1)^2 + \pi^-(k^- - 1)^2] \, dt, \quad (9)$$

in the case where k is constant. If $\pi^- = 0$ the process has limited liability, but if $\pi^- > 0$ there is a positive probability that it will go into default. To preserve limited liability we would, therefore, also have to specify a non-negative lower barrier for S. Taking the diffusion limit of (8) as with (6) (see footnote 1), we obtain

$$dS = \mu S dt + \sigma dz, \quad (10)$$

where μ and σ are given by (9). This process would thus characterize a firm whose increments in value have a constant variance. To impose limited liability, we let the origin be an absorbing barrier, and consider (10) as governing the stock value only as long as this point is not reached. There would again be a positive probability of bankruptcy during any period.

3. Option valuation theory

The structure of the hedging arguments used to obtain valuation formulas for options can be illustrated in a fairly general setting. The first step is to choose a particular stochastic process to govern the price movement of the underlying asset, say a stock with price, S. Let us assume that we can write the random differential movement in S as

$$dS = \mu_S dt + \sigma_S dx_S. \quad (11)$$

As in the examples of section 2, μ_S and σ_S are taken to be functions of the current state of the world, which for simplicity is supposed to be summarized by S and t alone. The (non-anticipating) stochastic term $\mathrm{d}x_S$ is assumed to be either a Wiener diffusion term, $\mathrm{d}z$, or a unit Poisson variable $\mathrm{d}\pi$. If $\mathrm{d}x_S$ is a Poisson term, then we interpret σ_S in (11) to be the random jump amplitude given a jump.

The next step in the argument is to take an instrument whose value is dependent on S, say an option written on the stock, and assume that a sufficiently regular price function exists, $P(S, t)$, which is the option value at time t, given that the stock price at t is equal to S. Postulating such a function permits us (given that μ_S, σ_S and P are sufficiently well behaved mathematically) to derive the differential movement in the option value,

$$\mathrm{d}P = \mu_P \mathrm{d}t + \sigma_P \mathrm{d}x_S. \tag{12}$$

The functions μ_P and σ_P now depend on the unknown function P and the known values of S and t. If $\mathrm{d}x_S$ follows a unit Poisson process σ_P may be a random function whose values depend on the function P and the jump size, σ_S, and it need not be proportional to σ_S.

The economic argument that leads to a formula for pricing the option is based on the presence of a third asset that earns a riskless instantaneous interest rate, r, which we will take to be a constant rate at which individuals can borrow and lend freely. We also will assume that the stock, S, can be sold short with the seller receiving the proceeds, and that there are no transactions costs or taxes. Most importantly, we make the competitive assumption that agents act as though they cannot influence r or any price. Under these assumptions it is easy to show that all riskless assets must earn the riskless rate, r, to prevent arbitrage.

While it is possible to solve option problems for random jumps to more than one value as in the birth and death process of (6) when $\pi^+, \pi^- \neq 0$, to do so requires the introduction of additional stocks either to support the hedging argument as in Cox and Ross (1975b), or the use of Ross's (1973) arbitrage argument to obtain an approximate formula as in Merton (1975). To avoid either of these possibilities we will further assume that if $\mathrm{d}x_S$ is a Poisson process, the jump amplitude σ_S (and σ_P) is a non-random function at a jump. It follows that there is a hedge portfolio of the stock, S, and its option, P, such that

$$\alpha_S \sigma_S (\mathrm{d}x_S/S) + \alpha_P \sigma_P (\mathrm{d}x_S/P) = 0,$$

or

$$\alpha_S(\sigma_S/S) + \alpha_P(\sigma_P/P) = 0, \tag{13}$$

where α_S and α_P are the portfolio weights in the stock and the option respectively. Such a hedge portfolio is riskless and must have a rate of return

$$\alpha_S(\mu_S/S) + \alpha_P(\mu_P/P) = (\alpha_S + \alpha_P)r, \tag{14}$$

the return at the riskless rate. From (13) and (14) we obtain the fundamental option valuation equation

$$(\mu_P - rP)/\sigma_P = (\mu_S - rS)/\sigma_S. \tag{15}$$

The valuation equation, thus, reduces to the familiar statement that the risk premium divided by the scale of risk has to be the same for the stock and its option. As a mathematical matter, eq. (15) is usually a differential-difference equation and together with the terms of the option we can hopefully apply some available mathematical techniques to solve it.

For example, with the Black and Scholes log-normal diffusion (1), the valuation eq. (15) takes the form

$$\tfrac{1}{2}\sigma^2 S^2 P_{SS} + rSP_S - rP = -P_t. \tag{16}$$

Using the boundary condition for a European call option

$$P(S, T) = \max\{S - E, 0\},$$

where E is the exercise price, Black and Scholes were able to transform (16) to the heat equation of physics and solve it in closed form.

In Cox and Ross (1975a), however, a systematic technique for solving the valuation equation was introduced that exploits the economic structure of the problem and provides further insight into the structure of option valuation problems in general. The fact that we could use a hedging argument to derive (15) and the argument that $P(S, t)$ exists uniquely means that given S and t the value of the option, P, does not depend directly on the structure of investors' preferences. Investors' preferences and demand conditions in general enter the valuation problem only in so far as they determine the equilibrium parameter values. No matter what preferences are, as long as they determine the same relevant parameter values, they will also value the option identically. In the Black and Scholes case, for example, (16) does not depend on μ and the only relevant parameters for the pricing problem are r and σ. To solve (15), then, we need only find the equilibrium solution for P in some world where preferences are given and consistent with the specified parameter values; the solution obtained will then be preference free.

A convenient choice of preferences for many problems (although one can envision problems where another preference structure might be more suitable) is risk neutrality. In such a world equilibrium requires that the expected returns on both the stock and the option must equal the riskless rate. For the stock, then

$$E\left\{\frac{S_T}{S_t}\,\middle|\, S_t\right\} = e^{r(T-t)}. \tag{17}$$

Similarly, if we are considering a general European option with boundary value,

$$P(S, T) = h(S), \tag{18}$$

then, at time t,

$$E\left\{\frac{P(S_T, T)}{P} \,\middle|\, S_t\right\} = \frac{1}{P} E\{h(S_T) \mid S_t\} = e^{r(T-t)},$$

or

$$\begin{aligned} P(S, t) &= e^{-r(T-t)} E\{h(S_T) \mid S_t\} \\ &= e^{-r(T-t)} \int h(S_T) dF(S_T, T \mid S_t, t), \end{aligned} \tag{19}$$

where $F(S_T, T \mid S_t, t)$ is the probability distribution of the stock price at time T, S_T, given the stock price at time $t < T$, S_t. Eq. (19), with (17), provides the solution to the option valuation problem. Eq. (17) is used to satisfy any special features of the parameter set that are implied by the hedging equation.[2]

From (19) it is apparent that if we know the cumulative probability distribution of the stock process we can value the option. The converse is generally true as well. In the case of European calls, for example, the general option pricing formula (19) for arbitrary exercise prices, E, involves knowing all of the right semi-moments of the terminal stock distribution, given that (17) is satisfied. This is, however, equivalent to knowing the distribution itself.[3] In other words, the option valuation problem is really equivalent to the problem of determining the distribution of the stock variable, S, whose movement is governed by the postulated process (11). This establishes an important link between the option valuation problem and the fundamentals of stochastic processes.

It is well known that the probability transition functions, $F(S_T, T \mid S_t, t)$, satisfy two central equations, the forward (or Fokker–Planck) equation and the Kolomogorov backward equations [see Feller (1966)]. The backward equations

[2]Some awareness of this technique appears in previous work. Black and Scholes, in an earlier version of their seminal paper, first found the solution to (16) by setting $\mu = r$ in Sprenkle's (1961) formula for the option value. Merton, in Samuelson (1973), also noted that setting $\alpha = \beta = r$ in Samuelson's $\alpha - \beta$ model gave the Black and Scholes solution.

[3]We can sketch a formal proof of this proposition. We only need to show that the semi-moments determine the distribution. Suppose that two distributions, F and G, have the same semimoments, or equivalently, the same option values for all exercise prices, E. The family of functions, $f_E(S) = \max\{S-E, 0\}$, generates a lattice, K (closed under addition and multiplication by constants), on compact sets on the line which contains the constant functions and separates points. The lattice structure is immediate and for $E' > E$, $f_E(S) - f_{E'}(S) = E' - E$, $S \geqq E'$, i.e., a constant. By the Stone–Weierstrass theorem, then, on compact sets, the lattice, K, is dense in the continuous functions and since F and G agree on K, it follows from the Helly–Bray lemma that they agree on all continuous functions.

describe the way in which $F(S_T, T \mid S_t, t)$ is altered as the initial time, t, is changed. For example, the backward equation for the diffusion process (1) is given by

$$\tfrac{1}{2}\sigma^2 S^2 F_{SS} + \mu S F_S + F_t = 0, \tag{20}$$

where $S_t = S$, and $F(S_T, T \mid S, t)$ must satisfy (20) for all values of (S_T, T). In a risk-neutral world, from (17), the drift on the stock $\mu = r$. Suppose, then, we consider the backward equation (20) with $\mu = r$. Transforming this equation by substituting (19) we obtain (16), the Black and Scholes option valuation equation. In general, if (17) can be satisfied, the option valuation equation (15), is the transform (19) of the Kolmogorov backward equation for the transition probability function, F. The operational significance of these observations is simply that we can solve the option valuation problem only for those cases where we know the probability distribution of the terminal stock value.

The next sections illustrates these techniques by applying them to the option valuation problems for the stochastic processes introduced above. In the final section we are able to obtain an important new result, the valuation of options on stocks paying dividends, by the application of these techniques to the square root process (7).

4. Option valuation problems

4.1. Alternative jump processes

In this section we will explore the option valuation problem for some of the jump processes considered in section 2. As in section 3 we restrict the general form (3) to the case of a single post jump value, $k(S, t)$.

Our problem is to value a call option on S with an expiration date T at which time the holder receives max $\{S_T - E, 0\}$. We will initially assume that the stock pays no dividends so that it would never be optimal to exercise an American call before the expiration date T and it will, therefore, be valued as a European call [see Merton (1973)]. To solve this problem we specialize the hedging argument to the jump case. The local return on the stock is given by (3) and the option follows a perfectly dependent process

$$\mathrm{d}P = \begin{cases} \xrightarrow{\lambda S \mathrm{d}t} P(S+k-1, t) - P(S, t), \\ \xrightarrow[1-\lambda S \mathrm{d}t]{} P_t \mathrm{d}t + \mu P_S \mathrm{d}t, \end{cases} \tag{21}$$

where λ is an arbitrary function.

By forming a hedge portfolio of the stock and the option with weights α_S and α_P respectively chosen so that

$$\alpha_S\left[\frac{k-1}{S}\right]+\alpha_P\left[\frac{P(S+k-1,t)-P(S,t)}{P(S,t)}\right] = 0, \tag{22}$$

the hedge position will be riskless. It follows that if r is the (instantaneous) riskless rate of interest, then

$$\alpha_S\left(\frac{\mu}{S}\right)+\alpha_P\left(\frac{P_t+\mu P_S}{P}\right) = (\alpha_S+\alpha_P)\, r, \tag{23}$$

i.e., the hedge must be equivalent to a riskless short bond to prevent arbitrage possibilities. Combining (22) and (23) we have that $P(S,t)$ must satisfy the difference-differential equation version of (15),

$$\mu P_S+\left[\frac{\mu-rS}{1-k}\right]P(S+k-1,t)+\left[\frac{r[k-1+S]-\mu}{1-k}\right]P = -P_t, \tag{24}$$

where μ and k are functions of S and t.

An important feature of (24) and, consequently, the resulting option formulas is that they are independent of the choice of λ, the process intensity. This characteristic feature of option valuation formulas for jump processes was first shown for process (2) [see Cox and Ross (1975a)], and it is easy to see by the hedging argument that the intensity, quite generally, plays no role in the valuation since the hedge position depends only on the jump size. In fact, by setting $\mu(S,t) = \mu S$ and $k(S,t) = S(k-1)+1$, (24) becomes the option pricing relation [equation (10) in Cox and Ross (1975a)] for process (2). We can, now, use (24) to study a variety of alternative jump processes.

Example 1

Consider, first, a pure birth process without drift,

$$\mathrm{d}S = \begin{cases} \xrightarrow{\lambda S \mathrm{d}t} k-1, \\ \xrightarrow[1-\lambda S \mathrm{d}t]{} 0. \end{cases} \tag{25}$$

In this case eq. (24) specializes to

$$r(k-1)^{-1}S[P(S+(k-1),t)-P(S,t)]-rP(S,t) = -P_t(S,t), \tag{26}$$

with

$$P(S,T) = \max\{S-E,0\}.$$

To solve (26) we use the technique described in section 3. [As a check, it is not difficult to verify that (26) is the transformed backward equation for the process (25).] In a risk-neutral world the expected returns on both the stock and the option must equal the riskless rate, and (17) becomes

$$E\left[\frac{S_T}{S_0}\right] = e^{\lambda(k-1)(T-t)} = e^{r(T-t)}, \tag{27}$$

or

$$\lambda(k-1) = r,$$

where we have used a familiar result from the theory of birth processes. To obtain the expected return on the option we have to use the distribution function for S_T, which is simply the distribution for a scaled pure birth process [see, e.g., Feller (1966)]. It follows that,

$$\begin{aligned} E\left[\frac{P_T}{P}\right] &= \frac{1}{P} E[\max\{S_T - E, 0\}] \\ &= \frac{1}{P} \sum_{S_T \geqq E} (S_T - E) \begin{bmatrix} \dfrac{S_t}{k-1} - 1 \\ \dfrac{S_t}{k-1} - 1 \end{bmatrix} (e^{-r(T-t)})^{S_t/(k-1)} \\ &\quad \times (1 - e^{-r(T-t)})^{(S_T - S_t)/(k-1)}, \end{aligned} \tag{28}$$

and using (27) and the required equality with the riskless return, we obtain

$$\begin{aligned} P(S,t) &= S \sum_{j \geqq [E/(k-1)+2]} B\left(j; \frac{S}{k-1} + 1, e^{-r(T-t)}\right) \\ &\quad - Ee^{-r(T-t)} \sum_{j \geqq [E/(k-1)+1]} B\left(j; \frac{S}{k-1}, e^{-r(T-t)}\right), \end{aligned} \tag{29}$$

where

$$B(j; x, q) = \binom{j-1}{x-1} q^x (1-q)^{j-x},$$

the negative binomial density, $\binom{j-1}{x-1}$ denotes $\Gamma(j)/\Gamma(x)\Gamma(j-x+1)$, and $[y]$ is the largest integer not exceeding y. This example illustrates the way in which (17) is used in the solution technique. From the hedging argument the intensity λ does not affect the option valuation. In a risk-neutral market $\lambda = r/(k-1)$, which allows us to eliminate λ from the option valuation (29). It is important to realize that this does not imply that we are only solving the valuation problem when

(27) is satisfied. On the contrary, for a given r and k the solution is independent of λ and for any λ the solution will be identical to the solution when (27) holds.

This example also reveals an important feature of solutions to valuation problems in general and jump problems in particular. At points where (29) and the solutions below are not differentiable they cannot, of course, satisfy differential equations of the form of (26). The paradox is resolved by modifying (26) appropriately. At points of non-differentiability, P_t, for example, will not in general capture the true time component of the change, or gradient, in option value. The hedging argument, on the other hand, will use this time gradient and the result is a slight generalization of the differential equations. Our solutions are everywhere correct for these generalized equations. This point is discussed in greater detail in Cox and Ross (1975a and b).

Unfortunately, though, there is no general solution for (24) available, and our technique of evaluating the solution for a risk-neutral world cannot avoid this difficulty. As a consequence, even seemingly straightforward generalizations of the results we do have can become formidable.

Example 2

Suppose we try to extend our option valuation results to the case of the pure jump process, (25), augmented by a proportional drift term, μS, as in (4). This is an important extension because by the techniques employed in footnote 1, (4), like a birth and death process, can be made to converge to the square root diffusion, (7).

To apply our technique to obtain the solution for the differential valuation equation, (24), requires us to know the distribution of S_T/S_t so as to be able to calculate the semi-moment $E\{\max\{S_T-E, 0\}\}$, which gives the option value. Unfortunately, though, the addition of the deterministic drift term greatly complicates this problem. The reason is that the process is now non-homogeneous in time in the sense that the probability of a jump in the next instant depends not only on the number of past jumps, but also on when they occurred, i.e., their timing. Without going into the messy details it can be shown, though, that, given (4), the density function of S_T is

$$\operatorname{Prob}\{S_T \varepsilon (x, x+\mathrm{d}x)\} = \sum_{n=0}^{\infty} \left(\frac{\lambda(k-1)}{\mu}\right)^n \mathrm{e}^{(\lambda/\mu)[S_t + n(k-1) - x]} \times \int_{A_n} \prod_{i=1}^{n} \left(S_t - \sum_{j=1}^{i=1} x_j\right) x_i^{-2} \mathrm{d}x_{ij}, \tag{30}$$

where

$$A_n \equiv \{(x_1, \ldots, x_n) \mid \sum_i x_i = S_t - x\mathrm{e}^{-\mu(T-1)}, -(k-1) \leqq x_1 \leqq \ldots \leqq x_n \leqq -(k-1)\,\mathrm{e}^{-\mu(T-1)}\}.$$

We can now use (19) and (30) to evaluate the option value, but we will no longer have a closed form solution. [The integrals in (30) do not appear to be readily available in closed form, but (30) can be approximated for computation purposes.]

Example 3

As a final jump example that illustrates one of the hazards of applying the solution technique consider applying it to the option valuation problem for the absolute process (8) without drift. To avoid limited liability problems and to permit one stock hedging suppose that $\Pi^{+} = 1$, so that this is a pure growth jump. Simply solving (17), and using the fact that the number of jumps in $[t, T]$ is Poisson distributed, would give

$$E\left\{\frac{S_T}{S_t}\right\} = \frac{\lambda(k-1)}{S_t}(T-t) = e^{r(T-t)},$$

which solves for the omitted parameter, λ, as a function of S_t, the current stock value. This, however, violates the originally postulated absolute process with λ independent of current stock value. In other words, the assumed process is inconsistent in a risk neutral market. Nevertheless, we can still value an option on such a process by noting that the hedging differential equation is given by (26) just as for the pure birth process. This must be the case, since the intensity parameter plays no role in the valuation, other than through (27). It follows, then, that the solution to this problem will be the same as that for the birth process, (29) without drift, and can be found from (30) with a drift term. Even though the absolute process is inconsistent in a risk-neutral market, the differential valuation equation is the same as that for the birth process which is consistent with risk neutrality. This permits us to value the absolute process given whatever structure of market preferences and other assets which will support it in equilibrium. This inconsistency with risk neutrality does not apply to an absolute process with a symmetric two point jump and proportional drift, but consideration of this two jump case cannot be done in the context of single stock hedging.

We now turn to the option problems for the diffusion limits introduced in section 3.

4.2. Alternative diffusion processes

The first step is to derive the differential equation which the option value must follow for all diffusion processes and then specialize for our two cases.[4] In this section we will explicitly consider a stock or firm which makes payouts.[5]

[4]This development follows along the lines given by Black and Scholes and Merton (1974) for the diffusion process (1).

[5]Payouts can also be readily introduced into the jump processes, but this may in some cases greatly complicate the solution.

Suppose that the stock price is governed by

$$\mathrm{d}S = \mu(S, t)\,\mathrm{d}t + \sigma(S, t)\,\mathrm{d}z, \tag{31}$$

where $\mu(S, t)$ and $\sigma^2(S, t)$ are, respectively, the instantaneous mean and variance of the diffusion process. Applying Ito's lemma [see McKean (1969)], the option price will follow,

$$\mathrm{d}P = [P_t + \mu(S, t)P_S + \tfrac{1}{2}\sigma^2(S, t)P_{SS}]\,\mathrm{d}t + P_S\sigma(S, t)\,\mathrm{d}z. \tag{32}$$

Suppose also that each unit of the stock pays out in dividends the continuous stream $b(S, t)$. Consider a portfolio in which we hold a unit of the option, some fraction α_S of a unit of stock, and some amount of borrowing or lending such that the aggregate investment is zero. If we choose α_S to be $-P_S$ then the portfolio will have no stochastic component and to prevent arbitrage its local mean must be zero.

This means that in each instant the three sources of change in the portfolio, the deterministic part of the price changes in the stock and option, the risk-free return on the lending (or borrowing), and payouts received (or made in restitution in the case of short sales) must exactly offset each other. From the above we have that the net deterministic price change component is $\frac{1}{2}\sigma^2(S, t)P_{SS} + P_t$, the return on the bond position in $rSP_S - rP$, and the restitution required for dividend payments made to the stock while held short is $-b(S, t)P_S$. Collecting these terms yields the differential equation form of (15),

$$\tfrac{1}{2}\sigma^2(S, t)P_{SS} + [rS - b(S, t)]P_S - rP = -P_t. \tag{33}$$

With the diffusion processes, then, the stochastic assumptions enter the valuation equation only in the determination of the coefficient of the second derivative term, as would be expected from the earlier discussion about the relation between the valuation equation and the Kolmogorov backward equation for the process in question. Also we can note the convenience of the choice of risk-neutral preferences is not affected by payouts, since the risk neutrality would simply require that the instantaneous mean total return on the stock be rS, so that the required mean price change would be $\mu(S, t) = rS - b(S, t)$.

In the following we will consider only payout functions of the form $b(S, t) = aS + c$ since this will provide a satisfactory representation for most problems. Also we will consider only European options, although for many constant dividend policies equivalent American options would have the same value, since premature exercising would never be optimal.

Example 4

Let us first examine the case (7) where the variance is proportional to the stock price. From (23), the differential valuation equation becomes

$$\tfrac{1}{2}\sigma^2 SP_{SS}+[(r-a)S-c]P_S-rP = -P_t. \tag{34}$$

We could attack this problem directly by standard analytic methods but it is easier to apply the solution technique used above if the terminal density (in a risk-neutral setting) is already known. Fortunately, this is the case since Feller (1951a, b), in his work on birth and death processes, was led to studying the limiting diffusion case. The density of S_T conditional on S_t is given for $S_T > 0$ by

$$\begin{aligned} f(S_T, T; S_t, t) &= \left(\frac{2(r-a)}{\sigma^2(\mathrm{e}^{(r-a)(T-t)}-1)}\right)\left(\frac{S_t\mathrm{e}^{(r-a)(T-t)}}{S_T}\right)^{\frac{1}{2}(1+2c/\sigma^2)} \\ &\quad\times \exp\left[-\frac{2(r-a)(S_t\mathrm{e}^{(r-a)(T-t)}+S_T)}{\sigma^2(\mathrm{e}^{(r-a)(T-t)}-1)}\right] \\ &\quad\times I_{1+2c/\sigma^2}\left[\frac{4(r-a)(S_T S_t\mathrm{e}^{(r-a)(T-t)})^{\frac{1}{2}}}{\sigma^2(\mathrm{e}^{(r-a)(T-t)}-1)}\right], \end{aligned} \tag{35}$$

where $I_q(\cdot)$ is the modified Bessel function of the first kind of order q.[6]

Integrating (35) over the range $S_T > 0$ results in a probability of less than unity. The remaining mass is the probability that $S_t = 0$ for some $t \leqq T$, in which case S was 'absorbed' and remains at zero. Applying our technique we take the expectation of max $(S_T-E, 0)$ and discount it to time t as in (19) to obtain the valuation formula

$$\begin{aligned} P(S, t) &= S\mathrm{e}^{-a(T-t)} \sum_{n=0}^{\infty} \frac{(n+1)\mathrm{e}^{-y}y^{n+2c/\sigma^2}G(n+2, \theta E)}{\Gamma[n+2+2c/\sigma^2]} \\ &\quad -E\mathrm{e}^{-r(T-t)} \sum_{n=0}^{\infty} \frac{\mathrm{e}^{-y}y^{n+1+2c/\sigma^2}\, G(n+1, \theta E)}{\Gamma[n+2+2c/\sigma^2]}, \end{aligned} \tag{36}$$

where

$$\theta = \frac{2(r-a)}{\sigma^2[\mathrm{e}^{(r-a)(T-t)}-1]},$$

$$y = \theta S\mathrm{e}^{(r-a)(T-t)}, \qquad G(m, x) = [\Gamma(m)]^{-1}\int_x^{\infty} \mathrm{e}^{-z}z^{m-1}\mathrm{d}z,$$

[6]It is a difficult mathematical question to decide whether a stochastic differential equation can be solved for a non-trivial stochastic process in cases where the coefficients do not have bounded derivatives. In this case, however, (7) was actually derived from the stochastic process given by (35) and no such problems arise. More generally, if we are given the process itself, any increasing transform of it (like P) will itself be a well-defined process with instantaneous mean, $\mu(S,t)P_S+\frac{1}{2}\sigma^2(S,t)P_{SS}+P_t$, and instantaneous variance, $\sigma^2(S,t)P_S{}^2$, if it is C^2, and derivable even if it is not [see Feller (1966, p. 326)]. This approach permits us to bypass the Ito processes and any additional regularity conditions they might require.

the complimentary standard gamma distribution function. The value of an option at $S = 0$ is implied by the description of the process and no additional restrictions need to be made. For a process with an absorbing barrier at zero we will obviously have $P(0, t) = 0$.

Example 5

Turning now to (10) where the variance is independent of the price, eq. (33) is specialized to

$$\tfrac{1}{2}\sigma^2 P_{SS} + (r-a)SP_S - rP = -P_t. \tag{37}$$

As with (34) this problem could be handled directly, for example by transformation to the heat equation. It is again easier and more illuminating however to make use of knowledge of the terminal stock distribution. Inspecting the equation we note that it is analogous to the backward equation of the Ornstein–Uhlenbeck process, whose physical origins lay in the study of particles in Brownian motion in the presence of an elastic force. It makes little economic sense for a price with limited liability to reach zero if it can subsequently become positive, so we would wish to use the Ornstein–Uhlenbeck process with an absorbing barrier at zero as with the square root process. In the above we have looked only at the specialization $c = 0$, i.e., only at proportional payouts, since otherwise the corresponding density is not known (and the transformation to the heat equation leads to an as yet unsolved time-dependent boundary problem). For the case considered, the density of S_T conditional on S_t is, for $S_T > 0$,

$$f(S_T, T; S_t, t) = (2\pi Z)^{-\frac{1}{2}} \left[\exp\left(-\frac{[S_T - S_t e^{(r-a)(T-t)}]^2}{2Z} \right) - \exp\left(-\frac{-[S_T + S_t e^{(r-a)(T-t)}]^2}{2Z} \right) \right],$$

where

$$Z = \left[\frac{\sigma^2}{2(r-a)} \right] [e^{2(r-a)(T-t)} - 1]. \tag{38}$$

Applying (19) yields the valuation formula,

$$\begin{aligned} P(S, t) = {} & (Se^{-a(T-t)} - Ee^{-r(T-t)})N(y_1) \\ & + (Se^{-a(T-t)} + Ee^{-r(T-t)})N(y_2) \\ & + v[n(y_1) - n(y_2)], \end{aligned} \tag{39}$$

where $N(\cdot)$ is the cumulative unit normal distribution function, $n(\cdot)$ is the unit normal density function, and

$$v = \sigma\left(\frac{e^{-2a(T-t)}-e^{-2r(T-t)}}{2(r-a)}\right)^{\frac{1}{2}},$$

$$y_1 = \frac{Se^{-a(T-t)}-Ee^{-r(T-t)}}{v},$$

$$y_2 = \frac{-Se^{-a(T-t)}-Ee^{-r(T-t)}}{v}.$$

The comparative statics associated with parameter changes in (36) and (39) are tedious, but fairly intuitive, and we defer then to subsequent work.

4.3. Applications to other securities

While we have focused on options above these same techniques can be applied to a wide range of financial instruments. A convenient approach to valuing corporate securities is to assume that the total value of the firm, V, follows a particular stochastic process and then consider individual securities as functions of the value of the firm and time. The value of the individual securities of any firm whose total value follows a diffusion process, for example, must, then, satisfy an equation of the same form as (33). Unlike options, though, most corporate securities, F, receive payouts, $b'(V, t)$, and eq. (33) must be modified to include this return,

$$\tfrac{1}{2}\sigma^2(V,t)F_{VV}+[rV-b(V,t)]F_V-rF+b'(V,t) = -F_t. \tag{40}$$

The securities of a given firm can be distinguished by their terminal conditions and payouts received. As a concrete example, consider a firm with one stock issue and one bond issue. The bond would have a terminal value of min (B, V), where B is the maturity value of the bond, and would receive a constant payout, say c'. The stock would have a terminal condition of max $(V-B, 0)$ and would receive in dividends $aV+c''$, where $c'+c'' = c$, the total constant portion of payouts.[7]

To value such securities it will be useful to think of the total value of any security as being the value the security would have if it received no payouts, i.e., it only received its terminal return, plus the value of the payouts it will potentially receive. In terms of eq. (40) these two components would correspond,

[7]For the log-normal process (1), Merton (1974) has studied the problem of valuing the pure discount funds of a firm which makes no payouts ($a = c = 0$) and Ingersoll (1975) has discussed a model with proportional payouts ($c = 0$).

respectively, to (i) the solution of (40) without the inhomogeneous term $b'(V, t)$ but with the proper terminal conditions for the security, and (ii) the solution of the full eq. (40) with a zero terminal condition $[F(V, T) = 0]$. If we restrict our attention to payout policies of the form $aV+c$, then we can further break down (ii) into the value of the proportional payout and the value of the constant payout. It is easy to see that the sum of these solutions is the complete value of the security.

Applying our technique, the solution to (i) for any security is simply given by eqs. (19) and (17). Having found the solution to (i) for all securities, by the Modigliani–Miller theorem we can find the value of the total payout stream, $aV+c$, by subtracting the sum of these solutions from V. If the payout received by each security j can be written as a proportion of the total payout $k_j(aV+c)$, $(\sum k_j = 1)$, then it is evident from (40) that the value of (ii) for each security j will be k_j times the value of the total payout to all securities. We can then obtain a complete solution without having to solve (ii) separately. This technique can be used, for example, if $a = 0$, which would be the case of a stock that received constant dividends, or $c = 0$, i.e., the bond was a pure discount bond. In general, though, the securities of the firm receive different proportions of the constant payout, c, and the proportional payout, aV, and it is necessary to have a direct solution to (ii) to value such securities. However, we would only need to value separately the total proportional component and the total constant component, since from (40) the value of the payouts to individual securities can be written as a linear combination of these two terms.

To solve problem (ii) by our techniques note that the value of each point in a payout stream in a risk-neutral world must be its expected value discounled to the present. The total value of the stream can then be obtained in the usuat way by integrating over all points in the stream. Once again, since we have established the hedging eq. (40), this solution will be the correct solution in general, not simply in a risk-neutral world. The expected value of any point in the constant stream, say, at time q, will be c times the probability that the payment will be received. This will be the probability, conditional on the current $(t < q)$ value of the firm, that the firm will not be bankrupt at time q. We get this probability by replacing T with q in the terminal density of the value of the firm and then integrating this density with respect to $V_q > 0$. For our process (7), this probability can be obtained from (35) as

$$\sum_{n=0}^{\infty} \frac{e^{-y} y^{n+1+2c/\sigma^2}}{\Gamma[n+2+2c/\sigma^2]} = 1 - G[1+2c/\sigma^2, y], \tag{41}$$

where in y, q replaces T and V replaces S. The value of the entire stream will then be given by integration from t to T, giving

$$\int_t^T c e^{-r(q-t)}[1 - G(1+2c/\sigma^2, \theta V e^{(r-a)(q-t)})] \mathrm{d}q. \tag{42}$$

If we knew the solution to (i) for all securities and the solution to (ii) for the constant component, we could value the proportional component by simply subtracting these from V. It is instructive, though, to value the proportional part of the payout stream directly. The expected value of the stream aV_q at each point q can again be obtained from the density and then discounted back to the present. Alternatively, the discounted expected value could be obtained directly in each of our cases from (36) or (39) by replacing S with V and T with q, and setting the exercise price, $E = 0$. We could then find the total value of the proportional component of the stream at time t by integration with respect to q from t to T.

For the case with variance proportional to value, the solution for the proportionate payout is

$$\int_t^T aVe^{-a(q-t)}\left[\sum_{n=0}^{\infty}\frac{(n+1)e^{-y}y^{n+2c/\sigma^2}}{\Gamma[n+2+2c/\sigma^2]}\right]dq, \tag{43}$$

where, again, in y, V replaces S and q replaces T. When $c = 0$ the expression in square brackets equals one, and (43) reduces to simply

$$\textstyle\int_t^T aVe^{-a(q-t)}dq = V[1-e^{-a(T-t)}]. \tag{44}$$

Applying the analysis to the absolute diffusion (10) where $c = 0$, we find that (44) solves this case as well. In fact, inspection of (40) shows that when only proportional payouts are being made, (44) is the proper valuation for the payout stream for any diffusion process. However, as we have seen, when constant payouts are being made, the valuation of the proportional component will depend on the process being considered.

5. Summary and conclusion

The type of stochastic process determining the movement of the stock is of prime importance in option valuation. At present the workhorse of the option pricing literature has been the log-normal diffusion process. This paper introduced several alternative jump and diffusion processes, and provided solutions for the limiting diffusion cases and for the single-stage forms of the jump processes. The explicit solutions presented have potential empirical applications and a comparative study of them should give additional insight into the structure of security valuation. Aside from the intrinsic value of studying alternative admissible processes, though, a number of important problems involving payouts and bankruptcy which remain intractable for the log-normal are, nevertheless, solvable for some other processes. Throughout, the paper developed and used an economically interpretable technique for solving option problems which has intuitive appeal and should facilitate the solution of other problems in this field.

References

Black, F. and M.J. Scholes, 1973, The pricing of options and corporate liabilities, Journal of Political Economy 81, no. 3, 637–654.

Cootner, P.H., ed., 1964, The random character of stock market prices (M.I.T. Press, Cambridge, Mass.).

Cox, J.C. and S.A. Ross, 1975a, The pricing of options for jump processes, Rodney L. White Center Working Paper no. 2–75 (University of Pennsylvania, Philadelphia, Penn.).

Cox, J.C. and S.A. Ross, 1975b, The general structure of contingent claim pricing, mimeo. (University of Pennsylvania, Philadelphia, Penn.).

Feller, W., 1951a, Diffusion processes in genetics, Proceedings of the Second Berkeley Symposium on Mathematical Statistics and Probability, 227–246.

Feller, W., 1951b, Two singular diffusion problems, Annals of Mathematics 54, 173–182.

Feller, W., 1966, An introduction to probability theory and its applications, vols. I and II (Wiley, New York).

Ingersoll, Jr., J., 1975, A theoretical and empirical investigation of the dual purpose funds: An application of contingent-claims analysis, M.I.T. Working Paper no. 782–75 (M.I.T., Cambridge, Mass.).

McKean, H.P., 1969, Stochastic integrals (Academic Press, New York).

Merton, R.C., 1973, The theory of rational option pricing, Bell Journal of Economics and Management Science 4, no. 1, 141–183.

Merton, R.C., 1974, On the pricing of corporate debt: The risk structure of interest rates, The Journal of Finance 29, no. 2, 449–470.

Merton, R.C., 1975, Option pricing when underyling stock returns are discontinuous, M.I.T. Working Paper no. 787–75 (M.I.T., Cambridge, Mass.).

Modigliani, F. and M.H. Miller, 1958, The cost of capital, corporation finance, and the theory of investment, American Economic Review 48, no. 3, 261–297.

Ross, S.A., 1973, The arbitrage theory of capital asset pricing, Rodney L. White Center Working Paper no. 2–73, forthcoming in the Journal of Economic Theory.

Samuelson, P.A., 1965, Rational theory of warrant pricing, Industrial Management Review 6, no. 2, 13–31.

Samuelson, P., 1973, Mathematics of speculative price, with Appendix: R.C. Merton, Continuous time speculative prices, SIAM Review 15, no. 1.

Sprenkle, C.M., 1961, Warrant prices as indicators of expectations and preferences, Yale Economic Essays 1, no. 2, 178–231.

Journal of Financial Economics 5 (1977) 177–188. © North-Holland Publishing Company

AN EQUILIBRIUM CHARACTERIZATION OF THE TERM STRUCTURE

Oldrich VASICEK*

Wells Fargo Bank and University of California, Berkeley, CA, U.S.A.

Received August 1976, revised version received August 1977

The paper derives a general form of the term structure of interest rates. The following assumptions are made: (A.1) The instantaneous (spot) interest rate follows a diffusion process; (A.2) the price of a discount bond depends only on the spot rate over its term; and (A.3) the market is efficient. Under these assumptions, it is shown by means of an arbitrage argument that the expected rate of return on any bond in excess of the spot rate is proportional to its standard deviation. This property is then used to derive a partial differential equation for bond prices. The solution to that equation is given in the form of a stochastic integral representation. An interpretation of the bond pricing formula is provided. The model is illustrated on a specific case.

1. Introduction

Although considerable attention has been paid to equilibrium conditions in capital markets and the pricing of capital assets, few results are directly applicable to description of the interest rate structure. The most notable exceptions are the works of Roll (1970, 1971), Merton (1973, 1974), and Long (1974). This paper gives an explicit characterization of the term structure of interest rates in an efficient market. The development of the model is based on an arbitrage argument similar to that of Black and Scholes (1973) for option pricing. The model is formulated in continuous time, although some implications for discrete interest rate series are also noted.

2. Notation and assumptions

Consider a market in which investors buy and issue default free claims on a specified sum of money to be delivered at a given future date. Such claims will be called (discount) bonds. Let $P(t, s)$ denote the price at time t of a discount bond maturing at time s, $t \leqq s$, with unit maturity value,

$$P(s, s) = 1.$$

*The author wishes to thank P. Boyle, M. Garman, M. Jensen, and the referees, R. Roll and S. Schaefer for their helpful comments and suggestions.

The yield to maturity $R(t, T)$ is the internal rate of return at time t on a bond with maturity date $s = t+T$,

$$R(t, T) = -\frac{1}{T}\log P(t, t+T), \qquad T > 0. \tag{1}$$

The rates $R(t, T)$ considered as a function of T will be referred to as the term structure at time t.

The forward rate $F(t, s)$ will be defined by the equation

$$R(t, T) = \frac{1}{T}\int_t^{t+T} F(t, \tau)\mathrm{d}\tau. \tag{2}$$

In the form explicit for the forward rate, this equation can be written as

$$F(t, s) = \frac{\partial}{\partial s}[(s-t)R(t, s-t)]. \tag{3}$$

The forward rate can be interpreted as the marginal rate of return from committing a bond investment for an additional instant.

Define now the spot rate as the instantaneous borrowing and lending rate,

$$r(t) = R(t, 0) = \lim_{T\to 0} R(t, T). \tag{4}$$

A loan of amount W at the spot rate will thus increase in value by the increment

$$\mathrm{d}W = Wr(t)\mathrm{d}t. \tag{5}$$

This equation holds with certainty. At any time t, the current value $r(t)$ of the spot rate is the instantaneous rate of increase of the loan value. The subsequent values of the spot rate, however, are not necessarily certain. In fact, it will be assumed that $r(t)$ is a stochastic process, subject to two requirements: First, $r(t)$ is a continuous function of time, that is, it does not change value by an instantaneous jump. Second, it is assumed that $r(t)$ follows a Markov process. Under this assumption, the future development of the spot rate given its present value is independent of the past development that has led to the present level. The following assumption is thus made:

(A.1) The spot rate follows a continuous Markov process.

The Markov property implies that the spot rate process is characterized by a single state variable, namely its current value. The probability distribution of the segment $\{r(\tau), \tau \geqq t\}$ is thus completely determined by the value of $r(t)$.

Processes that are Markov and continuous are called diffusion processes. They can be described [cf. Itô (1961), Gikhman and Skorokhod (1969)] by a stochastic differential equation of the form

$$dr = f(r, t)dt + \rho(r, t)dz, \tag{6}$$

where $z(t)$ is a Wiener process with incremental variance dt. The functions $f(r, t)$, $\rho^2(r, t)$ are the instantaneous drift and variance, respectively, of the process $r(t)$.

It is natural to expect that the price of a discount bond will be determined solely by the spot interest rate over its term, or more accurately, by the current assessment of the development of the spot rate over the term of the bond. No particular form of such relationship is presumed. The second assumption will thus be stated as follows:

(A.2) The price $P(t, s)$ of a discount bond is determined by the assessment, at time t, of the segment $\{r(\tau), t \leqq \tau \leqq s\}$ of the spot rate process over the term of the bond.

It may be noted that the expectation hypothesis, the market segmentation hypothesis, and the liquidity preference hypothesis all conform to assumption (A.2), since they all postulate that

$$R(t, T) = E_t\left(\frac{1}{T}\int_t^{t+T} r(\tau)d\tau\right) + \bar{\pi}(t, T, r(t)),$$

with various specifications for the function $\bar{\pi}$.

Finally, it will be assumed that the following is true:

(A.3) The market is efficient; that is, there are no transactions costs, information is available to all investors simultaneously, and every investor acts rationally (prefers more wealth to less, and uses all available information).

Assumption (A.3) implies that investors have homogeneous expectations, and that no profitable riskless arbitrage is possible.

By assumption (A.1) the development of the spot rate process over an interval (t, s), $t \leqq s$, given its values prior to time t, depends only on the current value $r(t)$. Assumption (A.2) then implies that the price $P(t, s)$ is a function of $r(t)$,

$$P(t, s) = P(t, s, r(t)). \tag{7}$$

Thus, the value of the spot rate is the only state variable for the whole term structure. Expectations formed with the knowledge of the whole past development of rates of all maturities, including the present term structure, are equivalent to expectations conditional only on the present value of the spot rate.

Since there exists only one state variable, the instantaneous returns on bonds of different maturities are perfectly correlated. This means that the short bond and just one other bond completely span the whole of the term structure. It should be noted, however, that bond returns over a finite period are not correlated perfectly. Investors unwilling to revise the composition of their portfolio continuously will need a spectrum of maturities to fulfil their investment objectives.

3. The term structure equation

It follows from eqs. (6), (7) by the Itô differentiation rule [cf., for instance, Itô (1961), Kushner (1967), Åström (1970)], that the bond price satisfies a stochastic differential equation

$$\mathrm{d}P = P\mu(t,s)\,\mathrm{d}t - P\sigma(t,s)\,\mathrm{d}z, \tag{8}$$

where the parameters $\mu(t,s) = \mu(t,s,r(t))$, $\sigma(t,s) = \sigma(t,s,r(t))$ are given by

$$\mu(t,s,r) = \frac{1}{P(t,s,r)}\left[\frac{\partial}{\partial t} + f\frac{\partial}{\partial r} + \tfrac{1}{2}\rho^2\frac{\partial^2}{\partial r^2}\right]P(t,s,r), \tag{9}$$

$$\sigma(t,s,r) = -\frac{1}{P(t,s,r)}\,\rho\,\frac{\partial}{\partial r}P(t,s,r). \tag{10}$$

The functions $\mu(t,s,r)$, $\sigma^2(t,s,r)$ are the mean and variance, respectively, of the instantaneous rate of return at time t on a bond with maturity date s, given that the current spot rate is $r(t) = r$.

Now consider an investor who at time t issues an amount W_1 of a bond with maturity date s_1, and simultaneously buys an amount W_2 of a bond maturing at time s_2. The total worth $W = W_2 - W_1$ of the portfolio thus constructed changes over time according to the accumulation equation

$$\mathrm{d}W = (W_2\mu(t,s_2) - W_1\mu(t,s_1))\,\mathrm{d}t - (W_2\sigma(t,s_2) - W_1\sigma(t,s_1))\,\mathrm{d}z \tag{11}$$

[cf. Merton (1971)]. This equation follows from eq. (8) by application of the Itô rule.

Suppose that the amounts W_1, W_2 are chosen to be proportional to $\sigma(t,s_2)$, $\sigma(t,s_1)$, respectively,

$$W_1 = W\sigma(t,s_2)/(\sigma(t,s_1) - \sigma(t,s_2)),$$

$$W_2 = W\sigma(t,s_1)/(\sigma(t,s_1) - \sigma(t,s_2)).$$

Then the second term in eq. (11) disappears, and the equation takes the form

$$\mathrm{d}W = W(\mu(t, s_2)\sigma(t, s_1)-\mu(t, s_1)\sigma(t, s_2))(\sigma(t, s_1)-\sigma(t, s_2))^{-1}\mathrm{d}t. \quad (12)$$

The portfolio composed of such amounts of the two bonds is instantaneously riskless, since the stochastic element dz is not present in (12). It should therefore realize the same return as a loan at the spot rate described by eq. (5). If not, the portfolio can be bought with funds borrowed at the spot rate, or otherwise sold and the proceeds lent out, to accomplish a riskless arbitrage.

As such arbitrage opportunities are ruled out by Assumption (A.3), comparison of eqs. (5) and (12) yields

$$(\mu(t, s_2)\sigma(t, s_1)-\mu(t, s_1)\sigma(t, s_2))/(\sigma(t, s_1)-\sigma(t, s_2)) = r(t),$$

or equivalently,

$$\frac{\mu(t, s_1)-r(t)}{\sigma(t, s_1)} = \frac{\mu(t, s_2)-r(t)}{\sigma(t, s_2)}. \quad (13)$$

Since eq. (13) is valid for arbitrary maturity dates s_1, s_2, it follows that the ratio $(\mu(t, s)-r(t))/\sigma(t, s)$ is independent of s. Let $q(t, r)$ denote the common value of such ratio for a bond of any maturity date, given that the current spot rate is $r(t) = r$,

$$q(t, r) = \frac{\mu(t, s, r)-r}{\sigma(t, s, r)}, \qquad s \geqq t. \quad (14)$$

The quantity $q(t, r)$ can be called the market price of risk, as it specifies the increase in expected instantaneous rate of return on a bond per an additional unit of risk.

Eq. (14) will now be used to derive an equation for the price of a discount bond. Writing (14) as

$$\mu(t, s, r)-r = q(t, r)\sigma(t, s, r),$$

and substituting for μ, σ from eqs. (9), (10) yields, after rearrangement,

$$\frac{\partial P}{\partial t}+(f+\rho q)\frac{\partial P}{\partial r}+\tfrac{1}{2}\rho^2\frac{\partial^2 P}{\partial r^2}-rP = 0, \qquad t \leqq s. \quad (15)$$

Eq. (15) is the basic equation for pricing of discount bonds in a market characterized by Assumptions (A.1), (A.2), (A.3). It will be called the term structure equation.

The term structure equation is a partial differential equation for $P(t, s, r)$. Once the character of the spot rate process $r(t)$ is described and the market price of risk $q(t, r)$ specified, the bond prices are obtained by solving (15) subject to the boundary condition

$$P(s, s, r) = 1. \tag{16}$$

The term structure $R(t, T)$ of interest rates is then readily evaluated from the equation

$$R(t, T) = -\frac{1}{T}\log P(t, t+T, r(t)). \tag{17}$$

4. Stochastic representation of the bond price

Solutions of partial differential equations of the parabolic or elliptic type, such as eq. (15), can be represented in an integral form in terms of an underlying stochastic process [cf. Friedman (1975)]. Such representation for the bond price as a solution to the term structure equation (15) and its boundary condition is as follows:

$$P(t, s) = E_t \exp\left(-\int_t^s r(\tau)\mathrm{d}\tau - \tfrac{1}{2}\int_t^s q^2(\tau, r(\tau))\mathrm{d}\tau + \int_t^s q(\tau, r(\tau))\mathrm{d}z(\tau)\right), \qquad t \leqq s. \tag{18}$$

To prove (18), define

$$V(u) = \exp\left(-\int_t^u r(\tau)\mathrm{d}\tau - \tfrac{1}{2}\int_t^u q^2(\tau, r(\tau))\mathrm{d}\tau + \int_t^u q(\tau, r(\tau))\mathrm{d}z(\tau)\right),$$

and apply Itô's differential rule to the process $P(u, s)V(u)$. Then

$$\begin{aligned}
\mathrm{d}(PV) &= V\mathrm{d}P + P\mathrm{d}V + \mathrm{d}P\mathrm{d}V \\
&= V\left(\frac{\partial P}{\partial t} + f\frac{\partial P}{\partial r} + \tfrac{1}{2}\rho^2\frac{\partial^2 P}{\partial r^2}\right)\mathrm{d}u + V\frac{\partial P}{\partial r}\rho\mathrm{d}z + PV(-r - \tfrac{1}{2}q^2)\mathrm{d}u \\
&\quad + PVq\mathrm{d}z + \tfrac{1}{2}PVq^2\mathrm{d}u + V\frac{\partial P}{\partial r}\rho q\mathrm{d}u \\
&= V\left(\frac{\partial P}{\partial t} + (f + \rho q)\frac{\partial P}{\partial r} + \tfrac{1}{2}\rho^2\frac{\partial^2 P}{\partial r^2} - rP\right)\mathrm{d}u + PVq\mathrm{d}z + V\frac{\partial P}{\partial r}\rho\mathrm{d}z \\
&= PVq\mathrm{d}z + V\frac{\partial P}{\partial r}\rho\mathrm{d}z,
\end{aligned}$$

by virtue of eq. (15). Integrating from t to s and taking expectation yields

$$E_t(P(s,s)V(s)-P(t,s)V(t)) = 0,$$

and eq. (18) follows.

In the special case when the expected instantaneous rates of return on bonds of all maturities are the same,

$$\mu(t,s) = r(t), \qquad s \geqq t,$$

(this corresponds to $q = 0$), the bond price is given by

$$P(t,s) = E_t \exp\left(-\int_t^s r(\tau)\,\mathrm{d}\tau\right). \tag{19}$$

Eq. (18) can be given an interpretation in economic terms. Construct a portfolio consisting of the long bond (bond whose maturity approaches infinity) and lending or borrowing at the spot rate, with proportions $\lambda(t)$, $1-\lambda(t)$, respectively, where

$$\lambda(t) = (\mu(t,\infty)-r(t))/\sigma^2(t,\infty).$$

The price $Q(t)$ of such portfolio follows the equation

$$\mathrm{d}Q = \lambda Q(\mu(t,\infty)\mathrm{d}t-\sigma(t,\infty)\mathrm{d}z)+(1-\lambda)Qr\,\mathrm{d}t.$$

This equation can be integrated by evaluating the differential of $\log Q$ and noting that $\lambda(t)\sigma(t,\infty) = q(t,r(t))$. This yields

$$\begin{aligned}\mathrm{d}(\log Q) &= \lambda\mu(t,\infty)\mathrm{d}t-\lambda\sigma(t,\infty)\mathrm{d}z+(1-\lambda)r\,\mathrm{d}t-\tfrac{1}{2}\lambda^2\sigma^2(t,\infty)\mathrm{d}t\\ &= r\,\mathrm{d}t+\tfrac{1}{2}q^2\,\mathrm{d}t-q\,\mathrm{d}z,\end{aligned}$$

and consequently

$$\frac{Q(t)}{Q(s)} = \exp\left(-\int_t^s r(\tau)\mathrm{d}\tau-\tfrac{1}{2}\int_t^s q^2(\tau,r(\tau))\mathrm{d}\tau+\int_t^s q(\tau,r(\tau))\mathrm{d}z(\tau)\right).$$

Thus, eq. (18) can be written in the form

$$P(t,s) = E_t Q(t)/Q(s), \qquad t \leqq s. \tag{20}$$

This means that a bond of any maturity is priced in such a way that the same portion of a certain well-defined combination of the long bond and the riskless asset (the portfolio Q) can be bought now for the amount of the bond price as is expected to be bought at the maturity date for the maturity value.

Equivalently, eq. (20) states that the price of any bond measured in units of the value of such portfolio Q follows a martingale,

$$\frac{P(t, s)}{Q(t)} = E_t \frac{P(\tau, s)}{Q(\tau)}, \qquad t \leqq \tau \leqq s.$$

Thus, if the present bond price is a certain fraction of the value of the portfolio Q, then the future value of the bond is expected to stay the same fraction of the value of that portfolio.

In empirical testing of the model, as well as for applications of the results, it is necessary to know the parameters f, ρ of the spot rate process, and the market price of risk q. The former two quantities can be obtained by statistical analysis of the (observable) process $r(t)$. Although the market price of risk can be estimated from the defining eq. (14), it is desirable to have a more direct means of observing q empirically. The following equality can be employed:

$$\left.\frac{\partial R}{\partial T}\right|_{T=0} = \tfrac{1}{2}(f(t, r(t)) + \rho(t, r(t)) \cdot q(t, r(t))). \tag{21}$$

Once the parameters f, ρ are known, q could thus be determined from the slope at the origin of the yield curves. Eq. (21) can be proven by taking the second derivative with respect to s of (18) (Itô's differentiation rule is needed), and putting $s = t$. This yields

$$\left.\frac{\partial^2 P}{\partial s^2}\right|_{s=t} = r^2(t) - f(t, r(t)) - \rho(t, r(t)) \cdot q(t, r(t)). \tag{22}$$

But from (1),

$$\left.\frac{\partial^2 P}{\partial s^2}\right|_{s=t} = r^2(t) - 2\left.\frac{\partial R}{\partial T}\right|_{T=0}. \tag{23}$$

By comparison of (22), (23), eq. (21) follows.

5. A specific case

To illustrate the general model, the term structure of interest rates will now be obtained explicitly in the situation characterized by the following assumptions: First, that the market price of risk $q(t, r)$ is a constant,

$$q(t, r) = q,$$

independent of the calendar time and of the level of the spot rate. Second, that the spot rate $r(t)$ follows the so-called Ornstein–Uhlenbeck process,

$$\mathrm{d}r = \alpha(\gamma - r)\,\mathrm{d}t + \rho\,\mathrm{d}z, \tag{24}$$

with $\alpha > 0$, corresponding to the choice $f(t, r) = \alpha(\gamma - r)$, $\rho(t, r) = \rho$ in eq. (6). This description of the spot rate process has been proposed by Merton (1971).

The Ornstein–Uhlenbeck process with $\alpha > 0$ is sometimes called the elastic random walk. It is a Markov process with normally distributed increments. In contrast to the random walk (the Wiener process), which is an unstable process and after a long time will diverge to infinite values, the Ornstein–Uhlenbeck process possesses a stationary distribution. The instantaneous drift $\alpha(\gamma - r)$ represents a force that keeps pulling the process towards its long-term mean γ with magnitude proportional to the deviation of the process from the mean. The stochastic element, which has a constant instantaneous variance ρ^2, causes the process to fluctuate around the level γ in an erratic, but continuous, fashion. The conditional expectation and variance of the process given the current level are

$$E_t r(s) = \gamma + (r(t) - \gamma)\mathrm{e}^{-\alpha(s-t)}, \qquad t \leqq s, \tag{25}$$

$$\mathrm{Var}_t r(s) = \frac{\rho^2}{2\alpha}(1 - \mathrm{e}^{-2\alpha(s-t)}), \qquad t \leqq s, \tag{26}$$

respectively.

It is not claimed that the process given by eq. (24) represents the best description of the spot rate behavior. In the absence of empirical results on the character of the spot rate process, this specification serves only as an example.

Under such assumptions, the solution of the term structure equation (15) subject to (16) [or alternatively, the representation (18)] is

$$P(t, s, r) = \exp\left[\frac{1}{\alpha}(1 - \mathrm{e}^{-\alpha(s-t)})(R(\infty) - r) - (s-t)R(\infty) - \frac{\rho^2}{4\alpha^3}(1 - \mathrm{e}^{-\alpha(s-t)})^2\right], \qquad t \leqq s, \tag{27}$$

where

$$R(\infty) = \gamma + \rho q/\alpha - \tfrac{1}{2}\rho^2/\alpha^2. \tag{28}$$

The mean $\mu(t, s)$ and standard deviation $\sigma(t, s)$ of the instantaneous rate of return of a bond maturing at time s is, from eqs. (9), (10),

$$\mu(t, s) = r(t) + \frac{\rho q}{\alpha}(1 - e^{-\alpha(s-t)}),$$

$$\sigma(t, s) = \frac{\rho}{\alpha}(1 - e^{-\alpha(s-t)}),$$

with $t \leqq s$. It is seen that the longer the term of the bond, the higher the variance of the instantaneous rate of return, with the expected return in excess of the spot rate being proportional to the standard deviation. For a very long bond (i.e., $s \to \infty$) the mean and standard deviation approach the limits

$$\mu(\infty) = r(t) + \rho q/\alpha,$$

$$\sigma(\infty) = \rho/\alpha.$$

The term structure of interest rates is then calculated from eqs. (17) and (22). It takes the form

$$R(t, T) = R(\infty) + (r(t) - R(\infty))\frac{1}{\alpha T}(1 - e^{-\alpha T})$$

$$+ \frac{\rho^2}{4\alpha^3 T}(1 - e^{-\alpha T})^2, \qquad T \geqq 0, \tag{29}$$

Note that the yield on a very long bond, as $T \to \infty$, is $R(\infty)$, thus explaining the notation (28).

The yield curves given by (29) start at the current level $r(t)$ of the spot rate for $T = 0$, and approach a common asymptote $R(\infty)$ as $T \to \infty$. For values of $r(t)$ smaller or equal to

$$R(\infty) - \tfrac{1}{4}\rho^2/\alpha^2,$$

the yield curve is monotonically increasing. For values of $r(t)$ larger than that but below

$$R(\infty) + \tfrac{1}{2}\rho^2/\alpha^2,$$

it is a humped curve. When $r(t)$ is equal to or exceeds this last value, the yield curves are monotonically decreasing.

Eq. (29), together with the spot rate process (24), fully characterizes the behavior of interest rates under the specific assumptions of this section. It provides both the relationship, at a given time t, among rates of different maturities, and the behavior of interest rates, as well as bond prices, over time. The relationship between the rates $R(t, T_1)$, $R(t, T_2)$ of two arbitrary maturities can be determined by eliminating $r(t)$ from eq. (29) written for $T = T_1$, $T = T_2$. Moreover, (29) describes the development of the rate $R(t, T)$ of a given maturity over time. Since $r(t)$ is normally distributed by virtue of the properties of the Ornstein–Uhlenbeck process, and $R(t, T)$ is a linear function of $r(t)$, it follows that $R(t, T)$ is also normally distributed. The mean and variance of $R(\tau, T)$ given $R(t, T)$, $t < \tau$, are obtained from (29) by use of (25), (26). The calculations are elementary and will not be done here. It will only be noted that eqs. (24), (29) imply that the discrete rate series,

$$R_n = R(nT, T), \qquad n = 0, 1, 2, \ldots,$$

follows a first-order linear normal autoregressive process of the form

$$R_n = c + a(R_{n-1} - c) + \varepsilon_n, \tag{30}$$

with independent residuals ε_n [cf. Nelson (1972)]. The process (30) is the discrete elastic random walk, fluctuating around its mean c. The parameters c, a, and $s^2 = E\varepsilon_n^2$ could be expressed in terms of γ, α, ρ, q. In particular, the constant a, which characterizes the degree to which the next term in the series $\{R_n\}$ is tied to the current value, is given by $a = \mathrm{e}^{-\alpha T}$.

Also, eq. (29) can be used to ascertain the behavior of bond prices. The price $P(\tau, s)$ given its current value $P(t, s)$, $t \leqq s$, is lognormally distributed, with parameters of the distribution calculated using eqs. (1), (25), (26), and (29).

The difference between the forward rates and expected spot rates, considered as a function of the term is usually referred to as the liquidity premium [although, as Nelson (1972) argues, a more appropriate name would be the term premium]. Using eqs. (3) and (25), the liquidity premium implied by the term structure (29) is given by

$$\begin{aligned}\pi(T) &= F(t, t+T) - E_t r(t+T) \\ &= \left(R(\infty) - \gamma + \tfrac{1}{2}\frac{\rho^2}{\alpha^2}\mathrm{e}^{-\alpha T}\right)(1 - \mathrm{e}^{-\alpha T}), \qquad T \geqq 0.\end{aligned} \tag{31}$$

The liquidity premium (31) is a smooth function of the term T. It is similar in form to the shape of the curves used by McCulloch (1975) in fitting observed estimates of liquidity premia. Its values for $T = 0$ and $T = \infty$ are $\pi(0) = 0$, $\pi(\infty) = R(\infty) - \gamma$, respectively, the latter being the difference between the yield on the very long bond and the long-term mean of the spot rate. If $q \geqq \rho/\alpha$, $\pi(T)$ is a monotonically increasing function of T. For $0 < q < \rho/\alpha$, it has a humped shape, with maximum of $q^2/2$ occurring at

$$T = \frac{1}{\alpha} \log\left(\frac{\rho/\alpha}{\rho/\alpha - q}\right).$$

If the market price of risk $q \leqq 0$, then $\pi(T)$ is a monotonically decreasing function.

References

Åström, K.J., 1970, Introduction to stochastic control theory (Academic Press, New York).
Black, F. and M. Scholes, 1973, The pricing of options and corporate liabilities, Journal of Political Economy 81, 637–654.
Friedman, A., 1975, Stochastic differential equations and applications (Academic Press, New York).
Gikhman, I.I. and A.V. Skorokhod, 1969, Introduction to the theory of random processes (W.B. Saunders, Philadelphia, PA).
Itô, K., 1961, Lectures on stochastic processes (Tata Institute, Bombay).
Kushner, H.J., 1967, Stochastic stability and control (Academic Press, New York).
Long, J.B., 1974, Stock prices, inflation, and the term structure of interest rates, Journal of Financial Economics 1, 131–170.
McCulloch, J.H., 1975, An estimate of the liquidity premium, Journal of Political Economy 83, 95–119.
Merton, R.C., 1971, Optimum consumption and portfolio rules in a continuous-time model, Journal of Economic Theory 3, 373–413.
Merton, R.C., 1973, An intertemporal capital asset pricing model, Econometrica 41, 867–887.
Merton, R.C., 1974, On the pricing of corporate debt: The risk structure of interest rates, Journal of Finance 29, 449–470.
Nelson, C.R., 1972, The term structure of interest rates (Basic Books, New York).
Roll, R., 1970, The behavior of interest rates: The application of the efficient market model to U.S. treasury bills (Basic Books, New York).
Roll, R., 1971, Investment diversification and bond maturity, Journal of Finance 26, 51–66.

THE JOURNAL OF FINANCE • VOL XXXVI, NO. 4 • SEPTEMBER 1981

The Journal of FINANCE

VOL. XXXVI SEPTEMBER 1981 No. 4

A Re-examination of Traditional Hypotheses about the Term Structure of Interest Rates

JOHN C. COX, JONATHAN E. INGERSOLL, JR., and STEPHEN A. ROSS*

ABSTRACT

The term structure of interest rates is an important subject to economists, and has a long history of traditions. This paper re-examines many of these traditional hypotheses while employing recent advances in the theory of valuation and contingent claims. We show how the Expectations Hypothesis and the Preferred Habitat Theory must be reformulated if they are to obtain in a continuous-time, rational-expectations equilibrium. We also modify the linear adaptive interest rate forecasting models, which are common to the macro-economic literature, so that they will be consistent in the same framework.

THIS PAPER EXAMINES SOME traditional theories and hypotheses about the term structure of interest rates and discusses the implications of modern portfolio theory and the valuation of contingent claims under diffusion processes in this area of research.

A general equilibrium model of bond pricing which is the basis of further discussion is outlined in Section I. Section II examines the Expectations Hypothesis and concludes that tradition assigns it to three (or four) mutually contradictory "equilibrium" mechanisms. In Section III we prove that only one of these is consistent with a general equilibrium in continuous time. Sections IV and VI discuss the role of risk-neutrality in the Expectations Hypothesis. We show there that the Expectations Hypothesis will not in general describe equilibrium among uniformly risk-neutral investors. Section V looks at Hicksian Liquidity Preference and the Preferred Habitat Theory of Modigliani and Sutch. We find, unlike Hicks, that term premiums may be either positive or negative. Furthermore, we give an interpretation of this result different from that of Modigliani and Sutch. We show that it is not preference for consumption at different times which creates "habitats," but rather the degree of risk aversion. Sections VII and VIII examine the popular discrete-time linear interest rate forecasting models and show how these may be solved in continuous time.

* Stanford University, University of Chicago, and Yale University respectively. We are grateful for the helpful comments and suggestions of Merton Miller and many of our other colleagues, too numerous to mention. This research was supported in part by the Dean Witter Foundation, the Center for Research in Security Prices and the National Science Foundation.

I. Bond Pricing with Diffusion State Processes

In this section we develop a relation linking the expected rates of return on default-free pure discount bonds (single payment debt) of all maturities. Since any default-free coupon-bearing bond may be considered to be a portfolio of pure discount bonds, the derived relation holds for the former as well. We perform this analysis in a continuous-time framework since this would appear to be the only unambiguous choice for the "shortest time interval." Indeed, we shall see that certain characterizations regarding the term structure of interest rates can obtain only on an instantaneous basis.

The following assumptions are taken to characterize the economy:

A1. There is a set of N state variables $\{Y_n\}$ whose current values completely specify all relevant information for investors.

In general the state variables may include both exogenous information like the distribution of returns currently available on physical investment and endogenous information like investors' wealths. The assumption that only current state variable values are relevant does not imply that investors ignore useful historical information. For example, the current value of one or more state variables may be averages of past interest rates if such information is useful in forecasting the future. Since bonds are usually denominated in nominal terms, it may be assumed that the analysis here is carried out using nominal prices and returns. In this case the state variables would include the price(s) of the consumption good(s) or, if relevant, a price index. However, this assumption is only one of convenience, since the results obtained must describe real prices and returns as well for, possibly, a different set of state variables.

A2. The state variables are jointly Markov[1] with movements determined by the system of stochastic differential equations.

$$dY_n(t) = \mu_n(Y, t)\, dt + g'_n(Y, t)\, dz(t) \tag{1}$$

μ_n is the expected change per unit time for the nth state variable. $z(t)$ is a K-dimensional standardized Wiener process.[2] g_n is a K-dimensional vector measuring the response of the nth state variable to each of the $K \leq N$ sources of uncertainty in the economy. $g'_n g_m$ is the covariance of changes in the nth and m^{th} state variables. We assume that the variance-covariance matrix $\{g'_n g_m\}$ is positive semidefinite and of rank K (positive definite if $K = N$).[3]

For full generality we admit the possibility that some $(N - K)$ state variables, or linear combinations thereof, may be nonstochastic. This would arise, for example,

[1] The joint Markov assumption is not merely one of convenience, but is rather a logical necessity. If the state variables specify *all* relevant information, then a fortiori they must jointly describe their own future probability distributions.

[2] A K-dimensional standardized Wiener process is a set of K independent normal random variables, each with mean increment zero and unitary variance per unit time increment. See Arnold [1] for a full treatment.

[3] The matrix $\{g'_n g_m\}$ may have rank of less than K at isolated locations in (Y, t). This would occur, for example, at a natural reflecting or absorbing barrier for one of the state variables.

if one variable were a moving average of another. We examine systems of this type in later sections.

A3. *Investors are nonsatiated, strictly preferring more wealth to less. Investors are sufficiently risk tolerant that they are willing to hold the risky assets at finite expected rates of return.*

This is the only assumption required about investors' preferences. We do not require that they be risk-averse or even that they choose among alternatives on the basis of expected utility maximization. The first part of A3 is sufficient to assure that all assets are priced so that none are dominated (i.e., sell at the same or greater price and offer the same or lesser return under all circumstances as some portfolio made up of other assets). The second part of this assumption is a technical one only and assures that the market for risky assets can reach some equilibrium.

We also assume that the markets for assets are perfect and frictionless.

A4. *All investors believe the economy to be as described in* (A1) *and* (A2), *and have homogeneous assessments of the parameters.*

A5. *All markets are competitive, and each investor acts like a price taker.*

A6. *There is a market for riskless instantaneous borrowing and lending at the endogenously determined equilibrium interest rate r and markets for longer term borrowing and lending at endogenously set prices.*

A7. *There are no taxes, transactions costs, or other institutional sources of market friction. Markets are open continuously, and trading takes place only at equilibrium prices.*

Let $P(Y, t, T)$ denote the current (time t) price of a pure discount bond promising to pay one dollar at time T. The instantaneously realized percentage price change of this bond may be decomposed into the anticipated equilibrium rate of return and the unexpected variation in return due to the random changes in the underlying state variables.

$$dP(Y, t, T)/P(Y, t, T) = \alpha(Y, t, T)\, dt + \delta'(Y, t, T)\, dz(t) \tag{2}$$

α and $\delta'\delta$ are the expected rate of return and variance of return, respectively.

Using Ito's lemma,[4] the following relations can be established

$$\alpha(Y, t, T)P(Y, t, T) = \textstyle\sum_{n=1}^{N} P_{Y_n}\mu_n + \dfrac{1}{2}\sum_{n=1}^{N}\sum_{m=1}^{N} P_{Y_n Y_m} g'_n g_m + P_t$$

$$= L[P(Y, t, T)] + P_t \tag{3a}$$

$$\delta'(Y, t, T)P(Y, t, T) = \textstyle\sum_{n=1}^{N} P_{Y_n} g'_n \tag{3b}$$

where subscripts on P denote partial differentiation. $L[\cdot]$ is the Dynkin operator or differential generator over the state variables. The bond price's response to the kth source of uncertainty is, from (3b), $\delta_k = \sum P_{Y_n} g_{nk}/P$.

If the expected rate of return on bonds were a known function of the state

[4] See Arnold [1] for a statement and formal proof of Ito's lemma. See Merton [32] for a heuristic development.

variables, time, and maturity, then (3a) together with the no-default terminal condition $P(Y, T, T) = 1$ (and other boundary or regularity conditions as required) would form a well-posed problem whose solution completely described the market for default-free bonds, both discount and coupon. For example, if it were known that the expected rates of return on all bonds were equal to the current instantaneous rate of interest, i.e., one characterization of the Expectations Hypothesis held, then expected rates of return would be empirically observable as $\alpha(Y, t, T) = r(Y, t)$. However, if other propositions about expectations, liquidity preferences, or "habitat" behavior were valid, then the expected rate of return might vary with maturity and would require further specification.

As we show below, even when the expected rate of return does vary with maturity, strong restrictions can be placed on the functional form of this dependence. In this regard, consider the potential portfolio strategy[5] consisting of V dollars invested in $K + 1$ discount bonds with distinct (positive) maturities with proportional investment x_i in bond $P(Y, t, T_i)$. The realized rate of return on this portfolio is

$$\frac{dV}{V} = \sum_{i=1}^{K+1} x_i \frac{dP(Y, t, T_i)}{P(Y, t, T_i)} = \sum_{i=1}^{K+1} x_i \alpha(Y, t, T_i)\, dt + \sum_{i=1}^{K+1} x_i \delta'(Y, t, T_i)\, dz(t) \tag{4}$$

If the portfolio weights are selected so that each source of uncertainty vanishes, i.e.,

$$\sum_{i=1}^{K+1} x_i \delta_k(Y, t, T_i) = 0, \text{ all } k \tag{5}$$

then the portfolio will be (locally) riskless. In equilibrium, its expected rate of return must then be the currently prevailing spot rate. Thus, $\sum x_i \alpha(Y, t, T_i) = r(Y, t)$, or

$$\sum_{i=1}^{K+1} x_i [\alpha(Y, t, T_i) - r(Y, t)] = 0 \tag{6}$$

since $\sum x_i = 1$.

Combining (5) and (6), we derive the equilibrium condition

$$\begin{pmatrix} \alpha(Y, t, T_1) - r, \cdots, \alpha(Y, t, T_{K+1}) - r \\ \{\delta(Y, t, T_1)\}, \cdots, \{\delta(Y, t, T_{k+1})\} \end{pmatrix} \begin{pmatrix} x_1 \\ \cdot \\ \cdot \\ x_{K+1} \end{pmatrix} = (0) \tag{7}$$

Since a nonzero linear combination of the columns of this $K + 1$ square matrix equals zero, the matrix must be singular. It follows then that the rows are linearly dependent. Furthermore, since the choice of maturities of the bonds was arbitrary, the linear relation among the rows cannot depend upon maturity. Thus, for some vector function $\hat{\lambda}'(Y, t)$ independent of maturity T,

$$\begin{aligned} \alpha(Y, t, T) &= r(Y, t) + \hat{\lambda}'(Y, t)\delta(Y, t, T) = r + \textstyle\sum_{k=1}^{K} \hat{\lambda}_k \delta_k \\ &= r(Y, t) + \textstyle\sum_{n=1}^{N} \lambda_n P_{Y_n}(Y, t, T)/P(Y, t, T) \end{aligned} \tag{8}$$

where $\lambda_n = \sum_{k=1}^{K} \hat{\lambda}_k g_{nk}$ is also independent of maturity.

[5] We confine our attention to portfolios which satisfy certain technical restrictions on rebalancing strategies. See Harrison and Kreps [21] or Dothan and Williams [14] for a detailed discussion of these restrictions and their interpretation.

Since nowhere in the derivation of (8) was it required that the assets forming the portfolio be discount bonds, this equilibrium condition applies to default-free coupon-bearing bonds as well. Indeed, Equation (8) describes the expected rates of return on all assets whose values depend only on these N state variables and, in this sense, is equivalent to the valuation equation exposited by Garman [20]. The derivation here, it is hoped, gives a stronger understanding of the economics underlying the equilibrium in outlining the course of action an investor could take by forming a portfolio to realize excess returns if the equilibrium did not hold.

While the derivation above is complete and requires no additional assumptions beyond those stated, the valuation equation is as it stands virtually an empty mathematical shell. A determination of what the relevant state variables are and the form of the factor risk premiums requires an embedding equilibrium. In work on contingent claims analysis, such as option pricing, it is common, and to a first approximation reasonable, to insist only on a partial equilibrium between the prices of the primary and derivative assets. For something as fundamental as the rate of interest, however, a general equilibrium model is to be preferred. Cox, Ingersoll, and Ross [9] provide one such model and in a subsequent paper [10] discuss some problems which can arise when equilibrium modeling is ignored.

The equilibrium condition in (8) may be given the following characterization. The term premium, i.e., excess expected rate of return,[6] on any bond is given by a linear model with K factors, one for each relevant source of uncertainty. Each component in the premium is the product of a measure of the quantity of type-k risk the bond exhibits, δ_k, and the equilibrium compensation for bearing one unit of this risk, $\hat{\lambda}_k$. By choosing K bonds, forming a basis which spans the set of investment opportunities, $\hat{\lambda}$ can be elimintated from the returns relation and (8) can be written as a multifactor CAPM-type model. Define the vector of expected returns on the basis bonds to be $\alpha_B' \equiv (\alpha(Y, t, T_1), \cdots, \alpha(Y, t, T_K))$ and the matrix of risk factors $\Delta' \equiv (\delta(Y, t, T_1), \cdots, \delta(Y, t, T_K))$. Then, solving for $\hat{\lambda} = \Delta^{-1}(\alpha_B - r\mathbf{1})$, we can write (8) for the nonbasis bonds as

$$\alpha(Y, t, T) = r(Y, t) + \delta'(Y, t, T)\Delta^{-1}(\alpha_B - r\mathbf{1}) \tag{9}$$

Returning to the bond valuation problem, we obtain the general bond pricing equation by substituting (8) into (3a)

$$\tfrac{1}{2} \textstyle\sum_{n=1}^{N} \sum_{m=1}^{N} g_n' g_m P_{Y_n Y_m} + \sum_{n=1}^{N} P_{Y_n}(\mu_n - \lambda_n) - rP + P_t = 0 \tag{10}$$

A comparison of (3a) and (10) shows that the latter would be the valuation equation for an economy in which the expected rate of return on each bond was equal to the prevailing spot rate and investor's expectations of the changes in the state variables were altered to $\mu_n - \lambda_n$.[7] One important implication of this

[6] Throughout this paper, the phrase "term premium" will mean the excess of the expected rate of return over the spot rate of interest, and not the meaning sometimes given to it of the excess of the yield to maturity ofer the spot rate.

[7] This adjustment in both the state variables' drifts and the asset's discount rate is similar to the technique in option pricing of employing an equivalent "risk-neutral" economy. The interpretation here must be different. The equivalent economy is not risk neutral as we show in Section IV. In fact, even though (10) is mathematically identical to (3a), we have not shown that there is any equivalent economy for which the beliefs $\mu_n - \lambda_n$ exhibit rational expectations. In particular, interpretation

equivalency for empirical work is that any test for term premiums conducted by comparing average rates of return is equivalent to some test comparing *properly adjusted* forward rates with actual future rates.[8]

II. The Expectations Hypothesis: Alternate Forms[9]

Many theories have been proposed to explain the relation among the returns on bonds of various maturities. One of the earliest was the Expectations Hypothesis. This theory of the term structure cannot be attributed to any one individual. Rather, it has developed over much of this century. Certainly the proposition that investors' expectations about future spot rates affect the level of current long rates dates back (at least) to Irving Fisher [18]. However, most of the theory underlying the Expectations Hypothesis was not developed until the late 1930s by, notably, Hicks [22] and Lutz [27].

The traditional expectations theory has led these and other authors to set out a number of economic propositions about the relation between short and long rates. For example, Lutz [27, pp. 37, 49] states: "An owner of funds will go into the long market if he thinks the return he can make there over the time for which he has funds available will be above the return he can make in the short market over the same time, and vice versa," and "... a lender who wants to invest for only one year is in principle prepared to buy ... a bond of any other maturity and sell it again after the first year."

The broadest interpretation of these propositions would lead to the conclusion that equilibrium is characterized by an equality among expected holding period returns on all possible default-free bond investment strategies over all holding periods. That is, for any holding period t_0 to t_n, the return on any feasible series of investments must have the same expectation:

$$E\left[\frac{\tilde{P}(t_1, T_1)}{P(t_0, T_1)} \cdot \frac{\tilde{P}(t_2, T_2)}{\tilde{P}(t_1, T_2)} \cdot \ldots \cdot \frac{\tilde{P}(t_n, T_n)}{\tilde{P}(t_{n-1}, T_n)}\right] = \phi(t_n, t_0) \tag{11}$$

where we have suppressed the bonds' dependence on the state variables for convenience of notation. In (11), the expected return ϕ must be independent of the arbitrary reinvestment times t_i ($t_0 < t_1 < \cdots < t_n$) and the bonds selected, as denoted by their maturity dates T_i ($T_i \geqslant t_i$).

It is an easy matter to prove that Equation (11) cannot be generally valid since it demands too much. For example, (11) requires that the expected return on a bond maturing at t_2 over the period (t_0, t_1) must equal the certain return on a

problems may arise if one or more of the state variables has a specified boundary behavior (e.g., the nonnegativity of the nominal interest rate) which is satisfied with the beliefs μ_n but not with $\mu_n - \lambda_n$. There might also be a problem when a state variable dynamics were subject to some control (e.g., wealth) and the beliefs $\mu_n - \lambda_n$ could only be interpreted as suboptimal behavior.

[8] Even with no term premiums an adjustment is required to correct for the difference due to Jensen's inequality. This issue is discussed in the next section.

[9] Some of the results of the next two sections could differ for a discrete-time model. The appendix restates these results. Readers who are not familiar with continuous-time models may prefer to read the appendix before continuing.

bond maturing at t_1

$$\frac{1}{P(t_0, t_1)} = \frac{E[P(t_1, t_2)]}{P(t_0, t_2)} \tag{12}$$

Furthermore, the return expected over (t_0, t_2) on a bond maturing at t_1 rolled over at maturity into a bond maturing at t_2 must equal the guaranteed return on the bond maturing at t_2,

$$\frac{1}{P(t_0, t_2)} = \frac{1}{P(t_0, t_1)} E\left[\frac{1}{P(t_1, t_2)}\right] \tag{13}$$

Together, (12) and (13) imply that

$$E\left[\frac{1}{P(t_1, t_2)}\right] = \frac{P(t_0, t_1)}{P(t_0, t_2)} = \frac{1}{E[P(t_1, t_2)]} \tag{14}$$

But by Jensen's inequality, (14) cannot be true except in the case of certainty. Thus, all expected returns for all holding periods can never be equal in equilibrium.

This contradiction can be avoided if it is postulated that expected holding period returns are equal only for one specific holding period. The natural choice of holding period is the next basic (i.e., "shortest") interval. This interpretation of the Expectations Hypothesis has only recently come into favor, particularly in the field of finance. Under this assumption, equilibrium is characterized by

$$\frac{E[dP(Y, t, T)]}{P(Y, t, T)} = r(t)\,dt \tag{15}$$

Since there are no term premiums in this formulation, many authors have been lured into referring to it as the "Risk-Neutral Expectations Hypothesis." In fact, (15) is not a consequence of universal risk-neutrality, as is demonstrated in Section IV. To avoid possible confusion, we shall refer to this equilibrium as the Local Expectations Hypothesis (L-EH) because (15) asserts equality of local expected rates of return.

Relying on the isomorphic relation between differential and integral equations, (15) can be rewritten as

$$P(Y, t, T) = E\left[\exp\left(-\int_t^T r(s)\,ds\right) \middle| Y(t)\right] \tag{16}$$

where the bond's current price is the expected discounted value of the promised unit payment.[10] Equation (16) states the common sense result that if there is no term premium, then the rate of discount to be used at each instant is the prevailing spot rate.

Traditionally, the equilibrium relation of the Expectations Hypothesis has been stated in a different fashion. It is often assumed, as implied by Lutz's first quote above, that the guaranteed return from holding any discount bond to maturity is

[10] For a proof of the equivalency of (15) and (16) see Cox, Ingersoll, and Ross [9] Lemma 3 or 4.

equal to the return expected from rolling over a series of single-period bonds; i.e.,[11]

$$\frac{1}{P(Y, t, T)} = E\left[\exp\left(\int_t^T r(s)\,ds\right) \middle| Y(t)\right] \tag{17}$$

Some authors make a similar assumption about equality of expected yields. For example, Malkiel [28, p. 20] states that "... all differentials in anticipated holding period yields [are] completely eliminated ..."; i.e.,

$$\frac{-1}{T-t}\ln[P(Y, t, T)] = E\left[\frac{1}{T-t}\int_t^T r(s)\,ds \,|\, Y(t)\right] \tag{18}$$

To distinguish these two equilibrium conditions from (15), we shall refer to (17) and (18) as the Return-to-Maturity Expectations Hypothesis (RTM-EH) and the Yield-to-Maturity Expectations Hypothesis (YTM-EH), respectively.

In other cases it is assumed that forward rates are unbiased estimates of future interest rates. In the words of Malkiel [p. 23]: "Forward rates and expected spot rates are driven to equality." i.e.,

$$\frac{-\partial P(Y, t, T)/\partial T}{P(Y, t, T)} = E[r(T) \,|\, Y(t)] \tag{19}$$

For this final conjecture we employ the traditional name, the Unbiased Expectations Hypothesis (U-EH). Integrating (19) and applying the condition $P(Y, T, T) = 1$ gives

$$-\ln[P(Y, t, T)] = \int_t^T E[r(s) \,|\, Y(t)]\,ds \tag{20}$$

Therefore, in a continuous-time framework these last two conditions, (18 and 19) are tautological,[12] and we need not consider the Unbiased Expectations Hypothesis separately.

Many researchers are not precise in distinguishing among (16), (17), and (18), perhaps not realizing that these propositions are (pairwise) incompatible. If we define the random variable $\tilde{X} \equiv \exp(-\int_t^T r(s)ds)$, then (16) through (18) can be rewritten as

$$P = E[\tilde{X}] \tag{16'}$$

$$P^{-1} = E[\tilde{X}^{-1}] \tag{17'}$$

$$\ln(P) = E[\ln \tilde{X}] \tag{18'}$$

[11] For some stochastic processes, the expectation in (17) may not be bounded. This is true even if r has a well-defined (finite variance) steady-state distribution. For example, if the spot rate is governed by the Markov stochastic process utilized by Cox, Ingersoll, and Ross [10], $dr = K(\mu - r)\,dt + \sigma\sqrt{r}\,dz$, then, for $2\sigma^2 > K^2$, $E[\exp(\int_0^T r(t)\,dt)] = ([K\sin(\eta T) + 2\eta\cos(\eta T)]/2\eta)^{-2K\mu/\sigma^2}\exp(K^2\mu T/\sigma^2 + [\eta\cot(\eta T) + K/2]^{-1}r)$ where $\eta \equiv \sqrt{2\sigma^2 - K^2}$. This expectation exists only for $T < (2/\eta)\cot^{-1}(-K/\eta)$ (where the inverse function is interpreted to give a positive angle in the interval $(\pi/2, \pi)$). At this point the two terms in brackets become zero and the expectation is infinite. In cases such as these, (17) obviously cannot serve as a useful equilibrium condition.

[12] In a discrete-time model the equivalent relations are not tautological and, in general, are even inconsistent. See the appendix for details.

By invoking Jensen's inequality, it is clear that if Equation (18) describes equilibrium, then the yield on $T-t$ period bond will be greater than the value given in (16) and less than the value given in (17). On the other hand, if equilibrium condition (16) (condition (17)) is valid, then Equations (17) and (18) (Equations (16) and (18)) give long yields which are too large (small).

In summary, the Expectations Hypothesis has (at least) three distinct forms. Only the local version (16) is characterized by the absence of term premiums in the expected instantaneous rates of return on long bonds.[13] In the other three versions, term premiums are positive.

III. The Expectations Hypotheses and Equilibrium

In the previous section we saw that the Expectations Hypothesis is in fact a set of three distinct propositions. In this section, we examine each version using the equilibrium relation (8) to determine if it demonstrates rational expectations. We prove that only the Local Expectations Hypothesis, expected instantaneous rates of return on all bonds are equal, can be sustained in equilibrium (except under certain interest rates when all three propositions are identical). The other versions are incompatible not only with whatever economy supports the L-EH, but with any continuous-time rational expectations equilibrium whatsoever. In the next section, we show sufficient conditions to support the Local Expectations Hypothesis.

The equilibrium condition (8) is stated in terms of risk (term) premiums. So, to establish the possibility of sustaining equilibria for these expectations theories, the premiums must be extracted from the appropriate partial differential pricing equations. From (15) it is clear that the Local Expectations Hypothesis obtains in an economy if there are no premiums, $\lambda' = O'$. As we saw in the previous section, term premiums under the other traditional forms of the Expectations Hypothesis will be positive. In our continuous-time model we can derive the exact form of these premiums.

Applying Ito's lemma and using the price dynamics in (2), the reciprocal of the bond price evolves according to

$$d(1/P) = (-\alpha + \delta'\delta)(1/P)\,dt - (1/P)\delta'\,dz \tag{21}$$

But under the RTM Expectations Hypothesis the expected change in the reciprocal of the bond price is, from (17), $E[d(1/P)] = -r(1/P)\,dt$; hence

$$\alpha(Y, t, T) = r(Y, t) + \delta'(Y, t, T)\delta(Y, t, T) \tag{22}$$

and the premium of each bond is equal to its variance of returns.

Applying Ito's lemma again, the log of the bond price evolves according to

$$d(\ln P) = (\alpha - \tfrac{1}{2}\delta'\delta)\,dt + \delta'\,dz \tag{23}$$

Under the Unbiased Expectations Hypothesis or the YTM-EH, the expected

[13] The unbiased expectations hypothesis is characterized by an absence of "premiums" in the forward rates and yields-to-maturity. The traditional version has no premiums in holding period returns.

change in the log of the bond price is, from (18) or (20), $E[d(\ln P)] = rdt$; thus

$$\alpha(Y, t, T) = r(Y, t) + \tfrac{1}{2}\delta'(Y, t, T)\delta(Y, t, T) \tag{24}$$

To show that neither of these two hypotheses can be sustained in equilibrium, we compare the expected rates of return under these two hypotheses, as given in (22) and (24), with the general expression for the equilibrium expected rate of return in (8). For expression (22) or (24) to yield equilibrium results, it is necessary that

$$\hat{\lambda}'(Y, t)\delta(Y, t, T) = a\delta'(Y, t, T)\delta(Y, t, T) \tag{25}$$

where $a = 1$ for the RTM Expectations Hypothesis and $a = \tfrac{1}{2}$ for the YTM- (or U-) Expectations Hypothesis.

Now it is certainly possible to construct an example for which (25) holds for a particular state at a given point of time, but we require that this relation be true in *all* states at *all* times. The state variables Y are driven by a set of K independent sources of uncertainty (the Wiener processes). However, to impose (25) at both times t and $t + dt$ requires that there be a functional relation among the K realizations of the Wiener processes. Since by definition they are independent, this is impossible.

To clarify this reasoning, consider the case when there is exactly one relevant source of uncertainty (with one or more state variables); then $\delta(T)$ is a scalar function and from (25), $\delta(T) = \hat{\lambda}/a$. Since $\hat{\lambda}$ and a do not depend upon the maturity of the bond in question, δ must be independent of maturity as well. But maturing bonds are riskless over the last instant of their life, $\delta(Y, t, t) = 0$, so if δ is to be constant, it must be identically zero. In this case, bond prices are nonstochastic, violating the assumption that there was one relevant source of uncertainty. Consequently, if one of the traditional forms of the Expectations Hypothesis held (and bonds were not riskless), excess (nonequilibrium) profits would be possible. To demonstrate, consider two discount bonds, with $\delta(T_1)\delta(T_2) > 0$,[14] combined in a portfolio with weights $x_1 = \delta_2/(\delta_2 - \delta_1)$ and $x_2 = 1 - x_1$. By construction, this portfolio will be riskless and have an expected and therefore guaranteed rate of return of

$$\alpha_P = r + a(x_1\delta_1^2 + x_2\delta_2^2) = r + a\delta_1\delta_2 > r \tag{26}$$

which exceeds the fair (riskless) return.

We have proved that the RTM, YTM, and Unbiased Expectations Hypotheses are not sustainable in a continuous-time rational expectations equilibrium. In the next section we consider the Local Expectations Hypothesis. We show that while it can obtain as an equilibrium condition, it does not do so in the generally cited case of universal risk-neutrality unless interest rates are nonstochastic or other special circumstances obtain.

IV. Risk-Neutrality and the Local Expectations Hypothesis

The development of the expectations theory has relied heavily on earlier models of interest rate behavior under certainty. It is well known that all forms of the

[14] This condition can be imposed with no loss of generality. For any three risky bonds with different values of $\delta(T)$ at least two of them must have $\delta(T)$ of the same sign.

Expectations Hypothesis are equivalent under certainty, and the relations given in the previous sections all must hold identically to ensure that arbitrage possibilities do not exist.

As all students of economics learn, certainty models can, in many cases, be adapted to uncertainty by the judicious use of expectations of the uncertain quantities if investors are risk-neutral. Unfortunately, uncertainty concerning interest rates is not one of these cases. In this section we examine the connection between the Local Expectations Hypothesis and risk neutrality. (Given the analysis of the previous section, only this form of the Expectations Hypothesis need be considered.) We find, despite the assumptions and claims of many,[15] that the Expectations Hypothesis is not a natural consequence of universal risk neutrality, except in the uninteresting case when interest rates are nonstochastic.

To illustrate this point, we consider two distinct market economies. The first is a pure exchange economy of the type studied by Lucas [26] and the second is a production-exchange economy of the Cox, Ingersoll, Ross [9] type. As we shall see, there are some substantive differences between the two types. In the three subsections below we show that: (a) in a risk-neutral pure exchange economy interest rates must be nonstochastic. All forms of the Expectations Hypothesis are therefore sustained but only in the singular sense of a certainty model; (b) in a risk-neutral production-exchange economy interest rates may be either certain or stochastic. In the first case, the Expectation Hypotheses hold (again in the singular sense); in the latter case the Local Expectations Hypothesis does not generally obtain; and (c) there are for each type of economy nontrivial conditions under which the Local Expectations Hypothesis does obtain for risk-averse agents.

A. Risk Neutrality in Pure Exchange Economies

Following Lucas, we assume that the quantity of the consumption good available each period is determined exogenously and if not consumed perishes. Suppose initially that the risk-neutral investors have homogeneous expectations, equal endowments, and the same time preference. For an economy of identical investors, prices will be set as if markets were complete, regardless of their actual scope. Thus the equilibrium allocation is characterized by

$$U_1(C_0, t_0) = \pi(s, t; s_0, t_0)U_1[C(s, t), t]/p(s, t; s_0, t_0) \tag{27}$$

where $\pi(s, t; s_0, t_0)$ is the probability as assessed at t_0 in state s_0 that state s will occur at time t, $p(s, t; s_0, t_0)$ is the price prevailing in state s_0 at time t_0 for one unit of the consumption good numeraire at time t in state s and $U_1(C, t)$ denotes the partial derivative $\partial U/\partial C$.

Using (27) and risk-neutrality, $U(C, t) = f(t)C$, we can write the price of a unit

[15] See, for example, Meiselman [29] and Richard [36]. We consider only single-good, time-additive functions, for which risk neutrality is defined as utility of the form $\sum f(t)C_t$. It could be argued, perhaps, that this description is incomplete and that other utility functions, such as $\prod f(t)C_t$, are also "risk-neutral." Certainly the time-additive form given would fit in virtually any definition of risk neutrality, and, as we are looking for its "natural consequences," it suffices to consider only this generally accepted case. Richard [36, footnote 13] explicitly considers this form, claiming it leads to the Local Expectations Hypothesis.

discount bond maturing at t as

$$P(s_0, t_0, t) = \int_S p(s, t; s_0, t_0)\, ds = \frac{f(t)}{f(t_0)} \int_S \pi(s, t; s_0, t_0)\, ds = \frac{f(t)}{f(t_0)} \qquad (28)$$

So bond prices are state independent and hence nonstochastic. If investors display a constant rate of time preference $f(t) = e^{-\rho t}$, then the yield curve is flat as well with a constant interest rate of ρ. In this world the Expectations Hypothesis characterizes the bond market, but it does so simply by arbitrage because there is no interest rate uncertainty.[16, 17]

If investors' initial endowments differ, these results are unchanged because the competitive equilibrium in an economy of risk-neutral investors is independent of the original allocation of wealth if they are otherwise identical. On the other hand, if the investors differ in beliefs *or* time preference, then no unconstrained equilibrium is possible. An investor would willingly supply (purchase) an infinite quantity of any Arrow-Debreu security whose price exceeded (was less than) his utility-discounted personally assessed probability for that state [i.e., $p(s, t; s_0, t_0) > (<) \pi_i(s, t; s_0, t_0) f_i(t)/f_i(t_0)$]. In such a situation it is meaningless to examine the proposed equilibrium relation.

B. Risk Neutrality in Production-Exchange Economies

We now extend the model to include production by assuming that any of the good unconsumed can be invested to provide for future consumption. If the investment opportunities are stationary or change deterministically over time, then results similar to those in the pure exchange model will obtain. Consequently, we shall assume that the investment opportunities evolve stochastically over time as governed by the state variables Y. As shown by Cox, Ingersoll, and Ross [9], the (representative) investor's consumption-investment decision is characterized by the derived utility of wealth function $J(W, Y, t)$ which is the solution to the partial differential equation

$$U(C, t) + J_t + [\alpha_W(Y, W, t)W - C]J_W + \tfrac{1}{2}\sigma_W^2(Y, W, t)W^2 J_{WW} + \textstyle\sum_{n=1}^{N} \sigma_{nW}(Y, W, t) W J_{WY_n} + L[J] = 0 \qquad (29)$$

[16] Leroy [25] has independently derived the same result. However, he considers only exchange economies. As we demonstrate below, in a risk-neutral production economy interest rates may be stochastic. But in this case the expectations hypothesis generally does not obtain. Neither is it true that the expectations hypothesis is approximately correct for, in Leroy's terminology, "near risk-neutrality."

[17] This result is not unique to risk-neutrality. Under certain assumptions, other preferences can also result in nonstochastic interest rates (and, a fortiori, the expectations hypothesis), even in a risky economy. For example, for identical investors with state-dependent power utility, equilibrium bond prices will be

$$P(s_0, t_0, t) = \frac{f(t)}{f(t_0)} \int_S \pi(s, t; s_0, t_0) \left(\frac{C(s)}{C(s_0)}\right)^{\gamma - 1} ds$$

If percentage changes in aggregate consumption are assumed to be independently distributed, then the distribution of $C(s)/C(s_0)$ is independent of the current state, and bond prices and interest rates are again nonstochastic.

where α_W and σ_W^2 are the state dependent expected return and variance of return on optimally invested wealth (the market portfolio), σ_{nW} is the covariance of change in the nth state variable with the return on wealth, and $L[\cdot]$ is the differential generator defined in (3).[18] The equilibrium interest rate in this economy is

$$r(W, Y, t) = \alpha_W - \frac{-WJ_{WW}}{J_W}\sigma_W^2 - \sum_{n=1}^{N}\frac{-J_{WY_n}}{J_W}\sigma_{nW} \tag{30}$$

To solve (29), the first order condition for a maximum, $U_C = J_W$, is generally imposed; however, for risk-neutral investors, $U(C, t) = f(t)C$, utility is not concave and an interior solution is not guaranteed. Under risk neutrality, investors must solve a singular control problem. There are three possibilities to consider: (1) investors are not currently consuming and $U_C = f(t) < J_W$; (2) investors are consuming at an infinite rate, completely exhausting their wealth and $f(t) > J_W$; and (3) investors are consuming at some finite rate with $J_W = f(t)$. Let us assume for the moment that conditions are such that this third case is always valid. Then integrating once gives

$$J(W, Y, t) = f(t)W + g(Y, t) \tag{31}$$

Substituting (31) into (29)

$$f(t)C + f'(t)W + g_t + (\alpha_W W - C)f(t) + L[J] = 0 \tag{32}$$

The third and fifth terms do not depend upon wealth; therefore, we require

$$\alpha_W(Y, W, t) = -f'(t)/f(t) \tag{33}$$

The time preference factor $f(t)$ is exogenous and state-independent, so Equation (33) can only be satisfied if α is deterministic. This will be true only if it does not depend upon the state variables or if one or more of the state variables is subject to sufficient control by investors such that the equality in (33) can be maintained. For example, if there are decreasing returns to scale in physical investment, wealth will then be one state variable and $\partial\alpha/\partial W < 0$. Then if α_W is less than $-f'(t)/f(t)$ at the current level of wealth, investors could consume more until (33) was satisfied.

If, as we have been assuming, the economy is such that this equilibrium is always achieved, then the expected rate of return on wealth is nonstochastic. Furthermore, $J_{WW} = J_{WY} = 0$, so from (30) $r = \alpha_W$ and the interest rate is nonstochastic as well. As in the Lucas-type model above, the Expectations Hypothesis will obtain, but only because there is no interest rate uncertainty.

If α_W does not depend upon wealth but only exogenous state variables or the economy is otherwise such that the equilibrium characterized in Case (3) cannot be achieved, then the interest rate will be stochastic. Analyzing the consumption-investment problem in this case requires a determination of the conditions under which investors will switch from investing their entire wealth to consuming it.

[18] If wealth is one of the relevant state variables included in Y, then it should *not* be included in $L[\cdot]$ here or subsequently in this section, since the dynamics for wealth are explicitly given.

Solving this "optimal stopping time" problem would lead us far astray from our original purposes and little of a general nature would be learned since investor behavior would depend upon the assumed dynamics of the state variables. However, a related problem suffices to show that the Local Expectations Hypothesis will not be generally valid.

Suppose that the risk-neutral investors consume only at a single point of time in the future, τ, i.e.,

$$U(C, t) = 0 \quad t \neq \tau$$
$$U(C, \tau) = C \tag{34}$$

The problem to be solved is formally identical to that in (29) with C and $U(C, t)$ set to zero. At time τ all wealth will be consumed so the appropriate boundary condition is $J(W, Y, \tau) = W$. Solving (30) for α_W and substituting into (29) yields

$$J_t + rWJ_W - \tfrac{1}{2}\sigma_W^2(Y, t)W^2J_{WW} + L[J] = 0$$
$$J(W, Y, \tau) = W \tag{35}$$

As a trial solution to (35), take $J(W, Y, t) = WQ(Y, t)$, then

$$Q_t + rQ + L[Q] = 0$$
$$Q(Y, \tau) = 1 \tag{36}$$

A formal solution to (36) is[19]

$$Q(Y, t) = E_t\left[\exp \int_t^\tau r(Y, s)\, ds\right] \tag{37}$$

So at any point of time the marginal utility of wealth is equal to the expected terminal value of one dollar earning the prevailing spot rate of interest.

As we have shown elsewhere [9, Equation (20)], the expected rate of return on a default-free bond in this continuous-time production economy of investors with isoelastic utility is given by

$$\alpha(Y, t, T)$$
$$= r + \textstyle\sum_{n=1}^N (P_{Y_n}/P)\left[-\dfrac{WJ_{WW}}{J_W}\sigma_{Wn} + \textstyle\sum_{m=1}^N -\dfrac{J_{WY_m}}{J_W}\operatorname{Cov}(Y_m, Y_n)\right] \tag{38}$$

For risk-neutral investors $J_{WW} = 0$; therefore, the covariance of the bond's return with that of the "market" portfolio, $\sum (P_{Y_n}/P)\sigma_{Wn}$, does not contribute to its risk premium. In some models, such as the CAPM in finance, a positive market covariance is the only cause for premium returns; however, such is not the case here. In (38) there also is a premium due to the final sum which measures the extra compensation, positive or negative, for each bond's potential to hedge against shifts in the investment opportunity set. Substituting for $J(\cdot)$ Equation

[19] See Friedman [19, Theorem 5.2]. For some stochastic processes, the integral in (36) may be undefined. See footnote 11.

(38) simplifies to

$$\alpha(Y, t, T) = r - \sum_{n=1}^{N} \sum_{m=1}^{N} (Q_{Y_m}/Q)(P_{Y_n}/P)\text{Cov}(Y_m, Y_n)$$

$$= r - \text{Cov}\left(\frac{dQ}{Q}, \frac{dP}{P}\right) \tag{39}$$

From the last line in (39) and the definition of Q in (37), the premium on a bond can be expressed as a single term which is the negative of the covariance of the bond's return with the percentage change in the expected value of a dollar compounded up to the consumption date τ by the time path of future instantaneous riskless interest rates. Only if this covariance is uniformly zero does the Local Expectations Hypothesis hold. While it might be possible to construct examples for which these terms are uncorrelated, there is no obvious reason for this to be the case unless interest rates are deterministic.

In the particular case when the spot rate of interest is the only relevant state variable, the covariance is negative since $Q_r > 0$ and $P_r < 0$.[20] In this economy term premiums will be positive and an increasing function of maturity.

C. The Local Expectations Hypothesis without Risk Neutrality

Since the Expectations Hypothesis is not a consequence of risk-neutrality, it is natural to ask if there are any conditions for which it does obtain. The answer is yes. There are two distinct cases, outlined below, corresponding to each of the models examined here, and a third case for uncertain inflation discussed in Section VI.

In a single-good pure exchange economy when the dynamics of aggregate consumption are locally certain, a default-free bond will not command a premium if utility of consumption is state-independent. This result follows immediately from the observation by Breeden [4] that at each instant any asset's risk premium is proportional to its instantaneous covariance with aggregate consumption. Clearly all these covariances and, thus, the risk premiums on all assets must be zero if consumption is locally certain. A fortiori there are no term premiums. Nevertheless, in a model of this type, the spot interest rate and hence bond prices can be locally stochastic if investors are risk-averse and changes in the rate of growth of consumption are locally stochastic.

In a production-exchange economy, universal state-independent Bernoulli-logarithmic utility of consumption is the primary requirement for the Local Expectations Hypothesis. For log utility, it is known that the derived utility of wealth function is separable $J(W, Y, t) = f(t)\ln W + q(Y, t)$. Hence, log utility investors' portfolio decisions are completely myopic being made with no regard for hedging against changes in the state variables since $J_{WY} = 0$. From (38), then, an additional condition sufficient for the Local Expectations Hypothesis is that returns on physical capital be uncorrelated with changes in the state variables.

[20] For a Markov interest rate process with a continuous sample path an increase in the current spot rate holding the realizations $dz(s)$ fixed will increase the value of the random variable $\int_t^T \tilde{r}(s)ds$. Thus, $Q_r > 0$, from (37).

V. Liquidity Preference and Preferred Habitats

As mentioned previously, the Expectations Hypothesis would appear to be a straightforward application of certainty results to a world of uncertainty. This "naive" approach has incurred it a substantial amount of criticism. The earliest attack was made by Hicks [22] and has developed into what is usually known as the Hicksian Liquidity-Preference Model. Building on the Keynesian notion of "normal backwardation," it was generally argued that the forward spot rate will normally exceed the expected spot rate. Equivalently, the expected rate of return on a long bond must exceed that on a short bond by a premium which compensates the lender for assuming the increased risks of price fluctuation.

Hicks [22, pp. 138–46] made his argument in three parts. First, "to hedge their future supplies of loan capital ··· [borrowers] will have a strong propensity to borrow long." Second, because of "the desire to keep one's hands free to meet ··· uncertainty ··· most people (and institutions) would prefer to lend short." Finally, "speculators" will offset this "constitutional weakness" in the supply of long funds by borrowing short and lending long; however, they must receive a premium return as "compensation for the risk they are incurring."

Culbertson [11] in his market segmentation hypothesis argued that individuals have strong maturity preferences and that bonds of different maturities trade in distinct markets. In their Preferred Habitat Theory, Modigliani and Sutch [34, pp. 183–84] began with the same approach. They defined an investor to have an n-period habitat if "he has funds which he will not need for n periods and which, therefore, he intends to keep in bonds for n periods." However, recognizing the implied inefficiency, they did not go so far as to assume that this investor considers only n-period bonds. Investors can be "tempted out of their natural habitats by the lure of higher expected returns."

In terms of its implications, the Liquidity-Preference Model can be considered a special case of the Preferred Habitat Theory, namely that case in which all investors have a habitat equal to the shortest holding period. This permits us to restrict our attention to the latter theory. Under what conditions, then, will investors' habitats affect the size or, more to the point, the sign of bond premiums?

To simplify the analysis, we shall assume that each investor has a strict τ-period habitat. That is, utility is derived from consumption only at a single point in time currently τ periods in the future and that all bonds are in zero net supply. In this economy, τ-period bonds are the "safest" and the Preferred Habitat Theory predicts that at the same expected return all investors would purchase them exclusively. Alternatively, as there is no net supply of these (or any other) bonds, their equilibrium expected return should be forced below that on all other bonds.

To illustrate this point, consider a simple CIR production economy with a single commodity, identical investors, and one production opportunity. Investment in this opportunity is riskless and yields its output instantaneously. Although production is (locally) riskless, its rate of return changes stochastically over time in a Markov fashion. We choose to examine the case of riskless production to emphasize that the resulting premiums are due only to investors' desires to hedge interest rate changes and are not systematic risk or beta premiums.[21]

In the simple economy just described, the state of nature is completely described by the per capita supply of the single commodity (per capita wealth) W and the currently available rate of return on production. Because production is riskless and must be engaged in, its rate of return will set the interest rate. The dynamics for this economy are

$$dW = rW\,dt \tag{40a}$$

$$dr = \mu(r)\,dt + g(r)\,dz \tag{40b}$$

where μ and g^2 are the drift and variance of the state variable as in (1).

Substituting these dynamics into the equation for the derived utility of wealth function (35) gives

$$J_t + rWJ_W + \tfrac{1}{2}g^2(r)J_{rr} + \mu(r)J_r = 0 \tag{41}$$

Bond risk premiums are from (38)

$$\alpha(r, t, T) - r = -\frac{P_r}{P}\frac{J_{Wr}}{J_W}g^2(r) \tag{42}$$

In the special case when utility is isoelastic $U(W(\tau)) = W^\gamma/\gamma$, the derived utility of wealth function is separable $J(W, r, t) = Q(r, t)W^\gamma/\gamma$ so the ratio of partial derivatives required in (42) is $J_{Wr}/J_W = Q_r/Q$. The function Q is determined as the solution to

$$O = Q_t + \gamma rQ + \mu(r)Q_r + \tfrac{1}{2}g^2(r)Q_{rr} \tag{43}$$

subject to $Q(r, \tau) = 1$. A formal solution to (43) is

$$Q(r, t, \tau) = E_t\left[\exp\left(\gamma\int_t^\tau r(s)\,ds\right)\right] \tag{44}$$

provided the expectation exists.

For a continuous-time economy in which $r(t)$ follows a continuous Markov process, an increase in its current value will increase all future interest rates for a fixed time path of random realizations on dz. Thus, an increase in $r(t)$ unequivocally increases the random variable $\int_t^T r(s)\,ds$. From (44), Q_r then has the same sign as γ. Also in this continuous-time economy P_r is negative. Q is clearly positive from (44) and P is also positive. Therefore, term premiums as given in (42) have the same sign as γ which may be positive or negative

$$\text{sgn}[\alpha(T) - r] = \text{sgn}[-(Q_r/Q)g^2(r)(P_r/P)] = \text{sgn}(\gamma) \gtrless 0 \tag{45}$$

Logarithmic utility ($\gamma = 0$) is the dividing point. Investors whose relative risk aversion is less than unity ($\gamma > 0$) demand positive term premiums. Investors

[21] A positive covariance between returns on physical investment and returns on bonds would contribute positively to term premiums. This feature, although a paradigm in risky asset pricing, has often been ignored in the analysis of "riskless" default-free bonds.

who are more risk-averse require only negative premiums. Furthermore, the more risk-averse the investors, the smaller (in algebraic value) need the premium be.

In an economy of investors who all desired to consume at only one fixed point in the future, it would be expected that the more risk-averse would lend to the less risk-averse in return for a guaranteed payment, since the former perceive a higher cost of bearing risk. The result here certainly suggests this behavior, but it contains an additional surprise. Investors who are sufficiently risk-tolerant (although still globally risk-averse) will at the same expected rate of return actually prefer the risk involved in a series of short-term bonds to the safety of a single bond maturing on the date they desire to consume.

This result may at first seem counterintuitive; however, there is a simple explanation. In portfolio choice, we define a risk premium as the required expected (arithmetic mean) return above the interest rate. This is natural, since, in a portfolio, risk (covariances) add together. However, in a multiperiod investment when the uncertainty is realized period by period, the risk does not add but compounds. Thus, a term premium is the required expected (geometric mean) return above the spot rate. Furthermore, just as linear utility is risk-neutral toward (arithmetic) mean zero gambles, logarithmic utility is risk-neutral toward (geometric) mean unity gambles.[22] Utility functions which are "less concave" than is the logarithmic (e.g., isoelastic with $\gamma > 0$) are, therefore, risk preferring in this context. Consequently, an investor with a τ-period horizon and relative risk aversion less than unity will actually seek the risk involved in rolling over a series of short bonds, unless he is bribed to hold the safe τ-period bond through receiving a higher expected return.

As the example above indicates, a τ-period habitat for consumption, even on the part of all investors, is insufficient to cause a smaller required return on τ-period bonds. Nevertheless, the result presented above is consistent with the Preferred Habitat Theory, provided we reinterpret a "habitat" as a stronger or weaker tendency to hedge against changes in the interest rate as suggested by Merton [31]. To see this interpretation, note that the derived utility and marginal utility of wealth are given by

$$J(W, r, t) = Q(r, t) W^{\gamma}/\gamma$$
$$J_W(W, r, t) = Q(r, t) W^{\gamma-1} \tag{46}$$

where $Q(\cdot)$ is defined in (44). An increase in the interest rate will always increase utility, since $\text{sgn}[\partial Q/\partial r] = \text{sgn}(\gamma)$. The obvious interpretation is that an increase in the physical rate of return will, ceteris paribus, increase future wealth and hence current utility. However, an increase in the interest rate will increase

[22] A unit geometric mean gamble, is one in which the logarithm of the proportion of final wealth to initial wealth has an arithmetic expectation of zero. i.e., $\tilde{W} = W_0 e^{\tilde{x}}$ and $E[\tilde{x}] = 0$. Since $E[\ln(\tilde{W})] = \ln W_0$, a log utility investor would be indifferent about undertaking this gamble. However, individuals with isoelastic utility with $\gamma > 0$ are "risk-prefering" with respect to the same gamble

$$E[\tilde{W}^{\gamma}/\gamma] = (W_0^{\gamma}/\gamma)E[e^{\gamma\tilde{x}}] > W_0^{\gamma}/\gamma(e^{\gamma\bar{x}}) = W_0^{\gamma}/\gamma$$

The second step above follows from Jensen's inequality. For $\gamma < 0$ the inequality would be reversed as utility is negative.

(decrease) *marginal* utility of wealth if γ is positive (negative). Therefore, an investor with positive (negative) γ will desire to sell short (purchase) long-term bonds whose price would fall, causing an offsetting change in marginal utility.[23]

VI. Risk Premiums for Nominal Bonds

In deriving the results in the two previous sections it was explicitly assumed that bond payments were riskless in terms of the consumption good. Unfortunately, most bonds are denominated in nominal terms. Indeed, inflation uncertainty comprises the predominant portion of interest rate risk at least for short term bonds.[24] Consequently, in this section we examine term premiums in an economy with uncertain inflation. Through the use of a simple model it is established that uncertain inflation is a third general case which can result in the Expectations Hypothesis with random interest rates. Furthermore, in this one case risk-neutrality does have a somewhat special role.

We add "money" to the previously developed single-good model by assuming that it is used only to denominate the payments on bonds and other nominal contracts. It is not required for transactions purposes or when undertaking real investment; neither does it enter the direct utility function of consumption. To permit concentration on the effects of inflation, we further assume that the real yield curve is flat and nonstochastic. Conditions sufficient for this assumption to obtain are that the real investment opportunity set be constant over time and that the common utility function be time additive with a constant rate of time-preference, and isoelastic. Given these assumptions, it is straightforward to show that any investor's derived utility function is also isoelastic and depends only on his real wealth and time.

Although the real yield curve is flat, the state variables other than wealth do affect the prices of nominal contracts through the distribution of future inflation. The expected real rates of return on nominal contracts will depend upon the remaining N state variables. From (39)

$$\alpha(Y, t, T) = r + \textstyle\sum_{n=1}^{N} (P_{Y_n}/P)(1 - \gamma)\sigma_{Wn} \tag{47}$$

where r is the (constant) real interest rate, σ_{Wn} is the covariance of real returns on optimally invested wealth and changes in the nth state variable, and P is the nominal bond's real price. The valuation equation (10) can then be written as

$$\tfrac{1}{2} \textstyle\sum_1^N \sum_1^N P_{Y_n Y_m} g_n' g_m + \sum_1^N [\mu_n - (1 - \gamma)\sigma_{Wn}] P_{Y_n} + P_t - rP = 0 \tag{48}$$

subject to the condition that at maturity $P(Y, T, T) = 1/\pi(Y, T)$ where π is the price level.

Although not necessary, it will be convenient for the analysis to assume that

[23] From footnote 21 we see that an increase in wealth to xW ($x > 1$) provides a greater (lesser) gain in utility than a decrease to W/x if γ is positive (negative). Thus, a given infinitesimal increase in the interest rate increases utility by more (less) than the same decrease in r would decrease it. Consequently, investors with $\gamma > 0$ are willing to gamble for interest rate increases, while investors with $\gamma < 0$ will buy long bonds to hedge against interest rate decreases.

[24] See Fama [17].

the price level is the first state variable and that its evolution is locally multiplicative. i.e.,

$$d\pi = \mu_1(Y, t)\, dt + g_1'(Y, t)\, dz$$
$$\equiv \pi\hat{\mu}\, dt + \pi\hat{g}'\, dz \qquad (49)$$

where the expected rate and variance of inflation, $\hat{\mu}$ and $\hat{g}'\hat{g}$ may depend upon time and all the state variables except the price level itself.

In this case the nominal valuation equation can be determined from (48) by substitution of the bond's nominal price $P^* = P\pi$. This gives

$$\tfrac{1}{2}\sum_2^N\sum_2^N P^*_{Y_nY_m}g_n'g_m + \sum_2^N[\mu_n - (1-\gamma)\sigma_{Wn} - \hat{g}'g_n]P^*_{Y_n}$$
$$+ P_t^* - (r + \hat{\mu} - (1-\gamma)\hat{\sigma}_{W\pi} - \hat{g}'\hat{g})P^* = 0 \qquad (50)$$

where $\hat{\sigma}_{W\pi} \equiv \sigma_{W\pi}/\pi$ is the covariance of real returns on wealth with the percentage change in the price level. (This valuation equation is to be solved subject to the condition at maturity $P^*(Y, T, T) = 1$.) The last term in (50) is the price multiplied by the nominal rate of interest[25]; therefore, the nominal factor risk premium for the nth state variable is

$$\lambda_n = (1-\gamma)\sigma_{Wn} + \hat{g}'g_n \qquad (51)$$

The first term in (51) is relative risk-aversion multiplied by the covariance of real returns on wealth with changes in the state variable. The second term is the covariance of inflation with changes in the state variable.

In the economy described above, the term structure of real interest rates will be nonstochastic. To prevent arbitrage the real returns on index bonds, those with payoffs denominated in the real numeraire, must all be equal and all forms of the Expectations Hypothesis will hold. However, nominal interest rates will be stochastic, and nominal bonds of different maturities may have different expected nominal rates of return.

The Local Expectations Hypothesis, but not the other forms unless inflation is nonstochastic, will obtain for nominal rates only if each factor risk premium is zero. A sufficient, but not necessary, condition for this is that each nominal state variable (i.e., excluding real wealth) be uncorrelated with the real return on aggregate wealth and realized inflation. If investors are risk-neutral, the latter alone is sufficient (since $\gamma = 1$). This, or similar cases, appears to be the only

[25] It is by now well known that the nominal rate of interest is not simply the real rate plus the expected rate of inflation. In a continuous-time-state model these two factors overstate the nominal rate by the variance of inflation and a wealth related risk premium for inflation. To prove that the four term expression in (50) is the nominal rate we write the nominal price as $P^* = \exp[-R(Y, t, T)(T - t)]$. Then

$$P_Y^* = (t-T)R_YP^*$$
$$P_{YY}^* = (t-T)R_{YY}P^* + (t-T)R_Y R_Y P^*$$
$$P_t^* = [R + (t-T)R_t]P^*$$

Substituting these expressions into (50) and taking the limit as T approaches t gives the nominal spot rate $R(Y, t, t) = r + \hat{\mu} - (1-\gamma)\hat{\sigma}_{W\pi} - \hat{g}'\hat{g}$.

situation in which risk-neutrality is compatible with both the Expectations Hypothesis and stochastic interest rates, and it obtains only because inflation has no real consequences within the economy.

VII. A Continuous-Time Formulation of a Class of Popular Discrete-Time Interest Rate Models

While any observable characteristic of importance in the economy could be selected as a state variable, a large body of literature has relied on models, recently surveyed by Dobson, Sutch, and Vanderford [13], which use only the current and lagged values of interest rates. Typically in these models the assumed equilibrium yield-to-maturity on a pure discount bond of maturity T is

$$R(t, T) = \frac{1}{T-t} \sum_{i=0}^{T-t} E_t[r_{t+i}] + h(t, T) \tag{52}$$

where h captures the effects of any premium. The forecasts required in (52) are generated by

$$E_t[r_{t+1}] = w_0\mu + \sum_{i=1}^{\infty} w_i r_{t+1-i} \tag{53}$$ [26]

Using the properties of conditional expectations to evaluate (53) recursively permits a reexpression of the long rates in (52) as a linear function of observable past rates

$$R(t, T) = x_0(T-t) + \sum_{i=1}^{\infty} x_i(T-t) r_{t+1-i} \tag{54}$$

Different choices for the forecast weights in (53) can lead to a wide variety of shapes for the yield curve for the same history of interest rates. Nevertheless, all of the resulting models can be easily studied due to the simple linear structure of (54). For these two reasons, numerous studies have employed models of this type in both theoretical and empirical research. Unfortunately, in light of the discussion in the previous sections of this paper, these models must be re-evaluated. The continuous-time equivalent of (52) is very similar to (20), the Unbiased Expectations Hypothesis, which we have demonstrated to be invalid as an equilibrium specification. Consequently, the form of the term premium in (52) must be carefully chosen to ensure a tenable model. Nevertheless, since the simple linear structure of these models makes them so useful, the formulation of a consistent model with this same property is desirable.

The continuous-time equivalent of the forecasting equation (53) is

$$E_t[r(t+dt)] = \left[w_0\mu + w_1 r(t) + \int_0^{\infty} w(s) r(t-s)\, ds \right] dt \tag{55}$$

In general (55) cannot be transformed into a simple diffusion model since the

[26] Typically, strong regularity conditions are imposed on the set of weights w_i, and they are usually assumed to be constant over time. In addition, the constant term $w_0\mu$ is often set to zero. For stationarity of the model it is required that $w_0 \neq 0$, $\sum w_i = 1$, and $\sum w_i^2 < \infty$. In this case μ represents the steady state mean of the spot rate of interest.

implied interest rate model is not Markov but depends upon an uncountable infinity of "state variables," all past levels of the interest rate. Nevertheless, if the weighting function $w(s)$ is sufficiently well behaved, a diffusion representation is possible.

One particularly simple formulation is the elastic random walk or autoregressive model with $w(s) = 0$. This model places no predictive weight on any values of the interest rate other than its current level. That is, the spot rate follows a Markov process. Equation (55) expressed in difference form becomes

$$dr = k(\mu - r)\,dt + \sigma(\cdot)\,dz \tag{56}$$

where $k = w_0 = 1 - w_1$ and σdz is the forecast error. This model of interest rate dynamics dates back, at least in spirit, to the Keynesian [1930] concept of a "return to a normal level" of interest rates, and is characterized by the following behavior. Over the next period, the interest rate when above (below) its usual level is expected to fall (rise) by an amount proportional to the current deviation from normal.

Cox, Ingersoll, and Ross [10] have examined this model and demonstrated that it gives long rates which are a linear function of the spot rate if and only if the uncertainty term is linear in the spot rate, $\sigma^2(r) = a + br$.[27] This finding indicates that models which ignore the inherent uncertainty in predictions are misspecified and can reach erroneous conclusions about the shape of the yield curve. Nevertheless, the model does demonstrate that the desired linear property can be incorporated into a continuous-time equilibrium model. Unfortunately, it does not have the same flexibility to incorporate the variety of yield curves that the general formulation in (54) does. We can, however, increase the scope of the model by an expansion of states.

In this regard, we introduce a state variable $x(t; \beta)$ which is an exponentially smoothed average of past spot rates

$$x(t; \beta) \equiv \beta \int_0^\infty e^{-\beta s} r(t-s)\,ds \tag{57a}$$

$$= \beta e^{\beta t} \int_{-\infty}^{t} e^{\beta t} r(\tau)\,d\tau \tag{57b}$$

From (57b) the dynamics of x can be derived as

$$dx = \beta(r - x)\,dt \tag{58}$$

so local changes in x are nonstochastic and no additional uncertainty is added to the model.[28]

[27] The risk compensation factor, λ, must also be linear in the interest rate. Furthermore if $b \neq 0$ equilibrium requires that $\lambda(r)$ be proportional to the variance $\lambda(r) = \lambda(a + br)$. Richard [35] and Vasicek [37] examined special cases of this model with $a = 0$ and $b = 0$, respectively. Merton [30] and Dothan [14] looked at the pure random walk, $k = 0$, for $\sigma^2(r) = \sigma^2$ and $\sigma^2(r) = \sigma^2 r^2$. In the latter case long rates are not linear in the short rate.

[28] All forecasting models of this type share this important feature. Regardless of the number of state variables (smoothed averages of the interest rate) there is but a single source of uncertainty in each period. An intuitive explanation of this feature is that once "next period's" spot rate is observed, no further information is required to update all the state variables.

A simple model incorporating this state variable is the choice $w_0 = 0$, $w_1 = 1 - b$, $w(s) = b\beta e^{-\beta s}$ which can be written as the two-state variable Markov process

$$dr = b(x - r)\,dt + \sigma(\cdot)\,dz$$

$$dx = \beta(r - x)\,dt \tag{59}$$

Here we have replaced the constant μ of model (56) with the moving average x.

From (57a) we can see that the state variable x is equivalent to a geometric average of discrete observations. Malkiel [28] proposed the discrete time equivalent of the model in (59) by using a moving average[29] as a "normal range" for the interest rate, a substitute for the Keynesian concept of a normal level

$$E_t[r_{t+1}] = (1 - b)r_t + bB \sum_{s=0}^{\infty} (1 - \beta)^s r_{t-1-s} \tag{60}$$

Bierwag and Grove [2] and Mincer [33] have suggested generalizations of this model in which the "normal range" is a convex combination of geometric averages. The extension of these models to a continuous-time framework is immediate. The drift of r includes additional terms with additional state variables, and each new state variable evolves in a locally nonstochastic fashion similar to (58).

Duesenberry [16] and others have challenged the hypothesis of an autoregressive evolution of the spot rate. Instead they suggest that the interest rate might be expected to continue to evolve along recent trends. The forecasting structure in (59) can also accommodate this hypothesis if $b < 0$. Now, if the interest rate has moved above (below) its recent average level, it will tend to go even higher (lower). The extrapolative nature of this model becomes clearer if we adopt an alternate state variable description. This description will also prove useful in empirical applications of the model.

We define the new state variable $u \equiv r - x$. Then, using Ito's lemma, (59) can be written as

$$dr = -bu\,dt + \sigma(\cdot)\,dz \tag{61a}$$

$$du = -\delta u\,dt + \sigma(\cdot)\,dz \tag{61b}$$

where $\delta = b + \beta$. From (61b) we see that u is an exponentially smoothed average of past forecast errors[30]

$$u(t) = \delta \int_0^{\infty} e^{-\delta s}\sigma(\cdot)\,dz(t - s) \tag{62}$$

The empirical advantage of this specification is that with a little formal manip-

[29] In many studies the moving average $\beta' \sum_{s=0}^{\infty} (1 - B')^s r_{t-s}$ is used in place of the one defined in (60). Even though this state variable is stochastic, the statement in footnote 28 remains valid. No additional uncertainty is added to the model since the error term in r and X' are exactly proportional $\Delta X'_{t+1} = B'(r_{t+1} - X'_t) = B'(r_t - x'_t) + B'\Delta r_{t+1}$.

[30] An intuitive explanation of (61a) is that if the interest rate has risen unexpectedly in the recent past so that $u > 0$, there will be a tendency for it to fall for the autoregressive model ($b > 0$) or to rise further for the extrapolative model ($b < 0$).

ulation (61a,b) can be written as[31]

$$dr(t + dt) = (1 - \delta\, dt)\, dr(t) - [1 - (\delta - b)\, dt]\sigma\, dz(t) + \sigma\, dz(t + dt) \qquad (63)$$

which will be recognized as the continuous-time equivalent of a Box Jenkins model, specifically an ARMA (1,1) process in the first difference, dr. In this form the empirical techniques developed for Box Jenkins models can now be employed.

Just as the models of Mincer [33] and Bierwag and Grove [2] could be extended to continuous-time by using more than one weighted average, multiple-variable extrapolative models and combined extrapolative-regressive models can also be formulated. In principle, even the completely generalized model in Equation (55) can be written using only the current spot rate and state variables which are exponentially smoothed averages of past spot rates.

Consider the weighted "sum" of state variables $\int \omega(\beta)x(t;\beta)\, d\beta$. Since $x(t;\beta)$ has weight $\beta e^{-\beta s}$ at lag s, we can match the general model (55) by choosing ω to satisfy:

$$w(s) = \int_0^\infty \beta e^{-\beta s}\omega(\beta)\, d\beta \qquad (64)$$

The right-hand side of (64) is the Laplace transform of $\beta\omega(\beta)$, so matching can be achieved for all weighting functions $w(s)$ which decay sufficiently for large lags. (For models which have been proposed, this requirement will always be met.) Furthermore, any weighting can be matched to any desired degree of accuracy by the choice of a finite number of state variables which are exponentially smoothed past spot rates by choosing an approximation

$$w(s) \cong \textstyle\sum_{m=1}^{M} \beta_m e^{-\beta_m s}\hat{\omega}(\beta_m) \qquad (65)$$

VIII. Bond Pricing Models with Linearly Related Interest Rates

If the relevant state variables for the term structure consist of only the spot rate and smoothed averages of the spot rate, then for the dynamics introduced in the previous section the bond valuation Equation (10) becomes

$$\tfrac{1}{2}\sigma^2(r, X)P_{rr} + [\textstyle\sum_0^N b_i(x_i - r) - \lambda(r, X)]P_r - rP + \textstyle\sum_1^N \beta_i(r - x_i)P_{x_i} - P_\tau = 0 \qquad (66)$$

where X is a vector of the smoothed averages, $\tau \equiv T - t$ is the time to maturity, and x_0 is a degenerate moving average ($\beta_0 = 0$) with a constant value. For the desired result that long-term discount rates be linear in the state variables the present value function must be expressible as

$$P(r, X, \tau) = \exp[B(\tau)r + \textstyle\sum_0^N C_i(\tau)x_i] \qquad (67)$$

with $B(0) = C_i(0) = 0$.

[31] Using (61b) write $u(t) = (1 - \delta\, dt)u(t - dt) + \sigma\, dz(t - dt)$. Solve (61a) for $u(t - dt) = -[dr(t) - \sigma\, dz(t)]/b\, dt$ and substitute these two expressions into (61a).

Substituting (67) into (66) gives

$$\tfrac{1}{2}\,\sigma^2(\cdot)B^2 + \left[\textstyle\sum_0^N b_i(x_i - r) - \lambda(\cdot)\right]B - r + \textstyle\sum_1^N \beta_i(r - x_i)C_i - rB' - \textstyle\sum_0^N x_i C_i' = 0 \qquad (68)$$

Equation (68) can be uniformly satisfied if and only if $\sigma^2(\cdot)$ and $\lambda(\cdot)$ are linear functions of the state variables[32]

$$\sigma^2(\cdot) = \sigma_0^2 + \sigma^2 r + \textstyle\sum_1^N \sigma_i^2 x_i$$

$$\lambda(\cdot) = \lambda_0 + \lambda r + \textstyle\sum_1^N \lambda_i x_i \qquad (69)$$

In this case by equating the constant terms and those multiplying r and x_i each to zero, (68) can be rewritten as a set of simultaneous, first-order ordinary differential equations with constant coefficients

$$x_0 C_0' = \tfrac{1}{2}\,\sigma_0^2 B^2 + (b_0 x_0 - \lambda_0)B \qquad (70a)$$

$$B' = \tfrac{1}{2}\,\sigma^2 B^2 - \left(\textstyle\sum b_i + \lambda\right)B - 1 + \textstyle\sum \beta_i C_i \qquad (70b)$$

$$C_i' = \tfrac{1}{2}\,\sigma_i^2 B^2 + (b_i - \lambda_i)B - \beta_i C_i. \qquad (70c)$$

One primary advantage of postulating linearity is now apparent. The ordinary differential equations in (70) are more tractable than the general partial differential equation of valuation in its original form. If, for example, the interest rate variance is constant, $\sigma = \sigma_i = 0$, then an analytical solution may be easily obtained as outlined below. On the other hand, if numerical techniques are required for solution, it will be much less costly to apply them to (70) than to (66).[33]

As a practical matter, we desire a parsimonious fit which requires relatively few additional state variables. Most past research has assumed that the weighting function $w(s)$ introduced in the previous section was either strictly decreasing (regressive models) or unimodal (extrapolative-regressive models). These char-

[32] The proof of the "if" clause is verified by the constructive solution technique in (70). To prove "only if" consider a regular point r_0 of both $\sigma^2(\cdot)$ and $\lambda(\cdot)$ where the Taylor series expansions

$$\frac{1}{2}\sigma^2(\cdot) = a_0 + a_1(r - r_0) + a_2(r - r_0)^2 + \cdots$$

$$\lambda(\cdot) = b_0 + b_1(r - r_0) + b_2(r - r_0)^2 + \cdots$$

exist. Then by equating terms of r^2 in (68) we conclude that $a_2B^2 - b_2B = 0$. This implies that (1) $a_2 = b_2 = 0$; (2) $B(\tau) \equiv 0$; or (3) $B(\tau) \equiv b_2/a_2$. Since a_2 and b_2 do not depend upon the maturity of the bond, condition (3) implies that B is constant and hence zero since $B(0) = 0$. But if $B \equiv 0$ in (3) or (2) then r is not a relevant state variable contrary to assumption. Thus, (1) must hold. But a_2 and b_2 are proportional to the second derivatives of σ^2 and λ at r_0 and only for a linear function is the second derivative zero at each regular point. A similar analysis shows that σ^2 and λ must be linear in each x_i.

[33] Brennan and Schwartz [6, 7] discuss numerical solutions to partial differential equations such as (66). Both the implicit and explicit methods increase in time required exponentially with the number of state variables. Equations (70) should require computation time which is linear in the number of state variables.

acteristics can be captured with only two smoothed averages. We also permit regression towards a constant mean. The forecasting model is[34]

$$dr = [b_0(\mu - r) + b_1(x_1 - r) + b_2(x_2 - r)]\,dt + \sigma(\cdot)\,dz$$

$$dx_i = \beta_i(r - x_i)\,dt,\ i = 1, 2 \tag{71}$$

If $b_1 > 0 > b_2$, then the first factor would promote regression to a moving mean and the second extrapolation. Although not required, typically $\beta_2 > \beta_1$ as extrapolation is generally considered the shorter-term effect. Under these conditions, the weighting function is uniformly positive and strictly decreasing if $\beta_1^2 b_1 + \beta_2^2 b_2 \geqslant 0$.Otherwise there is a single peak at lag

$$s = \frac{1}{\beta_2 - \beta_1} \ln\,[-b_2\beta_2^2/b_1\beta_1^2] \tag{72}$$

The model in (71) can also be written using two smoothed averages of past forecast errors as[35]

$$dr = [\alpha_0(\mu - r) + a_1u_1 + a_2u_2]\,dt + \sigma(\cdot)\,dz$$

$$du_i = -\alpha_i u_i\,dt + \sigma(\cdot)\,dz,\ i = 1, 2 \tag{73}$$

The model in (73) can be solved in closed form for a constant variance under the Local Expectations Hypothesis. The discount bond price is then

$$P(r, u_1, u_2, \tau) = \exp\{-\mu\tau + (r - \mu + s_1u_1 + s_2u_2)\phi(\tau; \alpha_0)$$
$$- s_1u_1\phi(\tau; \alpha_1) - s_2u_2\phi(\tau; \alpha_2) + \tfrac{1}{2}\,\sigma^2 \textstyle\sum_0^2 \sum_0^2 s_is_j(\alpha_i\alpha_j)^{-1}[\tau - \phi(\tau; \alpha_i)$$
$$- \phi(\tau; \alpha_j) + \phi(\tau; \alpha_i + \alpha_j)]\} \tag{74}$$

where

$$\phi(\tau; \alpha) \equiv -(1 - e^{-\alpha\tau})/\alpha$$
$$s_i \equiv a_i/(\alpha_i - \alpha_0) \quad i = 1, 2$$
$$s_0 \equiv 1 - s_1 - s_2$$

[34] Forecasting models of the type presented here are generally used in an empirical context and little concern is placed on finding a consistent embedding equilibrium. The issue of why past interest rates are plausible state variables in a rational expectations equilibrium is ignored. One possible justification arises when investment is not readily reversible so that past "interest rates" are still reflected in the current production function. Changes in the interest rate will then be affected by past rates as these investments disappear or are abandoned. Such a situation might be modeled as in (71). A somewhat less satisfying model also providing this justification can be built upon the economy outlined in Equation (40). If one method of production is locally riskless, as in (40a), but its physical rate of return is changing over time, as modeled in (71) rather than (40b), then the interest rate will also behave as in (40b), provided that this riskless production opportunity is always employed.

[35] The models in (71) and (73) are related as follows

$$2\nu_1 \equiv \alpha_2 + \alpha_1 + a_2 + a_1 \qquad \nu_2 \equiv (\nu_1^2 - \alpha_1\alpha_2 - \alpha_1a_2 - \alpha_2a_1)^{1/2}$$

$$\beta_1 \equiv \nu_1 + \nu_2 \qquad \beta_2 \equiv \nu_1 - \nu_2$$

$$b_0 \equiv \alpha_0\alpha_1\alpha_2/\beta_1\beta_2$$

$$b_1 \equiv -(\alpha_2 - \alpha_1)^2a_1a_2(\alpha_0 - \beta_1)[2\nu_2\beta_1(\alpha_2 - \beta_2)(\alpha_1 - \beta_2)]^{-1}$$

$$b_2 \equiv (\alpha_2 - \alpha_1)^2a_1a_2(\alpha_0 - \beta_2)[2\nu_2\beta_2(\alpha_2 - \beta_1)(\alpha_1 - \beta_1)]^{-1}$$

If the Local Expectations Hypothesis does not hold, but factor risk premiums are linear in the state variables, then a similar solution with modified parameters is obtained.[36]

IX. Conclusion

The Term Structure of Interest Rates has a long and checkered history in the field of financial economics. In this paper, many of the traditional propositions and hypotheses in this area are reexamined by employing recent advances in the theory of dynamic equilibrium valuation and contingent-claims pricing.

In discussing the Expectations Hypothesis we show that it must be considered to be a theory of several mutually incompatible propositions. We prove further that only one of these propositions can obtain in a continuous-time, rational-expectations equilibrium. This version, which we term the Local Expectations Hypothesis, holds that the instantaneous expected rates of return on all bonds are equal to the prevailing spot rate of interest. Since, by assumption, bonds earn no risk premiums in this equilibrium, tradition has long assigned a special role to risk neutrality as a potential justification. We demonstrate that this connection does not exist. In general universal risk neutrality results in nonzero bond premiums. In fact, the one type of utility which seems to be most strongly related to the Expectations Hypothesis and zero risk premiums is logarithmic utility.

This finding also serves as a basis for analysis of the Preferred Habitat Theory of Modigliani and Sutch. In Section V we provide a partial corroboration for this theory; however, we give a decidedly different interpretation to habitats. It is an investor's risk aversion and not his rate of time preference or desire to consume at a particular point of time which is the determinant.

In the final two sections we consider the linear adaptive interest rate forecasting models found throughout the macroeconomic literature. We show that these models are incomplete because the functional form of the forecast error, which is traditionally unspecified, influences the form of the resulting equilibrium. We complete and adapt these models to a continuous-time framework in such a way that they are readily tractable and retain the desired linearity properties.

Appendix

The Expectations Hypotheses in Discrete Time

In a discrete-time model, the four forms of the expectations hypothesis are in general distinct. The Local Expectations Hypothesis, which holds that expected single period returns are equal for all bonds, can be written as

$$\frac{E_t[P(t+1, T)]}{P(t, T)} = 1 + R_t \tag{A.1}$$

Here we have used R to denote the effective single period rate to distinguish it

[36] For example, if term premiums are linear in the interest rate, $\alpha(r, X, \tau) = r + (\lambda_0 + \lambda r)\delta(r, X, \tau)$ then in the modified dynamics for (71) $b_0' \equiv b_0 + \lambda\sigma$ and $\mu' \equiv (b_0\mu - \lambda_0\sigma)/b_0'$. In (73), the same modified μ' is used and $\alpha_0' \equiv b_0'\beta_1\beta_2/\alpha_1\alpha_2$ replaces α_0.

from the continuously-compounded rate r used throughout the text. Evaluating (A.1) recursively leads to the statement of equilibrium

$$P(t, T) = E_t[[(1 + R_t)(1 + \tilde{R}_{t+1}) \cdots (1 + \tilde{R}_{T-1})]^{-1}] \tag{A.2}$$

Under the Return-to-Maturity Expectations Hypothesis, the guaranteed return from holding any discount bond to maturity is equal to the return expected from a series of single-period bonds

$$1/P(t, T) = E_t[(1 + R_t)(1 + \tilde{R}_{t+1}) \cdots (1 + \tilde{R}_{T-1})] \tag{A.3}$$

If this equality is to be valid instead for the expected yields from these two strategies (the Yield-to-Maturity Expectations Hypothesis), then

$$[P(t, T)]^{-1/(T-t)} = E_t[[(1 + R_t)(1 + \tilde{R}_{t+1}) \cdots (1 + \tilde{R}_{T-1})]^{1/(T-t)}] \tag{A.4}$$

As in the continuous-time models each of these propositions is incompatible with the other two. Defining $\tilde{X} \equiv [(1 + R_t)(1 + \tilde{R}_{t+1}) \cdots (1 + R_{T-1})]^{-1}$ Equations (A.2) through (A.4) can be rewritten as

$$P = E[\tilde{X}]$$

$$P^{-1} = E[\tilde{X}^{-1}]$$

$$P^{-1/(T-t)} = E[\tilde{X}^{-1/(T-t)}] \tag{A.5}$$

Jensen's inequality assures us that at most one of these relations can be valid.

For the Unbiased Expectations Hypothesis, forward rates are equal to expected future spot rates.

$$P(t, T)/P(t, T + 1) = E_t[1 + R_T] \tag{A.6}$$

A recursive evaluation of (A.6) gives the equilibrium condition

$$1/P(t, T) = (1 + R_t)E_t(1 + R_{t+1}) \cdots E_t(1 + R_{T-1}) \tag{A.7}$$

In the continuous-time model the Unbiased Expectations Hypothesis is equivalent to the YTM-Expectations Hypothesis (A.4). Here, as we show below, it is not.[37] It is equivalent to the RTM-EH (A.3) if the *levels* of future interest rates are uncorrelated. However, this is at odds with the empirical evidence, which indicates that changes in the spot rate are close to uncorrelated. If interest rate levels are positively autocorrelated and (A.3) describes equilibrium, then forward rates are biased high.

To see that the Unbiased Expectations Hypothesis (A.7) is incompatible with the other two forms (A.2) and (A.4), note that for a two-period bond the former implies both

$$P(t, t + 2) = [(1 + R_t)E_t(1 + R_{t+1})]^{-1} < E_t[(1 + R_t)^{-1}(1 + R_{t+1})^{-1}] \tag{A.8a}$$

$$[P(t, t + 2)]^{-1/2} = [(1 + R_t)E_t(1 + R_{t+1})]^{1/2}$$

$$> E_t[(1 + R_t)^{1/2}(1 + r_{t+1})^{1/2}] \tag{A.8b}$$

[37] If yields and forward rates are re-expressed as continuously compounded interest rates over a single period, then the Unbiased and the Yield-to-Maturity Expectations Hypotheses are equivalent as in continuous-time models.

In each case the inequality follows by Jensen's inequality. (A.8a) conflicts with (A.2) while (A.8b) contradicts (A.4).

In the body of this paper we proved that only the Local Expectations Hypothesis could obtain in a continuous-time, continuous-state equilibrium. The same types of models, e.g., logarithmic utility, will also support this form of the expectations hypothesis in discrete time. However, it is also possible for the Return-to-Maturity and Unbiased Expectations Hypotheses to obtain in discrete time as we now outline.

Consider a complete-markets pure-exchange economy with identical investors. The quantity of the consumption good available each period is a random variable independent of all past realizations. As investors are identical, individual consumption will also be independent period to period. From the investor's first-order conditions for an optimal portfolio we can derive the state prices

$$p(s_T, s_t) = \pi(s_T, s_t)U_1[C(s_T), T]/U_1[C(s_t), t] \tag{A.9}$$

where π is the probability of state s_T and $U_1(\cdot)$ is marginal utility of consumption.

We denote $U_1[C(\tilde{s}_t), t]$ by $\tilde{u}_t$. From the assumed intertemporal independence of consumption, $\tilde{u}_t$ are also independent of past state realizations, so

$$E[\tilde{u}_T \mid s_t] = \bar{u}_T \quad \text{all} \quad t < T \tag{A.10}$$

Discount bond prices are given by

$$P(s_t, t, T) = \int_S p(s_T, s_t)\, ds_T = \bar{u}_T/u_t \tag{A.11}$$

Future interest rates are

$$1 + R(s_t, t, t+1) = u_t/\tilde{u}_{t+1} \tag{A.12}$$

which are also intertemporally independent.

Using (A.10) through (A.12), it is a simple matter to verify that the Unbiased Expectations Hypothesis (A.7) obtains. Substituting (A.12) into (A.7), the definition of the Unbiased Expectations Hypothesis, and using (A.10) gives

$$\begin{aligned} 1/P(t, T) &= (1 + R_t)E_t(1 + R_{t+1}) \cdots E_t(1 + R_{T-1}) \\ &= (u_t/\bar{u}_{t+1})E_t(\tilde{u}_{t+1}/\tilde{u}_{t+2}) \cdots E_t(\tilde{u}_T) \\ &= (u_t/\bar{u}_{t+1})(\bar{u}_{t+1}/\bar{u}_{t+2}) \cdots (\bar{u}_{T-1}/\bar{u}_T) \\ &= u_t/\bar{u}_T \end{aligned} \tag{A.13}$$

which is (A.11), the previously determined equilibrium. Since interest rates are intertemporally uncorrelated, the Returns-to-Maturity Expectations Hypothesis is valid as well.

The differences between discrete-time and continuous-time models are generally a matter of form rather than substance. Indeed, most results in either type of model can be mimicked in the other. Therefore, the demonstration above of a RTM-EH equilibrium might be disturbing, for we proved in Section III that no such equilibrium could obtain in a continuous-time, continuous-state economy. Fortunately, when we examine the continuous-time limit of the model presented here, this discrepancy is reconciled.

Using (A.11) and (A.12) and defining the length of a single period to be Δt, discount bond prices can be rewritten as

$$P(s_t, t, T) = [1 + R(s_t, t, t + \Delta t)]^{-1}\bar{u}_T/\bar{u}_{t+\Delta t} \quad \text{(A.14)}$$

But $R(\cdot)$ is the effective single-period interest rate expressed on a per-period basis. In the limit, then, as $\Delta t \to 0$, $R(\cdot) \to 0$ as well, and the first factor in (A.14) does not affect bond prices. This is the case in all continuous-time models. However, here the prevailing interest rate does not affect the quotient $\bar{u}_T/\bar{u}_{t+\Delta t}$ either. Therefore, each realization of the interest rate can have only a vanishingly small effect on bond prices, and they are, in the limit, certain. Thus, in the continuous-time limit of the model presented above, the RTM-EH holds, but only in the singular sense of a certainty model.

REFERENCES

1. L. Arnold. *Stochastic Differential Equations.* New York: John Wiley & Sons, Inc., 1974.
2. G. O. Bierwag and M. A. Grove. "A Model of the Term Structure of Interest Rates." *Review of Economics and Statistics* (February 1967), pp. 50–62.
3. G. Box and G. Jenkins. *Time Series Analysis: Forecasting and Control.* San Francisco: Holden-Day, 1976.
4. D. Breeden. "An Intertemporal Asset Pricing Model with Stochastic Consumption and Investment Opportunities." *Journal of Financial Economics* (September 1979), pp. 265–96.
5. D. Breeden and R. Litzenberger. "Prices of State-Contingent Claims Implicit in Option Prices." *Journal of Business* (October 1978), pp. 621–52.
6. E. Brennan and E. Schwartz. "Savings Bonds, Retractable Bonds, and Callable Bonds." *Journal of Financial Economics* (August 1977), pp. 67–88.
7. M. Brennan and E. Schwartz. "Finite Difference Methods and Jump Processes Arising in the Pricing of Contingent Claims." *Journal of Financial and Quantitative Analysis* (September 1978), pp. 461–74.
8. D. Cox and H. Miller. *The Theory of Stochastic Processes.* London: Methuen and Co., 1970.
9. J. Cox, J. Ingersoll, and S. Ross. "An Intertemporal Asset Pricing Model with Rational Expectations." Unpublished working paper, Stanford University, 1980.
10. J. Cox, J. Ingersoll, and S. Ross. "A Theory of the Term Structure of Interest Rates." Unpublished working paper, Stanford University, 1980.
11. J. Culbertson. "The Term Structure of Interest Rates." *Quarterly Journal of Economics* (November 1957), pp. 485–517.
12. F. De Leeuw. "A Model of Financial Behavior." In J. S. Duesenberry et al. (eds.), *The Brookings Quarterly Econometric Model of the United States,* pp. 465–530. Chicago: Rand McNally, 1965.
13. S. Dobson, R. Sutch, and D. Vanderford. "An Evaluation of Alternative Empirical Models of the Term Structure of Interest Rates." *Journal of Finance* (September 1976), pp. 1035–65.
14. L. U. Dothan. "On the Term Structure of Interest Rates." *Journal of Financial Economics* (March 1978), pp. 59–69.
15. L. U. Dothan and J. Williams. "Term-Risk Structures and the Valuation of Projects." Unpublished working paper, Northwestern University, 1979.
16. J. Duesenberry. *Business Cycles and Economic Growth.* New York: McGraw-Hill, 1958.
17. E. Fama. "Inflation Uncertainty and Expected Returns on Treasury Bills." *Journal of Political Economy* (June 1976), pp. 427–48.
18. I. Fisher. "Appreciation and Interest." *Publications of the American Economic Association* (1896), pp. 23–29 and 88–92.
19. A. Friedman. *Stochastic Differential Equations and Applications.* Vol. I. New York: Academic Press, 1975.
20. M. Garman. "A General Theory of Asset Valuation under Diffusion State Processes." Unpublished working paper, IBER no. 50, University of California at Berkeley, 1976.

21. M. Harrison and D. Kreps. "Martingales and the Valuation of Redundant Assets." Unpublished working paper IMSSS no. 261, Stanford University, 1978.
22. J. Hicks. *Value and Capital.* London: Oxford University Press, 1939.
23. J. Ingersoll, J. Skelton, and R. Weil. "Duration Forty Years Later." *Journal of Financial and Quantitative Analysis* (November 1978), pp. 627–50.
24. T. Langetieg. "A Multivariate Model of the Term Structure." *Journal of Finance* (March 1980), pp. 71–98.
25. S. LeRoy. "Securities Prices under Risk-Neutrality and Near Risk. Neutrality." Unpublished working paper, University of California, Santa Barbara, 1979.
26. R. Lucas. "Asset Prices in an Exchange Economy." *Econometrica* (November 1978), pp. 1429–45.
27. F. Lutz. "The Structure of Interest Rates." *Quarterly Journal of Economics* (1940–41), pp. 36–63.
28. B. Malkiel. *The Term Structure of Interest Rates: Expectations and Behavior Patterns.* Princeton: Princeton University Press, 1966.
29. D. Meiselman. *The Term Structure of Interest Rates.* Englewood Cliffs, N. J.: Prentice-Hall, 1962.
30. R. Merton. "A Dynamic General Equilibrium Model of the Asset Market and Its Application to the Pricing of the Capital Structure of the Firm." Sloan School of Management, M.I.T. working paper, 1970.
31. R. Merton. "An Intertemporal Capital Asset Pricing Model." *Econometrica* (September 1973), pp. 867–87.
32. R. Merton. "On the Mathematics and Economic Assumptions of Continuous Time Models." In W. F. Sharpe (ed.), *Financial Economics: Essays in Honor of Paul Cootner.* Amsterdam: North-Holland, forthcoming.
33. J. Mincer. "Models of Adaptive Forecasting." In J. Mincer (ed.), *Economic Forecasts and Expectations: Analysis of Forecasting Behavior and Performance*, pp. 83–111. New York: National Bureau of Economic Research, 1969.
34. F. Modigliani and R. Sutch. "Innovations in Interest Rate Policy." *American Economic Review* (May 1966), pp. 178–97.
35. S. Richard. "An Arbitrage Model of the Term Structure of Interest Rates." *Journal of Financial Economics* (March 1978), pp. 33–58.
36. J. Van Horne. "Interest-Rate Risk and the Term Structure of Interest Rates." *Journal of Political Economy* (August 1965), pp. 344–51.
37. O. Vasicek. "An Equilibrium Characterization of the Term Structure." *Journal of Financial Economics* (November 1977), pp. 177–88.
38. J. Wood. "The Expectations Hypothesis, the Yield Curve and Monetary Policy." *Quarterly Journal of Economics* (August 1964), pp. 457–70.

[17]

A THEORY OF THE TERM STRUCTURE OF INTEREST RATES[1]

By John C. Cox, Jonathan E. Ingersoll, Jr., and Stephen A. Ross

This paper uses an intertemporal general equilibrium asset pricing model to study the term structure of interest rates. In this model, anticipations, risk aversion, investment alternatives, and preferences about the timing of consumption all play a role in determining bond prices. Many of the factors traditionally mentioned as influencing the term structure are thus included in a way which is fully consistent with maximizing behavior and rational expectations. The model leads to specific formulas for bond prices which are well suited for empirical testing.

1. INTRODUCTION

The term structure of interest rates measures the relationship among the yields on default-free securities that differ only in their term to maturity. The determinants of this relationship have long been a topic of concern for economists. By offering a complete schedule of interest rates across time, the term structure embodies the market's anticipations of future events. An explanation of the term structure gives us a way to extract this information and to predict how changes in the underlying variables will affect the yield curve.

In a world of certainty, equilibrium forward rates must coincide with future spot rates, but when uncertainty about future rates is introduced the analysis becomes much more complex. By and large, previous theories of the term structure have taken the certainty model as their starting point and have proceeded by examining stochastic generalizations of the certainty equilibrium relationships. The literature in the area is voluminous, and a comprehensive survey would warrant a paper in itself. It is common, however, to identify much of the previous work in the area as belonging to one of four strands of thought.

First, there are various versions of the expectations hypothesis. These place predominant emphasis on the expected values of future spot rates or holding-period returns. In its simplest form, the expectations hypothesis postulates that bonds are priced so that the implied forward rates are equal to the expected spot rates. Generally, this approach is characterized by the following propositions: (a) the return on holding a long-term bond to maturity is equal to the expected return on repeated investment in a series of the short-term bonds, or (b) the expected rate of return over the next holding period is the same for bonds of all maturities.

The liquidity preference hypothesis, advanced by Hicks [**16**], concurs with the importance of expected future spot rates, but places more weight on the effects of the risk preferences of market participants. It asserts that risk aversion will cause forward rates to be systematically greater than expected spot rates, usually

[1] This paper is an extended version of the second half of an earlier working paper with the same title. We are grateful for the helpful comments and suggestions of many of our colleagues, both at our own institutions and others. This research was partially supported by the Dean Witter Foundation, the Center for Research in Security Prices, and the National Science Foundation.

by an amount increasing with maturity. This term premium is the increment required to induce investors to hold longer-term ("riskier") securities.

Third, there is the market segmentation hypothesis of Culbertson [7] and others, which offers a different explanation of term premiums. Here it is asserted that individuals have strong maturity preferences and that bonds of different maturities trade in separate and distinct markets. The demand and supply of bonds of a particular maturity are supposedly little affected by the prices of bonds of neighboring maturities. Of course, there is now no reason for the term premiums to be positive or to be increasing functions of maturity. Without attempting a detailed critique of this position, it is clear that there is a limit to how far one can go in maintaining that bonds of close maturities will not be close substitutes. The possibility of substitution is an important part of the theory which we develop.

In their preferred habitat theory, Modigliani and Sutch [25] use some arguments similar to those of the market segmentation theory. However, they recognize its limitations and combine it with aspects of the other theories. They intended their approach as a plausible rationale for term premiums which does not restrict them in sign or monotonicity, rather than as a necessary causal explanation.[2]

While the focus of such modern and eclectic analyses of the term structure on explaining and testing the term premiums is desirable, there are two difficulties with this approach. First, we need a better understanding of the determinants of the term premiums. The previous theories are basically only hypotheses which say little more than that forward rates should or need not equal expected spot rates. Second, all of the theories are couched in ex ante terms and they must be linked with ex post realizations to be testable.

The attempts to deal with these two elements constitute the fourth strand of work on the term structure. Roll [29, 30], for example, has built and tested a mean-variance model which treated bonds symmetrically with other assets and used a condition of market efficiency to relate ex ante and ex post concepts.[3] If rationality requires that ex post realizations not differ systematically from ex ante views, then statistical tests can be made on ex ante propositions by using ex post data.

We consider the problem of determining the term structure as being a problem in general equilibrium theory, and our approach contains elements of all of the previous theories. Anticipations of future events are important, as are risk preferences and the characteristics of other investment alternatives. Also, individuals can have specific preferences about the timing of their consumption, and thus have, in that sense, a preferred habitat. Our model thus permits detailed predictions about how changes in a wide range of underlying variables will affect the term structure.

[2] We thank Franco Modigliani for mentioning this point.

[3] Stiglitz [35] emphasizes the portfolio theory aspects involved with bonds of different maturities, as do Dieffenbach [9], Long [18], and Rubinstein [31], who incorporate the characteristics of other assets as well. Modigliani and Shiller [24] and Sargent [33] have stressed the importance of rational anticipations.

The plan of our paper is as follows. Section 2 summarizes the equilibrium model developed in Cox, Ingersoll, and Ross [6] and specializes it for studying the term structure. In Section 3, we derive and analyze a model which leads to a single factor description of the term structure. Section 4 shows how this model can be applied to other related securities such as options on bonds. In Section 5, we compare our general equilibrium approach with an alternative approach based purely on arbitrage. In Section 6, we consider some more general term structure models and show how the market prices of bonds can be used as instrumental variables in empirical tests of the theory. Section 7 presents some models which include the effects of random inflation. In Section 8, we give some brief concluding comments.

2. THE UNDERLYING EQUILIBRIUM MODEL

In this section, we briefly review and specialize the general equilibrium model of Cox, Ingersoll, and Ross [6]. The model is a complete intertemporal description of a continuous time competitive economy. We recall that in this economy there is a single good and all values are measured in terms of units of this good. Production opportunities consist of a set of n linear activities. The vector of expected rates of return on these activities is α, and the covariance matrix of the rates of return is GG'. The components of α and G are functions of a k-dimensional vector Y which represents the state of the technology and is itself changing randomly over time. The development of Y thus determines the production opportunities that will be available to the economy in the future. The vector of expected changes in Y is μ and the covariance matrix of the changes is SS'.

The economy is composed of identical individuals, each of whom seeks to maximize an objective function of the form

$$(1) \qquad E\int_t^{t'} U(C(s), Y(s), s)\, ds,$$

where $C(s)$ is the consumption flow at time s, U is a Von Neumann-Morgenstern utility function, and t' is the terminal date. In performing this maximization, each individual chooses his optimal consumption C^*, the optimal proportion a^* of wealth W to be invested in each of the production processes, and the optimal proportion b^* of wealth to be invested in each of the contingent claims. These contingent claims are endogenously created securities whose payoffs are functions of W and Y. The remaining wealth to be invested in borrowing or lending at the interest rate r is then determined by the budget constraint. The indirect utility function J is determined by the solution to the maximization problem.

In equilibrium in this homogeneous society, the interest rate and the expected rates of return on the contingent claims must adjust until all wealth is invested in the physical production processes. This investment can be done either directly by individuals or indirectly by firms. Consequently, the equilibrium value of J is given by the solution to a planning problem with only the physical production processes available. For future reference, we note that the optimality conditions for the proportions invested will then have the form

$$\Psi = \alpha W J_W + GG'a^* W^2 J_{WW} + GS' W J_{WY} - \lambda^* 1 \leq 0 \tag{2}$$

and $a^{*\prime}\Psi = 0$, where subscripts on J denote partial derivatives, J_{WY} is a $(k \times 1)$ vector whose ith element is J_{WY_i}, 1 is a $(k \times 1)$ unit vector, and λ^* is a Lagrangian multiplier. With J explicitly determined, the similar optimality conditions for the problem with contingent claims and borrowing and lending can be combined with the market clearing conditions to give the equilibrium interest rate and expected rates of return on contingent claims.

We now cite two principal results from [6] which we will need frequently in this paper. First, the equilibrium interest rate can be written explicitly as

$$\begin{aligned} r(W, Y, t) &= \frac{\lambda^*}{W J_W} = a^{*\prime}\alpha + a^{*\prime}GG'a^* W\left(\frac{J_{WW}}{J_W}\right) + a^{*\prime}GS'\left(\frac{J_{WY}}{J_W}\right) \\ &= a^{*\prime}\alpha - \left(\frac{-J_{WW}}{J_W}\right)\left(\frac{\text{var } W}{W}\right) - \sum_{i=1}^{k}\left(\frac{-J_{WY_i}}{J_W}\right)\left(\frac{\text{cov } W, Y_i}{W}\right), \end{aligned} \tag{3}$$

where (cov W, Y_i) is the covariance of the changes in optimally invested wealth with the changes in the state variable Y_i, with (var W) and (cov Y_i, Y_j) defined in an analogous way; note that $a^{*\prime}\alpha$ is the expected rate of return on optimally invested wealth. Second, the equilibrium value of any contingent claim, F, must satisfy the following differential equation:

$$\begin{aligned} &\tfrac{1}{2}a^{*\prime}GG'a^* W^2 F_{WW} + a^{*\prime}GS' W F_{WY} + \tfrac{1}{2}\operatorname{tr}(SS'F_{YY}) \\ &\quad + (a^{*\prime}\alpha W - C^*)F_W + \mu' F_Y + F_t + \delta - rF \\ &= \phi_W F_W + \phi_Y F_Y, \end{aligned} \tag{4}$$

where $\delta(W, Y, t)$ is the payout flow received by the security and

$$\begin{aligned} \phi_W &= (a^{*\prime}\alpha - r)W, \\ \phi_Y &= \left(\frac{-J_{WW}}{J_W}\right)a^{*\prime}GS'W + \left(\frac{-J_{WY}}{J_W}\right)' SS'. \end{aligned} \tag{5}$$

In (4) subscripts on F denote partial derivatives; F_Y and F_{WY} are $(k \times 1)$ vectors and F_{YY} is a $(k \times k)$ matrix. The left hand side of (4) gives the excess expected return on the security over and above the risk free return, while the right hand side gives the risk premium that the security must command in equilibrium. For future reference, we note that (4) can be written in the alternative form:

$$\begin{aligned} &\tfrac{1}{2}(\text{var } W)F_{WW} + \sum_{i=1}^{k}(\text{cov } W, Y_i)F_{WY_i} + \tfrac{1}{2}\sum_{i=1}^{k}\sum_{j=1}^{k}(\text{cov } Y_i, Y_j)F_{Y_iY_j} \\ &\quad + [rW - C^*]F_W + \sum_{i=1}^{k}\left[\mu_i - \left(\frac{-J_{WW}}{J_W}\right)(\text{cov } W, Y_i)\right. \\ &\quad \left. - \sum_{j=1}^{k}\left(\frac{-J_{WY_j}}{J_W}\right)(\text{cov } Y_i, Y_j)\right]F_{Y_i} + F_t - rF + \delta = 0. \end{aligned} \tag{6}$$

To apply these formulas to the problem of the term structure of interest rates, we specialize the preference structure first to the case of constant relative risk aversion utility functions and then further to the logarithmic utility function. In particular, we let $U(C(s), Y(s), s)$ be independent of the state variable Y and have the form

$$(7) \qquad U(C(s), s) = e^{-\rho s}\left[\frac{C(s)^{\gamma}-1}{\gamma}\right],$$

where ρ is a constant discount factor.

It is easy to show that in this case the indirect utility function takes the form:[4]

$$(8) \qquad J(W, Y, t) = f(Y, t)U(W, t) + g(Y, t).$$

This special form brings about two important simplifications. First, the coefficient of relative risk aversion of the indirect utility function is constant, independent of both wealth and the state variables:

$$(9) \qquad \frac{-WJ_{WW}}{J_W} = 1-\gamma.$$

Second, the elasticity of the marginal utility of wealth with respect to each of the state variables does not depend on wealth, and we have

$$(10) \qquad \frac{-J_{WY}}{J_W} = \frac{-f_Y}{f}.$$

Furthermore, it is straightforward to verify that the optimal portfolio proportions a^* will depend on Y but not on W. Consequently, the vector of factor risk premiums, ϕ_Y, reduces to $(1-\gamma)a^{*\prime}GS' + (f_Y/f)SS'$, which depends only on Y. In addition, it can be seen from (3) that the equilibrium interest rate also depends only on Y.

The logarithmic utility function corresponds to the special case of $\gamma = 0$. For this case, it can be shown that $f(Y, t) = [1-\exp[-\rho(t'-t)]]/\rho$. The state-dependence of the indirect utility function thus enters only through $g(Y, t)$. As a result, ϕ_Y reduces further to $a^{*\prime}GS$. In addition, the particular form of the indirect utility function allows us to solve (2) explicitly for a^* as

$$(11) \qquad a^* = (GG')^{-1}\alpha + \left(\frac{1-1'(GG')^{-1}\alpha}{1'(GG')^{-1}1}\right)(GG')^{-1}1$$

when all production processes are active, with an analogous solution holding when some processes are inactive.

In the remainder of the paper, we will be valuing securities whose contractual terms do not depend explicitly on wealth. Since with constant relative risk aversion neither the interest rate r nor the factor risk premiums ϕ_Y depend on wealth, for such securities the partial derivatives F_W, F_{WW}, and F_{WY} are all equal to zero and the corresponding terms drop out of the valuation equation (4).

[4] This type of separability has been shown in other contexts by Hakansson [**15**], Merton [**22**], and Samuelson [**32**].

By combining these specializations, we find that the valuation equation (4) then reduces to

$$\tfrac{1}{2}\operatorname{tr}(SS'F_{YY})+[\mu'-a^{*\prime}GS']F_Y+F_t+\delta-rF=0. \tag{12}$$

Equation (12) will be the central valuation equation for this paper. We will use it together with various specifications about technological change to examine the implied term structure of interest rates.

3. A SINGLE FACTOR MODEL OF THE TERM STRUCTURE

In our first model of the term structure of interest rates, we assume that the state of technology can be represented by a single sufficient statistic or state variable. This is our most basic model, and we will examine it in some detail. This will serve to illustrate how a similarly detailed analysis can be conducted for the more complicated models that follow in Sections 5 and 6.

We make the following assumptions:

ASSUMPTION 1: *The change in production opportunities over time is described by a single state variable,* $Y(\equiv Y_1)$.

ASSUMPTION 2: *The means and variances of the rates of return on the production processes are proportional to Y.*[5] *In this way, neither the means nor the variances will dominate the portfolio decision for large values of Y. The state variable Y can be thought of as determining the rate of evolution of the capital stock in the following sense. If we compare a situation where* $Y=\bar{Y}$*, a constant, with a situation in which* $Y=2\bar{Y}$*, then the first situation has the same distribution of rate of return on a fixed investment in any process over a two-year period that the second situation has over a one-year period. We assume that the elements of* α *and G are such that the elements of* a^* *given by* (11) *are positive, so that all processes are always active, and that* $1'(GG')^{-1}\alpha$ *is greater than one.*[6]

ASSUMPTION 3: *The development of the state variable Y is given by the stochastic differential equation*

$$dY(t)=[\xi Y+\zeta]\,dt+v\sqrt{Y}\,dw(t), \tag{13}$$

where ξ *and* ζ *are constants, with* $\zeta\geq 0$*, and* v *is a* $1\times(n+k)$ *vector, each of whose components is the constant* v_0.

[5] Although our assumptions in this section do not satisfy all of the technical growth restrictions placed on the utility function and the coefficients of the production function in [6], they do in combination lead to a well-posed problem having an optimal solution with many useful properties. The optimal consumption function is $C^*(W,Y,t)=[\rho/(1-\exp(-\rho(t'-t))]W$ and the indirect utility function has the form $J(W,Y,t)=a(t)\log W+b(t)Y+c(t)$, where $a(t)$, $b(t)$, and $c(t)$ are explicitly determinable functions of time.

[6] The condition $1'(GG')^{-1}\alpha>1$, together with (13) and (14), insures that the interest rate will always be nonnegative. If $1'(GG')^{-1}\alpha<1$, the interest rate will always be nonpositive.

This structure makes it convenient to introduce the notation $\alpha \equiv \hat{\alpha} Y$, $GG' \equiv \Omega Y$, and $GS' \equiv \Sigma Y$, where the elements of $\hat{\alpha}$, Ω, and Σ are constants.

With these assumptions about technological change and our earlier assumptions about preferences, we can use (3) to write the equilibrium interest rate as

$$r(Y) = \left(\frac{1'\Omega^{-1}\hat{\alpha} - 1}{1'\Omega^{-1}1} \right) Y. \tag{14}$$

The interest rate thus follows a diffusion process with

$$\text{drift } r = \left(\frac{1'\Omega^{-1}\hat{\alpha} - 1}{1'\Omega^{-1}1} \right)(\xi Y + \zeta) \equiv \kappa(\theta - r), \tag{15}$$

$$\text{var } r = \left(\frac{1'\Omega^{-1}\hat{\alpha} - 1}{1'\Omega^{-1}1} \right)^2 \upsilon\upsilon' Y \equiv \sigma^2 r,$$

where κ, θ, and σ^2 are constants, with $\kappa\theta \geq 0$ and $\sigma^2 > 0$. It is convenient to define a new one-dimensional Wiener process, $z_1(t)$, such that:

$$\sigma\sqrt{r}\, dz_1(t) \equiv \upsilon\sqrt{Y}\, dw(t); \tag{16}$$

this is permissible since each component of $w(t)$ is a Wiener process. The interest rate dynamics can then be expressed as:

$$dr = \kappa(\theta - r)\, dt + \sigma\sqrt{r}\, dz_1. \tag{17}$$

For κ, $\theta > 0$, this corresponds to a continuous time first-order autoregressive process where the randomly moving interest rate is elastically pulled toward a central location or long-term value, θ. The parameter κ determines the speed of adjustment.[7]

An examination of the boundary classification criteria shows that r can reach zero if $\sigma^2 > 2\kappa\theta$. If $2\kappa\theta \geq \sigma^2$, the upward drift is sufficiently large to make the origin inaccessible.[8] In either case, the singularity of the diffusion coefficient at the origin implies that an initially nonnegative interest rate can never subsequently become negative.

The interest rate behavior implied by this structure thus has the following empirically relevant properties: (i) Negative interest rates are precluded. (ii) If the interest rate reaches zero, it can subsequently become positive. (iii) The absolute variance of the interest rate increases when the interest rate itself increases. (iv) There is a steady state distribution for the interest rate.

The probability density of the interest rate at time s, conditional on its value at the current time, t, is given by:

$$f(r(s), s; r(t), t) = c\, e^{-u-v} \left(\frac{v}{u} \right)^{q/2} I_q(2(uv)^{1/2}), \tag{18}$$

[7] The discrete time equivalent of this model was tested by Wood [**38**], although, being concerned only with expectations, he left the error term unspecified.

[8] See Feller [**12**].

where

$$c \equiv \frac{2\kappa}{\sigma^2(1-e^{-\kappa(s-t)})},$$

$$u \equiv cr(t)\, e^{-\kappa(s-t)},$$

$$v \equiv cr(s),$$

$$q \equiv \frac{2\kappa\theta}{\sigma^2} - 1,$$

and $I_q(\cdot)$ is the modified Bessel function of the first kind of order q. The distribution function is the noncentral chi-square, $\chi^2[2cr(s); 2q+2, 2u]$, with $2q+2$ degrees of freedom and parameter of noncentrality $2u$ proportional to the current spot rate.[9]

Straightforward calculations give the expected value and variance of $r(s)$ as:

$$E(r(s)|r(t)) = r(t)\, e^{-\kappa(s-t)} + \theta(1-e^{-\kappa(s-t)}),$$

$$\text{var}\,(r(s)|r(t)) = r(t)\left(\frac{\sigma^2}{\kappa}\right)(e^{-\kappa(s-t)} - e^{-2\kappa(s-t)}) + \theta\left(\frac{\sigma^2}{2\kappa}\right)(1-e^{-\kappa(s-t)})^2. \tag{19}$$

The properties of the distribution of the future interest rates are those expected. As κ approaches infinity, the mean goes to θ and the variance to zero, while as κ approaches zero, the conditional mean goes to the current interest rate and the variance to $\sigma^2 r(t)\cdot(s-t)$.

If the interest rate does display mean reversion ($\kappa, \theta > 0$), then as s becomes large its distribution will approach a gamma distribution. The steady state density function is:

$$f[r(\infty), \infty; r(t), t] = \frac{\omega^\nu}{\Gamma(\nu)} r^{\nu-1}\, e^{-\omega r}, \tag{20}$$

where $\omega \equiv 2\kappa/\sigma^2$ and $\nu \equiv 2\kappa\theta/\sigma^2$. The steady state mean and variance are θ and $\sigma^2\theta/2\kappa$, respectively.

Consider now the problem of valuing a default-free discount bond promising to pay one unit at time T.[10] The prices of these bonds for all T will completely determine the term structure. Under our assumptions, the factor risk premium in (12) is

$$\left[\hat{\alpha}'\Omega^{-1}\Sigma + \left(\frac{1-1'\Omega^{-1}\hat{\alpha}}{1'\Omega^{-1}1}\right)1'\Omega^{-1}\Sigma\right]Y \equiv \lambda Y. \tag{21}$$

[9] Processes similar to (17) have been extensively studied by Feller. The Laplace transform of (18) is given in Feller [12]. See Johnson and Kotz [17] for a description of the noncentral chi-square distribution. Oliver [27] contains properties of the modified Bessel function.

[10] A number of contractual provisions are sufficient to preclude default risk and make the value of a bond independent of the wealth of its seller. For example, the terms of the bond could specify that the seller must repurchase the bond at the price schedule given by (23) whenever his wealth falls to a designated level.

By using (15) and (21), we can write the fundamental equation for the price of a discount bond, P, most conveniently as

$$\tfrac{1}{2}\sigma^2 rP_{rr} + \kappa(\theta - r)P_r + P_t - \lambda rP_r - rP = 0, \tag{22}$$

with the boundary condition $P(r, T, T) = 1$. The first three terms in (22) are, from Ito's formula, the expected price change for the bond. Thus, the expected rate of return on the bond is $r + (\lambda rP_r/P)$. The instantaneous return premium on a bond is proportional to its interest elasticity. The factor λr is the covariance of changes in the interest rate with percentage changes in optimally invested wealth (the "market portfolio"). Since $P_r < 0$, positive premiums will arise if this covariance is negative ($\lambda < 0$).

We may note from (22) that bond prices depend on only one random variable, the spot interest rate, which serves as an instrumental variable for the underlying technological uncertainty. While the proposition that current (and future) interest rates play an important, and to a first approximation, predominant role in determining the term structure would meet with general approval, we have seen that this will be precisely true only under special conditions.[11]

By taking the relevant expectation (see Cox, Ingersoll, and Ross [**6**]), we obtain the bond prices as:

$$P(r, t, T) = A(t, T)\, e^{-B(t,T)r},$$

where

$$A(t, T) \equiv \left[\frac{2\gamma\, e^{[(\kappa+\lambda+\gamma)(T-t)]/2}}{(\gamma+\kappa+\lambda)(e^{\gamma(T-t)} - 1) + 2\gamma}\right]^{2\kappa\theta/\sigma^2},$$

$$B(t, T) \equiv \frac{2(e^{\gamma(T-t)} - 1)}{(\gamma+\kappa+\lambda)(e^{\gamma(T-t)} - 1) + 2\gamma}, \tag{23}$$

$$\gamma \equiv ((\kappa+\lambda)^2 + 2\sigma^2)^{1/2}.$$

The bond price is a decreasing convex function of the interest rate and an increasing (decreasing) function of time (maturity). The parameters of the interest rate process have the following effects. The bond price is a decreasing convex function of the mean interest rate level θ and an increasing concave (decreasing convex) function of the speed of adjustment parameter κ if the interest rate is greater (less) than θ. Both of these results are immediately obvious from their effects on expected future interest rates. Bond prices are an increasing concave function of the "market" risk parameter λ. Intuitively, this is mainly because higher values of λ indicate a greater covariance of the interest rate with wealth. Thus, with large λ it is more likely that bond prices will be higher when wealth is low and, hence, has greater marginal utility. The bond price is an increasing

[11] In our framework, the most important circumstances sufficient for bond prices to depend only on the spot interest rate are: (i) individuals have constant relative risk aversion, uncertainty in the technology can be described by a single variable, and the interest rate is a monotonic function of this variable, or (ii) changes in the technology are nonstochastic and the interest rate is a monotonic function of wealth.

concave function of the interest rate variance σ^2. Here several effects are involved. The most important is that a larger σ^2 value indicates more uncertainty about future real production opportunities, and thus more uncertainty about future consumption. In such a world, risk-averse investors would value the guaranteed claim in a bond more highly.

The dynamics of bond prices are given by the stochastic differential equation:

$$dP = r[1-\lambda B(t, T)]P\,dt - B(t, T)P\sigma\sqrt{r}\,dz_1. \tag{24}$$

For this single state variable model, the returns on bonds are perfectly negatively correlated with changes in the interest rate. The returns are less variable when the interest rate is low. Indeed, they become certain if a zero interest rate is reached, since interest rate changes are then certain. As we would intuitively expect, other things remaining equal, the variability of returns decreases as the bond approaches maturity. In fact, letting t approach T and denoting $T-t$ as Δt, we find that the expected rate of return is $r\Delta t + O(\Delta t^2)$ and the variance of the rate of return is $O(\Delta t^2)$ rather than $O(\Delta t)$, as would be the case for the returns on an investment in the production processes over a small interval. It is in this sense that the return on very short-term bonds becomes certain.

Bonds are commonly quoted in terms of yields rather than prices. For the discount bonds we are now considering, the yield-to-maturity, $R(r, t, T)$, is defined by $\exp[-(T-t)R(r, t, T)] \equiv P(r, t, T)$. Thus, we have:

$$R(r, t, T) = [rB(t, T) - \log A(t, T)]/(T-t). \tag{25}$$

As maturity nears, the yield-to-maturity approaches the current interest rate independently of any of the parameters. As we consider longer and longer maturities, the yield approaches a limit which is independent of the current interest rate:

$$R(r, t, \infty) = \frac{2\kappa\theta}{\gamma+\kappa+\lambda}. \tag{26}$$

When the spot rate is below this long-term yield, the term structure is uniformly rising. With an interest rate in excess of $\kappa\theta/(\kappa+\lambda)$, the term structure is falling. For intermediate values of the interest rate, the yield curve is humped.

Other comparative statics for the yield curve are easily obtained from those of the bond pricing function. An increase in the current interest rate increases yields for all maturities, but the effect is greater for shorter maturities. Similarly, an increase in the steady state mean θ increases all yields, but here the effect is greater for longer maturities. The yields to maturity decrease as σ^2 or λ increases, while the effect of a change in κ may be of either sign depending on the current interest rate.

There has always been considerable concern with unbiased predictions of future interest rates. In the present situation, we could work directly with equation (19), which gives expected values of future interest rates in terms of the current rate and the parameters κ and θ. However, in the rational expectations model we have constructed, all of the information that is currently known about the future movement of interest rates is impounded in current bond prices and the term structure. If the model is correct, then any single parameter can be determined from the term structure and the values of the other parameters.

This approach is particularly important when the model is extended to allow a time-dependent drift term, $\theta(t)$. We can then use information contained in the term structure to obtain $\theta(t)$ and expected future spot rates without having to place prior restrictions on its functional form.

Now, the future expected spot rate given by (19) is altered to:

$$E(r(T)|r(t)) = r(t)\, e^{-\kappa(T-t)} + \kappa \int_t^T \theta(s)\, e^{-\kappa(T-s)}\, ds. \tag{27}$$

The bond pricing formula (30), in turn, is modified to:

$$P(r, t, T) = \hat{A}(t, T)\, e^{-B(t,T)r}, \tag{28}$$

where

$$\hat{A}(t, T) = \exp\left(-\kappa \int_t^T \theta(s) B(s, T)\, ds \right), \tag{29}$$

which reduces to (23) when $\theta(s)$ is constant.

Assuming, for illustration, that the other process parameters are known, we can then use the term structure to determine unbiased forecasts of future interest rates. By (28), $\hat{A}(t, T)$ is an observable function of T, given the term structure and the known form of $B(t, T)$, and standard techniques can be invoked to invert (29) and obtain an expression for $\theta(t)$ in terms of $\hat{A}(t, T)$ and $B(t, T)$. Equation (27) can now be used to obtain predictions of the expected values of future spot rates implicit in the current term structure.

Note that these are not the same values that would be given by the traditional expectations assumption that the expected values of future spot rates are contained in the term structure in the form of implicit forward rates. In a continuous-time model, the forward rate $\hat{r}(T)$ is given by $-P_T/P$. Then, by differentiating (28):

$$\begin{aligned} \hat{r}(T) &= -P_T(r, t, T)/P(r, t, T) \\ &= rB_T(t, T) + \kappa \int_t^T \theta(s) B_T(s, T)\, ds. \end{aligned} \tag{30}$$

Comparing (27) and (30), we see they have the same general form. However, the traditional forward rate predictor applies the improper weights $B_T(s, T) \neq e^{-\kappa(T-s)}$, resulting in a biased prediction.

A number of alternative specifications of time dependence may also be included with only minor changes in the model. One particularly tractable example leads to an interest rate of $\bar{r}(t) + g(t)$, where $\bar{r}(t)$ is given by (17) and $g(t)$ is a function which provides a positive lower bound for the interest rate. The essential point in all such cases is that in the rational expectations model, the current term structure embodies the information required to evaluate the market's probability distribution of the future course of interest rates. Furthermore, the term structure can be inverted to find these expectations.

Other single variable specifications of technological change will in turn imply other stochastic properties for the interest rate. It is easy to verify that in our model if α and GG' are proportional to some function $h(Y, t)$, then the interest rate will also be proportional to $h(Y, t)$. By a suitable choice of $h(Y, t)$, $\mu(Y, t)$, and $S(Y, t)$, a wide range of a priori properties of interest rate movements can be included within the context of a completely consistent model.

4. VALUING ASSETS WITH GENERAL INTEREST RATE DEPENDENT PAYOFFS

Our valuation framework can easily be applied to other securities whose payoffs depend on interest rates, such as options on bonds and futures on bonds. This flexibility enables the model to make predictions about the pricing patterns that should prevail simultaneously across several financial markets. Consequently, applications to other securities may permit richer and more powerful empirical tests than could be done with the bond market alone.

As an example of valuing other kinds of interest rate securities, consider options on bonds. Denote the value at time t of a call option on a discount bond of maturity date s, with exercise price K and expiration date T as $C(r, t, T; s, K)$.[12] The option price will follow the basic valuation equation with terminal condition:

$$C(r, t, T; s, K) = \max[P(r, T, s) - K, 0]. \tag{31}$$

It is understood that $s \geq T \geq t$, and K is restricted to be less than $A(T, s)$, the maximum possible bond price at time T, since otherwise the option would never be exercised and would be worthless. By again taking the relevant expectations, we arrive at the following formula for the option price:

$$\begin{aligned} C(r, t, T; s, K) &= P(r, t, s)\chi^2\left(2r^*[\phi + \psi + B(T, s)]; \frac{4\kappa\theta}{\sigma^2}, \frac{2\phi^2 r e^{\gamma(T-t)}}{\phi + \psi + B(T, s)}\right) \\ &\quad - KP(r, t, T)\chi^2\left(2r^*[\phi + \psi]; \frac{4\kappa\theta}{\sigma^2}, \frac{2\phi^2 r e^{\gamma(T-t)}}{\phi + \psi}\right), \end{aligned} \tag{32}$$

where

$$\gamma \equiv ((\kappa + \lambda)^2 + 2\sigma^2)^{1/2},$$

$$\phi \equiv \frac{2\gamma}{\sigma^2(e^{\gamma(T-t)} - 1)},$$

$$\psi \equiv (\kappa + \lambda + \gamma)/\sigma^2,$$

$$r^* \equiv \left[\log\left(\frac{A(T, s)}{K}\right)\right] / B(T, s),$$

[12] Since the underlying security, a discount bond, makes no payments during the life of the option, the analysis of Merton [23] implies that premature exercise is never optimal, and, hence, American and European calls have the same value.

and $\chi^2(\cdot)$ is the previously introduced noncentral chi-square distribution function. r^* is the critical interest rate below which exercise will occur; i.e., $K = P(r^*, T, s)$.

The call option is an increasing function of maturity (when the expiration date on which the underlying bond matures remains fixed). Call options on stocks are increasing functions of the interest rate, partly because such an increase reduces the present value of the exercise price. However, here an increase in the interest rate will also depress the price of the underlying bond. Numerical analysis indicates that the latter effect is stronger and that the option value is a decreasing convex function of the interest rate. The remaining comparative statics are indeterminate.

5. A COMPARISON WITH BOND PRICING BY ARBITRAGE METHODS

In this section, we briefly compare our methodology to some alternative ways to model bond pricing in continuous time. It is useful to do this now rather than later because the model of Section 3 provides an ideal standard for comparison.

Our approach begins with a detailed description of the underlying economy. This allows us to specify the following ingredients of bond pricing: (a) the variables on which the bond price depends, (b) the stochastic properties of the underlying variables which are endogenously determined, and (c) the exact form of the factor risk premiums. In **[21]**, Merton shows that if one begins instead by imposing assumptions directly about (a) and (b), then Ito's formula can be used to state the excess expected return on a bond in the same form as the left-hand side of (4). If the functional form of the right-hand side of (4) were known, then one could obtain a bond pricing equation. For example, if one arbitrarily assumed that bond prices depend only on the spot interest rate r, that the interest rate follows the process given by (17), and that the excess expected return on a bond with maturity date T is $Y(r, t, T)$, then one would obtain

$$(33)\quad \tfrac{1}{2}\sigma^2 rP_{rr} + \kappa(\theta - r)P_r + P_t - rP = Y(r, t, T).$$

If there is some underlying equilibrium which will support the assumptions (a) and (b), then there must be some function Y for which bond prices are given by (33). However, as Merton notes, this derivation in itself provides no way to determine Y or to relate it to the underlying real variables.

An arbitrage approach to bond pricing was developed in a series of papers by Brennan and Schwartz [3], Dothan [**10**], Garman [**14**], Richard [**28**], and Vasicek [**37**]. Arguments similar to those employed in the proof of Theorem 2 of Cox, Ingersoll, and Ross [**6**] are used to show that if there are no arbitrage opportunities, Y must have the form

$$(34)\quad Y(r, t, T) = \psi(r, t)P_r(r, t, T),$$

where ψ is a function depending only on calendar time and not on the maturity date of the bond. This places definite restrictions on the form of the excess expected return; not all functions Y will satisfy both (33) and (34).

There are some potential problems, however, in going one step further and using the arbitrage approach to determine a complete and specific model of the term structure. The approach itself provides no way of guaranteeing that there is some underlying equilibrium for which assumptions (a) and (b) are consistent. Setting this problem aside, another difficulty arises from the fact that the arbitrage approach does not imply that every choice of ψ in (34) will lead to bond prices which do not admit arbitrage opportunities. Indeed, closing the model by assuming a specific functional form for ψ can lead to internal inconsistencies.

As an example of the potential problem, consider (33) with Υ as shown in (34). This gives the valuation equation

$$(35)\quad \tfrac{1}{2}\sigma^2 rP_{rr}+\kappa(\theta-r)P_r+P_t-rP=\psi(r,t)P_r,$$

which is identical to (22) apart from a specification of the function ψ. We could now close the model by assuming that ψ is linear in the spot rate, $\psi(r,t)=\psi_0+\lambda r$. The solution to (35) is then

$$(36)\quad P(r,t,T)=[A(t,T)]^{(\kappa\theta-\psi_0)/\kappa\theta}\exp[-rB(t,T)],$$

and the dynamic behavior of the bond price is given by

$$(37)\quad dP=[r-(\psi_0+\lambda r)B(t,T)]P\,dt-B(t,T)\sigma\sqrt{r}P\,dz_1.$$

The linear form assumed for the risk premium seems quite reasonable and would appear to be a good choice for empirical work, but it in fact produces a model that is not viable. This is most easily seen when $r=0$. In this case, the bond's return over the next instant is riskless; nevertheless, it is appreciating in price at the rate $-\psi_0B(t,T)$, which is different from the prevailing zero rate of interest.[13] We thus have a model that guarantees arbitrage opportunities rather than precluding them. The difficulty, of course, is that there is no underlying equilibrium which would support the assumed premiums.

The equilibrium approach developed here thus has two important advantages over alternative methods of bond pricing in continuous time. First, it automatically insures that the model can be completely specified without losing internal consistency. Second, it provides a way to predict how changes in the underlying real economic variables will affect the term structure.

6. MULTIFACTOR TERM STRUCTURE MODELS AND THE USE OF PRICES AS INSTRUMENTAL VARIABLES

In Section 3, we specialized the general equilibrium framework of Cox, Ingersoll, and Ross [6] to develop a complete model of bond pricing. We purposely chose a simple specialization in order to illustrate the detailed information that such a model can produce. In the model, the prices of bonds of all maturities depended on a single random explanatory factor, the spot interest rate. Although the resulting term structure could assume several alternative shapes, it is inherent

[13] As stated earlier, the origin is accessible only if $\sigma^2>2\kappa\theta$. Somewhat more complex arguments can be used to demonstrate that the model is not viable even if the origin is inaccessible.

in a single factor model that price changes in bonds of all maturities are perfectly correlated. Such a model also implies that bond prices do not depend on the path followed by the spot rate in reaching its current level. For some applications, these properties may be too restrictive. However, more general specifications of technological opportunities will in turn imply more general bond pricing models. The resulting multifactor term structures will have more flexibility than the single factor model, but they will inevitably also be more cumbersome and more difficult to analyze.

To illustrate the possibilities, we consider two straightforward generalizations of our previous model. Suppose that in our description of technological change in (13) and (15), the central tendency parameter θ is itself allowed to vary randomly according to the equation

(38) $$d\theta = \nu(Y - \theta)\,dt,$$

where ν is a positive constant. That is, we let $\theta \equiv Y_2$ and $\mu_2 = \nu(Y_1 - Y_2)$. The value of θ at any time will thus be an exponentially weighted integral of past values of Y. It can then be verified that the interest rate r is again given by (14) and that the bond price P will have the form

(39) $$P(r, \theta, t, T) = \exp[-rf(t, T) - \theta g(t, T)],$$

where f and g are explicitly determinable functions of time. In this case, both the yields-to-maturity of discount bonds and the expected values of future spot rates are linear functions of current and past spot rates.[14]

As a second generalization, suppose that the production coefficients α and GG' are proportional to the sum of two independent random variables, Y_1 and Y_2, each of which follows an equation of the form (13). Then it can be shown that the spot interest rate r will be proportional to the sum of Y_1 and Y_2 and that bond prices will again have the exponential form

(40) $$P(r, Y_2, t, T) = f(t, T)\exp[-rg(t, T) - Y_2 h(t, T)],$$

where f, g, and h are other explicitly determinable functions of time. In this model, price changes in bonds of all maturities are no longer perfectly correlated.

Each of these generalizations gives a two factor model of the term structure, and the resulting yield curves can assume a wide variety of shapes. Further multifactor generalizations can be constructed along the same lines.

In each of the models considered in this section, one of the explanatory variables is not directly observable. Multifactor generalizations will typically inherit this drawback to an even greater degree. Consequently, it may be very convenient for empirical applications to use some of the endogenously determined prices as instrumental variables to eliminate the variables that cannot be directly observed. In certain instances, it will be possible to do so. Let us choose the spot rate, r,

[14] Studies which have expressed expected future spot rates as linear combinations of current and past spot rates include Bierwag and Grove [2], Cagan [4], De Leeuw [8], Duesenberry [11], Malkiel [19], Meiselman [20], Modigliani and Shiller [24], Modigliani and Sutch [25], Van Horne [36], and Wood [38]. Cox, Ingersoll, and Ross [5] examine this issue in a diffusion setting.

and a vector of long interest rates, l, as instrumental variables. In general, each of these interest rates will be functions of W (unless the common utility function is isoelastic) and all the state variables. If it is possible to invert this system globally and express the latter as twice differentiable functions of r and l, then r and l can be used as instrumental variables in a manner consistent with the general equilibrium framework.

For the purposes of illustration, suppose that there are two state variables, Y_1 and Y_2, and that utility is isoelastic so that the level of wealth is immaterial. Then, for instrumental variables r and l, a scalar, direct but involved calculations show that the valuation equation (4) may be rewritten as:

$$\begin{aligned}(41)\qquad & \tfrac{1}{2}(\operatorname{var} r)F_{rr}+(\operatorname{cov} r, l)F_{rl}+\tfrac{1}{2}(\operatorname{var} l)F_{ll}+[\mu_r-\lambda_r(r, l)]F_r \\ & +[\mu_l-\lambda_l(r, l)]F_l-rF+F_t+\delta=0.\end{aligned}$$

The functions λ_r and λ_l serve the role of the factor risk premiums in (5). They are related to the factor risk premiums, ϕ_Y, by:

$$\lambda_r(r, l)=\left[\psi_1\frac{\partial g}{\partial l}-\psi_2\frac{\partial f}{\partial l}\right]\Big/\Delta,$$

$$\lambda_l(r, l)=\left[\psi_2\frac{\partial f}{\partial r}-\psi_1\frac{\partial g}{\partial r}\right]\Big/\Delta,$$

where

$$\begin{aligned}(42)\qquad & Y_1\equiv f(r, l, t), \qquad Y_2\equiv g(r, l, t), \\ & \phi_{Y_1}(Y_1, Y_2, t)\equiv\psi_1(r, l, t), \qquad \phi_{Y_2}(Y_1, Y_2, t)\equiv\psi_2(r, l, t),\end{aligned}$$

and

$$\Delta\equiv\frac{\partial f}{\partial r}\frac{\partial g}{\partial l}-\frac{\partial f}{\partial l}\frac{\partial g}{\partial r}.$$

Thus far we have not used the fact that l is an interest rate, and the transformation of (4) to (41) can be performed for an arbitrary instrumental variable if the inversion is possible. The advantage of choosing an interest rate instrument is that the second risk factor premium λ_l and the drift μ_l can be eliminated from (41) as follows.

Let Q denote the value of the particular bond for which l is the continuously compounded yield-to-maturity. Denote the payment flow from the bond, including both coupons and return of principal, by $c(t)$. In general, this flow will be zero most of the time, with impulses representing an infinite flow rate when payments are made. Since by definition $Q\equiv\int_t^T c(s)\exp[-l(s-t)]\,ds$, we can write:

$$\begin{aligned}(43)\qquad & Q\equiv\Lambda_0(l), \quad Q_l=\Lambda_1(l), \\ & Q_{ll}=\Lambda_2(l), \quad Q_t=-c(t)+l\Lambda_0(l)=-\delta+l\Lambda_0(l), \\ & Q_r=Q_{rr}=Q_{rl}=0,\end{aligned}$$

where

$$\Lambda_n \equiv \int_t^T (t-s)^n c(s)\, e^{-l(s-t)}\, ds,$$

and the integral is to be interpreted in the Stieltjes sense. If (43) is substituted into (41), we then obtain:

$$(44) \qquad \mu_l - \lambda_l(r, l) = \frac{(r-l)\Lambda_0(l) - \frac{1}{2}(\operatorname{var} l)\Lambda_2(l)}{\Lambda_1(l)},$$

and the unobservable factor risk premium may be replaced by the observable function in (44). If Q is a consol bond with coupons paid continuously at the rate c, then $\Lambda_0 = c/l$, $\Lambda_1 = -c/l^2$, $\Lambda_2 = 2c/l^3$, and (44) may be written as:[15]

$$(45) \qquad \mu_l - \lambda_l(r, l) = \frac{(\operatorname{var} l)}{l} + l(l-r).$$

These representations may be a useful starting point for empirical work. However, it is important to remember that they cannot be fully justified without considering the characteristics of the underlying economy. In the next section, we examine some additional multiple state variable models, all of which could be reexpressed in this form.

7. UNCERTAIN INFLATION AND THE PRICING OF NOMINAL BONDS

The model presented here deals with a real economy in which money would serve no purpose. To provide a valid role for money, we would have to introduce additional features which would lead far afield of our original intent. However, for a world in which changes in the money supply have no real effects, we can introduce some aspects of money and inflation in an artificial way by imagining that one of the state variables represents a price level and that some contracts have payoffs whose real value depends on this price level. That is, they are specified in nominal terms. None of this requires any changes in the general theory.

Suppose that we let the price level, p, be the kth state variable. Since we assume that this variable has no effect on the underlying real equilibrium, the functions α, μ, G, S, and J will not depend on p. Of course, this would not preclude changes in p from being statistically correlated with changes in real wealth and the other state variables. Under these circumstances, the real value of a claim whose payoff is specified in nominal terms still satisfies equation (4). All that needs to be done is to express the nominal payoff in real terms for the boundary conditions. Alternatively, the valuation equation (4) will also still hold if p is a differentiable function of W, Y, and t.[16]

[15] See Brennan and Schwartz [3] for this representation.

[16] If one wished to make real money balances an argument in the direct utility function U, it would be straightforward to do so in our model. A utility-maximizing money supply policy would depend only on the state variables, real wealth, and time, so the induced price level would depend only on these variables as well.

We can illustrate some of these points in the context of the model of Section 3. Let us take a second state variable to be the price level, $p(\equiv Y_2)$, and consider how to value a contract which will at time T pay with certainty an amount $1/p(T)$. Call this a nominal unit discount bond, and denote its value at time t in real terms as $N(r, p, t, T)$. Suppose that the price level p moves according to

$$(46) \qquad dp = \mu(p)\,dt + \sigma(p)\,dw_{n+2}(t)$$

and that it is uncorrelated with W and Y_1. Assume also that the coefficients in (45) are such that $E[p^{-1}(s)]$ exists for all finite s.

We would then have the valuation equation for N

$$(47) \qquad \tfrac{1}{2}\sigma^2 rN_{rr} + \tfrac{1}{2}\sigma^2(p)N_{pp} + [\kappa\theta - (\kappa+\lambda)r]N_r + \mu(p)N_p + N_t - rN = 0$$

with terminal condition $N(r, p, T, T) = 1/p(T)$. It can be directly verified that the solution is

$$(48) \qquad N(r, p, t, T) = P(r, t, T) \underset{p(t),t}{E} [1/p(T)]$$

where P is the price of a real discount bond given in (23).

In this formulation, the expected inflation rate changes only with the price level. For the commonly assumed case of lognormally distributed prices, however, $\mu(p) = \mu_p p$, $\sigma(p) = \sigma_p p$, and

$$(49) \qquad N(r, p, t, T) = e^{-(\mu_p - \sigma_p^2)(T-t)} P(r, t, T)/p(t),$$

so in this case the price of a nominal bond in nominal terms, $\hat{N} \equiv p(t)N$, would be independent of the current price level. With lognormally distributed prices, the expected inflation rate is constant, although of course realized inflation will not be.

As a somewhat more general example, we can separate the expected inflation rate factor from the price level factor and identify it with a third state variable. Again no change in the general theory is necessary. Label the expected inflation rate as y. We propose two alternative models for the behavior of the inflation rate: (i) Model 1,

$$(50) \qquad dy = \kappa_1 y(\theta_1 - y)\,dt + \sigma_1 y^{3/2}\,dz_3;$$

(ii) Model 2,

$$(51) \qquad dy = \kappa_2(\theta_2 - y)\,dt + \sigma_2 y^{1/2}\,dz_3$$

with the stochastic differential equation governing the movement of the price level being in each case

$$(52) \qquad dp = yp\,dt + \sigma_p p y^{1/2}\,dz_2$$

with $(\text{cov}\ y, p) \equiv \rho\sigma_1\sigma_p y^2 p$ in Model 1, $(\text{cov}\ y, p) \equiv \rho\sigma_1\sigma_p yp$ in Model 2, and $\sigma_p < 1$. Here, as in (17), we have for convenience defined $z_2(t)$ and $z_3(t)$ as the appropriate linear combinations of $w_{n+2}(t)$ and $w_{n+3}(t)$.

Model 1 may well be the better choice empirically, since informal evidence suggests that the relative (percentage) variance of the expected inflation rate increases as its level increases. Model 1 has this property, while Model 2 does not. However, the solution to Model 2 is more tractable, so we will record both for possible empirical use. In both models the expected inflation rate is pulled toward a long-run equilibrium level. Both models also allow for correlation between changes in the inflation rate and changes in the price level, thus allowing for positive or negative extrapolative forces in the movement of the price level.

The valuation equation for the real value of a nominal bond, specialized for our example with Model 1, will then be

$$\begin{aligned}(53)\qquad &\tfrac{1}{2}\sigma^2 rN_{rr}+\tfrac{1}{2}\sigma_1^2 y^3 N_{yy}+\rho\sigma_1\sigma_p y^2 pN_{yp}+\tfrac{1}{2}\sigma_p^2 p^2 yN_{pp}+[\kappa\theta-(\kappa+\lambda)r]N_r\\ &+\kappa_1 y(\theta_1-y)N_y+ypN_p+N_t-rN=0\end{aligned}$$

with $N(r, y, p, T, T)=1/p(T)$. The solution to equation (53) is

$$N(r, y, p, t, T)=\frac{\Gamma(\nu-\delta)}{\Gamma(\nu)}\left[\frac{c(t)}{y}\right]^{\delta} M\left(\delta, \nu, -\frac{c(t)}{y}\right)P(r, t, T)/p(t),$$

where

$$\begin{aligned}&c(t)\equiv\frac{2\kappa_1\theta_1}{\sigma_1^2(e^{\kappa_1\theta_1(T-t)}-1)},\\ (54)\qquad &\delta\equiv[[(\kappa_1+\rho\sigma_1\sigma_p+\tfrac{1}{2}\sigma_1^2)^2+2(1-\sigma_p^2)\sigma_1^2]^{1/2}-(\kappa_1+\rho\sigma_1\sigma_p+\tfrac{1}{2}\sigma_1^2)]/\sigma_1^2,\\ &\nu\equiv 2[(1+\delta)\sigma_1^2+\kappa_1+\rho\sigma_1\sigma_p]/\sigma_1^2,\end{aligned}$$

$M(\cdot, \cdot, \cdot)$ is the confluent hypergeometric function, and $\Gamma(\cdot)$ is the gamma function.[17]

Proceeding in the same way with Model 2, we obtain the valuation equation:

$$\begin{aligned}(55)\qquad &\tfrac{1}{2}\sigma^2 rN_{rr}+\tfrac{1}{2}\sigma_2^2 yN_{yy}+\rho\sigma_2\sigma_p ypN_{yp}+\tfrac{1}{2}\sigma_p^2 yp^2 N_{pp}+[\kappa\theta-(\kappa+\lambda)r]N_r\\ &+\kappa_2[\theta_2-y]N_y+ypN_p+N_t-rN=0\end{aligned}$$

with $N(r, y, p, T, T)=1/p(T)$. The corresponding valuation formula is:

$$\begin{aligned}(56)\qquad &N(r, y, p, t, T)\\ &=\left(\frac{2\xi e^{[(\kappa_2+\rho\sigma_2\sigma_p+\xi)(T-t)]/2}}{(\xi+\kappa_2+\rho\sigma_2\sigma_p)(e^{\xi(T-t)}-1)+2\xi}\right)^{2\kappa_2\theta_2/\sigma_2^2}\\ &\times\exp\left(\frac{-2(e^{\xi(T-t)}-1)(1-\sigma_p^2)y}{(\xi+\kappa_2+\rho\sigma_2\sigma_p)(e^{\xi(T-t)}-1)+2\xi}\right)P(r, t, T)/p(t),\end{aligned}$$

where

$$\xi\equiv[(\kappa_2+\rho\sigma_2\sigma_p)^2+2\sigma_2^2(1-\sigma_p^2)]^{1/2}.$$

[17] Slater [34] gives properties of the confluent hypergeometric function.

The term structure of interest rates implied by (54) and (56) can assume a wide variety of shapes, depending on the relative values of the variables and parameters. More complex models incorporating more detailed effects can be built along the same lines.

Throughout our paper, we have used specializations of the fundamental valuation equation (6). This equation determines the real value of a contingent claim as a function of real wealth and the state variables. For some empirical purposes, it may be convenient to have a corresponding valuation equation in which all values are expressed in nominal terms.

In our setting, this is given by the following proposition. In this proposition, we let nominal wealth be $X \equiv pW$, the indirect utility function in terms of nominal wealth be $V(X, Y, t) \equiv J(X/p, Y, t) \equiv J(W, Y, t)$, and the nominal value of a claim in terms of nominal wealth be $H(X, Y, t) \equiv pF(X/p, Y, t) \equiv pF(W, Y, t)$. As before, we let p be the kth element of Y.

PROPOSITION: *The nominal value of a contingent claim in terms of nominal wealth, $H(X, Y, t)$, satisfies the partial differential equation*

$$\begin{aligned}(57)\qquad & \tfrac{1}{2}(\operatorname{var} X)H_{XX} + \sum_{i=1}^{k} (\operatorname{cov} X, Y_i)H_{XY_i} + \tfrac{1}{2}\sum_{i=1}^{k}\sum_{j=1}^{k} (\operatorname{cov} Y_i, Y_j)H_{Y_iY_j} \\ & + (\iota X - pC^*)H_x + \sum_{i=1}^{k}\left[\mu_i - \left(\frac{-V_{XX}}{V_X}\right)(\operatorname{cov} X, Y_i)\right. \\ & \left. - \sum_{j=1}^{k}\left(\frac{-V_{XY_j}}{V_X}\right)(\operatorname{cov} Y_i, Y_j)\right]H_{Y_i} + H_t + p\delta - \iota H = 0,\end{aligned}$$

where the nominal interest rate, ι, is given by

$$(58)\qquad \iota = \alpha_X - \left(\frac{-V_{XY}}{V_X}\right)\left(\frac{\operatorname{var} X}{X}\right) - \sum_{i=1}^{k}\left(\frac{-V_{XY_i}}{V_X}\right)\left(\frac{\operatorname{cov} X, Y_i}{X}\right)$$

and α_X is the expected rate of return on nominal wealth,

$$(59)\qquad \alpha_X = a^{*\prime}\alpha + \left(\frac{\mu_p}{p}\right) + \left(\frac{\operatorname{cov} p, X}{pX}\right) - \left(\frac{\operatorname{var} p}{p^2}\right).$$

PROOF: Ito's multiplication rule implies that

$$(\operatorname{var} W) = (1/p^2)(\operatorname{var} X) - (2X/p^3)(\operatorname{cov} X, p) + (X^2/p^4)(\operatorname{var} p),$$

$$(\operatorname{cov} W, p) = (1/p)(\operatorname{cov} X, p) - (X/p^2)(\operatorname{var} p),$$

$$(\operatorname{cov} W, Y) = (1/p)(\operatorname{cov} X, Y) - (X/p^2)(\operatorname{cov} p, Y),$$

and

$$\alpha_X = a^{*\prime}\alpha + (\mu_p/p) + (1/pX)(\operatorname{cov} X, p) - (1/p^2)(\operatorname{var} p).$$

With

$$J(W, Y, t) \equiv J(X/p, Y, t) \equiv V(X, Y, t),$$

we have

$$(J_{WW}/J_W) = p(V_{XX}/V_X),$$
$$(J_{WY_i}/J_W) = (V_{XY_i}/V_X), \qquad \text{and}$$
$$(V_{Xp}/V_X) = -(1/p) - (X/p)(V_{XX}/V_X).$$

Equation (57) follows by writing the derivatives of $F(W, Y, t)$ in terms of those of $H(X, Y, t)$ and substituting all of the above into (6). The nominal interest rate can then be identified as the nominal payout flow necessary to keep the nominal value of a security identically equal to one, which is ι as given in (58).

Q.E.D.

A comparison of (57) and (58) with (6) and (3) shows that the interest rate equation and the fundamental valuation equation have exactly the same form when all variables are expressed in nominal terms as when all variables are expressed in real terms. By using the arguments given in the proof of the proposition, the nominal interest rate can be expressed in terms of real wealth as

$$(60) \qquad \iota = r + \left(\frac{1}{p}\right)\left[\mu_p - \left(\frac{-J_{WW}}{J_W}\right)(\text{cov } W, p) - \sum_{i=1}^{k}\left(\frac{-J_{WY_i}}{J_W}\right)(\text{cov } Y_i, p) - \left(\frac{\text{var } p}{p}\right)\right],$$

where r, the real interest rate, is as given by equation (3). The term (μ_p/p) is the expected rate of inflation. The remaining terms may in general have either sign, so the nominal interest rate may be either greater or less than the sum of the real interest rate and the expected inflation rate.[18]

8. CONCLUDING COMMENTS

In this paper, we have applied a rational asset pricing model to study the term structure of interest rates. In this model, the current prices and stochastic properties of all contingent claims, including bonds, are derived endogenously. Anticipations, risk aversion, investment alternatives, and preferences about the timing of consumption all play a role in determining the term structure. The model thus includes the main factors traditionally mentioned in a way which is consistent with maximizing behavior and rational expectations.

By exploring specific examples, we have obtained simple closed form solutions for bond prices which depend on observable economic variables and can be tested. The combination of equilibrium intertemporal asset pricing principles and appropriate modelling of the underlying stochastic processes provides a powerful tool for deriving consistent and potentially refutable theories. This is the first

[18] For a related discussion, see Fischer [13].

such exercise along these lines, and the methods developed should have many applications beyond those which we considered here.

In a separate paper, Cox, Ingersoll, and Ross [5], we use our approach to examine some aspects of what may be called traditional theories of the term structure. There we show that some forms of the classical expectations hypothesis are consistent with our simple equilibrium model and more complex ones, while other forms in general are not. We also show the relationship between some continuous time equilibrium models and traditional theories which express expected future spot rates as linear combinations of past spot rates.

Massachusetts Institute of Technology
and
Yale University

Manuscript received September, 1978; revision received October, 1984.

REFERENCES

[1] BEJA, A.: "State Preference and the Riskless Interest Rate: A Markov Model of Capital Markets," *Review of Economic Studies*, 46(1979), 435-446.

[2] BIERWAG, G. O., AND M. A. GROVE: "A Model of the Term Structure of Interest Rates," *Review of Economics and Statistics*, 49(1967), 50-62.

[3] BRENNAN, M. J., AND E. S. SCHWARTZ: "A Continuous Time Approach to the Pricing of Bonds," *Journal of Banking and Finance*, 3(1979), 133-155.

[4] CAGAN, P.: "The Monetary Dynamics of Hyperinflation," in *Studies in the Quantity Theory of Money*, ed. by M. Friedman. Chicago: University of Chicago Press, 1956.

[5] COX, J. C., J. E. INGERSOLL, JR., AND S. A. ROSS: "A Re-examination of Traditional Hypotheses about the Term Structure of Interest Rates, *Journal of Finance*, 36(1981), 769-799.

[6] ———: "An Intertemporal General Equilibrium Model of Asset Prices," *Econometrica*, 53 (1985), 363-384.

[7] CULBERTSON, J. M.: "The Term Structure of Interest Rates," *Quarterly Journal of Economics*, 71(1957), 485-517.

[8] DE LEEUW, F.: "A Model of Financial Behavior," in *The Brookings Quarterly Econometric Model of the United States*, ed. by J. S. Duesenberry et al. Chicago: Rand McNally, 1965.

[9] DIEFFENBACH, B. C.: "A Quantitative Theory of Risk Premiums on Securities with an Application to the Term Structure of Interest Rates," *Econometrica*, 43(1975), 431-454.

[10] DOTHAN, L. U.: "On the Term Structure of Interest Rates," *Journal of Financial Economics*, 6(1978), 59-69.

[11] DUESENBERRY, J. A.: *Business Cycles and Economic Growth*. New York: McGraw-Hill, 1958.

[12] FELLER, W.: "Two Singular Diffusion Problems," *Annals of Mathematics*, 54(1951), 173-182.

[13] FISCHER, S.: "The Demand for Index Bonds," *Journal of Political Economy*, 83(1975), 509-534.

[14] GERMAN, M. B.: "A General Theory of Asset Valuation Under Diffusion Processes," University of California, Berkeley, Institute of Business and Economic Research, Working Paper No. 50, 1977.

[15] HAKANSSON, N. H.: "Optimal Investment and Consumption Strategies under Risk for a Class of Utility Functions," *Econometrica*, 38(1970), 587-607.

[16] HICKS, J. R.: *Value and Capital*, 2nd edition. London: Oxford University Press, 1946.

[17] JOHNSON, N. L., AND S. KOTZ: *Distributions in Statistics: Continuous Univariate Distributions—2.* Boston: Houghton Mifflin Company, 1970.

[18] LONG, J. B.: "Stock Prices, Inflation, and the Term Structure of Interest Rates," *Journal of Financial Economics*, 1(1974), 131-170.

[19] MALKIEL, B. G.: *The Term Structure of Interest Rates: Excpectations and Behavior Patterns.* Princeton, New Jersey: Princeton University Press, 1966.

[20] MEISELMAN, D.: *The Term Structure of Interest Rates*. Englewood Cliffs, New Jersey: Prentice Hall, 1962.

[21] MERTON, R. C.: "A Dynamic General Equilibrium Model of the Asset Market and Its Application to the Pricing of the Capital Structure of the Firm," Massachusetts Institute of Technology, Sloan School of Management, Working Paper No. 497-70, 1970.

[22] ———: "Optimum Consumption and Portfolio Rules in a Continuous Time Model," *Journal of Economic Theory*, 3(1971), 373-413.

[23] ———: "Theory of Rational Option Pricing," *Bell Journal of Economics and Management Science*, 4(1973), 141-183.

[24] MODIGLIANI, F., AND R. J. SHILLER: "Inflation, Rational Expectations and the Term Structure of Interest Rates," *Economica*, 40 N.S. (1973), 12-43.

[25] MODIGLIANI, F., AND R. SUTCH: "Innovations in Interest Rate Policy," *American Economic Review*, 56(1966), 178-197.

[26] NELSON, C. R.: *The Term Structure of Interest Rates*. New York: Basic Books, Inc., 1972.

[27] OLIVER, F. W. J.: "Bessel Functions of Integer Order," *Handbook of Mathematical Functions*, ed. by M. A. Abramowitz and I. A. Stegun. New York: Dover, 1965.

[28] RICHARD, S. F.: "An Arbitrage Model of the Term Structure of Interest Rates," *Journal of Financial Economics*, 6(1978), 33-57.

[29] ROLL, R.: *The Behavior of Interest Rates*. New York: Basic Books, Inc., 1970.

[30] ———: "Investment Diversification and Bond Maturity," *Journal of Finance*, 26(1971), 51-66.

[31] RUBINSTEIN, M. E.: "The Valuation of Uncertain Income Streams and the Pricing of Options," *Bell Journal of Economics*, 7(1976), 407-425.

[32] SAMUELSON, P. A.: "Lifetime Portfolio Selection by Dynamic Stochastic Programming," *Review of Economics and Statistics*, 51(1969), 239-246.

[33] SARGENT, T. J.: "Rational Expectations and the Term Structure of Interest Rates," *Journal of Money, Credit, and Banking*, 4(1972), 74-97.

[34] SLATER, L. J.: "Confluent Hypergeometric Functions," in *Handbook of Mathematical Functions*, ed. by M. Abramowitz and I. A. Stegun. New York: Dover, 1965.

[35] STIGLITZ, J. E.: "A Consumption-Oriented Theory of Demand for Financial Assets and the Term Structure of Interest Rates," *Review of Economic Studies*, 37(1970), 321-351.

[36] VAN HORNE, J. C.: "Interest-Rate Risk and the Term Structure of Interest Rates," *Journal of Political Economy*, 73(1965), 344-351.

[37] VASICEK, O. A.: "An Equilibrium Characterization of the Term Structure," *Journal of Financial Economics*, 5(1977), 177-188.

[38] WOOD, J. H.: "The Expectations Hypothesis, the Yield Curve and Monetary Policy," *Quarterly Journal of Economics*, 78(1964), 457-470.

[18]

AN INTERTEMPORAL GENERAL EQUILIBRIUM MODEL OF ASSET PRICES[1]

BY JOHN C. COX, JONATHAN E. INGERSOLL, JR., AND STEPHEN A. ROSS

This paper develops a continuous time general equilibrium model of a simple but complete economy and uses it to examine the behavior of asset prices. In this model, asset prices and their stochastic properties are determined endogenously. One principal result is a partial differential equation which asset prices must satisfy. The solution of this equation gives the equilibrium price of any asset in terms of the underlying real variables in the economy.

1. INTRODUCTION

IN THIS PAPER, we develop a general equilibrium asset pricing model for use in applied research. An important feature of the model is its integration of real and financial markets. Among other things, the model endogenously determines the stochastic process followed by the equilibrium price of any financial asset and shows how this process depends on the underlying real variables. The model is fully consistent with rational expectations and maximizing behavior on the part of all agents.

Our framework is general enough to include many of the fundamental forces affecting asset markets, yet it is tractable enough to be specialized easily to produce specific testable results. Furthermore, the model can be extended in a number of straightforward ways. Consequently, it is well suited to a wide variety of applications. For example, in a companion paper, Cox, Ingersoll, and Ross [7], we use the model to develop a theory of the term structure of interest rates.

Many studies have been concerned with various aspects of asset pricing under uncertainty. The most relevant to our work are the important papers on intertemporal asset pricing by Merton [19] and Lucas [16]. Working in a continuous time framework, Merton derives a relationship among the equilibrium expected rates of return on assets. He shows that when investment opportunities are changing randomly over time this relationship will include effects which have no analogue in a static one period model. Lucas considers an economy with homogeneous individuals and a single consumption good which is produced by a number of processes. The random output of these processes is exogenously determined and perishable. Assets are defined as claims to all or a part of the output of a process, and the equilibrium determines the asset prices.

Our theory draws on some elements of both of these papers. Like Merton, we formulate our model in continuous time and make full use of the analytical tractability that this affords. The economic structure of our model is somewhat similar to that of Lucas. However, we include both endogenous production and

[1] This paper is an extended version of the first half of an earlier working paper titled "A Theory of the Term Structure of Interest Rates." We are grateful for the helpful comments and suggestions of many of our colleagues, both at our own institutions and others. This research was partially supported by the Dean Witter Foundation, the Center for Research in Security Prices, and the National Science Foundation.

random technological change. Since we allow for randomly changing investment opportunities, the intertemporal effects noted by Merton apply to our model and play an important role in our results.

In independent work, Brock [**4, 5**] and Prescott and Mehra [**22**] have also developed intertemporal models of asset pricing. The general approach of their papers is similar to ours, but the methods used and the issues addressed are quite different. Other related work includes papers by Breeden [**3**], Constantinides [**6**], Donaldson and Mehra [**9**], Huang [**14**], Richard and Sundaresan [**24**], Rubinstein [**26**], and Stapleton and Subrahmanyam [**28**].

Our paper is organized in the following way. In Section 2, we develop the model and characterize the equilibrium interest rate and equilibrium rates of return on assets. Section 3 presents our fundamental valuation equation and interprets its solution in a number of ways. Section 4 shows the relationship of our model to the Arrow-Debreu model and discusses the role of firms. In Section 5, we provide some concluding remarks and discuss several possible generalizations of our results.

2. AN EQUILIBRIUM VALUATION MODEL

This section will develop a model of general equilibrium in a simple economic setting. The following assumptions characterize our economy.

ASSUMPTION A1: *There is a single physical good which may be allocated to consumption or investment. All values are expressed in terms of units of this good.*

ASSUMPTION A2: *Production possibilities consist of a set of n linear activities.*[2] *The transformation of an investment of a vector η of amounts of the good in the n production processes is governed by a system of stochastic differential equations of the form:*[3,4]

$$(1) \qquad d\eta(t) = I_\eta \alpha(Y, t)\,dt + I_\eta G(Y, t)\,dw(t),$$

[2] We consider a pure capital growth model by assuming that labor is unnecessary in production (or that there is a permanent labor surplus state). This provides a more streamlined setting for the issues which we wish to stress. There is no essential difficulty in expanding the analysis to include labor inputs and nonlinear technologies.

[3] In describing the probabilistic structure of the economy, we will be implicitly referring to an underlying probability space $(\Omega, \mathcal{B}, \mathcal{P})$. Here Ω is a set, $\mathcal{B}$ is a σ-algebra of subsets of Ω, and $\mathcal{P}$ is a probability measure on $\mathcal{B}$. Let $[t, t']$ be a time interval and M be a separable complete metric space. By a stochastic process z, we mean a function from $[t, t'] \times \Omega$ into M such that z is measurable with respect to $\mathcal{B}$ and the σ-algebra of Borel subsets of M. We will take M to be R^n, n-dimensional Euclidean space. A stochastic process is said to be continuous if its possible realizations, or sample paths, are continuous with probability one. A real valued process w on $[t, t']$ is a Wiener process if: (i) w is a continuous process with independent increments, (ii) $w(s) - w(t)$ has a normal distribution with mean zero and variance $s - t$. A process is an n-dimensional Wiener process if its components are independent one-dimensional Wiener processes.

[4] Stochastic differential equations used in this paper are to be understood in the following way. Let $x(t)$ be an m-dimensional stochastic process which satisfies the system of stochastic differential equations

$$dx = a(x, t)\,dt + B(x, t)\,dw(t),$$

where $w(t)$ is an $(n+k)$ dimensional Wiener process in R^{n+k}, Y is a k-dimensional vector of state variables whose movement will be described shortly, I_η is an $n\times n$ diagonal matrix valued function of η whose ith diagonal element is the ith component of η, $\alpha(Y,t)=[\alpha_i(Y,t)]$ is a bounded n-dimensional vector valued function of Y and t, and $G(Y,t)=[g_{ij}(Y,t)]$ is a bounded $n\times(n+k)$ matrix valued function of Y and t. The covariance matrix of physical rates of return on the production processes, GG', is positive definite.[5]

System (1) specifies the growth of an initial investment when the output of each process is continually reinvested in that same process. It thus provides a complete description of the available production opportunities. It does not imply that individuals or firms will necessarily reinvest in this way. The production processes have stochastic constant returns to scale in the sense that the distribution of the rate of return on an investment in any process is independent of the scale of the investment.[6]

ASSUMPTION A3: *The movement of the k-dimensional vector of state variables, Y, is determined by a system of stochastic differential equations of the form:*

$$(2)\qquad dY(t)=\mu(Y,t)\,dt+S(Y,t)\,dw(t),$$

---

where $a(x,t)$ is an $m\times 1$ vector valued function and $B(x,t)$ is an $m\times n$ matrix valued function, and $w(t)$ is an n-dimensional Wiener process. A solution of this system with initial position $x(t)$ is a solution of the system of integral equations

$$x(s)=x(t)+\int_t^s a(x(u),u)\,du+\int_t^s B(x(u),u)\,dw(u),$$

where the latter integral is defined in the sense of Ito.

We assume, in reference to (1), (2), and (3), that a and B are measurable on $[t,t']\times R^m$ and satisfy the following growth and Lipschitz conditions:

(i) There exists a constant k_1 such that for all (x,s) in $[t,t']\times R^m$,

$$|a(x,s)|\leq k_1(1+|x|)\quad\text{and}\quad |B(x,s)|\leq k_1(1+|x|).$$

(ii) For any bounded $Q\subset R^m$ there exists a constant k_2, possibly depending on Q and s, such that for all $x,y\in Q$ and $t\leq s\leq t'$,

$$|a(x,s)-a(y,s)|\leq k_2|x-y|,$$
$$|B(x,s)-B(y,s)|\leq k_2|x-y|.$$

Detailed information on all of these topics can be found in Fleming and Rishel [**10**], Friedman [**11**], and Gihman and Skorohod [**12**].

[5] When discussing stochastic differential equations as given in footnote 4, we will refer to $a(x(t),t)$ as the vector of expected returns (or changes) of x and $B(x(t),t)B'(x(t),t)$ as the covariance matrix of returns (or changes) of x. Similarly, if I_x is a diagonal matrix with the ith component of x as its ith diagonal element, then $I_x^{-1}a$ is the vector of expected rates of return (or rates of change or percentage changes) of x and $I_x^{-1}BB'I_x^{-1}$ is the covariance matrix of rates of return (or rates of change or percentage changes) of x.

[6] This formulation allows for quite general probabilistic behavior by the capital stock. However, since the stochastic differential equations are driven by Wiener processes, sudden discontinuous changes in the capital stock are precluded. Note that the incremental return on an investment in any production process can be negative, thus reflecting random physical depreciation.

where $\mu(Y,t)=[\mu_i(Y,t)]$ *is a k-dimensional vector and* $S(Y,t)=[s_{ij}(Y,t)]$ *is a* $k\times(n+k)$ *dimensional matrix. The covariance matrix of changes in the state variables,* SS', *is nonnegative definite. We will assume that Y has no accessible boundaries. Note that* (2) *need not be a linear homogeneous system, and that both Y and the joint process* (η, Y) *are Markov.*

This framework includes both uncertain production and random technological change. The probability distribution of current output depends on the current level of the state variables Y, which are themselves changing randomly over time. The development of Y will thus determine the production opportunities which will be available to the economy in the future. In general, opportunities may worsen as well as improve.

Unless GS' is a null matrix, changes in the state variables will be contemporaneously correlated with the incremental returns on the production processes. Indeed, when S is identically equal to G, they are perfectly correlated and the value of Y at any time will be completely determined by the previous returns on the production processes. Consequently, our description of technological change can easily represent situations in which the random shocks to any individual production process are correlated over time.[7]

Y may also include state variables which do not affect production opportunities but are nevertheless of interest to individuals. We postpone further discussion of these variables until a suitable context is developed later in the paper.

ASSUMPTION A4: *There is free entry to all production processes. Individuals can invest in physical production indirectly through firms or directly, in effect creating their own firms. We will adopt the second interpretation, with some remarks about the first. Individuals and firms are competitive and act as price takers in all markets.*

ASSUMPTION A5: *There is a market for instantaneous borrowing and lending at an interest rate r. The market clearing rate, as a function of underlying variables, is determined as part of the competitive equilibrium of the economy.*

ASSUMPTION A6: *There are markets for a variety of contingent claims to amounts of the good. These are securities which are issued and purchased by individuals and firms. The specification of each claim includes a full description of all payoffs which may be received from that claim. These payoffs may depend on the values of the state variables and on aggregate wealth. The values of the claims will in general depend on all variables necessary to describe the state of the economy. We can write the stochastic differential equation governing the movement of the value of claim i,* F^i, *as*

(3) $$dF^i=(F^i\beta_i-\delta_i)\,dt+F^ih_i\,dw(t)$$

[7] As a simple example, suppose $k=n$, $\alpha=-Y$, $\mu=-Y$, and $S=G$, where G is a constant diagonal matrix. Then Y is an n-dimensional first-order autoregressive process and (1) can be rewritten as $d\eta(t)=I_n\,dY(t)$.

where h_i is a $1\times(n+k)$ vector valued function. In (3) *the total mean return on claim i, $\beta_i F^i$, is defined as the payout received, δ_i, plus the mean price change, $\beta_i F^i - \delta_i$. The variance of the rate of return on claim i is $h_i h_i'$. Ito's formula implies a specific relationship of β_i and h_i to the partial derivatives of the value of the claim and the instantaneous means and covariances of the variables on which it depends, but for the moment,* (3) *should be considered as providing only a notation for entities which will be examined in detail later.*[8] *It does not imply that the movement of a price is being specified exogenously. The equilibrium β_i and r are stochastic processes which are to be determined endogenously.*

ASSUMPTION A7: *There are a fixed number of individuals, identical in their endowments and preferences. All individuals agree that the production opportunities and state variables are as described. Each individual seeks to maximize an objective function of the form:*[9,10]

$$E\int_t^{t'} U[C(s),\, Y(s),\, s]\, ds. \tag{4}$$

In (4), *E is an expectation operator conditional on current endowment and the state of the economy, $C(s)$ is the consumption flow at time s, and U is a von Neumann–Morgenstern utility function. We assume that U is increasing, strictly concave, twice differentiable, and satisfies the condition $|U(C(s), Y(s), s)| \leq k_1(1+C(s)+|Y(s)|)^{k_2}$ for some positive constants k_1 and k_2.*

ASSUMPTION A8: *Physical investment and trading in claims take place continuously in time with no adjustment or transactions costs. Trading takes place only at equilibrium prices.*

We will begin our analysis of this economy by considering the individual's allocation problem. In the presence of contingent claims, the individual portfolio selection problem will in general not have a unique solution. Consequently, it is convenient to choose a basis for the set of investment opportunities, including both production processes and contingent claims. A basis is defined as the set

[8] Let $dx = a(x,t)\,dt + B(x,t)\,dw(t)$, let $a_i(x,t)$ be the ith element of a, and let $b_{ij}(x,t)$ be the i, jth element of B. Ito's formula can be stated in the following way. If $f(x,t)$ is a continuous function with continuous partial derivatives f_t, f_x, f_{xx} on $[t,t']\times R^m$ then

$$df(x(t),t) = \left[f_t(x,t) + \sum_{i=1}^{m} f_{x_i}(x,t)a_i(x,t) + \tfrac{1}{2}\sum_{j,k=1}^{m} f_{x_k x_j}(x,t)\sum_{i=1}^{m} b_{ki}(x,t)b_{ji}(x,t)\right]dt + \sum_{i=1}^{n}\sum_{j=1}^{m} f_{x_j}(x,t)b_{ji}(x,t)\,dw_i(t).$$

[9] We adopt a finite-horizon formulation to allow consideration of the effects of horizon length on contingent claim values. A bequest function assigning utility to terminal wealth could easily be added. The infinite-horizon case proceeds along the same lines with appropriate technical modifications.

[10] It should be stressed that the role of the state variables in our subsequent propositions is in no way due solely to their presence in the direct utility function, *U*. The only simplifications that would result from a state independent direct utility function are noted in equations (28), (29), and (30).

of production processes and a set of contingent claims, with row vectors h_i, as in (3), forming the matrix H, such that for any other contingent claim j, h_j can be written as a linear combination of the rows of G and H. Equation (3) will now be interpreted as referring to the claims in the basis. The explicit construction of the basis over time is not of importance as long as its dimension remains unchanged, which we assume to be the case. Any creation or expiration of contingent claims which causes a change in the dimension of the basis will cause a change in the hedging opportunities available to an individual. For simplicity we assume that the basis consists of the n production activities and k contingent claims.

It is sufficient for both individual choice and equilibrium valuation to determine the unique allocation resulting when the opportunity set is restricted to the basis. Any allocation involving nonbasis claims could be replicated by a controlled portfolio of claims in the basis.[11] Since any of these choices would give the individual the same portfolio behavior over time and the same consumption path, he would be indifferent among them. In this scheme of things there is no reason for nonbasis contingent claims to exist, but there is no reason for them not to exist either, and we may assume that in general there will be an infinite number of them, each of which must be consistently priced in equilibrium.[12]

After defining the opportunity set in this way, an individual will allocate his wealth among the $(n+k)$ basis opportunities, and the $(n+k+1)$st opportunity, riskless borrowing or lending. Make the following definitions: W is the individual's current total wealth, $a_i W$ is the amount of wealth invested in the ith production process, and $b_i W$ is the amount of wealth invested in the ith contingent claim. The individual wishes to choose the controls aW, bW, and C which will maximize his expected lifetime utility subject to the budget constraint:[13]

$$dW = \left[\sum_{i=1}^{n} a_i W(\alpha_i - r) + \sum_{i=1}^{k} b_i W(\beta_i - r) + rW - C\right] dt \tag{5}$$

$$+ \sum_{i=1}^{n} a_i W\left(\sum_{j=1}^{n+k} g_{ij}\, dw_j\right) + \sum_{i=1}^{k} b_i W\left(\sum_{j=1}^{n+k} h_{ij}\, dw_j\right)$$

$$\equiv W\mu(W)\, dt + W \sum_{j=1}^{n+k} q_j\, dw_j.$$

We now make an assumption of a purely technical nature which enables us to apply standard results from stochastic control theory to this problem.

[11] For further details, see Merton [20], which contains a complete description of this concept. It is implicit in the earlier work of Black and Scholes [2] and Merton [18]. See also Harrison and Kreps [13].

[12] This would be the case, for example, for bonds with a continuum of maturity dates or options with a continuum of exercise prices. One could then describe individual holdings in terms of a measure on the admissible set, thus allowing finite holdings at points as well as over intervals.

[13] For a detailed explanation of the form of the budget constraint, see Merton [17].

ASSUMPTION A9: *In maximizing* (4), *the individual limits his attention to a class of admissible feedback controls, V. An admissible feedback control, v, is a Borel measurable function on* $[t, t') \times R^{n+k+1}$ *satisfying the growth and Lipschitz conditions given in footnote* 4. *Furthermore, admissible disequilibrium* β *and r are bounded and satisfy the Lipschitz conditions given in footnote* 4.

Measurability implies the natural restriction that the control chosen at any time must depend only on information available at that time.

Define

$$(6) \qquad K(v(t), W(t), Y(t), t) = \underset{W,Y,t}{E} \int_t^{t'} U(v(s), Y(s), s)\, ds$$

where $v(t)$ is an admissible feedback control, and let $L^v(t)K$ be the differential generator of K associated with this control,

$$(7) \qquad L^v(t)K = \mu(W)WK_W + \sum_{i=1}^{k} \mu_i K_{Y_i} + \tfrac{1}{2}W^2 K_{WW} \sum_{i=1}^{n+k} q_i^2 + \sum_{i=1}^{k} WK_{WY_i} \sum_{j=1}^{n+k} q_j s_{ij} + \tfrac{1}{2} \sum_{i=1}^{k} \sum_{j=1}^{k} K_{Y_iY_j} \sum_{m=1}^{n+k} s_{im}s_{jm}.$$

We can now state the following basic optimality condition for the individual's control problem:

LEMMA 1: *Let* $J(W, Y, t)$ *be a solution of the Bellman equation*

$$(8) \qquad \max_{v \in V} [L^v(t)J + U(v, Y, t)] + J_t = 0$$

for $(t, W, Y) \in \mathcal{D} \equiv [t, t') \times (0, \infty) \times R^k$, *with boundary conditions*

$$(9) \qquad J(0, Y, t) = \underset{Y,t}{E} \int_t^{t'} U(0, Y(s), s)\, ds \quad \text{and} \quad J(W, Y, t') = 0,$$

such that J, its first partial derivatives with respect to t, W, Y, and its second partial derivatives with respect to W, Y are continuous on $\mathcal{D}$, *J is continuous on* $\bar{\mathcal{D}}$, *the closure of* $\mathcal{D}$, *and* $|J(W, Y, t)| \leq k_1|W, Y|^{k_2}$ *for some constants* k_1 *and* k_2. *Then*: (i) $J(W, Y, t) \geq K(v, W, Y, t)$ *for any admissible feedback control v and initial position W, Y*; (ii) *if* $\hat{v}$ *is an admissible feedback control such that*

$$(10) \qquad L^{\hat{v}}(t)J + U(\hat{v}, Y, t) = \max_{v \in V} [L^v(t)J + U(v, Y, t)]$$

for all $(t, W, Y) \in \mathcal{D}$, *then* $J(W, Y, t) = K(\hat{v}, W, Y, t)$ *for all* $(t, W, Y) \in \mathcal{D}$ *and* $\hat{v}$ *is optimal.*

PROOF: See Fleming and Rishel [10, p. 159].

Our interest is in characterizations of equilibrium, so to avoid further technicalities we now assume:[14]

ASSUMPTION A10: *There exists a unique function J and control $\hat{v}$ satisfying the Bellman equation and the stated regularity condition.*

The following lemma verifies that J, the indirect utility function, inherits some of the qualitative properties of the direct utility function, U.

LEMMA 2: *J is an increasing, strictly concave function of W.*

PROOF: Suppose an individual has current wealth $W_2 > W_1$. Since the feasible set V is convex, he could choose $\hat{C}(W_1)+\hat{C}(W_2-W_1)$, $\hat{a}(W_1)W_1+\hat{a}(W_2-W_1)(W_2-W_1)$, $\hat{b}(W_1)W_1+\hat{b}(W_2-W_1)(W_2-W_1)$. Hence $J(W_2)\geq K(\hat{v}(W_1)+\hat{v}(W_2-W_1), W_2)>K(\hat{v}(W_1), W_1)=J(W_1)$, and J is an increasing function of W. Now suppose the individual has current wealth $\lambda W_1+(1-\lambda)W_2$. Since he could certainly choose the control $\lambda\hat{C}(W_1)+(1-\lambda)\hat{C}(W_2)$, $\lambda\hat{a}(W_1)W_1+(1-\lambda)\hat{a}(W_2)$, $\lambda\hat{b}(W_1)W_1+(1-\lambda)\hat{b}(W_2)W_2$, we have

$$
\begin{aligned}
J(\lambda W_1+(1-\lambda)W_2) &\geq K(\lambda\hat{v}(W_1)+(1-\lambda)\hat{v}(W_2), \lambda W_1+(1-\lambda)W_2)\\
&>\lambda K(\hat{v}(W_1), W_1)+(1-\lambda)K(\hat{v}(W_2), W_2)\\
&=\lambda J(W_1)+(1-\lambda)J(W_2).
\end{aligned}
$$

Hence, J is a strictly concave function of W. *Q.E.D.*

The portfolio proportions a_i represent investment in physical production processes, so they must be nonnegative. Similarly, negative consumption has no meaning. With these constraints, necessary and sufficient conditions for the maximization of $\psi\equiv L^v J+U$ as a function of C, a, b are

(11a) $\psi_C = U_C - J_W \leq 0,$

(11b) $C\psi_C = 0,$

(11c) $\psi_a = [\alpha - r1]WJ_W + [GG'a + GH'b]W^2J_{WW} + GS'WJ_{WY} \leq 0,$

(11d) $a'\psi_a = 0,$

(11e) $\psi_b = [\beta - r1]WJ_W + [HG'a + HH'b]W^2J_{WW} + HS'WJ_{WY} = 0,$

where β is a $(k\times 1)$ vector whose ith element is β_i, J_{WY} is a $(k\times 1)$ vector whose ith element is J_{WY_i}, and 1 is a $(k\times 1)$ unit vector.

By solving (11) for $\hat{C}$, $\hat{a}$, $\hat{b}$ in terms of W, Y, t, and partial derivatives of J and substituting back into (8) we obtain a partial differential equation for J. By substituting the solution for J from this equation back into $\hat{C}$, $\hat{a}$, $\hat{b}$ we obtain

[14] For some results on the existence of solutions to equations of this type see [10]. It can also be shown that in our context any sufficiently smooth indirect utility function must satisfy (8).

them as functions of only W, Y, and t. W and J are, respectively, the current wealth and indirect utility function of the representative individual.

The individual chooses $\hat{C}$, $\hat{a}$, $\hat{b}$ taking r, α, and β as given. Equilibrium in the economy determines the market clearing interest rate, the equilibrium expected returns on the contingent claims, the total production plan, and the total consumption plan. In aggregate the net supply of contingent claims and riskless lending must be zero. Formally, we have the following definition:

DEFINITION: An equilibrium is defined as a set of stochastic processes $(r, \beta; a, C)$ satisfying (11) and the market clearing conditions $\sum a_i = 1$ and $b_i = 0$ for all i.

As will soon be apparent, this is equivalent to defining equilibrium in terms of a set of stochastic processes $(r, F; a, C)$. The existence and uniqueness of an equilibrium, and its characterization by the fundamental equation of dynamic programming, are in effect assumed in Assumption A10. In this homogeneous society, an equilibrium is clearly Pareto optimal since for any (r, β) all individuals have the opportunity of attaining the optimum of a corresponding planning problem with no borrowing or lending and no contingent claims.

Suppose now that investment is done through competitive value-maximizing firms. Assume for simplicity that each firm invests in only one process, and let an industry be the collection of all firms using a process. With free entry and stochastic constant returns to scale, there will be no incentive for firms to enter or leave the industry if and only if the returns on the shares of each firm (the terms on which it can acquire capital) are identical to the technologically determined physical returns on that process. The equilibrium scale of each industry would then be determined by the supply of investment, which would be the same as the equilibrium with direct investment by individuals. In other words, in this simple economy the solution to the planning problem will be equivalent to the competitive equilibrium.

Let us now turn to the determination of the equilibrium values of a, r, and β. It is evident that the equilibrium solution for these in terms of J is partially separable. With $b = 0$, (11c, d) determines a and r. With a and r determined, (11e) is a linear system in β. This does not imply, however, that consumption and investment decisions are separable, since J must be determined jointly. As this separability suggests, we can gain insight into the equilibrium by examining two related problems: (i) the planning problem with the same physical production opportunities but with no borrowing and lending and no contingent claims, and (ii) the analogous problem with borrowing and lending but no contingent claims.

Consider the optimal physical investment policy, a^*, optimal consumption policy C^*, and the corresponding indirect utility function, J^*, of an individual facing the planning problem (i). The portfolio allocation component can be written as a quadratic programming problem:

$$(12) \qquad \max_a \; a'\gamma + a'Da$$

subject to:

$$a'1 = 1,$$

$$a \geqslant 0,$$

where γ is $\alpha WJ^*_W + GS'WJ^*_{WY}$, D is $\frac{1}{2}GG'W^2J^*_{WW}$, and 1 is a unit vector. Since a^* is optimal, then by the Kuhn-Tucker theorem, there exists a λ^* such that

$$(13) \qquad \gamma - \lambda^* 1 + 2Da^* \leqslant 0,$$

$$a^{*\prime}\gamma - \lambda^* a^{*\prime}1 + 2a^{*\prime}Da^* = 0.$$

Consider now problem (ii), with borrowing or lending at r^*, and with indirect utility function J^{**}. Inspection shows that if $J^{**} = J^*$ and $r^* = \lambda^*/WJ^*_W$, then (r^*, a^*, C^*) is the equilibrium for problem (ii). This equilibrium interest rate r^* is proportional to the Lagrangian multiplier associated with the constraint $1'a = 1$. Hence, in equilibrium in our economy $J = J^* = J^{**}$, $\hat{a} = a^*$, $\hat{C} = C^*$, and $r = r^*$.

We will first discuss some properties of the equilibrium interest rate, and then turn to the equilibrium rates of return on contingent claims. The equilibrium interest rate can be written explicitly as

$$(14) \qquad r(W, Y, t) = \lambda^*/WJ_W = a^{*\prime}\alpha + a^{*\prime}GG'a^* W\left(\frac{J_{WW}}{J_W}\right) + a^{*\prime}GS'\left(\frac{J_{WY}}{J_W}\right)$$

$$= a^{*\prime}\alpha - \left(\frac{-J_{WW}}{J_W}\right)\left(\frac{\text{var } W}{W}\right) - \sum_{i=1}^{k}\left(\frac{-J_{WY_i}}{J_W}\right)\left(\frac{\text{cov } W, Y_i}{W}\right),$$

where (cov W, Y_i) stands for the covariance of changes in optimally invested wealth with changes in the state variable Y_i, and similarly for (var W) and (cov Y_i, Y_j).[15]

$a^{*\prime}\alpha$ is the expected rate of return on optimally invested wealth. The equilibrium interest rate r may be either less or greater than $a^{*\prime}\alpha$, even though all individuals are risk averse to gambles on consumption paths. Although investment in the production processes exposes an individual to uncertainty about the output received, it may also allow him to hedge against the risk of less favorable changes in technology. An individual investing only in locally riskless lending would be unprotected against this latter risk. In general, either effect may dominate.[16]

The following theorem provides a more intuitive interpretation of the equilibrium interest rate. We first make one further technical assumption which will be needed only in the proof of Theorem 1.

[15] If a locally riskless production process exists, then its return would be a lower bound for the interest rate. The interest rate would be at this lower bound whenever the locally riskless process is used in equilibrium. It is easy to verify that (14) still holds.

[16] The presence of risk aversion suggests that the certainty equivalent rate of return on physical investment, $\bar{r}$, should exceed the interest rate. Consider a single locally riskless production process whose return is such that individuals would receive the same utility for investing their wealth in this process as they would from optimally investing it in the original n processes. The rate of return on this process is by definition $\bar{r}$. Inspection of (10) shows that

$$\bar{r}(W, Y, t) = r(W, Y, t) + \frac{1}{2}\left(\frac{-J_{WW}}{J_W}\right)\left(\frac{\text{var } W}{W}\right).$$

ASSUMPTION A11: *J_{WW}, J_{WY_i}, $J_{Y_iY_j}$, J_t, a_i^*, and C^* have one continuous derivative with respect to W on $\mathcal{D}$.*

THEOREM 1: *In equilibrium we have*

(15) r = −(*expected rate of change in the marginal utility of wealth*)
= (*expected rate of return on wealth*)
+ (*covariance of the rate of return on wealth with the rate of change in the marginal utility of wealth*).

PROOF: By Ito's formula, J_W will satisfy the stochastic differential equation

$$dJ_W = (J_{Wt} + LJ_W)\,dt + [J_{WW}a^{*\prime}GW + J'_{WY}S]\,dw(t), \tag{16}$$

where L is the differential generator defined in (7). Hence, the expected rate of change in marginal utility is $(J_{Wt} + LJ_W)/J_W$. By differentiating (8) with respect to W, using (11), and rearranging, we find that

$$\begin{aligned} r &= \left[a^{*\prime}\alpha - \left(\frac{-J_{WW}}{J_W}\right)\left(\frac{\text{var } W}{W}\right) - \sum_{i=1}^{k}\left(\frac{-J_{WY_i}}{J_W}\right)\left(\frac{\text{cov } W, Y_i}{W}\right)\right] \\ &= -\Bigg[\tfrac{1}{2}(\text{var } W)J_{WWW} + \sum_{i=1}^{k}(\text{cov } W, Y_i)J_{WWY_i} \\ &\quad + \tfrac{1}{2}\sum_{i=1}^{k}\sum_{j=1}^{k}(\text{cov } Y_i, Y_j)J_{WY_iY_j} + [a^{*\prime}\alpha W - C^*(W, Y, t)]J_{WW} \\ &\quad + \sum_{i=1}^{k}\mu_i(Y)J_{WY_i} + J_{Wt}\Bigg]\Bigg/ J_W = -(J_{Wt} + LJ_W)/J_W, \end{aligned} \tag{17}$$

which proves the first part. Recall that

$$dW = [a^{*\prime}\alpha W - C^*]\,dt + a^{*\prime}GW\,dw(t)$$

and

$$dY = \mu\,dt + S\,dw(t). \tag{18}$$

We then find that the covariance of the rate of return on wealth with the rate of change in the marginal utility of wealth, $(\text{cov } W, J_W)/WJ_W$, is

$$\begin{aligned} \left(\frac{\text{cov } W, J_W}{WJ_W}\right) &= \left(\frac{1}{J_W}\right)[J_{WW}a^{*\prime}GW + J'_{WY}S][a^{*\prime}G]' \\ &= -\left[\left(\frac{-J_{WW}}{J_W}\right)\left(\frac{\text{var } W}{W}\right) + \sum_{i=1}^{k}\left(\frac{-J_{WY_i}}{J_W}\right)\left(\frac{\text{cov } W, Y_i}{W}\right)\right]. \end{aligned} \tag{19}$$

The expected rate of return on wealth is $a^{*\prime}\alpha$. Combining these and comparing with (14) confirms the second part. *Q.E.D.*

When $U(C(s), Y(s), s) = e^{-\rho s}U(C(s), Y(s))$, then the first expression on the right hand side of (15) can be written as ρ minus the expected rate of change in the undiscounted marginal utility of wealth. These interpretations of course reduce to standard results when there is no uncertainty.

We now turn to the equilibrium expected return on contingent claims. Our second theorem gives these equilibrium expected returns in terms of the underlying fundamental variables.

THEOREM 2: *The equilibrium expected return on any contingent claim, say the ith, is given by*

$$(20)\qquad (\beta_i - r)F^i = [\phi_W \quad \phi_{Y_1} \quad \cdots \quad \phi_{Y_k}][F^i_W \quad F^i_{Y_1} \quad \cdots \quad F^i_{Y_k}]',$$

where

$$\phi_W = \left[\left(\frac{-J_{WW}}{J_W}\right)(\text{var } W) + \sum_{i=1}^{k}\left(\frac{-J_{WY_i}}{J_W}\right)(\text{cov } W, Y_i)\right],$$

$$\phi_{Y_i} = \left[\left(\frac{-J_{WW}}{J_W}\right)(\text{cov } W, Y_i) + \sum_{j=1}^{k}\left(\frac{-J_{WY_j}}{J_W}\right)(\text{cov } Y_i, Y_j)\right].$$

PROOF: Substituting a^* and r into (11e) gives

$$(21)\qquad \beta(W, Y, t) = (a^{*\prime}\alpha)1 + \left(\frac{1}{J_W}\right)[(a^{*\prime}GS'J_{WY})1 - HS'J_{WY}] + \left(\frac{WJ_{WW}}{J_W}\right)[(a^{*\prime}GG'a^*)1 - HG'a^*].$$

By using Ito's formula to give H explicitly and then rearranging terms, the expected return on any contingent claim in the basis, say the ith, can be rewritten as

$$(22)\qquad \beta_i F^i = rF^i + F^i_W\left[\left(\frac{-J_{WW}}{J_W}\right)(\text{var } W) + \sum_{i=1}^{k}\left(\frac{-J_{WY_i}}{J_W}\right)(\text{cov } W, Y_i)\right] + \sum_{i=1}^{k} F^i_{Y_i}\left[\left(\frac{-J_{WW}}{J_W}\right)(\text{cov } W, Y_i) + \sum_{j=1}^{k}\left(\frac{-J_{WY_j}}{J_W}\right)(\text{cov } Y_i, Y_j)\right],$$

which can be abbreviated as

$$(23)\qquad (\beta_i - r)F^i \equiv [\phi_W \quad \phi_{Y_1} \quad \cdots \quad \phi_{Y_k}][F^i_W \quad F^i_{Y_1} \quad \cdots \quad F^i_{Y_k}]'.$$

The equilibrium expected rates of return of contingent claims not in the basis are uniquely determined by the equilibrium expected rates of return of those in the basis. Recall that it is possible to construct a controlled portfolio from basis assets which would exactly duplicate the payout pattern of any non-basis contingent claim, $\bar{F}$. In equilibrium the initial value and expected rate of return on $\bar{F}$ must be equal to that of the controlled portfolio. Let θ_i be the number of units of F^i held in the controlled portfolio. Let F^1 be optimally invested wealth and let F^{k+2} be a unit investment in locally riskless lending, so $F^{k+2} \equiv 1$. Thus we have $\bar{F}=\sum_{i=1}^{k+2}\theta_i F^i$ and $\bar{\beta}\bar{F}=\sum_{i=1}^{k+2}\theta_i\beta_i F^i$. Combining these and using $\beta_{k+2}=r$ gives

$$(24)\qquad (\bar{\beta}-r)\bar{F}=[(\beta_1-r)F^1\,(\beta_2-r)F^2\cdots(\beta_{k+1}-r)F^{k+1}][\theta_1\,\theta_2\cdots\theta_{k+1}]'$$

$$=[\phi_W\quad\phi_{Y_1}\cdots\phi_{Y_k}]\begin{bmatrix}F^1_W & \cdots & F^{k+1}_W\\ F^1_Y & \cdots & F^{k+1}_{Y_1}\\ \vdots & & \vdots\\ F^1_{Y_k} & \cdots & F^{k+1}_{Y_k}\end{bmatrix}\begin{bmatrix}\theta_1\\ \theta_2\\ \vdots\\ \theta_{k+1}\end{bmatrix},$$

with the second line following from (23). By again using Ito's formula we can write θ explicitly as

$$(25)\qquad \begin{bmatrix}\theta_1\\ \theta_2\\ \vdots\\ \theta_{k+1}\end{bmatrix}=\begin{bmatrix}F^1_W & \cdots & F^{k+1}_W\\ F^1_{Y_1} & \cdots & F^{k+1}_{Y_1}\\ \vdots & & \vdots\\ F^1_{Y_k} & \cdots & F^{k+1}_{Y_k}\end{bmatrix}^{-1}\begin{bmatrix}\bar{F}_W\\ \bar{F}_{Y_1}\\ \vdots\\ \bar{F}_{Y_k}\end{bmatrix}.$$

Combining (24) and (25) gives

$$(26)\qquad (\bar{\beta}-r)\bar{F}=[\phi_W\quad\phi_{Y_1}\quad\cdots\quad\phi_{Y_k}][\bar{F}_W\quad\bar{F}_{Y_1}\quad\cdots\quad\bar{F}_{Y_k}]',$$

which confirms that (20) holds for all contingent claims. *Q.E.D.*

The equilibrium expected return for any contingent claim can thus be written as the riskfree return plus a linear combination of the first partials of the asset price with respect to W and Y. While these derivatives depend on the contractual provisions of the asset, the coefficients of the linear combination do not, and are the same for all contingent claims.

The coefficients of the linear combination in (20) can be given in terms of equilibrium expected rates of return on particular securities or portfolios. From (14), we see that $\phi_W=(a^{*\prime}\alpha-r)W$, the expected excess return (over the risk free return) on optimally invested wealth. The coefficient of ϕ_{Y_j} is the excess expected return on a security constructed so that its value is always equal to Y_j. Equation (31) below can be used to give the contractual terms required in this construction. ϕ_{Y_j} could also be expressed as a function of the expected rate of return on any other security or portfolio whose value depends only on Y_j.

In [**25**], Ross shows that if security returns are generated by a linear factor model, then under quite general conditions, the equilibrium excess expected rate of return of any security can be written as a linear combination of the factor risk premiums. The risk premium of the jth factor is defined as the excess expected rate of return on a security or portfolio which has only the risk of the jth factor. Although our underlying model is much more fully developed, the coefficients ϕ_W and ϕ_{Y_j} are Ross factor risk premiums and can be interpreted in this way.

The proof of the second part of Theorem 1 established that ϕ_W is the negative of the covariance of the change in wealth with the rate of change in the marginal utility of wealth. A similar argument shows that ϕ_{Y_i} is the negative of the covariance of the change in the ith state variable with the rate of change in the marginal utility of wealth. By using Ito's formula to write out (3) explicitly, as in the proof of Theorem 2, it then follows that

$$\beta_i - r = -(\operatorname{cov} F^i, J_W)/F^i J_W. \tag{27}$$

That is, the excess expected rate of return on the ith contingent claim is equal to the negative of the covariance of its rate of return with the rate of change in the marginal utility of wealth. Just as we would expect, individuals are willing to accept a lower expected rate of return on securities which tend to pay off more highly when marginal utility is higher. Hence, in equilibrium such securities will have a lower total risk premium.

If the direct utility function U does not depend on the state variables Y, and if both U and the optimal consumption function C^* possess the required derivatives, then it follows from applying Ito's formula to the marginal utility of consumption $U_C(C^*)$ that

$$dU_C = [LU_C + U_{Ct}]\,dt + U_{CC}[C^*_W a^{*\prime} GW + C^*_Y S]\,dw(t), \tag{28}$$

where C^*_W is the partial derivative of C^* with respect to W and C^*_Y is a $(1 \times k)$ vector whose ith element is $C^*_{Y_i}$, the partial derivative of C^* with respect to Y_i. If in addition optimal consumption is always positive, then $U_C(C^*)$ always equals J_W. By differentiating (11a) to obtain $J_{WW} = U_{CC} C^*_W$ and $J_{WY_i} = U_{CC} C^*_{Y_i}$ and using (28), we can rewrite the factor risk premiums as

$$\phi_W = \left(\frac{-U_{CC}(C^*)}{U_C(C^*)} \right)(\operatorname{cov} C^*, W), \tag{29}$$

$$\phi_Y = \left(\frac{-U_{CC}(C^*)}{U_C(C^*)} \right)(\operatorname{cov} C^*, Y),$$

where $(\operatorname{cov} C^*, W)$ denotes the covariance of changes in consumption with changes in wealth and $(\operatorname{cov} C^*, Y)$ is defined in a similar way. It then follows that

$$(\beta_i - r)F^i = \left(\frac{-U_{CC}(C^*)}{U_C(C^*)} \right)(\operatorname{cov} C^*, F^i), \tag{30}$$

so the expected excess return on any security is proportional to its covariance with optimal consumption.[17]

Two final observations on Theorem 2 deserve mention. Notice, first, that as preferences tend to risk neutrality over consumption paths all of the factor risk premiums do not vanish. Individuals who are risk neutral over consumption paths would not be neutral to uncertainty about changes in technology, and the factor risk premiums would reflect their desire to hedge away this uncertainty.[18] Second, we could rewrite (20) so that the equilibrium expected rate of return on any contingent claim, or on any active production process, is stated in terms of the equilibrium expected rate of return on other claims or portfolios. In this way

[17] For related observations in other contexts, see Breeden [3] and Brock [4, 5].

[18] We are grateful to Fischer Black for this observation.

one can write an expression for relative rates of return which does not explicitly involve preferences.[19]

3. THE FUNDAMENTAL VALUATION EQUATION AND ITS INTERPRETATION

We can now use the developments of the previous section to give one of the main results of the paper. This is the fundamental valuation equation for contingent claims, stated in the following theorem.

THEOREM 3: *The price of any contingent claim satisfies the partial differential equation*

$$\begin{aligned}(31)\qquad &\tfrac{1}{2}(\text{var } W)F_{WW}+\sum_{i=1}^{k}(\text{cov } W, Y_i)F_{WY_i}+\tfrac{1}{2}\sum_{i=1}^{k}\sum_{j=1}^{k}(\text{cov } Y_i, Y_j)F_{Y_iY_j}\\ &+[r(W,Y,t)W-C^*(W,Y,t)]F_W\\ &+\sum_{i=1}^{k}F_{Y_i}\left[\mu_i-\left(\frac{-J_{WW}}{J_W}\right)(\text{cov } W, Y_i)-\sum_{j=1}^{k}\left(\frac{-J_{WY_j}}{J_W}\right)(\text{cov } Y_i, Y_j)\right]\\ &+F_t-r(W,Y,t)F+\delta(W,Y,t)=0,\end{aligned}$$

where $r(W, Y, t)$ is given from equation (14) *as*

$$r(W,Y,t)=a^{*\prime}\alpha-\left(\frac{-J_{WW}}{J_W}\right)\left(\frac{\text{var } W}{W}\right)-\sum_{i=1}^{k}\left(\frac{-J_{WY_i}}{J_W}\right)\left(\frac{\text{cov } W, Y_i}{W}\right).$$

PROOF: Ito's formula tells us that the drift of $F(W, Y, t)$ is given by

$$\begin{aligned}(32)\qquad \beta F-\delta=&\tfrac{1}{2}(\text{var } W)F_{WW}+\sum_{i=1}^{k}(\text{cov } W, Y_i)F_{WY_i}\\ &+\tfrac{1}{2}\sum_{i=1}^{k}\sum_{j=1}^{k}(\text{cov } Y_i, Y_j)F_{Y_iY_j}\\ &+(a^{*\prime}\alpha W-C^*(W,Y,t))F_W+\sum_{i=1}^{k}\mu_iF_{Y_i}+F_t.\end{aligned}$$

On the other hand, Theorem 2 tells us that in equilibrium, the expected return on F must be

$$\begin{aligned}(33)\qquad \beta F=&rF+F_W\left[\left(\frac{-J_{WW}}{J_W}\right)(\text{var } W)+\sum_{i=1}^{k}\left(\frac{-J_{WY_i}}{J_W}\right)(\text{cov } W, Y_i)\right]\\ &+\sum_{i=1}^{k}F_{Y_i}\left[\left(\frac{-J_{WW}}{J_W}\right)(\text{cov } W, Y_i)+\sum_{j=1}^{k}\left(\frac{-J_{WY_j}}{J_W}\right)(\text{cov } Y_i, Y_j)\right].\end{aligned}$$

Combining (32) and (33) gives (31). *Q.E.D.*

[19] In other contexts, relationships of this kind are given in the static capital asset pricing models of Sharpe [27], Lintner [15], and Mossin [21], in the generalization of these models in Merton [19], in the consumption-based model of Breeden [3], and in the arbitrage model of Ross [25].

The valuation equation (31) holds for any contingent claim. The form of δ and the appropriate terminal and boundary conditions are particular for each claim and are given by the contractual provisions. In general, F is defined on $[t, T) \times Z$, where $Z \subset (0, \infty) \times R^k$ is an open set and ∂Z is its boundary. Let $\hat{\partial} Z$ be the closed subset of ∂Z such that $(W(\tau), Y(\tau)) \in \hat{\partial} Z$ for all $(W(t), Y(t))$, where τ is the time of first passage from Z. That is, $\hat{\partial} Z$ is the set of all accessible boundary points. So (31) holds for all $(s, W(s), Y(s)) \in [t, T) \times Z$, with the contractual provisions determining the boundary information[20]

$$
\begin{aligned}
&F(W(T), Y(T), T) = \Theta(W(T), Y(T)), && W(T), Y(T) \in Z, \\
&F(W(\tau), Y(\tau), \tau) = \Psi(W(\tau), Y(\tau), \tau), && W(\tau), Y(\tau) \in \hat{\partial} Z.
\end{aligned} \tag{34}
$$

In other words, the contingent claim F entitles its owner to receive three types of payments: (i) if the underlying variables do not leave a certain region before the maturity date T, a payment of Θ is received at the maturity date, (ii) if the underlying variables do leave the region before T, at time τ, a payment of Ψ is received at that time, and (iii) a payout flow of δ is received until time T or time τ, whichever is sooner. The boundaries of the region may be specified in the contract or may be chosen by the owner to maximize the value of the claim. All of our results will apply in either case. This formulation thus includes most securities of practical interest.

The existence and uniqueness of a solution to the fundamental valuation equation can be established under some additional regularity conditions.[21] To interpret the solution, consider the following two systems of stochastic differential equations: System I,

$$
\begin{aligned}
dW(t) &= [a^{*\prime}\alpha W - C^*]\, dt + a^{*\prime} G W\, dw(t), \\
dY(t) &= \mu(Y, t)\, dt + S(Y, t)\, dw(t);
\end{aligned} \tag{35a}
$$

and System II,

$$
\begin{aligned}
dW(t) &= [a^{*\prime}\alpha W - \phi_W - C^*]\, dt + a^{*\prime} G W\, dw(t), \\
dY(t) &= [\mu(Y, t) - [\phi_{Y_1} \quad \cdots \quad \phi_{Y_k}]']\, dt + S(Y, t)\, dw(t),
\end{aligned} \tag{35b}
$$

[20] It is important to distinguish between boundary conditions for the contingent claims F and those for the indirect utility function J. The results of the preceding section are unaffected by the boundary conditions which are imposed on any particular claim. However, if Y has accessible boundaries, then conditions will have to be imposed on J at these boundaries. Also, if these boundaries are contained in Z, then the value of F will not necessarily be given by the terms of the contract, and additional conditions on F at these boundaries may have to be determined from further economic considerations. For example, if Y_i can reach an instantaneously reflecting barrier at d, then the absence of arbitrage opportunities will normally require $F_{Y_i}(W, \ldots Y_{i-1}, d, Y_{i+1} \ldots, t) = 0$.

[21] To establish the existence and uniqueness of a solution to (31), we make some additional technical assumptions and continue them throughout the paper. Let Z be bounded and $(0, Y) \notin \bar{Z}$, the closure of Z. Let every point of ∂Z have a barrier, where a barrier $f_y(x)$ at the point $y \in \partial Z$ is a continuous nonnegative function in $\bar{Z}$ that vanishes only at the point y and for which $Lf_y(x) \leq -1$. Also assume: (i) δ is uniformly Hölder continuous on $(W, Y, s) \in \bar{Z} \times [t, T]$, (ii) Θ is continuous on $\bar{Z}$, (iii) Ψ is continuous on $\hat{\partial} Z \times [t, T]$, and (iv) $\Psi(W(T), Y(T), T) = \Theta(W(T), Y(T), T)$ if $(W(T), Y(T)) \in \hat{\partial} Z$. Previous assumptions imply that the coefficients of F and LF are uniformly Lipschitz continuous in $(W, Y, s) \in \bar{Z}$. Then from Friedman [11, p. 138], there exists a unique solution to (31) with boundary conditions (34).

where the processes solving (I) and (II) are defined on the same probability space and start from the same initial position. System (I) describes the actual movement of $W(t)$, $Y(t)$ until the first passage to $W=0$, while System (II) describes the movement of a similar process when the drifts are altered by the factor risk premiums. Assume that the coefficients are extended from $(0,\infty)\times R^k$ into R^{k+1} in any arbitrary way such that the regularity conditions of footnote 4 are satisfied and positive values of W are inaccessible from a nonpositive initial position. Our interest will be limited to the behavior of I and II in Z. Each of the processes j, $j=1, 2$, induces a probability Π_j on (C_T^{k+1}, Q_T), where C_T^{k+1} is the space of continuous functions $f(s)$ from $[t, T]$ into R^{k+1} and Q_T is the σ-algebra generated by the sets $(f(s)\in B)$, where B is any Borel set in R^{k+1} and $s\in[t, T]$.

Systems I and II can be used to give probabilistic interpretations of the solution to the valuation equation (31). These are contained in the following two lemmas.

Lemma 3: *The unique solution to* (31) *with boundary conditions* (34) *is given by*

$$F(W, Y, t, T) = \underset{W,Y,t}{E}\Bigg[\Theta(W(T), Y(T)) \times\left[\exp\left(-\int_t^T \beta(W(u), Y(u), u)\,du\right)\right] I(\tau \geqslant T) + \Psi(W(\tau), Y(\tau), \tau) \times\left[\exp\left(-\int_t^\tau \beta(W(u), Y(u), u)\,du\right)\right] I(\tau < T) + \int_t^{\tau\wedge T} \delta(W(s), Y(s), s) \times\left[\exp\left(-\int_t^s \beta(W(u), Y(u), u)\,du\right)\right] ds\Bigg], \tag{36}$$

where E denotes expectation with respect to System I, $I(\cdot)$ is an indicator function, and τ is the time of first passage to $\hat{\partial}Z$.

Proof: Recall that $LF+F_t+\delta=\beta F$ by Ito's formula and the definition of β, and then use Theorem 5.2 of Friedman [**11**, p. 147].

The expression in (36) clarifies the intuitive idea of discounting with respect to a randomly varying rate of return. However, it does not provide a constructive way of finding F unless the equilibrium expected rate of return, β, of that security is known explicitly in advance. In contrast, the next lemma requires only the interest rate and the factor risk premiums for a constructive solution, and these are common to all securities.

LEMMA 4: *The unique solution to* (31) *with boundary conditions* (34) *is also given by*

$$F(W,Y,t,T)=\hat{E}_{W,Y,t}\Bigg[\Theta(W(T),Y(T))\times\left[\exp\left(-\int_t^T r(W(u),Y(u),u)\,du\right)\right]I(\tau\geq T)$$
$$+\Psi(W(\tau),Y(\tau),\tau)\times\left[\exp\left(-\int_t^\tau r(W(u),Y(u),u)\,du\right)\right]I(\tau<T)$$
$$+\int_t^{\tau\wedge T}\delta(W(s),Y(s),s)\times\left[\exp\left(-\int_t^s r(W(u),Y(u),u)\,du\right)\right]ds\Bigg], \tag{37}$$

where $\hat{E}$ *denotes expectation with respect to System II, and* $I(\cdot)$ *and* τ *are as defined in* (36).

PROOF: Apply Theorem 5.2 of Friedman [**11**, p. 147] to equation (31).

Equation (37) says that the equilibrium price of a claim is given by its expected discounted value, with discounting done at the risk free rate, when the expectation is taken with respect to a risk-adjusted process for wealth and the state variables. The risk adjustment is accomplished by reducing the drift of each underlying variable by the corresponding factor risk premium.

4. THE RELATIONSHIP TO THE ARROW-DEBREU MODEL AND THE ROLE OF FIRMS

The model presented here is consistent with the framework of Arrow [**1**] and Debreu [**8**], and the following theorem verifies that the solution of (31) can be interpreted in terms of marginal-utility-weighted expected values. In the course of its proof, we recall the definition of L from (7) and define χ as the $(k+1)\times 1$ vector

$$\chi'\equiv\left[\left(\frac{-J_{WW}}{J_W}\right)\left(\frac{-J_{WY_1}}{J_W}\right)\cdots\left(\frac{-J_{WY_k}}{J_W}\right)\right]$$

and Σ as the $(k+1)\times(n+k)$ matrix

$$\Sigma\equiv\begin{bmatrix}a^{*\prime}GW\\ \cdot\ \dot{S}\ \cdot\end{bmatrix}.$$

Assume that $E_{W,Y,t}\exp(\lambda|\chi'(s)\Sigma(s)|^2)\leq d$, for some $\lambda>0$, $d>0$, and all s, $t\leq s\leq T$.

THEOREM 4: *The price of any contingent claim is given by*

$$F(W,Y,t,T)=\underset{W,Y,t}{E}\Bigg[\Theta(W(T),Y(T))\times\left(\frac{J_W(W(T),Y(T),T)}{J_W(W(t),Y(t),t)}\right)I(\tau\geqslant T)+\Psi(W(\tau),Y(\tau),\tau)\left(\frac{J_W(W(\tau),Y(\tau),\tau)}{J_W(W(t),Y(t),t)}\right)I(\tau<T)+\int_t^{\tau\wedge T}\delta(W(s),Y(s),s)\left(\frac{J_W(W(s),Y(s),s)}{J_W(W(t),Y(t),t)}\right)ds\Bigg], \tag{38}$$

where, again, E denotes expectation with respect to System I, and $I(\cdot)$ and τ are as defined in (36).

PROOF: By Ito's formula,

$$\left(\frac{J_W(W(s),Y(s),s)}{J_W(W(t),Y(t),t)}\right)=\exp\left[\log J_W(W(s),Y(s),s)-\log J_W(W(t),Y(t),t)\right]=\exp\left[\int_t^s\left(L(\log J_W(u))+\frac{\partial(\log J_W(u))}{\partial t}\right)du+\int_t^s(-\chi'\Sigma)\,dw(u)\right].$$

Now

$$L\log J_W=\left(\frac{1}{J_W}\right)LJ_W-\tfrac{1}{2}(\text{var }W)\left(\frac{-J_{WW}}{J_W}\right)^2-\sum_{i=1}^{k}(\text{cov }W,Y_i)\left(\frac{-J_{WY_i}}{J_W}\right)\left(\frac{-J_{WW}}{J_W}\right)-\tfrac{1}{2}\sum_{i=1}^{k}\sum_{j=1}^{k}(\text{cov }Y_i,Y_j)\left(\frac{-J_{WY_i}}{J_W}\right)\left(\frac{-J_{WY_j}}{J_W}\right)=\left(\frac{1}{J_W}\right)LJ_W-\tfrac{1}{2}\chi'\Sigma\Sigma'\chi=\left(\frac{1}{J_W}\right)LJ_W-\tfrac{1}{2}|\chi'\Sigma|^2.$$

Furthermore, from Theorem 1,

$$\left(\frac{1}{J_W}\right)(LJ_W+J_{W_t})=-r(W,Y,t).$$

Thus the expression

$$\left(\frac{J_W(W(s),Y(s),s)}{J_W(W(t),Y(t),t)}\right)$$

can be written as

$$(39)\quad \left(\frac{J_W(W(s),\,Y(s),\,s)}{J_W(W(t),\,Y(t),\,t)}\right)$$
$$=\left[\exp\left(-\int_t^s r(W(u),\,Y(u),\,u)\,du\right)\right]$$
$$\times\left[\exp\left(\int_t^s(-\chi'\Sigma)\,dw(u)-\tfrac{1}{2}\int_t^s|\chi'\Sigma|^2\,du\right)\right].$$

It then follows directly from Girsanov's theorem as stated in Friedman [**11**, p. 169] that (38) is the same as (37), which was shown to be the solution to (31). *Q.E.D.*

In the context of Arrow and Debreu, $C_{t'}^{k+1}$ is the state space. The state-space pricing system is a measure π, nonnegative but not generally a probability, on $(C_{t'}^{k+1}, Q_{t'})$. π is absolutely continuous with respect to the actual system probability π_1, and the Radon-Nikodym derivative of π with respect to π_1 is $d\pi/d\pi_1 = J_W(s)/J_W(t)$.

Equations (38) and (39) say that the value of any payment is equal to the expectation of the product of its random amount, a time-discount factor, and a risk-adjustment factor. The time-discount factor represents the accumulated effect of locally anticipated percentage changes in the marginal utility of wealth. The risk-adjustment factor in turn captures the accumulated effect of locally unanticipated percentage changes in the marginal utility of wealth, and is thus a martingale. This is suggestive of procedures which make separate sequential adjustments for time and uncertainty, but it does not imply this, since in general neither term can be brought outside the expectation. Another way to state the results is that if values are measured in utility terms, as quantities times the planning price J_W, then all contingent claims are priced so that their expected rate of return over any holding period is equal to zero.

A similar interpretation applies when investment is made through value-maximizing firms. We can without loss of generality consider firms which confine their investment to a single production process. As mentioned earlier, such firms will have an incentive to expand or contract their investments in each process unless the aggregate allocation corresponds to that with direct investment by individuals.

To see this in the context of the valuation equation, consider an aggregate allocation with the proportion of physical wealth invested in each process given by the vector $\bar{a}$. The shares of the firms can be valued in the same way as other contingent claims. However, their net supply will be positive rather than zero. The expected rate of return on the shares of firms in the ith industry, β_i, would then be given by the hypothetical value of α_i which would solve (11c) and (11d) with $a=\bar{a}$. The strict concavity of J implies that this β_i will differ from the actual technologically determined α_i whenever $\bar{a}$ differs from a^*.

The amount of the good held by a firm continually reinvesting its output in the ith process could then be taken as an additional state variable having an expected rate of return of α_i. By applying the valuation equation to this firm, we find that its market value is equal to the physical amount of the good it holds plus the value of a continual payout stream of $\alpha_i - \beta_i$. The market value of a firm will thus differ from the physical amount of the good that it holds whenever $\alpha_i \neq \beta_i$. Consequently, all firms will be in equilibrium, with no incentive to expand or contract their investments, only when $\bar{a} = a^*$.

5. CONCLUDING COMMENTS

In this paper, we have developed a general equilibrium model of a simple but complete economy and used it to study asset prices. One of our principal results was a partial differential equation which asset prices must satisfy. The solution of this equation determines the equilibrium price of a given asset in terms of the underlying real variables in the economy. By combining this solution with probabilistic information about the underlying variables, one can answer a wide variety of questions about the stochastic structure of asset prices.

We have intentionally kept our model as streamlined as possible in order to concentrate on the most important issues. A number of additional features could be added in a straightforward way. For example, we could introduce multiple goods or nonlinear production technologies. As another example, we could examine how the tradeoff between labor and leisure would affect asset prices by including labor in the production function and leisure in the direct utility function.

A further generalization follows from the fact that we are free to introduce state variables which do not affect production opportunities but are nevertheless of interest to individuals. There is no reason why the movement of these additional state variables could not be influenced by individual consumption decisions. Consequently, we could define the state variables as particular functions of past consumption. For example, if we specified $dY_j(t) = C(t)\,dt$, then the change in Y_j over any period would be the integral of consumption over that period. Further flexibility could be obtained by including a state-dependent utility of terminal wealth function, $B(W(t'), Y(t'))$. As a simple example, the specification $U(C(s), Y(s)) = 0$, $B(W(t'), Y(t')) = \gamma Y_j(t')$, and $dY_j(t) = [\gamma \log C(t)]Y_j(t)\,dt$, with γ a constant less than one, would correspond to the multiplicative utility functions studied in Pye [**23**]. In this way, we could introduce many types of intertemporal dependencies in preferences while still maintaining the tractability of our basic model.

Massachusetts Institute of Technology
and
Yale University

Manuscript received September, 1978; revision received October, 1984.

REFERENCES

[1] ARROW, K. J.: "The Role of Securities in the Optimal Allocation of Risk Bearing," *Review of Economic Studies*, 31(1964), 91-96.

[2] BLACK, F., AND M. SCHOLES: "The Pricing of Options and Corporate Liabilities," *Journal of Political Economy*, 81(1973), 637-654.

[3] BREEDEN, D. T.: "An Intertemporal Asset Pricing Model with Stochastic Consumption and Investment Opportunities," *Journal of Financial Economics*, 7(1979), 265-296.

[4] BROCK, W. A.: "An Integration of Stochastic Growth Theory and the Theory of Finance, Part I: The Growth Model," in *General Equilibrium, Growth, and Trade*, ed. by J. R. Green and J. A. Scheinkman. New York: Academic Press, 1979.

[5] ———: "Asset Prices in a Production Economy," in *The Economics of Information and Uncertainty*, ed. by J. J. McCall. Chicago: University of Chicago Press, 1982.

[6] CONSTANTINIDES, G. M.: "Admissible Uncertainty in the Intertemporal Asset Pricing Model," *Journal of Financial Economics*, 8(1980), 71-86.

[7] COX, J. C., J. E. INGERSOLL, JR., AND S. A. ROSS: "A Theory of the Term Structure of Interest Rates," *Econometrica*, 53(1985), 385-407.

[8] DEBREU, G.: *The Theory of Value*. New York: John Wiley, 1959.

[9] DONALDSON, J. B., AND R. MEHRA: "Comparative Dynamics of an Equilibrium Intertemporal Asset Pricing Model," *Review of Economic Studies*, 51(1984), 491-508.

[10] FLEMING, W. H., AND R. W. RISHEL: *Deterministic and Stochastic Optimal Control*. New York: Springer-Verlag, 1975.

[11] FRIEDMAN, A.: *Stochastic Differential Equations and Applications*, Volume 1. New York: Academic Press, 1975.

[12] GIHMAN, I. I., AND A. V. SKOROHOD: *Stochastic Differential Equations*. New York: Springer-Verlag, 1972.

[13] HARRISON, J. M., AND D. M. KREPS: "Martingales and Arbitrage in Multiperiod Securities Markets," *Journal of Economic Theory*, 20(1979), 381-408.

[14] HUANG, C.: "Information Structure and Equilibrium Asset Prices," *Journal of Economic Theory*, forthcoming.

[15] LINTNER, J.: "The Valuation of Risky Assets and the Selection of Risky Investments in Stock Portfolios and Capital Budgets," *Review of Economics and Statistics*, 47(1965), 13-37.

[16] LUCAS, R. E., JR.: "Asset Prices in an Exchange Economy," *Econometrica*, 46(1978), 1426-1446.

[17] MERTON, R. C.: "Optimum Consumption and Portfolio Rules in a Continuous Time Model," *Journal of Economic Theory*, 3(1971), 373-413.

[18] ———: "Rational Theory of Option Pricing," *Bell Journal of Economics and Management Science*, 4(1973), 141-183.

[19] ———: "An Intertemporal Capital Asset Pricing Model," *Econometrica*, 41(1973), 867-887.

[20] ———: "On the Pricing of Contingent Claims and the Modigliani-Miller Theorem," *Journal of Financial Economics*, 5(1977), 241-249.

[21] MOSSIN, J.: "Equilibrium in a Capital Asset Market," *Econometrica*, 34(1966), 768-783.

[22] PRESCOTT, E. C., AND R. MEHRA, "Recursive Competitive Equilibrium: The Case of Homogeneous Households," *Econometrica*, 48(1980), 1365-1379.

[23] PYE, G.: "Lifetime Portfolio Selection in Continuous Time for a Multiplicative Class of Utility Functions," *American Economic Review*, 63(1973), 1013-1016.

[24] RICHARD, S. F., AND M. SUNDARESAN: "A Continuous Time Equilibrium Model of Forward Prices and Futures Prices in a Multigood Economy," *Journal of Financial Economics*, 9(1981), 347-371.

[25] ROSS, S. A.: "The Arbitrage Theory of Capital Asset Pricing," *Journal of Economic Theory*, 13(1976), 341-360.

[26] RUBINSTEIN, M. E.: "The Valuation of Uncertain Income Streams and the Pricing of Options," *Bell Journal of Economics*, 7(1976), 407-425.

[27] SHARPE, W. F.: "Capital Asset Prices: A Theory of Market Equilibrium under Conditions of Risk," *Journal of Finance*, 19(1964), 425-442.

[28] STAPLETON, R. C., AND M. G. SUBRAHMANYAM: "A Multiperiod Equilibrium Asset Pricing Model," *Econometrica*, 46(1978), 1077-1096.

[19]

Journal of Banking and Finance 3 (1979) 133–155. © North-Holland Publishing Company

A CONTINUOUS TIME APPROACH TO THE PRICING OF BONDS

Michael J. BRENNAN and Eduardo S. SCHWARTZ*

University of British Columbia, Vancouver, BC, Canada

This paper develops an arbitrage model of the term structure of interest rates based on the assumptions that the whole term structure at any point in time may be expressed as a function of the yields on the longest and shortest maturity default free instruments and that these two yields follow a Gauss–Wiener process. Arbitrage arguments are used to derive a partial differential equation which must be satisfied by the values of all default free bonds. The joint stochastic process for the two yields is estimated using Canadian data and the model is used to price a sample of Government of Canada bonds.

1. Introduction

A theory of the term structure of interest rates is intended to explain the relative pricing of default free bonds of different maturities. Complete theories of the term structure take as given the exogenous specifications of the economy: tastes, endowments, productive opportunities, and beliefs about possible future states of the world; then the prices of default free bonds of different maturities are derived from these exogenous specifications.[1] However, most extant theories of the term structure are partial equilibrium in nature and take as given beliefs about future realizations of the spot rate of interest, which are combined with simple assumptions about tastes to derive yields to maturity on discount bonds of different maturities.

The theory of the term structure has been cast traditionally in terms of the relationship between the forward rates which are inherent in the term structure and the corresponding expected future spot rates of interest. Thus the typical version of the pure expectations hypothesis asserts that forward rates are equal to expected future spot rates.[2] In contrast to the pure expectations hypothesis stands the liquidity premium hypothesis which

*The authors are grateful to Peter Madderom of the U.B.C. Computing Centre for extensive programming assistance, to R. Solanki for research assistance, and to M. Brenner for helpful comments. Earlier versions of the paper have been presented at seminars at Berkeley, U.C.L.A., the University of Washington and the meetings of the European Finance Association, Bad Homburg, 1977. The authors retain responsibility for remaining errors.

[1]For example, Stiglitz (1970), Rubinstein (1976), and Roll (1970).

[2]It is now realized that this assumption is incompatible with universal risk neutrality, the assumption on which this version of the pure expectations hypothesis is usually based. See Merton (1973), Brennan and Schwartz (1977), Cox, Ingersoll and Ross (1977).

asserts that forward rates always exceed the corresponding expected future spot rates by a liquidity premium, which is required to compensate investors for the greater capital risk inherent in longer-term bonds. The market segmentation hypothesis can be regarded as a modification of the liquidity premium hypothesis to allow for positive or negative liquidity premia on longer-term bonds: this hypothesis recognizes that long-term bonds are not necessarily more risky than short-term bonds for investors who have long-term horizons, so that the prices of bonds of different maturities are determined by the preferences of investors with different horizons, with the result that forward rates may bear no systematic relationship to expected future spot rates. A major limitation of both liquidity premium and market segmentation hypotheses is their lack of specificity: since the relationship of liquidity premium to maturity is not specified, there are as many undetermined parameters in the model as there are bond maturities considered.

More recently it has been recognized that, if assumptions are made about the stochastic evolution of the instantaneous rate of interest in a continuous time model, much richer theories of bond pricing can be derived, which constrain the relationship between the risk premia on bonds of different maturities. Thus Merton (1973), Brennan and Schwartz (1977), and Vasicek (1976) have all assumed that the instantaneous spot rate of interest follows a Gauss–Wiener process. Then the arbitrage arguments, which are familiar from the option pricing literature, may be adduced to show that the prices of riskless bonds of all maturities must obey the same partial differential equation which contains only a single utility-dependent function. Since the whole term structure may be derived by solution of this partial differential equation, it follows that the liquidity premia for all maturities must depend upon this single function.

A significant deficiency of this arbitrage model of the term structure is the unrealism of the assumption about the stochastic process for the interest rate. It is assumed that since the instantaneous interest rate follows a Markov process, all that is known about future interest rates is impounded in the current instantaneous interest rate, so that the value of a default free bond of any maturity may be written as a function of this instantaneous interest rate and time. This implies that, apart from deterministic shifts over time in tastes, the whole term structure of interest rates may be inferred from the current instantaneous interest rate. This is clearly at odds with reality.

In this paper we take a step towards a more realistic approach to the relative pricing of bonds of different maturities by allowing changes in the instantaneous interest rate to depend not only on its current value but also on the long-term rate of interest, so that the long-term rate and the instantaneous rate follow a joint Gauss–Markov process. This expansion of the state space from one rate of interest to two is intended to reflect the assumption, which is the basis of both the pure expectations hypothesis and the liquidity premium hypothesis, that the current long-term rate of interest contains information about future values of the spot rate of interest. It should be clear that the model developed here, viewed simply as a model of the term structure, is less ambitious than the single state variable models referred to above: where they derive the long-term rate of interest, we take it as exogenous and attempt to explain only the intermediate portion of the yield curve in terms of its extremities. On the other hand, we avoid the objectionable implication of the above models that the long rate is a deterministic function of the current instantaneous interest rate. It is anticipated that the major contribution of the model developed here will be for the pricing of interest dependent contingent claims which contain an option element, such as savings bonds, retractable bonds and callable bonds. Then, just as the original Black–Scholes (1973) model determines the price of a call option in terms of the price of the underlying stock, without considering how the price of the underlying stock itself is determined, this model will permit the pricing of interest dependent claims in terms of the two exogenously given interest rates. However, before advancing to the more ambitious task of pricing bonds with an option element, it is useful to evaluate the ability of the model to price straight bonds of different maturities and this is the major objective of this paper: a subsidiary task is the estimation of the utility dependent function in the partial differential equation.

In two contemporaneous papers Richard (1976), and Cox, Ingersoll and Ross (1977) have also developed models of the term structure which incorporate two state variables. While our model takes these as the instantaneous rate and the long-term rate, their models take the state variables as the instantaneous real rate of interest and the rate of inflation, changes in which are assumed to be independent: from these state variables they are able to derive the long-term rate of interest. The advantage of their models then lies in the endogeneity of the long-term rate of interest, but this is obtained at the cost of introducing two utility dependent functions into the partial differential equation for bond prices, which considerably complicates the problems of empirical estimation. Our model avoids the need for one of the utility dependent functions by taking as the second state variable the long-term rate of interest which is inversely proportional to an asset price, the price of the consol bond: the risk associated with this state variable may then be hedged away. Both Richard and Cox, Ingersoll and Ross avoid the estimation problems posed by the two utility dependent functions in the partial differential equation by making explicit assumptions about the tastes of the representative investor: Richard considers both linear and logarithmic utility functions while Cox, Ingersoll and Ross consider only the logarithmic case. We assume that the utility dependent functions are constants and estimate their values from the data at hand.

In the following section the partial differential equation which must be satisfied by the value of any default free discount bond is derived. In section 3 the parameters of the assumed stochastic process for interest rates are estimated using data on Canadian interest rates. Section 4 reports the results of using the model to price a sample of Government of Canada bonds.

2. The pricing equation for discount bonds

Letting r denote the instantaneous rate of interest and l the long-term rate of interest which is taken as the yield on a consol bond which pays coupons continuously, it is assumed that r and l follow a joint stochastic process of the general type,

$$\begin{aligned} dr &= \beta_1(r,l,t)dt + \eta_1(r,l,t)dz_1, \\ dl &= \beta_2(r,l,t)dt + \eta_2(r,l,t)dz_2, \end{aligned} \tag{1}$$

where t denotes calendar time and dz_1 and dz_2 are Wiener processes with $E[dz_1]=E[dz_2]=0$, $dz_1^2=dz_2^2=dt$, $dz_1dz_2=\rho dt$. $\beta_1(.)$ and $\beta_2(.)$ are the expected instantaneous rates of change in the instantaneous and long-term rates of interest respectively, while $\eta_1^2(.)$ and $\eta_2^2(.)$ are the instantaneous variance rates of the changes in the two interest rates. ρ is the instantaneous correlation between the unanticipated changes in the two interest rates. Equation system (1) describes a situation in which changes in the instantaneous and long-term rates of interest are partially interdependent: both the expected change and the variance of the change in each interest rate may depend on the value of the other interest rate as well as on its own value. It is reasonable to suppose that the expected change in the instantaneous rate of interest will depend on the long-term rate of interest insofar as the long-term rate carries information about future values of the instantaneous rate; further, the expected change in the long rate must also depend on the current instantaneous rate if the expected rate of return on consol bonds is to be related to the rate of return on instantaneously riskless securities. In addition, (1) allows the unanticipated changes in the two interest rates to be correlated. While the degree of correlation is an empirical matter which will be addressed below, one may envisage the instantaneous rate changing as expectations of the instantaneous rate of inflation change, while the long rate responds to changing expectations about the long-run rate of inflation: it seems reasonable to suppose that changes in these expectations will be correlated but not perfectly so.

The price of a default free discount bond promising \$1 at maturity is assumed to be a function of the current values of the interest rates, r and l, and time to maturity, τ, which we write as $B(r,l,\tau)$. Applying Itô's Lemma, the stochastic process for the price of a discount bond is

$$dB/B=\mu(r,l,\tau)dt+s_1(r,l,\tau)dz_1+s_2(r,l,\tau)dz_2, \tag{2}$$

where

$$\mu(r,l,\tau)=(B_1\beta_1+B_2\beta_2+\tfrac{1}{2}B_{11}\eta_1^2+\tfrac{1}{2}B_{22}\eta_2^2+B_{12}\rho\eta_1\eta_2-B_3)/B,$$

$$s_1(r,l,\tau)=B_1\,\eta_1/B,$$

$$s_2(r,l,\tau)=B_2\,\eta_2/B,$$

and

$$B_1=\partial B/\partial r,\quad B_2=\partial B/\partial l,\quad B_3=\partial B/\partial\tau\quad\text{etc.}$$

To derive the equilibrium relationship between expected returns on bonds of different maturities, consider forming a portfolio, P, by investing amounts x_1, x_2, x_3 in bonds of maturity τ_1, τ_2, τ_3 respectively. The rate of return on this portfolio is[3]

$$\begin{aligned}dP/P=&[x_1\mu(\tau_1)+x_2\mu(\tau_2)+x_3\mu(\tau_3)]dt\\&+[x_1s_1(\tau_1)+x_2s_1(\tau_2)+x_3s_1(\tau_3)]dz_1\\&+[x_1s_2(\tau_1)+x_2s_2(\tau_2)+x_3s_2(\tau_3)]dz_2.\end{aligned} \tag{3}$$

The rate of return on the portfolio will be non-stochastic if the portfolio proportions are chosen so that the coefficients of dz_1 and dz_2 in (3) are zero. That is, so that

$$\begin{aligned}&x_1s_1(\tau_1)+x_2s_1(\tau_2)+x_3s_1(\tau_3)=0,\\&x_1s_2(\tau_1)+x_2s_2(\tau_2)+x_3s_2(\tau_3)=0.\end{aligned} \tag{4}$$

Then, to avoid the possibility of arbitrage profits, it is necessary that the rate of return on this portfolio be equal to the instantaneous riskless rate of interest, r, so that

$$x_1(\mu(\tau_1)-r)+x_2(\mu(\tau_2)-r)+x_3(\mu(\tau_3)-r)=0. \tag{5}$$

The zero risk conditions (4) and the no arbitrage condition (5) constitute a set of three linear homogeneous equations in the three portfolio proportions. They will possess a solution if and only if

$$\mu(\tau)-r=\lambda_1(r,l,t)s_1(\tau)+\lambda_2(r,l,t)s_2(\tau), \tag{6}$$

[3]The arguments, r and l, are omitted from the functions $\mu(\cdot)$, $s_1(\cdot)$ and $s_2(\cdot)$ for the sake of brevity; they are to be understood.

where the functions $\lambda_1(\cdot)$ and $\lambda_2(\cdot)$ are independent of maturity, τ. Eq. (6) is an equilibrium relationship which constrains the relative risk premia on bonds of different maturities. It expresses the instantaneous risk premium on a discount bond of any maturity as the sum of two elements: these are proportional to the partial covariances of the bond's rate of return with the unanticipated changes in the instantaneous and long term rates of interest, $s_1(\cdot)$ and $s_2(\cdot)$ respectively. $\lambda_1(\cdot)$ and $\lambda_2(\cdot)$ may then be regarded as the market prices of instantaneous and long term interest rate risk and will depend upon the utility functions of market participants. If the expressions for $\mu(\cdot)$, $s_1(\cdot)$ and $s_2(\cdot)$ are substituted in (6) the result will be a partial differential equation for the price of a discount bond, $B(r,l,\tau)$, which will contain the two utility dependent functions $\lambda_1(\cdot)$ and $\lambda_2(\cdot)$.[4] However, by making use of the fact that l is a function of the price of an asset which we assume to be traded, a consol bond, it can be shown[5] that $\lambda_2(\cdot)$ is given by

$$\lambda_2(r,l,t) = -\eta_2/l + (\beta_2 - l^2 + rl)/\eta_2. \tag{7}$$

Eq. (7) expresses $\lambda_2(\cdot)$ in terms of the two rates of interest and the parameters of the stochastic process for the long-term rate of interest. It therefore enables us to eliminate this utility dependent function from the partial differential equation for the price of a discount bond, so that substitution in the equilibrium relationship (6) of the expressions for $\mu(\tau)$, $s_1(\tau)$ and $s_2(\tau)$, and use of eq. (7) to eliminate $\lambda_2(\cdot)$, permits us to re-write the equilibrium relationship (6) as the partial differential equation

$$\begin{aligned}&\tfrac{1}{2}B_{11}\eta_1^2 + B_{12}\rho\eta_1\eta_2 + \tfrac{1}{2}B_{22}\eta_2^2 \\ &+ B_1(\beta_1 - \lambda_1\eta_1) + B_2(\eta_2^2/l^2 + l^2 - rl) - B_3 - Br = 0.\end{aligned} \tag{8}$$

Given the stochastic process (1) for the two interest rates r and l, (8) is the basic partial differential equation for the pricing of default free discount bonds. This equation, together with the boundary condition specifying the payment to be received at maturity, say $B(r,l,0)=1$, may be solved to yield the prices of discount bonds of all maturities from which the whole term structure of interest rates may be inferred. The term structure at any point in time will depend upon the current values of the state variables r and l, as well as upon the unknown function $\lambda_1(\cdot)$. The prices of regular coupon bonds may be obtained by treating them as portfolios of discount bonds; alternatively, if coupons are paid continuously at the rate c, then c should be added to the left-hand side of the partial differential eq. (8). In addition, this

[4]This would be identical to the partial differential equation obtained by Richard (1976) if the variable l is interpreted as the rate of inflation rather than as the long term rate of interest.

[5]See appendix.

equation is valid for all types of default free interest dependent claims, so that it may be applied for example to the pricing of saving bonds or callable bonds by the introduction of the appropriate boundary conditions defining the payoffs on the claims.

It is interesting to note that the partial differential equation is not only independent of $\lambda_2(\cdot)$, the market price of long-term interest rate risk, it is also independent of $\beta_2(\cdot)$, the drift parameter for the long term interest rate, so that the solution is independent of the expected rate of return on the consol bond. This result is analogous to the finding within the simple Black–Scholes (1973) model for the pricing of stock options that the function expressing the equilibrium price of the option in terms of the price of the underlying stock is independent of the expected rate of return on the underlying stock. The reason for the two results is the same: there exists an asset for which the partial derivatives of its value with respect to all of the state variables is known: in this case the consol bond, and in the Black–Scholes case the stock. It can be shown that in general the number of unknown utility dependent parameters left in the partial differential equation will be equal to the number of state variables, excluding time, less the number of assets for which the partial derivatives of the value function are known: in the Black–Scholes case this is zero and in the present case it is one. The time variable is excluded since the pure reward for the passage of time is equal to the interest rate. This proposition is illustrated more formally in the appendix.

The coefficients of the partial differential eq. (8) are the utility dependent function, $\lambda_1(\cdot)$, and the parameters of the underlying stochastic process for the two interest rates, (1). Empirical application of the model requires that the parameters of this stochastic process be estimated and this is taken up in the next section.

3. Estimation of the stochastic process

3.1. *The form of the stochastic process*

Estimation of the stochastic process for interest rates (1) presupposes some stronger assumptions about the form of the process than we have made hitherto. The first restriction comes from the requirement that the excess of the expected rate of return on the consol bond over the instantaneous rate of interest be commensurate with the degree of long-term interest rate risk of the consol. This requirement is expressed in eq. (7): solving this equation for $\beta_2(\cdot)$, we find

$$\beta_2(r,l,t)=l^2-rl+\eta_2^2/l+\lambda_2\eta_2. \qquad (9)$$

For empirical tractability it is assumed that $\lambda_2(\cdot)$, the market price of long-term interest rate risk, is constant.

The only other a priori restrictions which can be imposed on the stochastic process derive from the requirement that dominance by money be avoided, so that neither of the interest rates can be allowed to become negative. This possibility is avoided by assuming that

$$\eta_1(r,l,t)=r\sigma_1, \qquad \eta_2(r,l,t)=l\sigma_2, \tag{10}$$

and requiring that

$$\beta_1(r,l,t)\geqq 0. \tag{11}$$

Eqs. (10) and (11) jointly imply that $\beta_2(r,l,t)\geqq 0$. Eq. (10) specifies that the standard deviation of the instantaneous change in each interest rate is proportional to its current level.

To reflect the premise that the long-term rate contains information about future values of the instantaneous rate, it is assumed that the instantaneous rate stochastically regresses towards a function of the current long-term rate. This assumption and conditions (10) and (11) are satisfied by taking as the stochastic process for the logarithm of the instantaneous rate

$$\mathrm{d}\ln r=\alpha[\ln l-\ln p-\ln r]\mathrm{d}t+\sigma_1\mathrm{d}z_1, \tag{12}$$

which is equivalent to the assumptions that

$$\beta_1(r,l,t)=r[\alpha\ln(l/pr)+\tfrac{1}{2}\sigma_1^2], \tag{13}$$

$$\eta_1(r,l,t)=r\sigma_1. \tag{14}$$

The coefficient α represents the speed of adjustment of the logarithm of the instantaneous rate towards its current target value, $\ln(l/p)$, and p is a parameter relating the target value of $\ln r$ to the current value of $\ln l$.

Finally substituting for $\beta_2(\cdot)$ and $\eta_2(\cdot)$ from (9) and (10) in eq. (1), the stochastic process for the long-term rate of interest is

$$\mathrm{d}l=l[l-r+\sigma_2^2+\lambda_2\sigma_2]\mathrm{d}t+l\sigma_2\mathrm{d}z_2. \tag{15}$$

3.2. The linearized form of the stochastic process

Eqs. (12) and (15) constitute a non-linear system of stochastic differential equations governing the behaviour of the two interest rates. In order to estimate the system it is necessary first to linearize it, and to this end we approximate l and r by linear functions of $\ln l$ and $\ln r$. Thus, writing l and r

as functions of $\ln l$ and $\ln r$, and expanding in Taylor series about the mean sample values, $e^{\overline{\ln l}}$ and $e^{\overline{\ln r}}$,

$$l-r=e^{\overline{\ln l}}-e^{\overline{\ln r}}$$
$$\approx e^{\overline{\ln l}}(1-\overline{\ln l})-e^{\overline{\ln r}}(1-\overline{\ln r})+e^{\overline{\ln l}}\ln l-e^{\overline{\ln r}}\ln r. \qquad (16)$$

Then using Itô's Lemma to obtain the stochastic process for $\ln l$ from (15), and substituting for $(l-r)$ from (16), the linearized stochastic differential equation for the logarithm of the long-term rate may be written as

$$\mathrm{d}\ln l=[q-k_1\ln r+k_2\ln l]\mathrm{d}t+\sigma_2\mathrm{d}z_2, \qquad (17)$$

where

$$q=e^{\overline{\ln l}}(1-\overline{\ln l})-e^{\overline{\ln r}}(1-\overline{\ln r})+\tfrac{1}{2}\sigma_2^2+\lambda_2\sigma_2,$$

while we may write the stochastic differential equation for the logarithm of the instantaneous rate as

$$\mathrm{d}\ln r=\alpha[\ln l-\ln r-\ln p]\mathrm{d}t+\sigma_1\mathrm{d}z_1. \qquad (18)$$

This linearized system of stochastic differential equations for the logarithms of the two interest rates is written in matrix notation as

$$\mathrm{d}y(t)=Ay(t)\mathrm{d}t+b\mathrm{d}t+\mathrm{d}\xi(t), \qquad (19)$$

where

$$y(t)=\begin{pmatrix}\ln r(t)\\ \ln l(t)\end{pmatrix},\qquad d\xi(t)=\begin{pmatrix}\sigma_1\,\mathrm{d}z_1(t)\\ \sigma_2\,\mathrm{d}z_2(t)\end{pmatrix},$$

$$A=\begin{pmatrix}-\alpha & \alpha\\ -k_1 & k_2\end{pmatrix},\qquad b=\begin{pmatrix}-\alpha\ln p\\ q\end{pmatrix}.$$

3.3. *The exact discrete model*

While (19) is a system of linear stochastic differential equations, the data on interest rates which are required to estimate it are available only at discrete intervals. One approach to estimation when there are prior restrictions on the parameters[6] has been proposed by Bergstrom (1966). This involves first substituting finite differences for differentials and averages of beginning and end of period values for the time dated vector $y(t)$, and then

[6] k_1 and k_2 are known and the coefficients of the two variables in the first equation are known to be equal in magnitude but opposite signs.

estimating the resulting linear equations by standard simultaneous equations methods. Unfortunately, as Phillips (1972) points out, the undesirable feature of this approach is the specification error which causes the resulting parameter estimates to be asymptotically biased. A more efficient and elegant procedure is to obtain the exact discrete model corresponding to (19) and to estimate the parameters from this model.

The exact discrete model corresponding to (19) is[7]

$$y(t)=e^{A}y(t-1)+A^{-1}[e^{A}-I]b+\zeta(t), \tag{20}$$

where

$$\zeta(t)=\int_{t-1}^{t} e^{(t-s)A}\,\mathrm{d}\xi(s),$$

and the variance covariance matrix of errors is

$$E[\zeta(t)\zeta'(t)]=\int_{0}^{1} e^{sA}\Sigma e^{sA'}\,\mathrm{d}s, \tag{21}$$

where Σ is the instantaneous variance-covariance matrix with elements σ_1^2, σ_2^2, $\rho\sigma_1\sigma_2$.[8]

The matrix e^{A} is defined by

$$e^{A}\equiv Te^{\Lambda}T^{-1}, \tag{22}$$

where

$$e^{\Lambda}=\begin{pmatrix} e^{v_1} & 0 \\ 0 & e^{v_2}\end{pmatrix},$$

and v_1 and v_2 are the characteristic roots of the matrix A, while T is the matrix of characteristic vectors. In this case the characteristic roots are

$$\begin{aligned} v_1&=(k_2-\alpha+\sqrt{(k_2-\alpha)^2-4(k_1-k_2)})/2,\\ v_2&=(k_2-\alpha-\sqrt{(k_2-\alpha)^2-4(k_1-k_2)})/2, \end{aligned} \tag{23}$$

and the matrix of characteristic vectors is

$$T\equiv\begin{pmatrix} 1 & 1 \\ \dfrac{k_1}{k_2-v_1} & \dfrac{k_1}{k_2-v_2}\end{pmatrix}. \tag{24}$$

[7]See Bergstrom (1966), Phillips (1972), Wymer (1972).

[8]It can be shown that $\int_0^1 e^{sA}\Sigma e^{sA'}\mathrm{d}s\approx\Sigma$, so that the variance covariance matrix of errors from (20) provides good estimates of σ_1,σ_2 and $\sigma_{12}=\rho\sigma_1\sigma_2$.

Inverting A and carrying out the appropriate matrix multiplications in (20) the exact discrete model to be estimated is

$$\begin{aligned}
y_1(t) = {} & \frac{1}{v_1 - v_2}\left[e^{v_2}(k_2 - v_2) - e^{v_1}(k_2 - v_1)\right] y_1(t-1) \\
& + \frac{1}{k_1(v_1 - v_2)}\left[(k_2 - v_1)(k_2 - v_2)(e^{v_1} - e^{v_2})\right] y_2(t-1) \\
& + \frac{1}{(k_1 - k_2)(v_1 - v_2)}\{\ln p[k_2[e^{v_1}(k_2 - v_1) - e^{v_2}(k_2 - v_2) + v_1 - v_2] \\
& - \alpha k_1(e^{v_1} - e^{v_2})] + q[k_2(k_2 - v_1)(k_2 - v_2)(e^{v_1} - e^{v_2})/\alpha k_1 \\
& - e^{v_1}(k_2 - v_2) + e^{v_2}(k_2 - v_1) + v_1 - v_2]\} + \zeta_1(t).
\end{aligned} \tag{25}$$

$$\begin{aligned}
y_2(t) = {} & \frac{k_1}{v_1 - v_2}(e^{v_2} - e^{v_1}) y_1(t-1) + \frac{1}{v_1 - v_2}\left[e^{v_1}(k_2 - v_2) - e^{v_2}(k_2 - v_1)\right] y_2(t-1) \\
& + \frac{1}{(k_1 - k_2)(v_1 - v_2)}\{\ln p[k_1[e^{v_1}(k_2 - v_1) - e^{v_2}(k_2 - v_2) + v_1 - v_2] \\
& - \alpha k_1(e^{v_1} - e^{v_2})] + q[(k_2 - v_1)(k_2 - v_2)(e^{v_1} - e^{v_2})/\alpha \\
& - e^{v_1}(k_2 - v_2) + e^{v_2}(k_2 - v_1) + v_1 - v_2]\} + \zeta_2(t).
\end{aligned} \tag{26}$$

Summarizing the analysis to this point, the system of stochastic differential equations (1) was first specialized by assuming that the standard deviation of the unanticipated instantaneous changes in each interest rate is proportional to the current level of that rate (10); by requiring that the instantaneous expected rate of return on a consol bond be commensurate with its degree of long-term interest rate risk (9), where $\lambda_2(\cdot)$, the market price of long-term interest rate risk, is taken as constant; and by requiring that the logarithm of the instantaneous interest rate stochastically regress towards a target value which depends on the current value of the long-term rate (12). The resulting system of stochastic differential equations, (12) and (15), was then linearized to yield the system (19), where $y_1(t)$ and $y_2(t)$ are the logarithms of the instantaneous rate and the long-term rate respectively. Finally, since the equation system is to be estimated using data on r and l at discrete time intervals, the exact discrete model, (25) and (26), corresponding to the linearized form (19) was found.

3.4. *Empirical results*

The three coefficients of the equation system (25), (26) to be estimated are α, $\ln p$ and q. In addition we require an estimate of the variance-covariance matrix Σ, since the elements of this matrix appear as coefficients in the partial differential eq. (8) for the value of a bond. The estimation was carried out using a non-linear procedure described by Malinvaud (1966) and employed by Phillips (1972) in a similar context. The data for the instantaneous rate of interest were the yields on 30-day Canadian Bankers' Acceptances converted to an equivalent continuously compounded annual rate of interest, while the long-term rate of interest was the continuously compounded equivalent of the average yields to maturity on Government of Canada bonds with maturities in excess of 10 years. Both interest rates series are mid-market closing rates on the last Wednesday of each month from January 1964 to December 1976.[9]

The estimated equation system is

$$\begin{aligned} \mathrm{d}\ln r &= \underset{(0.0050)}{0.0701}[\ln l/r - \underset{(0.0050)}{0.0599}]dt + 0.0736\,\mathrm{d}z_1, \\ \mathrm{d}\ln l &= [\underset{(0.0020)}{0.0060} - 0.0051\ln r + 0.0058\ln l]\mathrm{d}t + 0.0250\,\mathrm{d}z_2, \end{aligned}$$

where the standard errors of the estimated coefficient are in parentheses and the coefficients of $-\ln r$ and $\ln l$ are the computed values of k_1 and k_2. The estimated correlation between the errors in the two equations, ρ, is 0.3747, and the adjustment coefficient of 0.0701 in the first equation implies that half of the adjustment in the instantaneous rate occurs within 10 months.

In terms of the coefficients of the basic partial differential eq. (8) for the pricing of discount bonds, the parameter estimates imply

$$\begin{aligned} &\eta_1 \equiv r\sigma_1 = 0.0736\,r, \quad \eta_2 \equiv l\sigma_2 = 0.0250\,l, \quad \rho = 0.3747, \\ &\beta_1(r,l,t) = r[\alpha\ln(l/pr) + \tfrac{1}{2}\sigma_1^2] \\ &\qquad = r[0.0701(\ln l/r - 0.0599) + \tfrac{1}{2}(0.0736^2)]. \end{aligned}$$

4. Bond pricing and the term structure of interest rates

Re-writing the partial differential eq. (8) to take account of the specific stochastic process for r and l assumed in the previous section, we have, substituting for $\beta_1(\cdot)$, $\eta_1(\cdot)$ and $\eta_2(\cdot)$,

$$\begin{aligned} &\tfrac{1}{2}B_{11}r^2\sigma_1^2 + B_{12}rl\rho\sigma_1\sigma_2 + \tfrac{1}{2}B_{22}l^2\sigma_2^2 \\ &+ B_1 r[\alpha\ln(l/pr) + \tfrac{1}{2}\sigma_1^2 - \lambda_1\sigma_1] + B_2 l[\sigma_2^2 + l - r] - B_3 - Br = 0. \end{aligned} \tag{27}$$

[9]Taken from the Bank of Canada Review, Cansim Series 2560.33 and 2560.13.

Then the value of a discount bond promising \$1 at maturity, $\tau=0$, is given by the solution to eq. (27) subject to the boundary condition

$$B(r,l,0)=1. \tag{28}$$

Using the values of α, $\ln p$, ρ, σ_1 and σ_2 estimated in section 3, eq. (27) with boundary condition (28) was solved[10] for values of λ_1, the market price of instantaneous interest rate risk, of -0.04, 0.0, 0.09. The resulting values of $B(r,l,\tau)$ are present value factors: for a given value of $\lambda_1, B(r,l,\tau)$ is the present value of \$1 payable with certainty in τ periods when the instantaneous and long-term rates of interest are r and l respectively.

A sample of 101 Government of Canada bonds was priced using the present value factors computed for each of the three values of λ_1. The bonds were priced on the last Wednesday of each quarter from January 1964 to January 1977 by applying the present value factors appropriate to the prevailing instantaneous and long-term rates of interest to the promised coupon and principal payments for each bond. The sample includes all Government of Canada bonds with maturities less than 10 years for which prices were available in the Bank of Canada Quarterly Review and which were neither callable nor exchangeable. The root mean square price prediction error was calculated for each of the three values of λ_1, and quadratic interpolation was used to estimate the value of λ_1 which minimizes the root mean square prediction error.[11] This estimated value of λ_1 was 0.0355 and the bonds were then priced for this value of λ_1.

In addition, for each of the four values of λ_1, yields to maturity were calculated based on the predicted bond values each quarter and these predicted yields to maturity were compared with the actual yields to maturity. The comparison of actual and predicted bond values and yields to maturity is reported, for each value of λ_1, in table 1: in this table all bonds are treated as having a par value of 100. Thus for the estimated value of $\lambda_1 = 0.0355$, the root mean square prediction error for bond prices is 1.56 and the mean error is -0.17. For the same value of λ_1, the root mean square prediction error for yields to maturity is 0.67% and the mean error is 0.24%. It is to be anticipated that the model will be less successful in predicting yields to maturity than in predicting bond prices, since a small error in the predicted bond price will cause a very large error in the predicted yield to maturity for short dated bonds.

[10]The solution procedure is described in the appendix.

[11]That is, a quadratic curve was fitted to the three pairs of RMSE and λ_1, and the RMSE minimizing value of λ_1 was computed. When the bonds were priced using this value of λ_1 the RMSE agreed with the interpolated value. This non-linear estimation procedure leads to a maximum likelihood estimator under the usual assumption of normal, independent, homoscedastic errors. A more efficient estimator which would allow for a generalized error structure was contemplated but ruled out on the basis of computational cost.

For both bond prices and yields to maturity, the actual values were regressed on the predicted values and the resulting regression statistics are reported in table 1 also. For unbiased predictions the intercept term (α) should be zero, and the slope coefficient (β) should be equal to unity. The actual slope coefficients for $\lambda_1 = 0.0355$ are 0.93 for bond prices and 0.79 for yields to maturity. While these regression results should be treated with caution since there is no assurance that the errors are either independent or normally distributed, it is encouraging to observe that there is a strong, though certainly not perfect, correspondence between the actual and predicted values.

Tables 2 and 3 report the results of predicting bond values and yields to maturity for the last Wednesday of each January from 1964 to 1977. These results are representative of those obtained for the other quarters for which predictions were made. While there is reasonable stability in the relationship between actual and predicted bond values, the relationship between actual and predicted yields to maturity is much more erratic. This reflects the greater difficulty in predicting this variable, referred to above, and also suggests that there are factors which are not encompassed in our model which determine the shape of the term structure.

Table 1

Predicted and actual bond prices and yields to maturity for alternative values of λ_1 (t-ratios in parentheses).

	Values of λ_1			
	−0.04	0.0	0.0355	0.09
Bond prices				
RMSE	1.95	1.65	1.56	1.74
Mean error	−1.05	−0.59	−0.17	0.41
α	13.44 (21.44)	10.01 (15.40)	7.28 (10.46)	4.12 (5.04)
β	0.87 (134.04)	0.90 (134.44)	0.93 (129.57)	0.95 (114.23)
R^2	0.93	0.93	0.93	0.91
Yields to maturity				
RMSE (%)	0.81	0.72	0.67	0.64
Mean error (%)	0.52	0.37	0.24	0.06
α (%)	1.12 (18.40)	1.15 (18.24)	1.18 (18.23)	1.25 (18.40)
β	0.77 (90.63)	0.78 (87.61)	0.79 (84.44)	0.80 (79.56)
R^2	0.86	0.86	0.85	0.83

Table 2

Predicted and actual bond prices by period for $\lambda_1 = 0.0355$ (α, β are the coefficients from the regression of actual values on predicted values).

Year (last Wednesday of January)	No. of observations	RMSE	Mean error (pred.–actual)	α (*T-stat.*)	β (*T-stat*)	R^2	Instantaneous interest rate	Long-term interest rate
1964	17	1.09	0.61	4.62 (0.43)	0.95 (8.68)	0.82	3.69%	5.17%
1965	16	1.04	0.39	23.29 (2.91)	0.76 (9.59)	0.86	3.81	4.69
1966	20	2.15	1.63	37.75 (3.24)	0.61 (5.23)	0.59	4.00	5.41
1967	21	0.91	−0.58	9.49 (1.10)	0.91 (10.44)	0.84	5.85	5.60
1968	22	1.64	0.93	−37.57 (−4.60)	1.38 (16.38)	0.93	6.40	6.54
1969	28	0.97	0.46	−14.97 (−3.53)	1.15 (26.39)	0.96	6.60	7.16
1970	31	1.06	0.07	−10.98 (−5.52)	1.11 (53.39)	0.99	8.90	8.31
1971	30	2.01	−1.61	−0.45 (−0.10)	1.02 (22.66)	0.95	6.00	6.67
1972	32	1.36	0.43	−7.84 (−1.67)	1.07 (23.17)	0.95	3.95	6.73
1973	28	0.46	−0.06	−0.22 (−0.13)	1.00 (59.39)	0.99	4.75	7.16
1974	24	1.95	−1.84	2.42 (1.19)	0.99 (46.00)	0.99	8.75	7.75
1975	22	3.37	−2.84	17.04 (3.32)	0.85 (15.86)	0.92	7.00	8.30
1976	22	1.71	−1.44	5.32 (2.02)	0.96 (33.76)	0.98	9.00	9.29
1977	16	0.99	−0.94	3.70 (1.18)	0.97 (30.88)	0.98	8.33	9.09

Table 3

Predicted and actual yields to maturity by period for $\lambda_1 = 0.0355$ (α, β are the coefficients from regression of actual values on predicted values).

Year (last Wednesday of January)	No. of observations	RMSE	Mean error (pred.–actual)	α (T-stat.)	β (T-stat.)	R^2	Instantaneous interest rate	Long-term interest rate
1964	17	0.21%	−0.16%	−1.56 (−2.86)	1.40 (11.05)	0.88	3.69%	5.17%
1965	16	0.25	0.01	−5.26 (−6.13)	2.22 (11.15)	0.89	3.81	4.69
1966	20	0.53	−0.50	−1.52 (−2.06)	1.44 (9.02)	0.81	4.00	5.41
1967	21	0.64	0.50	13.93 (10.38)	−1.57 (−6.58)	0.68	5.85	5.60
1968	22	0.39	−0.12	35.38 (5.09)	−4.54 (−4.16)	0.45	6.40	6.54
1969	28	0.24	−0.06	−27.45 (−8.36)	5.05 (10.44)	0.80	6.60	7.16
1970	31	0.79	0.42	16.66 (11.44)	−1.00 (−5.88)	0.54	8.90	8.31
1971	30	0.85	0.76	−18.70 (−4.40)	3.86 (5.70)	0.53	6.00	6.67
1972	32	0.35	−0.04	−0.66 (−0.95)	1.13 (8.69)	0.71	3.95	6.73
1973	28	0.20	0.05	−0.48 (−1.24)	1.07 (16.64)	0.91	4.75	7.16
1974	24	1.20	1.04	11.04 (14.58)	−0.51 (−5.37)	0.56	8.75	7.75
1975	22	1.11	1.05	2.52 (0.98)	0.53 (1.57)	0.10	7.00	8.30
1976	22	0.75	0.68	6.80 (0.88)	0.17 (0.198)	0.00	9.00	9.29
1977	16	0.52	0.49	7.55 (1.35)	0.04 (0.06)	0.00	8.33	9.09

One factor which has been neglected in the model developed in this paper is the role of income taxes and their differential impact on coupon income and capital gains. To test whether income taxes cause the coupon stream of a bond to be valued less highly than the principal repayment at maturity, the predicted value of the principal payment was subtracted from the actual bond price and the difference was regressed on the predicted value of the coupon stream. If income taxes are important in the pricing of bonds, the resulting regression coefficient should be less than unity, the difference between unity and the estimated regression coefficient measuring the effective tax rate on coupon income. The regression results are reported in table 4 for the different values of λ_1. The evidence presented in this table suggests that the effect of income taxes is slight: for the estimated value of $\lambda_1 = 0.0355$, the estimated tax rate is only 4 %, and even for $\lambda_1 = 0.09$ the estimated tax rate is only 8 %.

Table 4

The influence of taxes on bond prices: (bond price − predicted value of principal) $= \alpha + \beta$ (predicted value of coupons).

	Values of λ_1			
	−0.04	0.0	0.0355	0.09
α	0.62 (8.03)	0.67 (9.11)	0.71 (10.04)	0.78 (11.28)
β	1.03 (249.33)	0.99 (254.09)	0.96 (256.38)	0.92 (256.24)
R^2	0.98	0.98	0.98	0.98

5. Conclusion

In this paper we have developed a theory of the term structure of interest rates based on the assumption that the value of all default free discount bonds may be written as a function of time and two interest rates, the instantaneous rate and the long-term rate, which follow a joint Markov process in continuous time. This assumption permitted us to derive in section 2 a partial differential equation which must be satisfied by the values of all default free discount bonds. The partial differential equation contains two utility dependent functions, $\lambda_1(\cdot)$ and $\lambda_2(\cdot)$, but $\lambda_2(\cdot)$ was eliminated by making use of the assumption that there exists a traded asset, a consol bond, which corresponds to one of the state variables, the long-term rate of interest.

In section 3 the stochastic process for the two interest rates was specialized and estimated using data on Canadian interest rates. The partial differential equation was then solved using the estimated parameters and selected values for the market price of instantaneous interest rate risk, λ_1, to find the value of λ_1 which minimized the price prediction errors for a sample of Canadian government bonds, and the predictive ability of the model was evaluated: the root mean square prediction error for bond prices was of the order of 1.5%.

It is anticipated that models of this type will have application in the management of bond portfolios and studies of the efficiency of bond markets. Perhaps the most interesting application is to the pricing of bonds which contain an option such as callable bonds and saving bonds. The latter are default free securities allowing the holder the right of redemption prior to maturity at a predetermined series of redemption prices. While instruments of this type are common in North America and several European countries, including France, Germany, Italy and the United Kingdom, they have received virtually no attention to date from financial economists. Work is currently in progress to apply the model developed in this paper to Canadian savings bonds.

This model should be seen as a first step in the application of a new approach to the term structure of interest rates and the pricing of default free securities. Further work is required on the specification and estimation of both the stochastic process for the interest rates and the market price of interest rate risk.

Appendix

A.1. The market price of long-term interest rate risk, $\lambda_2(r,l,t)$

It is shown here that if there exists a consol bond, the utility dependent market price of long-term interest rate risk may be expressed in terms of the two interest rates and the parameters of the stochastic process for the long-term rate of interest. Let $V(l)$ denote the price of a consol bond paying a continuous coupon at the rate of $1 per period. Then the long-term rate of interest is defined by

$$V(l)=l^{-1}, \tag{29}$$

so that, applying Itô's Lemma, the stochastic process for the price of a consol bond is

$$\mathrm{d}V/V=(\eta_2^2/l^2-\beta_2/l)\mathrm{d}t-(\eta_2/l)\mathrm{d}z_2. \tag{30}$$

Then, defining $s_1(\infty)$ and $s_2(\infty)$ as the partial covariances of the consol's bond's rate of return with the unanticipated changes in the two interest rates, it follows from eq. (30) that $s_1(\infty)=0$, $s_2(\infty)=-\eta_2/l$. Further, defining $\mu(\infty)$

as the expected instantaneous rate of return on the consol bond including both the expected capital gain which is obtained from (30) and the rate of coupon payment per dollar of principal,

$$\mu(\infty)=\eta_2^2/l^2-\beta_2/l+l. \tag{31}$$

Now the expected rate of return on the consol bond must also satisfy the equilibrium risk premium equation, (6), so that substituting in this equation for $\mu(\infty)$, $s_1(\infty)$ and $s_2(\infty)$ and solving for $\lambda_2(\cdot)$, we obtain

$$\lambda_2(r,l,t)=-\eta_2/l+(\beta_2-l^2+rl)/\eta_2, \tag{32}$$

which is eq. (7) of the text.

A.2. Asset prices and state variables

This section illustrates for eq. (6) that the number of utility dependent functions left in the partial differential equation is equal to the number of state variables, excluding time, less the number of assets for which the partial derivatives of the value functions are known. Substitute in the equilibrium condition (6) the expressions for $\mu(\cdot)$, $s_1(\cdot)$ and $s_2(\cdot)$ to obtain

$$\begin{aligned}&B_1\beta_1+B_2\beta_2+\tfrac{1}{2}B_{11}\eta_1^2+\tfrac{1}{2}B_{22}\eta_2^2+B_{12}\rho\eta_1\eta_2-B_3-rB\\&=\lambda_1B_1\eta_1+\lambda_2B_2\eta_2.\end{aligned} \tag{33}$$

Now suppose that there exists an asset with value G, all of whose partial derivatives with respect to the state variables are known. The value of the asset must also satisfy the same partial differential equation,

$$\begin{aligned}&G_1\beta_1+G_2\beta_2+\tfrac{1}{2}G_{11}\eta_1^2G_{22}\eta_2^2+G_{12}\rho\eta_1\eta_2-G_3-rG\\&=\lambda_1G_1\eta_1+\lambda_2G_2\eta_2.\end{aligned} \tag{34}$$

Then to eliminate λ_2 and β_2 eq. (34) is multiplied by B_2/G_2 and subtracted from (33) to yield

$$\begin{aligned}&(B_1-B_2G_1/G_2)\beta_1+\tfrac{1}{2}(B_{11}-B_2G_{11}/G_2)\eta_1^2\\&+\tfrac{1}{2}(B_{22}-B_2G_{22}/G_2)\eta_2^2+(B_{12}-B_2G_{12}/G_2)\rho\eta_1\eta_2\\&-(B_3-B_2G_3/G_2)-r(B-B_2G/G_2)\\&=\lambda_1(B_1-B_2G_1/G_2)\eta_1.\end{aligned} \tag{35}$$

Since G and all of its partial derivatives are known functions, (35) contains only a single utility dependent function, $\lambda_1(\cdot)$, and the drift parameter for the corresponding state variable, β_1. If G is the consol bond, then substitution of the appropriate partial derivatives in (35) will yield our partial differential eq. (8). It should be clear that if G_1 were not zero, it would have been possible to eliminate λ_1 and β_1 instead of λ_2 and β_2, and that if a second distinct asset exists whose partial derivatives are known it will be possible to eliminate all four parameters.

A.3. Solution of the partial differential equation

Since there is no known analytic solution to the differential eq. (27) we apply a finite difference solution procedure. This requires that the equation be transformed to take advantage of the natural boundary conditions which occur as the interest rates approach zero and infinity.

To transform the equation, define the new state variables u_1 and u_2 where[12]

$$u_1 = 1/(1+nr), \quad u_2 = 1/(1+nl),$$

and let $B(r,l,\tau) \equiv b(u_1,u_2,\tau)$.

Writing the partial derivatives of $B(\cdot)$ in terms of those of $b(\cdot)$, we have

$$\begin{aligned}
B_1 &= -nu_1^2 b_1, \quad B_2 = -nu_2^2 b_2, \\
B_{11} &= n^2u_1^4 b_{11} + 2n^2u_1^3 b_1, \quad B_{22} = n^2u_2^4 b_{22} + 2n^2u_2^3 b_2, \\
B_3 &= b_3.
\end{aligned}$$

Substituting for r, l and the derivatives of $B(\cdot)$ in (27), we obtain the transformed equation

$$\begin{aligned}
&\tfrac{1}{2}b_{11}u_1^2(1-u_1^2)\sigma_1^2 + b_{12}u_1u_2(1-u_1)(1-u_2)\rho u_1u_2 + \tfrac{1}{2}b_{22}u_2^2(1-u_2^2)\sigma_2^2 \\
&+ b_1u_1(1-u_1)[\sigma_1^2(\tfrac{1}{2}-u_1) - \alpha(\ln u_1(1-u_2)/pu_2(1-u_1)) + \lambda_1\sigma_1] \\
&+ b_2u_2(1-u_2)[-\sigma_2^2u_2 - (1-u_2)/nu_2 + (1-u_1)/nu_1] \\
&- b_3 - b(1-u_1)/nu_1 = 0. \qquad (36)
\end{aligned}$$

The solution to this differential equation must satisfy the maturity boundary condition which is defined by assuming that the bond pays \$1 at maturity:

[12]The parameter n was chosen so that approximately one half of the range of u_1 and u_2 (0, 1) relates to the relevant range of interest rates, 0–20%, in which solution accuracy is required, i.e. $n=40$.

$$b(u_1, u_2, 0) = 1. \tag{37}$$

In addition we have the following natural boundaries obtained by letting u_1, u_2 approach zero and one[13] in the differential eq. (36):

(i) For $r = \infty (u_1 = 0)$, $l = \infty (u_2 = 0)$.

Multiply (36) by nu_1 and let u_1 and u_2 approach zero to obtain

$$b(0, 0, \tau) = 0. \tag{38}$$

(ii) For $r = \infty (u_1 = 0)$, $l \neq \infty$.

Multiply (36) by nu_1 and let u_1 approach zero to obtain the ordinary differential equation

$$b_2(0, u_2, \tau) u_2 (1 - u_2) - b(0, u_2, \tau) = 0.$$

Solving this equation and imposing the requirement that $b(0, u_2, \tau) \leqq 1$, we have

$$b(0, u_2, \tau) = 0. \tag{39}$$

(iii) For $l = \infty (u_2 = 0)$, $r \neq \infty$.

Divide (36) by $\ln u_2$ and let u_2 approach zero to obtain

$$\alpha u_1 (1 - u_1) b_1 (u_1, 0, \tau) = 0,$$

and since $b(0, 0, \tau) = 0$ from (38), this implies that

$$b(u_1, 0, \tau) = 0. \tag{40}$$

The boundary conditions (38)–(40) state that if either interest rate is infinite, the value of the bond is zero.

(iv) For $r = 0$ $(u_1 = 1)$, $l = 0$ $(u_2 = 1)$.

Setting u_1 and u_2 equal to unity in (36),

$$b_3(1, 1, \tau) = 0.$$

Combining this with the maturity value boundary, (37), we obtain

$$b(1, 1, \tau) = 1. \tag{41}$$

[13]This corresponds to letting the interest rates r and l approach infinity and zero respectively.

(v) For $r=0$ $(u_1=1)$, $l\neq 0$.

Taking the limit in (36) as $u_1\to 1$,

$$\tfrac{1}{2}b_{22}u_2^2(1-u_2^2)\sigma_2^2+b_2u_2(1-u_2)[-\sigma_2^2u_2-(1-u_2)/nu_2]-b_2=0. \tag{42}$$

$b(1,u_2,\tau)$ is obtained as the solution to (42) subject to the boundary conditions (37), (40) and (41).

(vi) For $l=0$ $(u_2=1)$, $r\neq 0$.

Divide (36) by $\ln(1-u_2)$ and let $u_2\to 1$ to obtain

$$\alpha u_1(1-u_1)b_1(u_1,1,\tau)=0. \tag{43}$$

The solution to (43) subject to the boundary (40) is

$$b(u_1,1,\tau)=1. \tag{44}$$

The finite difference approximation to (36) is obtained by defining $b(\cdot)$ at discrete intervals.

$$\begin{aligned} b(u_{1i},u_{2j},\tau_k)&\equiv b(hi,hj,gk)\\ &\equiv b_{i,j,k},\qquad i,j=0,\ldots,m,\quad k=0,\ldots,K, \end{aligned} \tag{45}$$

where h and g are the step sizes for the interest rates and time to maturity respectively; since u_1 and u_2 are defined on the interval (0, 1), $hm=1$. Then writing finite differences in place of partial derivatives, (36) may be approximated by

$$\begin{aligned} &c_1^{i,j}b_{i-1,j-1,k}+c_2^{i,j}b_{i-1,j,k}+c_3^{i,j}b_{i-1,j+1,k}\\ &+c_4^{i,j}b_{i,j-1,k}+c_5^{i,j}b_{i,j,k}+c_6^{i,j}b_{i,j+1,k}\\ &+c_7^{i,j}b_{i+1,j-1,k}+c_8^{i,j}b_{i+1,j,k}+c_9^{i,j}b_{i+1,j+1,k}\\ &=b_{i,j,k-1},\qquad i=1,\ldots,m-1,\quad j=1,\ldots,m-1, \end{aligned} \tag{46}$$

where $c_1^{i,j}$ etc. are coefficients derived from the parameters of the equation.

(46) is a system of $(m-1)^2$ equations in the $(m+1)^2$ unknowns $b_{i,j,k}$ $(i,j=0,1,\ldots,m)$; the remaining $4m$ equations are provided by the natural boundary conditions (i)–(vi) above.[14] The augmented system of equations may be solved recursively for the unknowns $b_{i,j,k}$ in terms of $b_{i,j,k-1}$, since the values

[14]Values of $b(1,u_2,\tau)$ are obtained by solving the finite difference approximation to (42).

$b_{i,j,0}$ are given by the maturity boundary condition (37). To take advantage of the structure of the coefficient matrix the equations were solved by the method of successive over-relaxation.[15]

[15]Westlake (1968).

References

Bergstrom, A.R., 1966, Non-recursive models as discrete approximations to systems of stochastic differential equations, Econometrica 34, 173–182.

Black, F. and M.J. Scholes, 1973, The pricing of options and corporate liabilities, Journal of Political Economy 81, 637–659.

Brennan, M.J. and E.S. Schwartz, 1977, Saving bonds, retractable bonds and callable bonds, Journal of Financial Economics 5, 67–88.

Cox, J. C., J. E. Ingersoll and S.A. Ross, 1977, Notes on a theory of the term structure of interest rates, Unpublished working paper.

Malinvaud, E., 1966, Statistical methods of econometrics (North-Holland, Amsterdam).

Merton, R.C., 1973, The theory of rational option pricing, Bell Journal of Economics and Management Science 4, 141–183.

Phillips, P.C.B., 1972, The structural estimation of a stochastic differential equation system, Econometrica 40, 1021–1041.

Richard, S.F., 1976, An analytical model of the term structure of interest rates, Working paper no. 1976-77 (Carnegie-Mellon University, Pittsburgh, PA).

Roll, R., 1970, The behaviour of interest rates (Basic Books, New York).

Rubinstein, M., 1976, The valuation of uncertain income streams and the pricing of options, The Bell Journal of Economics 7, 407–425.

Stiglitz, J.E., 1970, A consumption-oriented theory of the demand for financial assets and the term structure of interest rates, Review of Economic Studies.

Vasicek, O., 1976, An equilibrium characterization of the term structure, Unpublished manuscript.

Westlake, J.R., 1968, A handbook of numerical matrix inversion and solution of linear equations (Wiley, New York).

Wymer, C.R., 1972, Econometric estimation of stochastic differential equation systems, Econometrica 40, 565–577.

[20]

Econometrica, Vol. 60, No. 1 (January, 1992), 77–105

BOND PRICING AND THE TERM STRUCTURE OF INTEREST RATES: A NEW METHODOLOGY FOR CONTINGENT CLAIMS VALUATION[1]

BY DAVID HEATH, ROBERT JARROW, AND ANDREW MORTON[2]

This paper presents a unifying theory for valuing contingent claims under a stochastic term structure of interest rates. The methodology, based on the equivalent martingale measure technique, takes as given an initial forward rate curve and a family of potential stochastic processes for its subsequent movements. A no arbitrage condition restricts this family of processes yielding valuation formulae for interest rate sensitive contingent claims which do not explicitly depend on the market prices of risk. Examples are provided to illustrate the key results.

KEYWORDS: Term structure of interest rates, interest rate options, contingent claims, martingale measures.

1. INTRODUCTION

IN RELATION TO the term structure of interest rates, arbitrage pricing theory has two purposes. The first, is to price all zero coupon (default free) bonds of varying maturities from a finite number of economic fundamentals, called state variables. The second, is to price all interest rate sensitive contingent claims, taking as given the prices of the zero coupon bonds. This paper presents a general theory and a unifying framework for understanding arbitrage pricing theory in this context, of which all existing arbitrage pricing models are special cases (in particular, Vasicek (1977), Brennan and Schwartz (1979), Langetieg (1980), Ball and Torous (1983), Ho and Lee (1986), Schaefer and Schwartz (1987), and Artzner and Delbaen (1988)). The primary contribution of this paper, however, is a new methodology for solving the second problem, i.e., the pricing of interest rate sensitive contingent claims given the prices of all zero coupon bonds.

The methodology is new because (i) it imposes its stochastic structure directly on the evolution of the forward rate curve, (ii) it does not require an "inversion of the term structure" to eliminate the market prices of risk from contingent claim values, and (iii) it has a stochastic spot rate process with multiple stochastic factors influencing the term structure. The model can be used to consistently price (and hedge) all contingent claims (American or European) on the term structure, and it is derived from necessary and (more importantly) *sufficient* conditions for the absence of arbitrage.

The arbitrage pricing models of Vasicek (1977), Brennan and Schwartz (1979), Langetieg (1980), and Artzner and Delbaen (1988) all require an

[1]Formerly titled "Bond Pricing and the Term Structure of Interest Rates: A New Methodology."

[2]Helpful comments from P. Artzner, F. Delbaen, L. Hansen, an anonymous referee, and from workshops at Berkeley, Columbia University, Cornell University, Dartmouth College, Duke University, New York University, Stanford University, U.C.L.A., University of Illinois at Chicago, and Yale University are gratefully acknowledged.

"inversion of the term structure" to remove the market prices of risk when pricing contingent claims. This inversion is required due to the two-step procedure utilized in these papers to price contingent claims. The first step is to price the zero coupon bonds from a finite number of state variables. Given these derived prices, the second step is to value contingent claims. It is the first step in this procedure that introduces the explicit dependence on the market prices of risk in the valuation formulae. The equilibrium model of Cox, Ingersoll, and Ross (1985), when used to value contingent claims, also follows this same two-step procedure. To remove this dependence, for parameterized forms of the market prices for risk, it is possible to invert the bond pricing formula after step one, to obtain the market prices for risk as functions of the zero coupon bond prices.

This "inversion of the term structure" removes the market prices for risk from contingent claim values, but it is problematic. First, it is computationally difficult since the bond pricing formulae are highly nonlinear. Secondly, as will be shown later, the spot rate and bond price processes parameters are not independent of the market prices for risk. Hence, arbitrarily specifying a parameterized form of the market prices for risk as a function of the state variables can lead to an inconsistent model, i.e., one which admits arbitrage opportunities. This possibility was originally noted by Cox, Ingersoll, and Ross (1985, p. 398).

A second class of arbitrage pricing models, illustrated by Ball and Torous (1983) and Shaefer and Schwartz (1987) avoids this two-step procedure by taking a finite number of initial bond prices and bond price processes as exogenously given. Unfortunately, Schaefer and Schwartz's model requires a constant spot rate process, and as shown by Cheng (1987), Ball and Torous' model is inconsistent with stochastic spot rate processes and the absence of arbitrage.

The model of Ho and Lee (1986) also avoids the two-step procedure by taking the initial bond prices and bond price processes as exogenously given. Unlike all the previous models, however, they utilize a discrete trading economy. In this economy, the zero coupon bond price curve, in contrast to a finite number of bond prices, is assumed to fluctuate randomly over time according to a binomial process. Unfortunately, it is only a single factor model, so bonds of all maturities are perfectly correlated. Furthermore, to implement their model, they estimate the parameters of the discrete time binomial process including the risk neutral probability. For large step sizes, as shown by Heath, Jarrow, and Morton (1990), the parameters are not independent. This makes estimation problematic, as the dependence is not explicitly taken into account. The continuous time version of this model, which is studied below as a special case, is not subject to this same estimation difficulty.

We generalize the Ho and Lee model to a continuous time economy with multiple factors. Unlike the Ho and Lee model, however, we impose the exogenous stochastic structure upon forward rates, and not the zero coupon bond prices. This change in perspective facilitates the mathematical analysis and it should also facilitate the empirical estimation of the model. Indeed, since zero coupon bond prices are a fixed amount at maturity, their "volatilities" must change over time. In contrast, constant forward rate volatilities are consistent with a fixed value for a zero coupon bond at maturity.

The model in this paper takes as given the initial forward rate curve. We then specify a general continuous time stochastic process for its evolution across time. To ensure that the process is consistent with an arbitrage free economy (and hence with some equilibrium), we use the insights of Harrison and Kreps (1979) to characterize the conditions on the forward rate process such that there exists a unique, equivalent martingale probability measure. Under these conditions, markets are complete and contingent claim valuation is then a straightforward application of the methods in Harrison and Pliska (1981). We illustrate this approach with several examples.

An outline of this paper is as follows: Section 2 presents the terminology and notation. Section 3 presents the forward rate process. Section 4 characterizes arbitrage free forward rate processes. Section 5 extends the model to price interest rate dependent contingent claims. Sections 6 and 7 provide examples. Section 8 relates the arbitrage pricing approach to the equilibrium pricing approach, while Section 9 summarizes the paper and discusses generalizations.

2. TERMINOLOGY AND NOTATION

We consider a continuous trading economy with a trading interval $[0, \tau]$ for a fixed $\tau > 0$. The uncertainty in the economy is characterized by the probability space (Ω, F, Q) where Ω is the state space, F is the σ-algebra representing measurable events, and Q is a probability measure. Information evolves over the trading interval according to the augmented, right continuous, complete filtration $\{F_t\colon t \in [0, \tau]\}$ generated by $n \geqslant 1$ independent Brownian motions $\{W_1(t), W_2(t), \dots, W_n(t)\colon t \in [0, \tau]\}$ initialized at zero. We let $E(\cdot)$ denote expectation with respect to the probability measure Q.

A continuum of default free discount bonds trade with differing maturities, one for each trading date $T \in [0, \tau]$. Let $P(t, T)$ denote the time t price of the T maturity bond for all $T \in [0, \tau]$ and $t \in [0, T]$. We require that $P(T, T) = 1$ for all $T \in [0, \tau]$, $P(t, T) > 0$ for all $T \in [0, \tau]$ and $t \in [0, T]$, and that $\partial \log P(t, T)/\partial T$ exists for all $T \in [0, \tau]$ and $t \in [0, T]$. The first condition normalizes the bond's payoff to be a certain dollar at maturity. The second condition excludes the trivial arbitrage opportunity where a certain dollar can be obtained for free. The last condition guarantees that forward rates are well-defined.

The instantaneous *forward rate* at time t for date $T > t$, $f(t, T)$, is defined by

$$(1) \qquad f(t, T) = -\partial \log P(t, T)/\partial T \quad \text{for all} \quad T \in [0, \tau], \quad t \in [0, T].$$

It corresponds to the rate that one can contract for at time t, on a riskless loan that begins at date T and is returned an instant later. Solving the differential equation of expression (1) yields

$$(2) \qquad P(t,T) = \exp\left(-\int_t^T f(t,s)\,ds\right) \quad \text{for all} \quad T \in [0,\tau], \quad t \in [0,T].$$

The *spot rate*[3] at time $t, r(t)$, is the instantaneous forward rate at time t for date t, i.e.,

$$(3) \qquad r(t) = f(t,t) \quad \text{for all} \quad t \in [0,\tau].$$

3. TERM STRUCTURE MOVEMENTS

This section of the paper presents the family of stochastic processes representing forward rate movements, condition (C.1). This condition describes the evolution of forward rates, and thus uniquely specifies the spot rate process and the bond price process. Additional boundedness conditions, (C.2) and (C.3), are required to guarantee that the spot rate and the bond price process are well-behaved.

C.1—A FAMILY OF FORWARD RATE PROCESSES: *For fixed, but arbitrary* $T \in [0,\tau]$, $f(t,T)$ *satisfies the following equation*:

$$(4) \qquad f(t,T) - f(0,T) = \int_0^t \alpha(v,T,\omega)\,dv + \sum_{i=1}^{n} \int_0^t \sigma_i(v,T,\omega)\,dW_i(v) \quad \textit{for all} \quad 0 \leqslant t \leqslant T$$

where: (i) $\{f(0,T)\colon T \in [0,\tau]\}$ *is a fixed, nonrandom initial forward rate curve which is measurable as a mapping* $f(0,\cdot)\colon ([0,\tau], B[0,\tau]) \to (R,B)$ *where* $B[0,\tau]$ *is the Borel* σ*-algebra restricted to* $[0,\tau]$; (ii) $\alpha\colon \{(t,s)\colon 0 \leqslant t \leqslant s \leqslant T\} \times \Omega \to R$ *is jointly measurable from* $B\{(t,s)\colon 0 \leqslant t \leqslant s \leqslant T\} \times F \to B$, *adapted, with*

$$\int_0^T |\alpha(t,T,\omega)|\,dt < +\infty \quad \text{a.e. } Q, \quad \textit{and}$$

(iii) *the volatilities* $\sigma_i\colon \{(t,s)\colon 0 \leqslant t \leqslant s \leqslant T\} \times \Omega \to R$ *are jointly measurable from* $B\{(t,s)\colon 0 \leqslant t \leqslant s \leqslant T\} \times F \to B$, *adapted, and satisfy*

$$\int_0^T \sigma_i^2(t,T,\omega)\,dt < +\infty \quad \text{a.e. } Q \quad \textit{for} \quad i = 1,\ldots,n.$$

In this stochastic process n independent Brownian motions determine the stochastic fluctuation of the *entire* forward rate curve starting from a fixed initial

[3] This is equivalent to $r(t) = \lim_{h \to 0}[1 - P(t,t+h)]/P(t,t+h)h = f(t,t)$.

curve $\{f(0,T)\colon T \in [0,\tau]\}$. The sensitivity of a particular maturity forward rate's change to each Brownian motion is reflected by differing volatility coefficients. The volatility coefficients $\{\sigma_i(t,T,\omega)\colon T \in [0,\tau]\}$ for $i = 1,\ldots,n$ are left unspecified, except for mild measurability and integrability conditions, and can depend on the entire past of the Brownian motions. Different specifications for these volatility coefficients generate significantly different qualitative characteristics of the forward rate process. The family of drift functions $\{\alpha(\cdot,T)\colon T \in [0,\tau]\}$ is also unrestricted (at this point), except for mild measurability and integrability conditions.

It is important to emphasize that the only substantive economic restrictions imposed on the forward rate processes are that they have continuous sample paths and that they depend on only a finite number of random shocks (across the entire forward rate curve).

Given condition (C.1), we can determine the dynamics of the spot rate process:

$$(5)\qquad r(t) = f(0,t) + \int_0^t \alpha(v,t,\omega)\,dv + \sum_{i=1}^{n}\int_0^t \sigma_i(v,t,\omega)\,dW_i(v) \quad \text{for all} \quad t \in [0,T].$$

The spot rate process is similar to the forward rate process, except that both the time and maturity arguments vary simultaneously.

For the subsequent analysis, it is convenient to define an accumulation factor, $B(t)$, corresponding to the price of a money market account (rolling over at $r(t)$) initialized at time 0 with a dollar investment, i.e.,

$$(6)\qquad B(t) = \exp\left(\int_0^t r(y)\,dy\right) \quad \text{for all} \quad t \in [0,\tau].$$

Given the dynamics of the spot rate process, we need to ensure that the value of the money market account satisfies

$$(7)\qquad 0 < B(t,\omega) < +\infty \quad \text{a.e. } Q \quad \text{for all} \quad t \in [0,\tau].$$

This is guaranteed by condition (C.2).

C.2—Regularity of the Money Market Account:

$$\int_0^{\tau} |f(0,v)|\,dv < +\infty \quad \textit{and} \quad \int_0^{\tau}\left\{\int_0^t |\alpha(v,t,\omega)|\,dv\right\} dt < +\infty \quad \text{a.e. } Q.$$

Next, we are interested in the dynamics of the bond price process. The following condition imposes sufficient regularity conditions so that the bond price process is well-behaved.

C.3—REGULARITY OF THE BOND PRICE PROCESS:

$$\int_0^t \left[\int_v^t \sigma_i(v, y, \omega)\, dy\right]^2 dv < +\infty \quad \text{a.e. } Q$$

$$\textit{for all} \quad t \in [0, \tau] \quad \textit{and} \quad i = 1, \ldots, n;$$

$$\int_0^t \left[\int_t^T \sigma_i(v, y, \omega)\, dy\right]^2 dv < +\infty \quad \text{a.e. } Q$$

$$\textit{for all} \quad t \in [0, T], \quad T \in [0, \tau], \quad i = 1, \ldots, n;$$

and

$$t \to \int_t^T \left[\int_0^t \sigma_i(v, y, \omega)\, dW_i(v)\right] dy \quad \textit{is continuous a.e. } Q$$

$$\textit{for all} \quad T \in [0, \tau] \quad \textit{and} \quad i = 1, \ldots, n.$$

It is shown in the Appendix that under conditions C.2–C.3, the dynamics of the bond price process (suppressing the notational dependence on ω) are

$$\text{(8)} \qquad \ln P(t,T) = \ln P(0,T) + \int_0^t [r(v) + b(v,T)]\, dv - (1/2) \sum_{i=1}^n \int_0^t a_i(v,T)^2\, dv + \sum_{i=1}^n \int_0^t a_i(v,T)\, dW_i(v) \quad \text{a.e. } Q$$

where

$$a_i(t,T,\omega) \equiv -\int_t^T \sigma_i(t,v,\omega)\, dv \quad \text{for} \quad i = 1, \ldots, n \quad \text{and}$$

$$b(t,T,\omega) \equiv -\int_t^T \alpha(t,v,\omega)\, dv + (1/2) \sum_{i=1}^n a_i(t,T,\omega)^2.$$

A straightforward application of Ito's lemma to expression (8) yields $P(t,T)$ as the strong solution to the following stochastic differential equation:

$$\text{(9)} \qquad dP(t,T) = [r(t) + b(t,T)]P(t,T)\, dt + \sum_{i=1}^n a_i(t,T)P(t,T)\, dW_i(t) \quad \text{a.e. } Q.$$

In general, the bond price process is non-Markov since the drift term $(r(t,\omega)+b(t,T,\omega))$ and the volatility coefficients $a_i(t,T,\omega)$ for $i=1,\ldots,n$ can depend on the history of the Brownian motions. The form of the bond price process as given in expression (9) is similar to, but more general than, that appearing in the existing literature (see, for example, Brennan and Schwartz (1979) or Langetieg (1980)), because it requires less regularity assumptions and it need not be Markov.

We define the relative bond price for a T-maturity bond as $Z(t,T)=P(t,T)/B(t)$ for $T\in[0,\tau]$ and $t\in[0,T]$. This is the bond's value expressed in units of the accumulation factor, not dollars. This transformation removes the portion of the bond's drift due to the spot rate process. As such, it is particularly useful for analysis. Applying Ito's lemma to the definition of $Z(t,T)$ yields

$$\begin{aligned}(10)\qquad \ln Z(t,T) = \ln Z(0,T) + \int_0^t b(v,T)\,dv - (1/2)\sum_{i=1}^{n}\int_0^t a_i(v,T)^2\,dv \\ + \sum_{i=1}^{n}\int_0^t a_i(v,T)\,dW_i(v) \quad \text{a.e. } Q.\end{aligned}$$

Again, the relative bond price at date t may depend on the path of the Brownian motion through the cumulative forward rate drifts and volatilities. In general, it cannot be written as a function of only the current values of the Brownian motions.

4. ARBITRAGE FREE BOND PRICING AND TERM STRUCTURE MOVEMENTS

Given conditions C.1–C.3, this section characterizes necessary and sufficient conditions on the forward rate process such that their exists a unique, equivalent martingale probability measure.

C.4—EXISTENCE OF THE MARKET PRICES FOR RISK: *Fix $S_1,\ldots,S_n\in[0,\tau]$ such that $0<S_1<S_2<\ldots<S_n\leqslant\tau$. Assume there exists solutions*

$$\gamma_i(\cdot,\cdot;S_1,\ldots,S_n):\Omega\times[0,S_1]\to R \quad \text{for} \quad i=1,\ldots,n \qquad \text{a.e. } Q\times\lambda$$

to the following system of equations:

$$(11)\qquad \begin{bmatrix} b(t,S_1)\\ \vdots \\ b(t,S_n)\end{bmatrix} + \begin{bmatrix} a_1(t,S_1)\ldots a_n(t,S_1)\\ \vdots \\ a_1(t,S_n)\ldots a_n(t,S_n)\end{bmatrix}\begin{bmatrix}\gamma_1(t;S_1,\ldots,S_n)\\ \vdots \\ \gamma_n(t;S_1,\ldots,S_n)\end{bmatrix} = \begin{bmatrix}0\\ \vdots \\ 0\end{bmatrix}$$

which satisfy

$$(12.a)\quad \int_0^{S_1} \gamma_i(v; S_1, \ldots, S_n)^2\, dv < +\infty \quad \text{a.e. } Q \quad \textit{for} \quad i = 1, \ldots, n,$$

$$(12.b)\quad E\left(\exp\left\{\sum_{i=1}^{n} \int_0^{S_1} \gamma_i(v; S_1, \ldots, S_n)\, dW_i(v) - (1/2) \sum_{i=1}^{n} \int_0^{S_1} \gamma_i(v; S_1, \ldots, S_n)^2\, dv\right\}\right) = 1,$$

$$(12.c)\quad E\left(\exp\left\{\sum_{i=1}^{n} \int_0^{S_1} [a_i(v, y) + \gamma_i(v; S_1, \ldots, S_n)]\, dW_i(v) - (1/2) \sum_{i=1}^{n} \int_0^{S_1} [a_i(v, y) + \gamma_i(v; S_1, \ldots, S_n)]^2\, dv\right\}\right) = 1$$

$$\textit{for} \quad y \in \{S_1, \ldots, S_n\}$$

where λ *is Lebesgue measure.*

The system of equations in expression (11) gives $\gamma_i(t; S_1, \ldots, S_n)$ for $i = 1, \ldots, n$ the interpretation of being the *market prices for risk* associated with the random factors $W_i(t)$ for $i = 1, \ldots, n$, respectively. Indeed, to see this, we can rewrite expression (11) for the T-maturity bond as

$$(13)\quad b(t, T) = \sum_{i=1}^{n} a_i(t, T)(-\gamma_i(t; S_1, \ldots, S_n)).$$

The left side of expression (13) is the instantaneous excess expected return on the T-maturity bond *above* the risk free rate. The right side is the sum of (minus) the "market price of risk for factor i" times the instantaneous covariance between the T-maturity bond's return and the ith random factor for $i = 1$ to n. It is important to emphasize that the solutions to expression (11) depend, in general, on the vector of bonds $\{S_1, \ldots, S_n\}$ chosen.

The following proposition shows that condition C.4 guarantees the existence of an equivalent martingale probability measure.

PROPOSITION 1—Existence of an Equivalent Martingale Probability Measure: *Fix* $S_1, \ldots, S_n \in [0, \tau]$ *such that* $0 < S_1 < S_2 < \ldots < S_n \leqslant \tau$. *Given a vector of forward rate drifts* $\{\alpha(\cdot, S_1), \ldots, \alpha(\cdot, S_n)\}$ *and volatilities* $\{\sigma_i(\cdot, S_1), \ldots, \sigma_i(\cdot, S_n)\}$ *for* $i = 1, \ldots, n$ *satisfying conditions C.1–C.3, then condition C.4 holds if and only if there exists an equivalent probability measure* $\tilde{Q}_{S_1, \ldots, S_n}$ *such that* $(Z(t, S_1), \ldots, Z(t, S_n))$ *are martingales with respect to* $\{F_t \colon t \in [0, S_1]\}$.

Proof: In the Appendix.

This proposition asserts that under conditions C.1–C.3, condition C.4 is both necessary and sufficient for the existence of an equivalent martingale probability measure $\tilde{Q}_{S_1,\ldots,S_n}$. The key argument in the proof is Girsanov's Theorem, and it identifies this probability measure as

$$(14) \qquad d\tilde{Q}_{S_1,\ldots,S_n}/dQ = \exp\left\{ \sum_{i=1}^{n} \int_0^{S_1} \gamma_i(v; S_1,\ldots,S_n)\, dW_i(v) - (1/2) \sum_{i=1}^{n} \int_0^{S_1} \gamma_i(v; S_1,\ldots,S_n)^2\, dv \right\}.$$

Furthermore, it can also be shown that

$$(15) \qquad \tilde{W}_i^{S_1,\ldots,S_n}(t) = W_i(t) - \int_0^t \gamma_i(v; S_1,\ldots,S_n)\, dv \quad \text{for} \quad i = 1,\ldots,n$$

are independent Brownian motions on $\{(\Omega, \tilde{Q}_{S_1,\ldots,S_n}, F), \{F_t\colon t \in [0, S_1]\}$.

Although condition C.4 guarantees the existence of an equivalent martingale probability measure, it does not guarantee that it is unique. To obtain uniqueness, we impose the following condition:

C.5—Uniqueness of the Equivalent Martingale Probability Measure: *Fix* $S_1,\ldots,S_n \in [0,\tau]$ *such that* $0 < S_1 < S_2 < \ldots < S_n \leqslant \tau$. *Assume that*

$$\begin{bmatrix} a_1(t,S_1) & \ldots & a_n(t,S_1) \\ \vdots & & \vdots \\ a_1(t,S_n) & \ldots & a_n(t,S_n) \end{bmatrix} \quad \textit{is nonsingular a.e. } Q \times \lambda.$$

The following proposition demonstrates that condition C.5 is both necessary and sufficient for the uniqueness of the equivalent martingale measure.[4]

Proposition 2—Characterization of Uniqueness of the Equivalent Martingale Probability Measure: *Fix* $S_1,\ldots,S_n \in [0,\tau]$ *such that* $0 < S_1 < S_2 < \ldots < S_n \leqslant \tau$. *Given a vector of forward rate drifts* $\{\alpha(\cdot, S_1),\ldots,\alpha(\cdot, S_n)\}$ *and volatilities* $\{\sigma_i(\cdot, S_1),\ldots,\sigma_i(\cdot, S_n)\}$ *for* $i = 1,\ldots,n$ *satisfying conditions C.1–C.4, then condition C.5 holds if and only if the martingale measure is unique.*

Proof: In the Appendix.

Conditions C.1–C.5, through the functions $\gamma_i(t; S_1,\ldots,S_n)$ for $i = 1,\ldots,n$ impose restrictions upon the drifts for the forward rate processes

[4] For the case of a single Brownian motion, condition C.5 simplifies to the statement that $\sigma_1(t, S_1) > 0$ a.e. $Q \times \lambda$.

$\{\alpha(\cdot, S_1), \ldots, \alpha(\cdot, S_n)\}$. It imposes just enough restrictions so that there is a unique equivalent martingale probability measure for the bonds $(Z(t, S_1), \ldots, Z(t, S_n))$ with $0 < S_1 < \ldots < S_n \leqslant \tau$. Both the market prices for risk and the martingale measure, however, depend on the particular bonds $\{S_1, \ldots, S_n\}$ chosen. To guarantee that there exists a unique equivalent martingale measure simultaneously making *all* relative bond prices martingales, we prove the following proposition.

Proposition 3—Uniqueness of the Martingale Measure Across All Bonds: *Given a family of forward rate drifts* $\{\alpha(\cdot, T)\colon T \in [0, \tau]\}$ *and a family of volatilities* $\{\sigma_i(\cdot, T)\colon T \in [0, \tau]\}$ *for* $i = 1, \ldots, n$ *satisfying conditions C.1–C.5, the following are equivalent:*

(16) [$\tilde{Q}$ *defined by* $\tilde{Q} = \tilde{Q}_{S_1, \ldots, S_n}$ *for any* $S_1, \ldots, S_n \in (0, \tau\,]$ *is the unique equivalent probability measure such that* $Z(t, T)$ *is a martingale for all* $T \in [0, \tau]$ *and* $t \in [0, S_1]$];

(17) [$\gamma_i(t; S_1, \ldots, S_n) = \gamma_i(t, T_1, \ldots, T_n)$ *for* $i = 1, \ldots, n$ *and all* $S_1, \ldots, S_n, T_1, \ldots, T_n \in [0, \tau]$, $t \in [0, \tau]$ *such that* $0 \leqslant t < S_1 < \ldots < S_n \leqslant \tau$ *and* $0 \leqslant t < T_1 < \ldots < T_n \leqslant \tau$];

(18) [$\alpha(t, T) = -\sum_{i=1}^{n} \sigma_i(t, T)(\phi_i(t) - \int_t^T \sigma_i(t, v)\, dv)$ *for all* $T \in [0, \tau]$ *and* $t \in [0, T]$ *where for* $i = 1, \ldots, n$, $\phi_i(t) = \gamma_i(t; S_1, \ldots, S_n)$ *for any* $S_1, \ldots, S_n \in (t, \tau\,]$ *and* $t \in [0, S_1]$].

Proof: From Proposition 2, for each vector $(S_1, \ldots, S_n)$ with $S_1 < S_2 < \ldots < S_n \leqslant \tau$, $\tilde{Q}_{S_1, \ldots, S_n}$ is the unique equivalent probability measure making $Z(t, S_i)$ a martingale over $t \leqslant S_1$ for $i = 1, \ldots, n$. These measures are all equal to $\tilde{Q}$ if and only if $\gamma_i(t; S_1, \ldots, S_n) = \gamma_i(t, T_1, \ldots, T_n)$ for $i = 1, \ldots, n$ and all $S_1, \ldots, S_n, T_1, \ldots, T_n \in [0, \tau]$ and $t \in [0, \tau]$ such that $0 \leqslant t < S_1 < \ldots < S_n \leqslant \tau$ and $0 \leqslant t < T_1 < \ldots < T_n \leqslant \tau$. To obtain the third condition, by expression (13) and the fact that $(\phi_1(t), \ldots, \phi_n(t))$ is independent of T, one obtains $b(t, T) = -\sum_{i=1}^{n} a_i(t, T)\phi_i(t)$. Substitution for $b(t, T), a_i(t, T)$ for $i = 1, \ldots, n$ and taking the partial derivative with respect to T gives (18). *Q.E.D.*

This proposition 3 asserts that the existence of a unique equivalent probability measure, $\tilde{Q}$, making relative bond prices martingales (condition (16)) is equivalent to the condition that the market prices for risk are independent of the vector of bonds $\{S_1, \ldots, S_n\}$ chosen (condition (17)). Furthermore, condition (17) is also equivalent to a restriction on the drift of the forward rate process (condition (18)). We discuss each of these conditions in turn.

The martingale condition (16) implies that

$$(19) \qquad P(t,T) = B(t)E\left(\exp\left\{\sum_{i=1}^{n}\int_0^T \phi_i(t)\, dW_i(t) - (1/2)\sum_{i=1}^{n}\int_0^T \phi_i(t)^2\, dt\right\}\Big/B(T)\,\Big|\,F_t\right).$$

Expression (19) demonstrates that the bond's price depends on the forward rate drifts $\{\alpha(\cdot,T)\colon T\in[0,\tau]\}$, the initial forward rate curve $\{f(0,T)\colon T\in[0,\tau]\}$, and the forward rate volatilities $\{\sigma_i(\cdot,T)\colon T\in[0,\tau]\}$ for $i=1,\dots,n$. All of these parameters enter into expression (19) implicitly through $\phi_i(t)$ for $i=1,\dots,n$, the market prices for risk and $B(T)$, the money market account.

Condition (17) of Proposition 3 is called the *standard finance condition* for arbitrage free pricing. This is the necessary condition for the absence of arbitrage used in the existing literature to derive the fundamental partial differential equation for pricing contingent claims (see Brennan and Schwartz (1979) or Langetieg (1980)).

Last, for purposes of contingent claim valuation, the final condition contained in expression (18) will be most useful. It is called the *forward rate drift restriction*. It shows the restriction needed on the family of drift processes $\{\alpha(\cdot,T)\colon T\in[0,\tau]\}$ in order to guarantee the existence of a unique equivalent martingale probability measure. As seen below, not all potential forward rate processes satisfy this restriction.

5. CONTINGENT CLAIM VALUATION

This section demonstrates how to value contingent claims in the preceding economy. As this analysis is a slight extension of the ideas contained in Harrison and Kreps (1979) and Harrison and Pliska (1981), the presentation will be brief. More importantly, it also provides the unifying framework for categorizing the various arbitrage pricing theories in the literature (i.e., Vasichek (1977), Brennan and Schwartz (1979), Langetieg (1980), Ball and Torous (1983), Ho and Lee (1986), Schaefer and Schwartz (1987), Artzner and Delbaen (1988)) in relation to our own.

Let conditions C.1–C.5 hold. Fix any vector of bonds $\{S_1,\dots,S_n\}\in[0,\tau]$ where $0<S_1<S_2<\dots<S_n\leqslant\tau$. By Proposition 2, there exists a unique $\tilde{Q}_{S_1,\dots,S_n}$ making all $Z(t,S_i)$ martingales for $i=1,\dots,n$. The uniqueness of $\tilde{Q}_{S_1,\dots,S_n}$ implies that the market is *complete* (Harrison and Pliska (1981; Corollary 3.36, p. 241)), i.e., given any random variable $X\colon\Omega\to R$ which is nonnegative, F_{S_1} measurable with $\tilde{E}_{S_1,\dots,S_n}(X/B(S_1))<+\infty$ where $\tilde{E}(\cdot)_{S_1,\dots,S_n}$ denotes expectation with respect to $\tilde{Q}_{S_1,\dots,S_n}$, there exists an admissible[5] self-financing trading strategy $\{N_0(t),N_{S_1}(t),\dots,N_{S_n}(t)\colon t\in[0,S_1]\}$ such that the

[5]For the definition of an admissible self-financing trading strategy, see Harrison and Pliska (1981).

value of the portfolio satisfies

$$N_0(S_1)B(S_1) + \sum_{i=1}^{n} N_{S_i}(S_1)P(S_1, S_i) = X \quad \text{a.e. } Q. \tag{20}$$

The random variable X is interpreted as the payout to a *contingent claim* at time S_1. Harrison and Pliska (1981) define an arbitrage opportunity and show, in the absence of arbitrage, that the time t price of the contingent claim to X at time S_1 must be given by

$$\tilde{E}_{S_1,\ldots,S_n}(X/B(S_1)|F_t)B(t). \tag{21}$$

Substituting expression (20) into (21) yields

$$\tilde{E}_{S_1,\ldots,S_n}\left(N_0(S_1) + N_{S_1}(S_1)/B(S_1) + \sum_{i=2}^{n} N_{S_i}(S_1)Z(S_1, S_i)|F_t\right)B(t). \tag{22}$$

To value this contingent claim, expression (22) demonstrates that we need to know the dynamics for $r(t)$ and $Z(t, S_i)$ for $i = 1, \ldots, n$, all under the martingale measure; that is,

$$r(t) = f(0,t) + \int_0^t \alpha(v,t)\,dv + \sum_{i=1}^{n} \int_0^t \sigma_i(v,t)\,d\tilde{W}_i^{S_1,\ldots,S_n}(v) + \sum_{i=1}^{n} \int_0^t \gamma_i(v; S_1, \ldots, S_n)\sigma_i(v,t)\,dv \quad \text{a.e. } Q \tag{23}$$

and

$$Z(t,u) = Z(0,u)\exp\left\{-(1/2)\sum_{i=1}^{n}\int_0^t a_i(v,u)^2\,dv + \sum_{i=1}^{n}\int_0^t a_i(v,u)\,d\tilde{W}_i^{S_1,\ldots,S_n}(v)\right\} \quad \text{a.e. } Q \tag{24}$$

for $u \in \{S_1, \ldots, S_n\}$. Therefore, we need to know $\gamma_i(v; S_1, \ldots, S_n)$ for $i = 1, \ldots, n$, the market prices for risk. These enter through the dynamics of the spot rate process in expression (23). This is true even though the evaluation proceeds in the risk neutral economy under the martingale measure.

All other bonds of differing maturities $u \in [0, \tau]$ are assumed to have values at time S_1, through expression (8), which are F_{S_1} measurable. Since $\tilde{E}_{S_1,\ldots,S_n}(P(S_1,u)/B(S_1)) < +\infty$ for all $u \in [0, \tau]$ and the market is complete, every other bond can be duplicated with an admissible self-financing trading strategy involving only the n bonds $\{S_1, \ldots, S_n\}$ and the money market account. Thus, one can price *all* the remaining bonds and all contingent claims. These are the two purposes for the arbitrage pricing methodology as stated in the introduction.

As expressions (23) and (24) make clear, the dynamics for the bond price process, spot rate process, and the market prices for risk cannot be chosen independently. Independently specifying these processes will in general lead to inconsistent pricing models. This is the logic underlying the criticism of the arbitrage pricing methodology presented in Cox, Ingersoll, and Ross (1985, p. 398).

The model, as presented above, captures the essence of all the existing arbitrage pricing models. To see this, let us first consider Vasicek (1977), Brennan and Schwartz (1979), Langetieg (1980), and Artzner and Delbaen (1988). Since all four models are similar, we focus upon that of Brennan and Schwartz. Brennan and Schwartz's model has $n = 2$. Instead of specifying the two bond processes for $\{S_1, S_2\}$ directly as in expression (24), they derive these expressions from other assumptions. First, they exogenously specify a long rate process and a spot rate process. Second, they assume that *all* bond prices at time t can be written as twice-continuously differentiable functions of the current values of these long and short rates. In conjunction, these assumptions (by Ito's lemma) imply condition (24). The analysis could then proceed as above, yielding contingent claim values dependent on the market prices for risk.[6,7]

Along with the framework for categorizing the various models, an additional contribution of our approach is to extend the above analysis to eliminate the market prices for risk from the valuation formulas. Intuitively speaking, this is done by utilizing the remaining information contained in the bond price processes to "substitute out" the market prices for risk. For this purpose, we add the following condition:

C.6—COMMON EQUIVALENT MARTINGALE MEASURES: *Given conditions C.1–C.3, let C.4 and C.5 hold for all bonds* $\{S_1, \ldots, S_n\} \in [0, \tau]$ *with* $0 < S_1 < \ldots < S_n \leqslant \tau$. *Further, let* $\tilde{Q} = \tilde{Q}_{S_1, \ldots, S_n}$ *(on their common domain).*

To remove the market prices for risk from expression (23), we assume condition C.6. Proposition 3, the no arbitrage condition (expression (18)) gives

$$\text{(25)} \qquad \int_0^t \alpha(v,t)\,dv = -\sum_{i=1}^{n} \int_0^t \sigma_i(v,t)\phi_i(v)\,dv + \sum_{i=1}^{n} \sigma_i(v,t) \int_v^t \sigma_i(v,y)\,dy\,dv.$$

[6]Brennan and Schwartz (1979), however, didn't use this martingale approach. Instead, they priced based on the necessary conditions given by the partial differential equation satisfied by a contingent claim's value under condition (17). Artzner and Delbaen (1988) use the martingale approach.

[7]Ball and Torous (1983) and Schaefer and Schwartz (1987) exogenously specify two bond price processes $\{P(t, S_1), P(t, S_2)\}$ directly. They price contingent claims based on necessary, but not sufficient conditions, for the absence of arbitrage. Unfortunately, both the Ball and Torous model (as shown by Cheng (1987)) and the Schaefer and Schwartz model can be shown to be inconsistent with stochastic spot rate processes and the absence of arbitrage.

Substitution of this expression into expression (23) for the spot rate yields

$$r(t)=f(0,t)+\sum_{i=1}^{n}\int_0^t \sigma_i(v,t)\int_v^t \sigma_i(v,y)\,dy\,dv \tag{26}$$
$$+\sum_{i=1}^{n}\int_0^t \sigma_i(v,t)\,d\tilde{W}_i(v).$$

The market prices for risk *drop out* of expression (23) and they are replaced with an expression involving the volatilities across different maturities of the forward rates, i.e., a "term structure of volatilities." Thus, contingent claim values can be calculated independently of the market prices for risk. We further illustrate this abstract procedure with concrete examples in the next two sections.

6. EXAMPLES

This section presents two examples to illustrate and to clarify the analysis in Section 5. One example, a continuous time limit of Ho and Lee's (1986) model (see Heath, Jarrow, and Morton (1988)), may prove useful in practical applications due to its computational simplicity.[8]

We assume that forward rates satisfy the stochastic process from condition C.1 with a single Brownian motion and the volatility $\sigma_1(t,T,\omega)\equiv\sigma>0$, a positive constant. We let the initial forward rate curve $\{f(0,T)\colon T\in[0,\tau]\}$ be measurable and absolutely integrable (as in condition C.2). Given a particular, but arbitrary stochastic process for the market price of risk, $\phi\colon[0,\tau]\times\Omega\to R$ which is predictable and bounded, we also assume that the forward rate drift condition (18) is satisfied:

$$\alpha(t,T)=-\sigma\phi(t)+\sigma^2(T-t) \tag{27}$$
$$\text{for all}\quad T\in[0,\tau]\quad\text{and}\quad t\in[0,T].$$

It is easy to verify that conditions C.1–C.6 are satisfied. This implies, therefore, that contingent claim valuation can proceed as in Section 5. Before that, however, we analyze the forward rate, spot rate, and bond price processes in more detail.

Under the equivalent martingale measure, and in terms of its Brownian motion (see expression (15)), the stochastic process for the forward rate is

$$f(t,T)=f(0,T)+\sigma^2t(T-t/2)+\sigma\tilde{W}(t). \tag{28}$$

Under condition (28), forward rates can be negative with positive probability.

The stochastic spot rate process under the equivalent martingale measure is

$$r(t)=f(0,t)+\sigma\tilde{W}(t)+\sigma^2t^2/2. \tag{29}$$

Spot rates can also be negative with positive probability.

[8] The example in this section is similar to a model independently obtained by Jamshidian (1989).

The dynamics of the bond price process over time is given by substituting expression (28) into expression (2):

$$(30)\qquad P(t,T) = [P(0,T)/P(0,t)]e^{-(\sigma^2/2)Tt(T-t)-\sigma(T-t)\tilde{W}(t)}.$$

Next, consider a European call option on the bond $P(t,T)$ with an exercise price of K and a maturity date t^* where $0 \leqslant t \leqslant t^* \leqslant T$. Let $C(t)$ denote the value of this call option at time t. The cash flow to the call option at maturity is

$$(31)\qquad C(t^*) = \max[P(t^*,T) - K, 0].$$

By Section 5, the time t value of the call is

$$(32)\qquad C(t) = \tilde{E}(\max[P(t^*,T) - K,0]B(t)/B(t^*)|F_t).$$

An explicit calculation,[9] using normal random variables, shows that expression (32) simplifies to

$$(33)\qquad C(t) = P(t,T)\Phi(h) - KP(t,t^*)\Phi\left(h - \sigma(T-t^*)\sqrt{(t^*-t)}\right)$$

where

$$(34)\qquad h = \left[\log(P(t,T)/KP(t,t^*)) + (1/2)\sigma(T-t^*)^2(t^*-t)\right] / \sigma(T-t^*)\sqrt{(t^*-t)}$$

and $\Phi(\cdot)$ is the cumulative normal distribution.

The value of the bond option is given by a modified Black-Scholes formula. The parameter, $\sigma(T-t^*)$, is not equal to the variance of the instantaneous return on the T-maturity bond, but it is equivalent to the variance of the instantaneous return on the forward price (at time t^*) of a T-maturity bond, $(P(t,T)/P(t,t^*))$.

For the second example, assume that forward rates satisfy condition C.1 with the volatilities $\sigma_1(t,T,\omega) \equiv \sigma_1 > 0$ and $\sigma_2(t,T,\omega) \equiv \sigma_2 e^{-(\lambda/2)(T-t)} > 0$ where $\sigma_1, \sigma_2, \lambda$ are strictly positive constants, i.e.,

$$(35)\qquad df(t,T) = \alpha(t,T)\,dt + \sigma_1\,dW_1(t) + \sigma_2 e^{-(\lambda/2)(T-t)}\,dW_2(t)$$

$$\text{for all}\quad T \in [0,\tau] \quad\text{and}\quad t \in [0,T].$$

Here, the instantaneous changes in forward rates are caused by two sources of randomness. The first, $\{W_1(t)\colon t \in [0,\tau]\}$, can be interpreted as a "long-run factor" since it uniformly shifts all maturity forward rates equally. The second, $\{W_2(t)\colon t \in [0,\tau]\}$, affects the short maturity forward rates more than it does long term rates and can be interpreted as a spread between a "short" and "long term factor."

[9]This calculation and the one in the next section can be found in Brenner and Jarrow (1992).

The volatility functions are strictly positive and bounded. Furthermore, the matrix

$$\begin{bmatrix} a_1(t,S) & a_2(t,S) \\ a_1(t,T) & a_2(t,T) \end{bmatrix} = \begin{bmatrix} -\sigma_1(S-t) + 2\sigma_2(e^{-(\lambda/2)(S-t)} - 1)/\lambda \\ -\sigma_1(T-t) + 2\sigma_2(e^{-(\lambda/2)(T-t)} - 1)/\lambda \end{bmatrix} \tag{36}$$

is nonsingular for all $t, S, T \in [0, \tau]$ such that $t \leqslant S < T$.

We arbitrarily fix two bounded, predictable processes for the market prices of risk, ϕ_i: $[0,\tau] \times \Omega \to R$ for $i = 1, 2$. To ensure the process is arbitrage free, we set

$$\begin{aligned} \alpha(t,T) = & -\sigma_1\phi_1(t) - \sigma_2 e^{-(\lambda/2)(T-t)}\phi_2(t) + \sigma_1^2(T-t) \\ & - 2(\sigma_2^2/\lambda)e^{-(\lambda/2)(T-t)}(e^{-(\lambda/2)(T-t)} - 1). \end{aligned} \tag{37}$$

The above forward rate process satisfies conditions C.1–C.6. Under the martingale measure $\tilde{Q}$ and its Brownian motions $\{\tilde{W}_1(t), \tilde{W}_2(t) \colon t \in [0, \tau]\}$, the forward rate process is

$$\begin{aligned} f(t,T) = & f(0,T) + \sigma_1^2 t(T - t/2) \\ & - 2(\sigma_2/\lambda)^2\left[e^{-\lambda T}(e^{\lambda t} - 1) - 2e^{-(\lambda/2)T}(e^{(\lambda/2)t} - 1)\right] \\ & + \sigma_1\tilde{W}_1(t) + \sigma_2\int_0^t e^{-(\lambda/2)(T-v)}\,d\tilde{W}_2(v). \end{aligned} \tag{38}$$

This expression shows that forward rates can be negative with positive probability. The spot rate follows the simpler process:

$$\begin{aligned} r(t) = & f(0,t) + \sigma_1^2 t^2/2 - 2(\sigma_2/\lambda)^2\left[(1 - e^{-\lambda t}) - 2(1 - e^{-(\lambda/2)t})\right] \\ & + \sigma_1\tilde{W}_1(t) + \sigma_2\int_0^t e^{-(\lambda/2)(t-v)}\,d\tilde{W}_2(v). \end{aligned} \tag{39}$$

As before, we can calculate the value of a European call option on the bond $P(t,T)$ with an exercise price of K and a maturity date t^* where $0 \leqslant t \leqslant t^* \leqslant T$. Let $C(t)$ denote the value of this call option at time t. By Section 5, the call's value is

$$C(t) = P(t,T)\Phi(h) - KP(t,t^*)\Phi(h-q) \tag{40}$$

where

$$\begin{aligned} h = & \left[\log(P(t,T)/KP(t,t^*)) + (1/2)q^2\right]/q, \\ q^2 = & \sigma_1^2(T - t^*)^2(t^* - t) \\ & + (4\sigma_2^2/\lambda^3)(e^{-(\lambda/2)T} - e^{-(\lambda/2)t^*})^2(e^{\lambda t^*} - e^{\lambda t}). \end{aligned} \tag{41}$$

7. A CLASS OF STOCHASTIC DIFFERENTIAL EQUATIONS

The previous section provides examples of forward rate processes satisfying conditions C.1–C.6. These processes have deterministic volatilities which are independent of the state $\omega \in \Omega$. This section provides a class of processes with the volatilities dependent on $\omega \in \Omega$. This class of processes can be described as the solutions (if they exist) to the following stochastic integral equation with restricted drift:

$$f(t,T) - f(0,T) = \int_0^t \alpha(v,T,\omega)\,dv + \sum_{i=1}^n \int_0^t \sigma_i(v,T,f(v,T))\,dW_i(v) \tag{42}$$

$$\text{for all} \quad 0 \leqslant t \leqslant T$$

where

$$\alpha(v,T,\omega) \equiv -\sum_{i=1}^n \sigma_i(v,T,f(v,T))\left[\phi_i(v) - \int_v^T \sigma_i(v,y,f(t,y))\,dy\right]$$

$$\text{for all} \quad T \in [0,\tau],$$

$\sigma_i: \{(t,S): 0 \leqslant t \leqslant S \leqslant T\} \times R \to R$ is jointly measurable and satisfies

$\int_0^T \sigma_i(t,T,f(t,T))^2\,dt < +\infty$ a.e. Q for $i = 1,\ldots,n$ and

$\phi_i: \Omega \times [0,\tau] \to R$ is a bounded predictable process for $i = 1,\ldots,n$.

We now study sufficient conditions on the volatility functions such that strong solutions to this class of stochastic differential equations exist. The continuous time analogue of Ho and Lee's (1986) model as given in expression (28) is a special case of this theorem. The example of a proportional volatility function is also provided below to show that additional hypotheses are needed.

A key step in proving the existence theorem is the following lemma, which asserts that the existence of a class of forward rate processes in the initial economy is guaranteed if and only if it can be guaranteed in an "equivalent risk neutral economy."

LEMMA 1—Existence in an Equivalent Risk Neutral Economy:

(43) *[The processes $\{f(t,T)$: $T \in [0,\tau]\}$ satisfy (42) with $\gamma_i(t; S_1,\ldots,S_n) = \phi_i(t)$ for all $0 \leqslant t < S < \ldots < S_n \leqslant \tau$ and $i = 1,\ldots,n$]*

if and only if

(44) *[The process $\{\tilde{\alpha}(\cdot,T)$: $T \in [0,\tau]\}$ defined by $\tilde{\alpha}(t,T) = \sum_{i=1}^n \sigma_i(t,T,f(t,T)) \int_t^T \sigma_i(t,v,f(t,v))\,dv$ for all $T \in [0,\tau]$ satisfies (42) with $\tilde{\alpha}(t,T)$ replacing $\alpha(t,T)$, $\tilde{W}_i(t)$ replacing $W_i(t)$ where $\tilde{W}_i(t) \equiv W_i(t) - \int_0^t \phi_i(y)\,dy$ is a Brownian motion with respect to $[(\Omega, F, \tilde{Q}), \{F_t$: $t \in [0,\tau]\}]$, and $\tilde{Q}$ replacing Q where $d\tilde{Q}/dQ = \exp\{\sum_{i=1}^n \int_0^T \phi_i(t)\,dW_i(t) - (1/2)\sum_{i=1}^n \int_0^T \phi_i(t)^2\,dt\}$].*

PROOF: A straightforward application of Girsanov's Theorem. *Q.E.D.*

Combined with this, the next lemma generates our existence theorem given in Proposition 4.

LEMMA 2—Existence of Forward Rate Processes: *Let* σ_i: $\{(t,s)\colon 0 \leqslant t \leqslant s \leqslant T\} \times R \to R$ *for* $i = 1, \ldots, n$ *be Lipschitz continuous in the last argument, nonnegative, and bounded. Let* $(\Omega, F, \tilde{Q})$ *be any equivalent probability space with* $\{\tilde{W}_1(t), \ldots, \tilde{W}_n(t)\colon t \in [0,\tau]\}$ *independent Brownian motions; then, there exists a jointly continuous* $f(\cdot,\cdot)$ *satisfying* (42) *with* $\tilde{W}_i(t)$ *replacing* $W_i(t)$ *and*

$$\tilde{\alpha}(t,T) = \sum_{i=1}^{n} \sigma_i(t,T,f(t,T)) \int_t^T \sigma_i(t,v,f(t,v))\, dv \qquad \textit{for all} \quad T \in [0,\tau]$$

replacing $\alpha(t,T)$.

The proof of this lemma is contained in Morton (1988). The hypotheses of Lemma 2 differ from the standard hypotheses guaranteeing the existence of strong solutions to stochastic differential equations due to the boundedness condition on the volatility functions.

PROPOSITION 4—Existence of Arbitrage-Free Forward Rate Drift Processes: *Let* ϕ_i: $[0,\tau] \times \Omega \to R$ *be bounded predictable processes for* $i = 1, \ldots, n$. *Let* σ_i: $\{(t,s)\colon 0 \leqslant t \leqslant s \leqslant T\} \times R \to R$ *for* $i = 1, \ldots, n$ *be Lipschitz continuous in the last argument, nonnegative, and bounded; then, there exists a jointly continuous forward rate process satisfying condition* (42).

By appending the nonsingularity condition C.5, this proposition provides sufficient conditions guaranteeing the existence of a class of forward rate processes satisfying conditions C.1–C.6. This set of sufficient conditions is easily verified in applications.

To show that the boundedness condition in Proposition 4 cannot be substantially weakened, we consider the special case of a single Brownian motion where $\sigma_1(t,T,f(t,T)) \equiv \sigma \cdot f(t,T)$ for a fixed constant $\sigma > 0$. This volatility function is positive and Lipschitz continuous, but not bounded.

For this volatility function, the no arbitrage condition of Proposition 4 with $\phi_i(t) \equiv 0$ implies that the forward rate process must satisfy

$$f(t,T) = f(0,T) \exp\left\{\int_0^t \int_u^T f(u,v)\, dv\, du\right\} \exp\{-\sigma^2 t/2 + \sigma W(t)\} \qquad \text{for all} \quad T \in [0,\tau] \quad \text{and} \quad t \in [0,T]. \tag{45}$$

Unfortunately, it can be shown (see Morton (1988)) that there is no finite valued solution to expression (45). In fact, it can be shown that under (45), in finite time, forward rates explode with positive probability for the martingale measure, and hence for any equivalent probability measure. Infinite forward rates generate zero bond prices and hence arbitrage opportunities.

The forward rate process given in (45) is in some ways the simplest model consistent with nonnegative forward rates. The incompatibility of this process with arbitrage free bond prices raises the issue as to the general existence of a drift process $\{\alpha(\cdot, T)\colon T \in [0, \tau]\}$ satisfying conditions C.1–C.6, *and* with non-negative forward rates. This existence issue is resolved through an example.

This example can be thought of as a combination of the two previous examples. When forward rates are "small" the process has a proportional volatility, and when forward rates are "large" it has a constant volatility. Intuitively, as shown below, rates cannot fall below zero nor explode. Formally, consider a single Brownian motion process with $\sigma_1(t, T, f(t, T)) = \sigma \min(f(t,T), \lambda)$ for $\sigma, \lambda > 0$ positive constants. This volatility function is positive, Lipschitz continuous, and bounded; thus, for an arbitrary initial forward rate curve Proposition 4 guarantees the existence of a jointly continuous $f(t,T)$ which solves

$$df(t,T) = \sigma \min(f(t,T), \lambda)\left(\int_t^T \sigma \min(f(t,s), \lambda)\, ds\right) dt + \sigma \min(f(t,T), \lambda)\, dW(t). \tag{46}$$

The following proposition guarantees that this forward rate process remains positive for any strictly positive initial forward rate curve.

PROPOSITION 5—A Nonnegative Forward Rate Process: *Given $f(t,T)$ solves expression* (46) *and given an arbitrary initial forward rate curve $f(0,t) = I(t) > 0$ for all $t \in [0, \tau]$, then with probability one, $f(t,T) \geqslant 0$ for all $T \in [0, \tau]$ and $t \in [0, \tau]$.*

PROOF: In the Appendix.

Since the forward rate process is a mixture of the constant volatility and proportional volatility models, it is easy to see (using expression (46)) that the forward rate drifts $\{\alpha(\cdot, T)\colon T \in [0, \tau]\}$ will be dependent upon the path of the Brownian motion. Another forward rate process consistent with nonnegative forward rates is provided in the next section.

8. THE EQUILIBRIUM PRICING VERSUS THE ARBITRAGE PRICING METHODOLOGY

The crucial difference between our methodology for pricing contingent claims on the term structure of interest rates and that of Cox, Ingersoll, and Ross (1985) (CIR) is the difference between the arbitrage free pricing methodology and that of equilibrium pricing, respectively. To clarify the relationship between these approaches, we illustrate how to describe (or model) the equilibrium determined CIR square root model in our framework. The CIR model is based on a single state variable, represented by the spot interest rate $r(t)$ for $t \in [0, \tau]$.

The spot rate is assumed to follow a square root process

$$(47)\qquad dr(t) = K(\theta(t) - r(t))\,dt + \sigma\sqrt{r(t)}\,dW(t)$$

where $r(0), K, \sigma$ are strictly positive constants, θ: $[0,\tau] \to (0, +\infty)$ is a continuous function of time, $\{W(t): t \in [0,\tau]\}$ is a standard Wiener process initialized at zero, and $2K\theta(t) \geqslant \sigma^2$ for all $t \in [0,\tau]$.

The condition that $2K\theta(t) \geqslant \sigma^2$ for all $t \in [0,\tau]$ guarantees that zero is an inaccessible boundary for spot rates. Although this stochastic differential equation has a solution (see Feller (1951)), an explicit representation is unavailable. In equilibrium, CIR show that the equilibrium bond dynamics are:

$$(48)\qquad dP(t,T) = r(t)\left[1 - \lambda\bar{B}(t,T)\right]P(t,T)\,dt - \bar{B}(t,T)P(t,T)\sigma\sqrt{r(t)}\,dW(t)$$

where λ is a constant,

$$\bar{B}(t,T) = 2(e^{\gamma(T-t)} - 1)/\left[(\gamma + K + \lambda)(e^{\gamma(T-t)} - 1) + 2\gamma\right],$$

$$\text{and}\quad \gamma = \left((K+\lambda)^2 + 2\sigma^2\right)^{1/2}.$$

The parameter λ is related to the market price of risk, $\phi(t) = -\lambda\sqrt{r(t)}/\sigma$. The market price of risk is restricted in equilibrium to be of this particular functional form. CIR solve for the bond price process, and from this one can deduce the forward rate process:

$$(49)\qquad f(t,T) = r(t)\left(\partial\bar{B}(t,T)/\partial T\right) + K\int_t^T \theta(s)\left(\partial\bar{B}(s,T)/\partial T\right)ds.$$

Given its parameters, CIR's model has a predetermined functional form for the forward rate process at time 0 given by expression (49). To match any arbitrary, but given initial forward rate curve, CIR suggest that one "inverts" expression (49) when $t = 0$ for $\{\theta(t): t \in [0,\tau]\}$ to make the spot rate process's parameters implicitly determined by the initial forward rate curve; see CIR (p. 395).

CIR never prove that such an inversion is possible, i.e., that a "solution" $\{\theta(t): t \in [0,\tau]\}$ exists to expression (49) with $t = 0$. In fact, if $\{\partial f(0,T)/\partial T: T \in [0,\tau]\}$ exists and is continuous, then there is a *unique* continuous solution.[10] Using standard procedures, one can show that the solution $\{\theta(s): s \in [0,\tau]\}$ to

[10] Let $\{f(0,T): T \in [0,\tau]\}$ be twice continuously differentiable. Note that $\bar{B}_T(t,T) \equiv \partial\bar{B}(t,T)/\partial T$ and $\bar{B}_{TT}(t,T) \equiv \partial^2\bar{B}_T(t,T)/\partial T$ are continuous on $0 \leqslant t \leqslant T \leqslant \tau$ with $\bar{B}(t,t) = 0$ and $\bar{B}_T(t,T) = 1$. Expression (49) with $t = 0$ is

$$f(0,T) = r(0)\bar{B}_T(0,T) + K\int_0^T \theta(s)\bar{B}_T(s,T)\,ds.$$

Differentiating with respect to T yields

$$\left[\partial f(0,T)/\partial T - r(0)\bar{B}_{TT}(0,T)\right]/K = \theta(T) + \int_0^T \theta(s)\left(K\bar{B}_{TT}(s,T)\right)ds.$$

This is a Volterra integral equation of the second kind with a unique continuous solution $\theta(\cdot)$ on $[0,\tau]$; see Taylor and Lay (1980, p. 200). *Q.E.D.*

equation (49) with $t=0$ can be approximated to any order of accuracy desired (see Taylor and Lay (1980, pp. 196–201)). Nonetheless, the CIR model is not consistent with all initial forward rate curves. This is due to the requirement that $2K\theta(t) \geqslant \sigma^2$ for all $t \in [0, \tau]$. Indeed, consider expression (49) initialized at $t = 0$. Substitution of the inaccessible boundary condition into it, and simplification yields

$$(50) \qquad f(0,T) \geqslant r(0)\partial \bar{B}(0,T)/\partial T + \sigma^2 \bar{B}(0,T)/2.$$

Not all initial forward rate curves will satisfy this expression.

Hence, in our framework we have that CIR's term structure model can be written as

$$(51) \qquad df(t,T) = r(t)K\big(\partial^2 \bar{B}(t,T)/\partial t \partial T - \partial \bar{B}(t,T)/\partial T\big)\,dt + \big(\partial \bar{B}(t,T)/\partial T\big)\sigma\sqrt{r(t)}\,dW(t)$$

where

$$r(t) = \left[f(t,T) - K\int_t^T \theta(s)\big(\partial \bar{B}(s,T)/\partial T\big)\,ds\right]\Big/\big(\partial \bar{B}(t,T)/\partial T\big),$$

$\{f(0,T)\colon T \in [0,\tau]\}$ is a continuously differentiable, fixed, initial forward rate curve, and $\theta\colon [0,\tau] \to (0, +\infty)$ is the unique continuous solution to expression (49) with $t = 0$.

To apply our analysis based on expressio (51), we need to guarantee that conditions C.1–C.6 are satisfied. Recall that conditions C.1–C.3 guarantee that the bond price process satisfies expression (8). Next, given expression (8), conditions C.4 and C.5 guarantee that for any vector of bonds $\{S_1, \ldots, S_n\}$ an equivalent martingale measure exists and is unique. Finally, condition C.6 ensures that the martingale measure is identical across all vectors of bonds. These conditions are sufficient to price all contingent claims when starting from forward rates.

Alternatively, CIR exogenously specify the spot rate process. Consequently, using different methods, they are able to guarantee that the bond price process satisfies expression (8). Hence, we don't need to check sufficient conditions C.1–C.3, since expression (8) is the starting point of our analysis. Next, given that the bond prices are generated by an equilibrium with a single Brownian motion, conditions C.4, C.5, and C.6 are easily verified. In fact, to check condition C.6 one can easily verify that expression (18) is satisfied.

Given the form of the CIR model as in expression (51), we can now proceed directly as in Section 5 to price contingent claims. This analysis will generate the *identical* contingent claim values as in CIR subject to the determination of $\{\theta(s)\colon s \in [0,\tau]\}$. Note that the forward rate's quadratic variation

$$\langle f(t,T)\rangle_t = \int_0^t \left[\big(\partial \bar{B}(s,T)/\partial T\big)\sigma\sqrt{r(s)}\right]^2 ds$$

depends on the parameters $\lambda, \sigma, K, r(0)$, and $\{f(0,T)\colon T \in [0,\tau]\}$. The parameter λ, however, is functionally related to the market price of risk. This makes contingent claim valuation explicitly dependent on this parameter as well (e.g., see CIR (expression (32), p. 396)).

With this analysis behind us, we can now discuss some differences between the two pricing approaches. First, CIR's model fixed a particular market price for risk and endogenously derived the stochastic process for forward rates. In contrast, our approach takes the stochastic process for forward rates as a given (it could be from an equilibrium model) and prices contingent claims from it.

9. SUMMARY

This paper presents a new methodology for pricing contingent claims on the term structure of interest rates. Given an initial forward rate curve and a mechanism which describes how it fluctuates, we develop an arbitrage pricing model which yields contingent claim valuations which do not explicitly depend on the market prices for risk.

For practical applications, we specialize our abstract economy and study particular examples. For these examples, closed form solutions are obtained for bond options depending only upon observables and the forward rate volatilities. These models are testable and their empirical verification awaits subsequent research.

The paper can be generalized by imbedding our term structure model into the larger economy of Harrison and Pliska (1981), which includes trading in alternative risky assets (e.g., stocks) generated by additional (perhaps distinct) independent Brownian motions. Our model provides a consistent structure for the interest rate process employed therein. This merging of the two analyses can be found in Amin and Jarrow (1989).

Operations Research and Industrial Engineering, Cornell University, Ithaca, NY 14853, U.S.A.

Johnson Graduate School of Management, Cornell University, Ithaca, NY 14853, U.S.A.

and

Department of Information and Decision Sciences, College of Business Administration, University of Illinois at Chicago, Chicago, IL 60680, U.S.A.

Manuscript received November, 1989; final revision received May, 1991.

APPENDIX

PROOF OF EXPRESSION (8): Before proving expression (8), we need to state a generalized form of Fubini's theorem for stochastic integrals. This proof of this theorem follows Ikeda and Watanabe (1981, p. 116) very closely, and is available from the authors upon request.

LEMMA 0.1: *Let (Ω, F, Q) be a probability space. Let (F_t) be a reference family satisfying the usual conditions and generated by a Brownian motion $\{W(t): t \in [0, \tau]\}$.*

Let $\{\Phi(t,a,\omega): (t,a) \in [0,\tau] \times [0,\tau]\}$ *be a family of real random variables such that:*

(i) $$((t,\omega),a) \in \{([0,\tau] \times \Omega) \times [0,\tau]\} \to \Phi(t,a,\omega)$$

is $L \times B[0,\tau]$ *measurable where* L *is the predictable* σ*-field;*

(ii) $$\int_0^t \Phi^2(s,a,\omega)\,ds < +\infty \quad a.e. \quad \text{for all} \quad t \in [0,\tau];$$

(iii) $$\int_0^t \left\{\int_0^T \Phi(s,a,\omega)\,da\right\}^2 ds < +\infty \quad a.e. \quad \text{for all} \quad t \in [0,\tau].$$

If $t \to \int_0^T \{\int_0^t \Phi(s,a,\omega) dW_s\} da$ *is continuous a.e., then*

$$\int_0^t \left\{\int_0^T \Phi(s,a,\omega)\,da\right\} dW_s = \int_0^T \left\{\int_0^t \Phi(s,a,\omega)\,dW_s\right\} da \quad \text{for all} \quad t \in [0,\tau].$$

COROLLARY 1: *Let the hypotheses of Lemma* 0.1 *hold. Define*

$$\Phi(s,a,\omega) = \begin{cases} 0 & \text{if } (s,a) \notin [0,t] \times [t,\tau], \\ \sigma(s,a,\omega) & \text{if } (s,a) \in [0,t] \times [t,\tau]. \end{cases}$$

Then

$$\int_0^y \left\{\int_t^T \sigma(s,a,\omega)\,da\right\} dW(s) = \int_t^T \left\{\int_0^y \sigma(s,a,\omega)\,dW(s)\right\} da \quad \text{for all} \quad y \in [0,t].$$

COROLLARY 2: *Let the hypotheses of Lemma* 0.1 *hold. Define*

$$\Phi(s,a,\omega) = \begin{cases} 0 & \text{if } (s,a) \notin [0,t] \times [0,t], \\ \sigma(s,a,\omega) 1_{s \leqslant a} & \text{if } (s,a) \in [0,t] \times [0,t]. \end{cases}$$

Then

$$\int_0^y \left[\int_s^t \sigma(s,a,\omega)\,da\right] dW(s) = \int_0^t \left[\int_0^{a \wedge y} \sigma(s,a,\omega)\,dW(s)\right] da \quad \text{for all} \quad y \in [0,t].$$

Now we can proceed with the proof of expression (8).

$$\ln P(t,T) = -\int_t^T f(0,y)\,dy - \int_t^T \left[\int_0^t \alpha(v,y)\,dv\right] dy - \sum_{i=1}^n \int_t^T \left[\int_0^t \sigma_i(v,y)\,dW_i(v)\right] dy.$$

Note that the integrals are well-defined by conditions C.1, C.2.

By condition C.2, we can apply the standard Fubini's theorem. By conditions C.1–C.3 we can apply Corollary 1 with $y = t$ to get

$$\ln P(t,T) = -\int_t^T f(0,y)\,dy - \int_0^t \left[\int_t^T \alpha(v,y)\,dv\right] dy - \sum_{i=1}^n \int_0^t \left[\int_t^T \sigma_i(v,y)\,dy\right] dW_i(v).$$

Adding and subtracting the same terms yields

$$= -\int_0^T f(0,y)\,dy - \int_0^t \left[\int_v^T \alpha(v,y)\,dy\right] dv - \sum_{i=1}^n \int_0^t \left[\int_v^T \sigma_i(v,y)\,dy\right] dW_i(v)$$

$$+ \int_0^t f(0,y)\,dy + \int_0^t \left[\int_v^t \alpha(v,y)\,dy\right] dv + \sum_{i=1}^n \int_0^t \left[\int_v^t \sigma_i(v,y)\,dy\right] dW_i(v).$$

But, expression (5) yields with Corollary 2 (by C.1–C.3) for $y = t$:

$$\ln P(t,T) = \ln P(0,T) + \int_0^t r(y)\,dy - \int_0^t \left[\int_v^T \alpha(v,y)\,dv\right] dy$$

$$- \sum_{i=1}^{n} \int_0^t \left[\int_v^T \sigma_i(v,y)\,dy\right] dW_i(v).$$

This completes the proof. *Q.E.D.*

PROOF OF PROPOSITION 1: This proposition is proved through the following two lemmas. The straightforward proofs of these lemmas are omitted.

LEMMA 1.1: *Assume C.1–C.3 hold for fixed* $\{S_1,\dots,S_n\} \in [0,\tau]$ *such that* $0 < S_1 < \dots < S_n \leqslant \tau$. *Define*

$$X(t,y) = \int_0^t b(v,y)\,dv + \sum_{i=1}^{n} \int_0^t a_i(v,y)\,dW_i(v)$$

$$\text{for all } t \in [0,y] \text{ and } y \in \{S_1,\dots,S_n\}.$$

Then $\gamma_i\colon \Omega \times [0,\tau] \to R$ *for* $i = 1,\dots,n$ *satisfies*:

(i) $$\begin{bmatrix} b(t,S_1) \\ \vdots \\ b(t,S_n) \end{bmatrix} + \begin{bmatrix} a_1(t,S_1) & \dots & a_n(t,S_1) \\ \vdots & & \vdots \\ a_1(t,S_n) & \dots & a_n(t,S_n) \end{bmatrix} \begin{bmatrix} \gamma_1(t) \\ \vdots \\ \gamma_n(t) \end{bmatrix} = \begin{bmatrix} 0 \\ \vdots \\ 0 \end{bmatrix} \quad \text{a.e. } \lambda \times Q;$$

(ii) $$\int_0^{S_1} \gamma_i(v)^2\,dv < +\infty \quad \text{a.e. } Q \quad \text{for } i = 1,\dots,n;$$

(iii) $$E\left(\exp\left\{\sum_{i=1}^{n} \int_0^{S_1} \gamma_i(v)\,dW_i(v) - (1/2)\sum_{i=1}^{n} \int_0^{S_1} \gamma_i(v)^2\,dv\right\}\right) = 1; \quad \text{and}$$

(iv) $$E\left(\exp\left\{\sum_{i=1}^{n} \int_0^{S_1} [a_i(v,y) + \gamma_i(v)]\,dW_i(v)\right.\right.$$

$$\left.\left. - (1/2)\sum_{i=1}^{n} \int_0^{S_1} [a_i(v,y) + \gamma_i(v)]^2\,dv\right\}\right) = 1$$

for $y \in S_1,\dots,S_n$ *if and only if*: *there exists a probability measure* $\tilde{Q}_{S_1\dots S_n}$ *such that*

(a) $$d\tilde{Q}_{S_1\dots S_n}/dQ = \exp\left\{\sum_{i=1}^{n} \int_0^{S_1} \gamma_i(v)\,dW_i(v) - (1/2)\sum_{i=1}^{n} \int_0^{S_1} \gamma_i(v)^2\,dv\right\};$$

(b) $\tilde{W}_i^{S_1\dots S_n}(t) = W_i(t) - \int_0^t \gamma_i(v)\,dv$ *are Brownian motions on*

$$\left\{\left(\Omega, F, \tilde{Q}_{S_1\dots S_n}\right), \{F_t\colon t \in [0,S_1]\}\right\} \quad \text{for } i = 1,\dots,n;$$

(c) $$\begin{pmatrix} dX(t,S_1) \\ \vdots \\ dX(t,S_n) \end{pmatrix} = \begin{pmatrix} a_1(t,S_1) & \dots & a_n(t,S_1) \\ \vdots & & \vdots \\ a_1(t,S_n) & \dots & a_n(t,S_n) \end{pmatrix} \begin{pmatrix} d\tilde{W}_1^{S_1\dots S_n}(t) \\ \vdots \\ d\tilde{W}_n^{S_1\dots S_n}(t) \end{pmatrix} \quad \text{for } t \in [0,S_1];$$

and

(d) $Z(t,S_i)$ *are martingales on* $\left\{\left(\Omega, F, \tilde{Q}_{S_1\dots S_n}\right), \{F_t\colon t \in [0,S_1]\}\right\}$ *for* $i = 1,\dots,n$.

LEMMA 1.2: *Assume C.1–C.3 hold for fixed* $\{S_1 \dots S_n\} \in [0, \tau]$ *such that* $0 < S_1 < \dots < S_n \leqslant \tau$. *Define*

$$X(t, y) = \int_0^t b(v, y)\, dv + \sum_{i=1}^{n} \int_0^t a_i(v, y)\, dW_i(v)$$

$$\textit{for all} \quad t \in [0, y] \quad \textit{and} \quad y \in \{S_1 \dots S_n\}.$$

There exists a probability measure $\bar{Q}$ *equivalent to* Q *such that* $Z(t, S_i)$ *are martingales on* $\{(\Omega, F, \bar{Q}), \{F_t: t \in [0, S_1]\}\}$ *for all* $i = 1, \dots, n$ *if and only if there exists* $\gamma_i: \Omega \times [0, \tau] \to R$ *for* $i = 1, \dots, n$ *and a probability measure* $\bar{Q}_{S_1 \dots S_n}$ *such that (a), (b), (c), and (d) of Lemma 1.1 hold.*

PROOF OF PROPOSITION 2: The proof of this proposition requires the following two lemmas.

LEMMA 2.1: *Fix* $S < \tau$. *Let* $\beta_i: \Omega \times [0, \tau] \to R$ *for* $i = 1, \dots, n$ *be such that* $\int_0^S \beta_i^2(v)\, dv < +\infty$ *a.e.* Q. *Define*

$$T_m \equiv \inf\left\{ t \in [0, S]: E\left(\exp\left\{ (1/2) \sum_{i=1}^{n} \int_0^t \beta_i(v)^2\, dv \right\} \right) \geqslant m \right\},$$

$$M^m(t) \equiv \exp\left\{ \sum_{i=1}^{n} \int_0^{\min(T_m, t)} \beta_i(v)\, dW_i(v) - (1/2) \sum_{i=1}^{n} \int_0^{\min(T_m, t)} \beta_i(v)^2\, dv \right\}.$$

Then

$$E\left(\exp\left\{ \sum_{i=1}^{n} \int_0^S \beta_i(v)\, dW_i(v) - (1/2) \sum_{i=1}^{n} \int_0^S \beta_i(v)^2\, dv \right\} \right) = 1$$

if and only if $\{M^m(S)\}_{m=1}^{\infty}$ *are uniformly integrable.*

PROOF: Define $\beta_i^m(v) \equiv \beta_i(v) 1_{\{v \leqslant T_m\}}$; then by Elliott (1982, p. 165),

$$M^m(t) = \exp\left\{ \sum_{i=1}^{n} \int_0^S \beta_i^m(v)\, dW_i(v) - (1/2) \sum_{i=1}^{n} \int_0^S \beta_i^m(v)^2\, dv \right\}$$

is a supermartingale. Since

$$E\left(\exp\left\{ (1/2) \sum_{i=1}^{n} \int_0^{T_m} \beta_i(v)^2\, dv \right\} \right) = E\left(\exp\left\{ (1/2) \sum_{i=1}^{n} \int_0^S \beta_i^m(v)^2\, dv \right\} \right) \leqslant m,$$

by Elliott (1982, p. 178) $E(M^m(S)) = 1$. Hence, $M^m(t)$ is a martingale. Note

$$\lim_{m \to \infty} M^m(S) = \exp\left\{ \sum_{i=1}^{n} \int_0^S \beta_i(v)\, dW_i(v) - (1/2) \sum_{i=1}^{n} \int_0^S \beta_i^2(v)\, dv \right\}$$

with probability one since $T_m \to S$ with probability one. Observe that $\{M^m(S)\}_{m=1}^{\infty}$ is a martingale with respect to $m = 1, 2, \dots$ because $\sup E(M^m(S)) = 1 < +\infty$ and $E(M^{m+1}(S) | F_{\min(S, T_m)}) = M^{m+1}(\min(S, T_m))$ by the Optional Stopping Theorem (since $T_m \leqslant S$, see Elliott (1982, p. 17)) $= M^m(S)$ by the definition of M^m.

Step 1: Suppose $\{M^m(S)\}_{m=1}^{\infty}$ are uniformly integrable; then

$$\lim_{m \to \infty} M^m(S) = \exp\left\{ \sum_{i=1}^{n} \int_0^S \beta_i(v)\, dW_i(v) - (1/2) \sum_{i=1}^{n} \int_0^S \beta_i(v)^2\, dv \right\}$$

in L^1 (see Elliott (1982, p. 22)), and thus

$$E\left(\exp\left\{ \sum_{i=1}^{n} \int_0^S \beta_i(v)\, dW_i(v) - (1/2) \sum_{i=1}^{n} \int_0^S \beta_i(v)^2\, dv \right\} \right) = \lim_{m \to \infty} E(M^m(S)).$$

But, $E(M^m(S)) = 1$. This completes the proof in one direction.

Step 2: Conversely, suppose

$$E\left(\exp\left\{\sum_{i=1}^{n}\int_0^S \beta_i(v)\,dW_i(v) - (1/2)\sum_{i=1}^{n}\int_0^S \beta_i(v)^2\,dv\right\}\right) = 1.$$

We know

$$E\left(\exp\left\{\sum_{i=1}^{n}\int_0^S \beta_i(v)\,dW_i(v) - (1/2)\sum_{i=1}^{n}\int_0^S \beta_i(v)^2\,dv\right\}\middle| F_{T_n}\right) = M^m(S),$$

hence $M^m(S)$ is uniformly integrable. Q.E.D.

LEMMA 2.2: *Assume conditions C.1–C.3 hold for fixed* $S_1,\dots,S_n \in [0,\tau]$ *such that* $0 < S_1 < \dots < S_n \leqslant \tau$. *Suppose conditions (i), (ii), (iii), and (iv) of Lemma 1.1 hold; then* $\gamma_i(t)$ *for* $i = 1,\dots,n$ *satisfying (i), (ii), (iii), and (iv) are unique (up to* $\lambda \times Q$ *equivalence) if and only if*

$$A(t) \equiv \begin{pmatrix} a_1(t,S_1) & \dots & a_n(t,S_1) \\ & \vdots & \\ a_1(t,S_n) & \dots & a_n(t,S_n) \end{pmatrix}$$

is singular with $(\lambda \times Q)$ *measure zero.*

PROOF: Suppose $A(t)$ is singular with $(\lambda \times Q)$ measure zero. Then, by condition (i) of Lemma 1.1, $\gamma_i(t)$ for $i = 1,\dots,n$ are unique (up to $\lambda \times Q$ equivalence).

Conversely, suppose $\Sigma \equiv \{t \times \omega \in [0,S] \times \Omega\colon A(t)$ is singular$\}$ has $(\lambda \times Q)(\Sigma) > 0$. We want to show that the functions satisfying conditions (i), (ii), (iii), and (iv) are not unique. First, by hypothesis, we are given a vector of functions $(\gamma_1(t),\dots,\gamma_n(t))$ satisfying (i), (ii), (iii), and (iv).

Step 1: Show that there exists a bounded, adapted, measurable vector of functions $(\delta_1(t),\dots,\delta_n(t))$ nonzero on Σ such that

$$A(t)\begin{bmatrix}\delta_1(t)\\ \vdots \\ \delta_n(t)\end{bmatrix} = \begin{bmatrix}0\\ \vdots\\ 0\end{bmatrix} \quad \text{and}$$

$$g(t) \equiv \exp\left\{\sum_{i=1}^{n}\int_0^t \delta_i(v)\,dW_i(v) - \sum_{i=1}^{n}\left(\int_0^t \delta_i(v)\gamma_i(v)\,dv\right) - (1/2)\sum_{i=1}^{n}\int_0^t \delta_i^2(v)\,dv\right\}$$

is bounded a.e. Q. Let $\Sigma_i = \{(t,w)\colon A(t)$ has rank $i\}$. Σ_i is a measurable set. Then $\Sigma = \cup_{i=1}^{n-1}\Sigma_i$ and $\Sigma_i \cap \Sigma_j = \varnothing$ for $i \neq j$. Fix $\eta > 0$. On each set Σ_i, set $\delta_i^\eta(t)$ for $i = 1,\dots,n$ equal to a solution to

$$A(t)\begin{bmatrix}\delta_1^\eta(t)\\ \vdots \\ \delta_n^\eta(t)\end{bmatrix} = \begin{bmatrix}0\\ \vdots\\ 0\end{bmatrix}$$

such that $\delta_i^\eta(t)$ are bounded by $\min(\eta, 1/\gamma_i(t)$ for $i = 1,\dots,n)$. Finally, let $\delta_i^\eta(t)$ be zero on Σ^c for $i = 1,\dots,n$. Note that we shall always interpret superscripts on δ as the upper bound on the process, and not as an exponent.

By construction, $\delta_i^\eta(t)$ are adapted, measurable, bounded by η, and

$$\left|\sum_{i=1}^{n}\int_0^t \delta_i^\eta(v)\gamma_i(v)\,dv + (1/2)\sum_{i=1}^{n}\int_0^t \delta_i^\eta(v)^2\,dv\right| \leqslant [2+\eta^2]\tau \quad \text{a.e. } Q.$$

Let $\alpha = \inf\{j \in \{1,2,3,\dots\}\colon (1/2)^{2j}S < 1\}$. Define inductively the stopping times:

$$\tau_1 = \inf\left\{t \in [0,S]\colon \sum_{i=1}^{n}\int_0^t \delta_i^{(1/2)^\alpha}(v)\,dW_i(v) \geqslant (1/2)\right\},$$

$$\tau_j = \inf\left\{t \in [0,S]\colon \sum_{i=1}^{n}\int_{\tau_{j-1}}^t \delta_i^{(1/2)^{2j+\alpha}}(v)\,dW_i(v) \geqslant (1/2)^j\right\} \quad \text{for } j = 2,3,4,\dots.$$

We claim that $Q(\lim_{j\to\infty}\tau_j = S) = 1$. Indeed,

$$Q\left(\tau_j < S \mid F_{\tau_{j-1}}\right) \leqslant Q\left(\left|\sum_{i=1}^{n}\int_{\tau_{j-1}}^{S}\delta_i^{(1/2)^{2j+\alpha}}(v)\,dW_i(v)\right| \geqslant (1/2)^j \mid F_{\tau_{j-1}}\right)$$

$$\leqslant \frac{1}{[1/2]^{2j}}\int_{\tau_{j-1}}^{S}\left(\delta_i^{(1/2)^{2j+\alpha}}(v)\right)^2 dv \quad \text{by Chebyshev's inequality,}$$

$$\leqslant \frac{1}{[1/2]^{2j}}\left([1/2]^{2j+\alpha}\right)^2 S < (1/2)^{2j} \quad \text{by choice of } \alpha.$$

Hence $E[Q(\tau_j < S \mid F_{\tau_{j-1}})] = Q(\tau_j < S) < (1/2)^{2j}$. Since

$$Q\left(\lim_{j\to\infty}\tau_j = S\right) = 1 - Q\left(\lim_{j\to\infty}\tau_j < S\right) \quad \text{and}$$

$$Q\left(\lim_{j\to\infty}\tau_j < S\right) < Q\left(\bigcap_{j=1}^{\infty}(\tau_j < S)\right) \leqslant \inf\left\{Q(\tau_j < S):\quad j = 1,2,3,\ldots\right\} = 0,$$

this proves the claim.

Set

$$\delta_i(t) = \sum_{j=0}^{\infty} 1_{[\tau_j,\tau_{j+1}]}^{(t)}\delta_i^{(1/2)^{2j+\alpha}}(t) \quad \text{for} \quad i = 1,\ldots,n.$$

$\delta_i(t)$ is bounded, adapted, and measurable and satisfies

$$A(t)\begin{bmatrix}\delta_1(t)\\ \vdots \\ \delta_n(t)\end{bmatrix} = \begin{bmatrix}0\\ \vdots \\ 0\end{bmatrix} \quad \text{a.e.} \quad \lambda \times Q.$$

Note that for all $t \in [0, S]$,

$$\left|\sum_{i=1}^{n}\int_0^t \delta_i(t)\,dW_i(t)\right| \leqslant \sum_{j=0}^{\infty}(1/2)^j = 2,$$

so

$$\exp\left\{\sum_{i=1}^{n}\int_0^t \delta_i(t)\,dW_i(t) - \sum_{i=1}^{n}\int_0^t \delta_i(v)\gamma_i(v)\,dv - (1/2)\sum_{i=1}^{n}\int_0^t \delta_i^2(v)\,dv\right\}$$

is bounded a.e. $\lambda \times Q$. This completes Step 1.

Step 2: Show that $(\gamma_1(t) + \delta_1(t),\ldots,\gamma_n(t) + \delta_n(t))$ satisfies conditions (i), (ii), (iii), and (iv) of Lemma 1.1. This step will complete the proof.

Conditions (i) and (ii) are obvious. To obtain condition (iii), define

$$T_m = \inf\left\{t \in [0,T]: E\left(\exp\left\{(1/2)\sum_{i=1}^{n}\int_0^t (\gamma_i(t) + \delta_i(t))^2\,dv\right\} \geqslant m\right)\right\},$$

$$M^m(t) = \exp\left\{\sum_{i=1}^{n}\int_0^{\min(T_m,t)}[\gamma_i(v) + \delta_i(v)]\,dW_i(v)\right.$$

$$\left. - (1/2)\sum_{i=1}^{n}\int_0^{\min(T_m,t)}[\gamma_i(v) + \delta_i(v)]^2\,dv\right\}.$$

By Lemma 2.1, we need to show that $M^m(S)$ is uniformly integrable. But

$$M^m(s) = \exp\left\{\sum_{i=1}^{n}\int_0^{\min(S,T_m)}\gamma_i(v)\,dW_i(v) - (1/2)\sum_{i=1}^{n}\int_0^{\min(S,T_m)}\gamma_i(v)^2\,dv\right\}\exp\left\{\sum_{i=1}^{n}\int_0^{\min(S,T_m)}\delta_i(v)\,dW_i(v) - (1/2)\sum_{i=1}^{n}\int_0^{\min(S,T_m)}\left[2\gamma_i(v)\delta_i(v)+\delta_i(v)^2\right]dv\right\}.$$

Since

$$\exp\left\{\sum_{i=1}^{n}\int_0^{\min(S,T_m)}\delta_i(v)\,dW_i(v) - (1/2)\sum_{i=1}^{n}\int_0^{\min(S,T_m)}\left[2\gamma_i(v)\delta_i(v)+\delta_i(v)^2\right]dv\right\}$$

is bounded,

$$0 \leqslant M^m(S) \leqslant K\exp\left\{\sum_{i=1}^{n}\int_0^{\min(S,T_m)}\gamma_i(v)\,dW_i(v) - (1/2)\sum_{i=1}^{n}\int_0^{\min(S,T_m)}\gamma_i(v)^2\,dv\right\} \quad \text{for some } K>0.$$

By Lemma 2.1 since $\gamma_i(t)$ satisfies (iii), the right hand side is uniformly integrable. By Kopp (1984, p. 29), it can be shown that $M^m(S)$ is uniformly integrable. Finally, an analogous argument used to prove (iii) shows (iv) holds as well. *Q.E.D.*

Proof of Proposition 5: Fix a T_0. Consider

$$\eta(t) \equiv -\sigma\min(f(t,T_0),\lambda)\int_t^{T_0}\sigma\min(f(t,s),\lambda)\,ds/\sigma\min(f(t,T_0),\lambda) = -\int_t^{T_0}\sigma\min(f(t,s),\lambda)\,ds.$$

Since $\sigma\min(f(t,s),\lambda)$ is bounded, $\eta(t)$ is bounded. Hence,

$$E\left(\exp\left\{(1/2)\int_0^{T_0}\eta(t)^2\,dt\right\}\right) < +\infty.$$

By Girsanov's theorem, there exists an equivalent probability measure $\overline{Q}$ and a Brownian motion $\overline{W}(t)$ such that $df(t,T_0)=\sigma\min(f(t,T_0),\lambda)\,d\overline{W}(t)$. Define $t_0=\inf\{t\in[0,T_0]\colon f(t,T_0)=0\}$. By Karlin and Taylor (1981, Lemma 15.6.2), zero is an unattainable boundary, i.e., $\overline{Q}\{t_0\leqslant T_0\}=Q\{t_0\leqslant T_0\}=0$. Since $f(t,T_0)$ has continuous sample paths, $f(t,T_0)>0$ a.e. Let $\{T_i\colon i=1,2,3,\ldots\}$ be the rationals in $[0,\tau]$:

$$Q\{f(t,T_i)=0 \text{ for some } T_i \text{ and some } t\in[0,T_i]\} = Q\left\{\bigcup_{i=1}^{\infty}\{f(t,T_i)=0 \text{ for some } t\ [0,T_i]\}\right\} \leqslant \sum_{i=1}^{\infty}Q\{f(t,T_i)=0 \text{ for some } t\in[0,T_1]\}=0.$$

By the joint continuity of $f(t,T)$, $Q\{f(t,T)\geqslant 0$ for all $T\in[0,\tau]$ and all $t\in[0,T]\}=1$. *Q.E.D.*

REFERENCES

AMIN, K., AND R. JARROW (1989): "Pricing American Options on Risky Assets in a Stochastic Interest Rate Economy," unpublished manuscript, Cornell University.

ARTZNER, P., AND F. DELBAEN (1987): "Term Structure of Interest Rates: The Martingale Approach," forthcoming, *Advances in Applied Mathematics*.

BALL, C., AND W. TOROUS (1983): "Bond Price Dynamics and Options," *Journal of Financial and Quantitative Analysis*, 18, 517–531.

BRENNAN, M. J., AND E. S. SCHWARTZ (1979): "A Continuous-Time Approach to the Pricing of Bonds," *Journal of Banking and Finance*, 3, 135–155.

BRENNER, R., AND R. JARROW (1992): "A Simple Formula for Options on Discount Bonds," forthcoming in *Advances in Futures and Options Research*, 6.

CHENG, S. T. (1987): "On the Feasibility of Arbitrage-Based Option Pricing when Stochastic Bond Price Processes are Involved," unpublished manuscript, Columbia University.

COX, J. C., J. E. INGERSOLL, AND S. A. ROSS (1985): "A Theory of the Term Structure of Interest Rates," *Econometrica*, 53, 385–407.

ELLIOTT, R. J. (1982): *Stochastic Calculus and Applications*. New York: Springer-Verlag.

FELLER, W. (1951): "Two Singular Diffusion Problems," *Annals of Mathematics*, 54, 173–182.

HARRISON, J. M., AND D. M. KREPS (1979): "Martingales and Arbitrage in Multiperiod Security Markets," *Journal of Economic Theory*, 20, 381–408.

HARRISON, J. M., AND S. PLISKA (1981): "Martingales and Stochastic Integrals in the Theory of Continuous Trading," *Stochastic Processes and Their Applications*, 11, 215–260.

HEATH, D., R. JARROW, AND A. MORTON (1990): "Bond Pricing and the Term Structure of Interest Rates: A Discrete Time Approximation," *Journal of Financial and Quantitative Analysis*, 25, 419–440.

HO, T. S., AND S. LEE (1986): "Term Structure Movements and Pricing Interest Rate Contingent Claims," *Journal of Finance*, 41, 1011–1028.

IKEDA, N., AND S. WATANABE (1981): *Stochastic Differential Equations and Diffusion Processes*. New York: North-Holland.

JAMSHIDIAN, F. (1989): "An Exact Bond Option Formula," *Journal of Finance*, 1, 205–209.

KARLIN, S., AND H. TAYLOR (1981): *A Second Course in Stochastic Processes*. New York: Academic Press.

KOPP, P. E. (1984): *Martigales and Stochastic Integrals*. New York: Cambridge University Press.

LANGETIEG, T. C. (1980): "A Multivariate Model of the Term Structure," *Journal of Finance*, 35, 71–97.

MORTON, A. (1988): "A Class of Stochastic Differential Equations Arising in Models for the Evolution of Bond Prices," Technical Report, School of Operations Research and Industrial Engineering, Cornell University.

SCHAEFER, S., AND E. SCHWARTZ (1987): "Time-Dependent Variance and the Pricing of Bond Options," *Journal of Finance*, 42, 1113–1128.

TAYLOR, A., AND D. LAY (1980): *Introduction to Functional Analysis*, 2nd Edition. New York: John Wiley and Sons.

VASICEK, O. (1977): "An Equilibrium Characterization of the Term Structure," *Journal of Financial Economics*, 5, 177–188.

[21]

Philip H. Dybvig
Washington University

Jonathan E. Ingersoll, Jr.
Stephen A. Ross
Yale University

Long Forward and Zero-Coupon Rates Can Never Fall*

In a model without frictions, default-free bonds can be priced as equivalent portfolios of pure discount or zero-coupon bonds. Equivalently, default-free bonds can be priced using the forward rates at a point in time. Specifying stochastic processes on one or several of the discount-bond yields or forward rates is a popular approach to building multiple factor models of the term structure of interest rates. In this article we prove that the absence of arbitrage restricts severely the behavior of these rates in the limit as maturity increases. Specifically, the limiting forward or discount rate can rise with some probability or even with certainty, but the limiting rate can never fall with positive probability. This result can be tested directly in any econometric model that allows us to extrapolate from the available finite-maturity data to test hypotheses about the limit. This result also serves as a caution that not every assumption about comovements of forward or discount rates is consistent with a coherent model of the term structure.

In frictionless markets having no arbitrage, the asymptotic zero-coupon rate never falls. The same is true of the long forward rate. The long par-coupon rate can rise and fall due to forward rate movements at short maturities. This article relates the three types of interest rate and formalizes and proves the impossibility results for falling asymptotic rates. These results can be tested in a parametric term structure specification that is rich enough to identify a time series of long rates. The results show that it is not possible to specify arbitrarily the long forward or zero-coupon rate process.

* We thank Bob Jarrow, Jeff Rosensweig, an anonymous referee, and especially Kerry Back and Hal Pedersen. This article has gone through many versions, including an early version entitled "Do Interest Rates Converge?"

(*Journal of Business*, 1996, vol. 69, no. 1)

0021-9398/96/6901-0001$01.50

Many economists would probably expect that it is possible to build a neoclassical model in which the (asymptotic) long forward and/or discount rate can move around over time. For example, assume that the expectations hypothesis is true. The expectations hypothesis asserts that today's forward rates are unbiased estimates of the unknown future spot rates. If the expectations hypothesis is true, then the forward rate today for a given future date will be today's expectation of the forward rate tomorrow for the same future date, because the change in the forward rate is an innovation in an optimal prediction.[1] Applying this implication of the expectations hypothesis to longer and longer maturities suggests that the (asymptotic) long forward rate, if it exists, should be the expectation today of what the long forward rate will be tomorrow. This article shows that this intuition is misleading: absence of arbitrage implies that today's long forward rate is no larger than the smallest long forward rate in tomorrow's distribution and, in fact, may be even smaller than that. The reason is that returns on longer and longer bonds are increasingly convex in the yields. If the long forward rate can fall, the potential loss on holding a long discount bond is limited by the purchase price, but the potential gain when the long forward rate falls becomes greater and greater as maturity increases. This implies that the long forward rate can never fall if there are no market frictions and expectations are rational.

This result becomes a testable restriction on the data once we assume a functional form for yield curves, and if the restriction is violated there is an obvious trading strategy that can be followed to exploit the arbitrage. Alternatively, the restriction can be tested nonparametrically if we are willing to assume how close zero-coupon rates at the longest maturity we observe are to the asymptotic rates. This testable restriction is especially important now that there are actively traded zero-coupon bonds (Treasury STRIPS) at long maturities. Theorists building term structure models should take the results as a caution about what assumptions can be made about interest rates in a no-arbitrage context. For example, assuming that either the long zero-coupon rate or the long forward rate follows a diffusion process necessarily implies arbitrage, so neither rate can be used as a factor in a multifactor diffusion term structure model.

Section I contains a collection of results about a single yield curve that can be derived from the absence of arbitrage and the definition of discount rates, zero-coupon rates, and par-coupon bond rates. Section II contains our main results on the behavior of long rates. Section III

1. Formally, the law of iterated expectations says that the expectation conditional on information today of the expectation conditional on information tomorrow of the future spot rate is equal to the expectation today of the future spot rate. Given the expectations hypothesis, this is just another way of saying that the expectation today of the forward rate tomorrow equals the forward rate today.

shows how our results apply to a particular term structure model of a sort described by Ho and Lee (1986). Section IV closes the article.

I. Results for a Single Yield Curve

In this section, we explore the relations among various interest rates that can be inferred solely from the absence of arbitrage in a single yield curve observed at one point in time. We assume that there are no taxes or transaction costs and that unlimited short sales are permitted. Note that in the absence of arbitrage, this implies that borrowing and lending rates are equal. To leave the application of our results open to real as well as nominal interest rates, we do not rule out negative interest rates a priori, and we will make explicit any assumption that interest rates cannot be negative. (Absence of arbitrage does imply that simple interest rates are greater than -100%, or else borrowing money would be an arbitrage.)

In our analysis, we will take as given zero-coupon (pure discount) bonds for all integer maturities. In a world where such assets do not exist but there is no arbitrage, these assets could be added with shadow prices as given by some version of the result that absence of arbitrage implies the existence of a positive linear pricing rule. However, to do so would take us unnecessarily far from where we want to go, and we simply assume that there are traded zero-coupon bonds of all integer maturities. We define $v(t, T)$ to be the discount bond price, that is, the price at t of receiving a unit payoff at a later time T.[2] As implied above, we are intentionally vague about whether these are real or nominal flows, given that we want our analysis to apply to both real and nominal bonds. We know that $v(t, T) > 0$ (the simple interest rate for borrowing from t to T must be greater than -100%); otherwise, selling short at t a discount bond maturing at T and holding it to maturity would be an arbitrage.

We consider three types of interest rates: zero-coupon rates, $z(t, T)$; forward rates, $f(t, T)$; and par-coupon bond rates, $c(t, T)$. The zero-coupon rate is the yield-to-maturity at t on a zero-coupon bond maturing at T. For $T > t$, the zero-coupon yield is defined implicitly by

$$v(t, T) = \frac{1}{[1 + z(t, T)]^{T-t}}. \tag{1}$$

2. Although we will consider limits of these interest rates as $T \uparrow \infty$, we will not have to make any assumption concerning bubbles or their absence since we will look only at arbitrages from holding finitely many assets. Nor do we need to define arbitrage over an infinite time horizon. This avoids potential paradoxes and messy issues such as what prevents agents from rolling over short borrowing indefinitely.

The forward rate $f(t, T)$, for $T > t$, is a rate at which we could contract at time t to borrow or lend money from T to $T + 1$. In the absence of arbitrage, the forward rate satisfies[3]

$$v(t, T) = [1 + f(t, T)]v(t, T + 1). \tag{2}$$

This follows because borrowing by shorting a bond maturing at T and going long an equal present value in a bond maturing at $T + 1$ is the same as borrowing forward directly (else borrowing long the cheaper way and lending long the dearer way would be an arbitrage).

Next we want to define coupon rates. Of course, coupon bonds with the same maturity but different coupons can (and typically will) have different yields. To select a unique rate we choose the yield-to-maturity of the coupon bond that is selling at par. By the absence of arbitrage, the par-coupon rate $c(t, T)$ at t on a bond maturing at T is given implicitly by

$$1 = v(t, T) + c(t, T) \sum_{\tau=t+1}^{T} v(t, \tau). \tag{3}$$

If not, it would be an arbitrage to go long in either the coupon bond or the portfolio of zero-coupon bonds replicating it, whichever is cheaper, shorting the other, and holding both positions to maturity. Equations (1)–(3) are the basic definitions of interest rates on which all the analysis in the article is based.

Because we take the prices of zero-coupon bonds as primitive in deriving our results about interest rates, it is convenient to express the latter in terms of the former. The inverse relations of (1) and (2) are well known:

$$z(t, T) = v(t, T)^{-1/(T-t)} - 1, \tag{4}$$

$$f(t, T) = \frac{v(t, T)}{v(t, T + 1)} - 1. \tag{5}$$

3. We choose to work in discrete time for convenience. All of our results remain valid in continuous time provided suitable regularity conditions hold. For example, in continuous time, the forward rate is $f(t, T) = -\partial \log[v(t, T)]/\partial T$, so $v(\cdot)$ must be differentiable with respect to T. Note that differentiability with respect to t, which we would not expect to obtain in any model with locally unpredictable prices, need not hold. More subtly in a continuous-time model, an integral representation property of the pricing rule must exist. Without the integral representation property, the value of a continuous unit coupon would not necessarily equal the integral of the zero-coupon bond prices. Back and Pliska (1991) give an example in which there is no arbitrage but there is no integral representation of the pricing rule either. In their example, the linear pricing rule is finitely additive but not countably additive.

The inverse relation of (3) expressing the par-coupon rate can also be easily derived:

$$c(t, T) = \frac{1 - v(t, T)}{\sum_{\tau=t+1}^{T} v(t, T)}. \tag{6}$$

It will also be convenient to have expressions for the zero-coupon rates and par-coupon rates in terms of the forward rates. Again the former is a well-known relation while the latter can be derived with simple algebraic manipulations:

$$z(t, T) = \left(\prod_{\tau=t}^{T-1} [1 + f(t, \tau)]\right)^{1/(T-t)} - 1, \tag{7}$$

$$c(t, T) = \frac{\sum_{\tau=t}^{T-1} v(t, \tau + 1) f(t, \tau)}{\sum_{\tau=t}^{T-1} v(t, \tau + 1)}. \tag{8}$$

Equation (7) shows that one plus the zero-coupon rate $1 + z(t, T)$ is the (equally weighted) geometric average of one plus the forward rate $1 + f(t, \tau)$ for times t through $T - 1$. Equation (8) shows that the par-coupon rate can be expressed as a positively weighted average of forward rates. In other words, (7) and (8) show that the zero-coupon rate and par-coupon rate are (types of) averages of the forward rates up through their maturities. These averages provide us with the following useful lemma. Its proof is immediate from (7), (8), and the positivity of $v(t, T)$.

Lemma 1. At any time t, the zero-coupon rate and the par-coupon rate for maturity T lie within the range of forward rates over the maturity interval $[t, T - 1]$. That is,

$$\inf_{s \in [t, T]} f(t, s) \leq z(t, T) \leq \sup_{s \in [t, T]} f(t, s)$$

and

$$\inf_{s \in [t, T]} f(t, s) \leq c(t, T) \leq \sup_{s \in [t, T]} f(t, s).$$

Proof. Immediate from (7), (8), and the positivity of $v(t, T)$. Q.E.D.

Our primary concern in this article is to analyze the behavior of the limiting values of these interest rates as the time to maturity goes to infinity. We define the *long forward rate*, the *long zero-coupon rate*, and the *long par-coupon rate*, respectively, by

$$f_L(t) \equiv \lim_{T \uparrow \infty} f(t, T), z_L(t) \equiv \lim_{T \uparrow \infty} z(t, T), c_L(t) \equiv \lim_{T \uparrow \infty} c(t, T). \quad (9)$$

Of course, each definition makes sense only if the corresponding limit exists. We will refer to this existence in the usual informal way. For example, the statement that $f_L(t)$ exists means that the limit in (9) defining $f_L(t)$ exists.

It is not obvious that the various long interest rates should exist. For example, forward rates might increase without bound, or more plausibly, the forward rates need not settle down to a limit. Our first theorem characterizes the relations among the three long interest rates and gives some existence results.

THEOREM 1: EXISTENCE AND PROPERTIES OF LONG INTEREST RATES.

1. If $v(t, T)$ is uniformly bounded across T, then $c_L(t)$ exists.

2. If $f_L(t)$ exists, so do $z_L(t)$ and $c_L(t)$. Furthermore $z_L(t) = f_L(t)$, but $c_L(t)$ need not and typically does not equal $f_L(t)$.

3. If both $f_L(t)$ and $c_L(t)$ exist, with $f_L(t) > c_L(t)$ (respectively $f_L(t) < c_L(t)$), then $c(t, T)$ is increasing in T (respectively decreasing in T) for T sufficiently large.

Proof. 1. By monotone convergence, either the denominator in (6) increases without bound as T increases, implying $c_L(t) = 0$ (since the numerator is bounded by assumption), or the denominator converges, implying that $\lim_{T \uparrow \infty} v(t, T) = 0$. In this case, $c_L(t)$ is equal to one divided by the limit of the denominator.[4]

2. From (7), one plus the zero-coupon rate is a geometric average of one plus the forward rates. The long zero-coupon rate must equal the long forward rate since the relative weight on forward rates before any given maturity approaches zero as $T \uparrow \infty$. From (8), each par-coupon rate is a positively weighted average of forward rates. Therefore, as above, if the long forward rate exists, then so does the long par-coupon rate.

3. From equation (8) $c(t, T + 1) = \alpha f(t, T) + (1 - \alpha)c(t, T)$, where $0 < \alpha \equiv v(t, T + 1)/\Sigma_{\tau=t}^{T} v(t, \tau + 1) < 1$. Therefore, $c(t, T + 1)$ is between $f(t, T)$ and $c(t, T)$ for all T, and for T sufficiently large the par-coupon yield curve will slope toward $f_L(t)$. Q.E.D.

The last two parts of theorem 1 assume the existence of the long forward rate. The long forward rate may not exist if the probability

4. More structure would be required to make this argument in continuous time. The continuous-time equivalent of (6) is $c(t, T) = [1 - v(t, T)]/\int_t^T v(t, \tau)d\tau$. The integral in the denominator can converge even if the integrand does not. An additional assumption is required. One assumption that would suffice is "All forward rates are nonnegative." A weaker but less intuitive assumption is "$v(t, T)$ has bounded variation across all $T > t$, not just on compact sets."

that the spot interest rate can become unbounded is sufficiently great. Cyclical interest rates are another hindrance to the existence of the long forward rate. Intuitively, if there is any persistent cyclical feature to short-term interest rates (e.g., rates are higher on average on Wednesdays or lower in election years),[5] then forward rates should also cycle, and the long forward rate will not exist.[6]

If the long forward rate exists, then the long zero-coupon rate exists and equals the long forward rate. For the same reason, if the forward rate is increasing and unbounded in T, so will be the zero-coupon rate and neither long rate will exist. However, the long zero-coupon rate also exists in some cases when the long forward rate does not. For example, the long zero-coupon rate exists with pure (identical) bounded cycles in forward rates because one plus the long zero-coupon rate will simply equal the geometric average of one plus the forward rate over one complete cycle. Nevertheless, bounded forward rates are insufficient to guarantee the existence of the long zero-coupon rate (if only in the context of the sorts of models we usually analyze).

For example, let the forward rate be 10% for 1 period, then 20% for 1 period, 10% for 2 periods, 20% for 2 periods, 10% for 4 periods, 20% for 4 periods, and so forth, each time doubling the length of the two cycles. By (7), the zero-coupon rate is $\sqrt{1.1 \cdot 1.2}$ after a stretch of 20% rates, and after many strings tends[7] to $1.1^{2/3}1.2^{1/2} - 1 \approx 13\%$ after a stretch of 10% rates. Because the stretches of constant interest rate get longer and longer, this example seems implausible, but it does provide an example in which the long zero-coupon rate does not exist even though forward rates are uniformly bounded.

Interestingly, our analysis does not imply that the long par-coupon rate will equal the long zero-coupon or forward rates if all exist, because the relative weight on early forward rates in (8) remains significant as $T \uparrow \infty$. We can say, however, that a yield curve of par-coupon rates will always slope toward the forward rate at any maturity, that is, $c(t, T + 1)$ is between $f(t, T)$ and $c(t, T)$. This result is useful for interpreting "textbook" yield curves based on coupon bonds. Suppose we infer from a textbook yield curve that the par-coupon rates ap-

5. Taken literally, this does assume implicitly that we know what calendar will be used for all future human endeavor and that our existing institutions will survive forever. This is a characteristic of most (if not all) models employed, even if it is not literally true.

6. For example, if the interest rate pattern for all future history is known now, the forward rate $f(t, T)$ must be the same as the known future spot rate $z(T, T + 1)$, by absence of arbitrage. Therefore, any cycles in the future spot rates are exactly reflected in today's forward rates. In most stochastic models, forward rates reflect any anticipated future cycles, but more structure is required to prove this.

7. The zero-coupon rate is $1.1^{(2^i-1)/(3 \cdot 2^{i-1}-2)}$ after the ith string of 10% rates. The exponents converge to ⅔ and ⅓ as $i \uparrow \infty$.

proach 10% from below as $T \uparrow \infty$. Then we can conclude that the long zero-coupon and forward rates (which are equal) exceed 10%.[8]

We have now proven and discussed the results in theorem 1, and we are prepared to turn to our main new results.

II. Results for a Pair of Yield Curves

The single-yield-curve results in the previous section do not seem like asset pricing results in the usual sense, because there is no uncertainty involved. In this section, we consider the relation between the yield curve at one point in time t and the distribution of potential yield curves at some later time s. To avoid cumbersome notation based on conditional expectations, all distributions we consider will be taken as conditional on the information available at the earlier time t, from the perspective of whatever information set (individual, public, or some subset) is relevant for the problem at hand. We write, for example, $z(s, T; \omega)$ for the zero-coupon rate at s for maturity T in state ω, and $z_L(s; \omega)$ for the long zero-coupon rate at s in state ω. These conventions are without loss of generality. Note that focusing on two dates does not rule out continuous-time models, since our results apply to trade at any two dates in a continuous-time model. All that is important is that there are traded discount bonds at both dates for some unbounded set of maturities.

To prove our main results, we want to be a bit more formal about what we mean by an arbitrage opportunity. In a model with finitely many states, the definition implicit in Section I is fine, while with infinitely many states we want to include some notion of continuity, which allows us to say when a sequence of trading strategies admits arbitrage in the limit. Here is a definition of arbitrage that will serve our purposes.[9]

Definition. An arbitrage opportunity is a sequence of net trades (allowing free disposal),[10] such that either (i) the price tends to zero

8. Of course, this involves leaps of faith for extrapolation to the limit, for bypassing data problems, and for assuming the long zero-coupon rate exists.

9. Our definition makes absence of arbitrage a weaker assumption than the more common assumption of no arbitrage in mean-variance or L^2 (or L^p for $p \in [1, \infty)$) limits as in Harrison and Kreps (1979), Harrison and Pliska (1981), Kreps (1981), and Chamberlain and Rothschild (1983). The more common definition of no arbitrage would also suffice for our results, because it implies our sense of no arbitrage. Note that our definition of the absence of arbitrage would be too weak for their purposes, because our definition implies continuous positive linear pricing over L^∞ but not over L^p for any $p < \infty$. In fact, risk-neutral probabilities need not exist given our assumptions, as in Back and Pliska (1991).

10. Free disposal, the subtraction of an arbitrary nonnegative random variable, is needed in general for technical reasons. Otherwise a sequence of larger and larger payoffs would not converge and therefore would not qualify as an arbitrage. The eco-

but the payoff tends uniformly to a nonnegative random variable that is positive with positive probability or (ii) the price tends to a negative number (you are paid to enter the position) but the payoff tends uniformly to a nonnegative random variable.

This definition of arbitrage is general enough to permit completely general probability spaces, and in particular our results apply to any two dates in a continuous-time model. This includes, but is not limited to, models in which the interest rate processes are diffusions, jump processes, or general stochastic integrals.

One main result of our study is that we have enough structure to prove that the long zero-coupon rate cannot fall over time.

THEOREM 2: THE LONG ZERO-COUPON RATE CAN NEVER FALL. Let $t < s$ and assume there is no arbitrage. Suppose that the long zero-coupon rate $z_L(t)$ exists at time t and that the long zero-coupon rate $z_L(s)$ exists at time s with probability one. Then $z_L(t) \leq z_L(s; \omega)$ for a set of states ω at time s having probability one.

Proof. The general structure and proof are in the appendix. Here we present a considerably simpler proof along similar lines for finitely many states.

Let ω be a typical state that might occur at time s. Without loss of generality (since we are proving a "probability one" result), we restrict attention to states ω that happen with positive probability. Since there are finitely many states, we can choose ω^* to be a state in which the long zero-coupon rate at time s achieves its smallest value, that is, $z_L(s; \omega^*) = \min_\omega z_L(s; \omega)$. We then want to show that $z_L(t) \leq z_L(s; \omega^*)$.

Suppose to the contrary that $z_L(t) > z_L(s; \omega^*)$. Then we want to show that there is arbitrage. Consider the net trade of buying at t and selling at s the default-free claim maturing at T with face value $[1 + z_L(s; \omega^*)]^{T-s}$. The arbitrage we seek will be the sequence of net trades for any increasing unbounded sequence of times T. We will show that such a sequence of net trades has an initial cash flow tending toward zero yet has a limiting payoff that is nonnegative and positive with positive probability. For each T, the net trade's cash flow at t (= $-$claim's price) is given by

$$-\frac{[1 + z_L(s; \omega^*)]^{T-s}}{[1 + z(t, T)]^{T-t}}, \tag{10}$$

nomic meaning of an arbitrage opportunity is that it is a "money pump" that any agent would want to pursue at arbitrarily large scale, and this suggests that something that dominates an arbitrage should be an arbitrage, too. This is not an issue for the finite-state case analyzed in the proof of theorem 2 given in the text, but it is an issue in the general proof given in the appendix.

which tends to 0 as $T \uparrow \infty$ because $\lim_{T\uparrow\infty} z(t, T) = z_L(t) > z_L(s; \omega)$. The proceeds from sale of the claim at s are given by

$$\frac{[1 + z_L(s; \omega^*)]^{T-s}}{[1 + z(s, T; \omega)]^{T-s}}. \tag{11}$$

As $T \uparrow \infty$, the value of this ratio at time s tends to 1 in states ω such that $z_L(s; \omega) = z_L(s; \omega^*)$ and it tends to 0 in states ω such that $z_L(s; \omega) > z_L(s; \omega^*)$. (By definition of ω^*, it cannot be that $z_L(s; \omega) < z_L(s; \omega^*)$.) Since statewise (almost sure) convergence is equivalent to uniform convergence when there are finitely many states, this is an arbitrage under our definition of arbitrage which is a contradiction. Q.E.D.

The proof showed that if well-defined long zero-coupon rates can fall, then there is arbitrage in the limit. When there are finitely many states, the set of feasible net trades is a closed subspace of L^∞ and therefore any arbitrage in the limit must also be available directly. See Berk (1990) for a construction of the direct arbitrage (without resorting to a sequence) in a finite economy in which long zero-coupon rates can fall.

The following corollary shows that well-defined long forward rates can never fall.

Corollary 2.1: The Long Forward Rate Can Never Fall. Let $t < s$ and assume there is no arbitrage. Suppose that the long forward rate $f_L(t)$ exists at time t and that the long forward rate $f_L(s)$ exists at time s with probability one. Then $f_L(t) \leq f_L(s; \omega)$ for a set of states ω having probability one.

Proof. By theorem 1, the long forward rate is equal to the long zero-coupon rate whenever the long forward rate exists. Therefore, this corollary follows directly from theorem 2. Q.E.D.

We have proven that the long forward rate can never fall. Can it rise over time? The answer to this question is yes as illustrated by the following example.

Example 1. Suppose it is known that the spot rate will be r_1 from t to s, and that at time s it will be revealed to either shift to r_2 forever or to remain at r_1 forever. If the two states have equal risk-neutral probabilities[11] of ½, the price at t of a discount bond maturing at $T > s$ is

11. Risk-neutral probabilities are used for pricing by expected discounted value, where discounting is at the rolled-over instantaneous spot rate. Existence of risk-neutral probabilities with the same possible events as actual probabilities implies absence of arbitrage. Conversely, existence of consistent risk-neutral probabilities follows from absence of arbitrage in a finite-state economy but requires a bit more structure in general. Dybvig and Ross (1987) contains an elementary exposition of these results for finitely many states.

$$
\begin{aligned}
v(t, T) &= \frac{1}{2}(1 + r_1)^{-(T-t)} + \frac{1}{2}(1 + r_1)^{-(s-t)}(1 + r_2)^{-(T-s)} \\
&= \frac{1}{2}(1 + r_1)^{-(T-t)} + \frac{1}{2}(1 + r_2)^{-(T-t)}\left(\frac{1 + r_2}{1 + r_1}\right)^{s-t}.
\end{aligned} \tag{12}
$$

For large T, the first term dominates if $r_1 < r_2$, while the second term dominates if $r_1 > r_2$. For any values of r_1 and r_2, $f_L(t) = z_L(t) = \min(r_1, r_2)$ which implies that the long rate cannot fall and rises if $r_1 \neq r_2$ and the larger of the two is realized at time s.

In example 1, the long forward and zero-coupon rates at time t are both equal to the smallest value they can take on at the later date s. This result makes intuitive sense given that we know from theorem 2 and corollary 2.1 that the long rates cannot fall, and it seems unlikely that we would know for sure that the long rate today is bounded away from the support of the possible values tomorrow. Unfortunately, while this intuition holds when there are finitely many states, it does not hold in general. We close the section with a theorem, its corollary, and an example that together formalize the observations that the long forward and discount rates must be equal to the smallest realizable value in the probability distribution at a future time if there are finitely many states but, in general, might be bounded (above) away from the range of possible values at some future time.

THEOREM 3: THE LONG ZERO-COUPON RATE EQUALS ITS MINIMUM FUTURE VALUE WITH FINITELY MANY STATES. Let $t < s$ and assume there is no arbitrage. Suppose that the long zero-coupon rate $z_L(t)$ exists at time t, that the long zero-coupon rate $z_L(s)$ exists at time s with probability 1, and that there are finitely many states of nature at time s. Then $z_L(t) = \min_\omega \{z_L(s; \omega)\}$ where we are including only states of positive probability in the minimum.

Proof. From theorem 2, $z_L(t) \leq z_L(s; \omega^*)$. Therefore, it suffices to show that $z_L(t) \geq z_L(s; \omega^*)$. Suppose to the contrary that $z_L(t) < z_L(s; \omega^*)$. Consider a net trade of selling short at t and liquidating at s the claim indexed by $T > s$ paying $[1 + z(t; T)]^{T-t}$ for sure at time T. The claim has a value of 1 for all T, and therefore a limiting value of 1, which is also the limiting value of the proceeds from the short sale. But the cash flow at time s from liquidating the short sale is given by

$$
-\frac{[1 + z(t, T)]^{T-t}}{[1 + z(s, T; \omega)]^{T-s}}, \tag{13}
$$

which tends to 0 in every state because as $T \uparrow \infty$, $z(s, T; \omega) \rightarrow z_L(s; \omega) \geq z_L(s; \omega^*) > z_L(t)$. Since statewise convergence implies uniform convergence with finitely many states, this sequence of net trades represents an arbitrage opportunity. Q.E.D.

Corollary 3.1: The Long Forward Rate Equals Its Minimum Future Value with Finitely Many States. Let $t < s$ and assume there is no arbitrage. Suppose that the long forward rate $f_L(t)$ exists at time t, that the long forward rate $f_L(s)$ exists at time s with probability 1, and that there are finitely many states of nature. Then $f_L(t) = \min_\omega f_L(s; \omega)$ (where we are including only states of positive probability in the minimum).

Proof. Immediate given theorem 3 and item 2 of theorem 1. Q.E.D.

It should be noted that this corollary (like the previous theorem) relates the long rate to its own possible future values. It makes no claim that the long rate must equal the minimum possible spot rate in the future. Typically it will exceed this. For example, if the spot rate, r, is distributed independently and identically each period under the risk-neutral probabilities, then for all $T > t$,

$$\frac{1}{1 + f_L(t)} = \left(\hat{E}\left[\prod_{s=t}^{T-1} \frac{1}{1 + r_s}\right]\right)^{1/(T-t)} = \hat{E}\left[\frac{1}{1 + r}\right], \tag{14}$$

where r has the shared distribution of the r_s's under the risk-neutral probabilities for which expectations are indicated by $\hat{E}$.[12] Clearly the long forward and zero-coupon rates will exceed the minimum spot rate if there is any dispersion in the distribution.

If there are infinitely many states at time s, then the above theorem and its corollary are no longer valid. In some models the long rates may be strictly less than their smallest possible values at a later date. This striking result is illustrated in the next example.

Example 2. Let the spot rate be r_1 from time t until time $s + \theta$ and let it be r_2 for all time after $s + \theta$, where θ is a nonnegative random variable conditional on information at t and known for sure at time s. Conditional on information at t, θ has a geometric distribution, and the probability of any nonnegative integer value of θ is $p(1 - p)^\theta$ for some known probability parameter $p \in (0, 1)$. The random variable θ has the same distribution as the number of tails before the first heads in a sequence of flips of a coin having probability p in each flip of coming up heads. The realization of θ is learned at time s, and since θ is known then $v(s, T) = (1 + r_1)^{-\theta}(1 + r_2)^{-(T-\theta-s)}$ for all $T \geq s + \theta$. Now, $z_L(s) = r_2$ independent of θ because long zero-coupon rates are not affected by the "temporary" effect of r_1 up to time $s + \theta$.[13]

12. For a finite state space, this expectation exists provided only that $r > -100\%$ in all states with positive probability.

13. More formally,

$$\begin{aligned} z_L(s) &= \lim_{T\uparrow\infty} v(s, T)^{-1/(T-s)} - 1 \\ &= \lim_{T\uparrow\infty} (1 + r_1)^{\theta/(T-s)}(1 + r_2)^{(T-s-\theta)/(T-s)} - 1 \\ &= (1 + r_1)^0(1 + r_2)^1 - 1 = r_2. \end{aligned}$$

To determine $z_L(t)$, we denote by $\hat{E}_t$ expectations under the risk-neutral probabilities conditional on information at time t, and we use the following convention. Let 1_S denote the indicator function that is 1 when the statement S is true and 0 when S is false. Then

$$\begin{aligned} v(t, T) &= \hat{E}_t\left[\frac{1_{s+\theta<T}}{(1+r_1)^{\theta+s-t}(1+r_2)^{T-s-\theta}} + \frac{1_{s+\theta\geq T}}{(1+r_1)^{T-t}}\right] \\ &= \sum_{\theta=0}^{T-s-1} \frac{p(1-p)^\theta}{(1+r_1)^{s+\theta-t}(1+r_2)^{T-s-\theta}} + \sum_{\theta=T-s}^{\infty} \frac{p(1-p)^\theta}{(1+r_1)^{T-t}} \\ &= \frac{p}{(1+r_1)^{s-t}(1+r_2)^{T-s}}\left[1-\frac{(1-p)(1+r_2)}{1+r_1}\right]^{-1} \\ &\quad + \frac{(1-p)^{T-s}}{(1+r_1)^{T-t}}\left[1-p\left(1-\frac{(1-p)(1+r_2)}{1+r_2}\right)^{-1}\right]. \end{aligned} \tag{15}$$

If $1 + r_2 < (1 + r_1)/(1 - p)$, then for large T the first term dominates and $z_L(t) = r_2$, while if $1 + r_2 > (1 + r_1)/(1 - p)$, then for large T the second term dominates and $z_L(t) = (1 + r_1)/(1 - p) - 1$. In general, the long forward and zero-coupon rates in the example are given by $f_L(t) = z_L(t) = \min[r_2, (1 + r_1)/(1 - p) - 1]$. When $1 + r_2 < (1 + r_1)/(1 - p)$, the long zero-coupon rate $(1 + r_1)/(1 - p) - 1$ at t is strictly less than the smallest (and only) possible zero-coupon rate r_2 at the later time s. It is striking that the long forward and zero-coupon rates at s are nonstochastic and therefore known at the earlier time t, but nonetheless strictly less than the corresponding long rates at t.

To understand the example, it is useful to think about pricing in an abstract way. With only slight loss of generality, we can write pricing given countably many states ω at time s as

$$v(t, T) = \sum_{\omega} p_\omega \frac{1}{[1 + z(s, T; \omega)]^{T-s}}, \tag{16}$$

where p_ω is the state price at time t of the state ω at time s. If there is a single state in which $z_L(s, T; \omega)$ is smallest, then that state will dominate $v(t, T)$ as T gets large. However, if the smallest long forward rate is not actually realized except in the limit along some sequence of states, then it may be that different states are most important in the expectation as maturity increases. For example, if in each state ω the short interest rate will be zero until some critical date and very high forever afterward, then $v(s, T; \omega)$ will approximate a step function with value one until the critical date and value zero afterward. Since any decreasing function can be approximated by the weighted average of step functions, this puts no restriction beyond nonnegativity on the long zero-coupon rate at t, although in each state ω at time s the long zero-coupon rate is very high.

In most popular term structure models, the long forward and zero-coupon rates neither fall nor rise, but are constant. This is true of Vasicek's (1977) "absolute" variance model with mean reversion, the "square root" and "three-halves" models proposed by Cox, Ingersoll, and Ross (1985), and many multifactor generalizations of these models. Theorem 3 and examples 1 and 2 provide the intuition for why this must be true. The long rates at times t_1 and t_2 are each equal to the minimum possible long rate at some later time s. The long rate can rise only if the state at time s with the minimum long rate has become impossible between times t_1 and t_2.

It is interesting to ask when the long discount rate not only cannot fall, as shown by our results, but also cannot rise and is therefore constant as in many of the popular models of the term structure. One sufficient condition is that the economy is Markov and all states are recurrent, since if long discount rates cannot fall and they must return again and again to this level, they cannot rise either in the interim. Unfortunately, for technical reasons it is not reasonable to think that the entire state of the economy or even the entire state of the term structure (outside of a single factor world) is recurrent, that is, that it will return again and again to its current value.[14] However, a weaker and more reasonable condition suffices. On economic grounds, it is hard to imagine that we will ever learn enough about how the economy works to ensure that the long discount rate can never subsequently return to today's value. Given that (as we have proven) the long discount rate cannot fall, this is enough to prove it is constant. Therefore, we should think of the ordinary situation as one in which the long discount rate is constant.

14. For example, with probability one, a nondegenerate diffusion in two or more dimensions never returns to its starting place. An example illustrates why it is possible for even a diffusion model to have a nonconstant long zero-coupon rate. Consider a diffusion model with the short rate r as the single state variable. The drift and standard deviation of the interest rate process are C^1 in r. The standard deviation is positive except for $r = 5\%$ and $r = 10\%$, where it is zero. The drift is positive at 10% but negative at 5%. (With minor technical assumptions the stochastic integral defining rates will have unique solution and all the long rates will exist.) Then, if the interest rate starts between 5% and 10%, it will wander around within this region initially, but it will hit 5% or 10% at some finite time. If it hits 5%, the interest rate will be stuck below 5% forever (given the negative drift and zero variance at 5%), and the long forward rate will be forever after below 5%. If the interest rate hits 10%, the interest rate will remain forever above 10%, and the long forward rate will be forever after above 10%. (There is almost enough structure here so that the long forward rate is constant for all time if the interest rate ends up below 5% and jumps up once if the interest rate ends up above 10%, but that depends on things like the boundary classification at zero and the asymptotic properties at infinity.) In general, even with the special structure of a multivariate diffusion and nonzero variance, there is not an obvious general result, due to potential absorbing boundaries.

In our theorems and examples we have proved that the long zero-coupon rate cannot fall over time though it may increase. How has this rate actually behaved? Because neither the long zero-coupon nor forward rate is directly observable, we cannot answer this question with certainty; however, it may be possible to make some deductions by examining the yield curve of U.S. Treasury STRIPS. The Treasury has been stripping zeros from its coupon bonds since February 1985. Commencing in 1987 they began reconstituting the STRIPS into coupon bonds upon request. Beginning in 1989, the market for STRIPS became sufficiently active to have price quotes in the *Wall Street Journal*.

Figure 1 shows the zero-coupon yield curves of U.S. Treasury STRIPS on June 30 for each year since 1989. Both the 1989 and 1990 yield curves have slight downward slopes for maturities in excess of 15 years. For the last 4 years the yield curves have been upward sloping through about 20 years to maturity and then had a slightly more pronounced downward slope. If the 30-year rate is a valid proxy for the long zero-coupon rate, then theorem 2 has obviously been violated by the decreases in this rate from 1991 to 1992 and 1992 to 1993.

Of course, it is possible that the zero-coupon yield curve has not reached its asymptotic value even by a maturity of 30 years. All of the curves have distinct negative slopes after 20 years to maturity. Furthermore, in each case the negative slope appears to be increasing in absolute value, indicating that an asymptotic value is not near. An alternative, and more likely, explanation is there is some unusual clientele effect at the very long end perhaps related to tax effects and the expense of short selling.

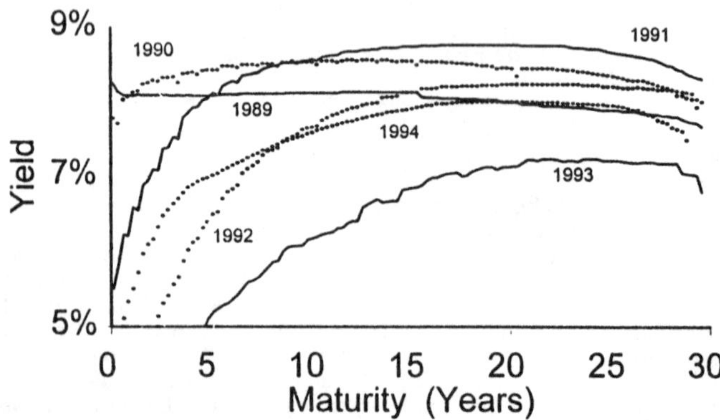

FIG. 1.—Zero-coupon yields from U.S. Treasury STRIPS

III. The Behavior of Long Coupon Rate

In the previous section we learned that the long forward and zero-coupon rates could not fall over time. Indeed for popular term structure models which all exhibit recurrence, these long rates neither rise nor fall but are constant. How does the long par-coupon rate behave?

Working with the diffusion interest rate model, $dr = \mu r^2 dt + \sigma r^{3/2} d\omega$, Cox, Ingersoll, and Ross (1980) derived the price for a consol bond which is inversely proportional to the instantaneous interest rate. For this model the long par-coupon rate will be proportional to the instantaneous rate of interest. Obviously, we cannot, therefore, construct any general theorem that prohibits a decrease (or increase) in the long par-coupon rate. As we shall see, this property is ubiquitous. The long coupon rate must be random in essentially any stochastic model of the interest rates where there is no arbitrage.

For the purposes of this section, we assume there exists a unit consol bond (perpetuity) paying a coupon of one per period and having an ex-coupon price at time t equal to $P(t) = \Sigma_{T=t+1}^{\infty} v(t, T)$.[15] Then, provided $v(t, T)$ is bounded in T, it is easy to show that the long par-coupon rate $c_L(t)$ equals the yield, $1/P(t)$, on the unit consol, and we have the following theorem.

THEOREM 4: THE LONG PAR-COUPON RATE FOLLOWS A DETERMINISTIC PROCESS IF AND ONLY IF THE SHORT RATE IS DETERMINISTIC OVER TIME. If $z(s, s + \tau)$ is known for all s and τ at time t, then $c_L(s)$ is known at time t for all s. Conversely, if conditional on information at time t, the long par-coupon, $c_L(s)$, is known for all future times $s > t$, then all future zero-coupon rates, $z(s, s + \tau)$, must also be known at time t.

Proof. If the interest rate is deterministic, then so is the long coupon rate, $c_L(t)$, which equals $1/P(t)$; namely,

$$P(t) \equiv \sum_{T=t+1}^{\infty} v(t, T) = \sum_{T=t+1}^{\infty} \left[\prod_{s=t}^{T-1} (1 + r(s)) \right]. \tag{17}$$

Conversely, given that the long coupon rate, $c_L(t)$, is deterministic, so is the price of the consol, $P(t) = 1/c_L(t)$. The rate of return from holding the consol for 1 period

15. We normally think the consol can be priced just from an absence of arbitrage, but this depends on the particular model and the definition of arbitrage. Quite generally the consol's price must be at least as large as $\Sigma_{T=t+1}^{\infty} v(t, T)$ (or else a simple arbitrage can be constructed with finitely many assets held for a finite time). However, the price of the perpetuity can be larger than this sum in some models. One example is Back and Pliska (1991), in which it is feasible to hold more than finitely many assets at a time.

$$\frac{1}{P(t)} + \frac{P(t+1) - P(t)}{P(t)}, \tag{18}$$

is then also deterministic. By the absence of arbitrage this rate of return must equal the risk-free rate. Since $c_L(t)$, and hence $P(t)$, is known for all time, the short rate, $r(t)$, must also be known for all time. The forward rates must equal these short rates, $f(t, T) = r(T)$, and the zero-coupon rates can be determined from (7). Q.E.D.

Even though the long coupon rate must be random in any stochastic economy, it is still possible it may never fall over time with the uncertainty being only about how much it will increase. The following example illustrates this point.

EXAMPLE 3. Let $R \equiv 1 + r$ be one plus the single-period interest rate. Suppose that each period R increases to θR with a risk-neutral probability of p or remains unchanged with a risk-neutral probability of $1 - p$. Then

$$v(R, t, T) = \frac{1}{R}[pv(\theta R, t+1, T) + (1-p)v(R, t+1, T)]. \tag{19}$$

The solution to this recursion problem is $v(R, t, T) = R^{-(T-t)}(p/\theta + 1 - p)^{T-t-1}$. The price of a consol is

$$P(R) = \sum_{\tau=1}^{\infty} R^{-\tau}[p/\theta + 1 - p]^{\tau-1} = \frac{1}{R - 1 + p - p/\theta}. \tag{20}$$

The long par-coupon rate is equal to the consol's yield which is the reciprocal of its price

$$c_L(t) = R_t - 1 + p - p/\theta. \tag{21}$$

Since the interest rate can only increase, the long par-coupon rate will similarly never fall but will increase along with all zero-coupon rates.

Figure 2 illustrates the par-coupon rates constructed from Treasury STRIPS over the past 5 years. The most notable feature is that the yield curves are "flatter" than those of the zero-coupon rates. This is to be expected since the par-coupon rates are averages of the zero-coupon rates. The final tailing off of the curves is also much less noticeable (though there is still some evidence of a clientele effect at extreme maturities).

IV. Classes of Examples

In most popular term structure models, the long zero-coupon rate is constant.[16] On the other hand, Vasicek's absolute model without mean

16. Throughout this section, we will work with the long zero-coupon rate. If the long forward rate exists, it has the same properties by theorem 1.

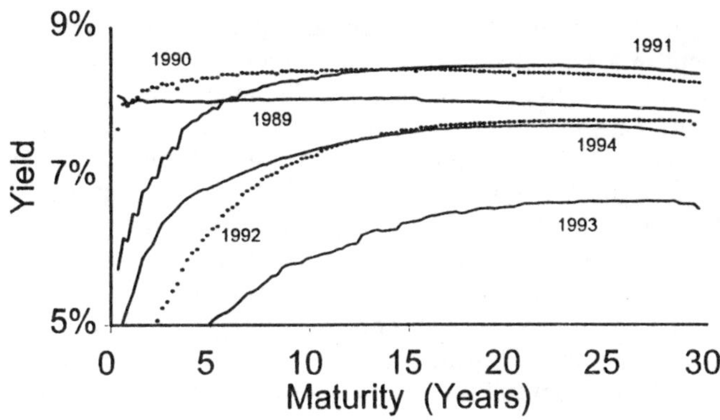

FIG. 2.—Par-coupon yields from U.S. Treasury STRIPS

reversion has the property that zero-coupon rates tend to $-\infty$ as maturity increases, and therefore the long zero-coupon rate does not exist. This section explores two simple classes of term structure models with more interesting long rate behavior: the long zero-coupon rate exists in these models (at least initially), but shocks are permanent and the long zero-coupon rate is not constant. This was also true in examples 1 and 2 in the previous section. However, these examples were obviously "cooked" to illustrate specific points and were not rich enough to merit serious consideration as models to use in applications. The two classes of models analyzed in this section have been used in practice, and the qualitative results would be the same in other models fitting the initial yield curve and having permanent shocks.

The two classes are the discrete time binomial class of models proposed by Ho and Lee (1986) and the continuous-time analogs of these models (which look like the absolute model without mean reversion but with a deterministic time-dependent drift). Interestingly, the two cases are qualitatively different. In the discrete-time model of Ho and Lee, the long zero-coupon rate always exists but jumps upward when the short rate gets a positive shock, while in the continuous-time version the long zero-coupon rate never exists beyond the initial instant.[17]

Ho and Lee (1986) provide a class of binomial one-factor models of the term structure of interest rates. The models in this class have the feature that any desired initial yield curve can be replicated by some element of this class. For example, a flat yield curve at any particular

17. For a critical discussion of these models, see Dybvig (1989). A number of other authors have also studied multifactor and/or translated versions of Vasicek's model, like the continuous-time class we are studying.

rate can be chosen. In addition, uncertain interest rate movements are permanent in a sense to be made more precise below. For these reasons, we use the Ho and Lee model to illuminate our results because on the surface it may seem to be inconsistent with our results.

In the Ho and Lee model, there is a single Bernoulli factor that affects the term structure in a given period. Indirectly it is assumed that changes in this factor have a permanent effect in the sense that a current shock has the same impact on a distant future yield curve as the same shock just before the distant future date.[18]

Ho and Lee showed that absence of arbitrage and their other assumptions imply the following process for the vector of discount bond prices. In the risk-neutral probabilities, at time t we have a probability π of an up move with new zero-coupon bond prices,

$$v(t, T; u) = h(T - t)\frac{v(t - 1, T)}{v(t - 1, t)}, \tag{22}$$

and a probability $1 - \pi$ of a down move with new zero-coupon bond prices,

$$v(t, T; d) = h^*(T - t)\frac{v(t - 1, T)}{v(t - 1, t)}, \tag{23}$$

where

$$h(T - t) = \frac{1}{\pi + (1 - \pi)\delta^{T-t}}, \quad h^*(T - t) = \frac{\delta^{T-t}}{\pi + (1 - \pi)\delta^{T-t}}, \tag{24}$$

and δ is a parameter greater than one.[19] The two possible yield curves are "parallel" so the shock is felt equally along the entire range of maturities, although the slope and curvature of the yield curve change over time.[20]

Assume the long zero-coupon rate exists at time $t - 1$. In the up

18. The explicit assumption is that an "up" move followed by a "down" move gives the same term structure as a "down" move followed by an "up" move from any given starting point. By induction, this says that the final effect of a sequence of shocks depends only on the number of up and down shocks, not on their order.

19. The parameter δ must be positive for $v(\cdot)$ to be positive. Without loss of generality, assume that $\delta > 1$ (or else replace δ by δ^{-1} and switch the two state designations). With this specification the "up" state corresponds to larger interest rates than the down state.

20. In particular,

$$\frac{1 + z(t, T; u)}{1 + z(t, T; d)} = \left[\frac{v(t, T; u)}{v(t, T; d)}\right]^{-1/(T-t)} = \left[\frac{h(T - t)}{h^*(T - t)}\right]^{-1/(T-t)} = \delta,$$

so that the difference between the two possible continuously compounded zero-coupon rates is $\log[1 + z(t, T; u)] - \log[1 + z(t, T; d)] = \log \delta$, independent of $T - t$. Note that neither resulting yield curve is "parallel" to the existing yield curve at time, $z(t - 1, T)$.

state, one plus the long zero-coupon rate at time t is given by

$$\begin{aligned} 1 + z_L(t; u) &\equiv \lim_{T \uparrow \infty} [v(t, T; u)]^{-1/(T-t)} \\ &= \lim_{T \uparrow \infty} \left(\frac{v(t-1, T)}{v(t-1, t)} h(T-t) \right)^{-1/(T-t)} \\ &= [1 + z_L(t-1)] \lim_{T \uparrow \infty} h(T-t)^{-1/(T-t)} \\ &= [1 + z_L(t-1)]\delta > 1 + z_L(t-1). \end{aligned} \tag{25}$$

Similarly in the down state,

$$\begin{aligned} 1 + z_L(t; d) &= [1 + z_L(t-1)] \lim_{T \uparrow \infty} h^*(T-t)^{-1/(T-t)} \\ &= 1 + z_L(t-1). \end{aligned} \tag{26}$$

This model is illustrated in figure 3. The initial yield curve at time 0 is indicated by the horizontal line. The two possible yield curves at time 1 (dotted lines) and the three possible yield curves at time 2 (solid lines) are also indicated. The yield curves at time 1 are "parallel," as are those at time 2.

If there is a "down" shock at time 1, then as shown in the lower dotted line, the long rate does not change while the short rate falls. If there is an "up" shock, then as shown in the upper dotted line, all interest rates increase with the largest increase in the longest rate. The same is true for shocks at time 2.

The short rate moves up or down, but the long rate can only increase. Over time, the long rate will increase without bound with probability one. Furthermore, any one of these shocks has a permanent effect in the sense that the order in which they occur does not matter. The solid yield curve in the middle is the result after either an "up" shock followed by a "down" shock or vice versa.

Our result that the long zero-coupon rate can never fall is upheld in this model, even though interest rate shocks are permanent. What is happening is that while the difference in zero-coupon rates in the up and down states is the same at all maturities, the average change is large enough at long maturities to overcome the largest possible decrease in rates.

Our second class of examples contains continuous-time analogs of the models in the Ho-Lee class. The default-free instantaneous short rate process under the risk-neutral probabilities is given by

$$r_t = \sigma W_t + F_t, \tag{27}$$

where W is a standard driftless Wiener process and F_t is a function of time alone. This is analogous to the Ho-Lee discrete time model be-

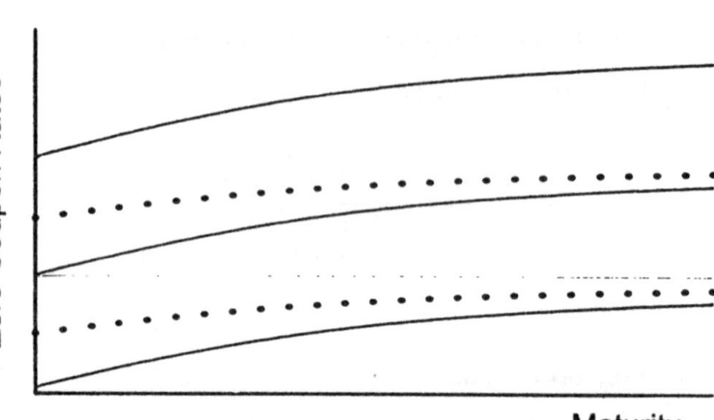

FIG. 3.—Yield curves for "Ho-Lee" models

cause in that model the short rate process under the risk-neutral probabilities is a random walk with independent increments plus a time-dependent deterministic drift. Letting $\hat{E}_t$ denote expectations under the risk-neutral probabilities, discount bond prices are given by

$$\begin{aligned} v(t, T) &\equiv \hat{E}_t\left[\exp\left(-\int_t^T r_\tau d\tau\right)\right] \\ &= \exp\left[-\sigma W_t(T-t) - \int_t^T F_\tau d\tau + \frac{(T-t)^3\sigma^2}{6}\right], \end{aligned} \tag{28}$$

where the details are standard for these models and we have used the normal moment generating function for the second equality.[21] In a moment, it will be useful to have on hand the expression

$$\begin{aligned} \log[v(t, T; W_t)] = \log[v(0, T)] - \sigma W_t(T-t) + \int_0^t F_\tau d\tau \\ - \frac{(3T^2t - 3Tt^2 + t^3)\sigma^2}{6}, \end{aligned} \tag{29}$$

which follows directly from (28).

Suppose that the long zero-coupon rate exists at time zero. Then

21. These are similar to calculations in sec. 3 of Dybvig (1988). Since r is Gaussian, so is its integral, which is why we can use the normal moment generating function, once we use standard methods to compute the mean and variance of $\int_t^T r_\tau d\tau$ conditional on information available at t.

the long zero-coupon rate at any $t > 0$ is given by

$$
\begin{aligned}
z_L(t; W_t) &= \lim_{T \uparrow \infty} -\frac{\log[v(t, T; W_T)]}{T - t} \\
&= \lim_{T \uparrow \infty} \frac{1}{T - t}\Big[-\log[v(0, T)] - \sigma W_t(T - t) \\
&\qquad + \int_0^t F_\tau d\tau - \frac{\sigma^2}{6}(3T^2 t - 3Tt^2 + t^3)\Big] \qquad (30) \\
&= z_L(0) + \sigma W_t - 0 + \lim_{T \uparrow \infty} \frac{(3T^2 t - 3Tt^2 + t^3)\sigma^2}{6(T - t)} = +\infty,
\end{aligned}
$$

or the long zero-coupon rate does not exist. In this model, an initial yield curve with finite long zero-coupon rate can be fit initially by careful choice of F_t. However, the long zero-coupon rate must be infinite for all subsequent time. This is consistent with the discrete model in the sense that no finite deterministic increase in the average long zero-coupon rate is sufficient to cover the largest possible decline in rates from the Wiener term over a fixed time interval.[22]

The net pragmatic effect of these examples is probably to reinforce previous arguments (as in Dybvig 1989) why these classes are not reasonable models. However, the examples do illuminate the results of this study. Also, questions of reasonableness should ultimately be determined by the data, and the two classes of examples given here are interesting alternatives to models in which the long zero-coupon rate is constant.

V. Conclusion

We have shown that long forward and zero-coupon rates can never fall in the absence of arbitrage. These results show that frictionless competitive models cannot have arbitrary behavior of long interest rates. Therefore, it is not permissible, for example, to specify a term

22. A different continuous-time model for which the long rate can exist both before and after it rises is given in Ingersoll, Skelton, and Weil (1978). In this model, which is the continuous-time analog of that in example 3, random Poisson events cause the entire yield curve to shift by a fixed amount δ. The continuously compounded yield-to-maturity at time t on a zero-coupon bond maturing at time T is

$$z(t, T) = r(t) + \lambda - \frac{\lambda}{\delta(T - t)}[1 - e^{-\delta(T-t)}],$$

where $r(t)$ is the current instantaneous spot rate and λ is the (risk-neutral) probability per unit time of the Poisson event. If interest rates jump up, $\delta > 0$, then the long rate exists, $z_L(t) = r(t) + \lambda$, and increases as the spot rate increases over time. If the rates can only jump down, $\delta < 0$, then the long rate is $z_L(t) = -\infty$ initially and cannot decrease.

structure model with a stochastic factor which is the long (asymptotic) end of the zero-coupon yield curve (unless this factor can only increase over time). In a similar fashion, empirical fittings of yield curves, using, for example, splines, may wish to constrain the asymptote to be constant (or nondecreasing). Furthermore, these results can be tested directly in parametric term structure models possessing enough structure to permit identification of long forward or discount rates. If we are willing to make further realistic assumptions, then these and similar results can be helpful in deriving practical implications for the pricing of long (but finite) maturity bonds as shown by Dybvig and Marshall (1995).

Appendix

General Proof of Theorem 2: Long Zero-Coupon Rates Can Never Fall

The general proof does not assume a finite state space. It follows the same idea as the finite state space proof, but with two new technical problems. First, the lowest (more formally essential infimum, defined below) of the long zero-coupon rates at time s need not be achieved with positive probability. Second, statewise (almost sure) convergence does not imply uniform convergence in general. To sidestep these problems requires a more careful proof, and it also requires invoking free disposal (which was not needed in the earlier proof). In particular, free disposal is used to truncate payoffs that fail to converge because they are exploding and more subtly to throw away the payoff in some states to convert almost-sure convergence to uniform convergence.

As a preliminary, we define some of the formal notation. Let (Ω, F, P) be the probability space on which payoffs at time s are defined. Conditional on all information at time t (which we are taking as fixed), Ω is the set of primitive states, F is a sigma-algebra of sets of events knowable at time s, and P is the probability measure. Then $z(s, T; \omega)$ and $z_L(s; \omega)$ will be F-measurable random variables that are well defined for all $\omega \in \Omega$ and $T > s$. We also will use the notion of essential infimum, which is the analogue for general state spaces of the minimum in finite states. The essential infimum of a random variable $x(\omega)$ is ess $\inf[x(\omega)] \equiv \sup\{y \in \mathbb{R} | P(y > x) = 0\}$. If x is essentially unbounded below (i.e., the set $\{y \in \mathbb{R} | P(y > x) = 0\}$ is empty), the essential infimum is defined formally to be $-\infty$, which is an object that is taken to be less than any real number.

Proof of theorem 2. Suppose the statement of this theorem is not true. Then $z_L(t) > z_L(s; \omega)$ with positive probability, but there is no arbitrage. Since $z_L(t) > z_L(s; \omega)$ with positive probability, we can choose $\bar{z}$ such that ess $\inf[z_L(s, \omega)] < \bar{z} < z_L(t)$. We will look at a typical claim, indexed by T, that pays off $(1 + \bar{z})^{T-s}$ for sure at time T. The sequence of net trades giving an arbitrage will involve any unbounded increasing sequence of times T. A typical net trade T involves purchase of claim T at time t and liquidation at time s with some free disposal that ensures uniform convergence without eliminating the money pump in the limit.

Our first task is to compute the particular pattern of free disposal that will serve our purpose. First, use free disposal to reduce any value at time s that exceeds 1. This yields a payoff at time s equal to

$$v_1(s, T; \omega) \equiv \min\left(1, \frac{(1+\bar{z})^{T-s}}{[1+z(s, T; \omega)]^{T-s}}\right).$$

In every state ω with $z_L(s, T; \omega) < \bar{z}$, the second term in the minimum goes off to $+\infty$ as $T \uparrow \infty$, and consequently there exists a smallest critical value $T^*(\omega) \geq s$ such that $v_1(s; \omega) = 1$ for all $T > T^*(\omega)$. By choice of $\bar{z}$, the set $\Omega_1 \equiv \{\omega | z_L(s, T; \omega) < \bar{z}\}$ of states ω on which $T^*(\omega)$ is defined is a measurable set of positive probability. Also, because the variables defining $T^*(\omega)$ on Ω_1 are measurable, $T^*(\omega)$ is a measurable function on Ω_1. Choose any $\bar{T} >$ ess $\inf\{T^*(\omega) | \omega \in \Omega_1\}$. Then the set $\Omega_2 \equiv \{\omega \in \Omega_1 | T^*(\omega) \leq \bar{T}\}$ is a set of positive probability.

The typical net trade T in the arbitrage is defined by purchase of the claim T at time t, with liquidation at time s, with free disposal to 0 in $\Omega \backslash \Omega_2$ and free disposal to 1 in Ω_2 whenever the claim exceeds 1. The price of claim T is

$$\frac{(1+\bar{z})^{T-s}}{[1+z(s, T; \omega)]^{T-t}},$$

which tends to 0 as $T \uparrow \infty$. The value at time s, for all $T \geq \bar{T}$, is given by 1 on Ω_2 and by 0 on the complement $\Omega \backslash \Omega_2$. Therefore, the cash flow to the net trade at time s converges uniformly (in fact, at finite $T = \bar{T}$) to the random variable that is 1 on Ω_1 and 0 on $\Omega \backslash \Omega_1$. Since Ω_2 is a set of positive probability, this is an arbitrage, which is a contradiction. Q.E.D.

References

Back, Kerry, and Pliska, Stanley. 1991. On the fundamental theorem of asset pricing with an infinite state space. *Journal of Mathematical Economics* 20:1–18.

Berk, Jonathan. 1990. The yield on a long bond can never fall: A constructive example. Working paper. New Haven, Conn.: Yale University.

Chamberlain, Gary, and Rothschild, Michael. 1983. Arbitrage, factor structure, and mean-variance analysis on large asset markets. *Econometrica* 51 (September): 1281–1304.

Cox, John C.; Ingersoll, Jonathan E., Jr.; and Ross, Stephen A. 1980. An analysis of variable rate loan contracts. *Journal of Finance* 35 (May): 389–403.

Cox, John C.; Ingersoll, Jonathan E., Jr.; and Ross, Stephen A. 1985. A theory of the term structure of interest rates. *Econometrica* 53 (March): 385–407.

Dybvig, Philip H. 1988. Inefficient dynamic portfolio strategies or how to throw away a million dollars in the stock market. *Review of Financial Studies* 1 (Spring): 67–88.

Dybvig, Philip H. 1989. Bond and bond option pricing based on the current term structure. Working paper. St. Louis: Washington University.

Dybvig, Philip H., and Marshall, William J. 1995. Pricing long bonds: Pitfalls and opportunities. Working paper. St. Louis: Washington University.

Dybvig, Philip H., and Ross, Stephen A. 1987. Arbitrage. In J. Eatwell, M. Milgate, and P. Newman (eds.), *The New Palgrave: A Dictionary of Economics*. New York: Stockton.

Harrison, J. Michael, and Kreps, David. 1979. Martingales and arbitrage in multiperiod securities markets. *Journal of Economic Theory* 20 (June): 381–408.

Harrison, J. Michael, and Pliska, Stanley. 1981. Martingales and stochastic integrals

in the theory of continuous trading. *Stochastic Processes and Their Applications* 11:215–60.
Ho, Thomas S. Y., and Lee, Sang-Bin. 1986. Term structure movements and pricing interest rate contingent claims. *Journal of Finance* 41 (December): 1011–29.
Ingersoll, Jonathan E., Jr.; Skelton, Jeffrey; and Weil, Roman L. 1978. Duration forty years later. *Journal of Financial and Quantitative Analysis* 13 (November): 627–48.
Kreps, David. 1981. Arbitrage and equilibrium in economies with infinitely many commodities. *Journal of Mathematical Economics* 8 (March): 15–35.
Vasicek, Oldrich. 1977. An equilibrium characterization of the term structure. *Journal of Financial Economics* 5 (November): 177–88.

Name Index

Abbott, C.C. 98
Almon, S. 87
Amin, K. 524
Amsler, C. 135
Ando, A. 153, 167
Arnold, L. 405–6
Arrow, K.J. 475, 477
Artzner, P. 503, 513, 515
Asay, M. 319, 323
Åström, K.J. 395

Bachelier, L. 327
Back, K. 532, 535, 539, 547
Backus, D. 167
Ball, C. 503–4, 513, 515
Begg, D.K.H. 153
Beltratti, A. 231
Benninga, S. 149
Bergstrom, A.R. 488–9
Berk, J. 541
Bicksler, J.L. 288
Bierwag, G.O. 101, 144, 160, 426–7, 449
Bischoff, C. 78, 87
Black, F . 98, 271, 327–8, 331–2, 339, 342, 364, 370–72, 378–9, 384, 392, 463, 471, 482, 486
Bliss, R.R. 154, 162, 226–7, 229, 233
Bohm-Bawerk, E.V. 142
Booth, D. 296
Bose, R.C. 299
Boyle, P. 392
Brainard, W.C. 167
Breeden, D. 243, 266–7, 297, 312, 418, 459, 471–2
Breit 27
Brennan, M.J. 150, 242, 428, 447, 451, 480–81, 503, 509, 513, 515
Brenner, M. 480
Brenner, R. 517
Brock, W.A. 459, 471
Brown, S. 151, 163, 247
Bryan, W.R. 102
Buse, A. 102, 151
Buser, S. 296

Cagan, P. 99, 108, 112, 290, 449
Campbell, J. 125, 141–2, 145, 152, 154–5, 161, 165–6, 221–7, 229, 231, 237, 239, 241, 246, 256, 315–16
Cargill, T.F. 160
Carleton, W.T. 102, 135
Chamberlain, G. 539
Chambers, D.R. 135
Chen, A.H.Y. 342
Chen, E.T. 171
Chen, N. 241, 296
Cheng, S.T. 504, 515
Churchill, R.V. 353, 361
Clark, J.B. 142
Clark, T.A. 164
Conard, J.W. 65, 143
Constantinides, G. 296, 459
Cootner, P.H. 349, 365, 370
Cox, J.C. 144–5, 148, 150–51, 221, 241–4, 266, 268, 307, 315, 372, 374, 377–8, 381, 383, 408, 410–11, 414–15, 425, 437, 443, 447–9, 456, 458, 480, 482, 504, 515, 521, 545, 547
Culbertson, J. 65, 83, 112, 143, 156, 419, 436

David, H.A. 107
De Leeuw, F. 64, 81, 85–8, 90–91, 167, 449
De Scitovszky, T. 65
Debreu, G. 475, 477
Delbaen, F. 503, 513, 515
Dettman, J.W. 353, 361
Dieffenbach, B.C. 436
Diller, S. 99, 151
Dingle, M.E. 33
Dobson, S. 160, 424
Donaldson, J.B. 459
Dothan, L.U. 150, 407, 425, 447
Duesenberry, J. 86, 426, 449
Durand, D. 65, 72–3, 135, 151
Dybvig, P. 134, 151, 163, 247, 541, 549, 552–4

Elliott, R.J. 527
Engle, R.F. 166

Fama, E.F. 98, 107, 154, 162, 166, 223, 226–7, 229, 233, 241–2, 246, 248, 252, 258, 260, 264–6, 269, 288, 293, 296–8, 301, 309, 312, 349, 422
Feller, W. 375, 379, 382, 386, 441–2, 522
Fellner, W. 64
Ferson, W. 241, 246, 256, 296
Fischer, S. 455

Fisher, I. 4, 32, 64, 142–3, 149, 271, 276, 283–4, 286, 289, 409
Fisher, L. 136
Flavin, M. 157–8, 160
Fleming, W.H. 460, 464
Fong, H.G. 135, 138, 171
French, K.R. 241
Friedman, A. 397, 417, 460, 473–5, 477
Friedman, B. 125, 151–2, 167
Friedman, M. 290
Froot, K.A. 156, 221, 226

Garman, M. 392, 408, 447
Garren, D. 271
Gibbons, M. 241, 246, 248, 256, 296
Gihman, I.I. 460
Gikhman, I.I. 394
Goldberger, A.S. 114
Goldman, B. 365
Goldstein, H. 64
Gonedes, N. 271
Grossman, S.J. 165
Grove, M.A. 64, 101, 144, 160, 426–7, 449

Hakansson, N.H. 439
Haley, B. 64
Hall, R. 78, 88, 150, 241
Hamao, Y. 315–16
Hamburger, M.J. 288
Hansen, L. 161, 227, 241–2, 246, 256, 503
Hardy, G.H. 367
Harrison, J.M. 407, 463, 505, 513–14, 524
Hart, B.I. 106
Hartley, H.O. 107
Harvey, C. 241
Hawtrey, R.G. 4, 32, 64, 68
Heath, D. 315, 504, 516
Hendershott, P.H. 167
Hentschel, L. 239
Hess, P.J. 288
Hickman, W.B. 33, 143
Hicks, J.R. 4, 14–15, 33, 64, 68, 82, 113, 135–7, 143, 146–8, 150, 286, 404, 409, 419, 435
Ho, T.S.Y. 315, 503–4, 513, 516, 519, 534, 549–50
Hodrick, R.J. 224, 227, 235, 241, 246, 256
Holthausen, R. 296
Homer, S. 135
Hopewell, M. 136
Horwich, G. 64
Hsieh, D. 251, 296
Huang, C. 459
Huberman, G. 241
Huizinga, J. 241, 257
Hurd, M. 285

Ibbotson, R.G. 298
Ikeda, N. 524
Ingersoll, J. 125, 134, 137, 144–5, 148, 150–51, 221, 241–4, 266, 268, 307, 315, 388, 408, 410–11, 414–15, 425, 437, 443, 447–9, 456, 458, 480, 482, 504, 515, 521, 545, 547, 553
Itô, K. 394–5, 460

Jagannathan, R. 241
Jamshidian, F. 516
Jarrow, R. 315, 504, 516–17, 524, 532
Jensen, M. 271, 370, 392
Johnson, N.L. 244, 442
Johnston, J. 72
Jones, D.S. 166
Jordan, J.V. 135
Jung, J. 125

Kaldor, N. 137
Kandel, S. 241
Kane, E.J. 99, 119–20, 125, 152
Karlin, S. 530
Kassouf, S.T. 355
Kaufman, G. 136
Keim, D.B. 166, 241
Kennickell, A. 153
Kessel, R. 74, 85, 98–9, 102, 108, 113, 143, 165, 296
Keynes, J.M. 7, 27, 32–3, 64, 68, 85, 146–7, 163
Kikugawa, T. 314, 319, 323
Kim, S. 125, 164
Kimoto, N. 323
Klein, J.J. 290
Koch, K. 31
Kool, C.J.M. 314
Kopp, P.E. 530
Kotz, S. 244, 442
Kreps, D. 407, 463, 505, 513, 539
Krieger, R. 323
Kushner, H.J. 348, 395

Laffer, A. 271
Langetieg, T.C. 150, 503, 509, 513, 515
Lay, D. 522–3
Lee, S-B. 315, 503–4, 513, 516, 519, 534, 549–50
Leiderman, L. 257
Leonard, R.J. 364
LeRoy, S. 125, 144–5, 148–9, 157, 415
Lilien, D.M. 166
Lindahl 4
Lindahl, E. 137
Lintner, J. 297, 312, 472
Litterman, R. 323
Liviatan, N. 88

Long, J. 113, 370, 392, 436
Lucas, R. 414, 458
Luckett, D.G. 65
Lutz, F.A. 33–4, 64–5, 143, 146, 148, 409–10

Macaulay, F.R. 4, 8, 135–7, 141, 143, 155, 164
MacBeth, J. 271
Madderom, P. 480
Malinvaud, E. 491
Malkiel, B. 85, 99, 119–20, 142, 144, 152, 160, 411, 426, 449
Mankiw, N.G. 154, 162–5, 226, 235, 239
Marsh, T.A. 150, 243
Marshall, W.J. 554
Matsunaga, Y. 323
McCulloch, J.H. 98–9 101–2, 108, 112–13, 120, 125–7, 134–5, 137–9, 141, 159, 170–71, 222, 227, 296–7, 402
McDermott, S. 323
McKean, H.P. 348, 350, 353, 357, 359, 385
McKinnon, R.I. 285
Meginnis, J. 98
Mehra, R. 459
Meiselman, D. 65, 67–70, 83, 85, 99, 143–4, 151, 296, 414, 449
Melino, A. 165
Merton, R.C. 297, 312, 327–9, 331–2, 347–50, 354, 357, 364–5, 370, 377, 379–80, 384, 388, 392, 395, 400, 406, 421, 425, 439, 446–7, 458–9, 463, 472, 480–81
Merton, R.K. 327
Meyer, R.A. 160
Michaelsen, J.B. 70
Miller, M. 98, 102, 112, 271, 329, 338–9, 370–71, 404
Miller, R.G. 299–300
Mills, E.S. 64
Mincer, J. 426–7
Miron, J. 125, 162, 164
Mishkin, F.S. 153, 166, 226, 241, 257
Modigliani, F. 99, 148, 153, 159, 166–7, 286, 294, 329, 338–9, 370–71, 404, 419, 430, 436, 449
Moore, G.H. 266
Morrison, D.F. 299
Morton, A. 315, 504, 516, 520
Mossin, J. 472

Nelson, C. 98–9, 108, 135, 151, 165–6, 271, 402
Newey, W.K. 230

Okun, A.M. 167
Oldfield, G.S. 243–4
Oliver, F.W.J. 442
Orr, D. 112

Pearson, E.S. 107
Pedersen, H. 532
Pesando, J.E. 153
Phillips, L. 153
Phillips, P.C.B. 489, 491
Pinkus, S. 323
Pippenger, J. 153
Pliska, S. 505, 513–14, 524, 535, 539, 547
Porter, R.D. 157
Praetz, P.D. 107
Prescott, E.C. 459
Press, S.J. 107
Protopapadakis, A. 149
Pye, G. 478

Ramaswamy, K. 241, 248
Rice, J.R. 102
Richard, S. 144, 150, 244, 414, 425, 447, 459, 482, 485
Richardson, M. 224, 235
Riefler, W.W. 4, 13, 32, 64
Rishel, R.W. 460, 464
Roberts, H. 271
Robins, R.P. 166
Robinson, J. 125
Rogalski, R.J. 243–4
Roley, V.V. 166–7
Roll, R. 99, 102, 107, 112, 153, 271, 284, 288, 296, 392, 436, 480
Rosenfeld, E.R. 243
Rosensweig, J. 532
Ross, S.A. 134, 144–5, 148, 150–51, 221, 241–4, 266, 268, 307, 315, 372, 374, 377–8, 381, 383, 408, 410–11, 414–15, 425, 437, 443, 447–9, 456, 458, 470, 472, 480, 482, 504, 515, 521, 541, 545, 547
Rothschild, M. 335, 354, 366, 539
Roy, S.N. 299
Rubinstein, M. 243, 267, 436, 459, 480

Sakellaris, P. 125
Samuelson, P. 78, 101, 136, 288, 327–8, 331, 335, 342, 347–9, 351, 353–5, 357, 359, 370, 379, 439
Santomero, A.M. 285
Sargent, T.J. 161, 164, 284, 436
Say, J.B. 31, 142
Scadding, J. 285
Schaefer, S. 135, 392, 503–4, 513, 515
Schoenholtz, K.L. 141–2, 152, 154–5, 166, 221, 223–4, 226–7, 229
Scholes, M. 102, 327–8, 331–2, 339, 342, 364, 370–72, 378–9, 384, 392, 463, 482, 486
Schwartz, A.J. 290

Schwartz, E. 150, 242, 428, 447, 451, 480–81, 503–4, 509, 513, 515
Schwert, G.W. 241, 296
Scott, R.H. 167
Shapiro, E. 78
Shapiro, M.D. 235
Sharpe, W.F. 285, 297, 312, 472
Shea, G.S. 135
Shikano, Y. 315
Shiller, R.J. 99, 141–2, 145, 151–5, 157–66, 170–71, 221–7, 229, 231, 237, 239, 436, 449
Shirakawa, H. 315
Sidgwick, H. 31, 142
Siegel, A.F. 135
Singleton, K.J. 157, 241–2, 314–15, 319, 323
Sinquefield, R. 296, 298
Skelton, J. 137, 553
Skinner, E.B. 133
Skorohod, A.V. 460
Skorokhod, A.V. 394
Slater, L.J. 453
Smith,G. 167
Snyder, G.L. 361
Solanki, R. 480
Sprenkle, C.M. 347, 353, 379
Stambaugh, R. 166, 235, 241, 296
Stapleton, R.C. 459
Startz, R. 241, 296–7, 312
Stiglitz, J.E. 101, 144, 152, 332, 335, 339, 354, 366, 436, 480
Stigum, M. 133
Stock, J.H. 224, 235
Stoll, H.R. 342
Stulz, R. 241
Subrahmanyam, M.G. 459
Summers, L.H. 226, 239
Sundaresan, M. 459
Sutch, R. 99, 148, 153, 160, 167, 286, 294, 404, 419, 424, 430, 436, 449

Tatom, J.A. 314
Tauchen, G. 261
Taylor, A. 522–3
Taylor, H. 530
Telser, L.G. 98, 108
Thorp, E.O. 355
Tobin, J. 167
Torous, W. 503–4, 513, 515
Tsubouchi, K. 323

Upton, C. 271

Van Horne, J. 108, 332, 335, 449
Vanderford, D. 160, 424
Vasicek, O. 135, 138, 150, 171, 244, 425, 447, 481, 503, 513, 515, 545, 548–9
Vogel, R.C. 290
Volterra, V. 141
Von Weizsacker, C.C. 144, 152

Waldman, D.W. 135
Walker, C.E. 65, 166
Wallace, N. 106, 167
Watanabe, S. 524
Weil, D.N. 162
Weil, R.L. 137, 553
Weingartner, H.M. 102
West, K.D. 230
Westlake, J.R. 502
White, H. 227, 251
Williams, J. 4, 7, 14–15, 101–2, 143, 407
Winn, W.J. 65
Wood, J.H. 65, 441, 449
Woodward, S. 150
Wymer, C.R. 489

Zarnowitz, V. 266